Nineteenth-Century Literature Criticism

Guide to Gale Literary Criticism Series

For criticism on	Consult these Gale series
Authors now living or who died after December 31, 1999	*CONTEMPORARY LITERARY CRITICISM (CLC)*
Authors who died between 1900 and 1999	*TWENTIETH-CENTURY LITERARY CRITICISM (TCLC)*
Authors who died between 1800 and 1899	*NINETEENTH-CENTURY LITERATURE CRITICISM (NCLC)*
Authors who died between 1400 and 1799	*LITERATURE CRITICISM FROM 1400 TO 1800 (LC)* *SHAKESPEAREAN CRITICISM (SC)*
Authors who died before 1400	*CLASSICAL AND MEDIEVAL LITERATURE CRITICISM (CMLC)*
Authors of books for children and young adults	*CHILDREN'S LITERATURE REVIEW (CLR)*
Dramatists	*DRAMA CRITICISM (DC)*
Poets	*POETRY CRITICISM (PC)*
Short story writers	*SHORT STORY CRITICISM (SSC)*
Literary topics and movements	*HARLEM RENAISSANCE: A GALE CRITICAL COMPANION (HR)* *THE BEAT GENERATION: A GALE CRITICAL COMPANION (BG)* *FEMINISM IN LITERATURE: A GALE CRITICAL COMPANION (FL)* *GOTHIC LITERATURE: A GALE CRITICAL COMPANION (GL)*
Asian American writers of the last two hundred years	*ASIAN AMERICAN LITERATURE (AAL)*
Black writers of the past two hundred years	*BLACK LITERATURE CRITICISM (BLC)* *BLACK LITERATURE CRITICISM SUPPLEMENT (BLCS)* *BLACK LITERATURE CRITICISM: CLASSIC AND EMERGING AUTHORS SINCE 1950 (BLC-2)*
Hispanic writers of the late nineteenth and twentieth centuries	*HISPANIC LITERATURE CRITICISM (HLC)* *HISPANIC LITERATURE CRITICISM SUPPLEMENT (HLCS)*
Native North American writers and orators of the eighteenth, nineteenth, and twentieth centuries	*NATIVE NORTH AMERICAN LITERATURE (NNAL)*
Major authors from the Renaissance to the present	*WORLD LITERATURE CRITICISM, 1500 TO THE PRESENT (WLC)* *WORLD LITERATURE CRITICISM SUPPLEMENT (WLCS)*

ISSN 0732-1864

Volume 270

Nineteenth-Century Literature Criticism

Criticism of the
Works of Novelists, Philosophers, and Other
Creative Writers Who Died between 1800
and 1899, from the First Published Critical
Appraisals to Current Evaluations

Lawrence J. Trudeau
Editor

GALE
CENGAGE Learning

Detroit • New York • San Francisco • New Haven, Conn • Waterville, Maine • London

Nineteenth-Century Literature Criticism, Vol. 270

Layman Poupard Publishing, LLC

Editorial Directors: Richard Layman,
Dennis Poupard

Editorial Production Manager: Janet Hill

Permissions Manager: Kourtnay King

Quality Assurance Manager:
Katherine Macedon

Production Technology Manager:
Natalie Fulkerson

Content Conversion, Data Coding,
Composition: Apex CoVantage, LLC

Advisors to LPP:
Ward W. Briggs
James Hardin
Joel Myerson

Volume Advisors:
James Hardin, Distinguished Professor
Emeritus, University of South Carolina
(for "Johann Wolfgang von Goethe")
Susan Adams Delaney, Ithaca College
(for "Adah Isaacs Menken")
William Baker, Northern Illinois University
(for "Sir Walter Scott")

For product information and technology assistance, contact us at
Gale Customer Support, 1-800-877-4253.
For permission to use material from this text or product,
submit all requests online at **www.cengage.com/permissions.**
Further permissions questions can be emailed to
permissionrequest@cengage.com

While every effort has been made to ensure the reliability of the information presented in this publication, Gale, a part of Cengage Learning, does not guarantee the accuracy of the data contained herein. Gale accepts no payment for listing; and inclusion in the publication of any organization, agency, institution, publication, service, or individual does not imply endorsement of the editors or publisher. Errors brought to the attention of the publisher and verified to the satisfaction of the publisher will be corrected in future editions.

Gale
27500 Drake Rd.
Farmington Hills, MI, 48331-3535

LIBRARY OF CONGRESS CATALOG CARD NUMBER 84-643008

ISBN-13: 978-1-4144-8532-4
ISBN-10: 1-4144-8532-8

ISSN 0732-1864

Printed in Mexico
2 3 4 5 6 7 22 21 20 19 18

Contents

Preface

Since its inception in 1981, *Nineteenth-Century Literature Criticism* (*NCLC*) has been a valuable resource for students and librarians seeking critical commentary on writers of this transitional period in world history. Designated an "Outstanding Reference Source" by the American Library Association with the publication of its first volume, *NCLC* has since been purchased by over 6,000 school, public, and university libraries. The series has covered more than 500 authors representing 38 nationalities and over 28,000 titles. No other reference source has surveyed the critical reaction to nineteenth-century authors and literature as thoroughly as *NCLC*.

Scope of the Series

NCLC is designed to introduce students and advanced readers to the authors of the nineteenth century and to the most significant interpretations of these authors' works. The great poets, novelists, short story writers, playwrights, and philosophers of this period are frequently studied in high school and college literature courses. By organizing and reprinting commentary written on these authors, *NCLC* helps students develop valuable insight into literary history, promotes a better understanding of the texts, and sparks ideas for papers and assignments. Each entry in *NCLC* presents a comprehensive survey of an author's career, an individual work of literature, or a literary topic, and provides the user with a multiplicity of interpretations and assessments. Such variety allows students to pursue their own interests; furthermore, it fosters an awareness that literature is dynamic and responsive to many different opinions.

Volumes 1 through 19 of *NCLC* feature author entries arranged alphabetically by author. Beginning with Volume 20, every fourth volume of the series is devoted to literary topics. These topics widen the focus of the series from the individual authors to such broader subjects as literary movements, prominent themes in nineteenth-century literature, literary reaction to political and historical events, significant eras in literary history, prominent literary anniversaries, and the literatures of cultures that are often overlooked by English-speaking readers. With *NCLC*, Volume 243, the series returns to a standard author approach, with some entries devoted to a single important work of world literature and others devoted to literary topics.

NCLC is part of the survey of criticism and world literature that is contained in Gale's *Contemporary Literary Criticism* (*CLC*), *Twentieth-Century Literary Criticism* (*TCLC*), *Literature Criticism from 1400 to 1800* (*LC*), *Shakespearean Criticism* (*SC*), and *Classical and Medieval Literature Criticism* (*CMLC*).

Organization of the Book

An *NCLC* entry consists of the following elements:

- The **Author Heading** cites the name under which the author most commonly wrote, followed by birth and death dates. Also located here are any name variations under which an author wrote, including transliterated forms for authors whose native languages use nonroman alphabets. If the author wrote consistently under a pseudonym, the pseudonym will be listed in the author heading and the author's actual name given in parenthesis on the first line of the biographical and critical information. Uncertain birth or death dates are indicated by question marks. Single-work entries are preceded by a heading that consists of the most common form of the title in English translation (if applicable) and the name of the author.

- The **Introduction** contains background information that introduces the reader to the author, work, or topic that is the subject of the entry.

- The list of **Principal Works** is ordered chronologically by date of first publication and lists the most important works by the author. The genre and publication information of each work is given. In the case of foreign authors, a translation of the title is provided as an aid to the reader; the translation is a published translated title or a free translation provided by the compiler of the entry. In the case of foreign authors whose works have been translated into English, the **Principal English Translations** focuses primarily on twentieth-century translations, selecting those works most commonly considered the best by critics. Unless otherwise indicated, dramas are dated by first performance, not first publication, and the location of the first performance is given, if known. Lists of **Representative Works** by different authors appear with topic entries.

- Reprinted **Criticism** is arranged chronologically in each entry to provide a useful perspective on changes in critical evaluation over time. The critic's name and the date of composition or publication of the critical work are given at the beginning of each piece of criticism. Unsigned criticism is preceded by the title of the source in which it appeared. All titles by the author featured in the text are printed in boldface type. Footnotes are reprinted at the end of each essay or excerpt. In the case of excerpted criticism, only those footnotes that pertain to the excerpted texts are included. Criticism in topic entries is arranged chronologically under a variety of subheadings to facilitate the study of different aspects of the topic.

- A complete **Bibliographical Citation** of the original essay or book precedes each piece of criticism. Citations conform to recommendations set forth in the Modern Language Association of America's *MLA Handbook for Writers of Research Papers*, 7th ed. (2009).

- Critical essays are prefaced by brief **Annotations** describing each piece.

- An annotated bibliography of **Further Reading** appears at the end of each entry and suggests resources for additional study. In some cases, significant essays for which the editors could not obtain reprint rights are included here. Boxed material following the further reading list provides references to other biographical and critical sources on the author in series published by Gale.

Citing *Nineteenth-Century Literature Criticism*

When citing criticism reprinted in the Literary Criticism Series, students should provide complete bibliographic information so that the cited essay can be located in the original print or electronic source. Students who quote directly from reprinted criticism may use any accepted bibliographic format, such as University of Chicago Press style or Modern Language Association style.

The examples below follow recommendations for preparing a works cited list set forth in the Modern Language Association of America's *MLA Handbook for Writers of Research Papers*, 7th ed. (2009); the first example pertains to material drawn from periodicals, the second to material reprinted from books:

Franklin, J. Jeffrey. "The Victorian Discourse of Gambling: Speculations on *Middlemarch* and *The Duke's Children*." *ELH* 61.4 (1994): 899-921. Rpt. in *Nineteenth-Century Literature Criticism*. Ed. Jessica Bomarito and Russel Whitaker. Vol. 168. Detroit: Gale, 2006. 39-51. Print.

Frank, Joseph. "*The Gambler*: A Study in Ethnopsychology." *Freedom and Responsibility in Russian Literature: Essays in Honor of Robert Louis Jackson*. Ed. Elizabeth Cheresh Allen and Gary Saul Morson. Evanston: Northwestern UP, 1995. 69-85. Rpt. in *Nineteenth-Century Literature Criticism*. Ed. Jessica Bomarito and Russel Whitaker. Vol. 168. Detroit: Gale, 2006. 75-84. Print.

The examples below follow recommendations for preparing a bibliography set forth in *The Chicago Manual of Style*, 15th ed. (2003); the first example pertains to material drawn from periodicals, the second to material reprinted from books:

Franklin, J. Jeffrey. "The Victorian Discourse of Gambling: Speculations on *Middlemarch* and *The Duke's Children*." *ELH* 61, no. 4 (winter 1994): 899-921. Reprinted in *Nineteenth-Century Literature Criticism*. Vol. 168, edited by Jessica Bomarito and Russel Whitaker, 39-51. Detroit: Gale, 2006.

Frank, Joseph. "*The Gambler*: A Study in Ethnopsychology." In *Freedom and Responsibility in Russian Literature: Essays in Honor of Robert Louis Jackson*, edited by Elizabeth Cheresh Allen and Gary Saul Morson, 69-85. Evanston, Ill.: Northwestern University Press, 1995. Reprinted in *Nineteenth-Century Literature Criticism*. Vol. 168, edited by Jessica Bomarito and Russel Whitaker, 75-84. Detroit: Gale, 2006.

Suggestions are Welcome

Readers who wish to suggest new features, topics, or authors to appear in future volumes, or who have other suggestions or comments are cordially invited to call, write, or fax the Product Manager:

Product Manager, Literary Criticism Series
Gale
Cengage Learning
27500 Drake Road
Farmington Hills, MI 48331-3535
1-800-347-4253 (GALE)
Fax: 248-699-8884

Acknowledgments

The editors wish to thank the copyright holders of the criticism included in this volume and the permissions managers of many book and magazine publishing companies for assisting us in securing reproduction rights. Following is a list of copyright holders who have granted us permission to reproduce material in this volume of *NCLC*. Every effort has been made to trace copyright, but if omissions have been made, please let us know.

COPYRIGHTED MATERIAL IN *NCLC*, VOLUME 270, WAS REPRODUCED FROM THE FOLLOWING PERIODICALS:

Comparative Literature, v. 10.3, 1958. Public domain.—*Deutsche Vierteljahrsschrift für Literaturwissenschaft und Geistes-geschichte,* v. 58.2, 1984; v. 68.1, 1994. Copyright © 1984, 1994 J. B. Metzlersche Verlagbuchhandlung und Carl Ernst Poes Chel Verlag GmbH. Reproduced by permission of the publisher.—*German Quarterly,* v. 32.3, 1959. Public domain; v. 55.1, 1982; v. 69.1, 1996; v. 77.4, 2004. Copyright © 1982, 1996, 2004 American Association of Teachers of German. All reproduced by permission of the publisher.—*Goethe Yearbook: Publications of the Goethe Society of North America,* v. 5, 1990; v. 14, 2007. Copyright © 1990, 2007 Goethe Society of North America. Both reproduced by permission of Boydell and Brewer, Ltd.—*Legacy: A Journal of American Women Writers,* v. 15.1, 1998. Copyright © 1998 by The Pennsylvania State University. Reproduced by permission of the University of Nebraska Press.—*Louisiana Literature: A Review of Literature and Humanities,* v. 17.1, 2000. Copyright © 2000 *Louisiana Literature.* Reproduced by permission of the publisher.—*Modern Language Notes,* v. 28.8, 1913; v. 30.1, 1915; v. 59.8, 1944. All public domain.—*Modern Language Studies,* v. 31.1, 2001. Copyright © 2001 Northeast Modern Language Association. Reproduced by permission of the Northeast Modern Language Association and the University of South Carolina Press.—*New York Times,* 21 Oct. 1868. Public domain.—*New-York Daily Tribune,* 29 Sept. 1868. Public domain.—*Nineteenth Century Studies,* v. 17, 2003. Copyright © 2003 Nineteenth Century Studies Association. Reproduced by permission of the publisher.—*Nineteenth-Century Fiction,* v. 27.4, 1973. Copyright © 1973 by the Regents of the University of California. Reproduced by permission of the University of California Press.—*North Dakota Quarterly,* v. 61.4, 1993 for "Adah Isaacs Menken: An American Original" by Barbara Foster and Michael Foster. Copyright © 1993 Barbara Foster and Michael Foster. Reproduced by permission of the authors.—*PMLA: Publications of the Modern Language Association of America,* v. 71.3, 1956. Public domain; v. 121.1, 2006. Copyright © 2006 by The Modern Language Association of America. Reproduced by permission of the copyright holder, The Modern Language Association of America.—*Poetica: An International Journal of Linguistic-Literary Studies,* v. 61, 2004. Copyright © 2004 Toshiyuki Takamiya. Reproduced by permission of Shubun International Co. Ltd.—*Publications of the English Goethe Society,* v. 56, 1987. Copyright © 1987 Maney Publishing. Reproduced by permission of Maney Publishing, www.maney.co.uk/journals/ceu, www.ingentaconnect.com/content/maney/ceu.—*Quarterly Review,* v. 15, 1816. Public domain.—*Representations,* v. 82.1, 2003. Copyright © 2003 The Regents of the University of California. Reproduced by permission of the publisher.—*Studies in Romanticism,* v. 40.1, 2001. Copyright © 2001 *Studies in Romanticism.* Reproduced by permission of the publisher.—*Studies in Scottish Literature,* v. 11.4, 1974. Copyright © 1974 G. Ross Roy. Reproduced by permission of *Studies in Scottish Literature.*—*Virginia Woolf Miscellany,* v. 70, 2006 for "'Slaves of the Imagination': Sir Walter Scott in the Works of Virginia Woolf" by Jennifer Parrott. Copyright © 2006 Jennifer Parrott. Reproduced by permission of the author.

COPYRIGHTED MATERIAL IN *NCLC*, VOLUME 270, WAS REPRODUCED FROM THE FOLLOWING BOOKS:

Bahr, Ehrhard. From *Reflection and Action: Essays on the Bildungsroman.* Ed. James Hardin. University of South Carolina Press, 1991. Copyright © 1991 University of South Carolina. Reproduced by permission of the University of South Carolina Press.—Bahr, Ehrhard. From *The Novel as Archive: The Genesis, Reception, and Criticism of Goethe's* **Wilhelm Meisters Wanderjahre.** Camden House, 1998. Copyright © 1998 Ehrhard Bahr. Reproduced by permission of Camden House, Inc.—Barclay, G. Lippard. From *The Life and Remarkable Career of Adah Isaacs Menken, The Celebrated Actress.* Barclay, 1868. Public domain.—Brooks, Daphne A. From *Recovering the Black Female Body: Self-Representations by African American Women.* Ed. Michael Bennett and Vanessa D. Dickerson. Rutgers University Press, 2001. Copyright © 2001 Daphne A. Brooks. Reproduced by permission of Rutgers University Press.—Buckley-Fletcher, Carolyn. From *Nonfictional Romantic Prose: Expanding Borders.* Ed. Steven P. Sondrup, Virgil Nemoianu, and Gerald Gillespie. John Benjamins, 2004. Copyright © 2004 John Benjamins B.V./Association Internationale de Littérature Comparée. Reproduced by permission of John

Advisory Board

The members of the Advisory Board—reference librarians from public and academic library systems—represent a cross-section of our customer base and offer a variety of informed perspectives on both the presentation and content of our literature products. Advisory board members assess and define such quality issues as the relevance, currency, and usefulness of the author coverage, critical content, and literary topics included in our series; evaluate the layout, presentation, and general quality of our printed volumes; provide feedback on the criteria used for selecting authors and topics covered in our series; provide suggestions for potential enhancements to our series; identify any gaps in our coverage of authors or literary topics, recommending authors or topics for inclusion; analyze the appropriateness of our content and presentation for various user audiences, such as high school students, undergraduates, graduate students, librarians, and educators; and offer feedback on any proposed changes/enhancements to our series. We wish to thank the following advisors for their advice throughout the year.

Wilhelm Meister's Travels
Johann Wolfgang von Goethe

The following entry provides criticism of Goethe's novel *Wilhelm Meisters Wanderjahre oder Die Entsagenden* (1821, revised 1829; *Wilhelm Meister's Travels; or, The Renunciants*). For additional information about Goethe, see *NCLC,* Volume 4; for additional information about the novel *Die Leiden des jungen Werthers* (*The Sorrows of Young Werther*), see *NCLC,* Volumes 22 and 247; for additional information about the play *Faust,* see *NCLC,* Volumes 34 and 154; for additional information about the novel *Wilhelm Meisters Lehrjahre* (*Wilhelm Meister's Apprenticeship*), see *NCLC,* Volume 90; for additional information about the novel *Die Wahlverwandtschaften* (*Elective Affinities*), see *NCLC,* Volume 266.

INTRODUCTION

Wilhelm Meister's Travels is Goethe's final novel. Chapters of this formally experimental work were initially published in 1810. The first full edition appeared in 1821 and a heavily revised second version was included in Goethe's collected writings in 1829. More than any of the author's other major works—save for, perhaps, his tragedy *Faust—Wilhelm Meister's Travels* rejects the ideals of Classical unity that characterize Goethe's earlier writing, installing in their place a sprawling, digressive collection of aphorisms, poems, and novellas that undercut any expectation of linearity and have drawn much critical attention to the presumedly chaotic structure of the novel. Regardless of critical opinion about the success or failure of the overall structure, it is generally agreed that several of the interpolated novellas, particularly "Der Mann von funfzig Jahren" ("The Man of Fifty Years"), rank among Goethe's most imaginative and powerful works.

Wilhelm Meister's Travels follows the action of the earlier *Wilhelm Meisters Lehrjahre* (1795-96; *Wilhelm Meister's Apprenticeship*), and Goethe's journals and letters indicate that he had planned to complete the *Wilhelm Meister* series with a volume on the protagonist's *Masterjahre* (Master Years). The titles of the novels draw upon a medieval European tradition, still alive in Goethe's time, of craftsmen beginning their study as apprentices (the *Lehrjahre*), then undertaking a journey over a period of three years before establishing their own practices as masters of their trade. *Wilhelm Meister's Travels* depicts the middle phase of this metaphorical progression, the self-imposed "wandering" of Wilhelm as he moves toward both greater self-knowledge and the adoption of a craft. In comparison to *Wilhelm Meister's Apprenticeship,* however, in which the

narrative is relatively straightforward and highly focused on Wilhelm, the basic story of *Wilhelm Meister's Travels* is often interrupted or suspended for many pages. The narrator frequently pauses with Wilhelm, looking over his shoulder at a literary work that appears within the novel's world, or steps out of the action of the story to address the reader directly. Partly for this reason, the book has provided fertile ground both for subsequent novelists, who have prized its risk-taking and all-inclusive form, and theorists of narrative, who have considered the work structurally ahead of its time.

PLOT AND MAJOR CHARACTERS

Book One begins with the title character writing to his betrothed, Natalie, explaining his vow not to rest more than three days under any one roof. With his son, Felix, as a constant traveling companion, Wilhelm sets out on his journey. The two eventually arrive at a castle, where they meet the young Hersilie, with whom Felix becomes infatuated. Hersilie, in turn, asks Wilhelm to visit her aunt Makarie and to find her cousin, Lenardo, who has promised to return to his family. Bound by his pledge to wander, Wilhelm agrees to both requests and learns that Lenardo is in anguish over the fate of Valerine, a woman he once loved. Although Wilhelm is able to inform Lenardo that Valerine is alive and well, Lenardo soon realizes that the woman he remembers is actually named Nachodine. Given that he must continue to travel anyway, Wilhelm proceeds to search for Nachodine as well. In Book Two the journeyman visits the Pedagogical Province, a semi-fantastic region where he absorbs the principles of a sound education based on current pedagogical theory, such as that expressed in the works of the Swiss educator Johann Heinrich Pestalozzi, as interpreted by Goethe. Wilhelm leaves Felix in the care of the tutors of the province and resumes his wandering. He next takes up the study of medicine, which, along with the exchange of letters with Hersilie, is the central activity of Book Three. Meanwhile, Felix has confessed his affections for Hersilie, drawing the gradually coalescing love triangle of the novel into sharp relief. Believing himself rejected by Hersilie, the young man rides off on horseback, falls, and almost drowns in a river, but Wilhelm, using his newly acquired expertise as a doctor, rescues and resuscitates him.

Interspersed with the narrative, which accounts for about half of the novel, are seven novellas (which often speak to the themes of the larger frame story), miscellaneous poems, and chapter-length collections of aphorisms ostensibly coined by the characters of the novel. The work progressively blurs the boundaries between the outer "frame story" of Wilhelm's wandering, the real world of Goethe's age, and the contents of stories referring to works by other writers. In Book Two, Wilhelm meets a painter who has read *Wilhelm Meister's Apprenticeship* and developed an obsession with a character from that text, the mysterious and tragic figure of Mignon. Even when the novellas are clearly fictional from Wilhelm's perspective, they often serve to mirror situations in the main plot of the novel. The most frequently discussed example of this technique is "Die pilgernde Törin" ("The Pilgrim Fool") which tells of a young noblewoman driven mad by the infidelity of her lover. She eventually finds her way to the estate of Herr von Revanne, and both the nobleman and his son soon fall in love with her, presenting a potentially dangerous dilemma. On its own, the novella is Goethe's updated version of a well-known French tale, but when it is provided as bedtime reading for Wilhelm by Hersilie—who, according to the narrator, translated the work herself—the story acquires clear overtones of irony and admonition.

MAJOR THEMES

As literary critics have frequently noted, *Wilhelm Meister's Travels* is in many ways a novel about the acts of writing and reading. Throughout the book Goethe used symbols in a way that calls attention to the constructed nature of his work. One of the most famous of these is the locked casket that Felix discovers early in the book, the key to which does not appear until considerably later. On one level Goethe made it clear that the casket represents the undeveloped relationship between Felix and Hersilie. But it does more than this: its presence throughout the novel serves as a symbol for symbols themselves and for the desire, evinced by both Wilhelm and Felix, to arrive at a conclusive meaning. Likewise, the "alphabet" of rocks collected by Wilhelm's geologist friend Jarno suggests both the arbitrariness and the potential folly of the meanings humans assign to natural (and, given that these are fictional rocks, textual) objects.

Goethe called further attention to the process of "compiling" the novel by assuming the role of an editor who happens upon a set of disparate documents—transcripts, letters, poems, and novellas—and has the task of making them into a unified whole. Finally, the publication history of the novel itself contributes to its being read as a commentary on the literary process, as Goethe's heavy revisions of the *Wilhelm Meister's Travels,* coupled with an insistence that it was still the same book, challenged contemporary notions of what constituted an original literary text and what could be considered a mere reprinting. Birgit Baldwin (1990) provided a thorough survey of the argument that *Wilhelm Meister's Travels* is a "novel about

reading novels," and Andrew Piper (2006) examined the ideals of contemporary print culture as revealed by Goethe's editorial practices.

CRITICAL RECEPTION

Since it was essentially rediscovered as an object of literary study in the 1950s, *Wilhelm Meister's Travels* has been the subject of diverse, lively, and largely inconclusive scholarly discussion. Critics have seen in the novel a blend of disillusionment and hope regarding both contemporary artistic and social circumstances and humanity as a whole. Goethe occasionally took the opportunity to satirize the perceived excesses of a younger generation of artists. As Gabrielle Bersier (1999; see Further Reading) noted, the opening episodes of the novel are essentially a literal application of the principles of the Nazarene painters, whose work Goethe found inappropriately nostalgic. He was more optimistic regarding the North American continent, whose immigrant peoples he saw as comparatively free of the burden of history. In *Wilhelm Meister's Travels,* he drew upon multiple accounts of life on the American frontier. Nicholas Saul (2002) detailed Goethe's response to the sometimes-sensational novels of James Fenimore Cooper. Goethe was evidently fascinated by the utopian communities of religious immigrants who in his day were traveling to America; his revision of 1829, according to Karl J. R. Arndt (1958), incorporates emerging accounts of the originally German Harmony Society, whose members had settled in Pennsylvania and Indiana.

Though not widely read until the latter half of the twentieth century, Goethe's final novel exerted a considerable influence on the work of later authors both in Germany and abroad. Comparatists have eagerly sought out the many traces of the *Wilhelm Meister's Travels* (and of the *Wilhelm Meister* series as a whole) in other nineteenth-century works. Richard A. Zipser (1974; see Further Reading) observed that the fragile, romantic Mignon informs an array of similar figures in the English writing of the Romantic and Victorian eras, with her progeny especially numerous in the works of Edward Bulwer-Lytton. According to Stephen Prickett (1990; see Further Reading), Goethe's transposition of the concerns of character development beyond the "limitations of conventional realism" may also have served as an antecedent for George MacDonald's 1858 fantasy novel *Phantastes.*

More than any individual episode within its pages, however, the overall form of the novel has attracted critics' attention. Numerous theories and formulations have been developed to account for Goethe's purpose in assembling such an open-ended work. A vocal minority of readers has argued that the novel is the result of slapdash composition, with the poems, novellas, and maxims included simply to fill out the volume. Marlis Mehra (1983; see Further Reading), however, suggested that this attitude is tied to the

Classical aesthetic that characterizes Goethe's earlier work and that Goethe had rejected this outlook by the time he composed the novel. Frederick Amrine (1982) similarly remarked that, in terms of the romance genre, the "polyphonic" or "interlaced" quality of the novel is a virtue, aiming as it does at the expression of "unity-in-diversity." Alexander Gelley (1984) maintained that the sheer variety of the text makes a search for "what the story is about" potentially frustrating and futile but that the interrelationships of the various side stories, the "how" and "why" of their arrangement and inclusion, are fertile ground for critical inquiry. Addressing the status of truth in a novel of so many layers, William Larrett (1987) theorized that a useful epistemological maxim can be found elsewhere in Goethe's poetry, where he declared that "nature has neither core nor shell." Read in this way, the novel, like nature, becomes—despite its superficial fragmentation—a seamless entity that can be understood only gradually and incompletely. For Steve Dowden (1994), this implicit emphasis on the reader's responsibility to strive for understanding has an ethical overtone, with Goethe's novel presenting irony and multiplicity as testing grounds for the reader's own attitudes.

Scholars have also discussed the political implications of Goethe's choice of form. Ehrhard Bahr (1991) suggested that the "archival novel," departing so markedly from the more conventional plot of the *Wilhelm Meister's Apprenticeship,* was one way in which Goethe addressed the rapid social change he witnessed in European society toward the end of his life. Laura Martin (1993; see Further Reading), on the other hand, argued that portions of the novel anticipate a feminist critique. Focusing on "The Pilgrim Fool," she contended that the incorporation of a strong, unrestrained, and even vindictive female voice serves as a confession of the "mistakes and inequities of the patriarchy," even as Goethe elsewhere continued to give preference to the deeds and thoughts of men. Robin A. Clouser (2007) further associated the "wise fool" of this novella with a tradition in medieval and Renaissance literature of voicing important truths through supposedly mad characters. The truth, in this case, is a complicated one, but it reflects very unfavorably on a society that makes excuses for male infidelity and possessiveness.

In light of these concerns, virtually every distinguishing feature of the novel has been scrutinized as a potential interpretive hint. For Goethe's literary biographers, even the "To Be Continued" at the book's end offers multiple potential avenues of meaning. There is evidence in Goethe's private writings that he fully intended to write a third novel, but many have instead seen the phrase as a bit of bleak humor on the part of the octogenarian author, who had taken nearly two decades to set down the finalized *Wilhelm Meister's Travels.*

Michael J. Hartwell

PRINCIPAL WORKS

Neue Lieder in Melodien gesetzt [*Songs with Melodies*]. Leipzig: Breitkopf, 1770. (Poetry)

Brief des Pastors zu *** an den neuen Pastor zu ***: Aus dem Französischen [*Letter from the Pastor of *** to the New Pastor of ****]. Frankfurt am Main: n.p., 1773. (Theology)

Götz von Berlichingen mit der eisernen Hand [*Goetz of Berlichingen with the Iron Hand*]. Darmstadt: n.p., 1773. (Play)

Von deutscher Baukunst [*On German Architecture*]. Frankfurt am Main: n.p., 1773. (Essay)

Clavigo. Leipzig: Weygand, 1774. (Play)

Die Leiden des jungen Werthers [*The Sorrows of Young Werther*]. Leipzig: Weygand, 1774. (Novel)

Claudine von Villa Bella [*Claudine of Villa Bella*]. Berlin: Mylius, 1776. (Play)

Stella. Berlin: Mylius, 1776. (Play)

Proserpina. N.p.: n.p., 1778. (Play)

Die Geschwister [*The Sister*]. Leipzig: Göschen, 1787. (Play)

Iphigenie auf Tauris [*Iphigenia in Tauris*]. Leipzig: Göschen, 1787. (Play)

Der Triumph der Empfindsamkeit [*The Triumph of Sensibility*]. Leipzig: Göschen, 1787. (Play)

Goethes Schriften [*Goethe's Writings*]. 8 vols. Leipzig: Göschen, 1787-90. (Plays and poetry)

Egmont. Leipzig: Göschen, 1788. (Play)

Faust: Ein Fragment [*Faust: A Fragment*]. Leipzig: Göschen, 1790. (Play)

Torquato Tasso. Leipzig: Göschen, 1790. (Play)

Versuch die Metamorphose der Pflanzen zu erklären [*Goethe's Botany: The Metamorphosis of Plants*]. Gotha: Ettinger, 1790. (Essay)

Beiträge zur Optik [*Contribution towards Optics*]. 2 vols. Weimar: Industrie-Comptoir, 1791-92. (Essay)

Der Groß-Cophta [*The Grand Kofta*]. Berlin: Ungar, 1792. (Play)

Der Bürgergeneral [*The Citizen-General*]. Berlin: Ungar, 1793. (Play)

Reineke Fuchs [*Reynard the Fox*]. Berlin: Ungar, 1794. (Poetry)

Wilhelm Meisters Lehrjahre [*Wilhelm Meister's Apprenticeship*]. 4 vols. Berlin: Ungar, 1795-96. (Novel)

Venetianische Epigramme [*Venetian Epigrams*]. Berlin: Ungar, 1796. (Poetry)

Xenien [*Goethe's and Schiller's Xenions*]. With Friedrich von Schiller. Weimar: n.p., 1797. (Poetry)

Hermann und Dorothea [*Herman and Dorothea*]. Berlin: Vieweg, 1798. (Poetry)

Die natürliche Tochter [*The Natural Daughter*]. Tübingen: Cotta, 1804. (Play)

Winckelmann und sein Jahrhundert [*Winckelmann and His Century*]. Ed. Johann Wolfgang von Goethe. Tübingen: Cotta, 1805. (Biography)

Faust. Tübingen: Cotta, 1808. (Play)

Die Wahlverwandtschaften [*Elective Affinities*]. 2 vols. Tübingen: Cotta, 1809. (Novel)

Pandora. Vienna: Geistinger, 1810. (Unfinished play)

Zur Farbenlehre [*Theory of Colors*]. 2 vols. Tübingen: Cotta, 1810. (Essay)

Aus meinen Leben: Dichtung und Wahrheit [*The Autobiography of Goethe: Truth and Poetry from My Own Life*]. 2 vols. Stuttgart: Cotta, 1811-13. (Autobiography)

Des Epimenides Erwachen [*The Awakening of Epimenides*]. Berlin: Duncker, 1815. (Play)

Sonnette [*Sonnets*]. Stuttgart: Cotta, 1815. (Poetry)

Italienische Reise [*Travels in Italy*]. 2 vols. Stuttgart: Cotta, 1816-17. (Travel essay)

Über Kunst und Altertum [*Art and Antiquity*]. Ed. Goethe. 6 vols. Stuttgart: Cotta, 1816-32. (Criticism)

Zur Morphologie [*On Morphology*]. Ed. Goethe. 2 vols. Stuttgart: Cotta, 1817-23. (Essay)

West-östlicher Divan [*West-Eastern Divan*]. Stuttgart: Cotta, 1819. (Poetry)

Wilhelm Meisters Wanderjahre oder Die Entsagenden [*Wilhelm Meister's Travels; or, The Renunciants*]. Stuttgart: Cotta, 1821. (Novel)

Die Campagne in Frankreich 1792 [*Campaign in France in the Year 1792*]. Stuttgart: Cotta, 1822. (History)

Trilogie der Leidenschaft [*Trilogy of Passion*]. Stuttgart: Cotta, 1827. (Poetry)

*Werke: Vollständige Ausgabe letzter Hand. 60 vols. Vols. 41-60. Ed. Johann Peter Eckermann and Friedrich Wilhelm Riemer. Stuttgart: Cotta, 1827-42. (Poetry, plays, essays, novels, novellas, short stories, criticism, history, biography, autobiography, letters, and librettos)

Briefwechsel zwischen Schiller und Goethe [*Correspondence between Goethe and Schiller, 1794-1805*]. Stuttgart: Cotta, 1828. (Letters)

Novelle [*Novella*]. Stuttgart: Cotta, 1828. (Novella)

Faust II [*Goethe's Faust: Part II*]. Stuttgart: Cotta, 1832. (Play)

Gespräche mit Goethe in den letzien Jahren seines Lebens: 1823-1832 [*Conversations with Goethe in the Last Years of His Life*]. With Eckermann. 3 vols. Leipzig: Brockhaus, 1836-48. (Conversations)

Goethe's sämmtliche Werke [*Goethe's Collected Works*]. 40 vols. Stuttgart: Cotta, 1853-58. (Poetry, plays, essays, novels, novellas, short stories, criticism, history, biography, autobiography, letters, and librettos)

Goethe's Faust in ursprünglicher Gestalt nach der Göchhausenschen Abschrift herausgegeben [*Goethe's Urfaust*]. Weimar: Bühlau, 1888. (Play)

Wilhelm Meisters theatralische Sendung [*Wilhelm Meister's Theatrical Mission*]. Zürich: Rascher, 1910. (Unfinished novel)

Werke [*Goethe's Work*]. Ed. Erich Trunz. 14 vols. Hamburg: Wegner, 1952-60. (Poetry, plays, novels, novellas, short stories, autobiography, biography, criticism, essays, and history)

Principal English Translations

Wilhelm Meister's Travels; or, The Renunciants. Trans. Thomas Carlyle. Edinburgh: Tait, 1827. Print. Trans. of *Wilhelm Meisters Wanderjahre oder Die Entsagenden.*

†*Goethe's Collected Works.* Ed. Victor Lange, Eric Blackall, and Cyrus Hamlin. 12 vols. New York: Suhrkamp/ Insel, 1983-89. Print.

*This work includes: *Novelle* [*Novella*]. Vol. 15. 1828; *Wilhelm Meisters Wanderjahre oder Die Entsagenden* [*Wilhelm Meister's Travels; or, The Renunciants*]. Rev. and expanded ed. Vols. 21-3. 1829; *Faust: Eine Tragödie. Zweyter Theil in fünf Akten* [*Faust: A Tragedy. Second Part in Five Acts*]. Vol. 41. 1832; and *Aus meinem Leben: Dichtung und Wahrheit. Vierter Theil* [*The Autobiography of Goethe: Truth and Poetry from My Own Life*]. Vol. 48. 1833.

†Comprises: *Selected Poems.* Trans. and ed. Christopher Middleton, Michael Hamburger, David Luke, J. F. Nims, and V. Watkins. Vol. 1. 1983; *Faust I and II.* Trans. and ed. Stuart Atkins. Vol. 2. 1984; *Essays on Art and Literature.* Trans. E. von Nardhoff and E. H. von Nardhoff. Ed. John Gearey. Vol. 3. 1986; *From My Life: Poetry and Truth; Campaign in France 1792; Siege of Mainz.* Trans. Thomas Saine and R. Heitner. Ed. Saine and Jeffrey Sammons. Vols. 4 and 5. 1987; *Italian Journey.* Trans. Heitner. Ed. Saine and Sammons. Vol. 6. 1989; *Early Verse Drama and Prose.* Trans. R. M. Browning, Hamburger, Cyrus Hamlin, and F. Ryder. Ed. Hamlin and Ryder. Vol. 7. 1989; *Verse Plays and Epic.* Trans. Hamburger, Luke, and

H. Hannum. Ed. Hamlin and Ryder. Vol. 8. 1987; *Wilhelm Meister's Apprenticeship*. Trans. Eric Blackall and Victor Lange. Ed. Lange. Vol. 9. 1989; *Wilhelm Meister's Journeyman Years*. Trans. Krishna Winston, J. van Heurck, and Jane K. Brown. Ed. Brown. Vol. 10. 1989; *The Sorrows of Young Werther; Elective Affinities; Novella*. Trans. Lange and J. Ryan. Ed. D. Wellbery. Vol. 11. 1988; and *Scientific Studies*. Trans. and ed. D. Miller. Vol. 12. 1988.

CRITICISM

George C. Buck (essay date 1956)

SOURCE: Buck, George C. "The Pattern of the Stowaway in Goethe's Works." *PMLA* 71.3 (1956): 451-64. Print.

[*In the following essay, Buck examines Goethe's tendency to incorporate enigmatic elements in his works, focusing on* The Sorrows of Young Werther *and the* Wilhelm Meister *volumes. With regard to* Wilhelm Meister's Travels, *Buck claims that in an attempt to stretch the manuscript, Goethe added a set of aphorisms and a recently composed poem—stowaway material—that were not placed where he initially intended, and that subsequent editors and critics, attempting to rationalize the added text, raised for themselves a problem that "is probably insoluble" because it was created by an afterthought on Goethe's part.*]

The purpose of this paper is to analyze one particular aspect of Goethe's creative process which manifests itself throughout his artistic career, a strange and as yet unexplained motivation which prompted him at times to incorporate in his works enigmatic elements which puzzled his contemporaries and continue to confound scholars. Toward the end of *Werther* [*Die Leiden des jungen Werthers*], for example, we find several pages of a translation from *Ossian*. The sixth book of *Wilhelm Meisters Lehrjahre* is purportedly a manuscript entrusted to a doctor by a mysterious aunt and which bears a title of its own: **"Die Bekenntnisse einer schönen Seele."** Obviously this chapter made a singular impression on the public at that time, because in 1806 an otherwise unknown author by the name of Friedrich Buchholz wrote a novel with this same title and it was reviewed by Goethe.[1] Goethe's chapter has even been issued in a separate edition by the theologian Hermann Dechent.[2] Not many novels contain chapters which can exist independent of their matrix.

Two more examples may be found in *Faust I.* "Oberon und Titanias goldene Hochzeit" has excited little professional interest because it so obviously violates the usual standards of artistic integration. A few years ago Oskar Seidlin challenged the right of the "Vorspiel auf dem Theater," genetically, to a place at the beginning of Goethe's greatest work with the claim that it was written for Goethe's *Zauberflöte Zweiter Theil*,[3] although his

arguments have subsequently been weakened somewhat by Momme Mommsen.[4]

Appended to several chapters of *Die Wahlverwandtschaften* there is a diary, kept by Ottilie. This is perhaps not quite as unusual as the previous examples, but it does contain a number of elements which do not harmonize with Ottilie's nature.[5] In the second chapter of *Dichtung und Wahrheit* [*Aus meinen Leben: Dichtung und Wahrheit*] (pub. 1811), we find a complete short story, **"Der neue Paris."** The last volume, containing Books XVI-XX, is filled with odds and ends, taken from Lavater, Ulrich von Hutten, et al.

In the 1820's these odd-shaped chips from the master's lathe are scattered about at random in the *Wanderjahre* [*Wilhelm Meisters Wanderjahre*], the *Ausgabe letzter Hand* [*Werke: Vollständige Ausgabe letzter Hand*], and in his journal *Über Kunst und Altertum* (1816-32). Although most of these features are known to a certain extent, up to now no one has attempted to examine them and to relate them to the pattern of Goethe's creative methods. We feel that a thorough grasp of this situation would aid toward a better understanding of Goethe, the artist and the man. Furthermore, it would furnish a concrete basis for practical decisions which must be made in the editing of Goethe's works. At least three major Goethe editions are now being edited: the *Gedenkausgabe* [*Gedenkausgabe der Werke, Briefe und Gesprache*], by Ernst Beutler; the *Hamburger Ausgabe* [*Goethes Werke*], by Erich Trunz; and the *Mainzer-Goethe-Welt-Ausgabe* [*Werke*], by a number of scholars, including Kippenberg and Petersen.[6]

In accordance with a suggestion by Carl F. Schreiber I have chosen to call these incongruous elements "stowaways." A stowaway by definition is a fairly lengthy piece, written for its own sake, or for no particular purpose, and embodied within the framework of a larger work. In spite of their numbers and their frequency of occurrence, no two of these renegades can be regarded as equals although they all have some common elements and vary only in degree. It cannot be claimed, for example, that there is progressive degeneration in the technique employed (or lack of technique) but the general tendency is clearly toward a greater degree of freedom, or license, on the part of the author.

Within the scope of this paper only two extreme cases can be discussed: *Werther* and the *Wanderjahre.*

We can date Goethe's first interest in *Ossian* from a letter to Friederike Oeser in 1769.[7] Two years later he dedicated his translation of the "Songs of Selma" to Friederike Brion. The report of Jerusalem's death, which might be called the catalyst or even the bare nucleus of *Werther,* did not reach Goethe until November 1772—one year after the conclusion of the *Ossian* translation. It is quite clear that the two have nothing in common genetically. Yet two years later the "Songs of Selma" appear as an integral part of

Werther. It is just this sort of occurrence that enlivens our curiosity. We want to know whether the versions of his translations are identical, why Goethe put the first one where it is, what function it serves, and a host of other answers.

When we look into the translation question we discover that there are three versions: the manuscript sent to Friederike Brion, reprinted in Max Morris, *Der junge Goethe*; the *Werther* version of 1774; and a third variation in the second edition of *Werther* in 1787. Rudolf Horstmeyer has made a close comparison of the three versions which shows conclusively that the third version contains only relatively few stylistic variations over the second and in many cases they are "Verschlimmbesserungen"; the second, in turn, is widely removed in its polished excellence from the literal, often crude, version sent to Friederike.[8] In addition to the "Songs" there are a few sentences lifted out of the first paragraph of "Das Lied von Berrathon" (Book VII of *Ossian*). J. H. Merck and Goethe edited and published the first complete edition of *Ossian* in the original on the continent, a four-volume work which appeared between 1773-77. Goethe even made two etchings for the frontispieces. It is clear that he inserted every bit of the *Ossian* that he had in his files into *Werther* so that it wouldn't go to waste. In order to make it fit better, he added a few more lines from "Berrathon" which were probably still echoing in his ears. Without an intimate knowledge of *Ossian* it is quite impossible, on the basis of these fragments, to imagine the original situation in MacPherson's epic, but that is hardly their purpose. There is an obvious use to which these passages have been put by Goethe. Not only do their stormy, romantic lines contrast sharply with the quiet classicism of Homer and thus support the irrational relationship obtaining between Lotte and Werther, but they also bear within them the foreshadowings of things to come. When Lotte hears the lines: "Oft im sinkenden Monde sehe ich die Geister meiner Kinder, halb dämmernd wandeln sie zusammen in trauriger Eintracht,"[9] she bursts into tears. One might say that these are the shadowy shapes of children she will never bear. Werther doesn't exist for her in a practical sense—he is the idealized foil to her solid, practical husband, whose reality she would never relinquish in order to fulfill her unrealistic dreams. The final lines from "Berrathon" underscore the deeply tragic element in this relationship: "Aber die Zeit meines Welkens ist nahe, nahe der Sturm, der meine Blätter herabstört! Morgen wird der Wanderer kommen, kommen der mich sah in meiner Schönheit, ringsum wird sein Auge im Felde mich suchen, und wird mich nicht finden."[10] Both Lotte and Werther are completely shaken by the portent which they dimly sense in these lines. Artistically, Werther's suicide forms the anticlimax to these lines. From this time on Werther is dead—in a sense his physical suicide merely satisfies convention. The young Goethe apparently used all his craft to work this magnificent passage into the fabric of the novel. The basic extraneousness of the material has lost all its strangeness in these surroundings.

For the second example I have chosen the most vivid contrast imaginable and this too must be considered in the light of its origins. By a longer demonstration than is warranted here, it can be shown that Goethe overextended himself in promising the publisher Cotta enough material for forty volumes of his *Ausgabe letzter Hand.* A glance at the publication history will show that from 1786 on, a collected edition of Goethe's works appeared roughly every ten years, starting with Göschen and followed by Unger. (The "*Unger-Fraktur*" made its first appearance in this series.) The first edition of 1806 began the long and fruitful association of Goethe with the then Prince of Publishers, Cotta. The second Cotta edition of twenty volumes appeared from 1816-20 and was immediately pirated in Austria. Even before his contract ran out in 1823 Goethe began laying the groundwork for a new contract and suggesting the possibility of a new edition. This time, however, with some slight help from his son August, Goethe managed to secure for himself and family a copyright protection in Germany, Austria, and Switzerland. The Dutch negotiations were not immediately successful. Not only did this make the possession of an exclusive contract with Goethe a much more worthwhile proposition but obviously it had lasting international implications: the status of the writer was considerably elevated from this time on. The principle at stake was the valuation of, and exclusive rights to, intellectual property, as opposed to real property.

In order to capitalize on this enterprise to the full, Goethe had to make a new edition desirable. The numerous earlier editions led to extensive duplication within the collected editions and together with the pirated versions they flooded the potential markets. We must also remember that with the exception of *Werther, Hermann und Dorothea* or *Reinecke Fuchs,* it was rare that a work from the master's pen managed to capture the fickle public fancy. From a practical point of view we may say that those who admired Goethe probably owned his works already, since they belonged to an elite class, but five or even ten more smallish volumes would not constitute a sufficient inducement to subscribe. He had to promise new material in quantity. But where was it to come from? Goethe was seventy-five years old when he launched upon this venture. Reliable estimates of that day calculated that thirty-five volumes of creative material would be the very maximum he could hope for. In defiance of these opinions Goethe promised forty volumes and he had almost insurmountable difficulties in producing that amount. The first installment of the *Ausgabe letzter Hand* (Vols. I-V) offered a few new poems, some **"Zahme Xenien,"** and the "*Helena-act*" from *Faust* [*Faust II*]. The second installment (VI-X) was all old material. At that point complaints were heard and Goethe felt the danger that was threatening to reduce the subscription lists, which would mean curtailment of a provision for his immediate family. The *Ausgabe letzter Hand* was Goethe's only capital asset. To assuage criticism Goethe added to Vol. XII, which was to contain *Faust I,* about two thirds of **Part II** [*Faust II*], Act I. The text ends in the midst of nowhere and is temporarily sealed off with the admonition "Ist fortzusetzen." The installment (Vols. XI-XV) was concluded with the recently finished **"Novelle."** But the fourth installment (XVI-XX) was again made up of well-known items. The *Lehrjahre* [*Wilhelm Meisters Lehrjahre*], first published in 1795-96, spread over three volumes.

The criticisms which had momentarily been checked now burst forth with renewed vigor. This time Goethe felt he had a sound reply. He had quite thoroughly revised the *Wanderjahre,* which had first appeared in 1821, and was convinced it would produce three volumes instead of the announced two. While these were being printed, Goethe set Eckermann to the task of combing his files for aphorisms which would fit somewhere in the installment under the title **"Betrachtungen im Sinne der Wanderer."** The completed collection was topped off with a poem of recent vintage entitled **"Vermächtnis"** and sent off as an addition to Vol. XXII, which he vaguely felt was shorter than the other volumes. When the proof sheets arrived at the end of February, the old man must have been jolted out of his premature composure, for he soon discovered he had overestimated his MS by a wide margin, due to the lapidary scrawl of his amanuensis, John. For the next ten days Goethe and Eckermann were madly engaged in untying and tying up bundles of manuscript in search of material which was so badly needed to fatten the undernourished Vol. XXI. Between them they managed to fashion a hasty arrangement of aphorisms called **"Aus Makariens Archiv,"** which was made to simulate the earlier collection by adding an unpublished poem, called variously **"Im ernsten Beinhaus," "Schillers Schädel,"** or **"Schillers Reliquien."** The heterogeneous assortment was then bundled off to the printer Frommann for Vol. XXI, but the printer informed him that the press had already run off Vol. XXI. At the same time he asked whether Vol. XXIII wouldn't be a satisfactory repository. Goethe's true feelings toward this obvious padding are revealed in his ready acquiescence.[11] If he had felt that it was really an integral part of Vol. XXI, he surely would have insisted on a special arrangement with the press.

Now this sounds simple and clear, as if there could be only one interpretation, but such is not the case. This whole issue has been confounded by some of the most ingenious arguments conceivable. Eckermann, in what seems an honest attempt to report the situation, has lumped together the events of two and one-half months into fourteen days (*Gespräche* [*Gespräche mit Goethe in den letzien Jahren seines Lebens: 1823-1832*], 15 May 1831). He claims that both collections (**"Die Betrachtungen im Sinne der Wanderer"** = **"BSW"** and **"Aus Makariens Archiv"** = **"AMA"**) were assembled at the same time for the same purpose, namely to pad out the skinny volumes, and that each was capped off by the addition of a poem recently composed. But this statement has by no means been accepted as gospel. A counter direction which at least in print is the prevailing one today was initiated by Max Wundt.[12] The same direction essentially has been taken by Gerhardt Küntzel, Wilhelm Flitner, Paul Stöcklein, Erich Trunz, and some of the latter's students: namely, that the aphoristic collections must be regarded as an integral part of the *Wanderjahre.*

For the American scholar, however, the problem reached its most dramatic climax in the pages of this journal, when in the mid-1940's Professors Viëtor, Mautner, Feise, and Hohlfeld engaged in a stimulating round-robin, hinging ultimately on the meaning of Goethe's cryptic admonition, "Ist fortzusetzen," which appears at the end of Vol. XXIII of the *AlH* [*Werke: Vollständige Ausgabe letzter Hand*], (p. 286), immediately following the poem, **"Schillers Schädel,"** and printed in the same Roman type in contrast to the main body of the work which is of course printed in Gothic type.[13] In all subsequent editions of the *Wanderjahre* up to but not including that by Erich Trunz (*Hamburger Ausgabe,* Vol. VIII) this whole complex of aphorisms and poems along with the admonition has been removed from the context of the novel. The decision is presumably based on an oral report from Goethe to Eckermann and was first put into effect with the quarto edition of 1836 f. edited by Goethe's close friends (von Müller and Riemer).

The question on which the German investigations center is basically whether the later editors were justified in accepting the pattern established in the quarto edition. The Americans, on the other hand, are concerned with the meaning of "Ist fortzusetzen," which occurs twice in all of Goethe's works.[14] Feise and Mautner agree that it refers to a continuation of **"Schillers Schädel,"** which for different reasons they feel has not achieved the consummate perfection expected of a Goethe poem. Hohlfeld, on the basis of a remark ascribed to Chancellor von Müller, argues for a continuation of the novel. Viëtor takes the position that the poem is perfect but that there is the promise of an unfulfilled lyric cycle in it.[15] Heinrich Henel, in his review of A. R. Hohlfeld's book (*Fifty Years with Goethe,* Madison, 1954), has recently given us a succinct résumé of the question and has expressed the opinion that the problem is probably insoluble.[16] In the sense that the solution cannot be proved with mathematical accuracy, I am in full accord with Henel's views, but I do think we can gain a clearer insight into the problem. Elsewhere I have developed my views on this subject at great length, but here it is sufficient to say that any explanation of "Ist fortzusetzen" must accommodate itself to both occurrences of the phrase, since they would hardly be unique. In order to introduce some new material which has a bearing on this problem and which has led me to my present position, I should like to sketch briefly the historical development of this phase of the problem.

Max Wundt asserted that even as a "Primaner" he felt the aphorisms were an integral part of the *Wanderjahre* and he accordingly set out to disprove Eckermann's statement.[17] In 1923-25 Julius Petersen succeeded in casting doubt on some of Eckermann's dates (*Die Entstehung der Eckermannschen Gespräche und ihre Glaubwürdigkeit*). However, his acid-tongued colleague, the polemically minded H. H. Houben, rose magnificently to Eckermann's rescue in a two-volume work (1925-28) in which he disputed practically all of Petersen's figures and unearthed a great deal more evidence for Eckermann's unusual talents.[18] Wundt, however, out of an inordinate dislike for Eckermann, insisted that his story is all a fabrication. Early in the *Wanderjahre* the narrator does say he may be disposed at some time to print some of these sayings elsewhere ("Die Papiere, die uns vorliegen, gedenken wir an einem andern Orte abdrucken zu lassen," Book I, Ch. X). Letters of Goethe and other pronouncements indicate that he at one time was planning an archive for the novel although I believe he was forced by pressure of activities to give up the idea.[19] By paraphrasing each aphorism Wundt tries to invest the aphorisms with a greater significance than is warranted and to represent them as reflecting Goethe's broad interests (pp. 457 ff.).

This line of argument overlooks certain basic factors. Goethe was an old man when he contracted to edit his life's works, a man who was already burdened with far more responsibilities than he could handle. In addition he had made the mistake of overestimating what he could accomplish. His diaries for 29 December 1828 to March 1829 give us a clear and unmistakable picture of what must have transpired. Goethe first handed Eckermann a large batch of aphoristic material and asked him to arrange the better ones for the *Wanderjahre*. Short conferences were held almost daily on this material until 21 February 1829, when the "Einzelnheiten" were sent off for Vol. XXII; thus the fifth installment (XXI-XXV) was completed. From then until 2 March 1829 there is a complete silence in the diaries on the aphorisms. Goethe has turned to the *Farbenlehre* and to his other interests. On 2 March however, we read the entry: "Mittags Dr. Eckermann. Wir deliberirten über einen zu besorgenden Nachtrag." No one has ever asked what this means. Why did he feel an addition was necessary? After a great deal of searching I came upon the innocent little entry: "Aushängebogen von Augsburg" (27 February 1829). In order to appreciate this properly, one must be fully aware of the actual collation of the *Ausgabe letzter Hand*. (In the duodecimo format of the "Taschenausgabe" even a full volume would look puny.) The contract with Cotta called for twenty-two signatures per volume and Vol. XXI had only 14.2 sig. When Goethe began to examine these proofsheets, probably shortly after 27 February, he was unpleasantly startled to discover that his meager, skimpy volume was well below the average stipulated length. Furthermore he must have been aware that the volumes XXII and XXIII had suffered in like manner,

since they were all copied in the same large hand: they do in fact contain 13.1 and 14.8 sigs. respectively. He had to work fast if he was to avoid another outburst of bitter criticism from disappointed subscribers and a reflection thereof at the sales counter. For the next two weeks Goethe and Eckermann conferred daily until they managed to scrape together just enough maxims to match the first collection *exactly,* plus a poem which was not "gerade vollendet," as Eckermann claimed, but which had probably been written in 1826 though suppressed while Karl August was still alive.[20] Archives as a general rule are not symmetrical! It is certainly no accident that these two collections are identical in length and in construction. "Makariens Archiv" was sent as an addition to Vol. XXI but, since it was sent in too late, Reichel had it put at the end of XXIII, which is as far away from the discussion of "Makariens Archiv" in the novel as is physically possible. That in itself is a devastating blow to the school of critics who like to claim an unusual degree of integration for this bit of padding.

The purpose here is merely to prove beyond any doubt that "Makariens Archiv" is an afterthought, and that in fact it owes its very existence to an act of chance. My own feeling on the subject, without becoming involved in the esthetic problem, is that if the novel could just as well have appeared without the collection as with it, then it cannot have been very tightly "integrated" in the common acceptation of this term. The facts of the diaries and letters have been open for all to read for a long time. It may be that they are misleading or do not admit of one clear interpretation, but there is still another way to verify and validate this picture. That is by a study of the two collections themselves.

In the back of his edition Max Hecker has listed all the known information on the dating of each Goethe maxim. If we compare the dates of each collection carefully, we discover that the latter collection, "AMA," has dipped down more deeply into the files than the former. It contains several maxims which at one time had been considered for the *Lehrjahre* but had then been discarded (p. 351). Furthermore the distribution of the dates throughout the two groups yields two distinctly different patterns. The older group shows an even spacing throughout, indicating a slower, more painstaking selection. "Makariens Archiv," on the other hand, betrays the haste of its origin in the piling up of dates. The maxims come in large clusters from the early period (ca. 1796) and from the very late period (ca. 1828).

Another feature of the latter collection which affects the artistic quality to some extent, and which should also be considered in our picture of haste, may be found in the direct quotations. All of the direct quotations, lifted from other sources and merely translated or in some cases printed in the original language, are in the latter collection, which surely indicates that they have not gone through the usual digestive process that gives a Goethean aphorism an individual stamp. But the most convincing feature of this proof is to be found in Goethe's own psychological attitude, which slowly becomes clear in analyzing the stowaway problem. Let us see how that is revealed in a specific case.

In 1826 Goethe was interested enough in Laurence Sterne to write a short essay about him for his own journal. In March 1828, just one year before **"Makariens Archiv"** was assembled, he had been reading a book called the *Koran* by Richard Griffiths but falsely attributed to Sterne. A number of maxims are quoted directly from this book.[21] In January of 1826 he had been reading Sterne's letters, from which he had also excerpted several maxims. We already know that he kept his files chronologically, and so if Eckermann were to start at the "open" end and work backward toward the older material, he would take out the *Koran* maxims first, and then the Sterne maxims. Now it so happens that this is exactly the way they are arranged in the *AlH.* Furthermore, it was not Eckermann who thought of the Sterne maxims, but Goethe himself. On 6 March 1829, as this wise but weary old man was getting desperate for material, he must have racked his brains for something to assist the methodical and not very resourceful Eckermann. Suddenly he remembered his recent Sterne readings which Eckermann must have rejected while making the first collection, for on that day we find the entry: "Einiges über Sterne." Later on the same day after the secretary had copied these off, Goethe handed the manuscript to Eckermann, which the latter took just as it was. If we inspect the arrangement of these maxims, we can readily see that they are in the worst possible order. The maxims lead us helter-skelter through the *Koran* and into Sterne's odd thoughts, but not until very late (#773) do we finally come upon his dates and some facts about his life which obviously should have been the starting point.

There are many scholars who claim that there is a highly artistic arrangement in these aphorisms. To my knowledge no one has pointed to the lack of order in these odds and ends. Even Max Hecker, who has come the closest to this problem, admits his helplessness when he tries to define what principle holds them together, although he speaks of a "carefully devised plan" (p. xxviii). There are no convincing demonstrations of the careful articulation of this formless lump. In fact, there is nothing beyond an outright statement that the arrangement is masterful.[22] As far as can be determined, there is no evidence to support this contention. Eckermann may have been wrong on a few of the details, but the spirit of his argument, that the maxims were collected as space fillers, has not been vitiated. Goethe wanted to be reimbursed for the effort he had spent in reading so many books. His energies were rarely wasted. He wanted to get into print all the material he could exhume from his vast and uncharted holdings without going to too much trouble. He took the most recent things

he had available, whenever possible. His embarrassment over this matter shows up in letters and conversations where he attempts to justify his actions. The aphorisms and poems constitute a stowaway in the fullest sense of the word.[23]

In a few short paragraphs I would like to bring these two lines of inquiry, i.e., **Werther** and **Wanderjahre,** together into a sort of pattern which is clear and distinguishable. The examples I have discussed are spaced more than fifty years apart. If we try to find what they have in common, we discover a relationship which might be compared with coal and the diamond. They are both composed of the same element but in the one case there is a more felicitous union. We may further consider that both products represent expended effort which would never have been repaid unless Goethe had hit upon this manner of use. A partial translation has little commercial value and another person's maxims have even less. In a certain sense both are originally the products of another's pen, though each, to a varying degree, has undergone a transformation at Goethe's hands.

Goethe was a relatively efficient human being. He rarely wrote letters or made requests of his superiors until he was sure they would bring results. However, it was not until relatively late in life that his efforts were nourished and ripened until they yielded a cash return. Even though his price for **Hermann und Dorothea** was considered exorbitant at the time, his reward was not nearly commensurate with that reaped by its various publishers. But as he grew older his somewhat difficult and improvident family made it imperative that he seek a proper return for the expenditure of his energy. In many people this would not be a basic motivating force because under pressure they could always shirk the responsibility, just as many Bohemian artists have done. Goethe, however, represents an extreme in the loyalties he showed his friends and family. I do not wish to overstress this extra-artistic consideration but in Goethe's case it cannot be ignored, especially toward the end of his life. But more important for us than this desire for financial stability in Goethe's motivation is the earnest and more wide-spread endeavor to rescue "these bits of self from the waters of Lethe," as he expresses it. Both of our examples exemplify this desire for self-preservation.

How do they differ? Regardless of one's standards, there is a quantitative difference in the amount of poetic craft required to produce the two results. We can compare the original maxims and Goethe's translations of them. In the case of *Ossian* we have Horstmeyer's comparison of all three translations, which leaves no doubt of the improvement. There is also a visible and measurable effort to integrate the *Ossian* into the **Werther** (e.g., "Berrathon"), whereas any such claim for the **Wanderjahre** maxims would be patently in contradiction to the facts. One decision was at least partially dictated by artistic necessity, while the other can only be regarded as the result of a physical expedient.

In retrospect, we can see that at least one clue to this engaging problem is to be found in seemingly extraneous biographical detail. Along one great wall in the Goethe-Schiller Archive are ranged row after row of cardboard filing cases which were added after the effects in the Goethe house became a national possession. Where Goethe kept the contents in his own house must remain a guess, but it is clear that he had a household retainer gather up all the incoming mail, say, from January through June, and then had the conglomerate mass stitched loosely or "spindled." An examination of the contents reveals that everything which came into the "Goethe-Haus am Frauenplan" in the form of letters, bills, circulars, and other printed material was included in these spindled bundles. It is most significant to note here that the very first one is dated January 1797.

If we inspect Goethe's early diaries, we perceive that they are riddled with gaps and often gather several months into one entry: that is, until 1797, when they are systematically kept with entries for nearly every day. There are of course supplementary sources for the earlier years such as *Dichtung und Wahrheit, Italienische Reise,* and *Campagne in Frankreich* [*Die Campagne in Frankreich 1792*], but even so there are many years which have not otherwise been treated. The *Annalen,* or as Goethe first called them, *Tag- und Jahreshefte als Ergänzung meiner sonstigen Bekenntnisse,* were an attempt to fill some of these gaps. They were first published in 1830; but again it is significant to note that when Goethe first began toying with the idea in 1820 he started with the years 1797-98.[24] Goethe's life and works are surely among the most thoroughly documented in history. There are probably many explanations for the developments we have discussed, but it may not be overstating the case to say that one of them lies in the fact that at about this time—that is, 1797—Goethe began to realize he was not only extremely talented (he had known that at least since 1774, when *Werther* appeared) but that he had achieved an elevation rarely vouchsafed to mortal man—in other words, he was a genius. It is this realization as much as anything else which shaped the course of his subsequent publications. From this time on Goethe regarded everything he wrote, said, or did as important in some way and worthy to be preserved for posterity. This feeling has left a visible precipitate in his works which we have chosen to call stowaways.

At the very outset of this paper are listed items which fit under the rubric: "strange cargo." If we subject each one of them to the same kind of analysis, it soon becomes clear that Goethe must have felt a powerful urgency about getting as much of his material as possible out of its state of suspended animation and into lasting printed form before he himself would no longer be able to take a personal part in the matter. As we probe each successive instance, we cannot avoid observing how this tendency grows progressively more obsessive as Goethe realizes more clearly the place he occupies in world letters until, at the end, especially in his journal, *Über Kunst und Altertum* (1816-32), he has shed all literary scruples in yielding the upper hand to this urge.

From a modern point of view, it seems as if the artist has surrendered more and more artistic integrity. Even if this were true, Goethe could be excused on purely human grounds. What more natural instinct than to protect one's loved ones? But we need not yield to mawkish sentiment. First of all, each of these aphoristic collections is clearly separated from the body of the novel, though the former (**"BSW"**) does interrupt the flow of the narrative by its very position between Vols. II and III (i.e., XXII and XXIII). We must also not forget that Goethe's generation had a much different conception of a novel's structure than is currently popular. As yet no one has found a clear formulation for Goethe's artistic theories,[25] but Robert Riemann (*Goethes Romantechnik,* Leipzig, 1902) has presented sufficient evidence to dispel the notion that Goethe's somewhat bold or whimsical procedure is entirely unique. The sovereign license exercised in the instance we have discussed is admittedly daring but in the looser standards of an older period by no means shocking or even disturbing.

Our delineation has been presented with an eye toward historical fact—to illustrate the impact of everyday necessity and the self-realization of historical importance on artistic considerations. Actually, the problem of artistic integration, as understood by our modern scholars, does not seem to have been a vital issue in Goethe's time. It certainly does not detract from his magnificent art, even if one may feel that the novel was weakened by the inclusion of the aphoristic material, and full accord may well be given to Eckermann's report that Goethe wanted it removed from any further edition to a more suitable location.

A recognition of the "stowaway-principle" leads to several important considerations. First of all, that the editors of today might well continue with the 120-year-old tradition, started by Riemer, Chancellor von Müller, and Eckermann in the quarto edition of Goethe's works (1836 f.), of removing the two collections of aphorisms with their respective poems from the context of the *Wanderjahre.* Those who persist in their viewpoint to the contrary (e.g., Trunz and Stöcklein) should at least be logically consistent and print the two poems along with them. Secondly, as a byproduct of this study, structural studies of the *Lehrjahre* (because of **"Die Bekenntnisse einer schönen Seele"**) and *Die Wahlverwandtschaften* (because of **"Ottiliens Tagebuch"**) are certainly suggested. If the statements by Max Wundt, Gerhardt Küntzel, Paul Stöcklein, Wilhelm Flitner, Erich Trunz, and others concerning the organicity of the maxim collection can now be regarded as inadequate, by the same token one must reassess their studies of Goethe's works. It seems evident that there is an ever-widening breach between the textual critic of today and the historical scholar of the late nineteenth century. Both have made excellent contributions but someone has to combine these two directions if we are to avoid errors. A third possibility suggested by this study is the inspection of all Goethe's works to see whether this principle operates in miniature as well. For example, what sort of process lies behind the use of Meyer's description of the Swiss spinners and weavers in the *Wanderjahre*? Or are the short stories of the *Wanderjahre* really as carefully integrated as Deli Fischer-Hartmann would have us believe?[26]

There is something both glorious and pathetic in the figure of the old Goethe trying desperately to rescue all the loose ends before surrendering to a higher power. Some of his actions are perhaps not beyond reproach by modern standards, and yet there is a warmly human quality about them during this hectic chapter of his life which helps to melt some of the frigid Olympianism with which scholars have gradually estranged Goethe from a public he so richly deserves. Answers to the critical questions posed in the preceding paragraphs might bring Goethe still closer to his public.

Notes

1. *Bekenntnisse einer schönen Seele, von ihr selbst geschrieben* (Berlin, 1806). Rev. by Goethe: WA 1, XL, 367 ff. (WA = Weimar ed.; JA = Jubilee ed.; AlH = *Ausgabe letzter Hand*).

2. *Goethe's Schöne Seele Susanna Katharina v. Klettenberg* (Gotha, 1896).

3. "Is the Prelude in the Theatre a Prelude to *Faust*?" *PMLA,* LXIV (June 1949), 462-470.

4. "Zur Entstehung und Datierung einiger Faust-Szenen um 1800," *Euphorion,* XLVII (1953), 295-330.

5. Cf. maxims numbered 3, 16, 23, 31, 45 in Max Hecker, *Goethe: Maximen und Reflexionen* (Weimar, 1907).

6. Paul Stöcklein has advocated printing the maxims with the *Wanderjahre,* but when faced with the practical decision for Vol. IX of the *Gedenkausgabe* (Beutler ed.), he chose to let them follow on the heels of the novel accompanied with a footnote which explains the historical relationship. Erich Trunz is thus far the only scholar with the fortitude to follow his own convictions. In Vol. VIII of his *Hamburger Ausgabe* he actually reprints the maxims in the original sequence as they occurred in the *Ausgabe letzter Hand.* However, even he omits the poems, which surely seems a methodological error.

7. 13 Feb. 1769: Max Morris, *Der junge Goethe,* I, 323.

8. *Die deutschen Ossian-Übersetzungen des XVIII. Jahrhunderts* (Diss. Greifswald, 1926).

9. WA 1, XIX, 175.

10. Ibid., pp. 175 f.

11. See letter from Reichel to Goethe, 15 March 1829, in WA 4, XLV, 402 f. and Goethe's reply of 19 March 1829: "Ew. Wohlgeboren Vorstellung und Wünschen füge mich um so lieber, als der letzte Band auch nicht stark ist und es hauptsächlich darauf ankommt, daß diese übersendeten Aphorismen mit gegenwärtiger Lieferung [i.e., Vols. XXI-XXV] in's Publicum treten. Hiernach käme das Nachgesendete: *Aus Makariens Archiv* an's Ende des dritten Bandes der Wanderjahre [i.e., Vol. XXIII]."

12. *Goethes "Wilhelm Meister" und die Entwicklung des modernen Lebensideals* (Berlin and Leipzig, 1913; 2nd ed., 1932). Also, "Aus Makariens Archiv. Zur Entstehung der Aphorismensammlungen in den Wanderjahren," *Germanisch-Romanische Monatschrift,* VII (1915-19), 177-184.

13. *PMLA,* LIX (Dec. 1944), 1156-62 (Mautner); 1162-66 (Feise); 1166-72 (Viëtor); LX (June 1945), 399-420 (Hohlfeld); 421-426 (Viëtor).

14. It occurs first in *AlH,* XII, 313, i.e., on the last page of the volume, immediately following the fragment of *Faust II,* Act I. Its final occurrence is in *AlH,* XXIII, 286, where it is printed out of esthetic reasons in the same Roman type font as the poem, "Schillers Schädel."

15. Curtis Vail has pointed out to me that the most recent scholar to accept the latter view is Paul Friedländer, *Rhythmen und Landschaften im zweiten Teil des "Faust"* (Weimar, 1953), p. 107, n. 1.

16. *Monatshefte,* XLV (Oct. 1953), 333.

17. *Meister,* p. xi: "Seit ich als Primaner ..."

18. *J. P. Eckermann: Sein Leben für Goethe* (Leipzig, 1925-28).

19. George C. Buck, *Goethe and His Stowaways* (diss. Yale, 1954), pp. 360 ff.

20. The MS is no longer extant. The question has been debated at great length in the articles cited above by the late Karl Viëtor and A. R. Hohlfeld in *PMLA,* LIX (Dec. 1944) and LX (June 1945).

21. Hecker, p. 361.

22. E.g., Wundt, p. 453; Paul Stöcklein, *Wege zum spälen Goethe* (Hamburg, 1949), p. 165; Wilhelm Flitner, "Aus Makariens Archiv. Ein Beispiel Goethescher

Spruchkomposition" in *Goethe-Kalender des Frank-furter Goethe-Museums auf das Jahr 1943* (Leipzig, 1942), p. 126.

23. Before leaving this rather intricate business, I should like to subjoin my own interpretation of Goethe's procedure which cannot be developed in detail here. The "Ist fortzusetzen" is a mild imperative which seems to contain the author's promise to the reader that he will continue to freight down future install-ments of the *Ausgabe letzter Hand,* in answer to his critics who claim there is nothing "new" in the new edition, thus making its purchase worthwhile, even for those who already have editions of his works. (The irony becomes evident when one actually de-termines the amount of duplication for which the reader had to pay double and the amount of new material. Of course Goethe did not evaluate his ad-ditions by the pound or page.) To my way of think-ing, then, the aphorisms and poems are not an integral part of the novel but a form of customer appeasement which is loosely added to the end of a volume. The choice of volume was dictated by edi-torial necessity. The practice of stowing away irrel-evant material of this sort continues sporadically throughout the whole 40 volumes of the *AlH.*

24. JA, xxx, vii.

25. We may expect something along these lines in René Wellek's forthcoming book on the history of literary criticism, two volumes of which have already ap-peared.

26. *Goethes Altersroman: Studien über die innere Ein-heit von "Wilhelm Meisters Wanderjahren"* (Halle, 1941).

Karl J. R. Arndt (essay date 1958)

SOURCE: Arndt, Karl J. R. "The Harmony Society and *Wilhelm Meisters Wanderjahre." Comparative Literature* 10.3 (1958): 193-202. Print.

[In the following essay, Arndt describes similarities between the Harmony Society (a utopian religious move-ment) and its fictional counterparts in Wilhelm Meister's Travels. *Arndt observes that the 1829 rewriting of the novel includes an increased emphasis on emigration as a response to political problems, and he highlights Goethe's reliance on numerous contemporary texts that depicted America as a land of liberty attended by great practical challenges.]*

The subject of this paper, the influence of George Rapp's Harmony Society on the "Auswandererstaat" in Goethe's *Wilhelm Meisters Wanderjahre,* would undoubtedly have been thoroughly explored long ago, except for two circum-

stances—inadequate knowledge of the institutions and history of the society and neglect of the *Wanderjahre* by Goethe scholars.

Our information concerning the Harmony Society has been fragmentary because complicated legal and political problems have prevented the full examination of its ex-tensive archives, and scholars have had to depend largely on visitors' reports, which tend to confuse Rapp's society with Robert Owen's New Harmony.[1] The neglect of the *Wanderjahre* seems to be due principally to its obscurity and the frightening effect of its tedious style, even on devoted students of Goethe.[2] All studies of the work begin with an apology for its form, though they may urge the reader not to be deterred from pressing on to find the buried gold.

Goethe's interest in the Harmony Society and the possible importance of the society for the understanding of the *Wanderjahre* have been suggested though not pursued. Erich Küspert, in his *New Harmony: Ein historischer Vergleich zwischen zwei Lebensanschauungen* (Nurem-berg, 1937), calls attention to Goethe's interest in the society; his study is, however, based almost exclusively on the *Reise Sr. Hoheit des Herzogs Bernhard zu Sachsen-Weimar-Eisenach durch Nord-Amerika in den Jahren 1825-1826* (1828) and on *The New Harmony Commun-ities* (1905) by George Browning Lockwood, who knew no other source than the accounts of Bernhard and other travelers.

In addition to Küspert, who wrote for economists and sociologists, two others scholars have suggested a possible relation between the Harmony Society and the *Wander-jahre.* Walther Linden, in his revision of Bielschowsky's *Goethe, sein Leben und seine Werke* (Munich, 1928), suggests the influence of Robert Owen's New Harmony, but without realizing that New Harmony was the second settlement of the Harmonists, that they had sold this set-tlement to Robert Owen, and that the founder of the Harmonists, a contemporary and countryman of Schiller, had been Owen's teacher. Robert Hering comes closest to the problem in his extremely detailed and careful study, *Wilhelm Meister und Faust und ihre Gestaltung im Zei-chen der Gottesidee* (Frankfurt, 1952). He raises the ques-tion whether Goethe's and George Rapp's paths might not have crossed in Württemberg before Rapp emigrated to America, but he does not pursue it further. Perhaps he would have done so, had he lived to finish his studies. If he had had time or opportunity for further study of the Har-mony Society, Hering certainly would not have described the "Auswandererstaat" as

... das Wunschbild eines Gemeinwesens, das die Aus-
wanderer mit hinüber in die neue Welt nehmen, um es dort
der Verwirklichung entgegenzuführen, die entsprechend
ihrem Gesellenstand, nicht mehr Aufgabe der Wanderjahre sein kann, sondern den Meisterjahren, wenn es

solche überhaupt geben kann, vorbehalten bleiben mußten.

[p. 395]

This statement is for the most part correct; but Goethe's reading about America before writing the last eight chapters of the *Wanderjahre* gave him too realistic a knowledge of such a "Gemeinwesen" already in existence in America to allow the plan to be called a "Wunschbild," an ideal similar to the "pädagogische Provinz" which he presented without consideration of the obstacles which might prevent its realization. Apart from other sources of information, Goethe was at the time considerably interested in Lord Byron's *Don Juan,* and Lord Byron had become so fascinated by the reports in England of the Harmony Society that he wrote these lines about it in Canto XV of the work, which Goethe reviewed in *Kunst und Altertum* [*Über Kunst und Altertum*]:

XXXV

When Rapp the Harmonist embargo'd marriage
In his harmonious settlement—(which flourishes
Strangely enough as yet without miscarriage,
Because it breeds no more mouths than it nourishes,
Without those sad expenses which disparage
What Nature naturally most encourages)—
Why call'd he "Harmony" a state sans wedlock?
Now here I've got the preacher at a dead lock.

XXXVI

Because he either meant to sneer at harmony
Or marriage, by divorcing them thus oddly.
But whether reverend Rapp learn'd this in Germany
Or no, 'tis said his sect is rich and godly,
Pious and pure, beyond what I can term any
Of ours, although they propagate more broadly.
My objection's to his title, not his ritual,
Although I wonder how it grew habitual.

XXXVII

But Rapp is the reverse of zealous matrons,
Who favour, malgré Malthus, generation—
Professors of that genial art, and patrons
Of all the modest part of propagation;
Which after all at such a desperate rate runs,
That half its produce tends to emigration,
That sad result of passions and potatoes—
Two weeds which pose our economic Catos.

Emigration, of course, was very much in the mind of Englishmen and Germans at this time, and, as these lines reflect the seriousness of the problem, so does the entire revision of the *Wanderjahre.* As an Entwicklungsroman, *Wilhelm Meister* reflects the changing spirit of an age, and a study of its genesis from the *Theatralische Sendung* [*Wilhelm Meisters theatralische Sendung*] to the revised *Wanderjahre* reveals Goethe's decreasing faith in the future of Europe and his growing faith in America. The *Sendung* does not even mention America, while the *Lehr-*

jahre [*Wilhelm Meisters Lehrjahre*] pictures America as a land of temporary adventure from which Lothario returns with the conviction, "Hier oder nirgends ist America."

It was between 1821 and 1829 that the "Americanization" of *Wilhelm Meister* set in, and the *Wanderjahre* changed completely from a work concerned with "Wandern" to one concerned with "Auswandern." If the *Lehrjahre* is "amerikamüde," then the revised *Wanderjahre* is "europamüde,"[3] conforming to the Old World weariness which Goethe expressed in his well-known poem, **"Amerika Du hast es besser als unser Kontinent, das Alte."** Goethe in these years saw in America the hope for the individual of the future, provided he were willing to make the necessary practical adjustments. And it was in these years that he struggled against time to round out the last eight chapters of the revised *Wanderjahre,* the chapters sketching his "Auswandererstaat," and, as a concession to those few unable to break with the old homeland, the project of developing a backward area in the Old World. Both have their parallels in the history of the Harmony Society.

Apart from suggestions from Byron and from the personal contacts with Americans who came to pay homage in these years, what influences may have had an effect on the revision of the *Wanderjahre*? We find the answer in the records of the Grand Ducal Library, in Goethe's diaries and letters, and in the works on America in his private library. Goethe, we learn, was reading the works of James Fenimore Cooper, Ludwig Gall's *Meine Auswanderung nach den Vereinigten Staaten in Nord Amerika im Frühjahr 1819 und meine Rückkehr nach der Heimath im Winter 1820* (Trier, 1822), Fearon's *Sketches of America* (London, 1818), Morris Birkbeck's *Bemerkungen auf einer Reise in Amerika von der Küste von Virginien bis zum Gebiete von Illinois,* W. MacClure's *Observations on the Geology of the United States,* Moritz von Fürstenwärther's *Der Deutsche in Nord Amerika* (Stuttgart, 1818), Schoolcraft's *Wanderungen in den Vereinigten Staaten,* W. H. Keating's *Reise durch Nord Amerika,* and the *Reise Sr. Hoheit des Herzogs Bernhard ... durch Nord-Amerika* (Weimar, 1828).

All these works except Cooper's are factual reports; and Cooper's influence on Goethe is to be found in the *Novelle* rather than the *Wanderjahre.* Aside from Cooper and MacClure, all of these books present the great advantage of organizing emigration and settlement societies and extoll the Harmony Society as the model of models. And MacClure, whom Duke Bernhard met at New Harmony, had close personal connections with the society. We do not know Goethe's reactions to all of these works, but we do know what he thought of Gall and Bernhard.

In *Kunst und Altertum* (XIV, 380 f.) at the very time he was working on the "Auswandererstaat" Goethe published a very illuminating discussion of Gall's *Meine*

Auswanderung, recommending the book and American themes to young writers searching for new material. In this article he outlines a plot for a novel suggested by Gall's account of America. The plot actually sketches the history of the Harmony Society, without mentioning its name, from the time of its organization in Schiller's homeland to its settlement in America. Goethe proposes as the central character a Protestant minister who leads his people to the sea and then across, a man who would in his experiences often call to mind Moses in the wilderness—incidentally, a comparison which Rapp, the Protestant minister and leader of the Harmonists, often used in speaking of himself. In an exact parallel to George Rapp, Goethe's plot pictures this central character as one driven on by his ruling passion to carry out his plan to the end, when he has overcome an immeasurable lack of sense, averted a catastrophe, and established a decent living for his people. This is what happened to Rapp when he came to America and struggled to establish his first settlement. A great part of the story is told in Duke Bernhard's travels.

The plot which Goethe outlines, by the way, gives us an idea of the type of *Meisterjahre* he might have written, if he had had time to complete what he at least suggested at the end of the **Wanderjahre.** After apologizing to his readers for leaving them in the dark about the fate of so many of his characters who have already departed, he says: "Wir leben jedoch in der Hoffnung, sie dereinst in voller geregelter Tätigkeit, den wahren Wert ihrer verschiedenen Charaktere offenbarend, vergnüglich wieder zu finden" (VIII, 468). Goethe concludes his suggestions in the Gall review in a similarly promising tone:

> Was den Personenbestand betrifft, so hat weder ein epischer noch dramatischer Dichter je zur Auswahl einen solchen Reichtum vor sich gesehen. Die Unzufriedenen beider Weltteile stehn ihm zu Gebot, er kann sie zum Teil nach und nach zugrunde gehen, endlich aber, wenn er seine Favoriten günstig untergebracht hat, die Übrigen stufenweise mit sehr mäßigen Zuständen sich begnügen lassen. Ich behalte mir vor, die Lösung dieser Aufgaben, insofern ich sie erleben sollte, so gründlich als es mir nur möglich zu beurteilen, weil hier eine Gelegenheit wäre, von dem Werte des Stoffs, dem Verdienste des Gehalts, der Genialität der Behandlung, der Gediegenheit der Form hinlängliche Rechenschaft zu geben.
>
> [XIV, 381]

It is a pity that this review was not republished in connection with the Vietor-Hohlfeld controversy about the meaning of "Ist fortzusetzen" at the end of the **Wanderjahre**; for it certainly can be used to show what Wilhelm Meister's *Meisterjahre* would have been like if Goethe had had time to write it.[4]

Although Goethe thought so highly of Gall's work that he recommended it for study to young authors, he was even more interested in the observations on America which were sent to Weimar periodically by Duke Bernhard,

the first Weimarer to travel in the United States. Here were reports of a young man well known to Goethe, and the eagerness with which he read them may be judged from a letter of October 22, 1826 to Wilhelm von Humboldt:

> Das Bild eines recht lebendigen Weltlebens ist übrigens in dieser letzten Zeit in meine Klause gekommen, das mich sehr unterhält: das Journal des Herzogs Bernhard von Weimar, der im April 1825 von Gent abreiste und vor kurzem erst wieder bei uns eintraf. Es its ununterbrochen geschrieben, und da ihm sein Stand, seine Denkweise, sein Betragen in die höchsten Regionen der Gesellschaft einführten, er sich in den mittlern Zuständen behagte und die geringsten nicht verschmähte, so wird man auf eine sehr angenehme Weise durch die mannigfaltigsten Lagen durchgeführt, welche unmittelbar anzuschauen mir wenigstens von großer Bedeutung war.
>
> [XXI, 709]

These views are repeated in letters to C. F. Zelter and Graf von Sternberg. Goethe had, of course, been reading the journal in sections as it was received in Weimar even before Bernhard's return. It is mentioned frequently in the letters, where it is called "exciting," "highly interesting," and "very instructive." Upon Bernhard's return Goethe himself took an active part in seeing the journal through the press.

Like all travelers of the time, Bernhard visited the Harmony Society, and devotes a great deal of attention to it. What makes his report of particular value is the fact that he visited the third home of the society, as well as the second in Indiana which had just been sold to Robert Owen, who had only recently come from Scotland with his widely publicized "boatload of scholars" to establish his new world in the old Harmonist settlement. Earlier accounts had already been published in Europe and especially in Germany about the plans of the Harmonists to establish an "Auswandererstaat" on the Wabash. The Harmonists had spoken to Thomas Jefferson about the plan and the United States Congress had debated it at great length. They had purchased large areas of land on the Wabash and had sent a committee of elders to Württemberg to invite more Germans to migrate to this territory. They had suggested that Congress subsidize emigration in order to populate the wilderness. The migration threatened to become so heavy that the Württemberg government began a project of land development to hold back some of the people, just as Odoard does in the **Wanderjahre** (VIII, 438-443).[5]

In the ninth chapter of the third book of the **Wanderjahre,** Lenardo gives his great address on the reasons for and the advantages to be derived from group migration, a chapter which ends with the singing of the verse:

> Bleibe nicht am Boden heften,
> Frisch gewagt und frisch hinaus!
> Kopf und Arm mit heitern Kräften
> Überall sind sie zu Haus;

Wo wir uns der Sonne freuen
Sind wir jede Sorge los,
Daß wir uns in ihr zerstreuen
Darum ist die Welt so groß.

No group of people in the world at that time had given more practical evidence of the truth of these sentiments than the Harmonists, and, shortly before Duke Bernhard's arrival, they had with a very similar song taken leave a third time from homes they had created. Owen himself had been present at their orderly and solemn departure. Duke Bernhard heard Owen's account of the departure and was told about Owen's plans. Bernhard not only gives a vivid account of this visit and of his conversations with Owen, but also reprints the constitution and plans which Owen had so carefully and laboriously worked out for the communities which he tried to establish and which failed so completely and so soon.

Soon after his visit with Owen on the Wabash Duke Bernhard met George Rapp and his followers in their third settlement near Pittsburgh. He gives a full and detailed account of life in the community, of the trades practiced there, of the kind of factories in operation, of the good practical sense found throughout the colony. Comparing Rapp's practical success with Owen's more elaborate theories, Bernhard of Weimar concludes: "Herr Rapp hält aber seine Gesellschaft nicht allein durch diese Hoffnung zusammen, sondern auch durch das Band der Religion, welches bei Herrn Owen's Gesellschaft gänzlich fehlt. Die Resultate zeugen für Rapp's System" (II, 205). In view of the emphasis which Bernhard places on religion it is striking that religion is the first point Goethe mentions in the sketch of his "Auswandererstaat."

> Wilhelm ließ sich den Plan im allgemeinen vorzeichnen, und da man mit Landschaft und Gegend genugsam vertraut geworden, auch die Hoffnung besprochen war, in einem ausgedehnten Gebiete schnell eine große Anzahl Bewohner entwikkelt zu sehen, so wendete sich das Gespräch, wie natürlich, zuletzt auf das was Menschen eigentlich zusammenhält: auf Religion und Sitte ... Folgendes ergab sich als die Quintessenz dessen was verhandelt wurde:
>
> Daß der Mensch ins Unvermeidliche sich füge, darauf dringen alle Religionen, jede sucht auf ihre Weise mit dieser Aufgabe fertig zu werden.
>
> Die christliche hilft durch Glaube, Liebe, Hoffnung gar anmutig nach; daraus entsteht denn die Geduld, ein süßes Gefühl, welch eine schätzbare Gabe das Dasein bleibe, auch wenn ihm, anstatt des gewünschten Genusses, das widerwärtigste Leiden aufgebürdet wird. An dieser Religion halten wir fest, aber auf eine eigene Weise; wir unterrichten unsre Kinder von Jugend auf von den großen Vorteilen, die sie uns gebracht hat; dagegen von ihrem Ursprung, von ihrem Verlauf geben wir zuletzt Kenntnis. Alsdann wird uns der Urheber erst lieb und wert, und alle Nachricht die sich auf ihn bezieht wird heilig. In diesem Sinne, den man vielleicht pedantisch nennen mag, aber doch als folgerecht anerkennen muß, dulden wir keinen

Juden unter uns; denn wie sollten wir ihm den Anteil an der höchsten Kultur vergönnen, deren Ursprung und Herkommen er verleugnet?

[VIII, 433-434]

Like the Harmony Society, the "Auswandererstaat" is specifically described as a Christian society, and its admission policy is like that of the Harmony Society, which restricted membership to Christians and Christians only, but from all denominations. The Harmonists were pragmatic rather than historical in their approach to the religious instruction of their youth.

The "Sittenlehre" of Goethe's emigrant state is described as "rein tätig und wird in den wenigen Geboten begriffen: Mäßigung im Willkürlichen, Emsigkeit im Notwendigen." This was essentially the practice of the Harmonists and, as Goethe comments further, also provided "einen ergiebigen Text zu grenzenloser Ausführung."

Most visitors to the Harmony Society commented on its economy of time and the eagerness to use each hour to best advantage. To keep everyone aware of the passing hour the Harmonists first used a town crier, then a huge bell, made for their special needs in England and shipped up the Mississippi and Wabash to Harmony. At their third settlement they built a huge clock which struck each quarter hour, exactly as proposed in the "Auswandererstaat" and for the same reason noted there: "Der größte Respekt wird allen eingeprägt für die Zeit als für die höchste Gabe Gottes und der Natur und die aufmerksamste Begleiterin des Daseins" (VIII, 434). Both plans considered the proper division of time and its use as a basic point of "Sittenlehre."

Goethe's plan does not accept the Harmony Society's discouragement of propagation, but agrees completely in placing great weight upon life in the family circle. In the Harmony Society even single persons without family were placed in families, for the same reasons mentioned in the "Auswandererstaat." Like the Harmonists, Goethe called for mutual education: "eigentlich aber kommt alles darauf an, zu gleicher Zeit Lehrer und Schüler zu bilden" (VIII, 435).

Lenardo, like Rapp, is not a theorist but a practical man eager to get to the new home and down to work:

> wir alle sind ungeduldig das Geschäft anzutreten, munter und überzeugt, daß man einfach anfangen müße. So denken wir nicht an Justiz, aber wohl an Polizei. Ihr Grundsatz wird kräftig ausgesprochen: niemand soll dem andern unbequem sein; wer sich unbequem erweist wird beseitigt, bis er begreift wie man sich anstellt um geduldet zu werden.
>
> [VIII, 436]

This had always been the policy of the Harmony Society. Even the Biblical system of the stages of brotherly admonition, which the Harmonists observed, is taken into the "Auswandererstaat" with only slight modification.

Rapp and Goethe agree in their attitude toward the majority: "Wegen der Majorität haben wir ganz eigne Gedanken; wir lassen sie freilich gelten im notwendigen Weltlauf, im höhern Sinne haben wir aber nicht viel Zutrauen auf sie. Doch darüber darf ich mich nicht weiter auslassen" (VIII, 436). The Harmonists' view could not be stated better.

The "Auswandererstaat," like the Harmony Society, was planned to function in another country under another government. Rapp was determined to take to America only the advantages of the old culture, while Lenardo states: "Die Hauptsache bleibt nur immer daß wir die Vorteile der Kultur mit hinüber nehmen und die Nachteile zurücklassen. Branntweinschenken und Lesebibliotheken werden bei uns nicht geduldet" (VIII, 437). For their insistence on both of these points, especially the first, the Harmonists created much ill feeling among their neighbors, especially while they were on the Wabash.

Goethe was not interested in a state of religious communists, so he did not accept the pacifism and the community ownership of property which the Harmonists practiced. However, his proposed state was conceived along socialistic lines, and provision was accordingly made for a soak-the-rich taxation plan, as we may conclude from the words: "Wächst nach und nach der Besitz der Staatsbürger, so zwackt man ihnen auch davon ab, weniger oder mehr, wie sie verdienen daß man ihnen von dieser Seite wehe tue" (VIII, 437). These were the general points on which Lenardo reported agreement; but, in summarizing it all, he repeats: "Die Hauptsache wird aber sein, wenn wir uns an Ort und Stelle befinden." This had always been Harmonist policy in contrast to that of Robert Owen, as Duke Bernhard pointed out in his journal.

The greatest effect on Goethe of his reading of reports on America was the emphasis on practicality, "Tätigkeit." This becomes very apparent when we compare the "Pädagogische Provinz" with the "Auswandererstaat" and note the great changes Goethe makes in his main characters. Almost all are trained for a trade in America. The first version of the *Wanderjahre* knew nothing of the need to prepare for a definite "Metier," as Goethe called it in his outlines for the revision. The theme of practicality is introduced by Jarno-Montan with his vigorous criticism:

> Narrenpossen sind eure allgemeine Bildung und alle Anstalten dazu. Daß ein Mensch etwas ganz entschieden verstehe, vorzüglich leiste, wie nicht leicht ein anderer in der nächsten Umgebung, darauf kommt es an, und besonders in unserm Verbande spricht es sich von selbst aus.

[VIII, 305]

These words are spoken by Montan in the name of the now streamlined "Turm." Wilhelm follows Jarno-Montan's

advice and vigorous example. Goethe had to make many revisions in the *Wanderjahre* to fit Wilhelm's completely changed attitude into the novel.

The glorious cultural mission of the actor in the early *Theatralische Sendung* is now scorned as "Lebensgewackel und Geschnatter," and the revision is so drastic that Goethe interrupts the course of the narrative to say:

> Mag doch der Redakteur dieser Bogen hier selbst gestehen: daß er mit einigem Unwillen diese wunderliche Stelle durchgehen läßt. Hat er nicht auch in vielfachem Sinn mehr Leben und Kräfte als billig dem Theater zugewendet? und könnte man ihn wohl überzeugen, daß dies ein unverzeihlicher Irrtum, eine fruchtlose Bemühung gewesen?

[VIII, 280]

Wilhelm, partly under the influence of Jarno-Montan, has become so weary of academic learning that he is determined to take up medicine, but not as a profession, with all the academic study this would imply, but as a trade. He wants to become a "Chirurg," a glorified old-time barber, who will be useful in the New World. So it is with the rest. Philene becomes a pattern cutter, Lydie a seamstress and sewing teacher, Friedrich a practical secretary, while Felix is prepared for a life on the range as a cowhand. German scholars like Hering either are not sufficiently aware of the American background against which Goethe revised the *Wanderjahre* or want to cover their wounded European pride when they suggest that Felix is being trained to follow in the dignified footsteps of Frau von Stein's husband; but Goethe knew that the New World would have little patience with an "Oberstallmeister."

The most striking overall change in the revised *Wanderjahre,* then, is its utilitarianism. Except for the Abbé, who shrinks into the background, there is not a humanist, poet, painter, musician, actor, scholar, or academically trained person in the "Auswandererstaat." It is a state made up of "Handwerker," men prepared to practice useful trades. It is not the Robert Owen state with its famous boatload of scholars, about which Goethe had been so fully informed by Duke Bernhard's firsthand reports, but a state patterned after George Rapp's practical Harmonists, who had proved their ability to all the world—and to Duke Bernhard—by creating three successful communities in the wilderness. The members of Goethe's "Auswandererstaat" are men "von allem Wissensqualm entladen," suitable candidates for American citizenship. "Wo ich nütze," that is decisive. The final revision of *Wilhelm Meisters Wanderjahre* seems to be a denial of everything that Goethe himself had stood for, all of which helps explain the deep significance and perhaps bitter resignation of the subtitle, **"Die Entsagenden."**

Notes

1. Karl J. Arndt, "The Harmony Society from its Beginnings in Germany in 1785 to its Liquidation in the

United States in 1905," *Year Book of The American Philosophical Society,* 1953, pp. 188-191.

2. See Gerhard Künzel's introduction to the *Wanderjahre,* in the Artemis-Verlag memorial edition of Goethe's works, Zürich, 1948-54, VIII, 885. All quotations from Goethe in this article are from this edition. On the style of the work, see Arno Schmidt, *Aus dem Leben eines Fauns* (Hamburg, 1953), p. 97. An American, Charles Sealsfield, shortly after Goethe's death called the style an insult to German readers against which they should have rebelled. *Gesammelte Werke* (Stuttgart, 1846), VII, 9.

3. Ernst Willkomm, *Die Europamüden* (Leipzig, 1838); Ferdinand Kürnberger, *Der Amerikamüde* (Munich, 1856).

4. *PMLA,* LIX (1944), 142-183, 1157-1172; LX (1945), 399-426.

5. Theodor Steimle, *Die wirtschaftliche und soziale Entwicklung der württ. Brüdergemeinden Korntal und Wilhelmsdorf* (Korntal, 1929).

Mary Gies Hatch (essay date 1959)

SOURCE: Hatch, Mary Gies. "The Development of Goethe's Concept of the Calling in *Wilhelm Meisters Lehrjahre* and *Wanderjahre.*" *German Quarterly* 32.3 (1959): 217-26. Print.

[*In the following essay, Hatch expands on Thomas Mann's observation that Goethe's belief in one's obligation to the duties of his profession was one of the qualities that marked him as a representative of the middle class "with its inherent capacity to outgrow itself." Hatch contends that Meister Wilhelm's learning years and travel years demonstrate his march to maturity by recognizing his learning capacity, which he can trust to help him realize his potential, and most important "the crucial importance of occupation" in achieving his ends.*]

"Bürgerlich-überbürgerlich" is the expression which Thomas Mann used to designate the tendency of middle class culture to ennoble and transcend itself. In his address in commemoration of the hundredth anniversary of Goethe's death, Mann chose to regard Goethe not as representative of the classic-humanistic tradition, nor as the Olympian poet, but as representative of the middle class with its inherent capacity to outgrow itself. It was his thesis that Goethe's life and work represent the development of the universal out of the bourgeois: "Das Würdig-Bürgerliche als Heimat des Allmenschlichen, Weltgröße als Kind der Bürgerlichkeit—dies Schicksal von Herkunft und kühnstem Wachstum ist nirgends zu Hause wie bei uns ..."[1]

Among the qualities which characterized Goethe as representative of the German middle class of his time Thomas Mann emphasized devotion to the duties of one's profession. This devotion he designated as typical of the middle class with its Protestant religious orientation. After recalling the incident of Goethe's neglect of a social obligation in order to finish a certain task, Mann defined the religious sanction for fulfillment of occupational obligation: "Ein rührendes kleines Vorkommnis, und man kann bürgerlicher Ethik keine höhere Ehre erweisen, als indem man diese Fleißestreue bis zum letzten als bürgerlich anspricht. Man darf es wohl, denn die Liebe zu Mühe und Arbeit, der asketische Glaube daran ist ja auch von einer Soziologie, die die bürgerliche Geistesform religiös-protestantisch begründet, als seelisches Zubehör der Bürgerlichkeit gekennzeichnet worden."[2]

It is the purpose of this inquiry to trace the development of Goethe's concept of the calling as a factor in the life of the individual through the events of *Wilhelm Meisters theatralische Sendung, Wilhelm Meisters Lehrjahre,* and the *Wanderjahre* [*Wilhelm Meisters Wanderjahre*]. These novels, written over a period of some fifty years, reveal Goethe's emerging conviction that occupational achievement is of fundamental importance for personal productivity, for establishing significant relations with others, and for the attainment of self-knowledge. It is Wilhelm's task to learn what he can do and whom he can trust; it is the mark of maturity that he in some measure achieves this knowledge.

In order to evaluate the originality of Goethe's ultimate conception of the relationship between occupation and personality development, it will be useful to recall briefly the teachings of Lutheranism, the prevailing form of Protestantism in Germany, and the religion of Goethe's parents. Central to Luther's thought was the problem of how the individual might attain salvation in the next world. It became Luther's conviction that the inwardness of communion with God, or the possession of grace, was independent of the mediation of a priesthood. Luther had asserted that the individual could not earn salvation by performing "good works" in the sense of the medieval church; for him the important thing was the inward state of grace resulting from faith which enabled the individual to live acceptably to God. Luther regarded the secular world as the sphere of action appointed by God for all, and he believed that the faithful performance of occupational duties was not only a *remedium peccati,* but was the best proof of love of one's neighbor.[3] Luther declared that the social class system and the occupational system had been established by divine act, and he insisted that it was the duty of the individual to remain in the class into which he was born, and in the occupation of his parents.[4]

In comparing Goethe's ideas regarding the value of occupation with the traditional view of Lutheranism, emphasis has been placed upon the salient differences: choice of occupation, renunciation and challenge as aspects of productivity, and the relationship of the individual to others.[5]

CHOICE OF OCCUPATION

For the orthodox Lutheran the choice of occupation was no problem. Luther had said that God had created the existing social system with its social and occupational hierarchy, and that it was the duty of the Christian to demonstrate his faith by humbly submitting to the order of the world as he found it.

In the *Sendung* [*Wilhelm Meisters theatralische Sendung*] and in the *Lehrjahre* [*Wilhelm Meisters Lehrjahre*], Werner typifies the individual who is influenced in his pursuit of a vocation by a secularized Lutheran tradition. Werner is not troubled about earning salvation through the practice of worldly asceticism, it is true, but he is concerned with adherence to the tradition of the society of which he is part. He does not consider entering any other vocation than the family business, nor does he wish to rise above his social class. Not so Wilhelm. Wilhelm realizes that he has a talent for the theatre, and even after his disillusionment in Marianne, he can return to the family business only with grudging submissiveness. In both the *Sendung* and the *Lehrjahre* Wilhelm longs to find expression for his poetic and dramatic gifts. He scorns Werner's advice that he use his talent as a pastime. In the *Sendung,* Wilhelm is drawn half against his will into an association with a troupe of players under the direction of Madame de Retti. He is cajoled into acting a part in his own play. He reminds himself occasionally of his obligations to the family business, but just as frequently he is lured back to the stage. In the end, the Wilhelm of the *Sendung* is induced to join Serlo's company, but the "Ja denn" is a half-hearted consent, and his thoughts turn to the vision of the Amazon in the forest.

Likewise in the *Lehrjahre* Wilhelm tries to escape the family trade with its obligations and restrictions and find self-fulfillment among the players. His success in Serlo's production of *Hamlet* is at once the culmination of his artistic dreams and the proof of his inadequacy as an actor. Serlo's growing coolness and finally Jarno's merciless appraisal of his abilities convince Wilhelm that he can play only himself, that he possesses only a half-talent. At the end of the *Lehrjahre,* Wilhelm has found friends and he has found his betrothed. He has recognized with some bitterness what he cannot do, but he has not yet discovered what he can do.

Only in the *Wanderjahre* does Wilhelm find the profession suited to his abilities and useful to society. He realizes that he has always wanted to practice medicine, and he is now willing to subordinate himself to the demands of science: "Laß mich bekennen, . . . daß mir dies hundertmal eingefallen ist; es regte sich in mir eine innere Stimme, die mich meinen eigentlichen Beruf hieran erkennen ließ."[6]

As a surgeon he wholeheartedly devotes his time and ability to the fulfillment of the duties of his calling.

Occupational excellence, Goethe repeats in his discussion of education in the *Wanderjahre,* demands more than a half-talent. Everyone must have an occupation. This occupation should be of his own choice, but it should be more than a mode of self-expression. It must be appropriate to the natural endowment of the individual, and it must be of use to society.

Concern with this problem of personal inclination as a factor in choice of occupation appears throughout the discussion of the Abbé's educational methods and later in the exposition of the methods of the directors of the unique educational institution, *die pädagogische Provinz.* The Abbé permitted each of the four children in his charge to follow his own inclination in learning. It was his idea that, if given ample opportunity, each would discover his latent talent and voluntarily develop it to the fullest extent. Natalie remarks that this system of education was successful with Lothario and with herself, but not with Friedrich and her sister. She adds that the Abbé may have modified his theories in the light of experience.

PRODUCTIVITY THROUGH RENUNCIATION

If the Wilhelm of the *Wanderjahre* has become cold and uninteresting, it is to some extent because he has become one of the *Entsagenden.* The wayward, enthusiastic, often disillusioned Wilhelm is gone, and in his place is a silent, earnest, purposeful man. It has become Goethe's conviction that in order to be productive, the individual must learn to renounce all that stands in the way of the fullest use of his abilities.

Asceticism had never been an important aspect of Lutheranism. Unlike Calvinism and Pietism, Lutheranism did not prescribe forms of self-denial, and the individual Lutheran was expected to use a part of his earnings for his own pleasure. Goethe was acquainted with Lutheran acceptance of worldly pleasures as well as with the systematic asceticism of the Pietists and Calvinists. He could never accept either rigorous asceticism or passive indulgence as a way of life.

In the *Wanderjahre* there emerges a concept of renunciation quite different from the ascetic renunciation of any religious sect. Goethe is not concerned with foregoing such worldly pleasures as eating, drinking, or love-making. For Goethe, renunciation is the creative act of putting aside the unimportant in order to achieve the important. He is concerned with giving up self-deception, anger, futile regret,—all that interferes with personal growth.

In order to learn and practice his future profession, Wilhelm must subordinate his personal vanities to the demands of his profession. For him there can be no more indulgence of half-talents, no more aimless discussions, no more futile reminiscence.

PRODUCTIVITY THROUGH CHALLENGE OF OCCUPATION

Perhaps the most characteristic innovation in the concept of occupation in the life of the individual is Goethe's idea of the need for unceasing striving to improve oneself and to advance one's chosen profession. For Luther, devotion to a calling had been evidence of possession of grace. For him the work of the layman in his occupation was not unlike the service of the monk within the cloister. Each was bound to accept his given task, to fulfill his duties without question and thereby earn salvation. During subsequent centuries much of the original religious intention was lost, and the pursuit of the calling tended to become a ritualistic procedure for establishing the individual as a respected member of bourgeois society.

Werner appears as the ritualist for whom the performance of daily tasks has become an end in itself. The unexpected meeting between the two friends at Lothario's estate shows the contrast between the two men. "Der gute Mann [Werner] schien eher zurück als vorwärts gegangen zu sein. Er war viel magerer als ehemals, sein spitzes Gesicht schien feiner, seine Nase länger zu sein, seine Stirn und sein Scheitel waren von Haaren entblößt, ... seine farblosen Wangen ließen keinen Zweifel übrig, daß ein arbeitsamer Hypochondrist gegenwärtig sei."[7] Wilhelm remarks that Werner seems to be more interested in reckoning the possibility of marrying him off to a rich heiress than in renewing their friendship, and he protests against being treated as a salable commodity.

For Goethe, passive dedication was not enough, and no religious affirmation could give it sanction. It becomes a dominant idea of the *Wanderjahre* that the individual must strive within the duties of his occupation in order to live and grow. Wilhelm has made many mistakes, but he has grown through attempt and failure, through seeking and not always finding.

Wilhelm subordinates his poetic inclinations to the demands of medicine in order to become a surgeon, but he also has an opportunity to exercise a creative capacity through a new medium. He studies anatomy through the use of models. He seeks to test a suggested method of resuscitating the drowned through blood-letting.[8]

Among the other individuals who seek beyond the traditional limits of a science is the physician who is interested not only in the physical well-being of the individual, but in discovering the subtle relationship between mind and body. Lothario is concerned not only with the military defense, but with the organization of government in the colony. Jarno, the realist, investigates the possibilities of discovering mineral deposits through the sensitivity of certain peculiarly endowed individuals.

The idea of applying creative talent to the resolution of problems of daily work represents a basic difference between Lutheran teachings and Goethe's conception of *Beruf,*—between ritualism and genuine productivity.[9]

RELATIONSHIP OF THE INDIVIDUAL TO OTHERS

In the course of the **Wanderjahre,** Goethe defines a new kind of social organization based upon occupational achievement rather than upon hereditary social status.

Lutheran tradition had justified service in the calling as the expression of love for one's fellow man, but without concern for changing society or enlarging the opportunities of the individual. The occupational system, as an aspect of the class system, was regarded by Luther as having been instituted by divine authority. Hence the individual had no choice but to show love of God through submissiveness to authority, and love of his neighbor through faithful performance of occupational duties.

In both the **Sendung** and **Lehrjahre,** Wilhelm's association with the players is a mode of rebellion against his obligations to the family business and against his inherited social status. Actually Wilhelm is never able to reconcile his consciousness of middle class social status with the condition of a strolling player. During his adventures on the stage Wilhelm is repeatedly involved in situations which require that he conceal his identity. In the **Sendung** his friend, *Herr von C.,* is obliged to fight a duel to defend his intimacy with a player. As Wilhelm is aware of the distinction between himself and the players, so he is also aware of the social chasm which separates him from the nobility. He is deeply resentful of the narrow world in which he is confined: "Ich weiß nicht, wie es in fremden Ländern ist, aber in Deutschland ist nur dem Edelmann eine gewisse allgemeine, wenn ich sagen darf, personelle Ausbildung möglich. Ein Bürger kann sich Verdienst erwerben und zur höchsten Not seinen Geist ausbilden; seine Persönlichkeit geht aber verloren, er mag sich stellen, wie er will."[10]

Wilhelm's relationship to the group of strolling players under Melina's direction is highly personal. Like the other members of the troupe, Wilhelm is interested in realizing his own goals through membership in the group. Because he so greatly desires a medium for the exercise of his talent, Wilhelm endows the players with many attributes which they do not actually possess. He imagines them to be artists dedicated to the task of improving the German theatre. Wilhelm's attitude toward his fellow players is quite unrealistic; he makes them what he wishes them to be as a part of his highly idealized image of the theatre. When he at last realizes that each actor hopes to achieve his personal aims without regard for the welfare of the group, he is bitterly disappointed and complains: "Mit welcher Heftigkeit wirken sie gegen einander! und nur die kleinlichste Eigenliebe, der beschränkteste Eigennutz macht, daß sie sich mit einander verbinden. ... Immer bedürftig und immer ohne Zutrauen, scheint es, als wenn sie sich vor nichts so sehr fürchteten als vor Vernunft und gutem Geschmack, und nichts so sehr zu erhalten suchten als das Majestätsrecht ihrer persönlichen Willkür."[11]

In the *Wanderjahre,* the importance of the relationship of the individual to his occupation receives a new and different emphasis. The individual may identify himself with the occupational organization voluntarily, but as a member of the group he must subordinate his personal wishes to the goals of the group. *Das Band* is characterized by a minimum of authority, but so long as the individual is a part of the group, he must maintain a positive attitude toward the goals of the organization and toward his fellow workers.

The dilemma of the able individual whose aspirations are limited by class restrictions is solved in the *Wanderjahre.* Hereditary class status is here subordinated to personal qualities and to occupational achievement. Everyone must work,—men and women, commoners and noblemen. Every member must excel in a particular vocation, and the status of the individual is determined by his function within the organization.[12] "Das Bürgerliche besitzt eine gewisse geistige Transzendenz, in der es sich aufhebt und verwandelt"[13] concludes Thomas Mann, and in no respect is this more evident than in Goethe's development of the function of occupation in the life of the individual.

The problem of the hero of the *Sendung* and of the *Lehrjahre* was to find a way out of middle class society with its lack of social mobility and its high regard for ritualistic service in a traditional occupation. Wilhelm attempted to find recognition for his talents and freedom to develop his own personality without the restrictions of family position and expectation. The futility of such an attempt at escape is foreshadowed in the conclusion of the *Sendung,* and is emphasized in the close of the *Lehrjahre.* After the adventures and disillusionments detailed in the *Lehrjahre,* Wilhelm turns from rebellion against the existing occupational structure to innovation within it.

In the *Wanderjahre* Goethe recognized the crucial importance of occupation: through appropriate occupation the individual must unite with others for socially useful production, and through occupational discipline and challenge the individual is able to realize his own highest potential.

Notes

1. Thomas Mann, "Goethe als Repräsentant des bürgerlichen Zeitalters," *Leiden und Grösse der Meister, neue Aufsätze* (Berlin, 1935), p. 10.

2. *Ibid.,* pp. 23-24. Thomas Mann refers to the sociology which relates bourgeois attitude toward occupation with Protestant doctrine. In 1904-5, Max Weber's essay, "Die protestantische Ethik und der Geist des Kapitalismus" appeared in *Archiv für Sozialwissenschaft und Sozialpolitik,* Vols. XX and XXI. This essay developed the idea that religious beliefs and social institutions were different expressions of a common psychological attitude. A more detailed analysis of the social and economic teachings of Protestant groups appeared in *Die Soziallehren der christlichen Kirchen und Gruppen* by Ernst Troeltsch (Tübingen, 1912). For the purposes of this article, information concerning Lutheran doctrine has been taken from Troeltsch.

3. Tauler's sermons published in 1498 were an important influence upon Luther. Tauler declared that all honest labor was service to God, and that spinning and shoe-making were gifts of the Holy Spirit. Preserved Smith, *The Age of the Reformation* (New York, 1920), p. 31.

4. Ernst Troeltsch, *The Social Teaching of the Christian Churches,* trans. Olive Wyon (London, 1950), Vol. II, p. 473: "To put it briefly: this system of vocational organization is a stable class system of a patriarchal kind, fixed by Divine appointment in the Old Testament and by the Law of Nature, to which each individual belongs, in permanent categories, usually receiving at birth his assigned calling. Further, we must not forget that this immediate Divine character of Nature is due to a simple, positive decree of the Will of God, which a Christian must accept in a spirit of humble obedience without any attempt at understanding it ..." It might be added that Hans Sachs gives an orthodox Lutheran interpretation of the divine institution of the occupational system in *Die ungleichen kinder Eve.* The possibility that the motif for the poem was derived from an earlier Latin version suggests the similarity of Lutheran doctrine to the teachings of the medieval church.

5. It is well known that the theological idea of the importance of the pursuit of the calling is reflected in Luther's use of *Beruf* for worldly calling or vocation. Throughout the Middle Ages the clergy alone were regarded as having a "calling." Before Luther there was no word which corresponded to *Beruf* in its present meaning: "Die deutsche Mystik erkannte, daß Gottes Ruf an alle geht; ihm kann man auch außerhalb des Klosters folgen. Dies schloß sie aus 1. Kor. 7, 29, wo Luther übersetzt: *Ein jeglicher bleibe in dem beruf, darin er berufen ist.* (Die Augsburger Zainerbibel von 1475 hat hier *berüffung*) ... Die religiöse Schätzung der weltlichen Arbeit hob sich seitdem, und der Einfluß dieser neuen Betrachtungsweise ... ging so tief, daß auch der Sprachgebrauch sich danach umformte." Trübners *Deutsches Etymologisches Wörterbuch* (1939), I, 286f.

"Seit 1522 setzt Luther *Beruf* und *berufen* auch im weltlichen Sinn für 'Amt, Stand; tätig sein lasser,' entscheidend 1. Kor. 7, 20 … Damit ist Luther maßgebend noch für die heutige Schriftsprache, in der der hohe Klang des Wortes unverbraucht fortwirkt, etwa bei Arthur Schnitzler (1898) *Die Gefährtin …" Etymologisches Wörterbuch der deutschen Sprache,* Friedrich Kluge, Alfred Götze (Berlin, 1953), p. 70.

For the purposes of this inquiry *calling, occupation,* and *profession* are used for *Beruf.* Webster's *New Collegiate Dictionary* (1956) defines *calling* as "one's usual occupation; vocation; trade." Talcott Parsons, in his translation of Weber's essay, states that he makes use of *calling* and *profession* in translating *Beruf. The Protestant Ethic and the Spirit of Capitalism* (London, 1930), p. 194.

6. Goethe, *Wilhelm Meisters Wanderjahre* (Jubiläums-Ausgabe), XX, 46.

7. *Lehrjahre,* (J.A.), XIIX, 263.

8. There are indications that Goethe recognized the need for extending knowledge of the functioning of the human body. In his letter to Natalie, Wilhelm recalls that his own father had been influential in overcoming objections to vaccination against smallpox. Wihelm mentions his interest as a boy in the suggestion that the drowned boys might perhaps have been saved by blood-letting. (*Wanderjahre* [J.A.], 20, 43-44.) That Goethe recognized the traditional restrictions placed upon medical practice is evident. It is equally evident that he recognized the need for breaking away from the traditional in seeking sounder knowledge and new methods of treatment. The master who instructs Wilhelm in anatomy warns him that his work must be pursued in secret: "Es muß eine Schule geben, und diese wird sich vorzüglich mit Überlieferung beschäftigen; was bisher geschehen ist, soll auch künftig geschehen, das ist gut und mag und soll so sein. Wo aber die Schule stockt, da muß man bemerken und wissen; das Lebendige muß man ergreifen und üben, aber im stillen, sonst wird man gehindert und hindert andere." (*Ibid.,* 20, 70.) The idea of the endless possibilities in the study of physiology is suggested by Jarno: "Willst du dich ernstlich dem göttlichsten aller Geschäfte widmen, ohne Wunder zu heilen und ohne Worte Wunder zu tun, so verwende ich mich für dich." (*Ibid.,* 20, 47.) Similarly, the master urges Wilhelm to perfect his knowledge of anatomy: "Alles, worein der Mensch sich ernstlich einläßt, ist ein Unendliches; nur durch wetteifernde Tätigkeit weiß er sich dagegen zu helfen …" (*Ibid.,* 20, 69-70.) Goethe himself made a significant contribution to the study of anatomy through his demonstration that the intermaxillary bone was not missing in the human being.

9. A recent study of the working objectives of middle class men shows striking similarity with Goethe's conception of the importance of occupation in the life of the individual. "Thus a life without working to a man in a middle class occupation would be less purposeful, stimulating and challenging." Nancy C. Morse and Robert S. Weiss, "The Function and Meaning of Work and the Job," *American Sociological Review,* Vol. 20, No. 2 (April, 1955), p. 198.

10. *Lehrjahre* (J.A.), XVIII, 13.

11. *Ibid.,* XVIII, 185.

12. The importance of occupational achievement in determining status is recognized by students of modern social organization. Talcott Parsons concludes that in our present social system occupational achievement and personal qualities rank with kinship as determinants of social status. "An Analytical Approach to the Theory of Social Stratification," *American Journal of Sociology,* Vol. XLV, No. 6 (May 1940).

13. Thomas Mann, *op. cit.,* p. 46.

Frederick Amrine (essay date 1982)

SOURCE: Amrine, Frederick. "Romance Narration in *Wilhelm Meisters Wanderjahre." German Quarterly* 55.1 (1982): 29-38. Print.

[*In the following essay, Amrine suggests that, despite appearances to the contrary, Goethe actively worked to endow* Wilhelm Meister's Travels *with an ideal "Romance form" that could capture "unity-in-diversity." The novellas, asides, and aphorisms that fill the work are likened variously to counterpoint and polyphony in music and to interlaced motifs in the visual arts.*]

In a letter to Göttling of January 1829, Goethe compared the novel he was straining to complete to a "sisyphischer Stein" that he hoped soon to push over the summit and roll toward the public.[1] Predictably, Goethe's readers have for the most part merely scurried out of the way. Interpreters of the ***Wanderjahre*** [***Wilhelm Meisters Wanderjahre***], attempting to roll this great boulder of a novel back uphill to see whence it came, have all too often abandoned the Sisyphean task in utter frustration.

Numerous critics have turned to the ***Wanderjahre*** seeking a coherent formal or structural principle only to come away convinced that there is none to be found. In his history of the novel of the *Goethezeit,* H. H. Borcherdt has given the novel a chapter apart, as an anomaly;[2] Hermann Broch and Ehrhard Bahr have seen the ***Wanderjahre*** as an "experimental novel" anticipating modernism's total break with traditional genre forms.[3] The long-prevailing view of the *Wanderjahre* is presented succinctly by Emil Staiger, who suggests that the unity of the work lies somehow "jenseits des Romans" and is to be supplied by the reader, but also, less charitably, that the work's disunity represents "ein Zeichen des Verlusts an Kraft ... den das hohe Alter bringt. Die Energie reicht nicht mehr aus, ein weitgedehntes Ganzes bestimmt und folgerichtig durchzubilden."[4] He goes on to conclude that one can find grounds for reading any interpretation into the novel: all interpretations, and none, are justified in what Staiger sees as a situation of utter formal ambiguity and ambivalence.[5] Certain of Goethe's own pronouncements upon the two versions of the *Wanderjahre* (some of which Staiger quotes) might well seem at first glance to support such a contention.[6]

I would like to argue, however, that such statements on Goethe's part must not be taken as apologies for formlessness, but rather as descriptions of a kind of formal unity different from that which Goethe's contemporaries had come to expect in a novel: warnings that the form of the *Wanderjahre* was of a different order altogether, and that the novel thus had to be read in a different way. Contemporary readers also failed to find any unifying principle in the *Wanderjahre,* but Goethe himself saw it differently: he wrote of a "romantischer Faden" running through the work, weaving it together into a "wunderlich anziehendes Ganze."[7] To one correspondent who had criticized the "disunity" of the first version, Goethe replied rather defensively:

> Daß Sie ihre Ungeduld bei'm Wiederlesen der **'Wanderjahre'** gezügelt haben, freut mich sehr. Zusammenhang, Ziel und Zweck liegt innerhalb des Büchleins selbst; ist es nicht aus einem Stück, so ist es doch aus einem Sinn, und dieses war eben die Aufgabe, mehrere fremdartige äußere Ereignisse dem Gefühl als übereinstimmend entgegen zu bringen.[8]

Although the unity of the *Wanderjahre* was certainly not the simple, systematic unity of classical form, Goethe did insist that there was a unifying "Sinn" at work reconciling and conjoining seeming antitheses in the novel.

There has been a tendency within more recent interpretive work to take Goethe's cue and go in search of a unifying principle within the novel, but the result has been for the most part only vague intuitions. Eberhard Lämmert, for example, describes the *Wanderjahre*'s unusual mode of narrative integration merely as a "freizügige Verknüpfungsweise," while Wilhelm Emrich argues that formal "totality" is achieved in the novel "only indirectly," without ever explaining how.[9] Katharina Mommsen sees the selection of motives as an "equivalent" to formal unity amid formal license ("der Mangel formaler Einheit wird also ersetzt durch Einheitlichkeit der Motive"[10]), yet surely the unity of all motives must originate at a level

of formal organization more encompassing than the individual motif, which would then constitute a "formal unity." Claude David claims to have found the unifying principle of the *Wanderjahre*'s narration in the concept of "Zufall," which forces him, however, into some rather paradoxical statements, e.g.: "Man kann buchstäblich sagen, daß dem Zufall eine Art von Vernunft zugeschrieben wird"; and "Eine gewisse Unordnung kann dem Sinn des Ganzen nur zuträglich sein."[11] One might well wonder how chance—the ultimate "disunity-principle"—could serve as the basis for artistic unity. Explanations such as these seem rather to beg the question entirely.[12]

The few satisfying interpretations that have been put forth have been founded upon two very precise metaphors or formal analogs of the unifying principle in the novel: Goethe's own image of "wiederholte Spiegelungen," and that of musical polyphony. These subtle insights have indeed proved keys that unlock many of the novel's formal secrets. Yet I will attempt to show that these perspectives on the form of the *Wanderjahre* open out upon an even greater vista; that they can be fully understood only when seen as formal features characteristic of the Romance mode.[13] In this way it will become possible to define even more precisely the kind of formal "unity-in-diversity" achieved in the *Wanderjahre*'s narration and, more importantly, to place the novel for the first time within the literary-historical context of a distinct narrative tradition.

The transformation of narrative structure that occurs between the *Lehrjahre* [*Wilhelm Meisters Lehrjahre*] and the *Wanderjahre* is profound. The narrative situation of the *Lehrjahre,* in which one all-comprehending narrator looks down upon his narrative with complete insight and thus with complete control of tone, has disappeared. As Eduard Spranger has noted, the narrator of the sequel is no longer a "psychologischer Beobachter," but rather an editor of others' narratives.[14] Volker Neuhaus discerns approximately twenty different narrators in the *Wanderjahre,* exclusive of the authors of the various epigrams appended to Books II and III.[15] The one narrator who speaks directly to the reader has merely taken it upon himself to collect and organize others' narratives. Thus he characterizes himself as the "Sammler und Ordner dieser Papiere,"[16] as the "Redakteur dieser Bogen" (p. 258), and as a "treuer Referent" (p. 584).[17] Even the Wilhelm-plot, which seems initially to be narrated by the editor, is in fact (as Neuhaus has well argued) a transposition of Wilhelm's *Tagebuch* [*Wilhelm Meisters Tagebuch*] from the first into the third person.[18]

The tremendous refraction of attention and diversity of perspectives generated by the *Wanderjahre*'s multiple narration is typical of Romance form. In *The Nature of Narrative,* Scholes and Kellogg trace this device from Heliodorus, who first employed it extensively in his romances, through early Gothic romances and nineteenth-century works such as *Wuthering Heights* to more modern Romance writers such as Conrad, Faulkner and Isak Dinesen. As narrators are multiplied, "empiricism becomes romance."[19] The shift from single to multiple narration is accompanied by an analogous shift from a "simple linear plot" to a "multifoliate plot" (pp. 208 f.). In a similar vein, Gillian Beer lists as the traditional narrative techniques of prose romance "the prolific and apparently disorderly inclusiveness, the way in which events engender a whole range of disconnected happenings whose connections are yet felt though never pointed,"[20] the way in which story burgeons out of story, yielding a complexity close to that of life itself.[21] Beer seconds C. S. Lewis's suggestion that the organization of Romance works might best be described as "polyphonic narrative": as in polyphonic music, in which the various voices move independently yet harmonize, romance narration "moves freely while at the same time being interwoven to compose a congruent whole" (p. 20). Following Eugène Vinaver, Beer finds a further analogy to Romance polyphonic narration in the *entrelacement* of motifs and ornament in the visual arts of the Middle Ages (p. 21), a device that allows the romancers to intimate "the infinity which everywhere touches on the world they display" without resorting to overt allegory (p. 18).

Many interpreters have had recourse to the same, or very similar, analogies in their attempts to characterize the form of the **Wanderjahre.** In his book *Goethe and the Novel*, Eric Blackall entitles his interpretation of the **Wanderjahre** "Counterpoint in the Symbolic Mode," and describes the novel's rich formal texture as a composition of contrasting "themes and counterthemes," of "primary subjects and secondary subjects" in polar tension.[22] Like Lewis's medieval romances, the **Wanderjahre** resounds with a great array of antiphonal voices, seemingly independent in their movement yet continually yielding subtle harmonies when heard together. Victor Lange has also noted an essential formal principle in the **Wanderjahre** that reminds one precisely of Vinaver's "interlaced" Romance form, in which no one segment is meaningful in itself, but only in the context of its interweavings with other segments:

> The world through which Wilhelm and his son are led is pieced together from a multiplicity of details, each in itself important, but deriving its full force only from the light which they all, in turn, cast upon each other. What results, or what, at any rate, Goethe meant to produce, was an interlocking system of archetypal forms.[23]

Claude David likens the configuration of *Leitmotive* that run through the work to "ein symbolisches Filigran."[24] Yet none of these interpreters have seen that these characteristic structures are part of a long tradition of Romance narration.

Goethe seems to have worked quite consciously with these Romance narrative principles of "counterpoint" and "interlace" that together weave the narrative fabric of the

Wanderjahre. Like the Baronesse in his earlier **Unterhaltungen deutscher Ausgewanderten,** Goethe was intrigued by the possibilities for multiple reflection and refraction offered by "Parallelgeschichten."[25] Indeed, from the time that he began work on the novellas that would later be incorporated into the first version of the **Wanderjahre** right up until his death, Goethe was preoccupied with romance of every kind. An octavo *Notizheft* dating from Goethe's stay in Karlsbad of 1807, when he first conceived the **Wanderjahre,** offers much insight into what Goethe was reading and thinking at the time, and thus into possible antecedents and sources of the novel's form.[26] To a remarkable extent it reads like a synopsis of the major themes, motifs and specific literary works belonging to the mode of Romance. Goethe's **Tagebuch** also contains an extensive listing of the motifs in *Daphnis and Chloe* (the best known of the Greek romances, and Goethe's favorite work in later life),[27] and numerous entries from the same period of time (May-August 1807) such as that of 22 July: "Die romanhaften Motive zu den Wanderjahren überdacht." In later years Goethe's interest in Romance grew even stronger, as evidenced by his admiration for Scott's historical romances, Johnson's philosophical romance *Rasselas*[28] and the Chinese novels *Huan Chien Chi, Hau Kiou Choaan* and *Iu Kiao Li.* As both Stuart Atkins and Eric Blackall have noted, all three of these Chinese novels are romances.[29]

Within the **Wanderjahre,** this formal device of interweaving is "bared" by the fictive narrator precisely in the middle of the novel, in the "Zwischenrede":

> Wir haben in diesem zweiten Buche die Verhältnisse unsrer alten Freunde bedeutend steigern sehen und zugleich frische Bekanntschaften gewonnen ... Erwarten wir also zunächst, einen nach dem andern, sich verflechtend und entwindend, auf gebahnten Wegen wiederzufinden.

(p. 244)

Weaving is one of the great order-symbols for Goethe, both in the **Wanderjahre** and elsehwere:[30] the wonderfully ordered existence of the "Schöne-Gute" is symbolized by the weaving that her people perform, and in the **Lehrjahre,** at the moment of greatest insight into the ordering power of destiny, Wilhelm imagines his own life woven together with that of those around him by the flying shuttle of a great loom (*H.A.* [**Goethes Werke**] VII, 544). It is thus highly significant that this metaphor appears at the very center of the **Wanderjahre,** where the narrator momentarily unveils the principle according to which he has structured his narrative—an archetypal principle of Romance narration.

Eugène Vinaver's address *Form and Meaning in Medieval Romance* represents an extraordinarily subtle and precise characterization of this device as it appears in the medieval romances. Vinaver recounts in outline the efforts of late twelfth- and thirteenth-century writers to arrange the various Arthurian tales, legends and sagas into "a vast rational *ensemble*," a true "Arthurian cycle."[31] Their chief problem, according to Vinaver, was to find a way to narrate in coherent fashion adventures that had been transmitted haphazardly, and had thus lost whatever organic connection they might have once possessed. The device they eventually hit upon was to weave together the stories in such a way that none could stand alone, because each implied and was implicated with the others:

> ... namely the device of interweaving two or more separate themes. Far from being a mosaic from which any one stone could be removed without upsetting the rest, the Cycle turned out to be remarkably like the fabric of matting or tapestry; a single cut across it, made at any point, would unravel it all. And yet it was clearly not a unified body of material: it consisted of a variety of themes, independent of, but inseparable from, one another.
>
> (p. 10)

The result was "an eminently *acentric* composition, with as much internal cohesion as one would find in any centralized pattern" (p. 10), an entirely "un-Aristotelian" mode of unity. Such a Romance form is woven between the warp and woof of amplification or *digressio*, an "expansion or unrolling of a number of interlocked themes" (pp. 11f.) and *entrelacement*. The result is an ordered projection of the narrative threads, a stretching of the narrative fabric "until the reader loses every sense of limitation in time or space" (p. 12). The romance thus remains totally open-ended, yet each section represents a microcosm of the potential whole. Numerous themes can be pursued simultaneously by alternating them like threads in a woven tapestry: in this way each theme is implicated in the others, and all remain "constantly present in the author's and the reader's mind" (pp. 12f.). Vinaver finds analogs to this archetypal Romance formal principle in the basic patterns of Romanesque and early Gothic ornament, especially the interlace and the coiling spiral (p. 14). Unlike classical ornament, in which the design approaches and recedes from an imaginary center, this acentric medieval ornament moves toward "potential infinity," then returns whence it came (p. 14). Romance narrative is anything but chaotic: the subtle principles of its unity are merely less obvious.

An extremely apposite example of the interaction of these two principles, *digressio* and *entrelacement*, is offered by Wilhelm's own "narration within the narration," the letter to Natalie in which he attempts to relate why he has decided to become a surgeon.[32] Again and again he tries to come directly to the point, only to lapse into seemingly unrelated digressions.[33] He begins by telling the story of a lad who finds a rudder-pin upon the seashore; his interest awakened, the lad sets about to acquire first a full rudder, then a boat, mast, sails, etc. until finally, as an indirect result of his original chance find, he becomes the master of a great ship. But then Wilhelm halts and is forced to admit:

> Indem ich dich nun veranlasse, diese artige Geschichte wieder zu lesen, muß ich bekennen, daß sie nur im weitesten Sinne hierher gehört, jedoch mir den Weg bahnt, dasjenige auszudrücken, was ich vorzutragen habe. Indessen muß ich noch einiges Entferntere durchgehen.
>
> (p. 268)

Wilhelm goes on to discuss man's innate faculty for imitation; how the son frequently chooses the occupation of the father, although he sometimes lacks the father's talent; how those born into a "Familientalent" are perhaps the most fortunate. Yet this, too, proves to be a digression: "Da dieses aber nicht ist, was ich sagen wollte, so muß ich meinen Mitteilungen von irgendeiner andern Seite näher zu kommen suchen" (p. 269). Wilhelm laments that he cannot reproduce in writing the complicated intermediate steps that weave his thoughts together until a resolution is formed:

> Das ist nun das Traurige der Entfernung von Freunden, daß wir die Mittelglieder, die Hülfsglieder unserer Gedanken, die sich in der Gegenwart so flüchtig wie Blitze wechselseitig entwickeln und durchweben, nicht in augenblicklicher Verknüpfung und Verbindung vorführen und vorfahren können. Hier also zunächst eine der frühsten Jugendgeschichten.
>
> (p. 296)

He despairs of reproducing the fullness of reality, but hits upon a mode of narration that approximates this fullness: a series of seeming digressions that are actually subtly interrelated, or "interwoven," as Wilhelm's telling metaphor conveys.

There follows Wilhelm's relation of his childhood friendship with the so-called "Fischerknabe," the latter's drowning, and Wilhelm's passionate but unsuccessful attempts to revive him. Yet even this digression proves insufficient to attain the goal. Wilhelm apologizes for having to pursue such an "Umweg," and in the process employs yet another telling metaphor for the subtle, indirect mode of narration that his letter, and the novel in its entirety, display:

> Wenn ich nach dieser umständlichen Erzählung zu bekennen habe, daß ich noch immer nicht ans Ziel meiner Absicht gelangt sei und daß ich nur durch einen Umweg dahin zu gelangen hoffen darf, was soll ich da sagen! Wie kann ich mich entschuldigen! Allenfalls hätte ich folgendes vorzubringen: Wenn es dem Humoristen erlaubt ist, das Hundertste ins Tausendste durcheinanderzuwerfen, wenn er kecklich seinem Leser überläßt, das, was allenfalls daraus zu nehmen sei, in halber Bedeutung endlich aufzufinden, sollte es dem Verständigen, dem Vernünftigen nicht zustehen, auf eine seltsam scheinende Weise ringsumher nach vielen Punkten hinzuwirken, damit man sie in *einem* Brennpunkte zuletzt abgespielt und zusammengefaßt erkenne, einsehen lerne, wie die verschiedensten Einwirkungen den Menschen umringend

zu einem Entschluß treiben, den er auf keine andere
Weise, weder aus innerm Trieb noch äußerm Anlaß,
hätte ergreifen können?

(pp. 279f.)

Wilhelm likens his narrative to a set of mirrors arranged
around a periphery that are, however, unified in their
effect, in that they are all focused upon one central *Brenn-
punkt.* Goethe had used a similar image in a letter to the
orientalist Karl Iken in 1827: "Da sich manches unserer
Erfahrungen nicht rund aussprechen und direkt mitteilen
läßt, so habe ich seit langem das Mittel erwählt, durch
einander abspiegelnde Gebilde den geheimeren Sinn dem
Aufmerkenden zu offenbaren."[34] Numerous critics have
found this analogy of "wiederholte Spiegelungen" particularly apt in describing the form of the *Wanderjahre.*[35]
For our purposes, it is most important to realize that this
metaphor of "repeated mirrorings" is in every way the
equivalent of polyphony, weaving, and of digression and
interlace—the metaphors that Vinaver and others have used
to describe the unique texture of Romance narrative. In
Goethe's romance, as in all Romance, the ultimate goal is
to capture the infinite within the finite, a mimesis of potential infinity that is ideal, yet as complex, contradictory
and all-inclusive as one's experience of life itself—a kind
of realism subsumed beneath the ideal:

> Mit solchem Büchlein aber ist es, wie mit dem Leben
> selbst: es findet sich in dem Complex des Ganzen Not-
> wendiges und Zufälliges, Vorgesetztes und Ausgeschlos-
> senes, bald gelungen, bald vereitelt, wodurch es eine Art
> von Unendlichkeit erhält, die sich in verständige und
> vernünftige Worte nicht durchaus fassen, noch einschlie-
> ßen läßt.[36]

Wilhelm's letter to Natalie is an attempt to reproduce in
narrative the infinitely complicated yet immediate, and
thus timeless, workings of the mind in assessing its
own destiny. What Wilhelm has to convey is too subtle
for direct assertion, for immediate exposition. His decision
to become a surgeon is inseparable from the process
that has led up to it, yet no single phase of the process
would be meaningful in isolation, either. Only when all the
episodes are seen together do their "deep subliminal interrelationships" stand revealed.[37] The seeming digressions
actually interlace and interweave to form a subtle tapestry,
a narrative fabric just like that of the romance as described
by Vinaver. Wilhelm's letter to Natalie, which seeks to
make sense of his whole life's course, is a microcosm of
the entire novel, one that condenses and lays bare in a most
remarkable way the formal underpinnings of the *Wanderjahre* as a whole.

Here one might recall that the predominant structural
"counterpoint" in the novel, the mutual reflection and
interweaving of the novellas with their frame, is a form
that Northrop Fry has called "a modulation of the endless
romance."[38] One might even argue that the archetypal
"movement" of the *Wanderjahre,* with its digressive,

ever-expanding inclusiveness, is presented ideally in the
image of Makarie's spiralling journey out into the cosmos.
As Vinaver has shown, the spiral is an analogue of the
interlace, and thus an archetypal Romance form.

Finally, one notes a remarkable similarity between the way
in which the medieval romancers seek to unite the disparate Arthurian adventures into a single, cohesive narrative,
and the gestation process of the *Wanderjahre.* Eric Blackall describes in some detail the changes that the *Wanderjahre* underwent from its earliest, formative stages in 1807
through the first version of 1821 to the final version of
1829.[39] The version of 1821 was a true aggregate that
presented itself as an "archival novel": a fictive editor
presented the plethora of novellas, epigrams and isolated
incidents more or less "as he found them," leaving the
work of unifying them mentally to the reader. The 1829
version Goethe shaped into a coherent whole, a symbolic
novel with "a highly complex, but nevertheless unitary
structure" (p. 269). Through the twenty years during
which the *Wanderjahre* took shape, Goethe worked steadily toward the fulfillment of Romance form: complete
unity-in-diversity. Was this not one of the last and greatest
visions in Dante's greatest of romances, the vision of the
scattered sibyl's-leaves of the universe bound together in
one book by love?:

> Nel suo profondo vidi che s'interna,
>   legato con amore in un volume,
>   ciò che per l'universo si squaderna,
>
> sustanzia ed accidenti, e lor costume,
>   quasi conflati insieme per tal modo,
>   che ciò ch' io dico è un semplice lume.[40]

Notes

1. Letter to Göttling, 17 January 1829; H. Gräf, *Goethe
   über seine Dichtungen,* Pt. 1, II (Frankfurt: Rutten
   und Loenig, 1902), 1925 (hereafter: "Gräf").

2. H. Borcherdt, *Der Roman der Goethezeit* (Urach und
   Stuttgart: Port Verlag, 1949), pp. 559-97.

3. See E. Bahr, "Goethe's *Wanderjahre* as an Experimental Novel," *Mosaic,* 5 (1972), pp. 61-71.

4. E. Staiger, *Goethe* (Zürich: Atlantis Verlag, 1959), III,
   134-36. See also, e.g., A. Henkel, *Entsagung: Eine
   Studie zu Goethes Altersroman* (Tübingen, 1954), p.
   11; D. Fischer-Hartmann, *Goethes Altersroman:
   Studien über die innere Einheit von "Wilhelm Meisters Wanderjahren"* (Halle: Max Niemeyer Verlag,
   1941), p. 113f.; H.-J. Bastian, "Die Makrostruktur
   von 'Wilhelm Meisters Wanderjahren,'" *Weimarer
   Beiträge,* 14 (1968), p. 633; and K. Viëtor, *Goethe:
   Dichtung: Wissenschaft: Weltbild* (Bern: Francke Verlag, 1949), pp. 281-304.

5. Staiger, p. 137.

6. E.g., Goethe's letters to Zauper of 7 September 1821 (Gräf 1783), to Rochlitz of 28 July 1829 (Gräf 1941), to Boisserée of 2 September 1829 (Gräf 1943), as well as his conversation with Fr. v. Müller of 18 February 1830 (Gräf 1947).

7. *Tag- und Jahres-Hefte,* 1807—actually written January 1823 (Gräf 1807).

8. Letter to Zauper, 7 September 1821 (Gräf 1783).

9. E. Lämmert, *Bauformen des Erzählens* (Stuttgart: Metzler, 1955), p. 62; W. Emrich, "Das Problem der Symbolinterpretation im Hinblick auf Goethes 'Wanderjahre,'" *DVjs,* 26 (1952), p. 351.

10. K. Mommsen, *Goethe und 1001 Nacht* (Berlin: Akademie-Verlag, 1960), p. 121.

11. C. David, "Goethe's 'Wanderjahre' als symbolische Dichtung," *Sinn und Form,* 8 (1956), pp. 113-28. In this regard, see also K.-D. Müller, "Lenardos Tagebuch. Zum Romanbegriff in Goethes *Wilhelm Meisters Wanderjahre,*" *DVjs,* 53 (1979), pp. 275-99. The full spectrum of possible narrative forms that Müller advances as the basis of the *Wanderjahre*'s unity is surely not realized in the novel, and even if it were, the assumption that a plenum of narrative possibilities would unify a literary work seems dubious in the extreme.

12. Anneliese Klingenberg's attempt to explain the structure of the *Wanderjahre* in terms of Goethe's archetypal principles of "Polarität" and "Steigerung" is considerably more promising, but remains sketchy (*Goethes Roman "Wilhelm Meisters Wanderjahre oder die Entsagenden": Quellen und Komposition* [Berlin und Weimar: Aufbau-Verlag, 1972], pp. 150-64).

13. Since the word "romantic," capitalized or uncapitalized, represents an invitation to hopeless confusion, I will henceforth employ the term "Romance," both as noun and—admittedly inelegant—adjective, meaning thereby the narrative mode described by Northrop Frye in his *Anatomy of Criticism* (Princeton: Princeton University Press, 1957). As is well known, Frye employs the four modes of Tragedy, Satire and Irony, Comedy and Romances as compass-points to chart the literary universe. These four modes (or, as Frye also terms them, "*mythoi*") are "narrative pregeneric elements of literature," "generic (i.e., universal) plots," narrative categories that are "broader than, or logically prior to, the ordinary literary genres" (p. 162). In this they are analogous to tonalities in music (the circle of fifths comes immediately to mind): any number of distinct musical forms (e.g., a sonata, a symphony, an oratorio and a mass) may be composed in the same key.

Uncapitalized, the word "romance" refers to any of the several historical genres.

14. E. Spranger, "Der psychologische Perspektivismus im Roman," in his *Goethe: seine geistige Welt* (Tübingen: Rainer Wunderlich Verlag, 1967), p. 228. Unfortunately, Spranger confuses this editor with Goethe. See V. Neuhaus, "Die Archivfiktion in *Wilhelm Meisters Wanderjahren,*" *Euphorion,* 62 (1968), pp. 13-27.

15. Neuhaus, p. 25. On the multiplicity of narrative perspectives in the novel, see also J. Brown, *Goethe's Cyclical Narratives: Die Unterhaltungen deutscher Ausgewanderten and Wilhelm Meisters Wanderjahre* (Chapel Hill: University of N. Carolina Press, 1975), p. 78.

16. J. W. von Goethe, *Werke. Hamburger Ausgabe,* Ed. E. Trunz, 8th ed. (München: C. H. Beck, 1973), VIII, 408. All future references to the *Wanderjahre* will be to this edition and volume.

17. Trunz's contention that the narrator "clearly steps forth as an individual" (*CHA* VIII, p. 532) is, I think, unconvincing. All we know with certainty is that he has engaged in theatrical pursuits in the past, and now seems to regret it (p. 258). The editor cannot be assumed the author of the various fragments—especially since they originate in the circle around Makarie, of which the editor is not a part—and the remaining evidence that Trunz adduces to prove that the editor is aged (pp. 100, 6f. and 209, 16) is entirely inconclusive.

18. Neuhaus, p. 18ff. The *Tagebuch* itself is mentioned in Wilhelm's letter to Natalie (see p. 12); as Neuhaus shows (p. 19), this is a device that allows, among other things, descriptions of the *Auswanderergesellschaft* through Wilhelm's innocent eyes.

19. R. Scholes and R. Kellog, *The Nature of Narrative* (London: Oxford University Press, 1966), p. 262.

20. Remarkably close to Goethe's own description of the form of the *Wanderjahre*!: "... und dieses war eben die Aufgabe, mehrere fremdartige äussere Ereignisse dem Gefühle als übereinstimmend entgegen zu bringen" (Letter to Zauper, 7 September 1821 [Gräf 1983]).

21. G. Beer, *The Romance* (London: Methuen, 1970), pp. 76f.

22. E. Blackall, *Goethe and the Novel* (Ithaca: Cornell University Press, 1976), p. 236.

23. V. Lange, "Goethe's Craft of Fiction," *PEGS,* 12 (1953), pp. 31-63.

24. David, p. 114.

25. "Ich liebe mir sehr Parallelgeschichten. Eine deutet auf die andere hin und erklärt ihren Sinn besser als viele trockene Worte" (*HA* VI, 187).

26. J. W. von Goethe, *Werke. Weimarer Ausgabe* (Weimar: H. Böhlau, 1887-1912), I 25^2, 215. This *Notizheft* contains preliminary outlines for what was to become the *Wanderjahre,* as well as lists of themes and motifs culled from Goethe's readings at the time (the latter have been printed separately at I 53, 438-42). Katharina Mommsen argues convincingly (p. 307f.) that this notebook must date from Goethe's stay in Karlsbad in 1807—that is, precisely the time at which the first inspiration for the *Wanderjahre* came to him.

27. 22 July 1807. In the last chapter of *Goethe and the Novel,* Eric Blackall makes much of Goethe's interest in *Daphnis and Chloe,* and even compares that work to the *Wanderjahre* (p. 273).

28. See Blackall, *Goethe and the Novel,* pp. 195-96.

29. S. Atkins, "Wilhelm Meisters Lehrjahre: Novel or Romance?," in *Essays on European Literature: In Honor of Lieselotte Dieckmann,* ed. P. Hohendahl, H. Lindenberger and E. Schwarz (St. Louis: Washington University Press, 1972), pp. 45-52; Blackall, *Goethe and the Novel,* pp. 273-74 and Blackall, "Goethe and the Chinese Novel," in *The Discontinuous Tradition: Studies in Honor of Ernst Ludwig Stahl,* ed. P. Ganz (Oxford: Clarendon Press, 1971), pp. 29-53, where Blackall describes these works in some detail.

30. Cf. Blackall, *Goethe and the Novel,* p. 268.

31. E. Vinaver, *Form and Meaning in Medieval Romance* (Modern Humanities Research Association, 1966), p. 7.

32. I must disagree with A. G. Steer's interpretation of this passage (*Goethe's Science in the Structure of the Wanderjahre* [Athens: University of Georgia Press, 1979], pp. 68-73). Steer describes its structure as frame within frame within yet another frame. This implies that Wilhelm's main intent is to relate the story of the "Fischerknabe," and that the other narrative material is subordinate thereto. I feel that these can be described more accurately as a series of digressions and amplifications, narrative means to the end of depicting a complex process of inner resolve. Moreover, Steer's view necessitates seeing the tale of the "Fischerknabe" as framed in its very middle, which the author himself admits is "an unusual place to find framing material" (p. 69).

33. Cf. Lucidor in "Wer ist der Verräter?," who decides after repeated failures to attain his goal that the shortest distance between two points may be a crooked line after all. I am grateful to Maria Tatar for this insight.

34. Letter to Iken, 23 September 1827.

35. See especially L. Willoughby, "Literary Relations in the Light of Goethe's Principle of 'Wiederspiegelung,'" *CL,* 1 (1949), pp. 309-23 and L. Dieckmann, "Repeated Mirror Reflections: The Technique of Goethe's Novels," *Studies in Romanticism,* 1 (1961-62), pp. 154-74; but also E. Trunz's commentary, p. 530; Spranger, p. 196; Blackall, *Goethe and the Novel,* p. 262; David, pp. 124f.; and Brown, *passim.*

36. Goethe, letter to Rochlitz, 23 November 1829 (Gräf 1945). Cf. David, p. 115 and Lange, p. 60.

37. Bahr, p. 66.

38. N. Frye, *The Secular Scripture: A Study in the Structure of Romance* (Cambridge: Harvard University Press, 1976), p. 169.

39. Blackall, *Goethe and the Novel,* Chapters 10 and 11.

40. Dante, *Paradiso XXXIII,* 85-90. In Wicksteed's translation:

> Within its depths I saw ingathered, bound by love in one volume, the
>   scattered leaves of all the universe;
> Substance and accidents and their relations, as though together fused,
>   after such fashion that what I tell of is one simple flame.

Scott Abbott (essay date 1984)

SOURCE: Abbott, Scott. "'Des Maurers Wandeln/Es gleicht dem Leben': The Freemasonic Ritual Route in *Wilhelm Meisters Wanderjahre.*" *Deutsche Vierteljahrsschrift für Literaturwissenschaft und Geistesgeschichte* 58.2 (1984): 262-88. Print.

[In the following essay, Abbott calls for a closer examination of the correspondence between Wilhelm Meister's journey of initiation and the "ritual routes" important to Freemasonic ceremonies. Suggesting that Goethe's involvement with Freemasonry has too often been seen as irrelevant or embarrassing, Abbott highlights the recurrence of Masonic architecture in Wilhelm's travels.]

> Ich wette, Freund Voland liest da nicht einmal die Kirchenväter ... wie ... ich die Maurerreden in den deutschen Klassikern ... immer übersprungen habe.
>
> Mit einem ganz natürlichen Instinkt, lieber Dystra ... Sie haben wahrscheinlich immer gefühlt, daß diese Maurerreden in der That Dasjenige, was wir an Herder und Goethe bewundern, nicht ausdrücken ... Goethe vollends als Maurer hat sich im Großkophta selbst persiflirt, wie er sich im zweiten Teil des Faust als Minister persiflirte. Der

große allgewaltige Olympier, den wir in ihm bewundern, hat mit der Loge nichts gemein. Man zeigte mir einmal in Weimar Goethes Schurzfell; es hat mich nicht erbaut.

If this character in Karl Gutzkow's novel *Die Ritter vom Geist* (1850-51) is right, there is little need for the present study. "So what," he asks. We all know by now that Goethe was a Freemason. But didn't he himself make fun of the whole business in his anti-Masonic *Groß-Cophta*? Obviously this is nothing to be taken seriously.

While there may be some truth to what Gutzkow's character says—both proud Freemasons and zealous anti-Masons have waved Goethe's Masonic apron as if its existence alone proved something—we still have no right to simply burn the apron. Rather than dismiss the Freemasonic texts as trivial, as an embarassment, or as unenlightened hocus pocus, why not begin with the assumption that the text is perfect,[1] that the Freemasonic passages serve as context for the remaining text, and that understanding *Wilhelm Meister* depends on a careful reading of the very parts of the text Gutzkow's "enlightened" character chooses to skip. Before undertaking this task, let us consult the novel's own statements on how such passages should be read.

I

One of the poems introducing the 1821 version of the *Wanderjahre* [*Wilhelm Meisters Wanderjahre*] describes writing and reading the novel in terms of unearthing treasure, smelting metals, and coining coins:

> Und so heb' ich alte Schätze,
> Wunderlichst in diesem Falle;
> Wenn sie nicht zum Golde setze,
> Sind's doch immerfort Metalle.
> Man kann schmelzen, man kann scheiden,
> Wird gediegen, läßt sich wägen,
> Möge mancher Freund mit Freuden
> Sich's nach seinem Bilde prägen![2]

Besides offering a delightful invitation to a plurality of readings, the poem presents a novelist/treasure hunter ("setzen" is both a metalurgical and a printing term) seemingly untroubled at the thought that his treasures may not prove to be gold. Why the unexpected modesty, we might ask. Doesn't the reader deserve gold? We can tentatively answer these questions with reference to a statement about alchemy and gold in Goethe's *Farbenlehre* and to lines from the first scene of the *Wanderjahre.*

Goethe describes alchemy in the *Farbenlehre* as "der Misbrauch des Echten und Wahren, ein Sprung von der Idee . . . zur Wirklichkeit. . . ." Mankind, he writes, desires gold (along with health and long life) above all else. There is nothing intrinsically wrong with such wishes—unless, that is, we fall prey to the alchemists' promise to turn these wishes into reality through supernatural means. Goethe contrasts this jump from idea to reality with "die höchste

Bildung" through which our extravagant wish for Gold is tempered.[3]

The opening lines of the *Wanderjahre* likewise have gold as a theme. Wilhelm's son Felix picks up a stone and turns to this father:

> "Wie nennt man diesen Stein, Vater?" sagte der Knabe.
>
> "Ich weiß nicht," versetzte Wilhelm.
>
> "Ist das wohl Gold, was darin so glänzt?" sagte jener.
>
> "Es ist keins!" versetzte dieser, "und ich erinnere mich, daß es die Leute Katzengold nennen."
>
> "Katzengold!" sagte der Knabe lächelnd, "und warum?"
>
> "Wahrscheinlich weil es falsch ist und man die Katzen auch für falsch hält."
>
> (HA [*Goethes Werke*], VIII, 7)

The gold of the discussion between Wilhelm and Felix (and of the poem and passage on alchemy as well) is unreal, or at least unattainable. Bildung—analogical Bildung like that given here—is the real treasure. Felix is left holding a worthless stone, but he has had a lesson in simile. "Das will ich mir merken," he says.[4] Although the analogy proves more important than the supposed gold, without the gold there would have been no analogy. The novel will prove to be full of "alte Schätze," treasures the reader must simultaneously suspect as fool's gold and draw on metaphorically.

The poem about the novel as treasure is deleted in the 1829 version. In its stead appear two scenes in which we again see the novelist as treasure hunter or the novel as treasure.

Early in the book, Fitz leads Wilhelm, Felix, and Jarno to a charcoal burner's where "eine wunderlich verdächtige Gesellschaft" gathers around. The next morning Jarno takes Fitz to task for his aquaintance with some of these men:

> "Du bist überhaupt ein Schelm," sagte Jarno; "diese Männer heute Nacht, die sich um uns herum setzten, kanntest du alle. Es waren Holzhauer und Bergleute, das mochte hingehen; aber die letzten halt' ich für Schmuggler, für Wilddiebe, und der lange, ganz letzte, der immer Zeichen in den Sand schrieb und den die andern mit einiger Achtung behandelten, war gewiß ein Schatzgräber, mit dem du unter der Decke spielst."
>
> (HA, VIII, 41)

This last man, the most questionable, the one who writes signs in the sand and whom the others treat with a certain respect—this is the new embodiment of the poem's treasure-hunting novelist.

Jarno's discussion with Fitz continues, and we find that the treasure hunter has bought *Kreuzsteine* to help him find treasure (or, as novelist, to help him find the "alte Schätze" he needs as building blocks for his novel). Fitz describes the stones as "ein kostbares Gestein, ohne dasselbe läßt sich kein Schatz heben; man bezahlt mir ein kleines Stück gar teuer" (HA, VIII, 42). On one level, the *Kreuzsteine* are supposedly efficatious in supernatural undertakings; but on another level, these are natural metaphors the novelist must have to express the concepts he terms "treasures." In a letter to Zauper written while working on the **Wanderjahre,** Goethe says of nature that it can serve as a metaphorical key to self-understanding: "Die Natur, wenn wir sie recht zu fassen verstehen, spiegelt sich überall analog unserm Geiste; und wenn sie nur Tropen und Gleichnisse weckt, so ist schon viel gewonnen."[5] In the novel Jarno speaks of the *Kreuzsteine* as such natural figures:

> Man freut sich mit recht, wenn die leblose Natur ein Gleichniss dessen, was wir lieben und verehren, hervorbringt. Sie erscheint uns in Gestalt einer Sibylle, die ein Zeugniss dessen was von der Ewigkeit her beschlossen ist und erst in der Zeit wirklich werden soll, zum voraus niederlegt. Hierauf als auf eine wundervolle, heilige Schicht hatten die Priester ihren Altar gegründet.

> (HA, VIII, 35-36)

Others may use the *Kreuzsteine* to search for gold, but Jarno, understanding their true, metaphorical worth, goes so fas as to exchange gold for information about the stones: "'Nimm dein Goldstück,' versetzte Montan, 'du verdienst es für diese Entdeckung'" (HA, VIII, 35).

Jarno speaks of his study of geology in terms which again link the search for precious metals and reading a text: "'Wenn ich nun aber,' versetzte jener, 'eben diese Spalten und Risse als Buchstaben behandelte, sie zu entziffern suchte, sie zu Worten bildete und sie fertig zu lesen lernte, hättest du etwas dagegen?'" (HA, VIII, 34). He continues his lecture much later in the novel and contrasts a fruitless reliance on the supernatural with rational inquiry:

> Weil ich nun hier, wo nicht zu befehlen, doch zu raten habe, bemüht' ich mich, die Eigenschaft des Gebirgs kennen zu lernen. Man strebt leidenschaftlich nach den Metallen, die es enthält. Nun habe ich mir auch das Vorkommen derselben aufzuklären gesucht, und es ist mir gelungen. Das Glück tut's nicht allein, sondern der Sinn, der das Glück herbeiruft, um es zu regeln. Wie diese Gebirge hier entstanden sind, weiß ich nicht, will's auch nicht wissen; aber ich trachte täglich, ihnen ihre Eigentümlichkeit abzugewinnen. Auf Blei und Silber ist man erpicht, das sie in ihrem Busen tragen; ich weiß es zu entdecken: das Wie? behalt' ich für mich und gebe Veranlassung, das Gewünschte zu finden ... Sie haben mich in Verdacht, daß ich eine Wünschelrute besitze, sie merken aber nicht, daß sie mir widersprechen, wenn ich etwas Vernünftiges vorbringe, und daß sie dadurch sich den Weg abschneiden zu dem Baum des Erkenntnisses, wo diese prophetischen Reiser zu brechen sind.

> (HA, VIII, 263-64)

Jarno finds metal in the earth (lead and silver, not gold!) because he has learned the language of the mountains. Although some people suspect that a divining rod (or *Kreuzsteine,* or esoteric lore, etc.) leads him to the ore, he explains that that belief keeps them from the very rational knowledge which would unlock the secrets of geology.

But if rationality is given such priority, why does Fitz, a superstitious boy of questionable character, have possession of the *Kreuzsteine*? And why does the novelist appear as a disreputable treasure hunter?[6] Because the novel is full of "alte Schätze" which lend themselves to misuse as well as to metaphor. Without the treasures no metaphor, but without metaphor a fatal jump from idea to reality. In building his novel on an religious/occult symbolic foundation, the novelist works with an ambiguous, questionable, slippery medium. He indicates this and points his reader to a figurative reading by calling his own activity into question.

Fitz possesses the key to another treasure which likewise weaves together hermetic, tropic, and novellic motifs. In the Riesenschloß, which Wilhelm and Felix visit the day after their stay at the charcoal burner's (while Fitz has followed the lure of Jarno's gold), Felix finds a mysterious little box: "Endlich erhub sich der Verwegene schnell aus der Spalte und brachte ein Kästchen mit, nicht größer als ein kleiner Oktavband, von prächtigem alten Ansehn, es schien von Gold zu sein, mit Schmelz geziert" (HA, VIII, 43). Felix describes how he found the box in the corner of a larger, iron box: "zuletzt habe er den Kasten zwar leer, in einer Ecke desselben jedoch das Prachtbüchlein gefunden. Sie versprachen sich beiderseits deshalb ein tiefes Geheimnis" (HA, VIII, 44). The box seems to be gold and thus promises that which the occult treasures hunter seeks.

But this is no normal box—it is the size of an "Oktavband" and explicitly called a "Prachtbüchlein." The designations "Prachtbüchlein" and "Oktavband," added in the 1829 version, and the treasure hunter, who first appeared in 1829 as well, accomplish within the novel what the original poem did outside the narrative; that is, they identify the novel as treasure and the novelist and reader as treasure hunters. The 1829 version of the **Wanderjahre** was indeed an *Oktavband,* making the identification of the novel with the box/*Oktavband* even more convincing.

The key to the box/book, found later in Fitz's jacket, is depicted in the novel and has been linked by Emrich, in one of several readings, to Freemasonry:

> Es wäre einer besonderen Untersuchung wert, einmal den Schlüssel, den Goethe im Roman abbilden ließ, auf seine Form hin zu überprüfen, wobei freilich höchste Vorsicht bewahrt werden muß. Der untere Schlüsselteil mit seinen 'Haken' erinnert auffällig an ein griechisches CH, und der

obere geht wahrscheinlich auf Freimaurersymbole zurück (Quadrat mit drei Kreisen an den oberen Ecken, innerer durchkreuzter Kreis). Doch müßte eine solche Untersuchung sich vor eindeutigen Festlegungen und vor allem vor mystischen Auslegungen hüten.[7]

Ohly continues Emrich's careful speculation with discussion of a book Goethe read in July of 1819: August Kestner's *Die Agape oder der geheime Weltbund der Christen.* Kestner postulates a secret society of early Christians (with many Freemasonic aspects) through which Christianity supposedly achieved the unity and strength which enabled it to become a major religion. Comparing two secret signs depicted in Kestner's book with the key in the **Wanderjahre,** Ohly concludes that Emrich was right in seeing in the key a combination of Christian and "Freemasonic" symbols.[8] The key and the box/book have many functions in the novel, as Emrich points out;[9] but if we focus on the Freemasonic aspects just discussed, we find the attempts to get at the secrets of the seemingly golden box analogous to the reader's efforts to understand the novel with short-sighted reference to Freemasonry. When, for example, Felix turns the key with Freemasonic markings, in a fever to discover the mysteries within, the key breaks. It responds only to a more studied hand. The fact that the box ultimately remains closed to Wilhelm and Felix manifests the enigmatic quality of the novel, or, more importantly, the fact that the message lies not in the spurious secret, but rather in the figures pointing to the secret. The only person to open the box, in the end, is the goldsmith. He who daily works with gold understands the secrets of the trick key; but he counsels amateurs to leave the contents of the box untouched.

To summarize then: the poem of the 1821 version compares the novelist and reader to treasure hunters and the novel to a treasure. In the 1829 version the explicit comparison gives way to a more subtle manifestation in the person of the writing treasure hunter and in the form of the box/book. The mystery promised is not the gold of supernatural expectations, but the more useful metals of allegory, metaphor, and the like. The keys to buried treasure and to the *Prachtbüchlein* are, respectively, the *Kreuzsteine* and the key depicted in the novel (whose form originated in a book on a secret society of early Christians, a supposed forerunner of Freemasonry). Used as occult objects, the two keys are of questionable value. But when we view them allegorically, they indeed open up new perspectives. Their power to do so comes in part from their origin in the mysterious, secret, irrational, questionable world Fitz knows, a world known also by many eighteenth-century Freemasons. In addition, both keys relate to the problem of Wilhelm's and Felix's education and to the reading of the novel (or education of the reader). We shall proceed now to unearth a series of motifs best understood in the context of Freemasonry and shall seek to understand them figuratively, hopefully sidestepping the attraction of esoteric gold.

II

On February 13, 1780, having recently returned from a trip to Switzerland, Goethe wrote a letter to the head of the Freemasonic lodge Amalia in Weimar, explaining that social inconveniences encountered during his trip had intensified a long-standing wish to become a Freemason.[10] On the twenty-third of June of that same year he was taken into the lodge as an apprentice. Exactly one year later he was made a fellow, and on March 2, 1782, became a master mason. Writing to Kayser on June 14, 1782, Goethe ethusiastically claimed that a sub rosa tour of lodge rooms hitherto closed to him had given him unbelievable knowledge of the secrets of Freemasonry: "Im Orden heis ich Meister das heist nicht viel, durch die übrigen Säle und Kammern hat mich ein guter Geist extra-judizialiter durch geführt. Und ich weis das unglaubliche."[11] During this year Goethe also became a member of the Illuminati, recruited along with Karl August and Herder by the publisher and translator Bode. Within months, as the result of increasing quarrels between different Freemasonic systems, the lodge Amalia ceased operation.

In another letter to Kayser, several months after the closing of the lodge, Goethe showed early signs of distancing himself from Freemasonry:

> Die geheimen Wissenschaften haben mir nicht mehr noch weniger gegeben als ich hoffte. Ich suchte nichts für mich drinne, bin aber schon belehrt genug da ich sehe, was andere für sich drinne suchten, fanden, suchen und hoffen. Man sagt: man könne den Menschen beym Spiel am besten kennen lernen, seine Leidenschaften zeigten sich da offen und wie in einem Spiegel; so habe ich auch gefunden, daß in der kleinen Welt der Brüder alles zugeht wie in der großen, und in diesem Sinne hat es mir viel genützt diese Regionen zu durchwandern.[12]

Consistent with his later use of Freemasonry, Goethe here views the fraternal world as a kind of microcosm of the larger world. The final aphorism **"Aus Makariens Archiv"** echoes this earlier concept of education through analogy: "Wer lange in bedeutenden Verhältnissen lebt, dem begegnet freilich nicht alles, was dem Menschen begegnen kann; aber doch das Analoge und vielleicht einiges, was ohne Beispiel war" (HA, VIII, 486). Although failing to satisfy youthful desires for mystical wisdom ("das unglaubliche"), Freemasonry (like alchemy) provided Goethe with symbols, themes and structures for his literary endeavors.

In the following years Goethe expressed himself more and more negatively concerning the Freemasons and secret societies in general, writing, for example, in a letter to Karl August:

> Jena war, wie Sie wißen mit einer Loge bedroht … der Gedanke ein Collegium über das Unwesen der Geheimen Gesellschaft lesen zu laßen, ist trefflich. Ich habe den Direktoren der Litt. Zeitung auch einen Vorschlag gethan den sie angenommen haben, wodurch allen geheimen

Verbindungen ein harter Stoß versetzt wird. Sie werden es bald gedruckt lesen. Und so ist es gut daß man öffentlich Feindschaft setze zwischen sich und den Narren und Schelmen.[13]

Goethe expressed this antagonistic view of Freemasonry dramatically in *Der Groß-Cophta* (1791).[14]

It is understandable that Goethe developed such a bad opinion of Freemasonry. In the middle years of the eighteenth century, the original institution, very much a product of the Enlightenment, turned to exoticism of many sorts. Freiherr von Hund's establishment of the Strict Observance (in which the original three levels, apprentice, fellow, and master, multiplied, each succeeding level promising ever higher esoteric revelations) played an important role in the increasing disinterest and even hostility of men like Goethe. But even in these years Goethe drew on Freemasonry for his work.

Four years after the *Groß-Cophta*'s negative depiction of Masonic-like secret societies, Goethe finished *Wilhelm Meisters Lehrjahre,* in which a similar society has a more positive, if highly ambivalent, influence on Wilhelm Meister. In these years Goethe also worked on a sequel to *Die Zauberflöte,* Mozart's and Schickaneder's Freemasonic opera—to be called *Der Zauberflöte 2. Theil.*

Goethe's shifting relationship to Freemasonry took yet another turn in 1808, when, with his support, the lodge Amalia began functioning once again under a more rational system created by the Hamburg actor Friedrich Ludwig Schröder. For four years Goethe was fairly active as a Freemason; but in 1812 he asked to be relieved of all responsibilities vis-à-vis the lodge. Even after this date, however, he wrote occasional poetry for the lodge and participated in special occasions (e.g. the speech **"Zu brüderlichem Andenken Wielands"** which he gave in the lodge on the eighteenth of February, 1813; and the poem **"Symbolum,"** written in 1815 and first published in *Gesänge für Freimaurer,* Weimar 1816).[15]

III

Perhaps the most prominent feature of Freemasonry is its ritual, one aspect of which proves especially helpful in reading Goethe's "Freemasonic" works. In an article called "The Architecture of the Lodges: Ritual Form and Associational Life in the Late Enlightenment,"[16] Anthony Vidler points out the general belief of Enlightenment utopian writers that environmental form shapes man. Freemasonry, a kind of "lived utopia," Vidler says, developed an initiation ceremony which gradually came to include progression along a ritual route from a point of entry into the lodge past various symbolic objects to a final station where the initiate stood before officers of the lodge. At first the routes were traced in chalk on the floor, but as the rituals became more elaborate various floor coverings were used. These coverings most often represented the type of the Masonic lodge—Solomon's temple, and secondarily Egyptian temples and pyramids. As the actual ritual structures of the Egyptians were studied by Masonic iconographers, they were thought, Vidler writes, to have been "deliberately constructed to affect the succeeding states of mind of the aspirant by providing, as it were, a stage set for the initiation . . . The spacial organization of the initiatory sequence . . . becomes an agent of mental change."[17]

As increasingly occult Freemasonry spread through Europe, and as individual patrons of individual mystics emerged, new cultist lodges were established on secluded estates. Cagliostro, for example, built a lodge of "Regeneration" on the estate of the banker Sarasin near Basel in 1781. These "temples in the garden," as Vidler calls them,[18] represented an extention of the ritual routes into the landscape. A description of an initiatory sequence in such a "lodge," given by the English mystic and novelist, William Beckford, and quoted by Vidler, provides a good example of the practice.

In a letter to his sister dated 1784,[19] Beckford claimed to have been led by the architect Ledoux in a shuttered carriage through the streets of Paris to an outlying estate. Beckford was sworn to ask no questions concerning what he might see or hear. The two men got out before a stone wall, and, passing through gates, found themselves in a vast space occupied by wood-piles. Walking through a rude door in the largest of the piles, they entered a "gloomy vestibule, more like a barn than a Hall." The next door led them into a "plain room like the chamber of a cottage . . . overlooking a little garden." Passing through an apartment of better proportion and furnishing they then came into a "lofty square room" with more light, marble pilasters, and a sleeping cockatoo. A grand portal, its tapestry curtains open, invited them into a magnificent salon with a "coved ceiling, richly painted with mythological subjects." In front of a fire sat a "grim-visaged old man" with "most vivid and most piercing eyes." The old man suggested that he examine the works of art in the room, remarking that "'they merit a deliberate survey.'" Obeying, Beckford eventually came to an enormous bronze cistern filled with water in which he saw ghastly shadows. Hearing chanting from an adjoining room, all three men descended a stairway, passing into a tribune room from which they could see a large chapel in which a strange service was taking place. Here, Beckford writes, he faltered, and, in the words of the architect, "lost an opportunity of gaining knowledge which may never return." If he had undergone a slight ceremony he might have asked any question with the certainty of answer. But, the moment gone, Beckford and the architect retraced their steps, guided through the woodpiles by an "impish looking lad with a lanthorn," and found their way home.

It is easy to demonstrate that Goethe subscribed to the Enlightenment belief that environmental form shapes man, and that he artistically ordered the architectural symbols of ritual routes "to affect the succeeding states of mind of the aspirant." Take, for example, two stanzas from **"Die Geheimnisse,"** a fragmentary epic poem (1784/85) in which Bruder Markus is invited to enter into the secrets of the order:

> "Du kommst hierher auf wunderbaren Pfaden,"
> Spricht ihn der Alte wieder freundlich an;
> "Laß diese Bilder dich zu bleiben laden,
> Bist du erfährst, was mancher Held getan;
> Was hier verborgen, ist nicht zu erraten,
> Man zeige denn es dir vertraulich an;
> Du ahnest wohl, wie manches hier gelitten,
> Gelebt, verloren ward, und was erstritten.
>
> Doch glaube nicht, daß nur von alten Zeiten
> Der Greis erzählt, hier geht noch manches vor;
> Das, was du siehst, will mehr und mehr bedeuten;
> Ein Teppich deckt es bald und bald ein Flor.
> Beliebt es dir, so magst du dich bereiten:
> Du kommst, o Freund, nur erst durchs erste Tor;
> Im Vorhof bist du freundlich aufgenommen,
> Und scheinst mir wert, ins Innerste zu kommen."[20]

Here we have the architectural metaphor of passing through the first gate into the courtyard, and finally into the inner sanctum in search of ever greater knowledge. The phrase "Du scheinst mir wert, ins Innerste zu kommen," will be repeated several times in the course of the *Wanderjahre,* as will the "wunderbaren Pfaden," the paintings, the tapestry as a veil, and the successive gates or doors.

Goethe makes further use of such an architectural figure at the beginning of his **"Einleitung in die Propyläen"**:

> Der Jüngling, wenn Natur und Kunst ihn anziehen, glaubt mit einem lebhaften Streben bald in das innerste Heiligtum zu dringen; der Mann bemerkt, nach langem Umherwandeln, daß er sich noch immer in den Vorhöfen befinde.
>
> Eine solche Betrachtung hat unsern Titel veranlaßt. Stufe, Tor, Eingang, Vorhalle, der Raum zwischen dem Innern und Äußern, zwischen dem Heiligen und Gemeinen kann nur die Stelle sein, auf der wir uns mit unsern Freunden gewöhnlich aufhalten werden.[21]

With this description of ritual architecture, used to begin the introduction of his new periodical, Goethe demonstrates how well the movement from outside to inside, from entryway to antechamber to inner sanctum, serves as a figure for a gradual process of education. The Propyläen (the entry gate to the temples of the Acropolis in Athens, and now the title of Goethe's publication—meant to provide a forum, or rather Propyläum, for art-historical discussions) serves as an architectural figure for a station on the path of knowledge, whose end presumably lies in the temple of Athena. But it is not the mystical end which interests the man, as opposed to the youth. The man is content with moving along the path, with learning in the space between the inner and the outer, between the sacred and the profane.

This distinction between man and youth is similar to the definition of alchemy quoted above, "ein Sprung von der Idee, vom Möglichen, zur Wirklichkeit," for both alchemist and youth draw on true feelings but rush to false conclusions. Wisdom would eschew the mystery, would condemn the jump from idea to reality.

"Die Geheimnisse," based on Rosicrucian tradition (a rosy cross adorns the door of the monastery), and the introduction to the *Propyläen*, based on the architecture of Greek religion, belong tangentially in a discussion of Freemasonic architectural tradition, for Freemasonry borrowed freely from Egyptian rites, Eleusynian ritual, Solomon's temple, Rosicrucian lore, etc. But the poem **"Symbolum"** provides the most direct link between the Freemasonic initiatory route and Goethe's thinking concerning the same:

> Des Maurers Wandeln
> Es gleicht dem Leben,
> Und sein Bestreben
> Es gleicht dem Handeln
> Der Menschen auf Erden.
>
> Die Zukunft decket
> Schmerzen und Glücke.
> Schrittweis dem Blicke,
> Doch ungeschrecket
> Dringen wir vorwärts.
>
> Und schwer und schwerer
> Hängt eine Hülle
> Mit Ehrfurcht. Stille
> Ruhn oben die Sterne
> Und unten die Gräber.
>
> Betracht' sie genauer
> Und siehe, so melden
> Im Busen der Helden
> Sich wandelnde Schauer
> Und ernste Gefühle.
>
> Doch rufen von drüben
> Die Stimmen der Geister,
> Die Stimmen der Meister:
> "Versäumt nicht zu üben
> Die Kräfte des Guten.
>
> Hier winden sich Kronen
> In ewiger Stille,
> Die sollen mit Fülle
> Die Tätigen lohnen!
> Wir heißen euch hoffen."[22]

At the outset the poem proclaims a congruence between the development of the Freemason and the life of mankind, between his efforts and mankind's actions.[23] As the Freemason moves along his ritual route he approximates symbolically the stages of life. He walks forward, even while unaware of what awaits him. In so doing he draws closer to a covering which hangs "heavy and heavier" with *Ehrfurcht.*[24] The Mason contemplates God in the stars and death in the graves. Only then, after deep and serious feelings, can he pass on to the master who conducts the ceremony. The final exhortation is to action, to performance of good deeds, and a promise is made of reward to those who act. Again, we shall see this movement from Freemasonic symbol to action in the *Wanderjahre*. For the moment, however, let us simply note Goethe's explicit description of a Freemasonic ritual route as an allegory of life.

IV

In *Wilhelm Meisters Lehrjahre* (which preceded the final version of the *Wanderjahre* by more than thirty years) we find frequent reference to a kind of Freemasonry, to architectural pedagogy, and to the allegorical importance of the secret society—all of which are amplified in the *Wanderjahre.* The Tower Society, the organization whose members direct Wilhelm Meister's education in both novels, draws its name from a mysterious tower—part of what is described as "an altes unregelmäßiges Schloß mit einigen Türmen und Giebeln." An entire wing of this "wunderliches Gebäude," as it is called, remains closed to Wilhelm: "Zu gewissen Galerien und besonders zu dem alten Turm, den er von außen recht gut kannte, hatte er bisher vergebens Weg und Eingang gesucht" (HA, VII, 492-93).

Not long after Wilhelm realizes he has been excluded from these parts of the castle, he is taken aside by Jarno, who promises to show him the tower and introduce him to the secrets of its Society. The next morning, before sunrise, an initiation ceremony begins.

Jarno first leads Wilhelm from known parts of the castle to unknown rooms. A large, old door serves both actually and symbolically as an entryway into a new world. Inside a room once used for religious purposes, Wilhelm moves through a curtain from utter darkness to blinding sunlight. In this partially secularized space (a table covered with green cloth stands where once an altar stood), Wilhelm learns that members of the Society have carefully directed his education. They also introduce him to an extensive archive, to which he now, as an initiate, has free access. The Abbé gives him a *Lehrbrief* to further instruct him; and the scene ends as Felix, Wilhelm's son, appears and father and son move about the garden outside—Felix asking for the names of plants they see, Wilhelm somewhat lamely trying to teach him. This initiation ceremony, with movement through symbolic space as a major constituent, not only acts to further educate Wilhelm, but also marks the conclusion and the beginning of stages in that education.

In the irregular castle, in the tower, in the initiatory path (from room to room, through the large door and past the curtain to the brightly lit hall housing the archive, and finally in the garden), Wilhelm finds a symbolic architecture which acts to educate him. Most interesting here is the hall, which retains the stained glass and raised altar of a chapel, but which has been partially secularized. This new

Tower Society stands on a mystical base, the symbols of which still have value even if final assumptions are no longer shared. But as the *Lehrbrief* reiterates (in much the same language we quoted earlier from the *Farbenlehre*), impatience leads many to skip the progressive steps of education in an attempt to immediately grasp the mystery—"Die Höhe reizt uns, nicht die Stufen; den Gipfel im Auge wandeln wir gerne auf der Ebene" (HA, VII, 496). Finally, the *Lehrbrief,* after warning against the "Word" and the "Sign," describes an education by analogy, exactly the education the *Wanderjahre* thematicizes: "Der echte Schüler lernt aus dem Bekannten das Unbekannte entwickeln und nähert sich dem Meister."

The architectural pedagogy of the Tower continues as the novel nears its end and Wilhelm travels to the Oheim's estate. Having entered the courtyard, holding his sleeping son in his arms, Wilhelm "fand sich an dem ernsthaftesten, seinem Gefühle nach dem heiligsten Orte, den er je betreten hatte" (HA, VII, 512). The next morning, rising early, Wilhelm looks around the house which has so affected him: "Es war die reinste, schönste, würdigste Baukunst, die er gesehen hatte. 'Ist doch wahre Kunst,' rief er aus, 'wie gute Gesellschaft: sie nötigt uns auf die angenehmste Weise, das Maß zu erkennen, nach dem und zu dem unser Innerstes gebildet ist'" (HA, VII, 516). This contrasts with the asymmetrical house of Wilhelm's grandfather which originally held the art collection now in the Oheim's more symmetrical dwelling place (cf. also the disordered home of the Tower Society). Later, while walking in the garden, Natalie introduces Wilhelm to the "Hall of the Past," likewise an imposing architectural construction:

> Sie führte ihn durch einen geräumigen Gang auf eine Türe zu, vor der zwei Sphinxe von Granit lagen. Die Türe selbst war aufägyptische Weise oben ein wenig enger als unten, und ihre ehernen Flügel bereiteten zu einem ernsthaften, ja zu einem schauerlichen Anblick vor. Wie angenehm ward man daher überrascht, als diese Erwartung sich in die reinste Heiterkeit auflöste, indem man in einen Saal trat, in welchem Kunst und Leben jede Erinnerung an Tod und Grab aufhoben . . . Alle diese Pracht und Zierde stellte sich in reinen architektonischen Verhältnissen dar, und so schien jeder, der hineintrat, über sich selbst erhoben zu sein, indem er durch die zusammentreffende Kunst erst erfuhr, was der Mensch sei und was er sein könne.
>
> (HA, VII, 539-40)

Thus both the house and the "Hall of the Past" are said to represent an architecture so pure that it acts to educate the attentive viewer, raising him above his present level of education, teaching him of the measure according to which his most inner self corresponds.

While undergoing this increasingly orderly architectural education in the company of mentors and friends, Wilhelm witnesses Mignon's death and finds himself torn between Theresia and Natalie. He becomes bitter about the Tower Society and the way its members have mechanically structured his life. When Jarno tells him "alles, was Sie im

Turme gesehen haben, sind eigentlich nur noch Relequien von einem jugendlichen Unternehmen," Wilhelm cries out, "also mit diesen würdigen Zeichen und Worten spielt man nur . . . man führt uns mit Feierlichkeit an einen Ort, der uns Ehrfurcht einflößt . . . und wir sind so klug wie vorher" (HA, VII, 548), again the *Ehrfurcht* so prominent in the *Wanderjahre.* In answer, Jarno asks for the *Lehrbrief* and comments on various passages from it. He says that secrets, ceremonies, and grand words often attract young people with depth of character. The Society has kept its ceremonies, Jarno continues, to provide "'etwas Gesetzliches in unseren Zusammenkünften, man sah wohl die ersten mystischen Eindrücke auf die Einrichtung des Ganzen, nachher nahm es, wie durch ein Gleichnis, die Gestalt eines Handwerks an, das sich bis zur Kunst erhob. Daher kamen die Benennungen von Lehrlingen, Gehülfen und Meistern'" (HA, VII, 549). He continues to describe the archive they developed and finally says that because not all people are interested in their own education, some are held up and brushed aside with mystifications. The metaphor comes to seem real and thus becomes opaque.

Jarno here makes explicit what the secularized chapel depicted architecturally: that the original mystical impressions remain to point back to historical beginnings and thus to give order to the Society's meetings, and to act to separate serious seekers of education from enthusiasts. Even more interestingly, he also explains the assumption of a craft by the Society and its transformation into an art for figurative purposes. Although he does not mention which craft, the parallel to masonry/Freemasonry is clear. In Freemasonry the skills and tools of masons loose their concrete functions and gain figurative significance. Or, another example of figurative transformation of craft to art: in the occult, alchemical, Freemasonic-related *Gold-* and *Rosenkreutzer* of the late eighteenth century, the actual *Handwerk* of alchemy was practiced ("die ersten mystischen Eindrücke"); but when this *Handwerk* is raised to an art, the transformation of metals becomes a metaphor for education. Raising the *Handwerk* to art, then, as the Tower Society has done, does not mean, as Wilhelm first thinks, that he is led into a place which fills him with *Ehrfurcht* and then left with nothing, but rather, that he should come to the education he expects through the signs and symbols he sees, secularized or not. The Egyptian doorways, mysterious towers, and perfectly harmonious buildings serve not only as outward signs of Wilhelm's inward development—they are agents of the growth.

Through the "Handwerk . . . das sich bis zur Kunst erhob," through alchemy which becomes symbolic, through masonry that becomes Freemasonry, through architecture which becomes symbolic architecture, Wilhelm's education continues.

V

The first paragraphs of the sequel to the *Lehrjahre* [*Wilhelm Meisters Lehrjahre*] immediately sound themes which alert the reader that Wilhelm's travels are meant to provide a figural education and that each stage along his ritual route is important. As one of the poems preceding the 1821 edition states: "Die Wanderjahre sind nun angetreten / Und jeder Schritt des Wandrers ist bedenklich."[25]

The novel's first sentence places Wilhelm in meaningful surroundings: "Im Schatten eines mächtigen Felsen saß Wilhelm an grauser, bedeutender Stelle. . . ." Felix's question, "Wie nennt man diesen Stein, Vater?" links the novel at its outset with the scene, immediately following Wilhelm's initiation into the Tower Society, in which Felix asks for the names of plants growing in the garden. Felix's questions and Wilhelm's answers—the first explaining the name "Katzengold" by analogy to cats, and the second identifying part of a plant as a fir-cone by comparison of its scales or bracts with those of better known fir-cones—show Wilhelm's ability to think analogically, begin to teach Felix to do the same, and awaken in the reader a sensitivity to figures of all sorts. Wilhelm and the reader are thrust even further into this figurative mode when Joseph appears carrying the *Polieraxt* and *Winkelmaß* of a carpenter (HA, VIII, 9)—cf. the *Zirkel* and *Winkelmaß* of the mason/Freemason—leading a donkey bearing a woman in red and blue with a baby. Wilhelm is, of course, astonished to find the **"Flight to Egypt"** become reality in this mountain setting.

Wilhelm sends Felix with this wonderful family, and, as the day comes to a close, climbs the peak to retrieve his papers and pack. Climbing ever higher he once again sees the sun, "das himmlische Gestirn, das er mehr denn einmal verloren hatte" (HA, VIII, 11). He writes to Natalie that the mountains he is about to leave behind will act as a wall between them. The last sentence of the letter, written just as he leaves the border house high on the mountain, depicts him as a man about to die (and thus to leave behind the world of the *Lehrjahre* and to undertake a new life). The next morning he will descend the mountain and find a valley in which lies the monastery of St. Joseph, under whose broken altar the *Kreuzsteine* were found. These motifs (mountain, sun seen setting several times, valley, monastery, and cross) are precisely those encountered in the first stanzas of **"Die Geheimnisse,"** where Bruder Markus ascends a mountain near the end of day, the sun appears again as he reaches the top, he "ist wie neugeboren" when he hears a bell, and he finds a valley in which lies a monastery with a rosy cross on its door. These striking parallels make it clear that the Rosicrucian/Freemasonic substance of **"Die Geheimnisse"** continues here in the *Wanderjahre.*[26]

The half ruined, secularized monastery of St. Joseph is Wilhelm's first stop after leaving the mountain top. Religious services no longer take place here, but a religious spirit still pervades the atmosphere. Depictions of the life of St. Joseph line the walls. Wilhelm voices his surprise at the congruence between the paintings and his host's appearance, and receives the answer: "'Gewiß, Ihr bewundert die Übereinstimmung dieses Gebäudes mit seinen Bewohnern, die Ihr gestern kennenlerntet. Sie ist aber vielleicht noch sonderbarer, als man vermuten sollte: das Gebäude hat eigentlich die Bewohner gemacht. Denn wenn das Leblose lebendig ist, so kann es auch wohl Lebendiges hervorbringen'" (HA, VIII, 15). With this statement we stand again in the realm of architecture and education. Here is a building which has "made" its inhabitants. Influenced by artistic representations of St. Joseph as a carpenter and of fine carving on Herod's throne, the young man, who already bore the saint's name, also took on his craft. As we noted, Jarno talked in the **Lehrjahre** about the initiation rites as a "Handwerk das sich bis zur Kunst erhob," an art which, through its symbolic architecture and ceremonies, furthered Wilhelm's education. In the case of St. Joseph the Second, the craft raised to art in the paintings has led him to choose carpentry as his vocation. Thus the craft has become art and the art leads back to the craft. The circle continues as the young man uses his carpentry skills, which he rapidly develops into an art, to rebuild and restore the chapel housing the paintings. The craft becomes art which educates to craft which produces art, and so on. As a result of his visit to the monastery then, Wilhelm and the reader are explicitly reminded of the role symbolic architecture plays in "making the man," and of the role of the artisan/artist in making the work of art which makes the man.

After some conversation and a meal, Joseph finds Wilhelm worthy of further education: "'Es ist billig ... daß ich Ihre Neugierde befriedige ... ich fühle, daß Sie imstande sind, auch das Wunderliche Ernsthaft zu nehmen, wenn es auf einem ernsten Grund beruht'" (HA, VIII, 17). What is the serious foundation which allows a person to take the extraordinary appearance of Joseph and Mary seriously? Nothing other than Wilhelm's ability, demonstrated in the **Lehrjahre,** to recognize that no magic is at work here, changing idea to false reality, but rather that the paintings, the figures, have wrought such marvelous works. The real, satisfying, forming, educating magic lies in the paintings and the pedagogical treasures of the narrative.

As we have seen, Wilhelm's experiences at the monastery make him once again aware of the power of architecture/painting to educate, of the progression from *Handwerk* to *Kunst* to *Handwerk*. Leaving the monastery, Fritz leads Wilhelm and Felix to Jarno. Jarno lectures Wilhelm at length (there are connections here to the *Lehrbrief*) on the alphabet of nature, on a craft which, through art, becomes figurative, and on the *Kreuzsteine* as natural figures. As night approaches they all follow Fitz "durch wundersame Pfade" (HA, VIII, 37) to the *Kohlenmeiler* in the middle of the woods.

The night passes, and Jarno continues to lecture Wilhelm: "Wenn du es aber doch nicht lassen kannst und auf eine vollkommene Bildung so versessen bist, so begreif' ich nicht, wie du so blind sein kannst, wie du noch lange suchen magst, wie du nicht siehst, daß du dich ganz in der Nähe einer vortrefflichen Erziehungsanstalt befindest" (HA, VIII, 39). Wilhelm does not understand, so Jarno explains (using the *Kohlenmeiler* as a metaphor—raising the product of craft to art) that there the wood is not completely burned, but rather partially burned in a confining environment, with the result that the wood/charcoal becomes useful. Wilhelm learns from this that limitation is necessary and that he should become skilled in a trade. While this pedagogy takes place, a mysterious group of men—including the treasure hunter—gathers around the *Kohlenmeiler*; and the next morning Jarno accuses Fitz of being in league with them.[27]

Fitz and Jarno go their own way, and Felix and Wilhelm come to the *Riesenschloß*, a natural architectural wonder, where Felix finds the box/book already discussed. Fitz returns and leads them from the "geraden breiten, eingeschlagenen Weg" onto what seems a short-cut. They find themselves traveling rapidly downhill through a wood, "der, immer durchsichtiger werdend, ihnen zuletzt die schönste Besitzung, die man sich nur denken kann, im klarsten Sonnenlichte sehen ließ" (HA, VIII, 45). But such sudden vision achieved by taking the short-cut suggested by Fitz (the supplier of magic *Kreuzsteine*) proves false, for a deep ditch and a high wall separate them from the Oheim's estate (cf. alchemy as a similar short-cut). Fitz has anticipated this, and cannot conceal his Schadenfreude when Wilhelm recognizes what has happened.

In order to avoid a long detour, Fitz next suggests that they enter the estate through vaults built to allow rain water from the mountains to enter the estate in an ordered fashion. Just as Felix insisted on seeing the *Riesenschloß* and entering its caves, even when Fitz had counseled against it, he again wants to enter the vaults: "Als Felix von Gewölben hörte, konnte er vor Begierde nicht lassen, diesen Eingang zu betreten" (HA, VIII, 45). The three enter the vaults, climb down stairs, and find themselves now in the light, now in the dark. Suddenly a shot sounds and iron grates fall to imprison Wilhelm and Felix. Fitz escapes, leaving behind his coat, its arm caught in the fence.

Men from the estate appear and lead Wilhelm and Felix as prisoners up a circular staircase. At the top they find themselves in "einem seltsamen Orte; es war ein geräumiges, reinliches Zimmer, durch kleine, unter dem Gesimse hergehende Fenster erleuchtet, die ungeachtet der starken Eisenstäbe Licht genug verbreiteten ... es schien dem, der sich hier befand, nichts als die Freiheit zu fehlen" (HA, VIII, 46). Felix reacts violently to the restraining walls and the iron bars, beating on the strong doors with his fists. Wilhelm, seeing a seemingly enlightened inscription on the wall, tries to comfort the boy, but Felix immediately falls into a deep sleep.

An official enters the room, and after hearing Wilhelm's story and seeing his papers, helps him carry the still sleeping Felix into a beautiful garden room where refreshments await them. When the boy awakens they walk to the castle, fronted by trees which form a "Vorhalle des ansehnlichen Gebäudes." Inside the building, Wilhelm passes quickly through the vestibule, ascends a stairway and enters a main hall, seeing in each place certain paintings. The *Hausherr,* "ein kleiner, lebhafter Mann von Jahren," welcomes his guests, and asks them, pointing to the walls, whether Wilhelm knows the cities depicted there. Wilhelm replies, demonstrating a thorough knowledge of several of them. During the next two days Wilhelm finds his way into a gallery to look at portraits hanging there and finally is led by the Oheim into an inner room where he sees more portraits, relics, and manuscripts. "Zuletzt legte er Wilhelmen ein weißes Blatt vor mit Ersuchen um einige Zeilen, doch ohne Unterschrift; worauf der Gast durch eine Tapetentüre sich in den Saal entlassen und an der Seite des Kustode fand" (HA, VIII, 80). Wilhelm and Felix later leave the Oheim's to travel to Makarie's castle, and the route they trace will play an important role in a later phase of this discussion; but for now, let us review the route we have just described with William Beckford's ritual route in mind.

Beckford describes (1) his route from Paris, (2) the wall of the estate, (3) the wood piles, (4) the pyramidal entrance, (5) the "barnish hall," (6) the cottage and garden, (7) the antechamber, (8) the curtain, (9) the main salon with the grim-visaged old man who suggests that Beckford carefully observe the mythological paintings, laver, and fire, and (10) the chapel and tribune. In Vidler's schematization this appears as follows:

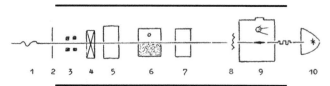

If we schematicize Wilhelm's route we find some remarkable similarities:

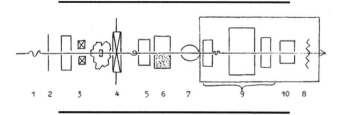

Wilhelm travels (1) the route from the *Lehrjahre* to (2) the mountains which act as a wall. The monastery of St. Joseph reminds him that the building makes the man, (3) the wood pile of the charcoal burner is a natural *Erziehungsanstalt,* and the *Riesenschloß* is nature's ruined temple with a secret at its center. (4) A vault serves as both an entrance and a trap, and from there Wilhelm and Felix walk up a spiral staircase to (5) a prison room. This

environment, oppressive to Felix, gives way to (6) a garden room and then to (7) a natural vestibule surrounded by trees. Inside the castle father and son move through (9) a series of rooms with paintings on the walls. In the main hall "ein kleiner, lebhafter Mann von Jahren," meets Wilhelm and asks him about the paintings on the walls. Finally Wilhelm moves through the gallery to (10) the inner room with its treasures. He leaves through (8) a curtained doorway.

Beckford's and Wilhelm's routes have in common (1) a path to the estate, (2) a wall, (3) woodpiles, (4) a pyramidal entrance, (5) a barnish hall/prison room, (6) a garden room, (7) a vestibule, (8) a curtain, (9) a hall with paintings and an old man who recommends observation of them, and (10) an inner room or chapel in which the final disclosure is or is not made.

Despite the remarkable congruence, there seems to be no way that Goethe could have known Beckford's description of his initiatory journey, written as a letter to his sister. But while this specific case may not be the source for Wilhelm's pedagogical journey, it provides information concerning the substance of such ritual routes, transferred from the floor-drawings of Freemasonic lodges into the gardens and buildings of estates. It also gives us a context in which we can more fully understand the *Wanderjahre.*

VI

We have come a long way since our suggestion that Goethe may have used Freemasonic ritual to help structure his last novel. We learned first to treat whatever esoteric lore we found in the novel as possible fools-gold and then pointed out the allegorical value of Freemasonry, alchemy, Christianity, etc. After discussing Freemasonic architecture and ritual routes we found several works in which Goethe employed a similar architectural/pedagogical strategy. We then turned to the *Lehrjahre* and noted the initiation rites and architectural pedagogy of the Tower Society. A reading of early scenes in the *Wanderjahre* established that once again Freemasonic architectural symbols played a substantive role in the text. Finally we found a remarkable congruence between Beckford's description of an initiatory route and the path Wilhelm follows in the early pages of the novel. This last discovery has value primarily in leading us to examine closely the various routes Wilhelm follows in the course of the *Wanderjahre.* If we take the architectural details seriously, as elements in an educational sequence inspired by Freemasonry, we have a new basis on which to compare and contrast different stages in Wilhelm's journey. These stages have been interpreted in various ways in the past—a look at two such interpretations will put our work in a little broader context.

Ohly, for example, draws on the teachings about *Ehrfurcht* in the pädagogische Provinz to examine the *Kloster,* the *Riesenschloß,* the Oheim's estate, and Makarie's realm as representative of "Ehrfurcht vor dem, was über uns ist," "Ehrfurcht vor dem, was unter uns ist," "Ehrfurcht vor dem, was uns gleich ist," and "Ehrfurcht vor dem, was in uns ist" respectively, and then finally the pädagogische Provinz as the "die geistig reine Mitte."[28] He is quite convincing, especially in his reading of the successive estates as symbolic regions, but in the end one has the feeling that the complexity of the novel calls for other perspectives as well. Why, for instance, should the pädagogische Provinz and its teachings be seen as the center of the novel?[29] And why does the final region Wilhelm enters, that of the Tower Society, not enter into the scheme of things?

Wilhelm Vosskamp likewise considers several of the regions, this time within the structure of utopias.[30] The Oheim's estate, the pädagogische Provinz, and the two groups of the Tower Society are convincingly considered as contrasting utopias. Vosskamp supports his argument with good textual analysis—for example, he notes that Wilhelm enters the Oheim's estate and the Provinz through gates which set the utopias off from the surrounding countryside. He does not, however, mention the doors/gates of each of the other realms of the novel, which likewise set them off. We are left with the question: Why deal with only four regions and leave others undiscussed? Again, the system used to examine the novel proves only partially successful.

In what follows, we shall build on Ohly's and Vosskamp's (and others') attempts to analyze the succesive regions along Wilhelm's route in his ***Wanderjahre***. While our understanding of this complex novel will also remain woefully fragmentary, we hope to begin to approach a more comprehensive interpretation. The method will be that suggested by the comparison of aspects of the ***Wanderjahre*** with what we know about Freemasonic ritual routes; for as we compare the stages along Wilhelm's route we find the similarities which allow us to group the realms together and subsequently find ourselves able to note the differences which characterize the individual realms.

Putting aside for the moment the fictional and biographical realms Wilhelm enters through reading and hearing the Novellen and stories, we find the following stages in his journey: St. Joseph's monastery, Montan's mountain realm (including the *Kohlenmeiler* and the *Riesenschloß*), the Oheim's estate, Makarie's house, the pädagogische Provinz, the Lago Maggiore, and finally the estate on which the Tower Society has gathered. There are other short stops along the way (the old house in the city, for instance, where Wilhelm leaves the box/book), but in the interest of economy we shall not include them.

The following chart makes clear the congruity of the various routes Wilhelm takes, as well as the incongruities:

	path	door	guide	hall/ paintings	worthy	curtain	archive treasure	garde
WML	493 durch Galerien	493 alte Tür	493 Jarno	493 Saal, Kapelle Gemälde	493 tiefer in Geheimnis	493 Teppich zum Licht	497 Archiv Lehrjahre	498 im Garten mit Felix
Joseph	13 Berg-Tal	14 offenes Tor	Joseph	14 Saal, Kapelle Gemälde	17 Neugierde befriedigen	X	Kreuzsteine	16 Ruinen Garten
Montan	30 ohne Pfad 37, 42	?	Fitz Jarno Bote	?	33, 36 *nicht*	X	43 box book	alles Natur
Oheim	44 steil oder breit	45 Gewölbe	49 Mann von Jahren	49, 64, 79 Saal Gemälde	49-50 79, 80	80 Tapentüre	80 Handschriften	48 Gefängnis zum Garten-Zimmer
Makarie	114	114 Tor Pforte, Tür	115 Astronom	115 Saal Gemälde	126 weiterführen	115 grüner Vorhang	124 Archiv	122 Sternwarte zum Garten
Provinz	149 nach Vorschrift	154-161 Tor, Pforte Portal, Pforte	154 die Drei	158 8-eck. Halle, Gemälde	165 zu Vertrauten gezählt	164 Schleier über Leiden	164 Heiligtum des Schmerzens	158 Galerie mit Garten
Lago M.	226 Berg-Tal	X	234 Reiseführer	234 Insel Gemälde	231 Pfeil zutraulich	X	239 Schmerz	alles Natur
Tower Society	310 Karte quer durchs Land 316	316 Schloßtore	316 der Vogt	311 Saal Buchstaben	311 aufgenommen	X	316 Gastmahl Schmerz	318 enden im Garten

We notice first that in every case the path to the respective estate is described. We also become aware that one region (Montan's) may actually have three parts, for we see the travelers making their way to the peak where Jarno works, to the charcoal burner's, and then to the *Riesenschloß* on another peak. The respective paths to these places are "ohne Pfad," "wundersame Pfade," and "beschwerlicher Pfad."

Second, each estate is separated from the outside world by at least one wall through which a door leads. Exceptions: the Lago Maggiore and Montan's realm. But entrance to the latter is gained when Jarno reaches his hand down to Wilhelm and lifts him up over the natural mountain wall.

Third, a guide (usually an old man) leads Wilhelm through the house or countryside to, fourth, a hall in which paintings hang. In each case Wilhelm studies the paintings. Sometimes he demonstrates his knowledge of the people or places depicted and thus wins the favor of his host, and sometimes the paintings are used explicitly as pedagogical tools. The various collectors are characterized by their collections as well. In Montan's realm there are no paintings, but in their place we find the analogies he uses to teach Wilhelm. Wilhelm's journey thus takes him to the paintings of the life of St. Joseph which so affect the modern Joseph and Mary, to the natural metaphors, the "letters of nature," to the Oheim's geographical representations and portraits (no painting with religious or mythical theme), to the historical paintings on Makarie's walls, to the eight-sided hall of the pädagogische Provinz with its paintings from the Old and New Testaments, to the landscapes of the painter in Italy, and finally to the complete absence of paintings in the temporary lodgings of the Tower Society. Here the constancy of the repetition brings us to ask a question we would otherwise not ask. Why are there no paintings in this last region? One answer lies in the secret part of the castle in the *Lehrjahre.* There, in the secularized chapel, instead of paintings, Wilhelm sees active figures from his past step through a frame. The men at the end of the *Wanderjahre* are likewise active men. Wilhelm's education ends in the years immediately following the Lago Maggiore when he learns the trade of *Wundarzt,* and now the absence of paintings signals that completion. To support this we might point out that after asking innumerable questions at each of the previous stages of his *Wanderjahre,* Wilhelm now, in the company of active men, of comrades from the Tower Society, is forbidden to ask questions. A second answer may be found in the letters Wilhelm sees in the *Vorsaal* of the *Wirtshaus:* "'Ubi homines sunt modi sunt.'" "Daß da, wo Menschen in Gesellschaft zusammentreten, sogleich die Art und Weise, wie sie zusammen sein und bleiben mögen, sich ausbilde," so translates the narrator. In each succeeding realm Wilhelm has seen a different way of life, in each case strictly ordered and ruled by a specific world view. The paintings, along with various declarations of values, have

given him insight into each. But now, at the end, we ask which realm is the final, the highest embodiment of Goethe's thought. Or are we simply to find a golden mean? On the contrary. The golden [!] letters leave Wilhelm free, leave the Tower Society free, to organize themselves as they will. Here we find no normative paintings—only various sorts of action.

Fifth, with amazing regularity Wilhelm gains permission to enter further into the marvelous and secret affairs of the respective hosts: "es wäre unbillig, wenn wir Sie nicht tiefer in unsere Geheimnisse einführen," "es ist billig … daß ich Ihre Neugierde befriedige," "der Hausherr, zufrieden, daß der Gast eine so reich herangebrachte Vergangenheit vollkommen zu schätzen wußte, ließ ihn Handschriften sehen," "wir dürfen Sie weiterführen," "dieser wird nun zu den Vertrauten gezählt," "der Gast sei angenommen." These statements lie at the heart of our assertion that Goethe makes use of the Freemasonic ritual route to complete Wilhelm's education. A notable exception: Wilhelm repeatedly asks Montan for information about the mineral world so he can instruct Felix, and Montan repeatedly turns him down ("gib das auf"—HA, VIII, 36, 260). Montan gives several reasons for his refusal to initiate Wilhelm into the secrets of nature, but we may decide, in the end, that the "Buchstaben der Natur," nature's archive, can only be opened by nature herself. This makes sense when we see the route approaching Montan's cliff. We find Wilhelm climbing "ohne einen Pfad vor sich zu haben" (HA, VIII, 30).

Sixth, each realm has a secret, a truth revealed only to those found worthy of initiation. In the traditional ritual route (as in Solomon's temple or the veil of Isis) the secret is covered by a curtain or veil. We find such curtains in several of the routes Wilhelm traverses. In the *Lehrjahre* he passed through a curtain to the bright light of the secularized chapel, the table/altar was covered with a green tapestry, and a curtain covered the empty frame. Before Wilhelm sees Makarie "ein grüner Vorhang zog sich auf." And in the pädagogische Provinz the depictions of Jesus' death are kept veiled: "wir ziehen einen Schleier über diese Leiden." But the most interesting of the curtains/veils is the one Wilhelm passes through at the Oheim's. Only *after* visiting the inner rooms where the Oheim keeps his treasures does Wilhelm go through a "Tapetentüre." There may be a veiled statement here about the worth of the Oheim's highly rational and empirical way of life.

Seventh, what treasures does Wilhelm find as he passes into the various inner rooms? In the *Lehrjahre* he finds an archive, a *Lehrbrief,* and then, turning from the empty word as the *Lehrbrief* suggested, discovers his son. At St. Joseph's, after being found worthy, Wilhelm hears Joseph's story of how the building with its paintings made the man. The *Kreuzsteine,* once under the altar there, natural metaphors, represent another treasure. In the *Riesenschloß* the treasure is the box/book. The Oheim shows Wilhelm relics and manuscripts. At Makarie's Wilhelm gains access to a very interesting archive (a collection of aphorisms, among other things) and learns the great secret about Makarie's wonderful ties to the cosmos. The secret of the Provinz lies in the suffering of Jesus on the cross, a "Heiligtum des Schmerzes" Wilhelm does not enter. The emotional high point of the Lago Maggiore scene lies in the suffering of the four as they contemplate leaving one another's company and remember, all too vividly, Mignon's suffering. And finally, with the Tower Society, Wilhelm takes part in a *Gastmahl,* often the end of a traditional ritual route and the culmination of Freemasonic ceremony. Here too the participants suffer deeply at the thought of parting, but like the four sufferers at the Lago Maggiore, have been "eingeweiht in alle Schmerzen des ersten Grades der Entsagenden," and pass through this potentially destructive mode to action. As we list these treasures a definite pattern appears. Four (or five, if we include Montan and his "Buchstaben der Natur") of the first regions have archives at their centers. The last three regions, however, share *Schmerzen* as their secret, *Schmerzen* overcome through *Entsagung.*

And finally, after all of these ritual routes leading to various central places and secrets, the garden appears as the last stage of the journey. After his initiation into the Tower Society Wilhelm takes Felix into a garden where they begin their educations anew. The *Wanderjahre* begin with Wilhelm and Felix in a natural setting. After observing Joseph's paintings Wilhelm goes out into a garden. Montans's realm is entirely natural. Wilhelm and Felix leave a prison room at the Oheim's and enter a garden room. After his miraculous dream on the *Sternwarte* at Makarie's Wilhelm goes into a garden. The Lago Maggiore is once again almost totally garden.[31] After the *Gastmahl* with the Tower Society, Wilhelm steps out into the castle gardens and overlooks a broad valley. And as the novel ends, Wilhelm and Felix once again lie in the arms of nature. No matter what secrets each region conceals at its center, the ultimate treasures lie in nature.

A final note on the successive realms: it seems that Wilhelm's stages alternate between the natural, unbounded, and the artifical, bounded. He moves from the mountain to the "umschlossenes Tal" of St. Joseph, from Montan's peak where he feels threatened to the "beschränkter Waldraum" of the charcoal burner, from the *Riesenschloß* on a wild peak to the extraordinary order of the Oheim's, from the frightening openess of Makarie and her tower to the pedantic order of the Provinz, and finally from the open Italian lake to the self-imposed order of the Tower Society.

Until now we have traced Wilhelm's various routes exclusively in the frame of the novel. The Novellen strewn through the novel, as others have pointed out, provide "wiederholte Spiegelungen" of motifs and actions in the frame. When we find such mirroring of our theme in the Novellen it gives us one more assurance of the productivity of our new perspective.

"Die Pilgernde Törin," the first of the Novellen, is given to Wilhelm by Hersilie to read during his stay at the Oheim's. When the young woman in question is brought to Revanne's castle, she proves her worthiness for such an environment through her reactions to the castle ("sie zeigt sich als eine Person, der die große Welt bekannt ist" HA, VIII, 54). After receiving refreshments she comments on the furniture, the paintings, the division of the rooms, and finally, in the library, shows that she knows good books. This, of course, mirrors almost precisely the process Wilhelm has just gone through with the Oheim (cf. HA, VIII, 49-50 and the pages after the story in which Wilhelm sees the Oheim's manuscript collection).

In **"Wer ist der Verräter?,"** again given by Hersilie to Wilhelm, Lucidor finds himself at one point in a hermitage with a Chinese roof. There he sees hundreds of paintings on the walls which disclose the historical inclinations of the old man who lives there from time to time. Later he is led through "lange, weitläufige Gänge des alten Schlosses" to a *Gerichtssal* in what was once a chapel. Locked in there, he finds an archive containing some of his own work. Next he is brought to a large hall where people await a festive announcement of his marriage. He flees into a garden hall where he finally, miraculously, finds the woman he loves. We immediately recognize considerable congruence between this story and the accounts we have described: the historical pictures on the walls mirror several halls, the movement through the castle hallways to an archive in a secularized chapel mirrors Wilhelm's initiation in the *Lehrjahre* to an astonishing degree, and the final flight to the garden finds a parallel in the many final garden scenes already discussed.

"Das nussbraune Mädchen" contains nothing especially interesting in our context, but **"Der Mann von fünfzig Jahren"** provides us with a very interesting reflection of ritual initiation. The actor brings with him a "Toilettenkästchen über allen Preis," which, with its promise of extended youth, mirrors the *Kästchen* Felix finds with its promise of a great secret. The way to the secret of youth, to the "höhere Geheimnisse," to the "Geheimnisse für Eingeweihten" leads, the man is told, over "Stufen und Grade." In the course of the story the man of fifty years loses a tooth and the arcane promise is called into question, just as we have questioned the gold of the box/book.

"Die neue Melusine" carries on the box/book/gold metaphor. We learn here the consequences of a passion for the secret (the box, the gold coins, and the gold ring). The metaphor of a little world in a box also deftly mirrors the box/book which is the novel. In the lines immediately following this story, Hersilie writes to Wilhelm about similar temptations she combats in the presence of the "Schatzkästchen": "Wünschelrutenartig zog sich die Hand darnach, mein bißchen Vernunft hielt sie zurück" (HA, VIII, 377).

"Die gefährliche Wette" and **"Nicht zu weit"** contain little of relevance for us; but the repeated mirrorings of the Novellen discussed give us added cause to consider the symbolic landscape and architecture in the context of Freemasonic ritual routes.

When Theodore Mundt reviewed *Wilhelm Meisters Wanderjahre* in 1830, he said that the novel is full of "Freimaurerische Geheimniskrämerei."[32] We have established that Freemasonry may, indeed, have strongly influenced the paths Wilhelm and Felix follow; but in so doing we have found the influence to be anything but *Geheimniskrämerei*. The remnants of Freemasonry we see in the novel—primarily the initiatory route the Masons use—give us cause to examine closely the routes to and through the various regions Wilhelm visits. Far from engaging in esoteric/hermetic games, Goethes here raises the *Handwerk* to art. He builds on the foundation of Freemasonry a building whose successive rooms figuratively teach Wilhelm and the reader Goethe's sense of the meaning of life.

Notes

1. Hans-Georg Gadamer, *Wahrheit und Methode* (2. Auflage, 1965), p. 278.

2. Goethe, *Wilhelm Meisters Wanderjahre oder Die Entsagenden* (Erster Theil, 1821). Also in the *Gedenkausgabe* (1949), VIII, 8.

3. *Goethes Werke, Hamburger Ausgabe in 14 Bänden* (6. Auflage, 1964), XIV, 78. Hereafter refered to in the text as HA, with roman numeral for volume and arabic numeral for page.

4. Felix immediately pulls out a kind of pine cone and asks what it is. Wilhelm's answer demonstrates his ability to extrapolate analogically ("eine Frucht ... und nach den Schuppen zu urteilen, sollte sie mit den Tannenzapfen verwandt sein"); but Felix's reply shows that he still needs to learn the skill ("das sieht nicht aus wie ein Zapfen, es ist ja rund").

5. 10 September 1823; *Goethes Briefe, Hamburger Ausgabe in 4 Bänden* (1967), IV, 90.

6. Cf. Goethe's poem "Der Schatzgräber" (1798), in which a poor man tries to sell his soul for the magic formula which will lead him to "dem alten Schatze." Fortunately (or unfortunately) for him, a "heavenly" messenger appears and counsels him to go back to work: "'Grabe hier nicht mehr vergebens! / Tages Arbeit, abends Gäste! / Saure Wochen, frohe Feste! / Sei dein künftig Zauberwort'" (HA, I, 265-66).

7. Wilhelm Emrich, "Das Problem der Symbolinterpretation im Hinblick auf Goethes *Wanderjahre*," *DVjs,* 26 (1952), 348.

8. Friedrich Ohly, "Goethes Ehrfuchten—ein ordo caritatis," *Euphorion,* 55 (1961), 419-423.

9. Cf. the quotations from Emrich in HA, VIII, 616-617.

10. *Goethes Briefe,* HA, I, 294. The facts concerning Goethe's relationship to Freemasonry are well known, but for the purpose of our argument they are repeated here.

11. *Goethes Werke, Weimarer Ausgabe* (1889), IV, 5, 342.

12. 15 March 1783; *Goethes Briefe,* HA, I, 422.

13. 6 April 1789; *Weimarer Ausgabe* (1891), IV, 9, 101.

14. In the play a Cagliostro figure swindles members of the French nobility with promises of spiritual visitations, the opening of all of nature's secrets, eternal youth, and constant health. He claims to have his secrets from ancient India and Egypt and belongs, he says, to a secret society of men scattered around the world. The Groß-Cophta leads his gullible followers through ritual dialogues, through ever higher levels until they reach his Egyptian lodge where the ultimate secret lies hidden. For the audience, the ultimate secret is obvious—it lies in the ability of a brilliant confidence man to dupe a public frantic for supernatural knowledge.

15. For a more complete account of Goethe and Freemasonry see Eugen Lennhoff, Oskar Posner, *Internationales Freimaurerlexikon* (unveränderter Nachdruck der Ausgabe 1932, 1980), p. 616-19; and Rosemarie Haas, *Die Turmgesellschaft in 'Wilhelm Meisters Lehrjahren'* (1975), Regensburger Beiträge zur deutschen Sprach- und Literaturwissenschaft, Reihe B, 7, 21-28. Although I emphasize Goethe's involvement in the Freemasonry of the Enlightenment, there is another side to the story. How deeply Goethe was influenced by the hermetic tradition—the Gold- and Rosenkreuzer—is made apparent by Rolf Christian Zimmermann in his two-volume *Das Weltbild des jungen Goethe: Studien zur hermetischen Tradition des deutschen 18. Jahrhunderts* (1969, 1979).

16. *Oppositions,* 5, Summer 1976.

17. Vidler, p. 87.

18. Vidler, p. 89.

19. J. W. Oliver, *The Life of William Beckford* (1937), pp. 172-81.

20. HA, II, 271-81.

21. HA, XII, 38.

22. HA, I, 340-41.

23. Trunz's notes in the HA point out the following Freemasonic allusions: "die Grade (*schrittweis*), der Teppich bzw. Vorhang (*Hülle*), der *Stern*, der Zuruf des 'Meisters vom Stuhl'; vielleicht auch die Gräber ..." (HA, I, 658).

24. *Ehrfurcht* proves to be an important lesson of the *Wanderjahre,* whose ritual routes we shall describe later. The covering here, identified with *Ehrfurcht*, bears symbolic representations of the stars above and the graves below. Compare, from the *Wanderjahre*: "Ehrfurcht vor dem, was über uns ist," and "Ehrfurcht vor dem, was unter uns ist."

25. Also found in the *Gedenkausgabe* (1949), VIII, 8.

26. Cf. Trunz's notes to "Die Geheimnisse": "Manches, was in den Geheimnissen unausgeführt blieb, kam in den Wanderjahren zur Sprache: Verschiedene religiöse Wege, die alle letztlich zum gleichen Ziele führen; bildliche Darstellungen, die symbolisch eine Urreligion aussprechen; ein Kreis weiser Männer, der solches esoterische Wissen bewahrt und pflegt" (HA, II, 595).

27. The charcoal burner's trade, like the mason's, is one long associated with secret societies. Cf. Italy's Carbonari.

28. Ohly, pp. 411-433.

29. Cf. the description of how Wilhelm judges the paintings in the Provinz's octagonal hall: "Er betrachtete diese Bilder zuletzt nur aus den Augen des Kindes, und in diesem Sinne war er vollkommen damit zufrieden" (HA, VIII, 161).

30. Wilhelm Voßkamp, "Utopie und Utopiekritik in Goethes Romanen *Wilhelm Meisters Lehrjahre und Wilhelm Meisters Wanderjahre,*" *Utopieforschung: Interdisziplinäre Studien zur neuzeitlichen Utopie,* ed. Wilhelm Voßkamp (1982), III, 227-249.

31. In the Provinz the only mention of a garden is in connection with a "Galerie ... die, an der einen Seite offen, einen geräumigen, blumenreichen Garten umgab. Die Wand zog jedoch mehr als dieser heitre, natürliche Schmuck die Augen an sich" (HA, VIII, 158). I am not sure how this fits into the scheme I have drawn here.

32. Quoted in Joseph Strelka, *Esoterik bei Goethe* (1980), p. 84, note 5. Originally in *Blätter für literarische Unterhaltung* Nr. 264-66, September 21-23, 1830.

Oskar Seidlin (essay date 1984)

SOURCE: Seidlin, Oskar. "Goethe's Vision of a New World." *Goethe Proceedings: Essays Commemorating the Goethe Sesquicentennial at the University of California, Davis.* Ed. Clifford A. Bernd et al. Columbia: Camden House, 1984. 23-34. Print.

[*In the following essay, Seidlin discusses the recurring allusions in Goethe's writings to a "new world" shaped by work and imagination—a world sometimes geographically remote and sometimes wholly imaginary. Seidlin traces the manifestations of this theme in Goethe's later revisions of earlier works, including* Wilhelm Meister's Travels *and* Faust.]

The aphorisms which Ottilie, the heroine of Goethe's ***Wahlverwandtschaften,*** jots down in her diary in the second part of the novel are hardly the fruit of her own insight and wisdom. It is quite frankly her creator, the poet himself, who speaks through her, nowhere more undisguised than at the point when he makes Ottilie proclaim: "We may turn any way we wish, we shall always conceive of ourselves as seeing creatures. It may be that man even dreams only so that he does not have to stop seeing."[1] For to Goethe, who has enriched our world by a wealth of things seen, living and seeing were almost the same, and the older he grew the more fervently he developed a piously religious veneration for the human eye, the precious door through which the images of the living universe enter our consciousness.

We cannot help seeing images; and therefore a clearly defined, concrete picture should provide a focus to our eyes when we are in danger of losing ourselves in the vast and limitless panorama which Goethe's life and work present to the viewer, and of which a tiny reflection at least ought to be conveyed by a commemorative address. Let us then fasten our eyes to a small radius of visibility: the tiny room upstairs in the manorial house on the Frauenplan in Weimar, furnished with a plain desk and a few simple book cases, a monk's cell rather than the study of a writer whom much of Europe reveres as the uncrowned ruler over the realm of the spirit. At this desk he is at work now, a very old man, over eighty years of age, holding himself quite erect, under a thin crown of white hair and a majestically high forehead a pair of dark eyes whose clarity, firmness and power have struck so many of his visitors as supranatural. He knows that death already awaits him at the threshold, that he has traversed almost to the end a life richer than that of many another mortal in experiences and in productive responses to these experiences. But he has yet to finish his greatest work, the dramatic poem of *Faust,* which has accompanied him through all his life. For he was an impetuous youngster of hardly more than twenty when the image of Faust first appeared before his mind; and now, sixty years later, he still lies chained to this poem of his. Faust has traveled with him through all the avenues of life, has partaken of his experiences: the passionate search for truth, the bliss of love, the agonies of suffering, error and sin, fulfillment and failure, loud worldly splendor and the serene devotion to beauty. For sixty years this creation of his has been at his side; and now the moment has come when, in the great poem, Faust's final hour has struck. And while the wing-beat of death already touches his own shoulder, Goethe, the old man in his eighties, takes leave of Faust, the old man of one hundred. Yet before the poet lowers the last curtain over Faust's earthly existence, he grants this child of his imagination a last vision. Once more Faust sees, no longer with his physical eyes, whose light old age and worry have extinguished; but before his inner eye a sight opens which transforms the moment of his death into the moment of highest triumph:

> A marsh extends along the mountain chain
> That poisons what so far I've been achieving:
> Could I that noisome pool now drain,
> 'Twould be the highest, last achieving.
> Thus space to many millions I will give
> Where, though not safe, yet free and active they may live.
> Green fertile fields where straightway from their birth
> Both man and beast live happy on the newest earth,
> Settled forthwith along the mighty hill
> Raised by a daring, busy people's will.
> Within: a land like paradise; outside:
> Up to the brink may rage the mighty tide,
> And where it gnaws and would burst through and sap
> A common impulse hastes to close the gap.
> Yes, to this thought I hold unswerving,
> To wisdom's final fruit, profoundly true:
> Of freedom and of life he only is deserving
> Who every day must conquer them anew.
> That there, by danger girt, the active day
> Of childhood, manhood, age will pass away.
> Aye, such a throng I fain would see,
> Stand on free soil, among a people free.
> Then I might say, that moment seeing:
> Oh linger on, thou art so fair!
> The traces of my earthly being,
> Can perish not in aeons—they are there.
> That lofty moment I now feel in this:
> I now enjoy the highest moment's bliss.

A new world, Faust's last vision, Goethe's last vision: not a peacefully sweet Utopia, but a world fought for, a world to be defended every day, soil won from the bottomless, destructive element, the water; not ready-made land into which we just have to move, but earth created by our own hands, made fertile by the rhythm of our work and life. Free people on free soil: free not by virtue of brief and seal, but free because this land is created out of the nothingness, and because these people are creating it.

A man whose life has been filled with work, a poet crowned with fame as no other in centuries, a human being who suffered more intensely than any other man—and now when the lights grow dim, there is no gloating over great achievements, there is no bitterness over great disappointments,

there is a vision of new living things, an echo of the words which, at about the same time, at the age of eighty-one, he spoke when he was told that his only son, his hope for the future, had died: "Over graves—onward!" And it might be that the example of the old man in his stately house in the city of Weimar holds a promise and a hope for all humanity, especially for a world which has stood before so many graves in wars, concentration camps and gulags, and a time which has become paralyzed by smugness or by fear and doubt.

We need not strain our eyes too much in order to recognize the rough outlines of Faust's envisaged new world, in order to give it an at least approximately correct name: a frontier and frontiersmen, land to be wrung from the hold of the unknown and dangerous, bulwarks built by the communal efforts of a new nation—who, and who in this country, could fail to call these people on free soil by their proper name? Indeed, from the beginning of the nineteenth century, Goethe was fascinated by the experiment whose name was America: and if we may dismiss as a whimsical jest the remark of the septuagenarian that he, were he only twenty years younger, would like to set sail and settle in this new world, there are indications aplenty that the older he became, the more attentively and curiously he watched this young nation which was growing up under his eyes. In the great novel of his old age, **Wilhelm Meisters Wanderjahre,** America, now called by its proper name, appears again as the vision of a new life and a new society, and we know how eagerly he listened to those young men who came to visit him from Massachusetts and Maryland, when they gave him information pertaining to their country. There is warmth in his voice whenever he speaks of America, a cordial and paternal "good luck to you," a joyful feeling as if these far-away people, who may never have heard of him, were his true children, going the way he wanted the new generation to go:

> America, you're better off
> Than our continent, the old.
> You have no castles which are fallen,
> No basalt to behold.
> You are not disturbed in your inmost being,
> In the very pulsation of life
> By useless remembering
> And unrewarding strife.
> Use well the present—and good luck to you!
> And when your children begin writing poetry,
> Let them guard well, in all they do,
> Against knight-, robber-, and ghost-story.

If we listen closely enough to this little congratulatory poem, we may be inclined to think that it contains a slightly lefthanded compliment. For what he finds so enviable and fortunate about this new country is not that it has things others don't have, but that it does not have things others, unfortunately, have. America has no memories, no spectres rising out of the twilight zone of the human heart and human history, no ghosts which haunt the living and make their hands tremble. Geologist that he is, he even believes (and we know that he was quite wrong in that) that the very earth upon which this new nation has grown holds no memories of violent volcanic outbursts by which old and hidden formations of the soil are vehemently thrown onto the surface, that the basalt, witness of such explosions, is lacking in the make-up of this "newest earth." The hour that strikes over this country is always morning, its illumination the light of early day. Newly opened spaces where expansive and active motion is still possible, newly born time not yet overshadowed by the broodings and memories of yesteryears—this is the bright vision for which Goethe found the name America.

It would be wrong and much too simple to explain Goethe's love for a youthful country, for youth altogether, as the yearning for freshness and vitality of one who knew himself to be—and very proudly at that—the focal point of traditions amassed and handed down through centuries, and who, at times, may have felt heavily burdened by the very riches which he represented for the entire world. His devotion to youth had nothing nostalgic about it at all: it was a salute to his own vitality, his pride in an inexhaustible fertility, which made the man of sixty-five call out like a youngster who sees his whole life still ahead of him: "My heritage, how splendid, rich and grand, / My property is time, and time my harvest land!" Time was a magic word for him, and that he was granted so much of it, eighty-three years of it, filled him with an exultant and charmingly naive delight. His harvest land—the ground on which he stood, the beloved medium in which things come to pass, the medium beloved because in it always new things may come to pass.

That things were in permanent flux, always beginning anew, and every end only the starting point for more and richer life—that was his profoundest conviction, and it was, the older he grew, the source of all his happiness. *Stirb und Werde!* 'Die and grow!'—this is the formula by which he expressed the secret of his own life, by which he tried to express the secret of life itself. And it was the very principle of stagnation that he embodied in the character of his devil Mephistopheles, the "Bastard, half hellfire and half dung," who raises his cold fist against the eternally creative power. Goethe may, at times, have been annoyed when the young generation turned against him, the great colossus, who, in the eyes of some, stood in the way of new principles and new forms of life. Yet again and again he acknowledged the right of those who traveled on roads alien to him, because they were the roads of a new era:

> An aged man is always like King Lear.
> Who shared your doings, hand in hand,
> Long since went down the highway;
> Who loved and grieved at your command
> Is courting in another byway.
> Just for its own sake youth is with us here;
> It would be folly to demand:
> Come, grow a little old with me, my dear.

Indeed, it would be folly—and worse. It would be an attempt to interfere with the organic rhythm of birth, growth, decay and rebirth which he not only worshipped in nature but which he observed and enjoyed in every single individual, in all manifestations of man's activities. It would be the most objectionable violation of what he recognized as man's highest duty. "And what is your duty?" he asks; and he answers himself: "The demand of the day!" The demand of the day, the challenge of the hour! When he was thinking of a new world, he thought of a humanity which listened obediently to what every hour expected of them and answered the call of the hour by an active response—by work. His devotion to work, to purposeful, practical activity, became with him more and more a religious credo, and it is not by chance that he wrote into the album of his grandson, then a little fellow hardly seven years old:

> The hour has sixty minutes in store,
> The day a thousand and more.
> Now figure out, my little son,
> All the things that can be done.

Only through work can man become real: only in his work can he recognize himself and become recognizable to others. What Goethe found at the bottom of nature, of art, was a secret creative force which knew only one end: to become visible in an innumerable variety of manifestations. This pattern man had to follow if he was not to miss his real vocation: to become visible, to press and to express all his potentialities in manifest symbols, to crystallize the dark and impalpable whirl of his energies into durable objects which would bear witness to his existence in the light of day. Without this work, man was for him an amorphous mass, something without contours, floundering in a twilight which is the twilight before the creation. A form—and a formless thing was for him a non-existent thing—a form man could find only in the work he did. It fulfilled the function every form has to fulfill: to free and to limit at the same time. To free: because through form alone inner impulses and forces can manifest themselves; and to limit: because form narrows down the vagueness of infinite possibilities to the one finite and distinguishable phenomenon. Work, then, the concrete answer to the concrete demands of every day, prevents man from being engulfed by the two extreme dangers: to atrophy in mute unexpressiveness, or to dissolve himself in the innumerable but shapeless potentialities of the infinite.

> This solves the great interrogation
> As to our second fatherland.
> For our work here, if it has duration,
> Ensures that we eternally shall stand.

Perhaps we can now distinguish more clearly the outline of the new horizons which open before Faust's inner eye at the moment of his death: a milling throng of people following the eternal rhythm of life, childhood, manhood, old age—working, and by working, lifting the concrete, the formed land, out of the chaotic shapelessness of the waters, fighting for it daily so that it will not slip back into the deadly silence of the unformed. If we asked under which form of government this new world would stand, Goethe would answer with a skeptical smile. The thing that really mattered to him was what he called the communal effort: the daily work of the common people for their common good. He did not believe in political slogans, no matter in which camp they had been formulated; he was highly suspicious of general principles, of grandiose ideas which, in spite of their solemn ring, could only divert man from his sole and primary duty: the demand of the hour. He had no use for missionaries who preached the salvation of man through a magic formula, be it even so bewitching a formula as "liberty, equality, fraternity," because the passionate fight for these principles, for any principles as a matter of fact, allowed man only to play hooky, to run behind the school, to neglect, while searching in the clouds, the concrete tasks with which our daily existence confronts us. "Grand ideas and great conceit," he remarked, "are always geared to bring about fearful misfortune."

We know what he meant by this "fearful misfortune": it was the French Revolution, whose sight frightened and upset him. When opposing the French Revolution, he did not defend any privileges, and certainly not the many which he himself considered unjust. What he feared was the dissolution of order, of form and shape in the socio-political field, the unleashing of chaotic forces which would burst through the dams and destroy—not only the guilty ones, but the innocent, plain, hard-working people as well. He anticipated—and he anticipated correctly—the Reign of Terror, the endless chain of Napoleonic Wars, an upheaval which would not only bury under its weight the "old regime" for which he held no particular brief, but which would endanger and obstruct the slow and laborious progress of mankind which was to be achieved only step by step, by a devoted application to the exigencies of each day, and not by running amuck under the spell of abstract ideas, no matter how noble they sounded.

It is quite revealing that in the little well-wishing poem to America there is not even a hint at a new political or social order, at representative government or majority rule or the like. What he saw was a country which would make good use of the present moment, without being blinded by the luring stars of a far-away eternity, a country which is not disturbed in the very pulsation of life by unrewarding quarrels, and whose very earth does not exhibit the scars and remnants of violent volcanic outbursts. In another document, however, he does make mention of the American form of government, and we cannot help being amused at the perspective from which he views it. In 1819, at the age of seventy, he sent upon request of his New England admirers a set of his collected works to the Harvard library. And this copy he dedicated "to the magnificent country which draws the eyes of the whole world upon herself by a solemnly lawful state of affairs which

promotes a growth hampered by no bounds." Aren't we startled, looking around in 1982, to hear our government called a "solemnly lawful state of affairs"? Be that as it may, he approved of it; and not because it rested on a set of political ideas which he may or may not have preferred to others—and to be quite frank, he hardly did—but because it promoted growth and whatever promoted growth was good in his eyes. Only order, only a concrete visible organization capable of warding off the onslaught of unruly impulses, of chaotic and shapeless elemental forces, can promote growth. What mattered in a new world as he saw it in his vision, was to permit the communal effort to come into play, to see to it that every individual could become real by being allowed to do his work, that everybody could stand firm on his own place, no matter how modest. Then indeed the body politic as a whole could not help being sound and healthy.

The communal effort—that is what counted in his eyes, the common fight against the dangers which threaten the community of men. And this community was for him indivisible and all-embracing. Every barrier which tried to cut up this indivisibility was to him a dangerous and meaningless abstraction. The idea of different nationalities became to him more and more a nebulous superstructure erected over the palpable, concrete life and activities of the individual within the community. The only citizenship he proudly claimed was that of a citizen of the world, and it was in is eighty-first year, at a time when Europe entered a phase of violent nationalism and imperialism, that he made a statement whose benevolent wisdom mankind has not yet learned a hundred and fifty years later: "All in all, it is a strange thing with national hatred. On the lowest level of culture you will always find it most strongly and violently. But there is a level where it disappears entirely, and where the good and bad fortune of one's fellow-nation is felt as keenly as if it had befallen your own. This level of culture corresponded to my own nature, and I had entrenched myself firmly on this level before I had reached my sixtieth year."

Indeed, Goethe does well to use the word "entrench," a word connoting labor and persistence. He was keenly aware that a steady and steadfast practice is required. It would not come easily to anybody, and it certainly did not come easily to him. More than anybody else he was threatened by the extremes which undermine the communal effort: on the one hand, a wild and reckless tendency toward self-assertion which destroys the communal spirit, on the other hand a longing for flight from reality, for the great and absolute calm in which no practical effort, no effort at all, can assert itself. He was exposed, and exposed until his very old age, to the passionate and storming beat of his insatiable heart which could not stop short of extreme self-fulfillment regardless of the ravages it might work. But he was equally exposed to the deadening lure of complete withdrawal, of losing himself in the irresponsible bliss of dreaming and forgetting, exposed to the yearning of forever-turning-away from what Orestes in his *Iphigenie* [*Iphigenie auf Tauris*] calls "life's fitful fever." The greatest achievement, the greatest glory of this man is not his poetry, his artistic and scientific endeavors, but the mainspring of his life, his refusal to go to pieces under the strain of conflicting tendencies, his perseverance in finding a balance on the razor's edge, his discipline—and what a severe discipline it was!—in training himself for the communal effort, for the great reconciliation which embraces at the same time self-limitation in service to and for others, and self-expression through free, personal creation.

Better than anybody else Goethe knew—or rather, more painfully than anybody else Goethe had experienced within himself—that it takes a long and laborious training to develop the attitude without which a new world cannot be born, an attitude which succeeds in balancing harmoniously man's rightful claim to independence and society's rightful claim to man's submission. The level must be found where man can save his own face, that individual face which Goethe loved so dearly, and still become a part of a larger whole, a community without whose shelter man destroys himself and his surroundings. It is, indeed, a most timely problem, and Goethe, citizen of a much less shaken world than ours, saw it in all its mercilessness and inevitability. Long before others, he was afraid of the rise of a mass civilization, of an anonymous uniformity in which the individual would lose his unmistakable face, and he knew very well that this danger could arise under any form of government, a democratic no less than an autocratic one. Yet he knew equally well the destructive results of a reckless individualism which would not only destroy all order, but would, at the same time, isolate man, transport him into a frigid loneliness in which the individual himself could not survive. To be sure, he did not care for the masses, this shapeless monster which blurred and gobbled up the distinguishing features of each individual; but he cared even less for those who believed that the only thing that mattered was to release and to realize their unbridled urge for personal freedom.

To achieve this balance where man does not abdicate before the demands of society, and where society is not ripped apart by man's rightful claim to self-realization—that is the task we have to fulfill if we want to bring about a new world. Goethe knew that it would never do to find an easy but superficial compromise between the two conflicting tendencies, a grudging give-and-take where, more often than not, the right hand does not know what the left hand is doing. A basic attitude had to be found, not a composite of two or more, but just one basic attitude which would at the same time comprise self-preservation and self-abandonment. This attitude was to be made the cornerstone upon which the education of a new man for a new world was to rest. He found it, and in the great novel of his old age, in **Wilhelm Meisters Wanderjahre** he describes the school in which the generation of the future is educated for the future. He leads us in this novel into his "pedagogical province," one of the most inspiring pedagogical utopias ever developed by Western man. But before he introduces us to the concrete curriculum of the school, he shows us the pupils' training in the basic attitude without which no curriculum and no program would be of any avail. And what is this attitude? Goethe calls it reverence, a reverence extending to three spheres: the reverence for that which is above us, the reverence for that which is around us, and the reverence for that which is underneath us. When speaking of "above, around and below" he does not only refer to the human and social structure, although in the case of the reverence for that which is underneath us, he takes pains to point specifically to the human level, to those who through suffering, social inequality, lack of strength, are being held in the lower regions. With his "above, around and below" Goethe wants to draw a much wider circle: he wants to point to all possible directions of the universe. Below: that is the very earth upon which we stand, the solid soil from which we and all nature derive our daily food, the forces under the surface which feed all vegetative life. Around: this is the human level, the sphere of man, man as our neighbor and equal. And above: this is the world of the spirit, of the stars into which our destiny is inscribed, the world of the spirit's Highest: of God. This is what the disciples of the pedagogical province learn as their first and basic lesson: that they owe reverence to the whole cosmos, the suprahuman, the human, and the subhuman.

Reverence, then, appears to Goethe as the proper attitude of a new man in a new world, for it is the human sentiment in which man's insistence on his independence and his recognition of his dependence on other powers are blended. It does not obliterate man's face, for reverence has nothing whatsoever to do with slavish submission, yet it does, at the same time, give proper due to everything which is outside our own ego, be it "above, around or below." The German word, the German equivalent for "reverence" that Goethe uses here, seems to define the attitude of which we are speaking much more clearly. The word is *Ehrfurcht*, a compound of two words: *Ehre*, meaning "honor," and *Furcht*, meaning "fear," or "awe." *Ehrfurcht*, then, is the human sentiment which permits man to show awe without losing his honor. This is exactly the way Goethe defined the word: "if man lets himself be governed by *Ehrfurcht*, he can keep his honor while rendering honor." In this sentiment, and in this sentiment alone, pride and modesty have become one and the same; it makes us great and small at the same time; it keeps us aware of the fact that we are faced with powers that determine us, but that we have the right and the duty to face these powers as free men. Not to be blindly overcome by the forces that are above, around and below us, nor on the other hand to burst into a reckless freedom that tries to break down all the barriers that are set to man—this is the problem we have to solve, and only reverence, only *Ehrfurcht* will enable us to solve it.

Not to be overcome by fear, not to abdicate, not to feel that we are only playthings in the hands of outside forces—

could there be a more timely lesson? And do we not remember in this connection the words of an American statesman which, quite unconsciously to be sure, sounds like an echo of Goethe's wisdom even if it is, more likely, the echo of a Thoreauean dictum: "The only thing we have to fear is fear itself." Yet this is only half the truth as Goethe saw it. Being wiser than the statesman in question, he would have continued: and the next worst thing we have to fear is absolute fearlessness, the denial of our limitations, the arrogant emancipation from the awe which we owe to the above, the around and the below. There is a sort of freedom, a rebellious blindness against everything that limits us, which is as disastrous as fear. Fear gives the powers outside ourselves complete control over our own existence, but recklessness makes us lose control over ourselves, transforms us into helpless puppets—not in the hands of others, but in our own hands. And who, in our days, in the days of a perniciously unfettered self-confidence, everybody blithely doing one's own thing, would not have to ponder Goethe's words: "Everything that liberates our mind without giving us control over ourselves is ruinous."

Liberty and control, being free and being bound at the same time—this in Goethe's eyes is the position man has to find. And therefore the disciples of the "pedagogical province," after having acquired the three forms of reverence, have yet to learn the highest type of reverence: reverence for oneself. Not to violate that honor of the self to which we, as human beings, are entitled, nor, on the other hand, to violate the limitations and conditions of our nature; not to become subject to the dark and instinctive drives in our souls, nor to hurt and suppress our innate, God-given constitution. This, then, would be wisdom's final fruit: to be true to self, yet never to become a slave of self.

This is Goethe's lesson, the lesson that is taught in the "pedagogical province." And who would deny that this conviction may have a meaning for our own lives and our own days, no matter how much the conditions of Goethe's world and ours may differ? A poet never tries to give answers which will hold good under all circumstances, and certainly no such attempt was made by Goethe, who, more fervently than anybody else, believed that every day has its own demands, and that, obviously, the demands of today cannot be met with the answers of yesterday. Nothing would have appalled him more than the sight of a humanity which would cling to a ready-made formula, even if it were his own. After all, it was he who told his contemporaries, all those who were so smugly satisfied with their own cleverness and who had found a permanent niche from which they did not care even to peep out,

> Get wise to yourself, now trot
> Out of this mucky groove,
> There is more to earth than this spot,
> Move! . . .

and he would have been the first one to protest if anyone had tried to elevate his own answers and his own intuitions

to the status of canonical laws, valid for all eternity. Yet he knew equally well that man's basic problems are always the same, and that we cannot do more than re-formulate the principal attitudes so that they will furnish us with a definite answer in a definite situation. "All intelligent thoughts," he said, "have already been thought; what is necessary is only to try to think them again." He tried—and he tried as sincerely and honestly as any man can. Once, when he was a very old man, a Frenchman came to see him, and after looking into this venerable face, furrowed by wisdom and sorrow, exclaimed: "Voilà un homme qui a eu de grands chagrins." Goethe liked these words and translated them, somewhat arbitrarily and incorrectly, as you will not fail to notice, by the words, "There is a man who has taken life seriously." Indeed, he had the right to confess that he never played with life, that he never shut himself against the sufferings, the doubts and arduous tasks which are man's lot. He accepted all of it, beauty and despair, joy and misery.

He knew the dangers, dangers in his own heart, and dangers approaching him from outside, yet he never lost hope that somehow he—and we—would pull through. One of his most beautiful poems he ends with the words: "We bid you hope"; and the old man of eighty stood in his little study, and while his life was drawing to a close, he put into the mouth of his dying Faust the hymn to a new life, to a new world. And this indeed Goethe would have wished the coming generations to learn from him: the hope and the faith that man's endeavors are not lost, that the vision of a new world can and must remain alive, even if darkness is closing in on us. He did not want to offer ready-made answers on how to do things tomorrow. But he hoped and wished that his whole life's work, the sum total of his existence, would strengthen future generations in their belief that there will *be* a tomorrow, and that our own daily work will bring it about. His whole existence, not this or that work of his, was to hold out hope for the future. And we cannot do him greater honor than by simply repeating the little song of gratitude which he addressed to a fellow-poet, to Schah Sedschaa, an old Persian sage and singer of the thirteenth century:

> And fear will seize us never
> While living with your song!
> Your life, may it last long,
> Your kingdom—ever!

Note

1. Some of the translations of the Goethe texts are my own, others by J. W. Priest (*Faust*), and, in the case of "Sprüche in Versen," B. Q. Morgan and Isidor Schneider (from *The Permanent Goethe*, ed. Thomas Mann, New York, 1948).

Alexander Gelley (essay date 1984)

SOURCE: Gelley, Alexander. "Frame, Instance, Dialogue: Narrative Structures in the *Wanderjahre.*" *Johann Wolfgang von Goethe: One Hundred and Fifty Years of Continuing Vitality.* Ed. Ulrich Goebel and Wolodymyr T. Zyla. Lubbock: Texas Tech UP, 1984. 61-78. Print.

[*In the following essay, Gelley examines the variety of narrative structures simultaneously at play in* Wilhelm Meister's Travels, *noting that the novel defies neat classification in this regard. Gelley also draws upon the narrative theories of Walter Benjamin and Mikhail Bakhtin to shift the discussion from "what the story is about" to how and why the numerous stories that compose* Wilhelm Meister's Travels *are told.*]

In relation to **Wilhelm Meisters Lehrjahre** (1796), the **Wanderjahre** [**Wilhelm Meisters Wanderjahre**], (first version, 1821, revised and expanded version, 1829) represents a marked divergence from the model of a *Bildungsroman,* that is, a narrative focused on a single protagonist and utilizing encounters and illustrative tales to mark the stages of his development. In the **Wanderjahre** the frame story, with Wilhelm at its center, is of course still operative, but instead of the teleological progression of the earlier novel, we now have a series of episodes and interpolated texts whose relation to the main strand is by no means self-evident. The very status of the frame has been put into question by the fact that many of the stories occupy an intermediate position, both inside and outside. In calling attention to the hybrid structure of the **Wanderjahre** I do not intend to make a value judgment but to explore ways of identifying and analyzing its diverse generic and formal elements.

The function of a story as *exemplum,* as illustration or instance, becomes problematic in a work like the **Wanderjahre** where the principal narrative strand, what should be the authoritative level of meaning, is ambiguous or weakly articulated. But such a problematization itself gives rise to a different kind of thematic focus, one involving the production and dissemination of narratives rather than their truth value or ethical import. Here Walter Benjamin's discussion of the storyteller is pertinent. Further, Mikhail Bakhtin's concept of the dialogic novel, of the medley of styles and attitudes that constitute the fabric of a certain kind of prose fiction, will help us to consider some of the narratives in the **Wanderjahre** not so much in terms of their content—what the story is about—but of their modes of enunciation and transmission—how they are told, by whom, and for what purpose. (AG)

> Mit solchem Büchlein aber ist es wie mit dem Leben selbst: es findet sich in dem Komplex des Ganzen Notwendiges und Zufälliges, Vorgesetztes und Angeschlossenes, bald gelungen, bald vereitelt, wodurch es eine Art von Unendlichkeit erhält, die sich in verständige und vernünftige Worte nicht durchaus fassen noch einschliessen läßt[1]

More than once Goethe spoke of the symbolic method of his later work in terms of a multiperspectivism, of

"contrastive and mutually reflective forms" designed to disclose a "more secret meaning" ("durcheinander gegenüber gestellte und sich gleichsam ineinander abspiegelnde Gebilde den geheimeren Sinn … zu offenbaren").[2] In statements like these regarding the method of his later work Goethe projects an ideally suited instance of reception, an audience or readership capable of penetrating the complexities of this body of work. Of course, such remarks should not be taken too strictly in a poetological sense. They were oriented to a specific correspondent or interlocutor, and may have expressed also a wish that Goethe saw little likelihood of being realized in the German public of the last twenty years of his life. Nonetheless, the formulations I have cited represent a useful heuristic model for the kind of reading of the **Wanderjahre** that I propose.

Many interpreters have sought to specify the kind of adequate reader that Goethe occasionally evoked (e.g., in such formulations as "der echte Leser," "der Aufmerkende," and "[der] einsichtige[ ] Leser"),[3] and to make this the basis of a determinate interpretation of the work, usually in terms of some thematic or philosophic thesis. But I would suggest that Goethe does not so much project a model of total comprehension, of crystallized meaning (at the level of the signified), but rather a process of signification (at the level of signifiers) that the work in itself cannot altogether anticipate or circumscribe. "Jede Lösung eines Problems ist ein neues Problem," he remarked to the Kanzler v. Müller in connection with the **Wanderjahre.**[4] And in the passage already cited where he ascribed to the work "eine Art von Unendlichkeit," we may take this not necessarily as a kind of infinity but as a principle of seriality, of propagation and dispersal.

This, I trust, will help to situate my method in what follows. Instead of drawing on a type of interpretation based largely on themes or ideas, or even a kind of formal analysis based on accredited genre concepts (for example, of the novella), I have tried to adapt elements of a narrative pragmatics, utilizing principles of communications theory and of a reader-oriented aesthetics.

* * *

Near the beginning of the **Wanderjahre,** in Wilhelm's first letter to Natalie, he mentions the obligation of his journeymanship as determined by the Society of the Tower, including the requirement that he change his locale every three days. It appears at this point that we may expect a continuation of the pattern of the **Lehrjahre** [**Wilhelm Meisters Lehrjahre**], that is, a period of searching and testing in which the chance experiences of the journey will serve as instruments of formation. But the impulse to journey is not long sustained. In Wilhelm's first encounter with a member of the Society, Montan-Jarno, he asks to be relieved of this obligation since he wants to devote himself to learning a craft, and his request is eventually granted. In spite of its title, the **Wanderjahre** is not, like *Don Quixote* or *Tom Jones,* structured in terms of the hero's peregrination. The road with its potential for incidents and encounters does not serve as an integrating narrative device. As a recent interpreter of the novel puts it, "Die Absage an den romantischen Wander-Topos ist unüberhörbar."[5]

Alternatively, a unifying principle for the novel has been sought in Wilhelm's personal project of growth and self-realization. Thus H. M. Waidson argues, "the structural centre of the *Wanderjahre* lies in Wilhelm's decision to become a surgeon in order to place his new skill at the disposal of the community. . . ."[6] Certainly, this decision is enunciated early in the work and two narrative segments mark stages of the project—the story of the drowning of the fisher boy, which Wilhelm gives as the earliest motivation for his choice of a profession; and the account of his anatomical studies in Book III. The concluding incident of the novel shows Wilhelm treating his son Felix after the youth has lost consciousness through an accidental fall, and this is undoubtedly meant to demonstrate what Wilhelm has achieved since the tragic episode of the fisher boy, when he could only embrace the body of the drowned boy in impotent grief. But a link between these episodes does not yet give us a means of unifying the work as a whole. It is true that in reworking the *Wanderjahre* for the second and final version between 1821 and 1829 Goethe took pains to elaborate the frame story, thus significantly transforming what had been more a collection of tales in the Boccaccian sense than a novel.[7] The relations among Hersilie, Felix, and Wilhelm, on the one hand, and Wilhelm's choice and attainment of the surgeon's craft, on the other, represent the major elements in this elaboration of the frame action. But these two strands, separately or in combination, are still far from integrating the diverse segments and themes of the novel, whether the unity is sought at the level of the novellas and other interpolations or of the figure of Wilhelm. Such a judgment could, of course, only be substantiated by means of a detailed interpretation of the whole work. I can do no more here than indicate the general tendency of the argument through a discussion of the fisher-boy story.

This incident stands out in the novel not only as the sole reminiscence on Wilhelm's part of his childhood, but also for the intensity of the recital (in a tone that recalls *Werther* [*Die Leiden des jungen Werthers*]) and the passionate nature of the experience itself. The reenactment of an overpowering childhood experience, the fused themes of friendship, erotic attraction, and death, the sense of proximity to a paradisic, preternatural state of being—all these give the episode a quality that is unique in the novel. "Unerwartet, in demselbigen Augenblick," Wilhelm writes, "ergriff mich das Vorgefühl von Freundschaft und Liebe" (p. 273).[8] And he goes on to underscore the direct link between this experience and the emotional and imaginative powers that will find an outlet in his theatrical career, "Das Bedürfnis nach Freundschaft und Liebe war aufgeregt, überall schaut' ich mich um, es zu befriedigen. Indessen ward

Sinnlichkeit, Einbildungskraft and Geist durch das Theater übermässig beschäftigt . . ." (p. 279). In the aftermath of the catastrophe, Wilhelm writes, he heard of forms of resuscitation that might have helped in such a case and he resolved then to learn about them. The letter goes on to justify his decision to abandon the journeymanship and to apply himself to the study of surgery. Here, however, Wilhelm's application of the fisher boy story is far from doing justice to the quality of the episode itself as he had delineated it earlier. What was revealed there was a psyche in a formative stage, open to the influences of a primal natural environment and of a spontaneous, still undifferentiated erotic drive. The encounter with Adolf (the fisher boy) represented, as Wilhelm puts it, "jenes erste Aufblühen der Außenwelt," and he identifies this with "die eigentliche Originalnatur . . . , gegen die alles übrige, was uns nachher zu den Sinnen kommt, nur Kopien zu sein scheinen . . ." (p. 273 f.). In the later part of the letter, when he draws a lesson from the episode, Wilhelm stresses the relative and indeterminate nature of any single motive in shaping his future. He has distanced himself from the intense childhood experience and, writing in a much cooler tone, seems intent on assimilating that episode to the requirements of a rational life plan. The letter itself reflects a shift from the sphere of "eigentliche Originalnatur" to that of "Kopien." Karl Schlechta has argued that after the attachment to Mariane early in the *Lehrjahre,* Wilhelm falls increasingly under the sway of a petrifying, authoritarian spirit, a spirit typified by members of the Society of the Tower.[9] This leads to a progressive suppression of Wilhelm's affective and imaginative impulses. While I cannot altogether subscribe to this position, Schlechta's study represents a serious challenge to any overly positive or unproblematic view of Wilhelm's career. As my discussion of the one letter has tried to show, there are striking shifts in perspective, in voice, and in narrative form that make it difficult to view the action in terms of a linear, teleological pattern.[10]

The evolving, cumulative form of self-consciousness that is characteristic for the *Bildungsroman,* and that is to some degree present in the *Lehrjahre,* is markedly absent in the *Wanderjahre.* Let us briefly sketch this pattern by way of contrast. What is typical for the protagonist of a story of growth and formation is that his most significant acts involve not what he does in direct commerce with individuals and circumstances but what he comes to know through a retrospective interpretation of his acts. Greimas and Courtès have put forward a structural narrative model that tries to establish a common ground for action and for the attainment of knowledge by narrative agents, an approach that is most pertinent to our topic.[11] They posit first an elementary level, a "simple narrative," where "there is no distance between the events and the knowledge about the events," and then proceed to develop various forms of "cognitive action" that constitute a second degree of narrative. This level may take the form of an interpretive investment on the part of the protagonist, an investment that adds the new function of being a recipient (of knowledge) to that already operative of being the agent of action (or "the subject of doing," in their terminology). The protagonist realizes that actions undertaken for apparently self-evident motives must be revised in the light of his new stage of self-understanding. But the earlier, unreflective agent of action is not thereby simply eliminated and supplanted. Rather, the split in the subject is itself now thematized and this brings about a transformation of the narrative form. The shift is from a first level of narrative whose pivots are the acts of a unified protagonist, a single "subject of doing," to a second order of pivots (such as dissimulation, self-deception, recognition, peripeteia) which specify the mode of action of the "cognitive subject." In adapting this model I have sought to identify the principal elements of a *Bildung* narrative in structural rather than historical terms. The model proves to be perfectly congruent with an analysis that Goethe offered regarding the *Lehrjahre.* In it he speaks of the errors and false turnings that seem to pursue his protagonist during his life, and concludes, "Und doch ist es möglich, daß alle die falschen Schritte zu einem unschätzbaren Guten hinführen: eine Ahnung, die sich im 'Wilhelm Meister' immer mehr entfaltet, aufklärt und bestätigt, ja sich zuletzt mit klaren Worten ausspricht: 'Du kommst mir vor wie Saul, der Sohn Kis, der ausging seines Vaters Eselinnen zu suchen, und ein Königreich fand.'"[12]

But in the *Wanderjahre,* Wilhelm, though involved throughout the frame action and privy to all of the interpolated texts, rarely assumes the function of a cognitive subject in the sense just discussed. In the letter to Natalie that includes the fisher boy story Wilhelm, of course, serves as narrator. More often his part in the action is rendered by a third-person narrator, but this does not bring a greater focus on stages of growth and self-awareness. Thus the diverse forms of aesthetic experience evoked in the episodes of Saint Joseph the Second, the trip on Lago Maggiore, and the visit to the Artists' Province do not seem to affect Wilhelm in a cumulative manner. He takes in the system of instruction in the Artists' Province without giving the slightest indication that, only a little earlier when he was in the company of the painter on Lago Maggiore, he had been in contact with a conception of art that represented its very antithesis.[13] One could almost speak of a kind of amnesia on Wilhelm's part, or at least of a disinterestedness which makes him eminently adaptable to the various situations in which he finds himself but, correspondingly, leaves him relatively immune to being strongly affected by them.

We do not find in the *Wanderjahre* the kind of passionate self-scrutiny and projection of purpose as in the long letter to Werner in the *Lehrjahre,* where Wilhelm stated, "Daß ich Dir's mit *einem* Worte sage: mich selbst, ganz wie ich da bin, auszubilden, das war dunkel von Jugend auf mein Wunsch und meine Absicht."[14] What corresponds to this in the *Wanderjahre* is perhaps the parable of the rudder peg

(*Ruderpflock*—see p. 268), though it projects a far more tenuous and indeterminate path. Though he is the nominal hero of the *Wanderjahre* Wilhelm does not provide the kind of unifying thread that we might expect from a general account of the frame story or from the antecedent patter of the *Lehrjahre.* Although the dispersal of personal identity is not so extreme in the *Wanderjahre* as in the second part of *Faust,* there is a marked loosening of structure in the second part of both works. Goethe's well-known characterization of Wilhelm as "armer Hund" was made in 1821 when he was just putting out the first version of the *Wanderjahre* and it seems more applicable to the Wilhelm of that work than of the *Lehrjahre*: "Wilhelm is freilich ein armer Hund, aber nur an solchen lassen sich das Wechselspiel des Lebens und die tausend verschiedenen Lebensaufgaben recht deutlich zeigen, nicht an schon abgeschlossenen festen Charakteren."[15] But while this remark supports us in not looking for a structuring principle for this novel at the level of character or psychology, it does not provide any indication of what to look for. We still need to find a way of converting "das Wechselspiel des Lebens und die tausend verschiedenen Lebensaufgaben," into a principle of narrative sequence and linkage, and for this we will do well to turn to a consideration of the narrative structure in its own right.

* * *

It is not easy to characterize the novellas in the *Wanderjahre* as a group. Most interpretations underline certain consolidating themes that tie them to one another and to the frame story.[16] But I would stress their open-ended, discontinuous features, their tendency to dispersal and fragmentation. Some break off unexpectedly. Some introduce new narrative strands that displace the original focus. Some cross over into the frame action in ways that leave one uncertain regarding the link between novella and frame. There are abrupt transformations in figures who appear in both a novella and in the frame action (for example, the Beautiful Widow). This is true too of figures who tell stories about themselves in which they appear very different than in the main strand (for example, Wilhelm, Odoard).

Telling a story about oneself rarely serves as a means of self-revelation (as in the fisher boy episode) but is more often a kind of strategy, a modus of behavior adapted to the given situation (for example, the burlesque romance that the Foolish Pilgrim sings as payment for her reception; the Barber's storytelling for the amusement of the company). We are not generally given finished life stories but images or episodes of a life in progress (for example, Leonardo, Makarie), and often the recital of such an episode itself contributes to the furtherance of a more general process whose outcome remains unarticulated. Leonardo's words at the beginning of **"Das nußbraune Mädchen"** have a more general application: "Ich darf Ihnen wohl vertrauen und erzählen, was eigentlich keine Geschichte ist" (p.

129). What he recounts is indeed not a unified narrative but the inaugural episode of a circuitous search involving mistaken identity, diversionary materials, and breaks in the manuscript.

The search is for a woman who herself undergoes a series of transformations, from the intense, passionately pleading child who first arrests Leonardo's attention to the shadowy, recessive figure dubbed "die Gute-Schöne." (This kind of fading from a proper name to an epithet says much about the conception of character in this novel.) Her eventual union with Leonardo is evoked but left unresolved and she is left in the end in the role of Makarie's assistant. Everything about her—the multiple names and epithets, the indeterminate fate—confirms Leonardo's impression of her as "die Ersehnte," (p. 416) the wished-for but never altogether palpable goal of his quest.

The *Wanderjahre* is composed of an assemblage of text forms that represent a great variety of language uses, and these uses or pragmatic functions cannot be readily reconciled to one another or made to depend on a single, authoritative narrative principle. To be attentive to the pragmatic dimension of a text means that we attempt to situate it in terms of its intended application, that we discern in its very form a directive or mode of transformation that implicates all the instances of a communicative process. Of course, the question of the application of a text, of its pragmatic dimension, is one that may be posed for all types of texts, fictive or non-fictive, narrative or nonnarrative. And we cannot overlook that the structure of the *Wanderjahre* is perplexing in part because it includes a great heterogeneity of textual forms—novellas, letters, monologues, collections of maxims, scientific discussions, aesthetic speculations, accounts of dreams, data regarding techniques and crafts, pedagogic theory, etc.[17] All these forms are, of course, to some extent modalized by their inclusion in the novel, and yet they may still be analyzed by means of pragmatic models appropriate to each of them.

Walter Benjamin sought to define the pragmatic dimension of storytelling—"die Kunst des Erzählens"—by underscoring its usefulness—"ihren Nutzen"—its tendency to convey what we would term home truths, words of wisdom—"Rat," "Weisheit."[18] What is basic to the traditional story in his sense is that it draws on a stock of communal experience—"Erfahrung"—and is thus capable of fashioning exemplary cases, that is, such as replenish and extend a communally accredited image of man. Benjamin's argument is designed to set off the traditional, orally-based story from one of its modern derivatives, namely, the novel, which is deprived of an exemplifying function through the solitude, the infertile inwardness of its protagonist. "Die Geburtskammer des Romans," he writes, "ist das Individuum in seiner Einsamkeit, das sich über seine wichtigsten Anliegen nicht mehr exemplarisch auszusprechen vermag, selbst unberaten ist und keinen Rat geben kann." The exemplary function that Benjamin as-

signs to the story, and which differentiates it from the novel in the modern sense, can help us to identify the *Wanderjahre* as a hybrid form occupying an intermediate place between *Novellenkranz* and novel.

The storyteller, Benjamin writes, "weiß Rat—nicht wie das Sprichwort: für manche Fälle, sondern wie der Weise: für viele." When Benjamin speaks of "Rat" as one of the effects of storytelling, he allows for a transformation of the exemplary function of narrative (in the traditional sense, the story as an illustration of proverb or maxim) into a more fluid principle of form. The level of proverbs, the explicit condensation of wisdom and good counsel, is obviously very important in the *Wanderjahre,* but we cannot always assume that the "truths" enunciated in this form are intended as propositional statements. There are in fact so many "truths" strewn through the multiple, interrelated stories that they contravene any fixed application. The overdetermination of the level of wisdom and good counsel becomes veritably dizzying if we include the extranarrative collections of aphorisms and notations, **"Betrachtungen im Sinne der Wanderer"** and **"Aus Makariens Archiv."** Within the narrative proper a saying often stands in an oblique relation to the action and may be enunciated primarily in order to be tested.

The clearest case involves the Uncle whose estate Wilhelm and Felix visit early in the book. This typical Enlightenment figure is in the habit of affixing maxims on the gates and entryways of his estate, a penchant that is wittily subverted by his niece, Hersilie. During a conversation between Wilhelm and the two sisters, Hersilie and Juliette, Wilhelm notices one of the maxims that the Uncle has had posted in the garden, "Vom Nützlichen durchs Wahre zum Schönen" (p. 65). And although we are told that Wilhelm undertakes to interpret it "in his manner" (which must be appropriately moralistic since it gains the approbation of the gentle Juliette), Goethe does not actually give us this interpretation but a much less orthodox view offered by Hersilie, an explicitly feminine exegesis:

> Wir Frauen sind in einem besondern Zustande. Die Maximen der Männer hören wir immerfort wiederholen, ja wir müssen sie in goldnen Buchstaben über unsern Häupten sehen, und doch wüßten wir Mädchen im Stillen das Umgekehrte zu sagen, das auch gölte, wie es gerade hier der Fall ist. Die *Schöne* findet Verehrer, auch Freier, und endlich wohl gar einen Mann; dann gelangt sie zum *Wahren*, das nicht immer höchst erfreulich sein mag, und wenn sie klug ist, widmet sie sich dem *Nützlichen,* sorgt für Haus und Kinder und verharrt dabei.
>
> (p. 66)

A feminine exegesis, as I have said, and at a number of levels: First, in that Hersilie takes a general rule, supposedly operative at a universal level, and demonstrates its specific applicability for a subclass of the social body, for a minority not usually taken account of in the principles of the Enlightenment. And then feminine also in the rhetorical sense—in the supple, ingratiating, yet basically subversive manner in which the language of authority is turned against itself.

Benjamin's study suggests that the "moral" of a story, its pragmatic point, may be understood not only as an effect of summation and closure but also as a kind of propagating energy that connects the single tale with a larger narrative current. This may take two forms. One involves the principle of linkage among stories, the network of what he terms narrative remembrance ("Gedächtnis") or "das Netz, welches alle Geschichten miteinander am Ende Bilden." And he goes on, "Eine schließt an die andere an, wie es die großen Erzähler immer und vor allem die orientalischen gern gezeigt haben. In jedem derselben lebt eine Scheherazade, der zu jeder Stelle ihrer Geschichten eine neue Geschichte einfällt." The other form this energy takes involves the formation of a body of auditors, "die Gemeinschaft der Lauschenden," a communality specifically constituted by its receptivity to the story. Here too Benjamin utilizes an image from textile manufacture. The art of telling stories, he writes, "verliert sich, weil nicht mehr gewebt und gesponnen wird, während man ihnen lauscht. Je selbstvergessener der Lauschende, desto tiefer prägt sich ihm das Gehörte ein. Wo ihn der Rhythmus der Arbeit ergriffen hat, da lauscht er den Geschichten auf solche Weise, daß ihm die Gabe, sie zu erzählen, von selber zufällt. So also ist das Netz beschaffen, in das die Gabe zu erzählen gebettet ist."

The association of spinning and weaving with the formation of stories is, of course, an ancient one—its mythological prototype is the three Fates. In the *Wanderjahre* we find more than one variant of this theme. In the case of the Beautiful Widow (in **"Der Mann von Fünfzig Jahren"**) it is adapted to the luxurious world of an eighteenth-century salon. The Widow, in connection with an elaborately embroidered portfolio she has made, speaks of her handiwork in these terms: "Als junge Mädchen werden wir gewöhnt, mit den Fingern zu tifteln und mit den Gedanken umherzuschweifen; beides bleibt uns, indem wir nach und nach die schwersten und zierlichsten Arbeiten verfertigen lernen . . ." (p. 189). The musing, uncommitted play of fancy expressed here suggest a Penelope function, the weaving of an endless tapestry, perhaps a metaphor for a proto-narrative source from which every story is derived and to which it refers through some loose ends, some trace of its connection to other stories, to all stories.

By drawing on Benjamin's analysis we have been able to relate certain formal elements of narrative to a communal practice that brings into play the circuit of narrative transmission. "So haftet an der Erzählung," Benjamin writes, "die Spur des Erzählenden wie die Spur der Topferhand an der Tonschale." Now this foreign element in the tale, the trace of its origin, of who made it and for what purpose, should be projected forward as well, toward the recipient. When this is done we have all of the constituents of narrative structure in a pragmatic sense—the telling, the listening, the passing on.

* * *

Recent theoretical work has shown that the narrating process is itself a modus of action within narrative forms, perhaps the most basic and pervasive of all. Far from placing it outside the form, as a kind of source or cause, critics have begun to demonstrate how this process (the "discours du récit," as the French structural critics term it) is perfectly assimilable to those signifying elements that have generally been considered the primary content or subject matter of narrative, such as action, character, or description. Since, in the *Wanderjahre,* the narrating instance is distributed among many figures, the circuit of narrative transmission[19] is complex and exceptionally significant for the work's structure. The novel includes, as I have already indicated, a great multiplicity of text forms, and not only does each one involve its distinct mode of enunciation, transmission, and reception, but their copresence within the same narrative further complicates the communicative circuit. This explains why I have been led to focus on the pragmatic dimension of the text—on the modes of transmission rather than on some definitive message.

Mikhail Bakhtin's work allows us to extend the notion of a narrative pragmatics by offering a model of dialogue or intertextuality designed specifically to account for the heterogeneous materials that enter into the structure of the novel. Of the various terms that Bakhtin utilizes, "heteroglossia" is perhaps the most suggestive for the medley of styles and attitudes that make up the fabric of prose fiction. In Bakhtin's view the multiplicity of discursive modes that make up a text are not simply citations or remnants of antecedent speech forms, as Barthes interprets them in the context of his "referential, endoxal" code.[20] Rather, Bakhtin underscores a dynamic interplay, a collision of singular, though not necessarily personal, "voices," and through the conjunction which the novel brings about a new form of meaning emerges, an authentic signifying operation. The dialogic novel, as he conceives it, has the capacity of assimilating these heterogeneous elements but without altogether normalizing them. They retain to some degree the force of their various origins. Furthermore, Bakhtin makes us particularly attentive to the specific stance, the intentional vector, one may say, encoded in every statement, the very quality that makes it a voice in an active dialogue. But to call it a voice does not mean to make it dependent on a character. The polyphony of voices derives from a prepersonal discourse level which frequently but not invariably utilizes anthropomorphic agents as instances of enunciation. The speech of characters in a novel represents a secondary operation and it presupposes a repertoire of registers, what has been termed "normative genres of discourse,"[21] whose ultimate basis is social and cultural.

What is especially relevant for us in Bakhtin's notion of dialogue is that every word, or speech segment, is to be taken not as an invariant unit of meaning but as enunciatory act, an act which betrays the pressure of other speech acts. "The word is not a thing," he writes, "but rather the eternally mobile, eternally changing medium of dialogical intercourse. It never coincides with a single consciousness or a single voice. The life of the word is in its transferral from one mouth to another, one context to another, one social collective to another, and one generation to another. In the process the word does not forget where it has been and can never wholly free itself from the dominion of the contexts of which it has been a part."[22]

Bakhtin's categories refer to different levels of the narrative process in ways that he himself did not fully indicate, thus any effort to apply his ideas to a work involves certain interpretive choices regarding the theory. I would suggest three ways in which the *Wanderjahre* exemplifies a dialogic practice: first, in destabilizing genre forms; then, in orienting representational devices toward the instance of reception; and finally, in thematizing the channels of communication as such.

Let us first examine heteroglossia at the level of genre, as a loosening of, a playing with a given generic formula. The pattern that Goethe had available in constructing the stories for the *Wanderjahre* was that of the Renaissance novella, a form in which exemplarity and entertainment, moral point and witty pointe, are subtly interwoven. As a background to this form we may take, as Karlheinz Stierle has argued,[23] the medieval fable, where the narrative sequence is unequivocally oriented toward an apothegm or maxim, a *sententia*. Conversely, this moral point may be viewed as the kernel that gives rise to a narrative expansion. Now in various Renaissance forms the expansion went well beyond the limits implicit in the didactic or moralistic kernel, without, however, altogether obliterating the initial pragmatic orientation. What is noteworthy about the Boccaccian novella, Stierle argues, is the way that the exemplum, the illustrative narrative, wins a certain autonomy, establishing an oblique relation to the pragmatic context on which it is based. The exemplum is overdetermined; its applicability in moral or social terms is no longer self-evident though the field of that applicability remains as a point of reference. The problematization of the exemplum in the novella may be viewed not only in terms of the narrative form (at the level of the sender) but also of the intended audience (or receptor). In fact, it is often the frame structure that makes this feature most explicit. "The new mode of representation of the novella," Stierle writes with respect to Boccaccio, "is thematized as a function of the self-understanding of the kind of society that is delineated in the frame."

One could find numerous instances in the *Wanderjahre* where the exemplifying function typical of the novella form is put into question, instances both at the level of the stories (as in **"Die gefährliche Wette,"** where a farce takes an unexpected tragic turning) and of the frame (as in various episodes where there is a disequilibrium between what we know of the speaker and what he recounts about himself—for example, the case of Wilhelm already discussed, or Odoard recounting **"Nicht zu weit"**). In a pioneering study Ernst Friedrich von Monroy showed that many of the novellas displace the basic narrative pattern by introducing contrastive devices characteristic of other literary forms, such as legend, comic drama, or fairy tale.[24]

A second way of approaching the dialogic mode in the *Wanderjahre* is to note the frequency of speech forms, whether in monologue or dialogue, that are markedly oriented toward their reception. This might be viewed as a thematization of the dialogic by means of dramatic or theatrical devices. In such utterances the intention to affect or influence the auditor is clearly exhibited by way of manner and gesture. But there is also in the substance of the enunciation a strategy aimed at forestalling and modifying the anticipated response. Bakhtin speaks of the "alien words" which inhabit all our utterances and which we, consciously or not, take account of in all communicative acts. This alien word, he writes, is "in the consciousness of the listener, of his apperceptive background, pregnant with responses and objections. And every utterance is oriented toward this apperceptive background of understanding, which is not a linguistic background but rather one composed of specific objects and emotional expressions."[25]

A number of episodes in the *Wanderjahre* hinge not on what is directly stated in a speech or dialogue, but rather on a strategy oriented to the act of reception. This is patent in instances where a speaker directly manipulates an interlocutor, as in the Foolish Pilgrim's half-veiled, deceiving intimations to Herr von Revanne and to his son that she has become pregnant through the other. But it is operative too in less overt instances where we become attentive less to the motives of the speaker than to the effects of the speaking—thus, in the Foolish Pilgrim's ballad, in Nachodine's plea to Leonardo, in Lucidor's monologues in **"Wer ist der Verräter?"** (whose plot turns on their being overheard), in the echo effects of the poems which Flavio and Hilarie exchange, not to mention the *Wechselgedichte* which they read together and which serve to kindle their love. Of course, each of these instances viewed in the context of its episode fulfils a traditional pattern of dramatized representation. But, through its repeated, cumulative use in the novel, this kind of strategic address in monologue and dialogue must be accounted a basic structuring principle, subverting the authority of a single narrative persona and shaping the reception of the work as a whole.

Finally, I see the dialogic principle operative in the *Wanderjahre* in a recurrent focus on the communicative channel as such, or rather on the interferences or blockages that impede the full circulation of narrative information. An important recent study of the novel is entitled *Wilhelm Meisters Wanderjahre oder, die Kunst des Mittelbaren; Studien zum Problem der Verständigung in Goethes Altersepoche.*[26] In it Manfred Karnick deals with what may be termed Goethe's communicative reticence, and he offers some excellent analyses of its implications for the mode of indirect and symbolic presentation characteristic of the *Wanderjahre.* What for him, however, are privative categories at a biographical, existential level—such as secrecy and hiddenness ("Verschlossenheit")—I would take more as strategic choices which open up new possibilities of form. I can only sketch what I have in mind by touching on the role of Hersilie in the action.

Hersilie provides her own character, and that of her household, in a consciously parodistic listing of the cast of characters that Wilhelm meets on the Uncle's estate: "ein wunderlicher Oheim, eine sanfte und eine muntere Nichte, eine kluge Tante, Hausgenossen nach bekannter Art . . ." (p. 68). She, of course is the "muntere Nichte." Her first letter to her aunt Makarie opens with a complaint that strikes us as singular when we consider the highly disciplined, well-nigh ritualistic pattern of intercourse practiced in her house. "Ich will und muß sehr kurz sein, liebe Tante," Hersilie writes, "denn der Bote zeigt sich unartig ungeduldig" (p. 75). How could a messenger from Makarie's household be so impertinent? Later in the letter she writes, "Der Bote! der Bote! Ziehen Sie Ihre alten Leute besser, oder schicken sie junge. Diesem ist weder mit Schmeichelei noch mit Wein beizukommen" (p. 76). We never hear again about this annoying courier. Now if we attempt to assign him a function in the action we hardly know what to do with him. He is a kind of noise, an intrusive, unassimilable element in the communicative circuit. But the insistent, thrice-reiterated reference to the messenger—"Der Bote! der verwünschte Bote!"—foregrounds a meta-narrative function that we cannot altogether ignore.

Later in the novel a young courier does in fact appear. This one bears a message ("eine Botschaft") from Felix, who at this point is in school in the Pedagogic Province. The whole episode is recounted by Hersilie in a letter to Wilhelm. (It's worth noting that her sole entry into the novel after her initial appearance at the Uncle's estate is by way of a series of letters which she addresses to Wilhelm, though we never learn that he replies to any of them.) What is it that the courier brings from Felix? A slate school tablet with the rudimentary inscription,

Felix
liebt
Herselien.
Der Stallmeister
kommt bald.

(p. 265)

Herselie is perturbed, baffled, uncertain how to reply. In the end the young itinerant merchant gives her a similar tablet on which she traces a response, a slightly askew mirroring of Felix's words designed both to satisfy him and to show her good-humored reception of his message,

Hersiliens
Gruß
an Felix.
Der Stallmeister
halte sich gut.

Goethe here undoubtedly alludes to far more exalted instances of a courtship carried on by an exchange of verse where each partner echoes the other—there is his own cycle, the *West-östlicher Divan,* and in this novel there is the exchange of poems between Flavio and Hilarie already mentioned. The exchange of messages on slate tablets between Hersilie and Felix appears to be a kind of parody of such a courtship.[27]

It serves, though, to introduce another courier figure, another passing intermediary—gypsy or Jew, perhaps, "etwas Orientalisches," is how Hersilie characterizes him. Typically, he is gone before she can get a clear image of him, and she muses, "Allerdings etwas Geheimnisvolles war in der Figur; dergleichen sind jetzt im Roman nicht zu entbehren, sollten sie uns denn auch im Leben begegnen? Angenehm, doch verdächtig, fremdartig, doch Vertrauen erregend; warum schied er auch vor aufgelöster Verwirrung? warum hatt' ich nicht Gegenwart des Geistes genug, um ihn schicklicherweise festzuhalten?" (p. 267).

Hersilie and the elusive courier—here is a motif that does not fill out into a story. It is a narrative kernel of indefinite mass. Hersilie, of course, is a figure who tries to resist typification. She knows the stereotypes of fiction all too well. Her own story, her attachment to Felix or to his father, never quite gets off the ground. She is the guardian of the mysterious little box that Felix had found, but she never gets to see what's in it, even when the key is finally restored to her. Her plea to Wilhelm regarding this box—"daß es ein Ende werde, wenigsten daß eine Deutung vorgehe, was damit gemeint sei, mit diesem wunderbaren Finden, Wiederfinden, Trennen und Vereinigen," (p. 378)—remains unanswered. If Makarie is the repository of everyone's secrets, the wise counselor, the secular mystic, what is Hersilie, who can't decide between father and son, whose letters go unanswered, who remains in posession of a mysterious box that she can't or won't open?

There seems to be a function in the communicative channel that facilitates narrative without being altogether part of it. We hardly have a name for it. Its agents have no great dignity in the roster of narrative roles. Perhaps we touch here on an emergent stage of the narrative impulse, one not yet fully conscious of itself, not yet informed by a narrative subject. If so, Hersilie names it since she is akin to it —"Der Bote! der verwünschte Bote!"

Notes

1. To Johann Friedrich Rochlitz, November 23, 1829. Cited in the edition of the *Wanderjahre* in *Goethes Werke*, Hamburger Ausgabe, ed. Erich Trunz (Hamburg: Christian Wegner Verlag, 1950) VIII, 578. Hereafter cited *GW*.

2. To Iken, September 23, 1827. Cited in *GW*, III, 448.

3. "Der echte Leser," *GW*, VIII, 575; "der Aufmerkende," *GW*, III 448; "Dem einsichtigen Leser," *GW*, VIII, 578.

4. June 8, 1821. Cited in *GW*, VIII, 574.

5. Heidi Gidion, *Zur Darstellungsweise von Goethes 'Wilhelm Meisters Wanderjahre'* (Göttingen: Vandenhoeck u. Ruprecht, 1969 [Palaestra, Bd. 256]), 27 f.

6. "Death by Water: or, The Childhood of Wilhelm Meister," *Modern Language Review*, 56 (1961), 44-53; this passage p. 50.

7. Cf. Hans Reiss, " 'Wilhelm Meisters Wanderjahre'— Der Weg von der ersten zur zweiten Fassung," *D.V.L.G.*, 39 (1965), 34-57.

8. All page numbers in the text from *GW*, VIII.

9. Karl Schlechta, *Goethes Wilhelm Meister* (Frankfurt a.M.: V. Klostermann, 1953). Cf. Arthur Henkel's review, *G.R.M.*, 36 (1955), N.F. 5, 85-89.

10. The overwhelming tendency of modern interpreters to understand the Wilhelm Meister novels in this progressive manner can be traced back at least to Max Wundt's *Goethes Wilhelm Meister und die Entwicklung des modernen Lebensideal* (Berlin and Lepzig: G. J. Göschen, 1913). But recent studies like those by Gidion (see note 5 above), Karnick (see note 26 below), Heinz Schlaffer ("Exoterik and Esoterik in Goethes Romanen," *Goethe Jahrbuch*, 95 [1978], 212-226), and Hans Vaget ("Recurrent Themes and Narrative Strategies in Goethe's Novels," a paper delivered at the Irvine Goethe Symposium, April 8, 1982, forthcoming in proceedings of the Symposium, Walter de Gruyter, Berlin) have moved in an opposite direction. Schlechta, in spite of the extreme thesis he maintains, can be viewed as their pioneer.

11. A. J. Greimas and J. Courtès, "The Cognitive Dimension of Narrative Discourse," *New Literary History*, 7 (1975-76), 433-47.

12. From *Tag- und Jahreshefte*. Cited in *GW*, VIII, 519.

13. Cf. Gidion, p. 30.

14. *GW*, VII, 290.

15. In conversation to Kanzler v. Müller, January 22, 1821. Cited *GW*, VIII, 519.

16. One of the most discerning studies in this vein is Arthur Henkel, *Entsagung, Eine Studie zu Goethes Altersroman* (Tübingen: Max Niemeyer, 1954 [Hermaea, Bd. 3]).

17. Hans Reiss's comparison of the style of the two versions of the *Wanderjahre* is illuminating. In contrast to the relative homogeneity of the first he lists some of the new stylistic registers of the second: "In der zweiten Fassung aber gibt es jene intensivierte Dichte der Makarie-Kapitel, wo wissenschaftliche Sprache und Darstellung in einer wohl höchsten Steigerung der Goetheschen Erzähler-Prosa verbunden sind. Es gibt außerdem noch eine an der Sturm und Drang erinnernde Sprache, in der Flavios leidenschaftliche Erregung geschildert wird; ... Außerdem gibt es noch den lakonisch abrupt konzentrierten Stil des zusammenfassenden Berichts, welcher, ähnlich wie in Goethes *Annalen* viele Ereignisse zusammenrafft und knapp angibt. Schließlich noch die prägnante Form der Sprüche und die symbolische Ausdrucksform der beiden weltanschaulichen Gedichte." Op. cit., p. 56 f.

18. "Der Erzähler," in *Gesammelte Schriften*, II, 2.

19. I adapt this notion from an analysis by Jean-François Lyotard that develops certain issues of the tradition of storytelling in a manner similar to Benjamin's essay. Lyotard suggests that one way a culture stores and transmits its customs and wisdom ("savoir") is through its techniques of narrative construction. "A generally acknowledged property of traditional knowledge," he writes, "is that the narrative positions or stances (sender, receptor, hero) are so distributed that the right to occupy that of the sender is based on the double condition of having occupied that of the receiver and of having been, by virtue of his name, already the object of a narrative, that is, placed in the position of a diegetic referent of other narrative occurrences." *La Condition post-moderne* (Paris: Editions of Minuit, 1979), p. 40. My translation.

20. See *S/Z—An Essay*.

21. John Frowe, "Voice and Register in *Little Dorrit*," *Comparative Literature*, 33 (1981), 263.

22. M. M. Bakhtin, *Problems of Dostoevsky's Poetics* (Ann Arbor: Ardis, 1973), p. 167.

23. "Geschichte als Exemplum—Exemplum als Geschichte—Zur Pragmatik und Poetik narrativer Texte," in *Text als Handlung* (Munich: W. Fink, 1975), pp. 14-48.

24. "Zur Form der Novelle in 'Wilhelm Meisters Wanderjahre,'" *G.R.M.,* 31 (1943), 1-19.

25. M. M. Bakhtin, *The Dialogic Imagination—Four Essays,* ed. Michael Holquist (Austin: University of Texas Press, 1981), p. 281. I have already spoken in connection with Benjamin and Lyotard of the ways that the context of reception is constitutive for the form of a narrative. For Bakhtin too a narrative event cannot be established in abstract terms, as part of some self-contained logic of narrative. There is an "evaluative function" encoded in the telling without which there would be no story. (I cite this phrase from the stimulating article by Rolf Kloepfer, "Dynamic Structures in Narrative Literature—'The Dialogic Principle.'" *Poetics Today,* [1979-80], 118.)

26. Manfred Karnick, *Wilhelm Meisters Wanderjahre oder, die Kunst des Mittelbaren: Studien zum Problem der Verständigung in Goethes Altersepoche* (Munich: W. Fink, 1968).

27. I note two recent essays focusing on the figure of Hersilie, though neither parallels my discussion: Marianne Jabs-Kriegsmann, "Felix und Hersilie," in *Studien zu Goethes Alterswerken,* ed. Erich Trunz (Frankfurt a.M.: Athenäum-Verlag, 1971); Françoise Derré, "Die Beziehung zwischen Felix, Hersilie and Wilhelm in 'Wilhelm Meisters Wanderjahre,'" *Goethe Jahrbuch,* 94 (1977), 38-48.

William Larrett (essay date 1987)

SOURCE: Larrett, William. "'Weder Kern Noch Schale': The 'Novel' Epistemology of Goethe's *Wilhelm Meisters Wanderjahre.*" *Publications of the English Goethe Society* 56 (1987): 38-55. Print.

[In the following essay, Larrett addresses the difficulty of finding a suitable model for the fundamental structure of Wilhelm Meister's Travels. *After surveying some alternative formulations, Larrett suggests that the novel portrays a Nature that, in Goethe's words, "has neither core nor shell" but is essentially a seamless unity, admitting of only partial and gradual understanding.]*

Wilhelm Meisters Wanderjahre was the only literary work of Goethe's to be published during his lifetime containing an illustration, though to call it an 'illustration' may be slightly misleading. What I am referring to is the picture, reproduced in Book III, Chapter 3, of the key to that mysterious box or casket which had been found earlier in a cave by Wilhelm's son, Felix (Book I, Chapter 4). This seemingly trivial detail derives provocative significance partly from its uniqueness within Goethe's oeuvre and partly from the delightful irony that this is precisely what this work lacks: a key to all its many secrets, including that of its form. Despite the drawing, this work is

hardly 'un roman à clef'; a view shared by the author himself for, as he said to Eckermann on 18 January 1825: 'Es gehört dieses Werk übrigens zu den inkalkulabelsten Produktionen, wozu mir fast selbst der Schlüssel fehlt.' Here it is interesting to note that 'dieses Werk' refers to a work simply entitled *Wilhelm Meister* which, however, through the immediate mention, in the same sentence, of Schiller's letters seems to indicate that he has ***Die Lehrjahre*** [*Wilhelm Meisters Lehrjahre*] in mind. Nevertheless, the omission of a more precise designation and the date 1825 suggest a blurring of the two works. One can make a similar claim for an earlier like-worded remark in the ***Tag- und Jahreshefte*** for 1796: 'Es bleibt daher dieses [*Wilhelm Meister*] eine der inkalkulabelsten Produktionen, man mag sie im ganzen oder in ihren Teilen betrachten; ja um sie zu beurteilen, fehlt mir beinahe selbst der Maßstab' (HA [***Goethes Werke***], x, 446). Of course, in the context of the named year '1796' this must refer to ***Die Lehrjahre,*** though surely, if he has only this novel in mind, it seems to be an exaggerated claim. But this is not a diary entry for 1796 but an opinion expressed with hindsight when the ***Tag- und Jahreshefte*** were compiled in the 1820s after the publication of the first version of ***Wilhelm Meisters Wanderjahre*** and during the period of intense revision and extension which the ***Wanderjahre*** underwent at that time. It seems to me that in both these statements Goethe is projecting back to ***Wilhelm Meisters Lehrjahre*** a view of the whole which he has gained from the experience of composing and revising the ***Wanderjahre.*** It also suggests that he sees greater homogeneity between the two works than most critics allow and that he regards the ***Wanderjahre*** as a genuine sequel to, and extension of, the earlier ***Lehrjahre,*** albeit one which contains a mystery which even eludes its creator. One cannot dismiss these remarks of Goethe's by saying that his own memory of the ***Lehrjahre*** was hazy, since we know he had re-read the earlier work—though skipping Books I and II (skipping, that is, everything up to the point where Melina forms his own theatre group)—in 1821, which had led him to stress the novel's symbolic content in a conversation reported by Kanzler von Müller (22 January 1821): 'Es mache ihm Freude und Beruhigung, zu finden, daß der ganze Roman durchaus symbolisch sei. ...' But having said all that, how do we as *readers* come to grips with ***Wilhelm Meisters Wanderjahre***?

Despite Goethe's scornful dismissal of any attempt on the part of the reader to construe and analyse the book systematically, saying as late as 18 February 1830, again in conversation with Kanzler von Müller, 'Das [ist] rein unmöglich, das Buch [gibt] sich nur für ein Aggregat aus,' part of the work's abiding fascination nevertheless resides in its challenge to the reader's natural desire to try and make sense of the work as a whole and to probe its opaqueness. We feel that to describe the work simply as an 'Aggregat' belies so much of what we know about the work's composition. At the same time, one must recognize that in employing a term like 'Aggregat' Goethe can also be ironically understating the narrative stance he has adopted consistently throughout, that is, that of editor and collector. We also know that as a collector Goethe was himself both voracious and systematic; in his will he wrote: 'Ich habe nicht nach Laune und Willkühr, sondern jedesmal mit Plan und Absicht zu meiner eignen folgerechten Bildung gesammelt und an jedem Stück meines Besitzes etwas gelernt.'[1] What I think Goethe is resisting when he rejects any systematic attempt at analysis of the *Wanderjahre* is the subversive urge on the part of the commentator to reduce the measure of mystery which is both appropriate to, and inheres in, a work of art as significant form, as symbol. It is what he felt he had to resist even in a mind as sophisticated and differentiating as Schiller's, when in connection with the *Lehrjahre* Goethe had to ward off his friend's wish for 'eine noch etwas deutlichere Pronunziation der Hauptidee' (Schiller to Goethe, 19 October 1796).

It is not my intention here to proclaim with Hersilie: 'Kurz und gut! Zu Ihrem Prachtkästchen ist das Schlüsselchen gefunden' (320),[2] and with this 'Eureka!' don a new neat formula like a certain emperor who once paraded in a new suit of clothes. What I hope to do is consider some of the issues raised, and problems posed, by the *Wanderjahre* and, whilst presenting much that will be familiar, to suggest a fresh arrangement and perspective, though even that seems an immodest claim in view of the work's complexity.

One of the problems, perhaps the chief problem, in any assessment of the *Wanderjahre* is how to get the emphasis right, how to avoid on the one hand a 'catch-all' model which runs the risk of too bland a formulation (and for all his sensitivity in its application, I think Professor Blackall's notion of counterpoint[3] demonstrates this risk), and how to avoid on the other hand the sort of formulation which can excite initially but soon proves rather brittle (as an example of this danger, I would refer to Ehrhard Bahr's distinction[4] between 'metaphorical' and 'metonymic,' a distinction I find too delphic, especially if one is to categorize the *Lehrjahre* as metaphoric and the *Wanderjahre* as metonymic—on reflection, how can 'metonymic' be applied to such a work in its entirety, unless, of course, 'metonymic' is used 'metaphorically'?).

When discussing *Wilhelm Meisters Wanderjahre* we fall—understandably—all too easily into the trap of emphasizing its disparate nature, of concentrating too much on that deceptive notion of an 'aggregate' which seems to suggest that the work's meaning is simply to be found in the sum total of its parts. But this is to ignore that other scientific sense of 'aggregate' which denotes a mixed and fused entity. After all, we are not dealing with a random structure, a chance assemblage of bits and pieces, caught coincidentally between two covers. The fact that *part* of its contents owes more to chance than to design (i.e. the

presence of two collections of maxims within the compass of the work and the final position of those maxims being determined more by a printer's schedule; and the fact that Goethe apparently left the choice of maxims to Eckermann), this fact, which is so often highlighted, diverts our attention away from the care with which Goethe revised and worked on the *Wanderjahre,* away from the emphasis put both within the work and in the relevant diary entries etc., on the shaping and the organizing of the material, on the activity of 'ordnen.' Arguably, if the maxims had appeared where first envisaged, that is: **'Aus Makariens Archiv'** between Books I and II, and **'Betrachtungen im Sinne des Wanderers'** between Books II and III, leaving the book to end with the scene where Felix, after his near drowning, is restored both to health and society by his father, the weight of critical stress might well have been on symmetry and unity and 'closed' form.

Similarly, no matter how difficult it may be to avoid a term like 'Rahmenhandlung,' useful as it is as a shorthand label, it nevertheless distorts our view of the kind of form with which we are confronted in *Wilhelm Meisters Wanderjahre.* Goethe himself as author/narrator/editor is at pains constantly to undermine such distinctions in a variety of ways. The organization of the work into books and chapters points in itself to a coherence, which overrides expected divisions. Why does the story **'Wer ist der Verräter?'** occupy Chapters 8 and 9 in Book I? Why is it divided at all? Why is the story **'Der Mann von fünfzig Jahren'** spread over three chapters in Book II, that is, Chapters 3, 4 and 5? Why is this division into three chapters nevertheless presented as providing a unity of narration which runs contrary to contemporary popular taste? Chapter 3 is introduced by the following remarks:

> Der Angewöhnung des werten Publikums zu schmeicheln, welches seit geraumer Zeit Gefallen findet, sich stückweise unterhalten zu lassen, gedachten wir erst, nachstehende Erzählung in mehrerer Abteilungen vorzulegen. Der innere Zusammenhang jedoch, nach Gesinnungen, Empfindungen und Ereignissen betrachtet, veranlaßte einen fortlaufenden Vortrag. Möge derselbe seinen Zweck erreichen und zugleich am Ende deutlich werden, wie die Personen dieser abgesondert scheinender Begebenheit mit derjenigen, die wir schon kennen und lieben, aufs innigste zusammengeflochten worden.

(167)

Dividing these stories into chapters and then numbering those chapters according to the overall numerical sequence of the books in which they are located inevitably serves to blur any notion of their separateness from the rest. Furthermore the above comment with which Chapter 3 opens is shot through with irony and seems to poke fun at contemporary preference for fragmentary modes of narration, and invokes immanent laws of coherence. Despite this, however, the story (**'Der Mann von fünfzig Jahren'**) is not complete by the end of Chapter 5, as its two main female characters are to meet up with Wilhelm in Chapter 7 and the final paragraph of the story is withheld to Book III, Chapter 14, one of the closing chapters of the work as a whole, where the author is quite candidly tying up loose ends.

Another way in which Goethe deliberately blurs and obscures his divisions lies in his use of names. Consider the names of his female characters: Natalie, Makarie, Hersilie, Hilarie, Lydie, Lucie, Julie, Juliette, Melusine, Valerine, Nachodine and Philine; and the male characters: Lenardo, Lothario, Jarno, Odoard, Friedrich, Felix, Fitz. It is almost as if Goethe were pulling his reader's leg, or at least the legs of those readers, who might smugly realize, before Lenardo tumbles to the fact, that he (Lenardo) has confused the identities of Valerine and Nachodine in his memory, only to find that they too, once they have put the book down, can no longer recall with certainty which character belongs where. (And if we were to play the names' game further, would we have been at all surprised to add Ottilie and Honorio to the list, the one from *Die Wahlverwandtschaften,* the other from *Novelle,* both of which pieces might have formed part of the 'Aggregat' of *Wilhelm Meisters Wanderjahre*?) It is as a pointer towards such shifting borders of context that I have included the phrase 'weder Kern noch Schale' in my title.

To talk of context is to talk of weaving, and in the *Wanderjahre* we are examining a literary work, whose author—half 'Textor'![5]—weaves weaving into the texture of his narrative. The main character of this episode is Nachodine, **'Das nußbraune Mädchen,'** a girl for whose fate Lenardo holds himself in part responsible. When he finds her again by chance—but not wholly by chance—she is a widow uncertain as to how to shape her future, not knowing whether she should marry again, whether she should emigrate, or whether she should stay and resist, or adapt to, the inevitable changes with which mechanization threatens weaving as a cottage industry. Her story is subtly narrated, this time 'stückweise,' spread over five stages, two of which take the form of Lenardo's diary of his travels, in the course of which he finds Nachodine, now known as Frau Susanne. The first part of his diary comprises Chapter 3 of Book III and consists entirely of a factual account of spinning and weaving in the Swiss mountain communities which Lenardo visits on what today might be called 'a fact-finding mission.' What is of especial significance for us here is that the account stems not from Goethe's pen but from that of his friend and collaborator, the Swiss Heinrich Meyer, who had provided Goethe with such an account—at Goethe's request—in 1810. Although from Meyer's pen, it is not wholly Meyer, for that irrepressible editor has rearranged the material. The form is Goethe's, the text verbatim Meyer; combined they produce an essentially discursive account which, according to Goethe's diary, they discussed again together on 13 November 1820. Whereas Goethe, as author, rearranged Meyer's report, Goethe as fictive narrator-cum-editor withholds the combination of Lenardo's diary from a curious Wilhelm, and thereby from the reader, with the following justification

> Hier endigte das Manuskript, und als Wilhelm nach der Fortsetzung verlangte, hatte er zu erfahren, daß sie gegenwärtig nicht in den Händen der Freunde sei. Sie ward, sagte man, an Makarien gesendet, welche gewisse Verwicklungen, deren darin gedacht worden, durch Geist und Liebe schlichten und bedenkliche Verknüpfungen auflösen solle.—Der Freund mußte sich diese Unterbrechung gefallen lassen und sich bereiten, an einem geselligen Abend, in heiterer Unterhaltung, Vergnügen zu finden.

(352)

Wilhelm will only get to see the continuation of Lenardo's diary when Makarie has had the chance to sort out some of the difficulties reported in that part of the diary. Note that the hoped-for resolution is couched in terms of unravelling and untying ('gewisse Verwicklungen schlichten'; 'bedenkliche Verknüpfungen auflösen'), a point to which I shall be returning presently.

Since he cannot provide us with the continuation of the diary at this point, the narrator/editor yields to another narrator, a character renowned for the silent execution of his trade—a virtue not normally found in a barber—and, conversely, for his skill as raconteur. The yarn that he spins is that of **'Die neue Melusine.'** (Is it too fanciful to hear in that name an echo and anagram of 'Musseline,' the fine muslin, the production of which has just been described in the preceding chapter, in part I of Lenardo's diary?)

When Wilhelm does eventually get to read the second half of Lenardo's diary, Makarie has had time to fulfil once more her function of bringing harmony and clarity to confused and tangled situations. What is interesting is that the solution to Frau Susanne's (Nachodine's) uncertainties will be found in her giving up her business and leaving home, but not in order to be free to emigrate but in order to become Makarie's companion. Thus Makarie, who has the metaphorical skills of weaving and unravelling, will be joined and aided by a professional weaver, as if an underlying aptitude of mind and temperament allows that manual skill and dexterity to become a craft of the spirit. Perhaps this is something that Lenardo has intuitively recognized when he names Nachodine alias Susanne 'die Gute-Schöne' (428), a designation of which the form is immediately reversed to remain then fixed as 'Die Schöne-Gute,' a sequence which might suggest an adjusted emphasis in favour of inner virtue. In any event the sequence of names ('das nußbraune Mädchen,' Nachodine, Susanne, 'Die Gute-Schöne,' 'Die Schöne-Gute') indicates a progressive development, almost a transfiguration, and when the narrator refers to her in Book III, Chapter 14 as 'Die Schöne-Gute, sonst das nußbraune Mädchen genannt' (446) we are reminded of a similar elevating formulation from the end of *Faust II* 'Una Poenitentium sonst Gretchen genannt.' This parallel designation (sonst—genannt) expresses essence and shell, distilled virtue and enclosing form. A capacity for such penetrating perception of this kind is what had struck Wilhelm when he first met the marvellous and puzzling figure of Makarie. We are told:

> Makarie sprach zu Wilhelm als einem Vertrauten, sie schien sich in geistreicher Schilderung ihrer Verwandten zu erfreuen; es war, als wenn sie die innere Natur eines jeden durch die ihn umgebende individuelle Maske durchschaute. Die Personen, welche Wilhelm nannte, standen wie verklärt vor seiner Seele, das einsichtige Wohlwollen der unschätzbaren Frau hatte die Schale losgelöst und den gesunden Kern veredelt und belebt.

(116)

Makarie, with such gifts of divination, gentle and patient judgement, and oracular utterance, is, like a high priestess, shrouded in mystery. Hers is a being of a different order, inhabiting, or at least having access to, other realms. Her astronomer's observations have led him to the conclusion that her spirit voyages through space in tune with the universe. The climax of the speculation about the true nature of Makarie is expounded with some understandable hesitation on the part of the narrator, for in this section he is not prepared to vouch for the complete veracity of his account, since the document upon which it is based was compiled from memory, 'aus dem Gedächtnis geschrieben und nicht, wie es in einem so merkwürdigen Fall wünschenswert wäre, für ganz authentisch anzusehen' (448f.). Surely, there is a tongue firmly in someone's cheek here! That being so, however, the narrator can indulge his fancy and, feigning modest scepticism, can proceed to plot the course of Makarie's spirit through the cosmos, expressing the hope, in terms more appropriate to the description of some benign comet, that she will return to the benefit of future generations.

Then, leaving Makarie's spirit to move outwards towards the peripheries of space, the narrator abruptly brings his readers down to earth from the realms of 'diese ätherische Dichtung' by directing their attention to another mysterious figure, the central character of what is hardly more than an anecdote, which nevertheless is given the ironic status of 'ein terrestrisches Märchen' by the narrator (452). The activity of this figure (Montan/Jarno's assistant), whilst of a similar kind to that of Makarie, functions at the opposite pole: whereas Makarie is aetherial, divining both spiritual and cosmic relationships, this person is terrestrial and, divining the secrets of the earth, can reveal where water and mineral deposits are to be found. In this section (451-53), however, both with regard to Makarie and this other unnamed person, Goethe as narrator is at his most mischievous and deft, inflating and deflating his heroes with a delicate touch. Here is 'Spiel' and 'Heiterkeit.' Here the narrator teases his reader with yet more secrets: in this instance, neither the sex nor the identity of this character is revealed, but remain masked by the convenient veil of German syntax, since the constant reference to 'Die Person' and the appropriate pronoun 'sie' reveal only grammatical gender. The reader is left to wonder why the third woman in Jarno's party (the others being his wife Lydie and Philine), though apparently 'eine Dienerin,' is never asked to assist the other two ladies with their toilette (a point the narrator comments on), and why 'she' can wield a spade with the energy of three (men being the implication), and the inference we must draw is that a man hides behind the female garb (a kind of inverse Amazon) —a man who just might be Fitz who was earlier associated with Jarno. In the course of this one brief passage (451-53) Goethe has playfully juxtaposed highfalutin spirituality and crude disguise and on both counts the reader is left with the feeling that the joke is on him, as the theme of 'inner' and 'outer' is given another twist.

For this theme, the phrase 'Kern und Schale' provides a handy and obvious label. As a theme it appears in a variety of guises: body and soul, body and clothing, identity and illusion, rocks and minerals, town and countryside, house and garden, public room and inner sanctum, revelation and concealment, propriety and candour, esoteric and exoteric as attributes, articulation and silence. Consider the following quotations:

> Schnell angekleidet standen wir uns noch immer unverhüllt gegeneinander, unsere Gemüter zogen sich an, und unter den feurigsten Küssen schwuren wir eine ewige Freundschaft.

(272)

> ... der Mensch ohne Hülle ist eigentlich der Mensch ... dem Reinen ist alles rein, warum nicht die unmittelbare Absicht Gottes in der Natur? Aber vom Jahrhundert kann man dies nicht verlangen, ohne Feigenblätter und Tierfelle kommt es nicht aus ...

(329)

> Die tätigen Männer, einer guten geglückten Handlung und des zu erwartenden reichlichen Lohns zum voraus sich erfreuend, hatten auf dem heißen Kies die Kleider des Jünglings schon so gut als getrocknet, um ihn beim Erwachen sogleich wieder in den gesellig anständigsten Zustand zu versetzen.

(460)

These three statements represent different aspects of the question of appropriate responses, in different contexts, to the valid claims (a) of shared intimacy which overcomes innocent individuality, (b) of artistic candour which challenges false modesty and reminds us of our naked shared humanity, (c) of conformity and decency which permit social intercourse and concerted action. The development of man's perception of these and other issues proceeds from childhood onwards through stages shaped and determined by the interplay between self and world, an interaction which grows ever more sophisticated and refined. Nevertheless, if he is to progress, man must never lose the innocence of a child, for Jarno says:

> In einem jeden neuen Kreise muß man zuerst wieder als Kind anfangen, leidenschaftliches Interesse auf die Sache werfen, sich erst an der Schale freuen, bis man zu dem Kerne zu gelangen das Glück hat.
>
> (33)

Only by preserving such a stance can one guard against the dangers, as Goethe saw them, inherent in the imposition of a precocious pattern upon observed phenomena. In the child, innocence is accompanied by impulse and spontaneity but in the man childlike innocence must be tempered by discretion, tact and reverence, resisting the urge to know too much too soon. Awe and reverence, themselves not innate virtues, are not to be acquired however at the expense of creative spontaneity; quite the opposite in fact, creative modes of perception are liberated by reverence: 'Staunen' allied to 'Ehrfurcht' goes hand in hand with 'Schauen.' If such thoughts are most explicitly enacted in the educational methods of 'Die pädagogische Provinz,' they are implicit in many other episodes and sections in the *Wanderjahre.*

One of the central symbols that relate to this major theme of mystery and curiosity, impulse and decorum, initiation and revelation is that of the 'Kästchen' which furnished me with my point of departure. In the *Wanderjahre* there are three such 'Kästchen,' all containing secrets: for the 'Man of Fifty' the 'Kästchen' contains the secrets of cosmetic rejuvenation; for the narrator of **'Die neue Melusine'** the 'Kästchen' contains the secret of love and a fabulous world; for Hersilie, and Wilhelm, the 'Kästchen' contains we know not what. In the first two cases, the secrets lead those who acquire them on false paths. The Major, flattered by both his own wishes and his niece's love, dons the mask—with the help of his actor friend—of 'der erste Liebhaber,' a role his professional friend can rightly assume and sustain on stage where the notion of 'sich von außen nach innen bilden' (175) is quite properly at home. But after an initial sense of well-being, both inward and outward, the Major feels he is no longer acting in character; distortion has taken place. Similarly in **'Die neue Melusine'** the hero can survive only temporarily in the land of dwarfs. Having betrayed his love and acquired forbidden secrets, he must either renounce his love for ever or assume the full consequences and follow her to her realm, surrendering his human existence. This he boldly does at first, but—like the Major—after his initial pleasure in his new life, he becomes ill at ease:

> Nun begriff ich zum ersten Mal, was die Philosophen unter ihren Idealen verstehen möchten, wodurch die Menschen so gequält sein sollen. Ich hatte ein Ideal von mir selbst und erschien mir manchmal im Traum wie ein Riese. Genug, die Frau, der Ring, die Zwergenfigur, so viele andere Bande machten mich ganz und gar unglücklich, daß ich auf meine Befreiung im Ernst zu denken begann.
>
> (375)

From this it is but a short step to one of Goethe's more difficult maxims which is included in **'Makariens Archiv'**:

> Man kann den Idealisten alter und neuer Zeit nicht verargen, wenn sie so lebhaft auf Beherzigung des einen dringen, woher alles entspringt und worauf alles wieder zurückzuführen wäre. Denn freilich, ist das belebende und ordnende Prinzip in der Erscheinung dergestalt bedrängt, daß es sich kaum zu retten weiß. Allein wir verkürzen uns an der andern Seite wieder, wenn wir das Formende und die sichere Form selbst in eine von unserm äußern und innern Sinn verschwindende Einheit zurückdrängen.
>
> (463f.)

The language the narrator of **'Die neue Melusine'** uses to describe his predicament shows a startling correspondence to that of the maxim: 'auf meine Befreiung im Ernst au denken' / 'sich kaum zu retten weiß'; 'gequält,' 'viele andere Bande' / 'bedrängt,' 'zurückdrängen'; and in both the 'Ideal' is held in a restricted and restricting form: the 'giant' confined within a dwarf is a literal embodiment of 'verkürzen' and 'eine verschwindende Einheit.' In both instances the import is the same: whilst too much emphasis on the form and the phenomenon disadvantages the ideal, too much emphasis on the ideal is detrimental to the form and thereby to our perception of the ideal inherent in the form. The avoidance of such distorting emphasis is only possible if a balance between the two is maintained and constantly checked. The balance may not be the same for all places and for all times but is one which is continually being relativized by context.

Insight into such truths is afforded only to the wise, and whilst Goethe flatters his readers in his *West-Östlicher Divan* by intimating that they are numbered among the select few ('Sagt es niemand, nur den Weisen …') he withholds such reassurance in the *Wanderjahre* and maintains the mystery that surrounds or—to put it more aptly—that lies within the casket that Felix had discovered in a cave. Into the secrets of this casket no-one is initiated. Even possession of the key does not grant immediate access, for the key itself has secrets. If used without finesse it 'breaks,' though the break is only a break to the inept. Magnetism holds the two halves together with enough strength to open the lock if the key is in the hands of the initiate. But even then, the possession of the key *and* the knowledge of its application does not mean that the box *should* or *must* be opened. The professional craftsman maintains a proper sense of the appropriate moment and of the dangers involved in an untimely violation of such mysteries: 'Der Mann tritt in einige Entfernung, das Kästchen springt auf, das er gleich wieder zudrückt: an solche Geheimnisse sei nicht gut zu rühren, meint er' (458). Its secret, whether sinister or sublime, remains intact. It might be Pandora's box; it might—like the 'Kästchen' in *Der Sammler und die Seinigen*—contain a beautiful reclining nude Venus; it might even be empty, in which case the mystery and its significance may be said to *surround* it, like some sacred casket. And—as is made clear in Goethe's poem **'Im ernsten Beinhaus…'**—even if empty and reduced to no more than 'eine dünne Schale,' such a receptacle can become, for the adept, 'Geheim Gefäß' imbued with a sense of the spiritual which, through its own unique activity, transforms and assimilates the phenomena of the material world and lends permanence to its own constructions. This late poem, written in 1826 and first published together with **'Vermächtnis'** in 1829 fittingly, at the end of the revised version of the *Wanderjahre,* closes with the lines:

> Was kann der Mensch im Leben mehr gewinnen,
> Als daß sich Gott-Natur ihm offenbare?
> Wie sie das Feste läßt zu Geist verrinnen,
> Wie sie das Geisterzeugte fest bewahre.

(HA, I, 367)

Within the *Wanderjahre* as a whole there are many instances of concealment and revelation, of explicit and implicit truths. They are embedded in the strata of the plot as plot and caught in the net of the language. The work abounds and delights in secrets and mysteries and the narrator plays with them on all registers, transposing from affected ignorance to tantalizing partial discovery or to information deliberately withheld. At times, pronouncements are made with authorial authority, at others the narrator shrinks almost coyly from such responsibility. In part, this is conscious 'deconstruction' and partly it is an overt assertion of artistic freedom. But, it is also to impart a feeling of genuine reverence for mystery that transcends literary gimmicks and relates to a vital aspect of any epistemological quest. It engages the reader both in his innocence and in his canniness and through its style the work encourages the one whilst educating the other. Even the way in which maxims function points in the same direction: 'Kurzgefaßte Sprüche jeder Art weiß ich zu ehren, besonders, wenn sie mich anregen, das Entgegengesetzte zu überschauen und in Übereinstimmung zu bringen,' says Wilhelm in Book I, Chapter 6 (70). Reversing the sense of a maxim is rather like turning it inside-out.

By now the significance of 'Kern und Schale' as a theme should be clear enough, but its modulation to 'weder Kern noch Schale' will require a little more time, although it has been implicit in much of what has gone before. To develop this further, we need to introduce a new strand derived from Goethe's scientific studies, in particular his work on morphology and his perception of growth and metamorphosis, and to see how far we are helped by the cross-fertilization of nature and art.

On 14 February 1819, Goether wrote as part of the *Tag- und Jahreshefte, Bis 1780*: 'Die Anfänge des *Wilhelm Meister* wird man in dieser Epoche auch schon gewahr, obgleich nur kotyledonenartig: die fernere Entwikkelung und Bildung zieht sich durch viele Jahre' (HA, x, 481). He may be talking of his early years in Weimar, but his language is that of the older botanist, whose works on morphology were published over the period 1817-1824 (during which time, of course, the *Wanderjahre* also first appeared). Thoughts about a continuation of the Wilhelm Meister story go back, not surprisingly, to the time when the *Lehrjahre* were completed, but work on the sequel proceeds rather curiously with Goethe apparently able to work on a number of threads simultaneously, spinning them out individually in parallel, before weaving them together in the completed work. As if to underline their initial independence, five of the stories of the eight finally included in the second version are published separately in their preliminary form between 1808 and 1817. They are: **'Die pilgernde Törin,' 'Sankt Joseph der Zweite,' 'Das nußbraune Mädchen,' 'Die neue Melusine,'** and **'Der Mann von Fünfzig Jahren.'** What I want to highlight here is the interaction between separate publication, revision and final location within the scope of the larger work. If these stories individually deal with, amongst other things, notions of 'inner' and 'outer,' what modification do they undergo when seen in relation to each other and to the whole? The reader moves through ever-changing dimensions, which expand and contract; the mind and the imagination pass from the familiar to the new and from the immediate to the distant in both space and time. What at one point is contextual, at another is central, dependent on the point of view of reader/observer, as determined at any one moment by his position. What has to be guarded against is the danger of solipsism implicit in the essential singleness of all vision, a corrective awareness of which informs so much of Goethe's thinking, feeling and writing. This is, I believe, one of the underlying reasons for those conglomerate works which confront the reader with shifting contexts and boundaries and diverse texts. *Wilhelm Meisters Wanderjahre* may be the extreme example but it is not the exception. The embryo form of the *Wanderjahre* can be seen 'kotyledonenartig'—to borrow Goethe's term—in *Werther* [*Die Leiden des jungen Werthers*]. Is not that work published and then revised? Does it not contain letters? Does it not include other stories which are developed to a lesser or greater degree? Does it not contain a translation? Is it not at times sententious? Is not part of the narrative taken verbatim from someone else's pen (Kästner's report of the suicide of Jerusalem)? And does not the author don the mantle of editor and narrator? One could go on: *Die Lehrjahre* contains eleven poems, Wilhelm's narrative of his childhood, the maxims of the 'Turmgesellschaft,' and *Die Bekenntnisse einer schönen Seele*; *Die Wahlverwandtschaften* includes one novella and extracts from Ottilie's diary; then there is the short configuration of *Der Sammler und die Seinigen,* a hybrid work of fiction, comprising letters, dialogue and theory (a work whose categories could be considered further in relation to this whole subject); and one should not forget the differing modes of diversity, collection and assembly in the *West-Östlicher Divan* and *Faust.* Similarly, Goethe's papers on morphology do not maintain fixed borders but include the first publication of a number of poems which later will be combined in a different context to form a different whole. Take, for instance, the three poems: **'Epirrhema'** (1819), **'Antepirrhema'** (also 1819), and **'Parabase'** (1820), which for *Die Ausgabe letzter Hand* [*Werke: Vollständige Ausgabe letzter Hand*] (1827) in the section 'Gott und Welt' Goethe rearranges and combines with two other poems to form the group: **'Parabase,' 'Die Metamorphose der Pflanzen'** (first published in 1799), **'Epirrhema,' 'Metamorphose der Tiere'** (written possibly in 1799 but not published until 1820) and **'Antepirrhema.'** Furthermore, we have only to consider some lines from these poems, to find the reasons that inspire such groupings, such 'Aggregate,' for they provide us with models, both semantic and stylistic, which are applicable to the form and themes of the *Wanderjahre*:

EPIRRHEMA

Müsset im Naturbetrachten
Immer eins wie alles achten;
Nichts ist drinnen, nichts ist draußen;
Denn was innen, das ist außen.
So ergreifet ohne Säumnis
Heilig öffentlich Geheimnis.

Freuet euch des wahren Scheins,
Euch des ernsten Spieles:
Kein Lebendiges ist ein Eins,
Immer ist's ein Vieles.

(HA, I, 358)

ANTEPIRRHEMA

So schauet mit bescheidenem Blick
Der ewigen Weberin Meisterstück,
Wie Ein Tritt tausend Fäden regt,
Die Schiff lein hinüber, herüber schießen.
Die Fäden sich begegnend fließen.
Ein Schlag tausend Verbindungen schlägt,
Das hat sie nicht zusammengebettelt,
Sie hat's von Ewigkeit angezettelt:
Damit der ewige Meistermann
Getrost den Einschlag werfen kann.

(HA, I, 358)

For all the diversity of its parts, the form of the *Wanderjahre* is likewise not 'zusammengebettelt' but 'angezettelt,' and—as I am endeavouring to show through the application of 'weder Kern noch Schale'—the work is a fictional re-enactment of Goethe's firm belief in appropriate modes of observation which allow for both unity and diversity and for the constant reappraisal of forms, context and content.

The poem **'Allerdings'** (appended in full, together with the relevant section of the Haller poem from which Goethe quotes, albeit misquoting slightly) to which I owe my text 'weder Kern noch Schale' dates from the same period, 1820, and was also first published in *Zur Morphologie* in

a short section entitled 'Freundlicher Zuruf.' The lines immediately preceding the poem, which here has no title, are:

> Ich fühle mich mit nahen und fernen, ernsten, tätigen Forschern glücklich im Einklang. Sie gestehen und behaupten: man solle ein Unerforschliches voraussetzen und zugeben, alsdann aber dem Forscher selbst keine Grenzlinie ziehen.

> Muß ich mich denn nicht selbst zugeben und voraussetzen, ohne jemals zu wissen wie es eigentlich mit mir beschaffen sei, studiere ich mich nicht immer fort, ohne mich jemals zu begreifen, mich und andere, und doch kommt man fröhlich immer weiter und weiter.

> So auch mit der Welt! Liege sie anfang- und endelos vor uns, unbegrenzt sei die Ferne, undurchdringlich die Nähe; es sei so; aber wie weit und wie tief der Menschengeist in seine und ihre Geheimnisse zu dringen vermöchte, werde nie bestimmt noch abgeschlossen.

> Möge nachstehendes heitere Reimstück [**'Allerdings'**] in diesem Sinne aufgenommen und gedeutet werden.

(HA, XIII, 34)

Note the posited acceptance of a seamless and infinite world, but note also the accompanying injunction with its implicit confident belief in the powers of man's mind, trust in the yielding resistance of Nature's secrets and tacit acknowledgement of the unfathomable aspect of even the very process of revelation itself. As Goethe wrote in 1829, in prose verging on poetry:

INDUKTION

Hab' ich mir nie, auch gegen mich selbst nicht erlaubt.
  Ich ließ die Fakten isoliert stehen
  Aber das Analoge sucht' ich auf.
  Und auf diesem Wege z.B. bin ich zum Begriff
der Metamorphose der Pflanzen gelangt.[6]

Observation, analysis, reflection, synthesis and hypothesis (correctly applied) will lead to a greater comprehension of the secrets of that mysterious entity 'Gott-Natur' (a hyphenated noun that fuses 'Kern' and 'Schale'). Yet no matter how many layers we penetrate in our research, no matter how much we feel we are in the inside, we always remain on the surface of the unknown. The artist, the poet, the image-maker, however, can help; he can provide analogies, can provide 'Vorbilder' to point the way. For the uninitiated in botany, the metamorphosis of plants can become more familiar and comprehensive when linked to the growth and flowering of human love; for the uninitiated in the mysteries of poetic creativity, the metamorphosis of plants can provide the model for the growth and flowering of the poetic process:

> Doch immer reift von innen
> Und schwillt der braune Kern,

Er möchte Luft gewinnen
Und säh' die Sonne gern.

Die Schale platzt und wieder
Macht er sich freudig los;
So fallen meine Lieder
Gehäuft in deinen Schoß.

(HA, II, 77)

'An vollen Büschelzweigen ...' (written 1815) is almost a précis of the longer elegy **'Die Metamorphose der Pflanzen.'** It combines abundance with surprise, and understanding with wonder at the process and the end result; the existence of 'Kern' and 'Schale' as part of that process guarantees both mysterious growth and marvellous revelation. The fruit returns to the earth, to the 'Schoß' from which it first emerged. The 'Kern' itself will in turn become 'Gefäß,' the vessel of new life.

It is such confident insight into the simple truths manifested and masked by the multifarious diversity of nature which allows Goethe through his art to produce such seemingly 'incalculable' (cf. 'alles ist sie mit einem Male') works as *Wilhelm Meisters Wanderjahre.* By presenting his readers with such models he involves them in the process of discovery by analogy and engages them through their creative participation in reciprocal activity, whilst issuing at every step the challenging 'Ultimatum':

Und so sag'ich zum letzten Male;
Natur hat weder Kern noch Schale;
Du prüfe dich nur allermeist,
Ob Du Kern oder Schale seist!

(HA, I, 306)

Appendix I

Wie unterscheidest du die Wahrheit und den Traum?
Wie trennt im Wesen sich das feste von dem Raum?
Der Cörper rauhen Stoff, wer schränkt ihn in Gestalten,
Die stäts verändert sind, und doch sich stäts erhalten?
Den Zug, der alles senkt, den Trieb, der alles dähnt,
Den Reitz in dem Magnet, wonach der Stahl sich sehnt,
Des Lichtes schnelle Fahrt, die Erbschaft der Bewegung
Der Theilchen ewig Band, die Quelle neue Regung,
Dieß lehre grosser Geist die schwache Sterblichkeit,
Worinn dir niemand gleicht und alles dich bereut.
Doch suche nur im Riß von künstlichen Figuren
Beym Licht der Ziffer-Kunst, der Wahrheit dunkle Spuren;
Ins innre der Natur dringt kein erschafner Geist,
Zu glücklich, wenn sie noch die äußre Schale weis't;
Du hast nach reiffer Müh, und nach durchwachten Jahren,
Erst selbst, wie viel uns fehlt, wie nichts man weiß, erfahren.

Albrecht von Haller,
extract from
'Die Falschheit menschlicher Tugenden' (1730)

(Quoted from *Gedichte des Herrn von Haller,*
seventh impression, Zürich, 1758, p. 65.)

ALLERDINGS

Dem Physiker

"Ins Innre der Natur—"
O du Philister!—
"Dringt kein erschaffner Geist."
Mich und Geschwister
Mögt ihr an solches Wort
Nur nicht erinnern:
Wir denken: Ort für Ort
Sind wir im Innern.
"Glückselig! wem sie nur
Die äußre Schale weist!"
Das hör' ich sechzig Jahre wiederholen,
Ich fluche drauf, aber verstohlen:
Sage mir tausend tausendmale:
Alles gibt sie reichlich und gern:
Natur hat weder Kern
Noch Schale,
Alles ist sie mit einem Male.
Dich prüfe du nur allermeist,
Ob du Kern oder Schale seist.

Goethe

Notes

1. Quoted from *Goethe-Handbuch,* edited by Julius Zeitler, Stuttgart, 1917, II, 405.

2. Textual quotations are taken from the *Hamburger Ausgabe,* Vol. VIII, with page numbers in brackets.

3. See Chapter 8 entitled 'Counterpoint in the Symbolic Mode' in Eric A. Blackall's *Goethe and the Novel,* Ithaca and London, 1976, pp. 236-69, where Blackall argues for coherence and unity through counterpoint.

4. In 'Revolutionary Realism in Goethe's *Wanderjahre,*' *Goethe's Narrative Fiction,* edited by William J. Lillyman, Berlin and New York, 1983, pp. 161-75, Ehrhard Bahr applies in too simple a fashion Roman Jakobson's use of metaphor and metonym to describe two modes of narrative writing, linking metaphor to classical realism—as exemplified in the *Lehrjahre*—and metonym to revolutionary realism, for which the *Wanderjahre* is paradigmatic. However, in my opinion, the latter novel is too complex a work for such reductive labels, because its focus of interest lies always in border areas, where formulae which differentiate and imply new entities and models of organization are more apposite. 'Weder Kern noch Schale' can be said to operate in the context as both metaphor and metonym, whilst at the same time its syntactical structure (weder/noch) denies not only the appropriateness of either noun but also the validity of its use as either metaphor or metonym.

5. Goethe's mother was the daughter of Johann Wolfgang Textor, whose family name three generations earlier had been 'Weber.'

6. JA, xxxix, 54. This was not published in Goethe's lifetime, but the manuscript bears the date 5 November 1829.

Birgit Baldwin (essay date 1990)

SOURCE: Baldwin, Birgit. "*Wilhelm Meisters Wanderjahre* as an Allegory of Reading." *Goethe Yearbook* 5 (1990): 213-32. Print.

[*In the following essay, Baldwin advances an interpretation of* Wilhelm Meister's Travels *as a "novel about reading novels." She presents a variety of evidence for this claim, including the author's (or, more accurately, the fictional editor's) direct remarks to the reader and the emphatic presence of tantalizing but "unreadable" symbols, such as Felix's casket and Jarno's rocks.*]

Hermann Broch's assessment of *Wilhelm Meisters Wanderjahre* as "[der] Grundstein der neuen Dichtung, des neuen Romans" suggests that Goethe's novel poses a challenge to theories of narrative.[1] This paper will examine the *Wanderjahre* as a novel about its own being as a novel. At issue are the ways in which this novel's plot seems to have more to do with how novels are read than with plots themselves, and the tension that arises as a consequence between these two aspects of narrative.

Secondary literature has not sufficiently stressed the fact that Goethe's novel explicitly privileges reading and writing. At the Oheim's estate, for example, Hersilie tells Wilhelm "daß bei uns viel gelesen wird." To prove it, she gives him the manuscript of the inserted novella **"Die pilgernde Törin"** for bedtime reading. She explains that from his reading he will be able to judge his new friends and participate in their circle: "Hiernach werden Sie uns beurteilen, hiernach teilnehmen, einstimmen oder streiten" (50).[2] Again, after having read the internal correspondence between the various members of that household, Wilhelm writes to Natalie: "Wie viel die Menschen schreiben, davon hat man gar keinen Begriff" (78), where *wie viel* has the force not only of factual description but also of rhetorical exclamation. This heightened emphasis on reading and writing could of course be partly explained by the constraints of the *Entsagung* plot, the fact that the characters, having renounced the company of their loved ones, are separated from one another and forced to wander, never remaining in the same place for more than three days. Nevertheless, we the readers are also constantly made aware of the fact that we are reading a novel. At one point the narrator even explains his own procedure in these terms: "Unsere Freunde haben einen Roman in die Hand genommen" (118).

The privileged status of textual issues is evident even in the opening scene of the novel, in which Wilhelm is already writing and the discussion centers around problems of naming and the relation of fiction to reality. Wilhelm is sitting in the shadow of a mighty rock, "an grauser, bedeutender Stelle": "Er bemerkte eben etwas in seine Schreibtafel, als Felix, der umhergeklettert war, mit einem Stein in der Hand zu ihm kam. 'Wie nennt man diesen Stein, Vater?' sagte der Knabe." Although Wilhelm does not know, he remembers that people call it *Katzengold,* presumably, as he explains, since it is false and so are cats. "Das will ich mir merken," says Felix (7). Felix's question deals with meta-critical issues: what does the metaphor of the stone's name signify? How do appearances which deceive fit into reality? These questions immediately take on a certain seriousness when, moments later, St. Joseph the Second passes by with his wife Mary and her baby on a mule. Wilhelm gets confused about reality and history, and asks what is under the circumstances a rather strange question: "ob ihr wirkliche Wanderer oder ob ihr nur Geister seid" (10). It is indeed an ominous spot, a "frightening, significant place," which allows Wilhelm to be more surprised and awed by real wanderers—who, although they may look like the holy family, are at least human—than by "mere ghosts."

In dealing with the novel as an allegory of reading, my paradigmatic example will be the *Kästchen,* taken as both impediment and impetus to reading. By reading this and other examples, I will try to elaborate a strategy of reading that would be capable of accounting for the self-reflexive status of the novel, beginning from the concept of renunciation referred to in the subtitle of the *Wanderjahre,* "oder *Die Entsagenden.*" The "renunciants" can be understood as model readers—readers willing to renounce the certainty that comes with assigning meanings to symbols. *Entsagung,* as a strategy of reading, would seek to maintain rather than to flatten out the conflicting clues the text offers for its interpretation. Such a model of reading can best be approached by dealing with irony, for, as I will argue, it is irony that makes the *Wanderjahre* a meta-text, and its constitutive refusal to lend stability to a reading is precisely what is at stake in what I mean by an allegory of reading. For the vehicle of renunciation, as well as its motive, is precisely irony, understood most generally as "a fundamental principle of discontinuity in the structure of literary language."[3]

The earliest reader of the novel, Hegel's student H. G. Hotho, characterized its richness in these terms:

> Dieser oft schroffe Wechsel gerade und diese Verschlingung scheinbar heterogener Elemente giebt unserem Romane jenen Reiz der Sprödigkeit, welcher ebenso anlockt als abstößt, und uns nur dann zu ungestörtem Genusse gelangen läßt, wenn wir ganz mit den Eigenheiten des Werkes vertraut geworden sind.[4]

It is in this power of simultaneously enticing and repelling that the novel's fascination lies. Hotho's eloquent description of Goethe's poetic treatment of his material also points to what continues to enchant readers: "Er schweigt ohne zu verschweigen, er zieht den Schleier, indem er ihn lüftet, nur verhüllender umher."[5] And what he says about those capable of truly enjoying the novel can stand as a challenge: "Nur Zartempfindende, vielseitig Gebildete, nachdenkend ein Kunstwerk zu reproduzieren Gewöhnte sind in der Lage diesen Roman zu genießen."[6]

* * *

Even a brief glance at the secondary literature shows the degree to which the mystery of the *Kästchen* has attracted the critical attention of scholars.[7] What is interesting about the symbolic function of the *Kästchen* is not just the numerous ingenious interpretations it has inspired, but the very fact that they arise in the first place. Indeed, I would argue that the prime fascination of the symbol is that it *has to* generate so much interpretation. This has to happen because it functions both as a symbol that produces narrative and as a symbol of symbol. While on the one hand it generates plot by imposing itself as a mystery on the characters in the novel, who have to deal with it in some manner, on the other hand, since the search for meaning is transferred to the readers, the *Kästchen* also allegorizes what readers are doing when they try to penetrate its secret—that is, when they read. The *Kästchen* demands interpretation, but radically refuses to deliver any final meaning—thus telling the story of what we are doing as readers when we try to "unlock" its secret. As this special kind of symbol, the *Kästchen* in turn allegorizes, in miniature as it were, the initial problem: the difficulty of being simultaneously a novel and a novel of novels.

The sporadic appearance of the *Kästchen* throughout the text forces the reader not only to pay attention to *how* connections are made while reading, and thus to speculate on possible interpretations for the symbolism, but also to attend to the fact *that* they are made. This may seem an obvious point, but in certain contexts it becomes truly perplexing. For example, because the **"Neue Melusine"** episode appears in close proximity to Hersilie's letter announcing that she now has both the key and the casket together and is impatient to solve the mystery, it is inevitable that the casket in the "fairy tale" should be linked with that of the "frame" story. Although some readers are willing to make that connection—producing interesting interpretations of how the various caskets and containers in the novel play off each other, and providing an astonishing variety of answers as to what all this means—no one has been willing to ask what happens to the various narrative levels themselves if and when the *Kästchen* produces such connections. I would suggest that the function of the *Kästchen* is to force such a meta-critical reading, a reading that would examine what it is that makes readers unwilling to question narrative artifices like the term "frame" and "fairy tale," even when the characteristics that are supposed to differentiate them seem unstable at best. The ease with which these categories can be reversed is apparent when the difference between a fairy tale and "real-life"

narrative is tested. The reader has merely to wonder how "realistic" in fact the frame *is* when what look like biblical representations turn out to be "real" people, where the landscape is strictly mythical, where a revered old aunt is both a revered old aunt and a star in the galaxy (to name just a few irregularities).

If categories like fantasy and reality are not so easy to keep apart in the novel, this may be understood as a consequence of the novel's emphasis on reading. The connection can be established by looking at the role of Hersilie, the self-conscious character in the novel who makes explicit her and the other characters' status as characters in a novel. Hersilie uses generic terms to describe the other members of her family as stock characters of novels and plays:

> [Unser Personal] ist das ewig in Romanen und Schauspielen wiederholte: ein wunderlicher Oheim, eine sanfte und eine muntere Nichte, eine kluge Tante, Hausgenossen nach bekannter Art; und käme nun gar der Vetter wieder, so lernte er einen phantastischen Reisenden kennen, der vielleicht einen noch sonderbarern Gesellen mitbrächte, und so wäre das leidige Stück erfunden und in Wirklichkeit gesetzt.

(67-68)

Certainly the reader should take note when Hersilie herself makes a distinction between something that has been invented and the reality into which it will be placed. But if she knows that she is a figure in a novel, is it necessarily safe to assume that what she is calling reality is still the fiction of the novel? Readers of the novel have remarked on the lively flesh-and-blood nature of Hersilie and wondered about her tragic fate, as she is unable to decide between the disinterested father who ignores her letters and the young son whose stormy struggle for immediate access to his passions overwhelms her. But it is worth pondering the paradox caused by this contamination of her reality (as text) with ours (as flesh and blood)—and in particular, about the fact that this most "real" character, after making some rather disturbing statements about reading and interpretation, then disappears out of the realm of experience lived by the other characters and exists for us solely in her letters to Wilhelm.[8]

Wilhelm may be able to ignore her there, but we cannot: for to ignore Hersilie would be to ignore the story of reading in the novel. Earlier in the scene quoted above, Hersilie makes a startling contribution to the discussion between Wilhelm and her comparatively conventional sister, Juliette. Hersilie offers a paradoxical reading of one of the "wise" maxims engraved over the doors at the Oheim's estate: "Vom Nützlichen durchs Wahre zum Schönen" (65). She prefaces her reading by saying:

> Wir Frauen sind in einem besondern Zustande. Die Maximen der Männer hören wir immerfort wiederholen, ja wir müssen sie in goldnen Buchstaben über unsern Häupten

sehen, und doch wüßten wir Mädchen im stillen das Umgekehrte zu sagen, das auch gölte, wie es gerade hier der Fall ist.

                                                    (66)

After providing her own alternate reading of the maxim taken in the opposite direction, as an allegory of the fate of a reasonable woman in the eighteenth century, she observes: "Wir Mädchen haben Zeit zu beobachten, und da finden wir meist, was wir nicht suchten" (66). She implies not so much that women are by definition better readers, but rather that time will allow any reader to come up with surprising readings. Her negative version of the Biblical "seek and ye shall find" is an invitation to explore the ambiguity of language as it manifests itself in narrative. A reversed reading, Hersilie will argue, may even make the saying more true, as is certainly the case here from her point of view as a woman. In a later conversation she praises her sister somewhat ironically for being able to interpret (*auslegen*) all the uncle's sayings, but counters: "Ich aber finde, daß man sie alle umkehren kann und daß sie dann ebenso wahr sind, und vielleicht noch mehr" (68). At this point, Wilhelm is willing to agree with the unconventional sister, adding: "Ich leugne nicht, [...] es sind Sprüche darunter, die sich in sich selbst zu vernichten scheinen." While Wilhelm is not quite saying the same thing as Hersilie, he acknowledges with Hersilie the irony of language that allows something to be and not to be at the same time.[9] This is what calls for reading.

The passage seems to set up a preliminary difference between reading and interpretation. Reading would be the name for what Hersilie does, letting the paradoxes in language stand as such while trying to make sense of the words against the grain; interpretation would be the name for Juliette's straightforward, commonsense laying out of the meaning. I do not want to press the distinction here, since reading *per se* is not mentioned; yet the distinction must remain posed as a crucial problem. That Juliette's method is threatened by "backwards" reading is clear from the defensive counter-proposal with which she answers a question posed by Wilhelm: "Umschreiben Sie die wenigen Worte, so wird der Sinn alsobald hervorleuchten" (68). Rather than reversing (*umkehren*) the order of the words to come up with a new or truer meaning, Juliette proposes to rewrite or to paraphrase (*umschreiben*) the words in order for the meaning to shine through. The juxtaposition puts in question the difference between these two kinds of rewriting. Is Juliette's *umschreiben* any more "faithful" to the maxims than Hersilie's seemingly radical *umkehren*? The optimism of Juliette's response seems inappropriate, not only in light of Hersilie's convincing "reversed" reading, but also in the context of the maxims offered by the novel in the chapters **"Betrachtungen im Sinne der Wanderer"** and **"Aus Makariens Archiv."** These wise sayings pose a massive challenge to a reading of the novel as a whole, a challenge that seems to be taken

up paradigmatically and proleptically by its characters. What does it mean for us readers when a self-conscious character in a novel herself provides a compelling reading of the same material we read? The maxims appear as a preliminary form of the stumbling block that will provide the ultimate focus for my reading, and the two sisters' approaches to these obstacles can be seen as exemplary versions of readers' reactions to difficult texts. Stumbling can be taken for granted; the difference between one instance and the other lies in the degree to which the stumbler notices the fall.

The point in stressing Hersilie's paradoxical reading is to insist that there is a great deal that is strange in this novel. Readers tend to want to explain away perplexing inconsistencies in order to make sense out of them—which is usually called reading. Yet why, or how is it that the well-meaning quest for meaning, pursued even by those who seem to allow for a residue of undecidability, usually ends up rather with a renunciation of reading in Hersilie's sense?

                                        * * *

The renunciation of reading and its relation to the confusion of narative levels can be seen in the "neue Melusine" episode. Here the normal authorial distancing mechanisms have been abandoned in order to tell this "wahrhafte Geschichte," something that happened to the narrator in his youth. As noted above, the placement of the fairy tale forces the reader to make connections between the caskets that appear both inside and outside the confines of the story. The *Kästchen* puts into question the ease with which inside and outside can be kept apart: as it glides between the fairy tale and the "real story,"[10] the casket makes these narrative artifices impossible to ignore, yet impossible to maintain. This unsettling feature of the narrative is irony at work.

In both provoking a reading that would put it to rest and calling for a reading that would renounce this desire, the *Kästchen* brings into play the double-bind that is constitutive of irony. Irony offers access to comprehensibility by means of the paradoxality of language, but this paradoxality at the same time radically challenges comprehension to the point where irony may seem to have more to do with incomprehensibility. The *Kästchen* sets up a scenario in which the reader comes face to face with an enactment—call it an allegory—of what it is to read: a scenario involving an attempt to counter the temptation to renounce making sense with the imperative to keep reading, to allow the paradoxes of language to remain in a no-man's land between comprehensibility and incomprehensibility. The double introduction to the "neue Melusine" episode brings us face to face both with renunciation and with the dialectic of enticing and distancing the reader. Already from the beginning there is a double movement within the double introduction. On the one hand, the narrator (and

Lenardo, as the one who grants him speech) wants to grab the reader or listener, to make the point that this is not just any made-up story but an "incredible but true" account. On the other hand, the double introduction helps to distance the story from those for whom it is destined: the story places time between itself and the reader, as the narrator claims that what is recounted happened to him some years ago (354). During the course of the telling, however, this time seems to vanish, since the last line of the story places the hero in a context in which he was found and befriended by those who are now listening to him (376). The temporal distance with which the narrator in the beginning of his story excuses his rash, youthful behavior, gets collapsed by the end of the account and can no longer serve as a protective device.

The reader's strange predicament—being at the same time courted and kept at a distance—is further problematized by the difficulties he or she may have in sympathizing with the narrator. Some critics praise the delightful qualities of the fairy tale, others criticize the wilfully self-destructive nature of the hero; but no one has remarked on how the narrative assumes the reader's sympathy with the main character, who is now telling the story of a youthful folly. The coercive thrust seems to suggest a threat: the listeners must enjoy the tale without raising any moral objections, or else they have the formidable narrator to contend with. The audience in the novel is thus clearly a captive audience, but the question remains whether readers of the novel do not face, in a different way, the same predicament. While the reader of the novel is surely not threatened in the same way that the reader in the novel is deprived of moral judgment vis à vis the narrator of **"Die neue Melusine,"** the "real" reader risks renouncing reading if coerced by the narrator's stance of incorrigibility, his reluctance if not refusal to learn anything from the unusual experiences he has narrated. Having escaped from the kingdom of the elves and regained his normal size, he stands "freilich um so vieles größer, allein, wie mir vorkam, auch um vieles dümmer und unbehülflicher" (375-76). Not only has he learned nothing, he has also lost something in the way of knowledge—which would correspond to his continually forgetting the lessons Melusine has been trying to teach him throughout the fairy tale, a forgetting which causes him to regress slightly every time he seems to have learned something, as he always again commits the same mistake, each time with slightly more serious consequences. The reader of the novel is in turn faced with the paradox of the regressing narrator who renounces nothing, except an understanding of his narrated life and of his interaction with the novel in its propagation of the virtue of renunciation.

It would be easy to see the narrator's failure to renounce merely as a counter-example to the general ethos of the novel, as some critics have claimed. But that would be to renounce reading the role of the *Kästchen*. The *Kästchen*, as the emblem of the mysterious that refuses to divulge its secret, puts us in the same position as the giant narrator:

since the contents of the casket are never revealed, we are no more enlightened at the end of the novel than he. "Wir sind so klug, wie wir am Anfang waren" is Karl Schlechta's resigned assessment of the reader's position vis à vis the persistent *Rätselnatur* of the secret.[11] What is disturbing is not that we do not learn the secret of the casket, but that our position of ignorance is comparable to the uncomfortable, regressively shifting place of the narrator within the novel. If the narrator of **"Die neue Melusine"** refuses to learn from his story, he is at least aware that he may have lost something in the experience. If we too realize that we are no smarter at the end than in the beginning, we cannot be sure we have not also lost something in the process. Losing knowledge seems to become part of the reading process. Resisting the temptation to renounce reading would then involve giving up the hope of certain knowledge about what the *Kästchen* means.

* * *

Critics have recognized the supernatural characteristics of the *Kästchen* in other aspects of the novel, particularly in the character of Hersilie. Bernd Peschken relates Hersilie's contradictory nature—her drive both to separate and to unite, her ability to read against the grain—to the demonic, understood as the monstrous and ungraspable.[12] He cites maxim 133 from the **"Betrachtungen im Sinne der Wanderer"** (303), in which existence is called monstrous (*ungeheuer*), in conjunction with a passage from *Dichtung und Wahrheit* [*Aus meinen Leben: Dichtung und Wahrheit*] where the monstrous is called demonic and equated with the ungraspable. A look at what form the ungraspable takes for Goethe in *Dichtung und Wahrheit* will facilitate further discussion of irony in the novel. Speaking in the third person, Goethe describes his youthful experience of the ungraspable:

> [...] und er glaubte mehr und mehr einzusehn, daß es besser sei, den Gedanken von dem Ungeheuren, Unfaßlichen abzuwenden. Er glaubte in der Natur, der belebten und unbelebten, der beseelten und unbeseelten, etwas zu entdecken, das sich nur in Widersprüchen manifestierte und deshalb unter keinen Begriff, noch viel weniger unter ein Wort gefaßt werden könnte. Es war nicht göttlich, denn es schien unvernünftig, nicht menschlich, denn es hatte keinen Verstand, nicht teuflisch, denn es war wohltätig, nicht englisch, denn es ließ oft Schadenfreude merken. Es glich dem Zufall, denn es bewies keine Folge, es ähnelte der Vorsehung, denn es deutete auf Zusammenhang. Alles, was uns begrenzt, schien für dasselbe durchdringbar, es schien mit den notwendigen Elementen unsres Daseins willkürlich zu schalten, es zog die Zeit zusammen und dehnte den Raum aus. Nur im Unmöglichen schien es sich zu gefallen und das Mögliche mit Verachtung von sich zu stoßen. Dieses Wesen, das zwischen alle übrigen hineinzutreten, sie zu sondern, sie zu verbinden schien, nannte ich dämonisch, nach dem Beispiel der Alten und derer, die etwas Ähnliches gewahrt hatten. Ich suchte mich vor diesem furchtbaren Wesen zu retten, indem ich mich, nach meiner Gewohnheit, hinter ein Bild flüchtete.[13]

Peschken regards this passage as a fitting description of Hersilie and of her relation to the casket, and certainly there are echoes in terminology. But the passage describes even more precisely the way the casket functions in the narrative as an impetus to reading. For the essence of the demonic, as the ungraspable, seems to be its contradictoriness. It is described as being neither one nor the other of the pair in several binary oppositions: it is a something that is at the same time a nothing. The demonic thus shares the philosophical position of irony, as it appears in Kierkegaard as "a nothingness which consumes everything and a something which one can never catch hold of, which both is and is not."[14] Indeed, the terms from this passage of **Dichtung und Wahrheit** would describe irony quite precisely, as a ghostly apparition that transcends binary oppositions and that defies categorizing.

The passage sets up a tension between seeing and understanding: "er glaubte mehr und mehr *einzusehn,* daß es besser sei, den *Gedanken* von dem Ungeheuren, Unfaßlichen *abzuwenden*" (my emphases). Thoughts have to turn away (in tropes) from what is monstrous and ungraspable, from that which, in this case, can only be grasped (if at all) through a process of elimination structured by personification. The text tries to give the ungraspable a shape by proceeding negatively through a series of contrasting characteristics that are ruled out one by one. Although one of these eliminated qualities is the human (*menschlich*), the text nevertheless tries to anthropomorphize this being (*Wesen*) by using such human attributes as reason (*Vernunft*) and spite (*Schadenfreude*), enjoyment (*sich gefallen*), well-meaning (*wohltätig*), and disdain (*Verachtung*). By naming it *dämonisch,* by taking refuge in the tradition of the ancients, Goethe seeks to flee this disturbing force which refuses all attempts at being defined.

Angus Fletcher, in his classic study of allegory, discusses this relation between the demon's power and its being named, adding: "It appears that to name a person is to fix his function irrevocably. This fact can be explained in terms of daemonology."[15] Insofar as demons are related to curses, they can only be invoked and empowered by being named. Goethe's text would be arguing for a reversal of this power-play, whereby naming would disarm the demonic. Yet in spite of this apparent trust in naming, the text makes explicit the problem of linking word with concept. It states that since this being manifests itself only by means of contradiction, it can be comprehended by no concept, still less by a word ("und deshalb unter keinen Begriff, noch viel weniger unter ein Wort gefaßt werden könnte"). The difficulty resides in the fact that the demonic is said to be something that can be "still less" grasped by a word, which would contradict the just-posited impossibility of subsuming it under a concept. Rather than relying on a presupposed correlation between word and concept, the text posits a split between the two, a split that cannot be recuperated by the demonic since it furnishes the evidence of such a rift in the first place. And yet Goethe's discussion

of the demonic, in discovering this split, at the same time ignores it by positing in the term "demonic" the same correlation between word and concept that the demonic makes impossible.

The demonic, as something that seems both to separate and to connect ("sie zu sondern, sie zu verbinden schien"), is described in the terms used in Hersilie's description of events concerning the casket as well as the reading process: she desperately needs to know "was damit gemeint sei, mit diesem wunderbaren Finden, Wiederfinden, Trennen und Vereinigen" (378). But the passage does more than describe irony or the demonic, the behavior of the *Kästchen* or how to read it; it also performs the subject of its narration. It tells the story of how someone (an *er* who becomes an *ich*) tries to save himself from a dreadful (*furchtbar*) being by calling it demonic and by escaping behind a picture or image ("hinter ein Bild flüchtete"). The relation between concept and word, already seen to be problematic, is thus played out at the end in a slightly different configuration: the narrator names the being with the *word* "demonic," but then tries to flee behind an *image.* The image that appears at the end as a supposedly safe haven seems not to be implicated in the concept/word problematics. Yet it is precisely an image (of the demonic) that the narrator has trouble providing. He has to describe the being negatively, and does so to such an extent that the only thing that becomes clear is that it refuses to be fixed as image. The only *Bild* to be found here is the word "Bild." This is not just because we are dealing with a text rather than with representational graphics, but because there can be no images if the demonic appears only as something that cannot appear. Since no word can contain the demonic, it is not likely that the word "Bild" will provide much of a hiding place for the narrator.

* * *

The flight from language to "Bild" that the demonic seems to initiate may shed some light on the infamous drawing of the key that is eventually found in the course of the **Wanderjahre.** The importance of this drawing should not be underestimated. Like the story of the *Kästchen,* this drawing of the key has provoked a variety of ingenious interpretations: symbols from Freemasonry and from Eleusinian festivals of fertility have been conjured forth and "Freudian" readings of erotic symbolism have been proffered.[16] The illustration of the key is rightly said to call attention to the limits of language.[17] Finally, the praise accorded to Sterne in Makarie's Archive suggests that the drawing of the key alludes to a similar instance in another novel of novels, the "arabesque" in *Tristram Shandy.* Hersilie has indeed asked the right question: "Hier aber, mein Freund, nun schließlich zu dieser Abbildung des Rätsels was sagen Sie?" (321).

Some readers have granted the key the meta-critical status of key to the whole novel, and have recognized how the casket and key, as a symbol of symbol, are reluctant to deliver their meaning.[18] Yet although some interpretations tolerate a certain residue of undecidability,[19] their respect for the impenetrability of the text remains a gesture because their argument is formulated in terms of unlocking a difficult, closed text that nonetheless (it is assumed) *can* be opened with the right critical tools. Once readers begin talking about keys, they assume the existence for their own use of some "skeleton key" like Melusine's. Since it is impossible to escape the strictures of terminology, a certain self-consciousness in using the idiom is especially crucial; one might add that this is all the more necessary when irony can be detected. An unselfconscious hermeneutic terminology of locks and keys may no longer be appropriate when it becomes entrapped in its own metaphors without being able to account for how this predicament comes about. The result in such a case is a renunciation of reading. The solution that is found—the "key"—is in truth the problem.

What then *is* there to say about a representation (*Abbildung*) of a key which is called a puzzle (*Rätsel*), when the key is supposed to unlock the casket that throughout the narrative has been called a secret (*Geheimnis*)? The first thing to say is that the key disturbs the distinction between secrets and riddles. The *Kästchen,* which appears in the novel only as a linguistic construct, has been called a secret, something that presumably could be manifested as either a physical or a linguistic object. The representation of the key, however, the sole non-linguistic entity in the text, is called a riddle, something that can exist only in language.[20] This contradictory behavior induced by the picture recalls the demonic. The demonic, as Goethe told us, can be grasped by neither concept nor word; and here on the page is just that, neither concept nor word, but a picture. If this picture were itself a manifestation of the demonic, Hersilie's bizarre hortatory exclamation after her two rhetorical questions would no longer be so odd: "Gott sei uns gnädig!" As the demonic, the picture would reinforce our suspicion that the image behind which the narrator of **Dichtung und Wahrheit** wants to flee is no safe haven from the demonic. Not only was there no *Bild* there—just the word "Bild"—but as it turns out, when a *Bild* appears, it may well be the demonic itself.[21] If the demonic can appear in all its contradictoriness as an *Abbildung,* the last place in which to seek refuge would be a *Bild.*[22]

The fact that the key, simultaneously symbol and the symbol of symbol, is represented in a non-linguistic way, presents reading with a seemingly insurmountable obstacle. Indeed, reading must come to a halt when faced with black marks that cannot be "read" in the strict sense. Yet the drawing, which cuts off the flow of words by sitting as an obstacle on the page, calls our attention back to reading as a subject of the narrative. The inherently secret nature of casket and key has throughout the novel

teasingly prodded the reader and the characters toward solving the riddle. But it is the drawing of the key that seems to elicit the most tenacious attempts to fix the meaning once and for all—perhaps because the manifest visual sign supposedly does not allow for ambiguity, whereas ambiguity is the hallmark of the linguistic sign. And yet it is no longer clear which of the two—the sleek, impenetrable visual sign or the ambiguous linguistic sign—is capable of arousing more interpretive insistence. It would be necessary to ask whether the two can be treated in the same manner, or whether they do not in fact insist on a differentiation between reading and interpretation.

The drawing causes reading to come to a halt, without however implying an end or closure. On the contrary, an allegorizing reading of the casket and key must leave open the possibility that meaning is always deferred.[23] When reading stops at this obstacle, it can start to reflect on how the various linguistic symbols function in ways that must be different from the unreadable drawing. Although it might seem that the drawing of the key is offered in the text as a final solution to the enigma of the casket, this key clearly opens up more possibilities than it closes. That these possibilities may be uncontrollable only makes reading all the more necessary. The imperative of reading becomes even more urgent when we focus on how the text itself provides the reader with excuses to renounce reading. Although the drawing causes reading to stop, it cannot, by the sheer force of its unreadability, prevent the resumption of reading. It would be astonishing if a novel of five hundred pages would allow for a renunciation of reading in the face of the "dumb presentation" of a drawing.[24] The massive obstacles to reading, however, present it with a stony front.

My insistence on the fact that the enigmatic casket and key call for, as well as call attention to continued reading does not condone a reticent respect for the aging Goethe's wish to keep certain secrets secret. The valorization of the secret as secret, which appears in various forms throughout the novel, is one way in which reading is actively discouraged. The reported opinion of the old jeweler, "an solche Geheimnisse sei nicht gut rühren" (458), is often cited in the scholarship as an excuse to stop pondering the mystery.[25] But these words could easily have the opposite effect on the reader. Nor do they seem to have calmed Hersilie into resigning herself to the fact that she does not belong to the initiated. Although the reader discovers—when it opens of its own accord after the jeweler has taken a few steps back from it—that only the initiated can open the casket, the mystery is still not solved but is instead aggravated by the possibility that it cannot be resolved by those who most pressingly want to do so.

What is solved by the jeweler, though perhaps not in a finalized way, is the mystery of the key that breaks when Felix, whose youthful impatience and desire for direct access to the world is at odds with the mediated aura around the casket, tries to open the casket by force. The old man shows Hersilie that the two halves of the key are magnetically bound together—thereby enacting, by means of the key in the story, the etymological meaning of symbol. This is not the first time the original meaning of symbol is acted out in the novel. In the first book, Wilhelm deposits the casket for safe keeping with the collector, who tells him not to force it open but rather to test his luck on it, adding: "Denn wenn Sie glücklich geboren sind und wenn dieses Kästchen etwas bedeutet, so muß sich gelegentlich der Schlüssel dazu finden, und gerade da, wo Sie ihn am wenigsten erwarten" (146). The collector, as one whose profession is to gather what belongs together, has seen other similar cases and hence has the authority to make such predictions. He shows Wilhelm an ivory crucifix that, over the course of thirty years, he has managed to reassemble with the original parts: the body, the cross, and finally the arms. He calls this achievement a "glückliches Zusammentreffen," seeing in it an allegory of the fate of Christianity, which "oft genug zergliedert und zerstreut, sich doch endlich immer wieder am Kreuze zusammenfinden muß." The story ends: "'Wer lange lebt,' sagte der Alte, 'sieht manches versammelt und manches auseinanderfallen'" (147). This vocabulary of separating and joining recurs throughout the novel on the level of plot. Maxim 133 of the **"Betrachtungen im Sinne der Wanderer"** could be seen as summing up the collector's thoughts in the same terms: "Ist das ganze Dasein ein ewiges Trennen und Verbinden, so folgt auch, daß die Menschen im Betrachten des ungeheuren Zustandes auch bald trennen, bald verbinden werden" (303). This aphorism is, of course, also a link to the demonic, which was said to divide and connect things simultaneously.

The activity of the symbol—separating and connecting—can be considered a way to describe the reading of the text. The casket has shown how reading has to do with the making and breaking of connections, what Wolfgang Staroste calls "das ungesagte In-Bezug-Setzen zweier bedeutender Gegenstände."[26] But what is meaningful (*bedeutend*) about such objects is not so much their intended meaning as the fact that they produce or destroy connections—that they call for *Deutung*. Early in the novel, in the passage just discussed, the collector projects hypothetically about Wilhelm's casket: "wenn dieses Kästchen etwas bedeutet"; and by the end, the casket has proven its meaningfulness, as Hersilie writes: "Das bedeutende Kästchen steht vor mir" (458). The collector's prediction about where the key will be found, "gerade da wo Sie ihn am wenigsten erwarten," echoes Hersilie's earlier formula for reading against the grain, as opposed to her sister's method of interpretation (*Auslegung*): "da finden wir meist, was wir nicht suchten." But later in the novel, when Hersilie's patience with paradox and openness has worn out, she herself calls for interpretation, *Deutung*: "daß es ein Ende werde, wenigstens daß eine Deutung vorgehe, was damit gemeint sei, mit

diesem wunderbaren Finden, Wiederfinden, Trennen und Vereinigen" (378).

* * *

If the **Wanderjahre** offers a "strategy of deferral," I would also claim that it thereby provides the incentive for a sustained effort at reading rather than an abdication. This is precisely what is at stake in a conception of renunciation as a strategy for reading. Yet we have also seen how the novel tries to persuade its reader to renounce reading. Because Goethe's text shifts continually between hiding and revealing, it is difficult to maintain the distinction between, on the one hand, reading as a renunciation of the desire to replace incomprehensibility with comprehensibility, and on the other hand, an interpretation that renounces reading when faced with impenetrable obstacles.

Depending on the reader's interests, this persistent vacillating provides incentive for both reading and giving up reading. The most compelling encouragement for renouncing reading is encountered in the "Steine des Anstoßes" passage. I quote the aphorism, which finds a place in almost every study of the **Wanderjahre,** in order to point out the danger of quoting it:

> Die Geheimnisse der Lebenspfade darf und kann man nicht offenbaren; es gibt Steine des Anstoßes, über die ein jeder Wanderer stolpern muß. Der Poet aber deutet auf die Stelle hin.
>
> (460)

The danger of the passage is that it works within the text in a way that is completely at odds with its own statement. The passage functions for readers *not* as one of these "Steine des Anstoßes" (a difficult stumbling block) but simply as a *Stein,* a smooth, polished stone or pearl of wisdom that poses no problem for reading because its meaning is so clear. The result is the same, however, whether the stones are smooth stones (like the transparent aphorism itself) or stumbling stones (like the subject of that aphorism). In both cases, the stones offer a way out of trying to make sense of them, either because they are too easy or because they are too difficult to understand. Yet in addition to allowing for a renunciation of reading, these stumbling blocks, as well as the passage in which they appear (which *should* be a stumbling block) are capable of forcing a reading to stumble, to slow down enough to become aware of the competing directions that the novel itself offers as possible options for resolving the incomprehensibility it poses. The built-in fullness of language— irony at work—would allow me to push on the word *Anstoß* and recall that outside the expression *Steine des Anstoßes* it means something that initiates, an impetus or inducement, which is precisely the role it should play in reading. The stones of contention, as it were, thus tolerate as well as foster some measure of incomprehensibility in the text and in the reading. The text's refusal to give up a certain opacity is a constant impetus to reading.

The dialogue between Wilhelm and Jarno about the geological book of nature is a crucial case in point. Wilhelm meets Jarno early in the novel, and they discuss such topics as knowledge and insight, the happiness of mankind, the relationship of words to sound, and the book of nature. Jarno values his "rigid rocks" (*starre Felsen*), he says, because they at least, in contrast to humans, do not have to be comprehended ("denn diese sind wenigstens nicht zu begreifen," 34). The dialogue, of which I shall quote only the final part, is extremely rich and could offer numerous possibilities for reading. I will limit myself to observations about how it crystalizes the issues that have been raised: the novel as an allegory of reading, and the differences between reading and interpretation in the context of a reading as renunciation.

Jarno makes a plea to be allowed to treat the cracks and fissures in the rock as letters of an alphabet that has to be learned like any other:

> "Wenn ich nun aber," versetzte jener, "eben diese Spalten und Risse als Buchstaben behandelte, sie zu entziffern suchte, sie zu Worten bildete und sie fertig zu lesen lernte, hättest du etwas dagegen?"—"Nein, aber es scheint mir ein weitläufiges Alphabet."—"Enger, als du denkst; man muß es nur kennen lernen wie ein anderes auch. Die Natur hat nur *eine* Schrift, und ich brauche mich nicht mit so vielen Kritzeleien herumzuschleppen. Hier darf ich nicht fürchten, wie wohl geschieht, wenn ich mich lange und liebevoll mit einem Pergament abgegeben habe, daß ein scharfer Kritikus kommt und mir versichert, das alles sei nur untergeschoben."—Lächelnd versetzte der Freund: "Und doch wird man auch hier deine Lesarten streitig machen."—"Eben deswegen," sagte jener, "red' ich mit niemanden darüber und mag auch mit dir, eben weil ich dich liebe, das schlechte Zeug von öden Worten nicht weiter wechseln und betrieglich austauschen."

(34)

Jarno insists that nature has only one way of writing and that therefore he does not have to fear, as he would with a normal text, the sharp critic who will pronounce his text "forged" or "misrepresented" (*untergeschoben*). When Wilhelm points out that nature's text is equally open to a contesting reading, Jarno agrees and explains his reluctance to discuss these matters. The fact that Wilhelm does not regard Jarno's valorization of the stones' incomprehensibility as sincere sets up, in miniature, an allegory of the reading of the novel: a privileging of opacity, a resistance to complete clarity and closure, and a resulting yearning for interpretation and comprehension. In this way, Jarno's incomprehensible stones function like the casket in the Felix-Hersilie-Wilhelm narrative strand: both offer the promise of demystification, yet ultimately refuse that very knowledge.

Jarno's paradox is that he not only values the stones for being incomprehensible, he also insists they can be comprehended if they are treated like an alphabet. Yet if nature's writing turns out to be just as vulnerable to instability as "real" writing, it is necessary to ask what the difference might be between *real* impediments to reading, like stones and drawings of keys—which nonetheless are interpretable in some sense—and enigmatic linguistic constructions which refuse ultimate interpretation, but in doing so also allow for a reading of this refusal. The novel highlights this crucial difference, and the reading process itself, by juxtaposing the two kinds of symbols, the linguistic casket and its pictorial key. At the same time it seems to want to produce these secrets only to have them be forgotten by the reader, who can rely on the poet to point in the right direction. Whatever differences might have existed are thus elided, and the text allows the reader a renunciation of ultimate meanings. Yet in this taunting proffering of an easy way out, the novel all the more emphatically demands to be read. A renunciation of ultimate meaning and a refusal of definite interpretability must be part of every such act.

The allegorization of reading so enigmatically enacted in the ***Wanderjahre*** seems therefore to be both the subject matter of the story and a reason to keep reading it. We recall how Juliette advocates exegesis (*Auslegung*), which corresponds to interpretation in the hermeneutical sense, the kind many readers of the novel practice in seeking the meaning behind the symbol of the key or the casket. We have seen how the novel encourages this kind of curiosity but at the same time blocks it with many unanswered mysteries, thus allowing for a certain kind of renunciation of understanding. By focusing on the *Kästchen* and the drawing of its key, we have been able to see how the novel allegorizes interpretation, but also how it allegorizes reading in Hersilie's sense of reading paradoxically or against the grain. Reading has been recognized as a kind of renunciation which differs decisively from the kind of interpretation that performs a renunciation by taking seriously the novel's excuses to stop looking for meaning. It is not so much concerned with finding meaning behind symbols, as rather with looking closely at how incomprehensibility's force is manifested in narrative, and how this is to be accounted for. The obstacles the text poses for interpretation and reading emphasize the difference between them: the drawing of the key can be interpreted but cannot finally be read, while the casket refuses ultimate interpretability yet must be read. Hersilie's call for closure and "at least" interpretation, in seeming to capitulate or renounce, only reinforces the distinction. Her fate attests to the difficulties of dwelling in paradoxality with the demonic, of which Goethe wrote in ***Dichtung und Wahrheit***: "Nur im Unmöglichen schien es sich zu gefallen."[27] This impossible place, a place both overfilled and empty at the same time, is that "gruesome, meaningful place" where the novel began, the only suitable place for a novel that is both a novel and a novel about reading novels.

Wilhelm, whose "silence" towards Hersilie's letters is the ostensible cause of her capitulation, and whose role in our account has hardly been titular, offers, in a letter to Natalie, the only possible answer to the questions raised here: "du mußt dich eben in Geduld fassen, lesen und weiter lesen" (280).

Notes

1. Hermann Broch, "James Joyce und die Gegenwart," *Essays* (Zürich: Rhein-Verlag, 1955) 1:206; quoted by Oskar Seidlin in "*Melusine* in der Spiegelung der *Wanderjahre*," in: *Aspekte der Goethezeit,* ed. Stanley A. Corngold, Michael Curschmann, and Theodore J. Ziolkowski (Göttingen: Vandenhoeck & Ruprecht, 1977) 146.

2. Here a certain initial epistemological equalizing takes place within the novel, since we as readers get to know the characters in the novel in precisely the same way as the characters themselves get to know each other: by reading internal narratives. A crucial difference remains, however, since several of these narratives are "written" or "translated" by some characters for the benefit of the others, not for the readers of the novel; thus the readers *in* the novel often seem to have certain advantages over the readers *of* the novel. Quotations from the *Wanderjahre* are taken from volume 8 of the Hamburger Ausgabe, ed. Erich Trunz; references are given parenthetically in the body of my text.

3. Cyrus Hamlin, "Platonic Dialogue and Romantic Irony: Prolegomenon to a Theory of Literary Narrative," *Canadian Review of Comparative Literature* 3 (1976): 5-26, here 25.

4. "Wilhelm Meisters Wanderjahre oder die Entsagenden," two-part review originally published in *Jahrbücher für wissenschaftliche Kritik* (Stuttgart and Tübingen, 1829-1830), reprinted in *Goethe und seine Kritiker,* ed. Oscar Fambach (Düsseldorf: Verlag L. Ehlermann, 1953) 314-66, here 333.

5. Hotho 339.

6. Hotho 362.

7. As Hotho states in his review article, "Man könnte Werke über dieß Werk schreiben" (362). The most important for my consideration of the *Kästchen* are: Eric A. Blackall, *Goethe and the Novel* (Ithaca: Cornell University Press, 1976); Stefan Blessin, *Die Romane Goethes* (Königstein/Ts.: Athenäum, 1979); Volker Dürr, "Geheimnis und Aufklärung: Zur pädagogischen Funktion des Kästchens in *Wilhelm Meisters Wanderjahren*," *Monatshefte* 74, 1 (1982); Wilhelm Emrich, *Die Symbolik von Faust II* (Berlin: Junker & Dünnhaupt, 1943) and "Das Problem der Symbol-interpretation im Hinblick auf Goethes 'Wanderjahre,'" in Emrich, *Protest und Verheißung: Studien zur klassischen und modernen Dichtung* (Frankfurt/Main: Athenäum Verlag, 1960); André

Gilg, *"Wilhelm Meisters Wanderjahre" und ihre Symbole* (Zürich: Atlantis Verlag, 1954); Friedrich Ohly, "Goethes Ehrfurchten—ein ordo caritas," *Euphorion* 55 (1961) and "Zum Kästchen in Goethes 'Wanderjahren,'" *Zeitschrift für deutsches Altertum* 91 (1961-1962); A. G. Steer, *Goethe's Science in the Structure of the "Wanderjahre"* (Athens: University of Georgia Press, 1979); and Joseph Strelka, *Esoterik bei Goethe* (Tübingen: Max Niemeyer Verlag, 1980). See also Stephan Broser's article on Freud, "Kästchen, Kasten, Kastration," *Cahiers Confrontation* 8 (1982) and Avital Ronell, *Dictations: On Haunted Writing* (Bloomington: Indiana University Press, 1986).

8. See Françoise Derré, "Die Beziehungen zwischen Felix, Hersilie und Wilhelm in 'Wilhelm Meisters Wanderjahren,'" *Goethe Jahrbuch* 94 (1977): 48.

9. Wilhelm's self-canceling maxims are strongly reminiscent of Kierkegaard's description of irony as "a nothingness which consumes everything and a something which one can never catch hold of, which both is and is not" (Søren Kierkegaard, *The Concept of Irony,* trans. with an introduction by Lee M. Capel [Bloomington: Indiana University Press, 1965] 171). This self-destructive aspect of language will recur in our discussion of the demonic.

10. I would have to disagree with Seidlin's statement (note 1) that this only *seems* to be so: "so als *wäre* es aus der eben gehörten Nebengeschichte in die Hauptgeschichte hinübergeglitten" (158-59, my emphasis). One might, however, commend Seidlin's description of the *Kästchen* as "vieldeutig und schwebend."

11. Schlechta, *Goethes Wilhelm Meister* (Frankfurt/Main: Klostermann, 1953) 149.

12. Peschken, *Entsagung in "Wilhelm Meisters Wanderjahren"* (Bonn: Bouvier, 1968) 43-44.

13. HA 10:175-76.

14. Kierkegaard (note 9) 171, 161.

15. Fletcher, *Allegory: The Theory of a Symbolic Mode* (Ithaca: Cornell University Press, 1964) 50.

16. See in particular Ohly, Steer, and Strelka (note 7).

17. See Gilg 135.

18. See in particular Emrich (note 7), "Das Problem der Symbolinterpretation" 64.

19. See Gilg, for example, who makes his tolerance explicit.

20. See Peschken (note 12) for an analysis of how, in Hersilie's letters, the words *Geheimnis* and *Rätsel* become *Schlüssel* and *Kästchen*.

21. This uncanny situation, in which one runs into the very thing one is out to avoid, would be the proper place to invoke Freud, rather than with respect to the phallic properties of the key.

22. Once the demonic (or the ironic) is recognized, nothing seems stable, locks and keys are no longer helpful tools, puns refuse to contain themselves. Hersilie writes that the drawing comes finally— *schließlich* rather than *endlich*—because she cannot flee the key: finality gets locked up with the activity of keys, *schließen,* closing and locking. Furthermore, the key is supposed to remind Wilhelm of an arrow with barbs ("Pfeile mit Widerhaken"). Very few readers have taken this suggestion seriously, although it has caused great exegetic irritation. Perhaps the barbed arrow irritates because *Widerhaken* means irritation, not because there are any *Widerhaken* in the picture. Rather than the picture recalling a "Pfeile mit Widerhaken," the word *Widerhaken* recalls other contrary words like *Widerspruch* (the only place the demonic is manifested) and *Widersinn* (which the key is capable of generating in its readers).

23. Cf. Clark Muenzer, *Figures of Identity: Goethe's Novels and the Enigmatic Self* (University Park: Pennsylvania State University Press, 1984) 101-29. Muenzer acknowledges the danger of relying on keys to unlock ultimate meanings: "In the spirit of the ideal scientific investigator, who can only postulate this or that point of reference, its 'renunciants' (as its ideal readers) will only find keys that must be relinquished because they cannot really open locks. [...] As Goethe's strategic distractions, the text's multiple interests become essential detours and serve as reminders of the need to renounce all ultimate meanings, even as they are pursued" (107). Renouncing "all ultimate meanings," though, does not necessarily mean renouncing reading.

24. Cf. Gilg's suggestion that the drawing points to something incapable of being uttered as/in language: "er [deutet] mit dem stummen Vorzeigen des Bildes auf ein Unaussprechliches" (135).

25. See in particular Marianne Jabs-Kriegsmann, "Felix und Hersilie," in Erich Trunz, ed., *Studien zu Goethes Alterswerken* (Frankfurt/Main: Athenäum Verlag, 1971) 75-98, here 90.

26. *Raum und Realität in dichterischer Gestaltung: Studien zu Goethe und Kafka* (Heidelberg: Lothar Stiehm Verlag, 1971) 23.

27. HA 10:175.

James Hardin (essay date 1991)

SOURCE: Hardin, James. "Carlyle's Translation of Goethe's *Wilhelm Meisters Wanderjahre*: An Introduction." *Goethe's* Wilhelm Meister's Travels. Trans. Thomas Carlyle. Columbia: Camden House, 1991. v-xvi. Print.

[*In the following essay, Hardin surveys several textual and historical aspects of the 1821 version of* Wilhelm Meister's Travels, *as translated in 1827 by Thomas Carlyle. Hardin provides a summary of the association between the young Carlyle and the aging Goethe, furnishes a brief editorial history of Goethe's novel, and discusses the few English translations to appear since Carlyle's.*]

Johann Wolfgang von Goethe's *Wilhelm Meisters Lehrjahre* (1795-96, translated as *Wilhelm Meister's Apprenticeship*) is the most influential German novel ever written. It is generally considered the prototypical Bildungsroman, and has had enormous literary impact not just on German but on world literature. Although Goethe's continuation of the novel, *Wilhelm Meisters Wanderjahre oder die Entsagenden* (1821 and 1829, *Wilhelm Meister's Travels*) has not been nearly as popular or influential as the *Apprenticeship,* it has attracted considerable attention in recent years among literary critics. This upsurge in interest has to do with the fact that some idiosyncrasies of the book that had earlier seemed daunting to the reader—its unconventional structure, its mixture of genres, its disregard for verisimilitude, its arbitrariness, its philosophical component—mark it precisely as a forerunner of the modern novel. Ehrhard Bahr, for example, has shown striking resemblances between the *Wanderjahre* and James Joyce's *Ulysses* in the inclusion in both works of detailed technical passages taken from the realm of the work world.[1]

The fame of *Wilhelm Meister* [*Wilhelm Meisters Lehrjahre*] as a Bildungsroman has assured it a place in world literature in spite of the skepticism with which some critics regard that literary term. It has been shown that the Bildungsroman (roughly, "novel of education") exists in far fewer exemplars than was thought earlier, that the number of novels that actually "fit" the usual descriptions of the genre are surprisingly scarce.[2] The problem may in part be a semantic one. Although it is careless to apply the term "Bildungsroman" indiscriminately to any novel that treats the life of a young man or woman who goes out into the world and comes into conflict with its "realities," it may also be unnecessarily restrictive to define the genre as a novel that describes the multifarious influences on a youth, portrays the unfolding of his inner life and confrontation with the sober demands of the world, and invariably ends at a point when the protagonist has achieved a modicum of wisdom based at least in part on a humanistic, enlightened, secular Weltanschauung. There are other possibilities, variants, as can be seen in what I would call variants on the Bildungsroman, such as *Le rouge et le noir* (no coming to terms with society there!) and the deeply tragic *Jude the Obscure.*

Whatever view one may have of the usefulness and descriptive quality of the literary term, the stature of Goethe's Wilhelm Meister novels remains unaffected. The slow-paced story of young Wilhelm's love affair with the actress Mariana and with the stage (in Goethe's original plan for the book Wilhelm would found a German National Theater) instantly entered the German literary canon and, through translation, attracted readers—not all of them enthusiastic about this unconventional and "immoral" novel—in America and most of Europe. Although it did not achieve the immediate, explosive success of *Die Leiden des jungen Werthers* (1774; *The Sufferings of Young Werther*) *Wilhelm Meister* was much read and debated in Germany and enjoyed by relatively large numbers of English and American readers from the time of Carlyle's translation, in 1824, to the present.

Wilhelm Meisters Wanderjahre oder die Entsagenden is a symbolic work, one of Goethe's last and most significant. It portrays not so much figures and the development of character as issues and forces. The rococo dalliances of the earlier books of the *Apprenticeship* have been replaced now by a sobering appraisal of the possibilities for human development in the second decade of the nineteenth century. It is a novel whose subtitle has not only to do with renunciation in personal involvements but also, with the profound historical changes that had occurred between the year of the inception of the *Lehrjahre* [*Wilhelm Meisters Lehrjahre*] 1777, and 1821, when the first version of its "sequel" appeared. The new age—immensely more complex than the odd admixture of Baroque and Enlightenment Goethe had known as a youth—demands specialization and group interaction. And thus the *Wanderjahre* is not a Bildungsroman in the same sense that its predecessor was. It has to do more with the Bildung, the education and formation, of society at large, and less to do with the development of individual aesthetic sensibilities.

* * *

Carlyle's long and fruitful connection with Goethe began after he learned sufficient German to read about a subject of great interest to him: geology.[3] He then became interested in German letters generally, read Schiller's *History of the Thirty Years' War* in the original, Goethe's *Faust I,* plays by the popular dramatist August von Kotzebue, Klopstock's religious epic *Der Messias* (1749), and a scattering of other works, when he happened on *Wilhelm Meister* in 1821. In his *Reminiscences* he reports that he was immediately taken by the book: "Grand, surely, harmoniously built together, far seeing, wise and true. When, for many years, or almost in my whole life before, have I read such a book?"[4] It was a strange attraction, between the dour mystic whose faith in traditional Christianity was failing, and the work of a widely travelled, sophisticated, free-thinking man of the world. He saw something in *Wilhelm Meisters Lehrjahre* that helped him overcome his pessimism. In Wilhelm's vicissitudes, as Carlyle understood

the book, the hero learned that there is something higher than happiness. It is "spiritual clearness."[5] He found the message of the novel to be that Meister found fulfillment in a life devoted to others. The pursuit of Bildung was scarcely noticed by him. Instead, as Howe puts it, Carlyle

> used the mildly pantheistic sage of Weimar to bolster up a shaky Presbyterian Christianity, and fastened upon the inferior [sic] second part of *Meister*—the *Wanderjahre*—. . . culling from it one of its least characteristic and most unimportant points, the "worship of sorrow" idea.[6]

It is, of course, well known that Carlyle consciously or unconsciously used Goethe's thought in *Wilhelm Meister* as he saw fit. Much more important is that Carlyle—for whatever reason—turned to Goethe, and ultimately translated the two *Wilhelm Meister* novels, thus opening English letters to the lasting influence of these very un-English works.

* * *

It may fairly be asked whether it is necessary to republish Thomas Carlyle's translation of Goethe's *Wilhelm Meisters Wanderjahre.* The language is dated, and it is well known that the translation is not always completely accurate. But I believe the present reprint edition will be welcomed for several reasons: first, as of this writing, it is the only one available. A recent accurate and indeed excellent translation by Krishna Winston[7] can be obtained only as part of the entire twelve-volume edition of Goethe's works. More significant, the language of Carlyle captures in a way no longer possible for the English translator the tone of the time in which it was read. The modern translator who attempted to use the language of the early nineteenth century would surely fail; the result would be a futile and pretentious rendering into a language that never lived. There is, therefore, in my view much to recommend the contemporary translation. Furthermore, it is Carlyle's translation that was most widely read in the nineteenth century; it was indisputably the most influential rendering, even though it was a translation of Goethe's *first* version of the *Wanderjahre,* that of 1821 rather than the final, much revised and expanded version of 1829. Although Carlyle certainly read the later work, he wrote in the preface to the 1839 edition of *Wilhelm Meister's Apprenticeship and Travels,* "revised and edited by Thomas Carlyle," that

> I have changed little or nothing: I might have added much; for the original since that time [of his translation of the first edition] was as it were taken to pieces by the author himself in his last years, and constructed anew; and in the Final Edition [**Ausgabe letzter Hand**] [*Werke: Vollständige Ausgabe letzter Hand*] of his works, appears with multifarious intercalations, giving a great expansion both of size and of scope. Not Pedagogy only, and Husbandry and Art and Religion And Human Conduct in the Nineteenth Century, but Geology, Astronomy, Cottonspinning, Metallurgy, Anatomical Lecturing, and much else, are typically shadowed forth in this second form of the *Travels*; which, however, continues a Fragment like the first,

significantly pointing on all hands towards infinitude; not more complete than the first was, or indeed perhaps less so. It will well reward the trustful student of Goëthe to read this new form of the *Travels*; and see how in that great mind, beaming in mildest mellow splendour, beaming if also trembling, like a great sun on the verge of the horizon, near now to its long farewell, all these things were illuminated and illustrated: but for the mere English reader there are probably in our prior edition of the *Travels* already novelties enough; for us, at all events, it seemed unadvisable to meddle with it farther at present.

Carlyle here touches on the fact that the work, especially in its later reworking, bewildered, even alienated contemporary readers. But it no longer need put off the attentive, participatory reader. We have now been better acclimated by the literature of our own time to appreciate the richness of the novel, and to see its remarkable affinities to such novels as Hermann Broch's *The Death of Vergil,* Musil's *Man without Qualities,* and James Joyce's *Ulysses.*[8]

Wilhelm Meister's Travels had either been received negatively or been misunderstood by most nineteenth-century critics. A new appreciation of the worth of the book can be said to have begun—so far as critical literature is concerned—with the appearance in 1913 of Max Wundt's *Goethes Wilhelm Meister und die Entwicklung des modernen Lebensideals.*[9] But even more important than Wundt's appreciation for the radically new aesthetic of Goethe's last novel was the emergence of the innovative novels of the early twentieth century. Goethe's arbitrary use of "archival" materials from the most disparate sources; of novellas that could exist independently and that are subtly linked to the fabric of the novel as a whole; his bold denial of the demands of verisimilitude and "realistic" portrayal of events in an ordered, chronological way; and, above all, his insistence that the reader order and interpret the sometimes conflicting or incomplete data presented all were characteristics that linked the work with the modern novel and that were recognized by Wundt and by the now better attuned reader.[10]

THE EDITORIAL HISTORY OF THE TWO VERSIONS OF *WILHELM MEISTERS WANDERJAHRE*

I have mentioned several times the fact that there are two German versions of Goethe's *Wanderjahre.* A few words on their relationship and the publishing history of the original works are in order.[11] The following stages can be distinguished:

1. Some of the novellas interspersed in the novel were published in the periodical *Taschenbuch für Damen* in 1809-10 and 1816-19. These include ***Die pilgernde Törin, Sankt Joseph der Zweite, Das nußbraune Mädchen, Die neue Melusine,*** and ***Der Mann von funfzig Jahren.***

2. The first, shorter edition appears in 1821. As Ehrhard Bahr points out, this first edition is not a mere "stepping stone" to the final version, "but a relatively independent work with its own unique aesthetic and philosophical qualities."[12]

3. The final version in Goethe's lifetime, 1829, in the ***Ausgabe letzter Hand,*** somewhat carelessly proofed and set by Cotta.

4. Subsequent editions in the nineteenth and well into the twentieth century attempted variously not only to correct obvious errors but to rearrange parts of the work and even to omit two poems and two collections of maxims placed by Goethe at the end of the second and third Books. This redactional violence was done on the authority of one of Goethe's secretaries and confidants, Johann Peter Eckermann, who erroneously claimed that the maxims were not actually planned to be part of the novel but were added to "fill out" the volumes.

5. Publication in 1926 of the so-called **"Festausgabe"** [***Goethes Werke. Festausgabe***].[13] Restoration of portions of the book excised after Goethe's death.

6. The Artemis edition of Goethe's works in 1949[14] and the Hamburg edition of 1950 reprinted the ***Wanderjahre*** again in its version of 1829 in the ***Ausgabe letzter Hand.***

7. The Reclam study edition of Bahr restores the introductory poem and maxims of the first version of 1821. These are not included in the popular Hamburg edition. Other passages from the first version—omitted in error in 1829—were restored. In general Bahr follows the aforementioned ***Festausgabe*** of 1926, which provides, unlike the Hamburg edition, all variants from the first version of 1821 as well as other corrections.

CHIEF DIFFERENCES IN THE TWO VERSIONS

The first version appeared under the title ***Wilhelm Meisters Wanderjahre oder Die Entsagenden. Ein Roman von Goethe. Erster Theil,*** and includes eighteen chapters with no division into books. Only the first part of the novella ***Der Mann von funfzig Jahren*** is included, which is Chapter 3 of Book II in the 1829 version. Chapters 4 and 5 are lacking. Some sections of version 1 were eliminated in version 2, and of course large sections were added in version 2, namely chapters 7 and 10 in Book I; 4 and 5 in II; 3-5, 7-8, 10-18 in Book III. Of all the revisions of Goethe, his reworking of the ***Wanderjahre*** was one of the most radical.[15]

THE TRANSLATION

As could be seen from his remarks to the revised edition, Carlyle was himself somewhat put off by the final form of the novel, and perhaps that is the reason he never translated it. Thus, it is the original translation of 1827 that was reprinted in dozens of editions in Great Britain and America over the next century.[16] The present edition provides the *first* English printing of the ***Wanderjahre*** from which all later editions of Carlyle's translation stem. Subsequent editions claim to be "new" or "revised," but the revisions were apparently few in number. Edward Dowden, "Professor of English Literature in the University of Dublin," wrote the following in his introduction to ***Goethe's Wilhelm Meister's Apprenticeship and Travels*** of 1890:

> Carlyle's translation of ***Wilhelm Meister's Apprenticeship*** and ***Wilhelm Meister's Travels*** have such high excellence as pieces of English narrative that it is not likely they will be soon displaced. Occasionally, but rarely, he has made a downright error in translation, occasionally he has needlessly departed from the exact sense of the original.[17]

Yet this very error, found in the ***Lehrjahre,*** is allowed to stand—in the 1890 edition—presumably with all the other "downright errors" alluded to by Dowden.[18]

TRANSLATIONS OF THE *WANDERJAHRE* AFTER CARLYLE

Apparently the most glaring omission in Carlyle's translation of the novel, in the view of the English-language readership, was the conclusion of the novella **"The Man of Fifty."** It was, for example, added in an appendix to the 1890 Chicago edition in a translation attributed to Edward Bell. Likewise included, as appendix B, is **"Odoard's Address."** Bell's translation had appeared in 1885 under the title ***Wilhelm Meister's Travels.*** By Johann Wolfgang Goethe. Translated from the later and enlarged edition of the German, and edited by Edward Bell. London: G. Bell and Sons, 1885. [= Bohn's Libraries, Volume IX of **Goethe's Works**]. The Bohn Library volumes were printed on extremely poor paper with a high wood content, and poorly bound, so that most of that edition appears to have vanished.

But even after the appearance of Bell's translation of the second version, Carlyle's translation of the first continued to dominate, as the list of editions on page xiiif. illustrates. A translation by R. O. Moon[19] is reported in 1947 but I have not been able to view a copy. The National Union Catalogue does not report a reprinting of this translation. The only other translation known to me is the important recent rendering of Krishna Winston. Clearly, the Carlyle translation has—until now—been decisive in forming the English-speaking world's understanding of Goethe's last novel. This reprint and new introduction to the first edition of that translation is provided in recognition of that fact.

Notes

1. See Bahr's *Nachwort* to the Reclam edition of Goethe's *Wilhelm Meisters Wanderjahre.* Stuttgart: Philipp Reclam jun., 1982, and his article, "Goethe's *Wanderjahre* as an Experimental Novel," *Mosaic* 5 (1972), Nr. 3, 61-71.

2. The most persuasive of these is Jeffrey L. Sammons, who points out that in his exhaustive reading of

German nineteenth century novels he found only a handful of scattered examples of the genre. See Sammons, "The Mystery of the Missing *Bildungsroman* or: What Happened to Wilhelm Meister's Legacy?" *Genre* 14 (1981): 229-46.

3. See Susanne Howe, *Wilhelm Meister and his English Kinsmen: Apprentices to Life.* New York: Columbia University Press, 1930, 82-93.

4. Quoted by Howe, *Wilhelm Meister and his English Kinsmen,* 86.

5. Quoted by Howe from Carlyle's 1838 shorthand report, *Lectures on the History of Literature,* 88.

6. Howe, 89.

7. Volume 10 in the 12-volume Suhrkamp edition of Goethe's works in English: *Conversations of German Refugees,* translated by Jan van Heurck in cooperation with Jane K. Brown; *Wilhelm Meister's Journeyman Years or the Renunciants,* translated by Krishna Winston, ed. by Jane K. Brown. New York: Suhrkamp, 1989. The notes to this volume do not take up the interesting and important matter of earlier translations of the works in question.

8. See Ehrhard Bahr's *Nachwort* to the Reclam edition of Goethe's *Wilhelm Meisters Wanderjahre.* Stuttgart: Philipp Reclam jun., 1982, and his article, "Goethe's *Wanderjahre* as an Experimental Novel," *Mosaic* 5 (1972), Nr. 3, 61-71.

9. Berlin and Leipzig: Göschen. See Bahr's *Nachwort* in the Reclam edition of the *Wanderjahre.*

10. See Bahr, Reclam edition of the *Wanderjahre,* 551-553.

11. For information on the genesis of the novel and its publishing history I am indebted to Ehrhard Bahr's excellent *Studienausgabe* of *Wilhelm Meisters Wanderjahre* (Stuttgart: Reclam, 1982), 527-564, and to Erich Trunz's indispensable edition of the *Wanderjahre* in the famous "Hamburg Edition" of Goethe's collected works. See especially Trunz's commentary and notes in volume 8, *Goethes Werke: Romane und Novellen III,* textkritisch durchgeschen und kommentiert von Erich Trunz. (Munich: C. H. Beck, 1982 [11th ed.]), 527-690.

12. Bahr, Reclam edition of the *Wanderjahre,* 527.

13. *Goethes Werke. Festausgabe.* Im Verein mit F. Bergermann, hrsg. von Robert Petsch. Vol. 12 ed. by Julius Wahle with an introduction by Oskar Walzel. Leipzig: Bibliographisches Institut, 1926.

14. *Gedenkausgabe der Werke, Briefe und Gespräche.* Hg. von Ernst Beutler. Vol. 8: *Wilhelm Meisters*

Wanderjahre—Wilhelm Meisters theatralische Sendung. Zurich: Artemis Verlag, 1949.

15. See Trunz, vol. 8 of the Hamburg Edition, 548-49.

16. The following prints are listed in National Union Catalogue: *Wilhelm Meister's Apprenticeship and Travels.* ... Philadelphia: Lea and Blanchard, 1840; *Wilhelm Meister's Apprenticeship and Travels.* ... London: Chapman and Hall, 1842; *Wilhelm Meister's Apprenticeship and Travels.* ... Boston: Ticknor, Reed, and Fields, 1851; *Wilhelm Meister's Apprenticeship and Travels.* ... London: Chapman and Hall, 1858; *Wilhelm Meister's Apprenticeship and Travels.* ... Boston: Ticknor and Fields, 1865; *Wilhelm Meister's Apprenticeship and Travels.* ... Boston: Ticknor and Fields, 1867; *Wilhelm Meister's Apprenticeship and Travels.* ... London: Chapman, 1868; *Wilhelm Meister's Apprenticeship and Travels.* ... London: Chapman and Hall; New York, Scribner Welford and Co., 1871; *Wilhelm Meister's Apprenticeship and Travels.* ... London: Chapman and Hall, 1874; *Wilhelm Meister's Apprenticeship and Travels.* ... New York: Scribner, Welford and Co., 1874; *Wilhelm Meister's Apprenticeship and Travels.* ... Boston: J. R. Osgood, 1876; *Wilhelm Meister's Apprenticeship and Travels.* ... Boston: Houghton, Osgood and Co., 1880; *Wilhelm Meister's Apprenticeship and Travels.* ... New York: American Book Exchange, 1881; *Wilhelm Meister's Apprenticeship and Travels.* ... Boston: S. E. Cassino, 1882; *Wilhelm Meister's Apprenticeship and Travels.* ... Chicago: Belford Clarke & Co., 1882; *Wilhelm Meister's Apprenticeship and Travels.* ... New York: Wm. L. Allison & Sons, 1882; *Wilhelm Meister's Apprenticeship and Travels.* ... New York: Hurst & Co., [ca.] 1882; *Wilhelm Meister's Apprenticeship and Travels.* ... New York: J. D. Williams, 1882; *Wilhelm Meister's Apprenticeship and Travels.* ... Boston: Estes and Lauriat, [ca] 1882; *Wilhelm Meister's Apprenticeship and Travels.* ... Boston: S. E. Cassino, 1884; *Wilhelm Meister's Apprenticeship and Travels.* ... New York: Wm. L. Allison, 1886; *Wilhelm Meister's Apprenticeship and Travels.* ... London: Chapman & Hall, Ltd. [1888]; *Wilhelm Meister's Apprenticeship and Travels.* ... Boston: Houghton, Mifflin, 189?; *Wilhelm Meister's Apprenticeship and Travels.* ... With a critical introduction by Edward Dowden. ... Chicago: A. C. McClurg & Co., 1890; *Wilhelm Meister's Apprenticeship and Travels.* ... London: Chapman and Hall, 1890; *Wilhelm Meister's Apprenticeship and Travels.* ... Complete in one volume. New York: A. L. Burt, [1893]; *Wilhelm Meister's Apprenticeship and Travels.* ... London: Chapman & Hall, 1894; *Wilhelm Meister's Apprenticeship and Travels.* ... Centenary edition. London: Chapman and Hall, 1899; *Wilhelm Meister's Apprenticeship and Travels.* ...

New York: A. L. Burt, [1899?]; *Wilhelm Meister's Apprenticeship and Travels.* ... Philadelphia: H. T. Coates, [1899?]; *Wilhelm Meister's Apprenticeship and Travels.* ... Illustrated cabinet ed. Boston: D. Estes, [1901]; *Wilhelm Meister's Apprenticeship and Travels.* ... Ed. with an introduction by Henry Duff Traill. New York: C. Scribner's Sons, 1901; *Wilhelm Meister's Apprenticeship and Travels.* ... London: Chapman and Hall, 1903; *Wilhelm Meister's Apprenticeship and Travels.* ... New York: Scribners, 1904; *Wilhelm Meister's Apprenticeship and Travels.* ... London: Chapman and Hall, 1907; *Wilhelm Meister's Apprenticeship and Travels.* ... New York: E. P. Dutton & Co., [1912]; *Wilhelm Meister's Apprenticeship and Travels.* ... London & Toronto: J. M. Dent & Sons; New York: E. P. Dutton & Co., [1925-26]; *Wilhelm Meister's Apprenticeship and Travels.* ... as previous item, 1930.

17. [This is a footnote in the original text. JH]

> One error of the translator must be noted, for it completely obscures the sense of the German: "He soon became a friend of the family; and finding in me, as he was pleased to say, a person free alike from the extravagance and emptiness of the great world, and from the narrowness and aridness of the still world in the country (*der Stillen im Lande*), he courted intimacy with me" (B[ook] vi. p. 385). Evidently, Carlyle was not aware that "Die Stillen im Lande" was the name given to the German Pietists of the seventeenth and eighteenth centuries.

18. The new, exemplary translation by Eric Blackall and Victor Lange renders the passage question more accurately but somewhat obscurely: "Neither the extravagance and vanity of high society nor the bloodless timidity of the conventiclers." *Goethe's Work* Volume 9. New York: Suhrkamp, 1989, 238.

19. *Wilhelm Meister, Apprenticeship and Travels.* London: G. T. Foulis, 1947.

Ehrhard Bahr (essay date 1991)

SOURCE: Bahr, Ehrhard. "*Wilhelm Meisters Wanderjahre, oder die Entsagenden* (1821-1829): From Bildungsroman to Archival Novel." *Reflection and Action: Essays on the Bildungsroman.* Ed. James Hardin. Columbia: U of South Carolina P, 1991. 163-94. Print.

[In the following essay, Bahr examines Goethe's development of an "archival novel" in the 1829 edition of Wilhelm Meister's Travels *and explores the relationship of the work's unusual form to its treatment of a society in transition. Bahr notes that the use of technical prose in select passages serves to underscore the prosaic world (and the corresponding representational challenge) inherited by modern novelists.]*

And we have, have we not, those priceless pages of
Wilhelm Meister?

James Joyce: *Ulysses*

In his essay "James Joyce and the Present" (1936) the
Austrian novelist Hermann Broch argued that Goethe established in *Wilhelm Meisters Wanderjahre, oder die
Entsagenden* (1829, translated as *Wilhelm Meister's
Journeyman Years, or The Renunciants*) the foundation
of modern literature and the new novel. Broch thought it
"quite possible, even probable" that Goethe presaged the
development of modern literature, especially the fundamental changes of consciousness within the modern novel.
Broch boldly hypothesized that Goethe's *Wanderjahre*
had already accomplished what James Joyce's *Ulysses*
(1922) did one hundred years later: the conception of
the modern world in a single work of art.[1] Broch substantiated his thesis with the Hegelian term "totality."[2] For
Broch, totality in a literary work of art constituted a view of
the world that compounded "all knowledge of infinite
human development into a single, simultaneous act of
recognition." This conception of the world stands in contradistinction to a "totality of being" that requires "entirely
new forms of expression" in the work of art. Broch argued
that the grasping of the totality was the task of literature
and art in general. The stronger this "totality of being" is
realized in the work of art, he said, "the more timeless the
work will prove itself to be." Thus, the "adequate totality
of form" plays a particular role for Broch in "the complete
command of all aesthetic means of expression, subordinated to the universality of content." He viewed Goethe's
Wanderjahre and *Faust* as "art works of totality" (*Total-
itätskunstwerke*). Both works realized this "adequate totality of form" insofar as they transcended the traditional
genre forms of the novel and drama.[3]

Without treating in detail the question of literary reflection, Broch placed special emphasis on the "periods of
destruction of values" (*Epochen des Wertzerfalls*), which
are characterized by the problem of "representation" (*Ab-
bildbarkeit*):

> The further the destruction of value continues ... the
> greater the artistic cost necessary to handle and manage
> the collection of powers; indeed, the cost will become so
> great and so complicated that the works of totality within
> the general production of art—in clear contrast with gen-
> uine periods of value—will not only become increasingly
> rare ... but also increasingly complicated and inaccessi-
> ble. This condition raises the problem of whether a
> world with constant destruction of value must not ulti-
> mately renounce its concept of totality in the work of
> art, in so doing becoming "nonrepresentational/" (*unab-
> bildbar*).[4]

In order not to fall into flat naturalism or fashionable "modernity," the "art work of totality" is rendered difficult to
understand by virtue of its "advanced reality" (*vorauseilende
Realität*). The "advanced reality" has the peculiar and characteristic property that it is a condition of totality unrecog-
nized by contemporaries, one that has been observed only
with the historical retrospection of a later period.

Accordingly, Goethe's *Wilhelm Meisters Lehrjahre* (*Wilhelm Meister's Apprenticeship*)[5] of 1795-96 was written in
a "value-centered" period in which the "niveau of totality,"
and with it, the "niveau of quality," were still determined by
a pervasive unity. In Broch's words, "the classical novel
[was content] to observe real and physical circumstances in
life, content to describe these circumstances by the means
of language."[6] But in the *Wanderjahre*, language and narration themselves became problematic. This novel clearly
fits Broch's definition of "period of destruction of values."
Although *Wilhelm Meisters Lehrjahre* of course was written at the time of the French Revolution, Goethe sought
to develop with this novel an alternative to the events
in France, that is, to provide new values.[7] Not until the
Wanderjahre did Goethe represent in the novel the break
and the change of consciousness resulting from the French
and industrial revolutions.

The destruction of values after the French Revolution was
reflected by the disintegration of narrative forms in the
traditional novel. The problematic nature of the *Wanderjahre* is clearly documented by the history of its reception.[8] The chain of misunderstandings and incorrect
interpretations of the *Wanderjahre* continued unabated
into the twentieth century. A reliable edition was, in
fact, not available until 1950; a complete, faithful English
translation not until 1989. Excepting the early socialist
interpretations between 1832 and 1852 (Varnhagen von
Ense, Hermann Hettner, Ferdinand Gregorovius, Karl
Grün, and others), and Broch's essay on Joyce, the "advanced reality" of this novel was not recognized until the
end of the 1960s.[9]

In Broch's interpretation the nineteenth century constituted a period of incubation, during which traditional
narrative forms could still be cultivated despite Goethe's
new concept of the novel. Old value systems remained, as
did the hope that theology and philosophy would answer
the "burning questions of the epoch." However, this hope
had dissipated by the end of the century. Philosophy and
the sciences had returned to a kind of Goethean skepticism.[10] These disciplines had given up trying to answer the
metaphysical and central mysteries that had existed since
time immemorial. Broch said of Goethe that "his intuition
and knowledge ... were one hundred years ahead of his
time." His successors in the nineteenth century—for example, Balzac, Zola, or Flaubert—were still tied to the age
of restoration: "They allowed themselves to be restricted,
indeed they had to restrict themselves, to the entertaining
and educating of their public." This was, so Broch writes,
no longer possible in the twentieth century, as the spirit of
this period did not allow this type of entertainment any

longer. In Broch's time the writer was compelled to "fulfill the Goethean challenge by approaching the legacy that human striving for knowledge had handed over to him." This legacy was "the philosophical comprehension of being in the universal representation of the world."[11]

Broch's bold hypothesis sheds a special light on the "adequate totality of form" in the _Wanderjahre_ and has frequently been alluded to by recent Goethe scholarship to demonstrate the modernity of the work.[12] Yet the direct comparison with James Joyce has yet to be fully appreciated, not even by Broch, who maintained that direct comparisons of modern works of art with those of Goethe were bound to be flawed. According to Broch modern literature had to reckon with the Goethean ambition of "raising the poetic to the level of knowledge (_Erkenntnis_)."[13]

In a comparison of Goethe with Joyce, two things may be kept in mind. First, the long development of the _Wanderjahre_ between 1798 and 1829 must be seen as a continuation of _Wilhelm Meisters Lehrjahre,_ that is, of a traditional epistolary novel, to an "archival novel." Second, a comparison of two works is quite problematic when they are separated by almost a century. Nevertheless, one may perhaps recognize some particular relationships that reveal similar applications of the technique and theory of the novel. Thus, the description of the cotton industry in Lenardo's diary in Goethe's _Wanderjahre_ (book 3, chapter 5, 333-42)[14] correlates with the description of Dublin's waterworks in the Ithaca chapter of _Ulysses._[15] In both cases, factual prose (_Sachprosa_) is laden with technical details and exact numbers. The passage in _Ulysses_ reads as follows:

> From Roundwood reservoir in County Wicklow of a cubic capacity of 2,400 million gallons, percolating through a subterranean aqueduct of filtre mains of single and double pipeage constructed at an initial plant cost of £5 per linear yard by way of the Dargle, Rathdown, Glen of the Downs and Callowhill to the 26 acre reservoir at Stillorgan, a distance of 22 statute miles, and thence, through a system of relieving tanks, by a gradient of 250 feet to the city boundary at Eustace bridge, upper Leeson street, though from prolonged summer drouth and daily supply of 12 1/2 million gallons the water had fallen below the sill of the overflow weir for which reason the borough surveyor and waterworks engineer, Mr Spencer Harty, C. E., on the instructions of the waterworks committee, had prohibited the use of municipal water for purposes other than those of consumption (envisaging the possibility of recourse being had to the impotable water of the Grand and Royal canals as in 1893) particularly at the South Dublin Guardians, notwithstanding their ration of 15 gallons per day per pauper supplied through a 6 inch meter, had been convicted of a wastage of 20,000 gallons per night by a reading of their meter on the affirmation of the law agent of the corporation, Mr Ignatius Rice, solicitor, thereby acting to the detriment of another section of the public, selfsupporting taxpayers, solvent, sound.

(655)

In the final edition of Goethe's _Wanderjahre,_ similar technical language accounts for some twenty pages. I will quote two passages.

> For right-spun yarn there are 25 to 30 to a pound; while for left-spun yarn 60 or 80, sometimes even 90. A loop on the winder will run about seven quarter-ells or slightly more, and my slim, diligent spinner claimed that she spun 4 or even 5 skeins a day on her wheel, which would be 5000 loops, amounting to 8 to 9000 ells of yarn.

(book 3, chapter 5, 336)

> An especially nimble and diligent weaver can, if she has help, produce a 32 ell piece of not particularly fine muslin in one week; that, however, is very rare, and if there are other household chores, it is usually two weeks' work. The beauty of the cloth depends upon the even operation of the treadles, on the even pressure of the beater, and also on whether the weft is laid in wet or dry. Completely even and strong tension also contributes, to which end the weaver of fine cotton cloth hangs a heavy stone from the nail of the cloth beam. If the cloth is pulled very tight during the weaving (the technical term is high tension), then it lengthens noticeably, by 3/4 of an ell on 32 ells and about 1 1/2 ells on 64. This excess is the property of the weaver; she is paid extra for it or she saves it for kerchiefs, aprons, etc.

(book 3, chapter 5, 341)

In both cases, the factual or technical language seems out of place in the novel. It is a clear break in style. For Joyce as well as for Goethe, the technical language functions as a kind of slice of reality in the novel, which remains largely unmediated in relation to the novel's plot. This plot, developed in the pertinent chapters by highly intimate forms of human seeking and returning home, stands in clear contrast to the objective, mathematically exact numbers in the passages cited. Bloom-Ulysses, while looking for his son, returns from ill-fated journeys through Dublin to his Ithaca at Number 7 Eccles Street, accompanied by his spiritual son Stephen-Telemachus, whom he serves the ritual meal of a cup of cocoa before the destruction of the suitors and reunion with his spouse Molly-Penelope. The description of the Dublin waterworks follows the question put by the anonymous narrator, whether the water flows ("Did it flow?"), as Bloom placed the kettle on the boiler in order to heat the water for the cocoa. In the _Wanderjahre,_ the young aristocrat Lenardo, the leader of a group of emigrants en route to America, seeks the love of his youth, Nachodine, now thought to be lost. At issue is a "love arising from a troubled conscience" (book 3, chapter 14, 409). Lenardo is erotically and guiltily tied to the tenant farmer's daughter, because she and her father were dismissed and driven off the land to finance Lenardo's education abroad. Lenardo stands just before the goal of his desires. How and in which situation he ultimately relocates his lover is not related until the diary continues some forty pages later in chapter 13. Chapter 5 restricts itself to the report of Lenardo's trip to the mountain as he recruits the spinners and weavers for the American project.

Here the descriptions of spinning and weaving stand in the foreground.

In *Ulysses* and the ***Wanderjahre,*** the technical language (*Sachprosa*), which has its own verifiable precision and authenticity, functions as a fictional part of the novel. Joyce probably appropriated his text from the daily press in 1904, while Goethe got his text from the painter Heinrich Meyer, of whom Goethe requested a "continued technical description" [fortgesetzte technische Beschreibung] of the Swiss cottage industry in 1810.[16] Goethe appropriated this description almost verbatim for Lenardo's diary in the ***Wanderjahre,*** as the following comparison shows:

Heinrich Meyer:

For right-spun yarn there are 25-30 to a pound. While for left-spun, 60, 80, even 90 skeins; for [so-called] "letter yarn" 120 and even more. A loop on the winder will run about one quarter ell or slightly more, and a diligent spinner can spin 4 or even 5 skeins, that is, 5000 loops, amounting to 8 to 9000 ells of yarn a day on her wheel.[17]

Goethe:

For right-spun yarn there are 25 to 30 to a pound; while for left-spun 60 or 80, sometimes even 90. A loop on the winder will run about seven quarter ells or slightly more, and my slim, diligent spinner claimed that she spun 4 or even 5 skeins a day on her wheel, which would be 5000 loops, amounting to 8 to 9000 ells of yarn.

(book 3, chapter 5, 336)

As Goethe wrote to Meyer on 3 May 1810, he had "studied cotton well" in Meyer's "primer."[18] Similarly, it is known that Joyce had conceived the Ithaca chapter as a form of "mathematical catechism."[19]

Both Goethe and Joyce disrupt the continuity of the novel's action in order to attain a higher degree of reality. This heightened reality serves above all to confirm the given reality, be it in the city of Dublin in 1904 or in the Swiss cottage industry in 1810. Such a precise reflection of the external reality, however, does not permit the depiction of the protagonists' inner world. For Joyce the non-technical aspects of the texts are only heightened by the repeated reports of nearly scientific precision. Explanations of phenomena other than technical data prove to be impossible. The reader gets no clue what is going on inside of Bloom-Ulysses or Stephen-Telemachus. For Goethe the objective language of the passage conceals the protagonists' emotional state. This narrative strategy succeeds especially well when Lenardo actually becomes interested in spinning and weaving and when he must accomplish the emigrants' mission. His remark that "we always mirror ourselves in everything we produce" (book 3, chapter 4, 332) still creates confusion for the reader, as the continuation of his diary in chapter 13 shows. Lenardo couches

himself and his reader—in this case Wilhelm Meister—behind the technical language.

The structural differences between both passages in the ***Wanderjahre*** and *Ulysses* are a matter of degree rather than kind. For Goethe the technical language is still integrated with Lenardo's introductory remarks to the novel's plot. As first-person narrator, Lenardo reports that he took "careful notes" and that he has decided "to use the time as well as possible" so as to be introduced "into the antechamber of the art of weaving" (book 3, chapter 5, 336 and 337). For Joyce, by contrast, the anonymous narrator's mechanical questions are simply followed by the Ithaca chapter. The technical language no longer has a mimetic function but merely presents itself as is. It retains a function in the frame of the novel's disintegrated plot only by virtue of the narrator's game of question-and-answer, while the continuity of plot is maintained by the analogy to the Ulysses myth.[20] By contrast, the mythological deep structure of the ***Wanderjahre*** is only sporadically realized. By that I mean that at one level mythological figures can be perceived in some of the novel's characters: for example, in Wilhelm and his son Felix, Castor and Pollux; in Natalie, Minerva; in Hilarie, Psyche; in Flavio, Orestes; and so on.[21] This fact alone requires a greater integration of plot in Goethe's novel, since the fundamental continuity of a single, underlying myth, as in Joyce's *Ulysses,* does not exist in ***Wanderjahre.***[22]

On the whole, we may agree with Hermann Broch's hypothesis regarding Goethe's poetics of the novel in the ***Wanderjahre***: the novel is the forerunner of a technique and theory whose perfection was achieved by Joyce in *Ulysses.* In both novels motivations and explanations of occurrences in the traditional sense are abandoned. By means of various types of nonfictional prose a more complete representation of various layers of reality and perceptions within literary fiction is achieved. This gain in the levels of reality and consciousness is paid with a loss in aesthetic unity, which we may associate with Goethe's concept of renunciation (*Entsagung*).

The double title, ***Wilhelm Meisters Wanderjahre, oder Die Entsagenden*** (***Wilhelm Meister's Journeyman Years, or The Renunciants***), is a conspicuous clue to the problematic meaning of this theme in the novel. The meaning is first expressed by the characters of the novel, because the protagonists learn and teach renunciation. For Goethe the concept of renunciation (*Entsagung*) is determined philosophically, ethically, and historically but is synonymous neither with resignation nor expediency.[23] Erich Trunz and Arthur Henkel have shown that Goethe's sense of renunciation is neither stoicism nor asceticism, although perhaps they have emphasized the "happiness of renunciation" too strongly.[24] However, speaking of a Goethean "misery of renunciation" is surely an exaggeration in the opposite direction, because Goethe understands renunciation in the Hegelian sense of being historically necessary.[25] As

Helmut Brandt has shown, the term "renunciation" originated from Goethe's stay in Italy and his second decade in Weimar, which was influenced by the French Revolution. According to Brandt, the timely development of the term belongs "among the really fruitful consequences of Goethe's response to the Revolution, if not of the Revolution itself."[26] Goethe had recognized that historical development could not be halted and that it even had a certain regularity. He anticipated the development of nineteenth-century bourgeois society without ever identifying himself with it or propagandizing for it. In many respects his picture corresponded to the developing society as posited in the Hegelian design of bourgeois society in *Grundlinien der Philosophie des Rechts* (*Basics of the Philosophy of Law*) of 1821.[27] Yet it appears that Goethe's reaction to this development was ambivalent, even critical. In his fiction he tried to portray alternatives for creatively overturning this development. In the *Wanderjahre* the project of the European resettlement as well as that of the emigration to America are such alternatives, presented nevertheless with ironic distance and guarded criticism.[28]

Given the figures and episodes within the novel, a simple formula informs the term *renunciation*: it always begins as rejection and then leads ultimately to compromise, wherever possible to a gain at another level. Renunciation is especially manifest in the area of eros, where it is first determined physically by the renunciation of possession of a loved one, then by a psychic compromise that means neither resignation nor surrender but continuation and transcendence in the Goethean sense. As the titular protagonist, Wilhelm Meister is the first to undertake, by means of the vow of the wandering years, the eventual renunciation of Natalie, who had been promised as his wife at the end of the first novel, *Wilhelm Meisters Lehrjahre.* With the injunction "not to remain more than three days under the same roof" and to leave no hostel without "travelling at least one mile from the spot" (book 1, chapter 1, 101), Wilhelm travels with his son Felix through the novel's landscape. While traveling to Mignon's homeland is depicted only as a subordinate goal, the purpose of the emigration to America remains indefinite and hazy in the background until the end of the novel.

The intermediate stations of longer duration are of greater importance, for they show Felix enrolled several years in the educational institute of the Pedagogic Province and Wilhelm undergoing his own education as a surgeon. For this purpose Wilhelm is released from his journeyman's vow of not staying more than three days under the same roof, although the physical separation from his wife Natalie continues. Even at the end of the novel there is no reunion. Rather, we are told that Natalie has already gone "to sea" on her way to America with the rest of the members of the Society of the Tower (book 3, chapter 14, 401). Nevertheless, Wilhelm is emotionally that much more drawn to Natalie in their many messages and letters. Ultimately, his last letter, documenting his life's con-

fession and release from the trauma of a fisherboy's drowning, reveals a major step in his development: he now realizes that his calling is that of surgeon.[29] Natalie's remoteness allows Wilhelm to sublimate his attraction for a friend from youth, erase a guilt-ridden homoerotic development, and insure his own identity, thus forming the relationship with Natalie anew so that for the first time a feeling of pride and real worth affects him (book 2, chapter 11, 283-294).

This gain at a higher level cannot be readily equated with traditional concepts of happiness or misery, as the following story involving Lenardo, aristocrat and Wilhelm's counterfigure, proves. Lenardo likewise seems to be separated from his lover. Like Wilhelm, he is bound to a life of wandering by an ethical failing. He hopes to find his lover again and to atone for his failure. Yet Wilhelm dissuades Lenardo from this passionate seeking with the advice of renunciation, so that Lenardo does not neglect his responsibility toward "the great life-task" (book 2, chapter 6, 254), that is, the emigration to America, because of his personal desires. Rather, Lenardo is able to unite mission and longing, as is manifest from his diary, so that he again finds his lover among the spinners and weavers whom he wishes to enlist for the emigration. Based on her previous marriage and the command her father gave them both on his death bed—namely, love each other "like brother and sister" (book 3, chapter 13, 399)—"a closer tie" between Lenardo and Nachodine does not occur, although it is not completely precluded in the distant future (book 3, chapter 14, 408). As with Wilhelm and Natalie, the prospect of a reunion beyond the borders of the novel is suggested. Lenardo maintains that he felt strengthened in his project mainly by the thought of summoning his lover to come over to America, "if not fetch[ing] her himself," once he has secured a foothold over there (book 3, chapter 14, 409).

A modified example of renunciation is found in the tale entitled **"Der Mann von funfzig Jahren"** (**"The Man of Fifty Years"**). There the titular protagonist rejects, for the benefit of his son Flavio, the possession of his cherished niece Hilarie, while he wins the hand of the beautiful widow, who had earlier dismissed the son as too stormy a lover. Refusal and painful rejection ultimately lead to marriage for the "man of fifty" and the widow, as well as for Flavio and Hilarie.

Not all figures in the novel succeed at renunciation: painful rejection is observable in the cases of the deranged pilgrim woman in the tale of the same name (**"Die pilgernde Törin"**), the barber cum narrator of the Melusina fairy tale (**"Die neue Melusine"**), and Odoard. However, Odoard's unsuccessful renunciation does not disqualify him from the European resettlement project. The only figures who seem to stand outside the spell of renunciation are Felix and Hersilie. In spite of the tempestuous dissolution of their relationship at the end of the novel and although they are not spared from pain and doubt, the hope for an union without renunciation is offered by the symbol of the mysterious casket and the undamaged key, which function in the text as a semiotic sign (book 3, chapter 2, 320-211; book 3, chapter 17, 416). The key, thought-to-be broken, which is held together invisibly by magnetism, is reproduced in the text (book 3, chapter 2, 321).[30] It is designed for the initiate to unlock the secret of the casket, signifying the future of the owners. Hersilie and Felix are not ready to unlock their immediate future—Felix actually believes he has broken the key during his last encounter with Hersilie and leaves her to kill himself—but the key is magnetically joined and the lovers are bound together by the mystery of the casket (book 3, chapter 17, 415-16). Because of Hersilie's desperate warning, Wilhelm Meister is able to save his son from self-destruction in a moving scene at the end of the novel, when father and son embrace as Castor and Pollux, reborn from death.

In its general form renunciation is expressed in the epistle or so-called paper (*Blatt*), summarizing Wilhelm's admonition to Nachodine-Susanna. In it the limitation of human beings is defined in three ways: existentially, epistemologically, and ethically as well as metaphysically. This paper is of central significance for the novel and at the same time functions as a pendant to Kant's three critiques: first, every human being is "continually limited, restricted in his [or her] position"; second, he or she "generally does not achieve clarity"; and third, he or she is referred to a "direct attention to the task of the day" to gain "a proper attitude toward the Sublime" (book 3, chapter 13, 393-94). Thus, renunciation is proscribed in the *Wanderjahre* in the sense of Kant's *Kritik der praktischen Vernunft* (*Critique of Practical Reason*).[31]

Much more important, if not as obvious, is renunciation as it is expressed in the novel's narrative technique and narrative theory. It first results from the changing narrative situation. The omniscient auctorial narrator of *Wilhelm Meisters Lehrjahre* is replaced by a fictitious editor in the *Wanderjahre.* Thus, the novel of education, or Bildungsroman—if, for heuristic reasons, one may satisfactorily use this term here—is superseded by the "archival novel."[32] Erich Trunz's earlier interpretive model of frame story and novellas as in *A Thousand and One Nights,* which Goethe greatly admired, does not do justice to the structure of the *Wanderjahre* in the same way as Volker Neuhaus's more recent model of the "archival novel."[33] Goethe's arrangement of single narratives within the frame story can be much more adequately explained by the model of the archival novel. As Neuhaus has shown, approximately twenty fictitious persons provide collected narratives, reports, drawings, diaries, letters and speeches for Makarie's archives and for the emigrants' archives. In addition, there are aphorisms from the collections **"Reflections in the Spirit of the Wanderers"** (294-312) and **"From Makarie's Archives"** (417-36), as well as from the philosophical instructional poems **"Vermächtnis"**

("Testament") and **"Im ernsten Beinhaus wars"** ("There was in the solemn burial vault"), also known as **"Lines Written upon the Contemplation of Schiller's Skull."**[34] The fictional editor includes these texts for the purpose of producing the fiction of the novel, because it is *about* a novel, as the editor explicitly assures his readers: "Our friends have taken a *novel* into their hands" (I 10, 176; emphasis mine). As Klaus Detlef Müller has indicated, the fictitious editor of the *Wanderjahre* stands in contrast to the eighteenth-century novel, in which the fictitious editor was intended as the verification of the "truth" of fiction, as, for example, in Wieland's *History of Agathon* or in the *Sorrows of Young Werther.* In the *Wanderjahre,* on the other hand, the editor is assigned the task of producing and preserving the fiction of the novel. Therefore, the editor in fact has no auctorial responsibility, but rather an editorial responsibility for the narrative ordering and sorting of isolated texts.[35]

The problem of the *Wanderjahre* is that the fiction of the editor, though tangible throughout, can be recognized as an edition only relatively late. Only at the end of the first book—page 118 of the Hamburg edition, page 176 of the English translation—does the first clearly editorial comment appear. Earlier interventions and commentaries go back to the traditional figure of an auctorial narrator. By contrast, the fictive editor in Goethe's *Werther* [*The Sorrows of Young Werther*] (1774) is introduced immediately in the foreword. For the first ten chapters of the *Wanderjahre,* the fiction of the editor is observable only in retrospect. This rejection of an immediately recognizable narrative structure informs the poetics of renunciation.

But as soon as the editor of the *Wanderjahre* intervenes for the first time, his responsibility is unmistakable. For example, he intervenes in order to spare the reader the reading of an oral report on mathematics at Makarie's and to reestablish the suspense of literary fiction. "We intend to have the papers at our disposal printed elsewhere," the editor explains, suggesting that on this occasion we "shall proceed with our history without further ado, since we ourselves are impatient to see the riddle before us finally explained" (book 1, chapter 10, 176). With the introduction of the narrative **"The Man of Fifty Years,"** editorial reasons are cited for "an uninterrupted presentation" instead of "a number of installments," although the story is not presented without interruption (book 2, chapter 3, 212). The duration of narrated time between Wilhelm's first and second visits to the Pedagogic Province is demarcated by an editorial "interpolation" that indicates "to the reader an intermission, and indeed one of several years," for which reason the editor would have liked "to end the volume here, had that been compatible with typographic conventions" [mit der typographischen Einrichtung] (book 2, chapter 7, 266-67). During the discussion of the dangers of the theater for the pupils of the Pedagogic Province, the editor intermediates, confessing "that he has allowed this odd passage to slip by with some reluctance."

Without addressing the time of narration in a longer discussion, the editor points to the continuation of literary fiction: "We have no time to dwell on such painful memories and afterthoughts, for our friend [Wilhelm Meister] is agreeably surprised to see one of the Three [supervisors of the Pedagogic Province] coming toward him" (book 2, chapter 8, 277). In spite of these editorial interruptions, the tension of literary fiction remains intact as the degree of reality in the fiction of the editor increases.

The editorial collation of texts, too, is unrecognizable at first reading. The prelude of the *Wanderjahre* under the titles **"The Flight into Egypt," "Saint Joseph the Second," "The Visitation"** and **"The Lily Stalk"** can be seen only in retrospect as a fictional transmission of Wilhelm's diary from the first-person narrative to an impersonal, third-person mode of narration. The reader learns only indirectly of the transposition of the text, with the insertion of Wilhelm's letters to Natalie in the introductory chapters.[36] During Odoard's narrative **"Nicht zu weit" ("Not Too Far")**, which is made available in a transcript by a stranger, the editorial intervention is more obvious, since the editor expressly states that he has "usurped the rights of the epic poet" to transform the text into a "passionate recital" (book 3, chapter 10, 371).

Two of the most important texts in the *Wanderjahre,* the American utopia (book 3, chapter 11, 378-80) and the "ethereal fiction" of Makarie's position in the solar system (book 3, chapter 15, 409-11), assume their full meaning only by way of editorial remarks. The editor apologizes for submitting the American utopia simply as the "quintessence" of a conversation between Wilhelm Meister and Friedrich. The brief document, however, is announced as "a rich text with limitless application" (book 3, chapter 11, 378), whereby the terse account of institutional anti-Semitism, as well as the twenty-four-hour police surveillance and the criminal justice of deportation and confiscation of property, is recommended for careful consideration by the reader. These statements are alarming in their implications for the controls over social, economic, and political life. Granted, the "merry Friedrich" cannot be regarded as a reliable informant, yet his account of the American utopia gives cause for deep concern about this future society.[37]

Makarie's "ethereal fiction" is presented by the editor as "a page from our archives," which cannot be regarded as entirely authentic, since it is "written from memory, long after its contents were communicated" (book 3, chapter 14, 409). The character of Makarie is one of the boldest fictions of the novel. She is a modern type of saint, representing cosmic love.[38] On the one hand, she appears as a good old aunt and "family confessor" in a wheelchair; on the other hand, as an entelechy on a planetal orbit, extending past the limits of the solar system. On the basis of astronomic computations it is concluded "that she had long since passed beyond the orbit of Mars and was nearing the orbit of Jupiter." Nevertheless, the hope is expressed that she will long to return, "in order to exercise her influence upon earthly life again, to the benefit" of those who seek her assistance. Even the anonymous author of this text voices some reservations about this figure (book 3, chapter 15, 411). By admitting to the utter fictitiousness of the text as a fairy tale, "suitable perhaps for a novel," the author is able to maintain its value as a "metaphor for the highest good" (book 3, chapter 14, 407). The contrasting of the sidereal saint with the good old aunt produces an ideal image that does not require a proof of truth.[39]

Near the end of the novel editorial interventions proliferate. The farce **"Die gefährliche Wette" ("The Perilous Wager")** is inserted because the editor fears that "we are unlikely to find room further on for irregularities of this sort" (book 3, chapter 8, 360). The novel's conclusion presents special problems for the editor, since "here the task of communicating, portraying, amplifying, and pulling together becomes ever more difficult." He decides on a form of simultaneous representation in order to summarize what "we knew or had learned of at that time, as well as of what we were later informed, and in this spirit to bring the solemn business we have undertaken, of being a faithful chronicler, to a fitting conclusion" (book 2, chapter 14, 400-01). He fulfills his task by editing the impersonal narration of Felix's salvation by his father, as well as by providing the aphorisms from Makarie's archives.

The fiction of the editor represents an important part of the poetics of renunciation. A realistic structure of sorting and combining the isolated passages is established after aesthetic integration has been rejected. Goethe had originally conceived the *Wanderjahre* as a frame story with inserted narratives, as his letter of 27-28 May 1798 to his publisher Johann Friedrich Cotta indicates.[40] For this purpose he had studied around 1807 narrative techniques in larger frame stories such as Boccaccio's *Decamerone,* the *Heptameron* of Margarete von Navarra, the *Cent nouvelles* of Antoine de la Sale, *A Thousand and One Nights,* as well as his own **Unterhaltungen deutscher Ausgewanderten (Conversations of German Refugees)**. At the same time, he began to publish in Cotta's *Taschenbuch für Damen* single narratives later used in the *Wanderjahre.*[41] But as early as 1821 he had abandoned the traditional model of a frame story with the publication of the first version of the *Wanderjahre,* as the fiction of the archive took its place. In the final version of 1829 the fiction of the archive was not strengthened but rather concealed, as can be seen by the deletion of several of the editor's mediating texts in the second version of 1829.[42]

However, the editor's technique represents only a part of the fiction of the archive. Based on the rejection of narrative integration and auctorial judgment, the other part of creating the fiction is assigned to the implied reader.[43] The fiction of the archive requires the reader's active participation. The demands placed on the reader's power of imagination in the ***Wanderjahre*** go far beyond the norms of the eighteenth-century art of narration and depict the other important point of the poetics of renunciation. Hans R. Vaget has wittily called the novel an exercise in reading.[44] Instead of being provided with signals for interpretation, readers are left to their own resources. They are forced to approach the text of the novel in the same way they empirically experience reality. The various types of text passages confront the readers with facts and processes of consciousness which they must assess to understand the novel. What Wolfgang Iser has said with regard to the means of interpreting literature applies to the reader of the *Wanderjahre*:

> The reader is meant to become aware of the nature of his or her faculties of perception, of his or her own tendency to link things together in consistent patterns, and even the whole thought process that constitutes his or her relations with the external world.[45]

The condition for this is posited in the ***Wanderjahre*** insofar as the novel no longer confines itself to telling a story but represents various types and levels of reality and of reflections of consciousness produced by the fiction of the archive. Thus the reader's expectations, formed by the auctorial novel of the eighteenth century, are disappointed and confused. The disparity of archival texts compels the reader to establish connections between perception and thought which, based on the complicated transmission of various types of text, require constant revision.

The reader's irritation begins with the novel's prelude. To one's consternation, one learns only from Wilhelm's second letter that the impersonally narrated story **"Saint Joseph the Second"** was written down by Wilhelm for Natalie and changed here and there by the anonymous editor for inclusion in the archive (book 1, chapter 3, 112). Thus the reader must consider layers of narrative perspective, emphasized by the double revision of the original first-person narrative of Saint Joseph the Second, without ever receiving reliable information with respect to the transmission of the text. This irritation continues with the secretive allusion to Wilhelm's fetish, "something that looked half like a wallet, half like a set of instruments," in conversation with Jarno-Montan (book 1, chapter 4, 120). Only nineteen chapters later does it become clear to the reader that it involves the surgeon's instruments in ***Wilhelm Meisters Lehrjahre,*** which Wilhelm had acquired as a memento and used now to justify his "true vocation" (book 2, chapter 11, 292). The reading of interrupted and isolated pieces of narrative and making the connection between the childhood experience of the fisherboy's drowning and the trivial objects of the surgeon's instruments reflect the process of analyzing a repressed trauma.[46] Another example is the mysterious casket with its magnetic key, which has the function of mediating the development of the relationship between Felix and Hersilie. Since the content of the box remains a secret, the

reader's imagination is provoked to speculate.[47] Numerous examples of things that irritate readers may be given, such as the overlapping of narrative perspectives and levels of reception, or the transcendence of linear narration and the withholding of information.[48]

The balance of reading freedom and reading control belongs to the traditional expectation of reading. While the effort to strike this traditional balance is unmistakable within the editorial comments regarding the American utopia and Makarie's fairy tale, reading freedom is increased in both collections of aphorisms. Here in the truest sense of the word one deals with texts with "limitless applications" (book 3, chapter 11, 378). The linear process of reading a novel is disrupted or abandoned via the discontinuity in reading the aphorisms, as in the **"Reflections in the Spirit of the Wanderers"** as well as in the aphorisms **"From Makarie's Archives."** The aphorisms require from the reader the ability to participate in the jump of thoughts in content and arrangement. While the rest of the texts in the novel remain bound to the ongoing plot despite the simultaneity of the archival fiction, the collections of aphorisms are presented as "coexisting compositions" in the novel's plot, in contrast to Lessing's definition of poetry in *Laokoon*.[49] In the tradition of the gnomic verses of classical antiquity, the reader is provided with psychological experiences, rules to life, as well as scientific, aesthetic, and philosophical information for infinite speculation and combination within the novel's action. Several aphorisms agree almost exactly with words in the novel's plot (book 2, chapter 9, 280 and 312; book 2, chapter 9, 260 and 429).[50] Here we find a peak in the poetics of renunciation. The raw material of the archive depicts a maximum of narrative disintegration. Yet with this rejection of narrative integration, a gain is again to be had: in this case, a maximum of reading freedom, namely "sagacity and penetration," so admired in the Irish novelist Laurence Sterne. "His sagacity and penetration are boundless," as it is quoted in an aphorism from **"Makarie's Archives"** (434). In this sense, perhaps the novel's last sentence, "Ist fortzusetzen" ("To be continued"), refers to the maximal liberation of the reader from the text.[51]

Goethe was quite conscious of the uniqueness of his work, as can be seen from remarks to his real readers. To Josef Stanislaus Zauper, a professor of rhetoric, he wrote on 17 September 1821,

> Coherence, aim and purpose lie within the little book itself; if it is not of One piece, then it is still of One meaning, and this was precisely the task: to bring strange external events together so that the reader may feel that they belong together.[52]

In a letter from 28 July 1829 Goethe explained to Johann Friedrich Rochlitz, a writer himself and music critic in Leipzig,

> A work like this one, which proclaims itself a whole by seeming to be in a certain sense only put together for the

purpose of linking disparate entities, permits and even demands more than another work, that each reader appropriates the work as he or she sees fit.[53]

And in a letter of 23 November 1829, following the same idea, Goethe wrote again to Rochlitz,

> Such a little book is like life itself: located in the complex of the whole are necessity and chance, preordination and adherence, now successful, now futile, through which it achieves a type of infinity that does not completely allow itself to be summarized in understandable and reasonable words.[54]

In conversation with Chancellor von Müller on 18 February 1830 Goethe characterized the form of the *Wanderjahre* as a "mere aggregate."[55] Goethe was especially conscious of the demands on the reader. Even in the *Lehrjahre* [*Wilhelm Meisters Lehrjahre*] he had indicated in a letter to Schiller of 26 June 1796 that the reader had "to supply something according to his or her intention." These demands increased considerably in the *Wanderjahre.* Goethe knew well that much would remain puzzling for readers, yet he hoped that "the genuine reader will again sense and think through everything."[56] He wrote to a reader in Berlin, expressing the hope that the *Wanderjahre* "provided much to mull over."[57] In response to the positive critique of his young friend Sulpiz Boisserée, a writer and collector of medieval art, Goethe answered with the following reference to form and effect:

> The serious and careful efforts will not remain hidden to the intelligent reader whereby I attempted this second experiment (*Versuch*) to unite, manipulate, and modulate such disparate elements, and I have to be happy when such a risky undertaking appears fairly successful to you.[58]

These letters provide the biographical argument for the complex poetics of the *Wanderjahre.* They show that Goethe had conceived that changing relationship of structure and reception which would grant the implied reader a maximum of freedom with the reduction of the form of the novel to an "aggregate." In the open form of the *Wanderjahre* the implied reader was given the opportunity to realize a total and, at the same time, individually conceived fictitious world.

This form corresponds to the concept of totality in Hegel's *Aesthetics.* There this concept serves first to characterize epic poetry, which is defined as "unified totality" (*einheitsvolle Totalität*). Then the term is applied to the novel as "modern bourgeois epic." With respect to the form of representation, it is also said that "the true novel, like the epic, requires totality as the basis of its view of the world and life, whose manifold materials and forms appear within the individual event, which supplies the focal center for the entire complex."[59] Goethe may have heard of Hegel's lectures on aesthetics or philosophy of art, but he did not read the *Aesthetics,* since it did not appear until 1835. On the other hand, the *Aesthetics* displays enough

examples to prove that Hegel was quite familiar with Goethe's work and that he developed his theory of the novel based on the model of *Wilhelm Meisters Lehrjahre.*

Goethe's thought in old age exhibits an affinity with Hegel's philosophy. His concept of totality is thoroughly grounded in the Hegelian sense, and in fact Goethe and Hegel corresponded.[60] Their most important meetings took place during the second working period of the *Wanderjahre* between 1821 and 1829. After Goethe's death an unopened copy of *Phänomenologie des Geistes* (*The Phenomenology of the Mind*) was found in his library. In 1821 Goethe sent Hegel a dedication with the words, "The primary phenomenon (*Urphänomen*) recommends itself most graciously for friendly reception by the absolute." Later Goethe declared that he agreed with Hegel's basic thought and sensibility and that "one could quite well approach and join each other in the mutual development and exchange of ideas."[61]

To Hegel the problem of the novel involved the "*original poetic condition of the world,*" out of which the epic originated. This "poetic condition of the world," however, is no longer present in modern times: "The novel in the modern sense presupposes a basis of reality already organized in its *prosaic* form." In the modern novel, therefore, poetry reclaims its lost right on the basis of prosaic conditions.[62] Nobody recognized this dilemma better than Goethe, who pointed out a solution with the example of technical prose from the *Wanderjahre,* as Hegel had described in the *Aesthetics.* Hegel stated, "One of the most common, and for the novel most fitting, collisions is therefore the conflict between poetry of the heart and the contrasting prose of external conditions antagonistic to it."[63] Exactly this was at hand when Goethe asked his friend Heinrich Meyer for the "technical description" of the Swiss cottage industry. He endeavored "to craft a lengthy realistic yarn into a poetic web." The weaving process is used as a metaphor for literary production. Still, Goethe was concerned whether "this interweaving of strictly dry technical matters and aesthetic and sentimental events could bring about a good effect."[64] According to Hegel, this conflict between technical factual prose and poetry of the heart is resolved.

> On the one hand, the characters who in the first instance contend with the ordinary course of life learn to recognize the genuine and substantial in the usual world order, coming to terms with their conditions and ready to cooperate with them; on the other hand, however, they strip off the prosaic aspect of all that they do and accomplish and thereby replace the prose with a reality allied and congenial to beauty and art which they have found there.[65]

These words can be read as an abstract explanation of Lenardo's and Nachodine-Susanna's individual fate. The prose of conditions is allowed to enter into the fiction of the novel with Susanna's concern about the dangers of the "increasing dominance of machine production." This passage holds an important aspect of totality in the ***Wanderjahre***: the impoverishment among spinners and weavers as a result of the industrial revolution is included in the novel. Goethe became familiar with this problem during his first decade in Weimar. Among his official duties was the supervision of the stocking manufacturers in Apolda. The manufacturing, which was based on the cottage industry, had been exposed to fluctuations in cotton prices and, therefore, tended to exploit the workers. In his diary Goethe noted in March 1779 that one hundred looms were not operating and that the people lived "from hand to mouth." Because of competition by the mechanized English textile industry, the situation became completely untenable. Uprisings among the weavers had to be suppressed with the help of the military in 1784 and 1797.[66]

While Goethe excluded the hungry "stocking weavers from Apolda" from the text of his drama ***Iphigenie auf Tauris*** (in order to, as he said, let the king of Tauris speak), the impoverishment of the Swiss spinners and weavers is taken up in the text of the ***Wanderjahre.*** The novel's totality is manifested in the fact that the novel is open to everyday reality. The artwork's totality in Goethe's post-Classical period, always consciously directed at recording and shedding light on the tendencies of the age, superseded the closed form of the Classical work of art, which always represents a loss of reality. We can recognize other problems in Goethe's achievement of the ***Wanderjahre***: problems having to do with bourgeois society, work, education, humanity and Christianity.[67]

The integration of events into the plot through the various documents of the archival novel clearly shows one of the problems Goethe had in mind when he wrote ***Wanderjahre,*** namely, the relationship between man as a private individual and as a member of society. This dualistic aspect has been the "fundamental problem of all modern theories of the state and society," as Karl Löwith has pointed out (232). For Rousseau this relationship was incongruous, true harmony between the private individual (*homme*) and the citizen (*citoyen*) being impossible. Goethe, on the other hand, tried to overcome this incompatibility in ***Wanderjahre*** through renunciation, thus establishing a balance between the two basic aspects of human existence in modern society. The function of society, as presented in one document by the collector and arranger of the papers in ***Wanderjahre,*** is "to maintain uniformity in the most important matters, and to let everyone have his own will in less crucial ones" (book 3, chapter 11, 380). This train of thought parallels that of Hegel, who in his *Grundlinien der Philosophie des Rechts* (*Basics of the Philosophy of Law*) of 1821 similarly tried to reconcile the principles of individuality and commonweal in his design of the modern state. Admittedly, some of Hegel's ideas are not devoid of authoritarianism. But then, the document about the American utopia in Goethe's ***Wanderjahre*** contains unmistakable characteristics of a police state. The utopia is described as consisting of people who "concern themselves not with justice but rather with police powers. ... Anyone who proves a nuisance shall be removed" (book 3, chapter 11, 379).

Other problems, discussed in various documents of ***Wanderjahre,*** concern work and education. Both, according to Karl Löwith, "become the substance of the life of bourgeois society" in the nineteenth century (260). The dangers of industrialization and the threat of unemployment are discussed in detail. Lenardo records the following statement by a manufacturer of linen goods in his diary:

> But what weighs on my mind is an economic problem, unfortunately not of concern for the moment, no, for the entire future. The increasing dominance of machine production torments and frightens me: it is rolling on like a thunderstorm, slowly, slowly; but it is headed this way, and it will arrive and strike. ... People think about it, people talk about it, and neither thinking nor talking can help. And who likes to picture such calamities!

> (book 3, chapter 13, 396)

The alternatives offered to industrialization are resettlement in Europe or emigration to America. In a speech before the emigrants their leader explains that people used to believe in "the high value of land ownership (*Grundbesitz*) and [made] us regard it as the first and best asset man can acquire." But this concept is replaced by the idea of work and achievement when the following statement is added: "Even though a man's property is of great worth, even greater worth must be ascribed to his deeds and achievements" (book 3, chapter 9, 364).

Education in ***Wanderjahre*** is related to work. In various conversations, documents and letters, the figures of the novel and hence the readers are urged to acquire a useful skill that can be applied for the common good. As Wilhelm reports in a letter to Natalie, he is told in no uncertain terms that "the day for specialization" has come: "Fortunate is he who comprehends this and labors in this spirit for himself and others. ... To restrict oneself to one craft is the best thing" (book 1, chapter 4, 118). Therefore, Wilhelm becomes a surgeon, a profession which at that time was still considered a craft. Liberal education is renounced in favor of specialization, which foreshadows the division of labor in industrial production.

Nineteenth-century criticism of religion, specifically of Christianity, is reflected in various documents of ***Wanderjahre.*** Religion is transformed into a kind of "secular piety" (*Weltfrömmigkeit*), as it is called in a letter of the abbé (book 2, chapter 7, 266). In the Pedagogic Province, attitudes of "reverence" (*Ehrfurcht*) are taught. Three types of religion are acknowledged: an ethnic religion based on reverence for what is above man; a philosophical religion, which is based on reverence for that which is equal to man; and the Christian religion, which is founded on reverence of that which is below man (book 2, chapter 1, 202-5). However, Christ's sufferings and death, the central component of Christianity, are withheld from the sight of the students of the Pedagogic Province, being hidden by a veil (book 2, chapter 2, 210). On the frescoes of the inner sanctum of the Pedagogic Province, Christ appears as "a true philosopher ... as a sage in the highest sense" (book 2, chapter 2, 209). Thus, Christianity becomes secularized and is transcended by philosophy, as in Hegel's writings, where religion, in fact, becomes the highest form of philosophy (Löwith 324-29).

All these problems, as they are presented by the fictional editor of the papers of the novel's archives, testify to the "advanced reality" of the *Wanderjahre.* The novel becomes a true representative of the tendencies affecting its century. With Goethe's striving for totality in thematics, structure, and reception, the *Wanderjahre* approaches the twentieth century to the extent that Hermann Broch was able to see this novel realize the demand expressed by him in his essay on "James Joyce and the Present": "to raise the poetic to the level of knowledge (*Erkenntnis*)."[68]

Notes

1. Hermann Broch, "James Joyce und die Gegenwart," in *Schriften zur Literatur 1: Kritik,* vol. 9/1 of the Kommentierte Werkausgabe, ed. Paul Michael Lützeler (Frankfurt am Main: Suhrkamp, 1975), 63-91. On Joyce's influence on Broch, see Heinz Politzer, "Zur Feier meines Ablebens," *Der Monat* 3, no. 36 (1951): 630-32; and Breon Mitchell, *James Joyce and the German Novel, 1922-1933* (Athens: Ohio UP, 1976), 151-74.

2. Broch 64ff., as well as Georg Wilhelm Friedrich Hegel, "Die Poesie," Part 3 of *Vorlesungen über die Ästhetik,* ed. Rüdiger Bubner (Stuttgart: Reclam, 1971), 158-78.

3. Broch, 87.

4. Broch, 66.

5. Johann Wolfgang Goethe, *Wilhelm Meister's Apprenticeship,* ed. and trans. by Eric A. Blackall in cooperation with Victor Lange, vol. 9 of *Goethe's Collected Works* (New York: Suhrkamp, 1989).

6. Broch, 77ff.

7. Hans R. Vaget, "Liebe und Grundeigentum in *Wilhelm Meisters Lehrjahren*: Zur Physiognomie des Adels bei Goethe," in *Legitimationskrisen des deutschen Adels, 1200-1900,* ed. Peter Uwe Hohendahl and Paul Michael Lützeler (Stuttgart: Metzler, 1979), 137-57; and Karl-Heinz Hahn, "Zeitgeschichte in Goethes Roman *Wilhelm Meisters Lehrjahre,*" in *Deutsche Klassik und Revolution,* ed. Paolo Chiarini and Walter Dietze (Rome: Ateneo, 1981), 169-94.

8. Hans Rudolf Vaget, "Johann Wolfgang Goethe: *Wilhelm Meisters Wanderjahre* (1829)," in *Romane und Erzählungen zwischen Romantik und Realismus: Neue Interpretationen,* ed. Paul Michael Lützeler (Stuttgart: Reclam, 1983), 136-42.

9. Klaus F. Gille, *Wilhelm Meister im Urteil der Zeitgenossen: Ein Beitrag zur Wirkungsgeschichte* (Assen: van Gorkum, 1971), 306-12.

10. This is a translation of Broch's term *Goethesche Skepsis,* referring to Goethe's rejection of pat answers of dogmatic theology and the traditional sciences to the problems of his time. Goethe favored skepticism as an approach over dogmatism in his scientific studies and writings.

11. Broch, 87.

12. Joseph Strelka, "Goethes *Wilhelm Meister* und der Roman des 20. Jahrhunderts," *German Quarterly* 41 (1968): 338-55; Heidi Gideon, *Zur Darstellungsweise von Goethes* Wilhelm Meisters Wanderjahre (Göttingen: Vandenhoeck & Ruprecht, 1969), 138-40; Ehrhard Bahr, "Goethe's *Wanderjahre* as an Experimental Novel," *Mosaic* 5, no. 3 (1972): 61-71; Bahr, "Realismus und Totalität: *Wilhelm Meisters Wanderjahre* als Roman des 19. Jahrhunderts," in *Formen realistischer Erzählkunst: Festschrift für Charlotte Jolles in Honour of Her 70th Birthday,* ed. Jörg Thunecke (Nottingham: Sherwood Press, 1979), 88-92; and Bahr, "Revolutionary Realism in Goethe's *Wanderjahre,*" in *Goethe's Narrative Fiction: The Irvine Symposium,* ed. William J. Lillyman (Berlin and New York: de Gruyter, 1983), 161-75.

13. Broch, 88.

14. *Wilhelm Meisters Wanderjahre* is hereafter cited parenthetically in the text by book and chapter and by the page numbers of the English translation by Krishna Winston, edited by Jane K. Brown, and published under the title *Wilhelm Meister's Journeyman Years or The Renunciants,* vol. 10 of *Goethe's Collected Works* (New York: Suhrkamp Publishers, 1989), 93-436.

15. The Joyce quotation is taken from *Ulysses* (New York: Modern Library, 1934), 655.

16. *Goethes Werke*: Hamburger Ausgabe, ed. Erich Trunz, 10th ed. (Munich: Beck, 1981), 8:520. Hereafter cited as HA.

17. *Werke,* Weimar edition, Part. 1, vol. 25/2 (Weimar: Böhlau, 1905), 264.

18. HA 8:520.

19. On the genesis of the Ithaca chapter, see Phillip F. Herring, "Zur Textgenese des *Ulysses*: Joyces Notizen und seine Arbeitsmethoden," in *James Joyces*

Ulysses: Neuere deutsche Aufsätze, ed. Therese Fischer Seidel (Frankfurt am Main: Suhrkamp, 1977), 80-104, especially 98-100; Wolfgang Iser, "Der Archetyp als Leerform: Erzählmodalitäten und Kommunikation in Joyces *Ulysses,"* in *Der implizite Leser* (Munich: Fink, 1972), 300-58; R. M. Adams, *Surface and Symbol: The Consistency of James Joyce's* Ulysses (Oxford and New York: Oxford UP, 1962); and Stuart Gilbert, *James Joyce's* Ulysses: *A Study* (New York: Vintage Books, 1955), 369-84.

20. Iser, 300-306.

21. Hannelore Schlaffer, *Wilhelm Meister: Das Ende der Kunst und die Wiederkehr des Mythos* (Stuttgart: Metzler, 1980), 166-74. See also review in *Goethe Yearbook* 2 (1984): 244ff.

22. Klaus Detlef Müller, "Lenardos Tagebuch: Zum Romanbegriff in Goethes *Wilhelm Meisters Wanderjahre,"* *Deutsche Vierteljahrsschrift für Literaturwissenschaft und Geistesgeschichte* 53 (1979): 275-99. Müller correctly objects to understanding Goethe's procedure as an "anticipation of modern montage technique." On the problem of mythological continuity in the modern novel, see Gregory L. Lucente, *The Narrative of Realism and Myth: Venga, Lawrence, Faulkner, Pavese* (Baltimore: Johns Hopkins UP, 1979).

23. Melitta Gerhard, "Ursache und Bedeutung von Goethes Entsagung," *Jahrbuch des Freien Deutschen Hochstifts* (1981): 110-15.

24. HA 8:536-38; Arthur Henkel, *Entsagung: Eine Studie zu Goethes Altersroman,* 2d ed. (Tübingen: Niemeyer, 1962), 142-68.

25. Thomas Degering, *Das Elend der Entsagung: Goethes* Wilhelm Meisters Wanderjahre (Bonn: Bouvier, 1982). See also the review in *Germanistik* 23 (1982): 803.

26. Helmut Brandt, "Entsagung und Französische Revolution: Goethes Prokurator- und Ferdinand-Novelle in weiterführender Betrachtung," in *Deutsche Klassik und Revolution,* ed. Paolo Chiarini and Walter Dietze (Rome: Ateneo, 1981), 198.

27. Georg Wilhelm Friedrich Hegel, *Grundlinien der Philosophie des Rechts oder Naturrecht und Staatswissenschaft im Grundrisse,* ed. Bernhard Lakebrink (Stuttgart: Reclam, 1970), 327-86; Degering, 61-105.

28. Ehrhard Bahr, *Die Ironie im Spätwerk Goethes: Diese sehr ernsten Scherze: Studien zum West-östlichen Divan, zu den* Wanderjahren *und zu* Faust II (Berlin: Erich Schmidt, 1972), 116 and 127ff. On the question of utopia, see Wilhelm Voßkamp, "Uto-pie und Utopiekritik in Goethes Romanen *Wilhelm Meisters Lehrjahre* und *Wilhelm Meisters Wanderjahre,"* in *Utopieforschung: Interdisziplinäre Studien zur neuzeitlichen Utopie,* ed. Wilhelm Voßkamp (Stuttgart: Metzler, 1983), 3:227-49.

29. Vaget, 155-57; K. R. Eissler, *Goethe: A Psychoanalytical Study, 1775-1786* (Detroit: Wayne State UP, 1963), 2:1448-57; H. M. Waidson, "Death by Water: or, the Childhood of Wilhelm Meister," *Modern Language Review* 56 (1961): 44-53.

30. Grete Ruthenberg, "Der Schlüssel in *Wilhelm Meisters Wanderjahre,"* *Erziehungskunst* 25 (1961): 370-73; A. G. Steer, *Goethe's Science in the Structure of* Wanderjahre (Athens: U of Georgia P, 1979), 126-40.

31. Bernd Peschken, "Das 'Blatt' in den *Wanderjahren,"* *Goethe* 27 (1965): 205-30; Peschken, *Entsagung in* Wilhelm Meisters Wanderjahren (Bonn: Bouvier, 1968), 67ff. and 282-83.

32. Since studies by Kurt May (1957) and Hans Eichner (1966) the debate about the *Bildungsroman* has been enlivened by the monographs of Monika Schrader (1975), Martin Swales (1978), Michael Beddow (1982), Ivar Sagmo (1982), and Klaus-Dieter Sorg (1983). For a brief survey, see Rolf Selbmann, *Der deutsche Bildungsroman* (Stuttgart: Metzler, 1984); Jürgen Jacobs and Markus Krause (eds.), *Der deutsche Bildungsroman: Gattungsgeschichte vom 18. bis zum 20. Jahrhundert* (Munich: Beck, 1989). For a contrastive view, cf. Jeffrey L. Sammons, "The Mystery of the Missing *Bildungsroman,* or What Happened to Wilhelm Meister's Legacy?," *Genre* 14 (1981): 229-46. Norbert Ratz has introduced the term *novel of identity* in his *Der Identitätsroman: Eine Strukturanalyse* (Tübingen: Niemeyer, 1988).

33. Volker Neuhaus, "Die Archivfiktion in *Wilhelm Meisters Wanderjahren,"* *Euphorion* 62 (1968): 12-27. Erich Trunz has stayed with the model of the frame story also in his tenth edition (HA 8: 527-32). By contrast, Eric A. Blackall has appropriated the model of the "archival novel" for his chapter on the *Wanderjahre* (*Goethe and the Novel* [Ithaca and London: Cornell UP, 1976], 224-35).

34. See "Prefatory Note" in *Wilhelm Meister's Journeyman Years,* vol. 10 of *Goethe's Collected Works,* page v, and Johann Wolfgang Goethe, *Selected Poems,* vol. 1 of *Goethe's Collected Works,* ed. Christopher Middleton (Boston: Suhrkamp, 1983), 256-59, 266-69. The English translation of *Wanderjahre,* vol. 10 of *Goethe's Collected Works,* translated by Krishna Winston, follows the example of the so-called Hamburger Ausgabe (HA) and does not print these two poems, which were included as part

of the novel in the original edition of 1829 (*Vollständige Ausgabe letzter Hand,* vols. 21-23 [Stuttgart and Tübingen: Cotta, 1829]). The Reclam edition of *Wanderjahre* (Stuttgart, 1982) follows the original edition in printing the poems: the first at the end of "Reflections in the Spirit of the Wanderers," and the second at the end of "From Makarie's Archives." The novel is concluded with the sentence "Ist fortzusetzen" ("To be continued") which is also missing from the Hamburg edition as well as from the English translation.

35. Müller, 280ff.

36. Vaget, 145; Neuhaus, 18-21.

37. Degering, 1-11; Gert Mattenklott, "Der späte Goethe," in *Vormärz: Biedermeier, Junges Deutschland, Demokraten,* vol. 6 of *Deutsche Literatur: Eine Sozialgeschichte,* ed. Horst Albert Glaser (Reinbek: Rowohlt, 1980), 296; Heinz Schlaffer, "Exoterik und Esoterik in Goethes Romanen," *Goethe Jahrbuch* 95 (1978): 224ff. Hans R. Vaget compares the *Wanderjahre* in mood to Franz Schubert's *Winterreise* (157).

38. For Eric A. Blackall, Makarie represents "the highest form of order presented in this novel" by virtue of the fact that she "both mirrors and figures in the cosmos" (*Goethe and the Novel,* 242). See also Clark S. Muenzer, *Figures of Identity: Goethe's Novels and the Enigmatic Self* (University Park and London: Pennsylvania State UP, 1984), 120-23.

39. Bahr, *Die Ironie im Spätwerk Goethes,* 127ff.

40. "Letters of a traveler and his pupil, under romantic [i.e., fictitious] conditions, next to Wilhelm Meister." Attached to a letter to Cotta on 27-28 May 1798, *Goethe and Cotta: Briefwechsel 1797-1832,* ed. Dorothea Kuhn, 3 vols. (Stuttgart: Cotta, 1980), 1:23.

41. Bahr, *Die Ironie im Spätwerk Goethes,* 101ff.; Katharina Mommsen, *Goethe und 1001 Nacht* (Berlin: Akademie-Verlag, 1960), 118-21.

42. See the *Wanderjahre* in Reclams Universal-Bibliothek, ed. Ehrhard Bahr (Stuttgart: Reclam, 1982), 205-8.

43. According to Wolfgang Iser, at issue here is not a typology of possible or fictitious readers, but the "text's strategies for the process of reading" (*Der implizite Leser,* 9). On the reader in the *Wanderjahre,* see Manfred Karnick, *Wilhelm Meisters Wanderjahre oder die Kunst des Mittelbaren* (Munich: Fink, 1968), 186-91; and Bahr, "Goethe's *Wanderjahre* as an Experimental Novel," 66-67. The author is indebted to Benjamin Bennett, who was the first to

apply convincingly Iser's theory to the *Wanderjahre* in a lecture at the MLA Convention in 1982.

44. Vaget, 142.

45. Iser, 10.

46. Eissler, 2:1448-57.

47. The function of the mysterious casket or little box as a Goethean symbol has often been overestimated. In my opinion the casket constitutes a form of metonymy. See my article "Revolutionary Realism in Goethe's *Wanderjahre*," 169; cf. Volker Dürr, "Geheimnis und Aufklärung: Zur pädagogischen Funktion des Kästchens in *Wilhelm Meisters Wanderjahren,*" *Monatshefte* 7 (1982): 11-29; and Wilhelm Emrich, "Das Problem der Symbolinterpretation im Hinblick auf Goethes *Wanderjahre,*" in *Protest und Verheißung* (Frankfurt am Main: Athenäum, 1960), 48-66. Steer 130-32 offers a good summary.

48. Gidion, 106-25.

49. I am indebted to Benjamin Bennett for the reference to Lessing's *Laokoon.*

50. See HA 8:638.

51. As previously pointed out, this sentence was deleted from the Hamburg edition and is also missing from the English translation of 1989. For comparison, cf. Reclam edition (Stuttgart, 1982), 525. See also Karl Viëtor, "Goethes Gedicht auf Schillers Schädel," *Publications of the Modern Language Association of America* 49 (1944): 142-83; Franz Mautner, "'Ist fortzusetzen': Zu Goethes Gedicht auf Schillers Schädel," *Publications of the Modern Language Association of America* 49 (1944): 1156-62.

52. "Zusammenhang, Ziel und Zweck liegt innerhalb des Büchleins selbst; ist es nicht aus Einem Stück, so ist es doch aus Einem Sinn; und dies war eben die Aufgabe, mehrere fremdartige äußere Ereignisse dem Gefühle als übereinstimmend entgegenzubringen" (HA 8:521).

53. "Eine Arbeit wie diese, die sich selbst als kollektiv ankündigt, indem sie gewissermaßen nur zum Verband der disparatesten Einzelheiten unternommen zu sein scheint, erlaubt, ja fordert mehr als eine andere, daß jeder sich zueigne, was ihm gemäß ist" (*Goethes Briefe,* ed. Karl Robert Mandelkow [Hamburg: Wegner, 1967], 4:339).

54. "Mit einem solchen Büchlein aber ist es wie mit dem Leben selbst: es findet sich in dem Komplex des Ganzen Notwendiges und Zufälliges, Vorgesetztes und Angeschlossenes, bald gelungen, bald vereitelt,

wodurch es eine Art von Unendlichkeit erhält, die sich in verständige und vernünftige Worte nicht durchaus fassen noch einschließen läßt" (HA 8:526).

55. *Goethes Gespräche,* ed. Flodoard von Biedermann (Leipzig: Biedermann, 1910), 4:217.

56. "Der echte Leser wird das alles schon wieder herausfühlen und -denken" (HA 8:522).

57. "[Ich hoffe, meine *Wanderjahre*] ... haben Ihnen mancherlei zu denken gegeben" (HA 8:525).

58. "Dem einsichtigen Leser bleibt Ernst und Sorgfalt nicht verborgen, womit ich diesen zweiten Versuch, so disparate Elemente zu vereinigen, angefaßt und durchgeführt, und ich muß mich glücklich schätzen, wenn Ihnen ein so bedenkliches Unternehmen einigermaßen gelungen erscheint" (HA 8:525-26).

59. "Der eigentliche Roman [fordert] wie das Epos die Totalität einer Welt- und Lebensanschauung, deren vielseitiger Stoff und Gehalt innerhalb der individuellen Begebenheit zum Vorschein kommt, welche den Mittelpunkt für das Ganze abgibt" (Hegel, *Vorlesungen über Ästhetik,* 3:178). Friedrich Spielhagen in 1864 was the first to apply the term *totality* to the *Wanderjahre,* followed by Max Wundt in 1913. See Anneliese Klingenberg, *Goethes Roman* Wilhelm Meisters Wanderjahre: *Quellen und Komposition* (Berlin: Aufbau, 1972), 22ff.

60. *Lexikon der Goethe-Zitate,* ed. Richard Dobel (Zurich: Artemis, 1968), 924: "... denn nur durch Zusammenstellen des Verwandten entsteht nach und nach eine Totalität, die sich selbst ausspricht und keiner weitern Erklärung bedarf" [Because only by arranging the related parts does a totality gradually come into existence, speaking for itself and needing no further explanation] (*Entwurf einer Farbenlehre,* 2d Part, 228) and "Es gestaltet sich gewiß immer wieder im Universum derselbe besondere Mensch ... damit es nie und zu keiner Zeit an diesem Supplement der Totalität fehle" [Certainly, the same special human being appears again and again in the universe ... , so that there is never a lack to provide totality with this supplement] (*Riemer,* 25 November 1824).

61. "Dem Absoluten / empfiehlt sich / schönstens / zu freundlicher Aufnahme / das Urphänomen /" (*Goethes Briefe* 3:694). "Daß ... man also in beiderseitigem Entwickeln und Aufschließen sich gar wohl annähern und vereinigen könne" (*Goethes Briefe* 4:260). See the afterword to the *Wanderjahre* edition in Reclams Universal-Bibliothek, 553ff.; and especially Karl Löwith, *From Hegel to Nietzsche: The Revolution in Nineteenth-Century Thought,* transl. David E. Green (Garden City: Doubleday,

1964), 2-28; and Hans Mayer, *Goethe: Ein Versuch über den Erfolg* (Frankfurt am Main: Suhrkamp, 1973), 134-60.

62. "Der Roman im modernen Sinne setzt eine bereits zur *Prosa* geordnete Wirklichkeit voraus" (Hegel, *Vorlesungen über die Ästhetik,* 3:177).

63. "Eine der gewöhnlichsten und für den Roman passendsten Kollisionen ist deshalb der Konflikt zwischen der Poesie des Herzens und der entgegenstehenden Prosa der Verhältnisse" (Hegel, *Vorlesungen über die Ästhetik,* 3:177).

64. HA 8:520.

65. "Einerseits [lernen] die der gewöhnlichen Weltordnung zunächst widerstrebenden Charaktere das Echte und Substantielle in ihr anerkennen ... , mit ihren Verhältnissen sich aussöhnen und wirksam in dieselben eintreten, andererseits aber von dem, was sie wirken und vollbringen, die prosaische Gestalt abstreifen und dadurch eine der Schönheit verwandte und befreundete Wirklichkeit an die Stelle der vorgefundenen Prosa setzen" (Hegel, *Vorlesungen über die Ästhetik,* 3:177f.).

66. Effi Biedrzynski, ed., *Mit Goethe durch das Jahr: Ein Kalender für das Jahr 1983* (Zurich: Artemis, 1982), 93.

67. See Bahr, "Goethe's *Wanderjahre* as an Experimental Novel," 68-71. A glance at Karl Löwith's analysis of nineteenth-century philosophy from Hegel to Nietzsche may suffice to show that Goethe conceptualized almost all tendencies of his age in *Wanderjahre.*

68. Broch, 88.

Steve Dowden (essay date 1994)

SOURCE: Dowden, Steve. "Irony and Ethical Autonomy in *Wilhelm Meisters Wanderjahre.*" *Deutsche Vierteljahrsschrift für Literaturwissenschaft und Geistesgeschichte* 68.1 (1994): 134-54. Print.

[*In the following essay, Dowden argues that the apparently "slapdash" structure of* Wilhelm Meister's Travels *is in fact a deliberate authorial attempt to shift interpretive responsibility to the reader. Dowden further suggests that Goethe shared with his eighteenth-century predecessors, including Laurence Sterne and Henry Fielding, a sense of the potential of irony in portraying the ambiguities of life.*]

Goethe ended the revised edition of his *Wanderjahre* [*Wilhelm Meisters Wanderjahre*] with a promise: "Ist Fortzusetzen." This twist came as a surprise to the novel's first readers, and it has continued to surprise. It poses an obvious question about a writer who is eighty years old. Did Goethe expect to live long enough to write a third Wilhelm Meister novel and so complete the series with a *Meisterjahre*? The matter has proved so vexing for his solemn editors that even major editions, such as the Hamburger Ausgabe, leave out Goethe's self-ironic jest. One supposes they thought it an editorial blunder, a sign of mental faculties enfeebled by advanced age, or of some other lapse in literary judgment. Whatever their individual reasons may have been, they seemed reluctant to take it seriously, or at least in the way that a good joke ought to be taken seriously.

The novel as a whole has not fared much better with readers than its parting words. Summing up the views of many, the founder of the *Goethe-Jahrbuch,* Ludwig Geiger, wrote this about the *Wanderjahre*: "Die Komposition und Darstellung ist wenig gelungen. Überall bemerkt man die Altersmüdigkeit, die Notwendigkeit, zu Ende zu kommen."[1] Contemporary commentators are more circumspect, of course, but the novel remains well outside of the canon. It is the province of specialists in the German-speaking world, outside of the German world it is scarcely known at all.

The bafflement of Goethe's editors over the question of "Ist Fortzusetzen" embodies the larger failure of literary critics in general to make sense of the novel's place in the tradition of the European novel. Goethe's ironic stance in the *Wanderjahre,* I will argue, belongs to an identifiable European tradition. As for the specific instance of the "Ist Fortzusetzen" jest, it seems likely to me that Goethe's promise to continue the novel was written in the spirit of high irony. If this is so, then the end of *Wilhelm Meisters Wanderjahre* deserves to be taken seriously as a parting gesture worthy of Goethe's imagination. In a novel whose main theme is "Entsagung," it should hardly come as a surprise that Goethe should grasp and be able to express his own finitude with a light, self-ironic touch. The experience that gave rise to his **'Trilogie der Leidenschaft'** lay only a few years behind him. And one of the *Wanderjahre*'s most prominent themes is the acknowledgement of human limitations. Death, obviously, is the ultimate limit of human striving. We think of Faust, old and blind, as death approaches. It would be strange indeed if Goethe were unwilling to admit this limitation as his own. His bit of drollery at the end of the *Wanderjahre* gives us the measure of human contingency, and with it the contingency of his narrative. There are natural limitations to his control over it. He turns it over to us, his readers, to "continue" it for him. Death undercuts his authority, both literally and symbolically. There is always more tale than he can tell. He invites us to apply our own imagination in order to fill in—to use Iser's term—the "Leerstellen."

I am proposing to view the novel from this standpoint: it was fitting that Goethe, master of metamorphosis and of becoming, finally resisted the closure of his last novel. Its

shifting center of gravity and ultimate openness suggest not infirmity of purpose or lack of control, but wit, depth, and complexity. Precisely these characteristics invite us to reevaluate the *Wanderjahre*'s place in the larger European tradition, and especially in its relationship to German modernism.

I

Closure is a feature of plot widely associated with the novel of the nineteenth century.[2] Goethe's contemporary, Jane Austen, ties up loose ends in a tidy knot at the end of her novels (usually a marriage knot). And certainly Goethe's **Werther** [*Die Leiden des jungen Werthers*] ends on an unequivocal note of finality. The *Wanderjahre,* by contrast, ends on a note of deliberate and provocative incompletion. The rescue of Felix provides a climax of sorts and various characters are married off to each other,[3] but the imminent American adventure strongly implies the story's continuation, even without the teasing addition of an *Ist fortzusetzen*. Moreover, Wilhelm has not been reunited with Natalie—he stands not at the end of an odyssey, but at the beginning of one. Felix's fortunes are anything but settled, and the mystery of the Kästchen remains a mystery.

Some commentators, especially Ehrhard Bahr,[4] have argued that one of Goethe's main links to modernism is the aim of his novel to achieve narrative "totality," a philosophical concern closely linked to closure. The supposed totality of Goethe's *Wanderjahre* forms the crux of Hermann Broch's argument about the novel's modernity. The novel genre, argues Broch, has taken over a quest for wholeness that religion and philosophy have renounced. But the claim reveals more about Broch's intention in his own writing than it does about the *Wanderjahre.*[5] Broch's preoccupation with totality echoes Hegelian philosophy and Wagner's aesthetic, but not Goethe's conspicuous preoccupation with the particular.[6]

Moreover, modernism is not so much concerned with the vast inclusiveness that Joyce had in common with Balzac. Our guide on this matter should not be Broch, but Samuel Beckett. His seminal essay on Proust clarifies the point. According to him, modern fiction concentrates the attention on a *progression in depth,* and not Balzacian breadth.[7] Beckett's work, as well as Kafka's, Bernhard's and many others', emphasizes concentration, specificity, and irony. This is because the grand unity of German idealism has given way in modernism to a world of distinct and competing realities. Truth is not unified and absolute in the pluralist universe of the moderns; instead local truths make separate and sometimes conflicting claims, depending on historical, political and social circumstance, point of view, and any number of other possible contingencies.

No one knows this better than Ulrich, Robert Musil's "Mann ohne Eigenschaften." For him reality is a contingent, ceaselessly mobile set of circumstances. To live in such a world, the individual must be adaptable, the self a congeries of possibilities. A modernist "man without qualities" radicalizes Goethe's injunction in the *Wanderjahre* that the self must always be adaptable to a multiplicity of possible lives, open to self-transformation.[8] There is no ideal totality that determines the order of things.

So totality is not the right word for the multidimensional, ironic complexity of Goethe's *Wanderjahre.* This is so mainly because the worldview of totality, rooted in the certainties of myth and ideology, presupposes closure. Irony is a most unwelcome mode of thought in the realms of myth and ideology. Goethe shows little affinity for the idiosyncratic idea of myth that Broch uses to frame his concept of narrative totality.[9] It is fairer to describe the *Wanderjahre* as a kaleidoscopic novel, one in which the writer intended to expound views and pose questions about many aspects of life—precisely because modern life is manifold, rich in paradox, ambiguity, and contradiction. Even Makarie, Goethe's outlandish personification of utopian wholeness, must, by virtue of her wildly implausible ideality, be taken with a grain of salt.[10] For Goethe, as for the modernists (we might think in particular of Broch's Mutter Gisson in *Die Verzauberung*), such perfection can only be posited ironically, as fiction. After all, the *Wanderjahre*'s basic theme is renunciation, itself a product of an ironic world view.[11] Perfection, total harmony, and wholeness are ideals that Wilhelm Meister (and all the rest of us) must learn to do without. Nor is there any compelling evidence that Goethe aimed for a comprehensive, mythologically legitimated embrace of his era's unified totality. In fact, the evidence points in the opposite direction. First, we should note that Goethe's mature habits of mind pivoted on the intellectual mode of ironic skepticism.[12] With our expectations thus framed, we can look with sharpened awareness into the details of the *Wanderjahre.*

An aphorism among those at the end of book two suggests Goethe's sense of discontinuity between fiction and life: "Literatur ist das Fragment der Fragmente; das wenigste dessen, was geschah und gesprochen worden, ward geschrieben, vom Geschriebenen ist das wenigste übriggeblieben":[13] between life and art there is no closure. In the *Wanderjahre* Goethe was interested in the kaleidoscopic bits and pieces that eventually add up to an aggregate artifice, not an organic whole. He is explicit in a much-quoted (but seldom appreciated) letter to Rochlitz about the primacy of the particular over the totality:

> Mit solchem Büchlein ... ist es wie mit dem Leben selbst: es findet sich in dem Komplex des Ganzen Notwendiges und Zufälliges, Vorgesetztes und Angeschlossenes, bald gelungen, bald vereitelt, wodurch es eine Art von Unendlichkeit erhält, die sich in verständige und vernünftige Worte nicht durchaus fassen noch einschließen läßt. Wohin ich aber die Aufmerksamkeit meiner Freunde gerne lenke ... sind die verschiedenen, sich voneinander absondernden Einzelheiten, die doch ... den Wert des

> Buches entscheiden. ... Das Büchlein verleugnet seinen kollektiven Ursprung nicht, erlaubt und fordert mehr als jedes andere die Teilnahme an hervortretenden Einzelheiten. Dadurch kommt der Autor erst zur Gewißheit, daß es ihm gelungen sei, Gefühle und Nachdenken in den verschiedensten Geistern aufzuregen.[14]

The philosophical and narrative dimensions of his novel point away from a "totalizing" intent. They suggest instead a studied attempt at a loosely organized composite in which pieces, not the whole, should seize the reader's imagination. Fragmentation, and not the nostalgia for a lost totality, is the defining feature of the *Wanderjahre.*

It makes more sense to speak of totality with regard to nineteenth-century realism. The realist illusion offers a vision of the world in which all the pieces fit. But the realist effect is first and foremost, as Goethe seems to have understood, the *illusion* of a world in which all the pieces fit. The *Wanderjahre* is neither realist nor illusionist. It is symbolic and self-consciously ironic, schooled on the eighteenth-century English novel, and especially on Laurence Sterne and Henry Fielding. Where the realist novel claims to be a mirror to the world, the ironic novel insists on a certain skeptical detachment from it.[15]

Modernist narrative characteristically insists on this ironic detachment of fiction from what it only seems to depict. The imagination does not describe a world so much as produce one. In evidence we might offer the first chapter of Musil's *Mann ohne Eigenschaften,* in which he demonstrates the narrator's power to envision the world any way he wants. From another perspective Kafka's fiction does the same thing. He imagines worlds that do not reproduce the one we live in, but he still manages to comment on our world in penetrating ways. The two realms are connected via myriad ironies. More obvious is Thomas Mann's irony, as in parodies such as *Der Zauberberg* or *Felix Krull,* Mann distances himself from what he and his contemporaries take to be the nineteenth-century tradition. In yet another register, Hofmannsthal's *Ein Brief* is also a variant of the modernist's characteristic distance from extraliterary experience. In it the emphasis falls on the ways in which language can mislead and distort. In all these cases, modernist irony drives a wedge between lived reality and narrative artifice.

The modernist taste for such irony is usually fixed in literary history as a turn away from the mimetic practices of the nineteenth century. No doubt this assessment is true, as far as it goes. But there is good reason to take the ironic mode of modernism as a partial return to the eighteenth-century novel and the possibilities it opens to the literary imagination. Above all it means affinities to the narrative forms of Laurence Sterne and Henry Fielding.[16] Goethe's *Wanderjahre* novel was influenced most plainly by Sterne, whom Goethe openly admired and to whom he alludes (in the aphorisms at the end of Book III,[17] and in Lenardo's speech to the prospective emigrants, III, 9). In a conversation of 1824 Goethe draws Eckermann's attention to Henry Fielding, claiming him as one of the most significant influences on German literature and therefore, we must also assume, on him.[18] Goethe was also an admirer of Diderot, whose ironic, self-conscious, theorizing *Jacques le Fataliste* was, as he wrote, a "most splendid work."[19]

It should be noted in passing that Goethe read Diderot's novel not long before the composition of **Wilhelm Meisters theatralische Sendung**. Nicholas Boyle doubts that his reading of *Jacques* induced Goethe to reflect on the nature of the novel.[20] He considers the narrative "awkwardness" of the **Sendung** to be the result of an informality and even indifference to design that reflect Goethe's growing awareness that there is "no logic to his story." Boyle is no doubt right about the story's shapelessness. It is a judgement that has traditionally weighed even more heavily against the **Wanderjahre**.[21] If the **Lehrjahre** [**Wilhelm Meisters Lehrjahre**] or the **Wanderjahre** lack the dramatic tension of realist fiction, it is because Goethe believes that life itself does not proceed according to such a pattern. It could be true (however unlikely it may seem) that Goethe composed **Wanderjahre** novel in a slapdash way. Commentators from Lewes to Walter Benjamin and Emil Staiger have leveled this charge. But it also seems unlikely that Diderot, Sterne, and Fielding did not leave their mark on his concept of narrative.

Let me stress that I am not suggesting a direct genealogy of influence from Sterne, Fielding, and Diderot via Goethe to the German modernists. What concerns us here are affinities. They disclose a shared sense of irony about the way life and fiction are related (and not related) that enters fiction at the level of structure and style. What is most striking about the Wilhelm Meister novels is the special emphasis that falls on structure and style, an emphasis that calls to mind the examples of Fielding, Sterne, and Diderot. What Goethe shares with them, and what they all together share with the modernists, is the ironic mode of seeing. Milan Kundera has usefully described novelistic irony as a clear-sighted view of ambiguity and uncertainty:

> Irony: Which is right and which is wrong? Is Emma Bovary intolerable? Or brave and touching? And what about Werther? Is he sensitive and noble? Or an aggressive sentimentalist, infatuated with himself? The more attentively we read a novel, the more impossible the answer, because the novel is, by definition, the ironic art: its "truth" is concealed, undeclared, undeclarable. "Remember, Razumov, that women, children and revolutionists hate irony, which is the negation of all saving instincts, of all faith, of all devotion, of all action," says a Russian woman revolutionary in Joseph Conrad's *Under Western Eyes*. Irony irritates. Not because it mocks or attacks but because it denies us our certainties by unmasking the world as ambiguity.[22]

From the beginning **Wilhelm Meisters Wanderjahre** has been a source of irritation to its readers. At least one of its very few early devotees, H. G. Hotho, was able to recognize what he called the novel's "Reiz der Sprödigkeit."[23] Yet only since the 1970s has the novel's ironic edge begun to receive the critical attention that is its due.[24]

II

There is every reason to believe that Goethe had his wits about him in his old age. The **Wanderjahre** were meant as a challenge to the imagination. In 1827 he assured Eckermann that his **Wahlverwandtschaften** was probably his easiest novel to understand, because a single "durchgreifende Idee" governs it. However, he refuses to elevate this kind of unity into a superior virtue of novels in general: "Der Roman [i.e., **Die Wahlverwandtschaften**] ist dadurch für den Verstand faßlich geworden; aber ich will nicht sagen, daß er dadurch *besser* geworden wäre. Vielmehr bin ich der Meinung: *je inkommensurabler und für den Verstand unfaßlicher eine poetische Produktion, desto besser.*"[25] When Schiller had complained to him years earlier about the confusion in the **Lehrjahre,** as Goethe famously recalled to Eckermann (18. Jan. 1825), his comment was similar: "Es gehört dieses Werk übrigens zu den inkalkulabelsten Produktionen, wozu mir fast selbst der Schlüssel fehlt."[26] Here he strongly recalls Sterne, who had once described *Tristram Shandy* as a book "made and formed to baffle all criticism."[27] Goethe goes on to add that seeking the novel's center is "schwer und nicht einmal gut. Ich sollte meinen, ein reiches mannigfaltiges Leben, das unsern Augen vorübergeht, wäre auch an sich etwas ohne ausgesprochene Tendenz, die doch bloß für den Begriff ist." The welter of thoughts and deeds—not a "center," which means also not Wilhelm himself—binds the novel into a narrative whole, but not an organic "totality" in the Hegelian philosophical sense that Lukács and Broch still took for granted.

What I want to stress now is this idea: Goethe invites our complicity in making sense of his protagonist's messy, basically defective an incomplete experience of the world. It is worth recalling at this point Goethe's famous comment to the historian Heinrich Luden in 1806. Luden was reporting to Goethe how annoying he found the **Faust** interpretations of Hegel, Schelling, and the Schlegels. He objected that they were turning Goethe's work to their own purposes, willfully ignoring its true meaning. He turned to Goethe for the true meaning and received instead something of a reproof: "Der Dichter soll nicht sein eigener Erklärer sein und seine Dichtung in alltägliche Prosa fein zerlegen; damit würde er aufhören Dichter zu sein. Der Dichter stellt eine Schöpfung in die Welt hinaus; es ist die des Lesers, des Ästhetikers, des Kritikers zu untersuchen, was er mit seiner Schöpfung gewollt hat."[28] If a reader fails to understand his book or poem or play, Goethe is not willing to spell it out as a closed, schematic system. The reason is plainly not that he was a careless writer, and it has nothing to do with authorial disdain for the reader. It must be because Goethe values something more than the reader's grasp of his meaning:

namely, that his readers should come to see these things for themselves. This gives the novel the character of a game; reading becomes a form of play.

But it is a purposeful game. By shifting onto his readers' shoulders the responsibility of interpretation, Goethe reveals that *moral autonomy* is a value at the heart of his conception of the novel. It is dialectical in the specific sense that Goethe solicits his reader's active participation in the creation of meaning. Goethe's late fiction and poetry have too often been misunderstood as a way of allegorizing ideas. He refused this didactic role, counting instead on the reader as an active participant in the construction of meaning. In one of the aphorisms from Makarie's archive, Goethe's view of Sterne could equally well apply to himself: "Er fühlte einen entschiedenen Haß gegen Ernst, weil er didaktisch und dogmatisch ist und gar leicht pedantisch wird, wogegen er den entschiedensten Abscheu hegte."[29] The thrust of **Wilhelm Meisters Wanderjahre,** like that of *Tristram Shandy,* is anti-dogmatic and anti-didactic. In its ironic posture (teaching by refusing to preach) lies its wisdom and moral strength.

Let me illustrate the ironic mode of Goethe's novel with a few salient examples. First, the so-called "archival fiction"[30] must be taken into account. Goethe interposes a narrator between us and his fictional world. This narrator is self-conscious, as the narrators in modernism tend to be (as in, for example, *Les Faux-Monnayeurs, Die Schlafwandler,* and *Der Mann ohne Eigenschaften,* or more recently, in Thomas Bernhard's *Das Kalkwerk*).[31] His importance lies in the distance that Goethe puts between the teller and the tale. He is not an all-knowing narrator. In fact, he is not a storyteller at all. Instead, he serves as a detached organizing consciousness, merely the "Sammler und Ordner dieser Papiere": comprising a miscellany of letters, stories, reports, diaries, technical treatises, and speeches he has at his disposal.[32]

In the novel's first version (1821) he informs us that he can do nothing more than try to put certain archival materials into a narrative order. If there are gaps in his tale, then it is because there are gaps in the material. In this way Goethe builds ambiguity and uncertainty into the structure of the novel. Ehrhard Bahr has usefully connected the narrative structure to the principal theme by calling attention to Goethe's "Poetik der Entsagung."[33] He actively renounces the convention of a unified plot.

Goethe's contemporaneous readers might have reasonably expected a narrator who serves to verify the story, as in Goethe's **Werther** or Wieland's *Geschichte des Agathon.*[34] Toward the end of book one, after we readers have had ample time to settle comfortably into the imaginary world of the book, we are suddenly and unexpectedly confronted by our hitherto invisible narrator. That we should meet him so far into the novel is neither a defect nor an oversight. It

is shrewdly calculated on the part of the author to give us a surprise, to disorient us a little and force us into a more reflective frame of mind. Everything we thought was coming to us first hand, from an author, turns out to be second hand, the handiwork of a fallible, and perhaps capricious, editor.

The scene occurs very much in the tradition of Laurence Sterne, famous for his chatty apostrophes to the reader.[35] The **Wanderjahre**'s narrator addresses us, abruptly puncturing the fictional bubble, in the middle of book I, chapter 10. As his scene is in full swing, just as one the fictional figures is about to read a mathematical treatise aloud, the narrator intrudes, into the narrative with this remark:

> Wenn wir aber uns bewogen finden, diesen werten Mann nicht lesen zu lassen, so werden es unsere Gönner wahrscheinlich geneigt aufnehmen, denn was oben gegen das Verweilen Wilhelms bei dieser Unterhaltung gesagt worden, gilt noch mehr in dem Falle, in welchem wir uns befinden. Unsere Freunde haben einen Roman in die Hand genommen, und wenn dieser hie und da schon mehr als billig didaktisch geworden, so finden wir doch geraten, die Geduld unserer Wohlwollenden nicht noch weiter auf die Probe zu stellen. Die Papiere, die uns vorliegen, gedenken wir an einem andern Orte abdrucken zu lassen und fahren diesmal im Geschichtlichen ohne weiteres fort, da wir selbst ungeduldig sind, das obwaltende Rätsel endlich aufgeklärt zu sehen.[36]

The tone is witty and light. The narrator feigns a stiff formality—his style is of the chancery—but it is undercut by the extraordinary surprise of his sudden intrusion into our view of the fictional world.

Goethe is having fun with us and with the fictional status of his book. He is ironizing his narrative by informing us that it is not the unmediated truth, but an artifice ("unsere Freunde haben einen Roman in die Hand genommen") with which he plans to entertain us, and does not wish to bore us with dry mathematical papers. We are made to realize this the novel has to be thought through more attentively than most. In **Werther** his narrator asked us to take the fiction at face value; in the **Wanderjahre** he warns us against it. We are asked to be both coolly detached and minutely attentive to indirections, omissions, and qualifications.

The trick, of course, is irritating and, as the history of this novel's reception has shown, it has not always been well received. But the ironic turn, properly understood, contributes to the entertainment of reading the book, if we are willing to join in the fun by responding in kind to Goethe's richly inventive imagination. In a limited way, this particular species of irony aligns him with the German romantics, who were great admirers of it in Cervantes and Sterne. When, in book 2 chapter 7 of the **Wanderjahre,** Wilhelm makes the acquaintance of an artist who has plainly read **Wilhelm Meisters Lehrjahre,** we know we are in the hands of a self-conscious ironist.[37] In most other ways, though, Goethe remains distinct from them. The romantics were advocates of closed, organic totalities. The fictional world as Goethe presents it is not whole. It is not a closed and absolute totality; it is a tentative construct of a single consciousness, a contingent world dependent for order upon an "editor," the metaphorically limiting image of the author. This links **Wilhelm Meisters Wanderjahre** and its challenging multiplicity to the poised ambiguity of the great modernists: James, Musil, Kafka, Joyce, Uwe Johnson. The world of modernism is always relative, contingent, broken up into fragments that can never be reassembled into the whole that the Romantics (and many romantic modernists) longed to return to or at least to re-create in imagination.

The numerous other intrusions of the editor into the text of the **Wanderjahre** are well known and need no special elaboration here.[38] The principle that I want to emphasize is Goethe's shrewd and intentional injection of ironic distance into his novel.[39] Its consequences are far-reaching. We might consider its bearing on what has traditionally been regarded as one of the novel's most important scenes, the one in which the some of the details of the immigration league's supposed utopia are elaborated (III, 11). At the outset of the chapter the editor warns us that he is presenting the gist of a conversation between Wilhelm and Friedrich. Thus he alerts us to his own detachment from their attitudes and opinions. As Erich Trunz has observed, Goethe positions the reader at a triple remove. "Der amerikanische Plan," he writes in his commentary to the Hamburger edition of the **Wanderjahre,** "erscheint wie durch drei Gläser gesehen: die Turmgesellschaft hat ihn formuliert, Friedrich hat davon berichtet, und nun erzählt ihn der Dichter als *Sammler und Ordner dieser Papiere*."[40] The gesture of distanciation is important. There has been a tradition of attributing this vision of utopia to Goethe himself.[41] The assumption sits uneasily because the supposed utopia is a police state from which Jews, books and alcohol are banished.

Was Goethe an advocate of institutionalized anti-Semitism? The question is especially relevant because it highlights the way in which irony and ethics are connected. If Goethe aims, as I have suggested, to involve the reader in his tale's kinetic system of puzzling ambiguities, this one is a good test case because so much is at stake ethically. Does Friedrich speak for Goethe, or is the passage informed by ironic skepticism? Two levels of evidence must be weighed: first, Goethe's attitude toward Jewry, and second, the specific context of the situation in the novel.

The evidence concerning Goethe's attitude toward Jewry is circumstantial. In a few letters and other writings there exists a smattering of evidence to suggest he may have approved of the society's decision to bar Jews from its proposed settlements. However, there is also just as much, or more, evidence to suggest the opposite.[42] In general,

Goethe's views on Jewry were more liberal than not.[43] Despite whatever anti-Jewish comments he may have occasionally made in private, in his public literary life he remained a liberal: he favored tolerance and help up of Jewry as emblematic of certain virtues. In this context we might especially consider remarks he published on *Nathan der Weise* in an 1813 survey of German drama: "Möge doch die bekannte Erzählung, glücklich dargestellt, das deutsche Publikum auf ewige Zeiten erinnern, daß es nicht nur berufen wird, um zu schauen, sondern auch, um zu hören und um zu vernehmen. Möge zugleich das darin ausgesprochene göttliche Duldungs- und Schonungsgefühl der Nation heilig und wert bleiben."[44]

As for the virtues he associated with Jewry, the instance that bears most directly on the present discussion is drawn from Wilhelm's visit to the Pedagogical Province. While visiting its gallery of religious art, Wilhelm asks why they have chosen to place special emphasis on "das israelitische Volk." The Elder answers that, though the Jews labor under the same vices and shortcomings as other peoples, they have distinguished themselves in this way: "Es ist das beharrlichste Volk der Erde, es ist, es war, es wird sein, um den Namen Jehova durch alle Zeiten zu verherrlichen. Wir haben es daher als Musterbild aufgestellt, als Hauptbild, dem die andern nur zum Rahmen dienen."[45] Many such passages can be culled from Goethe's writings.[46] Moreover, the implicit message of the Pedagogical Province's syncretic religious utopia is in no way hostile to Judaism. It stands as one of the three great world religions, and also as a model of autonomy.

In the context of the novel, then, the league's bias against Jews begins to look suspect, especially from the modern perspective. The plan to establish a colony across the Atlantic in which no Jews are allowed bears an ugly resemblance to the anti-Semitic emigration plan actually carried out by Elisabeth Nietzsche and her husband, Bernhard Förster. In the 1880s they established an "Aryan" colony in Paraguay.[47] Their project would seem to be an extension of the league of emigrants' own. Bigotry is central to both. However, Goethe seems well aware of this aspect. His reader must be attentive to the skepticism expressed in the novel's ironic structure.

Let me emphasize that the aim of my appeal to irony is not to rescue Goethe from the charge of bigotry. He may deserve it. The evidence is not clear enough to say one way or the other. Instead, my aim is to discover the meaning of his novel, which may well transcend its author's limitations and liabilities, or indeed his conscious intentions. Goethe's intent will remain beyond our reach. Even so, the ironic structure is too plain and too powerful to overlook.

The operative irony in the present question is this: a contradiction exists between the utopian spirit of the Pedagogical Province and the political praxis of the league of emigrants. In the novel's design, the Pedagogical Province's famous three reverences (for that which is above, that which is below, and that which is next to us) are embodied in the novel's three most prominent secondary figures.[48] The celestial Makarie belongs to that which is above; the tellurian Montan is drawn downward, toward what is below; and Lenardo, a practical and level-headed leader, is distinguished by his conspicuous reverence for his fellow man. His anxiety over his responsibility for Nachodine's fate particularizes this reverence, and his mission to act as a leader of the emigration to the New World is an extension of the same reverence. This perspective on the league brings into a clash between ideal and action. The province's ideal of reverence for one's fellow man is baldly contradicted in the league's anti-Jewish policy.

However, the question is not, "Which one speaks for Goethe, the league or the province?" Instead, the question should be, "What are we to make of the novel's internal contradiction?" Intentionally or not (and I believe it is deliberate) Goethe draws us into an ironic incongruity. In so doing, he shifts the burden of responsibility, a plainly moral responsibility, for interpretation onto the reader's shoulders. It is worth remembering here what Goethe wrote about the ethical responsibility of fiction in *Dichtung und Wahrheit* [*Aus meinen Leben: Dichtung und Wahrheit*]. He argues there that literature has no didactic moral purpose. It neither propagandizes nor vilifies, but must instead neutrally develop the consequences of attitudes and actions.[49] It is the reader who must discover their meaning.

Goethe's stance implies a dialectic that involves the reader in discriminating meanings and possibilities. The author does not simply spell things out. Thus the wary reader of the *Wanderjahre* should be doubly suspicious of the league's attitude toward Jews when it occurs alongside the other two odd elements of this supposedly ideal state: no books or alcohol. If the net were cast widely enough, a commentator could conceivably defend Friedrich's social engineering by arguing that there are precedents in Plato and Rousseau. Plato excludes the poet from his Republic, and Rousseau insists that the theater exerts a corrupting influence on society. Perhaps Goethe is suggesting that books and alcohol similarly overstimulate the imagination, leading simple folk astray. But that also would mean that almost nobody could read *Wilhelm Meisters Wanderjahre.*

What are we to make of a book that banishes books? Or a writer, noted for his prodigious consumption of wine, who forbids alcohol? He is either a hypocrite or an ironist. Maybe there was a bigoted side to Goethe; and maybe he really did envisage a happy new proletariat, blissfully spared the ravages of literature and wine—but it does not seem likely.[50] Goethe is more probably intentionally ironizing the colonists' utopian illusions. Still, the question cannot be decided with certainty. But thematic uncertainty, as Kundera makes clear in the passage cited earlier, is a

hallmark of the novel as a genre. Irony makes the novel permanently contemporary.

III

Apart from the central irony of the novel's archival fiction, I want to call attention to two other ironic devices at work in the *Wanderjahre.* One is structural and the other is thematic. A good example of the first is the interpolated novella **"Nicht zu weit"** (III, 10). It begins with the "editor" figure's ironic disclaimer: "Hier fand sich nun Odoard bewogen, nach und nach von den Angelegenheiten seines Geistes und Herzens fragmentarische Rechenschaft zu geben, deshalb denn auch von diesem Gespräche uns freilich nur unvollständige und unbefriedigende Kenntnis zugekommen."[51] He goes on to promise that later more will be told, but we hear no more about it later. The unfinished tale was a favorite device of Laurence Sterne and must have been a familiar one to Goethe.

The story tells of Odoard, leader of the colonists planning to resettle within Europe. With children waiting and dinner on the table, the unhappily married Odoard impatiently awaits the return of his wife from a birthday celebration being held in her honor. Albertine does not come and does not come. Believing her to be lingering in the arms of "der Hausfreund," Lelio, Odoard decides she has pushed him too far. He leaves in haste to see the worst for himself. He rushes to an inn where he compromises not his wife, but Sophronie, the married woman he loves. Meanwhile his wife has arrived home, delayed by a carriage accident which has revealed to her that her lover, Lelio, and her best friend, Florine, are having an affair.

Here the story breaks off. Naturally we would have been interested in the final confrontation between Odoard and Albertine. And how did Odoard come to join the league of emigrants? Perhaps his failed marriage has driven him to it. Is he in flight from his marital responsibilities? Can he and his wife be reconciled to the life they have shaped for themselves? Where is Albertine anyway? What has become of their children? Did harm come to Sophronie because of Odoard's indiscretion? The editor does not satisfy our curiosity. He leaves it for us to imagine, not delivering on his plan to tell us more later.

The tale seems to be mutilated, incomplete. Here, more emphatically than elsewhere, Goethe turns the story over to his readers. He enjoins us to think through the possibilities of action and meaning, character and moral responsibility. In it Goethe also shows a conspicuously modern preoccupation with fragmentation and various species of open-endedness. The story comes to us narrated second-hand and piecemeal by the "editor" figure, and it never even comes to a conclusion. Indeed, the novel itself ends with the phrase "To be continued." If one were to press the case hard enough, such elements could be made to suggest an anticipation of the epistemological questions that preoccupy the modernist imagination, from Hofmannsthal's Chandos letter to Uwe Johnson's Achim and Thomas Bernhard's Konrad.

"Nicht zu weit" is not a highly condensed version of the nineteenth-century novel of adultery in which wrongdoers are punished by society. Instead, Goethe chooses to explode the conventions by implying a multiplicity of points of view—in the narrative technique and, by extension, morally. The narrative complexity of Odoard's story has implications for Goethe's relationship to modernism. The modernist novel has been associated for the most part with the trend toward emphasis on a central, governing consciousness as opposed to outward social reality. The trinity of Joyce, Proust, and Kafka point toward Johnson and Bernhard, Frisch and Beckett. Goethe stood at the beginning of the "inward turn," as it has been called,[52] with his Werther.

The near solipsism of Werther's self-absorption gave center stage to the perceiving consciousness, but the later Goethe critically resisted the inward relocation of reality. He disperses reality into the multiple viewpoints of the *Wanderjahre.* No one figure, not even Wilhelm or the narrator, dominates the sense of reality. The world is mobile, plural, and open to discussion from differing perspectives that, in the end, may not converge.

Odoard's tale illustrates the tension between points of view. The various mediations of Odoard's story begin with the "editor" figure, who gives us his account of Friedrich's account of Odoard's account. Thus we are thrice divorced from the reality. It seems likely that Goethe was aware that an ironic narrator of the sort, for example, in Humean *Tristram Shandy* would shift the focus of reality from external events to the perceiving, narrating consciousness. In casting his narrator as an editor, Goethe retains his novel's concentration on external events while at the same time making them relative to a central, organizing intelligence. In this way he achieves a dynamic equipoise of subject and object, preserving the claims of each, not deciding in favor of the one or the other.

He seeks reality and truth in individual experience, here in the experience of Odoard—or so it seems at first. However, Goethe cunningly opens the narrative to multiple perspectives on individual experience. Odoard's individual experience is shown to be one voice in a complex fugue of individual perspectives.[53] The editor's account of Odoard, apart from being filtered through Odoard and Friedrich, comprises the viewpoint of multiple narrators, including Odoard, a respected servant in his household, and Albertine. Even the perspective of the two children is implied without being taken up explicitly. The medley of perspectives signifies a moral complexity without actually sorting it out for the reader into an neat Aesopian moral. Nor in the end does Goethe seem to support the status quo of sticking out a bad marriage. Odoard's presence among the emigrants suggests he and Albertine may have split up.

Goethe presents Odoard's story without using traditional authorial authority to impose moral judgments on it. He lets his characters exist as individuals, telling their story from their own points of view. Its title, **"Nicht zu weit,"** comes from the servant's warning (the servant is the voice of conventional piety) to Albertine that she had better not push Odoard "too far." But the title leaves open, indeed, it forces open, the question of which figures have gone too far and in what way. Obviously Albertine and Lelio have gone too far. But Odoard also went too far when he married a woman he did not love; he went too far again when he tried to humiliate his wife and succeeded only in jeopardizing Sophronie's reputation. Both Albertine and Odoard went too far for the good of their children. And, finally, the story itself does not go "too far" by spelling out a moral. Goethe leaves the puzzle to us.

It would no doubt be possible to pursue the moral implications of the little story in great detail. But my aim at present is only to indicate the nature of the irony at work in the *Wanderjahre.* **"Nicht zu weit"** is exemplary in its narrative and moral complexity. It gives in miniature a model that helps define the *Wanderjahre* as a whole. Goethe's vision in it embraces multiple realities which are, in themselves, not moral or immoral, but complexly ramified and open to interpretation. By refusing to moralize about his characters and their predicament in **"Nicht zu weit,"** Goethe more or less dares us to make judgments that are morally absolute. By refusing to complete the story, the novelist relinquishes control over the figures he invented. He gives them autonomy in their multivalent world of relationships, and he gives us the responsibility of pondering the ethical meaning of their situation. And the situation is not a single, objective world, but a world that arises out of a polyphony of individual, perhaps incommensurable voices.

In a more general way the theme of **"Nicht zu weit"** is uncertainty. Odoard acted on his belief that Albertine was in Lelio's arms, when in fact she was hurt in a carriage accident. A false sense of certainty pushed him into unfortunate set of actions. The theme of certainty plays an important role elsewhere in the novel, too. Or to be more exact, the opposite of certainty comes to the fore. Goethe presents the love affair between Hersilie and Felix as a *mystery,* a realm in which certainty is impossible.

Goethe embodies this mystery in the small, locked chest—the so-called Kästchen—that has justifiably excited much attention among commentators. It is an important symbolic image in the book. But it has also resisted definitive interpretations. The mystery of the box's content remains a mystery, and therein lies its thematic importance for the novel.

The facts of the case are these: the ornate box was found in a mountain cave in the strangely named "Riesenschloß" to which the mysterious and somewhat sinister boy Fitz led Felix; it is locked, but a key exists. Goethe gives plain signals that the box is a key symbol to the novel. Not the least of these signals is the fuss he and his characters make over its key. In a probable allusion to Laurence Sterne,[54] Goethe goes so far as to draw us a picture of it. The upshot of his efforts is to pass on a feeling that the box engenders large meanings. The plural is central. The box is not to be understood as the static allegory of an idea. Instead, it is the ambiguous, overdetermined vessel of many meanings. We think of Pandora's box, not only the myth but also Goethe's Pandora and, because of our historical vantage, Wedekind's, too. In a similar vein, the locked box of Hersilie's chastity and the penetrating key of Felix's love for her inevitably come to mind. And the key itself works on a principle of magnetism, which for Goethe certainly had connotations of "animal magnetism" that exists for us only as a cliché, a dim verbal memory of the sort we still invoke when we talk about the "chemistry" that takes place (or doesn't) between potential lovers.

As in **Die Wahlverwandtschaften** the erotic spell that binds lovers is mysterious, an invisible magnetism that draws opposites together. That the magnetic key snaps in two when it is used tells us that the "chemistry" is not right, or at least not yet. Magnetism will draw the two pieces of the key back together, a signal that at some later date the chemistry might work.

In a more general sense the box serves as a metaphor for the things that lie beyond representation. Feelings, love, even character lie outside the pale: "Vergebens bemühen wir uns, den Charakter eines Menschen zu schildern," writes Goethe, "man stelle dagegen seine Handlungen, seine Taten zusammen, und ein Bild des Charakters wird uns entgegentreten."[55] The character of feeling that draws Felix and Hersilie together is the secret of the box, or at least one of its secrets, and it can only be got at through the cumulative picture that their outward behavior offers. Given their failure to come to an arrangement, it is no wonder that the key snaps in two when it is put to the test.

The box is first and foremost a literary way of properly focusing the reader's attention. It is deployed not to simplify or define mimetically; instead it has an exploratory use, as an instrument in the process of cognitive discovery. The mystery chest calls to mind a few conspicuous antecedents. Parzifal's grail cannot be overlooked. Wolfram's reserve as to its appearance would seem to have to do with his reverence before the divine. Goethean and modernist tact in such matters may also have to do with a reverence before the divine. But it also has to do with the modern conviction that the nature of certain things is not fixed, and that they must therefore be approached obliquely in literature, "andeutungsweise" as Kafka put it.[56] Henry James's

golden bowl is an image with symbolic qualities akin to those of Goethe's Kästchen, so is Kafka's castle, if on a very different scale. The specific quality I have in mind is the ironic aim to symbolize something without actually "defining" it, i.e., falsifying its shifting and changing essence by attributing to it a static form. It is worth recalling Goethe's famous definition of the symbol as "die Sache, ohne die Sache zu sein, und doch die Sache."[57] Irony means having it both ways.

Goethe's **Wanderjahre** trafficks unwillingly in absolutes, essences, and abstractions. The **Wanderjahre** itself embodies this principle of seeking the concrete according to the demands of the moment. Its predecessor, **Wilhelm Meisters Lehrjahre,** was more or less predicated on the idea that the protagonist's Bildung will fulfill and finish him. That is the idea of the Bildungsroman. But the **Wanderjahre,** ironic in attitude, skeptical of social and individual perfectibility, takes the form of the great western novel of possibilities and potentialities: it is a road novel. Any day may, and probably will, bring new experiences, new challenges, new ideas and feelings. In this Goethe's **Wanderjahre** is the quintessentially modern novel.

Notes

1. Ludwig Geiger, *Goethes Leben und Werke,* Berlin 1904, 144.

2. For an even-handed discussion see Marianna Torgovnick, *Closure in the Novel,* Princeton 1981. See also Frank Kermode, *The Sense of an Ending,* New York 1966; Barbara Herrenstein Smith, *Poetic Closure,* Chicago 1968; Robert M. Adams, *Strains of Discord. Studies in Literary Openness,* Ithaca 1968; D. A. Miller, *The Novel and its Discontents. Problems of Closure in the Traditional Novel,* Princeton 1981.

3. Lothario and Therese, Hilarie and Flavio, the Major and the beautiful widow, Angela and Werner's assistant, Susanne's suitor marries a hard-working girl, and Montan says he will marry Lydie.

4. Ehrhard Bahr, "Wilhelm Meisters Wanderjahre oder die Entsagenden (1821/1829)," *Goethes Erzählwerk. Interpretationen,* eds. Paul Michael Lützeler, James E. McLeod, Stuttgart 1985, 363-396, here: 389-393.

5. On Broch's self-contradictory relationship to the idea of totality see my "Ornament, Totality, Kitsch and *The Sleepwalkers*," in: Dowden (ed.), *Hermann Broch: Literature, Philosophy, Politics,* Columbia, South Carolina 1988, 273-278.

6. For a clear assessment of the gulf that separates Goethe from Hegel and the Hegelians see Rüdiger Bubner, *Hegel und Goethe,* Heidelberg 1978.

7. Samuel Beckett, *"Proust" and "Three Dialogues with George Duthuit,"* London 1965, 11-93.

8. Musil, *Der Mann ohne Eigenschaften, Gesammelte Werke in 9 Bänden,* ed. Adolf Frisé, Reinbek 1978, II, 526, 527. For a fuller discussion of Musil see my "The Cloud of Polonius," *Sympathy for the Abyss. A Study in the Novel of German Modernism,* Studien zur deutschen Literatur 90, Tübingen 1986, 57-93.

9. Broch frames his argument from the perspective of myth, by which he means some all-encompassing, universal and absolute "value" (e.g. God in the Catholic middle ages). Thus he emphasizes not breadth in the novel, but depth, by which he means "primal symbols" that attempt to totalize and close the system. He offers Melville's white whale as a modern example, though he considers it impossible to recapture the lost totality. Post-classical Goethe, including the *Wanderjahre,* shows no such closure grounded in myth and symbol (*Hofmannsthal und seine Zeit,* Kritische Werkausgabe, ed. Paul Michael Lützeler, Frankfurt a.M. 1975, IX/1, 314-315).

10. In this context Gert Ueding speaks of Goethe's "ironische Gelassenheit." For him Makarie is a "gesteigerte Iphigenie," which seems to me to suggest too that she is an ironic intensification of the Iphigenie figure. But it is a gentle irony that does not mock. Instead, it is the kind of irony that offers an idea while denying its possibility: Goethe simultaneously offers Makarie as a mythic image of a grand unity and retracts it at the same time. The wish for myth and the knowledge that myth is impossible points toward the ironic stances of modernists such as Thomas Mann and Hermann Broch. Cf. Ueding, *Klassik und Romantik. Deutsche Literatur im Zeitalter der Französischen Revolution 1789-1815, Hansers Sozialgeschichte der deutschen Literatur,* ed. Rolf Grimminger, vol. IV, Munich and Vienna 1987, 450. Ehrhard Bahr also emphasizes the irony of Makarie in *Die Ironie im Spätwerk Goethes,* Berlin 1972, 128-129.

11. Without sorting through the multiple views of irony that Friedrich Schlegel offered during his career (and without exploring Goethe's attitude toward Schlegel), we should bear in mind the nearness of their attitudes toward irony and human limitations. What Goethe describes in the *Wanderjahre,* Schlegel writes abstractly in a late lecture (1829). True irony, he writes, "ist die Ironie der Liebe. Sie entsteht aus dem Gefühl der Endlichkeit und der eigenen Beschränkung, und dem scheinbaren Widerspruch dieses Gefühls mit der in jeder wahren Liebe mit eingeschlossenen Idee eines Unendlichen" (*Kritische Friedrich-Schlegel-Ausgabe,* ed. Ernst Behler in cooperation with Jean-Jacques Anstett and Hans Eichner, Munich 1969, X, 357).

12. Hans-Egon Hass, "Über die Ironie bei Goethe," *Ironie und Dichtung,* ed. Albert Schaefer, Beck'sche Schwarze Reihe 66, Munich 1970, 59-83.

13. *HA* VII, 294 (*HA* refers throughout to the Hamburger Ausgabe in 14 Bänden, ed. Erich Trunz, 10th rev. ed., Munich 1974). Bahr has noted that the aphorism collections in the novel themselves serve an ironic function. They do not pin down its meaning; instead they open it up. The aphorisms ambiguate the meaning of the novel and thereby add to its ironic texture. They force the reader into the role of an active, reasoning interpreter. I would add that the aphorisms open many possibilities of meaning and in so doing militate against closure. See Bahr (note 10), 100-101.

14. Letter of 23 November 1829 to Friedrich Johann Rochlitz, *WA* IV/46, 165-168.

15. The modernist vision of realism tends to oversimplify the realists' actual notion of how fiction relates to reality. For discussions of the nuances of self-consciousness and representation involved in German realism see Gail K. Hart, *Readers and their Fictions in the Novels and Novellas of Gottfried Keller,* Univ. of North Carolina Studies in Germanic Languages and Literatures 109, Chapel Hill 1989 and Robert C. Holub, *Reflections of Realism. Paradox, Norm, and Ideology in Nineteenth-Century German Prose,* Detroit 1991. See also Todd Kontje, *Private Lives in the Public Sphere. The German Bildungsroman as Metafiction,* University Park, Pennsylvania 1992.

16. Robert Alter, "Fielding and the Future of the Novel," *Fielding and the Nature of the Novel,* Cambridge, USA, 1968, 176-202. On Sterne and the modernists see Alter, *Partial Magic. The Novel as a Self-Conscious Genre,* Berkeley 1975, 30-56.

17. See also Goethe's essay of 1827 "Lorenz Sterne" which emphasizes Sterne's humane wit as a point of orientation for Goethe's own sense of tolerance and his literary use of his characters' "ruling passions," which Goethe calls "Eigenheiten" (peculiarities), in creating the sense of human individuality. The essay appeared in *Kunst und Altertum.* See also Harvey W. Thayer, *Laurence Sterne in Germany,* New York 1905, 97ff.; James Boyd, *Goethe's Knowledge of English Literature,* Oxford 1932, 108-113.

18. Johann Peter Eckermann, *Gespräche mit Goethe in den letzten Jahren seines Lebens,* ed. Regine Otto in collaboration with Peter Wersig, Berlin (East) 1982, 111. Indeed, English writers in general were popular with the reading public. It was not uncommon for German writers to attempt to pass off their own work as translations from the English in order better to

attract readers. Harvey W. Hewett-Thayer, *Laurence Sterne in Germany,* New York 1905, 5.

19. "Urteilsworte französischer Kritiker," *Über Kunst und Altertum,* 1820, II, 2.

20. Nicholas Boyle, *Goethe. The Poet and the Age,* Oxford 1991, I, 370.

21. Summarizing the received wisdom on the *Wanderjahre,* Gerhard Schulz writes: "Es ist ein Plan, der reich und bedeutend an Sinn ist, aber als epischer Vorwurf in sich selbst nur von mäßigem Interesse" (Schulz, *Die deutsche Literatur zwischen Revolution und Restauration, II: Das Zeitalter der napoleonischen Kriege und der Restauration 1806-1830, Geschichte der deutschen Literatur von den Anfängen bis zur Gegenwart,* eds. Helmut de Boor and Richard Newald, vol. VI/2, Munich 1989, 342).

22. Milan Kundera, "Sixty-three Words," *The Art of the Novel,* trans. Linda Ascher, New York 1986, 134.

23. Gustav Heinrich Hotho published a lengthy review in two installments in the *Jahrbücher für wissenschaftliche Kritik* 2/109 (December 1829), 863-891 and 1/41 (March 1830), 323-382.

24. I have in mind especially Ehrhard Bahr's study on the *Wanderjahre* in his *Die Ironie im Spätwerk Goethes* (note 10), 88-125; Bahr lays strong emphasis on Goethean irony as a "Schwebezustand" of ironic indeterminacy. See also Mathias Mayer, *Selbstbewußte Illusion. Selbstreflexion und Legitimation der Dichtung im "Wilhelm Meister,"* Beiträge zur neueren Literaturgeschichte, Folge 3, 93, Heidelberg 1989.

25. Eckermann supplied the emphasis here, presumably because Goethe stressed the point himself (*Gespräche mit Goethe,* 6 May 1827, 547).

26. Eckermann (note 18), 122.

27. Cited in Alter, *Partial Magic* (note 16), 30.

28. *Goethes Gespräche 1752-1817,* Gedenkausgabe, XXII, 400. From Luden's memoir *Rückblicke in mein Leben,* Jena 1847. On this point cf. also Bahr, *Die Ironie im Spätwerk Goethes* (note 10), 106-107.

29. *HA* VIII, 484. Cf. his comment of 1830 to Riemer: "Ich las in Tristram Shandy und bewunderte aber und abermal die Freiheit, zu der sich Sterne zu seiner Zeit emporgehoben hatte, begriff auch seine Einwirkung auf unsere Jugend. Er war der erste, der sich und uns aus Pedanterie und Philisterei emporhob" (*Goethes Gespräche 1817-1832,* Gedenkausgabe, XXIII, 750).

30. A way of describing the narrative strategy of the *Wanderjahre,* first developed by Volker Neuhaus, "Die Archivfiktion in *Wilhelm Meisters Wanderjahren,*" *Euphorion* 62 (1968), 13-27.

31. Mathias Mayer (note 24) has made a detailed study of self-consciousness in Goethe's *Meister* novels. On the tradition of self-conscious novel see Alter, *Partial Magic* (note 16).

32. *HA* VIII, 408.

33. Bahr (note 4), 379-389.

34. Klaus-Detlef Müller, "Lenardos Tagebuch. Zum Romanbegriff in *Wilhelm Meisters Wanderjahre,*" *DVjs* 53 (1979), 275-299, here: 280-281.

35. Viktor Shklovsky, "The Novel as Parody: Sterne's *Tristram Shandy,*" *Theory of Prose,* trans. Benjamin Sher, Elmwood Park, Illinois 1991, 147-170; a translation of the book's second edition (Moscow 1929).

36. *HA* VIII, 118.

37. *HA* VIII, 617.

38. Bahr (note 10), 381 ff.

39. We must note in passing that the ironic distance was even greater in the novel's 1821 edition. There, at the end of chapter 11, the narrator inserts a long "Zwischenrede" in which he warns the reader that certain gaps, confusions and even incompletions will inevitably result from the editing process: "Denn wir haben die bedenkliche Aufgabe zu lösen, aus den mannigfaltigsten Papieren das Werteste und Wichtigste auszusuchen, wie es denkenden und gebildeten Gemütern erfreulich sein und sie, auf mancher Stufe des Lebens erquicken und fördern könnte" (Johann Wolfang von Goethe, *Wilhelm Meisters Wanderjahre,* eds. Gerhard Neumann, Hans-Georg Dewitz, 1/10, Frankfurt a.M. 1989, 127).

40. *HA* VIII, 651.

41. Ehrhard Bahr, for example, evidently accepts Friedrich as Goethe's mouthpiece: The novel's "seemingly liberal design [...] shows some unmistakable traits of a police state. The American utopia in the *Wanderjahre* is highly regimented day and night by telegraphic time signals, and it is described as consisting of people who do not think about justice, but police: 'Wer sich unbequem erweist wird beseitigt'" (III, 11). Penalties consist of expropriation or of "separation from civil society." Ehrhard Bahr, "Revolutionary Realism in Goethe's *Wanderjahre,*" *Goethe's Narrative Fiction. The Irvine Symposium,* ed. William J. Lillyman, Berlin and New York 1983, 161-175, 173. In his *Goethe and the Novel* (Ithaca

1976) Eric A. Blackall takes a favorable view of Odoard's authoritarian rules (calling it an "ideal moral community") for his league of emigrants (252ff.). He rather disingenuously omits a discussion of its anti-Semitic implications in order, evidently, to put the best face he can on inadequately mediated reading. Blackall makes no allowance for Goethean irony. Goethe is sowing the seeds of disillusion and disorder in Lenardo's paradise. One of the most persuasive views of Goethe is that of Heinz Schlaffer, speaking here not of the *Wanderjahre* and its supposed utopia, but of Goethe's overall ironic strategy in his novels: "Exoterisch bestätigen Goethes Romane die jeweils zeitgenössischen Ideen: Freiheit, Bildung, Sittlichkeit, Fortschritt; esoterisch enthüllen sie, wie im Komplex der Zeit diesen zur Ideologie entstellten Ideen die Negation innewohnt: Illusion, Entleerung, Naturverfallenheit, Tod. Der Aufstieg der bürgerlichen Gesellschaft, der mit Goethes Lebenszeit zusammenfällt, verhinderte notwendigerweise das Verständnis für dessen ironische Skepsis gegenüber diesem Aufstieg" (Heinz Schlaffer, "Exoterik und Esoterik in Goethes Romanen," *Goethe-Jahrbuch* 95 [1978], 212-226, here: 225).

42. As a young lawyer Goethe was on good terms with his Jewish clients. Later, as a culture hero, he had cordial social and intellectual relationships with many Jews, including Rahel Levin and Felix Mendelssohn-Bartholdy. He even seemed aware that he was susceptible to the prejudices of his time and place. When he met the Jewish banker Simon von Laemel in Karlsbad, Goethe confessed that his childhood aversion to Jews had been the reflection of the Christian society into which he was born. It was an attitude he had outgrown (Gedenkausgabe, XXII, 639f.). On the darker side, Chancellor Müller reports that Goethe was strongly opposed to Arch-Duke Karl August's 1823 legalization of marriage between Christians and Jews. Worse yet, Goethe once praised a law that prohibited Jews from spending the night in Jena. On the other hand, as director of the Weimar theater he refused to allow anti-Semitic comedy and he rebuked a man named Köbele for anti-Semitic writings. See Wilfried Barner, "150 Jahre nach seinem Tod. Goethe und die Juden," *Bulletin des Leo Baeck Instituts* 63 (1982), 75-82, esp. 79; and Ludwig Geiger, *Die Juden in der deutschen Literatur,* Berlin 1910, 100.

43. Wilfried Barner, "Jüdische Goethe-Verehrung vor 1933," *Juden in der deutschen Literatur. Ein deutsch-israelisches Symposion,* eds. Stéphane Moses and Albrecht Schöne, Frankfurt a.M. 1986. For a polemical use of Goethe to support anti-Semitic cultural conservatism see Houston Stewart Chamberlain, *Goethe,* Munich 1912, 688-697; for a polemical defense of Goethe against Nazi exploitation see Mark Waldman,

Goethe and the Jews. A Challenge to Hitlerism, New York and London 1934.

44. *Deutsches Theater, Gesamtausgabe der Werke und Schriften,* II/15: *Schriften zu Literatur und Theater,* ed. Wolfgang Rehm, Stuttgart, n.d., 597.

45. *HA* VIII, 160.

46. For a detailed accounting, see Waldman's *Goethe and the Jews* (note 43).

47. Ben Macintyre, *Forgotten Fatherland. The Search for Elisabeth Nietzsche,* New York 1992.

48. Clark Muenzer, *Figures of Identity. Goethe's Novels and the Enigmatic Self,* University Park and London 1984, 110-129.

49. *HA* XI, 590.

50. For an opposing view see Rolf Grimminger, *Die Ordnung, das Chaos und die Kunst. Für eine neue Dialektik der Aufklärung,* Frankfurt a.M. 1986, 231ff. Grimminger either ignores or discounts Goethean irony: "Die Ordnungen des Rahmens 'dezentrieren' mit den Individuen auch das Erzählen und den Roman selbst, zentral ist das Lehrbuch und seine Didaktik. Ihr nüchternes Pathos des Allgemeingültigen und Nützlichen kann aber nur schmale Sinnorientierungen anbieten. Eine Welt, in der nur instrumentelles Handeln nach mechanisch befolgten Richtlinien zugelassen wird, droht zum Arbeitslager zu verkommen, sie wird nicht nur inhuman, sondern auch sinnlos eng" (236).

51. *HA* VIII, 393.

52. Erich Kahler, *The Inward Turn of Narrative,* trans. Richard and Clara Winston, Princeton 1973.

53. Cf. Gerhard Neumann, who comments at considerable length on "Nicht zu weit" in his edition of the *Wanderjahre*: "Indem Goethe die Verantwortung für die Wahrheit des Erzählten auf verschiedene Gewährsleute und Autoritäten verteilt, suspendiert er letztlich die Verantwortung des 'Autors' für die Wahrheit des Geschehens und macht sie durch Zersplitterung der Erzählinstanzen unkenntlich" (*Wilhelm Meisters Wanderjahre,* eds. Gerhard Neumann and Hans-Georg Dewitz, 1216-1231, here: 1223).

54. As Birgit Baldwin has pointed out in "*Wilhelm Meisters Wanderjahre* as an Allegory of Reading," *Goethe Yearbook* 5 (1990), 213-232, here: 223-226.

55. *HA* XIII, 315.

56. I have developed this more fully in an essay entitled "Robinson Crusoe's Banner. Quixotic Nihilism and

Moral Imagination in Franz Kafka," *Southern Humanities Review* 24 (1990), 15-30.

57. Goethe, Gedenkausgabe, XIII, 315.

Marc Redfield (essay date 1996)

SOURCE: Redfield, Marc. "The Dissection of the State: *Wilhelm Meisters Wanderjahre* and the Politics of Aesthetics." *German Quarterly* 69.1 (1996): 15-31. Print.

[*In the following essay, Redfield examines the activity of anatomical dissection in the novel as a "rhetorical allegory" for the aesthetic state—a concept, originating with Friedrich Schiller, that presents the search for beauty as a necessary condition for political progress. Redfield maintains that such aestheticism, like dissection (but unlike surgery), can neither kill nor revive but only manipulate the bodies on which it operates.*]

Gestell heißt auch ein Knochengeripppe.

—Heidegger

In recent years one frequently encounters the claim that aesthetics is an essentially, and disingenuously, political discourse. The project of cultural critique, versions of which figure so visibly in the landscape of contemporary criticism, might be summed up as the attempt to demonstrate that aesthetics not only fails to transcend the purposeful machinations of power, but reinforces these machinations through its very pretense to transcend them. This demystification of aesthetics has enjoyed considerable success at least in part because aesthetics, as an identifiable discipline, is so clearly a historical phenomenon, and one which consequently can be incorporated into political narrative. The vehemence with which conservative journalists and critics parody and decry the "politicization" of aesthetics is doubtless in large part a tribute to the force of the demystifying narrative; for as soon as one considers, from a sociological perspective, the emergence of the aesthetic sphere over the course of the eighteenth century, it rapidly becomes obvious—particularly in the German contexts in which aesthetics was first and most elaborately theorized—that the idea, the funding, and the upkeep of a "cultural sphere" served recognizable, and quite pressing, political and class interests. The disinterestedness of aesthetics thus provides as it were a detour or disguise for various and not necessarily complementary projects: the consolation and bureaucratization of a middle class within an absolutist state; the construction of an ideological base for an eventual middle-class hegemony; the diversion of revolutionary energies; and so on.[1]

Any attempt to recover a political mission for aesthetics, however, risks tendentiousness if it fails to recall and examine not just the unwitting external instrumentality of aesthetics, but also this discourse's inherent and frequently overt politicality. Schiller's assertion that we can only approach the "problem of politics" through the "problem of the aesthetic" ("weil es die Schönheit ist, durch welche man zu der Freiheit wandert" [8]) makes for a particularly dramatic moment in the early history of aesthetic thought, but is hardly an eccentric claim. The Schillerian development of Kantian themes into the narrative of an "ästhetische Erziehung des Menschen" in a sense merely unleashes the totalizing power implicit in the *Kritik der Urteilskraft*'s location of aesthetics in the process of formalization. Since, in Kant, the particular aesthetic experience, in its formality, claims subjective universality, aesthetic judgment easily comes to prefigure the universality of Schiller's "reine[m] idealischen Menschen" (4.2), whose full realization would take place as the emergence of the "Staat des schönen Scheins" (27.12). The acculturation or *Bildung* of an individual by definition models a political process, however overtly apolitical or "inward" *Bildung*'s orientation, and despite the nonreferentiality of the aesthetic moment per se. For if the nonreferentiality of the aesthetic demonstrates the essentially harmony and prescriptive universality of "man," aesthetic formalization is nonreferential only so as to guarantee "man" as a transcendental referent. And since aesthetics presupposes sensory realization, aesthetics incipiently involves the political production of "man" in the world, whether as the education of an individual or the evolution of a community, nation, or race. Despite Heidegger's hostility to aesthetics, his elaboration of the ancient thought of *poiesis* as a mode of bringing-forth (*Her-vor-bringen*) does not finally run counter to the aesthetic tradition, precisely insofar as aesthetics presupposes its own self-production. In this sense, aesthetics may be understood as a certain culmination of the notion of *poiesis,* though aesthetics may also, as we shall see, be linked to the "modern technology" that Heidegger opposes to *poiesis* as a violent "challenging" (*Herausfordern*) to a "bringing-forth." It is one of the tasks of this essay to suggest that the "politics of aesthetics" resides in the peculiar and fundamental relation of aesthetics to the technical.

At this point one needs to remark, however, that if aesthetics is a political model, the notion of "politics" has itself, since Plato, been conceptualized in relation to the mimetic arts, and, more generally, to *poiesis* as the production or formation of form. Tragedians are expelled from the city of philosophy because the polis itself is "a representation of the fairest and best life, which is in reality ... the truest tragedy" (*Laws* VII, 817b). Thus, Philippe Lacoue-Labarthe insists,

> the political (the City) belongs to a form of *plastic art,* formation and information, *fiction* in the strict sense. ...
> The fact that the political is a form of plastic art in no way means that the *polis* is an artificial or conventional formation, but that the political belongs to the sphere of *technè* in the highest sense of the term: the sense in

which *technè* is thought as the accomplishment and the revelation of *physis* itself.

(66)

As "fiction," the political is organic, as in the famous opening of Aristotle's *Politics,* in which "the state is a creation of nature and . . . man is by nature a political animal" precisely because "man is the only animal whom [nature] has endowed with the gift of speech" (*Politics,* I, ii [1253b]). One could say that, thanks to language, the political becomes the fulfilment of nature (*physis*) in the non-natural sphere of culture (*technè*). This not only means that the state is conceived as artwork, but that the community itself is organic in essence, and discovers itself as such in the *technè* of art: "If *technè* can be defined as the sur-plus of *physis*, through which *physis* 'deciphers' and presents itself . . . , political *organicity* is the *surplus* necessary for a nation to present and recognize itself. And such is the political function of art" (Lacoue-Labarthe 69, emphasis in original).

Mutatis mutandis, this constellation of assumptions can be traced through Renaissance humanism to the inverted Platonism of eighteenth-century aesthetics, and finally to the racial ideologies of the modern period.[2] Though, as Lacoue-Labarthe comments, nothing requires aesthetic politics to become grounded in the pseudo-biology of race, "it can very easily be taken in that direction once *physis* comes to be interpreted as *bios*," precisely because of the "*organic* interpretation of the political" (69). Lacoue-Labarthe's point—that racism is "primarily, fundamentally, an aestheticism" (69)—helps one appreciate the degree to which aesthetics, in the most general sense, shaped both the official culture and the ideological energy of Nazism, less in Hitler's or his party's relation—philistine at best—to the arts per se than in their understanding of politics as the community's autoproduction in and through the spectacle of a "natural" destiny. The political thus becomes the production of itself as the total work of art, and thus also becomes, as Lacoue-Labarthe and Jean-Luc Nancy have argued, a violent ideologization of "the absolute, self-creating Subject" of the metaphysical tradition, a subject that purports to embody itself in "an immediate and absolutely 'natural' essence: that of blood and race" ("The Nazi Myth" 310). These claims represent an effort to discover nonreductive relations between twentieth-century fascism and a Western tradition for which the fascist regimes had, to be sure, utter contempt, but in the absence of which they are also inconceivable. Lacoue-Labarthe's specific project consists, of course, in the negotiation of a relation to Heidegger, and an assessment of the differences and complicities that Heidegger's thought and career offer in relation to National Socialism. This project has as its primary rationale not the weighing of personal or even philosophical guilt, but the examination of a thought that "can enlighten us as to the real, or profound, nature of Nazism" (53), occasionally despite itself. As suggested in the citations above, Heidegger's meditations on *technè*

thus take on considerable importance, offering as they do a reminder and an analysis of the intimacy between politics and aesthetics.[3]

I propose to return to the question of *technè* and technology, as Heidegger asks it, via a route that at first glance may seem at best improbable. However, few texts address the interleaved questions of art, technics, and politics more overtly, closely, and strangely than does the odd parody of a sequel to **Wilhelm Meisters Lehrjahre** that Goethe published, in two different versions, in the 1820s as **Wilhelm Meisters Wanderjahre**.[4] Like the second part of **Faust**, this text has always been received as a social and political, if highly symbolic, narrative, so much so that from the 1830s to the present day readers have frequently pressed it into the service of straightforwardly political visions.[5] Thomas Mann, for instance, who in 1923 somewhat rashly discerned in the *Meister* cycle a "wunderbare Vorwegnahme deutschen Fortschreitens von der Innerlichkeit zum Objektiven, zum Politischen, zum Republikanertum," summed up its plot in terms that distill the essence of *Bildung* as a political principle: "Es beginnt mit individualistisch-abendteuerndem Selbstbildnertum und endet mit politischer Utopie. Dazwischen aber steht die Idee der *Erziehung*" (855-56, Mann's emphasis).[6] The movement of *Erziehung* as a progression from inwardness to action and from theory to praxis is the narrative of *Bildung* that the **Wanderjahre** represents as the elaboration of a notion of art as *technè*, in the course of which aesthetics emerges as a highly effective, and profoundly unstable, political force.

I

Before turning to the ways in which Goethe's novel associates aesthetic totalization with technical and political power, we should recall the extent to which the **Wanderjahre** at least appears to exceed and destabilize such associations before they can even be proposed. The plot line to which Mann refers—the story of the eponymous Wilhelm Meister—is a shred of *Bildung* woven into a complex and not in any way obviously unified tapestry, since the **Wanderjahre**'s mélange of novellas, letters, speeches, journal entries, technical writing, poetry, and aphorisms, not to mention its overall symbolic density and narrative fragmentariness, make it difficult to assimilate to any generic standard, even one as capacious as that provided by the Romantic idea of the novel. It is not even certain what ought to count as **Wilhelm Meisters Wanderjahre** and what ought not, since, according to Eckermann, Goethe attached collections of maxims to the second and third of the text's three books simply in order to have more material to give the publisher, and then attached poems to the collections of maxims because this seemed a convenient way to dispose of two available, and as yet unpublished, poems. Where the **Wanderjahre** can be said to end is consequently such a vexed issue that the two most widely-used scholarly editions of Goethe's works have decided the matter differently.[7] And if the border or frame of the text remains uncertain, the content, or what one chooses to count as "content," has proved impossible to pin down tonally or thematically, even (or especially) when the content has a political cast. Later I shall examine more closely the "Bund" with which Wilhelm becomes involved in the text's third book; for the moment I would like to note that while, on the one hand, this organization's announced program offers the twentieth-century reader all the sinister touchstones of organicist politics (the League will tolerate no Jews, since they repudiate the "Ursprung und Herkommen" of "höchsten Kultur" [405]),[8] on the other hand, the League's proposed legislation is so elastically cranky that at one point we are told by one of the group's two charismatic leaders that the new community will forbid the beating of drums and the ringing of bells (406). W. H. Bruford understandably comments that "it is hard to know how much of all this the author expects us to take seriously" (103): there is a hint of Groucho Marx's Freedonia to a political vision that we also have every reason to handle with care.[9]

These large obstacles to interpretation have not prevented the emergence of a considerable body of secondary literature on *Wilhelm Meisters Wanderjahre,* and we may take a first step toward a reading of the role of aesthetics in this novel by noting the way in which the text's unruly shape and tone has tended to be aestheticized in the critical tradition, subsequent to the professionalization of literary studies and the hypercanonization of Goethe in the German academy. As in the case of the omnibus texts of the modernist period to which Goethe's late work is often compared, critics have frequently sought a unifying principle for the *Wanderjahre*'s heterogeneity in notions of "symbolic" narrative.[10] Appeal is often made to Goethe's famous definition of the symbol: "Die Symbolik verwandelt die Erscheinung in Idee, die Idee in ein Bild, und so, daß die Idee im Bild immer unendlich wirksam und unerreichbar bleibt und, selbst in allen Sprachen ausgesprochen, doch unaussprechlich bliebe" (*HA* [*Goethes Werke*] 12, 470-71). Once identified as "symbolic," the *Wanderjahre*'s heterogeneity can be turned into a paradoxical ground of identity, to the extent that the gap between signifier and signified—the "unreachableness" of the idea—can become a transcendental signified, the signifier of the totality of an inexpressible world. Thus, Goethe wrote,

> Mit solchem Büchlein aber ist es wie mit dem Leben selbst: es findet sich in dem Complex des Ganzen Nothwendiges und Zufälliges, Vorgesetztes und Angeschlossenes, bald gelungen, bald vereitelt, wodurch es eine Art von Unendlichkeit erhält, die sich in verständige und vernünftige Worte nicht durchaus fassen noch einschließen läßt.[11]

The uncertain borders of the text become a sign of this endlessness, and the ambiguous difference between seriousness and play in the text's tonal and thematic registers becomes the mark of an *obscuritas* that Ehrhard Bahr, in an influential study of Goethe's late style, calls irony.

In various ways, the *Wanderjahre* proposes connections between the symbol's transcendental unknowability or obscurity and the operations effected by technical knowledge. This occurs most famously in and around the story of the little *Kästchen* discovered early in the narrative by Wilhelm's son Felix. Since the casket is "nicht größer als ein kleiner Oktavband" (43), and since its contents remain unknown throughout the novel, critics have understandably tended to interpret this mysterious *Kästchen* as a figure for the text itself as symbol. Associated with subterranean mystery—Felix discovers it in a cave—the casket is "bedeutend" (458) precisely because it remains a "Rätsel" or "Geheimnis," both for us and for the text's characters.[12] The casket's story, furthermore, unfolds as an allegory of the definition of the symbol as the gathering of "disparate elements" into a unity. Early on in the novel, Wilhelm deposits the casket for safekeeping with a professional collector who warns him against forcing it open: "Denn wenn Sie glücklich geboren sind und wenn dieses Kästchen etwas bedeutet, so muß sich gelegentlich der Schlüssel dazu finden, und gerade da, wo Sie ihn am wenigsten erwarten" (146-47). And the collector tells an exemplary story of an ivory crucifix, a fragment when he first acquired it, for which he has been able to recover the missing pieces—the arms, a portion of the cross, and so on. (In this "glückliches Zusammentreffen," he tells us, we recognize the destiny of the Christian religion, "die, oft genug zergliedert und zerstreut, sich doch endlich immer wieder am Kreuze zusammenfinden muß" [147].) As any reader of novels might expect, the key to the casket is eventually found. However, when the impulsive Felix inserts it into the lock, it breaks into two pieces—literalizing the etymology of "symbol," and in the process reconfirming the *symbolon*'s transcendental resistance to decoding. The casket's contents thus remain a mystery, but we do shortly learn something else: first, that a skilled craftsman can in fact unlock a symbol, and second, that one of the secrets to being a skilled craftsman is the skill of keeping secrets secret. In the wake of Felix's misguided attempt to possess the casket's meaning, a jeweler demonstrates that the two pieces of the key are "magnetisch verbunden," and "schließen nur dem Eingeweihten"; then, rather as though the key were an electronic door-opener, "der Mann tritt in einige Entfernung, das Kästchen springt auf, das er gleich wieder zudrückt: an solche Geheimnisse sei nicht gut rühren, meinte er" (458).

The symbol, by definition, is a gathering of itself unto itself, as exemplified by the recovery of the "dismembered and scattered" limbs of a holy body or icon. The role of the technician in this transcendental economy may be less obvious, but is certainly also of ancient provenance. Magic is practical knowledge, *technè,* and the jeweler a savant in the Masonic and hermetic tradition: a technician whose craft presents itself as both pragmatic and esoteric. The jeweler's antics are sufficiently exaggerated that, as so often in the **Wanderjahre,** it is hard to know how much "the author expects us to take seriously"; but this undecidably valorized scenario nonetheless dramatizes a relation between technics and renunciation central to the **Wanderjahre.** Technics is knowledge derived from the renunciation of knowledge, and this renunciation of knowledge links technical prowess to the transcendental unknowability of the symbol. The symbol turns out to be a pragmatic principle, as Goethe's definition of it as "wirksam und unerreichbar" suggests. And as we shall see, the symbol's melange of secrecy, technics, and formal totalization acquires political clout through the valorization of a pragmatic aesthetic, which the text calls *Handwerk.*

II

An emphasis on pragmatic knowledge characterizes the various utopic (or mockutopic) communities that ***Wilhelm Meisters Wanderjahre*** either portrays or has its characters describe or theorize, particularly the "Bund" mentioned earlier. The *Bund,* an organization charged with the founding of utopic communities in both the New and the Old worlds, is the new name and identity of the *Turmgesellschaft* of ***Wilhelm Meisters Lehrjahre*—**a pseudo-Masonic secret society that, in the **Lehrjahre,** has nothing better to do than to watch over and manipulate Wilhelm's life behind the scenes, until, his *Bildung* complete, he is fit to enter its ranks. The transformation of this Society into a colonizing venture would thus certainly seem to mark an explicit politicization of the ends of *Bildung*: a politicization linked in turn with the question concerning technics. Generally, though not always, the League, in good Romantic-agrarian fashion, is opposed to technology but celebratory of *technè*, "dem Maschinenwesen weniger günstig als der unmittelbaren Handarbeit, wo wir Kraft und Gefühl in Verbindung ausüben" (337). The group's members, consequently, are idealized *Handwerker,* while its leaders—and its financial backing—are of aristocratic origin.

Thus consistently, if ironically, the text's characters and narrators propose *Handwerk* as a value.[13] Lenardo and Odoard's vision of their *Bund* gives overt political shape to an idealization of craft that we have already seen at work (or play) in the encounter of the jeweler and the casket, and which particularly marks the plot line featuring Wilhelm Meister. Within this narrative strand, *Handwerk* represents the effect or outcome of the "Entsagung" characterizing true *Bildung*. When Wilhelm asks the Collector to whom he has consigned the mysterious casket to advise him where he might consign his son, the Collector recommends the Pedagogical Province as a place where students receive a limited, technical, and thus genuine education:

> Allem Leben, allem Tun, aller Kunst muß das Handwerk vorausgehen, welches nur in der Beschränkung erworben wird. Eines recht wissen und ausüben gibt höhere Bildung als Halbheit im Hundertfältigen. Da, wo ich Sie hinweise, hat man alle Tätigkeiten gesondert ...

(148)

And the father, like the son, will undergo *Bildung* under the aegis of technics: indeed, while Felix's training in the Pedagogical Province turns out to be considerably less focused and effective than the Collector's account might suggest,[14] Wilhelm's education will discover its ultimate rationale in his assumption of the manual trade of surgeon—a profession nearly as distant from the middle-class norms of the day as carpentry or weaving would be. In the **Lehrjahre** Wilhelm had had to renounce the possibilities for *Bildung* that the theatre had seemed to represent—the proto-bohemian hope of capturing aristocratic well-roundedness through the protean grace of the actor; now, in the 1829 **Wanderjahre,** he must renounce not just aristocratic pretension, but also bourgeois dilettantism. In itself, Wilhelm's seeming loss of social prestige holds limited interest, since on this point the **Wanderjahre** is as cheerily unrealistic as the **Lehrjahre** had been in casually betrothing its middle-class hero to an aristocrat, Nathalie, in its final chapters. In the symbolic universe of the *Meister* cycle, Wilhelm's *dérogation* is not an appreciably material sacrifice in anyone's eyes, least of all Wilhelm's. However, if the "Entsagung" at work in the "Beschränkung" that is *Handwerk* lacks socioeconomic consequence, it does have a fundamental relation to the political, and more specifically to the politics of aesthetics as pragmatism—a pragmatism that claims to overcome the problem of truth by declaring it unavailable. As Clark Muenzer writes in a fine recent study of the figure of *technè* in Goethe's thought, one can "reject self-presence as a delusion" (141), bracket the question of truth or reference, and pass on to practical matters. The gesture is a familiar one in post-Romantic thought, and frequently appears in both academic and popular circles in the form of arguments or manifestos "against theory."[15] Goethe's novel, however, demonstrates that such pragmatism is finally an exacerbated aestheticism.

If the aesthetic, in its post-Kantian formulation, brackets meaning in order to recuperate meaning as form, a pragmatized aesthetic reiterates this gesture to the second power. Meaning is sacrificed so as to be reborn as meaning-as-action, the "doing" of meaning. The aestheticism and the totalizing ambition of technical pragmatism are spelled out early in the **Wanderjahre** when Wilhelm's old friend Jarno delivers a speech on the virtues of specialization so eloquent that Wilhelm makes his decision to become a surgeon upon hearing it:

> Sich auf ein Handwerk zu beschränken, ist das Beste. Für den geringsten Kopf wird es immer ein Handwerk, für den besseren eine Kunst, und der beste, wenn er eins tut, tut er alles, oder, um weniger paradox zu sein, in dem einen, was er recht tut, sieht er das Gleichnis von allem, was recht getan wird.

(37)

The seductive power of the trope of *Handwerk* as renunciation is both exemplified and analyzed in this passage:

the figure is persuasive because it mingles the steely resolve of renunciation with the luxury of recompense. Art
has not really been renounced at all, since it returns as the
universality of that which has been "recht getan." At the
same time, the totalizing mirage of *Kunst* has been projected onto the world: Wilhelm will cut bodies instead of
staging representations as he did in the ***Lehrjahre,*** and the
Society of the Tower will build colonies instead of manipulating private lives, which is to say that any instability
inherent in the aesthetic system will now have increased
opportunity to work itself out on a political level. Thus, the
elements in the ***Lehrjahre***'s narrative of renunciation
undergo pragmatic intensification in the ***Wanderjahre***'s.
If the previous novel moves Wilhelm toward a renunciation of the aesthetic lure of the theatre, the ***Wanderjahre***
ironically allows its League to risk philistinism by having
it toy with a literal renunciation of art itself. The *Bund*'s
artists, we learn at one point, will be obtained from the
Pedagogical Province—where they have been properly
trained in the ethos of corporate art—but even so, the
Bund will accept "very few": "Die Künste sind das Salz
der Erde; wie dieses zu den Speisen, so verhalten sich jene zu
der Technik. Wir nehmen von der Kunst nicht mehr auf als
nur, daß das Handwerk nicht abgeschmackt werde" (242).

We may now step back and begin to resurvey the terrain of
aesthetics in the ***Wanderjahre,*** since, as these words of the
Abbé suggest, the hyper-aesthetic of pragmatism raises the
specter of curiously specific aesthetic problems. As soon
as *Handwerk* becomes the epitome of the aesthetic,
another sort of epitome, *Kunst,* appears as a force needing
to be controlled—but also as a homeopathic cure for a
Handwerk inexplicably threatened with being "abgeschmackt." A sense of the tensions at play in the aesthetic of
Handwerk emerges in Odoard's speech to the League late
in the text. On the one hand, handicraft and art share a
profound identity, while on the other, they need to be
sharply distinguished: "Sobald wir jenen bezeichneten
Boden betreten, werden die Handwerke sogleich für
Künste erklärt, und durch die Bezeichnung 'strenge
Künste' von den 'freien' entschieden getrennt und abge-
sondert" (411). And in fact, handicraft must give the
exemple to art ("zum Muster dienen"), since in *Handwerk*
more is at stake:

> Sehen wir die sogenannten freien Künste an, die doch
> eigentlich in einem höheren Sinne zu nehmen und zu
> nennen sind, so findet man, daß es ganz gleichgültig
> ist, ob sie gut oder schlecht betrieben werden. Die
> schlechteste Statue steht auf ihren Füßen wie die beste,
> eine gemalte Figur schreitet mit verzeichneten Füßen gar
> munter vorwärts, ihre mißgestalteten Arme greifen gar
> kräftig zu, die Figuren stehen nicht auf dem richtigen
> Plan, und der Boden fällt deswegen nicht zusammen.
> Bei der Musik ist es noch auffallender; die gellende Fiedel
> einer Dorfschenke erregt die wackern Glieder aufs kräf-
> tigste, und wir haben die unschicklichsten Kirchenmu-
> siken gehört, bei denen der Gläubige sich erbaute.

(412)

If *Kunst* had earlier been seen as mere salt to the food of
Handwerk, here the free arts are relegated to an even more
tenuous supplementarity: inessential in comparison to the
"rigorous arts," they have now also become the locus of a
potential tastelessness, the status of which is somewhat
peculiar. On the one hand, the "free arts" are subject to
degeneracy precisely because they are referentially free:
the floor does not cave in under the impact of misdrawn
figures because they have no power to negate the real. On
the other hand, art's irresponsibility does not in the least
seem to preclude its having effects upon the real: the ugly
statue stands, the misdrawn figure gestures, the screeching
fiddle "stirs stout limbs most powerfully," and the abomi-
nable church music "edifies" believers. Free art is not any
less effective for being either non-referential or badly
constructed. In fact, as the passage's repeated invocations
of force, *Kraft,* suggests, art's performative power might
be all the greater for being indifferent to referential and
formal constraints.[16]

If the "free" and the "rigorous" arts are both tributaries of
Kunst, the degeneracy of the former is possibly the visible
sign of a disease hidden in the latter. The transcendental
and pragmatic order of the symbol, in other words, might
be animated by a referential force irreducible to the world
of meaning it produces.[17] The secret that the jeweler re-
secretes in the casket is perhaps best left undisturbed for
this reason, but perhaps also for this reason it is inhabited
and constituted by disturbance. Neither the jeweler nor
anyone else can allow the symbol to rest embalmed in its
Kästchen, any more than pragmatism can keep from reiterating the ambitions and difficulties of the metaphysics
it abjures. ***Wilhelm Meisters Wanderjahre*** takes up this
problem most visibly in the orbit of its master-trope of
Handwerk, surgery.

III

If *Handwerk,* as limitation, is the privileged trope of
Entsagung, surgery renders the essence of *Handwerk-*
as-*Entsagung,* both in its etymology (the Greek root,
kheirourgia, translates literally as "handwork" [*kheir +
erg*]) and in its dialectical figure of the cut that heals.[18]
Appropriately, a scene of surgery grants enough formal
and metaphysical incisiveness to one of the ***Wander-***
jahre's numerous formal borders that Eric Blackall un-
hesitatingly, and understandably, refers to this episode as
"the real ending of the novel" (259). In the last chapter
before the epigram collection, Wilhelm and Felix reenter
the narrative line (from which they have been absent for
some time): thanks to his surgical know-how, Wilhelm
saves his son's life after Felix tumbles into a river. Wilhelm
thereby not only raises his son from apparent death ("kein
Zeichen des Lebens" remains when Felix is pulled out of
the water [459]), but also bandages the wound that had
created his desire to be a surgeon in the first place—for, if
we believe what Wilhelm tells his fiancée Nathalie at the
end of Book II, he first acquired this desire after losing a

childhood friend, whose death by drowning might have been averted if there had been a surgeon available to bleed the recovered body. In closing off the *Meister* plot, the **Wanderjahre** thus stages a therapeutic repetition: the father's knife heals the son, thereby healing the father. The religious and psychoanalytic intertexts which inevitably come to mind reinforce a figurative structure that the novel has built with considerable care. Surgery is the handwork of handwork, the renunciation of renunciation: its castrating cut seals the symbolic order, drawing the sting of time and death, healing past wounds in a present that excises all loss.

However, if surgery is the epitome of aesthetic *Handwerk* it is also the locus of corruption: a hyperbolically *abgeschmackte* version of Felix's resurrection unfolds in the third chapter of the **Wanderjahre**'s third book as Wilhelm recounts the story of his surgical education to members of the League. Wilhelm's narrative, which occupies most of the chapter and is what Bernd Peschken has in mind when he calls this chapter one of the most enigmatic ("*rätselhaften*") of the novel (119), tells the tale of a problem and its solution, both possessing an element of the bizarre. When Wilhelm begins surgical training he discovers its "Grundstudium" to consist in the art of dissection [*Zergliederungskunst*], and also finds out that the pragmatic bent of this paradoxical *Bildung*-through-*Zergliederung* has violent, even anarchic consequences. The cadavers required by the medical school are in short enough supply to inspire both state-sponsored and individual acts of terror, which in turn generates tension between the people and the state: "Solche, wo nicht hinreichend, doch in möglichster Zahl zu verschaffen, hatte man harte Gesetze ergehen lassen, nicht allein Verbrecher, die ihr Individuum in jedem Sinne verwirkt, sondern auch andere körperlich, geistig verwahrloste Umgekommene wurden in Anspruch genommen" (323). Simultaneously, grave-robbing flourishes, to the point that the body of the polis itself seems at the point of dismemberment: "Immer weiter aber stieg das Übel ... Kein Alter, keine Würde, weder Hohes noch Niedriges war in seiner Ruhestätte mehr sicher ..." (323). Indeed, we learn later in Wilhelm's story that "in dieser Stadt ... man gemordet [hat], um den dringenden, gut bezahlenden Anatomen einen Gegenstand zu verschaffen" (333). The motive force of this legal and illegal industry is the pragmatic thrust of surgical *Bildung*:

> ... junge Männer, die mit Aufmerksamkeit den Lehrvortrag gehört, sich auch mit Hand und Auge von dem bisher Gesehenen und Vernommenen überzeugen und sich die so notwendige Kenntnis immer tiefer und lebendiger der Einbildungskraft überliefern wollten.

(324)

Education generates an "unnatural" and socially disruptive cognitive desire: "In solchen Augenblicken entsteht eine Art von unnatürlichem wissenschaftlichen Hunger, welcher

nach der widerwärtigsten Befriedigung wie nach dem Anmutigsten und Notwendigsten zu begehren aufregt" (324).

This phase in Wilhelm's story reaches a climax when "ein sehr schönes Mädchen," believing herself jilted by her lover, drowns herself; to the consternation of the city, she is handed over to the anatomists by the authorities, "die soeben das Gesetz geschärft hatten, durften keine Ausnahme bewilligen." Wilhelm is given her severed arm to dissect, and he balks at the idea of "dieses herrliche Naturerzeugnis noch weiter zu entstellen" (325). A sculptor, a mysterious figure whom the medical students frequently see at their lectures, notices Wilhelm's moral dilemma and invites him home to his studio, where, as it turns out, the sculptor uses his *Kunst* to teach the *Handwerk* of surgery by substituting wax and wooden models for bodies. Despite the "grosse Kluft zwischen diesen künstlerischen Arbeiten und den wissenschaftlichen Bestrebungen von denen sie herkamen" (326), Wilhelm is persuaded of their utility—and he finds out that in this the *Bund* is ahead of him: Lothario and his colleagues have already made plans to ship the sculptor's models to their utopic colony in America (328).[19]

The emergence of *Wissenschaft* as the ground of *Handwerk* is not in itself surprising: as "rigorous art," *Handwerk*, unlike "free art," *Kunst*, must be epistemologically reliable. But since this reliability turns into a referential disease, free art stages a paradoxical return as "plastic anatomy," which offers to contain the referential drive of *Wissenschaft* within the frame of the aesthetic while anchoring knowledge to the world. The aesthetic is to heal the aesthetic in a homeopathic cure, as *Kunst* prevents *Handwerk* from becoming *abgeschmackt*. We may expect this solution to be a fragile one, since we have seen that *Kunst* is also possessed of unreliable referential power; and inded, complications emerge as the *Bildhauer* sums up the difference between old-fashioned dissection and his new plastic anatomy, in a phrase often taken to be the moral of the entire chapter: "Aufbauen mehr belehrt als Einreissen, Verbinden mehr als Trennen, Totes beleben mehr als das Getötete noch weiter töten" (326).[20] The maxim moves from the cleanly structured antonyms of building and destroying, binding and severing, to a counterintuitive opposition and semi-chiasmus: where one might have expected "giving life to the dead" to oppose "killing the living," the text rather insists that dissection be thought as "das Getötete noch weiter töten." And since the opposition is between giving life to the dead and killing the dead, the word "tot" becomes a defaced residue within this tropological structure, inhabiting and enabling the opposition without being assimilable to it. To be dead, in this Gothic fiction, is not to be so dead that one cannot continue to die.

The disfiguring figure "das Getötete noch weiter töten" (echoed when Wilhelm, confronted with the beautiful female arm, hesitates "dieses herrliche Naturerzeugnis noch weiter zu entstellen") sums up the essential (il) logic of dissection, as becomes clear when we examine more closely the political impact of this "unnaturlichem wissenschaftlichen Hunger." As an approach to the question of what dissection is, we may ask what law is in this story. A negative definition emerges immediately: *Verbrecher* are those who have "ihr Individuum in jedem Sinne verwirkt." Law is the generality of a social contract within which individuality is defined; lawbreakers lose their individuality in the very act of breaking the law. Simultaneously, the law presents itself as a generality oriented toward the future possibility of particular application in the mode of violence: in this sense, capital punishment would seem the essence of legal referentiality, since when the law refers, it does so by obliterating the particular *as* particular in relation to the whole. Law would thus essentially be the law of death. However, a closer look reveals that criminals, in becoming criminals, have "forfeited their individuality" through their own agency; in essence the criminal is a suicide, and capital punishment merely a literalization of the lawbreaker's self-annihilation. Thus, the "harsh laws" that criminalize suicide are merely reflexive intensifications of ordinary laws. Criminals and suicides are the most extreme sort of *Entsagenden* from a legal perspective; what the law punishes is in fact death itself—death, that is, understood as the self-consumption of the individual in an ultimate act of freedom. The "harsh laws" reveal that the law obtains no referential grip via capital punishment, and that, insofar as it wishes to have referential purchase, law must be dissection. For suicides can kill themselves but cannot dissect themselves: only through *Zergliederung* can the law inscribe itself on the world.[21]

The "dead" excess or excessive death (as "Zergliederung," as "das Getötete noch weiter töten"), which inhabits and disrupts the binary opposition of death and life, represents the symbol's inability to bracket reference and thus guarantee itself as a transcendental frame—the frame within which the pragmatic work of symbolic exchange would safely occur. The pragmatic need to "verify with hand and eye" generates both law and the violation of law, such that, as in the Chancellor's speech in **Faust,** "Das Ungesetz gesetzlich überwaltet / Und eine Weltdes Irrtumssich entfaltet" (*HA* 3: 151). However, if dissection is excessively referential, it is also excessively formal: a mechanical iteration performed on body after body, an act of memorization rather than learning, but a memorization which endlessly memorizes the same thing.[22] "Jeder Arzt," Wilhelm sums up near the end of his narrative, "... ist nichts ohne die genauste Kenntnis der äußern und innern Glieder des Menschen ... Täglich soll der Arzt, dem es Ernst ist, in der Wiederholung dieses Wissens, dieses Anschauens, sich üben ..." (331). In the service of this constant need to re-member through dismemberment, doctors will hire anatomists, and the disaster of which we know will unfold:

Je mehr man dies einsehen wird, je lebhafter, heftiger, leidenschaftlicher wird das Studium der Zergliederung getrieben werden. Aber in eben dem Maße werden sich die Mittel vermindern; die Gegenstände, die Körper, auf die solche Studien zu gründen sind, sie werden fehlen, seltener, teurer werden, und ein wahrhafter Konflikt zwischen Lebendigen und Toten wird entstehen ... Dieser Konflikt, den ich ankündige zwischen Toten und Lebendigen, er wird auf Leben und Tod gehen; man wird erschrecken, man wird untersuchen, Gesetze zu geben und nichts ausrichten.

(332)

It is in the wake of these comments that Wilhelm delivers his memorable and much-quoted imperative that "was jetzo Kunst ist, muß Handwerk werden, was im Besondern geschieht, muß im Allgemeinen möglich werden" (332). But we now see that this pragmaticist formalism emerges out of a violent proliferation of referential declarations. If the lopsided chiasmus of "das Getötete noch weiter töten" registered an excess of death, here there appears to be such an excess of life that the dead themselves cannot die. For whether one calls this endless residue "life" or "death" is indifferent, since as a trope for tropological residue either term is a catachresis.

Because dissection is the *Bildung* of surgery, the transcendental and pragmatic secret of the symbol may be said to emerge out of the referential predicament which dissection exemplifies. Thus, throughout Wilhelm's story, the *Bildhauer* will be associated with the symbol's secrecy—and its guilty conscience. We learn among other things that when the *Bildhauer* was an anatomy student he knowingly received a murdered corpse: "wir sahen vor uns hin und schwiegen und gingen ans Geschäft.—Und dies ist's, mein Freund, was mich zwischen Wachs und Gips gebannt hat; dies ist's, was gewiß auch Sie bei der Kunst festhalten wird ..." (333). No one knows much about this *Bildhauer* except that he is a sculptor (though possibly also a "Goldmacher"); much of his house is closed to visitors, and so on—and the narrative never seriously tries to explain why. We are told that that plastic anatomy must be pursued "im tiefsten Geheimnis," yet for reasons slender enough to seem secretive themselves: "denn Sie haben gewiß oft schon Männer vom Fach mit Geringschätzung davon reden hören" (326). Not only are anatomical models to be distributed "im stillen," but in a strange turn of phrase the *Bildhauer* sets forth the pedagogical ambitions of plastic anatomy in terms reminiscent of grave robbing or worse: "Es muß eine Schule geben ... das Lebendige muß man ergreifen und üben, aber im stillen ..." (328). It is inevitable that the plastic anatomist comes to resemble Burke and Hare, for *Handwerk* is the excess of law, an excess which the law in part recuperates as guilt, secrecy, and the symbol.[23]

IV

The recuperation of dissection's excess can only be partial and temporary, for reasons we have elaborated: if both

Kunst and *Handwerk* exploit, conceal, and suffer the effects of a referentially unreliable referential force, the homeopathic cure of the one through the other is doomed to fail. Thus, plastic anatomy cannot prevent the return of dissection: as the *Bildhauer* explains to Wilhelm, the *Bund*'s New World colony will also be a state geared toward the production of corpses. Criminals will once again provide the raw material:

> "Damit man aber nicht glaube," sagte der Meister, "daß wir uns von der Natur ausschließen und sie verleugnen wollen, so eröffnen wir eine frische Aussicht. Drüben über dem Meere, wo gewisse menschenwürdige Gesinnungen sich immerfort steigern, muß man endlich bei Abschaffung der Todesstrafe weitläufige Kastelle, ummauerte Bezirke bauen, um den ruhigen Bürger gegen Verbrechen zu schützen und das Verbrechen nicht straflos walten und wirken zu lassen. Dort, mein Freund, in diesen traurigen Bezirken, lassen Sie uns dem Äskulap eine Kapelle vorbehalten, dort, so abgesondert wie die Strafe selbst, werde unser Wissen immerfort an solchen Gegenständen erfrischt, deren Zerstückelung unser menschliches Gefühl nicht verletze, bei deren Anblick uns nicht, wie es Ihnen bei jenem schönen, unschuldigen Arm erging, das Messer in der Hand stockte und alle Wißbegierde vor dem Gefühl der Menschlichkeit ausgelöscht werde."

(330)

Whether this carceral humanism represents an ethical advance over the *ancien régime*'s Gothic cruelty is perhaps uncertain; nor does the *Wanderjahre*'s ironic treatment of its "utopias" encourage easy answers. A political critique nonetheless emerges from the rhetorical critique to the extent that this latter uncovers and dissects the story of the aestheticization of the political. As the state becomes more absolute in its claim to mimic and complete nature's harmony, to absorb into its *techne* the self-sufficiency of *physis,* its violence must take unacknowledged and thus always potentially more violent form. The state's laws no longer deal death; yet since these laws nonetheless have inscriptive, dissective force, the objects of legal violence must be all the more obsessively effaced. Incarceration, like plastic anatomy, seeks to draw a frame around the uncontrollable proliferation of dissection; in no case can dissection be halted, but one can hope for various practical, if always uncertain effects. Here, for instance, the state can hope that neither the *Volk* nor the occasional anatomist will rise to protest the obliteration of *Persönlichkeit,* since the objects of violence have been violently denied membership in the category of the "human" which imprisons and dissects them. They cannot die because they are not properly alive (that is, human) to begin with. The text has revealed this deathlessness to be a general predicament, that of language itself; but in the *Bildhauer*'s brave new world this endless dying will be repressed and its recurrence quarantined.

It is thus as a rhetorical allegory that ***Wilhelm Meisters Wanderjahre*** offers a critique of the Aesthetic State.

Though violence, and the violent effacement of violence, are certainly in no way specific to aesthetic humanism, the residue of a humanist universe takes deformed form as the *in-* or *non*-human, the human that is not human: more animal than human, but more inanimate than animal, since even animals are potentially alive and possibly even able to die. The criminals in the *Bildhauer*'s fantasy are the defaced repetition of the anatomical models, repeating humanism's repressed instability in the mode of inhumanity.[24] They are still being treated as useful pedagogical objects, rather than simply being "treated," like vermin or waste products, for this Aesthetic State is not yet an extermination camp. Yet without hyperbole, anachronism, or any notion of a German "destiny," one can and must read the operation of a certain exterminating logic in this narrative, a logic that the *Wanderjahre* critiques, or, in the figurative vocabulary of this text, dissects. The rationalist and utilitarian consumption of the in-human is a false ingestion, since these criminals are the excess of the very pragmatism that exploits them. In its extremity the Aesthetic State can only turn to more and more savagely displaced repetitions of its own disarticulation, and at the limit of its destructive course will need to obliterate its non-humans with the formal, mechanical violence of a purposeless, bureaucratic, technological operation—carried out "im tiefsten Geheimnis," in "ummauerte Bezirke." It should be emphasized that the ominousness of such tropes is in one sense profoundly false. The unspeakable of the Holocaust does not speak in this text; nor does the *Wanderjahre* "predict" Nazism. It is rather in destroying such aesthetic models of history as revelation and destination that this text offers a certain insight into the political aestheticism that Lacoue-Labarthe, at least, is willing to call the "real, or profound, nature of Nazism" (53): an aestheticism that is always also a "humanism" to the extent that the "human" represents the Subject's self-productive incarnation.[25]

Lacoue-Labarthe achieves his reading of the Nazis' technical, bureaucratic program of extermination as "the useless residue of the Western idea of art, that is to say, of *techne*" (46) through a reading of Heidegger, and we can close our present attempt to think the politics of aesthetics by returning to the question of technology as Heidegger asks it, and as the *Wanderjahre* allows it to be read. Heidegger, we recall, opposes the bringing forth of *poiesis* to the "Herausfordern" of modern technology, which "an die Natur das Ansinnen stellt, Energie zu liefern, die als solche herausgefördert und gespeichert weden kann" ("Frage" 22). The violence inherent in modern technology's mode of revealing lies not simply in its aggressive procedures of extraction, but in the fact that it extracts so as to store or stockpile: every technological action or object is for the sake of something else. Consequently, there is no *object* in the technological universe, but only "standing reserve," *Bestand.* Similarly, there is no "subject" of technology; however, since technology conceals its own essence by concealing "revealing" (*aletheia*) itself, humanity is led to imagine itself a subject in control of technology. Technology thus presents itself as metaphysics—the metaphysics of the subject—at the same time that it threatens to transform everything, not excluding humanity, into *Bestand.*

Heidegger calls the "herausfordernden Anspruch" which gathers man to modern technology "Ge-stell," a word he ventures "in einem bisher völlig ungewohnten Sinne zu gebrauchen":

> Nach der gewöhnlichen Bedeutung meint das Wort "Gestell" ein Gerät, z. B. ein Büchergestell. Gestell heißt auch ein Knochengerippe. Und so schaurig wie dieses scheint die uns jetzt zugemutete Verwendung des Wortes "Gestell" zu sein, ganz zu schweigen von der Willkür, mit der so Worte der gewachsenen Sprache mißhandelt werden. Kann man das Absonderlichkeit noch weiter treiben? Gewiß nicht. Allein dieses Absonderliche ist alter Brauch des Denkens.

("Frage" 27)

Compared with Plato's violent reappropriation of the word *eidos,* Heidegger concludes, his own "gewagter Gebrauch" of the word "Gestell" is "beinahe harmlos" ("Frage" 28). Heidegger says no more in this vein; but if his "eerie" "mishandling" of the word "Gestell" is "almost harmless," which is also of course to assert that it might be nonetheless ever so slightly harmful, this is perhaps because what Heidegger has named as the essence of modern technology bears a resemblance to language as a general rhetoric.[26] Language, in the Aristotelian tradition that Heidegger recalls and rewrites here, is *technè* in the highest sense—the essence of the human, and the completion of nature as *physis*—but the thought of *poiesis* cannot exhaust the problem of language, as ***Wilhelm Meisters Wanderjahre*** has confirmed. And the violent slippage with which, according to Heidegger, "language and thought" occur, bears a greater resemblance to *Gestell* than to *poiesis.*

In elaborating *Ge-stell* as an endless, mechanical dissection, ***Wilhelm Meisters Wanderjahre*** confirms the linguistic character of Heidegger's insight. Dissection is a killing machine that is equally an animating machine, precisely because it can never finish killing what it kills. It thereby figures an uncontrollable figurative process that dismembers yet also produces the symbol's divine corpse, exceeding and ruining the instances of reference it enables. Dissection, in this allegory, is *Bildung* as the construction and deconstruction of the *Glieder* which make bodies possible, including textual and political bodies. Commenting on its own irreducibility to the symbolic totalities it encourages, ***Wilhelm Meisters Wanderjahre*** diagnoses the violence of the Aesthetic State as the effect of a technicity which proves all the more haunting when this violence itself is aestheticized as pragmatism. In consequence, the possibility of cultural critique becomes paradoxically in-separable from that of the rigorously technical linguistic performances we call literature.

Notes

1. For a recent sociological account of the emergence of aesthetics in eighteenth-century Germany, see Woodmansee, and for an incisive definition of the project of cultural critique, see JanMohammed and Lloyd.

2. For a useful history of the notion of the "aesthetic state," see Chytry, esp. pp. xxxi-lxxiv.

3. I offer a brief version of my understanding of the value of Heidegger's thinking about technology at the end of the present essay. Lacoue-Labarthe's somewhat different—and to be sure, far more thorough—analysis sees significant continuities and differences between Heidegger's employment of *technè* as knowledge or science (*Wissen*) in the *Rektoratsrede* (published as *Die Selbstbehauptung der deutschen Universität*) and related texts of 1933, and as art in the "Ursprung des Kunstwerkes" in 1935. Heidegger's destruction of traditional aesthetics in favor of an understanding of art as *technè* allows one to understand the "essence" of Nazism as something at once proximate to, and very different from, Nazism: what Lacoue-Labarthe calls "national aestheticism," and which he analyzes as cited and described above. For a fuller discussion, see Lacoue-Labarthe 53-121.

4. The first version of the *Wanderjahre* appeared in 1821; a longer and extensively rewritten one appeared in 1829. The discussion presented here refers to the 1829 version; except where noted, I quote from volume 8 of the Hamburger Ausgabe, abbreviated where necessary as *HA.* Two other editions of Goethe's works will be cited occasionally in what follows: the "Artemis-Ausgabe," abbreviated as *AA* followed by volume and page number; and the "Weimarer Ausgabe," abbreviated as *WA* followed by section, volume, and page numbers.

5. For a recent and particularly emphatic association of this novel with Schiller's Aesthetic State, see Chytry, especially 62. An account of the enthusiastic reception accorded the *Wanderjahre* in certain Young Hegelian and Proudhonian circles of the 1830s and 1840s may be found in Sagave.

6. Cited in Bruford 88: see Bruford 226ff for a discussion of the political context of Mann's speech. Mann refers only to *"Wilhelm Meister"* and would seem to have both the *Lehrjahre* and the *Wanderjahre* in mind, with the latter, as Bruford notes, providing the "political utopia."

7. The editorial issue turns on whether or not to print the poems that Goethe attached to the maxim collections: the Artemis-Ausgabe prints them as part of the *Wanderjahre,* while the Hamburger Ausgabe, interpreting Goethe's final intentions differently, prints them with his collected poetry.

8. Near the end of the *Wanderjahre,* the League members respond to a speech by one of their leaders with a song possessing the rather ominous refrain, "Heil dir Führer! Heil dir Band!" (413).

9. Similar questions of tone or representational mode afflict the *Wanderjahre*'s portrayal of other utopic communities, most notably the Pedagogical Province, a fiefdom-sized boarding school into which Felix, Wilhelm's son, is deposited much against his will, and where he suffers the attentions of an educational system too bizarre and complex for summary, though see note 14 below.

10. See, e.g., Blackall; Brown; David; and Neuhaus. The generic issues raised by the *Wanderjahre* go far beyond the scope of this study. There has, for instance, been much discussion of the interpolated *Novellen* which account for more than two thirds of the narrative—though some of these narrative digressions are not technically *Novellen,* while, to make matters worse, the main narrative line itself is at least as close in spirit to the *Novelle* as to the *Roman,* and so on.

11. Goethe to Johann Friedrich Rochlitz, 23 November 1829 (*WA* IV, 46: 166). Comments of a similar nature appear in Goethe's correspondence in 1821 with regard to the first version of the *Wanderjahre:* see in particular letters to Sulpiz Boisserée, 23 July 1821 (*WA* IV, 35: 31-32) and to J. S. Zauper, 7 September 1821 (*WA* IV, 35: 73-77). It is also worth noting, however, that Goethe's comments on the *Wanderjahre* include many of the sort that *Wanderjahre* critics usually cite only in order to ignore, as when he described the text as a work undertaken only "zu dem Verband der disparatesten Einzelheiten" (Goethe to Rochlitz, 28 July 1829 [*WA* IV, 46: 27]). Variants of this phrase reappear in other letters of this period: see Goethe's letter of 2 September 1829 to Boisserée (*WA* IV, 46: 66). See also Goethe's characterization of the text as an unsystematizable "Aggregat" in a letter to F. von Müller, 18 February 1830 (*AA* 23: 667).

12. See in particular Peschken; see also Baldwin for a rigorous discussion of the rhetorical problems raised by the "symbolic" *Kästchen,* and a useful bibliography of the secondary criticism devoted to it.

13. On Goethe's ironization of *Handwerk* see Armstrong, who focuses on the *Wanderjahre*'s St. Joseph the Second episode in order to show that handicraft is persistently shadowed by anachrony and absurdity, and is thus by no means the reliable value it appears.

14. As noted earlier, the Pedagogical Province is not an easy institution to summarize. It places emphasis on authoritarian communality and practical knowledge—the students sing in chorus while they work, are taught unquestioning respect for all forms of authority, learn languages while tending to agricultural chores, and so on. Felix does not appear to emerge from this educational utopia with any particular skills. For discussions of the intellectual heritage and (uncertain) symbolism of the Province, see Brown 87-97, and Bruford 104-11.

15. See in particular the essays collected in Mitchell.

16. The rhetoricians of the *Bund* speak a great deal of power [*Kraft*], and of solutions that are pragmatic [*tätig*] and practical [*praktisch*]: see, e.g., 405.

17. Goethe's famous speculations on the "demonic" are worth recalling here: apart from the well-known passage in *Dichtung und Wahrheit* (*HA* 10:175-76), see Eckermann's entries for 28 February and 2 March 1831, where he records Goethe's sense of the demonic as a "geheime problematische Gewalt" external to, but determinative of, intention and meaning: "ich bin ihm unterworfen" (402, 405). For a fine discussion of the demonic in relation to the secret of the casket in the *Wanderjahre,* see Baldwin 220-23.

18. The metaphysics of the hand are elaborated by Odoard in the speech cited earlier on the distinction between "free" and "rigorous" arts (412-13). The question of the hand holds great interest for the question of technology in its Heideggerian inflection; and though I cannot develop this theme here, we might recall the importance Heidegger persistently grants the trope of *Handwerk,* particularly in *Was heisst Denken?*: "[Das Denken] ist jedenfalls ein Hand-Werk. Mit der Hand hat es eigene Bewandtnis ... Nur ein Wesen, das spricht, d.h. denkt, kann die Hand haben und in der Handhabung Werke der Hand vollbringen" (51). For an important reading of this and other passages, see Derrida, "La main de Heidegger."

19. And indeed, the *Bildhauer* might even be said to have sold his scheme to the author of the *Wanderjahre;* Goethe promulgated the virtues of "plastische Anatomie" with urgency in an essay written a few months before he died, referring his reader back to the "Halbfiction" of Wilhelm's reportage: see "Plastische Anatomie" (*WA* II, 49: 64-75, here 64). Goethe dated the essay 4 February 1832, and mailed it to the Staatsrat P. C. W. Beuth in Berlin, where it met with a polite but definitive rejection. The essay, an intriguing text in its own right, urges the adoption of medical models on grounds very close to Wilhelm's. The

persuasive force of Wilhelm's curious narrative, one might say, ruptures the uncertain frame of "fiction" itself.

20. For a reading of the chapter that takes this phrase as its moral, see Peschken 119-25.

21. Paul de Man writes in a not unrelated context that a law is "more like an actual text than a piece of property or a State" (268).

22. Compare this with the countermyth of mimesis, as represented by the *Handwerk* of plastic anatomy: "Geben Sie zu, daß der größte Teil von Ärzten und Wundärzten nur einen allgemeinen Eindruck des zergliederten menschlichen Körpers in Gedanken behält und damit auszukommen glaubt, so werden gewiß solche Modelle hinreichen, die in seinem Geiste nach und nach erlöschenden Bilder wieder anzufrischen und ihm gerade das Nötige lebendig zu erhalten. Ja, es kommt auf Neigung und Liebhaberei an, so werden sich die zartesten Resultate der Zergliederungskunst nachbilden lassen. Leistet dies ja schon Zeichenfeder, Pinsel und Grabstichel" (328). The pressure of metaphors of inscription in this and other passages on memory and dissection in this chapter returns us to Jacques Derrida's discussion of writing and memory in the *Phaedrus*: see "Plato's Pharmacy," in *Dissemination* 61-171.

23. Goethe's interest in "plastic anatomy" was no doubt exacerbated, as he himself suggests in his essay, by the Burke and Hare case and the publicity and the imitative crimes it generated, but his interest in the medical utility of sculpture goes back to his earliest studies of anatomy in 1781, as Trunz remarks in his notes to the *Wanderjahre* chapter (HA 8: 646-47). Goethe's biographer, Nicholas Boyle, has drawn my attention to a reference to a "wooden surrogate" that appears in Goethe's diary for 1807 in the context of the early plans for the *Wanderjahre,* which would lend additional specificity to Trunz's claim that the chapter dramatizes long-standing concerns. Dr. Boyle confirms that it is difficult to know whether the Burke and Hare case influenced the composition of this chapter. Burke was executed on the 28th of January 1829, and Goethe might easily have heard of the case through the French newspapers while he was writing or revising chapter 3, since Book III of the *Wanderjahre* was largely composed between September 1828 and the end of February 1829, and its first two-thirds were revised in January. "It is therefore possible that knowledge of the trial of Burke and Hare had some influence on the formulation of chapter 3, specifically on the reference near the end of the chapter to 'newspaper articles' about 'resurrection men,'" Dr. Boyle comments; however, "It strikes me as unlikely that the Burke and Hare affair was the sole inspiration for the idea of wax substitutes for cadavers," for the reasons given above. Furthermore, "there is an undated schema for this chapter in the Weimar Edition apparatus which envisages a much more detailed motivation of the need for these surrogates, but which does not contain any obvious allusions to Burke and Hare" (letter of 27 March 1994).

24. In the language of the *Meister* cycle the criminals are displaced puppets, since the anatomical models recall the marionettes that spark Wilhelm's interest in the theatre in *Wilhelm Meisters Lehrjahre*. Wilhelm's story of surgical *Bildung* is thus a repetition of the theatrical matrix of the *Lehrjahre*—to such an extent that he remarks at the outset of his narrative in chapter three of the *Wanderjahre* that he actually isn't learning anything: "Auf eine sonderbare Weise, welche niemand erraten würde, war ich schon in Kenntnis der menschlichen Gestalt weit vorgeschritten, und zwar während meiner theatralischen Laufbahn." On and behind the stage he has learned about the body's "äussern Teile," and for some unexplained reason has also even gained "ein gewisses Vorgefühl" of the "innern Teile" (323). Renunciation never quite works in the *Meister* cycle, and the *theatrum anatomicum* thus provides yet another version of the career that Wilhelm has had to give up. For an analysis of theatricality and *Bildung* in the *Lehrjahre* which examines the uncertain figurative status of Wilhelm's puppets, see Redfield.

25. Because Nazism is a "humanism" in this sense, its violence takes place as a dehumanization, which is why the figure of the puppet occasionally appears in the rhetoric of extermination. Claude Lanzmann's *Shoah* records that the extermination camp guards at Chelmno forced the Jews to refer to corpses as "Dreck" or "Figuren," which translates as "puppets" as well as "shapes" or "figures of speech." (And Hannah Arendt, speaking both of and against such de-humanization, writes at one point of the victims of the death camps as "ghastly marionettes with human faces" [455].) For a discussion of this moment in Lanzmann's film, see Felman 204-83. It would be interesting in this context to analyze the role of puppets in Hans-Jürgen Syberberg's *Hitler: A Film from Germany* (see especially 68-71, 106-14, 201-08).

26. See Weber for a reading of "Die Frage nach der Technik" which disinters a subtext in Heidegger's essay to this effect: "the unsettling effects of technics cannot be considered to be an exclusive aspect of its peculiarly modern form. Rather, the danger associated with *modern* technics is—as Heidegger explicitly asserts—a consequence of the goings-on of technics as such and in general as a movement of unsecuring" (985). ("Goings-on" is Weber's imaginative translation of "Wesen.")

Works Cited

Arendt, Hannah. *The Origins of Totalitarianism.* New Edition. New York: Harcourt, 1966.

Aristotle. *Politics.* Trans. Benjamin Jowett. *The Basic Works of Aristotle.* Ed. Richard McKeon. New York: Random House, 1941. 1113-1316.

Armstrong, Bruce. "An Idyll Sad and Strange: The St. Joseph the Second Section and the Presentation of Craft Work in Goethe's *Wilhelm Meisters Wanderjahre.*" *Monatshefte für deutschen Unterricht, deutsche Sprache und Literatur* 77.4 (1985): 415-32.

Bahr, Ehrhard. *Die Ironie im Spätwerk Goethes.* Berlin: Erich Schmidt, 1972.

Baldwin, Birgit. "*Wilhelm Meisters Wanderjahre* as an Allegory of Reading." *Goethe Yearbook* 5 (1990): 213-32.

Blackall, Eric. *Goethe and the Novel.* Ithaca: Cornell UP, 1976.

Boyle, Nicholas. Letter to the author. 27 March 1994.

Brown, Jane K. *Goethe's Cyclical Narratives: "Die Unterhaltung deutscher Ausgewanderten" and "Wilhelm Meisters Wanderjahre."* Chapel Hill: U of North Carolina P, 1975.

Bruford, W. H. *The German Tradition of Self-Cultivation: Bildung from Humboldt to Thomas Mann.* Cambridge: Cambridge UP, 1975.

Chytry, Josef. *The Aesthetic State: A Quest in Modern German Thought.* Berkeley: U of California P, 1989.

David, Claude. "Goethes *Wanderjahre* als symbolische Dichtung." *Sinn und Form* 8 (1956): 113-28.

de Man, Paul. *Allegories of Reading: Figural Langugage in Rousseau, Nietzsche, Rilke, and Proust.* New Haven: Yale UP, 1979.

Derrida, Jacques. *Dissemination.* Trans. Barbara Johnson. Chicago: U of Chicago P, 1981.

———. "La main de Heidegger." *Psyche: inventions de l'autre.* Paris: Galilée, 1987. 415-51.

Eckermann, Johann Peter. *Gespräche mit Goethe in den letzten Jahren seines Lebens.* Munich: C. H. Beck, 1984.

Felman, Shoshana. "The Return of the Voice: Claude Lanzmann's *Shoah.*" *Testimony: Crises of Witnessing in Literature, Psychoanalysis, and History.* Shoshana Felman and Dori Laub. London: Routledge, 1992. 204-83.

Goethe, Johann Wolfgang von. *Goethes Werke* ("Weimarer Ausgabe"). Weimar: H. Böhlau, 1887-1919.

———. *Sämtliche Werke* ("Artemis Ausgabe"). Zürich: Artemis, 1979.

———. *Werke* ("Hamburger Ausgabe"). Hamburg: Christian Werner, 1950.

Heidegger, Martin. "Die Frage nach der Technik." *Vorträge und Aufsätze.* Tübingen: Günther Neske, 1954. 13-44.

———. *Die Selbstbehauptung der deutschen Universität.* 1933. Ed. Hermann Heidegger. Frankfurt a. M.: Klostermann, 1983.

———. *Ursprung des Kunstwerkes.* Stuttgart: Reclam, 1960.

———. *Was heisst Denken?* Tübingen: Max Niemeyer, 1954.

JanMohammed, Abdul, and David Lloyd. "Introduction: Toward a Theory of Minority Discourse." *Cultural Critique* 6 (1987): 5-12.

Lacoue-Labarthe, Philippe. *Heidegger, Art, and Politics: The Fiction of the Political.* Trans. Chris Turner. Oxford: Basil Blackwell, 1990.

Lacoue-Labarthe, Philippe, and Jean-Luc Nancy. "The Nazi Myth." *Critical Inquiry* 16 (1990): 291-312.

Mann, Thomas. "Geist und Wesen der deutschen Republik" [1923]. *Reden und Aufsätze. Gesammelte Werke.* 12 vols. Oldenburg: S. Fischer, 1960. 11: 853-60.

Mitchell, W. J. T., ed. *Against Theory: Literary Studies and the New Pragmatism.* Chicago: U of Chicago P, 1985.

Muenzer, Clark S. *Figures of Identity: Goethe's Novels and the Enigmatic Self.* University Park: Penn State UP, 1984.

Neuhaus, Volker. "Die Archivfiktion in *Wilhelm Meisters Wanderjahren.*" *Euphorion* 62 (1968): 13-27.

Peschken, Bernd. *Entsagung in "Wilhelm Meisters Wanderjahren."* Bonn: Bouvier, 1968.

Plato. *Laws.* Trans. R. G. Bury. Cambridge: Harvard UP. 1961.

Redfield, Marc. "Ghostly *Bildung*: Gender, Genre, Aesthetic Ideology, and *Wilhelm Meisters Lehrjahre.*" *Genre* 26.4 (1993 [1995]): 377-407.

Sagave, Pierre-Paul. "*Les Années de voyage de Wilhelm Meister* et la critique socialiste (1830-1848)." *Etudes Germaniques* 4 (1953): 241-51.

Schiller, Friedrich. *On the Aesthetic Education of Man, in a Series of Letters.* Bilingual edition ed. and trans. Elizabeth M. Wilkinson and L. A. Willoughby. Oxford: Clarendon, 1967.

Syberberg, Hans-Jürgen. *Hitler: A Film from Germany.* Pref. Susan Sontag. Trans. Jochim Neugroschel. New York: Farrar, Straus, Giroux, 1982.

Weber, Samuel. "Upsetting the Set Up: Remarks on Heidegger's Questing after Technics." *MLN* 104.5 (1989): 977-91.

Woodmansee, Martha. *The Author, Art, and the Market: Rereading the History of Aesthetics.* New York: Columbia UP, 1994.

Ehrhard Bahr (essay date 1998)

SOURCE: Bahr, Ehrhard. "The Structure of the *Wanderjahre.*" *The Novel as Archive: The Genesis, Reception, and Criticism of Goethe's* Wilhelm Meisters Wanderjahre. Columbia: Camden House, 1998. 14-33. Print.

[*In the following essay, Bahr examines the 1821 and 1829 versions of Goethe's novel, arguing that the 1821 edition is a sequel to* Wilhelm Meisters Lehrjahre *and that the 1829 edition is what he calls an "archival novel" that, though more challenging, allowed for freer interpretation by the reader and laid the foundation for the modern novel.*]

The *Wanderjahre* [*Wilhelm Meisters Wanderjahre*] of 1821 and 1829 are two novels that are significantly different in conception. Therefore, we speak of the two *versions* rather than the two *editions,* although the terms have been used interchangeably in **Wanderjahre** scholarship. The first version can still be considered a traditional sequel to the *Lehrjahre* [*Wilhelm Meisters Lehrjahre*], whether one describes that version as a travel novel, an epistolary novel, a cycle of novellas, or a combination of all three. The second version takes the step toward the archival novel, leading Hermann Broch in his 1936 essay on "James Joyce and the Present," to express the belief that Goethe had established in the *Wanderjahre* the foundation of modern literature and the new novel. Broch thinks it "quite possible, even probable" that Goethe presaged the fundamental changes of consciousness within the modern novel, and he boldly hypothesizes that the *Wanderjahre* had already accomplished what Joyce's *Ulysses* (1922) would achieve 100 years later: the conception of the modern world in a single work of art (63-65, 87).

One does not have to agree with Broch to acknowledge that from Goethe's hand a work appeared whose "aggregate" structure, as he characterized it, could be defended to his contemporaries only with the greatest difficulty. His own apologetic remarks and pleas for "sympathetic participation" demonstrate the "incommensurability" and "incalculability of the production" to which he himself, as he confessed to Eckermann on January 18, 1825, "almost lacked the key." Goethe had achieved something whose far-reaching implications he could not fully comprehend; for this reason, he challenged his "true readers" to assume a greater "freedom of interpretation" (letter to Zelter, October 19, 1821). The difficulty of interpreting the *Wanderjahre* has been documented in the reception history of the

work, as I will show in chapter 4. The long chain of misunderstandings and misreadings of the *Wanderjahre* stretches into the mid-twentieth century. Broch coined the phrase "vorauseilende Realität" (realism ahead of its time) to characterize the modernism of the *Wanderjahre.* With the exception of the "socialist readings" of 1832 to 1852 and Broch's 1936 essay on Joyce, this unique modernity of the *Wanderjahre* was not recognized by scholarship until the 1950s.

The Münchner Ausgabe (Munich Edition) of 1989 and the Frankfurter Ausgabe (Frankfurt Edition) of 1991 contain detailed synopses of the first and second versions of the *Wanderjahre* (MA [*Sämtliche Werke nach Epochen seines Schaffens*] 17: 1066-1079; FA [*Sämtliche Werke, Briefe, Tagebücher und Gespräche*] I, 10: 1273-89; see also Gräf [*Goethe über seine Dichtungen*] I.2, 904-908), which give exact information concerning the distribution of the narrative matter, omissions, continuations, and expansions, including completely new material. Goethe had already planned, at the time of the publication of the first version, much of what would go into the second part of the first version—which, however, was never written. On this point the schemas and drafts do not give sufficient information. Not until there is a critical edition of the *Wanderjahre* that matches the current level of modern editing practices is there hope that the history of the text's genesis can be reliably reconstructed in detail. Gerhard Neumann has identified such an edition as a desideratum of Goethe philology and considers it "among the most difficult and most necessary task." In his opinion, the editors of the Weimarer Ausgabe failed in their attempt "to clear up the genetic dimension of the text" (FA I, 10: 970).

The first issue of the version stands out because it begins with two prefatory poems and does not indicate the title until the third page: *Wilhelm Meisters/Wanderjahre/oder/ Die Entsagenden./Ein Roman/von/Goethe./Erster Theil./* Stuttgard und Tübingen,/in der Cotta'schen Buchhandlung./1821./(**Wilhelm Meister's/Journeyman Years/or/ The Renunciants./A Novel/by/Goethe./First Part./** Stuttgart and Tübingen,/in Cotta's Publishing House./ 1821). After the title page there are nine more poems on unpaginated pages, with the first chapter not beginning until page 9. This arrangement was so extraordinary that the later-bound copies of the first printing of the first edition deviated from this order: copies in the Landesbibliothek Stuttgart and in the Special Collections department of the Research Library of the University of California, Los Angeles, show this variant, with the title on the first page. This variant is not listed in Waltraud Hagen's bibliography, *Die Drucke von Goethes Werken* (The Printing of Goethe's Works, second revised edition, 1983); it probably resulted from a mistake in the binding process, but it was followed by the Artemis-Ausgabe of 1949. Some of the poems of the first version were later included in the enlarged edition of the *West-östlicher Divan* in volume 5 (1827) of the *Ausgabe letzter Hand*

[*Werke: Vollständige Ausgabe letzter Hand*] (the first edition of the *Divan* [*West-östlicher Divan*] was printed in 1818 and appeared in the fall of 1819).

The first version of the *Wanderjahre* consists of eighteen chapters without division into books. It begins with the story **"Sankt Joseph der Zweite"** (**Saint Joseph the Second**), which Goethe had already published in 1809 under the title **"Wilhelm Meisters Wanderjahre. Erstes Buch"** in Cotta's *Taschenbuch für Damen auf das Jahr 1810.* In the first chapter Wilhelm announces the conditions of his journey:

> I am not to stay beyond three days under one roof. I am not to quit no inn without removing at least one league from it. These regulations are in truth calculated to make my life a life of Travel [true journeyman years], and to prevent the smallest thought of settlement from taking hold of me.

> (Carlyle [*Goethe's Wilhelm Meister's Travels*], 43-44; quoted from his 1827 translation of the first version; this text was not changed in the second version [see SE [*Goethe's Collected Works*] 10: 101])

These words present the "fundamental constellation of the plot as well as the agenda" of the first version (FA I 10, 970). It is based, as Gerhard Neumann has said, on the "idea of wandering" (FA I, 10: 970). At the beginning Wilhelm Meister is accompanied by his son, Felix. They encounter Jarno, the former courtier from the *Lehrjahre,* who appears here as a mining engineer under the name Montan (from Latin *montanus,* "belonging to the mountain" or "living in the mountains"). After Felix is left at an educational institution, the Pedagogic Province, Wilhelm makes the acquaintance of Lenardo, a young baron, who functions in this first version as his foil. What they have in common is "a pilgrimage toward their beloved women," as Neumann puts it (FA I, 10: 970). Wilhelm is longing to be reunited with Natalie, his wife from the *Lehrjahre,* while Lenardo is trying to locate the "nut-brown maid," a tenant farmer's daughter whom he promised, but failed, to protect from eviction from his uncle's estate. Both men are included among the Entsagenden (Renunciants), as the subtitles of both versions indicate. The renunciation on Wilhelm's part is shown in the fact that Natalie figures merely as his partner in correspondence; he is never reunited with her. At one point he spies her on top of a cliff across the valley; observing her through a telescope, he nearly falls off his own cliff, but a helpful hand grabs him and tears him away from "the greatest danger and the greatest happiness as well" (chapter 13). Similarly, Lenardo is searching for the nut-brown maid, whom he failed to protect on account of his hasty departure for his educational tour abroad; Wilhelm locates her but he believes that he will serve Lenardo better by helping him to repress his love rather than by telling him where she is (chapter 11). Later, Lenardo finds the nut-brown maid himself; his diary is not included in the text (chapter 17), and so no narrative evidence of a reunion with his beloved is provided.

Other characters whom Wilhelm encounters during his journeyman years, or who figure in the novellas that are inserted, include the Uncle; the Aunt; Hersilie; Juliette; the Overseer and Heads of the Pedagogic Province; the members of the Wanderers' Association; the carpenter, Joseph; his wife, Maria; and her children. Special attention must be paid to the characters who are first presented through the novellas—which serve as reading material for the protagonists of the novel—and are later introduced into the plot of the novel itself, such as the characters in **"The Nut-Brown Maid"** and **"The Man of Fifty Years."** Lenardo's search for his beloved nut-brown maid is first conveyed in a correspondence among Hersilie, Juliette and the Aunt, which is mailed to Natalie for her information. This search is then continued from an objective narrator's point of view, with Wilhelm and Lenardo as the protagonists. The story of **"The Man of Fifty Years"** is conveyed through Wilhelm's reading of the first part of the novella, which is given to him by Hersilie. Later he encounters Hilarie and the Beautiful Widow, the female characters of the novella, in Italy; Wilhelm, a young painter who has accompanied him, and the characters of the novella subject themselves to dangerous passions and undergo the test of renunciation during an excursion on the Lago Maggiore. The remainder of the novella, which could have given insight into the power of renunciation, is not provided in the first version of the *Wanderjahre.* Neumann points out that **"The Man of Fifty Years"** constitutes an "open experimental model" that is "strategically introduced by Hersilie" as an "incitement in Wilhelm's life story, in order to aid him in determining his future course of action" (FA I, 10: 974). With the novellas **"The New Melusine," "The Deranged Pilgrim,"** and **"Who Is the Traitor,"** there is neither a crossing over of the novella plot, a deconstruction of the story, nor a withholding of information about the ending. In these cases, the novella's only significance is to be found in its position within the novel's plot.

The characters of the novel represent the various social groups with whom Wilhelm comes into contact and through whom his "journeyman years" gain their meaning: there is the group around Saint Joseph the Second, the group around Montan, the group around the Uncle, the group around the Collector, the group at the Pedagogic Province, and, finally, the Wanderers' Association. Saint Joseph the Second represents the religious artisan class with its naive faith in the imitation of biblical role models as they are presented in art. Montan represents modern science and engineering, harnessing nature for the benefit of humanity without exploiting it. The Uncle, with his soundly administered country estate, represents the Enlightenment. The Collector, with his house in the city, stands for the cultural sphere of objets d'art and antiquities. The Pedagogic Province provides education for a life of "secular piety" (*Weltfrömmigkeit*), according to the "credo of the three reverences." The Wanderers' Association represents a new form of society in which membership is based not exclusively on property, as it was for the middle class and nobility of the eighteenth- and nineteenth-century, but also on labor. In his farewell speech, Lenardo comes to a conclusion about property that would have been considered radical by his contemporaries:

> And yet we may assert, that if what man possesses is of great worth, what he does and accomplishes must be of still greater. In a wide view of things, therefore, we must look on property in land as one small [a smaller] part of the possessions that have been given to us. Of these the greatest and the most precious part consists especially in what is moveable, and in what is gained by a moving life.
>
> (Carlyle, 341-342, quoted from chapter 18 of
> his 1827 translation of the first version;
> FA I, 10: 251; MA 17: 231; cf. SE 10, 364)

Afterwards Wilhelm is introduced to the Wanderers' Association and learns about their organization and way of life. At the end some of the remaining characters of the *Lehrjahre* make an appearance, such as Lothario, Werner, the Abbé, and Friedrich; all of these characters are active in the Wanderers' Association. In Wilhelm's journey through Mignon's homeland, and especially in the repeat performance of her famous song about Italy ("Kennst du das Land, wo die Zitronen blühn, / Im dunkeln Laub die Goldorangen glühn, ..." [Do you know the land where the lemon-trees blossom, / Where the golden oranges glow in the dark foliage]) the self-referential character of the *Wanderjahre* becomes manifest in that the reader is expressly directed toward the preceding novel, the *Lehrjahre.* The painter friend with whom Wilhelm undertakes his "pilgrimage" to Mignon's homeland shows him a series of watercolor landscapes that have the figure of Mignon in the foreground and that were conceived after the painter read the *Lehrjahre.* He joins Wilhelm on the journey to paint the "Knaben-Mädchen" (boy-girl) of the *Lehrjahre* by copying "from nature the scenes where she passed her early years, ... and thus to make her image, which lives in all tender hearts, present also to the sense of the eye" (Carlyle, 192, quoted from chapter 12 of his 1827 translation; FA I, 10: 129; MA 17: 118; cf. SE 10, 255).

The structural arrangement of motifs in the first version of the *Wanderjahre* is primarily based on the motif of casket and key, which is derived from the Gothic novel. There is also the more limited telescope motif, when Wilhelm spies Natalie on the facing cliff, which represents the long-distance though intense relationship with the beloved woman.

One of the conventions of the traditional eighteenth-century novel is the omniscient narrator. The *Lehrjahre* has such a narrator; in the first version of the *Wanderjahre,* however, the authority of the omniscient narrator is undermined by the introduction of a personalized narrative perspective, as well as by the introduction of an editor. The fictional editor—another device of the eighteenth-century novel, as found in Goethe's *Werther* [*Die Leiden des jungen Werthers*] (1774)—creates a higher degree of realism: first, by remarking on the compositional history of the novel (referring, for example, to the edition as "twenty years in the coming" [FA I, 10: 127; MA 17: 116]); second, through editorial interruptions; third, by introducing the texts of the novellas from Lenardo's and/or Makarie's archives; and finally, by "the suppression of information and secrecy," which is explained as "very suitable for a little book such as this" (chapter 16; FA I, 10: 198; MA 17: 182). This higher degree of realism produced by the editor includes the anchoring of the novel in the poems on the introductory pages; by means of these poems the novel is placed within Goethe's autobiography. The reader is informed in the first poem that "[d]ie Wanderjahre sind nun angetreten" (the Wanderjahre have now begun) and that "jeder Schritt des Wandrers ist bedenklich" (every step of the wanderer is full of doubt and danger), but in case of danger he will turn "ins eigne Herz und in das Herz der Lieben" (to his own heart and to the hearts that love him). In the third poem the speaker distances himself from any commitment to his individuality as author—"Wüßte kaum genau zu sagen, / Ob ich es noch selber bin" (Barely could I tell you rightly / Whether I am the same or not)—trusting only in his work, which may appear contradictory by frightening and delighting his readers but will ultimately "In soviel tausend Zeilen" (In so many thousands of lines), establish a synthesis. On the other hand, on the fifth page Goethe places a poem dedicated to his daughter-in-law, Ottilie von Goethe, establishing an autobiographical continuity by commenting on their lives' journey together: "Ehe wir nun weiterschreiten, / Halte still und sieh dich um" (Before we continue forward / Halt quietly and look behind you). The poem ends with an apostrophe to her loyalty and an almost incestual wish that she may bring "dem Vater in dem Sohne / Tüchtigschöne Knaben" (to the father in his son / Sound and handsome boys).

Since the second part of the first version of the *Wanderjahre* was never written, one can only speculate about what its narrative perspective would have been. It is impossible to tell whether the structure of the second version would have been present here or whether a restructuring of the narrative perspective took place only after Goethe started work on the second version. The redistribution of the narrative material in June 1825 and Goethe's schemata and drafts of 1825-1826, which juxtaposed both versions for the purpose of comparison (see Paralipomena in WA [*Goethes Werke*] I, 25.2: 209-15), favor the latter interpretation.

The last chapter contains Lenardo's farewell speech on the topic of wandering and the ethos of utility, in which the value of land-ownership is lowered and that of labor is raised. The Wanderers' Association is conceived as a "*Weltbund*" (world confederation), in which society is identified as man's highest need: "Alle brauchbaren Menschen sollen in Bezug untereinander stehen" (All useful men should stand in relation to one another). To the duties of journeyman are added tolerance of religion and forms of government, as well as "Sittlichkeit ohne Pedanterei und Strenge" (morality without pedantry and dogmatism) and the three reverences of the Pedagogic Province. The first version ends with the Wanderers' song, beginning with the lines: "Bleibe nicht am Boden haften" (Cling not to [your homeland's] soil).

In the second version, which appeared in the *Ausgabe letzter Hand* as volumes 21 to 23, the title and subtitle were preserved in volume 21 as *Wilhelm Meisters/Wanderjahre/oder/die Entsagenden,* though the indication of genre and author were deleted as superfluous. The page opposite the title pages contains publication information: *Goethe's/Werke./Vollständige Ausgabe letzter Hand*/Einundzwanzigster Band./Unter des durchlauchtigsten deutschen Bundes schützenden Privilegien./Stuttgart und Tübingen,/in der J. G. Cotta'schen Buchhandlung./1829. (**Goethe's Collected Works. Authorized Version,** Volume 21. Published under the Copyright Protection of the German Federation by J. G. Cotta in Stuttgart and Tübingen in 1829). The novel is made up of three books with collections of aphorisms following the second and third book—**"Betrachtungen im Sinne der Wanderer/Kunst, Ethisches, Natur"** (**Reflections in the Spirit of the Wanderers/Art, Ethical, Nature**), consisting of 177 aphorisms, and **"From Makarie's Archive,"** consisting of 182 aphorisms—in addition to the poems **"Testament"** and **"Reflections on Schiller's Skull."** The novel ends with the ambiguous sentence "Ist fortzusetzen" (To be continued), giving rise to speculation that another sequel was planned. The newly introduced narrative texts are **"Die gefährliche Wette"** (**The Perilous Wager**), a farce, and **"Nicht zu weit"** (**Not Too Far**), one of Goethe's boldest novellas. Expanded and brought to a conclusion are **"The Man of Fifty Years"** and **"The Nut-Brown Maid,"** the latter of which is brought to a close in **"Lenardos Tagebuch"** (**Lenardo's Diary**). **"The Man of Fifty Years"** now represents a model for the characters of the novel to follow because of its love-quadrangle structure and the renunciation that develops from it. The topic of renunciation is introduced by the Beautiful Widow and Hilarie when they encounter Wilhelm and the young painter in the idyll at the Lago Maggiore and prove themselves to be "Renunciants" in the sense of the novel's subtitle. Three novellas of the first version of 1821 now obtain new positions and thus gain new significance within the plot of the main narrative of the novel: **"The Nut-Brown Maid"** is divided into two chapters (book 1, chapters 4 and 11) and the title is placed to introduce chapter 11; **"The Deranged Pilgrim"** is transposed from the episode of the emigrants at the end of the novel to the Uncle's country estate at the beginning. The novella **"Wo stickt der Verräther?"** (**Where Does the Traitor Hide?**), with its slightly changed title **"Wo ist der Verräther?"** (**Where is the Traitor?**), now appears in book 1, 8. As a result of these shifts, the relationships of Wilhelm and Hersilie, Felix and Hersilie,

and Lenardo and the nut-brown maid at the beginning of the novel are problematized by their juxtaposition with the novellas, which reflect the constellations and conflicts of the characters of the main plot of the novel. The **"Fisherman's Son"** episode of book 2, chapter 11 is another novella added to the second version. This death-by-water episode provides the motivation for Wilhelm's decision to become a surgeon. Wilhelm narrates this childhood experience of first love, friendship, and death by drowning in a letter to Natalie.

Like the first version, the second begins with **"Saint Joseph the Second."** Although the number of chapters is condensed from four to two, the titles of the missing chapters (**"The Visitation,"** **"The Lily Stalk"**) are preserved as subtitles. The conditions of the journeyman years remain the same, as does the fundamental idea behind the *Wanderjahre.* Nevertheless, the goal of the journey undergoes some alteration. While in the first version emigration is described as a *"Grille"* (whim) and a "deceptive hope for a better situation," resulting in the renunciation of the idea of emigration in favor of a rededication to wandering (FA I, 10: 199; MA 17: 183), the plan to emigrate to America, which was announced in the *Lehrjahre,* is carried through in the second version. In book 3 a second project, one of internal migration within Europe, is introduced to counterbalance the emigration to America: the Society of the Tower, Lenardo, and a large part of the Wanderers' Association prepare themselves for the emigration to America, while for the rest of the Wanderers' Association, who want to continue their "allegiance to their native soil and fatherland for the coming time," a European colonization project "for some years to come" is offered (book 3, chapter 10). This idea was probably inspired by the colonization conducted by Frederick II of Prussia and Maria Theresa of Austria in Russia and Bessarabia respectively. For the sake of differentiation, Gustav Radbruch uses *Binnenwanderer* (immigrants) to characterize the participants of the European colonization project (quoted in HA [*Goethes Werke*] 8: 703); we shall use the terms *Emigrants' League* and *Immigrants' League* to distinguish between the groups.

Wilhelm's relationship with his son Felix is expanded further in the second version. Felix is still sent to the Pedagogic Province, but in the second version the son becomes Wilhelm's rival for Hersilie. At the end of the novel Wilhelm is the "recognizing and recognized" rescuer of his son (book 3, chapter 18). In the scene of reconciliation between father and son the image of the divine twin brothers, Castor and Pollux, is conjured up. With the establishment of a connection to Hersilie, the figure of the son is bound to erotic rivalry as well as to the transmission of experience, knowledge, and love from fathers to sons who acknowledge each other as brothers. This relationship between father and son is reflected in the continuation of the novella **"The Man of Fifty Years,"** in which father and son compete for the same woman. Similarly, Hersilie experiences an increase of her importance in the novel's deep structure as an Alcmene figure between Wilhelm and Felix, and in the plot as a foil to Hilarie, the young woman attracted to a much older man in **"The Man of Fifty Years."**

Lenardo's "journeyman years" are represented through the medium of **"Lenardo's Diary"** in Book 3, chapters 5 and 13, which also tells of his reunion with the nut-brown maid. Still, Lenardo's function as a foil for Wilhelm is minimized by the introduction of Odoard, who experiences in the prelude to his own story, the novella **"Not Too Far,"** a tragic form of renunciation and, in contrast to Lenardo, engages in the project of European colonization. According to Gerhard Neumann, Lenardo and Odoard are the "representatives of two competing principles of identification, emigration on the one hand, and the colonization of homelike territories on the other" (FA I, 10: 981).

One of the most important figures of the second version is Makarie, who is certainly the boldest creation in Goethe's late works. The Aunt in the correspondence of the first version, she is introduced here as the "first Sibyl," as a "Saint," and a "higher being" (SE 10: 138, 404, 409; HA 8: 65, 441, 448; FA I, 10: 325, 725, 732; MA 17: 298, 668, 675). The "dignified aunt" is the "guardian angel of the family." She is "withered by illness in the body," yet she is "blooming with health in spirit" and speaks as if "the voice of an ancient sibyl, ... spoke pure, divine words of the greatest simplicity about human affairs" (SE 10: 138; HA 8: 65; FA I, 10: 325; MA 17: 298). On Wilhelm's arrival in her circle she presides as hostess at the breakfast table. Expressing keen interest, she listens to the scientific lecture by the Astronomer, and with loving care she makes sure that Felix does not get bored. She is a female confessor to the family. All troubled souls "who have lost themselves and who wish to find themselves again but do not know how" turn to her (SE 10: 252; HA 8: 223; FA I, 10: 493; MA 17: 453). With a sober mind, she mediates between the confused couples. The marriages that are concluded near the end the novel are finalized by her intervention. Meanwhile, it turns out that she is actually a star in the sky and constitutes part of the solar system. Makarie not only carries "the entire solar system within herself" but also moves "spiritually within the solar system as an integral part" (SE 10: 183; HA 8: 126; FA I, 10: 391; MA 17: 358). Makarie is represented realistically as the good old aunt in her wheelchair, on the one hand, and, on the other hand, as a "saint" who is transposed into the mysterious world of dream and fairy tale. Her existence in this dream world is, however, confirmed by the mathematical evidence of astronomy: while Wilhelm dreams of Makarie as the morning star, reminding the reader of Raphael's Sistine Madonna (SE 10: 179; HA 8: 122; FA I, 10: 386; MA 17: 353 f.), the Astronomer calculates Makarie's star chart: "incredibly his calculations [were] confirmed by her own statements" (SE 10: 183; HA 8: 126; FA I, 10: 391; MA 17: 358). This myth surrounding Makarie is preserved, as though it were true, in a sealed file

in her archives with the inscription "Makarie's Characteristics." It is published "from the archives" as a piece of fiction written from memory. The editor says that it is taken from an anonymous article and that "enough is presented here to provoke thought and make the reader consider whether anything similar or approaching this has ever been observed or recorded" (SE 10: 409; HA 8: 449; FA I, 10: 733; MA 17: 676). Even the author of the article implies special caution, when he says of the article's content that "one barely dares to express it in words" (SE 10: 409). In the middle of his report he interrupts himself with the comment: "Here we dare go no further, for the unbelievable loses its value if one tries to examine it in greater detail. Yet this much we shall say—." The description follows of how Makarie, who unites all contradictions in her person, who has lifted herself above all earthly concerns and moves within the solar system, is striving on her stellar course "toward Saturn in finite space." At this point the anonymous author adds that

> no one's imagination can follow her that far, but we hope that such an entelechy will not withdraw entirely from our solar system, but when she reaches its boundary will long again to return, in order to exercise her influence upon earthly life again, to the benefit of our great-grandchildren

> (SE 10: 411; HA 8: 452; FA I, 10: 737; MA 17: 679)

After expressing the hope that Makarie, representing a cosmic "love ... from above" (*Faust II,* 11938-11939), will interact with this mundane life, the editor pleads for the indulgence of his readers and calls the text an "ethereal fiction" (SE 10: 412). It is characteristic of the narrative structure of the second version that Makarie is distanced from the real world as a sidereal saint in this interpolated protocol and then is returned to the realistic plot of the novel as the good old Aunt. In contrast to *Faust, Part II,* the "love ... from above" represented by Makarie in the *Wanderjahre* is not of Christian origin, but part of the universe. Even if the myth about Makarie is only an "ethereal fiction," according to the editor this "fairy-tale suitable perhaps for a novel" has great value for skeptical persons, such as Montan and the Astronomer, who "would be able to consider it a parable of our greatest desires" (SE 10: 407; HA 8: 445; FA I, 10: 729; MA 17: 672). The subjunctive mood, which is typical of the narrative stance of the novel, keeps the credibility of the myth of Makarie in suspension; its efficacy is preserved precisely because its amusing fairy-tale quality is acknowledged from the start.

In comparison to Makarie, most of the other characters who are introduced in the second version are of only peripheral significance—Angela, the Astronomer, the Mineral Diviner, the young Assistant and the spinners and weavers. An exception is Susanna-Nachodine, or the Beautiful-Good One, as the nut-brown maid is now called, who finally appears in the second version as the lost beloved with whom Lenardo is finally reunited. Moreover, some well-known characters from the *Lehrjahre* are reintroduced in the concluding chapters of book 3: Lothario, Friedrich, the Abbé, Philine, and Lydia are mentioned as preparing for the voyage to America and receiving Makarie's blessings before their departure.

In addition to the social groups that have significance for Wilhelm's "journeyman years," the second version presents two additional groups: the circle around Makarie and the workers in the cotton industry, which is being threatened by the Industrial Revolution. The cotton industry is presented in all of its technical detail in **"Lenardo's Diary."** Another occupation of central relevance in the second version is surgery, which is introduced in a narrative of Wilhelm's training as a surgeon in book 3, chapter 3. This narrative also deals with the use of anatomical models to replace the traditional training by dissecting human cadavers. Finally, there is the project of the American utopia, which is conceived in competition with the project of European colonization. The account of the American utopia is transmitted in an unreliable manner similar to the "ethereal fiction" concerning Makarie's position in the solar system. It consists of the "quintessence" of a conversation between Wilhelm and Friedrich, who has a reputation as an unreliable informant. The "results" that are passed on by the editor are described as a "fertile text with endless possibilities of interpretation." The negative characteristics of institutional anti-Semitism and the police-state surveillance, as well as the punishment of deportation and of forced expropriation, are of particular consequence.

Concerning the other groups from the first version, the realm of the Uncle is expanded to represent a showcase of an estate managed according to the more efficient methods of the Enlightenment, and the Wanderers' Association is transformed into an Emigrants' League and its counterpart, an Immigrants' League, a group of European colonizers under Odoard's leadership.

The second version has a highly developed structure of motifs and has been described as the "most interesting area of the revisions" of 1829 (FA I, 10: 976). The motif of the casket or treasure chest is one of the most important in the novel. As in the first version, the small casket is found by Felix in the Castle of the Giants (*Riesenschloß*) and kept safe by the Collector. The casket and the recovered key represent the secret of the love of Felix and Hersilie (see Emrich, 61). The key is the only one of Goethe's symbols ever to be shown in an illustration in a text (SE 10: 321; HA 8: 321; FA I, 10: 599; MA 17: 552); it has been connected to Goethe's phallus drawings (Steer, 129-131). But even without this evidence, the sexual symbolism of Felix's vain attempts at opening the casket, as well as of his despair when he breaks the key, is obvious, since they occur almost simultaneously with Hersilie's refusal of his embrace. That the break is not jagged but smooth, and

that the halves of the key are connected magnetically, symbolize the future development of this relationship. Felix rides into the world "until [he] dies" (SE 10: 415). Nevertheless, Wilhelm, his father and rival in love, rescues him and thereby shows himself to be the twin brother mythologically prefigured by Castor and Pollux (SE 10: 417). In addition to this classical prefiguration, there is also a biblical reference to rebirth and resurrection (Zenker, 1990, 253-256; Schwamborn, 1997, 161-164).

The casket from the Castle of the Giants is, however, not to be considered in isolation but must also be related to the other casket or chest motifs. Arthur Henkel points out, for instance, that the fairy tale **"The New Melusine"** in book 3, chapter 6 concludes with a section concerning a small key and coffer (*Schatulle* or *Kästchen*) and that the next chapter of the novel, which consists of a letter from Hersilie to Wilhelm, begins with a reference to the small key and small casket (*Kästchen*) in the hands of Hersilie. In this manner, "the fairy tale of Melusine and the Hersilie narrative" forms "a secret relationship within the contrapuntal composition of the aged poet" (Henkel, 1954, 90). In **"The New Melusine"** the Barber recognizes the secret of the casket; this discovery leads to his break-up with his beloved, a dwarf princess who lives in the casket. In the case of Felix and Hersilie, the secret of chest and key is preserved; as a result, their break-up is not final. Even the little dressing case or make-up chest (*Toilettenkästchen*) in the novella **"The Man of Fifty Years"** possesses a secret: the secret of rejuvenation, which is supposed to make the old Major attractive to his young niece, Hersilie. In each of these three examples the secret of the casket promises the power of sexual attraction and requires renunciation by the characters involved if they want to avoid a break-up.

Furthermore, the little caskets establish secret connections throughout the novel. In the novella **"Who Is the Traitor?"** a rival in love, named Antoni, stirs up jealousy in Lucidor by giving a small jewelry case to Lucidor's future father-in-law as a groom's gift for Lucinde or Julie, one of his two daughters. In **"The Man of Fifty Years"** a portfolio or small wallet, which is a kind of chest, has the same function in the relationship between the Major and the Beautiful Widow. By presenting him with the handmade portfolio, the Beautiful Widow hands over to the Major "some part of [her] self, ... though multifaceted and ineffable" (SE 10: 225). The Major, on account of this object, finds himself, "not without embarrassment, involved in a pleasant relationship" (SE 10: 230). Even Hersilie works on a portfolio, "without exactly knowing who should have it in the end, the father or the son, but certainly one of these two" (SE 10: 282). Thus, Hersilie's situation between Wilhelm and Felix is a reflection of the love triangles presented in both **"The Man of Fifty Years"** and **"The Deranged Pilgrim,"** where fathers become rivals of their sons in love. In an impulsive decision Hersilie sends the portfolio to the son, but, remaining confused, she confesses her ambiguous feelings to the father.

Finally, small chests preserve important memories. The surgeon's instrument bag, which appeared first in the *Lehrjahre* and is also a kind of small casket, has this function. The surgeon's bag that Wilhelm carries like a fetish reminds him of his first encounter with Natalie in the *Lehrjahre,* a scene in which she seemed to him to be a saintly figure on horseback. Furthermore, the surgeon's bag keeps alive his painful memory of the fisherman's son whom he could not save from dying and his long-suppressed desire to become a surgeon. These indirect relationships among small caskets establish a network of motifs throughout the novel. At first glance such a network appears to be pure happenstance, but as an example of Goethe's compositional principle of "repeated mirroring" (*wiederholte Spiegelungen*) it has a great deal of significance. In contrast, the telescope motif seems to be completely isolated. It is not integrated into any overall motif structure, unless it is related to the cotton industry as one of the negative effects of the Industrial Revolution.

The significance of renunciation for the *Wanderjahre* is announced in the subtitle of the novel. Goethe's concept of renunciation is a matter neither of escapism nor of resignation, which later became important themes for the nineteenth-century novel. The scholarly consensus is that renunciation is, for Goethe, neither stoicism nor asceticism. Although one cannot speak of a "happiness of renunciation," to speak of the "misery of renunciation," as Thomas Degering does in his iconoclastic monograph of 1982, is an exaggeration in the opposite direction. Goethe's concept of renunciation originated during his stay in Italy and was strongly influenced by the French Revolution. The development of his concept of renunciation belongs, as Helmut Brandt says, "to the truly productive consequences if not of the revolution but of Goethe's critical analysis of it" (198). Goethe anticipated the emancipation of the bourgeois society of the nineteenth century without identifying with it or considering it a positive achievement. The society of the future was to be a society of the Renunciants. Through the concept of renunciation Goethe attempted to grasp the historical developments he tried to represent in his fiction: the European land reclamation, the American emigration, and the Industrial Revolution. Goethe's idea of renunciation begins with sacrifice and develops into compensation for an unsatisfactory situation, resulting in a payoff on a different level. In the realm of Eros renunciation is the sacrifice of the purely physical possession of the beloved; in regard to this aspect, Henkel has coined the phrase "love without possession" (125-141). Nevertheless, this sort of renunciation often leads to an unexpected compensation, transforming renunciation into "love *with* possession" but on a different level (Bahr, 1972, 123-124). On account of his journeyman's oath Wilhelm Meister finds himself bound to a temporary separation from Natalie, the woman who was promised as his wife at the end of the *Lehrjahre.* Under the conditions that he stay "not more than three days . . . under *one* roof" and not leave any lodging without

"traveling at least one mile away" (book 1, chapter 1), Wilhelm journeys with his son, Felix, across the novel's landscape. His goal, the emigration to America remains vague until the end of the novel. Of much greater significance are the stops that are made as a result of the conditions of his journeyman years: the country estate of the Uncle, the circle around Makarie, the Pedagogic Province, and his training as a surgeon. In consideration of his wish to study medicine the strictures of the journeyman years are relaxed, though the condition of separation from Natalie is not. Even at the end of the novel, the reunion of the two that one might expect does not take place; it turns out that Natalie has left for America with the other members of the Society of the Tower. Nevertheless, Wilhelm is intensely bound to Natalie through letters and other messages. The best example for this bond is his confessional letter to her that enables him to extricate himself from the trauma of the death of the Fisherman's Son and to acknowledge his calling to be a surgeon. Despite his spatial distance from his beloved, Wilhelm is able to come closer to her and to work through his grief for the loss of his childhood friend, to whom he is bound by the guilt of erotic attraction. Only then can he assure himself of his own identity and reshape his relationship to Natalie. The mechanism of renunciation reassures him that he truly deserves his beloved Natalie (book 2, chapter 11).

This payoff that he receives at a new level of their relationship hardly fits into the traditional categories of happiness or unhappiness. The parallel story of Lenardo, the noble foil to Wilhelm, has the same point. As a result of his ethical failings he is bound to a journeyman's life similar to Wilhelm's. He hopes to reunite himself with his beloved nut-brown maid and to show her his true worth. Nevertheless, under the sign of renunciation this passionate search is thwarted so that his private passions do not interfere with his duties toward "the great business of his life," the emigration to America. On the other hand, Lenardo is able to bring duty together with desire: he rediscovers his beloved among the spinners and weavers whom he wants to enlist for the emigration to America. Because of an earlier marriage and her father's commandment that she and Lenardo live like brother and sister, a closer relationship between Susanna, as she is finally called, and Lenardo never takes place; they show themselves to be exemplary renunciants, though some future liaison is not out of the question. As in the case of Wilhelm and Natalie, a reunion of the two is promised beyond the boundaries of the novel. The structure of the Heliodorian novel is negated, and then is reaffirmed when the editor reports that Lenardo was more resolved on the enterprise of emigration to America by the thought that once he had secured a foothold in the New World he would send for his beloved (book 3, chapter 14).

A similar model of renunciation is found in the interpolated novella **"The Man of Fifty Years,"** where the Major gives up the promised possession of his niece, Hilarie, in favor of his son, Flavio; at the same time, he wins the hand of the Beautiful Widow, who had turned the son away for being too impetuous a lover. Rejection and sacrifice lead to a rearrangement of physical possession among the four individuals involved.

But not for all the characters of the novel is renunciation positive: for the title character in **"The Deranged Pilgrim,"** the Barber in **"The New Melusine,"** and Odoard in **"Not Too Far"** it is a painful sacrifice. The only figures who seem to stand outside the influence of renunciation are Felix and Hersilie. Despite the passionate break-up of their relationship at the end of the novel, the hope of a relationship free of renunciation is offered by the motif of the magnetic key. Still, Felix and Hersilie are not completely spared suffering, pain, and despair.

The omniscient narrator of the eighteenth-century novel, such as appears in the *Lehrjahre,* had already been abandoned by the time Goethe wrote the first version; his function was divided into a personal narrator and an editor. The negation of the authority traditionally attributed to the narrator is the most significant characteristic of the second version of the *Wanderjahre.* It is a matter of the "disappearance of the author's 'responsibility' in relation to the narratability of his subject, the ever increasing independence of the individual parts of the narrative," as Gerhard Neumann has so aptly described it (FA I, 10: 982). For the analysis of the complex narrative structure of the second version, the interpretive model presented by Erich Trunz in 1950 in the Hamburger Ausgabe, which divided the frame narrative from the novellas, is no longer sufficient; the model of the archival novel (*Archivroman*), developed by Volker Neuhaus in 1968, is more convincing. With this model a much more adequate explanation can be given of the bridging of the novellas into the frame narrative. As Neuhaus shows in his seminal article, the stories, novellas, reports, notes, diaries, letters, and speeches of approximately twenty fictional persons can be found in Makarie's archives and in the archives of the Wanderers' Association. In addition, there are the aphorisms in both collections, as well as the two philosophical poems. These texts are presented by the "Redaktor" (editor) to create the novel. Again and again the reader is reassured by a self-referential gesture, for example: "Our friends have taken a novel into their hands" (book 1, chapter 10). As Neuhaus writes: "By means of the editing procedure the work becomes a *novel,* a work of art in opposition to reality" (17). As a complement to this thesis, Klaus-Detlef Müller has demonstrated that the fiction of an editor is employed here in a way opposite to the way it is employed in the eighteenth-century novel, such as Christoph Martin Wieland's *Geschichte des Agathon* (History of Agathon, 1766-1767) or Goethe's *Die Leiden des jungen Werthers,* where it serves to authenticate the "truth" of the fictional tale. In contrast to these novels, the editor in the *Wanderjahre* is given the task of constructing the fiction of the novel. He is assigned not an authorial but an editorial

responsibility for the employment and organization of individual texts within the narrative (Müller, 280-281). The problem in the second version arises from the fact that the fiction of the editor is present throughout the novel, but this fact is revealed to the reader relatively late. Not until the end of book I does the first visible editorial intervention occur; earlier intrusions and commentaries could be ascribed to the traditional omniscient narrator. In contrast, the editors in Wieland's *Agathon* and Goethe's *Werther* are announced in the prefaces. For the first ten chapters of the *Wanderjahre* of 1829 the function of the editor can only be ascertained by rereading the novel; the first editorial intervention does not take place until the tenth chapter. From then on, the editor's responsibility for the text is obvious. For example, he interrupts the text to spare the reader an essay on mathematics that Makarie composed, thus releasing the reader again to the suspense of the literary fiction. With the introduction of **"The Man of Fifty Years"** editorial arguments are given for presenting the novella uninterrupted instead of in installments, but the novella is presented in three installments.

The passing of time between Wilhelm's first and second visits to the Pedagogic Province is noted in an editorial interpolation that even makes reference to the typographical setup of the novel: "We should have liked to end the volume here, had that been compatible with the typographic conventions. However, the space between two chapters will doubtless suffice to carry us over the appropriate span of time" (book 2, chapter 7; SE 10: 267; HA 8: 244; FA I, 10: 515; MA 17: 474). On another occasion the editor gets involved in a discussion of the dangerous influence of the theater on the students of the Pedagogic Province and disagrees because he had invested a lot of time and energy in the theater. But instead of taking up narrative time to dwell on his own memories or vent his own opinions, the editor continues the fictive plot by guiding his protagonist toward another encounter with the head of the Pedagogic Province: "Our wanderer could approach him with trust and feel his trust reciprocated" (book 2, chapter 8).

The editorial reworking of texts is not recognizable at first glance. The commencement of the *Wanderjahre* with the titles, **"Die Flucht nach Ägypten"** (**The Flight to Egypt**) and **"Saint Joseph the Second"** shows itself only in hindsight to be a fictional reworking of Wilhelm's diary, which was originally written from a first-person perspective. The only reference to the reader of this revision is to be found in Wilhelm's letters to Natalie in book 1, chapter 1 and 3 (see Neuhaus, 18-21; Müller, 280; Vaget, *Romane,* 145). In Odoard's story, **"Not Too Far,"** which is presented as a transcription by another person, editorial interference is obvious: the editor assumes "the right of the epic poet" to divide the plot of the various narrative situations among the protagonists, who tell their stories from a first-person perspective. Gerhard Neumann has characterized this staggeringly complex structure of the novella as the "plurality" and "multi-faceted nature" of the narrative function in the *Wanderjahre* (FA I, 10: 1224).

Two of the most important texts of the second version, the American utopia (book 3, chapter 11) and the "ethereal fiction" of Makarie's position in the solar system (book 3, chapter 15), receive their special value from editorial comment. The editor begs forgiveness for presenting the American utopia merely as the "quintessence" of a discussion between Wilhelm and Friedrich, mentioning "other dispositions which are still circulating as problems in the society." Presented as a work in progress, the text has the finality of a master plan for a future society but allows for possible changes to be made to offensive passages. The "ethereal fiction," which is supposed to explain the essence of Makarie's personality, is communicated by means of "a page from our archives," which is introduced as "not completely authentic." With this admission, concerning the fictional character of the text, however, its content is, at least, revalorized as a credible example or parable worthy of meditation. The editorial comments underscore its ethical function without resorting to claims of scientific truth.

Toward the end of the novel the editorial intrusions accumulate. The novel's conclusion presents the editor with numerous problems, since "the task of communicating, portraying, amplifying, and organizing is becoming increasingly difficult." He finally decides on a method of simultaneous presentation, summarizing the events "of which [he] knew or had learned of at that time, as well as [those] of which [he was] later informed, and in this spirit to bring the serious business which [he] has undertaken to a fitting conclusion" (book 3, chapter 14).

The device of a fictional editor represents only one aspect of the archival fiction. Because of the abandonment of narrative integration as well as of authorial control over the plot, the construction of fiction is shifted to the "implied reader" (see Iser, *Der implizite Leser*). The archival fiction requires the active participation of the reader (Klaus-Detlef Müller, 283). The demands placed on the imagination of the reader of the *Wanderjahre* go beyond the narrative norms of all other eighteenth-century fiction, with, perhaps, the exception of Laurence Sterne's *Tristram Shandy*. Hans R. Vaget was justified in characterizing the *Wanderjahre* as an "intellectual exercise for the reader" (*Romane*, 142). Being denied authorial interpretation, the reader is forced to develop means of appropriating the text that are similar to his or her means of appropriating empirical reality. The variety of texts confronts the reader with facts and thought processes over which he or she must gain control in order to comprehend the novel. What Wolfgang Iser has said of textual strategies in the twentieth-century novel is also relevant for the reader of the second version of the *Wanderjahre*:

> The reader is meant to become aware of the nature of his or her faculties of perception, of his or her own tendency

to link things together in consistent patterns, and even the whole thought process that constitutes his or her relations with the external world.

(10)

The disparateness of the archival texts forces the reader to construct meaningful connections.

The reader's irritation sets in almost at the novel's commencement. It is disconcerting to discover from Wilhelm's second letter to Natalie that the story **"Saint Joseph the Second"** which has been narrated from a third-person perspective, is something that Wilhelm has been writing for Natalie's benefit and that he needed to change around here and there (book 1, chapter 3). The irritation is continued by the mysterious mention in a conversation between Wilhelm and Jarno-Montan of a fetish that Wilhelm carries with him as if his life depended on it (book 1, chapter 4). Not until nineteen chapters later is the reader made to realize, by a letter from Wilhelm to Natalie, that the fetish has something to do with the surgical instruments from the *Lehrjahre* that Wilhelm acquired as a talisman and that make him "aware of his real calling" (book 2, chapter 11; SE 10: 293; HA 8: 281; FA I, 10: 554; MA 17: 510). The letter, which deals with the connection between Wilhelm's childhood memory of the drowned fisherman's son and this trivial object, results in a self-analysis of his suppressed trauma. Wilhelm's decision to become a surgeon is traced back to the moment he heard that surgical bleeding might have saved his boyhood friend. But his guilt over the death of his friend prevented him from acknowledging his youthful wish until he received permission from the Society of the Tower to begin training as a surgeon. Thus, Wilhelm's rescue of his son, Felix, by bleeding him in the last chapter of the novel is a fulfillment of a wish kept alive by the memory of the drowned fisherman's son whom he could not save and the mysterious fetish mentioned in book 1.

The surgical instruments play a similar role to that of the mysterious little casket, which has the function, along with the magnetic key, of tracing the development of the relationship between Felix and Hersilie. As long as the contents of the chest remain unknown to the reader, his or her curiosity about the relationship is titillated—especially by the obviously sexual undertones associated with box and key in folklore and popular psychology. (Goethe also employs the key as a phallic symbol in Faust's descent to the realm of the Mothers in *Faust II*.) While the content of the casket is never revealed, the reader is informed about the fate of the key: it is not broken by Felix's impulsive act—the two pieces are magnetically joined (book 3, chapter 17). Heidi Gideon has presented numerous other instances of suppression of relevant information and of overlapping of narrative functions (106-125).

Maintaining a balance between the freedom of the reader and the manipulation of the reader is an essential element of the traditional narrative strategy. Whereas the editor's effort to maintain this traditional equilibrium can be found in his comments on the American utopia and on the "ethereal fiction" of Makarie, it is negated in favor of the freedom of the reader in the two collections of aphorisms. Here it is a matter of the "unlimited interpretation" of texts. By means of the two collections of aphorisms, the linear process of reading a novel is interrupted by the disjunctive process associated with the reading of aphorisms. The aphorisms demand from their reader the ability to follow their leaps of logic as well as their organization. Whereas the other texts in the novel are bound to the unfolding plot, the two collections of aphorisms represent something like the "coexisting compositions" that, according to Lessing's *Laokoon,* eighteenth-century experts in aesthetics expected to find only in paintings but not in literature ("coexistence in space" versus "sequence in time"). In the manner of the maxims of classical antiquity, which were also collected in anthologies, the reader is presented with psychological experience, rules of social conduct, and scientific, aesthetic, and philosophical insights for "unlimited interpretation." A few aphorisms are almost identical with statements made by characters in the main narrative. This sacrifice of integration is rewarded with the same "sagacity and penetration" to be found in Laurence Sterne's novels, which, according to aphorism 164 from Makarie's archives, "are boundless." Benjamin Bennett (1993) has posited a special "community of readers" of the ***Wanderjahre*** that constitutes itself for the purpose of subversive readings of the text. He even speaks of a new "Social Contract" for the readers of the ***Wanderjahre*** which enjoins them to apply "radical irony" to the text (14-63, 307-26).

Goethe was aware of the challenges his novel presented to its readers. On June 26, 1796, while working on the ***Lehrjahre,*** he pointed out in a letter to Schiller that the reader must "supplement [*supplieren*] a number of things which were present in the text only as intention [but not yet articulated]." Goethe also applied the term *supplieren* to the reading of **Faust II.** The ***Wanderjahre*** posed considerably more challenges to readers than the ***Lehrjahre*** did. Goethe knew that many aspects of his novel would remain puzzling to his readers; still, he wrote to Zelter on October 19, 1821, he was convinced that there was "not a single line that was not felt or thought," and he hoped that "the true reader [would] once again be able to feel and rethink [each line]."

Abbreviations

Carlyle Carlyle, Thomas. *Goethe's* Wilhelm Meister's Travels: *Translation of the First Edition by Thomas Carlyle,* with an introduction by James Hardin. Columbia, SC: Camden House, 1991.

FA *Johann Wolfgang Goethe: Sämtliche Werke, Briefe, Tagebücher und Gespräche,* Frankfurter Ausgabe, 40 volumes projected, edited by Hendrik Birus et al. (Frankfurt am Main: Deutscher Klassiker Verlag, 1985 ff.).

Gräf Gräf, Hans Gerhard, ed., *Goethe über seine Dichtungen: Versuch einer Sammlung aller Äußerungen des Dichters über seine poetischen Werke,* Part 1, volume 2 (Frankfurt am Main: Rütten & Loening, 1902; reprinted Munich: Rütten & Loening, 1968).

HA *Goethes Werke,* Hamburger Ausgabe, 14 volumes, edited by Erich Trunz (Hamburg: Wegner, 1948-1964; tenth revised ed. Munich: Beck, 1981); citations from the revised edition are marked with an asterisk: e.g., HA 8: 257*. The pagination of the text of the *Wanderjahre* is identical in both editions, but the pagination of the commentaries is not.

MA *Johann Wolfgang Goethe: Sämtliche Werke nach Epochen seines Schaffens,* Münchner Ausgabe, 25 volumes projected, edited by Karl Richter et al. (Munich: Hanser, 1985 ff.).

SE *Goethe's Collected Works,* Suhrkamp Edition, 12 volumes, edited by Victor Lange, Eric Blackall, and Cyrus Hamlin (Cambridge, MA [New York]: Suhrkamp, 1983-1989; reprinted Princeton: Princeton UP, 1994 ff.).

WA *Goethes Werke,* Weimarer Ausgabe, 143 volumes in 4 parts, edited under commission by Grand Duchess Sophie von Sachsen (Weimar: Böhlau, 1887-1919; reprinted Munich: Deutscher Taschenbuch Verlag, 1987).

Works Consulted

EDITIONS OF THE *WANDERJAHRE*

Wilhelm Meisters Wanderjahre oder die Entsagenden. Ein Roman von Goethe. Erster Theil. Stuttgart & Tübingen: Cotta, 1821.

Wilhelm Meisters Wanderjahre: Ein Novellenkranz. Nach dem ursprünglichen Plan, edited by Eugen Wolff. Frankfurt am Main: Rütten & Loening, 1916.

Wilhelm Meisters Wanderjahre: Nach der I. Fassung des Jahres 1821, edited by Max Hecker. Berlin: Dom 1921.

Wilhelm Meisters Wanderjahre oder die Entsagenden: Urfassung von 1821, edited by Erhard März. Bonn: Bouvier, 1986 (text identical with Propyläen edition).

Vollständige Ausgabe letzter Hand, Taschenbuch-Ausgabe, volumes 21-23. Stuttgart & Tübingen: Cotta, 1829.

Vollständige Ausgabe letzter Hand, Oktavausgabe, volumes 21-23. Stuttgart & Tübingen: Cotta, 1830.

Gedenkausgabe der Werke, Briefe und Gespräche, Artemis- or Gedenkausgabe, edited by Ernst Beutler, volume 8, edited by Gerhard Küntzel. Zürich: Artemis, 1949.

Poetische Werke, Berliner Ausgabe, edited by Siegfried Seidel, Regine Otto, Jochen Golz, et al., volume 11, edited by Regine Otto, Annemarie Noelle, Günther Mieth, and Annemarie Mieth. Berlin: Aufbau, 1963.

Wilhelm Meisters Wanderjahre oder Die Entsagenden, Reclam-Ausgabe, by Ehrhard Bahr. Stuttgart: Reclam, 1982. An edition of the second version that includes selected parts of the first version.

Goethes Werke auf CD-ROM: Weimarer Ausgabe, Alexandria, VA: Chadwyck-Healey with the cooperation and support of Hermann Böhlaus Nachfolger, Weimar and the Deutsche Taschenbuch Verlag, Munich, 1995.

Wilhelm Meister's Journeyman Years or The Renunciants, Suhrkamp Edition, edited by Jane K. Brown, translated by Krishna Winston, in Goethe's Collected Works, volume 10. New York: Suhrkamp, 1989, 93-440 (including notes).

Wilhelm Meister's Travels; or, The Renunciants, A Novel, translated by Thomas Carlyle, in *German Romance: Specimens of Its Chief Authors; with Biographical and Critical Notices,* volume 4. Edinburgh: William Tait, 1827. Reprinted as *Goethe's Wilhelm Meister's Travels: Translation of the First Edition by Thomas Carlyle,* introduction by James Hardin. Columbia, SC: Camden House, 1991.

SECONDARY WORKS

Broch, Hermann. "James Joyce und die Gegenwart: Rede zu Joyces 50. Geburtstag [1936]." *Schriften zur Literatur 1: Kritik,* Kommentierte Werkausgabe. Ed. Paul Michael Lützeler. Frankfurt am Main: Suhrkamp, 1975. 63-94.

Trunz, Erich. "Anmerkungen des Herausgebers: Wilhelm Meisters Wanderjahre oder die Entsagenden," in *Goethes Werke,* edited by Trunz, Hamburger Ausgabe, volume 8. Hamburg: Wegner, 1950. 579-730.

Emrich, Wilhelm. "Das Problem der Symbolinterpretation im Hinblick auf Goethes *Wanderjahre,*" *Deutsche Vierteljahrsschrift,* 26 (1952): 331-52. Reprinted in Wilhelm Emrich, *Protest und Verheißung: Studien zur klassischen und modernen Literatur,* second edition Bonn: Athenäum, 1963. 48-66.

Henkel, Arthur. *Entsagung: Eine Studie zu Goethes Altersroman,* Hermaea, volume 3. Tübingen: Niemeyer, 1954 (second unrevised edition 1964).

Neuhaus, Volker. "Die Archivfiktion in *Wilhelm Meisters Wanderjahren,*" *Euphorion,* 62 (1968): 13-27.

Gideon, Heidi. *Zur Darstellungsweise von Goethes* Wilhelm Meisters Wanderjahre. Palaestra 256. Göttingen: Vandenhoeck & Ruprecht, 1969.

Bahr, Ehrhard. *Die Ironie im Spätwerk Goethes: "diese sehr ernsten Scherze": Studien zum* West-östlichen Divan, *zu den* Wanderjahren *und zu* Faust II. Berlin: Erich Schmidt, 1972. 88-130.

Iser, Wolfgang. *Der implizite Leser,* second edition Munich: Fink, 1979.

Müller, Klaus-Detlef. "Lenardos Tagebuch: Zum Romanbegriff in Goethes *Wilhelm Meisters Wanderjahre,*" *Deutsche Vierteljahrsschrift für Literaturwissenschaft und Geistesgeschichte,* 53 (1979): 275-99.

Steer, Alfred Gilbert. *Goethe's Science in the Structure of the* Wanderjahre. Athens: U of Georgia P, 1979.

Brandt, Helmut. "Entsagung und Französische Revolution. Goethes Prokuratorund Ferdinand-Novelle in weiterführender Betrachtung," in *Deutsche Klassik und Revolution,* edited by Paolo Chiarini and Walter Dietze. Rome: Ateneo, 1981, 195-227.

Degering, Thomas. *Das Elend der Entsagung: Goethes Wilhelm Meisters Wanderjahre.* Bonn: Bouvier, 1982.

Hagen, Waltraud. *Die Drucke von Goethes Werken,* second revised edition. Weinheim: Acta humaniora, 1983.

Vaget, Hans Rudolf. "Johann Wolfgang Goethe: Wilhelm Meisters Wanderjahre (1829)," in *Romane und Erzählungen zwischen Romantik und Realismus: Neue Interpretationen,* edited by Paul Michael Lützeler. Stuttgart: Reclam, 1983. 136-64.

Zenker, Markus. *Zu Goethes Erzählweise versteckter Bezüge* in Wilhelm Meisters Wanderjahre oder die Entsagenden. Epistemata, no. 56. Würzburg: Königshausen & Neumann, 1990.

Bennett, Benjamin. *Beyond Theory: Eighteenth-Century German Literature and the Poetics of Irony.* Ithaca, New York & London: Cornell UP, 1993.

Bahr, Ehrhard. "Wilhelm Meisters Wanderjahre oder die Entsagenden," in *Goethe-Handbuch,* edited by Theo Buch et al. Stuttgart & Weimar: Metzler, 1997. 3: 186-231.

Schwamborn, Claudia. *Individualität in Goethes Wanderjahren.* Paderborn: Schöningh, 1997.

Volker Dürr (essay date 2000)

SOURCE: Dürr, Volker. "Perspectives of *Wilhelm Meister's Travels* and Nietzsche's Perspectivism." *The Spirit of Poesy: Essays on Jewish and German Literature and Thought in Honor of Géza von Molnár.* Ed. Richard Block and Peter Fenves. Evanston: Northwestern UP, 2000. 176-92. Print.

[*In the following essay, Dürr explores the ways in which the form of Goethe's last novel anticipates the perspectivist outlook of Friedrich Nietzsche. Dürr contends that* Wilhelm Meister's Travels, *with its multitude of digressions and authorial viewpoints—including the fiction of an "editor" compiling the stories—reflects a philosophical discontent with the assumption of a single, shared objective reality.]*

"Could even he have been prenihilistic?" asked Gottfried Benn, who saw with the eyes of Nietzsche, after reading **Wilhelm Meister's Travels, or The Renunciants.** Surely it is not by chance that the essay in which the question flashes up bears the title "Pessimism." The ominous phrase was prompted by a pronouncement of Montan: "Once you know what truly matters, you cease to be loquacious."[1] A reading of the statement constitutes an interpretation. If one understood Goethe's words to mean "Once you know what is at stake, you cease to be loquacious," there is no suggestion of a prenihilistic disposition. However, Benn must have read the pronouncement in the sense of "Once you know what it's all about, you cease to be communicative." The consequences of Benn's insight are silence and loneliness, the very conditions under which Goethe had undertaken his last novel.

The loneliness of the old Goethe had several causes. One was biological, for he had outlived his friends and peers who shared his values. Thus, despite many visitors from the German states and abroad, including America, he had become intellectually and emotionally isolated. Time itself had bypassed him so that he was no longer able to reconcile his aesthetic predilections with recent cultural developments. Since his self had always sought to live in harmony with his surroundings, the new life apart constituted a reversal. Whether his disposition should be called indifference, resignation, pessimism, or prenihilism remains to be seen. In "Marginal Notes" Benn asserts, "Resignation leads its perspectives to the edge of darkness, but it maintains its composure even in [the face of] this darkness."[2] This statement performs the transition from resignation and prenihilism to perspectivism without any effort, although such a transition is not a necessity. However, according to empirical knowledge, perspectivism appears to be a consequence of resignation and prenihilism, which means nothing else than that perspectivism arises from such attitudes toward life.

Benn's comment seizes on an essential feature of **Travels** [**Wilhelm Meister's Travels**] and the tenor of its subtitle, **The Renunciants.** The darkness, with which this author surrounds life (as for instance in the poem "A Word" [Ein Wort]), is the premise of resignation. Concerning Goethe's last novel, he indeed ties "perspectives" or "perspectival perceptions" to the concept of resignation. For if any authorial measure distinguishes **Travels** from Goethe's preceding novels, it is the multi-perspectival modes of perception, narration, and presentation. The causes for this narratological revolution lie in the author's somber view of the world. The perspectives of **Wilhelm Meister's Travels** lead to the edge of darkness; the narrative does not form an aesthetic whole, nor does the world it presents constitute a totality. The failure of Goethe's efforts and

those of the romantics to fuse the self and the world in harmony once more was the decisive reason. His struggle with Newtonian physics had convinced Goethe that the instruments of "modern" science, such as the telescope and the microscope, led to an estrangement of man from his home, the sensuously perceivable world, and were about to create the institutions that allowed science to pursue its goal of ultimately dominating and exploiting nature, unfettered by a restraining sense of awe or reverence.

The result of the demystification of the world was the "prosaically ordered reality,"[3] which Hegel considered the very premise of the modern novel. Its essential conflict lies in the collision between the poetry of the heart and the prose of conditions. This very dichotomy Goethe had presented in **The Sufferings of Young Werther** (1774). In *The Theory of the Novel* the still thoroughly Hegelian Georg Lukács describes the representative narrative of the nineteenth century as "the novel of romantic disillusionment" and singles out Gustave Flaubert's *A Sentimental Education* (1869) as the most characteristic example.[4] Lukács could also have made his case with Eduard Mörike's *Painter Nolten* (1832) and Gottfried Keller's *Green Henry* (1853), in which romantic expectations are shattered by the resistance of the real. Mörike's great poem "Visiting Urach" [Besuch in Urach] clearly articulates the epochal post-romantic problem by recognizing the separation of the self from nature, or of man from the truth, since sensuous-personal experience no longer possesses general validity.[5] Because of its acknowledgment of the situation, the poem might as well be entitled "Resignation." Formally, Goethe's last novel is comparable to a collage, the action of which [Rahmenhandlung] is again and again breached and "retarded" by novellas, digressions, and collections of aphorisms.

The thought of Nietzsche seems to set in at the point where Goethe's reflections end, and he forges perspectivism into his foremost epistemological instrument, especially in the third part of his oeuvre. An understanding of the perspectivism of Nietzsche, in whose thinking it plays such a prominent role, will be helpful in comprehending the perspectives of **Travels.** Even the early Nietzsche of *Untimely Considerations* displays a kind of perspectivism that is similar to that of **Travels.** This applies in particular to the essay "On the Use and Disadvantage of History for Life" (1872) and is separated from the first version of **Travels** by half a century. Nietzsche's threefold division of historiography into monumental, antiquarian, and critical approaches is a modest enactment of perspectivism. Is it not surprising to find in the young Nietzsche and the old Goethe correspondences in their perceptions of the world, since the perspectivism of **Travels** emerges in the autumn of a long and singularly successful life? Parallels become even more transparent as Nietzsche continues writing.

Nietzsche's work is distinguished, more than any other philosopher's, by its sharp and ongoing contradictions. For example, he might say, "[O]nly as an aesthetic phenomenon is the world eternally justified," yet he turns around and questions the value of "aesthetic illusion." Comparable controversies rage throughout *Thus Spoke Zarathustra*: for example, are poets liars, or is the lie a precondition of the will to power? One is confronted here with irreconcilable oppositions, antinomies, or paradoxes, but Nietzsche even contradicts the principle of contradiction. As Karl Schlechta has observed, there is a "strange monotony in his pronouncements,"[6] which is to say that Nietzsche contradicts himself perpetually yet always says the same thing. Like Goethe, he was concerned with the whole, but also like Goethe, he did not believe that totality could be grasped, nor, for that matter, could the single "thing." According to Peter Pütz, comprehension is impeded in a double sense: "The beholder is dependent on the point of perception, and he can recognize only a part of the object."[7] Here is one of Nietzsche's own formulations to this effect: "All seeing is essentially perspectival, and so is all knowing."[8] Since one cannot comprehend the whole, cognition is reduced to single judgments which may contradict each other. Of course the multitude of judgments relativize each view. This relativizing also includes the three principal perspectives of determining reality: those of common sense, conceptual language, and the natural sciences.

When Goethe dictated the two versions of *Travels,* the dominant perspective was still that of common sense, although this mode of cognition was steadily losing ground to Newtonian science and its claim to objectivity. Nietzsche considered both equally illusory, for while common sense meets the needs of everyday life and relies on tradition, or what Flaubert called "idées reçes," the perspective of the natural sciences constitutes just another form of subjectivity masquerading as objectivity. Nevertheless (or because of this deception?), the natural sciences have succeeded in imprinting the tangible world and most minds with their perspective by means of their spectacular achievements. Yet Nietzsche, the underminer of all generally held assumptions, also proceeded to question this perspective, in *Beyond Good and Evil*:

> Today it is dawning on perhaps five or six minds that physics, too, is only an interpretation of the universe, an arrangement of it (to suit us, if I may be so bold!), rather than a clarification. Insofar as it builds on faith in sense-evidence, however, it is and shall long be taken for more—namely for a clarification. Physics has our eyes and fingers in its favor; it has eye-witness and handiness on its side. This has an enchanting, persuasive, and *convincing* effect on any era with basically plebeian tastes; why, it follows instinctively the canon of truth of forever popular sensualism.[9]

Moreover, as early as in the essay "On Truth and Lie in an Extra-Moral Sense," Nietzsche demonstrated that since Aristotle philosophical language relied on concepts thrice removed from the primordial truth and thus stood in its own way of accessing the "real." Truth is nothing but "a mobile army of metaphors, metonyms, and anthropomor-

phisms [. . .]; metaphors which are worn out and without sensuous power; coins which have lost their pictures and now matter only as metal, no longer as coins."[10] As to conceptual language, it is forged by disregarding individuality and the concrete, by equating things that are not equal: "Concepts [are the] graveyard of concrete thought."[11] Taken together with his depreciation of common sense and the natural sciences, the questioning of conceptual language means that these three perspectives are no more and no less than rival interpretations among other possible interpretations, all of which are equally valid and false. The most radical form of Nietzsche's perspectivism is expressed in a posthumously published dictum, "No, there are no facts, only interpretations. We cannot discern a fact 'in itself,' perhaps it is nonsensical to want something like that. 'Everything is subjective,' you say, but even that already constitutes interpretation [. . .] 'Perspectivism.'"[12] The notion that there are no facts, no "thing in itself" and no "world in itself" apart from interpretations is the gist of radical perspectivism. It is radical in the sense that it does not acknowledge any "real"-world structure against which the truth of the various interpretations could be verified. Nietzsche even asserts,

> [T]he world which we have not reduced to our being, our logic, and psychological prejudices, does not exist as world "in itself"; essentially it is a world of relations, and under certain circumstances it presents a different face from every point; its being is essentially different at every point; [. . .] and these summations are in every sense wholly *incongruent.*[13]

Since every perspective is subjective, it must be related to the conditions of existence of the one whose perspective it is.[14]

These late-nineteenth-century perceptions about the self and the real contribute significantly to an illumination of the spirit in which *Travels* is written and its narrative devices. Concerning the opening chapters, Jane Brown offers this reading:

> The implied multiplicity of narrative perspectives suggests new perspectives on the same object or event, and simultaneously calls the validity of any perspective into question. The problematic relationship between an imitation or image and its object further places the validity of any given perception into question. The perception of reality is thus very much a problem in these opening chapters.[15]

Brown goes on to relate the disparate narrative forms of the novel to its multiple perspectives. "The variety suggests a formal parallel to the variety of perspectives that has been developed as a basic philosophical standpoint of the novel."[16] Regrettably, this "philosophical position" is not elucidated, since the cited study's approach is positivistic and tends to disregard questions about authorial motivations. Moreover, Nietzsche as the generally recognized exponent of perspectivism is not mentioned. It is evident that Goethe, who at the time he took up *Travels* was in his seventies, appeared no longer inclined to fashion a narrative that, as a unified whole, would have reflected a coherent world. In *The Elective Affinities* (1810) he broke with the aesthetics of illusion of his own classicism. Thus, the narrative of his old age does not transmit the image of a pretended world unity; instead, the world is presented in the way the author perceived it: as a stage of disjointed and often contradictory phenomena. Goethe's perspectival mode of narration gives eloquent testimony to this assessment, as does his calling the novel an "aggregate."[17]

Travels is undoubtedly one of Goethe's most puzzling works, and its reception has continuously engendered a critical cacophony. Sometimes even the individual reader arrives at contradictory assessments, as, for instance, the public and private Thomas Mann did. In "Goethe and Tolstoi," Mann, also the author of *Der Zauberberg, Lotte in Weimar, Doctor Faustus, Felix Krull,* and a volume of essays on Goethe, praises the novel's clairvoyant prophecy that training in a specific trade or profession will be more helpful than a liberal education, whereas in a letter to Hermann Hesse he describes the narrative as a "highly fatigued, dignified-sclerotic medley."[18] The meaning of the whole or its thrust has been no less elusive, for traditional interpreters such as Erich Trunz understand *Travels* as a continuation of *Apprenticeship* [*Wilhelm Meister's Apprenticeship*] and save it for the genre of the novel by assigning to its "frame" the function of carrying the novelistic action with the goal of making Wilhelm a useful member of the group of emigrants. The inserted novellas, written earlier, are seen as spontaneous tales that enliven the sober and subdued mood of the frame. Yet is *Travels* indeed an extension of *Apprenticeship* even though, as Friedrich Hebbel believed, the principal figures are utterly different from their namesakes in the classical Bildungsroman? "When Goethe lets the *Meister*-figures reappear in *Travels* [...], it is about the same as if a deranged father wrote with chalk pasquils on his children's backs and considered them thereby organically recast."[19]

Or is *Travels,* as Hannelore Schlaffer contends, a battleground between the *spokesmen* of usefulness with their international economic safety net and the spirit of poetry, whose incarnations, Mignon and the harper, are eliminated at the end of *Apprenticeship*? For Mignon reasserts herself at the occasion of Wilhelm's pilgrimage to Lago Maggiore, her home. In addition, Schlaffer perceives in the constant mythological allusions emanating from several principal figures a return of myth in which poetry regains its rights.[20] Although this thesis seems to be pushed too far (for instance in the case of Philine, who supposedly embodies important features of Aphrodite, the Fates, and Persephone), Schlaffer is correct in assuming that the resurgent spirit of poetry relativizes the somewhat pompous seriousness with which the leaders of the emigrants conduct themselves and their affairs.

According to another recent study, the spatial "side-by-side" of *Travels* does have a unifying feature in that many of its topographical units [Bezirke] are constructed in a similar manner. Whether one looks at the secularized monastery of St. Joseph the Second, the estate of the uncle, the Pedagogical Province, or Makarie's property, all are separated from the rest of the world by a wall or some sort of demarcation line, and they contain an "innermost" which is accessible through a portal that may, however, remain unopened.[21] Thus, the various topographical units, and there are just about a dozen, are closed upon themselves yet accessible at the same time. They constitute modes of living, if not of being; they are not integrated with one another but exist autonomously side by side (although some of them are connected by family ties). Each one is a small world in itself, and while it objectifies a certain Weltanschauung, it also contains within the contradiction of its own ideology. This built-in tension endows the unit with life and the capability to change. St. Joseph the Second, for instance, who conducts his life "in imitatio,"[22] is nonetheless sufficiently independent from his model to become a real father instead of only a foster parent, and he upholds a principle contradicting strict imitation: "Life belongs to the living, and he who lives must be prepared for change" (111). In an analogy, the inhabitants of the uncle's estate counteract the proprietor's program and the subtitle of the entire novel. As Juliette candidly observes, "From this you can see that we exercise great care not to be taken into your order, the community of the renunciants" (152).

The narrative could also be seen as a succession of tensions between efforts to enlighten the novelistic figures and the reader and to preserve the mystery of life, for according to Goethe, *Wilhelm Meister's Travels* is a book of "hidden meanings" and "open secrets."[23] Other antinomies, which could readily serve as topics for interpreting the text, are preservation and beginning anew, rest and motion, thinking and doing, and so on, not to speak of narratological aspects. The infinite possibilities of approaching this work are due to its perspectivism, for while any object can be perceived from many perspectives, *Travels* actually prompts perspectival readings because of its own perspectival structure. Nietzsche contended that no perspective is privileged over another (e.g., should one try to weigh the merits of the anatomist against those of the interior colonists?), and since the novel comprises about a dozen topographical units or small worlds with their own perspectives, multiple interpretations are inevitable.

However, the perspectivism of *Travels* sets in with the act of narration itself, for Goethe divides himself into three personae: author, narrator, and editor [Redaktor]. The narrator is quite close to the author, including the feature of advanced age: "We would not presume to describe the scene that must have taken place, for fear we might lack the requisite youthful ardor" (242). Occasionally, the narrator presents views which may not be in accord with Goethe's own. He is not always in complete control of how his materials are presented, for frequently he does not determine where matter is inserted. Such decisions are often left to the editor, whose role has been reduced in comparison with his role in the first version of *Travels*; in particular, he provides fewer explanations, a measure that enhances the autonomy of the different narrative units. With a narrator limited in his representational range yet close to the author, and an additional editor, we thus have, as far as narratorial positions are concerned, three perspectives outside the topographical units, the titular hero, the novellas, the diaries, the letters, the conversations, and the soliloquies. In the terminology of Gérard Genette, the narrative can

> regulate the information it delivers [...]; with the narrative adopting or seeming to adopt what we ordinarily call the participant's "vision" or "point of view"; the narrative seems in that case [...] to take on, with regard to the story, one or another *perspective.* "Distance" and "perspective" [...] are the two chief modalities of that regulation of narrative information.[24]

Through the device of dividing himself into three personae, Goethe distanced himself from his own narrative. While the splitting of narratorial tasks could serve the cause of verisimilitude, as for instance in Emily Brontë's *Wuthering Heights* (1847), it achieves the opposite effect in *Travels.* In his characterization of Goethe's last works, Nietzsche seizes on essential features without concerning himself with narratorial technicalities.

> No individuals, but more or less ideal masks; no reality, but allegorical generality; characteristics of the time and local colors toned down almost to invisibility and made mythical; the current sensibility and the problems of contemporary society condensed into the simplest forms, stripped of their alluring, exciting, pathological qualities and made ineffective in every sense but the artistic one; no new materials and characters, but the old, long accustomed ones forever reenlivened and transformed; this is art as Goethe *understood* it in his later years.[25]

The art practice Nietzsche ascribes to the old Goethe is antirealistic and mediated;[26] it is filtered through several prisms. Since Goethe did not like the German sociopolitical reality of the 1820s and 1830s, he saw no reason to imitate it. It certainly was not worthy of being transposed into aesthetic permanence (as Stifter attempted with his strange "realism" in *Indian Summer*). Nevertheless, as an artist of his time, he had to capture its contradictory spirit and diverging currents, not by mimetic re-presentation, but by the more abstract conventions approaching allegory, a mode toward which he was also tending in the last two books of *Apprenticeship.*[27] Thus he reduces problems of contemporary society to simple forms, and he offers ways to conduct life. The multitude of topographical units and perspectives does not allow their specification through the characteristic detail. The toning down of actuality and local color enables the reemergence of the mythical (Schlaffer focuses on this feature), to which the return of familiar figures, changed as they are, also contributes. By defining Goethe's art, Nietzsche describes his own philosophizing:

no new materials, but the old ones are taken up again and again, reformulated, and given new life.

In his notes from 1795-96, when he was writing ***Wilhelm Meister's Apprenticeship,*** Goethe called the protagonist his "aesthetic-ethical dream,"[28] a conception he tried to realize in the two concluding utopian books of the Bildungsroman. In *Travels,* though, this aesthetic-ethical dream can no longer be actualized, for the vocation of a "surgeon" [Wundarzt], which Wilhelm chooses, lacks the aesthetic component.[29] One could counter this objection by proclaiming Wilhelm to be the embodiment of one of the principal ideas of Friedrich Schiller's essay "On the Aesthetic Education of Man in a Series of Letters," according to which the individual must first become aesthetic, that is, "free" before he or she can conduct his or her life ethically.[30] Yet how could Wilhelm's experience of a decade with the theater be brought to bear on his new vocation? Does a "surgeon" have to be "free" in Schiller's sense in order to be effective? Is Wilhelm indeed free, or does he continue to be guided by the Tower? Here is one major difference between Goethe's classical Bildungsroman and *Travels.* About *Apprenticeship* Schiller wrote, "[E]verything happens to and around Wilhelm, but really not through him,"[31] precisely because things around him constitute energies, whereas in *Travels* nothing happens to him anymore, nor does he initiate anything. Instead, the sober spirit of the later novel reduces the protagonist to an instrument of perception and mediation of different and contrasting perspectives.

The Wilhelm of *Travels* has become a pale figure without much character who readily becomes assimilated to every environment he enters. As a prism of the many perspectives he encounters, he cannot be distinct. He also has been thoroughly desensualized, a process that is most obvious in his erotic ossification. Schlaffer has pointed out that the titular hero experiences the stages of *quinquae lineae* [the road to erotic fulfillment] in reverse order. He begins with sexual intercourse (Mariane, with whom he begets Felix; and Philine), which is followed by the forbidden kissing of the married countess, his ambivalent relationship with Mignon (lover, protector, father), the extensive conversations with Aurelie, the marriage proposed to Therese on the grounds of reason, and finally the correspondence with the distant fiancée whom he adores in the way one adores a saint.[32] In *Travels* he never gets to see Natalie; his encounter with Hersilie is a platonic dalliance. By that time he must be in his mid-thirties. Yet in his paleness, the new Wilhelm is no exception, for all figures—except for Felix and Hersilie—are "flat" (in the sense of E. M. Forster's definition)[33] and incapable of surprising the reader as "round" characters could and would. Nor are they "types" in the sense of the Marxist Georg Lukács: they do not present an entire class or thousands of individuals in similar psychosocial situations (e.g., Flaubert's pharmacist Homais, the archbourgeois, or Emma Bovary, the quixotic wife who weeps in every French village). Another salient feature of the "characters" of *Travels* is the fact that, as Waltraud Maierhofer has pointed out, they talk, listen to monologues, engage in discussion, write letters, and read epistles[34] (a convention, I should add, of the "idle" eighteenth century as far as the upper classes are concerned), so that little time is left for action.

Makarie and Montan are not only essentially different from the other figures of the novel; they also embody opposite modes of experiencing the world and of realizing themselves. They are unique and follow vocations that appear awe-inspiring to their contemporaries. Both are called wise and are, in addition, coordinated on account of their polar pursuits; her contemplative disposition complements Montan's *vita activa*. As to their natures, the narrator explains, "If one may assume that beings, insofar as they are corporeal, strive toward the center, while insofar as they are spiritual, they strive toward the periphery, then our friend belongs to the most spiritual" (410). One speaks of Makarie only in superlatives. According to her assistant, the astronomer, mathematician, and philosopher, she is a woman of whom it is said "that she not only carried the entire solar system within her, but also that she moved within it as an integral part" (183). In contrast to her astrospheric flights, Montan penetrates "the depth of the earth." While Makarie is described as "the most taciturn of all women" (252), although she turns out to be a loquacious mediator of interpersonal disputes, Montan is indeed the silent one because he knows too much.

> "I am thoroughly convinced that everyone must cherish for himself, with utmost seriousness, that which he holds dearest, which is to say, his convictions." [. . .] Challenged by Wilhelm's response, Montan explained further: "Once you know what truly matters, you cease to be loquacious." "But what does truly matter?" inquired Wilhelm impulsively. "That is easily said," the other replied. "Thought and action, action and thought, that is the sum of all wisdom, known from time immemorial, practiced from time immemorial, not realized by all."
>
> (280)

The most striking features about Montan's dramatized monologue are its sententious affirmations, which could just as well form part of **"Maxims and Reflections."** As such they constitute unmediated formulations of Goethe's wisdom and make Montan, as Nietzsche suggested, a "mask" of the author. This passage also contains the sentence, "Once you know [. . .]," which prompted Benn to ask whether Goethe, too, might have been prenihilistic. Instead of being as loquacious as most of the figures in *Wanderjahre,* Montan proposes "thought and action," that is, to go thoughtfully and without verbal ado about one's tasks.

The antithetical and additive structure of *Travels,* which is the formal expression of its perspectival conception, also manifests itself in Makarie's and Montan's assistants. They differ in gender and age from their superiors, and they embody contrastive epistemological approaches. Thus, the narrator attributes to Montan's female helper

> quite *remarkable* faculties and a peculiar affinity for everything that might be called rock, mineral, indeed any kind of element. This companion could sense not only a certain emanation from underground streams, deposits, and veins of metals, as well as coal and whatever else might be massed together, but what was more *amazing* still, would feel different with every change of place.
>
> (406)

Undoubtedly the woman at Montan's side possesses psychosomatic qualities that enable her to perceive things that would remain inaccessible to the rationalistic Montan. To draw attention to the otherness of the young woman, the narrator resorts to the adjective and adverb "wundersam" and "wunderbar" ([remarkable] and [amazing]) to define her abilities. Moreover, she performs her miraculous discoveries in a taciturn manner, a trait she shares with her patron. Makarie and the astronomer form a comparable team, though in reverse. In this case Makarie embodies the intuitive approach raised to the highest kind of spirituality, while the astronomer is primarily there to confirm her intuitions by means of the natural sciences.

It should be noted that these four figures constitute a crosswise constellation consisting of mature female and male principals with younger assistants of the opposite gender who perform their work by marshaling contrastive epistemological forces. In both pairs the female partners are the vessels of intuition and thus of apparently superior knowledge. Together Makarie's and Montan's helpers form a perfect whole of ethereal spirituality and sensuous intuition. Another example of superior female intuition manifests itself in the love triangle Felix-Hersilie-Wilhelm, which is closely tied to the mysterious golden casket. In this case, too, it seems to be Hersilie who knows best.[35] I say "seems to be" because it is a characteristic of Goethe's last novel and its perspectivism that assertions are taken back almost immediately after they have been made or fictively enacted. The examples of Makarie's and Montan's perspectives, the discussion of which leads to yet another perspective, disclose Goethe's procedure. After a conversation among themselves, Wilhelm, Montan, and Makarie's astronomer agree that one could descend into the deepest chasms of the earth and discover that even there "human nature contains something analogous to what is crudest and most rigid" (406), or that like Makarie one could withdraw beyond the extreme limits of our solar system to gain knowledge about the real constitution of our earth. Hence the participants of the talk arrive at two preliminary resolutions: First of all, neither Montan's nor Makarie's extreme positions are required to impress upon man as an inhabitant of the earth the necessity of taking action. In the second place, the narrator suddenly declares the vocation of the terrestrial Montan and the heaven-bound Makarie to be fairy tales [Märchen], or "a metaphor of the highest good" (407). The comparison suggests that as in the fairy tale, the wondrous can occur in everyday life, and thus the prose of "modernity," too, can be punctured by seemingly supernatural occurrences, although they may find scientific explanations.

Travels not only presents side by side different ways of life but also objectifies in some of the topographical units the epochal scientific controversy of how the self is actually formed. The dispute of the time pitted the adherents of preformation against those of epigenesis.[36] If *Apprenticeship* or the Bildungsroman is the enactment per se of the idea of epigenesis, Goethe seems to have taken back his predilection for self-formation as seen in *Elective Affinities,* an unredeemable world of poor judgment, guilt, and woe. And *Wilhelm Meister's Wanderjahre*? A comparison of passages treating the same theme, that is, the relationship of the individual and the outer world, illuminates the difference between the two Wilhelm Meister novels. In a conversation with the Beautiful Soul, her uncle affirms in book 6 of *Apprenticeship*:

> The whole universe lies before us, like a great quarry before the master-builder, who only deserves this name if he can put together with the greatest economy, purposiveness and firmness these chance natural masses according to a primeval image formed in his own mind. Everything apart from ourselves consists only of elements, indeed I may say everything about us; but there lies deep within us this creative force which is able to call into being what is to be and does not let us pause and rest until we have given expression to it outside ourselves, in one way or another.[37]

The message is a clear and firm commitment to self-formation, pronounced by a mature man whose life has been successful though not without profound grief. The uncle nevertheless believes, most likely as the author's spokesman, that the external world and the facticity of the self are "elements" or potentials to be shaped according to original images projected by our own creativity.

The collection of aphorisms at the end of the second book of *Travels,* **"Reflections in the Spirit of the Wanderers,"** contains the following entry:

> Every man sees the finished and regulated, formed, complete world only as an element from which he is to create a particular world suitable to him. Capable people set to without hesitation and try to manage as best they can. Others waver on the brink; some even doubt of its existence. Anyone imbued with this basic truth would quarrel with no one, but would simply regard the other's way of thinking, as well as his own, as a phenomenon.
>
> (310)

This reflection also appears to make a case for epigenesis in that all individuals are said to consider the preformed world as raw material from which they create worlds of their own that suit them. Of course this maxim "in the spirit of the Wanderers" applies to the "emigrants"

[Aus-wanderer] as well as to the interior colonists around Odoard who set out to create new human habitats and societies, although a number of strict regulations prescribe the colonists' future way of life in America even before they have departed. But how does the aphorism relate to the opening chapters of the novel concerning St. Joseph the Second or the world of the collector whom Wilhelm visits before entering the Pedagogical Province? Were there ever more preformed lives than these? Or does the life of this "holy family" no longer possess any validity since it is mere imitation of the outer trappings of an ideal whose substance it no longer possesses? Why should anyone turn back eighteen hundred years to adopt a role model while new machines are about to dislodge the weavers in the mountains? The positivistic philosopher Feuerbach would have criticized St. Joseph the Second for living in images rather than the concrete world. But Goethe had a sincere appreciation of "naive imitation"[38] and may have been willing to make concessions even to an imitative life.

While the images and the story of the "holy family" (**"The Flight to Egypt"**) open up the perspectivism of *Travels,* the second part of the uncle's reflection discloses new vistas. Its "basic truth" [Grundwahrheit] is the fact that individuals take different approaches to the offerings of the world. We know of Goethe's esteem for "upright" and "competent" people, yet we have also learned in the discussion of *Hamlet* in **Wilhelm Meister's Apprenticeship** that he was rather sympathetic to the wavering Shakespearean hero. And did he not muster empathy for even those who doubted the existence of a structured world, for it was he who secured a university position for the philosopher J. G. Fichte while later playfully referring to him as "the great Ego" in Jena. All three modes of perceiving and responding to the world are also Goethe's own perspectives, for was he himself not "competent" in the sense of answering the challenges of the day? Was his toned-down alter ego Wilhelm (in comparison to the hero of *Theatrical Mission* [*Wilhelm Meister's Theatrical Mission*]) not playing Hamlet so convincingly because he himself was Hamlet? And finally, did Goethe not harbor Faust and Mephisto in his bosom, the latter the eternal negator (of the world) and hence another "great Ego"? In short, Goethe had many and large sympathies that he objectified in *Travels.*

The aphorism from **"In the Spirit of the Wanderers"** [**"Reflections in the Spirit of the Wanderers"**] triggers another observation. While the last sentence is a plea for tolerance, the entire passage seems to be an elucidation of the connection between epigenesis and perspectivism. The latter could not possibly unfold in a preformed society; rather, the triumph of epigenesis was a precondition for its emergence. For indeed, is the creation of multitudes of individual worlds that run according to their own norms and rules, worlds coexisting side by side, not the premise of societal perspectivism, if not multiculturalism, within a given society? In the light of this, it seems only reasonable to conclude that the multiperspectival structure of *Travels,* with its narratorial machinery of author, narrator, editor, and its multiple topographical units, would have been inconceivable without the ideological foundation of epigenesis. However, there are also Makarie and Montan, who cannot be explained with either concept. These extraordinary figures live beyond space, time, and causality, as do figures of the fairy tale.

Throughout the narrative the editor's arrangement of the materials contributes to highlighting the multiperspectival conception of the novel. Thus, immediately after their encounter with the backward-looking St. Joseph the Second and his family, Wilhelm, Felix, and the reader meet Montan, one of the most knowledgeable and future-oriented figures. Such juxtapositions of contrary perspectives typify the structure of *Travels* and culminate in the miners' festival (book 2, chapter 9). Here a discussion takes place about the question of which elemental force or forces were responsible for giving the earth the form we know.

At the outset of the disputation, the Neptunic theory finds its most fervent detractors in the adherents of vulcanism and fire. To these two conceptions about the shaping of the surface of the earth, which were the dominant ones in Goethe's time, a third is added, which can be described as "dynamic-eruptive": "mighty formations already completed in the bowels of the earth had been extruded through the earth's crust by irresistible forces; and in the course of these convulsions various pieces of them had been scattered and strewn near and far" (279). There remain two other schools of thought about the formation of our planet. One was the "atmospherics," if one can call them that, who are convinced that several conditions of the surface of the earth could never be explained "unless it was allowed that greater and lesser segments of mountain could have fallen from the sky and covered great broad stretches of the landscape" (279). The fifth and last position upholds the theory of the ice age, which supposedly saw "glaciers descended from the highest mountain ranges far into the land, forming in effect slides for ponderous masses of primeval rock which were propelled farther and farther over the glassy track" (279). At this point the narrator delivers an ironical blow against so much sanguine theorizing by stating: "The general opinion was that it was far more natural to have the world be created with colossal crashes and upheavals, wild raging and fiery catapulting. And since the heat of the wine was now adding its strong effect, the glorious celebration might almost have ended in fatal clashes" (279).

There was hardly anything stranger to Goethe than theorizing individuals who upheld their views or prejudices with the utmost intolerance. In such a situation Montan, who knows what he is talking about when he talks, remains silent. He keeps his own understanding of geology to himself, although he is convinced, as Erich Trunz writes, that "the earth was formed by the cooperation of

various forces, all theories contained some truth, yet most work had been performed by the water."[39] We do not know how Trunz arrived at this finding. He simply must have seen Montan as Goethe's mouthpiece, and for Goethe the Neptunic theory was the most congenial since he preferred measured and steady developments to eruptive leaps and bounds or revolutions (as is obvious from the narrator's comment above). Instead of presenting the author's views directly, the narrator allows Wilhelm to remark after the heated dispute: "'[T]here are so many contradictions, and we are always told that the truth lies in the middle.' 'By no means,' Montan answered. 'The problem lies in the middle, unfathomable perhaps, perhaps also accessible, if you give it a try'" (280). In the controversy about how the surface of the earth was shaped, only Wilhelm is thinking of biblical genesis; but then, at the beginning of *Travels* this former incarnation of self-formation (*Apprenticeship,* book 5, chapter 3) had already empathized with St. Joseph the Second and his preformed life.

The most important point of this statement is Montan's belief that in case of contradictory claims it is not the truth that remains lying in the middle, but the problem itself, that is, the controversy about the formation of the earth. In Goethe's terminology, the phenomenon is not the "thing in itself" but the perceived object, in other words, a fusion of the object and the beholding subject. Although he does his utmost to exclude empirical variants and chance from the cognitive process, and although he writes, for instance, in **"Maxims and Reflections,"** "[One] phenomenon or one experiment cannot prove anything; it is a link in a long chain, and it is valid only in context," there always remains an inexpungeable element of subjectivity: a perspective. While this situation is almost identical with Nietzsche's assertion "[A]ll seeing is essentially perspectival, and so is all knowing," Goethe also believes with Nietzsche, "[W]here object and subject come together, there is life."[40] As I have shown, Nietzsche occasionally claims that there was no world outside human perception, but this is only the logical consequence of his perspectival premise. His more habitual inclination is to acknowledge a real world, an amorphous entity, an "undifferentiated original Oneness (Ureines)."[41] For Goethe, too, despite all perspectival activity, the world remains lying in the middle while, just as in Nietzsche, the sum of voiced perspectives does not constitute a coherent image.

The miners' festival is but one example of Goethe's perspectivism; another would be the presentation of the three basic religious forms in the Pedagogical Province—ethnic, philosophical, Christian—whereby once again no common ground is established. To investigate the religious perspectivism of the Pedagogical Province would require another essay. (This might be a task for you, Géza, on entering your silvery age.) Suffice it to say for the purpose of this essay that the narrator presents no more than what he considers three basic "Western" religious attitudes and leaves it at that. In the 1820s Goethe can foresee a number of developments in the nineteenth century and the modern age, but not all of them. He finds his own present highly complex, if not ultimately elusive, and he has his reservations about it, as exemplified by the utterly unconventional structure of **Travels.** He also expresses this apprehension in verse:

> Why should we be alarmed
> About the future? when
> The present already surpasses
> Human understanding.

With these lines from "Life is [. . .]" the old Goethe returns once again to the free rhythms of his youthful hymns of the 1770s, but in this instance the four verses are built around concepts, whereas metaphors made his early lyrics sparkle. This kind of epigrammatic poetry is also a form of resignation.

The author of **Travels** sees in everything taking place around him a threat to the world in whose creation he played a major role and to which he affixed his signature. It was a world built on harmonious agreements between the given and the projected, the real and the imaginary, the rational and the irrational. In old age, though, Goethe finds himself confronted with the demands of "modernity," which he can meet only with perspectivism. Montan's silence resounds louder than the marching songs of the emigrants, yet he keeps, in Benn's words, his countenance. In all deference to Goethe's genius, it is quite apparent that the perspectivism of **Wilhelm Meister's Travels** is conditioned by the political, social, and cultural climate of the Restoration. While the same epochal malaise engenders the perspectival plays and novels by the romantics Ludwig Tieck, Clemens Brentano, and E. T. A. Hoffmann, their and Goethe's perspectivism prepare the ground for that of Nietzsche. In all of them perspectivism is inseparable from irony, the distinguishing mark of a culture questioning itself.

Notes

Citations from Goethe's *Wilhelm Meisters Wanderjahre oder die Entsagenden* are taken from *Wilhelm Meister's Journeyman Years, or The Renunciants,* trans. Krishna Winston, ed. Jane K. Brown (New York: Suhrkamp, 1989). Although I use the title *Travels,* the page numbers I provide with citations in the text refer to this translation.

1. Gottfried Benn, *Gesammelte Werke,* ed. Dieter Wellershoff (Munich: Deutscher Taschenbuch Verlag, 1975), 3:921-22 (my translation).

2. Ibid., 3:961 (my translation).

3. G. W. F. Hegel, *Vorlesungen über die Ästhetik III, Werke,* ed. Eva Moldenhauer and Karl Markus Michel (Frankfurt am Main: Suhrkamp, 1986), 15:392.

4. Georg Lukács, *Die Theorie des Romans,* 3d ed. (Neuwied: Luchterhand, 1965), 114-34. Originally published in 1916.

5. With this poem Mörike confirms his closeness to the old Goethe, although some recent scholars, above all Harold Bloom, deny the existence of such "happy," productive relationships.

6. Karl Schlechta, "Nachwort" to *Friedrich Nietzsche, Werke in drei Bänden,* ed. Karl Schlechta, 8th ed. (Munich: Hanser, 1977), 3:1435 (my translation).

7. Peter Pütz, *Friedrich Nietzsche,* 2d ed. (Stuttgart: Metzlersche Verlagsbuchhandlung, 1967-75), 26 (my translation).

8. Nietzsche, *The Birth of Tragedy and the Genealogy of Morals,* trans. F. Golfing (Garden City, N.Y.: Doubleday/Anchor Books, 1956), 255.

9. Nietzsche, *Beyond Good and Evil,* trans. Marianne Conan (South Bend, Ind.: Gateway, 1955), 15.

10. Nietzsche, *The Portable Nietzsche,* selected, edited, and translated by Walter Kaufmann (Harmondsworth: Penguin, 1976), 46-47.

11. Nietzsche, *Werke in drei Bänden,* 3:319 (my translation; this passage was deleted by Kaufmann).

12. Ibid., 3:903 (my translation).

13. Ibid., 3:769 (my translation).

14. See also Arthur Danto, "Nietzsche's Perspectivism," in *Nietzsche: A Collection of Critical Essays,* ed. Robert C. Solomon (Garden City, N.Y.: Anchor Press, 1973), 29-57.

15. Jane Brown, *Goethe's Cyclical Narratives: Die Unterhaltungen deutscher Ausgewanderten and Wilhelm Meisters Wanderjahre* (Chapel Hill: University of North Carolina Press, 1975), 43.

16. Ibid., 48.

17. Goethe in conversation with Chancellor von Müller, February 18, 1830, in *Goethes Gespräche,* ed. Ernst Beutler, 2d ed. (Zurich: Artemis, 1966), 2:667.

18. Thomas Mann, "Goethe und Tolstoi," in *Adel des Geistes* (Stockholm: Bermann-Fischer BA, 1967), 263; and Thomas Mann, *Briefe 1937-1947,* ed. Erika Mann (Weimar, 1965), 424 (my translation).

19. Friedrich Hebbel, *Werke,* ed. Gerhard Fricke, Werner Keller, and Karl Pörnbacher. (Munich: Hanser, 1967), 5:174 (my translation).

20. See Hannelore Schlaffer, *Wilhelm Meister: Das Ende der Kunst und die Wiederkehr des Mythos* (Stuttgart: J. B. Metzlersche Verlagsbuchhandlung, 1989).

21. Heidi Gidion, *Zur Darstellungsweise von "Wilhelm Meisters Wanderjahre"* (Göttingen: Vandenhoeck and Ruprecht, 1969), 63, 71 (my translation).

22. The St. Joseph the Second chapters might have been inspired by Thomas à Kempis's *De imitatione*

Christi (1441), which regained currency at the beginning of the nineteenth century, especially among the Nazarenes. The book also plays a role in some of George Eliot's novels.

23. See also Volker Dürr, "Geheimnis und Aufklärung: Zur pädagogischen Funktion des Kästchens in *Wilhelm Meisters Wanderjahren*," *Monatshefte* 74 (1982): 11-19.

24. Gérard Genette, *Narrative Discourse,* trans. E. Lewin, (Ithaca, N.Y.: Cornell University Press, 1990), 162.

25. Nietzsche, *Werke in drei Bänden,* 1:580-81 (my translation).

26. See Manfred Karnick, *"Wilhelm Meisters Wanderjahre" oder die Kunst des Mittelbaren* (Munich: Fink, 1968).

27. See Volker Dürr, *"Wilhelm Meisters Lehrjahre*: Hypotaxis, Abstraction and the Realistic Symbol," in *Versuche zu Goethe: Festschrift für Erich Heller,* ed. Volker Dürr and Géza von Molnár (Heidelberg: Stiehm, 1976), 201-11.

28. Goethe, *Notizbuch* (1793), cited in *Goethes Werke,* Hamburger Ausgabe, ed. E. Trunz (Munich: C. H. Beck, 1982), 8:518 (my translation).

29. In her cited study, Hannelore Schlaffer presents medicine as an art and thereby not only justifies Wilhelm's career in the theater but also saves art for *Travels.* However, her argument is not wholly convincing.

30. Friedrich von Schiller, "Über die ästhetische Erziehung des Menschen in einer Reihe von Briefen," in *Sämtliche Werke* (Munich: Hanser, 1977), 5:646 (my translation).

31. Schiller to Goethe, in *Briefe an Goethe,* ed. Karl Robert Mandelkow (Hamburg: Wegner, 1965), 1:263 (my translation).

32. Schlaffer, *Wilhelm Meister,* 140 (my translation).

33. E. M. Forster, *Aspects of the Novel* (1927; reprint, New York: Harcourt, Brace, and World, 1954), 68-78.

34. Waltraud Maierhofer, *"Wilhelm Meisters Wanderjahre" und der Roman des Nebeneinander* (Bielefeld: Aisthesis Verlag, 1990), 118-19. Actually this observation is owed to Anneliese Klingenberg, *Wilhelm Meisters Wanderjahre oder die Entsagenden: Quellen und Komposition* (Berlin: Aufbau Verlag, 1972), 133.

35. Hersilie tells Wilhelm, "But the casket must first stand unopened between you and me, and then, once opened, decree what should follow. I hope there will be nothing inside [...]" (321). Indeed, between Hersilie and Wilhelm the casket remains

shut throughout the novel, just as their relationship does not gain momentum.

36. Helmut Müller-Sievers, *Epigenesis* (Paderborn: Schöningh, 1993), 17-52.

37. Goethe, *Wilhelm Meister's Years of Apprenticeship,* trans. H. M. Waidson (London: John Calder, 1978), 2:173.

38. Goethe, "Einfache Nachahmung der Natur, Manier, Stil," in *Goethes Werke,* 12:30-34.

39. Erich Trunz, "Nachwort," in *Goethes Werke,* 8:676 (my translation).

40. Goethe, reported by Gustav Friedrich Parthey, August 28, 1827, in *Goethes Werke,* Artemis Gedenkausgabe ed. Ernst Beutler (Zurich: Artemis, 1966), 33:492 (my translation).

41. Danto, "Nietzsche's Perspectivism," 56.

Virgil Nemoianou (essay date 2001)

SOURCE: Nemoianou, Virgil. "From Goethe to Guizot: The Conservative Contexts of *Wilhelm Meisters Wanderjahre*." *Modern Language Studies* 31.1 (2001): 45-58. Print.

[*In the following essay, Nemoianou suggests that Goethe maintained a conservative political philosophy, but he cautions against equating such a position with "'servility' and traditionalism." Nemoianou demonstrates that Goethe's counterreaction to a revolutionary age was shared by the French political thinker François Guizot, who rose to prominence in the years immediately after Goethe's death.*]

I

In this essay I intend to outline briefly some general features of Goethe's political philosophy. I believe that the elusive nature of this philosophy becomes clearer when placed in a European context and when focused on one of his latest works. I am now inclined to join the majority that regards Goethe as a conservative writer, like so many other great writers that we can think of, in fact. However the label itself is not very helpful unless thoroughly qualified: whether we look around us or look toward the past, we notice immediately the multiplicity of conservative modes.

For the sake of clarity, I will begin by stating that in my opinion there are *four* separate contexts that ought to be taken into consideration and these in turn will lead us to integrate Goethe in a broader European context that contains figures such as Chateaubriand, Mme de Staël, Guizot, Burke, Adam Smith, Tocqueville, Scott, perhaps Southey or Cobbett also, Jaime Balmes, Rosmini, with unavoidable similarities and differences. To my knowledge this has been done rarely, if ever.

These four contexts of conservatism (or "conservatism") which I regard as the most useful in explaining Goethe's mode of thinking are the following: 1) the influence of Justus Möser, 2) the connection with and serving of his own Duke Karl-August, 3) the delicate and intricate dialectics of Goethe's rapport with Metternich and Metternich's Europe, 4) (and most important in my view) the way in which the elder Goethe found himself on the same wavelength with François Guizot, and through him with the vast network of above-mentioned European intellectuals who, while accepting of the precipitated changes that became apparent around 1800, did so with some reluctance, hesitation, regrets, or warnings. They themselves saw this attitude as part of a search for moderation and "due process." Hence I place Goethe under the name of "Goethe Cunctator."

I also believe, to put the cards on the table from the beginning, that the very form of *Wilhelm Meisters Wanderjahre* (or the "formlessness" of which it was so often accused) expresses Goethe's struggle for a solution to the dilemmas of the new age and really makes it quite relevant to the turn of the 20th century (in the same way in which *Faust II* is quite relevant). In some ways it is the focus and the answer to the whole matter.

II

Let me briefly enumerate and describe these four modes. Justus Möser (1720-1794) influenced, as is well known[1] the young Goethe, whose views had been marked by lability. While Herder also exerted some influence, it seems to me that some specific features of the political philosophy of the wise old man of Osnabrück set a mark on Goethe that was to remain indelible all the way into his old age. Part of this was an early option for the "British political and historical mode of change" which Möser had understood much earlier than later (post-1789) converts. Let us remember that Osnabrück was in all respects close to the English political and intellectual life: in some ways it had the status and ways of thinking of the American possessions. In fact Möser several times times praised and offered as example the Pennsylvania Dutch community[2] (here Goethe's fascination with what we can call "the American solution" of his older age may have had its remote sources). In any case, despite his "patriotic" gesturing, Möser was closer to the English 18th-century intellectual environment than to the German (and "Frenchified," in the neo-classical version) one.

Additionally Goethe liked the "organicist" metaphor for history that Burke (a Whig to the end of his life) was soon to theorize and thus spread throughout Europe. Furthermore the emphasis of Möser was on *decentralization,* a kind of early form of the doctrine of "subsidiarity."[3] He struggled vigorously against centralizing levelling, expansion of taxes, division of the population into castes, rationalistic politics, and in favor of individual or, as he called it, "genuine," ownership. Möser defended the patchwork of legal rules and tiny privileges inherited from the Middle Ages, as being more reliable and authentic defenses

against tyranny than general laws and political dogmas. (Again, I see in *Wilhelm Meisters Wanderjahre* with its micro-societies and its archipelagoes of property a remote echo of these theories.)

Finally, perhaps as a detail, I will refer to the much-debated "technical description" of textile home-production, which so many critics have regarded as a total aesthetic breakdown.[4] Two things are to be said here. The first is that Goethe seems to be a forerunner: many novels in many languages during the 19th and 20th century resort to the same narrative technique. Second, Möser was a thorough connoisseur and apologist of this kind of textile production. There is no doubt in my mind that Goethe's careful description owes much to Möser's essays such as "Schreiben uber die Kultur der Industrie,"[5] in which Möser points out that one can recognize the origin and texture of cloth on the basis of the senses and of the production philosophy of families and/or communities.

III

Let us now turn to the *second* issue, that of the long service of Goethe under Duke Karl-August. Increasingly, we have come to recognize that Goethe took his administrative duties seriously and that he *did* contribute to political-managerial activities.[6] Without unduly expanding into biographical details let me just dwell on two points.

First I should record my disagreement with the overemphasis on Goethe's "servility" and traditionalism. He was indeed a convinced monarchist, and he also was clearly in favor of "law and order" whether in the tiny principality where he was active, or in the broader European society. By no stretch of the imagination can we say however that Goethe was a fanatic of any rigorous class division or of general stagnation. For every quotation in one direction one can easily adduce a quotation in a different direction.[7] Most specifically the conclusion of *Faust II,* along with *Wilhelm Meisters Wanderjahre* in its entirety, speak to a system of general prosperity, civil rights and freedoms, progress, and social mobility (horizontal certainly, but also vertically).[8] Second I am increasingly opposed to the Marxist-Leninist terminology of "feudalism," "capitalism," and so forth, which I find hollow and meaningless.[9] In fact, it is precisely the type of relationship between Goethe and Karl-August that proves my point: a relationship formally respectful and ceremonious, in reality egalitarian, even with an edge to Goethe.

The *third* contextual level (one that flows naturally out of the previous one) is the uneasy and delicate relationship between Goethe and Metternich's Europe (or even Prince Metternich personally). They met in person only twice (1818 and 1819, both times in Karlsbad), but Goethe maintained indirect contact with well-accredited representatives such as Gentz and others.[10] During the "Age of Restoration," Goethe was, and this should not be hidden, cautiously, but undoubtedly, a foe of the revolutionary movements, and he was glad to notice a re-establishment of order. From here we do not have to jump immediately to the conclusion that he approved in all details the measures and the structures of the re-organized society. We know very well that Goethe firmly kept a certain distance toward the powerful statesman, who would have gladly drawn him in his circle of adherents. We ought to underline that Goethe's influence and activity even inside Sachsen-Weimar-Eisenach diminished after 1815 and that he was much more of a private person than he had been earlier.[11]

There is another aspect here that, in my opinion, has not been discussed enough. In the period 1815-1848 (and even somewhat later) liberalism and nationalism went hand in hand in Germany, as well as in the rest of Europe. Nationalism (even racism) were the property of "the Left": the argument went that equality and fraternity grew out of *national* commonalities and could thus beneficially overthrow long-standing and legally entrenched class separations. Grim ethnic separations emerged quite easily later on, following this train of thought, but this happened chiefly in the *second* half of the 19th century.

It seems to me that to the extent to which Goethe rejected the radicalism of the "students" (as well as of other groups) this was due largely, if not exclusively, to his disgust toward their nationalism, which was categorically alien to Goethe's cosmopolitan humanism. Under these circumstances, Metternich's way of thought and action was simply the lesser evil. Any full identification between Goethe and the Metternich political structuring of Europe would be very extremely difficult to prove on a practical level. In fact it would be much easier to demonstrate substantial distinctions. Therefore, although I do not place myself in opposition to commentators[12] who argue that Goethe approved of Restorationist Europe, I maintain that he felt less than comfortable when he observed some of its ruling methods.

IV

These distinctions become even more obvious when we approach what I described as *level four* of Goethe's conservatism. At a certain point (actually in the very middle of the Metternichian age!) Goethe seems to have become aware of an alternative solution. This solution crystallized for him a kind of political "middle of the road": in other words, a way of finding (in and between the extremes that he instinctively disliked!) the outline of a framework compatible with his political philosophy.[13] This was at least the thinking (since Goethe was too old to experience the actual political practice) of François Guizot: at the very doors of Germany, and well integrated in the European world that Goethe had always tried to promote.[14]

A few words on Guizot are in order here. He clearly descended ideologically from Tocqueville[15] and (slightly less clearly) from Benjamin Constant, that is to say from figures of impeccable liberal credentials, indeed "Founders" of classical liberalism, one might say. In a more speculative mood we may well describe Guizot as intellectually akin with Goethe's good friend Wilhelm von Humboldt. His library contained books or pictures of Leibniz (one of the fundamental *spiritual* roots of liberalist Enlightenment and a close philosophical relative of Goethe's), Mme. de Staël, Chateaubriand and similar figures.[16] According to Guizot, these all had argued in favor of "une révolution sans devenir révolutionaires."[17]

Furthermore, Guizot can be defined as the equivalent of Sir Robert Peel in England. (As I suggested before, the actual political influence and power of both Guizot and Peel came to the fore immediately *after* Goethe's demise.) Still, this later point remains important. The emergence in political Europe of a "leftist" conservatism, or "rightist" liberalism, to use some very approximate terms, was for Goethe a reason of euphoria: he certainly approved of them and saw in them the vindication and the best formulation of his own combinative and ambiguous thinking.[18] Guizot described himself several times (particularly after 1830) as belonging to the "party of resistance"—i.e. resistance against the radicalization of change and progress. Does this turn him somehow into the equivalent of Metternich? After all, both statesmen lost power as a result of the 1848 revolutionary movements. Nevertheless the proposition is doubtful and, to my knowledge, has never been put forward as a credible argument. True, Metternich was much less of a "reactionary" than he was thought at his time (and than he is described and thought of nowadays). I think that nobody characterized him better than Henrich von Srbik, namely as a belated Enlightenment figure, who tried (after Romanticism and Revolution) to introduce or maintain its values.[19] Nevertheless, Metternich (and many of his equivalents in Russia, in the France of Louis XVIII, and particularly of Charles X), in the England of Canning, Wellington and Castlereagh and elsewhere did not (I am firmly convinced!) satisfy the desires of Goethe. Actually, despite his pretense of calm and indifference, Goethe was often in the claws of fear and of anger.

The enthusiastic reading of Guizot was a tremendous relief for him. Goethe found in Guizot's writings a political model that was theoretically much better structured than he had ever been able to articulate himself.[20]

It might be tempting to go into the complicated issue of how, when, and/or whether specifically **Wilhelm Meisters Wanderjahre** was influenced by the reading of Guizot or not; I fondly wish that somebody would do it, sooner, rather than later. The point is that there are significant parallels. Let me mention some of them. Guizot considered Peel (and this may well be seen as a self-description) as "un conservateur acquis aux changements et non [...] un libéral venu à la politique conservatrice."[21] or, to quote Guizot directly, "Un bourgeois chargé de soumettre à de dures reformes une puissante et fière aristocratie, un libéral sensé et modéré, mais vraiment libéral, trainant à sa suite les vieux tories et les ultras protestants."[22]

Like Scott, Guizot "est [...] le prophète de la montée en puissance politique de la bourgeoisie. Il a travaillé à lui donner une culture politique, à lui forger une mémoire, à la faire entrer dans l'âge politique." He is a kind of "Lénine de la bourgeoisie."[23] In a Biedermeier spirit Guizot proceeds to solve (and this is what intensely preoccupied Goethe, particularly in *Wilhelm Meisters Wanderjahre,* but elsewhere also) "Comment rester attaché aux resultats generaux de la révolution sans être aucunement révolutionnaire?"[24] The opposition between revolution and tradition can be solved only if we understand the former as a kind of hidden, unachieved tradition; only revolution "condenses" tradition into history seen as both act and narration.[25]

The issue for Scott, Goethe, and Guizot was that of "transfer of values"—preserving some essential spiritual principles and behaviors under categorically modified historical circumstances. This would allow progress of a constructive, not destructive nature, a kind of building on solid and historically well-tested foundations. At the same time it would mean a certain deceleration. Guizot's "Enrichissez-vous!"[26] would have allowed Goethe to maintain a class structure that he considered just, while modifying it at the same time.

One other important parallel should be mentioned here. While Goethe was struggling with the aporias of a comprehensive humanization, Europe after 1815 was witnessing a truly extraordinary religious revival, one of those *massive* changes that Catholicism (but not only Catholicism) seems to undergo once every couple of hundred of years. I say, not only Catholicism, because in the early 19th century we recognize such a change in various branches of Protestantism, to some extent in Eastern Orthodox Christianity, as well as in Judaism as developed inside Europe. A few short references will suffice as reminders. During much of the 18th century it seemed sometimes that the fate of Judaeo-Christian belief (or beliefs) was sealed. The intellectual and educated layers had turned toward atheism or, at best, toward vague convictions of a deist or pantheist tinge. More fundamentalist believers sought refuge in mystical and esoteric systems, enthusiastic piety devoid of a rationalist backbone: Methodism, Hassidism, Pietism, let alone the traditions of Swedenborg or Jakob Boehme.

If we are to choose *one* turning point (even though there had been several of the kind), that would have to be the work of Chateaubriand *Le Génie du christianisme* (1802) which, in a bold, even stunning, gesture decided that Christianity could find a rationally credible support in the beautiful, as it had relied on the true and the good in the past. Immediately thereafter, sometimes synchronically, we notice the work of Lamennais, the late Mme de

Staël and the enormous impact of Hannah More on both sides of the Atlantic. To this must be added the huge systems (polemical, but constructive also) of Rosmini and Balmes, the circle of German literary and philosophical stars around Archbishop Clemens Maria Hofbauer in Vienna, the Tractarians (Anglican, Anglo-Catholic, and Roman Catholic), Alois Gügler in Switzerland. Guizot, who was a Protestant by birth, devoted the last part of his long life to the cause of ecumenicism and to the unification of churches. My argument is that Goethe places himself in rhyme with most of these people, whether he knew them or not. This can be seen in *Wilhelm Meisters Wanderjahre,* and in the ending of *Faust II.* From the very beginning of Goethe's *Wilhelm Meisters Wanderjahre,* intriguing parallels (immediately noticed by readers and critics) abound. The most famous is at the very beginning, in Meister's first letter to Natalie in connection with the **"St. Joseph II"** episode. It has been less often noticed that the "St Joseph" location is similar to all those Californian centers that, religiously founded and named, became, in an ironic turnover, highly secular locations. Like them, it is a former place of prayer and meditation that has been turned in a center of labor and production. But is this not exactly what Emperor Joseph II (the symmetrical opposite of St. Joseph and at the same time his corresponding rhyme, as the craftsman/technologist) had been doing in his domains? Had he not liquidated monasteries and religious activities that did not correspond to the practical/utilitarian duties of his Empire? In a word, *Wilhelm Meisters Wanderjahre* begins as a work of secularization while maintaining heavy religious overtones. I regard this as Goethe's response to and integration in the religious revival-network that he oberved growing around him.

V

In the long run all these succesive levels of conservative context to Goethe's work and activity have to be connected to the ferment of responses to "modernization" alluded to earlier: urbanization and alienation, communication and rationalization, transactional modes of contact, historical acceleration and the prevalence of social and ethnic amalgamations. The self-consciousness of these changes, as emerging a few decades before and after 1800 led to an enormous number of interesting responses, many (perhaps *most*) of which continue to be relevant to us nowadays and to shape our thinking and action, directly or indirectly.[27] In the *Wanderjahre* [*Wilhelm Meisters Wanderjahre*] Goethe approaches the depth and the tortured effort to "absorb modernization" that we recognize more easily in *Faust.*[28]

Goethe, like many of his most brilliant contemporaries (political scientists, religious apologists, poets and philosophers) was wrestling mightily with this process of socioeconomic (better: existential!) "modernization" which had been pressing the West for several centuries, but was now becoming conscious for most people and was also expanding on a planetary scale.[29] His hero roams the world seeking (and finding!) islands of normality and organic intelligence that still survive in a chaotic world.

In *Faust II* (no less than in *Faust I*) we recognize a *gleaning* gesture, an effort to save and redeem, to bring back together all the values of the past. But is this, and I am now coming to the the conclusion of my argument, a *mere* "conservative" gesture and activity? My conviction is that it is *not*.

Why not? It seems to me that, in choosing out of all the features of this "modernization," Goethe was preoccupied (at a more or less conscious level) with the issue of *increased information*: the accumulation of knowledge, the informational on-rush that tended to break the dams of order, harmony, predictability. This explains the peculiar stylistics of *Wilhelm Meisters Wanderjahre.*

Many characters there are preoccupied by the issue of emigration, of a new beginning as a *replacement* for revolution and utopia, in a way analogous to Chateaubriand and Tocqueville. (Let us not forget that Chateaubriand embarked upon his famous expedition to the newly-independent United States at the very beginning of the French Revolution in order to evade his own ambiguous sentiments toward this historical event, and that Tocqueville went to the United States a generation later curious to find out what a democratic system in action, and likely to represent the future of his own homeland, might look like. Both were trying to explore alternatives to violent socio-historical overthrow.) Here we have on the one hand the beginnings of an understanding of exile as a key condition of modernity; however in Goethe's typical moderating fashion it should be an exile that is freely chosen and freely assumed.

In a more specifically literary fashion the book *has* to acquire an "archival" and discontinuous style. The discontinuities of the plot are a faithful mirror to the historical discontinuities that Goethe was discovering with more than a little vexation. Far from being a sign of senility, the disjointed structure of the book announces things to come: one might even say, only partly tongue-in-cheek, that the book is one of the earliest post-modernist exercises in European prose.[30] Documentary and digressionary techniques were in any case to become more and more frequent in the 19th and, again, particularly the 20th century. *Wilhelm Meisters Wanderjahre* constitutes a trait of continuity between the "romances" of the 16th and 17th centuries and the stylistics of the novel in the 20th century. Meister and his son travel (between deliberation and randomness) amongst islands of happiness, and quiet prosperity: discontinuities of contentedness and peace that crystallized into social constructs rising over and beyond, I dare say, the actual "pedagogical province." In its turn, the informational avalanche could be "accommodated" by the relative disorder or discordance of the plot stylistics. By choosing

the special organization of *Wilhelm Meisters Wanderjahre* Goethe argues, in my opinion, for the multiplicity and pluralism of a future society. His main strategy in *Wilhelm Meisters Wanderjahre* remains, as in *Faust,* one of gleaning, of selecting and bringing together genres, modes, ideas, themes. However, Goethe seems here much more convinced of the justification of disorder. The constitutional arrangements of the projected colony are part of a much more chaotic, but also exciting future.

The subtitle **"Die Entsagenden"** does not suggest to me primarily resignation, but rather *restraint.*[31] Goethe suggests not only a kind of slowing down as the "cunctator" that he was, but also kinds of voluntary limitation and renunciation for the sake of happiness. The conflict between freedom and happiness (as formulated a century after *Wilhelm Meisters Wanderjahre* by Aldous Huxley) was to become crucial for the ideologies and policies of the 19th and particularly of the 20th century. The renunciation or restraint in *Wilhelm Meisters Wanderjahre* is above all not an ethical, nor even a political one, it is an aesthetic one. This brings us back to the archival organization of *Wilhelm Meisters Wanderjahre.*

Notes

1. Goethe had read the *Patriotische Phantasien* (1775-1786) probably as soon as they came out and expressed enthusiasm about them. Cf. Claassen (1936:182 ff) or Kass (1909). Mommsen (1948:29-34) thinks this influence is to be recognized particularly in *Gotz von Berlichingen* but I see it as much more pervasive.

2. E.g. Möser (1944-1968: III, 20 or I, 31).

3. "Subsidiarity" is a term that was coined in Papal encyclicals (particularly in 1931) where it meant that every social activity ought to be fulfilled at the lowest possible level: something that the family can take care of must not be assigned to the school or the city, in turn whatever may be accomplished by the neighborhood community or the county must not be taken over by the state government and so on. The term was soon adopted by secular political theory and practice in Europe, particularly in the last two decades. However as Millon-Delsol shows, only the term as such was coined, the concept had existed in one form or another for many centuries, notably developed by the Calvinist administrator Johannes Althusius in his *Politica* (first published in 1603, later developed in the 1610 and 1614 editions).

4. Walter Benjamin, Thomas Mann, Spranger, Gundolf among others, earlier Burckhardt, Mundt, and Scherer. See in a more specifically scholarly vein Emil Staiger (1952-1959: III, 181-187). Equally puzzling for some was Goethe's "synthesis" of the

scientific and the literary. For a balanced treatment see Alfred G. Steer, 1979.

5. Möser (1944-1968: V, 110-114). Corresponding passage in Goethe's *Wilhelm Meisters Wanderjahre* (1829: III, 5).

6. Tümmler, 1976; Armin, 1987; Cape (1991: 10-16, 36-46, 127-144).

7. A nice general review in Gille, 1979. See also Flitner, 1947; Wergin, 1980; Lukacs, 1947; Witte et al (1996: III, 217-231) This stands in sharp contrast to most German Romantics; among many conclusive anthologies see Beiser, 1996.

8. Zenker, 1990. Thielicke, 1982.

9. Even somebody as knowledgeable and objective as Friedrich Sengle uses "Spätfeudalismus" in the subtitle of his excellent recent book (1993).

10. We can skip here the relationship between Goethe and Napoleon, although the motives were complex and even fascinating. Goethe's vanity was touched by Napoleon's attention, certain amounts of prudence and of anxiety in the face of a powerful dictator must also be assumed, additionally Goethe's well-known Francophilia undoubtedly played a certain role there.

11. Sengle (1993: 375-491).

12. Rothe (1998: 7-11, 49-61, 76-77, 92-107, 124-129, 134-189). Even earlier Mommsen (1948: 7-18, 28-34, 108-116, 166-280).

13. In fact one could almost argue that the whole of Goethe's later career is concentrated on this issue and returns to it in a stubborn and melancholy way. This was noticed early on. See Wundt, 1913 or (later) Bergstraesser, 1962; Schlechta (1982: 27-33, 47-53, 75-91, 228-235); Karnick, 1968; Schwamborn, 1997.

14. Guizot wrote his most important theoretical works in the 1820s, but exerted much more political influence in the 1830s and particularly the 1840s when he was almost without interruption a cabinet minister and the ideologue of King Louis-Philippe's regime.

15. Broglie (1990: 410, 413-413, 102).

16. Broglie (1990: 403-404, 62).

17. Broglie (1990: 116).

18. E.g. Goethe's conversations with Eckermann on February 17, April 2, 3, 6, 1829; cf. Broglie (1990: 102, 272).

19. Srbik, 1925.

20. I would argue, although this is probably not the place to do it, that Goethe's delighted reading of Walter Scott's early novels was due to equivalent sentiments. I say this because I know very well that Goethe's sophisticated aesthetic preferences would have made him reserved toward Scott. However here too the threads are tightly interwoven. French historians and critics (Mignet, Thierry, and in fact Guizot himself etc.) correctly read Scott as an author of "histoire démocratique," "le romancier des peuples," a political novelist etc. Cf. Rosanvallon (1985: 200).

21. Broglie (1990: 428), cf. also ibid., 343, 237.

22. Ibid., 426.

23. Rosanvallon (1985: 185, 171).

24. Rosanvallon (1985: 77).

25. Rosanvallon (1985: 287).

26. His most famous, but historically dubious sentence. See a detailed discussion in Broglie (1990: 333-335). See *Wanderjahre* (1829: I, 6). Cf. also Mommsen (1948: 264).

27. Let us also say that, although in speaking about the 19th-century novel in Europe, we think usually of Balzac and Flaubert, Tolstoy and Dostoyevsky, Austen, Dickens and George Eliot, German contributions on a realistic level (Fontane), or on a sentimental one (Raabe and Storm), or on a philosophical one (Goethe in particular) do contribute to the intellectual debates of the century and to its processes of self-definition.

28. For a more detailed discussion see Nemoianu (1994: 1-16). A somewhat materialistic but rather accurate reading in Jessing, 1991. Also Beller, 1995, an excellent and clear interpretation of the literary thematization of the process of "modernization." Mayer, 1989 openly declares at the very beginning of his book that his thesis is that the novel gives "eine bislang kaum gewürdigte Antwort ... auf die Frage nach der Existenzmöglichkeit von Kunst in einer von Ökonomie und Technik beherrschten Welt."

29. Following wiser and more competent thinkers, I have pointed this out in Nemoianu (1996: 43-73) and in 1995: 261-271. See also ed. Witte et al. (1996: III, 15, 203).

30. Scholarly arguments in Brown, 1975; Bennett, 1993.

31. For a meticulous discussion of the issue see Peschken (1968: 213-215). Also Bahr (1983: 161-175). Needless to add, I disagree entirely with Degering, 1982. For a brilliant alternative interpretation see Schlaffer, 1980.

Works Cited

Armin, Peter, *Goethe als Manager. Eine Führungslehre* (Hamburg: Steintor, 1987).

Bahr, Ehrhard, "Revolutionary Realism in Goethe's *Wanderjahre*" in W. J. Lillyman, *Goethe's Narrative Fiction* (Berlin and New York: 1983), 161-75.

Beiser, Frederick, ed. *Early German Romantic Political Writings* (Cambridge: Cambridge University Press, 1996).

Beller, Walter, *Goethes "Wilhelm Meister"-Romane: Bildung fur eine Moderne* (Hannover: Revonnah, 1995).

Bennett, Benjamin, *Beyond Theory: Eighteenth-Century German Literature and the Poetics of Irony* (Ithaca, NY: Cornell University Press, 1993).

Bergstrasser, Arnold, *Goethe's Image of Man and Society* (Freiburg: Herder, 1962).

Broglie, Gabriel de, *Guizot* (Paris: Perrin, 1990).

Brown, Jane K., *Goethe's Cyclical Narratives: "Die Unterhaltungen deutscher Ausgewanderten" und "Wilhelm Meisters Wanderjahre"* (Chapel Hill, NC: University of North Carolina Press, 1975).

Cape, Ruth, *Das französiche Ungewitter: Goethes Bildersprache zur französischen Revolution* (Heidelberg: C. Winter, 1991).

Claassen, Peter, *Justus Möser* (Frankfurt: 1936).

Degering, Thomas, *Das Elend der Entsagung: Wilhelm Meisters Wanderjahre* (Bonn: Bouvier, 1982).

Flitner, Wilhelm, *Goethe im Spätwerk: Glauben, Weltbild und Ethos* (Hamburg: Claassen und Goverts, 1947).

Gille, Klaus, ed. *Goethes Wilhelm Meister: zur Rezeptionsgeschichte der Lehr- und Wanderjahre* (Königstein: Athenäum, 1971).

Jessing, Benedikt, *Konstruktion und Eingedenken: zur Vermittlung von gesellschaftlicher Praxis und literarischer Form in Goethes "Wilhelm Meisters Wanderjahre."* (Wiesbaden: Deutscher Universitatsverlag, 1991).

Karnick, Manfred, *"Wilhelm Meisters Wanderjahre" oder die Kunst des Mittelbaren* (München: Wilhelm Fink, 1968).

Kass, Georg, *Möser und Goethe* (Berlin: B. Paul, 1909).

Lukacs, George, *Goethe und seine Zeit* (Bern: Francke, 1947).

Mayer, Mathias, *Selbstbewusste Illusion: Selbstreflexion und Legitimation der Dichtung im "Wilhelm Meister"* (Heidelberg: C. Winter, 1989).

Millon-Delsol, Chantal, *L'état subsidiaire. Ingerence et non-ingerence de l'état: le principe de subsidiarité aux fondements de l'histoire européene* (Paris: P.U.F., 1992).

Mommsen, Wolfgang, *Die politischen Anschauungen Goethes* (Stuttgart: DVA, 1948).

Nemoianu, Virgil, "Absorbing Modernization: the Dilemmas of Progress in the Novels of Scott and in *Faust II*" in *Interpreting Goethe's Faust Today,* ed. Jane K. Brown, Meredith Lee, and Thomas Saine (Columbia, SC: Camden House, 1994), pp. 1-16.

———, "Globalism, Multiculturalism, and Comparative Literature" in *Council of National Literatures World Report* (1996: 43-73).

———, "J. F. Cooper, East European, and African-American Intellectuals: Relativizing Cultural Relativism" in *Journal of Intellectual Studies* 11 (December 1995), 3-4: 261-271.

Peschken, Bernd, *Entsagung in "Wilhelm Meisters Wanderjahren"* (Bonn: Bouvier, 1968).

Rosanvallon, Pierre, *Le Moment Guizot* (Paris: Gallimard/ NRF, 1985).

Rothe, Wolfgang, *Der politische Goethe. Dichter und Staatsdiener im deutschen Spätabsolutismus* (Gottingen: Vandenhoeck und Ruprecht, 1998).

Schirmeyer, Ludwig, Kohlschmidt Werner et al., *Mösers samtliche Werke. Historischkritische Ausgabe,* 14 vols. (Berlin: Stalling, 1944-1968).

Schlaffer, Hannelore, *Das Ende der Kunst und die Wiederkehr des Mythos* (Stuttgart: Metzler, 1980).

Schlechta, Karl, *Goethes Wilhelm Meister* (1953; Frankfurt a.M.: Vittorio Klostermann, 1982).

Schwamborn, Claudia, *Individualität in Goethes "Wanderjahren"* (Paderborn: Schoningh, 1997).

Sengle, Friedrich, *Das Genie und sein Fürst. Die Geschichte der Lebensgemeinschaft Goethes mit dem Herzog Carl-August von Sachsen-Weimar-Eisenach. Ein Beitrag zum Spätfeudalismus und zu einem vernachlässigten Thema der Goetheforschung* (Stuttgart: Metzler, 1993).

Srbik, Heinrich von, *Metternich. Der Staatsman und Mensch,* 2 vols. (München: Bruckmann, 1925).

Staiger, Emil, *Goethe,* 3 vols. (Zurich: Atlantis, 1952-1959).

Steer, Alfred, *Goethe's Science in the Structure of the "Wanderjahre"* (Athens, GA: University of Georgia Press, 1979).

Thielicke, Helmut, *Goethe und das Christentum* (Munchen: Piper, 1982).

Tummler, Hans, *Goethe als Staatsmann* (Gottingen: Musterschmidt, 1976).

Wergin, Ulrich, *Einzelnes und Allgemeines. Die aesthetische Virulenz eines geschichtsphilosophischen Problems* (Heidelberg: C. Winter, 1980).

Witte, Bernd et al., *Goethe-Handbuch,* 4 vols. (Stuttgart: Metzler, 1996).

Wundt, Max, *Goethes Wilhelm Meister und die Entwicklung des modernen Lebensideals* (Berlin und Leipzig: Göschen, 1913).

Zenker, Markus, *Zu Goethes Erzählweise versteckter Bezüge in "Wilhelm Meisters Wanderjahre, oder, die Entsagenden"* (Würzburg: Konigshausen und Neumann, 1990).

Nicholas Saul (essay date 2002)

SOURCE: Saul, Nicholas. "Goethe and Colonisation: The *Wanderjahre* and Cooper." *Goethe and the English-Speaking World: Essays from the Cambridge Symposium for His 250th Anniversary.* Ed. Nicholas Boyle and John Guthrie. Rochester: Camden House, 2002. 85-98. Print.

[*In the following essay, Saul examines Goethe's response to the work of American author James Fenimore Cooper. While Goethe's best-known appraisal of America's cultural potential is in his brief 1827 poem "Amerika, du hast es besser," * Wilhelm Meister's Travels *also briefly takes up the issues of colonization, conquest, and utopianism addressed in Cooper's novels.*]

The *Wanderjahre* [*Wilhelm Meisters Wanderjahre*] is perhaps Goethe's most awkward text. It deals in pioneering fashion with still current problems: technology and industrialisation, fragmentation of personality, the new utopian orders of mass society and culture, and the role of art in this. Yet with its decentered authorial perspective, lack of narrative unity or closure, complex symbolism of contrastive mirrorings, and all the other numerous demands on the reader's initiative, the *Wanderjahre* frustrates conclusive readings.

Above all, there is the matter of America's deeply ambiguous role as utopian reference point of the novel's logical perspective. America was of course already that in the *Lehrjahre* [*Wilhelm Meisters Lehrjahre*], as the major focus of the colonising efforts of the Society of the Tower. Lothario had fought in the American Wars of Liberation on the American side. But later, in Europe and from the perspective of the "Turmgesellschaft," he decides: *"Hier oder nirgend ist Amerika!"* (*HA* [*Goethes Werke*] 7, 431),[1] so that America becomes more of a metaphor or an ideal than a real place, or at least as real in Europe as it was across the Atlantic. The utopian conditions that America alone, as a kind of *tabula rasa,* had seemed to fulfil for a fresh social, economic, and cultural start seem thereby to be disqualified. All the more confusing, then, when

another member of the Society, Jarno, decides for entirely pragmatic reasons of mutual security (*HA* 7, 564) to take his part of the "Turmgesellschaft" back to the States (563-64), while leaving Wilhelm and Lothario behind in utopian Europe and sending the Abbé off to the utopian Russia of Catherine the Great. If this is problematic, the *Wanderjahre* appears to take us little further in understanding the value of America for Goethe's utopian thought. Here, as was the spirit of the age, utopian organisations proliferate. The "Turmgesellschaft" is joined by the patriarchal Enlightenment demesne of the Oheim, the Pädagogische Provinz, Lenardo's Emigrants League, and Odoard's inner European colonisers. The Oheim is actually a third-generation American by birth, yet he follows the Goethean principle whereby the son contradicts the father, prefers the ancient culture of Europe and political accommodation with monarchy to the task of establishing the American nation like another Orpheus or Lycurgus (*HA* 8, 82), and returns to found his own European utopia. His nephew Lenardo, of course, tends in the opposite direction. Lenardo, as his address to the Emigrants League shows (384-92), is committed to the existential, indeed God-given (386) doctrine of continuous emigration and colonisation. Thus the Oheim has donated his old American estate: "ein bisher vernachlässigter Familienbesitz in jenen frischen Gegenden" (142; compare 439). To this place Lenardo will lead the mountain weavers and spinners made destitute by the march of technology and over-population (242). Links are established between the Society of the Tower, which still aims at American colonisation, and Lenardo's group. Lothario's American territory and that of Lenardo are to be linked by a canal for mutual benefit (142, 242). Moreover, links are forged between this alliance and the Pedagogic Province. Wilhelm sends Felix there for a year (167), and there too Lothario recruits suitable artisans (242-44). All this is done in the name of the practical, useful, selfless, universalising activity of the renouncers that the Abbé calls "Weltfrömmigkeit" (243). Thus, when the leading members of the Society of the Tower take ship (436), Lenardo's motto "Gedenke zu wandern!" (318) might seem to infuse the entire work, at least in its practical dimension, with the idea of America—except that of course the text contains counter-indicators undermining this reading.

The first is the unreliably reported and confessedly provisional blueprint (404-8) of Lenardo's new society, the depiction of which we know to have been influenced by Robert Owen's ideas, which in turn Goethe probably encountered through Duke Bernhard's report of his American journey in 1825.[2] I am only reporting the scholarly consensus when I say that this is a very mixed bag of ideas. It contains some likely sounding practical ideas for a pioneering society, such as a relatively informal system of jurisdiction and moderate taxation. On the other hand, there is the lack of a capital (which must hinder the new society's self-understanding and cultural development), also the positively industrialised way they use time, and the apparently anti-Semitic constitution. Secondly, there is

Odoard's inner European colonisation project (392-93, 408-13). This is obviously intended to relativise the American project, yet it too is unattractive. Odoard has total control over a distant province, he has a concept and is recruiting disciplined artisans from whom he requires only utmost skill and commitment. The political dimension seems to be covered by the refrain of the communal song: "Heil dir Führer! Heil dir Band!" (413), and with that the regressive, potentially dystopian quality of the project is revealed.

All this still leaves us with America as the perspective of the utopian strivings recorded in the archival novel. What America actually *means,* however, given all the ambivalence and all the transatlantic ditherings, remains unspecified. One way of responding to this challenge to the reader's initiative is to locate the implicit character of the American utopia safely in the dialectic of "Denken und Tun, Tun und Denken" (263) that Montan enunciates, and that characterises in a nutshell the structural principle of the novel, oscillating as it does between reflection and example in both framework and embedded texts of various types. Another way of responding is that of Gerhard Schulz in his most recent essay on the *Wanderjahre,* which is to declare the America theme of subordinate interest.[3] Nevertheless, leaving on one side the well-explored but frustratingly refractive area of Goethe's use of his wide knowledge of American social and economic affairs,[4] there is one further aspect of Goethe's encounter with America, in the years when he was recasting the *Wanderjahre,* that recent scholarship encourages us to explore,[5] that of American letters. I am referring to Fenimore Cooper and the *Wanderjahre,* a question that from Ernst Beutler to Erich Trunz and (most recently) Wynfried Kriegleder has become something of a topos, albeit unresolved. This I wish to explore, and to say something decided about it. American letters and Goethe might be examined under the rubric of "Weltliteratur" that, after all, an epigram from Makarie's Archive admonishes Germans to ignore at their peril (483, No. 151). In his collection of utterances on the notion of "Weltliteratur,"[6] Goethe, it must be noted, omits American literature. This is not, however, in itself a reliable guide. Persian and Chinese literatures are also passed over there, yet the *West-östlicher Divan* and the *Chinesisch-Deutsche Jahres- und Tageszeiten* provide compelling evidence of Goethe's practical intercultural engagement with these literatures. Indeed, it turns out that Goethe, despite his silence at the level of theory, was both formidably well informed about American affairs in general, and deeply interested in the progress of American letters. Here, for example, is something we all know:

> Amerika, du hast es besser
> Als unser Continent, das alte,
> Hast keine verfallene Schlösser
> Und keine Basalte.
> Dich stört nicht im Innern,
> Zu lebendiger Zeit

> Unnützes Erinnern
> Und vergeblicher Streit.
> Benutzt die Gegenwart mit Glück!
> Und wenn nun eure Kinder dichten,
> Bewahre sie ein gut Geschick
> Vor Ritter-, Räuber- und Gespenstergeschichten.

> (*HA* 1, 333)

These lines, written down on 21 June 1827,[7] are usually taken to apply one of Goethe's favourite natural-scientific analogies (the basalt) to the question of America's general social and cultural development. Scholars usually point to a pre-text of this poem in some notes by Goethe on Neptunism from 18 September 1819,[8] with which you are probably also familiar: "Nord Amerikaner glücklich keine Basalte zu haben. / Keine Ahnen und keinen klassischen Boden." Basalt, Goethe scholarship tells us, is a peculiar type of rock that in the scholarship of the day was once taken to be young but was increasingly discovered in older formations, and since then it became identified in Goethe's mind with fruitless controversy.[9] America is blessed with no basalt, and therefore, as a country unencumbered with useless reflection on its nonexistent past, can focus all its vitality on the present.

While that may be so, however, it should be pointed out that the last three lines extend the argument explicitly to cover America's future literary development. In fact, another source of Goethe's makes this plain. He had received a visit from one of his many learned American friends, the Harvard mineralogist J. C. Cogswell, at Weimar in May 1819, around the time of the speculation on basalt. On 11 May 1819 we find, however, the laconic journal entry "Zustand der Litteratur von Cogswell" (*WA* [*Goethes Werke*] 3, 7, 46), a work that Goethe later praises highly in a letter to Cogswell of 11 August 1819: "[. . .] die schönsten Aufschlüsse [. . .], so daß man ihn nicht genug lesen und wiederlesen kann. Man lernt bedeutende, sich auf eigne naturgemäße Art entwickelnde Zustände kennen" (*WA* 4, 31, 246). The Weimar editors kindly refer us to *Blackwood's Edinburgh Magazine* of March 1819, and there we find an essay by Cogswell (in fact, one of two) "On the State of Learning in the United States of America."[10] The essay is a masterly apologetic presentation and explanation of the state of American letters in general. Cogswell notes proudly that America is strong in "practical cleverness and businessmen" (Cogswell, 641), but also frankly admits that "learning, in its limited and appropriate sense, is not to be found in America" (641), and concedes the "low literary reputation of America" (642): "Franklin is their only philosopher whose discourses have been of much importance to mankind; and if the whole stock of their literature were set on fire tomorrow, no scholar would feel the loss" (646). Cogswell's point, though, is not so much to acknowledge "American barrenness in creative literature" (646), as to defend American creative intellect in principle against the extraordinary imputations widely made by naturalists and cultural anthropologists following Buffon in the latter half of the eighteenth century, and which are amusingly recorded in the opening chapters of James Ceasar's recent book *Reconstructing America*.[11] These held, in Cogswell's words, that "the human mind has suffered a deterioration by being transported across the Atlantic" (647), so that the admitted defects of American letters are due not to circumstantial factors but to the intrinsic "inferiority of the American intellect" (641). The present low state of letters in America, says Cogswell, is due rather to two extrinsic things: first, the "demand for active talent" (647) in practical activity is so great and so well rewarded, that it must for the present divert energies away from learning and writing. Furthermore, while Americans do indeed possess their fair share of native genius, it does not yet receive that stimulation from American life and nature that it needs, so that its development for the present is halted:

> There is nothing to awaken fancy in that land of dull realities; it contains no objects that carry back the mind to contemplation of early antiquity; no mouldering ruins to excite curiosity in the history of past ages; no memorials, commemorative of glorious deeds, to call forth patriotic enthusiasm and reverence; it has no tradition and legends and fables to afford materials for romance and poetry; no peasantry of original and various costume and character for the sketches of the pencil and the subjects of the song; it has gone through no period of infancy; no pastoral state in which poetry grows out of the simplicity of the language, and beautiful and picturesque descriptions of nature are produced by the constant contemplation of her. The whole course of life is a round of practical duties; for every day there is a task for every person; all are pressing forward in the hurry of business; no man stops to admire the heavens over his head, or the charms of creation around him; no time is allowed for the study of nature, and no taste for her beauties is ever acquired.
>
> (647)

America will, however, exhibit these (literary) "powers of a higher order" when in due course "a more improved and refined state of society shall bring them into action" (649). In this, she will equal England (649). Goethe's **"Amerika du hast es besser,"** we can now see, echoes not only his own earlier reflection on basalt, but also the early lines of this last extract from Cogswell, which he read around the same time: "[N]o objects that carry back the mind to contemplation of early antiquity; no mouldering ruins to excite curiosity in the history of past ages"—lines, let us note, which contain the promise of an eventual American contribution to "Weltliteratur" following "auf eigne naturgemäße Art." This parallel, then, underscores the emphatically literary function of the otherwise decidedly odd last three lines of Goethe's poem. In June 1827 Goethe evidently recalled his reading of Cogswell from 1819, just as he recalled the speculation on Neptunism from the same year in order to write **"Amerika, du hast es besser"** for the *Ausgabe letzter Hand* [*Werke: Vollstän-*

dige Ausgabe letzter Hand], and he uses it to give the American writers *in spe* a friendly warning to leave out the adventure novels and get on with the "Weltliteratur" as soon as possible. Moreover, it is clear from this extract that Goethe is not only well apprised of the degenerative paradigm widely applied to American nature and culture in the latter half of the eighteenth century, but also that he (on his own natural analogy) prefers the progressivist model of Cogswell.

That said, why should Goethe choose in 1827 to echo Cogswell's vindication of America's potential literary genius from 1819? It may be noted that the day after writing **"Amerika, du hast es besser,"** if the journal is to be believed, Goethe started his final revision of the second, definitive version of the ***Wanderjahre*** (*WA* 3, 11, 74), beginning as it does in basalt-rich European mountains. But perhaps a better reason is that in those intervening years there appeared the first major phenomenon of American letters, James Fenimore Cooper. Between 30 September 1826 and 29 January 1828,[12] Goethe read no less than six historical novels by Cooper. This represents all of Cooper's novels then in existence save the very first, the unrenowned novel of manners *Precaution* (1821). The most intensive phase of engagement stretches from 30 September to 4 November 1826,[13] when Goethe read, in this order: *The Pioneers, or the Sources of the Susquehanna* (1823), Cooper's third novel and the first Leatherstocking novel; *The Last of the Mohicans* (1826), Cooper's fourth novel and the most famous Leatherstocking novel; *The Spy* (1821), Cooper's second novel and first historical novel, which involves the Major John André case (Benedict Arnold's co-conspirator) and George Washington; and *The Pilot* (1824), a historical novel of the sea involving John Paul Jones. Finally, in June 1827, Goethe reads *The Prairie* (1827), the third Leatherstocking novel, which features Natty Bumppo's death; and in January 1828 *The Red Rover* (1827), another sea novel. These latter novels he seems to have read as soon as they were translated.

Such a pattern of reading suggests at least an unusual measure of enthusiasm and interest on Goethe's part for this first great manifestation of American literature. If we follow the laconic entries in his journal, Goethe is indeed impressed by Cooper's work. He reads and rereads the beginning of *The Pioneers*—a virtuoso presentation of an incident-packed forest sleigh-ride that skilfully introduces all the main characters, themes, and issues of the novel—and copies out the *dramatis personae*. "Auch das Kunstreiche daran näher betrachtet, geordnet und fortgesetzt" (*WA* 3, 10, 251; 1 October 1826), he writes. As he is finishing *The Prairie*, he notes: "bewunderte den reichen Stoff und dessen geistreiche Behandlung. Nicht leicht sind Werke mit so großem Bewußtseyn und solcher Consequenz durchgeführt als die Cooperschen Romane" (*WA* 3, 11, 76). This is little enough to go on and fairly general at that, but it is at least clear that Goethe has recognised not only Cooper's art of form, but also his content and meaning: the richness of material that Cooper treats ("reichen Stoff"), his intellectual stature ("mit so großem Bewußtseyn"), and the power of the arguments that run through his works ("Nicht leicht [...] mit solcher Consequenz durchgeführt"). Set against the background of Cogswell's remarks "On The State of Learning in the United States of America," which we know Goethe knew, they make still more interesting reading. If Cogswell had lamented the allegedly unpoetic quality of the American landscape, with its monotonous mountain ranges, featureless prairies, and oceanic forests, then we should recall that one of the triumphs of Cooper's writing achievement is precisely to have supplemented this alleged deficiency with inventions such as the great standing rock, centre of the action in *The Prairie,* the impressively allegorical Glens Falls in *The Last of the Mohicans,* or indeed the symbolically charged forest (or Glimmerglass Lake) in *The Pioneers* (to name but a few).

None of this covers the most striking feature of Cooper's novels, however, if we judge them against another of Cogswell's observations of 1819. Cogswell not only laments the absence of picturesque nature populated with interesting peasants; he also laments the absence of an American past or tradition, historical or legendary. America is paradoxically an adult nation without an infancy—grown up, but lacking the orientation and self-understanding that come from leaving childhood behind. Cooper's novels are of course that very paradoxical thing, historical novels of a nation seemingly without a history, but designed as such to supplement precisely these deficiencies. In a sense, they seek to satisfy in America the conditions Goethe himself set out in ***Litterarischer Sansculottismus*** for the establishment of a classic national German literature, and are presumably also those of a literature admissible to the canon of "Weltliteratur."

Let us look briefly, then, at some characteristic features of these novels by Cooper. I shall concentrate, because of the confines of this paper, on the landlocked ones, since three of them (*The Last of the Mohicans, The Pioneers,* and *The Prairie*) deal with Cooper's major creation, the semi-mythical figure of Natty Bumppo, at various stages of his career, and *The Spy* is of particular interest concerning the question of American identity. In all of these texts, Cooper supplements missing history in varying degrees with romance, and explores the problem of American identity by setting the romantic action in the transitional zones between two or more orders. In *The Last of the Mohicans,* which features the Leatherstocking as the youthful forty-year-old Hawk-eye in the service of the British in 1757, we are in the primeval forests between the British and French domains, but also between the Mohicans (Chingachgook and the last Mohican Uncas) and the Hurons (Magua). In *The Pioneers,* we are in a literary figuration of the town of Cooper's birth, Templeton, in 1793, where a rough-hewn new town is being established in the area at the sources of the Susquehanna,

where forest and settled land merge in a battle of colonisation and the winner is certain. Natty, still bonded with Chingachgook (who is himself now technically the last of the Mohicans), leads a frugal life on the fringe of the struggle between law and nature. This struggle ultimately focuses on his right to hunt on the land its owner and lawgiver, Judge Temple, claims. Traditionally, the land was that of the Indians. While Chingachgook dies as the white man finally usurps his ancient rights at the end of this novel, *The Prairie* takes us to the end of Bumppo's life, now known simply as the Trapper, in 1804. Here he has given up his right and will to hunt, accepted the onward march of civilisation, or colonisation, and moved further west to the prairies to lead a solitary existence among the warring Sioux and Pawnee. He discovers, however, that Ishmael Bush's ruthlessly exploitative settlers are claiming the prairie too, and bidding fair to reach the west coast beyond the Rockies. Even the wilderness will be subjected to the immigrants, he realises; an age has passed, and he, also the last of a particular race, dies. *The Spy* is set in 1780 and the War of Independence, in West-Chester, Neutral Ground between the American and British lines, where the conventional rules of war are suspended. It exploits even more than the others the ambiguity of crossed borders. The Whartons live deep in the Neutral Ground. Mr Wharton is an American whose loyalty, however, is to Britain. Daughter Sarah loves the American Major Dunwoodie and supports the Americans. Son Henry is a British Captain. The house is frequented by both parties—provided that they are uniformed. Nearby dwells Harvey Birch, universally despised as a British spy, but in fact an American double agent. His true loyalty must remain secret till his death, when a note from George Washington reveals the truth. While Birch is the spy of the title and symbol of inextinguishable American identity in adversity and even when it is positively mis-recognised, the plot revolves around Captain Wharton, who, though not a spy, ill-advisedly visits his family in disguise, and is taken. Only the united powers of the heroic Americans Birch, Dunwoodie, and Washington can eventually save the Briton from his own folly.

In terms of substantive argument, *The Spy* shows an authentically American identity emerging painfully from the crisscrossing of family and national loyalties, which have genealogies stretching back across the Atlantic. More significantly in this process of finding identity through history, the Leatherstocking novels also invent a history for the nation, but this time in another place—on American soil—and, paradoxically, in the shape of another race—the native American Indians.[14] In each of the three novels sketched here, Cooper sings a sentimental song of the necessary downfall of the Red Indian before the onward march of white colonisation. He is sentimentally unsparing in his criticism of the behaviour of the white colonists, in figures such as Judge Temple of Templeton in *The Pioneers,* whose law, strictly speaking, is based on a crime, the initial taking of the land from those who dwelt there untold thousands of years; or Ishmael Bush, whose colonisation in *The Prairie* consists in shameless preda-tory despoiling of Indians and whites alike. Cooper is also a sentimental ecologist. *The Pioneers* contains gruesome prophetic images of the white man's slaughter of the passenger pigeon. Billy Kirby, the manic forest feller of *The Pioneers,* is attacked for his ignorance of the conse-quences of his deeds. It is no coincidence that he is deputed to arrest Natty for the killing of the buck belonging to Judge Temple in the opening scene Goethe so admired, so that poor Natty, who kills only to survive, must defend himself before the white man's law. The Mohicans, Chingachgook and Uncas, or the Pawnee Hard-Heart in *The Prairie,* are veritable paradigms of the noble savage; they live in har-mony with nature, they rescue Cora and Alice Munro or Inez and Ellen, and the white race must bear forever the guilt of their destruction. On the other hand, as Stafford argues (Stafford, 243, 256-7, 259), there is no sense that Cooper, in his invented history of the American colonists, ever has more than passing regret for the dispossession and decimation of the Red nations. The "good" Indians are more than counterbalanced by the "bad," Magua and Mah-toree. The Indians, though picturesque and admirable in their own way and formidable in the forest arts, are never shown as being able even to resist white invasion, still less assimilate. As Chingachgook passes from being Chingach-gook to Mohegan to Indian John and finally willed self-destruction in Templeton, he is impressively pathetic, yet there is no sense that a cultural integration is possible for him. An amalgam of Indian and white culture seems to be the privilege of the white man Natty, who speaks all the languages, mediates fully between the religions and the cultures, and—apart from his privileged status—represents as fine an example of cultural hybridity as Homi Bhabha could wish for.[15] Yet it is precisely this hybrid status that makes Natty an outsider. These novels then, are sentimen-talist monuments to the passing of the native Americans, but their deeper purpose is to legitimise the colonists' history and identity as pioneers, with all their faults and virtues. The novels achieve this, but in terms of the theories of race of the day, by presenting the Indians as inferior, and also at the price of destroying the myth of America as a new country.

There are diverse thematic links between Cooper's and Goethe's works. We know, for example, that Goethe, in his meditation on culture and nature, *Novelle* (1795-1827), exploited both the puma episode from *The Pioneers* and the (Ossian-influenced) Indian mourning ritual from *The Last of the Mohicans.*[16] I can add that there is a noteworthy parallel between Goethe's well-known criticism of analytic medicine (with its rejection of dis-secting techniques) in the *Wanderjahre* and Cooper's gruesome corpse-chasing dissector Dr Sitgreaves in *The Spy.* But where might traces of Cooper's central problem, the fascinating construction of American identity and his-tory, with its sentimentally tragic legitimisation of white colonisation, be found in Goethe's late work? Can they be found, for example, in the images of America in the

Wanderjahre? Goethe is not blind to the moral problems and racial conflict of American colonisation. The Amer-ican Oheim supports his decision to return to Europe by arguing (with obvious rhetorical emphasis) that accom-modation with feudal monarchs is preferable to a situation in which "ich mich mit den Irokesen herumschlage, um sie zu vertreiben, oder sie durch Kontrakte betriege, um sie zu verdrängen aus ihren Sümpfen, wo man von Moskitos zu Tode gepeinigt wird" (*HA* 8, 82). It is noteworthy, how-ever, that this, the site of Lenardo's colony, and that of Lothario's neighbouring colony, are later presented as already settled (by tenants, 439). Both are situated "mitten in der vollkommensten bürgerlichen Einrichtung" (439) and next to a desert ("die noch unangebaute Wüste," 439; "unbebautes und unbewohntes Land," 242), through which the canal will be built and next to which the weavers and spinners will be established (242). Under these con-ditions the Cooperian issues of legitimisation, dispossess-sion and genocide do not for the Emigrants League and the Society of the Tower seem to arise—or at least not im-mediately. Goethe does not entirely evade the buried, yet fundamental issues of colonisation. In his speech to the Emigrants League (which predates the reading of Cooper), Lenardo notes: "Haben wir doch den Nordosten gesehen sich gegen Südwesten bewegen, ein Volk das andere vor sich hertreiben, Herrschaft und Grundbesitz durchaus ve-rändert. Von überbevölkerten Gegenden her wird sich ebendasselbe in dem großen Weltlauf noch mehrmals ereignen. Was wir von Fremden zu erwarten haben, wäre schwer zu sagen" (385). He later enjoins the Emi-grants "jeden Gottesdienst" und "alle Regierungsformen in Ehren zu halten" (391). Even so: in Lenardo's later provisional design of the colony (404-8), the focus of regulation is entirely internal and colony-centred—unless we count Lothario's offensive-defensive military manoeu-vres, or the ban on alcohol consumption (406). There is no place for a Natty Bumppo, and still less an Indian John, in the New Harmony of Lenardo and Lothario. Thus Lenar-do's design for the new colony does not—not yet, at least—have the intercultural generosity that Goethe expresses under the heading "Τυχη, das Züfallige" in the commen-tary on "Urworte. Orphisch": "[...] europäische Nationen, in andere Weltteile versetzt, legen ihren Charakter nicht ab, und nach mehreren hundert Jahren wird in Nordamerika der Engländer, der Franzose, der Deutsche gar wohl zu erkennen sein; zugleich aber auch werden sich bei Durchk-reuzungen die Wirkungen der Tyche bemerklich machen, wie der Mestize an einer klärern Hautfarbe zu erkennen ist" (*HA* 1, 404). The painful issues of cultural hybridity, legit-imisation, dispossession, and genocide so prominent in these, the first American novels of stature, which Goethe so eagerly read in 1826-27 as he recast the *Wanderjahre,* are in fact marginalised in that book: perhaps because of the colonisers' Goethean need to focus on the present; perhaps to underline just how Eurocentric Lenardo's vision still is, and how much European history he carries with him; perhaps to underscore just how literally Utopian their allegedly American utopia really is. Or has this dimension been positively written out?

This isn't quite the end of the story, however. I mentioned earlier how little evidence there seemed to be for Goethe's practical-intercultural engagement with Cooper (if we admit him to the canon of "Weltliteratur") on the lines of his engagement with Hafiz in the *Divan* [*West-östlicher Divan*]. But there is something, produced in one of Goethe's whimsical moments. In *Über Kunst und Altertum* in the spring of 1827, the high point of his engagement with Cooper, Goethe published a piece of advice for promising German poets under the title "Stoff und Gehalt, zur Bearbeitung vorgeschlagen."[17] Many talented writers today, he laments, waste their gift by treating fashionable, yet unworthy subjects. He offers three subjects from books recently published that merit profounder treatment than they received in their current form, and one of them is the Protestant pastor Ludwig Gall's *Auswanderung nach den Vereinigten Staaten* of 1822, a self-pitying 800-page "lament" about a failed emigration project.[18] The precondition of this re-writing exercise, says Goethe, is "das vorzüglichste Talent" (296) coupled with the ability to acquire extensive and deep knowledge of the material:

> Der Bearbeitende müßte den Stolz haben, mit Cooper zu wetteifern, und deßhalb die klarste Einsicht in jene überseeische Gegenstände zu gewinnen suchen. Von der frühesten Colonisation an, von der Zeit des Kampfes an, den die Europäer erst mit den Urbewohnern, dann unter sich selbst führten, von dem Vollbesitz an des großen Reichs, das die Engländer sich gewonnen, bis zum Abfall der nachher vereinigten Staaten, bis zu dem Freiheitskriege, dessen Resultat und Folgen: diese Zustände sämmtlich müßten ihm überhaupt gegenwärtig und im Besonderen klar sein. In welche Epoche jedoch er seine Behandlung setzen wolle, wäre mancher Überlegung werth.

(296)

Goethe leaves the choice of epoch (mirroring as it does those selected by Cooper for his novels) up to the writer, but he does suggest plot and mode for the new work. The main figure, the emigrant pastor, is to be a cross between Moses, leading his people into the desert, and Dr. Primrose (the Vicar of Wakefield), with his disproportionate combination of culture and naivety. Thus the plot will move through comic disaster to a tolerable solution back in Europe, and this will necessarily involve the depiction of a vast panoply of (usually dissatisfied) characters from both sides of the Atlantic. All Goethe does is promise to pass judgement according to his best ability on the results, but it seems clear to me that this is a concept for a great unwritten intercultural German-American comic novel. If I may borrow Suzanne Zantop's felicitous neologism, it would have been a kind of prose Occidentalist[19] equivalent to the Orientalist *Divan,* and might have provided a useful counterweight to the history of

nineteenth-century German literary misapprehensions of North America from Sealsfield to May, reconstructed by Jeffrey Sammons.[20] We can only wish that Goethe himself had had time to write it.

Abbreviations

HA   *Goethes Werke* (Hamburger Ausgabe). Edited by Erich Trunz. 14 vols. Munich: Beck, 1948-60.

WA   *Goethes Werke* (Weimarer Ausgabe). 133 vols. Weimar: Böhlau, 1887-1919.

Notes

1. On utopias in *Wilhelm Meisters Lehrjahre* and *Wilhelm Meisters Wanderjahre* see especially Wilhelm Voßkamp, "Utopie und Utopiekritik in Goethes Romanen in *Wilhelm Meisters Lehrjahre* und *Wilhelm Meisters Wanderjahre*," in *Utopieforschung. Interdisziplinäre Studien zur neuzeitlichen Utopie.* ed. W. V. 3 vols. (Stuttgart: Metzler, 1982), vol. 3, 228-49.

2. This included a description of Owen's American colony New Harmony, which sought after New Lanark to realise the vision of Owen's *New View of Society*; see too: *Reise des Herzogs Bernhard zu Sachsen-Weimar durch Nord-Amerika,* ed. H. Luden, 2 vols. (Weimar, 1828); on Goethe and America see Ernst Beutler, "Von der Ilm zum Susquehanna. Goethe und Amerika in ihren Wechselbeziehungen," in E. B., *Essays um Goethe*. Fifth edition. (Bremen: Schünemann, 1957), 580-629; Wynfried Kriegleder: "Wilhelm Meisters Amerika. Das Bild der Vereinigten Staaten in den *Wanderjahren*," *Jahrbuch des Wiener Goethe-Vereins* 95 (1991): 15-32; Waltraud Maierhofer, "Perspektivenwechsel: Zu *Wilhelm Meisters Wanderjahre* und dem amerikanischen Reisetagebuch Bernhards von Sachsen-Weimar-Eisenach," *Zeitschrift für Germanistik,* N.S. 3 (1995): 508-22; for an up-to-date overview: Ehrhard Bahr, *The Novel as Archive. The Genesis, Reception, and Criticism of Goethe's "Wilhelm Meisters Wanderjahre"* (Columbia, SC: Camden House, 1998).

3. "Zwar ist der Plan der Auswanderung nach Amerika ein Handlungsfaden im Hintergrund des Buches, und es ist gerade für das Deutschland des frühen 19. Jahrhunderts ein geschichtlich sinnreicher epischer Vorwurf, aber er bleibt letztlich unausgeführt [...] Das eigentlich poetische Leben des Buches liegt in einer Reihe von Erzählungen, die dann ihrerseits in den Zusammenhang des Buches überlaufen." Gerhard Schulz, *Exotik der Gefühle* (Munich: Beck, 1998), 133.

4. Leaving aside mineralogical works, he studied amongst numerous other similar works: D. B. Warden, *Statistical, Political and Historical Account of the United States of North America* (Edinburgh, 1819)

(*WA* 3, 7, 46-7); and David Ramsay: *Geschichte der Amerikanischen Revolution aus den Acten des Congresses* (Berlin, 1795) (*WA* 3, 10, 261-62); William H. Keating: *Narrative of an Expedition to the Source of St. Peter's River, Lake Winnipeek [...]* 2 vols. (Philadelphia, 1824) (*WA* 2, 10, 165); Henry Bradshaw Fearon: *Scizzen von America, entworfen auf einer Reise durch die Vereinigten Staaten in den Jahren 1817 und 1818* (Jena, 1819) (*WA* 3, 8, 198).

5. See Kriegleder, "Wilhelm Meisters Amerika," 29, Note 70; also: James Boyd, *Goethe's Knowledge of English Literature* (Oxford, 1932), 266-68; Erich Trunz, commentary on *Wilhelm Meisters Wanderjahre, HA* 8, 675 (Nachtrag).

6. On "Weltliteratur": Fritz Strich, *Goethe und die Weltliteratur* (Bern: Francke, 1946); most recently: Henrik Birus: "Am Schnittpunkt von Komparatistik und Germanistik. Die Idee der Weltliteratur heute," in H. B. ed., *Germanistik und Komparatistik. DFG-Symposion 1993* (Stuttgart, Weimar: Metzler, 1995), 439-57.

7. *WA* 4, 42, 378 (draft letter to Zelter).

8. *WA* 2, 13, 314.

9. Trunz, *HA* 1, 653; compare *WA* 2, 9, 183-95; 10, 273.

10. *Blackwood's Edinburgh Magazine,* no. 24 (March 1819): 641-49; compare: "On the Means of Education, and the State of Learning, in the United States of America," *Blackwood's Edinburgh Magazine,* no. 23 (February 1819): 546-53.

11. James W. Ceasar, *Reconstructing America. The Symbol of America in Modern Thought* (New Haven, London: Yale UP, 1998).

12. See Boyd, 266-9.

13. September-October 1826 was clearly a period of renewed intense study of America. Around this time we find Goethe reading not only the four Cooper novels, but also Warden, *Statistical, Political and Historical Account* (vol. 3, 10, 249, passim), Ramsay: *Geschichte der Amerikanischen Revolution* (*WA* 3, 10, 261-62); he also re-read and pondered the publication plans of Duke Bernhard's American travel journal (*WA* 3, 10, 253-54, 6 October 1826; 259, 19 October 1826, passim).

14. See Fiona J. Stafford, *The Last of the Race. The Growth of a Myth from Milton to Darwin* (Oxford: OUP, 1994), esp. 232-60.

15. Homi Bhabha derives his concept of hybridity in part from Goethe's concept of "Weltliteratur." See H. B.,

The Location of Culture (London, New York: Routledge, 1994), 11-12.

16. See Jane K. Brown, "The Tyranny of the Ideal: The Dialectics of Art in Goethe's *Novelle." Studies in Romanticism* 19 (1980): 217-31, esp. 227-28, note 21, 229-30. Also commentary in Goethe, *Werther. Die Wahlverwandtschaften,* ed., Waltraud Wiethölter and Christoph Brecht (*FA* I/8: 1054-55, 1080-81).

17. *WA* 1, 41.2, 293-97, dated Weimar, 28 February 1827 (*WA* 1, 42.1, 264).

18. *Meine Auswanderung nach den Vereinigten-Staaten in Nord-Amerika im Fruehjahr 1819 und meine Rueckkehr nach der Heimath im Winter 1820* (Trier: Gall, 1822).

19. On the phenomenon of German Occidentalism see Susanne Zantop, *Colonial Fantasies. Conquest, Family and Nation in Precolonial Germany, 1770-1870* (Durham, London: Duke UP, 1997).

20. Jeffrey Sammons, *Ideology, Mimesis, Fantasy: Charles Sealsfield, Friedrich Gerstäcker, Karl May, and Other German Novelists of America* (Chapel Hill, London: U of North Carolina P, 1998).

Karin Schutjer (essay date 2004)

SOURCE: Schutjer, Karin. "Beyond the Wandering Jew: Anti-Semitism and Narrative Supersession in Goethe's *Wilhelm Meisters Wanderjahre." German Quarterly* 77.4 (2004): 389-407. Print.

[*In the following essay, Schutjer situates the arguably anti-Semitic content of Goethe's novel in the context of an "ideal of wandering." Lenardo and his utopian emigrants construe the Jewish people as emblematic of an eternal, subversive tendency to wander; they seek to replace this variety of wandering with their "cosmopolitan, open-ended" and, at least potentially, Christian interpretation of the same activity.*]

One of the persistent interpretive challenges for readers of Goethe's late novel ***Wilhelm Meisters Wanderjahre***[1] is to make sense of its several anti-Semitic passages. These passages range in their vehemence from studied indifference to a stance of complete separatism toward the Jews. One of the strongest pronouncements, for example, comes up in a plan developed by the league of emigrants heading to America: the new society is to remain culturally bound to the figure of Christ, and therefore "wir dulden keine Juden unter uns" (FA [***Sämtliche Werke***] I.10: 687).

What is a reader of an author as complex as Goethe to do with such passages? Past criticism provides no clear answers. While Goethe's ambivalent relationship to Judaism has received substantial scholarly attention recently, studies tend to draw on a range of historical and biographical materials rather than on his works of a strictly literary nature.[2] This critical reserve toward Goethe's literary representations of Judaism stems perhaps from a recognition of the profound, often systemic irony of much of his writing. And indeed, nowhere is the irony more pervasive and the interpretive dilemma more acute than in the *Wanderjahre* [*Wilhelm Meisters Wanderjahre*]. Interpreters of this novel have long been wary of any readings that seek to cut across the contradictory contexts, disparate perspectives, and playful insertions—what Swales calls the novel's "postmodern universe of pantextuality"[3]—in order to arrive at a unified interpretation.

Among readers who emphasize the novel's fundamentally disparate character, Benjamin Bennett is perhaps unique in his effort to integrate these anti-Semitic passages into a view of the novel's overarching ironic strategies. Bennett understands the novel as radically subversive, in fact as *"nothing but subversive* with respect to anything that might be claimed as its content" (emphasis in original).[4] The logical outcome of this all-pervasive irony is our ultimate identification as readers with the excluded category—the Jews. Bennett reasons that: "... only the Jews—precisely in being unequivocally (and arbitrarily) rejected—can operate as a sign for the actual reading community."[5] Yet for many readers, Bennett's argument may not counter the blunt force of some of these passages. Indeed, critics such as Bahr and Dowden, who also emphasize the novel's thoroughgoing irony, still express their strong consternation towards these apparently anti-Semitic instances.[6]

I propose a reading of the novel that takes account of its representational sophistication but does not dissolve the anti-Semitic moments into a sea of irony. While I appreciate and will not seek to refute the evidence for a radically perspectivist approach to this work, I nevertheless read across the novel, culling my material from diverse contexts in order to describe an overarching pattern. I begin by assuming that wandering, as a complex, variegated, existential condition, functions as a meta-ideal in the novel. That is, even the novel's irony, its semiotic indeterminacy, its narrative perspectivism, anti-essentialism, and cosmopolitanism fall under the trope of the wanderer. I argue further that a major impetus behind the novel's anti-Semitism is a competition between the Goethean ideal of existential wandering and wandering as a philosophical posture associated with Jews.

This potential for competition with the Jews over the status of wanderer is made quite explicit in Lenardo's speech to the League of Emigrants. The League's ideal of wandering must be set apart from the eternal activity of the Jews, which is aimed to trick and surpass others:

> Was soll ich aber nun von dem Volke sagen, das den Segen des ewigen Wanderns vor allen andern sich zueignet und durch seine bewegliche Tätigkeit die Ruhenden zu überlisten und die Mitwandernden zu überschreiten versteht?

Wir dürfen weder Gutes noch Böses von ihnen sprechen; nichts Gutes, weil sich unser Bund vor ihnen hütet, nichts Böses, weil der Wanderer jeden Begegnenden freundlich zu behandeln, wechselseitigen Vorteils eingedenk, verpflichtet ist.

(FA I.10: 668)

Lenardo's attempt to distance his group from "[das] ewige[ ] Wandern[ ]" plays into a broader narrative subtext in the novel: Wilhelm is a Wandering Jew who becomes redeemed by his decision to become a surgeon [Wundarzt]. At the beginning of the novel, Wilhelm must travel under conditions imposed upon him by the Society of Renunciants: he must not stay in one place for more than three nights and, when leaving a place, he has to cover at least a mile's distance. In a letter to the Abbé, he asks to be relieved of the restriction, "die ihn zum ewigen Juden stempelte" (FA I.10: 408). Once freed from this relentless mobility, he is able to undertake training as a surgeon which allows him to achieve a more profound relationship to suffering, temporality, and other human beings. This new outlook on life, I will argue, is associated in the novel with Christianity.

My thesis is, therefore, that this competition over an ideal of wandering plays itself out through an implicit narrative of supersession in the novel. Judaism or, more precisely, Jewish wandering is to be overcome in the name of a new culture of wandering that is relativistic, ironic, cosmopolitan, open-ended—but can nevertheless be associated with Christianity.[7] This association may seem controversial given Goethe's deep ambivalence toward conventional Christianity. In at least one case, Goethe's rejection of Christian dogmatism caused him to identify himself with a Jewish victim of Christian zeal, Moses Mendelssohn. In *Dichtung und Wahrheit* [*Aus meinen Leben: Dichtung und Wahrheit*], Goethe portrays himself as like Mendelssohn an unhappy target of the aggressive evangelism of J. K. Lavater. Indeed, if Lavater pressed the issue, Goethe thought he might just choose atheism over Christianity (FA I.14: 661). Yet, around the same period in his early career, he decided he could not be robbed of a certain affection for aspects of Christianity and "so bildete ich mir ein Christentum zu meinem Privatgebrauch" (FA I.14: 692). Half a century later, *Wilhelm Meisters Wanderjahre* continues this religious reinvention. Here, Goethe presents an idiosyncratic version of Christianity that is cultural and existential rather than theological and metaphysical in its orientation. On its deepest level, what the novel attempts to supersede—and simultaneously appropriate—is a signifying tradition, an ethical orientation, and an historical outlook that Judaism can claim for itself.

* * *

As he reports in *Dichtung und Wahrheit*, Goethe became acquainted early on with the traditional legend of the

Wandering Jew as told in the old chapbooks (FA I.14: 692). This Christian myth of Ahasverus, while it had many earlier sources and precedents, was first circulated in 1602 in the anonymous "Kurtze Beschreibung und Erzehlung von einem Juden mit Namen Ahasverus." According to the story, Ahasverus was a shoemaker in Jerusalem who cursed Christ when Christ leaned up against his house while carrying the cross on his way to his crucifixion. Ahasverus was then condemned to leave his wife and child and wander through the ages seeking redemption and testifying to Christ's suffering.[8] According to later versions of the myth, Ahasverus is not able to stay in one place more than three days.[9] In 1774, Goethe began his own epic **"Der ewige Jude,"** which remained unfinished but is sketched out in his autobiography. Several elements of this early interpretation of the myth, as he relates it in ***Dichtung und Wahrheit,*** find resonance in his late novel. First, within Goethe's account, Christ rather than Ahasverus functions as the original model of the wanderer. Ahasverus is repeatedly represented as a stationary figure in front of his workshop, while Christ is "de[r] Vorbeigehende []" (FA I.14: 692). Indeed Ahasverus tries to discourage Christ's transient way of life: "Er lag daher Christo sehr inständig an ... nicht mit solchen Müßiggängern im Lande herumzuziehen, nicht das Volk von der Arbeit hinweg an sich in die Einöde zu locken ..." (FA I.14: 692-93). Within this story, then, Goethe reverses the traditional typological relationship between Judaism and Christianity that serves as a staple of Christian biblical hermeneutics. According to the typological model, one might expect an example of Jewish wandering—say Moses in the wilderness—to prefigure the itinerary of Christ. Here, however, Christ is the original model, which the sinful Ahasverus is forced to imitate in a confused and unproductive way.

Aspects of Ahasverus's character in the early work are also significant for the later work. Ahasverus's resistance to Christ's message and lifestyle is evidence of a literalist, utilitarian, hardheaded mentality. While he develops a relationship and an affection for Christ, with whom he frequently converses, he is incapable of grasping the higher meaning of Christ's words and deeds because of his prosaic mindset: "[Sein] Sinn [war] bloß auf die Welt gerichtet" (FA I.14: 692). Finally, central to Ahasverus's crime in Goethe's version of the story is his complete lack of compassion. Ahasverus not only feels no sympathy for the suffering Christ on the road to execution, but also shows no understanding for Judas's anguish after betraying Christ and so drives Judas to suicide. Thus, in his sketch of the early work, Goethe draws fundamental distinctions between a higher Christian wandering and a derivative, disoriented Jewish wandering resulting from hard-headedness and a failure to sympathize.

These religious typologies are in play from the very beginning in ***Wilhelm Meisters Wanderjahre.*** The term "wanderer" first appears in the novel in reference to the "holy family"—a father and mother with newborn, who con-

sciously style themselves after images of Joseph, Mary and baby Jesus on the flight to Egypt (FA I.10: 265). These holy Christian wanderers become models of imitation for Wilhelm. Just as "St. Joseph II," as the young father is called, explicitly takes on the role of Christ's adoptive father, Wilhelm takes on the role of "St. Joseph II," by supplying words for him in a letter to Natalie (FA I.10: 265). Later, in the Pedagogical Province, the boarding school to which Wilhelm entrusts his son, Christ's conduct or life journey [Wandel] is held up as an explicit model for human behavior (FA I.10: 429). Yet, Christ's wandering is of a particular sort: "[Christus] steht auf seinem Punkte fest; er wandelt seine Straße unverrückt." This conjunction of two opposing moments—of staying put and moving—is key to both the semiotics and the existential ideal of the novel. It is the core of a meaningful, oriented sort of wandering.

Meanwhile, the novel also holds out the danger of a deficient, radically disoriented, even destructive sort of wandering, identified with terms such as errancy [Verirrung] and confusion [Verwirrung].[10] While the novel clearly attributes a productive potential to errancy, it makes clear that error, as an extreme, unmoored form of mobility, leads nowhere. This risk is expressed in the collection of aphorisms **"Betrachtungen im Sinne der Wanderer"**: "Das Wahre fördert; aus dem Irrtum entwickelt sich nichts, er verwickelt uns nur" (FA I.10: 581).

The motif of the Jewish wanderer or Wandering Jew clearly belongs to the category of a deficient, non-developmental wandering in the novel.[11] In the passage quoted earlier, Lenardo characterizes the Jews as seeking to trick and surpass [überschreiten] other wanderers: clearly, this competitive out-maneuvering is without ethical progress or value. In the Pedagogical Province, Jews receive ambivalent praise as "das beharrlichste Volk der Erde" (FA I.10: 425). Jews, acccording to Wilhelm's guide, have few virtues as a people other than sheer persistence. Jewish history is cast in the novel as continuous movement without direction.

This disorientation is also Wilhelm's starting point in the novel. As noted, Wilhelm explicitly compares his status in the beginning of the novel to that of a Wandering Jew. Like Ahasverus, he is separated from his wife and—for most of the novel—his child. As in many popular versions of the myth, he is not permitted to stay in one place more than three days. While obviously no supernatural or divine curse is at work, the conditions of Wilhelm's constant mobility are cast in vaguely religious terms. These commandments [Gebote] (FA I.10: 268) are both self-imposed and issued by the Tower Society, as represented by a figure known only by his religious title—the "Abbé." While no specific sin is identified that has condemned Wilhelm to this itinerant lifestyle, the terms of his letter to Natalie suggest past mistakes and a vague underlying guilt.[12] He regards the document that bears the conditions of his wandering as "Zeugnis meiner letzten Beichte, meiner letzten Absolution" (FA I.10: 268).

Yet, the decision that frees him of the conditions that "mark him as a Wandering Jew," transforms rather than ends his wandering. His choice to become a surgeon has Christian overtones in the novel: the Pedagogical Province characterizes Christianity as a reverence for that which lies below us, including "d[a]s Widerwärtige[ ], Verhaßte[ ], Fliehenswerte[ ]" (FA I.10: 430), and emphasizes Christ's attention to sickness, suffering and pain. Clearly, Wilhelm's care of wounded bodies expresses a commitment to compassion in its most concrete and practical form and therefore a redemption from the original sin of the Wandering Jew. Wilhelm's final act in the novel of resurrecting the dead (his own son who appears lifeless after falling into the river) completes his transformation from Wandering Jew to a wanderer in a Goethean-Christian mode.

* * *

Goethe forges a conception of Christianity that is semiotically and epistemologically complex. In both its concreteness and its elusiveness, Christianity takes on the function of symbolic meaning in general. The paradigmatic Goethean symbol in the novel, so frequently cited by critics, is the casket [Kästchen] which reappears throughout the main plot of the novel and also emerges in different guises in a couple of the interpolated novellas.[13] The collector, with whom Wilhelm confers about having the casket forcibly opened, suggests Wilhelm wait to see if a key turns up. In making this argument, he compares the casket to a piece of an old crucifix he once owned, to which the other missing pieces eventually surfaced. The collector sees in this happy coincidence the fate of the Christian religion, "die oft genug zergliedert und zerstreut, sich doch endlich immer wieder am Kreuze zusammenfinden muß" (FA I.10: 412).

Crucial to the symbolic character of the casket is that it withholds any final meaning or epiphany. When at last the key turns up, and a goldsmith, who understands the mechanism, successfully opens the box, he immediately presses it closed again with the comment that it is better to leave such secrets be. If one pursues the collector's analogy between the casket and the fate of Christianity, this is also a Christianity without final epiphany. Dismembered and dispersed elements collect together around the *cross*— the image of earthly suffering; they are not necessarily made whole in an ultimate scene of resurrection or apotheosis. Indeed, when Wilhelm revives his own son in the final scene, this resurrection is but a moment in an inevitable sequence of new injuries and new recoveries: "'Wirst du doch immer aufs neue hervorgebracht, herrlich Ebenbild Gottes!' rief [Wilhelm] aus, 'und wirst sogleich wieder beschädigt, verletzt von innen oder von außen'" (FA I.10: 745). The Christianity identified with symbolic meaning in this novel thus contents itself with local in-

juries and local resurrections. It renounces any immanent metaphysical wholeness or chiliastic fulfillment.

To appreciate how, within the novel, these Christian semiotics stand in opposition to Judaism, requires a closer examination of the structure of the symbol in Goethe's work. Todorov identifies two aspects or "phases" in the Goethean symbol. First, the symbol has its own being. It is in this sense, opaque and intransitive. (The particular body, one might say, is a particular body.) Yet, to quote Todorov further: "[The symbol] is and it signifies at the same time."[14] In the second phase, the symbol points to something ineffable and inexpressible beyond itself.

Wilhelm Meisters Wanderjahre is full of this semiotic motion, which Blackall aptly calls "contrapuntal."[15] Some of the contrapuntal pairs identified by Blackall are movement and rest, stones and stars, and particular and general.[16] To those oppositions, one could add: inner and outer, center and periphery, coming together and coming apart, matter and spirit. Thus, the novel constantly alternates between a focus on local, concrete experience and a gesture towards something larger, even ineffable. This motion, which develops into an underlying rhythm in the novel, is well described by the term "schaukeln," which appears in a crucial scene in the very center of the novel. Rocking refers to both the physical motion of the renunciant friends in a boat on Lago Maggiore as well as their emotional states as they find themselves alternately drawn together and pulled apart. (FA I.10: 504).

This contrapuntal dynamic is also associated with Christ. Wilhelm's guide in the Pedagogical Province emphasizes Christ's twofold orientation toward both the lowly and the divine:

> … indem [Christus] das Niedere zu sich heraufzieht, indem er die Unwissenden, die Armen, die Kranken seiner Weisheit, seines Reichtums, seiner Kraft teilhaftig werden läßt und sich deshalb ihnen gleichzustellen scheint, so verleugnet er nicht von der andern Seite seinen göttlichen Ursprung; er wagt, sich Gott gleichzustellen, ja sich für Gott zu erklären.

> (FA I.10: 429)

The ideal of a Christian wandering thus contains within itself persistent, indissoluble oppositions, including the opposition between Christ's stasis and movement cited earlier.

At the very heart of the novel's semiotics and its version of Christianity stands at last a negation. The oscillations that structure the symbol imply an act of renunciation. As the novel rocks indecisively between the concrete and the indefinite, it renounces any fantasy of epiphanic fulfillment. Goethe's symbol, as it emerges in this novel, is therefore fundamentally a negative form of signification.

What does this have to do with Judaism? Goethe's notion of the symbol is, of course, based on an opposition with allegory. According to a guide in the Pedagogical Province, allegory is the appropriate mode for representing Jewish history after the fall of the temple (FA I.10: 427). It is, therefore, necessary to consider what it would mean for Judaism to be associated with allegory in opposition to Christian symbolism. In one of his most famous formulations, dating from 1822, Goethe describes the different relationships that symbol and allegory strike between the particular and general:

> Es ist ein großer Unterschied, ob der Dichter zum Allgemeinen das Besondere sucht oder im Besondern das Allgemeine schaut. Aus jener Art entsteht Allegorie, wo das Besondere nur als Beyspiel, als Exempel des Allgemeinen gilt; die letztere aber ist eigentlich die Natur der Poesie, sie spricht ein Besonderes aus, ohne ans Allgemeine zu denken oder darauf hinzuweisen.

(FA I.13: 368)

While poetry resides in the particular character of the symbolic sign, the particularity of the allegorical sign is of little consequence. To use Todorov's term, the allegorical sign is transitive: "In allegory there is an instantaneous passage through the signifying face of the sign toward knowledge of what is signified."[17] A later pronouncement by Goethe contrasts what the two signs are capable of signifying: symbol reaches toward an inexpressible idea, whereas allegory designates a mere concept.[18]

And yet, Goethe's opposition between symbol and allegory, like his implicit distinction between Christian and Jewish wandering, is distinctly unstable. Walter Benjamin, for example, has long since illuminated that the allegorical sign, precisely in its arbitrariness and subordinate position, can appear as estranged materiality and particularity. Furthermore, in its radical concreteness and disjunction, allegory can function paradoxically as a negative sign of something ineffable. By foregrounding its own semiotic deficiency, the allegorical sign can gesture to that which lies outside the sphere of representation. Thus, allegory, too, can operate in two phases—the sign is radically particular; and the sign, in its estrangement and insufficiency, points beyond itself.

An analogous signifying dynamic can be found in Hegel's *Vorlesungen über die Aesthetik* under the category of "Die Symbolik der Erhabenheit." Moreover, Hegel explicitly identifies this dynamic with Judaism.[19] On the one hand, according to Hegel, the sublime sign points beyond itself to an independent meaning. This incommensurability between sign and signified is in effect the content of the sublime: "Eben nichts als dieses Hinaussein und Hinausgehen [kommt] zur Darstellung."[20] On the other hand, the sublime brings with it a new emphasis on finitude: "So erhält sowohl die natürliche als auch die menschliche Existenz jetzt die neue Stellung, eine Darstellung des Göttlichen nur dadurch zu sein, daß ihre Endlichkeit an ihr selber hervortritt."[21] For Hegel, the two elements that

would be united in a genuine symbol remain separate in the sublime—the abstract "Fürsichsein" of God and the concrete "Dasein" of the world.[22] While Hegel's contrastive dynamic of individuality/materiality versus transcendent meaning may not be identical to the contrapuntal movement observed in Goethe's novel, it is certainly akin. Yet, Goethe's novel seems to formulate a Christian semiotics, whereas Hegel connects this two-phase form of signification with the Jewish ban on images, which denies that any material image is adequate to represent God.

It is evident by now that any semiotic distinction between Judaism and Christianity must slice through very complex and murky territory. Even if one were to treat as stable Goethe's 1822 equation of symbol with particularity and allegory with the general, it remains very difficult to pin these terms on to Christianity and Judaism, as Jeffrey Librett points out. Hence, one finds oneself confronted with the following apparent undecidability. Allegory seems Jewish because its abstract character coincides with the abstraction with which Judaism is identified insofar as Judaism is seen as a radically anti-idolatrous monotheism. Accordingly, symbol seems Christian because, just as symbolic art privileges concretion, so does Christianity (in the forms of the embodiment of God in humanity, the Eucharist, the iconic traditions, and so forth). On the other hand, allegory seems Christian because it, like Christianity, is radically spiritual; and symbol thus seems Jewish because of the worldly materiality and even literal realism it shares with the ostensibly Jewish fetishism of the legalistic letter.[23] I contend that *Wilhelm Meisters Lehrjahre* simplifies the task of constructing a Christian semiotics by misrepresenting its competition with Judaism. The images in the halls of the Pedagogical Province amount to a systematic degradation of the Jewish ban on images. On the whole, Judaism is relegated to a concrete and literal realm without capacity to signify something higher or greater. In the Pedagogical Province, Judaism is identified as an ethnic and furthermore *pagan* religion. The characterization of Judaism as pagan is debasing precisely because it carries the implication of idolatry. The guide concedes, however, that *among all the pagan religions* Judaism has the greatest advantages, one of which is its prohibition on embodying God in any form. The guide continues: "[die israelitische Religion] [läßt] uns die Freiheit, [Gott] eine würdige Menschengestalt zu geben, auch im Gegensatz die schlechte Abgötterei durch Tier- und Untiergestalten zu bezeichnen" (FA I.10: 426). The Jewish ban on images amounts, then, to little more than an intermediate step—a refusal to represent the divine in animal or monster form as other pagan religions do, thus paving the way for Christianity to represent God as human. The sublimity of mind that Hegel, and before him Kant, associate with the Jewish ban on images is completely denied.[24]

The murals concerning Judaism also differ in kind from those of Christianity in the next gallery. They are described as "sinnlich" and lacking the inwardness [Inneres] of the Christian murals (FA I.10: 426, 427). Wilhelm is glad to think that for his son, who will be raised among the murals, these exemplary events in Jewish history might become real and alive (FA I.10: 426). They do not evoke something inexpressibly deeper or higher as do the representations of Christian miracles and parables in the next gallery. Goethe denies Judaism here any kind of greater signifying trajectory and confines it to the literal realm. As noted, in the gallery devoted to Judaism, events after the destruction of the temple are represented through allegory, which in Goethe's lexicon is already a degraded form of representation. Allegory, the guide explains, is appropriate here, because the events depicted would fall outside the limits of true art (FA I.10: 427). This amounts to an inversion of the traditional *Bilderverbot*: the referent is too lowly not too lofty to allow for a direct representation.

The leaders of the Pedagogical Province come closest to associating something like a Goethean symbol with Jews when they praise the Hebrew holy books, which from the most foreign elements create "ein täuschendes Ganze" (FA I.10: 426). That "das Ganze" is modified by "täuschend" suggests, however, a signifying trajectory that nevertheless falls short. The described impact of the Hebrew Bible on its reader seems more transitory and physiological than far-reaching or profound: the holy books are complete enough to satisfy [befriedigen], fragmentary enough to stimulate [anreizen], barbaric enough to challenge [auffordern], and tender enough to calm [besänftigen] (FA I.10: 426). The character of the Hebrew bible is thus at most *proto*—symbolic and clearly surpassed by Christianity, as presented in the final gallery on Wilhelm's tour.

* * *

The semiotic contrast between Christianity and Judaism corresponds to an ethical opposition, in which again the Jews come up short. Lenardo, as previously mentioned, characterizes Jewish wandering as an attempt to trick and outmaneuver others. Wilhelm's guide in the Pedagogical Province prefaces his praise for the toughness and persistence of the Jews with the claim: "Das isrealitische Volk hat niemals viel getaugt, wie es ihm seine Anführer, Richter, Vorsteher, Propheten tausendmal vorgeworfen haben; es besitzt wenig Tugenden und die meisten Fehler anderer Völker" (FA I.10: 425).

Meanwhile, the novel develops a practical ethics linked to Christianity's reverence for the earthly and to Christ as healer. As Wilhelm frees himself from his status as Wandering Jew and acquires the practical surgical training to aid suffering bodies, he becomes a kind of secular, nonmetaphysical Christ-figure. Muenzer and more recently Redfield have pointed out that technical knowledge and local action in the novel take on a semiotic character. Redfield writes, "Technics is knowledge derived from the renunciation of knowledge, and this renunciation of

knowledge links technical prowess to the transcendental unknowability of the symbol."[25] The practical activity of the surgeon is a negation of, and thereby a reference to, an unknowable universal truth. Again, Goethe is suggesting here a pragmatic Christianity wrested free of all theological claims.

Yet, it is arguably Judaism rather than Christianity that anticipates this epistemological and ethical conception of local action.[26] In *Jerusalem oder über religiöse Macht und Judentum* (1783), Mendelssohn offers the ritual action prescribed by Jewish law as an alternative to the faith in revealed doctrine demanded by Christianity. Mendelssohn writes, "Unter allen Vorschriften und Verordnungen des Mosaischen Gesetzes, lautet kein Einziges: *Du sollst glauben! oder nicht glauben; sondern alle heissen: du sollst thun, oder nicht thun!*"[27] At the heart of Mendelssohn's critique of doctrinal revelation is, of course, the ban on images. Ritual actions are less likely than signs to lead to idolatry because they are themselves ephemeral and temporal. These actions are supposed to give rise to thinking about eternal truths but in no way claim to represent the unrepresentable. Furthermore, while in a narrow sense Mendelssohn's discussion concerns ceremonial laws and practices, in a broader sense he is attributing to Judaism a fundamentally social and practical orientation. Indeed, because of their transitory character, ceremonial rites promote social interaction:

> Die Handlungen der Menschen sind vorübergehend, haben nichts Bleibendes, nichts Fortdauerndes, das, so wie die Bilderschrift, durch Mißbrauch oder Mißverstand zur Abgötterey führen kann. Sie haben aber auch den Vorzug vor Buchstabenzeichen, daß sie den Menschen nicht isolieren, nicht zum einsamen, über Schriften und Bücher brütenden Geschöpfe machen. Sie treiben vielmehr zum Umgange, zur Nachahmung und zum mündlichen, lebendigen Unterricht. Daher waren der geschriebenen Gesetze nur wenig, und auch diese ohne mündlichen Unterricht und Überlieferung nicht ganz verständlich, und es war verboten, über dieselbe mehr zu schreiben.[28]

Further significant differences exist between Mendelssohn and Goethe's treatment of religion: Mendelssohn sees reason as a reliable source of eternal truth shared by all religions and all human beings. Without this ultimate appeal to reason, Goethe's skepticism towards revelation leads him into much deeper agnostic territory. Yet, the link developed in the **Wanderjahre** between epistemological renunciation and local action is clearly incipient in *Jerusalem*.

Even Nathan, Mendelssohn's fictional counterpart in Lessing's *Nathan der Weise,* makes this connection between ethical social action and a ban on idolatry. In the first act, Nathan's daughter Recha has become convinced—with the encouragement of her fanatical Christian nursemaid Daja—that the being who rescued her from a burning house was no mere mortal but an angel. To conflate sensory objects or persons with the supersensible realm in this way is a clear example of idolatry (or what Kant would call dogmatic metaphysics). Indeed, Nathan strives to convince his daughter that this fantasy runs the risk of "Gotteslästerung."[29] In attributing divine powers to this human being, Recha furthermore overlooks her rescuer's concrete needs and the real aid she can offer him. Nathan seeks to make Recha aware of the distinction between an idolatrous "Schwärmen" and a practical "Handeln": ". . . Begreifst du aber, / Wieviel andächtig schwärmen leichter, als / Gut handeln ist?[30] Recha's *Jewish* mentor Nathan teaches her to hold rigorously to the ethical demands of life in this world, while her *Christian* mentor Daja allows her to sink into otherworldly dreams. Lessing echoes a familiar enough complaint among intellectuals in Goethe's period: that Christianity substitutes metaphysical speculation (i.e., idolatry) for ethical engagement.[31]

* * *

There is one further respect in which Wilhelm's ideal of wandering claims to overcome an "eternal" Jewish wandering: it promises a new relationship to time. When Wilhelm is relieved of the conditions that "stamp him as a Wandering Jew," it alters his experiences of the passage of time. Now, his wandering acquires meaning in relationship to a purpose:

> [Er] gab nunmehr Rechenschaft von der Anwendung seiner Zeit, seitdem er die Vergünstigung erlangt, die auferlegte Wanderschaft nicht nach Tagen und Stunden, sondern dem wahren Zweck einer vollständigen Ausbildung gemäß einzuteilen und zu benutzen.
>
> (FA I.10: 537)

In the previous stage, by contrast, time was marked off in repetitive units—in days and hours—without orientation towards a goal. The eternity of "der ewige Jude" thus amounts to empty, relentless duration. This interpretation of the myth is explicit in Göschel's 1824 book on Goethe's *Faust*: "Insofern jene Sage in ihrer Allgemeinheit aufgefaßt wird, zeigt sie auf der Außenseite die Nichtigkeit der Zeit in allen ihren Dimensionen ... die Wesenlosigkeit des Gewesenen ... das Nichts der *Gegenwart*, ... die bodenlose Leerheit der *Zukunft*" (emphasis in original).[32]

This view of the temporal condition of the Wandering Jew has echoes elsewhere in the novel. As previously noted, in the Pedagogical Province Jews are praised, in the absence of any other virtue, for their historical perseverance. Jewish history is represented in these galleries as a series of real, external events belonging to the annals of world history, but without any connection to the events of Christ's life and teaching. When Wilhelm wonders why Christ is missing from the chain of events depicted before the destruction of the temple, his guide explains:

> Was Völkermassen und ihren Gliedern öffentlich begegnet, gehört der Weltgeschichte, der Weltreligion, welche wir für die erste [Religion] halten. Was dem Einzelnen

innerlich begegnet, gehört zur zweiten Religion, zur Religion der Weisen: eine solche war die, welche Christus lehrte und übte, so lange er auf der Erde umherging. Deswegen ist hier das äußere abgeschlossen und ich eröffne euch nun das Innere.

> (FA I.10: 427)

And thus the guide opens for Wilhelm a new gallery of an entirely different character, reflecting a new inner orientation.[33]

The experience of the past as an incessant chain of external events, here attributed to the Jews, may tie in to a persistent anxiety in the *Wanderjahre* about the trajectory of modernity. This uneasiness is most apparent in the section **"Betrachtungen im Sinne der Wanderer."** An aphorism on the culture of journalism laments that "our" time lets nothing ripen but rather consumes the present in persistent activity: ". . . man [verspeis't] im nächsten Augenblick den vorhergehenden, [vertut] den Tag im Tage, und [lebt] so immer aus der Hand in den Mund, ohne irgend etwas vor sich zu bringen" (FA I.10: 563). In the subsequent aphorism, this relentless modern velocity is cast in economic terms: "Die Lebhaftigkeit des Handels, das Durchrauschen des Papiergelds, das Anschwellen der Schulden, um Schulden zu bezahlen, das alles sind die ungeheuern Elemente, auf die gegenwärtig ein junger Mann gesetzt ist" (FA I.10: 563). While there is no allusion to Judaism or Jews in these passages, the description of vicious cycles of debt and credit easily plays into long-worn anti-Semitic stereotypes of usurious Jewish financiers. Indeed, as we have seen, Lenardo distances his group of wanderers from the Jews precisely because of their ruthless pace, through which they strive to trick and out-step their fellow wanderers (FA I.10: 668). Thus the novel, while developing an ideal of an adaptive, pragmatic, existential wandering, opposes itself to a frenetic, disoriented, modern acceleration, which is tied implicitly and explicitly to the Jews.

Wilhelm's task as Renunciant is indeed to overcome both the heavy burden of the past and the persistent pressure toward the future. Jarno reminds Wilhelm that the Renunciants are obligated to speak neither of the past nor the future but to focus entirely on the present (FA I.10: 296). After his visit with Makarie's astronomer friend, Wilhelm announces how one can counter the pull of an infinite time with a focus on the present:

> Das Resultat unsres heutigen Abends löst ja auch das Rätsel des gegenwärtigen Augenblicks. Wie kann sich der Mensch gegen das Unendliche stellen, als wenn er alle geistigen Kräfte, die nach vielen Seiten hingezogen werden, in seinem Innersten, Tiefsten versammelt, wenn er sich fragt: "Darfst du dich in der Mitte dieser ewig lebendigen Ordnung auch nur denken, sobald sich nicht gleichfalls in dir ein beharrlich Bewegtes, um seinen reinen Mittelpunkt kreisend, hervortut? Und selbst wenn es dir schwer würde, diesen Mittelpunkt in deinem Busen aufzufinden, so würdest du ihn daran erkennen,

daß eine wohlwollende, wohltätige Wirkung von ihm ausgeht und von ihm Zeugnis gibt.

(FA I.10: 382-83)

Wilhelm's solution to the relentless passing of time is for each individual to find and define his center of orientation. This internal orientation is also offered in the aphorisms cited above as the antidote to modern temporality: a measured, calm sense, or guiding will can counter this restless "Tagesgeist" (FA I.10: 563). As Wilhelm's guide in the Pedagogical Province explained, the expression of inwardness is precisely what distinguishes the images in the Christian from those in the Jewish galleries.

It is important, however, to note Wilhelm's agnosticism about the nature of this internal center. In the above quote, Wilhelm allows that it may be difficult to discover this center in oneself: only its outward, beneficial effects make it manifest. Thus, Wilhelm makes no claim about the nature or existence of a transcendent soul. His pronouncement here is perfectly compatible with a performative, non-essentialist notion of the self. The guiding internal principle retains the status of hypothesis: one gains access to it only through outward-directed activity. The self, therefore, remains thoroughly temporal in character even as it resists the all-engulfing press of time.[34]

Once again, to the extent that a concept of Christianity is in play here, it is a deeply existential one. That is precisely what places it in competition with Judaism: elsewhere Goethe explicitly identifies Jews with endeavours that are earthly, temporal, and directed towards the present moment: "Keiner, auch nur der kleinste geringste Jude, der nicht entschiedenes Bestreben verriethe, und zwar ein irdisches, zeitliches, Augenblickliches" (FA I.13: 273).[35] Consequently, what stands out in this novel is a drive to distinguish a productive focus on life in this world claimed for Christianity, from an earthly temporality associated with the Jews. Goethe achieves this, I contend, by trivializing the role of history for the Jews.

This emphasis on the role of history is evident in the passage in which the emigrant leaders conclude that no Jews will be tolerated in their colony. This declaration is not attributed to one character but presented as a more or less consensual outcome of a conversation between Friedrich and Wilhelm, which presumably involved previous consultation with Lenardo and others. The logic that leads to this pronouncement is deeply perplexing:

> An [der christlichen] Religion halten wir fest, aber auf eine eigne Weise; wir unterrichten unsere Kinder von Jugend auf von den großen Vorteilen, die sie uns gebracht hat; dagegen von ihrem Ursprung, von ihrem Verlauf geben wir zuletzt Kenntnis. Alsdann wird uns der Urheber erst lieb und wert, und alle Nachricht, die sich auf ihn bezieht, wird heilig. In diesem Sinne, den man vielleicht pedantisch nennen mag, aber doch als folgerecht anerkennen muß, dulden wir keinen Juden unter uns, denn wie

sollten wir ihm den Anteil an der höchsten Kulter vergönnen, deren Ursprung und Herkommen er verleugnet?

(FA I.10: 686-87)

According to this pedagogical strategy, Christianity is taught to children first as a set of values—faith, hope, love, endurance of suffering—rather than as historical revelation. Early instruction brackets out the figure of Christ as the originator of the Christian religion.

Indeed, throughout the novel and in many variations, origins appear ambiguous, inaccessible, or subordinate to a more pragmatic perspective. For example, at the "Bergfest" Wilhelm listens to a lively debate about the origin of the world. He hears many geological hypotheses and wonders about their relationship to the biblical account of the earth's genesis. When he turns to his friend Montan for an opinion, Montan shows no interest in arriving at the true answer. He concerns himself only with the present character of the mountains: "Wie diese Gebirge hier entstanden sind, weiß ich nicht, will's auch nicht wissen; aber ich trachte täglich ihnen ihre Eigentümlichkeit abzugewinnen" (FA I.10: 536).

And yet, even though the emigrants' approach to religion seems to share this more pragmatic orientation, it ultimately bans Jews on the basis of biblical origins. According to the above strategy, once youth have learned the advantages of Christianity, they come to love and cherish its founder, and regard the gospel of his life as "holy." Because Jews deny this religious origin and genealogy, they must be excluded from the colony's "highest culture." Given the apparent subordination of Christian origins to practical Christian values in the passage, this categorical exclusion of Jews seems gratuitous and unmotivated. The group acknowledges the pedantry of its logic, even while insisting on its consistency.

What are we to make of this strange justification for religious intolerance? Is the forced logic of this passage simply intended to draw our attention to the arbitrariness of the whole emigrant undertaking? Bennett views the "logical failure" in this passage as indeed self-conscious. In his view, it serves as further evidence of the deep and thoroughgoing irony of the novel, including its attitude toward Jews.[36] For Bennett, this failure consists in the fact that the valuable religious principles that the emigrants hope to gain from Christianity originate in the Hebrew Bible, in Ecclesiastes: "The allusions to Ecclesiastes, in fact, remind us that even that supposedly Christian 'reverence' (if we think back to the pedagogical province, and think of Ecclesiastes as a whole) can be derived from *Jewish* writings."[37] Yet, Bennett's own observation here could serve as a further instance of the pattern that I am identifying: the attribution to Christianity of principles and perspectives to which Judaism has a prior claim.

I read the emigrant group's argument not as self-canceling but as indeed—as the passage maintains—logically consistent [folgerecht]. This logic works, however, rather indirectly. The exclusion of the Jews, I contend, is not entailed by the pragmatic "Christian" view of origins endorsed by the colony and developed elsewhere in the novel; it is a consequence rather of the literalist conception of history that the novel attributes by contrast to the Jews. That is to say, the group judges the Jews incapable of participating in the highest culture of the colony, not just because they deny the historical Christ, but implicitly because *they* are so peculiarly and narrowly attached to historical events. As the guide in the Pedagogical Province explains," ethnic religions" such as Judaism are directly bound to history: "Der Gehalt [der ethnischen Religion] findet sich in der Weltgeschichte, so wie die Hülle derselben in den Begebenheiten" (FA I.10: 424). The emigrants thus have it both ways: they retain for Christianity a sophisticated irony towards history *and* reject Jews for their skepticism toward the revelatory claims of Christian history. Christianity, thereby, assumes the mantle of tolerance: indeed, Lenardo emphasizes in his speech his group's strong commitment to honor all forms of religious worship (FA I.10: 672)—by which he apparently means all forms of Christianity.

The emigrants' argument against the Jews hardly merits refutation. Nevertheless, one need only cast another glance toward Mendelssohn to find a very different Jewish conception of history that supports tolerance and exchange across religious faiths. (A version of this interfaith model was widely popularized in Lessing's *Ringparabel.*) In *Jerusalem,* Mendelssohn distinguishes between the role of historical and eternal truths in Judaism. Historical truths rest on evidence, cultural transmission, and authority and may involve revelations that are constitutive for a people, but they do not prescribe doctrine. Eternal truths are rational, according to Mendelssohn, and thus equally accessible to all human beings, regardless of culture or creed. One can certainly recognize in this division the logic of the *Bilderverbot,* that an eternal, universal absolute does not appear incarnate in human history. History is not, however, thereby devoid of meaning. Mendelssohn makes it clear that precisely because truth eludes permanent fixation in human signs, it is proper for religion to evolve historically through interpersonal transmission.[38] One could perhaps go a step beyond Mendelssohn's argument to further suggest why a history without final epiphany could nonetheless assume religious weight: as we saw in Hegel's paradox concerning the sublime, precisely through its negative and renunciatory relationship towards the absolute, finitude takes on meaning as a counterpart to the unrepresentable.

Mendelssohn's argument allows him to remain deeply committed to his own cultural history and tradition without insisting upon its absolute character. Separate cultures can thus share common ground and mutual respect. Mendelssohn quotes Rabbi Hillel's one-line summary of the Jewish

law, "Liebe deinen Nächsten wie dich selbst,"[39] which Jesus also identifies as a core commandment (Mt 22:39). Furthermore, as Hess argues, in *Jerusalem* Mendelssohn paints Jesus as an essentially Jewish thinker who supports the continued authority of Jewish law *for those born into it.* That is to say, according to Mendelssohn, Jesus does not overcome Judaism but rather endorses its continued existence. In this view, Jesus stands for precisely the Jewish model of religious tolerance that Mendelssohn himself advances.[40]

There is a further historical irony to the emigrant argument against the Jews, of which Goethe must have been aware. The group's logic rests on the supposition that a sophisticated Christian stance towards origins is incompatible with the dogmatic historical literalism of the Jews. In the Lavater affair, these two religions occupied opposite positions. Lavater seized upon an occasion on which Mendelssohn privately expressed philosophical and moral respect for Christ to publicly try to force Mendelssohn to convert In this well-known instance, then, *Jewish openness* towards the founding figure of Christianity was met with aggressive and relentless *Christian dogmatism.* As pointed out earlier, on this occasion, Goethe identified with Mendelssohn.

Indeed, at the root of the anti-Semitism in the novel there appears to lie an odd, distorted identification with the Jews. Goethe's vision in the **Wanderjahre** of epistemological renunciation and existential orientation places him much closer to Jewish than Christian tradition. Yet, just as Wilhelm strives to overcome his status as Wandering Jew, the novel strives to supersede its relationship to Judaism with its own brand of Christian existentialism. The novel achieves this by systematically downplaying the profound meaning of the Jewish *Bilderverbot* for semiotics, ethics, and historical consciousness. Meanwhile, the negative semiotics of the *Bilderverbot* are recuperated within the novel's own philosophy of renunciation. Thus, the exclusion of Jews from the novel's fundamental ideal of an ontological wandering does not seem accidental or merely ironic. Rather, it appears to be the foundation upon which the novel's own anti-foundationalism rests.

Notes

1. My discussion addresses the final, 1829 version of the novel. Parenthetical citations "FA" refer to Johann Wolfgang Goethe, *Sämtliche Werke: Briefe, Tagebücher und Gespräche,* ed. Dieter Borchmeyer et al., 48 vols. to date (Frankfurt am Main: Deutscher Klassiker Verlag, 1985-).

2. Two recent volumes represent the trend towards a more critical reassessment of Goethe's relationship to Judaism: Annette Weber, ed., *"Außerdem waren sie ja auch Menschen." Goethes Begegnung mit Juden und Judentum* (Berlin: Philo, 2000); and Klaus L.

Berghahn and Jost Hermand, eds. *Goethe in German-Jewish Culture* (Rochester: Camden House, 2001). The first volume is a particularly rich resource on the social, political, and religious context of Goethe's relationship to Judaism; the second volume is very strong on the history of Goethe's reception within German-Jewish culture. Yet, with the exception of Jürgen Stenzel's essay on the imagery of Goethe's "Judenpredigt" in Weber's volume, there are no detailed or sustained analyses of Goethe's representation of Jews and Judaism in a literary context. In the "Introduction" to his volume, Klaus Berghahn briefly refers to the passage from the *Wanderjahre* with which I opened, but only to suggest that one must read it in relationship to other passages in the novel (7-8).

3. Martin Swales, "Goethe's prose fiction," *The Cambridge Companion to Goethe,* ed. Lesley Sharpe (Cambridge: Cambridge UP, 2002) 145. But Swales notes an opposite tendency in the novel as well. That is, there *are* consistent socio-economic and pedagogical themes within the novel. He writes. "... the *Wanderjahre* exhibits a strange combination of postmodern irony with a kind of hectoring pedagogy in the service of self-discipline and renunciation" (145).

4. Benjamin Bennett, *Beyond Theory: Eighteenth-Century German Literature and the Poetics of Irony* (Ithaca: Cornell UP, 1993) 61.

5. Bennett 62.

6. "What the modern reader has to understand about the *Wanderjahre* is that it is not Goethe who is speaking. [...] This fact does not make the methods of discipline and punishment, and the institutional anti-Semitism, to be implemented by this utopian police state, less offensive. Nor does it relieve Goethe of his responsibility for the potential consequences of this text" (101). According to Bahr, the troubling passages in the novel present "an ethical challenge to the reader" and provide "space for the problematic subject matters of the period" (102). Ehrhard Bahr, *The Novel as Archive: The Genesis, Reception, and Criticism of Goethe's* Wilhelm Meisters Wanderjahre (Columbia, SC: Camden House, 1998). Steven Dowden also acknowledges some of the novel's anti-Semitic moments but maintains, "[Goethe's] reader must be attentive to the skepticism expressed in the novel's ironic structure." Dowden continues: "Let me emphasize that the aim of my appeal to irony is not to rescue Goethe from the charge of bigotry. He may deserve it. The evidence is not clear enough to say one way or the other. Instead, my aim is to discover the meaning of his novel, which may well transcend its author's limitations and liabilities, or indeed his conscious intentions." Steven Dow-

den, "Irony and Ethical Autonomy in *Wilhelm Meisters Wanderjahre*," *Deutsche Vierteljahresschrift* 68.1 (1994): 148.

7. In this sense, Goethe novel's participates in the broader competition between Christianity and Judaism to claim the mantle of modernity that Jonathan Hess has so well traced in the eighteenth century. See *Germans, Jews and the Claims of Modernity* (New Haven: Yale UP, 2002). I also thank Jonathan Hess for his input on this article.

8. For a general history of the myth, see George K. Anderson, *The Legend of the Wandering Jew* (Providence: Brown UP, 1966). Mona Körte's more recent literary history of Ahasverus includes a chapter on Mignon and the Harpist in *Goethe's Wilhelm Meisters Lehrjahre; Die Uneinholbarkeit des Verfolgten. Der Ewige Jude in der literarischen Phantastik* (Frankfurt: Campus, 2000).

9. See for example, Heinrich August Ottkar Reichard, *Der ewige Jude. Geschicht- oder Volksroman, wie man will* (Riga: im Hartknochschen Verlage 1785) 10, and *Der ewige Jude. Eine komische Geschichte aus dem 18. Jahrhundert* (Leipzig: Anton Doll, 1800) 86. K. F. Göschel notes this parallel in the *Wanderjahre: Uber Göthe's Faust und dessen Fortsetzung. Nebst einem Anhange von dem ewigen Juden* (Leipzig, Hartmann, 1824) 292. While Göschel's book was published between the two versions of Goethe's novel, thus before Goethe had made the comparison between Wilhelm and the Wandering Jew explicit in the 1829 version, he nevertheless picks up on the Wandering Jew motif and seems to anticipate Goethe's later emphasis.

10. The play on these terms is particularly evident in the novella "Der Mann von funfzig Jahren" in reference to Flavio's wandering in mental confusion (FA I.10: 474, 483, 484).

11. A connection between unbridled mobility and the Wandering Jew also appears in the novella, "Wer stickt der Verräter." Because of their insatiable *wanderlust*, Lucidor calls Antoni and Julie, respectively, "de[r] ewige[ ] Jude" and "das zapplige Quecksilber" (FA I.10: 354). Yet, by the end of the story, this mobility appears safely contained—consisting of comfortable outings in a pleasure park. Julie teases Lucidor for his earlier insult: "das gestehen Sie doch, der ewige Jude, der unruhige Anton Reiser, weiß noch seine Wallfahrten bequem genug einzurichten, für sich und seine Genossen: es ist ein sehr schöner bequemer Wagen" (FA I.10: 373).

12. Wilhelm's pilgrimage to Mignon's birthplace in the middle of the novel may link this vague sense of guilt to her fate. His failure to comprehend and sympathize with her suffering appears to hasten her illness

and death in *Wilhelm Meisters Lehrjahre.* Thus, Wilhelm's sin would be, like Ahasverus's, a failure of compassion.

13. Bahr challenges the tradition of criticism that sees the *Wanderjahre* as a symbolic novel and instead makes a case for metonymy as the organizing trope. Certainly, there is much to support Bahr's view that the novel is structured through unessential contiguous relationships. Nevertheless, as Bahr himself acknowledges, one trope does not rule out another. "Revolutionary Realism in Goethe's *Wanderjahre," Johann Wolfgang von Goethe,* ed. Harold Bloom (Philadelphia: Chelsea House, 2003) 41.

14. Tzvetan Todorov, *Theories of the Symbol,* trans. Catherine Porter (Ithaca: Cornell UP, 1982) 206.

15. Eric Blackall, *Goethe and the Novel* (Ithaca, Cornell UP, 1976) 236-69.

16. Blackall 237, 239, 242.

17. Todorov 201.

18. Todorov 205-06. Also, FA I.13: 207.

19. It would be very hard to read Goethe's semiotics in the novel as in direct conversation with Hegel's aesthetics. Hegel's lectures were delivered in 1823, 1826, and 1829 and published posthumously. While the novel's contrastive emphasis on Judaism was strengthened in the 1829 version of the novel— when, for example, Goethe added the explicit comparison between Wilhelm and the Wandering Jew— many of the passages on which I am drawing in my discussion of symbol and allegory, including the discourse on religion in the Pedagogical Province, appear already in the 1821 version of the novel. Thus, I am merely presenting Hegel's views as a contemporary point of comparison, with which Goethe may or may not have been familiar. Of course, the connection between sublimity and the Jewish ban on images was already established in Kant's aesthetics, published 1790. See n. 24 below.

20. G. W. F. Hegel, *Werke* 13 (Frankfurt: Suhrkamp, 1986) 479.

21. Hegel 482.

22. Hegel 481.

23. Jeffrey S. Librett, *The Rhetoric of Cultural Dialogue: Jews and Germans from Moses Mendelssohn to Richard Wagner and Beyond* (Stanford: Stanford UP, 2000) 33.

24. In his discussion of the sublime in the Third Critique, Kant writes, "Vielleicht gibt es keine erhabenere Stelle im Gesetzbuche der Juden, als das Gebot: Du sollst dir kein Bildnis machen, noch irgend ein Gleichnis, weder dessen was im Himmel, noch auf der Erden, noch unter der Erden ist u.s.w." Immanuel Kant, *Werkausgabe,* ed. Wilhelm Weischedel, vol. 10 (Frankfurt: Suhrkamp, 1974) 201.

25. Marc Redfield, *Phantom Formations: Aesthetic Ideology and the* Bildungsroman (Ithaca: Cornell UP, 1996) 105. Redfield refers to arguments made by Muenzer. See Clark Muenzer, *Figures of Identity: Goethe's Novels and the Enigmatic Self* (University Park, PA: Pennsylvania State UP, 1984) esp. 127-28.

26. While traditional Lutheran theology places primary emphasis on faith over works, Pietist theologians such as Gottfried Arnold, who was influential for Goethe as a young man in Frankfurt, placed greater emphasis on deeds for the Christian life. (On Arnold, see F. Ernest Stoeffler, *German Pietism during the Eighteenth Century* [Leiden: Brill, 1973] 179-80.) Yet, in his portrayal of "die schöne Seele" in *Wilhelm Meisters Lehrjahre,* a character based on his Pietist mentor Susanna von Klettenberg, Goethe clearly critiques Pietism as still insufficiently engaged with the external world.

27. Moses Mendelssohn, *Gesammelte Schriften. Jubiläumsausgabe,* ed. Alexander Altmann et al., 23 vols. to date (Bad Cannstatt: Friedrich Fromman Verlag, 1971-) 8.2: 166. Emphasis in original.

28. Mendelssohn 184.

29. Gotthold Ephraim Lessing, *Werke,* ed. Wilfried Barner et al., 12 vols. (Frankfurt: Deutscher Klassiker Verlag, 1985-90) 9: 495.

30. Lessing 497.

31. Compare Fichte's critique of Christianity in his *Reden an die deutsche Nation.* Johann Gottlieb Fichte, *Sämmtliche* Werke, ed. J. H. Fichte, 8 vols. (Berlin: Veit und Comp, 1846) 7: 378-79. In fact, one can easily recognize this critique elsewhere in Goethe's works as well. For example, Werther's fantasies of life after death with Lotte, which themselves constitute a sort of dogmatic metaphysics, help propel him toward suicide.

32. Göschel 230.

33. This contrastive depiction of the historicity of Christianity and Judaism may be related to the challenge Christianity faced with the rise of historical biblical criticism. Hess explains: "As German scholars subjected the Bible to historical critique, approaching it as an artifact that reflected its time and place of origin and its various human authors, they found themselves facing the task of salvaging Christianity for the modern world. They had to demonstrate, that is, not just the historical dimensions of scripture but also how Christianity *transcended* its concrete, historical

origins. The typical corollary of this project was a vision of Judaism as the historical religion *par excellence,* a religion that made little sense outside the historical framework that originally gave rise to it" (12). (Emphasis in orginal.)

34. Cf. Muenzer, who also sees in this passage the "infinite deferral of the true self" (109).

35. Quoted by Neumann and Dewitz in their textual commentary to the novel (FA I.10: 1235).

36. Bennett 62.

37. Bennett 62fn.

38. Mendelssohn 168-69.

39. Mendelssohn 168.

40. Hess 121-24.

Andrew Piper (essay date 2006)

SOURCE: Piper, Andrew. "Rethinking the Print Object: Goethe and the Book of Everything." *PMLA* 121.1 (2006): 124-38. Print.

[*In the following essay, Piper shows how Goethe's late works call into question the ideals of "monumentality" and "completeness" in the print culture of his day.* Wilhelm Meister's Travels, *published in various forms from 1810 to 1829, is viewed as an example of Goethe's understanding of publication as a "process" rather than an event fixed in time.*]

> Indeed, I wanted to write that my work consists of two parts: that which lies here before me and that which I have not written. And it is precisely this second part that is the more important.
>
> —Ludwig Wittgenstein

FORTRESSES OF THE SPIRIT

On Sunday, 28 June 1896, a ceremony was held to mark the completion of a new building for the recently established Goethe and Schiller Archive in Weimar. It was a day of extreme optimism: reverent speeches were delivered, Beethoven's Ninth Symphony was played, and newspapers around the world made grand pronouncements, comparing the archive to the library of Alexandria, calling Weimar the Athens on the Ilm, and anointing the new structure a "fortress of the spirit [*Geistesburg*]," a "temple," "hall of honor," "palace," and "citadel" (Golz 37).[1] Even the *Chicago Times Herald* reported the story, remarking, "The whole may well be named the Pantheon of German Literature—the most unique and valuable in the whole history of literature" (Golz 35). Standing imperiously on a hill overlooking, indeed dwarfing, the small town below it, the imposing new structure visually

articulated the cultural hierarchy it was intended to bring about. At the core of this architectural and institutional edifice was the emerging textual monument to be known as the Weimar edition.

The edition was initiated nine years earlier, only two years after the death of Goethe's last living relative, Walter Wolfgang von Goethe, who in 1885 bequeathed Goethe's entire *Nachlaß* or posthumous papers to the Großherzogin Sophie von Sachsen-Weimar. The transference of Goethe's manuscripts from private to public hands was a sensation in philological circles, and the duchess quickly assembled a team of six editors and over seventy assistants to begin producing a new critical edition. Thirty-two years and 143 volumes later, the project reached its conclusion.

The edition not only functioned as a kind of "Parallelaktion," in Dieter Borchmeyer's words (230), to the founding of the German nation—the spiritual edifice on which rested the new *Kulturnation*—it also represented the culmination of the twin nineteenth-century literary ideals of personality and totality. In his foreword to the first volume of the Weimar edition, the editor Hermann Grimm wrote, "One knew the poet, but now one wanted to know more about *the writer* and *the man. Everything about everything* of the man who was so dear to every German's heart" (xi; emphasis added). And Bernhard Suphan, the director of the project, wrote in his preface, "This edition shall represent in its *purity* and *completeness* the *entirety* of Goethe's literary activity along with *everything* that has been left behind of his *personal essence,* a project that has for the first time become achievable now that his posthumous papers have become accessible to scholarly treatment" (xvii-xix; emphasis added). As this proliferating vocabulary of material completeness and personal essences indicated, the exhaustive empirical recovery of the author's life along with its complete and conclusive representation in print was to provide the foundation for all future interpretation. One wanted "everything about everything" of the individual life, and the textual production was to represent the "purity" and "completeness" of this biographical data.

The Weimar edition, then, not only captured a theory of literature—that its meaning depended on knowledge of its author—but also a theory of print: that it was capable of producing timeless and unchanging objects, objects that were totemically capable of organizing or holding together the social form of the nation. In the hands of the editors of the Weimar edition, Goethe would no longer be a fluctuating network of publications and interpretations but would become something bound and complete, like the stone walls of the new archive that housed his literary remains. The Goethe of the Weimar edition—and indeed the format of the collected edition itself—was to provide the spiritual edifice that strengthened the walls of the national *Burg.*

RETHINKING THE PRINT OBJECT

The Weimar edition marked the culmination of an ideal of literature that emerged as part of a larger cultural and material reorientation beginning around the turn of the nineteenth century. By making the author and his life the central organizing principle of literary works—and by extension literary history—the Weimar edition was concluding a process that arguably began with C. M. Wieland's landmark collected works edition of the 1790s and achieved its most formidable expression in Goethe's ***Ausgabe letzter Hand*** [***Werke: Vollständige Ausgabe letzter Hand***] or Walter Scott's *Magnum Opus* edition of the late 1820s.[2] In response to the overwhelming proliferation of printed books in the early nineteenth century, the "collected works" had become one of the most—if not the most—effective vehicles for regulating, institutionalizing, and stabilizing the category of literature in the nineteenth century. Like the popular nineteenth-century format of the miscellany, the collected works had the capacity to group extraordinary textual diversity under a single heading. Yet unlike the miscellanies with their accompanying ethos of sharing and shared literary property, the collected works established the boundaries of an author's work as inviolable. The collected works thus not only responded to, and in part repaired, the spatial disorganization of the literary system in the nineteenth century, it also addressed the crisis of *traditio,* the problem of literature's temporal durability in an age of mass-reproduced objects. In its capacity to stabilize and pass on a literary canon over time, the collected works seemed to embody the arguments of pioneering book historians like Elizabeth Eisenstein and Alvin Kernan that print contributed to the standardization and the stability of cultural knowledge. And in its cultlike value to nineteenth-century projects of nation building, the collected edition offered a vivid example of Benedict Anderson's theory of print nationalism, as the operations to the textual body were intended to be symbolically performed on the national body as well.

The Weimar editors were thus largely continuing, or completing, a material practice that was launched in the age of Goethe and that Goethe himself, not uncharacteristically, played a substantial role in initiating. With the ***Ausgabe letzter Hand*** as the textual basis of their edition, the Weimar editors were re-collecting Goethe, who, toward the end of his life, had been hard at work collecting himself. After overseeing the creation of a personal archive for his lifetime of writing—a move of self-administration that must mark a first in literary history—Goethe used this personalized institution as the basis of his last edition of his works. In a real sense, Goethe's archivization preceded the architectural foundation of the Goethe Archive several decades later. At the same time that Goethe was contributing to his own private institutionalization, he was also working toward the public institutionalization of his works by applying to the Bundesversammlung, the parliamentary

body of the German states, for a "Privileg" for his edition (Fröbe). It was an anachronistic gesture that pointed back in time to the early modern system of the royal privilege—to the origins of print literature, in other words[3]—as well as forward to a time when a national system of copyright might exist to protect against the vigorous industry of piracy that beset the German book market. Most of all, it was intended to declare the sovereignty and the nationality of this final publication, that the boundaries of the book fixed the boundaries of the author's property as well as the cultural boundaries of the German nation that did not yet exist.[4] The privilege, like the archive, like the collected edition, was intended to institutionalize and nationalize the individual writer. It is easy to understand how the Weimar edition could imagine itself as the legitimate heir, indeed the apotheosis, of these dual authorial and national projects.

* * *

And yet this is only part of the story of publishing Goethe and Goethe publishing. If we look more closely at Goethe's late publishing practices that concluded in his final collected edition, we can see that, far from affirming these author- and nation-building projects, they yield a different set of literary ideals. I do not wish to imply that the Weimar edition was somehow a misguided practice or that it has not proved to be a tremendously valuable resource for Goethe scholarship. But I do want to suggest that its production rested on a set of assumptions about literature, about the function that the printed book had in maintaining these literary ideals, and ultimately about Goethe's privileged place in the continuation of this literary system.[5] Its production rested, in other words, on a way of reading Goethe that had become institutionalized in the nineteenth century, a perspective that depended on an understanding of what literary work was and thus where it could take place.

Thus in the same way that a particular mode of reading Goethe was used to underwrite a larger disciplinary program in the nineteenth century (and indeed for long after), close attention to his publishing practices can, I argue, underwrite the disciplinary convergence of book history and literary history that we are seeing today. Under what one could call an ideology of the hand—in their exclusive focus on Goethe's final collected edition, the ***Ausgabe letzter Hand,*** or their tireless attention to the unpublished manuscripts—the Weimar editors understood publication as a form of degradation, as a disruption to the economy of consolidation on which authorial identity and literary culture came to depend in the nineteenth century. Goethe's relation to print, however—the process of his actual publishing practices—necessarily remained overlooked. Yet as recent book historians, publishers, and bibliographers such as Siegfried Unseld, Waltraud Hagen, Dorothea Kuhn, and Wolfgang Bunzel have shown, few writers exhibited a greater concern for the intersections of literature and publication than Goethe did during his late period. We now have a much clearer idea of how varied, extensive, and calculated his relation was to categories like publication, print, and the book. There is a remarkable overlap between the formal operations in his late works and the media operations that surrounded the publication of these works. The meaning of Goethe's late work is always deeply and self-consciously intertwined with the changing conditions of communication in which it was produced.

In returning to those material and narrative spaces that were marginalized by the manuscriptural-biographical perspective canonized by the Weimar editors, I will look beyond markers like the *Privileg* and focus instead on the complex diffusion of Goethe's works in print that surrounded and ultimately concluded in the final collected edition. At the same time, I will try to illustrate how Goethe's use of language and narrative also contributed to what we might call a particular media imaginary. His fictions, too—most prominently on display in his last major prose work, **Wilhelm Meisters Wanderjahre (Wilhelm Meister's Journeyman Years)**—played a pivotal role in addressing the rules and protocols of print communication. When taken together, Goethe's uses of print, publication, and narrative, far from establishing and solidifying the regulatory system that was emerging in the nineteenth century, in fact strongly resisted this program. The values of personality, sovereignty, nationality, totality, and permanence that suffused the Weimar edition and that were at the heart of literature's classificatory system in the nineteenth century were, in Goethe's own collected edition, distinctly posited as problems.

In its divergence from such norms, Goethe's late work discloses a moment when categories like print, the book, and the work—all essential to the organization of the modern literary system—were still spaces of extreme fluctuation. It suggests that the pioneering work of an earlier generation of book historians, whose aim was to establish the essence of such categories, now needs to be revised. Recent works by Adrian Johns, Leah Price, Meredith McGill, Paul Keen, and Clifford Siskin are some of the many projects that have begun this endeavor of revision, to show how historically variable such categories were. My essay is thus conceived as part of this larger ongoing project, which addresses a simple question that yields surprisingly diverse answers: how did users use print to make literature?

As the proliferation and distribution of print objects accelerated around the turn of the nineteenth century, numerous writers were participating in the struggle to regulate, define, and stabilize the literary system. Goethe's late work assumes importance because of the way it imagined things differently. In place of the book as a spiritual fortress, it prioritized values like transformation, diffusion, and connectivity. It attempted to refashion literary communication within, and not against, the conditions of reproducibility

and mobility that were print technology's most salient features. It aimed to establish protocols for the control of communication that were crucially based on principles of decreasing control. Most important, it challenged and expanded the categories on which the literary system had come to depend. In thinking about the nature of the book, Goethe was thinking about the nature of literature.

LITERATURE UNBOUND

In what was labeled "Anzeige von Goethe's sämmtlichen Werken vollständige **Ausgabe letzter Hand**" ("Advertisement for Goethe's Complete Final Authorized Edition of His Collected Works"), printed in the popular daily newspaper *Morgenblatt für gebildete Stände* in July 1826, Goethe defined the key terms of his final literary project. "Nun mögte von so Manchem, was hier noch zu sagen wäre, nur zu berühren seyn, wie man der gegenwärtig angekündigten Ausgabe die Prädikate von *sämmtlich, vollständig* und *letzter Hand* zu geben sich veranlaßt gefunden" ("Of what remains to be said, it shall only be touched upon how one had occasion to give the present forthcoming edition the predicates *collected* [or complete], *complete*, and *final authorized*"). Here, one expects Goethe to authorize the model of monumentality that would later inform the Weimar edition. Yet something different happens in this short advertisement. In Goethe's words, *sämmtlich* is defined as "sodann Alles, was vorerst werth schien, aus den Papieren des Verfassers mitgetheilt zu werden" ("everything that appeared worth sharing from the papers of the author"). What has been collected is based on a criterion of value ("werth") that defines the act of collection first and foremost as one of selection. Instead of stressing the likeness or the unity of the collection's parts, this definition of "everything" emphasizes what has been left out. Goethe goes on to define his next term by arguing that *vollständig* represents, on the one hand, "des Verfassers Naturell, Bildung, Fortschreiten" ("the author's nature, formation, and progress") and, on the other hand, his "vielfaches Versuchen nach allen Seiten hin" ("multifaceted striving in all directions"). Completeness encompasses both the temporal evolution of the writer ("Fortschreiten") as well as the spatial diffusion or diversity of his work ("Versuchen nach allen Seiten"). The edition's completeness is a function of both time and space, but Goethe's use of gerunds (*Fortschreiten*, not *Fortschritt; Versuchen*, not *Versuche*) emphasizes process over completion. Finally, on the term *letzter Hand*, Goethe writes, "Der Ausdruck letzter Hand jedoch ist vorzüglich vor Mißverständniß zu bewahren. Wo er auch je gebraucht worden deutet er doch nur darauf hin, daß der Verfasser sein Letztes und Bestes gethan, ohne deshalb seine Arbeit als vollendet ansehen zu dürfen" ("It is principally important, however, to protect the expression *letzter Hand* against misunderstanding. Wherever it has been used, it only signifies that the author has done his last and best, without allowing his work to be seen as concluded"; 762). The works are complete (*vollständig*) without being concluded (*vollendet*). They extend beyond the work of the author's hand.

The advertisement thus constructs a fiction of the collected edition significantly different from the one created by the privilege on the title page of the edition. Set apart and at a distance to the physical edition, the advertisement emphasizes the a-partness of the writer's works. It underscores their diffusion, not their unity. Far from advancing the Weimar editors' ideals of nationality and monumentality, in Goethe's hands the collected works becomes a vehicle for negotiating the contradictory energies of transformation and preservation that were at the heart of the spreading culture of print. Instead of imagining the "purity" and the "completeness" of the print edition as something timeless, national, and monumental, Goethe was attempting to represent the paradoxical idea of the incompletion of completion of the print object. Publication is understood as a process or an event, not a fixed or fixable moment.

The advertisement suggests that the collected edition should be seen in a larger continuum, pointing not only to the forms that might come after it but to the elements that came before it and that also belong to it, even if at a distance. Goethe's practice of collection, while claiming to be a totality ("vollständig"), did not aim to reproduce that totality in the closed textual confines of the collected edition. The exclusion of texts was in fact a way of including them. By making simultaneous claims to totality and to openness, Goethe was refashioning the collected edition as something that included precisely that which was beyond its own textual borders. And it was this attention to the outside and the elsewhere that generated the most contemporary criticism of Goethe's undertaking. In his *Kritik der neuesten Cotta'schen Ausgabe von Goethe's Werken* ("Critique of the Latest Cotta Edition of Goethe's Works" [1828]), Friedrich Schütz, the author of a seven-volume work on Goethe's philosophy, queried, "Is it enough to lament that of the 'hitherto dispersed publications' that Goethe invokes, only 'some things' and not, as one would very much desire, 'everything' is included in this *Ausgabe letzter Hand*!" (44). The status and the location of "everything" was at stake in the construction of the collected edition, and the friction that the advertisement generated for contemporary readers was in the edition's redefinition of what "everything" meant and where it was located.

As a way of approaching what this new book of everything might look like, I will focus on the publication history of a single work from the final collected edition: Goethe's last major prose fiction, *Wilhelm Meisters Wanderjahre* (1808-29), which was conceived as a sequel to his popular bildungsroman *Wilhelm Meisters Lehrjahre* (*Wilhelm Meister's Apprenticeship* [1796]). As part novella collection, epistolary novel, and travel novel, the *Wanderjahre* has always posed classificatory challenges to literary scholars.[6] If one can speak of an interpretive consensus

regarding this novel today, it would surround the importance of what Volker Neuhaus first identified as the "archival fiction" at the novel's heart. Drawing on a Bakhtinian notion of the novel as the genre of multiple genres and discourses, numerous recent works of scholarship have highlighted the way the novel seems to register as many linguistic points of contact with the world as possible (Dane; Herwig; Schößler). As Ehrhard Bahr writes in his *The Novel as Archive*, "The problems of the *Wanderjahre* consist of the plurality of discourses and their discontinuity, instability, and transience" (99). However productive such readings have been, as a category to model the novel the archive is ultimately, in my view, far too static to account for the importance of the way information moves in the novel. In the words of information theorists, it privileges processing over transmission, where transmission seems equally, if not more, important to the novel's structure.

When we take into consideration the elaborate publishing strategy that constituted the novel in print, such questions of transmission become even more pronounced.[7] To discuss the *Wanderjahre* is to discuss a textual system that appeared in different versions in various early-nineteenth-century print formats over the course of two decades during Goethe's lifetime, from the newspaper to the miscellany to the novel to the collected edition. At the same time, a vast majority of Goethe's work on the second version of the *Wanderjahre,* which has become the version scholars most often refer to when they discuss the novel, was undertaken during Goethe's production of the *Ausgabe letzter Hand.*[8] There is a concrete overlap between the creative energies invested in assembling and editing his collected works and assembling and writing this major work. In addition, the second version of the *Wanderjahre* was never published as a stand-alone work but only as part of the collected works. It is specifically inscribed into the textual universe of the edition. Finally, like the collected works, the *Wanderjahre* was composed of numerous other works that had been previously published. From its inception, the *Wanderjahre* was surrounded by questions of collection that were at the heart of the collected works. It appears as a microcosm of the collection, a work about the works and thus about literary work itself.

"IF THE *MONA LISA* IS IN THE LOUVRE, WHERE IS *HAMLET*?"—F. W. BATESON

In the spring of 1822, following the publication of the first version of *Wilhelm Meisters Wanderjahre* one year earlier, Goethe published an essay in the *Morgenblatt* entitled **"Geneigte Theilnahme an den Wanderjahren"** (**"Inclined Participation in the *Journeyman Years*"**). It was offered as a response to an ongoing literary debate about the merits of the *Wanderjahre* as a novel. Of the many reasons why the reception of Goethe's latest work had been so rancorous, arguably the most significant was the appearance of a second *Wilhelm Meisters Wanderjahre,* written by Johann Pustkuchen and published almost simultaneously to Goethe's (Wolf). The instability of reception to which Goethe's intervention in print one year later was a response was thus due in large part to the problem of repetition that surrounded the *Wanderjahre* as a text: there were too many *Wanderjahre*s. The appearance of a second *Wanderjahre* was not, however, a unique event (and thus could not be written off as a literary coincidence or nuisance) but was indicative of the larger role repetition played in the *Wanderjahre*'s textual life. The *Wanderjahre* was not only conceived as a sequel, it also consisted of numerous works that had been previously published in pocketbook miscellanies. Pustkuchen's reuse of the title *Wilhelm Meisters Wanderjahre* was not to be understood as a parody, then, but as a representation of a reading experience that had overwhelmingly come to define the title of *Wilhelm Meisters Wanderjahre,* an amplification of the increasingly vague boundaries that seemed to constitute this literary "work."

The strategy of republication that was amplified by the *Wanderjahre*'s double appearance in 1821 dated back to 1808 with the publication of the novella **"Die pilgernde Törin"** (**"The Foolish Woman on a Pilgrimage"**), the first of several novellas that were individually published in Johann Friedrich Cotta's pocketbook miscellany, the *Taschenbuch für Damen* (*Ladies' Pocketbook*) and that were later included in the *Wanderjahre.* **"Die pilgernde Törin"** was a translation from an anonymously written French story, and thus the first work to appear in print that would later appear again in the *Wanderjahre* was a translation—a text that, like the sequel into which it would later be incorporated, pointed to preexisting material. This problematization of the boundaries of the *Wanderjahre* was further underscored when Goethe published the first four chapters of the *Wanderjahre* in Cotta's *Taschenbuch* in 1810, chapters that were framed in the miscellany by the novel's title, *Wilhelm Meisters Wanderjahre. Erstes Buch* (*Wilhelm Meister's Journeyman Years: Book One*). Where **"Die pilgernde Törin"** had pointed backward to another text from which it derived, the publication of material in 1810 pointed forward to a work that did not yet exist. Wolfgang Bunzel has argued that "these prepublications [*Vorabdrucke*] were components of a directed strategy of publication to gain readers" ("'Das ist'" 36). Certainly, but this strategy does more work than simple advertising. Even Bunzel's term *Vorabdrucke* makes an interpretive choice by determining that the novellas are part of the *Wanderjahre,* that they are not separate works. Yet it is this (a)partness—how they relate to the larger whole—that Goethe plays with in how they appear in print.

The first four chapters of the *Wanderjahre* published in 1810 were not only framed by a title page with the words *Wilhelm Meisters Wanderjahre. Erstes Buch,* they were also paginated in roman numerals. They were typographically set off from the rest of the pocketbook, a choice that

we know was Goethe's, not Cotta's (Bunzel, "'Das ist'" 45). The roman numerals marked the integrity and the apartness of the *Wanderjahre* from the rest of the miscellany. At the same time, however, chapter 1, **"Die Flucht nach Aegypten"** (**"The Flight to Egypt"**), concluded not the way it would conclude in the *Wanderjahre* but with the words

> Hier folgt im Original ein Brief an Natalien, wodurch die **Wanderjahre** eingeleitet und an die **Lehrjahre** [*Wilhelm Meisters Lehrjahre*] angeknüpft werden.
>
> (*Taschenbuch* viii)
>
> Here follows in the original a letter to Natalie, through which the *Wanderjahre* is introduced and connected to the *Lehrjahre.*

Thus the integrity that was typographically achieved through the roman numerals was simultaneously undermined through the parentheses that marked off a space that referred somewhere else. The excerpt, itself an indication of something incomplete, was here explicitly made incomplete. It was in essence an excerpt of an excerpt. The entirety of the first book that the title page announced was thus undermined by the parenthetical invocation of another textual space ("in the original"). At the same time, this other textual space—the original and thus origin—did not yet exist, upending the notion of originality on which the category of the excerpt depended. Finally, it was crucial to the logic of this publication that the part that was missing was framed as the introduction to the *Wanderjahre and* as the connection to its prequel, the *Lehrjahre.* The other textual space denoted by the parentheses—called the "original"—was supposed to mark both a beginning and a continuation of another work. It was deeply divided, in other words, between marking an origin and erasing the condition of originality. What we find in these two initial publications is the steady accumulation of texts that point to other texts through pointers that oscillate between the delineation and violation of textual boundaries.

This strategy continued right up until the publication of the first version of the *Wanderjahre* in 1821. In 1815, Goethe published an advertisement in the *Morgenblatt* (**"Antwort auf eine Anfrage über *Wilhelm Meisters Wanderjahre*"** [**"Answer to an Inquiry about *Wilhelm Meister's Journeyman Years*"**]) that apologized for the absence of the *Wanderjahre* from the German book market. The advertisement did not announce the pending appearance of a work, thus amplifying the work's presence, as an advertisement should, but instead substituted itself for a work that would not appear for another five years, indicating once more a text's absence. This advertisement was followed over the course of the next few years by the publication in Cotta's miscellany of portions of novellas that would all later be included in the *Wanderjahre*: the first part of **"Das nußbraune Mädchen"** (**"The Nut-Brown Maid"**); the first half of **"Die neue Melusine"** (**"The**

New Melusina"), with a preface that was not included in the *Wanderjahre*; **"Der Mann von funfzig Jahren"** (**"The Man of Fifty"**), an incomplete novella; and finally, the second half of **"Die neue Melusine."** In other words, the prepublications of the *Wanderjahre* consisted of a translation, an incomplete excerpt, an advertisement for an absent book, half of a novella, half of another novella with an original preface, an incomplete novella, and then the concluding half of a novella that had appeared three years earlier in print. Did the second half of **"Die neue Melusine"** point backward to its first half or forward to the pending publication of the *Wanderjahre*? What was the status of the "pre" in these prepublications?

With almost half of the novel in print by the time the 1821 edition appeared, it was little wonder that readers were critical of the repackaging of already printed and remunerated works. The feuilletonist Ludwig Börne claimed that Cotta's son had told him that "Goethe pulled out all his old stuff just to fill up the book," and Friedrich Glover charged that the whole project was driven by "base financial speculation" (Bunzel, "'Das ist'" 68). For early-nineteenth-century readers, the *Wanderjahre* looked like nothing more than reprinted goods. The appearance of Pustkuchen's *Wanderjahre* simply underscored a problem that readers had come to associate with the work. The problem was that the publishing event of the *Wanderjahre*—an event that by 1821 had spanned over a decade and would last another eight years—did not fit under either of the available early-nineteenth-century rubrics of reception. It was neither an original work nor the reissue of a classic in the service of fashioning a national heritage. The *Wanderjahre* challenged the agreed-on calculus of originality and repetition that early-nineteenth-century readers had come to expect from print media.

This predicament of novelty and repetition was magnified in the 1820s when Goethe significantly rewrote the *Wanderjahre* in the course of the decade but then only republished it as part of his final collected edition. Like the excerpts that had appeared in Cotta's miscellany, the *Wanderjahre* as a whole was now framed by a larger textual apparatus. The ambiguous textual boundaries that surrounded the *Wanderjahre* in the collected edition were amplified by the ambiguous textual boundaries between the 1821 and the 1829 versions. As Goethe wrote next to the listing for the *Wanderjahre* in the advertisement to his collected edition,

> Die wunderlichen Schicksale, welche dieß Büchlein bey seinem ersten Auftreten erfahren mußte, gaben dem Verfasser guten Humor und Lust genug, dieser Produktion eine doppelte Aufmerksamkeit zu schenken. Es unterhielt ihn, das Werklein von Grund aus aufzulösen und wieder neu aufzubauen, so daß nun in einem ganz Anderen Dasselbe wieder erscheinen wird.

("Anzeige" 759)

The marvelous fate that this small book experienced on its first appearance gave the author both the desire and good mood to give this production renewed attention. He found it entertaining to undo the work from the bottom up and rebuild it anew, so that in something totally different the same thing will appear.

Goethe informed his readers that the *Wanderjahre* in the collected works was indeed going to be something new ("to undo the work from the bottom up and rebuild it anew"), at the same time that he continued to challenge any claim to originality and autonomy for this "new" work ("so that in something totally *different* the *same* thing will appear"). What we find in Goethe's late work is the way the *version* (*Fassung*) captured something essential about the new condition of communication in which the author saw himself working, the increasing diffusion and connectivity of print media. The new media landscape allowed for the greater dissemination of a work at the same time that it made it possible to draw tighter connections between parts. Where the literary work under Goethe's aegis seemed to fuse claims to novelty and sameness, it simultaneously asserted the centrality of material expansion to the literary project. Whether it was in the form of prepublishing the fragmentary novellas or republishing the novel only as part of the collected works, we can see how the *Wanderjahre* enacted a paratextual program that redefined the location of the literary work, that continually transgressed and expanded the work's boundaries so that the demarcation of the text became increasingly problematic. And yet as we saw in Goethe's publications in the miscellanies, material deployment was only half of the equation of thinking about literature and the book. The changes Goethe made at the level of language and narrative from version to version crucially affected the imaginative reception of this increasingly diffuse work.

THE ARROW AND THE MAP

In book 2, chapter 7, of the *Wanderjahre*, we find the novel's hero, Wilhelm, traveling to the Lago Maggiore in Italy. It is one of many spaces that Wilhelm will traverse in the course of the *Wanderjahre*'s three books, from the naturalism of the steep cliffs of the alps, to the domesticity of the uncle's bourgeois salon, to the didacticism of the pedagogical province, to the colonialism of the American settlement, to the cosmological projections of Makarie's abode. The Lago Maggiore is significant because it is here where we are told that Wilhelm will undergo an important transition in his life. Indeed, in the original plan for the novel—before Cotta's publishing conditions forced Goethe to transform the work from two to three volumes—the Lago Maggiore was to mark the end of the first volume. The biographical transition was to be amplified by the material caesura of the physical book.

And yet the Lago Maggiore's importance to the novel lies not so much in the way it marks a distinct transition but in the way this textual site is overwhelmingly defined through its references to numerous other textual spaces. Wilhelm's traveling companion, the painter, has read the *Lehrjahre*—the prequel to the novel we are reading—and is on a pilgrimage to the home of one of its most memorable characters (Mignon); the travelers later encounter characters from the novella **"The Man of Fifty"**; the widow from **"The Man of Fifty"** tells Wilhelm her story, which is the novella we have just read; the narrator informs us he has included excerpts from another text (a text by C. V. Meyer); and finally, the painter sings Mignon's song from the *Lehrjahre,* a song that leads to a narrative crisis that concludes his and Wilhelm's time on the Lago Maggiore.

Far from enacting a moment of leaving behind, then, the scene of the Lago Maggiore is much more about the problem of the new beginning. It is a strategy that undoubtedly owes much to the renewed popularity of Cervantes's *Don Quixote* in the early nineteenth century, and taken together such devices are in themselves not terribly remarkable. They do little to amplify or draw attention to the variety of Goethe's publishing practices that surrounded the text. But critics have never before noted an instance of intertextuality that I have so far omitted, one that is crucial for making sense of how the formal arrangement of the *Wanderjahre* participates in the late Goethe's thinking about writing and print.

When Wilhelm and his traveling companion at the Lago Maggiore decide to find the two women from the novella **"The Man of Fifty,"** the narrator describes their quest in the following way:

> Nun stellten sie Kreuz- und Querfahrten an, die Punkte wo der Freunde in dieses Paradies einzutreten pflegt beobachtend. Ihre Schiffer hatten sie mit der Hoffnung Freunde hier zu sehen bekannt gemacht, und nun dauerte es nicht lange, so sahen sie ein wohlverziertes Prachtschiff herangleiten, worauf sie Jagd machten und sich nicht enthielten sogleich leidenschaftlich zu entern. Die Frauenzimmer einigermaßen betroffen faßten sich sogleich, als Wilhelm das Blättchen vorwies und beide den von ihnen selbst vorgezeichneten Pfeil, ohne Bedenken, anerkannten. Die Freunde wurden alsbald zutraulich eingeladen das Schiff der Damen zu besteigen, welches eilig geschah.

> (501)

They now began crisscrossing the lake, observing the points where their friends tended to appear in this paradise. They had informed their skipper that they had hopes of seeing friends here, and it was not long before they saw a beautifully ornamented ship gliding toward them. They hurried after it and did not restrain themselves from passionately preparing to board it immediately. The two women, who were somewhat taken aback, quickly composed themselves as Wilhelm showed them the small piece of paper and they both recognized, without a second thought, the arrow, which they themselves had drawn. The men were speedily and warmly invited to board the women's ship, which occurred with great haste.

Putting aside other details of this scene, I would like to pause and look more closely at the arrow and the little piece of paper that play such an important and yet barely noticeable role. There is a certain logic to the idea that a piece of paper and an arrow could facilitate Wilhelm and the painter's entry into the women's nautical salon. There is nothing contradictory, in other words, about the function of paper and arrow as communicative devices. But on another level, these signs make little sense in the context of this scene. We have never before encountered the small piece of paper and the arrow in the second version of the *Wanderjahre*: there is an element that remains unexplained, indeed unexplainable, about them. We might say that they operate as empty signifiers, as objects that invite and yet stubbornly resist interpretation, much like the little casket that circulates throughout the novel and that no one can open.

When we turn to the equivalent scene in the first version of the *Wanderjahre,* however, we find these two signs amply described. We see how they functioned as a way of facilitating communication between characters at a distance. At the conclusion of **"The Man of Fifty"** in the first version, Hersilie tells Wilhelm in a postscript how he will be able to find the characters of the novella:

> Um Ihnen nun den Weg zu zeigen, wie Sie das liebenswürdige Paar auf Ihren Wanderungen treffen können, so ergreife ich ein wunderliches Mittel. Sie erhalten hiebei den kleinen Ausschnitt einer Landkarte; wenn Sie diesen auf die größere legen, so deutet die darauf gezeichnete Magnetnadel mit der Pfeilspitze nach der Gegend, wo die Suchenswerten hinziehen.

> (126)

> To show you how you can meet this lovely pair on your travels, I will turn to rather strange means. You are receiving in this letter a small excerpt of a map; when you place this piece on the larger map, the point of the magnetic needle that is drawn on it will direct you to the region where those you seek have gone.

In the first version, we learn how Hersilie has constructed an elaborate cartographic game. Wilhelm's task is to find where on the larger map this excerpted piece fits, and when he has done so, the arrow that is drawn on the excerpt will point him where to go on the larger map. Only through the combination of the excerpt with its larger original will the sign (the arrow) make sense.

Thus what is amply described in the first version is left underdescribed in the second. The first version's more specific moniker of the "excerpt" becomes the decidedly vaguer "piece of paper" in the second. Instead of arguing for these signs' opacity in the second version, then, we might be inclined to argue, as the editors of the Frankfurt critical edition have done, that this omission of an explanation in the second version could be identified as a "mistake." "Goethe overlooked," write the editors, "the need to include in the second version an explanation of this mention of the arrow and the little piece of paper, both here and at a later point" (Goethe, *Wilhelm Meisters Wanderjahre* 1129n). To argue that Goethe overlooked something (however probable) is to rely on a problematic hermeneutical model that distinguishes between intentional changes and accidental changes. How would we be able to reliably differentiate omissions that are meaningful from ones that are mistakes in the process of rewriting? In arguing that something has been overlooked, something is being overlooked. Like the invocation of the importance of ambiguity, invoking the act of overlooking is a consequence, I would suggest, of not reading the text in its material context. The significance of the absence of explanation in the second version only emerges when we take into account the media operations that surrounded the publication of the *Wanderjahre* and that led to this variation. Only then does this "mistake" or "non-sense" emerge as an allegory of reading and communication.

The arrow in the second version does not function as a mistake or an opaque sign, then, but instead *as an arrow,* literally pointing the reader somewhere else, a somewhere else that I would identify as the first version of the *Wanderjahre,* in which the arrow's meaning is explained. By not including the explanation of the arrow in the second version, Goethe has placed the reader in the same situation as Wilhelm. Just as Wilhelm had to place a piece of one map on top of a much larger map for the piece to make sense, we as readers are invited to perform the same cartographic operations on the second version—to conceive the second version as an excerpt and to lay it onto a much larger map (or textual space) that would include the first version. Only then do the sign (the arrow) and the text (the map) make sense. This crucial moment in the frame narrative of the second version does not frame the work as either new or definitive but merely as part of a larger textual unit. Both sign and text are critically reconceived as excerpts. They do not resist meaning but radically expand the location of meaning. According to the arrow and the map, the meaningful unit is always the composite, the compound, and the collected.

The crucial point of this operation is how elegantly it mirrors the publishing practices that surrounded the work. The scene—so central to Wilhelm's self-fashioning—constructs a reader capable of interpreting the material expansionism of Goethe's late literary work, an expansionism that significantly depended on manipulating and participating in the distributive and decentralizing energies of the expanding print technology. When the painter in the Lago Maggiore scene reveals himself to have read the novel's prequel, the *Lehrjahre,* we are meant to see how knowledge of such larger textual universes was becoming increasingly important to reading experiences in the early nineteenth century. Balzac's transition to thinking of the "work" as a massive, unified "oeuvre" a year after Goethe's

death in 1833 would arguably mark the highpoint of this move toward larger and larger literary systems, a tradition that one could see concluding, and unraveling, in Robert Musil's endless modernist novel, *Der Mann ohne Eigenschaften* (*The Man without Qualities*). The arrow and the map in the second version of the *Wanderjahre* apply this principle of intertextuality—the displacement of meaning to a textual space beyond a single work's boundaries—not from one work to another but from one version to another of the same work. Goethe's project anticipated in many ways other nineteenth-century projects of rewriting, most notably exemplified by Walt Whitman's *Leaves of Grass,* but Goethe's asked that one observe the entirety of this process so that that each subsequent version only made sense in relation to all earlier versions.

Nineteenth-century readers were critical of Goethe for not including the first version of the *Wanderjahre* in his *Ausgabe letzter Hand* because they felt that the two versions constituted two separate creations and that a truly complete collected edition should contain all Goethe's "works."[9] But this was just the inverse of the critique that readers had made against the inclusion of the previously published novellas in the novel—namely, that there was no difference between the novellas in the miscellanies and the novellas that appeared in the *Wanderjahre* and thus they should not have been reprinted. In either case, the works are either the same or they are absolutely different. They are conceived of as finite objects and finite reading experiences. What the arrow and the map performed with elegant concision was the problematization of this logic of sameness and difference, and they did so by arguing for the importance of the material location of literary work. They located literary work, and thus the work itself, not in some ideal and crucially immaterial space but instead in the material operations of circulation, distribution, and reproduction that accompanied and defined its reception. They oriented the reader's gaze to the mobile artifacts of literary life. There is an amazing coincidence, in other words, between the reader figured in the *Wanderjahre* and the reader that the discipline of book history aims to construct today.

THE WORK OF ART AS *TECHNO-PRÄPARAT*

If the arrow of the Lago Maggiore in the *Wanderjahre* refigured the work as something that evolved over time and that incorporated these prior moments into itself, there is a key scene in book 3 that points forward, that establishes the work as a kind of limitless futurity. At the moment that Wilhelm experiences another biographical turning point—this time a crisis in his anatomy training to become a doctor—a man intervenes and leads him into an adjacent room. The room's walls are adorned with artificial limbs that have been made by Wilhelm's new guide. It is, on the one hand, a space of pure prosthesis, a media chamber of technologized body parts. These objects, however, are not artificial substitutions for lost body parts but instead artificial representations of various layers of body parts, to be used in anatomical training. Of the numerous spatiotemporal reorientations that this scene performs, the most significant is the substitution of substitution itself as the "Surrogat" is reformulated as a "Präparat" (604), a word that refers to an object that has been chemically treated in preparation for anatomical observation. In a play on the prefix *pro* in the German *Prothese,* the "beneath" depicted in these anatomical prostheses now also represents the "before." The new supplement marks both a (chemical) compound and a preliminary stage.

The *Präparat* can thus be read as a powerful metaphor for the literary work.[10] Like the arrow of the Lago Maggiore, the anatomical prosthesis points to something that is not there. But unlike the arrow and the operations of map reading it implies, the prosthesis points forward instead of backward. The work that is conceived as a technological preparation not only encompasses its various past permutations but now also anticipates, and in some sense participates in, the production of itself in the future. Like Wittgenstein's assertion that the most important works were those he did not write, the technological *Präparat* incorporates into itself all the forms that the work has not yet assumed. According to the didactic space of the adjacent room of anatomical sculptures, the work is figured neither as an intact, organic corpus nor as a fundament to secure the walls of a spiritual or national fortress. Instead, the work is figured as a prophetic, radiant, technological compound. It transcends the author's control and transgresses spatiotemporal boundaries to allow for more fluid literary and cultural configurations.

The Weimar editors imagined that they were printing "everything about everything" in a single textual unit that was not only bound by an ultimately finite number of volumes but also a finite amount of time. Goethe's project of collecting everything, on the other hand, disaggregated the text from a single, unified material location and unbound the temporal horizon that constituted the "work" as well. Through the strategic deployment of a range of print formats—the newspaper, the pocketbook miscellany, the novel, the collected edition—Goethe's late work exhibited an intense interest in using print's power of reproducibility, transmittability, and depersonalization to radically transform the notion of what a work was and where literary work was to be located. In rethinking the nature of the printed book, Goethe was rethinking the nature of literary work. No longer confined to the immaterial space of the imagination or the confessional paradigm of articulating interiority, literature was powerfully reconceived in its intersection with material and social spaces of communication. If the printed book was reconfigured in the *Wanderjahre* as an endlessly regenerating system of texts, then the *Wanderjahre* itself was to be the key, or in more modern terms, the programming code to this system. According to Goethe's late work, literature's future and literature's meaning depended on a fundamental reimagination of what the printed book could do.

Notes

1. All undocumented translations in this essay are my own.

2. For a discussion of Wieland's collected edition, see Ungern-Sternberg; for Scott, see Millgate; and for Goethe, see Hagen, "Goethes Ausgabe."

3. In his letter to the Bundesversammlung, Goethe writes, "Das Mittel jedoch, einen anerkannten geistigen Besitz dem einzelnen Verfasser zu erhalten, hatte sich schon bald nach Erfindung der Buchdruckerkunst hervorgetan, indem, bei ermangelnden allgemeinen Gesetzen, man zu einzelnen Privilegien schritt" ("Nevertheless, the means for an individual author to maintain his acknowledged intellectual property emerged soon after the discovery of the printing press, whereby in the light of a general deficiency of laws, one turned to individual privileges"; *Briefe* 239).

4. Goethe's emphasis on the nationalizing function of the congress's act was made explicit in his letter: "Sollte nun aber gegenwärtig der erhabene Bundestag, der Verein aller deutschen Souveränitäten, nicht dergleichen als Gesamtheit auszuüben geneigt sein, was die Einzelnen vorher anzuordnen und festzusetzen berechtigt waren und noch sind, und wäre nicht durch einen solchen Akt das entschiedenste Gewicht auf deutsche Literatur und Geistesbildung kräftigst zu betätigen?" ("Should not the noble Bundestag, the union of all German sovereignties, be equally inclined to exercise itself as a totality today, in a similar fashion to the individuals who were and continue to be afforded such rights? And would not such an act powerfully exercise the most decisive influence on German literature and spiritual development?"; *Briefe* 239). The importance of the unifying function of this title-page moniker is further underscored by the fact that Goethe insisted on it even though it was a fiction: the Bundesversammlung did not have the legal authority to grant a federation-wide privilege (Fröbe).

5. For a lengthier discussion of the process of Goethe's canonization in the nineteenth century, see Hohendahl.

6. For a history of the novel's reception, see Bahr. For a discussion of the *Wanderjahre*'s relation to Goethe's other novels, see Vaget, Blackall, Brown, and Blessin.

7. For a discussion of the genesis of the *Wanderjahre,* see Bahr; Reiss; and Schellenberg, although Schellenberg's article curiously only focuses on the first

version and contains no new information but does contain factual errors (the novellas are said to all be published in 1809) as well as interpretive misreadings (the 1829 version is referred to as a "new work").

8. See Erich Trunz, who demonstrates the way it was the *Wanderjahre* and not *Faust* that was Goethe's primary occupation ("Hauptgeschäft") during 1828-29.

9. Friedrich Schütz writes, "The old text would have to be reprinted in a complete edition of Goethe's collected works" (38).

10. Wilhelm's anatomical training is also the center of Marc Redfield's lucid reading of the *Wanderjahre,* which describes this scene's interrogation of *techne,* dissection, and unknowability as a critique of humanism and thus the ideals of the aesthetic state. By contrast, where I see the *Wanderjahre* articulating a particular political vision is through its endorsement of certain modes of technological communication that enable different and importantly nonnational political formations to take shape.

Works Cited

Anderson, Benedict. *Imagined Communities: Reflections on the Origin and Spread of Nationalism.* New York: Verso, 1991.

Bahr, Ehrhard. *The Novel as Archive: The Genesis, Reception and Criticism of Goethe's* Wilhelm Meister's Wanderjahre. Columbia: Camden, 1998.

Bateson, F. W. "Modern Bibliography and the Literary Artifact." *English Studies Today.* Ed. Georges A. Bonnard. Bern: Lang, 1961. 67-77.

Blackall, Eric A. *Goethe and the Novel.* Ithaca: Cornell UP, 1976.

Blessin, Stefan. *Goethes Romane. Aufbruch in die Moderne.* Paderborn: Schöningh, 1996.

Borchmeyer, Dieter. "Sophiens Reise von Weimar nach München." *Goethe-Jahrbuch* 106 (1989): 230-39.

Brown, Jane K. *Goethe's Cyclical Narratives.* Durham: U of North Carolina P, 1975.

Bunzel, Wolfgang. "'Das ist eine heillose Manier, dieses Fragmente-Auftischen.' Die Vorabdrucke einzelner Abschnitte aus Goethes *Wanderjahren* in Cottas *Taschenbuch für Damen."* *Jahrbuch des freien deutschen Hochstifts* (1992): 36-68.

———. *Poetik und Publikation. Goethes Veröffentlichungen in Musenalmanachen und literarischen Taschenbüchern. Mit einer Bibliographie der Erst- und autorisierten Folgedrucke literarischer Texte Goethes im Almanach (1773-1832).* Köln: Böhlau, 1997.

Dane, Gesa. *Die heilsame Toilette: Kosmetik und Bildung in Goethes "Der Mann von funfzig Jahren."* Göttingen: Wallstein, 1994.

Eisenstein, Elizabeth L. *The Printing Press as an Agent of Change: Communications and Cultural Transformations in Early-Modern Europe.* Cambridge: Cambridge UP, 1979. 2 vols.

Fröbe, Heinz. "Die Privilegierung der Ausgabe 'letzte Hand' Goethes sämtlicher Werke." *Archiv für Geschichte des Buchwesens* 2 (1960): 187-229.

Goethe, J. W. "Antwort auf eine Anfrage über *Wilhelm Meisters Wanderjahre."* Ed. Friedmar Apel. Goethe, *Sämtliche Werke* 19: 706.

———. "Anzeige von Goethe's sämmtlichen Werken vollständige Ausgabe letzter Hand." Ed. Anne Bohnenkamp. Goethe, *Sämtliche Werke* 22: 757-65.

———. *Briefe, Tagebücher und Gespräche 1823-1828.* Ed. Horst Fleig. Goethe, *Sämtliche Werke,* vol. 37.

———. "Geneigte Theilnahme an den *Wanderjahren."* Ed. Stefan Greif and Andrea Ruhlig. Goethe, *Sämtliche Werke* 21: 290-92.

———. *Sämtliche Werke. Briefe, Tagebücher und Gespräche.* 40 vols. Frankfurt am Main: Deutscher Klassiker, 1985-.

———. *Werke. Vollständige Ausgabe letzter Hand.* Stuttgart: Cotta, 1827-30. 40 vols.

———. *Wilhelm Meisters Wanderjahre.* Ed. Gerhard Neumann and Hans-Georg Dewitz. Goethe, *Sämtliche Werke,* vol. 10.

Golz, Jochen. "Das Goethe- und Schiller-Archiv in Geschichte und Gegenwart." *Das Goethe- und Schiller-Archiv 1896-1996.* Ed. Golz. Weimar: Böhlau, 1996. 13-70.

Grimm, Hermann. Vorwort [Foreword]. *Goethes Werke.* Vol. 1. Weimar: Böhlau, 1887. xi-xvii. 143 vols.

Hagen, Waltraud. *Die Drucke von Goethes Werken.* Berlin: Akademie, 1971.

———. "Goethes Ausgabe letzter Hand. Entstehung und Bedeutung." *Marginalien* 99 (1985): 1-22.

Herwig, Henriette. "Schule der Entsagung? Zur Kritik der moral-pädogogischen Instrumentalisierung von Goethes *Wanderjahren."* *Spuren-Signaturen-Spiegelungen. Zur Goethe-Rezeption in Europa.* Ed. Anke Bosse. Köln: Böhlau, 2000. 539-48.

Hohendahl, Peter Uwe. *Building a National Literature: The Case of Germany 1830-1870.* Ithaca: Cornell UP, 1989.

Johns, Adrian. *The Nature of the Book: Print and Knowledge in the Making.* Chicago: U of Chicago P, 1998.

Keen, Paul. *The Crisis of Literature in the 1790s: Print Culture and the Public Sphere.* Cambridge: Cambridge UP, 1999.

Kernan, Alvin. *Samuel Johnson and the Impact of Print.* Princeton: Princeton UP, 1989.

Kuhn, Dorothea, ed. *Goethe und Cotta: Briefwechsel 1797-1832.* Stuttgart: Cotta, 1979-83.

McGill, Meredith L. *American Literature and the Culture of Reprinting, 1834-1853.* Philadelphia: U of Pennsylvania P, 2003.

Millgate, Jane. *Scott's Last Edition: A Study in Publishing History.* Edinburgh: Edinburgh UP, 1987.

Neuhaus, Volker. "Die Archivfiktion in *Wilhelm Meisters Wanderjahre.*" *Euphorion* 62 (1968): 13-27.

Price, Leah. *The Anthology and the Rise of the Novel: From Richardson to George Eliot.* Cambridge: Cambridge UP, 2000.

[Pustkuchen, Johann]. *Wilhelm Meisters Wanderjahre.* Quedlinburg: Basse, 1821.

Redfield, Marc. *Aesthetic Ideology and the Bildungsroman.* Ithaca: Cornell UP, 1996.

Reiss, Hans. "*Wilhelm Meisters Wanderjahre.* Der Weg von der ersten zur zweiten Fassung." *Deutsche Vierteljahrsschrift* 39 (1965): 34-57.

Schellenberg, Renata. "The Genesis of Goethe's Last Novel: *Wilhelm Meisters Wanderjahre.*" *New German Review* 17 (2001): 47-63.

Schößler, Franziska. *Goethes Lehr- und Wanderjahre: Eine Kulturgeschichte der Moderne.* Tübingen: Francke, 2002.

Schütz, Friedrich. *Kritik der neuesten Cotta'schen Ausgabe von Goethe's Werken, nebst einem Plane zu einer vollständigen und kritisch geordneten Ausgabe derselben.* Hamburg: Nestler, 1828.

Siskin, Clifford. *The Work of Writing: Literature and Social Change in Britain, 1700-1830.* Baltimore: Johns Hopkins UP, 1998.

Suphan, Bernhard. Vorbericht [Preface]. *Goethes Werke.* Vol. 1. Weimar: Böhlau, 1887. xviii-xxv. 143 vols.

Taschenbuch für Damen auf das Jahr 1810. Stuttgart: Cotta, 1810.

Trunz, Erich. "Die *Wanderjahre* als 'Hauptgeschäft' im Winterjahr 1828/29." *Studien zu Goethes Alterswerken.* Frankfurt am Main: Suhrkamp, 1971. 99-121.

Ungern-Sternberg, Wolfgang von. "C. M. Wieland und das Verlagswesen seiner Zeit." *Archiv für Geschichte des Buchwesens* 14 (1974): 1213-1534.

Unseld, Siegfried. *Goethe und seine Verleger.* Frankfurt am Main: Insel, 1991.

Vaget, Hans. "Goethe the Novelist: On the Coherence of His Fiction." *Goethe's Narrative Fiction.* Ed. William J. Lillyman. New York: de Gruyter, 1983. 1-20.

Wolf, Thomas. *Pustkuchen und Goethe. Die Streitschrift als produktives Verwirrspiel.* Tübingen: Niemeyer, 1999.

Robin A. Clouser (essay date 2007)

SOURCE: Clouser, Robin A. "'Die pilgernde Törin': Genesis, Revaluation, and Mirroring in Goethe's *Wanderjahre.*" *Goethe Yearbook* 14 (2007): 171-206. Print.

[*In the following essay, Clouser provides a close reading of "The Pilgrim Fool," one of the novellas in* Wilhelm Meister's Travels. *Clouser's interpretation of the text reveals the young madwoman's status as a "wise fool" similar to King Lear's jester, presenting a timely intratextual lesson in the costs of jealousy and infidelity.*]

The critical revaluation of the structure and content of Goethe's ***Wanderjahre*** [***Wilhelm Meisters Wanderjahre***] in the past three decades has allowed most scholars to agree that the novel presents, not one narrative point of view, but many, indeed an "archive" of perspectives embodied in manuscripts and fragments from a wide cast of characters, assembled into the novel's present form by a fictional editor. Goethe is thereby credited with having anticipated the modern novel by his dispersal of the function of the author or narrator among a plethora of independently responsible narrators.[1] Because no particular narrator is privileged as authoritative, the "implied reader" is obliged to participate actively in appropriating and understanding the text, almost as if it were fragments of reality to be processed.[2] The primary structural principles by which Goethe organizes his materials and suggests ways for the reader to order and understand them are two: First, Wilhelm recedes as the center of attention and becomes a "string" on which to thread various stories and events that come to his attention.[3] Second, the various materials "mirror" each other—not necessarily in sequence or pairs but as pieces whose themes or motifs reinforce, recall, illuminate, relativize, or call into doubt the perspectives expressed in other "mirroring" pieces through the novel.[4]

As scholars reassess individual units of narrative in the ***Wanderjahre*** in light of this new paradigm of its archival structure, those elements, such as embedded novellas, that don't seem to "mirror" major plot lines, themes, or other narrative materials have tended to be devalued. **"Die** pilgernde Törin" is one such element. Although Goethe occupied himself with this novella off and on for a period of nearly 40 years, scholars have thus far linked it mainly to the love triangle of Hersilie-Felix-Wilhelm, which outwardly resembles the *Törin*'s situation between the elder and younger Revannes. The Hersilie triangle, however, turns out to be a dead end thematically: Wilhelm is already married, Hersilie sees only her own image in Felix's eyes, and the father-son relationship is in the end far more significant than either man's relationship with Hersilie.[5] It seems to me that **"Die pilgernde Törin,"** with its depiction of two noblemen in the main plot and a "noble youth" featured in her tragicomic song, in fact mirrors a much more significant element of the novel, the Lenardo saga. As Hans Vaget has pointed out, Goethe was preoccupied in all his novels with the reform of the nobility as the key to combating what he considered the ill effects of the French Revolution, and Lenardo becomes the primary vehicle of that theme in the *Wanderjahre*.[6] Issues of social class, personal responsibility, and treatment of women resonate in Goethe's handling of **"Die pilgernde Törin"** in ways that remind us of the social consciousness developed in the plot lines about Lenardo and "The Nut-Brown Maid." Lenardo serves as "the noble foil" to Wilhelm, one whose role, unlike Wilhelm's, grows more prominent in the novel, again making those narrative elements that mirror his themes important to our processing of the *Wanderjahre*.[7] The time has come for a critical revaluation of "Die pilgernde Törin" to flesh out its contribution to the chorus of voices in the *Wanderjahre*.

I. GENESIS AND EXTRATEXTUAL ARCHIVE

"Die pilgernde Thörinn" first appeared in German in the *Taschenbuch für Damen auf das Jahr 1809*.[8] It was one of Goethe's first ventures back into short fiction after the premature demise in 1795 of his framed-tale collection, ***Unterhaltungen deutscher Ausgewanderten.*** Later the tale was incorporated (spelled *Törin*) into both versions of the *Wanderjahre* (1821, 1829). The 1809 **"Thörinn"** looks both ways in Goethe's works. In its treatment of social strata, nonconformity, and sexual tartness, it would have fit nicely in the ***Unterhaltungen,*** whose announced topic was a frank discussion of how men and women disappoint and frustrate each other.[9] **"Die Thörinn"** was one of several tales slated for the ***Unterhaltungen*** before matronly protest in Weimar against Goethe's "piquant" taboo topics brought the series to an end.[10] **"Die pilgernde Törin"** also takes up themes of both *Wilhelm Meister* novels: love follies, wandering as a metaphor for intellectual and emotional growth, renunciation and self-control, and social reform. Yet despite its structural complexity, multiple voices, elegant finish, and pointed social commentary, this novella never received much critical attention even prior to the era of the archival paradigm. It was pigeonholed as "merely" a translation. Nevertheless, it is one of the best stories Goethe ever preserved for

posterity by embedding it in his own work. Erich Trunz recognized the tale as "ein Meisterwerk aus der Anfangszeit der neueren Novellistik."[11] Perhaps, however, it is too polished for its own good in an era when fragmentation has become one measure of "realism."

There are three major reasons for the tale's critical neglect: most scholars believe the tale is only a translation; they notice few "mirrorings" or parallels between the tale and other materials in the *Wanderjahre*; and they judge negatively the heroine's character and renunciation, a major point in a novel subtitled *Die Entsagenden.* Left almost entirely without comment are questions crucial to a basic understanding of the story and its relation to other materials: Is the tale to be considered realistic, a supernatural tale, or a satiric parable of social commentary? In what does the foolishness of the protagonist inhere? From what points of view is the reader invited to view her and other actors in the tale? Is she the chief fool or are the noblemen more foolish than she? Finally, how does this tale "mirror" other elements in the novel?

The French original of the **"Törin,"** "La folle en pèlerinage," appeared anonymously in H. A. O. Reichard's "Cahiers de lecture" in 1789 and enjoyed great popularity in Weimar; its author has never been discovered (HA [*Goethes Werke*] 8:568-69).[12] Goethe's secretary F. W. Riemer called Goethe's version "eine freie Übersetzung."[13] Because an overwhelming majority of scholars, however, regard Goethe's story as "merely a translation," it has been undeservedly neglected.[14] One scholar justifies ignoring it by saying Goethe could have written a better story himself; apparently unaware of the tradition in the novella, at least as old as Boccaccio's *Decameron,* of handing down choice tales, he charges that Goethe's use of the story borders on plagiarism.[15] One of the most recent commentators takes an earlier scholar's word on the "translation" and does not consult the source herself.[16] As recent research has shown for other tales reworked from French sources, however, Goethe made significant alterations to "La folle en pélerinage."[17] His changes sharpen the tale's social criticism, deepen its characters, and recapitulate themes about personal responsibility in matters of love that Goethe wrestled with all his life. Even if it were only a translation, the tale deserves analysis for what Goethe saw in it, for what it adds to the *Wanderjahre,* and for its droll commentary on men's and women's assumptions about each other in late eighteenth-century European society and how Goethe saw those roles changing in the nineteenth. By examining the changes Goethe made and the stages in his reaction to the original French tale, we can come to see what function Goethe believed it played in the *Wanderjahre* and why it preoccupied him for so long.

An idea of what Goethe liked about **"Die pilgernde Törin"** and the importance he attached to it is revealed by three changes between the 1821 and 1829 versions of the novel. First, he moved **"Die Törin"** forward, from sixth inset story (out of seven) in 1821—between **"Die neue Melusine"** and **"Wo stickt der Verräter"**—to second in 1829. By repositioning the social sophisticates of **"Die pilgernde Törin"** right after the arcadian **"Sankt Joseph der Zweite,"** Goethe shows the reader in quick succession at the start of his novel two highly contrasting views of love and its social function. Moreover, the self-centeredness of the Revannes stands out in greater contrast after the self-abnegation of "Sankt" Joseph.

Second, Goethe changed the narrators who introduce **"Die Törin."** In 1821 a minor character, the scapegrace Friedrich, gives it a deprecating lead-in: "Damit man sich recht durchdringen möge, welch ein Unterschied es sei zwischen einer verrückten Pilgerschaft, deren sich so manche in der Welt umhertreiben, und zwischen einem wohldurchdachten, glücklich eingeleiteten Unternehmen, wie das unsere. . . ."[18] Since Friedrich's own course through the *Meister*-novels is hardly "well-thought out" or "happily prepared" (he merely tags along with the others' grand plan to emigrate) his words are ironic, if not a joke at his own expense.[19] **"Die Törin"** depicts male as well as female foibles, another possible reason for Friedrich's antipathy. But Goethe's contemporary readers, especially the men, could easily miss or ignore the males' foibles and take Friedrich's opinion as Goethe's own. A desire to spotlight the tale's ironic view of irresponsible noblemen in a male-dominated world could account for why Goethe relocated the novella to so prominent a position in the final form of the *Wanderjahre*.[20]

In the 1829 version, a major and respected character, considered by several critics a locus of Goethe's sympathy, introduces the tale positively: Hersilie.[21] This cheerfully ironic young woman introduces **"Die pilgernde Törin"** by challenging Wilhelm to say if he has read many tales more artful than this: "Sie sollten sagen, ob Ihnen viel Artigeres vorgekommen ist" (51). Further, as a woman Hersilie endorses the sentiments of the heroine-fool: "Ein verrücktes Mädchen tritt auf! das möchte keine sonderliche Empfehlung sein, aber wenn ich jemals närrisch werden möchte, wie mir manchmal die Lust ankommt, so wär' es auf diese Weise" (51).[22] Instantly an alert reader would ask why young women would "want to go crazy." The patriarchal social situations of the novella provide an answer. As we have seen, the tale's plot also foreshadows Hersilie's own situation later in the novel; she too will be entangled romantically between a father and son. Hence the reader of the 1829 *Wanderjahre* is induced by Hersilie's charming empathy and implied similar suffering to think well of the "fool" in her favorite tale. If we agree that the time Hersilie has invested fictionally to translate the tale tells us something about her as a character, must we not also conclude that it tells us something about Goethe the author? He's the one who actually labored off and on for nearly two decades to re-work and translate various segments of it, and then fussed for two more decades to set

the tale properly in his novel. Only a tale that was important to him would have received such attention.

The third change from the 1821 to the 1829 edition, in contrast, eliminates a hint that calls the reader's attention to wandering, love-haunted fools. Bahr points out that the very first printing of the 1821 edition began with two poems that precede even the title page, followed by nine more poems on unpaginated pages before the first chapter.[23] One of those poems mentions a wanderer-fool:

Immer sehnt sich fort das Herz,
Ich weiss nicht recht ob himmelwärts;
Fort aber will es hin und hin
Und möchte vor sich selber fliehn.
Und fliegt es an der Liebsten Brust,
Da ruht's im Himmel unbewusst;
Des Lebens Strudel reisst es fort,
Und immer hängt's an Einem Ort;
Was es gewollt, was es verlor,
Es bleibt zuletzt sein eigner Tor.[24]

This 1821 epigraph alerts the reader of the *Wanderjahre* to any mention of a "fool"—a necessary strategy when **"Die Törin"** appeared at the end of the novel—and also to the theme of Wilhelm and Lenardo's pilgrimages, to "flee themselves" and their unfortunate previous actions, and make themselves worthy of "heaven" with their beloved Natalie and "Nut-Brown Maid."[25] The *Törin* similarly hopes that her noble fiancé will also someday reach self-knowledge and confess his own guilt in injuring her and the miller-maid; but the last she saw him, he was displacing his guilt onto others. Perhaps Goethe believed that a poetic signpost to be on the alert for fools was unnecessary in the 1829 edition, both because he had moved **"Die Törin"** to a more prominent position—thus serving itself as a red flag for that theme—and because Lenardo's saga had been brought to a more satisfactory "completion."

These 1821 poems remind us that when we think about what "mirrorings" and resonances were available to Goethe's contemporary readers, we have to remember who his audience was and that materials lying outside the covers of the *Wanderjahre* may have seemed to them to belong to their experience of Goethe's works, i.e., to the archive relevant to its interpretation. Bahr notes that the fictional editor of the 1821 edition says that it was "twenty years in the coming," thus inviting readers to remember both the *Lehrjahre* and other materials—novellas, relevant poems—that had been published in the interval. The eleven poems before and after the title page, Bahr notes, also serve to place the *Wanderjahre* "within Goethe's autobiography."[26] Vaget points out that "Goethe had no clearly identified public," no "large homogeneous reading public with fully developed forms of literary communication"; rather he wrote for "what was only a relatively small circle of friends" whom he needed to "educate . . . in the art of reading"[27]—and who were intimately familiar with prior stages of Goethe's treatment of **"Die Törin."** All the more reason why Goethe's contemporary readers—and we—are licensed to assume that previous materials related to **"Die Törin"** may also "mirror" themes in the *Wanderjahre* and be relevant to its interpretation.

II. THE EXTRATEXTUAL ARCHIVE ON "DIE TÖRIN"

The basic plot materials of **"Die pilgernde Torin"** play on the primacy of social caste in late eighteenth-century European courtship. The tale consists of two love-triangles. In the first, told in a flashback-like ballad sung by the *Törin,* the young noblewoman was a noble youth's "edles Liebchen" and fiancée (57), while a miller's daughter was the other object of his attention. In the second triangle, told in the narrative present of the tale, the well-born girl, now a mysterious wanderer, is courted by a "princely rich" father and son. How it happens that despite all these courtships the *Törin* still wanders alone in the world is the emotional burden of the tale.

Goethe's first response to the material after encountering it in 1789 was to try to translate the ballad. He did not succeed to his satisfaction until 1798. In the meantime he wrote three other ballads of his own to accompany it—a preoccupation that shows how deeply the material penetrated his authorial attention.[28] This ballad cycle forms, in effect, a prologue or *Vorgeschichte* to Goethe's version of the novella. Goethe even called it "einen kleinen Roman.[29]

In his ballads, Goethe is at pains to reveal the miller girl's point of view and motivate her eventual mysterious betrayal of the youth. Goethe's *Müllerin* is resentful of the reputation for promiscuity that peasant girls, especially millers' daughters, had in society. The theme of bad repute is present in the original French ballad, but the miller girl's indignation, possible virtue, and attitude toward the youth during their courtship remain unstated until Goethe's cycle. Goethe was especially sensitive to such a situation, having seen Duke Carl August's rather cavalier relations with young peasant women in Weimar-Saxony, and having himself been accused of deserting a high-born platonic love, Frau von Stein, for the lower-born Christiane Vulpius. Charlotte von Stein made her own translation of the French ballad, having apparently also been struck by the parallel.[30] Unlike Frau von Stein, Goethe shows sympathy for both young women, high born and low, in his ballads and tale.

Goethe's ballad cycle expands the social setting, characters and plot of the first love triangle. In **"Der Edelknabe und die Müllerin,"** the noble youth suggests to the miller's daughter that they hide in a bower at noon while she rests from haying; the *Müllerin* says, "Das gäbe Geschichten." He offers her his arms to rest in; she declines with an ironic word-play on her reputation and his fine dark clothes, evincing loyalty to her class and the view that

he is a rather perishable suitor: "Mitnichten! / Denn wer die artige Müllerin küsst, / Auf der Stelle verraten ist. / Euer schönes dunkles Kleid / Tät mir leid / So weiss zu färben. / Gleich und gleich! so allein ists recht! / . . . / Ich liebe mir den Müllerknecht; / An dem ist nichts zu verderben" (154-55). In **"Der Junggesell und der Mühlbach,"** the *Müllerin* sends the mill stream off to "wander" with a "joke" ("Sie lacht dich an und sagt im Scherz / Nun wandre!"; 156), prefiguring how she will pack the youth off on a "pilgrimage" with her trick in **"Der Müllerin Verrat"**—Goethe's version of the original French ballad and the third in his cycle. But in the fourth and last ballad, **"Der Müllerin Reue,"** Goethe has the young woman seek out the youth and declare, "Ich habe das nahe, das einzige Glück / Verscherzet" (161).

Thus Goethe resolves some of the mystery of the original ballad: He motivates the miller girl's rude, unheard-of treatment of her lover through class resentment, then softens her into a more sympathetic person who was touched by love after all, not the hard-hearted trickster her bitter lover thinks her when she turns him out. The ambivalence the *Müllerin* feels about a noble lover—accepting his favors, yet rejecting him before he can reject her (as she expects he eventually must)—becomes less cryptic in Goethe's ballad cycle.

We shall see more of Goethe's changes in **"Der Müllerin Verrat"** (or *"Romanze,"* as it is known in the tale). But to continue the gist of Goethe's ballad sequence and segue into the plot of the tale, this unheard-of novellistic event—a miller's daughter turning her nearly naked noble lover out in the snow after a love-night—made a tasty bit of gossip in the town and came to the ears of his fiancée (the future *Törin*). Rather than bear his infidelity in silence, as upperclass sweethearts and wives were expected to do in the days of Bourbon kings and marriages of convenience, the young lady does an unheard-of thing of her own. She refuses to feel forced by social example to accept her lover's behavior in silence, but instead feels "forced to bear her sorrows out into the world" ("Des raisons dont elle ne devoit compte á personne, la forçoient à promener ses douleurs dans le monde," 867;[31] "Ursachen, von denen sie niemand Rechenschaft schuldig sei, nötigten sie, ihre Schmerzen in der Welt herumzuführen," 53). The necessity, of course, lies in her own mind, in her self-respect and dignity of spirit. Like the socially alienated persona J. J. Rousseau created for himself, the young noblewoman stands up for true emotion and fidelity between the sexes and sets off walking. Dressed as if for a ball, she steps outside her decadent culture and becomes "une vagabonde," "eine Landstreicherin" (867; 52). The open countryside seems to her, for all its insecurities, less hurtful than the artificial world she left. Is she mad, or a droll-earnest commentator on mad times, like Rousseau? Given the diagrammatic starkness of the social context in the novella—enhanced by Goethe's ballads—it seems to me the *Törin* is to be taken as an affecting character in a satire or parable of social criticism, not a naturalistic person suitable for scholarly scolding.[32]

If for nothing else than the invention of these two female characters—the insubordinate *Müllerin* and the noble vagabond—the anonymous French author (male or female?) deserves the compliment Goethe paid by writing his own ballad cycle based on them and incorporating these two strong female characters into his own work.

As the *Müllerin* stands in an inferior social position to the youth, so the "foolish pilgrim" of the novella in the **Wanderjahre** is at a disadvantage vis-à-vis her wealthy father-and-son suitors. But in her case, the disadvantage is a chosen rather than an actual class disadvantage. Herr von Revanne is introduced as so wealthy in land, parks, manufactories and dependencies that he is a virtual prince in all but title (51). When she comes into his mansion, the beautiful pilgrim passes every test of social graces and gentility her host can muster. He is forced to admit that she shows all the subtle grace, charm, tact, wit, fine manners, and decorativeness of a lady of his own class (54, 56). As part of her "foolish" reaction to her fiancé's infidelity, however, she refuses to divulge the one datum necessary to certify her as "worthy" of Herr von Revanne's contemplated marriage proposal, or that of his similarly smitten son: her (presumably noble) family name.

On this insubstantiality, Revanne's courtship is wrecked. The pilgrim—as a lesson to the caste that formed her well and served her ill, or to evade any match since she still loves the youth—insists on being loved for who she is, not for her ancestry. She is "perfect" (52, 58) according to all their standards. Why then does she need a noble name? But Revanne is unable to see past the social forms, in spite of the lovely bride apparently within his grasp. When he finally deigns to suggest that his affection for the undocumented young lady could still lead to a closer tie, he destroys his own goal with an insulting offer of a "secret" though "legal" marriage, a "mistake" he later regrets (61).

Thus both Goethe's ballads and the adapted tale critique how class distinctions—or people's allowing such divides to influence them—hinder men and women from acting honestly and justly in love, from knowing their own hearts and acting on them—a bitter lesson that we later see Lenardo also working through in his own long pilgrimage to deserve his non-nobleborn "Nut-Brown Maid."

The French tale came so appositely to Goethe because he had long been exercised by the stresses of cross-caste romance. At age eighteen, in a letter of 3 Nov. 1767 to his friend Behrisch, Goethe threw himself into the state of mind of a prince contemplating the prospect of an arranged marriage, even as he rhapsodizes about a sweetheart (probably low-born) whom he cherishes for the sake of "love" rather than "interest": "O möchte ich doch ... mein eigner Herr seyn, um jener schröcklichen Verbindung entsagen

zu können die durch Interesse und nicht durch Liebe geknüpft ward. O wie hasse ich meine zukünftige Gemahlin. ... Sie mag gut seyn, ... aber Sie ist nicht du. ... Ich will sie heurahten, ich muss, aber mein Herz soll sie nicht haben. ..." Casting himself then as the prince married to his intended wife, Goethe in turn idealizes the noblewoman and thinks the prince must feel "ashamed" of his previous thoughts ("er muss sich doch manchmal schämen"). Goethe thinks that he would feel "crazy" and suicidal in such a position, that he had committed the equivalent of love's original sin: "So was, von so einer [edelen] Frau gesagt zu haben, würde mich toll machen, ich würde mich des Paradieses und meiner Eva unwürdig halten, und mich an den ersten Baum hängen. ..."

The *pilgernde Törin,* like the noble *Eva* Goethe imagined, feels the insult of exactly such a situation, and she reacts to it. Indeed, one could argue that she is the most sympathetic and three-dimensional noblewoman in either volume of *Wilhelm Meister,* the match of Hersilie and the *Schöne Seele,* who similarly comment on male vacillation and hypocrisy in love. The *Törin* achieves this roundedness by voicing and acting on her indignation about the social strictures that bind women more than men in eighteenth-century European society. She refuses to suffer in silence, nor to allow her hand and heart to be disposed of by men. Goethe sympathized with *all* sides in this social muddle. The torture of postponing love and sexual fulfillment to wait for a socially sanctioned mate, Goethe implies, led many a youth—at least those with a conscience—to feel that they ban themselves from "paradise" with their intended "Eve" if they meantime sought emotional sustenance from a more sexually available sweetheart. Society itself, Goethe implies, is out of joint. Artificial social constrictions contribute to people's folly in love.

Most scholars overlook the social criticism in **"Die pilgernde Törin,"** and instead fault the heroine for the tale's failure to culminate in that great society-affirming happy ending—marriage. But does this society deserve to be affirmed? (Do we criticize the **Wanderjahre** itself for not culminating in the reunion of all separated lovers?) Heinrich Düntzer set the tone: "Wie anmuthig auch die ganze Erzählung gehalten ist, so widerstrebt sie doch dem reinen Gefühle, da der Mangel an jeder weiblichen Zartheit und Scheu uns nothwendig verletzt."[33] Other critics follow him in condemning the pilgrim's "unfeminine" nonconformity. Arthur Henkel overlooks her courage in changing her passive status and insists she is emotionally static: "Die Treue der pilgernden Törin ist bloss gefrorene Leidenschaft und verhärtet überhaupt ihre Fähigkeit, zu lieben."[34] Hans Reiss considers her driven by only one motive: "Die Wanderschaft dieser Pilgerin geschieht nicht aus Entsagung, sondern aus Trotz; sie ist reine Torheit."[35] Meanwhile, no one scolds Wilhelm and Lenardo for staying true to their beloved women. Shouldn't the *Törin* be praised for continuing to hope her fiancé will reach a similar enlightenment on the "pilgrimage" he apparently set off on from the mill—even as she actively pursues her own pilgrimage of fidelity and social enlightenment?[36]

As the anonymous French author invokes and all literary critics ought to have recognized, there is a long literary tradition of "wise fools" who are not as foolish as they appear. Goethe knew, for example, Shakespeare's Falstaff and King Lear's Fool. Wise fools seem foolish because they don't follow convention, yet their nonconformity proves to be a deeper wisdom. They serve the literary function of challenging cultural assumptions and revealing the folly of supposedly sounder characters. The wise fool is often devoted to a substantive rather than an abstract ideal. In *Henry IV*, Part I, Falstaff ruminates on the emptiness of the word "honor" to one who is dead; he thinks life more precious than the bluster of honor (5.1:131-37). King Lear's Fool mocks his master's empty title after he has given away his authority: "Thou hadst little wit in thy bald crown when thou gav'st thy golden one away" (1.4:177-78). The *Törin* is devoted to the substance of fidelity, rather than the nominal show of noble marriage.

Like other wise fools, the *Törin* is not without personal weakness or fault. Yet by the accident of her fiancé's public scandal and by her strong sense of her own worth and rights, she has been distanced from her society's courtship rituals. Now she wanders the world as a sadly conscious satirist, trying to evoke some critical self-distance in her countrymen about their habits in love. Men cannot help being attracted to her beauty, but she has a message for them, as her last speech to the son makes clear. She is paradoxically both strongly detached from and attached to her society's ideals. She stands up for the ideal of emotional and sexual fidelity that society inculcated in her, even after she discovers that her beloved and the society don't apply it to themselves. By her exaggerated pilgrimage of fidelity, she reveals the bankruptcy of fidelity in her culture. The tale is a classic feminist critique of the folly of a double-standard sexist code of behavior, though those words didn't exist in Goethe's day.

The anonymous narrator gives us clues that we are to read the pilgrim as a "wise fool." On the one hand he characterizes her as "wahnsinning vor Treue" (62). On the other he subtly calls into question the very premise of her "foolishness" and relativizes the concept of *Torheit*: "Nun will ich die Torheit eines verständigen Frauenzimmers erzählen, um zu zeigen, dass Torheit oft nichts weiter sei als Vernunft unter einem andern Äussern" (60). Scholars have been quick to point out her "Torheit," but no one to date has discussed her "Vernunft," how she is a "sensible" or "intelligent" young woman. Similarly neglected is how other characters compare with her in wisdom or foolishness.

Goethe was attracted to the untraditional questions this tale raises: Is it "foolish" to expect fidelity from young men as well as young women in love? Should class and gender privileges define one's options in love and marriage? With this novella Goethe "mirrors" in both *Meister*-novels the problems that artificial social criteria impose on young men like Wilhelm and Lenardo when they fall in love, and the risks they take to fill socially proscribed emotional needs. *Müllerin* and *Törin* mirror the contrast between sexually available and exuberant actresses like Mariane or Philine, and emotionally straitened noblewomen like the *Gräfin* or Natalie whose husbands are chosen for them. Small wonder that Wilhelm spends his time puzzling over why he acts as he does in love and why he idealizes whom. Unlike the *Törin* and the young Goethe, however, the young Wilhelm lacks the social consciousness to arrive at a true analysis of his own feelings and his society. Lenardo develops that social consciousness only after his Grand Tour.[37] But both young men's reflections and puzzlement represent a virtue. Most of the *Meister*-novels' male characters, like the Revannes and Lothario, simply rationalize their folly and cruelty in love without reflecting on their assumptions, acts, or social culture. Looking back, we can see that Goethe has represented the persistent weakness of hubris even in a reform-minded character like Lothario by showing how cavalier he is with women: Lydie and Aurelie, for example.[38]

III. NARRATIVE VOICES: FRENCH AND GERMAN

Part of the wit of this novella (and perhaps why it has fooled critics) is that the pilgrim's critique of society is delivered not by her but through the men she baffles.[39] They quote her extensively, letting her strong voice be heard. But the bulk of the narration is divided largely between a man head over heels in love with her—Revanne—and an unnamed narrator (inherited by Goethe from the French), Revanne's confidante. This family friend also quotes and characterizes both the younger Revanne (52, 60-64) and the *Törin*. This narrator offers wry insight into his amorous friends' "mistakes," and even offers criticism. About the *Törin*, he is more insightful than the Revannes but still professes puzzlement—though that may be tact and a storyteller's finesse. The unnamed narrator thus explains the thoughts, emotions, and unconscious blunders of the Revannes, but leaves intact the aura of mystery around the enigmatic wanderer. Other voices also speak: The "noble youth" holds forth in the *Törin*'s song, we remember his and the *Müllerin*'s voices from Goethe's ballads, and the *Törin* herself rounds out the six voices of the tale.

The unnamed narrator begins the tale with a characterization of his noble friend. Herr von Revanne stands near the top of society's pyramid. He is described in the first paragraph as possessing a castle "worthy of a prince" and being, in person and power, a prince in all but name: "so ist er durch sein Ansehn und durch das Gute, das er stiftet, wirklich ein Fürst" (51). He is relatively enlightened, praised by the narrator for employing half the population for six miles around. He appears a model citizen, yet shortly shows himself a fool as well. Revanne is the second most important character in the tale, for he embodies the weaknesses and prejudices of his society, as well as its strengths. Despite his flaws, he claims at least some of our sympathy because of his urgent desire to be loved.

When we first meet Revanne, he is carrying a book and a rifle and strolling around his estate to the main road, where he plans to rest in a sheltered arbor by a spring. In an intriguing change, Goethe omits the original tale's double reference to winter in this opening scene. In the French, the arbor shelters travelers "even in winter when the leaves are down"; the grass and purling fountain "seem to warm the winter" as they refresh in hotter seasons:

> Une espèce de bocage où le voyageur ne peut s'empêcher de s'arrêter, l'hyver même où les arbres dépouillés offrent encore un abri contre les vents, & la fontaine qui coule entre leurs souches, encore des gasons & des eaux qui semblent rechauffer l'hiver, comme elles rafraichissent dans la belle saison.

(FA [*Sämtliche Werke*] 1.10:866)

These images are gratuitous in the French version as far as setting the scene is concerned, for it is not winter; there is "a half-light of verdure" ("le demi-jour de la verdure," FA 1.10:868). The images of winter are instead oblique references to the gentleman's age; they presage the melancholy failure of his courtship, late in life, of the pretty young wanderer he will shortly meet by the spring. Herr von Revanne will not be warmed in his old age by the sheltering and revivifying love of a young and bubbling nymph-like wife.

Goethe keeps most of this passage, even the later comparison of the pilgrim to a nymph, but not the winter references. Why did he not avail himself of this atmospheric imagery of old age and winter? Perhaps he wanted to avoid having his character suggest, even remotely, the classic stereotype of the *Senex,* the "old man" in Greek and Roman comedy, whose attempts to marry a young wife are inappropriate, bumblingly foolish, and predestined to defeat. As in **"Der Mann von fünfzig Jahren"** later in the *Wanderjahre,* Goethe wants us to take the older man seriously as a person, though not as a person beyond criticism. Revanne's foolishness is not simply that he wants to marry again at an older age; that, in Goethe's view, is not automatically a laughable motive. Revanne's folly lies elsewhere, and we are forced to suspend our judgment of Goethe's male protagonist until we see how Revanne behaves as a suitor.

The book and rifle are objects that tell us about Revanne's life and values. The book implies he is an educated and cultured man, traits that heighten the irony of his later irrationality. The rifle suggests his power, a masterful masculinity; it also hints of lurking danger and the need for caution. Yet Revanne's defenses, while adequate for highway robbers and wolves, ironically prove no match for the perils of meeting a highly attractive, cultured young lady along the road.

When Revanne first sees her, the narrator relates: "Sein Buch fiel ihm aus den Händen, überrascht wie er war" (52). Revanne's surprise is in response to her striking beauty and poise: "Die Pilgerin mit den schönsten Augen von der Welt und einem Gesicht, durch Bewegung angenehm belebt, zeichnete sich an Körperbau, Gang und Anstand dergestalt aus, daß er unwillkürlich von seinem Platze aufstand und nach der Straße blickte, um das Gefolge kommen zu sehen, das er hinter ihr vermutete." Startled by her unexpected appearance in this place, Revanne is depicted as physically out of control, first dropping his book, then jumping up "involuntarily." Turning the narration over temporarily to the afflicted one, the narrator quotes Revanne's confession that the beauty's sigh as she seated herself by the spring created an instant affinity in his breast: "Seltsame Wirkung der Sympathie! . . . dieser Seufzer ward in der Stille von mir erwidert." With no attendants to create a diversion to give him time to think nor a formal social context in which to approach her, Revanne falls into a self-admitted dither: "Ich blieb stehen, ohne zu wissen, was ich sagen oder tun sollte." Her beauty overwhelms his faculties: "Meine Augen waren nicht hinreichend, diese Vollkommenheiten zu fassen." From his words we gather he is literally staring. Idealistic projection is also evident in his summation: "Es war die schönste Frauengestalt, die man sich denken konnte!" (52). The wealthy, successful nobleman is immobilized, made speechless, rendered defenseless by one beautiful woman. Thus in spite of what the title leads us to expect, the narrator suggests that when the two main characters first meet, it is Herr von Revanne, not the poised and calm pilgrim, who suddenly finds himself losing self-control and acting the fool. Erotic attraction to her beauty has disarmed him. At once she and we know at least one of this great man's weaknesses.[40]

Revanne tries to size up the stranger from the evidence before him, though his critical faculties are clouded. He notes the discrepancy that her lovely clothes are more appropriate for a ball than for wandering: "Sie war angezogen, als wenn sie zum Balle gehen sollte. Auf eine Landstreicherin deutete nichts an ihr, und doch war sie's; aber eine beklagenswerte, eine verehrungswürdige" (52). On what basis other than appearance, not having even spoken to her at this point, does he judge her "worthy of sympathy and respect"? These words may be nostalgic as Revanne looks back on the episode, but like his responsive sigh, they suggest an irrational predisposition toward feminine beauty. Most of all, Revanne is astonished to find the young woman traveling by herself. He expects anyone dressed so daintily as a lady of privilege to be accompanied by an entourage and chaperone. This is his, and our, first evidence of the young woman's folly: she travels alone and undefended where, in Revanne's judgment, even a man might need a weapon.

Revanne manages to appear composed when he finally speaks, to ask if she travels alone. In her answer we hear the voice of one disillusioned with her supposed protectors: "Ja, mein Herr ... ich bin allein auf der Welt. ... Eltern hab' ich, und Bekannte genug; aber keine Freunde" (52). Revanne, however, at once disputes her view in a pseudo-compliment with a hidden sting: "Daran ... können Sie wohl unmöglich schuld sein. Sie haben eine Gestalt und gewiss auch ein Herz, denen sich viel vergeben lässt" (52). To have no friends and be reduced to wandering, he implies, she must be guilty of a considerable offense, since they would have forgiven her "much" for the sake of her beauty. But he also hides something from himself with his clever words. He thinks he neutralizes the power of her attraction over him by covertly insulting her, but instead he reveals his own weakness: that he too would probably forgive even a bad heart, a bad character, for the sake of a beautiful figure.

Since he sees the pilgrim is schooled enough in polite repartee to be "wounded" by his subtle reproach, Revanne prides himself that he has discovered she is "well-bred": "Sie fühlte die Art von Vorwurf, den mein Kompliment verbarg, und ich machte mir einen guten Begriff von ihrer Erziehung" (52-53). Cutting, convoluted language is thus ironically identified as a mark by which the upperclass recognize each other.

The pilgrim is forced to justify herself. At first she uses the advantage Revanne has already proved vulnerable to, as we see in his superlative-packed narration: "Sie öffnete gegen mich zwei himmlische Augen vom vollkommensten, reinsten Blau, durchsichtig und glänzend ..." (53). But the pretty pilgrim also meets (and by the end of the tale even exceeds) Revanne's skill at verbal jousting. Her reply is an odd mix of naïveté and strategy:

> Sie könne es einem Ehrenmanne, wie ich zu sein scheine, nicht verdenken, wenn er ein junges Mädchen, das er allein auf der Landstrasse treffe, einigermassen verdächtig halte. ... Sie habe gefunden, daß die Gefahren, die man für ihr Geschlecht befürchte, nur eingebildet seien und daß die Ehre eines Weibes, selbst unter Straßenräubern, nur bei Schwäche des Herzens und der Grundsätze Gefahr laufe.
>
> (53)

She probably underestimates the danger of traveling alone, but she is not simply naïve. She implies she knows what highwaymen might do and, by invoking them while calling her present companion a "man of honor," subtly challenges him to behave respectably.

The pretty pilgrim makes it a clear stipulation of any further acquaintance that Revanne not pry into her origins. Four times in thirty lines she repeats this message: "obgleich niemand das Recht habe, sie auszuforschen"; "Ursachen, von denen sie niemand Rechenschaft schuldig sei"; "Namen und Vaterland verberge sie"; "[sie] verhehle

nicht, daß sie über Vaterland und Familie nicht befragt sein wolle. Darauf bestimme man sich" (53). For the moment, Revanne (with politeness rather than sincerity, since he later presses her further) assures the stranger, "daß ich keineswegs an ihrem guten Herkommen zweifle, so wenig als an einem achtungswerten Betragen" (53). Nonetheless Revanne with tactless tact goes on to point out that a young woman who travels alone risks both her virtue and her reputation: "Ich versetzte ... daß ich, ungeachtet einer lebhaften Neugierde, nicht weiter in sie dringen wolle, vielmehr mich durch ihre nähere Bekanntschaft zu überzeugen wünsche, dass sie überall für ihren Ruf ebenso besorgt sei als für ihre Tugend" (53). Revanne insists on getting to know her even as he abjures curiosity; he challenges her to prove her virtue and good reputation through better acquaintance. Revanne seems to be posing a rational (although demeaning) task, but in fact he is revealing more the state of his heart than of his head.

The pilgrim answers that it is for reputation's sake that she conceals her name and origin, though she finds reputation a thing more suppositional than real: "Namen und Vaterland verberge sie, eben um des Rufs willen, der denn doch am Ende meistenteils weniger Wirkliches als Mutmaßliches enthalte" (53). Like a wise fool, she prefers substance to rumor or reputation. Certainly there is irony in a young woman's virtue being suspect when she puts herself in a position of relying on men's honor. Her "folly" seems consciously calculated to throw a burden of self-examination back onto any man she talks to. How will Revanne stand the test?

To show the pilgrim's verbal defenses is not to deny the folly of her risk, if we consider the narrative for a moment as realistic. Her belief in her fellow human beings is touching, even perhaps philosophically admirable, but dangerous. Still, she isn't so credulous as not to take precautions: "Übrigens gehe sie nur zu Stunden und auf Wegen, wo sie sich sicher glaube, spreche nicht mit jedermann und verweile manchmal an schicklichen Orten ..." (53). Though she has been safe so far, she does not estimate fully the danger of traveling alone. Her second folly is her decision, after only a brief conversation, to accept the invitation of a stranger to go home with him: "Sie macht keine Schwierigkeit, sie geht mit ..." (54). Perhaps she feels that after her fiancé's betrayal, no other potential injury matters. Or she trusts in her own ability to judge character.

Revanne's naïveté is also evident in this decision. After the briefest of interviews, on the slimmest information ("Ohne daher die Sache viel näher zu betrachten"; 54), he invites an eccentric stranger home, potentially endangering life, hearth, and family should she turn out to be, say, an arsonist or madwoman. Based on her repartee and protests of innocence ("Äußerungen dieser Art ließen keine Geistesverwirrung bei der schönen Abenteurerin argwohnen"; 54), he judges her not dangerous. Is it any less foolish for a man to invite an odd stranger home than for a woman to travel alone? Revanne makes a judgment call that she is of sound character. She does the same about him. They are both judging on appearances, trusting their ability to size each other up correctly after a few minutes of banter. Herr von Revanne, however, takes the greater risk because he has more to lose and endangers more people than just himself.

When the narrator takes over again, he suggests with the insight of a fellow male that Revanne is not at all making a calm, rational judgment of character, but is driven emotionally by beauty, competitive male instincts, fear, and an overheated imagination. The narrator recreates Revanne's internal irrational train of thought: "Herr von Revanne ... vermutete nun, daß man sie vielleicht gegen ihre Neigung habe verheiraten wollen. Hernach fiel er darauf, ob es nicht etwa gar Verzweiflung aus Liebe sei; und wunderlich genug, wie es aber mehr zu gehen pflegt, indem er ihr Liebe für einen andern zutraute, verliebt er sich selbst und fürchtete, sie möchte weiterreisen" (54). Jealousy of this "other," whom the beauty (perhaps) desperately loves, precipitates Revanne's falling in love with her himself, even though it seems a bit early for that. His competitive male urges—against an altogether hypothetical rival—contribute to his haste and folly, and he "fears" to lose the opportunity to win her. The narrator emphasizes how common such emotional non sequiturs are: "und wunderlich genug, indem es aber mehr zu gehen pflegt. ..." He shows how Revanne's imagination inflates her beauty: "Er konnte seine Augen nicht von dem schönen Gesicht wegwenden. ... Niemals zeigte, wenn es je Nymphen gab, auf den Rasen sich eine schönere hingestreckt; und die etwas romanhafte Art dieser Zusammenkunft verbreitete einen Reiz, dem er nicht zu widerstehen vermochte" (54). The references to myth and romantic fiction reveal the extent to which Revanne is in the grip of his own fantasies—as well as the narrator's articulate ironic distance from those genres. In short, Revanne's critical faculties have been rendered inoperative by his libido. "Ohne daher die Sache viel näher zu betrachten, bewog Herr Revanne die schöne Unbekannte, sich nach dem Schloße führen zu lassen" (54). Though Revanne "prevailed upon" her, the beautiful stranger is more in control of self and events than he.

Male vulnerability to beauty is a weakness Goethe is aware of throughout the *Lehr-* and *Wanderjahre,* so this tale and its gentle ridicule of Revanne's avidity came welcome to his purpose. Goethe's version emphasizes the pilgrim's beauty in Revanne's eyes even more than the original. While the French describes her as having "un visage agréablement animé par la fatigue" (FA 1.10:866), Goethe removes any hint of fatigue and lets her physical fitness make her more attractive: she is "durch Bewegung angenehm belebt" (52). In the French, Revanne "has eyes only for her" ("n'ayant que des yeux pour la regarder"); Goethe escalates even this intensity so that Revanne's eyes are "inadequate" to her "perfections": "Meine Augen waren nicht hinreichend,

diese Vollkommenheiten zu fassen" (52). M. Revanne leads home "l'inconnue" (FA 1.10:869), Herr von Revanne "die schöne Unbekannte" (54).

Goethe carefully frees the pilgrim from one accusation often directed at beauties by smitten men. The French text frequently uses "charming" and "charms" to describe her (FA 1.10:866, 868, 869, 872, 874). Goethe substitutes "liebenswürdig," "schön," or "mit aller Anmut begabt" for these; he uses "die Anmut ihres Wesens" (59) for "les charmes de sa figure" (873), and instead of "qui m'a charmé" (874), has Revanne say, "die mich ganz eingenommen hatte" (60). These locutions have etymologies not tied to witchcraft; they avoid imputing a sorceress's spell-casting wiles and guilt to the pilgrim, and leave the responsibility for male adoration to the male.

Only twice in the novella does Goethe use "charming," and they occur in cases where other factors besides the pilgrim contribute to the "magic." When narrating how the "fictionlike quality of their meeting spread a charm that [Revanne] couldn't resist," Goethe uses "Reiz" (54) to translate "charme" (868); it is clear that Revanne's imagination collaborates in this spell. During her musical performance, Goethe renders "sa voix vraiment enchanteresse" (872) quite exactly as "ihre Stimme war wirklich bezaubernd" (57); it is not solely her voice but also the magic power of music that charms Revanne here. Goethe's banishment of the idea that either sex might unfairly entrap the other extends to the younger Revanne, who is not allowed, as he does in the French, to try to "charm" the pilgrim ("Il s'attacha discrettement à charmer l'Inconnue," 874), but must try to "win" her: "Erst suchte er vorsichtig die Unbekannte zu gewinnen ..." (60).

Goethe also frees Herr von Revanne from certain malign overtones in the original. Twice Goethe changes a reference to Revanne's "flattering" himself (872, 874) into "hoping" (58, 60), making him seem less pompous. Another change clears him of a more serious character flaw. When M. Revanne relates how he "again wounded" the pilgrim by raising the subject of her "virtue," his reference to her as "my pilgrim" sounds offensively possessive: "Ma Pèrlerine parut encore blessée de ces derniers mots ..." (FA 1.10:868). M. Revanne implies, however unconsciously, that she is his to abuse. Goethe avoids such proprietary feelings and the *Schadenfreude* by having Herr von Revanne say simply, "Diese Worte schienen sie abermals zu verletzen" (53), leaving open at least the possibility that Revanne is surprised his words cut so deeply.

At Revanne's home the pretty pilgrim proves that his judgment and her protests of good character were justified: "sie ... zeigt sich als eine Person, der die grosse Welt bekannt ist" (54). Revanne cites the unmistakable signs of a lady: She accepts refreshments "ohne falsche Höflichkeit und mit den anmutigsten Dank ... bemerkt nur, was Auszeichnung verdient, ... kennt die guten Bücher und spricht darüber mit Geschmack und Bescheidenheit. Kein Geschwätz, keine Verlegenheit. Bei Tafel ein ebenso edles und natürliches Betragen. ... [I]hr Charakter scheint so liebenswürdig wie ihre Person" (54). When she repays her debt for dinner by playing the piano, he concludes: "Man zweifelte nicht mehr, daß sie ein Frauenzimmer von Stande sei, ausgestattet mit allen liebenswürdigen Geschicklichkeiten" (55). Later, after she has brought a wonderful new order and efficiency to the management of the house, Revanne avers: "Gewiß war es ein Frauenzimmer, gebildet, einem großen Hause vorzustehn; und doch schien sie nicht älter als einundzwanzig Jahre" (59).

Paradoxically, the pilgrim is made inebriating to Revanne not alone by her ladylike virtues, but also by a certain unladylike quality. This trait is most evident in her stubborn independence and travel and in the daring ballad she sings at the close of her piano concert. In the original French, this enticing trait is called "gaiety, mirth, cheerfulness": "Après le diner, un petit air de gaieté la rend encore plus belle" (FA 1.10:869); her song is called a "Romance burlesque" (870), a "gaillardise" (869)—a farcical, jolly or risqué song. In the 1809 **"Thörinn,"** Goethe translated this trait quite exactly as "ein kleiner lustiger Zug"; in all versions, he calls the ballad a "burleske Romanze" and a "Possen" (55, 57), a farce or practical joke. But in the 1821 version (retained in 1829), he made a psychologically astute change and rendered the trait with a word that conveys *willful* frivolity or mischievousness: "Nach der Tafel machte sie ein kleiner mutwilliger Zug noch schöner ..." (54).

Goethe's word "mutwillig" (from Mutwille, "ahd. muotwillo = eigener, freier Entschluss," *Duden: Wörterbuch der deutschen Sprache,* 1978) conveys the free will of the pilgrim, and with that he hits the heart of the matter: This young woman has taken her life and sexual fate into her own hands and become her own woman. Independence makes the pilgrim more alluring—to Revanne and many other men, if not to all critics. The Amazon Queen Penthesilea is more attractive to Achilles in her freedom and strength than the modest immured Greek maidens. Natalie is more attractive to Wilhelm in the *Lehrjahre* as an "Amazon" in a man's coat in the forest than in a dress among her marble statues and submissive to her brother's matchmaking. A woman of free will is more dangerous to a man but also more interesting, the anonymous French author and Goethe suggest. The French text *implies* this wisdom about relations between the sexes; Goethe's directly *names* it in that word "mutwillig."

By becoming sexually a free agent in her public image (though privately she remains true to her fiancé), the pilgrim takes on a *soupçon* of those free and saucy qualities that the noble youth found attractive in the *Müllerin,* and that Wilhelm finds enticing in his actress friends.[41] The pilgrim is a new type, a composite of noblewoman and free woman. Is this yet another foolish risk, since her

sauciness may be dangerously misinterpreted? Yes. Is this a new feminine wisdom for surviving in a society of easily distractable men and making the playing field between the sexes a more even one? Yes again.

Goethe makes two other changes to assure that the *Törin* cannot be easily labeled and dismissed. The French text says she plays "comically" as well as with "skill" ("Quoi qu'elle touchât comiquement, sa science n'étoit pas moins admirable"; FA 1.10:871-72). Goethe says: "Sie spielte neckisch, aber mit Einsicht" (57). Impudent chaffing is part of her allure, Goethe is not afraid to say so, but her "insight" counteracts any idea that she is "just" a tease. The French narrator's later groping attempt to explain her odd behavior as possible coquetry—"l'esprit fût-il égaré par la coquetterie ou par une folie véritable" (875)— becomes in Goethe's version: "hätte sich auch der Geist durch Eitelkeit oder wirklichen Wahnsinn verirrt" (61). Goethe prefers that his narrator theorize that the pilgrim may be vain (not a surprising weakness considering her effect on men), rather than have her dismissed as a coquette. This is no mere breaker of hearts, but a serious young woman with serious social intent.

The ballad itself, or "Romanze," contains numerous Goethean alterations to his purpose. He expands the song from seven to ten strophes, enlarges it in detail and emphasis, and stresses the mysteries of its story by asking in the first stanza five questions that are absent or at best latent in the French. The second of these questions, not even suggested in the source, ironically compares the young man's hasty decamping from the mill to "a pilgrimage": "Hat wohl der Freund beim scharfen Winde / Auf einer Wallfahrt sich erbaut?" (55). By using this key word, Goethe and the "pilgernde Törin" invite us to compare her pilgrimage of fidelity with the involuntary, ridiculous "pilgrimage" of her faithless lover—and the noble youth's with the *Wanderungen* of Wilhelm and Lenardo.

In the French original, the youth is compared to the man chased naked from "cet Eden" because he too has culled "une pomme / Pomme de vingt ans" (the miller girl). Goethe expands the biblical allusion, calling the youth "Beinah wie Adam bloss und nackt," and has the pilgrim sing a sixth question she must have often wanted to ask: "Warum auch ging er solche Wege / Nach jenem Apfel voll Gefahr, / Der freilich schön im Mühlgehege / Wie sonst im Paradiese war!" This trope underlines the archetypal seriousness of the offense. As in Goethe's letter to Behrisch, the youth's vagrancy is love's original sin. Although the youth does not know it yet, he has lost not only paradise at the mill but also the paradise of his intended marriage.

Thus even more than the original, the opening stanzas of Goethe's ballad caution us to have distance from the youth before he speaks. Paradoxically, Goethe's singer also expresses more sympathy for the youth in these early stanzas than the original singer: "L'ami" becomes "Der arme

Freund"; "Le manteau . . . / Le préserva de quelque injure" becomes the more empathetic "Und wenn er nicht den Mantel hätte / Wie grässlich wäre seine Schmach!" The singer seems to take his side by calling the *Müllerin* a knave for deceiving him: "So hat ihn jener Schalk betrogen" (55). Yet close after this comes her sixth question, which throws the responsibility of his Edenic free choice back on him. As in the tale, the male point of view is allowed full expression. But just as the anonymous narrator shows distance from Revanne, the singer cautions that the "complaining" youth may be unreliable, just as the ballad cycle stays in the back of our heads to remind us of the unfair social advantage that the youth had over the miller's daughter. The reader must keep all points of view in suspension. The young woman still loves the youth, and Goethe does not see their tale as a black-and-white issue.

Prepared by these lead-in stanzas narrated by the *Törin,* the narration is then taken over by the voice of the youth. Goethe increases the irony of the pending reversal of perspective and sympathy in the ballad by having the youth bemoan at greater length than in the French the miller girl's betrayal: "Ich las in ihren Feuerblicken / Doch keine Silbe von Verrat! / Sie schien mit mir sich zu entzücken / Und sann auf solche schwarze Tat!" He accuses her hyperbolically of being "assassin-like": "Konnt ich in ihren Armen träumen / Wie meuchlerisch der Busen schlug?" (56). Instead of the impersonal "twelve witnesses" ("douze témoins") summoned by the miller in the original, Goethe has the youth name a whole catalog: "Da drang ein Dutzend Anverwandten / Herein, ein wahrer Menschenstrom! / Da kamen Brüder, guckten Tanten, / Da stand ein Vetter und ein Ohm!" (56). The relatives not only make the scene more graphic, but his naming them boomerangs on the youth in its effect: The list makes even clearer than the original that there are familial implications to this, as any, seduction. Not only is the family at the mill affected, so also is the pilgrim's, soon to be deprived of their daughter, and probably the youth's as well.

But the headstrong youth doesn't see these implications. Like a trapped animal, he rages and sees the relatives as opposing beasts (instead of pirates in the French) when they demand from him—not money from his purse under threat of torture, as the raging youth in the original reports—but, in rather comic juxtaposition with their "monstrous" cries, significations of intent to marry: "Das war ein Toben, war ein Wüten! / Ein jeder schien ein andres Tier. / Da forderten sie Kranz und Blüten / Mit grässlichem Geschrei von mir." Their demand asserts that the *Müllerin* was a virgin, a claim the youth greets incredulously and (unlike the French youth) with a self-righteous assertion of his own innocence: "Was dringt ihr alle wie von Sinnen? / Auf den unschuld'gen Jüngling ein! / Denn solche Schätze zu gewinnen, / Da muss man viel behender sein" (56). The youth sees only his own self-perceived guiltlessness toward the miller girl, whose promiscuity he takes for granted, and conveniently forgets his guilt toward his fiancée in the larger context.

But at this vulnerable moment Goethe springs a bit of information that undercuts the youth's case for innocence even with the *Müllerin.* One of Goethe's most significant changes in the ballad is the miller girl's age. The youth in the original ballad rationalizes seducing her by arguing that a twenty-year-old virgin miller maid is as improbable as "a race of white crows": "Ditesmoi quand on vit en France / Une race de corbeaux blancs; / Et seulement une apparence / De Meûnière fille à vingt ans?" (FA 1.10:871). Goethe delays mention of the miller girl's age until the youth starts his rationalizations: "Weiss Amor seinem schönen Spiele / Doch immer zeitig nachzugehn: / Er lässt fürwahr nicht in der Mühle / Die Blumen sechzehn Jahre stehn" (56). By lowering her age from twenty to sixteen, Goethe renders it more credible that she could be a virgin; hence her seduction is the more objectionable. Certainly, too, the image of a flower being plucked is more tender and evocative of sympathy for the *Müllerin* than the ugly image of the crows. The irony of the ballad is palpable: the betrayed youth who complains loudest is at once the betrayer of two young girls: the miller girl and the pilgrim. His own words undercut him.

After absolving himself, the youth fights and curses and thunders his way out from "this low rabble" ("Gesindel"), as he calls the miller family (56). But even after all these bitter complaints, the youth in Goethe's ballad (unlike the French youth) pauses in the middle of his escape to look back at the *Müllertin*: "Ich sah noch einmal die Verruchte, / Und ach! sie war noch immer schön" (57). Both the youth and Revanne reveal the same weakness for beauty. And both interpret any unconventional, independent female will as "crazy"—and also alluring. But the disposition still to love even in circumstances they don't understand also redeems these two male characters from seeming unworthy of any sympathy.[42]

To make the transition back to the injured female pilgrim's point of view, the French ballad distances us from the youth with his repulsive image of the crows. Goethe uses a misogynistic passage that was placed earlier and in shorter form in the French (four lines to Goethe's eight). Though the youth had just sighed for her beauty, he now hyperbolically characterizes not only the *Müllerin,* but all country girls, city girls, and noblewomen as "practiced" "skinners" of men, while implicitly absolving men as merely women's "servants": "Man soll euch Mädchen auf dem Lande / Wie Mädchen aus den Städten fliehn! / So lasset doch den Fraun von Stande / Die Lust, die Diener auszuziehn! / Doch seid ihr auch von den Geübten / Und kennt ihr keine zarte Pflicht, / So ändert immer die Geliebten, / Doch sie verraten müßt ihr nicht" (57). The gross overgeneralization obviously discredits him. But his closing words, "if you have to change lovers all the time, you don't have to betray them," disclose that he doesn't understand the very changing of lovers as a betrayal. To his selfish, culturally conditioned eyes, only the miller's daughter giving *him* away to her family registers as betrayal.

At the close of the ballad when the perspective shifts and the *Törin* sings again in her own voice, Goethe adds a phrase of moral judgment to the French strophe. "Ich lache seiner tiefen Wunde, / *Denn wirklich ist sie wohlverdient*; / So geh' es jedem, der am Tage / Sein edles Liebchen frech belügt / Und nachts, mit allzu kühner Wage, / Zu Amors falscher Mühle kriecht" (57; my emphasis). Do we agree with her, or not, that the youth deserves his "wounds"? Goethe's changes make it easier to see the wrongs committed by the youth.

Some readers have felt that the pilgrim's song is too indecent to be sung by a virtuous young woman, and thus must distance us from her. Nevertheless she has respectable literary antecedents. As Gertrud Haupt notes, Shakespeare's Ophelia and Goethe's Gretchen also lament their lovers' faithlessness and hypocritical behavior by singing risqué or suggestive ballads.[43] After Ophelia is abandoned by Hamlet, she sings the bawdy "Saint Valentine's Song" with the following conclusion, though she remains a maid: "Quoth she, 'Before you tumbled me, / You promis'd me to wed.' / 'So would I ha' done, by yonder sun, / An thou hadst not come to my bed'" (4.5:63-66). Gretchen sings lines of graphic sexual longing in "Meine Ruh ist hin": "Mein Schoos! Gott! drängt / Sich nach ihm hin / Ach dürft' ich fassen / Und halten ihn / Und küssen ihn / So wie ich wollt / An seinen Küssen / Vergehen sollt" (*Urfaust,* Gretchens Stube, 1098-1105). The *Törin* shares with Ophelia and Gretchen the wretched experience of being aroused by a man who claims to love but then betrays her.

The pilgrim's song differs from theirs not in explicitness so much as in broader social awareness and a brave comic front. Only one song before the comic ballad, she had vented a deep sorrow: "Dann ging sie zu ernsten Tönen über, zu Tönen einer tiefen Trauer, die man zugleich in ihren Augen erblickte. Sie netzten sich mit Tränen, ihr Gesicht verwandelte sich, ihre Finger hielten an" (55). The pilgrim feels deep sadness, but not the despair into which Ophelia and Gretchen sink. Should she not be commended for saving her spirit with comic distance from her lover's folly? Is this not wisdom in a fool's cap?

After her performance, Revanne takes over the narration. His first thought is whether the ballad is not so out of place in the drawing room as to suggest the pilgrim's mind is unstable. But since she shows herself just as poised afterward as before, they decide her risqué sally was only entertainment: "Sie habe nur den Augenblick der Verdauung erheitern wollen" (57). Still, they watch her carefully for any outbreak of madness, even as they hasten to invite her to stay. But instead of craziness, they find her to

be "reason itself": "Sie verleugnete sich nicht einen Augenblick: sie war die Vernunft, mit aller Anmut begabt" (58). After another encomium to her gifts, Revanne sums up their bafflement at the mysterious mix in her character: "Daß wir nicht mehr wußten, wie wir jene Sonderbarkeiten mit einer solchen Erziehung vereinigen sollten" (58). So strange is an independent woman!

But in the world of the **Wanderjahre,** a person should be useful as well ornamental, not exist solely for oneself, but for the community. This is a prime value that Wilhelm evolves in his travels. Originally Revanne intended to offer the pilgrim "work" in his house—part of his rationalization for urging her to stay, to cover his attraction. But after he promenades her about, shows her off to visitors and feels "admiration" for her, he confesses: "Ich wagte wirklich nicht mehr, ihr Dienstvorschläge für mein Haus zu tun" (58)—even though she herself had mentioned "earning her keep by service" both at the spring and after the first dinner (53-55). Revanne's sister covers his embarrassment by inviting the pilgrim to manage the household together with her. It is interesting to see how Revanne reacts to her "serving" in this way. First he is deeply touched that she stoops even to "hand labor"; for this humbleness, he calls her (in a Goethean addition) by the affectionate, fatherly phrase "the good child": "Hier ließ sich das gute Kind öfters bis zur Handarbeit herunter . . ." (58). Then he marvels at how the pilgrim's management brings a higher "order" to the household that they never even missed before (58). Her "service" is of both high and humble distinction.

Next Revanne says, "Nun muß ich freilich gestehen, daß mich das Schicksal dieses Mädchens innigst zu rühren anfing. Ich bedauerte die Eltern, die wahrscheinlich eine solche Tochter sehr vermißten; ich seufzte, daß so sanfte Tugenden, so viele Eigenschaften verloren gehen sollten" (58). In what sense does he mean that her traits are "lost"? She "serves" his family and apparently others before, bringing order and delight into their midst. She also pleases herself and, as Bielschowsky suggests, calms her hurt psyche: "[die Geschichte zeigt wie die Törin] in diesem Verzicht [auf Elternhaus, Bequemlichkeit, Sicherheit] und in der Tätigkeit die Ruhe ihres Gemütes findet. . . ."[44] Like the *schöne Seele* in the **Lehrjahre** who freely elects not to marry Narziss but to serve instead as head of an institution, the *Törin* has found a happy, useful niche for herself. To Revanne, however, if she is not married, filling the position she was brought up to fill, and (perhaps the key point, anticipating the crisis of the tale) if she is not bearing children to inherit her "good traits" (and preferably his), then her virtues are "lost," go for naught. Her freedom bothers him.

Though she has lived with them "many months," Revanne still burns with curiosity about her past and "hopes the confidence they have tried to inspire in her would bring her secret to her lips" (58). Either he hasn't yet deciphered the ballad, or he understands it but rejects the distance that her indirect communication keeps between them. In bemoaning "her fate" and the "loss" of her virtues, Revanne slips into assuming that she has committed a "mistake" that his intervention could rectify. "War es ein Unglück, wir konnten helfen; war es ein Fehler, so ließ sich hoffen, unsere Vermittelung, unser Zeugnis würden ihr Vergebung eines vorübergehenden Irrtums verschaffen können" (58-59). Revanne wants to exercise his power to get her back "where she ought to be"; he thinks of this as benevolence and fails to see from her demeanor that it is not.

Revanne believes that hers is only a "passing errancy," but it is in fact existential. What the Revannes perceive as the pilgrim's "error" or "madness" ("Irrtum"; "une erreur," FA 1.10:873) is only her wandering, her exit from convention. Goethe carefully keeps all the original stems in his renderings of these words (Indo-European "ers = to be in motion," Latin "errare = to wander," *American Heritage Dictionary,* 1996; "mhd. *irre* = sich schnell, heftig, oder ziellos bewegend," *Duden,* 1978). No other part of her conduct can they criticize, except that she has left the established system—and that in itself is construed by Revanne and his culture as "madness," "Irrtum." But pilgrimage is a time-honored refuge for non-mainstream sensibilities; a healthy society allows such outlets. And there is a devotional quality to this wanderer. Not for nothing is she called a pilgrim. The *Törin,* like other explorers of the **Wanderjahre,** is not without a goal or guiding principle: she is on a pilgrimage for something new between men and women, and she brings a message to Revanne, his son, and the readers of her tale. If this be foolish or mad, it is an admirable grand folly, revealing hope for long-term rather than immediate change.

Such restlessness, however, is hard for those highest and most powerful in the status quo to understand. The narrator noted this of Revanne when he first met the pilgrim: "Herr von Revanne, der einen solchen Entschluß, in die Welt zu laufen, nicht gut begreifen konnte..." (54). By articulating this, the narrator implies that he, in contrast to Revanne, does understand, and thus expresses a subtle sympathy for the pilgrim.

The run up to the dénouement of the tale shows the powerful not at their best. Revanne becomes more and more impatient at the pilgrim's refusal to admit a mistake or confide in him. Forgetting her stipulations, forgetting that confidence cannot be forced, he pries, then complains that she doesn't answer: "Alle unsere Freundschafts-versicherungen, unsre Bitten selbst waren unwirksam" (59). Goethe omits another phrase in the French, "toute notre adresse" (873), "all our tact or shrewdness," for it is clear Revanne is neither tactful nor hiding his motive. The *Törin* deflects him with maxims: "Bemerkte sie die Absicht, einige Aufklärung von ihr zu gewinnen, so versteckte sie sich hinter allgemeine Sittensprüche, um sich zu rechtfertigen, ohne uns zu belehren" (59).[45] Revanne

wants the intimacy of a direct confession, but she resists his leading hints, using proverbs as her shield. Like Makarie, like Goethe, the *Törin* collects *Sprüche.*

Revanne is mistaken about how much her proverbs reveal. Just as her song told the double betrayal at the mill, the maxims tell her story and emotions since that shock. Like Lear's Fool, Ophelia, and the characters of near-eastern tales, the pilgrim speaks in platitudes, one of Goethe's favorite means in the **Wanderjahre** to veil-unveil a truth.[46] The proverbs in the tale, like the emphasis on "service," are another way in which the anonymous French tale perfectly suits Goethe's theme and techniques in the novel.

When Revanne and his family (he often hides his curiosity by using his sister as cover) try to draw the pilgrim into talking about "her misfortune" in love, she retreats behind a stoic biblical proverb, but also adds a psychically revealing trope: "Das Unglück ... fällt über Gute und Böse. Es ist eine wirksame Arzenei, welche die guten Säfte zugleich mit den üblen angreift" (59). She seems to picture herself and the youth as one body, one flesh, like the metaphor for man and wife. Misfortune, like strong medicine, may cure the "bad humors" in this body (the youth's infidelity), but it also attacks the good ones (their love for each other) that she is trying to sustain.

When the Revannes ask why she fled her father's house, she compares her movements to an innocent deer's: "Wenn das Reh flieht ... so ist es darum nicht schuldig" (59). They ask if she has been "pursued" or persecuted, and she gives an interesting perspective on her supposedly advantageous status: "Das ist das Schicksal mancher Mädchen von guter Geburt, Verfolgungen zu erfahren und auszuhalten. Wer über eine Beleidigung weint, dem werden mehrere begegnen." Does a girl denied free choice see suitors as pursuing persecutors? Heaping insults on a person already weeping over an offense seems cruel, yet perhaps "well-born maidens" were so treated if they wept over having no voice in marriage. The Revannes are deaf to these and earlier hints that members of her own class have most hurt the pilgrim; instead they ask how she can expose herself to the "rawness of the mob"—as if only unrefined folk could hurt her. She laughs and, in a marvelously compact aphorism, suggests that after living by her wits and seeing how the world looks to a poor person, she has a different view of the rich; she doesn't think of herself as a victim, but as a clever victor to be at their table: "Dem Armen, der den Reichen bei Tafel begrüsst, fehlt es nicht an Verstand" (59). Thus she defends her new position and privacy from intrusive benefactors.

Frustrated by her verbal dexterity, Revanne finally abandons all pretense and uses a "joking" moment to skewer the pilgrim point-blank with a blunt question: "ob sie den frostigen Helden ihrer Romanze nicht kenne?" (59). Instantly it is clear he has overstepped the line of good taste and kindness. The question "seems to pierce her through," and she turns on Revanne a look so earnest and severe that Revanne's eyes cannot sustain it. The French refers to "deux yeux severes," (873). Goethe's "ein Paar Augen so ernst und streng" (59) is softer and shows more empathy with her. Dropping his gaze is a graphic admission of Revanne's misdeed.[47]

It is the turning point in their relationship. But Revanne, if he realizes his fault, quickly forgets it. He seems surprised after this breach of trust that the pilgrim evinces "depression" of body and spirit whenever the subject of love comes up: "Sooft man auch nachher von Liebe sprach, so konnte man erwarten, die Anmut ihres Wesens und die Lebhaftigkeit ihres Geistes getrübt zu sehen. Gleich fiel sie in ein Nachdenken, das wir für Grübeln hielten und das doch wohl nur Schmerz war" (59). Seeing that his blunt question had so bad an effect, a kind person who cared for her would never bring up the topic of love again. Not only does Revanne test this result repeatedly, he judgmentally thinks her reaction is regret or self-criticism ("Grübeln"), only later recognizing it as pain.

Underlining his blind blundering, Revanne describes the retreating object of his obsession, but without attaching any meaning to her new reserve: "Doch blieb sie"—Goethe uses "remained," pointing back to Revanne's affront, instead of the French "elle étoit" (FA 1.10:873)—"im ganzen munter, nur ohne grosse Lebhaftigkeit ... gerade ohne Offenherzigkeit ... eher duldsam als sanftmütig, und mehr erkenntlich als herzlich bei Liebkosungen und Höflichkeiten" (59). As she retreats before our eyes, he, blind to her change, shows his own preoccupation by pronouncing her fit to head a great house (59). He could have understood her "inexplicableness" better if he were less self-absorbed.

After blithely narrating this crisis between them, Revanne prepares us for the story's dénouement and what he calls the pilgrim's strangest folly: "So zeigte sich diese junge unerklärliche Person, die mich ganz eingenommen hat, binnen zwei Jahren, die es ihr gefiel bei uns zu verweilen, bis sie mit einer Torheit schloss, die viel seltsamer ist, als ihre Eigenschaften ehrwürdig und glänzend waren" (60). Unable to see or admit that his own greatest folly is also about to be related, Revanne skips the "closing" event and abruptly jumps to its emotional aftermath: "Mein Sohn, jünger als ich, wird sich trösten können; was mich betrifft, so fürchte ich, schwach genug zu sein, sie immer zu vermissen" (60). This is the closest Revanne comes to admitting any "weakness." Goethe makes the hiatus in Revanne's narration even more obvious by omitting a terse sentence that intervenes and sums up the event in the French: "Nous l'avons perdue" (874). In fact she was never theirs to lose. On this note of "weakness" and a defeat incomprehensible to him, Revanne's narration ends.

The anonymous narrator now takes over. Before relating the climax, he restates his own interpretation of the two main characters. First, though Revanne has just spoken of the pilgrim's "most unusual folly," the narrator contradicts this judgment: "Nun will ich die Torheit eines verständigen Frauenzimmers erzählen, um zu zeigen, daß Torheit oft nichts weiter sei als Vernunft unter einem andern Äußern" (60). He concedes that in the end she resorted to a "comical strategem" that seems "stangely inconsistent" with her "noble character," but he stands by his assessment of her basic "understanding" and "reason," saying that we already knew her "irregularities": "Es ist wahr, man wird einen seltsamen Widerspruch finden zwischen dem edlen Charakter der Pilgerin und der komischen List, deren sie sich bediente; aber man kennt ja schon zwei ihrer Ungleichheiten, die Pilgerschaft selbst und das Lied" (60). The narrator shows, and invites, tolerance for eccentricity, nonconformity.

As for characterizing Revanne, the narrator recurs to his *leitmotif* about his friend, as if throwing up his hands about the infatuated one: "Es ist wohl deutlich, daß Herr von Revanne in die Unbekannte verliebt war." He then takes us on another tour of the older man's psyche:

> Nun mochte er sich freilich auf sein fünfzigjähriges Gesicht nicht verlassen, ob er schon frisch und wacker aussah als ein Dreissiger; vielleicht aber hoffte er, durch seine reine, kindliche Gesundheit zu gefallen, durch die Güte, Heiterkeit, Sanftheit, Grossmut seines Charakters; vielleicht auch durch sein Vermögen, ob er gleich zart genug gesinnt war, um zu fühlen, dass man das nicht erkauft, was keinen Preis hat.

(60)

His virtues, however, are ones that Revanne has not always shown the pilgrim—and the narrator agrees Revanne should not try to win her with his fortune. Goethe aptly substitutes this mercantile formulation for the French focus on honor—"quoiqu'il eût l'ame trop délicate pour acheter un triomphe, & déshonorer par-là une femme qu'il auroit aimée" (874)—for Revanne resorts to just such a base appeal.

The return home of Revanne's young, hot-blooded son is what precipitates the end. The son's interest in the pilgrim heightens his father's competitive passions just as the mere prospect of a rival had done earlier. Unaware of his father's love for the pilgrim, the younger Revanne plunges in, showing, the narrator notes, a paternal likeness: "Aber der Sohn ... liebenswürdig"—an adjective never applied to Revanne senior—"zärtlich, feurig, ohne sich mehr als sein Vater zu bedenken, stürzte sich über Hals und Kopf in das Abenteuer" (60). The pilgrim's attempt to discourage him with "severity" only "inflames" him: "Ihre Strenge mehr als ihr Verdienst und ihre Schönheit entflammte ihn" (60).

The narrator says the older Revanne knows better than to forsake his gentlemanly principles to achieve his goal: "Er kannte sich, und als er seinen Rival erkannt hatte, hoffte er nicht, über ihn zu siegen, wenn er nicht zu Mitteln greifen wollte, die einem Mann von Grundsätzen nicht geziemen" (60). Yet to such "unseemly means" he resorts in the very next sentence: "Dessenungeachtet verfolgte er seinen Weg ..." (60-61). Revanne is willing to win even by dishonoring himself as he defines it, even realizing that if she chose him, it would be "by calculation" ("mit Vorbedacht" [61]) of his wealth, not for love. The narrator follows this devastating central collapse in Revanne's character with the sentence: "Auch machte Herr von Revanne noch andere Fehler, die er später bereute" (61). After the mistake of betraying his own principles and self-respect, he twice demeans his intended beloved, first with the offer of a "secret tie" ("von einer dauerhaften, geheimen, gesetzmäßigen Verbindung"), and second, with a complaint of mistreatment and "ingratitude" when she rejects him—as if she owed him her hand in exchange for shelter in his house. The narrator shows his own understanding of the pilgrim and his embarrassed distance from Revanne by commenting, "Gewiß kannte er die nicht, die er liebte, als er eines Tages zu ihr sagte, daß viele Wohltäter Übles für Gutes zurückerhielten" (61).[48] Love as Herr von Revanne practices it has nothing to do with actually "knowing" the object of his love. Goethe (staying true to the French) underlines Revanne's blindness by ironically referring to her as "die Unbekannte" in the next sentence.

The pilgrim refutes Revanne's accusation of ingratitude with a maxim that epitomizes the social politics of the tale. Superbly concrete but with broad theoretical import, her retort contains both a mercantile metaphor—laying bare the baseness of Revanne's complaint—and a soaring political assertion that sets their dispute on an entirely different plane. Goethe translates her maxim almost verbatim from the French, a tribute to the strength of the original author's phrasing. But he strengthens *how* the pilgrim delivers it: instead of the ambiguous "avec simplicité" (FA 1.10:871), which could signify "with plainness" or "simplemindedly," Goethe substitutes "mit Geradheit"—which has only positive implications: straightness, uprightness and rectitude. "Ihm antwortete die Unbekannte mit Geradheit: 'Viele Wohltäter möchten ihren Begünstigten sämtliche Rechte abhandeln für eine Linse'" (61). The pilgrim's proverb recalls Ophelia's words when she returns Hamlet's trinkets: "Take these again, for to the noble mind / Rich gifts wax poor when givers prove unkind" (3.1:100-101).

While the father is abandoning his dignity to woo with his fortune, the son presses his suit by threatening suicide, "wie gebräuchlich," the narrator sighs. Between the two men's follies the embarrassed narrator can distinguish only with a comical double-negative: the senior Revanne is "etwas weniger unvernünftig" (61). The son commits errors of judgment, the father errors of the heart. We expect more of Revanne senior because of his age, but he doesn't see his own unkindness. The narrator rues that both men justify their "violent," "insolent" wooing by "the purity of their honorable intent" and takes the young lady's side:

"Sie war in der Gewalt zweier Liebenden, welche jede Zudringlichkeit durch die Reinheit ihrer Absichten entschuldigen konnten, indem sie im Sinne hatten, ihre Verwegenheit durch ein feierliches Bündnis zu rechtfertigen" (61). Is their behavior less foolish for not being directly so labeled?

Then the label is passed. Only the "beautiful stranger" (not called *Törin*) keeps her head and tries to "spare everyone their follies": "Die schöne Fremde ... scheint keine andere Absicht gehabt zu haben, als sich und andern alberne Streiche zu ersparen" (61). She could have set herself up for life since both men sincerely want to marry her (61), but instead she shows an unmercenary selflessness by extricating herself from between them. In this act we see most clearly her wisdom. She puts the welfare of the Revanne family and future relations between father and son above her own interest, while the two men think only of their own egos and passion. Calmly the wise fool devises a plan—admired by the narrator—that preserves everyone else's reputation while temporarily endangering her own: "Sie kommt nicht aus der Fassung, sie erdenkt ein Mittel, jedermann seine Tugend zu erhalten, indem sie die ihrige bezweifeln läßt" (62). The "foolish pilgrim" alone remains true to her "virtues."

She is calm but ecstatic in her practical idealism. The narrator follows the sentence about saving the Revannes' virtue with a tribute to her "crazy fidelity" and "sacrifices": "Sie ist wahnsinnig vor Treue, die ihr Liebhaber gewiß nicht verdient, wenn er nicht alle die Aufopferungen fühlt, und sollten sie ihm auch unbekannt bleiben" (62). Why does the narrator say "even if her sacrifices remain unknown to him"—for, of course, her fiancé can't know—unless he includes Revanne senior and junior in the category of a "lover who doesn't deserve her fidelity unless he feels all her sacrifices"? The son is called her "lover" only two paragraphs later. Does either Revanne learn to "feel" her sacrifices, as the narrator implies? One does.

Thus far, the narrator has expressed subtle but clear sympathy for the female point of view in these misunderstandings between the sexes. Through the *Törin*'s predicament, he sees how men in positions of social power frustrate and disappoint the women dependent on them. Now that the pilgrim, however, is forced by the Revannes' pressure to resort to a subterfuge—one that the narrator has already pronounced beneficial to all in the long run—he allows the men's complaints about women and their feminine wiles to be aired in the period of deception before her motive is clarified. Having seen the female point of view, we understand better why women employ the deceptions and theatrics that the Revannes complain of, and we also realize that men like Revanne senior don't see how they contribute to the problem. Overall, the narrator pronounces the pilgrim a "model" of "honesty" in love, the opposite of a cruel coquette who toys with men: "An dem Beispiele dieses Mädchens mögen die Frauen lernen, daß ein redliches

Gemüt . . . die Herzenswunden nicht unterhält, die es nicht heilen will" (61).

Here is the dénouement that Herr von Revanne can't bring himself to narrate. One day when he "returns too vigorously the friendship and gratitude she shows him," the "foolish pilgrim" "suddenly assumes a naïve manner" and lets him infer, with seeming confusion, that she is pregnant by his son. Not only the inference, but her naïve demeanor and the tears she "brings forth" exasperate Revanne. The narrator reports Revanne's misogynistic reaction: "denn niemals fehlt es Frauen an einer Träne bei ihren Schalkheiten, niemals an einer Entschuldigung ihres Unrechts" (62). The last phrase is ironic, for excusing one's own injustices is a talent of Revanne's.

Revanne shows instantaneous hauteur and sarcasm toward unauthorized motherhood, even in the woman he "loves": "So verliebt Herr von Revanne war, so musste er diese neue Art von unschuldiger Aufrichtigkeit unter dem Mutterhäubchen bewundern" (62). Revanne is unable to focus on anything but how her situation makes him look: "Dies klärt mich auf! Ich sehe, wie lächerlich meine Forderungen sind" (62). He sees not the pain of her position, but only his own embarrassment and pain and that which he promises his rival: "Als einzige Strafe für den Schmerz, den Sie mir verursachen, verspreche ich Ihnen von seinem Erbteile so viel, als nötig ist, um zu erfahren, ob er Sie so sehr liebt als ich" (62). In implying that she is materialistically motivated, the elder Revanne continues to misjudge her, and the nature of love.

Revanne informs his son of the supposed pregnancy, a message that has a similar impact on him. Just as the elder Revanne's first response was to defend his ego and his second to pay her off, so the younger Revanne: "Gehen Sie, Mademoiselle, . . . wenigstens sollte man rechtmässige Kinder nicht enterben; es ist schon genug, sie anzuklagen. . . . ich durchdringe Ihr Komplott mit meinem Vater. Sie geben mir beide einen Sohn, und es ist mein Bruder, das bin ich gewiß!" (63). No sympathy in the worst predicament a young woman can confront, no concern or love. Both Revannes focus only on protecting their own egos and material status. They cannot even show love for a coming child that is supposed to be related to them, though they professed mad love for the mother shortly before. She knew their character, knew they would react so; her stratagem relied on it. As she tells the son, "die Katze weiß wohl, wem sie den Bart leckt" (63). But it is sad to see them fail this test of their hearts.

Throughout this scene, the "beautiful empty-head," as the son thinks her ("l'aimable Insensée," FA 1.10:877; "die schöne Unkluge," 63) maintains a feminine imperturbability that annoys him as much as her tears angered his father: "'Nun, was denn, mein Herr?' sagte sie mit einem Lächeln, das bei einer solchen Gelegenheit zum Verzweifeln bringen kann" (63). "Mit ebenderselben ruhigen und heitern Stirne" (63), so maddening to men and so expressive of her confidence in the rightness of her defense of her sex, she delivers the heart of her message to the one male she believes capable of hearing it.

Denying his smug certitude that she is carrying his "brother," we now hear the depth of her hurt: "Von nichts sind Sie gewiß; es ist weder Ihr Sohn noch Ihr Bruder. Die Knaben sind bösartig; ich habe keinen gewollt; es ist ein armes Mädchen, das ich weiterführen will, weiter, ganz weit von den Menschen, den Bösen, den Toren und den Ungetreuen" (63). For the first and only time we hear the misanthropy life has taught her: that young girls need protection from men, villains, fools, and faithless boys. And finally putting the label where it belongs, Goethe translates "sots" ("des hommes, des méchans, des sots & des infidelès," FA 1.10:877) as "Toren," echoing the title of the story in a way the original does not and thus changing who the real fools of the story are.

But even now the "foolish pilgrim" shows forgiveness and generosity to the young Revanne and gives him wise advice. She calls him "lieber Revanne," says she believes "Sie haben mich aufrichtig geliebt," and, in Goethe's version, pays him the same compliment the narrator paid her: "Sie haben von Natur ein redliches Herz" (63; instead of the French "Vous êtes bien né," FA 1.10:877). She warns him not to surrender his "principles" as his father did: "erhalten Sie die Grundsätze der Aufrichtigkeit" (63).

Then in a series of maxims of New Testament cadence ("Wer sein Leben findet, der wird es verlieren," Math. 10:39, etc.), the *Törin* gives the young Revanne a sermon about young women, himself, his father, and men in general:

> Wer die Bitte bekümmerter Unschuld verachtet, wird einst selbst bitten und nicht erhört werden. Wer sich kein Bedenken macht, das Bedenken eines schutzlosen Mädchens zu verachten, wird das Opfer werden von Frauen ohne Bedenken. Wer nicht fühlt, was ein ehrbares Mädchen empfinden muß, wenn man um sie wirbt, der verdient sie nicht zu erhalten. Wer gegen alle Vernunft, gegen die Absichten, gegen den Plan seiner Familie, zugunsten seiner Leidenschaft Entwürfe schmiedet, verdient die Früchte seiner Leidenschaft zu entbehren und der Achtung seiner Familie zu ermangeln.
>
> (63)

Her voice is strong, like the last judge. This is no lament, no plea for justice by a weak person. It is an apocalyptic warning, the rhetoric of truth: We reap what we sow, between the sexes as elsewhere.

Finally the enigmatic wanderer reveals her ruse and shows that she knows what her own folly is. She has not been unchaste, nor unfaithful to her fiancé ("Sie wissen, ob ich untreu bin, Ihr Vater weiß es auch," 63). Nor does she regret her extraordinary fidelity to her first love. She hopes he will someday be wise enough to appreciate her, "der mich vielleicht wieder sieht, wenn sein Herz rein genug sein wird, zu vermissen, was er verloren hat" (64). She has not yet found the man who can appreciate her, a man with a kind and faithful heart. But she admits that in grief she exposed herself to dangers: "Ich gedachte durch die Welt zu rennen und mich allen Gefahren auszusetzen" (63-64). She also makes explicit what she hinted to the Revannes before, that of those dangers, "Gewiß diejenigen sind die größten, die mich in diesem Hause bedrohen" (64).

Like Lear's Fool, Goethe's *Törin* speaks truth to power, "crazy" as it sounds, and even though none—including many readers—may be clear-headed enough to hear it. Like Lear, the Revannes were blinded by their patriarchal pretentions to infallibility and benevolence.

The *Törin* gives her greatest insight, the distilled wisdom of her life, to the son just before she departs. "Aber weil Sie jung sind, sage ich es Ihnen allein und im Vertrauen. . . ." With these words she heralds one last maxim for young Revanne and the reader alike, reaffirming her belief that with his "honest, sincere heart" the son can change, though his father is hopelessly set in male blinders. Making more concrete and direct the language from his French source ("dans les deux sexes, on n'est infidèle que volontairement," FA 1.10:877), Goethe's wise fool underlines the role of "will" in fidelity: "Männer und Frauen sind nur mit Willen ungetreu" (64). Only the will—self-control—can prevent the follies of unbridled emotion, social hubris, and self-rationalization, as the youth at the mill and the elder Revanne demonstrate. The themes of self-control and lack of control, renunciation and self-indulgence in the French novella suits Goethe's **Wanderjahre** as if he had written it himself.[49]

The blindness falls from young Revanne's eyes—opened by tears of sympathy. Instead of hearing only his own ego, now he cannot get enough of hearing her: "Der junge Revanne hörte noch zu, da sie schon ausgesprochen hatte. Er stand wie vom Blitz getroffen; Tränen öffneten zuletzt seine Augen, und in dieser Rührung lief er zur Tante . . ." (64). The image of Zeus's stunning thunderous enlightenment ("Il demeuroit comme un homme frappé de la foudre," 877) is continued as the young man runs to his family to report that Mademoiselle is leaving, "Mademoiselle sei ein Engel, oder vielmehr ein Dämon, herumirrend in der Welt, um alle Herzen zu peinigen" (64). Perhaps in her ecstatic folly, her "craziness for fidelity," the *Törin* is indeed a *daimon,* one of Goethe's favorite Greek notions: an uncannily intense human spirit who, in this case, painfully draws men to strive toward a higher potentiality: a "Mittelwesen zwischen Mensch und Gott" (*Duden,* 1977) who hurts us by opening our eyes to our follies even as she enacts her own passionate folly with an impunity suggesting divine protection.

Father and son are finally "enlightened" by her revelatory ruse and message and by the impulse to reconcile that she

has given them: "Als Vater und Sohn sich erklärt hatten, zweifelte man nicht mehr an ihrer Unschuld, ihren Talenten, ihrem Wahnsinn" (64; the French has "expliqués" instead of Goethe's resonant "erklärt"). But unlike the son whose tears of sympathy "open his eyes," the elder Revanne never gains "the least enlightenment" about her: "So viel Mühe sich auch Herr von Revanne seit der Zeit gegeben, war es ihm doch nicht gelungen, sich die mindeste Aufklärung über diese schöne Person zu verschaffen . . ." (64; French "la moindre lumière," FA 1.10:878).

Goethe's final change from his French source comes at the end of the tale when he omits the concluding paragraph: "Je sens bien qu'elle n'est pas assez extravagante pour figurer parmi les folles du moment; mais, avec tant de vertus & tant d'amour pour la fidélité, je pense qu' elle peut pourtant paroître assez folle aujourd'hui" (878). These lines have a tacked-on, apologetic tone as if the author or editor were aware that the tale's follies may seem mild in comparison with scandals like the "Diamond Necklace" affair or rumblings of the revolution itself in the year of its publication in 1789. With good judgment about keeping to what is integral to the tale, Goethe omits these lines.

Instead, Goethe chose to end his tale of disappointed love. by having the *Törin* slip from the fingers of two unkind suitors just as she did from her faithless lover before the novella began. She becomes an unattainable, evanescent ideal to the men. The story ends with the elder Revanne comparing her to an angel, echoing his son's words: "[Es war Herrn von Revanne] doch nicht gelungen, sich die mindeste Aufklärung über diese schöne Person zu verschaffen, die so flüchtig wie die Engel und so liebenswürdig erschienen war" (64). Revanne's fruitless search suggests that although he doesn't understand what happened, he has finally realized her value. He has already told us he "will always miss her" (60).

We know that Wilhelm read this tale from Hersilie's hands. Did Lenardo, the cousin who returns troubled from his grand tour, also perhaps read and agree with its critique of society? Even if Lenardo missed it, Goethe placed this master novella early in the **Wanderjahre** as a mirror which alert readers might remember when they see the later lovelorn pilgrimages of the novel. The tale he labored on for so long speaks with many of Goethe's words as well as with the voices of its characters and French author. Through her unorthodox behavior and verbal talent, the *Törin* does her best to enlighten three men—and many readers—about the dangers of a scleratic social caste system. It is not her fault if so many male and female readers, like Herr von Revanne, have not wanted to look into that mirror.

Notes

1. First to comment on the link between *Wanderjahre* and the modern novel was Hermann Broch, "James

Joyce und die Gegenwart: Rede zu Joyces 50. Geburtstag [1936]," rpt. *Schriften zur Literatur 1: Kritik* (Frankfurt/Main: Suhrkamp, 1975) 63-94; see especially 86-90. First to discover the fictional editor was Arthur Henkel, *Entsagung: Eine Studie zu Goethes Altersroman* (Tübingen: Niemeyer, 1964) 13-19. First to describe the novel's structure as an "archive" was Volker Neuhaus, "Die Archivfiktion in *Wilhelm Meisters Wanderjahren,*" *Euphorion* 62 (1968): 13-27. A magisterial overview of *Wanderjahre* scholarship in the past three decades is given by Ehrhard Bahr, *The Novel As Archive: The Genesis, Reception, and Criticism of Goethe's* Wilhelm Meisters Wanderjahre (Columbia, SC: Camden House, 1998); see especially xv, 101, and 77: "Goethe, as author, disappears in the various author functions," leading to "the disintegration of the traditional author into a multitude of authors." "In hindsight, it is not difficult to pick the approximate period at which the process began that led to the disappearance of the author function in German literature: it must be associated with the publication of the second version of the *Wanderjahre* in 1829, a point that precedes Foucault's date, connected with the life and work of Stéphane Mallarmé (1842-1989), by approximately thirty years." See also Ehrhard Bahr, "Revolutionary Realism in Goethe's *Wanderjahre,*" *Goethe's Narrative Fiction: The Irvine Goethe Symposium,* ed. William J. Lillyman (1983): 170-71.

2. Bahr, *Archive,* 30-31: "Because of the abandonment of narrative integration as well as of authorial control over the plot, the construction of fiction is shifted to the 'implied reader' (see Iser, Der implizite Leser). ... The disparateness of the archival texts forces the reader to construct meaningful connections"; see also 77. See also Hans Rudolf Vaget, "Goethe the Novelist: On the Coherence of His Fiction," *Goethe's Narrative Fiction: The Irvine Goethe Symposium,* ed. Wm. J. Lillyman (New York: Walter de Gruyter, 1983) 11.

3. Bahr, "Realism," 165-66: "Wilhelm Meister is no longer the center of attention as an individual as in *Lehrjahre,* but he becomes a novelistic device connecting a number of small, self-contained narrative units which are independent of one another yet also affect each other." Bahr grounds this reading on Goethe's comment to Eckermann regarding Faust "that he had used 'die Fabel eines berühmten Helden bloss als eine Art von durchgehender Schnur, um darauf aneinanderzureihen, was er Lust hat.'" See also Bahr, *Archive,* 84.

4. Many scholars have noted and profitably used Goethe's words about his structural technique of "mirroring" in a letter to Carl Jocob Ludwig Iken on Sept. 27, 1827: "Da sich gar manches unserer Erfahrungen nicht rund aussprechen und direkt mitteilen lässt, so habe ich seit langem das Mittel gewählt, durch einander gegenübergestellte und sich gleichsam ineinander abspiegelnde Gebilde den geheimeren Sinn dem Aufmerkenden zu offenbaren." *Goethes Briefe,* 2nd edition, ed. Karl Robert Mandelkow (Hamburg: Wegner, 1976) 250; future references to this edition are identified simply by date in my text and endnotes. For examples of critics who cite this mirroring technique, see Neuhaus 13; Vaget 7-10; Bahr, *Archive,* 26, 85. For a discussion of the imagery and theory of mirroring in the *Wanderjahre* as a device for creating multiple perspectives, see Jane K. Brown, *Goethes Cyclical Narratives*: Die Unterhaltungen deutscher Ausgewanderten *and* Wilhelm Meisters Wanderjahre (Chapel Hill: U of North Carolina P, 1975) 45-47, 53, 57.

5. See Françoise Derre, "Die Beziehungen zwischen Felix, Hersilie und Wilhelm in "Wilhelm Meisters Wanderjahren," *Goethe Jahrbuch* 94 (1977): 38-48, for an attempt to clarify the exquisitely indefinite emotions among these three characters. Derre's reading seems to me based too much on the symbol of the casket and not enough on Hersilie's actions—regularly turning from Felix and writing to Wilhelm. At the climactic embrace, she sees not Felix but her own image in the mirror of his eyes—not, it seems to me, a woman in love with this man.

6. Vaget 16-20: "Goethe's peculiar understanding of the French Revolution clearly suggests that we can gain a more adequate perspective on the ideological profile of his novels by considering his portrayal of the nobility rather than his image of the middle class"; "in the final version of the novel Lenardo appears to be the central character next to Wilhelm ... he also provides the focus for the central socio-historical diagnosis in this reputedly unfocused book."

7. See Bahr, *Archive,* 16, 22, 27, for comments on Lenardo as a foil for Wilhelm.

8. Bahr, *Archive,* 36-37, gives a chronology of the early publications for the *Wanderjahre* novellas. "Die pilgernde Törin" was the first of the *Wanderjahre* novellas to be published. The volume was actually printed in late 1808, but by convention it is referred to as 1809.

9. "Sie behandeln ... gewöhnlich die Empfindungen, wodurch Männer und Frauen verbunden oder entzweiet, glücklich oder unglücklich gemacht, öfter aber verwirrt als aufgeklärt werden" (HA 6:143).

10. Robin A. Clouser, *Love and Social Contracts: Goethe's* Unterhaltungen deutscher Ausgewanderten (Bern: Peter Lang, 1991) 19-23, 66-68, 135-47.

11. Erich Trunz, *Anmerkungen,* HA 8:568-69. All references to the 1829 version of Goethe's novella and Trunz's editorial apparatus are to this edition, with page numbers given parenthetically in the text.

12. In mid-1798 Schiller provided Goethe with a copy of the original tale that Goethe had first read in 1789. Goethe then secured his own somewhat altered and flawed handwritten copy, and went on to rework the story for the 1808/09 *Taschenbuch.* The manuscript copy of the French tale, by an unknown copyist, is in the *Goethe und Schiller Archiv* in Weimar, with penned-in corrections by another unknown hand. Cf. Trunz's comments on Goethe's use of this manuscript (HA 8:569). I am indebted to Prof. Dr. Gerhard Schmid, Director of the Archive, for his kind assistance in making this manuscript available to me, as well as to Dr. Konrad Kratzsch, assistant director of the *Zentralbibliothek der deutschen Klassik in Weimar,* for access to the 1789 version in "Cahiers de lecture."

13. Friedrich Wilhelm Riemer, *Mittheilungen über Goethe* (Berlin: Duncker and Humbler, 1841) 615. Also in GA 15:1110.

14. Quote from J. G. Robertson, *Life and Work of Goethe* (London: Rutledge, 1932) 271. E. K. Bennett, *A History of the German Novelle* (Cambridge UP, 1974) 32-33, skips "Die pilgernde Törin" in his discussion of the embedded *Novellen* in the *Wanderjahre.* Johannes Klein, *Geschichte der deutschen Novelle von Goethe bis zur Gegenwart,* 4th ed. (Wiesbaden: Steiner, 1960) 72, devotes fewer than ten lines to it, mainly to compare the "Törin" to the "Prokurator" in the *Unterhaltungen.* More recent Goethe scholars also slight the tale, discussing its meaning and impact as if the *Wanderjahre* were an allegory. For example, Manfred Karnick, "*Wilhelm Meisters Wanderjahre* *oder Die Kunst des Mittelbaren: Studien zum Problem der Verständigung in Goethes Altersepoche* (Fink: Munich, 1968) 73, 75-79, believes the *Törin* represents "Verschlossenheit" and contrasts her with Lenardo: "Wahrend es Lenardo um die verdeckte Ermittlung einer Sache ging, erstrebt die wunderliche Heldin der 'verrückten Pilgerschaft' deren völligen Entzug." Ignoring the pilgrim's aphoristic and lyric self-revelations as well as her contributions to her benefactors' society, Karnick compares her to Montan the misanthrope, who completely withdraws from social life. Anneliese Klingenberg, *Goethes Roman* 'Wilhelm Meisters Wanderjahre oder die Entsagenden': *Quellen und Komposition* (Berlin: Aufbau, 1972) 128-31, compares the tale with all six of the other inset *Novellen* as illustrations of the conflicts that result from passion and emotional confusion, but gives the pilgrim little credit for self-control or renunciation. Jane Brown

53-58, finds the tale "less directly accessible" than other tales in the *Wanderjahre* "since it is an inserted translation with almost no variation from the French original. ..." Brown compares the pilgrim to the fairy Melusine, but draws no significance, other than a tone of mystery and fantasy that Hersilie loves, from the supernatural elements; nevertheless she finds echoes of the tale's themes in many other parts of the novel. Hannelore Schlaffer, *Wilhelm Meister: Das Ende der Kunst und die Wiederkehr des Mythos* (Stuttgart: Metzler, 1980) 51-59, strains to compare the gentle, witty, still hopeful *Törin* with the violent, bitter Aurelie in the *Lehrjahre* and with the mythical Philomena who loses her tongue.

15. A. G. Steer, Jr., in *Goethe's Science in the Structure of the* Wanderjahre (Athens: U of Georgia P, 1979) 35, declares that "the novella is just what Hersilie said it was, a translation from the French," and asks, "Why should he have 'borrowed' (not to say plagiarized) a fifteen-page piece of foreign literature ... ? He could have turned out a better piece of original material. ..."

16. Laura Martin, "Who's the Fool Now? A Study of Goethe's Novella 'Die pilgernde Törin' from His Novel *Wilhelm Meisters Wanderjahre*," *German Quarterly* 66 (1993): 431-50, offers a thorough analysis of the numerous narrative voices in the tale and how it privileges the female point of view. Nevertheless, Martin follows Jane Brown's judgment on the nature of Goethe's changes to the French text (433-34).

17. See Clouser (n. 10) for reinterpretations of other Gallic-Goethean tales. Only a few scholars have thoroughly compared Goethe's text with his French source. The earliest and most thorough comparison of the French and German texts is by Gertrud Haupt, *Goethes Novellen: Sankt Joseph der Zweite, Die pilgernde Thörin, Wer ist der Verräther?* (Greifswald: Adler, 1913) 37-64. Haupt takes a full fifteen pages to detail Goethe's hundreds of changes in the tale from the original, his corrections of the French text, omissions, and subtle alterations of French meanings. But Haupt does not explore the impact of these changes on the meaning of the story, nor does she interpret it, and she still considers the tale a translation. Jane Brown 53-58, notes changes made by Goethe in the opening and closing of the tale which she believes make the tale more mysterious and less satiric; she also offers an interpretation of the tale and connects it with other threads of the novel; yet I believe Brown misses the fundamental satire of the Revannes and of the youth's position between miller-maid and noble fiancée. Norbert Oellers, in a useful article on the tale's publication history, "Goethes Novelle 'Die pilgernde Thörinn' und

ihre französische Quelle," *Goethe-Jahrbuch* 102 (1985): 88-104, says that Goethe's version of the tale is "ja selbstverständlich zugleich eine Bearbeitung und Deutung der französischen Geschichte," but he too avoids any attempt at interpretation (93).

18. This and all other quotations from the 1821 *Wanderjahre* are from the Dom Verlag edition, ed. Max Hecker (Berlin/Leipzig: Dom, 1921) vol 4; Friedrich's remark is on 247.

19. I concur with Martin (n. 16), who comments: "The change of plan here [from male to female introducer of the "Törin"] is quite significant, for this story as told by a man, concerned as it is with the relationship between the sexes, must be very different from it as being told by a woman" (434).

20. I disagree with Ehrhard Marz, who prefers Goethe's 1821 introduction to "Die pilgernde Törin": "Im Gegensatz zur Spätfassung, wo die Erzählung dem Romanganzen wenig überzeugend eingegliedert ist, wird sie hier organisch in das Rahmengeschehen integriert," *Goethes Rahmen-Erzählungen (1794-1821): Untersuchungen zur Goetheschen Erzählkunst* (Frankfurt/Main: Lang, 1985) 158. Presumably the parallel "wandering" themes of inset novella and main narrative are what Marz finds organically apposite. But I find the male-female commentary in the novel a far more primary theme than the scheme of emigration.

21. See Trunz 576, quoting G. Radbruch: "Goethe hat das nicht ausgesprochen, aber er lächelt mit verborgener Ironie auf die Selbsttäuschungen des Oheims hinunter und hat sichtliche Freude an dem munteren Spott, welchen seine Nichte, die anmutig launenreiche Hersilie, eine von den zärtlichen Empfindungen des alternden Dichters umgebene Lieblingstochter seiner schöpferischen Kraft, gegen den prinzipienfesten Oheim wagt."

22. Martin (n. 16) interprets this quote by saying that Hersilie "not only presents this story as a way of acquainting Wilhelm Meister with her personality through ... her interests and occupations ... , but she also makes explicit claims to the story as representing her own ideas on some things" (434); Martin believes that Hersilie "is very nearly reflected in [the tale's] unnamed main character" (431).

23. Bahr, *Archive,* 15.

24. Quoted from the Dom Verlag reprint of the 1821 edition, "Mit einer Nachbildung der ersten vier Seiten der Originalausgabe," ed. Max Hecker, 1921.

25. Cf. Bahr, *Archive,* 16: "What [Wilhelm and Lenardo] have in common is "a pilgrimage toward their beloved women,' as Neumann puts it" (FA 1.10: 970).

26. Bahr, *Archive,* 18-19: "The fictional editor ... creates a higher degree of realism ... by remarking on the compositional history of the novel. ... This higher degree of realism produced by the editor includes the anchoring of the novel in the poems on the introductory pages; by means of these poems the novel is placed within Goethe's autobiography."

27. Vaget (n. 2) 4.

28. Both Oellers (n. 17) 88-92, and Haupt (n. 17) 37-38, give accounts of how Goethe tried unsuccessfully to translate the ballad after it first appeared in the tale in February of 1789. Then in mid to late 1797, without having the original at hand, he wrote three other "Müllerin" poems. In June of 1798 he finally succeeded in recasting the French ballad from "La folle"—from memory. Shortly afterwards Schiller provided him a copy of the original tale and ballad.

29. The Weimar edition of Goethe's works reprints his three ballads together in WA 1.1:187-98, with brief commentary (407-8). All four are printed together in *J. W. Goethe: Gedichte,* ed. Emil Staiger (Zurich: Manesse, 1949) 1:153-62. All further quotes from the ballad cycle are from the Staiger edition with pages in parentheses in the text. Staiger's commentary (463-64) points out Goethe's letter to Schiller of 12 September 1797, where he refers to the ballad cycle as "einen kleinen Roman." In the inset ballad or "Romanze," Gertrud Haupt (56) sees enough Goethean changes from the French to make it something other than a translation: "In seiner 'Pilgernden Thörin' hat Goethe, seinem französischen Vorbild folgend ... eine Romanze eingeschaltet, die aber keine Übersetzung, sondern eine freie Nachdichtung des Originals ist."

30. For accounts of the goings-on in Weimar, see Richard Friedenthal, *Goethe: His Life and Times* (Cleveland: World, 1965) 204-15, 254-66, and Clouser (n. 10) 29-38, 226-27. Oellers (89) reprints Charlotte von Stein's version of the French ballad.

31. For the French text, see FA 1.10:866-78; this reprint is not exactly identical to either of Goethe's sources (the 1789 "Cahiers de lecture" and the manuscript copy extant in the *Goethe-und-Schiller-Archiv*) but it is in all essentials correct. For ease of scholarly access, all quotations from the French source are from this edition; page numbers are given parenthetically in the text.

32. For a scholar who reads the novella's "pilgrimage" in medieval Christian terms rather than in the context of eighteenth-century social reform and enlightenment, see Henriette Herwig, *Das ewig Männliche zieht uns hinab: "Wilhelm Meisters Wanderjahre"* (Basel: Francke, 1997) 56-69. Although Herwig tries mightily to measure this story by church requirements, I

believe she misses the secular context of the tale, in both French and German versions, and of the *Wanderjahre* itself. Herwig nevertheless credits the *Törin* with achieving an "ethical" and "quasi-religious" conception of love: "Für sie ist die Treue zwischen Mann und Frau eine ethische Grundtugend, fast im alten Sinne eines rechtlich bindenden Vertragsverhältnisses oder eines Gelübdes, das quasi-religiöse Weihe hat, ein unhintergehbarer absoluter Wert" (68).

33. Heinrich Düntzer, *Erläuterungen zu den deutschen Klassikern* (Jena: Hochhausen, 1857) 1.4:58.

34. Henkel (n. 1) 82.

35. Hans Reiss, *Goethes Romane* (Bern: Francke, 1963) 248.

36. Some critics are even more explicit in their bias for the males' point of view. See Ehrhard Marz ([n. 20] 160); Maria Bindschedler ("Goethe und die kokette Frau," *Neue Schweizer Rundschau* [1949]: 380-81, 384, Jane Brown ([n. 4] 57); and Erich Trunz (570). Scholars have also noted the irony in the story's title and plot and sympathize with the pilgrim. See Albert Bielschowski (*Goethe: Sein Leben und seine Werke,* 36th ed. [Munich: Beck, 1919], 2:525); Emil Krüger (*Die Novellen in* 'Wilhelm Meisters Wanderjahren' [Rügenwalde: Albert Mewes, 1926] 18); Deli Fischer-Hartmann (*Goethes Altersroman: Studien über die innere Einheit von* 'Wilhelm Meisters Wanderjahren' [Halle: Max Niemeyer, 1941] 15, 43-46); Ernst Friedrich von Monroy ("Zur Form der Novelle in 'Wilhelm Meisters Wanderjahre,'" *Germanisch-Romanische Monatsheft* 31 [1943]: 3; Fritz Lockemann (*Gestalt und Wandlungen der deutschen Novelle: Geschichte einer literarischen Gattung im neunzehnten und zwanzigsten Jahrhundert* [Munich: Hueber, 1957] 44-45; Hellmuth Himmel (*Geschichte der deutschen Novelle* [Bern: Francke, 1963] 56). Scholars have also acknowledged both genders' contradictions, designations, and folly. See respectively Christine Träger, *Novellistisches Erzählen bei Goethe* (Berlin: Aufbau, 1984) 153-59; and Henry H. H. Remak, "Goethe and the Novella," in *Johann Wolfgang von Goethe: One Hundred and Fifty Years of Continuing Vitality,* ed. Ulrich Goebel and Wolodymyr T. Zyla (Lubbock: Texas Tech UP, 1984) 151; and Laura Martin (n. 16) 432.

37. In "Johann Wolfgang Goethe: *Wilhelm Meisters Wanderjahre,*" *Romane und Erzählungen zwischen Romantik und Realismus: Neue Interpretationen,* ed. Paul Michael Lützeler (Stuttgart: Reclam, 1983) 149-53, Vaget analyzes the psychic, social, erotic, and emotional complexities that underlie Lenardo's feelings about the "Nut-Brown Maid," feelings that lead him to "radikalen Massnahmen ... zu einem prinzipiellen Neubeginn, d.h. zur Auswanderung und Gründung eines neuen Gemeinwesens. Man wird also den entscheidenden Antrieb zur Auswanderung Lenardos ... zu sehen haben in seinem persönlichen Schuldkomplex, den er als eine Art Kollektivschuld seiner ganzen Klasse empfindet" (152). In this essay Vaget also addresses the theme of "Missheirat" between members of different social classes, noting that in the case of Lenardo, "Immerhin wird der Möglichkeit einer Vereinigung Lenardos mit der geliebten Frau in bestimmteren Worten Ausdruck gegeben als im Falle Wilhelms und Natalies" (152).

38. Vaget (n. 2) 18-20, analyzes Goethe's depiction of various noblemen in his novels as signs of his rising and falling hopes for reform of the aristocracy. Lothario in the *Lehrjahre* shows "eagerness to reform the existing social order by renouncing certain privileges of the nobility," yet Eduard in the *Wahlverwandtschaften* is "devoid of any sense of social responsibility for the common weal." At that point Goethe seemingly "wrote off for good the high hopes for social reform he had pinned on the Lotharios of the German nobility." With Lenardo, however, who "has left his aristocratic past behind," Vaget shows that Goethe's hope for reform seemed to have revived.

39. For a detailed and insightful analysis of the narrative levels of "Die pilgernde Törin" in the *Wanderjahre,* see Martin, passim. John Blair, *Tracing Subversive Currents in Goethe's* Wilhem Meister's Apprenticeship (Columbia, South Carolina: Camden House, 1997), does a similar narrative analysis of the *Lehrjahre.*

40. Brown (n. 4; 53-56) and Martin (n. 16; 433-34) argue that the satiric tone of the French original has been removed from Goethe's version. I cannot but find Herr von Revanne's graceless and stunned demeanor, his hyperbolic overreaction praising the wanderer's beauty, satiric in intent and effect for a man who has just been described as a prince.

41. Goethe had already created a heroine who is an actual sexual free agent in the first story of his *Unterhaltungen deutscher Ausgewanderten* (1795). "Antonelli" or "Das Märchen vom klingenden Gespenst," reworked from the *Mémoires d'Hippolyte Clairon,* is a frank embodiment of a woman's declaration of sexual independence and her disappointment with male double standards. For exegesis of the three French-originated stories in the *Unterhaltungen* and their testimony to Goethe's unortho-doxy about relations between men and women, see Clouser (n. 10) 69-96, 109-33.

42. Brown (56-57) also believes that Goethe shows more sympathy for the youth than the French original. But

Brown finds the youth a "warm-blooded innocent" and believes that "the young man's voice takes up too much of the poem, so that he shows equally well that he was mistreated. His perspective is not properly subordinated to hers, but takes on equal weight. Both these perspectives, then, must be taken into account. ..." Brown asks: "Why does Goethe give the perspective of the faithless friend equal validity to that of the girl who has renounced all the pleasures and comforts of family life to prove the existence of true fidelity ... ? The answer lies in the mistaken character of her renunciation." Brown somehow misses the satiric social commentary in the youth's compromised position—and the fact that the *Törin* frames her song—performed, we surmise, in other noble houses besides Revanne's—not solely as a message to her fiancé but as a social critique to all noblemen in her society.

43. Haupt (n. 17) 58.

44. Bielschowsky (n. 40) 2:525.

45. Martin (n. 16) 432, 445-47 analyzes how Hersilie and the *Törin,* like other socially powerless persons, subvert the "gold-lettered proverbs written on house walls" and other stylized elements of male-dominated language and turn them into a means of self-defense.

46. Katharina Mommsen traces Goethe's love of maxims to his reading of the *Thousand and One Nights*: "Derartige Sprüche, Maximen und Lebensregeln, auch Gedichte, in goldenen Buchstaben über der Tür anzubringen, ist speziell orientalische Sitte. Goethe wird hierauf bei seinen Divan-Studien aufmerksam geworden sein. Ausführlich spricht der Dichter in dem 1825 (zweite Jahreshälfte) entstandenen 6. Kapitel des 1. Buches [der *Wanderjahre*] über diese Sitte, und dabei wird auch ausdrücklich erwähnt, daß sie aus dem Orient stamme. ... Auch 1001 Nacht kennt solche Spruchinschriften." *Goethe und 1001 Nacht* (Frankfurt/Main: Suhrkamp, 1961) 148.

47. The pilgrim's deep emotional reaction here belies several critics' interpretation that she has no feeling, love, or sensitivity to others left. Like Revanne, these critics mistake her fidelity to her fiancé and unavailability to Revanne for lack of passion, whereas her instant hurt at Revanne's mention of the youth at the mill declares her passion quite active. These critics seem to resent her rejection of Revanne as much as he does. Besides Henkel's declaration (n. 1; 82) that her fidelity "ist bloss gefrorene Leidenschaft," Reiss asserts (n. 35; 248): "Die Pilgerin entsagt nicht nur den Gefühlen, sie lässt diese so weit absterben, dass sie bereit ist, anderen Menschen Übles zuzufügen, ganz wie jene beleidigte Schöne von der Mühle."

When it comes to "doing evil to others," Revanne is no slouch in torturing the pilgrim to show him more intimacy than she feels. The pilgrim's methods of extricating herself from his prying are tactful by comparison: first her maxims, then a retreat into herself so subtle he doesn't even notice. It seems to me Reiss forgives too easily the hurt or "evil" done by Revanne and the youth at the mill and fails to credit the pilgrim and the miller's daughter with being just as sensitive to rejection as the men are.

48. Himmel (n. 45; 56) is the only critic to note that the narrator distances himself from Revanne's confused, passion-clouded view of the pilgrim: "Mit diesem Absatz distanziert er [der Erzähler] sich von dem leidenschaftsgetrübten Blick des Herrn von Revanne, dem er vorher das Wort erteilt hatte." Klingenberg (n. 14; 130) criticizes Revanne for "mangelnde Achtung vor der begründeten Entscheidung des anderen, die der Törin schließlich das Recht gibt, den Knoten auf höchst merkwürdige Art zu lösen, indem sie Vater und Sohn zum Narren hält" and notes (131): "Als 'reicher Privatmann' war Ravenne [*sic*] ... offenbar nicht gewohnt, sich etwas zu versagen. ..." But Klingenberg considers the pilgrim equally misled by passion (130): "Daß Herr von Ravenne [*sic*] seine Werbungen trotz der Ablehnung der Törin und in bewusster Rivalität zu seinem Sohn fortsetzt, kennzeichnet ihn als in ebenso leidenschaftlicher Subjektivität beschränkt wie die Pilgerin selbst. Nachdenken über das ihm Gemässe scheint ihm ebenso abzugehen wie die Fähigkeit, sich zu bescheiden. ..."

49. Reiss (n. 35; 248) is very critical of the pilgrim and Hersilie for their "willfulness" and credits neither for their resigned adjustment to not finding fulfillment in love: "Als wir Hersilie kennenlernen, ist sie noch viel zu mutwillig, um zu den Entsagenden gehören zu wollen. Dies verrät die Novelle 'Die pilgernde Törin,' die sie erwählt. Die Wanderschaft dieser Pilgerin geschieht nicht aus Entsagung, sondern aus Trotz; sie ist reine Torheit." Reiss apparently never notices Revanne's willfulness and lack of self-control in pursuing his passion for the pilgrim.

Himmel (n. 45; 56), in contrast, credits both the pilgrim and Hersilie with self-control, renunciation, and bringing out the "virtues" in others: "Es gelingt ihr, 'jedermann seine Tugend zu erhalten, indem sie die ihrige bezweifeln lässt.' Dadurch erscheint sie der Welt als 'Törin'; diese Torheit ist aber, wie der Erzähler betont, 'Vernunft unter einem andern Außern.' ... Motiviert wird ihr Verhalten durch ihre Pilgerschaft, welche selbst wieder als Torheit anzusehen, Hersiliens Wort an Wilhelm verbietet: '... wenn ich jemals närrisch werden möchte, wie mir manchmal die Lust ankommt, so wär' es auf diese Weise.' Auch daß man sie im Roman aus den Augen verliert, spricht dafür, dass ihr Leben bereits Entsagung geworden ist." Like Himmel and Radbruch, I take Hersilie to be a far more credible character in the *Wanderjahre* than do Reiss and Brown (52-55). Hersilie's intimation that she too sometimes feels an impulse to go mad implies to me that prior to meeting Wilhelm she had already suffered a disappointment in love, about which she is already exercising the same kind of self-control and renunciation that the pilgrim shows. Thus in both tale and novel, Goethe allows the almost invisible willpower of the women to contrast ironically with many of the men's passionate lack of control.

FURTHER READING

Bibliographies

Glass, Derek. *Goethe in English: A Bibliography of the Translations in the Twentieth Century.* Ed. Matthew Bell and Martin H. Jones. Leeds: Maney Publishing for the English Goethe Soc. and the Modern Humanities Research Assn., 2005. Print.

> Contains a thorough list of English translations of Goethe's works published between 1900 and 1999, with commentary.

Hagen, Waltraud. *Die Drucke von Goethes Werken.* Berlin: Akadamie, 1971. Print.

> Bibliography of works by Goethe. Available only in German.

Kuhn, Dorothea, ed. *Goethes Werke (Hamburger Ausgabe).* Vol. 14. 7th ed. Munich: Beck, 1982. Print.

> One of the standard editions of the works of Goethe and easily accessible. The volume cited contains a select bibliography of materials (published up to 1980) that is adequate for most scholarly purposes. Available only in German.

Pyritz, Hans, Heinz Nicolai, and Gerhard Burkhardt. *Goethe-Bibliographie.* 2 vols. Heidelberg: Winter, 1965-68. Print.

> Includes more than 10,500 entries, systematically arranged in fourteen categories covering Goethe's early development as well as his contributions to science, art, theater, poetry, and other fields. The bibliography of criticism is in all major languages, although the majority is in German.

Seifert, Siegfried. *Goethe-Bibliographie 1950-1990.* 3 vols. Munich: Saur, 2000. Print.

> The most extensive bibliography of Goethe studies for the period, covering critical works in all major languages.

Biographies

Boyle, Nicholas. *Goethe: The Poet and the Age.* 2 vols. to date. Oxford: Clarendon P, 1991- . Print.

> The most detailed and sophisticated treatment of Goethe's life in English, covering the author's life to 1803.

Fairley, Barker. *A Study of Goethe.* Oxford: Clarendon P, 1947. Print.

> Provides an enlightening portrait of Goethe from the viewpoint of a distinguished Germanist. Fairley's biography appeared before the post-World War II worldwide resurgence of interest in Goethe.

Gajek, Bernhard, and Franz Götting, eds. *Goethes Leben und Werk in Daten und Bildern.* Frankfurt am Main: Insel, 1966. Print.

> Contains a useful table listing Goethe's activities and works year by year, as well as several hundred illustrations (monotone) of Goethe and his homes, friends, and travels. Available only in German.

Lewes, George Henry. *The Life and Works of Goethe: With Sketches of His Age and Contemporaries, from Published and Unpublished Sources.* 2 vols. London: Nutt, 1855. Print.

> The earliest biography of Goethe in English and still one of the most influential. Lewes was familiar with the Weimar setting and with people who knew Goethe.

Williams, John R. *The Life of Goethe: A Critical Biography.* Oxford: Blackwell, 1998. Print.

> A "critical account of [the] writer's creative works set in the context of his life and times." Williams translates all German quotations for the English-language reader.

Criticism

Bersier, Gabrielle. "Goethe's Parody of 'Nazarene' Iconography: The Joseph Story in *Wilhelm Meisters Wanderjahre.*" *Goethe Yearbook* 9 (1999): 264-77. Print.

> Draws attention to Goethe's detailed portrait of a secular, anachronistic "Saint Joseph" figure early in *Wilhelm Meister's Travels.* Bersier argues that earlier critics largely missed the satirical overtones of this passage and that Goethe, as an art critic, was mocking the tendencies of the Nazarene school of Romantic painters to imitate primitive Christian art.

Brown, Jane K. *Goethe's Cyclical Narratives*: Die Unterhaltungen Deutscher Ausgewanderten *and* Wilhelm Meisters Wanderjahre. Chapel Hill: U of North Carolina P, 1975. Print.

> Analyzes two works by Goethe that are linked by their complex structures. Brown discusses in detail heretofore unnoticed contemporary influences on *Wilhelm Meister's Travels* and explores the parodic aspects of the work. She examines the theme of renunciation that

runs through the novel and how it relates to Goethe's theory of history.

Maierhofer, Waltraud. Wilhelm Meisters Wanderjahre *und der Roman des Nebeneinander.* Bielefeld: Aisthesis, 1990. Print.

Compares Goethe's novel with contemporary works by Karl Immermann and Karl Gutzkow that have similarly complex structures. Available only in German.

Martin, Laura. "Who's the Fool Now? A Study of Goethe's Novella 'Die pilgernde Törin' from His Novel *Wilhelm Meisters Wanderjahre.*" *German Quarterly* 66.4 (1993): 431-50. Print.

Examines "The Pilgrim Fool," noting its origin in a French novella, the changes made in Goethe's translation, and the valuable perspective lent to *Wilhelm Meister's Travels* by the young woman in the novella who finds in her supposed madness a partial "escape [from] the mistakes and inequities of the patriarchy."

Mehra, Marlis. "The Aesthetics of Imperfection in Goethe's Last Novel." *Studies in Eighteenth-Century Culture* 12 (1983): 205-11. Print.

Argues against the common assumption that Goethe retained the Classical aesthetics that characterize his work from around 1800 throughout his life. Mehra suggests that, instead, Goethe later embraced an anti-Classical "aesthetics of imperfection," according to which the sprawling and fragmentary *Wilhelm Meister's Travels* is a greater achievement than his earlier, more obviously coherent works.

Prickett, Stephen. "Fictions and Metafictions: *Phantastes, Wilhelm Meister,* and the Idea of the *Bildungsroman.*" *The Gold Thread: Essays on George MacDonald.* Ed. William Raeper. Edinburgh: Edinburgh UP, 1990. 109-25. Print.

Describes the ways in which Wilhelm Meister prefigures Anodos, the hero of George MacDonald's 1858 fantasy novel *Phantastes.* Observed similarities in character and plot details lead to Prickett's suggestion

that Goethe, like MacDonald, tested the "limitations of conventional realism" as a means of depicting spiritual growth.

Schellenberg, Renata. "The Genesis of Goethe's Last Novel: *Wilhelm Meisters Wanderjahre* (1821)." *New German Review* 17 (2001-02): 47-63. Print.

Provides a brief historical account of the less-discussed 1821 version of *Wilhelm Meister's Travels,* summarizing the early printings of the interpolated novellas common to both editions of the work and noting the scandalous appearance of an anonymous "false" *Wilhelm Meister's Travels* that was passed off as Goethe's.

Tantillo, Astrida Orle. *Goethe's Modernisms.* New York: Continuum, 2010. Print.

Treats Goethe's *Faust, The Sorrows of Young Werther,* and the *Wilhelm Meister* novels. Tantillo's analysis of *Wilhelm Meister's Travels* concentrates on the educational theory in the novel and its possible relevance to modern pedagogical practices.

Waidson, H. M. "Death by Water: or, The Childhood of Wilhelm Meister." *Modern Language Review* 56.1 (1961): 44-53. Print.

Takes up a traumatic episode from Wilhelm Meister's early years: a childhood friend drowns, launching Wilhelm on his long and circuitous path to becoming a surgeon. Waidson cites the symbolic recurrence of this event as evidence that, despite the novel's myriad digressions, "what happens to Wilhelm . . . is the main concern of the *Wanderjahre* as a whole."

Zipser, Richard A. "Bulwer-Lytton and Goethe's Mignon." *Modern Language Notes* 89.3 (1974): 465-68. Print.

Traces the occurrence of characters very similar to Mignon (a character from *Wilhelm Meister's Apprenticeship* whose presence haunts *Wilhelm Meister's Travels*) in four works by the English Romantic novelist Edward Bulwer-Lytton. Bulwer-Lytton is credited with popularizing the Mignon archetype—a victimized but precocious maiden—in the English-language writing of his time.

Additional information on Goethe's life and works is contained in the following sources published by Gale: *Concise Dictionary of World Literary Biography: German Writers; Dictionary of Literary Biography,* **Vol. 94;** *DISCovering Authors; DISCovering Authors: British Edition; DISCovering Authors: Canadian Edition; DISCovering Authors Modules: Dramatists, Most-Studied Authors,* **and** *Poets; DISCovering Authors 3.0; Drama Criticism,* **Vol. 20;** *European Writers,* **Vol. 5;** *Gale Contextual Encyclopedia of World Literature; Gothic Literature: A Gale Criticial Companion,* **Vol. 2;** *Literary Movements for Students,* **Vol. 1;** *Literature and Its Times Supplement,* **Vol. 1;** *Literature Resource Center; Nineteenth-Century Literature Criticism,* **Vols. 4, 22, 34, 90, 154, 247, 266;** *Poetry Criticism,* **Vol. 5;** *Reference Guide to World Literature,* **Eds. 2, 3;** *Short Story Criticism,* **Vols. 38, 141;** *Twayne's World Authors;* **and** *World Literature Criticism,* **Vol. 3.**

Adah Isaacs Menken
1835-1868

(Born Adelaide McCord or Ada Berthe [or Bertha] Theodore; wrote under the pseudonyms Dr. Edwin F. B. Price and possibly Indigena) American actress and poet.

INTRODUCTION

One of the most notorious and successful actresses of her era, Menken lived a protean life, constantly reinventing the facts (or fictions) of her biography and the personae of her poetry. Add to this the gender-bending title role in the play *Mazeppa* (1861) that made her famous, along with her unconventional offstage behavior, and it is understandable that few of Menken's critics or biographers claim to know the "real" Menken, and that several speak of a "mask" or a "veil" in even her most deeply confessional documents. Menken, encouraged this sense of mystery, projecting an aura of ebullience in person even as her poetry, relatively little of which appeared before her death, told a quite different story. If Menken was the most famous (and surely the most highly paid) actress of the 1860s, she was also a disconsolate poet. Her single posthumous volume of verse, *Infelicia* (1868), is a study in deep unhappiness.

For many literary critics of Menken's time her theatrical career eclipsed her poetic aspirations so thoroughly that reviews of her book became referenda on her public appearances. Others were startled by the spirituality and sensitivity of her verse, which they imagined to be at odds with her audacious and "immoral" conduct. This view led many early biographers to minimize the importance of Menken's poetry, despite her lifelong association with such authors as Mark Twain and Walt Whitman. Toward the end of the twentieth century, a renewed critical appreciation of Menken's work as both poet and actress led to studies treating the two as part of a larger, lifelong artistic project. Yet in attempting to apply Postmodern notions of identity to Menken, scholars often found that she seems to have anticipated them, having learned over a century ago the power of a deliberately crafted persona.

BIOGRAPHICAL INFORMATION

The details of Menken's early life are impossible to reconstruct with certainty, as the poet herself provided reporters with multiple conflicting versions of her birth and parentage. In one of the more widely accepted accounts written soon after her death by G. Lippard Barclay (1868), Menken was born Adelaide McCord in the small town of Milneburg, Louisiana (now part of New Orleans), on 15 June 1835. A more recent account by Michael Foster and Barbara Foster (2011; see Further Reading) supports the birth name Ada Berthe Theodore. Menken added a variety of flourishes to her biography over the years, some of which survived as entirely alternate biographies. She identified herself at different times as being of Jewish, Irish, African-American, and Spanish descent, among others. The Fosters present evidence that she had an African-American background and was "passing" as white. As a girl she might have had a brief stage career, though her fame as an actress did not come until considerably later.

The public record of Menken's life began in 1855 with her short-lived marriage to the musician W. H. Kneass. By 1856 she had married the musician Alexander Isaac Menken. She initially found comfort and support not only in her husband's family but also in the larger Cincinnati Jewish community to which the Menkens belonged, and she set about establishing a Jewish identity for herself through the study of Hebrew and the publication of poems and essays championing "our people." In at least one interview, she contended that she was born Jewish. However, Menken's burgeoning career as an actress soon placed her at odds with the conservative views of Alexander's family. The two divorced in 1859, and she soon married the prizefighter John C. Heenan, but this marriage was brief and unhappy. After a period of depression, Menken experienced a marked change in fortune when she took the title role in *Mazeppa,* a stage show adapted from Lord Byron's poem of the same name. She played a Tartar prince who, betrothed to a daughter of his Polish enemies, attempts to reunite with her in disguise. The plot of the production, however, was largely secondary to the spectacle of Menken wearing a nude-toned bodysuit and strapped to a "fiery steed" that ran across the stage. Menken would take her *Mazeppa* performance on tour throughout the American West and later, to great acclaim, in London.

Some of Menken's poems play on widely circulated "tall tales" now recognized as factually unlikely. In one especially memorable anecdote, a party of Native Americans in Texas captures Menken. She communicates in Spanish with an "Indian maiden" named Laurelack, who helps Menken escape at the cost of her own life. Menken immortalized this brief friendship in her poem "A Memory." In another tale, Menken claims to have posed as a man and enlisted in the Confederate cause. Several of her poems invoke the imagery of Civil War battlefields, and at least one clearly adopts the persona that Menken claimed to have inhabited. What can be corroborated of her later life is, by the standards of her time and culture, almost as outlandish: witnesses in newspapers and magazines noted they were aghast to find that the actress frequently dressed in male evening clothes and visited cigar dens and brothels.

Menken's theater critics, including most famously Twain, were almost unanimous in their judgment that she lacked genuine acting ability. Her letters beg to differ, noting that the scandal of her multiple marriages effectively obviated a career in serious theater. To the audiences of the time, Menken became the famous "naked lady" whose dangerous equestrian spectacle shocked moralists and enthralled onlookers. Her volume of poetry, compiled shortly before her death, would for many years prove insufficient to overcome this caricature. Menken died in Paris on 10 August 1868 from complications of riding injuries, her health also possibly weakened by tuberculosis.

MAJOR WORK

Menken's collection of verse, *Infelicia* (Latin for "unhappy one"), appeared one week after her death. The work is, as the title indicates, characterized by varying degrees of melancholy, rage, despair, and doom. Two of the most widely discussed poems in *Infelicia* are "Infelix" and "Judith." The former, reflecting bitterly on the transience of life, asks in *ubi sunt* fashion (a motif from medieval poetry that muses on the question "Where are those who were before us?") where "the promise of my years" has fled and insists that all that remains is a triad of malevolent "sister powers": Evil, Sorrow, and Deceit. Critics have seen "Infelix" as reminiscent of the lyrical work of Edgar Allan Poe in its conventional pattern of meter and end rhyme. "Judith," by contrast, abandons rhyme and meter, combining elements of the devout Jewish verse that Menken wrote for the Cincinnati *Israelite* with a freer, more erotically charged persona than that of her earlier work. The poem tells of the deeds of the Old Testament heroine Judith, who seduced and beheaded the enemy general Holofernes and thereby saved her people from conquest. Menken's "Judith" seems to revel in the murder of Holofernes, "starving for" the "feast" of the slain general's blood.

Apart from *Infelicia*, Menken wrote approximately sixty known poems, many of which were published in the *Israelite* in the late 1850s and the New York *Sunday Mercury* in 1860-61. Notably, it has been established that she plagiarized several poems during this time, presenting the verse of well-known Jewish poet Penina Moïse as her own. The majority of Menken's poems, however, were not published in her lifetime, and previously unknown work attributed to her continues to be discovered. Among the most sought after: the *Dictionary of National Biography* reported that in about 1856 Menken published a volume of poems under the pseudonym Indigena called *Memories*, but no copy has been located.

CRITICAL RECEPTION

Contemporary reactions to Menken's poetry were largely determined by public impressions of her as an actress first and a writer second (if at all). Typical of these are two 1868 reviews of *Infelicia* in prominent New York newspapers, the *Daily Tribune* and the *Times*. The reviewer for the *Times* attributed "the interest of this little volume of poems" mainly to "the character and career of the author," while the *Daily Tribune* commentator noted that "the smell of foot-lights and burnt rosin pervades the whole composition, leaving the impression that stage-effect rather than sorrow is the source of her inspiration." Both appraised the book in largely negative terms; neither was able to reconcile what the *Tribune* refers to as the "jovial, rollicking adventuress" of the stage with the broader emotional range of her written work.

Both of these early reviewers also indicated (with disapproval) the connection between Menken's style and that of Whitman, at that time hardly the revered figure of American literature he later became. The *Tribune* reviewer cited Whitman as one of several "suspicious models" whose influence is detectable, while the *Times* reviewer disparaged Menken's free verse as "prose cut in lengths of varying measure, in the manner rendered familiar" by Whitman. This claim has been explored at length by later critics, including Gregory Eiselein (2002), who found detailed echoes of *Leaves of Grass* not only in Menken's prosody but also in her diction, use of repetition, and choice of imagery. Others, including Barbara Foster and Michael Foster (1993), pointed out that Menken was the only female poet of her century to attempt the rolling, catalogue-rich style of free verse for which Whitman was notorious. Moreover, her portrayal of Judith led the Fosters to assert "a kind of déjà vu in reverse" upon comparing Menken's work to that of the twentieth-century confessional poet Sylvia Plath. "Menken," they noted, "raged a full century before Plath."

Feminist critics found a similar prescience in Menken's life and work. Daphne A. Brooks (2001) regarded Menken as a case study in the politics of female resistance to the patriarchal gaze and considered the actress's spectacular displays to be a means of reasserting control over her publicly visible body. Similar arguments have been extended to Menken's poetry, in which she gave vent to a host of feelings unavailable in the "shape actress" roles that won her fame and wealth. Where the *Tribune* reviewer suggested that "a charitable father-confessor might discern the accents of unhoping penitence" in Menken's published work, Noreen Barnes-McLain (1998; see Further Reading) contended that it is just such a discourse that Menken hoped to subvert with her poetry—far from repenting of her actions as though they constituted a moral evil, Menken often seemed to celebrate and affirm transgressions of social norms, following her own advice to "swim against the current."

The "Jewish phase" of Menken's work attracted the attention of a few modern critics, who saw in her poetic devoutness a tension between the ideals of her (native or adoptive) religious community and the restless spirit that made her so memorable among her literary friends. The question of her plagiarism of Moïse proved something of a puzzle in this regard, because Menken chose a widely read and highly regarded poet to copy. Eiselein (2004) suggested that such an act "epitomized Menken's self-doubt and her anxieties and uncertainties about being a poet, a Midwesterner and a wife; they were symptoms of a certain undoing of identity." Menken gave evidence of a similar "undoing" in several other appropriations, along with compositions under a handful of pseudonyms, such as "Dr. Edwin F. B. Price," who wrote with fond admiration to Heenan. This practice has made the identification of Menken's poetry a challenging project. As Peter Dollard (2000) noted in his essay announcing six "new" Menken poems, the famous actress and forgotten poet seemed determined, even from beyond the grave, to confound those seeking certainty about the facts of her life.

Michael J. Hartwell

PRINCIPAL WORKS

Infelicia. New York: Williams, 1868. (Poetry)

Infelicia *and Other Writings.* Ed. Gregory Eiselein. Peterborough: Broadview, 2002. (Poetry and prose)

CRITICISM

New-York Daily Tribune (review date 1868)

SOURCE: Rev. of *Infelicia,* by Adah Isaacs Menken. *New-York Daily Tribune* 29 Sept. 1868: 6. Print.

[*In the following review, the critic takes exception to Menken's work, largely because of its "unscrupulous" and theatrical quality. The reviewer notes the formal resemblance of Menken's work to the poetry of Walt Whitman but expresses dissatisfaction with the poems on grounds of "rhyme and reason."*]

The notoriety of the author's life will awaken a degree of interest in this volume [**Infelicia**] to which it is not entitled by any poetical merit. It is little more than an echo of Walt Whitman, Ossian, and other suspicious models, with no assuring proof of originality or even of sincerity. As a record of personal feeling, it might challenge curiosity, did not the melodramatic character of the writer prevent any reliance on the truthfulness of its effusions. She unveils the secrets of her experience as unscrupulously as she went through the displays of the theater, but in both

cases, one will detect a morbid love of publicity, inflamed by a passion for admiration and a thirst for gain. Hence her disclosures have no value as studies in human nature, or as illustrations of abnormal passion. The tone of the volume is for the most part sad, often cynical, even desperate, but the smell of foot-lights and burnt rosin pervades the whole composition, leaving the impression that stage-effect rather than sorrow is the source of her inspiration. The expression of tender or lofty sentiment by such a jovial, rollicking adventuress has only a ludicrous aspect, even in the eyes of those who have the most faith in man,—or fast-riding Mazeppa women. There are perhaps occasional revelations of the self-conscious soul, that give transient glimpses of "the angel in the devil," like the closing piece in the volume, in which a charitable father-confessor might discern the accents of unhoping penitence, though he would not venture to describe a face that wears a perpetual mask.

INFELIX

Where is the promise of my years;
　　Once written on my brow?
Ere errors, agonies, and fears
Brought with them all that speaks in tears,
Ere I had sunk beneath my peers;
　　Where sleeps that promise now?

Naught lingers to redeem those hours,
　　Still, still to memory sweet!
The flowers that bloomed in sunny bowers
Are withered all; and Evil towers
Supreme above her sister powers
　　Of Sorrow and Deceit.

I look along the columned years,
　　And see Life's riven fane,
Just where it fell, amid the jeers
Of scornful lips, whose mocking sneers,
For ever hiss within my ears
　　To break the sleep of pain.

I can but own my life is vain
　　A desert void of peace;
I missed the goal I sought to gain,
I missed the measure of the strain
That lulls Fame's fever in the brain,
　　And bids Earth's tumult cease.

Myself! alas for theme so poor
　　A theme but rich in Fear;
I stand a wreck on Error's shore,
A spectre not within the door,
A houseless shadow evermore,
　　An exile lingering here.

This is better both in rhyme and reason than most of the contents of the volume, which is made up of sonorous rhapsodies in which prose takes the form of poetry without its spirit.

New York Times (review date 1868)

SOURCE: Rev. of *Infelicia,* by Adah Isaacs Menken. *New York Times* 21 Oct. 1868: 6. Print.

[In the following review, the critic expresses sympathy for Menken's work, noting its pathos and "evident sincerity," but concludes that the poems lack polish and owe their notoriety largely to Menken's fame as an actress. The reviewer also interprets Infelicia *as evidence of Menken's contrition for her unconventional way of life.]*

The interest of this little volume [**Infelicia**] of poems arises chiefly, to say solely would be hardly too strong, from their association in the reader's mind with the character and career of the author. Unpolished, crude in matter and in form, most of them would have been consigned to speedy oblivion had they emanated from the mind of any one less known, in the peculiar manner in which her notoriety was obtained, than ADAH ISAACS MENKEN. Though one of the most common experiences in the world, people were really astonished to learn that the most notorious representative of the "nude drama," a woman who in her own person had cast aside all the conventionalities and most of the moralities of society, had moments of serious thought, of poignant mental suffering, of regret, of yearning after better things, of aspirations for a higher life. The evident sincerity of her writings, as well as the contrast between these moods and her actual life, goes far to win our sympathy and disarm criticism. We need not spare the character of MISS MENKEN in judging of these poems. She never spared herself, was never modest for herself, nor asked others to be shame-faced for her. Her whole life was passed in violation of social law, yet these poems show that there was left in her this grace of virtue, that she never set up her life as a protest against society, nor claimed to be anything other than what she was; that she was conscious of the better way, and oftentimes, in the wildest delirium of her career, had thoughts "too deep for tears" and inexpressible in words.

Few of her poems display the finish of an artist. Most of them are hardly more than prose cut in lengths of varying measure, in the manner rendered familiar by WALT WHITMAN, whose style she admired and imitated. We quote a few lines from the poem called **"Resurgam"**:

> Why did I die?
> O love! I waited—I waited years and years ago.
> Once the blaze of a far-off edge of living Love crept up my
>   horizon, and promised a new moon of Poesy.
> A soul's full life!
> A soul's full love!
> And promised that my voice should ring trancing shivers
>   of rapt melody down the grooves of this dumb earth.
> And promised that echoes should vibrate along the purple
>   spheres of unfathomable seas, to the soundless folds of
>   the clouds.
> And promised that I should know the sweet sisterhood of
>   the stars.
> Promised that I should live with the crooked moon in her
>   eternal beauty.
> But a Midnight swooped down to bridegroom the Day.
> The blazing Sphynx of that far-off, echoless promise,
>   shrank into a drowsy shroud that mocked the crying
>   stars of my soul's muttered song.

> And so I died,
> Died this uncoffined and unburied Death.
> Died alone in the young May night.
> Died with my fingers grasping the white throat of many a
>   prayer.

Though disfigured by extravagant and incoherent phraseology, there is a great deal of genuine pathos in these lines, and the imagery is original and poetic. Here is an extract from another poem, called **"Into the Depths"**:

> Out of the depths have I cried unto thee, O Lord
> Weeping all the night-time—
> Weeping sad and chill through the lone woods—
> Straying 'mong the ghostly trees—
> Wandering through the rustling leaves—
> Sobbing to the moon, whose icy light wraps me like a
>   shroud;
> Leaning on a hoary rock, praying to the mocking stars.
> With Love's overwhelming power startling my soul like
>   an earthquake shock.
> I lift my soul above the low howl of the winds to call my
>   Eros to come and give me light and life once more.
> His broad arms can raise me up to the light, and his red
>   lips can kiss me back to life.
> I need not the storm of the world, nor the clashing of its
>   steel.
> I wait—wait—wait!

Still more pathetic is the poem called **"Drifts That Bar My Door,"** from which we take the opening lines:

> O, Angels! will ye never sweep the drifts from my door?
> Will ye never wipe the gathering rust from the hinges?
> How long must I plead and cry in vain?
> Lift back the iron bars, and lead me hence.
> Is there not a land of peace beyond my door?
> Oh, lead me to it—give me rest—release me from this
>   unequal strife.
> Heaven can attest that I fought bravely when the heavy
>   blows fell fast.
> Was it my sin that strength failed?
> Was it my sin that the battle was in vain?
> Was it my sin that I lost the prize? I do not sorrow for all
>   the bitter pain and blood it cost me.
> Why do ye stand sobbing in the sunshine?
> I cannot weep.
> There is no sunlight in this dark cell. I am starving for light.
> O, angels! sweep the drifts away—unbar my door!

The most beautiful, most touching, most highly finished poem in the volume is the one with which it closes, and with which we take leave of it. The verses ought to be engraved on the author's tombstone, as the appropriate epitaph of a wasted life. They are called

INFELIX

> Where is the promise of my years;
>   Once written on my brow?
> Ere errors, agonies and fears
> Brought with them all that speaks in tears,
> Ere I had sunk beneath my peers;
>   Where sleeps that promise now?

Naught lingers to redeem those hours,
　　Still, still to memory sweet!
The flowers that bloomed in sunny bowers
Are withered all; and Evil towers
Supreme above her sister powers
　　Of Sorrow and Deceit.

I look along the columned years,
　　And see Life's riven fane,
Just where it fell, amid the jeers
Of scornful lips, whose mocking sneers,
For ever hiss within mine ears
　　To break the sleep of pain.

I can but own my life is vain
　　A desert void of peace;
I missed the goal I sought to gain,
I missed the measure of the strain
That lulls Fame's fever in the brain,
　　And bids Earth's tumult cease.

Myself! alas for theme so poor
　　A theme but rich in Fear:
I stand a wreck on Error's shore,
A spectre not within the door,
A houseless shadow evermore,
　　An exile lingering here.

G. Lippard Barclay (essay date 1868)

SOURCE: Barclay, G. Lippard. *The Life and Remarkable Career of Adah Isaacs Menken, The Celebrated Actress.* Philadelphia: Barclay, 1868. 19-55. Print.

[*In the following essay, Barclay, who calls himself the editor, weaves the apologetic story of Menken's life and career from various secondhand accounts, making liberal use of her poetry, as well. He concludes with the expressed hope that the " 'ill-fed, foul-mouthed, cross-eyed reporters,' who have lately vied with each other in making the most slanderous reports of the late Adah Isaacs Menken's life and death will cease to put forth their weak articles teeming with the largest words from 'Webster's and Johnson's vocabulary.' "*]

It has been the aim of many biographers in writing the life of a woman, who during her "short allotted hours upon this earth," has been an actress, to "fill in" imaginary incidents, both ungentlemanly in the writer, and insulting to the subject of his remarks. "How little one half the world knows what the other half is doing," *and has done.* There are thousands to-day who look upon the theatre with perfect abhorrence imagining that, "behind the scenes, Satan himself is on the rampage." If these persons were allowed the privilege of a peep into the "greenroom" of any first class theatre, what a change would "come o'er their dreams."

Adah Isaacs Menken was born in the town of Milneburg, north of, and within a few miles of New Orleans, Louisiana. It was, at the time of Adah's birth, known as Chartrain, the lake of that name being in the immediate vicinity. Adah was born in the year 1835, June 15th, and was the eldest of three children, there being a boy and another girl. The sister was named Josephine. At the time of Adah's birth, her father, Mr. James McCord, was a merchant of eminent standing. When she was about seven or eight years of age, her father died, and as he, previous to his death, was in very straightened circumstances, the family were left wholly dependent upon themselves to procure a livelihood; this was by no means an easy thing to accomplish. Mr. McCord had been, during his life, an ardent admirer of the art of dancing, and at an early age the sisters had been placed under the instruction of a French master. Mrs. McCord, after the death of her husband, as a last resource, applied to the manager of the opera, then in New Orleans, for a position in the ballet for her little girls; they were accepted, and immediately entered upon their new life. They became, in a short time, great favorites with the company. The natures of the sisters were entirely different; that of Adah was naturally lively. She was arch and piquant, much better formed than her sister, and upon the stage seemed as if "native and to the manor born." Josephine did not possess the assurance of her sister. She was of a passive nature—shy and retiring. Adah adopted the name of Bertha Theodore for the stage.

During her career as *danseuse,* she mastered the French and Spanish languages. When about thirteen years of age she devoted considerable time to the translation of "Homer's Illiad," and as remarkable as it may appear, completed her arduous undertaking with triumph. About this time Adah played a very successful engagement as *danseuse* at the Tacon theatre, Havana. She became an immense favorite, and was called by the *habitues,* "Queen of the Plaza." After this she visited Texas and Mexico and played an engagement at the leading opera house in Mexico, which was a success both pecuniarily and artistically. She then proceeded to Port Lavaca, Texas, and here met with an adventure very stirring in nature, and which nearly deprived the theatrical world of its "Mazeppa." A hunting expedition was proposed, and Adah, with her customary fearlessness, readily consented to accompany the party.

The following is her version of the adventure: Having got every thing in readiness, and the morning beautifully serene, we started on the hunt. I rode a splendid horse belonging to Captain P. Gonzalez, who kindly loaned it to me. Both the horse and myself were in excellent spirits, as indeed was the whole party, with one exception. A man named Gus Varney accompanied our party, and a more inveterate coward I have never seen. It appears that he had been induced through a wager to join us, the betting party asserting that Varney was afraid to do so. We had scarcely proceeded fifteen miles when this Varney commenced to show evident signs of his noted cowardice, hinting as to the probability of Indians being in the vicinity. Several ladies became greatly alarmed at his suggestions, and I confess that I did not feel quite assured that such was not the case. The men attempted to make sport of Varney's fears, but his cowardice was greatly predominant over his sense of shame, and consequently had not the desired effect. A young man in the party, a practical joker of the worse kind, proposed to his companions to raise a cry of 'Indians are coming,' to frighten Varney, and then ridicule him, and try to convince him that his fears were groundless. Having communicated their plan to us, we consented to act our parts well by screaming and pretending to be greatly alarmed. At a given signal our joker cried: 'Run for your lives, the Indians are coming.' I was about to do as directed, when a sight that I never shall forget was presented me. There over the hill were plainly visible, not mere spectres, but solid and matter of fact bodies; a large number of Indians. I am not naturally a coward, but the sight of those savages sent a cold chill through me, whilst a perspiration came over me, outwardly; I lost my balance at the same time, my consciousness left me, and I remembered no more until I awoke within a wigwam, with a dusky 'son of the feather' gazing intently upon me.

'Pretty squaw—make me—good—like to much?' murmured the Indian in broken sentences.

All the heroines that I had ever read about, upon awakening from unconsciousness, repeated the well-known 'where am I,' consequently I said the same thing. His reply was as follows:—

'Big woods—my wigwam; you mine now—me big chief.'

'Was any of my friends captured?' I asked.

'Little Mole, he big coward, no fight.'

I understood from this that Varney had been caught as well as myself, and that had I at the time been perfectly conscious, I would have escaped with the rest of the party, as we were all well mounted, and the Indians being afoot, pursuit on their part would have been fruitless.

'Want see little Mole?' asked my captor.

At first I was disgusted at the idea, but having thought that Varney might possess a knowledge which would assist us in our escape, I consented to see him.

The Indian gave a peculiar signal, which was immediately answered in person by a young Indian girl. In appearance she did not possess any refined beauty, but there was something that drew me toward her; there was certainly something grand about her, as with stately step she answered the Indian's summons.

'Why am I called?' asked she.

'Laulerack is more proud than ever,' said the Indian. 'Bring hither the white man'; he spoke the Spanish language this time. She glanced toward me with a look of pity, I thought, and then, as if the act was a condescension on her part, obeyed the Indian's command.

'Is the maiden your wife?' I asked in Spanish. The Indian started as if some immortal power had addressed him, as I heretofore had only spoken English to him.

'No,' answered he bitterly; 'as each moon passes she grows more proud than ever, and although I am determined that she shall be so, she is if possible more determined not to wed me.'

'If you would wed her, why do you wish that I too should be your wife.'

'The white beauty in summer, the red beauty in winter,' replied he.

I saw that it were useless to try to divert his mind from having two wives at once. As the Indian did not seem inclined to converse further, I sat meditating upon the possibility of my escape, when Varney entered. Here was a caricature, if J. S. Clarke had been there at the time he would have learned that his low comedy motions were not perfection. His eyes reminded me of a case of 'stage fright' I had once seen. His body was doubled up like Quilp's in one of Dickens' novels. He possessed great facial expression, and at the time it was suggestive of Clarke's 'Bob Acres duel scene in the Rivals,' whilst his legs would put to shame that comedian's 'bend' in Toodles. In spite of my position I laughed heartily, and even on the Indian's face there lingered a smile, mingled with contempt for the cowardly being before him.

'Oh, Miss Theodore,' cried Varney, in piteous accents, 'we're gone up, as good as dead and buried. I shall be burned at the stake, I know I shall. Even the little devils and their inhuman mothers delight in torturing me. They hunt for pins in my coat, and then when the barbarians find them, they stick me most unmercifully.' The last five words were uttered with groans, and rolling eyes like a calf about to be slaughtered.

I perceived that it were useless to attempt to concoct a plan, and expect any assistance from Varney in regard to what means we should adopt to escape. My thoughts naturally turned toward the plausibility of asking the assistance of the Indian maiden. I resolved that it should be so, as this was my last and only hope.

'Oh, Miss Theodore,' said Varney, 'if there be any chance of getting away, name it. I'll do any thing but fight these darned heathens.' This was all spoken in a whisper, with timid glances toward our guard, who stood with the natural stoicism of his race, saying nothing, but endeavoring to catch each word. 'Think of some means whereby *I* can escape,' added Varney, 'and then if I get to Lavaca, I'll send out armed men to rescue you.'

The natural selfish nature of the man was predominant, and I made up my mind that before I would assist, in any way, a being so incapable to all the true requisite feelings of a man, I would rather remain in captivity. I did not speak my mind to Varney, but at the time felt very much like doing so. Varney, finding me in no mood to converse with him, retired. And I shortly afterwards expressed a desire to speak with Laulerack, which my dusky captor consented to comply with. She entered, and at the same time the Indian, understanding that we would be alone, stationed himself outside of the wigwam.

'What does my pale sister wish,' asked Laulerack, in a much more pleasant voice than she had used in addressing her Indian admirer.

'Thy sister's name is Bertha,' said I in Spanish, 'and although I have seen you but once before, I already love you.'

'My white sister has my pity.'

'And pity in a woman,' I quickly added, 'amounts to, or soon turns to love.'

'My sister is right,' Laulerack answered, 'and my pity has thus soon become a love.'

'Thanks, thanks,' I muttered.

'No thanks to me, but to the *Great Spirit who has willed it so.*'

'Yes, but if my sister had not a pure and loving nature, belonging more to the other world than this, the Great Spirit would not influence her to love her pale face sister, or be instrumental in causing her to harbor within her heart, a feeling of pity for the maiden torn from her friends and home, to be held captive in a wilderness, where each visible thing strikes terror, as the thrust of an enemy's bayonet does to the fallen and wounded warrior.'

'The Great Spirit,' said Laulerack, 'has given thee the power of speaking in winning speech, and thy words have much import to the red maiden.'

I perceived the advantage gained, and immediately followed it up. 'Then will you not, my sister, help me in my escape? Think of what I suffer in thus being retained. My friends perhaps mourn me as dead.' Laulerack's eyes shone with unusual brilliance, as she made answer and said:

'What are the pale sister's sufferings, when compared with mine? As the child's troubles are to those of their parents. Listen, and you shall hear my story. As thirteen moons are counted the year, so have four times that many moons passed since I have lost a father's protection, a mother's care. My father was then the chief of a powerful tribe; one cursed day he was prevailed upon to go to battle with another tribe equally as powerful. My father's tribe was victorious, and many captives were taken. A guard was appointed to watch, but being so worn out and moreover thinking of the glory they had but just achieved, they fell to

dreaming. In the meantime, the enemy, although fairly beaten, were not entirely subdued, and their chief warrior, a man of wise thought, resolved upon an attack, well knowing the condition of his opponents. His tribe were also much worn out, but stimulated by the hopes of regaining their lost honors, gladly consented to assist and stand by their leader. The canopy of darkness was chosen as the time of attack. In the stillness of night they moved on, and can you guess? Were successful. My father did all in his power to repulse the enemy, but they were completely mastered. An horrible massacre followed; my father was scalped upon the spot, and my mother tomahawked. Such a fate would surely have been mine, but for the young warrior who stands outside of the wigwam, Eagle Eye by name. He saw me, and claimed me as his captive, brought me to his tribe, wished to wed me, but I have resisted his attempts, and as I have since become a favorite with the other warriors, he dare not force me. But if I had a home elsewhere not one moon would see me here.'

I was touched by the plaintive manner in which the Indian maiden told her story, and said to her, 'If we could but escape together, you should always be my dear sister, and share with me my home.'

'We can but try,' said she. 'With the darkness to-night, we will wend our way towards your home, and ere the moon rises shall be far on the wilderness' winding path.' Bidding me prepare, she quitted the wigwam, having first placed her finger upon her lips as a warning to act silently. Night came at last, but oh, how long seemed the time. Although but a few hours, it seemed as if days had passed. I could feel my heart beat as a footstep sounded near the wigwam. It was now nearer than ever. I was sure it was she, and with a bound I sprang to meet her. A cold chill came over me as I beheld not Laulerack but my captor, Eagle Eye.

'The pale face maiden seems anxious to meet me,' said he.

'I thought it was Laulerack come to converse with me, as I am so lonely.'

'Eagle Eye would gladly stay with you,' the Indian answered.

'I love Laulerack and have not yet learned to love you.' I said this in order to get rid of him.

'Does the pale face maiden wish for any thing?' asked he.

'Nothing.'

He then, with a smile, which he intended for a loving one, but which in my eyes appeared hideous, left the wigwam. A long time elapsed ere Laulerack made her appearance, and I had almost given up all hopes of escape, for that night at least, when chancing to look up I was startled, for there directly in front of me stood Laulerack.

'Listen. I have kept my word; follow me quickly but quietly,' was all she said, and I followed her out into the open air. I felt as if I were free indeed, and with joyous feelings went with the bounding step usual to one who has realized their greatest vision of success. But oh, how little we know what one short hour may bring forth. We had proceeded quite a distance when sounds of pursuit followed us.

'Keep behind me and run,' said Laulerack.

I did as directed, but found myself scarcely equal to keep up to the Indian maiden, who ran more like a deer than a human being. I was consequently far behind, when she stumbled over a stone, directly before her. As I came up I was about to stoop and assist her to her feet, but she said:

'Do not stop for me, but run for your life.' She was not so badly hurt as I supposed, and presently came within hailing distance.

'On, on,' she cried, and I with a dreadful pain in my side endeavored to quicken my pace, but found it impossible to scarcely run at all. By this time we could hear guns firing, and I, expecting to be shot down, expressed my fears to Laulerack, who only laughed, as she said, between breath:

'They would not fire *at* us, but up in the air. It is merely to intimidate us.'

Explicitly believing all she said I ran for dear life. Laulerack, owing to a sprain received in falling, was unable to catch up to me, and remained quite a distance behind. I know not how long we had been running, when we suddenly came in view of an encampment, and had scarcely come near enough to distinguish if it were our friends, when a voice shouted, 'The Indians! They come!' and then dashed towards the encampment. The alarm was echoed as if by a hundred voices. I knew that these were white men, and shouted, 'A white maiden seek your protection,' but had scarcely got one word out when a volley of musket shots were fired in our path, and Laulerack, who had by this time got in front of me, was shot, and I at the time thought fatally. I really believe that had I been foremost that I would have received the shot. Laulerack, in a faint voice, called out to me to drop, which I did accordingly. The Rangers, (for such they afterwards proved to be,) finding all quiet advanced cautiously, and speaking in a loud, clear voice, I said, 'There are no enemies, but a white woman, and an Indian maiden, whom I fear you have killed.'

'Wall now I am gollderned if I wouldent 'eve sworn as how there was Ingins in ambush,' said a rough voice and presently he was joined by others, who came towards us, and lifting Laulerack carefully from the ground, carried her to the encampment.

'How did this 'ere happen,' said one who seemed to be leader.

'There is no time for explanation now, the enemy are in pursuit.'

'Wall I guess as how we'll revarse the action and make ourselves in pursuit of the derned red skins,' said the same man who had spoken before.

'Their village is but a short distance from here, and they hold a white man prisoner, who will soon be burned at the stake,' I said, forgetting that Varney did not deserve the blood that might be spilled by these brave men.

'By the living Austin,' said the leader, 'he shall be rescued, or not a man of us will go home to tell of the failure. Ain't I right, boys?'

'In course you is,' answered the men.

'Here, Bill Johnson, Ike Winsor, and Guy Gillingham, you remain and perteckt the wimmen.'

'If you please, I'd rather go and fight the Ingins,' said the last named individual.

'So would I,' said each of the others.

'Well, dern it, you've got to be martyrs this ere time.'

All being ready to follow their leader they immediately set out to meet the Indians.

'My white sister,' said Laulerack, 'my life is fast ebbing away.'

'Say not so,' I muttered. 'You will get well and then we will never leave each other.'

'No! It cannot be so, the Great Spirit has willed it otherwise.'

'And this was all my fault, had I not asked you to endanger your life by assisting me to escape, all would have been well.'

'No! No! fair maiden, it was no fault of yours, for I, may the Great Spirit forgive, had resolved to take my own life. But I will soon be with my father and mother in the great Hunting Ground, far, far beyond. Farewell, sister. May the Great Spirit watch over and protect you.'

'Oh, you cannot, must not die,' I cried, for I had learned to love this red maiden. The three men left to protect us from danger, now came near, and bending down, raised their hats, and looking up to heaven I said—'To thee we consign her soul,' and the men in solemn voices repeated it after me. Here was a living picture, true to the nature and yet more vivid than the imagination could conceive and paint upon canvas. Three stalwart sons of the forest kneeling with hats in hand, and uplifted faces. I sat motionless as a statue, but tears were coursing down my cheek; within the circle lay the now inanimate body of Laulerack. The moon shone through the trees, and God seemed to say: 'I have only taken her from earth—She is not dead.'

'I know not how long we sat thus, and probably it would have been much longer had we not been startled by the sound of many voices, which told us that our friends had returned.'

'Heigho, Gilly, what's the matter?' said the one whom I have mentioned as the leader.

'Sam, less noise' said Gillingham, 'the Indian maiden has been shot as you know, and you also know in mistake, but the murder lies between us. I hope to God it was no bullet from my musket that did the deed, and may God have mercy on the man who fired the shot that killed her.' 'Amen,' responded the men, as each and every one uncovered his head and looked up towards heaven.

After my grief had somewhat subsided, I listened to the plan of the attack, and capture of some four or five Indians, and rescue of Varney, whom I saw conversing with the rangers, relating his wonderful experience. Having discovered me in conversation with the leader, he came forward and expressed his immense gratification at seeing me safe and sound. Amongst the captives was 'Eagle Eye,' who was deeply affected at the death of Laulerack, and upon hearing Varney, came toward me, and in Spanish said:

'White man lie. Says he is glad to see you. He it was who gave the alarm when you escaped, in hopes of gaining his own liberty.'

I did not dare to translate this to the rangers, who seemed anxious that I should do so, as I knew their tempers were of a violent nature, and that Varney would swing for it. After a weary march of many miles we arrived at Austin, where I was kindly taken care of by General Harney, who was stationed there for three months.

Here ends her story, as given to my friend Mr. Wm. Wallis of the Arch Street Theatre, whilst he was on a visit to Paris. To him I am also indebted for many incidents occurring during her sojourn in Paris, of these, anon.

Adah soon left Austin, and returned to New Orleans, determined to give up the stage, and turn her attention to Literature. She commenced by studying assiduously the German language, and reading the Classic Authors.

One day she conceived the idea of collecting some of her poetic writings, and publishing them. She carried out her plans to perfection, and shortly afterwards they appeared in one volume, under the title of **"Memories."** These Poems gained for her considerable popularity throughout the South.

Among other short "squibs" there appeared the following:

Milton wrote a letter to his lady love,
    Filled with warm and keen desire—

He sought to raise a flame, and so he did,
    The lady cast his nonsense in the fire.

Here is another entitled

WOUNDED

Let me lie down!
Just here in the shade of this cannon torn tree
Here, low in this trampled grass, where I may see
The surge of the combat, and where I may hear
The glad cry of victory, cheer upon cheer,
    Let me lie down.

Oh, it was grand!
Like the tempest we charged, in the triumph to share;
The tempest—its fury and thunder were there,
On, on, o'er intrenchments, o'er living and dead,
With the foe underfoot and the flag overhead.
    Oh, it was grand!

Weary and faint,
Prone on the soldier's couch, ah! how can I rest
With this shot-shattered head and sabre-pierced breast?
Comrades at roll-call, when I shall be sought,
Say I fought where I fell, and fell where I fought,
    Wounded and faint.

Oh, that last charge!
Right through the dread host tore the sharpnel and shell,
Through, without faltering—clear through with a yell—
Right in their midst, in the turmoil and gloom
Like heroes we dashed, at the mandate of doom.
    Oh, that last charge!

But I am dying at last!
My mother, dear mother, with meek, tearful eye,
Farewell! and God bless you, forever and aye!
Oh, that I now lie on your pillowing breast,
To breathe my last sigh on the bosom first prest!
    I am dying, dying at last.

A remarkable feature in her poems was that no two were ever found to correspond with each other, their style being almost entirely different. Adah's professional name as a *Danseuse*—as I have already stated, was Adah Bertha Theodore, and on the 3rd of April 1856 she was married to Alexander Isaacs Menken.

"There is a destiny that shapes our ends." etc. She now resolved to adopt the theatrical profession, and during the season of 1856-7, made her *debut* at the Varieties Theatre, New Orleans, in the play of "Fazio." Her pretty face and a well formed figure created quite a *furore,* and although in her acting of the part there was nothing great, still she afterwards showed such a decided improvement, that she was retained, and played throughout the week with considerable success. Shortly after she was tendered a complimentary benefit, and the stockholders presented her with a magnificent set of diamonds. From other admirers she received a splendid golden goblet.

The night of her *debut* she showed no signs, as is usual with novices on their first appearance, of nervousness, and not until she had appeared before the large assemblage present did she realize her position. For some time it was an utter impossibility for her to speak. The loud and prolonged plaudits of her friends, served to awaken her from the lethargy into which she had fallen, and she put forth all her enegy to create an impression by her acting, as she had previously done by her face and figure. She accomplished her task, and as the curtain fell was an established favorite, from that time forward. You that have never made a "first appearance upon any stage" know not with what difficulty the thing is accomplished.

From New Orleans she went to Wood's Theatre, Cincinnati, Ohio, and from there to Lousisville, Kentucky. Next we find her as leading lady with Mr. W. H. Crisp's dramatic company on a tour through the Southern States. She supported James Murdoch, Edwin Booth, Neafie, and James Hackett, all first class actors. Mr. Murdoch in conversation with her one day, said:—"Adah, why not adopt the sensational line? Make 'Mazeppa' a speciality; you have a pretty face and a good form, and possess grace enough to cope with Celeste in the 'French Spy.'" At the time Adah was rather miffed than otherwise at "Merry James's" suggestion, thinking that he wished to insinuate that as an actress she would not do as well in the "pantomine business." Her engagement being fulfilled, she again resolved to leave the stage which she accordingly did. Be not surprised, dear reader, when I inform you that she found another occupation. She entered the studio of her friend Mr. T. D. Jones, at Columbus, Ohio; whilst here she wrote for several journals. Proceeding to Cincinnati she became the principal contributor to the Israelite, the leading Jewish paper in America. Her great reply to the "Churchman" in defence of Baron Rothchild's admission to Parliament, was extensively copied in England, and from Mr. Frank Queen, editor of the New York Clipper, the only reliable Theatrical journal in this country, I learn that the article was even translated into French and German, appearing in most of the leading papers throughout France and Germany. The baron sent her an autograph letter in which he praised her greatly, calling her the inspired Deborah of her adopted race.

Those that have for a long time appeared upon the stage, become restless when off, sometimes for one night even. I could mention several prominent ones, who have enough to "live at ease" all the rest of their lives, but who will persist in going on the stage every now and then. I have witnessed the "farewell to the stage" of one actor in the same city "four times," and yet he actually appeared again. This was the case with Adah Isaacs Menken.

Returning to the stage, and while in Dayton. Ohio, the theatrical world is surprised by the intelligence that Adah Menken, the actress, has been elected "captain of the Light Guard" of that place, owing to her proficiency in military exercises, exhibited by the beautiful manner in which she drilled the Dayton Corps.

It is said of a friend of mine, Mr. Stuart Robson, an eccentric comedian, that upon hearing of Adah's last acqusition, he exclaimed:—

"By the living jingo, what next? In case of female suffrage," he added, "Adah Isaacs Menken will be nominated for the presidency—yes, and be elected too."

Adah, in 1859, came near adding the art of "self-defence" to the many others already acquired. But no, she did not go quite so far. Instead of marrying the science, she came to look with favorable eyes upon an exponent of it, one John C. Heenan, better known as the "Benicia Boy." She was married to him on the 3d of April, 1859, by the Rev. J. S. Baldwin, at an inn on the Bloomingdale road, near New York City. Here were two natures entirely different "linked together" for life, I am not allowed to say, as an Indiana court choose to look upon the thing in an entirely different light, and Adah having applied to that "learned body" for a divorce; it was granted her; this was in 1862. "The atmosphere not being healthy" as "Artemas" used to say, they were made two, or in other words quoted from one of "Ward's" lectures, "they was disjointed and no more bone of one bone, nor birds of feather flockin' together, homeward bound for a home on the salty deep." As one of the parties of this "ill assorted union" still survives, it would, perhaps, be wise for me to refrain from any remarks to the why, and wherefore, and furthermore, said surviving party being "on the muscle," and much "bigger than I," he might challenge me to "put up or shut up." Now at the present time I can neither put up my "mauleys" in a "twenty-four foot ring" with the requisite amount of money, nor can I find any persons to back me, as regards the "filthy lucre." There is one thing I can do—shut up. "Mum's the word."

Adah Isaacs Menken made her first appearance in New York City, at the National Theatre, under Mr. Purdey's management. Her first engagement at the "Old Bowery" in that city commenced March 19th, 1860, and lasted six nights. Her second engagement at the "Old Bowery" was April 30th of the same year: this time she appeared as Mrs. J. C. Heenan. She next travelled through the South and West as a star. On her return to New York City she was engaged for the "New Bowery Theatre"; during this engagement she was married to Robert Newell, or "Orpheus Kerr," well-known as a writer of juvenile works. They were married I believe in October, 1861, and yet she at the time was not divorced from Heenan. However, after the course of law had been gone through with, the couple departed for California on the 13th of July, 1863. She made her debut in San Francisco, August 24th, at the Opera House, opening to a $1,640 house, the prices of admission being raised to one dollar and fifty cents to dress circle and parquet. The management, for this enterprise, were rewarded by crowded houses, which continued week after week, and was only brought to a close by Adah's illness; she was re-engaged, and commenced on Christmas eve in the "French Spy," and terminated her engagement January 24th, 1864.

She chose the character of "Mazeppa" for her debut in the gold State. "Render unto Cæsar what belongs to Cæsar." Mr. Murdoch's advice had been heeded. Her life was indeed an eventful one.

On the 22nd of April, 1864, she sailed from California to England, and was immediately secured for Astley's Theatre, London, where she made her debut under E. T. Smith's management, October 3d, in her specialty of "Mazeppa." This proved to be one of the greatest successes of the British stage. During the latter part of 1865 Mr. John Brougham wrote for her a play entitled the "Child of the Sun." The play was withdrawn after a run of six or seven weeks. It appears that she was more fortunate in her choice of plays, than that of a husband, for in October 1865 she was again divorced by an Indiana court. This time from Robert Newell. ("Orpheus Kerr.") She returned to New York in March, 1866, and made her debut on Broadway, at Wood's Theatre, April 30th, in her original character of "Mazeppa." On May 25th she was obliged to terminate her engagement abruptly, owing to sickness. After this she made a brief tour through the West, which was a decided success. Returning to New York she was married on the 21st of August 1866 to Mr. James Barclay, ("no relation to me,") at the Bleak House in that city.

Again she sailed for England, and after fulfilling an engagement in Liverpool, proceeded to Paris, making her debut there December 30th at the theatre De-le-Gaite, in a new *role* written expressly for her by Ferdinand Dugue, and Anicet Berugeois, in the play of "Les Pirates De la Savanne." She made one of the greatest hits ever known in Paris, being called out nine times the first night. Her performances were witnessed by the crowned heads of France. During this engagement she played before Prince Jerome and Prince Lucien Bonaparte, and the princesses of those royal houses, from whom she received great commendation. Prince Jerome presented her with a magnificent diamond ring. The receipts for the first eight representations amounted to three hundred and forty-six thousand francs. She concluded her one hundred nights' engagement with great *eclat* and was the only American actress that ever played a successful engagement in Paris. On her last night there were present Napoleon III; the King of Greece; the Duke of Edinburgh; and the Prince Imperial.

Adah Isaacs Menken was not a perfect woman; far from it; but where can you direct me to one that is. To me such a woman would indeed be a curiosity, and yet the press of this country have vied with each other in seeking after all her little faults, and converting them into errors of the greatest magnitude. During her life she was continually the object of articles appearing in the different New York journals, "bearing slander written in each and every line." What did these writers know of her? Ah! they have a great deal to answer for. One to my certain knowledge has gone to "that immortal bourne." May God have mercy on his soul, for any man that will relentlessly slander a woman, upon no other authority than empty rumor, has certainly no place among honest men, either in this world or the one to come. That she had faults, and many, perhaps, I will not dispute. Who has not?

> If to her share some female errors fall,
> Look in her face and you'll forget them all.

The friends and personal acquaintances of Adah Menken, are well aware of the falsity of the many indiscretions attributed to her. She was kind to a fault, but her biographers never classified this as among the rest. Churches or hospitals might have profited in the disposal of her estate, had not her heart told her that to give to those at the time of need, was a greater blessing, than leaving her money to public institutions after her death, and thereby having it recorded in the columns of the newspapers throughout the world that, Adah Isaacs Menken, the actress, had bequeathed to this institution, so many thousand dollars, and to that one, so much. She assisted many a poor and needy sister and brother professional, who sought her aid, either in this country, or Europe. She was a lady of great intellectual endowments, and high literary attainments. Her prose and poetry were alike redolent of bright and beautiful thoughts. She also possessed a keen sense of the ridiculous, and would often copy down laughable incidents occurring under her observation! The following is copied from a diary kept by her, during her sojourn in England—"Oct. 22d." "Visited the police court in company with my agent, out of curiosity. The class of people brought before the judge varied. Among the first was a man who gave the name of Warburton. He stated that his occupation was that of a poet. Mr. Warburton had reached the last stages of shabby gentility. Time had told sadly on his garments, originally of fine material, and fashionable cut. His black curly hair was whitened out by contact with whitewash, and his nose had become a garden for the culture of blossoms, by far more common than they are proper. But Mr. Warburton, despite the reverses which he had evidently suffered, stood proudly erect. If the external man was in a state of dilapidation, the spirit was unhurt. He smiled gracefully (perhaps his repeated 'smiling' the night before had made him a successful 'smiler,') when the judge addressed him and told him that he was charged with having been arrested in a state of drunkenness. Officers McClintop and Muldohn were the witnesses against Mr. Warburton. They stated that about one o'clock that morning, Warburton had been found by them in a muddled state of intoxication, standing in a barrel used for slop, extemporizing doggerel to an imaginary audience. They insisted upon his stopping, when Mr. Warburton told them that it was a violation of etiquette to interrupt a gentleman when he was delivering a poem before the Alumni of a college. Messrs. Clintop and Muldohn transmogrified it into 'Alum College,' which caused considerable laughter. He was evidently laboring under a 'hallucination,' as Mr Muldohn expressed it, and they thought for his own safety, that they had better bring him to the 'Lock-up.'

The following dialogue was entered upon by Warburton and the Judge.

JUDGE:

Mr. Warburton, you have heard what the officers state about your eccentric course of conduct; how did you happen to get drunk?

WARBURTON:

'Twas midnight, and gloomy darkness had her ebon veil unfurled, and nought remained but gaslight to light up this 'ere world. The heavens frowned, the twinkling orbs, with silvery light endowed, were all occult on 'tother side a thunderin' big black cloud. Pale Luna, too, shed not her beams upon the motley groups which gaily were standing round like new disbanded troops———

JUDGE:

It's not to hear such nonsense that I occupy this seat.

WARBURTON:

A deathlike stillness o'er prevailed on alley, pier, and street.

JUDGE:

To listen to such stuff sir, I can't sacrifice my time.

WARBURTON:

Don't discombobilate my thought, and interrupt my rhyme; I think that when misfortune is placed upon its defence, poetic justice, logic, law, as well as common sense, demand its story all be heard, unless *ex parte* proof is to send poor friendless cusses underneath the prison's roof. Shall I proceed?

JUDGE:

Proceed; but don't make your tale too long.

WARBURTON:

I'll make it as short as a 'sonnet,' and heed your words, depend upon it. I own that I was wrong in rushing head-long as I did into inebriation, but let me question now the court. Is it not a palliation of the depth of human guilt, if malice don't incite to break in divers fragments, state laws, wrong or right, and when only human appetite, uncontrolled by reason, leads men of genius, oftentime, the dish of life to season with condiments which *pro tem* the mental palate tickle, yet very often in the end put human joys in a pickle which ain't so cussed funny; though all the expense of grub and the *et ecteras* the public pays for; hence I ask this court (believing that its feelings are not hampered) if justice should not ever be with human mercy tempered?

JUDGE:

Perhaps. Now tell me, Warburton, where you bought your liquor.

WARBURTON:

Anon, I'll tell you. Last week, Judge, prostrate was I, far sicker than to me's agreeable with the diarrhœa chronic,

and sympathizing friends advised that I should take some tonic. I asked them what, at once they said, 'get some lager beer.' 'Twas got. Drink freely, boy, said they, 'nothing need you fear, but you'll be up and on your legs.' The lager beer 'was took'; soon every object in my sight had a very drunken look. Lager beer (to German ears the words may be euphonic). Tonic, certainly, it was, but decidedly too—tonic. Abnormal thirst excited it, and I went to great excesses (the statement's quite superfluous, my nose the fact confesses). Last night, attracted by the scenes which London's streets present, I dressed myself in sombre clothes, and out of doors I went; to quench my thirst did I imbibe the more of lager beer at Shirley's on the corner, several squares from here. No more know I, 'cept in the morn I wakened from my sleep, and having sowed perhaps, I'll learn that likewise I must reap.

JUDGE:

Have you got ten dollars?

WARBURTON:

Tis true, I hain't a red; I suppose the words unpleasant which next to me'll be said; that because by my imprudence my pocket book's collapsed, in prison drear must I remain till ten days have elapsed.

JUDGE:

I'll let you go this time.

WARBURTON:

Ha, say you so? Then ne'er till I fail to see through thin or thick will I forget to mention you as a perfect living brick.

Mr. Warburton left the room amid shouts of laughter, in which Judge and Jury joined."

Adah Menken was as gentle a woman as ever lived, and, as "old mother Stanton" remarked in a number of the Revolution, of which she is editress, "she *might* have been an honor to her sex." Let me ask, is "mother Stanton" an honor to her sex? If so in what way? Adah Menken was the constant recipient of notes begging an interview. But listen and mark my words—"*She kept virtuous.*" How would Mrs. Stanton's giddy mind receive such notes. But I doubt if there is that man living, possessing the sense of *sight,* who would ever address a love letter to her. If there is such a man, I pity his taste. Adah was now in the gay Paris. When will the world, old and young, tire of reading about Paris? From early boyhood the description of its old and narrow streets and of its modern and beautiful boulevards, has enchanted all of us. The city of ancient history and of modern times—of Mabile and Notre Dame—of great taste, but of great naughtiness—of brave men and of bad men,—of that worst of all, bad women—when will the name of Paris cease to have an interest? The traveler of the present day finds great improvements here during the last decade. The old Cathedral of Notre Dame is no longer approached by streets so narrow that "opposite neighbors can shake hands"; but wide boulevards sweep around its course. The offal is no longer thrown from windows; but cleanliness reigns throughout. The streets are no longer paved with huge blocks, but a macadamized road rolls you along like a ball on a ten-pin alley—one horse performing in *pleasant weather* the work of two or three Philadelphia or New York animals. I say in *pleasant weather*; for after a rain the principal boulevards abound, first in very slippery mud, then in annoying dust. The omnibus companies offered to take up the turnpike and to repave with large blocks at their own expense—and well they might, for a bad day lays up or destroys over a hundred horses, but the government refused the petition, for small stones and wide streets are a poor basis for barricades, and can be effectually swept by artillery. "Paris by gaslight" is the name of a new guide-book published, as announced, for the "Greenhorns." But the stranger needs no guide save the gaslight, which leads him to the Champs Elysee by its increasing glare, and then bewilders him by his manifold multiplications. An avenue twice the width of Broad street, Philadelphia; Bowery, New York; or State street, Chicago. It is lighted for several miles with a blaze of fire, which seems to speak of some other, and that not a better, world. At the sides, scarcely concealed by trees and shrubbery, are concert saloons, or small gardens, still more brilliantly illuminated—admission free—save that the visitor is expected to order, if he do not drink, some villainous beer and pay therefor twenty cents a glass. In some of these gardens can be witnessed dances, which most men would condemn, yet which all will go to see—some of them defy description. The principal feature of one of these dances, consisted in the grasping of the heel of the danseuse and extending her limb to to the position of a musket in "shoulder arms," and the whirling of herself round in that attitude. With pleasantries like these a brave people are beguiled of their liberties. They can do every thing but vote; they can be every thing but citizens.

Adah had scarcely been in the city three or four days, when she received the following:

MADEMOISELLE MENKEN,

Please accept the enclosed diamond ear-rings, and wear them for the donor's sake. I love you. My palace is at your disposal. I can not tell you my love by letter. You shall be my mistress, my all. Meet me at the Rue de Palle, after the performance.

Adieu, love, till then.
LORD ALBERT AVON.

Adah immediately despatched the following answer, written in the best of French.

Theatre de la Gaite.

TO LORD AVON:—

Monsieur,

Your note was received. I shall wear the diamond earrings, not for the 'donor's sake,' but in hopes that their magnificence may create an impression upon the audience of the 'Theatre de la Gaite.' As for accepting your Palace as a home, I can only say that my hotel is preferable. Go to your friends and tell them that Adah Isaacs Menken is an American woman, there is no French in her blood, and that all further attempts at *intrigue* are useless.

A. I. MENKEN.

"All nonsense," said Lord Avon, that evening, upon receiving Adah's response. "She will soon become used to French society, and then she's mine. I shall boast that such is the case, already."

"Never count your chickens you know, nor put all your eggs into one basket," said a young man at Lord Avon's elbow, in very bad French.

"Do you mean to insult me?" said Avon.

"Oh, no, far from it, I only wished to give you a piece of advice."

"It is neither solicited nor wanted," said Lord Albert as with a frown he turned upon his heel.

The American, for such he was, muttered something, the import of which was: "We shall meet when least you expect it, my lord," and then he too left the cafe. He had scarcely proceeded half the distance toward his hotel, when he perceived that he was followed by a man who seemed in great haste to overtake him. Accordingly he made a full stop, and the valet came up hurriedly, exclaiming:—

"Is monsieur the personage with whom my master, Lord Avon, was in conversation with at the cafe a few minutes since?"

The young American gentleman having responded in the affirmative, the servant handed him a note, which he ascertained, upon opening, was a challenge.

"Tell your master to call at the hotel De Garcon at eight this evening."

"I will Monsieur."

"So, so, this confounded interference of mine has served to bring me into a 'pretty pickle,'" said Lawrence, for so we must call him. "However," he added, "come what may, I'll see the end of it." That evening at precisely eight o'clock, there appeared a gentleman at the hotel De Garcon who enquired for Lawrence.

"Send him up," was the order given to the porter.

"Have I the honor of addressing Monsieur Lawrence?"

"You have, replied that personage. But I don't understand this; why did not Lord Avon appear in person?"

"Oh, monsieur is unacquainted with these little affairs. I am Lord Albert Avon's second and representative."

"I see clearly now. I thought Lord Avon sick," (and inwardly he wished that such was the case).

"Never better in his life, monsieur; but where will you fight?"

"Any where, damn it. I might as well be killed in one place as another," he added aside.

After the usual preliminaries had been gone through, the grounds weapons, etc., chosen, Lord Avon's second left the hotel with a benign smile upon his florid countenance.

Through Adah's intercession, however, the duel never came off. How she came to know of the affair I do not presume to say.—A laughable incident occurred during Adah's engagement at the "Theatre de la Gaite." A pantomime was given as an after-piece. The "trap" R. E. was used as "Demons' pit-hole," and the utility man engaged to do the demon, being taken sick one night, the "Ballet master" was prevailed upon to be hoisted up through the trap at the proper time. Monsieur having got in readiness, and the signal given, he goes into the "regions above." So far, very good, but monsieur being of a very restless nature, moved somewhat out of position, and when he suddenly makes his exit into the infernal regions, "horror of horrors" his nose comes in contact with the sides of the trap!—Of course it was dreadfully painful, and monsieur made the mimic hell below, a hell in reality by his cursing. "By damn," said he, "I no more be one damn demon, for any body." "But," expostulated the stage manager, "why did you move out of place? Did I not warn you of this?" "Oui you did, monsieur, but how can you expect me to do *my bizeness without ze paper.* This caused roars of laughter among the employees of the theatre who construed a *very different meaning* out of monsieur's sentence. Of course by "*ze paper*" he meant "the part." I find that I have not the space to go more fully into the details of Adah's Paris engagement. The senior partner of the firm of Barclay & Co., (publishers of this book,) suggested to me the idea of writing a life of Adah Isaacs Menken, saying at the same time, "I'll publish it, and I hope for the sake of the profession which you have adopted, that you will write of her *nothing but the truth.*" "I don't believe half that's said against her," he further added. During her residence at the Wesminster Hotel, in London, she was one of the lustres among the literary and professional stars of the house. Among her daily visitors, were to be found the most eminent literary men of England, Charles Dickens, Charles Read, Watts Phillips, John Oxenford, the Duke of Hamilton, Flecher, and many others of note, who gathered at her sociables to listen to the sparkling wit of one who must have been possessed of great genius to have entertained such brilliant persons. In Paris, Vienna, Berlin, in fact in every city that she visited, the most distinguished men of the day were numbered among her friends.

Mr. Henry B. Farnie who was with her during the period of illness, preceding her death, writes the following letter which he wishes published.

After reading several notices of the late Adah Isaacs Menken's last illness and death, more distinguished for uncharitable surmise than correct information, I cannot refrain from asking you to allow me a little space upon the same subject. A feeling of '*Comarderie*' alone—putting common charity out of the question, impels me to this course. I was engaged by the administration of the Chatelet to write a drama for Miss Menken, in June last, the date of her arrival in Paris; and from that time until her death, in August, I had frequent opportunities of seeing her. She had only attended two rehearsals of the 'Pirates de la Savanne,' in which she was to open at the Chatelet in the beginning of July, when she was prostrated by the painful illness which eventually killed her. The medical men at Paris were puzzled at first with the symptoms; and Miss Menken herself believed that it was inflammatory rheumatism. Later on, it was discovered to be caused by an abscess under the left side. This abscess was supposed by her medical attendants to have been of at least three or four years' growth, and from the moment of its discovery they gave up all hopes of saving her life. I can bear witness to the exquisite suffering she endured for these three months, and of the resignation and patience she invariably showed. Food she scarcely tasted, and she drank nothing but iced water. Once, and only once, she rose from her bed in the Rue Caumartin, and that was to try the effect of change of air at a pretty little village up the Seine at Baugival, a few miles from Paris. Accompanied by her maid, myself, and another friend, she managed to make the little journey; but the effort was too much for her enfeebled frame and immediately on arrival she went to bed very ill and there continued till her return to Paris two days afterwards.

* * *

This melancholy excursion has, I perceive, been described as 'an Orgie,' 'a scene of unbridled dissipation, etc.' How different the fact was let the kindly *patronne* of the 'Hotel des deux Ponts' at Baugival testify. Miss Menken died in the possession of the Jewish faith, and was attended by ministers of that religion. This I will say without violating sanctity of death, that however stormy her life may have been, the end was peaceful and serene. 'So may she rest, her faults lie gently on her.' I am sure, sir, that you will allow me, in conclusion, to protest against the ghastly pleasantries which are bandied over that poor, dear woman by certain portions of the Press. Surely the noble maxim, 'Of the dead naught but good,' is lesson enough to guide us still in such matters. Tennyson has said:

We cannot be kind to each other here for an hour,

and the accounts of Menken's death have only served to point the bitter truth. She was a woman of an excellent heart—somewhat careless and prodigal, it is true, but ever unselfishly. As Dumas, the great author, said to me at Havre, when I told him of Menken's death,

Poor girl, why was she not her own friend?

Very truly yours,
HENRY B. FARNIE

P. S. One point, I find, I have omitted, the paucity of mourners at her death. There were nearly a hundred present at *Pere la Chaise,* and there would have been three times that number had time permitted; but the French law compels interment within forty-eight hours, and it was exceedingly difficult for her kind friends, Sprent and Phipps, and others who helped in the arrangements, to get at the addresses of friends and acquaintances.

H. B. F.

The above is the greater portion of his letter. May God bless him for thus putting before the public the whole undivided truth

Adah Isaacs Menken, died in Paris on the 11th day of August 1868, and her tombstone bears the simple

"THOU KNOWEST"
Inscribed by her own orders.

The following excellent poem, I copy from the New York Clipper.

What news is this, that lightning sped,
    Had filled our hearts with strange dismay?
Read:—"Adah Isaacs Menken's dead—"
    She died in Paris, yesterday

This old, old mystery of death!
The failing voice, the parting breath,
The brief farewell, the quick drawn sighs,
Some visions of more sunny skies,
And then the pallid, hard-drawn face,
    The glassy coldness of the eyes,
And this is all; so ends the race,
The race of life which each must run,
Tho' all be vain when all is done

In distant lands she lies asleep,
    She does not heed the words we speak,
Her slumbers are serenely deep;
    On rose-red mouth, and peach-down cheek
The signet seal of death is press'd;
So, strewing lilies on her breast,
We leave her to her final rest!

To her 'twas given to charm the world
    By dashing power of genius born,
E'en while against its rules she hurled
    The pointed arrows of her scorn.
Her's was a mastery complete;
A thousand hearts obedient beat
At her behest. A thousand eyes
Followed her piquant witcheries,
While half the *ton* of gallant France
Owned to the magic of her glance.

The old German legends tell
Of fays who wove a wondrous spell,
Whereby, through practice of strange arts,
They traversed earth to capture hearts.
That power was also hers. She threw
    Out slyly, yet with care discreet,
The silken chains of love which drew
    Unwilling captives to her feet.

To higher realms, where few aspire,
    She dauntless soared and boldly sought

To steal the old Promethean fire
    Of knowledge from the gods of thought.
Her skill evoked from poetry's lyre
Such tender strains, such thrilling songs,
Such bitter memories of old wrongs,
Such thoughtful words, such hopes, such fears
Such echoes of departed years,
That she has fairly won, I trow,
A laurel wreath for her cold brow.

Yet more—upon the stage she gained
    The fame which doth outlive her life,
For there a very queen she reigned.
    And battling in the mimic strife
She all the valorous nerve displayed
Which gave to Orleans' fearless maid
A name to stand till Time shall fade.
We see her now, bound to her horse,
Dashing down th' accustomed course,
Her full eyes flashing with the light
Of conscious power. Ah! 'tis a sight
To make strange contrast with the bed
So narrow where she lieth dead.

Stand back, cold-hearted Pharisee!
Make broad your own phylactery;
Don all the robes the righteous wear,
But in this presence do not dare
To curse the helpless girl who lies
With death's deep shadow in her eyes,
Pass on—she had her faults, and we
Have ours as well—if one be free
Let him upbraid but otherwise
    Veil all her sins in charity.

So, strewing lilies on her breast,
    We leave her to her final sleep,
And humbly trust that she's at rest
    Beyond the cold dark river deep.

The above Poem was written expressly for the New York Clipper and signed "H. J. D." It was headed—

IN MEMORIAM.

———

ADAH ISAACS MENKEN.
Died August 11th., MDCCCLXVIII.

———

"Judge not harshly, for ye one day will be numbered among the dead."

Adah Menken dedicated a volume of poems to Mr. Charles Dickens, and received the following autograph letter:—

Gad's Hill Place, *Higham by Rochester,*
Kent, England.
Monday Twenty-first, October 1867.

Dear Miss Menken.

I shall have great pleasure in accepting your Dedication, and I thank you for your portrait as a highly remarkable specimen of photography.

I also thank you for the verses enclosed in your note. Many such enclosures come to me, but few so pathetically written, and fewer still so modestly sent.

Faithfully yours,
Charles Dickens

The following is a selection of her poems—

DREAMS OF BEAUTY

Visions of Beauty, of Light and of Love,
    Born in the soul of a dream,
Lost like the phantom-bird under the dove,
    When she flies over a stream.

Come ye through portals where Angel wings droop,
    Moved by the heaven of sleep?
Or are ye mockeries, crazing a soul,
    Doomed with its waking to weep?

I could believe ye were shadows of earth.
    Echoes of hopes that are vain,
But for the music ye bring to my heart,
    Waking its sunshine again.

And ye are fleeting. All vainly I strive,
    Beauties like thine to portray;
Forth from my pencil the bright picture starts,
    And—ye have faded away.

Like to a bird that soars up from the spray,
    When we would fetter its wing;
Like to the song that spurns memory's grasp,
    When the voice yearneth to sing,

Like the cloud-glory that sunset lights up,
    When the storm bursts from its height;
Like the sheet-silver that rolls on the sea,
    When it is touched by the night.

Bright, evanescent, ye come and are gone,
    Visions of mystical birth;
Art that could paint you was never vouchsafed
    Unto the children of earth.

Yet in my soul there's a longing to tell
    All you have seemed unto me;
Than unto others a glimpse of the skies
    You in their sorrow might be.

Vain is the wish—better hope to describe,
    All that the spirit desires;
When through a cloud of vague fancies and schemes
    Flash the Promethean fires.

Let me, then, think of ye, Visions of Light,
    Not as the tissue of dreams,
But as realities destined to be
    Bright in futurity's beams.

Ideals formed by a standard of earth,
    Sink at reality's shrine,
Into the human and weak like ourselves,
    Losing the essence divine.

But the fair pictures that fall from above,
    On the heart's mirror sublime,
Carry a signature written in tints,
    Bright with the future of time.

And the heart, catching them, yieldeth a spark,
    Under each stroke of the rod,
Sparks that fly upward and light the new life,
    Burning an incense to God!

TO ADELINA PATTI

Thou Pleiad of the lyric world,
    Where Pasta, Garcia shone,
Come back with thy sweet voice again,
    And gem the starry zone.

Though faded still the vision sees,
    The loveliest child of night,
The fairest of the Pleiades,
    Its glory and its light.

How fell with music from thy tongue,
    The picture which it drew,
Of Lucia, radiant, warm, and young,
    Amina, fond and true.

Or the young Marie's grace and art,
    So free from earthly strife,
Beating upon the sounding heart,
    The gay tattoo of life!

Fair Florence! home of glorious art
    And mistress of its sphere,
Clasp fast thy beauties to thy heart,
    Behold thy rival here!

The following poem was written in memory of the Indian maiden,

LAULERACK

I see her yet, that dark-eyed one,
    Whose bounding heart God folded up
In His, as shuts when day is gone,
    Upon the elf the blossom's cup,
On many an hour like this we met,
    And as my lips did fondly greet her,
I blessed her as love's amulet:
    Earth hath no treasure, dearer, sweeter.

The stars that look upon the hill,
    And beckon from their homes at night,
Are soft and beautiful, yet still,
    Not equal to her eyes of light.
They have the liquid glow of earth,
    The sweetness of a summer even,
As if some Angel at their birth,
    Had dipped them in the hues of heaven.

They may not seem to others sweet,
    Nor radiant with the beams above,
When first their soft, sad glances meet
    The eyes of those not born for love;
Yet when on me their tender beams
    Are turned, beneath love's wild control,
Each soft, sad orb of beauty seems
    To look through mine into my soul.

I see her now, that dark eyed one,
    Whose bounding heart God folded up,
In His, as shuts when day is done,
    Upon the elf the blossom's cup,
Too late we met, the burning brain,
    The aching heart alone can tell,
How filled our souls of death and pain,
    When came the last sad word, *Farewell!*

ASPIRATION

Poor, impious soul! that fixes its high hopes
   In the dim distance, on a throne of clouds,
From the morning's mist would make the ropes
   To draw it up amid acclaim of crowds—
   Beware! that soaring path is lined with shrouds,
And he who braves it, though of sturdy breath,
May meet, half way, the avalanche and death!

O, poor young soul! whose year devouring glance
   Fixes in ecstasy upon a star,
Whose feverish brilliance looks a part of earth,
   Yet quivers where the feet of angels are,
   And seems the future crown in realms afar—
Beware! a spark *thou* art, and dost but see
Thine own reflection in Eternity!

It may not be known, generally, that the late Adah Menken was a good singer, as she seldom indulged in this accomplishment when in public. An intimate friend of hers in America sent her the popular songs as they appeared in this country, and among them the touching ballad of "Ring the Bell Softly." In acknowledging the receipt of the latter, she wrote:—

> How inexpressibly beautiful is the sentiment of this song, and what an eloquent simplicity of language! I have wept over it again and again, and never has a poem touched my heart-strings more deeply.

Poor, Adah! How well the lines apply to your own passing away to the summer land. The following are the lines of the song. They were written by Dexter Smith, of Boston:—

> Some one has gone from this strange world of ours,
> No more to gather its thorns with its flowers;
> No more to linger where sunbeams must fade,
> Where, on all beauty, death's fingers are laid;
> Weary with mingling life's bitter and sweet,
> Weary with parting and never to meet,
> Some one has gone to the bright, golden shore.
> Ring the bell softly, there's crape on the door!
> Ring the bell *softly,* there's crape on the door!
>
> Some one is resting from sorrow and sin,
> Happy where earth's conflicts enter not in;
> Joyous as birds, when the morning is bright,
> When the sweet sunbeams have brought us their light.
> Weary with sowing, and never to reap,
> Weary with labor and welcoming sleep,
> Some one's departed to Heaven's bright shore.
> Ring the bell softly, there's crape on the door!
> Ring the bell *softly,* there's crape on the door!
>
> Angels were anxiously longing to meet.
> One who walks with them in Heaven's bright street;
> Loved ones have whispered that some one is blest—
> Free from earth's trials, and taking sweet rest.
> Yes! there is one more in angelic bliss—
> One less to cherish, and one less to kiss;
> One more departed to Heaven's bright shore.
> Ring the bell softly, there's crape on the door!
> Ring the bell *softly,* there's crape on the door!

ONE YEAR AGO

In feeling I was but a child,
   When first we met, one year ago,
As free and guileless as the bird,
   That roams the dreary woodland through.

My heart was all a pleasant world
   Of sunbeams dewed with April tears;
Lire's brightest page was turned to me,
   And naught I read of doubts or fears.

We met, we loved, one year ago,
   Beneath the stars of summer skies;
Alas! I knew not then as now,
   The darkness of life's mysteries.

You took my hand, one year ago,
   Beneath the azure dome above,
And gazing on the stars you told
   The trembling story of your love.

I gave to you one year ago,
   The only jewel that was mine;
My heart took off her lovely crown,
   And all her riches gave to thine.

You loved me too when first we met,
   Your tender kisses told me so.
How changed you are from what you were
   In life and love, one year ago.

With mocking words and cold neglect,
   My truth and passion are repaid,
And of a soul once fresh with love,
   A dreary desert you have made.

Why did you fill my youthful life
   With such wild dreams of hope and bliss?
Why did you say you loved me then,
   If it were all to end in this?

You robbed me of my faith and trust
   In all life's beauty—love and truth,
You left me nothing—nothing save
   A hopeless, blighted, dreamless youth.

Strike if you will, and let the stroke
   Be heavy as my weight of woe;
I shall not shrink, my heart is cold,
   'Tis broken since one year ago.

The press of England were very enthusiastic in their approval of this poem. The "*Times*" said of it:—

> England is behind, America has shot ahead. Where in all England can you find a poetess who has ever produced such a sublime piece of poetry as Adah Menken's **'One Year Ago'**? To each and every poetess of our 'Sunny Isles,' we would say: 'Look to your laurels,' and not until you have fairly won, shall you dare to snatch the wreath which is so deservedly worn, from off the 'beautiful waving tresses' of Adah Isaacs Menken; and till then, fair Adah, we hail thee as Queen of 'soul touching poetry.'

KARAZAH TO KARL

Come back to me! my life is young,
   My soul is scarcely on her way,

And all the starry songs she's sung,
  Are prelude to a grander lay.
            Come back to me!

Let this song-born soul receive thee,
  Glowing its fondest truth to prove
Why so early didst thou leave me,
  Are our heaven-grand life of love?
            Come back to me!

My burning lips shall set their seal
  On our betrothal bound to-night,
While whispering murmurs will reveal
  How souls can love in God's own light.
            Come back to me!

Come back to me! The stars will be
  Silent witnesses of our bliss
And all the past shall seem to thee
  But a sweet dream to herald this!
            Come back to me!

Surely the woman who could write such poems as these, filled as they are with "poetic music in every line," could not have been a lover of "things unseemly." It is to be hoped that the "ill-fed, foul-mouthed, cross-eyed reporters," who have lately vied with each other in making the most slanderous reports of the late Adah Isaacs Menken's life and death, will cease to put forth their weak articles, teeming with the largest words from 'Webster's and Johnson's vocabulary, but being summed up, amount to a 'nothingness,' like the sound produced by speaking in a cave where the 'empty sound is echoed, and thus making true the proverb (the quotation being slightly altered) of 'slander, like chickens, will come home to roost.'"

Some of my readers will, perhaps, suppose that in my allusion to the reporters, I am going too far in calling them "ill-fed, foul-mouthed, and blear-eyed." But there is in "merry England," a person of the masculine gender, who will answer the description exactly. Upon hearing of the death of Adah Menken, this "cur" conceives the brilliant idea of writing to a certain paper published in a town in the State of New York, and called "The *Cur*-rier." Now said "Prodigal son of the quill," who is a disgrace to the profession, left said "little town" owing several small bills, which the holders would gladly sell at *five cents on the dollar*. He wrote about *one hundred* of the worst lies imaginable, which this disreputable paper published. I am happy to say that the editors of the paper do not belong to the "Press club." (Editor.)

Ethel Colburn Mayne (essay date 1925)

SOURCE: Mayne, Ethel Colburn. "Adah Isaacs Menken." *Enchanters of Men*. New York: Putnam's, 1925. 328-43. Print.

[*In the following essay, Mayne asks, "What is the mysterious drawing of some women always to the evil men?" In Mayne's account Menken was a victim seeking, after her failed marriages, a "real career" in the theater without success until* Mazeppa, *in which the "chief charm was the scanty costume of Miss Menken." Meanwhile, Mayne suggests, she sought solace and expression in her poetry.*]

I try to bloom up into the light ...

That motto of her own writing she might well have chosen for her own life, as she chose the words *Thou knowest* for her grave. "A striving, and a striving, and an ending in nothing"—the leading-phrase of pessimism comes back to us, as we read of Adah Isaacs Menken; another phrase, too, comes back—one which may be the last word of despair or triumph: *Character is Fate*. For nothing, no one, but herself could save her; and herself was the traitor always. What is that mysterious drawing of some women always to the evil men? Round this one, men thronged perpetually—those of every type. To her rooms in London came Dickens, Charles Reade, Watts-Phillips, John Oxenford, Algernon Charles Swinburne; to those in Paris, Théophile Gautier, Alexandre Dumas; and everywhere that she was came the Bohemian in all his incarnations—in his fineness, coarseness, goodness, badness. Genial brilliant fellows, with pipes for ever in their mouths and kindness for ever in their hearts, rough of speech sometimes, calling her "Menken" *tout court,* yet ready at any moment to stand by her in any trouble. ... Such men she had at command throughout her life; one man she had towards the end for whom no chivalrous deed, no gentle-hearted devotion, were too knightly—and from such friends or such lovers, she, as it were by fatality, must turn away to those at whom the imagination shudders: "Benicia Boys," Wall Street punchers (whatever that may be), and foul-mouthed "Johnnie Gideons," who would write of her after she was dead without a kindly thought, piling lie upon lie to make better—or worse—copy.

A circus-rider—and one whose performance was denounced in the papers as "at once a scandal and a sham" ... of such a woman we might say in our haste that surely the Johnnie Gideons were free to write what they liked! She was the notorious *Mazeppa* of Astley's in 1864, when all London streamed over Westminster Bridge to behold her—all male London, that is, "all elderly vicious London," say some chroniclers. It was the elderly men who filled the stalls, who leered from the boxes at the "shameless exhibition" ... So we read, and push the page away to find the small contemporary photographs: *Menken as Mazeppa.*[1] What do we see? In one, a little figure seated on a tiger-skin, the dark head bent, the hair parted boyishly, a sweet round face beneath—and a form so exquisite that our eyes linger gladly on the gracious curves, and we think we have seen "Menken," until we take up the next picture and behold her lying full length on the tiger-skin, the wonderful limbs outspread. ...

Thou wert fair in the fearless old fashion,
  And thy limbs are as melodies yet—

inevitably the lines drift into our memory, and others come along with them:

> When these are gone by with their glories,
>   What shall rest of thee then, what remain?
> O mystic and sombre Dolores,
>   Our Lady of Pain? ...

This much remains. Adah Dolores Isaacs Menken was the woman who inspired that magnificent lyric.

Such was her glory. She had no other. Notoriety she had, friends, admirers, lovers, she had, beauty of face and form, beauty too indeed of soul, mind, heart—and yet, what utter ruin! *I try to bloom up into the light*: that phrase, from all the welter of phrases in her *Infelicia,* is the one which brings the pang for us.

* * *

Her baptismal name was Adelaide: her father's name McCord. She was born on June 15th, 1835, near New Orleans, at a place then known as Chartrain, and now as Milneburg. Her father was well-off; there were three daughters, of whom she was the eldest. When she was eight years old, he died; reverses had come already, and now came almost destitution. What to do? The widow at first felt hopeless. Adelaide was clever, studious—piquante and fascinating as well, but she was only eight years old. It seemed somewhat early for her to begin the battle of life. Moreover, what could even brilliant little Adelaide do? ... Suddenly, inspiration came—and doubtless brought a pang with it; but the mother recognised the inevitable, recognised too, it may be, the predestination! McCord had loved above all other arts the art of dancing. All his little girls had been taught—and taught seriously; and all had made astonishing progress, Adelaide naturally being first. It must have been the day for infant prodigies in New Orleans, for Mrs. McCord actually succeeded in getting engagements for all three children, who soon became great favourites under the *soubriquet* of the Theodore Sisters.

That was the beginning. From the first, Adelaide knew the taste of popularity, for of the favourite three she was *the* favourite. And there too, in that early period, we find the double thread, for our eldest Theodore Sister was for ever at her books—studying Greek, Latin, Hebrew, German, Spanish, and "translating Homer's *Iliad*." That must have brought a great moment, for we read that the small person of twelve "completed her arduous task with triumph!" Somehow the little girls who do this sort of thing are never lucky. Adelaide McCord began her career as a grown-up by marrying at seventeen "a nobody whose very name has been forgotten, who treated her cruelly, and finally abandoned her." We incline to believe that marriage at seventeen may be reckoned, however it turn out, among misfortunes. Knowledge so soon is bad enough; disillusionment so soon—that hardly bears thinking of. ... But she had youth at any rate on her side; and she had beauty, courage, ardour. What did she do with all these? We

read of no anguish, we read indeed of immediate triumphs of the footlights: first, she flashes out as "Queen of the Plaza at Havana." The phrase makes its picture for us on the spot, a picture of sunlight, brown faces, dark eyes, mantillas, long lazy days, cigar-smoke—and the morality which goes with all that, drifting like the smoke, easy like the life. Then swiftly with another phrase, the picture changes: "Liberty, Texas—and a newspaper." Only two elements remain: the tobacco-smoke and the morality that drifted with it! The newspaper was short-lived, but she never lost her fancy for that form of activity—it seemed to represent in her mind an outlet, a way of escape, from those footlights where she failed always, despite her strange successes, to find any sort of happiness.

New Orleans, teaching French and Latin in a girls' school, and the publication of a volume of poems came next; then Texas again, and at Galveston, in 1856 (when she was twenty-one), marriage again: the one marriage, it would seem, with which, short-lived as the union was, there came some genuine happiness. For she kept his name, Isaac Menken, to the end, adding an "s" to the "Isaac"; she altered her own name of Adelaide to the Jewish Adah; most striking tribute of all, she adopted Menken's faith and died an ardent Jewess. "She must at that time," writes a friend of those days, one Celia Logan, "have been one of the most peerless beauties that ever dazzled human eyes"; Menken was remarkably handsome also, and moreover, remarkably talented—a musician, a composer. He had fallen desperately in love with her, and had married her against his family's desire. Mystery envelops the breaking of this bond, but the same friend tells us that "in after-years, whoever threw a stone at Adah, it was never Isaac Menken, and she always retained his name. ... so much of the glamour of first love hung over them both."

It was at this time that she wrote a "magnificent article" in the New York *Churchman* upon the admission of Baron Rothschild to Parliament, which was translated into several languages. Rothschild wrote himself to thank her for it, calling her "the inspired Deborah of her race." Thus, what with the translations and the Baron's glittering journalese, we see that Adah was tasting success again. She was plainly in full career of journalism, for at Cincinnati, she almost edited *The Israelite,* and there was another joy besides, the study of sculpture, which, when the *Mazeppa* days arrived, proved very useful for her poses. ... This we take to be the happiest time of her life. She was in the flower of her beauty: dark, moderately tall, graceful and most exquisitely fashioned, with great melancholy eyes, "which strike the beholder and charm him irresistibly." Yes, happy, one likes to think—although it could not last, for with her "nought could endure but mutability."

* * *

For three years we hear nothing definite, but it would seem that she returned to the stage, and plainly the Menken marriage was done with, for about this time, she met and married (on April 3, 1859) John C. Heenan, the "Benicia Boy," a prize-fighter, antagonist of Tom Sayers "in the desperate contest for the championship of the world in 1860." Adah's third attempt quite failed to keep the proverbial promise of good fortune. Two years later, we find her trying again with Robert H. Newell, "Orpheus C. Kerr" (Office-Seeker), the satirist of the American Civil War; and, nearly a year after, getting her divorce by an Indiana Court from Heenan, "who had treated her in a brutal and ignominious manner." Well! it was America, and she was "Menken," and one husband was a Benicia Boy . . . yet there are few records of free-love which offend the taste as this does. Two husbands at a time: "*deux maris à la fois*"—that refrain would have seemed scabrous even to Béranger! The endless-chain marriages of America—so to term them—drag very heavily, very wearisomely, upon the sense of humour, do they not?

The punning pseudonymist, "Office-Seeker," in his turn, failed to make her happy, and—shall we finish the husbands?—there came in 1866 the help of another Indiana Court, and (in this case, subsequently) another husband: James or Paul Barclay, "a noted Wall Street puncher."[2] He was very rich, but not long after their marriage, he "threw out," and deserted her. In addition to his punching-glories, James (or Paul) has another title to fame: he was Adah's Last Husband.

It is ill jesting, though very anger makes us jest. How to sympathise? Pity we can give; sympathy—? And alas! if anything from women were wanted, sympathy could alone have been that thing. But no woman's name comes into her life at all. Her sisters we never hear of again, after the childish days; her mother—one knows not! Possibly the best that women could give her *was* pity, and pity, we may be sure, she would have none of without sympathy. . . . Before we dismiss the husbands, let us speak of the jest which most frequently recurs on this subject. "Adah of the Seven Husbands": that is its original form; but the better to point the aptness of the *Dolores* poem, it is often insinuated that the sub-title, *Notre-Dame des Sept Douleurs,* has reference to her matrimonial trials. The humour of great poets not seldom has these crudities: on that score we are at least quiescent—but in all the writings about her which are scattered through the American and English Press, we have searched in vain for the record of more than five husbands! Unless the chroniclers lost count with Barclay, the too-symmetrical Number Seven must be renounced. We are inclined, ourselves, to be content with the five—all of whom were living at the time of her death.

It was in 1861 that her real career may be said to have begun. In the "legitimate" drama she was quite hopelessly bad. Queen of the Plaza she had been—Frenzy of 'Frisco, Darling of Dayton (where she was made Honorary Captain of the Light Guard);[3] streets in mining-towns, nay! the mining-companies themselves had been called by her name, silver lingots had been presented in one place, fifty shares in another, worth one hundred dollars a share.[4] . . . All this—without one rôle recorded! Plain is the inference, we fear; her own wild words confirm it.

> "My heritage!" it is to live within
> The marts of Pleasure and Gain, yet be
> No willing worshipper at either shrine;
> To think, and speak, and act, not for my pleasure
> But others'. . . . Fortune's toy!
> Mine to stand on the brink of life
> One little moment while the fresh'ning breeze
> Steals o'er the languid lip and brow, telling
> Of forest-leaf and ocean-wave, and happy
> Homes and cheerful toil; and bringing gently
> To this wearied heart its long-forgotten
> Dreams of gladness.

But turning the fevered cheek to meet the soft kiss of the winds, my eyes look to the sky, where I send up my soul in thanks. The sky is clouded—no stars—no music—the heavens are hushed.

> My poor soul comes back to me, weary and disappointed.

Thus, incessantly, interminably, she lamented. It is always the one wail, however the setting may vary. The incongruity of her fate with her aspirations obsessed her: she could think of nothing else, and she could *do* little else but think of it. Sometimes, turning the pages of the monotonous tiny book, one stirs impatiently, doubting if she ever "tried" at all, suspecting that when a mood came over her, Adah would thrust some money into someone's, anyone's, hands—for she was utterly reckless in her unbounded generosity—and then would go and write a poem:

> Lost—lost—lost!
> The little golden key which the first angel entrusted
>   to me . . .
> O! angels, will ye never sweep the drifts from my door?
> Will ye never wipe the gathering rust from the hinges? . . .

But then, the utter pathos of her impotence overwhelms us once more; for it was *she* who could not sweep away the drifts, who could not wipe the rust from the hinges—she of whom the great poet asked:

> Who gave thee thy wisdom? What stories
>   That stung thee, what visions that smote?
> Wert thou pure and a maiden, Dolores,
>   When desire took thee first by the throat?

We think of the terrible answering to that terrible questioning. . . . "It makes a goblin of the sun."

* * *

Mazeppa—her Mascot, as one might say, if luck had ever seemed to come to her—was first tried at Albany, in 1861. Hitherto a man had always played the part, but the Manager of the Green Street Theatre there was "tickled" by the notion of a woman-Tartar bound to the back of the fiery steed, and consented to give her a *début*. She arrived on the

Saturday before the performance; the company was gathered for rehearsal, and it was found that Miss Menken did not know one word of her part. (She never did learn the words of any of her parts.) So the company was dispersed; she was said to be very tired—and then, she and "Captain" Smith got to work. The trained Mazeppa-horse was called in its private life, "Belle Beauty"—an invention which gives us instantly a flashlight upon the literary quality of this travesty of Byron. And to Belle Beauty's back she was to be strapped, and the strap was to be run through a loop in the band that was securely fastened round the horse's body. The performer held the ends in her hands, and the closer they were drawn, the closer she was held to the horse; directly she let them go, she was free. Smith gave her an exhibition of how it was done: the horse sprang forward from the footlights up an eighteen-inch "run" upon a painted mountain. She watched the feat, all pale and trembling. "I'd give every dollar I am worth if I was sure I could do that." "No danger!" affirmed Smith, but she was not reassured. She begged that the horse, instead of starting from the footlights, should be led up to the "run." It seems extraordinary that Smith, who must have known his business, should have humoured her, but he did—with the appalling result that the disconcerted, trained animal went only part of the way up, then "with an awful crash, plunged off the planking on to the staging and timber beneath." Adah was lifted, almost lifeless, the blood streaming from her shoulder. By some miracle, she was not seriously injured, though a doctor, hastily summoned, forbade her to appear on Monday. "Not appear on Monday! I'm going on with the rehearsal *now,*" cries Mazeppa, and so she did—performing the feat quite safely; and, on Monday, rousing a packed house to enthusiasm.

Pittsburg, Cincinnati, St. Louis, New York, followed—then in 1864, London and Astley's.

London behaved most characteristically. Her advent was well heralded by ostentatious shuddering of the Press. There was at that time a prominent theatrical organ, *The Orchestra,* and it was in *The Orchestra's* pages that the ground was prepared for her notoriety. On August 20, 1864, it came out with the most effective shudder. "The Naked Drama": that abracadabra was well used. "There is a depth of degradation in the drama which England has not yet reached"—that also saw the light. "We hope that Mr. E. T. Smith will keep this exhibition from Astley's ... a performance which will be hooted everywhere, save in a Yankee audience or among kindred spirits in a Sepoy community." Nothing could be better! And when the following week, there was printed a noble, dignified letter from the Living Scandal herself: "I have been long a student of sculpture ... my attitudes are selected from the works of Canova. ... Will your critic suspend his judgment until he has seen me?" ... why! *The Orchestra's* young man must have felt that much had been accomplished, and Mr. E. T. Smith, that base corrupter of England, and our Mazeppa, that deep student of Canova, must

have pronounced it "bully for him"—and bullier still for themselves. When in the first week of October, 1864, the Naked Drama began, that smart young man on *The Orchestra* knew exactly the right attitude to assume. He must have been balked of his shudder—for really there was nothing at all shameless about Mazeppa's white linen *maillot*—but he knew a good deal better than to say so. "It is not so bad as it might be, but it is bad at best": that would do very well. A certain scorn was the note. The "fearful rocks" were very ordinary mountain passes; the steed's hoofs rang very hollow on the boards, and the fiery courser seemed mildly surprised at the torches waved in his face. The play was not lively; its chief charm was the scanty costume of Miss Menken. "The bill informs us that she ascends fearful precipices and fights fearful combats herself, which has hitherto been done by deputy. As she has nothing else to do, we cannot imagine any deputy acting for her." ... And then, next week, a villainous punning couplet:

> Lady Godiva's far outdone,
>   And Peeping Tom's an arrant duffer;
> Menken outstrips them both in one
>   At Astley's, now the Opera *Buffer.*

The brilliancy of this is so dazzling that nobody, we imagine, could attempt to explain it; so it may have been accounted a failure, and on October 29th appeared a masterly paragraph: "Probably American ladies and children could go to Astley's, but English ladies and children have weaker nerves." One knows what would happen nowadays after such a hint; in those days, the result was what we have already seen—to fill the boxes at Astley's with elderly gentlemen, who no doubt left discontented wives and daughters at home, wondering what "the creature" was like. ... But *The Orchestra* had not exhausted its ingenuity yet. Shortly there began to appear a serial entitled *Adah's Life,* founded upon the pamphlet issued by Smith before she appeared. The pamphlet was a mass of lies, and the *feuilleton* a mass of insults. Few things more objectionable have, we incline to think, been published in England: *The Hawk,* perhaps, or *The Bat,* or some such defunct rag, may have emulated, but scarcely excelled.

In a word, "the Press, one and all, condemned *Mazeppa*"—very skilfully indeed. Nevertheless, there soon appeared in *The Orchestra's* columns two little poems from "the creature's" pen—the verses to Adelina Patti (May 13, 1865), and a little lyric, there called **Never Forgotten**; in her book—**A Memory.** For long she had been writing, and publishing in American newspapers, rhymed lyrics and those strange, unrhymed effusions which form the greater part of the much-discussed volume, **Infelicia.** This is a tiny green book, with no publisher's name upon its title-page. It has been the subject of keen controversy; its contents have been attributed to two of her friends—one, a certain John Thomson, of whom we shall speak later; the other, Mr. Swinburne. How the latter supposition ever sprang into being in any mortal brain is beyond our comprehension.

Nowhere is the faintest trace of such great influence to be found. The rhymed lyrics do not call for any serious attention, although W. M. Rossetti included in his Anthology of American verse, those entitled *One Year Ago, Aspiration,* and *Infelix. One Year Ago* never rises above the level of the Poets' Corner in a provincial newspaper; *Aspiration* scarcely reaches that; *Infelix* has pathos, but little beauty either of expression or workmanship. One phrase, perhaps:

> I stand a wreck on Error's shore,
> *A spectre not within the door* . . .

for the rest, it is merely the old wail, expressed in terms threadbare before she was born. We think of Swinburne's music, richness, strength—the lyric joy and pain, as of the sun over a tossed sea . . . and amazement at the power of gossip to blind men's critical faculties is our dominant feeling! That these little tight, immovable verses, this outworn language and these feeble forms should be attributed to his influence is absurd enough; that they should be attributed to himself, is surely the last word of ineptitude in literary appreciation. W. M. Rossetti, indeed, abandoning that theory, speaks of Edgar Allan Poe. It is only less grotesque. Here is no melody at all—to stop short of Poe's melody! Of the unrhymed irregular forms, better things can be said. They have a certain undisciplined lyric quality. To Walt Whitman's influence they were inevitably traced back. But there is nothing of Walt Whitman, save the irregularity. His magnificent energy, and the magnificent rhythms which belong to it. . . . No! The cuttings from the American newspapers—"long before she came to England"—are superfluous: Swinburne did not write, nor help in writing, *Infelicia*; Poe did not influence, Whitman did not influence. What there is, is all her own.

Or possibly, John Thomson's—that devoted, chivalrous Bohemian of whom we have already spoken. Mr. Ellis H. Ellis, in a letter to the *Referee* (Dec. 27, 1903), says that Thomson "always bristled with poetry. . . . He breathes on every page: he, and he alone, wrote *Infelicia.*" This is categorical enough, but it would seem that Mr. Ellis was, partially at any rate, mistaken, for there is the testimony of the newspaper-cuttings (from American journals) of nearly every poem in the little green book. Mr. George R. Sims has a valuable collection of these, and also of the MSS. of *Infelicia*—most of them written in a difficult, pale, sprawling hand (which does not much resemble Adah Menken's), and one, the *Infelix* lyric which closes the volume, in an exquisite, meticulous script which is known to be John Thomson's. For ourselves, we feel convinced that Adah wrote them: everything that is known of her makes it probable. These wild, unlovely things express precisely the degree of culture, of expression, to which she had attained.

Thomson was at the time Mr. Swinburne's private secretary. He had been "discovered" in his mother's lodging-house by W. Savile Clarke (a lodger), reciting *Paradise Lost* to the black-beetles in the kitchen at midnight. "He went on for a quarter-of-an-hour"—a youth of eighteen, with black hair and big dark eyes: Savile Clarke listened, wondered, finally got tired, and went to bed. But he told Swinburne, who was interested, and engaged the boy as his private secretary. "John would recite quite suddenly, would give no warning. He knew more poetry by heart than ever man did before," says Mr. Sims in the *Referee*; "he was a Bohemian of the old school, the gentlest, most amiable man that ever lived." Thomson came in later life to know Adah Menken, and the result is easy to foresee. A romantic, poetry-stricken young man—a beautiful, passionate, misunderstood woman! The poetry-stricken youth is quickly the love-stricken; and the beautiful woman loved poetry too—she was among the first to recognise the genius of Mr. Swinburne. . . . All the rest follows as a matter-of-course. The young Swinburne comes to her rooms (with other brilliant men), meets her at Bohemian dinners, writes a dainty French trifle in her Album (she kept an Album for her distinguished men's contributions), calling it *Dolorida*:—

> Combien de temps, dis, la belle,
> Dis, veux-tu m'être fidèle?—
> Pour une nuit, pour un jour,
>   Mon amour.
>
> L'amour nous flatte et nous touche,
> Du doigt, de l'œil, de la bouche,
> Pour un jour, pour une nuit,
>   Et s'enfuit.[5]

And later came that haunting *Dolores* lyric, when the thought of the magnetic, unhappy creature mingled in his brain with the magic in his soul of his own unsurpassed song.

> Seven sorrows the priests give their Virgin,
> But thy sins, which are seventy times seven,
> Seven ages would fail thee to purge in,
> And then they would haunt thee in heaven. . . .
> O mystical rose of the mire,
> O house not of gold but of gain,
>   O splendid and sterile Dolores[6]
>   Our Lady of Pain!

Is there any need to enquire further?

* * *

"One of the most noble-hearted women I ever met in my whole life"—so wrote one friend of those days to Mr. George R. Sims in 1905. "And with warm pleasure I remember many many gentle, womanly acts of goodness and loving-kindness done by her." The letter lies before us as we write, with its further reference to "dear gentle John Thomson." . . . That is a little glory, too, is it not? to have such remembrance after thirty-seven years. *I try to bloom up into the light*: the poignant little phrase "came true" sometimes. She bloomed up into the light for the kindly hearts that never, never would she draw nearest to her own.

* * *

On a day in 1868, Thomson waited for her by appointment in John Camden Hotten's office, to consult further about some of the arrangements for the book, which Hotten was to publish for her—and did publish, though without his imprint, after her death. So she never saw the little green volume—another sadness, is it not? For she was so eager about it—so interested! Mr. Sims kindly allows us to copy two letters, given him by Mr. Andrew Chatto:

Wednesday

DEAR MR. HOTTEN,

I am much pleased with the interview between yourself and Mr. Ellington yesterday. Your ideas are all excellent, and I am confident that we will have a grand success! I will call at your office to-morrow about two o'clock, if you will be so kind as to be 'at home' to me. I am anxious to see the designs that are to be engraved; also, I would be glad if I might look over the later proofs again, as I was very ill when they were corrected for me.

You know I never really liked the idea of my portrait being printed, but I am willing to submit to your judgment in all pertaining to our mutual interest. The proofs of the portrait you sent me are wonderfully well engraved.

Believe me, dear Sir,
Yours truly,
MENKEN

(There is no A. and no I. !)

Again:

Wednesday

DEAR MR. HOTTEN,

I am glad we have found another copy of **'Answer Me,'** I hope you will get it a good place in the book. It is a poem that *I* like, and I believe you will. If you believe in my idea of omitting the **'Karayah to Carl,'** you might put **"Answer Me"** there. However I am sure you will do the best you can for it. Can you get **'Aspiration'** in? Do try. When are we to see the final proofs? I am anxious to get the book out. I fear you put others out before me. In that case, we shall certainly quarrel, and that would be vastly disagreeable *to me.* Do hurry those printers, and I shall like you better than I do now. When you have an idle day, let me come and see more of your wonderful old books.

Yours faithfully,
MENKEN

The signature is written in huge sloping letters: at its quaintness in style we have already hinted. ... No! she never saw the little book, with its gigantic facsimile *MENKEN* on the cover, and its dedication to Charles Dickens, and the letter from the great man: "Many such enclosures" (she had sent him some verses) "come to me, but few so pathetically written and fewer still so modestly sent." ...

Thomson waited two hours that day in 1868, then wrote a note to be given her when she called. She never called. Mr. Sims saw the note recently at Mr. Chatto's—the little tender letter that she never read. ... Did Thomson see her again? We know not. She had left England suddenly, mysteriously; had gone to Paris, to rehearse for a performance of a play called *Les Pirates de la Savane.* Consumption struck her down there: the seeds had long since been sown. She knew she was doomed some time before she died. A friend told her she looked ill. "Yes—I'm shot," she answered. By August 10, 1868, she was utterly vanquished. She never rallied, but died quite peacefully "in an attic on the fifth floor of a low lodging in the Rue de Bondy, opposite the stage-door of the Porte St. Martin"— watched through the night by a devoted friend, Thomas Buchanan Read, the American poet. They buried her in the Jewish cemetery at Mont-Parnasse; her grave is covered by a slab of grey stone, headed by a small grey monument. At the top is a funeral urn, on one side of it are the words of her favourite saying, *Thou knowest*: on the other, "Adah Isaacs Menken, born in Louisiana, U.S. of A. Died in Paris, August 10, 1868."

> No soul shall tell nor lip shall number
> The names and tribes of you that slumber,
>   No memory, no memorial.
> *"Thou knowest"*—who shall say thou knowest?
> There is none highest and none lowest,
>   An end, an end, an end of all.

In the exquisite *Ilicet* stands that phrase, so quoted—the phrase she long had chosen for her grave. ... But we think of her *I try to bloom up into the light*—and search the stanzas of that perfect music for a tenderer word.

> Good-night, good sleep, good rest from sorrow
> To these that shall not have good-morrow,
>   The gods be gentle to all these.

Notes

1. Lent by Mr. G. R. Sims from his collection of letters, MSS., and photographs of Adah Isaacs Menken.

2. We hope some of our readers may be able to translate "Johnnie Gideon" (*Era Almanack,* 1868), from whom we deferentially quote. We acknowledge our own entire ignorance.

3. "A full length portrait with sword and epaulettes (presented by soldiers) is actually to be seen there." ... (Pamphlet issued by E. T. Smith, at the time of her engagement at Astley's.)

4. The shares went up to 1000 dollars each!

5. The verses may be read, in a dainty vellum-bound volume, all by themselves—two short stanzas, and

the binding filled up with blank pages!—at the British Museum: *Stanzas in the Album of Adah Isaacs Menken* (privately printed).

6. We quote from the first edition of *Poems and Ballads*.

Barbara Foster and Michael Foster (essay date 1993)

SOURCE: Foster, Barbara, and Michael Foster. "Adah Isaacs Menken: An American Original." *North Dakota Quarterly* 61.4 (1993): 52-62. Print.

[*In the following essay, the Fosters provide a brief literary biography of Menken, tracing the effects of her association with notable writers (including Walt Whitman, Alexandre Dumas,* père, *and Algernon Charles Swinburne) on the form and content of her writing.*]

In the Victorian era, Adah Isaacs Menken (b. 1835), who considered herself primarily a poet, became the first world-class superstar, a love goddess both created and exploited by the media of her time. This innovative performer brought sexuality to the American stage while her peers emoted in hoop skirts. She can be considered the Marilyn Monroe of the Civil War era, and a theatrical poster in which she appears semi-nude became an object of fantasy—the first "pin-up"—for both Yankee and Confederate soldiers. Her violet eyes, curvy figure, and audacious talent packed theaters and started riots.

Dead at 33, a martyr to fame, in a few years time Menken had gone from stunning ingenue to "the world's delight" to a corpse buried in a pauper's grave at Père Lachaise cemetery. As an actress, she attained top billing in New York, San Francisco, London, and Paris. Kings courted her, men raved and women fainted at her performances. Invariably, Adah preferred the literary crowd, and in turn Walt Whitman, Bret Harte, Charles Dickens, Algernon Charles Swinburne, Dante Gabriel Rossetti, Dumas *père,* and George Sand appreciated her wit and originality.

Menken's sensational ride up a stage-set mountain while strapped to the back of a "fiery steed" made audiences gasp. She appeared to be naked, although she was wearing a sheer body stocking. Her role as a Cossack prince in *Mazeppa,* Lord Bryon's poem recast in play form, required that Menken dress in men's clothes, and this became a trademark. Off-stage she was known to frequent gambling dens garbed in a white tuxedo and black top hat with a flair not seen till Marlene Dietrich. But stardom brought with it a notoriety that incited moralistic journalists to hound her.

Mark Twain, her friend and admirer, observed Menken's charisma onstage in *Mazeppa.* He reviewed her performance for the September 17, 1863, issue of *Territorial Enterprise*: "A magnificent spectacle dazzled my vision—the whole constellation of the 'Great Menken' came flaming out of the heavens like a vast spray of gas jets, and shed a glory over the universe as it fell" (qtd. in Meltzer 62). Horace Greeley, a notorious prude, undertook a vendetta against the "Naked Lady" in his *Tribune* "for daring to shock decent people by exposing her body nude" (qtd. in Mankowitz 11). Preachers denounced her for smoking in public, cutting her hair short, and marrying five times—once, according to her second husband, bigamously.

Multicultural before the term was coined, Menken was a woman of color—part black on her mother's side, likely Jewish on her father's, with a dash of Irish tossed into the gumbo. Her early life in New Orleans was impoverished, a case of the absent father whose affection she extravagantly sought in lovers later on. Allen Lesser, a generally reliable biographer, substantiated from a careful analysis of her poems Menken's boasts that she had a classical education. In *Enchanting Rebel* Lesser wrote, "[S]he was familiar with the odes of Horace and the writings of Catullus, and we may safely assume that her education also included the usual school readings from Caesar and Cicero" (250). Lesser doubted her claim that she studied Homer in the original Greek and translated the *Iliad* into French.

To blot out her "wounded child," Menken perennially invented a new self. She concocted scenarios worthy of the reigning superstar she became. In one she was the daughter of a Spanish grandee; in another tale she descended from French nobility; in yet another, Comanche Indians captured and "educated" her. For Menken truth ultimately resided in her poetry where she expressed both her highest aspirations and the despair hid by her dazzling smile. Lesser discovered verses from the late 1850s that Menken wrote while living in Cincinnati, Ohio, with her second husband, Alexander Menken, a Jewish violinist.

Adah contributed poems to the *Israelite,* a weekly founded by the dean of Reformed Judaism Rabbi Isaac Wise. Local literary circles welcomed the flashy newcomer determined to play a role other than housewife. Menken's first published poem appeared about the same time she made her debut on the Midwestern stage. Both careers began together, but she bared her body before the footlights, her soul in her poetry. Menken herself later explained: "I have written these wild soul poems in the stillness of midnight and when waking to the world the next day they were to me the deepest mystery. I do not see in them as a part of myself; yet I know that the soul prompted every word and that every line is somewhere within me" (qtd. in Lesser, *Rebel* 215).

Menken's Cincinnati poetry, before she became Walt Whitman's disciple, developed Jewish themes. She identified with the Biblical Hebrews and expressed outrage at their historical victimization. Her impassioned defense of Baron Lionel de Rothschild's right to sit in the British House of Parliament as an elected member moved him to anoint her "the inspired Deborah of her people" (qtd. in Lesser, *Weave* 30). She embraced a mystical Judaism, mastered Hebrew, and envisioned a Messiah prepared to liberate the "chosen people." Her martial spirit is evident in an essay called **"The Kingdom of the Mind,"** published in the *Israelite*. The inspired prophet declared: "Oh Israel! sleep not! The time has come when you must be up and exploring the vast kingdoms you have inherited from the birth of the world" (qtd. in Lesser, *Weave* 29).

The Cincinnati poems reveal a Menken struggling to develop her poetic voice. Their tone is imperious, if still on the optimistic side. Brooding undertones lurk, but disillusionment did not consume Adah until her second marriage to John Heenan, the world champion boxer whose fan club outnumbered Menken's; he repudiated her in the press. Menken's marriage in New York on September 3, 1859, and her subsequent troubles became front-page news played up even bigger than Marilyn Monroe's marriage and divorce from Joe DiMaggio in the 1960s. The Irishman's caddish behavior less than a year after their wedding precipitated Menken into a crisis that produced poetry on the emotional edge, sometimes over.

Reporters who formerly praised Menken as an exciting new stage presence now blackened her name. The *Dayton Empire* dug up a love poem written to Alex Menken published in 1858, retitling it **"Come to Me"**—a salacious spin. The paper claimed the poem was meant for Heenan but also insinuated that Menken welcomed other suitors, or as the *Empire* put it, "**'Come To Me'** may now be taken, without doing violence to anybody, as a general invitation to 'go in'" (qtd. in Lesser, *Rebel* 47). The third stanza is, in fact, a statement of Menken's unabashed sexuality:

> My burning lips shall set their seal
>   On our betrothal bond to-night,
>   While whispering murmurs will reveal
>   How souls can love in God's own light.
>   Come back to me!

In a flourish of publicity Heenan abandoned Menken, then denied they ever were married. A vindictive Alex Menken accused Adah Menken of bigamy in the New York press; the trauma caused her to miscarry Heenan's child. Since no theater would hire a woman branded as immoral, Menken almost starved. In despair she attempted suicide, but she was mysteriously rescued by a male friend, possibly Walt Whitman. Metaphorically, the promising ingenue passed away and a chastened woman emerged, competent to examine her place in the world. Her poems, mainly written in 1860, the year of her ordeal, herald a full-fledged poetry. Erica Jong, in a review she wrote of Sylvia Plath's *Correspondence* in November 1975, pointed out that "Sylvia Plath's poetry was the first poetry by a woman to fully express the female rage." Jong is off by about one hundred years. Menken raged a full century before Plath.

Robert Lowell, in his 1966 forward to the American edition of the *Ariel* poems, wrote that Plath was "playing Russian roulette with six cartridges in the cylinder"—a still more apt description of Menken's life and work. In the fall of 1962, when Plath was abandoned by her husband, she replayed the Menken scenario by writing out her heart in an anguished poetic voice. Depression pervades the *Ariel* poems—eventually published to immense critical acclaim. A. Alvarez, who became an early proponent of Plath's work, dubbed her poetry "Extremist Art"—perceptions pushed to the edge by the poet's breakdown (Newman 67). Learning of Menken's response when her golden boy Heenan abandoned her and her world fell in creates a kind of déjà vu in reverse.

According to Lesser, "The poems Menken wrote during this storm and stress period of her life, more revealing than those which any other female American poet had ever dared publish, disclose her growing bewilderment, her indignation, and finally the crushing sense of humiliation that followed" (*Rebel* 62). In **"Drifts That Bar My Door,"** published in the *Sunday Mercury,* July 29, 1860, Menken begged Heenan to save her before it was too late:

> Despair hath driven back Death, and clasps me in his
>   black arms
>   And the lamp! See the lamp is dying out!
> Oh, angels! sweep the drifts that bar my door!—lift up the
>   bars!

> (*Infelicia* 71)

Moods of despair alternated with flurries of defiance. **"Judith,"** published in the *Mercury,* September 2, 1860, challenged Menken's enemies to do their worst; she equated them with the Biblical Philistines and cried:

> I am Judith!
> I wait for the head of my Holofernes!
> Ere the last tremble of the conscious death-agony shall have shuddered, I will show it to ye, with the long black hair clinging to the glazed eyes, and the great mouth opened in search of voice, and the strong throat all hot and reeking with blood, that will thrill me with wild unspeakable joy as it courses down my bare body and dabbles my cold feet!
> My sensuous soul will quake with the burden of so much
>   bliss!
> Oh, what wild passionate kisses I will draw up from that
>   bleeding mouth!
> I will strangle this pallid throat of mine on the sweet blood!
> I will revel in my passion.

> (*Infelicia* 20)

Images of death pervade Menken's poems. She signed them "Infelissimus," unhappiest one. In **"The Ship That Went Down,"** published in the *Mercury,* January 13, 1861, Menken graphically described herself as one who previously had "gone down, down, down, to soundless folds of the fathomless ocean" (*Infelicia* 37). Finally, in **"Myself,"** published in February 10, 1861, a reborn, cynical Menken accepted her fate—the theatrical success she was born for.

> Now I gloss my pale face with laughter, and sail my voice
>   on with the tide.
> Decked in jewels and lace, I laugh beneath the gaslight's
>   glare and quaff the purple wine.
> But the minor-keyed soul is standing naked and hungry
>   upon one of Heaven's high hills of light.

(Infelicia 50)

Walt Whitman supported Menken throughout her troubles. She and Whitman first met at Pfaff's, a celebrated Bohemian rendezvous on Broadway just above Bleeker Street. These precursors of the Algonquin round table drank German beer and disputed literary matters. Although the Pfaffians adopted Poe as their god, Lesser found Whitmanesque influences in Menken's poetry. He wrote:

> Heretofore she had shown a self-consciousness of form and an unevenness of expression that indicated her chaffing against the restrictions imposed by conventional metres. Whitman's poetic form, as she found it in *Leaves of Grass* ... brought her a medium in which she could express the full fire of her passion and emotion. Although she never became a slavish imitator of his free verse form, she was unquestionably the first and probably the only American poet at the time who dared to follow along the path Whitman had opened.

(Rebel 64)

At a time when Whitman was being roundly condemned for his "barbaric yawp," Menken regarded *Leaves of Grass* as her bible. She wrote a bold defense of his poetry called **"Swimming against the Current"** (1860), trumpeting Whitman's greatness. "Look at Walter Whitman, the American philosopher, who is centuries ahead of his contemporaries," wrote Menken imperiously. "He hears the Divine voice calling him to caution mankind against this or that evil and wields his pen, exerts his energies, for the cause of liberty and humanity" (qtd. in Lesser, *Weave* 34). She compared Walt to the idealists of the past "who have been drowned in the current of life, because they swam against the stream" (qtd. in Lesser, *Weave* 34).

Menken convinced Robert Henry Newell, the influential literary editor of the *Sunday Mercury,* whom she met in the early 1860s, to publish her essay on Whitman along with her own poems. However, he disclaimed all responsibility for Menken's "eulogium on that coarse and uncouth creature Walt Whitman" (qtd. in Lesser, *Rebel* 65). Under Menken's spell, he published another essay in favor of the emancipated woman. On October 7, 1860, Menken demanded that "daughters should be trained with higher and holier motives than that of being fashionable and securing wealthy husbands. There are other missions for women than that of wife or mother" (qtd. in Lesser, *Rebel* 69).

Newell believed that Menken wasted her poetic genius in the theater. During the Civil War, under the punning pseudonym of Orpheus C. Kerr, the newspaper editor attained nationwide prominence. He wrote satires about corrupt office seekers in Washington, which Lincoln supposedly chuckled over. On September 24, 1862, Menken took the slender, intellectual editor as her third husband, this time choosing brains over brawn. Menken's wild horse ride garbed in pink tights in *Mazeppa* had catapulted her to superstardom, and the European capitals wanted her at any price. Menken decided to make her fortune in California among the gold prospectors starved for the sight of a female.

Newell tagged along to San Francisco where Menken performed at the Opera House in a costume still more abbreviated. Her payment was one third of nightly gross receipts and fifty percent of every matinee and Friday night. Menken became the biggest star since Lola Montez and probably the highest paid entertainer in the world. As ever, her friends were literary men: Mark Twain, Bret Harte, and Joaquin Miller, the poet of the Sierras—all contributors to the *Golden Era,* an ambitious literary magazine.

The *Golden Era* staff made Menken, the "frenzy of Frisco," their muse, and happily published her poetry. Meanwhile, they patronized the tepid Newell whose pretensions were antithetical to Western dynamism. In March 1864 Menken brought *Mazeppa* to Virginia City, Nevada, where the miners literally threw gold dust and nuggets at her feet, renamed an entire mining district "the Menken," and in her honor, formed the "Menken Shaft and Tunnel Company" to issue illustrated stock certificates bearing the picture of a naked lady bound to a galloping stallion. On April 23, 1864, Menken left the West burdened with wealth, her marriage in shreds. Superficially, she pretended indifference. **"Infelix,"** a poem published on January 3, 1864, in the *Golden Era,* proved otherwise in cadences reminiscent of Poe.

> Myself! alas for theme so poor
>   A theme but rich in Fear;
> I stand a wreck on error's shore,
> A spectre not within the door,
> A houseless shadow evermore,
>   An exile lingering here.

(Infelicia 124)

Two of her late poems **"Aspiration"** and **"Resurgam,"** both published in the *Golden Era* (1863) announced Menken's resolve never to be dependent on a man again. However, in 1864 aboard a ship bound for England she met James Paul Barkley, a Confederate officer turned gambler. Barkley bombarded Menken with his Southern charm and expensive presents. They carried on a trans-atlantic romance, Barkley commuting between London and New York. She dubbed him her "Prince," but she refused to marry him until she became pregnant. On August 19, 1866, at her New York mansion, called Bleak House after her idol Dickens' novel, Menken married for the fourth and final time. The marriage lasted exactly three days. Barkley pressured Menken to give up her career, but stardom in Paris held more allure than domesticity in New York. She was determined to take by storm the most sophisticated capital in the world. The newlyweds' violent quarrel resulted in a wan Menken being bundled aboard the steamer *Java* after an overdose of sleeping pills.

Menken arrived in the Paris of the Second Empire in September 1866. Emperor Napoleon III and his beautiful Empress Eugenie, a style setter, carried on a court that resembled a carnival. Menken remained in seclusion until the birth of her baby in November 1866. George Sand, her crony, agreed to be godmother to the child—a shadowy presence who died in infancy. Sand and Menken shared literary gossip, wore matching trousers, smoked cigars, and, when apart, wrote intimate letters.

Menken hoped that her Paris vehicle would offer an opportunity to extend her acting range. Instead, her French producers mounted another horse drama called *Les pirates de la savane*. Audiences watched a mute Menken cavort undressed in a garish but exciting melodrama. Paris adored her, and *la belle Menken* sold out the Theatre de la Gaite for an unheard of 150 performances.

Alexandre Dumas *pére,* once a popular author, by 1866 a paunchy has-been ignored by the fickle public, became Menken's most ardent fan. She found herself drawn to the raconteur (also of mixed blood) who scraped by on his son's charity. Dumas attended Menken's salon, one of the most brilliant in Paris, drank her champagne, and guided her to quaint spots on the boulevards and in the country-side. She footed the bills for her "King of Romance," who repaid her by publishing pictures taken of them in a domestic pose, that is, Dumas in his shirtsleeves, Menken's face snuggled against his chest. The pictures showed up in shop windows accompanied by bawdy verses. Parisians chuckled that the stunning Menken was the mistress of a roué old enough to be her father—publicity that gave the aging Dumas a last bloom.

Menken, generous of heart, forgave Dumas, her child of gentleness and love. On a photograph she treasured in her autograph album, he wrote, "To the last love of my heart" (qtd. in Mankowitz 178). The hardened conniver had good reason to adore Menken. The attention derived from their affair motivated theater managers to revive his plays, and for one more season Dumas reigned over the Paris stage. A tired Menken returned to London, the scene of former triumphs in the "naked drama." Acting had the virtue of

keeping her from introspection—painful now that she no longer wrote poetry to heal herself. She complained that, "[My] body and soul don't fit each other; they are always in a scramble" (Letter 1867).

In 1867 Menken made a final bid for immortality, hopeful that if she published a collection of her poems, the literary world would acknowledge her greatness. To foster the mood, she struck Byronic poses, wore curls and an open shirt. She asked Charles Dickens to accept her dedication of **Infelicia** to him. Once Dickens agreed, Menken approached Algernon Charles Swinburne, the poet 19th-century English critics anointed Shelley's successor. Jean Overton Fuller, a Swinburne biographer allowed access to his intimate papers, asserted that Dante Gabriel Rossetti, one of the founders of the pre-Raphaelite brotherhood, bet Menken ten pounds that she could not seduce the notoriously woman-shy Swinburne.

Swinburne made no secret of his preference for flagellation or his visits to "whipping ladies" in the St. Johns Woods section of London. Yet Menken and Swinburne developed a sexual bond of some sort. His letters refer to their "terrible games." Fuller quoted a remark of Menken's complaining about the inadequacy of their relationship: "I can't make him understand that biting is no use" (qtd. in Henderson 131).

Briefly, it flattered Swinburne's ego to squire about town the most beautiful woman in Europe. Menken assumed that she was the inspiration for his long sado-masochistic poem "Dolores," after a name she used occasionally. Although "Dolores" appeared in *Poems and Ballads,* in July 1866—before Menken became intimately involved with Swinburne—he knew of her as did all Europe, and certain of its verses are suggestive that he at least fantasized about her. In the fourth stanza we find:

> O lips full of lust and laughter,
>   Curled snakes that are fed from my breast,
> Bite hard, lest remembrance come after
>   And press with new lips where you pressed.
> For my heart too springs up at the pressure,
>   Mine eyelids moisten and burn;
> Ah, feed me and fill me with pleasure,
>   Ere pain come in turn.

>   (1:54)

Predictably, Swinburne became bored with being Menken's courtier. The poet wrote a flippant verse in Menken's album in lieu of a banal goodbye, and he dedicated it to "Dolorida."

> For how long, say, my beautiful one,
> Will you be true to me?
> For one night for a day,
>   My beloved.

> Love flatters us and touches us
> On the finger, on the eye, on the mouth,

For one day and a night
And flies away.

(qtd. in Fuller 164)

Swinburne found Menken a publisher for **Infelicia,** but Lesser is insistent that he made no substantive modifications in her text. Menken, unwell from a bad fall off her "fiery steed," and sensing that her *Mazeppa* days were numbered, hectored the publisher to hurry up the printing of her book. She waffled about which poems to include (they numbered 31), the typeface, and her frontispiece portrait. Convinced that literary fame must be won in England, she became obsessive that the edition be perfect.

Lesser, who failed to mention that being a woman in itself presented a major handicap, pointed out that Menken was playing in the wrong arena: "She lacked the critical perspective to see that her poems expressed the very essence of the American spirit in their bold rhythms and lurid images. In their broad splashes of color and extravagant self-dramatizations they were completely alien to the trend toward decadence of contemporary English literature" (*Rebel* 215). Swinburne signed off on her proofs of **Infelicia.** "Lo, this is she that was the world's delight" (qtd. in Lesser, *Rebel* 212).

In May 1868 Menken left London for Paris. Although *Mazeppa* no longer pulled in the crowds, she hoped the French would acclaim her as before. Her poems, like Plath's *Ariel,* were to be published posthumously. Had she lived to personally promote **Infelicia,** the critics might have been kinder. The general consensus went against both Menken's morals and her poems. William Rossetti, the brother of Dante, included **"Aspiration"** and **"Answer Me"** in his groundbreaking American anthology. Swinburne initially praised **Infelicia,** but typically he changed to a negative opinion, an about-face he showed toward Whitman's *Leaves of Grass.* He told his friend Watts Dutton that Menken's poems were "the greatest rubbish ever written" (qtd. in Leser, *Rebel* 212). Yet Dante Rossetti called **Infelicia,** "really remarkable" (qtd. in Lesser, *Weave* 26). It's no wonder Menken failed to please the male establishment that wrote about and published one another. The public found value in Menken's collection— Lesser traced eight American editions, the latest in 1902.

Menken's hopes that she would open in Paris to thundering applause were dashed. One week after her arrival she fell ill and died soon afterwards, probably of tuberculosis. At the end, Henry Wadsworth Longfellow visited her bedside; he read poetry to her and wrote a verse in her album. The American poet proved to be her last contact with the literary world. She died at 33, on August 10, 1868, a rabbi on hand to say the proper prayers. Menken, philosophical at the end, sighed: "After all, I have lived more than one hundred years, so it is just that I go where they carry old people" (qtd. in Lesser, *Rebel* 235). Her epitaph she borrowed from Swinburne's "Ilicet": "Thou knowest."

Works Cited

Foster, Michael and Barbara. *A Dangerous Woman.* Guilford, CT: Lyons Press, 2011.

Fuller, Jean Overton. *Swinburne.* London: Chatto & Windus, 1975.

Henderson, Philip. *Swinburne: Portrait of a Poet.* New York: Macmillan, 1974.

Jong, Erica. "Letters Focus the Exquisite Rage of Sylvia Plath." *Los Angeles Times* 23 Nov. 1975, 1, 10.

Lesser, Allen. *Enchanting Rebel.* New York: Beechurst Press, 1947.

———. *Weave a Wreath of Laurel.* New York: Coven Press, 1938.

Mankowitz, Wolf. *Mazeppa.* New York: Stein and Day, 1980.

Meltzer, Milton. *Mark Twain Himself.* New York: Bonanza Books, 1960.

Menken, Adah Isaacs. Letter to Charles Warren Stoddard from Paris: 27 September 1867, Harvard Theatre Collection, Cambridge, MA.

———. *Infelicia.* London: Hotten, 1868.

Newman, Charles, ed. *The Art of Sylvia Plath.* Bloomington: Indiana UP, 1970.

Plath, Sylvia. *Ariel.* New York: Harper & Row, 1966.

Swinburne, Algernon Charles. *Collected Poetical Works.* 2 vols. New York: Harper & Brothers, 1924.

Daphne A. Brooks (essay date 1998)

SOURCE: Brooks, Daphne A. "Lady Menken's Secret: Adah Isaacs Menken, Actress Biographies, and the Race for Sensation." *Legacy* 15.1 (1998): 68-77. Print.

[*In the following essay, Brooks surveys the biographical evidence relating to Menken, attempting to sort out "the most assiduously" created and "perplexing mythography which further conceals the actress even as it seeks to reveal her." She concludes that "repeatedly Menken is reduced to her body," which has become "the text on which male authors seek to inscribe knowledge and fill in the gaps of her history."*]

In late 1856, a racially ambiguous actress took to the stage in Texas and embarked on a brief, yet astonishing, transcontinental career as an entertainer which spanned a decade, and which placed her for a time as the highest-paid actress working in England and America in the early 1860s. Although Menken allegedly never "went public" in her lifetime regarding her African American roots in Louisiana's antebellum Creole community, her ability to shift and mutate racial as well as gender identity in a series of notoriously high-profile lead roles on stage in America and Great Britain won her admirers such as Walt Whitman, Mark Twain, and Dante Gabriel Rosetti, and disputed lovers such as Algernon Swinburne and Alexandre Dumas. Menken assumed a series of powerful, sexually assertive characters in her performances, but she was always best known for playing Lord Byron's Mazeppa, a performance requiring several levels of masquerade and culminating in a ride across the stage, scantily clad and bound to a black stallion.

Myths and legends surrounding the actress are numerous and far-reaching, in part due to the rumors and tales which Menken herself perpetuated about her life. At present, the general consensus is that she was born in 1839 in New Orleans, the child of Auguste Theodore, a mulatto registered as a "free man of color," and his French Creole wife Magdaleine Jean Louis Janneaux. She was named Philomene Croi Theodore. Despite the increasing corroboration of this information, Menken remains a complex figure to identify. She assumed a half dozen pseudonyms throughout her life, identified five different men as her father, and claimed to have had at least five husbands in sixteen years. The public name that she kept for a major portion of her life came as a result of her marriage to her first (authenticated) husband, a Jewish musician and businessman-turned-theatre manager, Alexander Isaac Menken. As a result of her marriage to Menken, she converted for a time to Judaism, becoming a staunch activist within the Jewish community. Her career was officially launched upon her first appearance in the title-role of *Mazeppa* in Albany, New York, on the eve of the Civil War in 1861. She went on to perform the role in New York City, Baltimore, and San Francisco, as well as London and Paris, picking up husbands, friends, lovers, and literary mentors along the way. She died in 1868 and was buried in the Jewish section of Pere La Chaise before being moved a year later to Montparnesse under the direction of her devoted friend and confidant, Edwin James, who saw fit to take up a collection and erect a tomb for the actress.[1]

But as all good students of Menken biographical discourse well know, coming to some conclusion about what to deem as "accurate" in regards to her life—not to mention "textual" in relation to her theatrical performances—remains a significant obstacle. Indeed, despite the fact that there exist over a dozen full-length biographies of the actress, as well as numerous articles, essays, and portions of theatrical studies, very little primary material on Menken exists save for several files of letters and articles scattered throughout collections in the northeast and in England, as well as a full-length collection of poems, published posthumously in 1868 and entitled *Infelicia.* Menken's elusiveness as an historical figure clearly warrants a diverse and perhaps even an unconventional methodological approach. Menken biographies sustain a startling and at times troubling dialectic between performance culture on the one hand and the interconnected literary genres of nineteenth-century Anglo-American sensation narratives,

actress biographies, and biographical narratives of African American women on the other. Recontextualizing these long-standing representations of Menken allows us to consider both the types of cultural biases and conditions under which she performed in her lifetime and those with which she has been re-membered throughout the twentieth century. "Sensation" followed Menken throughout her life; yet, it is her biographers who have worked the most assiduously to create a perplexing mythography which further conceals the actress even as it seeks to reveal her.

Although the works on Menken differ in size, scope, range, and style, the majority of these texts, from Edwin James's paper-thin pamphlet on his actress friend in 1868 to Wolf Mankowitz's meticulously researched 1982 work, seem to be united generically by the influence of sensation. As many as eight of the full-length biographies on which I have focused in my research weave elements of the sensation genre and particularly the related genre of the detective-quest into their narrative structure. Essentially, one finds that a number of Menken biographers who sought to write about the actress distinctly place themselves at the center of a mystery. They describe themselves as dedicated to a project of recuperation, yet the representation of that project places the author firmly at the core of the textual narrative, at times displacing the figure of Menken altogether. Authors such as Mankowitz, who sub-titles his work a "biographical quest" and describes his project as a "search for all her selves," and Allen Lesser, who offers a second bracketed title for his biography, "The Secret of Adah Isaacs Menken," each construct and sustain an elaborate pursuit of knowledge and "truth" regarding Menken's life. In doing so, in attempting to uncover what one theatre critic calls the "real woman" behind the legend, these biographers ultimately contribute to a much larger and even more problematic trend in the discourse surrounding the actress—that of the role of the detective. Lesser's preface, for instance, sets up the quest of his text, like that of a private dick's: "No one," he explains, "could tell me who Adah Isaacs Menken, the most famous actress in the world of the 1860s, really was. ... Her secret she carried with her to the grave" (1). Critiquing his fellow biographers' attempts to sort facts as "vain," Lesser claims with narrative swagger to hold "a solution to the mystery" which he aims to reveal in the course of his text (11-12).

Mankowitz's "quest," Lesser's "solution"—each author sets himself a mission obsessed with issues of "authenticity" and identity; these writers continuously obsess over Menken's putative role in obscuring her personal history from public scrutiny throughout her lifetime. In this way more than any other, Menken biographies resemble Victorian sensation novels, such as Mary Elizabeth Maxwell's *Lady Audley's Secret* and Ellen Wood's *East Lynne,* narratives obsessed with the act of revealing concealed identities. As Jonathan Loesberg has convincingly pointed out, Victorian sensation fiction is "constantly concerned with identity and its loss" and, I would add, the recuperation from that loss (117). Christopher Looby also finds that in the American sensation fiction found in the dime novels of George Thompson, for instance, the key characteristic of the text is its unyielding movement toward "the unveiling or revealing of an ugly truth hidden behind sham surfaces" (653).[2] Revelatory "truth" is inextricably linked to identity in these narratives, and more often than not this search is consistently and conventionally bound up with the figure of the fleeting female, veiled in secrecy and egging both reader and protagonist-turned-detective to release and resolve her secrets.[3]

Menken biographers extend and complicate the nineteenth-century sensation novel's trope of the arcane and elusive female stranger by incorporating distinct elements of the turn-of-the-century American passing narrative and its fixation on the alluring yet dangerous mulatta character who dares to transgress social and cultural boundaries. Mark Twain's 1894 *Pudd'nhead Wilson,* for instance, pivots on the discovery of "authentic racial identity" which restores a sense of social, cultural, and communal order in the face of one biracial character's (Roxie's) attempts to thwart and render meaningless such categories. Eric Sundquist contends that as a result of the title character's faithful sleuthing, in "*Pudd'nhead Wilson* masks are removed and order restored where an inversion in the hierarchy of mastery has momentarily left the community in a state of crisis" (268). Clearly American texts such as Twain's are similar to Victorian sensation narratives in that they employ what Patrick Brantlinger calls their "novel-within-a-secret" structure and have sustained life "in several forms of popular culture," in "modern mystery, detective, and suspense fiction and films" (1).[4] I want to briefly discuss three key biographical Menken texts: John S. Kendall's 1938 *Louisiana Historical Quarterly* article, "The World's Delight," Noel Bertram Gerson's 1964 *The Queen of the Plaza,* and the most contemporary of the full-length works, Wolf Mankowitz's 1982 *Mazeppa: The Lives, Loves, and Legends of Adah Isaacs Menken,* in order to demonstrate how each foregrounds the role of the "detective" in "uncovering" the "real" Adah Isaacs Menken.

Kendall's piece situates the author in a tradition of American detective fiction stretching from Twain's *Pudd'nhead* to the modern Walter Mosely mystery *Devil in a Blue Dress*—each of which lurches toward the amateur sleuth's discovery of a transgressive "mulatta's" hidden truths regarding identity, social, and cultural positioning. In his essay, Kendall maintains that "there was much mystery about Adah Isaacs Menken" and he subsequently attempts to undo that "mystery" largely through a rigorously constructed exposure of the actress's racial lineage (847). Writing in the post-Faulknerian, Depression era of the 1930s U.S. South, Kendall essentially invokes the American, postbellum obsession with race and genealogy—as evidenced by "the grandfather clause" and the "drop of blood" genetic hysteria of the Jim Crow era—invoking it loudly here. He speculates, "was all this mystification

about her parentage adopted to conceal facts of which she had no reason to be proud, and which, if known, she felt might react unfavorably upon her professional standing?" He concludes that "her motive ... must have been concealment" (849).

Interestingly, Kendall's obsession with Menken's hidden "secret" gets channeled into a directed mission to reconstruct her genealogical history. This pursuit inevitably permeates the structure of Kendall's text, which underscores and consistently celebrates his role as researcher-turned-detective. Frequently, the author records his own efforts at Menken documentation and his arduous retracing of the actress's African American roots. Kendall describes in great detail his laborious attempts at mining public documents in New Orleans and his fortuitous discovery of city birth records listing colored families between the years 1835 and 1839 which, in his opinion, corroborate Menken's birth date. All these tasks lead to his broad and sweeping conclusion that

> if our suppositions be justified, there were abundant motives why Adah should thereafter avoid telling the truth about her origins, and why she should devise one fantastic tale after the other about her family. Perhaps, too, that explains her beauty as well as her stormy temperament, indomitable ambition, and sketchy morals; for the octoroon women of New Orleans were reputed to be almost uniformly lovely.
>
> (852)

Here, Kendall assumes, first, that Menken's treasured "secret" is one of racial identity and, second, that it provides a crystal-clear explanation for her shameful concealment, that hiding her lineage wards off any association with blackness and its "scar of shame." This, Kendall's "quest," and his hunt for knowledge of Menken takes up a quarter of his article; it is a text which foregrounds the sleuth-like skills of the author, enacting his agency through speculative observations about the actress, knee-jerk psychology regarding her emotional stability, and racial and sexual fantasies invested in the "octoroon" figure. His work best exemplifies the generic convergence of sensation fiction and turn-of-the-century race narratives centralizing the trials and tribulations of the "tragic mulatta" figure.

And his study, no doubt, confirms what Hortense Spillers has claimed, that the figure and the term "mulatta" "tells us little or nothing about the subject buried beneath [it], but quite a great deal more concerning the psychic and cultural reflexes that invent and invoke them" (166). Hence, Kendall's construction of Menken as possessing a "moody" and "violent temper" along with "sketchy morals" supports his preconceived hypothesis of the "octoroon" heroine and illustrates Spillers's contention that "a semantic marker, already fully occupied by a content and an expectation, America's 'tragic mulatto' exists for others—and a particular male other" (167). Indeed, the "mulatto/a" figure functions as "a creation myth" which names and celebrates patriarchal law and "phallic violence." The fastidious detail which Kendall's article pays to filling in the gaps of Menken's nebulous paternal history demonstrates the way that the "mulatta" figure serves as the sensational connection to a white, patriarchal phallus. Menken's very body bears/bares the symbolic traces of her own as well as the antebellum South's public "secrets" of miscegenation and the so-called "sins of the fathers." Menken's history, her "unspeakable" past, her literal figure sustains the traces of the public "secret" of New Orleans race relations.[5] Yet Kendall's research, which subsequent biographers have firmly upheld, confirms that it was probably Menken's father and not her mother who was a "free-born mulatta." With this sensational inversion of the absent father's conventional identity (from white to black), the white patriarchal figure who begets and reaps the benefits of his miscegenous fruits is temporarily displaced in Menken's genealogical history, only to return here discursively and allegorically in the form of the biographers' detective work.[6]

To "solve" the mystery of Menken's seductiveness and her "rare" and magnetic beauty, various biographers craft elaborate projects which impose fixed narratives onto the conundrum of her bodily text. Kendall's bid to reveal Menken's African American blood-ties, though convincing and influential in its scope and range, encompasses a level of zeal, what Spillers would read as "patriarchal prerogatives ... centered in notions that concern the domestication of female sexuality—how it is thwarted, contained, circumscribed, and above all, *narrated*" (172-73, emphasis in original). Moreover, Kendall and the majority of Adah Isaacs Menken biographers' texts find it necessary to impose a definitive racial category onto Menken, an organizational gesture which ultimately elides the complexities of the actress's identity politics. Seemingly, it remains crucial for these writers to read Menken according to some arbitrary racial category which explains away the mystique of her figure and eradicates what Marjorie Garber might call the "category crisis" which her body elicits. Kendall's relentless efforts to categorize Menken, to look through her ambiguity, enacts a kind of detective-like attempt at circumscribing and looking through Menken's complex identity politics in order to sustain narrative control over her potentially unreadable body (16-17).[7]

MENKEN HAS LEFT THE BUILDING

Inheriting Kendall's penchant for detective work, Noel Gerson's and Wolf Mankowitz's subsequent biographical forays strikingly and self-consciously invoke the tradition of the sensation mystery as well. The intertextuality of these two biographical discourses, though published eighteen years apart, in and of itself resembles the familiar struggle at work in classic Victorian narratives such as Wilkie Collins's *The Woman in White,* wherein multiple narrators weave and collide with one another in the unraveling of the plot. Despite the fact that Mankowitz has

called Gerson Menken's "most imaginative biographer," together the two authors have succeeded in committing an act of collusion which is both shameless and elaborate in its professional scope and range. Gerson's work seemingly serves as the catalyst for this event. Until Mankowitz's critically acclaimed project, Gerson's text was generally considered the standard contemporary biography on Menken. Cited in numerous articles on the actress, it revels in pathologizing Menken's sexuality, conflating—rather than displacing—her identity with that of her "nearly nude" *Mazeppa* character of the stage.

Gerson's effort to characterize the "deviance" of his biographical subject is particularly clear in the research which he, and he alone, claimed to have "discovered" regarding Menken's whereabouts between the ages of 16 and 19—years which previous biographers have had difficulty pinpointing in their work on the actress. Gerson maintains at the outset of his work that "the raw material of *Queen of the Plaza* comes from a primary source, Adah Isaacs Menken herself," and that "her Diary and the autobiographical prose fragment, which she intended to publish as her Memoirs, are in the Adah Isaacs Menken Collection [at] Harvard University" (295). According to Gerson, this "Diary" details the adventures of Menken as mistress and concubine to a wealthy Austrian noble, Baron Friedrich von Eberstadt, who in 1853 took her to Havana where they cavorted for several months before the Baron abandoned Menken to return to his invalid wife in the United States, leaving the teen-ager to make her way as a prostitute in the city for two years before returning to Louisiana, "a changed woman."

Gerson makes much of this remarkable information regarding Menken's "past" as a prostitute and (as a sort of 'bonus' gesture) attempts to lavishly apply a series of neatly superficial theories which read Menken as suffering from casebook sexually deviant symptoms throughout her life. His extended analysis of Menken's elusive yet legendary *Diary* builds on this construction of the actress's sexual identity by yoking twentieth-century psychological and clinical theories. In the text of the journal, Menken allegedly details a short-lived, youthful, and illicit romance with the Austrian Baron. Not surprisingly, Gerson theorizes that this relationship early in Menken's life represents the core of deep-seated sexual dysfunction. He observes that

> The Baron's love-making disappointed Adah. She didn't know what to expect, what she was supposed to feel, but she realized that whatever it was, she did not experience it ... in her *Diary* the gates of the physical remain firmly closed. It is impossible for the modern reader, endowed with a greater knowledge of the human psyche, to refrain from guessing that, in all probability, Adah was frigid. Like so many women, throughout history and down to the present day, who took many lovers, it is likely that she was incapable of finding complete physical and emotional satisfaction and release in sex relations.
>
> (40-41)

Gerson's relentless efforts at diagnosing Menken's condition demonstrate his desire to attain a kind of scientific, authorizing mastery over Menken's body. Though Gerson never specifically attributes Menken's complex sexual behavior to nymphomania, he does tend to apply a series of popular and shifting medical arguments regarding the condition which characterize female patients as hysterically oscillating between sexual voraciousness and inhibition. In his study, Menken morphs, like the tragically ailing female sex addict, into a victim who is inevitably "driven to prostitution to satisfy [her] desires."[8]

Along with the fact that this material suspiciously follows conventional nineteenth-century theories which systematically equated actresses with prostitutes, the larger problem in Gerson's detective work is that, despite his foregrounding of the "Diary" in his biography, it has remained conspicuously absent in the research of other scholars. As feminist theatre critic Claudia Johnson discovered in her own study on Menken, Harvard University and other academic librarians claimed no knowledge of the diary and its whereabouts, and Johnson, waxing completely mystified about this development in the footnotes to her 1984 historical study, *American Actress,* declares that after numerous attempts to jog the aging Gerson's memory as to where the memoirs or alleged Menken memorabilia collector J. Hibbard resides, she has been forced to leave Gerson the privilege of laying claim to the "Diary."[9] Mankowitz, however, has more luck, and in chapter twelve of his fifteen chapter book on the actress, after quoting Gerson's work extensively throughout, and including the entire ten-page Gerson narrative of Menken's "lost years" in Havana, Mankowitz details his own quest for the "Diary" and his subsequent shocking conclusion.

The details of Mankowitz's research are worth sharing here since they demonstrate how old and young biographers alike become the subjects of their own projects. Mankowitz, for instance, in his representation of the "Diary" controversy foregrounds his role as skillful detective, and he hedges toward focusing on an intellectual confrontation with Gerson. He describes how "I picked up my correspondence with Gerson and, having by now collected together all the quotations in his book from the 'Diary' and feeling that the material did not totally match with Menken's styles in either her letters or any of her other writings, rashly addressed my senior colleague in the quest for Menken" (189). Mankowitz represents his skepticism towards the authenticity of Gerson's text and he underscores his keen intuition as researcher and biographer. Yet he also discloses his own distrust of Gerson's credibility in the last quarter of his own biographical project, after citing Gerson's biography extensively. This alone is reason to suspect Mankowitz of sustaining a problematic and insidious role in the sensation of Menken biographical research. For his suspension of the "diary" information until the close of his project aligns him with both the sensation narrator and detective figure

who, to quote Patrick Brantlinger, in "withholding the solution to a mystery ... also loses authority or at least innocence, becoming a figure no longer to be trusted" (15). Both literary types seemingly merge in the figure of Mankowitz who, at this crucial moment in the text, reveals himself to be an unreliable narrator as well as the key detective figure in the search for information on Menken.[10]

Indeed Mankowitz ambiguously affirms both his camaraderie as well as his professional superiority to Gerson in a letter to the senior biographer which he includes in chapter twelve and which I quote here at length, if for no other reason than to demonstrate the extent of both writers' stunning hubris and audacity, which has had far-reaching effects on studies of Adah Isaacs Menken. In his letter, Mankowitz writes,

> I propose ... in my book, because she invented so much about herself and so much was invented around her ... I consider, part of the legend of the lady ... which made it possible for her as a writer and so many of the rest of us, to build material around her. So that it doesn't really matter to my purposes whether the Diary you quote from so extensively actually exists or not. I shall be referring to your book ... in my own and—as one old pro to another—let me give it to you straight. If you did, in fact, invent that *Diary,* I would simply consider it to be an achievement in fable-building which should be acknowledged for its creative force—and I am certain it would be so regarded by Mazeppa herself. So can I ask you quite directly—did you actually invent that *Diary* material?

(188-89)

In a sense, Mankowitz's decision to include his epistolary exchange is a bold and daring move which lays bare the politics of biographical research and the struggle for documentation in (re)constructing the events in his subject's life. But the positioning of the letter, as well as the tone and content of his address suggest a thoroughly self-aggrandizing agenda. One assumes that Mankowitz's decision to include this controversy in the biographical narrative as opposed to the preface of his study, for instance, comes as a result of his intention to demonstrate and "deal with the legendary aspect of [Menken's] personality." Yet placing the lengthy letter in a chapter which ostensibly focuses on the actress's brief and unsuccessful performances in Vienna shifts the focus of the text to again mirror the role of the sensation sleuth. Feminist critic Ann Cvetkovich reminds us that, "[o]stensibly the innocent observer of events, [the detective] becomes an active participant in the drama he unfolds. He seems to produce the crime in the process of investigating it" (60).

Chillingly, Mankowitz establishes a familiar yet cautious "old-boy" tone in his address to Gerson, affirming their equal, "old-pro" status as biographers and flat-out praising him for his "fable-building" achievement. Whether for the purposes of his gaining the truth from his suspect or truly in admiration of Gerson's act of literary fraud, Mankowitz celebrates the senior writer's imaginative skills in perpetuating and building on the myths of Menken. Lest we forget, the core of the myth that Gerson produced was one which elaborately portrayed Menken as an agreeable mistress and prostitute in her late teens. Thus, Mankowitz confirms what many feminist theatre critics have noted, that "the actress's sexuality" persists as "public commodity and for sale" (Straub 101).

Gerson's response (which is included in Mankowitz's text) is equally revealing in its language and focus. His much shorter and partially edited text reads as follows: "You have penetrated the iron wall, and all I can say is that it takes a pro to smell out a pro. After due consultation with the elusive Hibbard, I must confess to you that the AIM *Diary,* which proved to be irresistible to write, is the product of my own imagination. So be it. ... Do what you will with the Diary. It is time the hoax is exposed" (189). Gerson's mildly homoerotic imagery and his seeming delight at having had Mankowitz "penetrat[e] the iron wall" of his own secret suggests, if not an eroticized, at the very least an intimate bonding between the two authors in the unfolding of both their projects. Gerson confesses a self-absorbed pleasure in the "irresistible" nature of his own production and languishes in the thrill of the competition between "pros," even as he loses the battle.[11]

More than any other two biographers, Gerson and Mankowitz assume the role of the detective in their work on Adah Isaacs Menken. Their exchange parallels that of the sensation novel's reputed "use of women as means of exchange for relations between men" (Cvetkovich 64). What is finally affirmed in the end has less to do with Menken's life and career and more to do with the ultimate skill of the sleuth; for, as Brantlinger points out, the ability to withhold and uncover a secret is one of the most potent strategies to underscore narrative authority in the novel. As narrator and detective, Mankowitz is, one assumes, to be treated with extreme apprehension. He manipulates the expectations of the reader, just as Gerson does throughout, and then details his acumen in following clues and building a case, finally serving as the agent who restores the order of the Menken narrative. When Gerson congratulates Mankowitz as one "pro" to another, a gesture of good sportsmanship which secures a professional camaraderie over the body of one dead black actress, his words reflect how the figure of Menken has served almost obsessively as conduit of desire for white male biographers over the years. Repeatedly Menken is reduced to the status of her body; perhaps because of the absence of biographical discourse on the actress, her literal body has become the text on which male authors seek to inscribe knowledge and fill in the gaps of her history.

Notes

1. Much of this information has been pieced together out of consistent material from various biographical sources such as Wolf Mankowitz's *Mazeppa;* however, as this project aims to reveal, much of the background on Menken warrants complex contextualization for reasons which I argue below. See also "Menken, Adah Isaacs," *Black Women in America.*

2. Loesberg argues that "sensation novels evoke their most typical moments of sensation response from images of a loss of class identity. And this common image links up with a fear of a general loss of social identity as a result of the merging of classes" (117).

3. Ann Cvetkovich argues convincingly that many of the canonical Victorian sensations are predicated upon the question and the spectacle of the "mysterious woman." She maintains, for instance, that the mystery of the woman in white in Wilkie Collins's novel of the same name functions as the source of sensation in the text which yields so great an affective response in protagonist Walter Hartright that he presses forward in solving the mystery of hidden and dual identity in the narrative. See Ann Cvetkovich, *Mixed Feelings.*

4. Another example of this turn-of-the-century genre which takes a different approach to the politics of passing but which is informed by similar sensation elements is Pauline Hopkins's *Of One Blood.* In Hopkins's text, the heroine "passes" unknowingly in Anglo culture until she is detected and abducted by the villain of the novel.

5. Spillers contends that literally in the face of the mulatta character, "the deceits of a culture are mirrored; the deeds of a secret and unnamed fatherhood made known" (166-68). Historian Joel Williamson additionally points out that, in the wake of the Civil War, "some whites took up the special idea that miscegenation was the basic sin of the antebellum South and the reason why God had forsaken them and allowed them to lose the war" (92).

6. For a convincing argument which explores the white patriarch's displacement of black matrilineage in nineteenth-century narratives of, by, and about the mulatta figure, see P. Gabrielle Foreman, "'Who's Your Mama?'"

7. Garber contends that "the tendency on the part of many critics has been to look through rather than at the cross-dresser, to turn away from a close encounter with the transvestite, and to want to subsume that figure within one of the two traditional genders" (9). By arguing that Menken, in many of the biographies written on her, occupies a representational space similar to that of the transvestite, I do not mean to conflate the self-conscious act of cross-dressing with that of racial ambiguity, nor do I wish to suggest that reading a figure as "mulatta" or biracial is necessarily

more acceptable than imposing an arbitrary category onto that figure. Rather, I employ Garber's useful observations here to make the point that, like the figure of the transvestite, a "racially ambiguous" figure such as Menken produces social and cultural obstacles which force Kendall as well as other biographers to police her body as a means to their own narrative control.

8. See Carol Groneman, "Nymphomania: The Historical Construction of Female Sexuality" (235). Gerson organizes this chapter of his biography, entitled "Queen of the Plaza," in meticulous detail. The Baron's "seduction" is described as having begun in "mid-October, 1853" at which time Menken's "Diary" is said to "contai[n] a single, hastily scribbled line: 'F. von E. loves me!'" (38). The "courtship" section offers intimate anecdotes wherein Gerson quotes Menken as having said "blithely" that "'I have brought very little lingerie.'" Gerson claims also that, according to the "Diary," the "Baron's lovemaking disappointed Adah" (40). Upon the Baron's "abandonment" of Menken in Havana, Gerson reports that the Diary suggests that it "was silly to starve when all she had to do was smile at a man. And if one would buy her a hearty dinner, others would pay her rent. Without a qualm she became a professional prostitute" (46). Subsequently, Gerson reports that Menken's "journal" digresses into a record of her income, expenses, and sexual favors.

9. For more on the nexus between actress and prostitute iconography in the nineteenth century, see Claudia Johnson, *American Actress* (12-17). See also Tracy Davis, *Actresses as Working Women*. Both works reveal that this sort of a conflation was very much a trans-Atlantic cultural phenomenon. Johnson writes that "the controversy and uncertainty about the life of Adah Menken have affected current criticism of her life. Much new material about her appears in ... *Queen of the Plaza*. [Gerson] based his study on an unpublished diary kept by Adah and an autobiographical fragment. The fragment was widely published and is readily available; the diary is, however, another story. Unfortunately, Mr. Gerson's bibliographical note that the diary is held by Harvard University appears to be incorrect. Neither the diary nor the collection cited by G. Hibbard is, according to Harvard librarians, in any of their collections. Private correspondence with Mr. Gerson has failed to jog his memory about where he did use the diary. Harvard has not been able to locate it; it is not listed in catalogs of manuscript collections; and extensive correspondence with other collections has failed to reveal the location of the diary as of this writing. Until that document is located, the information about Adah taken from the diary has to be considered unsubstantiated ..." (189).

10. Brantlinger argues that the detective in Victorian sensation fiction plays the role of restoring social as well as narrative order in the wake of the less-than-forthright narrator. But he adds that "the detective, moreover, is not so much the antithesis of the narrator, trying to recover what the narrator secretes, as one of his personifications in the text, presiding over the plot and leading the reader down several false paths before discovering—or recovering—the true one" (19).

11. It is worth questioning, however, who actually "lost" this battle of the biographers. For the myth regarding Menken's past as a prostitute has lingered despite Mankowitz's discovery. Johnson's text, for instance, was published two years after Mankowitz's study; yet she refers only to Gerson's puzzling work. More recently, Misha Berson's text on the history of nineteenth-century San Francisco theatre includes an allusion to Menken's having "endured a youthful spell as a prostitute" (75).

Works Cited

Berson, Misha. *The San Francisco Stage: From Gold Rush to Golden Spike, 1849-1869, The San Francisco Performing Arts Library and Museum Journal* 2 (1989): 75-79.

Brantlinger, Patrick. "What is 'Sensational' about the 'Sensation Novel'?" *Nineteenth-Century Fiction* 37 (1982): 1-28.

Cvetkovich, Ann. *Mixed Feelings: Feminism, Mass Culture, and Victorian Sensationalism.* New Brunswick: Rutgers UP, 1992.

Davis, Tracy. *Actresses as Working Women: Their Social Identity in Victorian Culture.* New York: Routledge, 1991.

Foreman, P. Gabrielle. "'Who's Your Mama?': White Mulatta Genealogies and Louisa Picquet's *The Octoroon.*" Paper presented at The Nineteenth-Century American Women Writers Conference, Trinity College, Hartford, May 31, 1996.

Garber, Marjorie. *Vested Interests: Cross-Dressing & Cultural Anxiety.* New York: HarperPerennial, 1992.

Gerson, Noel Bertram [pseud. Paul Lewis]. *Queen of the Plaza: A Biography of Adah Isaacs Menken.* New York: Funk & Wagnalls, 1964.

Groneman, Carol. "Nymphomania: The Historical Construction of Female Sexuality." *Deviant Bodies: Critical Perspectives on Difference in Science and Popular Culture.* Ed. Jennifer Terry and Jacqueline Urla. Bloomington: Indiana UP, 1995.

Hopkins, Pauline. *Of One Blood. The Magazine Novels.* Ed. Hazel Carby. New York: Oxford UP, 1988.

Johnson, Claudia. *American Actress: Perspectives on the Nineteenth Century*. Chicago: Nelson-Hall, 1984.

Kendall, John S. "'The World's Delight': The Story of Adah Isaacs Menken." *Louisiana Historical Quarterly* (1938).

Lesser, Allen. *Enchanting Rebel* [*The Secret of Adah Isaacs Menken*]. New York: Beechhurst, 1947.

Loesberg, Jonathan. "The Ideology of Narrative Form in Sensation Fiction." *Representations* 13 (1986): 115-38.

Looby, Christopher. "George Thompson's 'Romance of the Real': Transgression and Taboo in American Sensation Fiction." *American Literature* 65 (1993): 651-72.

Mankowitz, Wolf. *Mazeppa: The Lives, Loves and Legends of Adah Isaacs Menken, A Biographical Quest*. New York: Stein and Day, 1982.

"Menken, Adah Isaacs." *Black Women in America: An Historical Encyclopedia*, 1993. Ed. Darlene Clark Hine.

Spillers, Hortense. "Notes On an Alternative Model—Neither/Nor." *The Difference Within: Feminism and Critical Theory*. Ed. Elizabeth Meese and Alice Parker. Philadelphia: Benjamins, 1989.

Straub, Kristina. *Sexual Suspects: Eighteenth-Century Players and Sexual Ideology*. Princeton: Princeton UP, 1992.

Sundquist, Eric J. *To Wake the Nations: Race in the Making of American Literature*. Cambridge: Harvard UP, 1993.

Williamson, Joel. *New People: Miscegenation and Mulattoes in the United States*. Baton Rouge: Louisiana State UP, 1995.

Peter Dollard (essay date 2000)

SOURCE: Dollard, Peter. "Six New Poems by Adah Isaacs Menken." *Louisiana Literature* 17.1 (2000): 97-106. Print.

[*In the following essay, Dollard introduces six previously undiscovered poems, some of which shed light on Menken's complicated romantic life. They also exemplify Menken's penchant for reworking material to suit a present need: in three of the poems, she recasts portions of the same verse to express affection for her brother-in-law, her husband, and a longtime female friend.*]

Adah Isaacs Menken, who spent the formative years of her girlhood in New Orleans, was an international show-biz superstar in the 1860s, drawing packed houses from New York to California and from London to Paris. Newspapers such as the *New Orleans Picayune* helped her become infamous by highlighting her sensational stage performances and her often scandalous private life in order to increase their readership. She managed this strong media interest so well that she may have earned more money than any American performer before her, and she may have been the most frequently photographed person of the Civil War era.

Whatever she may have lacked on stage in terms of sheer talent, she made up for with a magnetic, generous, and charming personality. She sang, danced, mimed, and joked her way through all the popular show-biz productions of her time and once drew a standing ovation in response to her very eccentric portrayal of Lady Macbeth opposite James Murdoch, a leading Shakespearean actor.[1] She befriended and fascinated journalists in every city she visited, dined with the likes of Twain, Whitman, Swinburne, and George Sand, published poetry and essays, married half a dozen times, and became particularly notorious by appearing stark naked (or so it seemed) in the horse-opera version of Byron's *Mazeppa*. Menken died in Paris in 1868, only thirty-three years old, perhaps as a consequence of internal injuries accumulated in the many falls she suffered while performing her dangerous horseback ride in *Mazeppa*.

There was a much sharper division in Menken's time than there is today between the "serious" and the "popular" theater. Women who performed in the popular theater were commonly presumed to be immoral, and Menken was judged to be even more flagrantly so since she often played men's roles. Early in the Civil War, Menken flaunted her Southern sympathies in the North to the consternation of her detractors. Her economic independence and Bohemian lifestyle, combined with her very public liaisons and marriages with a series of men, seemed only to confirm to the self-styled guardians of public morality that this scandalous woman was not only beneath serious attention but of the kind who are potential sources of consequential social harm. In 1865, for example, some people were quick to draw connections between the purportedly harmful social effects of the popular theater and the assassination of Lincoln in a theater by an actor.

Menken's self-promotional guile led her to create entertaining and romantic histories of her own life that played well at the box office but have left her biographers groping for facts. She claimed at various times that, by origin, she was Spanish, British, French, and several different kinds of American. It was established only nine years ago that Menken was born with the surname McCord and was given her stepfather's surname, Campbell, when her mother remarried and moved to New Orleans.[2] It is quite possible that she started her performing career in Texas as a horseback rider in touring circuses.[3] It is fairly certain that she and her younger sister danced together as the Theodore Sisters in New Orleans early in her career, although her use of the stage name Theodore has mystified her biographers. Her biographers are also mystified over her decision to add the name Bertha, calling herself Ada Bertha Theodore by the time she married Alexander Isaac Menken in 1856 at the age of twenty-one. She finally settled into the name by which she is now known by adding as *s* to Isaac.

As if Menken's tales about herself and her liberal use of different names were not enough, her biographers and commentators have created further confusion by accepting earlier Menken lore uncritically, too often making little use of such primary sources as Menken's essays, poems, and letters or the many contemporary accounts of her that were published in the newspapers of her day. In recent decades, things have improved. In *The Naked Lady* (1934), Bernard Falk was the first biographer to delve deeply into these primary sources. Falk quoted from them extensively, but he then dismissed the notion of documentation with the assertion that to show all the work he had done in writing his Menken biography would be a mere "exercise in vanity."[4] The consequence is a very readable but often uncertain and dated source on Menken. Allen Lesser's biography, *Enchanted Rebel* (1947), is the seminal biography of Menken, although Lesser's proclivity for presenting scenes, conversations, and thoughts about which he could at best only conjecture limits its reliability.[5] Noel Gerson's 1965 "biography" of Menken, *Queen of the Plaza,* is immense fun to read, but, unfortunately, Gerson based much of the most interesting parts of his "biography" on a Menken diary that he had fabricated.[6] Gerson's deceit was revealed in the best Menken biography, Wolf Mankowitz's *Mazeppa* (1982). As good as the work is, however, Mankowitz relies heavily on Lesser and Falk and even quotes the deceitful Gerson at length because of Gerson's high entertainment value.[7]

When we read Menken's poems and letters, we see explicitly that she desperately wanted to be recognized as more than the scandalous woman and theatrical sex object on which too many of her commentators tend to focus. She wanted to be known as an artist, as a person of mind and spirit. As she herself often observed, however, she had to support herself, and she succeeded in that quite well by creating a public persona that drew crowds to the theaters in which she performed. Consequently, it is not surprising that much of what has been written about her has concentrated on her stage career and often titillating public life. There has been little focus on her writings, even though her single volume of published poetry, *Infelicia,* remained in print into the twentieth century, and even though her poetry is still being anthologized to this day. A major roadblock to discussing Menken, in fact, is that there is no complete and authoritative collection of her writings and that some of her writings have yet to be identified.[8] Her output was small: thirty-one poems in her *Infelicia,* fifty-three other poems listed in Lesser's bibliography, one poem identified by Mankowitz, and the six identified here add up to a grand total of ninety-one known poems.[9]

Menken's life as a performer has proved to be a continuing source of analysis and speculation more than a century

after her death, but, I believe, we can better understand her if we expand beyond that focus and think of her as well as an interesting second-tier poet. The intent of this essay is to help create that broader focus by presenting six new Menken poems that I have discovered and relating those six poems to circumstances and details of Menken's life. More information about Menken's outer life should help us move toward a better understanding of both her inner life and the cultural/historical significance of her life. Coincidentally, these six poems provide snapshots of her at three distinct points in time: the first two were written early on during a disconsolate period of her early adult life, the next three were written during a turbulent period just before she broke through to stardom, and the sixth was written just as she reached the self-assured pinnacle of her career.

The subjects of the first two poems are two men who have been given very short shrift by her biographers: one was her brother, and the other was very likely a husband above and beyond the four husbands her biographers tell us she had.

"To My Brother Gus" was published under the pen name Ada Bertha in the 8 October 1855 *Liberty (Texas) Gazette,* when Menken was twenty years old. This is Menken's earliest known published work, appearing a full two years before any other previously identified work by her.

It is clearly a very conventional and sentimental poem, but it is competently handled and shows that Menken had already taken up a style of writing that was very much based on feelings, experiences, and thoughts just then at the forefront of her mind. This poem has biographical significance because Menken's biographers have almost entirely dismissed or ignored her occasional claims elsewhere that she had a brother.[10] The discovery of this poem makes it very likely that she actually did have such a brother since it was written years before she had begun heavily mythologizing her past. Given Menken's predilection for playing men's roles—and given her notorious string of relationships with a series of men—it would be interesting to know more about this particular man. But, just like Adah's sister, Annie, Gus seems to have disappeared from her life at about the time she began her rise to prominence.

The second new poem, **"I am Thine—to W.H.K.,"** also published under the pen name Ada Bertha, appeared a month later in the 5 November 1855 in the *Liberty Gazette.* The biographical interest of this poem is its support of Mankowitz's speculation that Menken married a man named W. H. Kneass before she married Alexander Menken. Mankowitz reproduced a marriage record that indicates that Menken had married W. H. Kneass, using the name Adda Theodore, in Galveston, Texas, on 6 February 1855.[11] The fact that Menken dedicated this second poem to a man with precisely the same initials as W. H. Kneass is surely more than coincidental. This poem, then, written some nine months after the marriage discovered by Mankowitz and just five months before she married Alexander Isaac Menken, supports Mankowitz's hunch. This second indication that Menken had been married before she married Alexander Menken suggests that her profession of shock a few years later when she was publicly accused of bigamy may have been altogether disingenuous.[12]

These first two poems were written during the time when Menken's relationship with Kneass was coming to an end. She was disconsolate during "sorrow's hour" in the first poem and yearns for a lost closeness in the second. In both poems, she is a model of feminine deference to her man. Nothing is yet known about Kneass himself, but there was a theatrical Kneass family at the time, and it seems fair to speculate that Kneass was a member of that family.

In the remaining three poems, we see Menken three to four years later suffering under the constraints of a very restrictive and conventional marriage, then throwing that life aside when she became infatuated with a handsome boxer. The third poem, **"Happiness,"** was published in the 13 August 1858 *Jewish Messenger.* Menken's long religious poems are the ones most commonly anthologized today, and this particular one, addressed to her brother-in-law, Nathan, provides support for the often-repeated observation that Menken was feeling stifled by the restraints imposed on her by a husband who wanted her to stay at home and abandon the stage altogether. In telling Nathan to pursue the good selflessly, she may in fact be trying to persuade herself to do so. Here, we have a former career woman advising Nathan that it is "vain to seek [happiness] in ambition's path." Stop looking for the "plaudits of the world," she says, and free yourself of "sordid selfishness." Of course, she was also a recent convert to Judaism and perhaps intent on proving the sincerity of her conversion to her husband and in-laws. Her active insistence on repressing ambition in this poem contrasts quite strongly with the deferential tone of the first two poems and her worship of ambition in **"Reply to Dora Shaw"** six years later.

The fourth rediscovered Menken poem is **"The World of Thought,"** published in the 8 October 1858 *Jewish Messenger.* Although the heliocentric universe we see here may be bad science, the stars and comets running "wild" in the sky remind us that the word *star* had as much show-biz significance for Menken as it does for us today. To be a star was to be assured of top billing and top dollar. Menken had wanted to be a theatrical "star" before her marriage to Menken, and here we see her, newly converted to Judaism, seemingly intent on proving the solidity of her religious devotion but simultaneously embedding, perhaps unconsciously, an allusion to the grand theatrical ambitions that she may have been trying to convince herself she had put aside.

The fifth new poem, **"To John C. Heenan,"** is a reworked version of her **"To Brother Nathan,"** a poem addressed to

her brother-in-law that she had published a year earlier in the 25 June 1858 *Cincinnati Israelite.*[13] Thirteen months after publishing **"To Brother Nathan,"** Menken's career had begun its slide into the notoriety that was to follow her the rest of her life. She had found a new love, had left her husband, and had returned to New Orleans to resume her theatrical career. She then returned to **"Nathan,"** changed a few words and the title, added two new stanzas, and published **"To John C. Heenan"** in the 16 July 1859 *New York Clipper* under the pseudonym Edwin F. B. Price, M.D. Her use of that pseudonym is an interesting example of the ease with which Menken could fabricate even her own name if it suited her purposes.

Menken was not well known at the time, but the John C. Heenan to whom this poem is addressed was one of America's best known personalities in 1859, getting heavy media coverage because of his upcoming prizefight with Tom Sayers, the English champion. He was a celebrity figure, followed avidly by the newspapers of the era, whose merging of sporting and theatrical coverage was seen as a very appropriate valuing of both the body and the mind. The guardians of public morality, of course, regarded prizefighters like Heenan as part of an unsavory lower class, given to gambling, drinking, and whore-mongering. Heenan's Irish descent only worsened that image. Menken and Heenan seem to have met in Cincinnati in December 1858, when Menken, still married to Alexander Menken, fell "recklessly and blindly in love with ... a man ... far removed from her in background and character."[14]

There is no trace of the ostensible author of this poem, Edwin F. B. Price, M.D., other than this poem and a second poem by Price entitled **"The Strong Arm and Brave Heart"** that was published in the 31 December 1859 *Clipper,* after Heenan had dumped Menken, and just before he left the country for his world championship boxing match in England.[15] Issues of the *Clipper* make it clear, however, that Heenan himself had a friend and colleague named Edmund E. Price (*Clipper,* 16 July 1859). Price was a native of England (*Clipper,* 25 June 1859) who was described at the time as "a man of superior education and attainments, speaking, reading and writing the French and Italian languages as readily and fluently as his native English" (*Clipper,* 5 October 1859). Price, who had had a run-in with the law and was jailed briefly for forging bank bills before Menken and Heenan had met (*Clipper,* 9 January 1858), was also a prizefighter, and he eventually wrote a book on boxing. Edmund E. Price, then, was a very literate boxing pal of Heenan's who would certainly have been thought capable at the time of addressing a poem to Heenan, although readers surely must have noted that the supposedly male author used unusual imagery, to say the least, while addressing himself to another man.

Menken wrote the **"Heenan"** [**"To John C. Heenan"**] poem in New Orleans during the interval between her private rabbinical divorce in July from Alexander Isaac

Menken and her secret marriage in September to John C. Heenan. Heenan was moving for weeks between New York and Boston at the time, but he and Menken corresponded, as suggested by the allusion in the last stanza to vowing their "friendship . . . pen to pen." Menken "was well aware that she was risking her entire career by marrying so soon after her divorce, and to a pugilist of all men. The public scandal that might follow would rob her of every shred of respectability and bar her from every legitimate stage in the country."[16] Her need to display her feelings for Heenan was not to be completely stifled, however. The solution was to use a variant of Price's name rather than her own and to take advantage of the fact that both the editor of the *Clipper*, Frank Queen, and one of the *Clipper*'s reporters, Ed James, were close personal friends. Heenan and Price would also have been in on this joke since it was published while the romance was still very active and since they too were good friends of Queen and James.

It is surprising that the sixth new Menken poem has not been previously identified. It is signed by Menken, was published in a major newspaper, and shows Menken at her self-confident pinnacle. **"Reply to Dora Shaw"** was published five years after the **"Heenan"** poem in the 24 September 1864 *New York Clipper*, just five weeks before Menken opened her first London engagement. Clearly, Menken has transformed the **"Heenan"** poem. She retained the essence of the first and last stanzas from it and wrote four entirely new stanzas to replace the middle ones. By this time, the very first version, the 1858 **"To Brother Nathan,"** had disappeared entirely.

The Dora Shaw of the poem's title is a somewhat obscure figure, rarely referred to in biographical/reference sources. One biographer described her as "brilliant, beautiful, but eccentric."[17] She was identified in the 19 October 1856 *New Orleans Picayune* as a "lady, poetess, and artist" who was born in New Orleans, "passed a portion of her girlhood" there, and made her stage debut within the year preceding late 1856. Menken, still at the early part of her own stage career, was also playing in and around New Orleans in late 1856.[18] Circumstantially, it seems quite possible that Menken and Shaw knew each other over many years. Menken had also lived in New Orleans in 1848, when both she and Shaw would have been young girls.[19] As adults, they traveled the same theatrical circuits. This congruence of temperament, profession, and background suggests they may have been long-term acquaintances. Such a long-standing acquaintance may account for Menken's decision to pull the **"Heenan"** poem out again and readdress it defiantly to a woman who had been a truer friend than Heenan had ever been.

Menken's life was very different in 1864 from what it had been only five years earlier. In July 1859, Menken was not well known, had not yet recovered professionally from her failed New York debut the previous March, and was not well off financially. By the summer of 1864, things had changed considerably. She had become known as the infamous "naked lady" because of her seemingly nude performances in *Mazeppa*. She had played to packed houses for several years, including a tremendously lucrative trip to California and Nevada. She was making a fortune, demanding and getting higher salaries than any performer before her.[20] She and her agents had become expert promoters, plastering towns, for example, with posters showing the "naked lady" strapped to the back of what was almost always called a "fiery steed." Having shed both Heenan and her next husband, Robert Henry Newell, she was now involved with James Barkley, an "elegant, handsome, wealthy, and somewhat mysterious Southern" gambler. She "was besieged by the famous, the wealthy, and the aristocratic" as she waited from April to October to make her London debut.[21]

The delay gave her the free time to promote herself, by making very public and flamboyant rides through fashionable parts of London (*Clipper*, 6 August 1864). She was also able to write and gain additional publicity by, for example, countering H. B. Farnie's unkind attack on her in "The Morals of American Art" (*The Orchestra*, 20 August 1864) with an eloquent response only a week later (*The Orchestra*, 27 August 1864). Although impatient to start performing again, she was doing quite well—and then, in August, Heenan reentered her life. Heenan, it must be pointed out, had used Menken quite cruelly five years earlier. Not only had he publicly denied that he had ever married her, but he publicly denied that he was the father of a baby Menken lost in childbirth. He simply left the United States for England, leaving her destitute and pregnant. It was the low point of Menken's life, a time when she nearly committed suicide.[22]

Things were quite different when Heenan resurfaced in 1864. He had been decisively beaten by Tom King, the new English champion, and was now merely a cash-short, ex-champion boxer who supported himself by bookmaking. He decided to try to rekindle his affair with Menken, despite her current involvement with Barkley. Although Menken received him into her company, she was frightened of him, expressing the fear that "he will knock me down in the street if he meets me."[23] Her friend Ed James reported years after the fact about concerns that Heenan's "hirelings might make trouble" on her London opening night.[24] In her poem **"One Year Ago,"** a poignant expression of the despair she had felt years earlier over her breakup with Heenan, Menken refers to her fear that he might beat her, saying, "Strike if you will, and let the stroke / Be heavy as my weight of woe."[25]

Menken may have "enjoyed the satisfaction of seeing her former husband suffer all the pangs of jealousy" since Barkley, her current love interest, was a constant presence. In a letter, Menken said that Heenan had "been the ruin of what might have been a splendid life. . . . [H]e . . . taught me to disbelieve in man. . . . Now . . . it is my turn to *inflict* suffering" on him.[26] Heenan's reappearance, then, may have reminded Menken of the loving poem she had written to him pseudononymously five years earlier. His reappearance must have inspired her to take that poem back so that she could assert her "fealty" to her life's dreams as well as her assurance that she had moved well beyond her old infatuation with him.

Throughout her career, Adah Isaacs Menken wanted to be respected by the artistic and intellectual community of her time as a fellow artist and intellectual, not just as a performer in the so-called sensation drama. In the last few months of her life, almost as though she anticipated the worst, she tried to turn the critical focus over to her artistry by collecting the poems for what turned out to be her posthumous volume of poetry. Nevertheless, she still died frustrated by her inability to gain the artistic respect she had so deeply wanted, a respect that is coming to her slowly now through the process of being anthologized. At her death, some of her enemies savaged both her career and the single volume of verse. More commonly, she was remembered fondly as a generous, if errant, soul. Elizabeth Cady Stanton memorialized Menken as follows:

> Poor Adah! when she died she left the world a book of poems that reveals an inner life of love for the true, the pure, the beautiful, that none could have imagined possible in the actress, whose public and private life were alike sensual and scandalous. Who can read ... [her verses] ... without feeling that this unfortunate girl, a victim of society, was full of genius and tenderness.[27]

Menken was buried originally in the Père Lachaise cemetery in Paris on 10 August 1868. Her remains were transferred to the Montparnasse cemetery on 13 April 1869,[28] where her grave was a popular shrine well into the 1920s. But she has confounded us once again. I discovered in 1997 that Menken's remains were transferred back to Père Lachaise eight years ago. Her remains are now in the Père Lachaise ossuary, piled up with the bones of a crowd of anonymous others.

Notes

1. James E. Murdoch, *The Stage; or, Recollections of Actors and Acting from an Experience of Fifty Years* (1880; reprint, New York: Benjamin Blom, 1969), 285.

2. John Cofran, "The Identity of Adah Isaacs Menken: A Theatrical Mystery Solved," *Theatre Survey* 31, no. 1 (1990): 47-54, 52.

3. Kate Wilson Davis, "Adah Isaacs Menken—Her Life and Poetry in America" (M.A. thesis, Southern Methodist University, 1944), 18.

4. Bernard Falk, *The Naked Lady*, rev. ed. (London: Hutchinson, 1952), 251.

5. Allen Lesser, *Enchanting Rebel* (Philadelphia: Jewish Book Guild, 1947).

6. Noel Bertram Gerson, *Queen of the Plaza* (London: Alvin Redman, 1965).

7. Wolf Mankowitz, *Mazeppa* (London: Blond & Briggs, 1982).

8. The most complete Menken bibliography is the one appended to Lesser's *Enchanting Rebel.*

9. Lesser, *Enchanting Rebel,* 265; Mankowitz, *Mazeppa,* 37. Mankowitz claimed that he had found three new Menken poems in the *Liberty (Texas) Gazette.* He quotes all of "New Advertisement," gives the title of a second one ("The Bright and Beautiful"), and gives no further information on the third poem. I could not find "The Bright and Beautiful" in the *Gazette,* but "To My Brother Gus" and "I Am Thine—to W.H.K.;" poems not mentioned by Mankowitz, are found there.

10. Cofran, "Identity," 52.

11. Mankowitz, *Mazeppa,* 32.

12. To complicate this bigamy issue even further, Menken's biographers have also dismissed Menken's claim (Adah Isaacs Menken, "Notes on My Life," *New York Times,* 6 September 1868, 3) that she had married Juan Clemente Zenea, the Cuban revolutionary poet. The fact is that Zenea wrote several poems to and about Menken just after her death and that his Cuban biographers assert that the two met in Havana in 1850, when Menken was only fifteen years old (Juan Clemente Zenea, *Poesia,* ed. José Lizama Lima [Havana: Editorial Nacional de Cuba, 1966], 291, 17). None of Zenea's poetry has yet been translated into English, and no critical or biographical English-language studies of Zenea exist, even though Zenea is regarded as Cuba's leading romantic poet.

13. "To Brother Nathan" is included in Lesser's bibliography.

14. Lesser, *Enchanting Rebel,* 43.

15. The quality, style, and content of this other "Price" poem make it obvious that Menken did not write it. Heenan's friend Price probably wrote it.

16. Lesser, *Enchanting Rebel,* 43.

17. John S. Kendall, *The Golden Age of the New Orleans Theater* (Baton Rouge: Louisiana State University Press, 1952), 305.

18. Bill Parsons, "The Debut of Adah Isaacs Menken," *Quarterly Journal of Speech* 46, no. 1 (1960): 8-13, 8-10.

19. Cofran, "Identity," 54.

20. Falk, *The Naked Lady,* 86.

21. Mankowitz, *Mazeppa,* 151.

22. Ibid., 75.

23. Lesser, *Enchanting Rebel,* 164.

24. Ed James, *Biography of Adah Isaacs Menken* (New York: E. James, 1881), 9.

25. Adah Isaacs Menken, *Infelicia* (London, 1868), 61.

26. Lesser, *Enchanting Rebel,* 165.

27. Elizabeth Cady Stanton, "Adah Isaacs Menken," *The Revolution,* 1 October 1868, 201-2, 201.

28. James, *Biography,* 13.

Daphne A. Brooks (essay date 2001)

SOURCE: Brooks, Daphne A. "'The Deeds Done in My Body': Black Feminist Theory, Performance, and the Truth about Adah Isaacs Menken." *Recovering the Black Female Body: Self-Representations by African American Women.* Ed. Michael Bennett and Vanessa D. Dickerson. New Brunswick: Rutgers UP, 2001. 41-70. Print.

[*In the following essay, Brooks considers the implications of Menken's performance in* Mazeppa, *which, Brooks contends, crossed gender and racial boundaries. Brooks compares Menken and her contemporary, Sojourner Truth, who in different ways resisted the objectification of female bodies on stage.*]

Less than three months after she was laid to rest in the summer of 1868, actress Adah Isaacs Menken's elusive personal history cemented itself in the public imaginary. In an effort to untangle the New Orleans-born entertainer's notoriously circuitous identity politics, journalist G. Lippard Barclay scrambled to publish a pamphlet on Menken; in his modest volume, he claimed with great moral conviction that his editor had sternly directed him to "write of her nothing but the truth" (43). Yet Barclay's efforts went largely ignored by a generation of scholars and media critics who approached documenting and researching the enigmatic actress's adventurous life and work with varying degrees of accuracy and integrity. Barclay's "truthful" agenda failed to quell the controversy and allure that blanketed Menken's short career, and it did little to discourage future generations of fallacious narratives about the actress. Tellingly, in the decades following her death and in the wake of events in which her remains were literally exhumed, transferred, and reburied, Menken's legendary body (of work) lingers as a hotly contested site of analysis, a corporeal conundrum that repeatedly surfaces as an object of textual appropriation in popular and scholarly projects (James 14-16).[1]

Menken dominated the spectacle-driven transatlantic theater circuit for much of the 1860s, until her untimely death from stage injuries and an infection. She initially gained global notoriety for performing the eponymous lead in the 1861 production of *Mazeppa.* Strapped to a black stallion and cutting a treacherous path across the stage in "flesh-colored" tights and a tunic before full-house audiences in the United States and Europe, Menken's at once voluptuous and yet ambiguously costumed figure launched a groundswell of pop cultural fascination. The spectacle of her "disrobing" in the cross-dressed role of a heroic rebel warrior evolved into the central attraction during this nightly extravaganza. Yet with so much attention paid to that which she "laid bare" on the stage, the facts of her personal life have largely remained a source of occlusion and contention. This controversy has, in part, led to theater historians' immortalization of Menken less for her roles as a thespian and more as an object of public curiosity who claimed at least half a dozen pseudonyms throughout her lifetime, named five different individuals to be her father, identified just as many husbands in sixteen years, and boasted a colorful array of alleged celebrity paramours and confidants ranging from Alexandre Dumas *père* to Algernon Charles Swinburne and Mark Twain. Perhaps the most provocative controversy in twentieth-century scholarship on the actress, however, revolves around genealogical politics—the increasing corroboration of Menken's African ancestry, her putative Creole cultural background, and her own attempts to publicly obfuscate family lineage.

An inventive participant in the elision and effacement of her own personal history, Menken spent a good deal of her career circulating narratives by print and word of mouth that complicated the public perception of her identity, in turn inspiring a generation's worth of feeble attempts to crack the code of her "authentic" racial past. This biographical obsession with "uncovering the secret" of Menken's cultural and racial genealogy has paradoxically obscured her subjectivity in the work of many scholars who collapse a reading of the "truth" of her identity into the scene of corporeal unveiling in her professional work. At least seven full-length biographies, as well as numerous journal articles and several works of fiction, foreground Menken's racially ambiguous body and situate her figure as an open corporeal text inviting circumscription by the sleuthlike biographer. Menken, in these projects, comes across not so much as a theatrical pioneer of the mid-nineteenth-century extravaganza genre but more as a hapless criminal beckoning apprehension; an unruly figure, she is drawn to the theater, these texts suggest, by her essentially libidinous role as "the naked lady." Look no further, these biographies assert, than at the body before you on the stage to find the "true" Adah Isaacs Menken.[2]

This suggestion, however, seems to grossly oversimplify the life and career of an entertainer who was, between 1861 and 1863, the highest paid actress in England and America. Indeed, what is missing from this remarkably extensive yet egregiously facile biographical and scholarly discourse on Menken is a critical and methodological approach that allows for a more complex reading of her performative agency. An actress who intervened in the representation of her own body politics both on and off of the stage, Menken remains a rich and unrecuperated site of contradictions and intersections in performance culture. Her work has rarely been considered in the context of critical feminist cultural analysis, and few scholars have attempted to map a connection between her manipulation of racial and gender categories and the nature of her work as a legendary "shape actress."[3] What would it mean, for instance, to explore the ways in which the labyrinths of Menken's identity performances complicate the terms of her "exposure" as a female entertainer? How, if at all, might we discuss her work in the racially marked contexts that she simultaneously invoked and confounded? Only by critically recontextualizing biographical as well as theatrical "scenes" in multiple Menken narratives do we come closer to a consideration of the interplay between her continuum of identity constructions and her equally volatile body politics.

I intend to read against popular and long-standing representations of Menken that fix and reduce her stage materiality. I attempt instead to resituate the actress in a black feminist theoretical context that allows us to read her as radically using her body as a performative instrument of subjectivity rather than existing merely as an object of spectral ravishment and domination. What concerns me here is the possibility of locating an "imaginary body" that ultimately functions as representational resistance and that equally problematizes the ways in which we conceive of racial, gender, and corporeal spectacle in nineteenth-century culture.[4] Reading across the gaze of the white male spectator, I am most interested in mining what we might call a politics of opacity that black feminist theory enables. Thus the first section considers the methodological quagmire that Menken's life and work poses. I question whether it is possible to articulate an interpretative strategy of reading that negotiates black feminist theory and performance, as well as the politics of the body. The remainder of the essay responds to this initial query by examining the nexus between corporeal subjectivity and cultural agency as it specifically comes to bear upon Menken. Here I argue that the opaque operates as a method of contestation and invention for the public, performative, and racially ambiguous nineteenth-century female figure. From this standpoint I aim to reposition Menken as an actress and a cultural figure deeply rooted in transatlantic theater culture. A phantasmagoric body of (un)truthfulness that exemplifies the power of performance as a site of (re)covering, Menken's spectacular figure disrupts the conventional relationship between audience and performer in nineteenth-century theater culture. This project picks up where Barclay and other Menken "detectographers" have left off in that it aims to interrogate this arcane cultural icon from the standpoint of a different kind of "truth" and takes the unlikely figure of Sojourner Truth, Menken's black feminist contemporary, as a critical and methodological

point of departure. For it is Truth's repeated and legendary characterization of her own black, female, and very public body that forces an overt consideration of the corporeal as a site of spectacularly resistant opacity.

THE TRUTH ABOUT MENKEN

I feel that if I have to answer for the deeds done in my body just as much as a man, I have a right to have just as much as a man.

—Sojourner Truth (Gage, "Address")

For this opacity ... must be considered in relation to the dominative imposition of transparency and the degrading hypervisibility of the enslaved, and therefore, by the same token, such concealment should be considered a form of resistance.

—Saidiya Hartman, *Scenes of Subjection*

When the landmark abolitionist and feminist activist Sojourner Truth claimed equality by virtue of the "deeds done" in her body, she articulated a means of rescuing that very body from nineteenth-century proscriptions of racial and gender abjection by locating agency precisely within her flesh. This sort of corporeal challenge draws unlikely yet nevertheless resonant comparisons of Sojourner Truth to her contemporary, Adah Isaacs Menken. Both Truth, born to slave parents of "unmixed" African ancestry in 1797, and Menken, born in 1839 a free Southern woman of putative African and European lineage, face the threat of functioning as circumscribed corporeal spectacles in some of their more prominent biographical narratives. Truth, for instance, has been canonized as an illiterate "Amazon" lecturer whose "witnessing" of slavery before all-white audiences depended upon a deployment of the "violated" slave woman's body, reconfigured as a site of "physical endurance" (Mullen 5). Similarly, studies of Menken often construct her as a mute yet perilously salacious stage diva who dominated theater circles with her notorious striptease.[5] However, recent efforts of contemporary feminist theorists to reappropriate Truth's body from these sorts of fetishistic agendas perhaps clear a space for considering the subversive power of "bodily deeds." Such efforts inform my own reading and recontextualization of Menken as both a biographical and a performative subject. Thus, I will initially turn to the criticism of Truth as a methodological point of departure in exploring Menken.

White abolitionist Frances Gage's influential memoir of Sojourner Truth historically canonized her as an "authentic" body of racial and gender knowledge who faithfully fulfilled the desires of the white spectral eye/I. This "tall, gaunt black" female figure who marches through Gage's "Reminiscences" from 1851 is both imposingly present in the body and suspiciously absent in her ability to enforce a narrative control over that body. Rather, according to Gage, the "deep tones" of her oratory, which rivet white

Northern spectators, serve to convert and deliver her audience from the moral bankruptcy of complicity with slavery. Having taken her audience of "streaming eyes, and hearts beating with gratitude" into "her strong arms" and having "carried [them] safely over the slough of difficulty" (1960), Gage's Truth relinquishes interiority in favor of preserving the full emotional conversion of her white audience.[6] This sort of problem wherein the black abolitionist is reduced to the serviceable corporeal perhaps has much to do with the fact that her discursive body is so limited. As with the crisis in Menken studies in which the actress left behind only the slightest "fragments" of autobiography, Truth's lifelong illiteracy and a scarcity of self-authored documents leave a void in critical work on her life and activism.[7]

As historian Nell Painter speculates, Truth's "biographical problem becomes a larger question of how to deal with people who are in History but who have not left the kinds of sources to which historians and biographers ordinarily turn" ("Sojourner Truth" 13). Like Menken biographies, which simultaneously document and reinvent the legend of the "free-loving" actress, the myths and false reports regarding Truth (for instance, as being prematurely deceased) are clearly "all the more valuable as a reflection of Truth's mid-nineteenth-century persona" (9).[8] I would argue further that the representation of the socially "deviant" woman's constructed persona in both these cases reinforces the ways in which racially marked female bodies occupy a vexed and contested terrain in scholarly (and not so scholarly) discourse. In turn, the conspicuous voids in discursive material on Truth and Menken have contributed to this intense privileging of their bodies as "authentic" texts of identity. The question becomes, then, what kinds of critical methodologies might be used to interrogate the subjectivity of historical figures such as Truth and Menken, figures who have been largely denied the right to claim discursive property as well as the patriarchal fantasy of "writing themselves into being"? Does the scene of performance offer itself as an avenue for these women of the flesh to instead *act* themselves into being, to act themselves into history?[9]

These questions continue to circulate in current critical debates that perpetuate the reduction of Truth into "authentic," corporeal knowledge, a source of labor for some other agenda. As black feminist critic Deborah McDowell cogently observes, Sojourner Truth is too often employed as a sign to "rematerialize" poststructuralist, epistemological theory, particularly in the work of contemporary white feminist scholars where she is frequently "summoned from the seemingly safe and comfortable distance of a historical past" and transformed into a material and iconographic bridge to "experiential" politics (253). Her points here extend Valerie Smith's influential work on this topic, as do Margaret Homans's recent critical responses. Smith finds that "it is striking that at precisely the moment when Anglo American feminists and male Afro-Americanists

begin to reconsider the material ground of their enterprise, they demonstrate their return to earth, as it were, by invoking the specific experiences of black women and the writings of black women" (45).[10] In response to Smith's observations, Homans, a white feminist critic, painstakingly conscious of racial and gender positionality politics, attempts to question what happens when black women make use of their own materiality within narratives in which they are the subjects; she attempts to make a distinction between an African American woman working *through* her body for her own discourse and Anglo-American feminists working black figures into their discursive projects. In her reading of texts by contemporary black women writers, Homans contends that when these writers "image their own bodies, they set up a constructive dialogue between poststructuralist and humanist views of identity rather than either reducing the black woman's body to sheer ground or matter or, to the contrary, using that body to validate disembodiment" ("Women" 87).

What is most interesting about Homans's analysis for my purposes of recontextualizing and reinterrogating the work of Menken is the significance of performance in this move toward manipulating the borders of the material and the epistemological in black feminist (self-) representation. In a Patricia Williams narrative passage on which Homans focuses, "staging" the self and employing one's body as a performative instrument are of central importance. Williams constructs a moment of seeing herself in a dream: "the me-that-is-on-stage is laughing loudly and long. She is extremely vivacious, the center of attention. ... She is not beautiful in any traditional sense ... like a claymation model of myself. ... I hear myself speaking: *Voices lost in the chasm speak from the slow eloquent fact of the chasm. They speak and speak, like flowing water*" (201). Williams here conjures multiple visions of herself onstage, while yet another self sits in the audience looking on at this "claymation model" who is "laughing loudly and long." Watching this constructed self perform and speak "like flowing water," the projected "voices" of this Other Williams surf into the "fact of the chasm," a void, a space, an aphotic opening. In this passage, where Williams assumes the role of both performer and spectator, Homans observes that "there are two Williamses but they collaborate to make possible the pleasure of voyeurism," and thus Williams celebrates what Homans reads as "embodiment and identity" with "the denaturalizing of identity" ("Women" 89). Performance is the vehicle that enables this process; the "scene," as it were, allows Williams to negotiate an epistemological trajectory from her spectacular "claymation" self onstage to her voyeur figure looking on.

We might, then, think of the "chasm" in the "dream" as a sphere where multiple voices are born, where multiple possibilities exist for the black female cultural producer. Her figure, in this context, is both spectacularly visible and imaginatively elusive in its ability to "denaturalize," bifurcate, and multiply. This "eloquent fact" of the chasm operates as the critical point of departure in black feminist performance and its authorial repossession of body politics. A dark point of possibility, the chasm functions as a figurative site for the opaque reconfiguration of the black and female body on display. This trope of darkness represents a kind of shrouding that allows for corporeal unveiling to yoke with the (re)covering of flesh. Indeed, I suggest that we think of this location as a metaphorical site where black feminist performance flourishes, as a space where opacity works to contest the "dominative imposition of transparency" (Hartman 36). Yet unlike the colonial invention of exotic "darkness" that has historically been made to envelop bodies and geographical territories in the shadows of global and hegemonic domination, this form of black performative opacity, as Hartman suggests convincingly of black song, has the potential to "enabl[e] something in excess of the orchestrated amusements of the enslaved" (36). In the cases of Truth and Menken, opacity has the potential to further liberate "free" yet socially, politically, and culturally circumscribed bodies.[11]

Thus I wish to read for the spectacular opacities rooted in this form of corporeal representation in order to discover the Truth about Menken. It seems increasingly imperative to consider this kind of narrative possibility in relation to black feminist theory as an alternative means to interrogating the work of women whose complex bodies have been trivialized in most critical discourses. If, as performance theorist Jeanie Forte has argued, there are "reasons why . . . it is crucial for Anglo American feminism, and particularly feminist performance theory, to focus on the body at this historical juncture" (249), then the same can be said within African American feminist contexts. Reading these particular negotiations of black feminist performance provides a means to recuperating a narrative strategy that, for nineteenth-century socially, politically, and culturally marginalized women in particular, circumvents the dichotomy between being visible and abject and being "pure" and disembodied. To locate the veiled corners of these female cultural producers' work perhaps allows us to locate the ways in which they strategized "bod[ies] in representation" (249).

This kind of a methodological approach is particularly significant in reexamining the discursive representations of Truth and Menken. Despite the obvious objectification of both women in past and present biographical discourses, a re-consideration of their bodies in performance might allow us to locate the ways in which the opaque potentially produces revisionist and transformative subjectivities. It is, however, critical to point out that in using Truth's performative representations as a springboard into exploring Menken's, I in no way intend to elide the vast complexities of their formidable differences. Rather, my effort to consider Menken in relation to Truth is driven by a critical desire to complicate the discourses surrounding the actress that, up to this point, have avoided exploring the convergence of race and gender as ideological constructs

in her life and career.[12] With this in mind, I wish to return in brief to the legendary scene of Sojourner Truth's body on display so as to examine the ways in which she re-strategized the public spectacle of her body through performance politics, transforming her corporeality into a contested terrain of social and cultural consumption. This potent moment in abolitionist history ultimately offers a critical model that might finally be applied to re-examining Menken's staged body.

The scene in which Sojourner Truth is forced to disrobe before an all-white audience in rural Indiana is canonized in American historical discourse. Yet the cultural familiarity with this moment depends on the imagery of an anonymous account of Dr. T. W. Strain's interrogation of Truth. A white man suspicious of Truth's sex, Strain demands that

> Sojourner submit her breast to the inspection of some of the ladies present, that the doubt might be removed by their testimony. There were a large number of ladies present, who appeared to be ashamed and indignant at such a proposition.
>
> Confusion and uproar ensued, which was soon suppressed by Sojourner, who immediately rising, asked them why they suspected her to be a man. The Democracy answered, "Your voice is not the voice of a woman, it is the voice of a man, and we believe you are a man." . . . Sojourner told them that her breasts had suckled many a white babe, to the exclusion of her own offspring and she quietly asked them, as she disrobed her bosom, if they, too, wished to suck! She told them that she would show her breast to the whole congregation; that it was not her shame that she uncovered her breast before them, but their shame.
>
> (Sterling 151-53)

In this passage, wherein Truth remains potentially buried in the discourse of a nameless spectator, her use of the corporeal as a narrative strategy amounts to a performative twist: her breasts relay a textual meaning articulating the history of a slave past and work in contestation of discursive circumscription here by her allusion to what she calls "the deeds done in [her] body" (Gage, "Address" 1962). These "deeds" simultaneously mark her violation as a slave woman and potentially (re)cover her flesh as unreadable to a "shamed" congregation forced to acknowledge their spectatorial and social complicity in her abjection. For the Northern audience to read Truth's figure as she deploys it here is to affirm the repressed atrocities of slavery that her body harbors and to face their own implicit role in that scene. Harryette Mullen observes pointedly that Truth's "shameless gesture denies social propriety, its oppressive power to define, limit, or regulate her behavior" (3). Truth's demand to have her audience "see" her body according to her own narrative framing also establishes a way to read for the opacity, or for what Elin Diamond might call the "non-truth," of the scene.[13]

Indeed, with this unveiling of Truth before her white audience there appears to be more than one black female figure meeting the gaze of Dr. Strain here. The moment of initial supposed transparency that enables Truth's male spectators to seemingly view the dominant script of the mammy figure whose breasts are made available for "suckl[ing]" immediately transforms into a point of visual excess and occlusion, a suggestion of the extraneous corporeal (sub) texts that the spectator cannot, in fact, see at all. In this scene where Truth rejects the spectator's gaze by reminding her audience of her own absent offspring whom she is denied the right to nurse, she splinters the security of the viewer's intimacy with her body. The hidden narrative of black "motherhood" rather than "mammyhood" operates as a looming disruption that Truth invokes, a specter of contradistinction to the (un)veiled black body of deception who speaks not like a woman. This voice alone calls attention to Diamond's extended refiguration of feminist mimesis-mimicry as a destabilizing "alienation-effect," a point "in which the production of objects, shadows, and voices is excessive to the truth/illusion structure of mimesis, spilling into mimicry, multiple 'fake off-spring'" (371). A kind of "excessive" representation that overturns the subjectivity of the viewer, Truth's appearance here simultaneously assumes the role of the exploited slave by stripping and rejects that role by offering to her "shamed" spectators a body that is a text of multiple social and historical inscriptions that double and cover over each other. From the darkness of the void that she herself creates, multiple Truths are put into play.

It would seem that a moment encapsulating Menken's disrobing could have little in common with the complex distillation of power at work in the moment of Truth's exposure. Separated from Truth by her class status and by a public construction of whiteness that protected the actress from the hardships of American racism (and that shielded her from slavery altogether), Menken approached corporeal representation from a standpoint of relative privilege. Yet in the context of nineteenth-century gender politics, she negotiated a deployment of her body as a canvas of narrative authority that, similar to Truth's efforts, went against the grain of self-abnegation. Wrapping her body in the mosaic of mythography that she shrewdly perpetuates, Menken stages a critical striptease that brings to fore the strategic elements of her performative acts. A well-circulated anecdote exemplifies this point; it concerns how Menken, upon meeting the French journalist Adrian Marx during her stint in Paris, "revealed" herself in several ways to him during an interview that followed one of her sold-out performances. Biographer Allen Lesser describes the scene:

> Menken nonchalantly stripped to her form-fitting tights and then put on her costume for the next act in full sight of her visitor . . . he was certain that she had stood completely nude before him. "She changed costume," he recalled, "and let me see, without modesty and without embarrassment, the marvelous beauty of her body." . . . In answer to a question about her childhood and youth, about which everyone was curious, she launched into a fantastic narrative compounded of every adventure story she had ever read. Indians had captured her in her youth, she said, bending down so that he could feel "the depth of the scar left on her head" by a tomahawk flung at her when she escaped. She had also fought for the south disguised as a soldier, she added, pulling her skirt up above her thigh to show him "the trace of the balls she had received in war."

(170)

The passage is extraordinary in the way that it initially showcases the spectacle of Menken's "completely nude" body standing "nonchalantly" before Marx's helplessly ogling gaze. He marvels over Menken's unchecked boldness and apparent candor at allowing him to sneak a peak, "without modesty and without embarrassment," at her naked frame. Marx, in this presumed moment of intimacy and bonding, presses onward with his interview, querying the actress in regard to her childhood. The disingenuous responses that Menken offers, a largely discounted captivity narrative as well as a cross-dressing war tale, are corroborated through the marks and scars inscribed as text onto her body. Here the initial scene of disrobing transforms into a moment of (re)covering as well. At this very moment in the anecdote we are made to bear witness to the way in which Menken uses her body, not as evidence of some "incontrovertible truth" but as an instrument of ontological deception, part of the performance of Menken's passing before a rapt and naive spectator.[14]

To be sure, the narrative manifests Amy Robinson's definition of passing, which considers "the apparatus of the pass" as a "spectatorial transaction" rather than one that is merely ontological. Robinson lobbies for a method to explore passing as the product of skillful reading on the spectator's part as opposed to the visual markers of the passer. She contends that "to read the apparatus of passing in the stead of an inviolate prepassing identity is to value telling over knowing because the availability of codes of deception does not predict access to the authenticity of the subject of deception" (723). The skill to read as well as the skill to perform the pass is ultimately what disrupts arbitrary definitions of identity, for this notion of "the pass" itself as a process, as an apparatus, "catalogues discontinuity and disjunction." Robinson's theory of passing is predicated upon performance, what she sees as a "triangular theater" composed of the passer, the hegemonic dupe, and the "literate member" of the passer's "in-group" community out of which the subject has transmigrated. The pass, she argues further, can only be successful when it is witnessed by the literate "in-group" member (723-28).

Building on Robinson's work, I wish to contend that, as readers of Menken's as well as Truth's biographical and performative narratives, we might, for a change, assume the role of the "in-group" member who knows the "lie" rather than the "truth" about these women and who, along with her contemporaries, as well as various biographers, participates in a "triangular theatre" that recontextualizes the performing female subject's pass(ages) from one body to the next. This type of analysis seems crucial particularly with respect to re-reading Menken, a racially vexing figure whose ambiguous identity generated legendary historical anecdotes such as one in which she was said to have proclaimed to her lover Dumas père that she too was "a quadroon" (Mankowitz 174). If we assume that Menken operates in her biographical canon as what Jennifer Brody would call a "mulattaroon" figure, an "unreal, impossible ideal whose corrupted and corrupting constitution inevitably causes conflicts in narratives that attempt to promote purity" (16), then the exigencies for this sort of critical methodology are all the more apparent.[15] Interrogating the negotiation and the site of the pass in the context of this mulattaroon actress's many varied performances forces us to read through and across not one, but potentially two hegemonic dupes—that is, those in the narratives of nineteenth-century public, racialized women and the biographers who manufacture their narratives. Hence, I demonstrate how Menken extends the efforts of Truth's reappropriation of the corporeal. I will reveal how, through her highly stylized, "seminude" performances, the actress stages a veiled redeployment of her own controversial materiality. In this sense, then, her work also represents a formidable and resourceful critical paradigm for contemporary black feminist theory and practice. Menken enacts a means to resistance through the performance of her own bodily deeds.

SHAPE AND SUBSTANCE: DRAG/RACING THE BODY OF ADAH ISAACS MENKEN

> Perhaps she did not belong so much to the theater as to the circus.
>
> —John S. Kendall, "The World's Delight"

> To be inauthentic is sometimes the best way to be real.
>
> —Paul Gilroy, "'... To Be Real'"

While competing in their research and racing to assert their pivotal roles as detectives in their studies of Adah Isaacs Menken, numerous biographers are uncharacteristically in agreement on one subject: Menken's weakness as an actress and the way in which the spectacle of her body functioned as a primary vehicle in her quest for professional success. Noel Gerson, Wolf Mankowitz, and Bernard Falk all take pains to retell the legend of Menken's introduction to her career as a world-renowned "shape actress" whose "pink fleshlings" overrode any salvageable acting skills. Each of these authors foregrounds a retelling of the tale in which Shakespearean actor James Murdoch, after performing in a haphazard production of *Macbeth* with the actress, is said to have offered the parting advice that Menken "search out for herself some 'sensational spectacle' in which 'your fine figure and pretty face will show.'"[16] Murdoch's suggestion, offered time and

again by subsequent researchers, presents itself as the ultimate "proof" of Menken's status as merely a passive "shape" exhibition as opposed to a stage performer of substance.

This opinion was largely canonized by the influential drama critic William Winter, who declared in his review of Menken's 1866 *Mazeppa* performance that she "has not the faintest idea of what acting is. She moves about the stage with no motive, and therefore, in a kind of accidental manner. ... in short [she] invites critical attention, not to her emotional capabilities, her intellectual gifts, or her culture as an artist, but solely to her physical proportions" (Lesser 175). Winter maintained that Menken lacked vision, analytical clarity, and command over her craft in the role that made her a celebrity. Fame came to her, he argued, as a result of alluring "physical proportions." On the West Coast as well, the actress was simultaneously a box-office success and the subject of journalistic skepticism. Her most famous dual critic and hard-won fan, Mark Twain, was ever reluctant to review a "shape actress" who apparently "didn't have any histrionic ability or deserve any more consideration than a good circus rider!" Winter and Twain each envisioned the spectacle of a powerless (female) body, divested of reason and voice and existing exclusively and basely in relation to materiality (Lyman 270, 276).

These kinds of critiques would persist throughout the actress's career, resurfacing most often during her repeated revival performances of *Mazeppa*. In this her most famous role, Menken was, more often than not, conceived of by both critics and biographers in reductive terms as a mere body, stripped, as it were, of representational complexity. The production itself seemed only to promote this perception. First adapted for the stage in 1830 by English playwright Henry Milner, the drama retells Byron's tale of royal Tartar heir Mazeppa who, upon falling in love with the Polish Castellan's daughter, Olinska, attempts to invade the Polish encampment in order to rescue his betrothed, only to have his plan fail. Captured, stripped, and tortured by the Poles, Mazeppa is forced to ride a wild black stallion across the rugged Tartar landscape. He is subsequently rescued by and reunited with his long-lost father, the elderly Abder Khan, who successfully plots with Mazeppa to seek vengeance upon the ruling Poles in a climactic battle scene tableau. As Lesser points out, from its origination as a stage production the "high point of the spectacle" in *Mazeppa* was "the scene in which the hero is 'stripped' onstage, lashed to the back of the wild horse and carried along a narrow runway up to the top of the theater" (77). However, until American theater entrepreneur E. T. Smith was said to have approached Menken, no woman had ever played the part, and no performer of either sex had actually ridden during the famous horse sequence, opting instead for a dummy to substitute. Smith in 1861 claims to have initially envisioned the concept of placing Menken's physical "beauty" properly in distress in the old equestrian drama as an extremely lucrative box-office venture.

For this reason, critics and scholars have frequently written off Menken's *Mazeppa* production as an insubstantial spectacle that carried an otherwise skill-less actress to worldwide fame in the 1860s. A transatlantic body of spectacularly real deception, Menken was widely perceived by the press, and particularly the British press, as manifesting the bawdy sensationalism of early-nineteenth-century theater.[17] *Mazeppa*'s connection to the popular and evolving extravaganza genre only contributed to this perception; visually, the production was perhaps closely linked to playwright Dion Boucicault's innovative contributions to the field of "realist" spectacle, with its sprawling scenery and elaborate stunts.[18] Menken's and Smith's *Mazeppa* clearly aspired to Boucicault's paradoxical method of representing "realism" through a distinct reliance on the spectacle of artifice. In *Mazeppa* this effort was enacted through and across the site of Menken's spectacularly "real" and curvaceous female body. Falk speculates that "before him the spectator saw a lovely female form traced in winning line by flesh-coloured tights. ... It was not unintentional that the path Menken scaled was zigzag, and required fifteen minutes ... to traverse, long enough to permit the eye a satisfying feast of a seductive form" (53). Mankowitz adds that the production included "a formidable array of theatrical illusions. But the two most sensational illusions of all were the voluptuous figure of Adah Isaacs Menken as Ivan Mazeppa, a sexual transformation requiring an extremely willing suspension of disbelief; and more sensational still, the nakedness of the star" (18-19). Here he characterizes this spectacle as rooted both completely and self-consciously in an artificial insistence on representing the conspicuously "female" figure of Menken in drag as the Tartar warrior and also passing that spectacle of her "nakedness" off as "authentic" despite the fact that the actress wore stockings to maintain the "illusion" of nudity. Spectacle, in any case, resided in the (in)authenticity of Menken's disrobed figure on the stage.

This morally bankrupt entertainment, what London theater critic H. B. Farnie lamented as being one of the "many corruptions from America" (Mankowitz 130-31), was thus repeatedly read as a predictable manifestation of popular codes on both sides of the Atlantic, which dually conflated the actress with the sexual availability of the prostitute and the figure of the black woman.[19] Moral anxiety concerning Menken's performances as *Mazeppa* could, for instance, be traced to the production's clear and frequent engagement with Victorian pornographic coding and imagery. In reviewing Menken's success in the role, theater critics have maintained that the "basis of Menken's popular appeal in *Mazeppa* was undoubtedly sensationalism and not a very subtle kind of pornography" (WPA 57). Her costume's combination of "loose folds of white linen" and "flesh-coloured tights" that traced her "lovely female

form" boldly referenced contemporaneous pornographic markers, which, as Tracy Davis describes, "flagrantly violated the dress codes of the street and drawing room" in Victorian culture, "flaunting the ankles, calves, knees, thighs, crotch and upper torso" ("Actresses" 106).

Although the rare review rallied to Menken's defense, such as the *London Era*'s claim that her "upper limbs" were "no more delicately exposed than those of ballet and burlesque ladies" (Mankowitz 135), Davis points out in her work on Victorian theatrical nudity that it was precisely the sorts of vestiary devices found in ballet and extravaganza productions that incorporated costuming traditions promoting a way of "seeing nudity" ("Spectacle" 323). Davis argues that while "Victorian designers did not divest actresses of their clothes, they invested considerable ingenuity in creating costumes that simulated nudity—or at least signified it, keeping the referential body to the fore" (326). The purpose of pink tights and white, tightly bound, gauzelike wrappings, then, was to simulate nudity through props and devices in order to lead spectators to believe that they were, in fact, witnessing a nude—and importantly, a nude "white"—female body like that displayed in pornographic postcards and publications.[20] Thus, to cultural as well as moral pundits of the period, Menken's *Mazeppa* costume placed her firmly in a tradition of the sexual commodification of the "white" female body in theater and popular Victorian subculture.

Even to the critic with a discerning eye, nothing was presumed to have been left uncovered in this display of sheer whiteness. As Lesser contends, for the "excited masculine imagination," her "'classic Dress' concealed none of the exotic delights to which they had looked forward" (134).[21] Even Menken fan and supporter Mark Twain actively pointed out that Menken had "but one garment on—a thin tight white linen one" and she "dressed like the Greek Slave." But unlike Hiram Powers's morally revered figure of classic sculpture, Twain assures, Menken's postures are "not so modest" (78). Indeed, the very putative sexual availability combined with the racial complexities of this white-looking body perhaps aligns Menken's *Mazeppa* more deeply and more problematically with the sensational imagery of John Bell's 1868 statue *The Octoroon* than with Powers's *Greek Slave*. In a critical analysis of the Bell Royal Academy sculpture that brings forth the visual and thematic similarities to Powers's work, Joseph Roach observes that the "octoroon repines unresistingly in the almost ornamental chains of her bondage," recalling the positioning of *The Greek Slave*. Roach concludes, however, that Bell's work panders to a public fascination with white-looking female bodies that, when stripped and chained, are excessively eroticized rather than morally transcendent (220)—a quality that Joy Kasson associates with Powers's work. Although Twain's association of Menken with *The Greek Slave* offers the potential to represent what Kasson reads as the sculpture's "suppressed possibility of resistance" through a spiritual transcendence of the body, most Menken critics suggest that the actress's career-making production of *Mazeppa* sustained a troubling and reductive insistence on the reification of the actress's body, not unlike the thematics of Bell's *Octoroon*.[22]

The racial ambiguity inherent in Bell's statue and Menken's Creole-to-Spanish-to-Jewish identity politics (dueling significations that Menken as well as many scholars have evoked for generations) complicates the politics of female exposure. Both sculptures shed light on the multiple and intersecting racial and gender codes that specifically affect white actresses and public black women in the nineteenth century. These two groups, as Sander Gilman has observed, are specifically aligned from a spectatorial standpoint in that both European and European American "public" women (such as actresses and prostitutes) and women of African descent were, more often than not, visually commodified through their bodies (256). The point here is not to suggest that the political and socioeconomic position of white women who supported themselves through the theater is at all equivalent to that of free black women who, beginning with Maria Stewart in the 1830s, risked ridicule and sometimes bodily harm in order to publicly speak in support of abolitionism, prohibition, and suffrage, among other causes. Rather, the fact that both groups were perceived as revealing and inhabiting bodies that were vulnerable and open to varying degrees of public possession provides a significant and challenging context when reconsidering Menken's performances of *Mazeppa*. For just as the white actress was expected to display "what is cloaked (anatomically and experientially), supposedly revealing truths about womanhood ... promulgating a mystery as deep and as artificial as the colonial photographer's penetration in the Oriental harem" (Davis, "Actresses" 121), so, too, was the black woman's body, according to Peterson, "always envisioned as public and exposed" (20).

Yet like the Bell sculpture with its opaque rendering of an unveiled body, Menken's *Mazeppa* hero/heroine rides a formidable continuum of double drag that ultimately complicates notions of racial and gender-marked corporeal exposure; her work insists on a complex form of counterintuitive viewership that paradoxically sensationalizes the way that the female figure is obscured. In other words, just as the Bell statue and an entire subculture of antebellum slave auctions promoted public fascination with the eroticized subjugation of "white-looking" black bodies, so, too, did Menken's *Mazeppa* entice and seduce audiences through a demand to gaze upon the spectacle of a body that is not what it appears to be—a body dressed as a man that one is expected to know is inherently female and a body that conveys "whiteness" but simultaneously professes the constructedness of race itself. Despite this layered imagery, the majority of Menken critics and scholars have overlooked the complexities of what she (un)veiled on stage. Her "problem," according to numerous biographers

and critics, was that the gaze of the male spectator and a production of heavily encoded nude imagery encouraged "the onlooker to trace the lines of the posed figure," an act that Falk argues was "bad for masculine morals and treachery to the feminine species" (14). The real "treachery," according to feminist theater historian Faye Dudden is that in spite of Menken's recognition of her body as a financial "asset" in an ever-expanding transatlantic theater market, she faced what Dudden sees as an "attenuation of the self" as a result of the production's insistence on her status as mere physical commodity.[23]

Dudden contends that Menken's theatrical experience and what she reads as popular exploitation are indicative of much larger gender problems in nineteenth-century American culture. To Dudden, Menken's theatrical career represents "the problem of the body" for nineteenth-century American actresses. She explains that "the actress has been equated with the whore so persistently that no amount of clean living and rectitude among actual performers has ever served to cancel the equation. Acting is linked to sexuality because it is an embodied art—in contrast to the relatively disembodied business of writing. ... To act you must be present in the body, available to be seen." Like Davis, Dudden ultimately reads the "crisis" of the actress and of all nineteenth-century public (white) women as being a "problem" that forces one to be "present in the body" and "taken as a sexual object against one's will." Clearly, however, Dudden's critical observations are couched in an oversimplified dichotomization that conceptualizes "acting" as an "*embodied* art," fundamentally at odds with other aesthetic spheres (2-3).[24] From a black feminist standpoint as well, women on the margins of culture by virtue of their race and class have always been seen/scene. From this perspective, the significance of performance resides in its ability to exacerbate that moment, to disrupt and obfuscate spectatorial desire precisely through a creative use of "embodied art."

In contrast to this position, Dudden's analysis problematically privileges the authority of the male spectator over the agency of the female performer. What is sorely missing from her study is a more critical consideration of what it meant for an actress to willfully engage in a theatrical relationship with audiences that foregrounds the body. Instead, she asserts that from the 1830s forward the "way that theatre evolved exacerbated the body problem by making male visual pleasure and the sexualized image a routine element of commerce and hence of public life" (4). Although she points to very real systems of social and political power in the nineteenth century that were predicated upon gender as well as racial stratification, Dudden's argument acquiesces to an uncomplicated reification of the female body in this equation. In other words, Dudden juxtaposes the hegemonic power of the male gaze with an unproblematized notion of women's bodies as authentically constructed. Indeed, she contends that this "body problem" is, no doubt, analogous to a "hall of mirrors" that "rob[s] women of any authentic sense of self" (4). In the process, what Dudden fails to consider is how Menken's visual representation is founded upon the ambiguity of the body as a site of knowledge not only in her biographical discourse but in her very performances as Mazeppa. She overlooks the larger possibility of the female performer's role in acting *through* the body as a site of resistance to the male gaze. Dudden might have considered the inauthenticity of the female body as represented in theater as a theoretical approach that opens up a space for reinterrogating the nineteenth-century actress's agency. This critical perspective offers a method to explore Menken's potential engagement in narrating her body imaginatively, resiliently, and opaquely in her *Mazeppa* performances.

As the Tartar heir, Menken assumed a drag, or "breeches," role that required her to strip to a costume that simulated her (female) nudity. This role was built on an endless series of falsities: Menken, an actress of African descent passing for "white,"—in drag as the Tartar hero who disguises himself in order to rescue Olinska but who is forced to reveal a decidedly, perhaps even exaggerated, "naked" female form in the end. Misha Berson observes that Menken's version of *Mazeppa* "tested the waters for a new kind of stage androgyny: a woman revealing her female sexuality through a male role" (57). Indeed, Berson's observation reinforces the notion in nineteenth-century transatlantic theater culture that gender cross-dressing for actresses only served to "highligh[t] rather than disguis[e] sexual difference" (Davis "Actresses" 106). Davis, in fact, warns that in the "Victorian theater, adult female performers were never sexless. . . . Femininity was intractable and the point was to reveal it" (107). Feminist critics have steadfastly contended that, for nineteenth-century women performers, the acting profession is never fundamentally concerned with masquerade but rather with upholding a paradoxical striptease wherein the female body is made bare through the spectacle of covering it. In retrospect, Menken biographer John S. Kendall could claim with confidence that Menken "had the kind of figure which never looked so alluringly feminine as when clad in male attire" (855).

But what of the transracial body who drags herself across the stage, as it were, through multiple layers of masquerade? Could a racially transgressive actress wearing pink tights suggest the metaphoric nature of race as a construct? Could this "flesh" that is made "nude" through costume/covering make use of the fakery of "whiteness" as yet another shield of obstruction at the very moment in which the female body undoes its gendered drag? Does the very notion of the mulattaroon's appropriation of Victorian pornography's fetishization of "white" female corporeality perhaps "unmask the performative nature of whiteness" and "expos[e] the construction" of racial purities (Brody 9)? Despite the complex questions that her acts clearly elicit, Menken's work is most often perceived as a reactionary product of nineteenth-century theater culture.

Davis, for instance, argues that the artifice of drag only enticed the male spectator to uncover the sexual disguise onstage, that "sexuality had its own narrative logic that distinguished . . . Mazeppa from Godiva, and Menken from Maddocks" (*Actresses* 114). Marjorie Garber critiques this perspective by examining the ways that the subversiveness of cross-dressing and the ambiguity of identity politics that accompany it have often been avoided by critics who choose "to look *through* rather than *at* the cross-dresser, to turn away from a close encounter with the transvestite, and to want instead to subsume that figure within one of the two traditional genders" (9). Garber suggests that the spectator who witnesses the cross-dresser or the drag performance attempts to control the potential transgressive power of such an act by imposing an organizational gaze onto the figure, disregarding the notion of liminality altogether.[25]

Yet the content of Menken's performances potentially complicates and resists this sort of tyrannical categorization. Menken's theatricality can also be read as a series of cultural exchanges that drew attention to artifice as constitutive of the actress's public persona and her body politic. In *Mazeppa,* Menken calls attention to her materiality through resourceful performative acts that subvert the Victorian sexual reification of her body.[26] The intersections of gender and racial drag function as key elements that contribute to these disruptive performance strategies. Like the deployment of "pink gauze" as a representation of "whiteness," the actress's legendary Tartar warrior costume disrupts the feminist critique of women in (male) drag that was believed to have ultimately underscored and exposed the actress's (female) sexuality. The apparent transparency and disposability of the male costuming instead levels a critique at the patriarchal fantasies the costume figuratively and literally embodies. As Garber points out, the tradition of male cross-dressing performance has "turned on the artifactuality of women's bodies" rather than questioning the presumed authenticity of the male body as the norm. Garber adds that "to deny female fetishism is to establish a female desire for the phallus on the male body as *natural*" (125). From this standpoint, both racial and gender cross-dressing, here manifested in the racially transgressive female's invocation of both the phallus and the coverage of whiteness, present a crucial critique of identity construction in nineteenth-century culture; the artifice of both "manhood" and "white" femininity are put into play and stripped of their arbitrary power. Menken's palimpsested and contradictory racial as well as gender identities thus reflect Judith Butler's influential claim regarding the inauthenticity of the body itself. Butler argues for a clearer understanding of the way in which "the body is a historical situation . . . and is a manner of doing, dramatizing, and reproducing a historical situation" ("Performative" 272). Put another way, Butler suggests that the body is also a theatrical situation, "stylized" and transformed through gendered appearances.[27]

My point here is not to disregard the very real body of Adah Isaacs Menken, a resilient figure who traveled the transatlantic divide and labored adventurously on the stage during the socially and juridically volatile period of the mid-nineteenth century. Rather, I wish to suggest that Menken's symbolic manipulation of the corporeal in her performances was, in itself, a means to theatricalize her body in socially and culturally disruptive ways that have not always been apparent to audiences and critics alike. She embraced a concept of vaudevillian chaos that ran the gamut of genre and production style, testing and challenging her audiences along the way, and wresting the power of the theatrical exchange from the spectator only to plant it firmly, richly, and darkly in that place between the audience and the performer. In this opaque performative space, the groundbreaking "naked lady" of theater reinvented the terms of racial and gender "exposure."

Notes

1. Menken was originally buried in Paris's Pere la Chaise Cemetery on 10 August 1868. In April 1869 Menken's friend and confidant Edwin James spearheaded the exhumation and transference of her remains to the Cemetery Montparnasse. Mankowitz 237-44; James 14-16.

2. For a study of the connections between Menken biographies, identity politics, and the literary genre of sensation, see my "Lady Menken's Secret." Recent contemporary studies of the actress tend to trace Menken's genealogical history back to New Orleans, where she is believed to have been born as Philomene Croi Theodore in 1839 to a "free man of color" and his French Creole wife. The public moniker that she kept for a major portion of her life came as a result of her marriage to her first (authenticated) husband, the musician and businessman-turned-theater manager Alexander Isaac Menken. The most recent biography of Menken, written by Wolf Mankowitz, focuses in detail on the actress's family history. See also Lesser, Falk, and Gerson.

3. Female entertainers who worked as "shape actresses" often performed in extravaganza productions called "leg shows," which specialized in the "show of leg" and other suggestive body parts in order to accentuate the sexualized female form. See Dudden.

4. I borrow the formulation of "imaginary bodies" from Gatens.

5. For more on the problematics of Menken biographical discourse, see my "Lady Menken's Secret." See also Mankowitz's controversial depiction of his relationship with biographer Noel Gerson (Mankowitz 185-89). Mankowitz's savvy work manifests a sophisticated awareness of the complexities of Menken's identity politics; yet he ultimately foregrounds

his own subjectivity as a biographer at the expense of the actress's position in the text.

6. For more on Truth's oratory, see Peterson 47-53.

7. Painter argues that the *Narrative*'s longevity as a mainstay and as an exclusive source of Truth is due primarily to a "virtual lack of autobiographical documents" and Truth's own life-long illiteracy ("Sojourner Truth" 13). For a more detailed study of Truth's life and iconography, see Painter *Sojourner Truth*. Menken's "Notes of My Life" first appeared posthumously in the 6 September 1868 edition of the *New York Times*. Lesser is the only biographer who includes the piece in its entirety in an appendix to his biography (253-64).

8. Harriet Beecher Stowe, for instance, weaves a string of inaccuracies in her article on Truth, claiming in an egregious error that Truth was deceased at the time of her writing. For an analysis of Stowe's article, see Yellin 81-87 and Painter, *"Sojourner Truth"* 8-12. See also Washington's note on editions of Sojourner Truth's *Narrative* (125-27). For an example of the machinations of Menken mythography, see Gerson's largely erroneous work, *Queen of the Plaza*.

9. In their introduction to *The Slave's Narrative*, Davis and Gates argue that "the slave narrative represents the attempts of blacks to *write themselves into being*" (xxiii). This historically male-dominated strategy of canon formation sets the stage, so to speak, for the yoking of black ontological politics with the erasure of the (female) corporeal. Homans examines this gendered bifurcation in African American literary and cultural criticism wherein "the body that is troped as female" in the poststructuralist theories of many black male scholars is one "whose absence . . . theory requires" ("Racial" 81).

10. See also duCille's important work "The Occult of True Black Womanhood," which takes to task the problem of black women's persistent role in contemporary academic discourse as "infinitely deconstructable 'othered' matter" (70).

11. In her study of the performance of blackness in antebellum culture, Hartman declares that her "task is neither to unearth the definitive meaning of song or dance nor to read song as an expression of black character as was common among nineteenth-century ethnographers but to give full weight to the opacity of these texts wrought by toil, terror, and sorrow and composed under the whip and in fleeting moments of reprieve" (36). My use of the term "opacity" here differs somewhat from the Irigarian theory that "women represent the sex that cannot be thought, a linguistic absence and opacity" (Butler *Gender* 9). Rather than arguing for representational absence, I

am instead suggesting that "opacity" in this context characterizes a kind of performance rooted in a layering and palimpsesting of meanings and representations. From this standpoint, "opacity" is never a mark of absence but is always a present reminder of black feminist agency and the body in performance.

12. At present, outside of the Kendall essay, there are very few critical works that have examined Menken at length in the context of blackness and the politics of racial ambiguity. See, for instance, Monfried. Her adopted "Jewishness" has, however, been a subject of provocative discussion, particularly in works such as Falk's *The Naked Lady* and in Mankowitz. In his 1957 historical study of San Francisco, Dickson makes passing reference to the likelihood of Menken's father being a "'free' Negro of Louisiana" (70). See also Cofran's short article on Menken's genealogy, which briefly notes that the actress's father was a "free man of color" (52). More recently, Menken has been recuperated into a nineteenth-century black women's canon of poetry. For instance, her posthumous collection of poems entitled *Infelicia* (1868) is included in the *Schomburg Library of Nineteenth-Century Women Writers* series supplement.

13. Here I build on Judith Butler's nearly canonical revelation that "gender proves to be performative" and "always a doing" constituted by "deeds" (Butler *Gender* 25). Yet I wish to draw a distinction between my reading of Truth's role as a performative subject in this scene and Butler's groundbreaking theories of performativity, which call into question the existence of "a doer behind the deed" in gender construction. As Patrick Johnson queries in his cogent work on blackness, sexuality, and performance theory, "the body might be a blunt field of 'matter' inscribed and reinscribed, a site of infinitesimal signifiers, but does not the body signify in specific historical and cultural ways?" Johnson calls for the specific theory and practice of black queer critical methodologies and contends that "the body, too, has to be theorized" to "not only describe the ways in which it is brought into being" but so as to also articulate "what it *does* once it is constituted and the relationship between it and the other bodies around it." Hence, my reading of Truth in this scene is driven by a concern to identify how she employs performance as a means to resituating her body in multiple social and historical situations. Rather than jettisoning Truth as the "doer" of her "deeds," I employ performance as a lens through which to locate the moments when Truth makes her body "matter," as it were, in crucial social and political ways. Diamond, in her work on feminist performance theory, interrogates the viability as well as the efficacy of performance as an intervention in forms of patriarchal mimesis that merely reproduce the abject female form. Invoking Luce Irigaray's

critical transmutation of the Platonic cave of illusions into a female womb/theater structure as a point of departure, Diamond suggests that feminist appropriations of mimesis in performance posit "an irreducible conundrum: the nontruth of truth-reality constructed as a shadow-and-mirror play" (371). For Diamond, this "resistant" mimesis transforms the female body into a site of trickery that draws the male spectator into the reflection of the woman. Modleski has explored the politics of mimetic art as well in the work of African American performer Anna Deavere Smith. Yet I find Modleski's study problematic in the way that it often elides and sometimes romanticizes the role of the black female body on the stage.

14. For the most recent and complete version of Menken's captivity narrative, see Mankowitz 41-44. The tale is assumed to be largely fictional since Menken was said to have claimed to have been raised partly in Texas when the incident occurred, and no documents corroborate such a claim. Terry and Urla contend that "the body has been understood to be given by nature, and thus to be real and objective, capable of overriding even the most abstruse attempts of an individual to disguise his or her true self" (6). Menken's actions here reveal how the body can, in fact, become part of an inauthentic "disguise."

15. Brody demonstrates persuasively how an "American invention and New World product, the mulattaroon was a blood vessel who could be described as being neither black nor white, yet also both white and black. Throughout most of the nineteenth century, the struggle to definitively define her unstable constitution . . . was a real concern. Although answers to the problem of her identity and her identifications varied, the mulattaroons usually served as an interstitial ideal whose complicated constitution both marked and masked the nineteenth century mésalliance known as miscegenation" (16).

16. Indeed, Mankowitz's opening chapter begins with this anecdote. Murdoch was said to have had to prompt the actress on her lines throughout the performance (Mankowitz 6; Gerson 115; Falk 49). Lesser, arguably the biographer most attentive to the details of Menken's career as an actress, at one point reductively asserts that her "contribution" to American theater was that "she offered the female figure unadorned" (75).

17. In anticipation of her 1864 London debut at Astley's theater, the *London Review* argued that she was "'a notorious woman from America, with no more real talent for the stage than an ordinary fish-hag might possess,' who had 'found a manager willing to let her stride about with pink legs, bare arms, and something

which looks like three-fourths of a shift'" (Falk 93). Others have lavished praise on Menken's creative involvement in the production. Rourke maintains, for instance, that "she indubitably transformed a tawdry equestrian play into something which meant a reversion to poetry" (44).

18. Gerson, in fact, argues that the famed playwright and producer's influence was far-reaching in East Coast theater culture by the time Menken debuted in Albany, New York, as the heroic Tartar. He states that "the hand of Boucicault was plainly evident. Any play that hoped to succeed in New York had to include two elements that had made Boucicault popular. Unabashed melodrama predominated, and somewhere during the performance a touch of realism on a grand scale was required. Audiences demanded a diet that would jolt the emotions and leave them round-eyed with wonder" (36). For more on Boucicault's innovations in Victorian theatre, see Booth.

19. For more on the equation of the theatre with sexual depravity, see Johnson 3-36. Ryan argues that between 1825 and 1850 in New York, "women engaged in sexual commerce found themselves in exotic and motley company" including actresses, jugglers, and even puppet show performers (1-8). See also Gilman.

20. The sheer, stark whiteness invoked in this kind of coding points to the odd contradiction of nineteenth-century popular culture wherein nudity was most often conceived of and idealized as white; yet clearly it was black female flesh that was most vulnerable to sudden and aggressive exploitation and violation.

21. Menken wrote a widely published rebuttal to theatre critic Farnie in which she defended her performances of *Mazeppa* on the moral grounds that it invoked classical Greek sculpture (Mankowitz 131).

22. Twain's allusion here to the 1840s statue *The Greek Slave* is a provocative one given the ostensible similarities between Powers's work, which foregrounds the spectacle of the naked female body in chains, and Menken's role in *Mazeppa*. In the original stage adaptation of *Mazeppa,* the Castellan of Laurinski orders his servants to "tear the garb" off of the captive Mazeppa, to "lash the traitor" and bind him in cords. See *Mazeppa* 4. Like the *Mazeppa* production, Powers's statue of a European woman taken into slavery by the Turks is meant to reference a tale of abduction and bondage through the spectacle and display of female nudity and submission. Kasson argues, however, that Powers's heroine successfully "redirected the viewer's gaze from the female subject's body to her face, stressing her emotions: anxiety,

fortitude, and resignation" (178). For an insightful reading of the racial politics of *The Greek Slave,* see Brody 67-71.

23. In a broad and oversimplified argument regarding Menken's career, Dudden maintains that the actress's theatrical work hit a precipitous decline as her body aged. Dudden argues in an almost punitive tone that, by the time of her death, "Menken had proved that displaying her body might be lucrative for a woman, but she also demonstrated that, given the realities of aging, the resulting career might be pathetically brief" (164). Although Menken is often said to have been less than thrilled with one of her final roles in Paris as a mute heroine in *Les Pirates de Savanne,* most biographical accounts report that she was nonetheless a box-office success through her final performances in the summer of 1868. See Mankowitz 231-38.

24. Dudden's characterization of writing as a "disembodied" art form overlooks a vast array of critical feminist works, particularly by French scholars, that interrogate the site of writing as inextricably linked to the (female) body. See, for instance, Moi. Dudden ultimately fails to consider the ways in which acting might itself serve as an art form offering a means to the "embodied subjectivity" that Grosz envisions in her important work on corporeal representation and feminist politics.

25. Indeed, as Butler points out in her work on the politics of passing, the surveillance of liminal bodies functions as both an act of fetishizing the other and reinforcing the hegemonic position of the spectator, for "the spectre of racial ambiguity . . . must be conquered" in the end (*Bodies* 172).

26. This method of foregrounding the body as a site of resistance is not unlike that employed by black women abolitionists such as Truth, who, Peterson argues, strategically "call[s] attention to the materiality of the black female body in both its productive and reproductive functions in order to subvert the dominant culture's construction of it" (22). Peterson contends that African American women lecturers had to function as "actresses" who constantly negotiated their self-representation in a bid to resist dominant racial and gender stereotypes.

27. See also Butler's *Gender Trouble.* In both a provocative and a problematic twist, Menken would later in her career become one of only a handful of women performing minstrelsy. Clearly, in one sense, her decision to don burned cork suggests an ultimate rejection and ridicule of blackness. Yet perhaps one might read her minstrel characters—like her cross-dressing as Mazeppa—as transgressing white

patriarchal circumscription from within its very borders rather than simplistically succumbing to it. One could perhaps contend that she, in fact, positioned what Eric Lott might call her mythologized "wench" persona in a "breeches" role, smoking cigars and cracking profane jokes while also invoking the show of her female physique as a way of potentially undoing the total subjugation of racially and gender abject bodies in minstrelsy.

Works Cited

Barclay, G. Lippard. *The Life and Career of Adah Isaacs Menken, the Celebrated Actress.* Philadelphia, 1868.

Berson, Misha. "The San Francisco Stage: From Gold Rush to Goldenspike, 1849-1869." *San Francisco Performing Arts Library and Museum Journal* 2 (1989): 75-79.

Booth, Michael R. *Victorian Spectacular Theatre: 1850-1910.* Boston: Routledge, 1981.

Brody, Jennifer DeVere. *Impossible Purities: Blackness, Femininity, and Victorian Culture.* Durham: Duke UP, 1998.

Brooks, Daphne A. "Lady Menken's Secret: Adah Isaacs Menken and the Race for Sensation." *Legacy: A Journal of American Women Writers* 15:1 (1998): 68-77.

Butler, Judith. *Bodies That Matter: On the Discursive Limits of "Sex."* New York: Routledge, 1993.

———. *Gender Trouble: Feminism and the Subversion of Identity.* New York: Routledge, 1990.

———. "Performative Acts and Gender Constitution: An Essay in Phenomenology and Feminist Theory." *Performing Feminisms: Feminist Critical Theory and Theatre.* Ed. Sue-Ellen Case. Baltimore: Johns Hopkins UP, 1990. 270-82.

Cofran, John. "The Identity of Adah Isaacs Menken: A Theatrical Mystery Solved." *Theatre Survey* 31 (May 1990): 47-54.

Davis, Charles T., and Henry Louis Gates Jr. "Introduction: The Language of Slavery." *The Slave's Narrative.* Ed. Davis and Gates. New York: Oxford UP, 1985.

Davis, Tracy. *Actresses as Working Women: Their Social Identity in Victorian Culture.* New York: Routledge, 1991.

———. "The Actress in Victorian Pornography." *Victorian Scandals: Representations of Gender and Class.* Athens: Ohio UP, 1992. 99-133.

———. "The Spectacle of Absent Costume: Nudity on the Victorian Stage." *New Theatre Quarterly* 5 (1989): 321-33.

Diamond, Elin. "Mimesis, Mimicry, and the 'True-Real.'" *Acting Out: Feminist Performances.* Ed. Lynda Hart and Peggy Phelan. Ann Arbor: U of Michigan P, 1993. 363-82.

Dickson, Samuel. *Tales of San Francisco.* Stanford: Stanford UP, 1957.

DuCille, Ann. "The Occult of True Blackwomanhood: Critical Demeanor and Black Feminist Studies." *The Second Signs Reader: Feminist Scholarship, 1983-1996.* Ed. Ruth-Ellen B. Joeres and Barbara Laslett. Chicago: U of Chicago P, 1996.

Dudden, Faye E. *Women in the American Theatre: Actresses and Audiences, 1790-1870.* New Haven: Yale UP, 1994.

Falk, Bernard. *The Naked Lady.* London: Hutchinson, 1934.

Forte, Jeanie. "Focus on the Body: Pain, Praxis, and Pleasure in Feminist Performance." *Critical Theory and Performance.* Ed. Janelle G. Reinelt and Joseph R. Roach. Ann Arbor: U of Michigan P, 1992. 248-62.

Gage, Frances. "Address to the First Annual Meeting of the American Equal Rights Association." Lauter et al. 1962-63.

———. "Reminiscences by Frances D. Gage of Sojourner Truth, for May 28-29, 1851." Lauter et al. 1959-61.

Garber, Marjorie. *Vested Interests: Cross Dressing and Cultural Anxiety.* New York: Harperperennial, 1992.

Gatens, Moira. *Imaginary Bodies: Ethics, Power and Corporeality.* New York: Routledge, 1996.

Gerson, Noel. *Queen of the Plaza: A Biography of Adah Isaacs Menken.* By Paul Lewis (pseud.). New York: Funk, 1964.

Gilman, Sander L. "Black Bodies, White Bodies: Toward an Iconography of Female Sexuality in Late Nineteenth-Century Art, Medicine, and Literature." *"Racing," Writing, and Difference.* Ed. Henry Louis Gates Jr. Chicago: University of Chicago Press, 1985. 223-61.

Gilroy, Paul. "'. . . To Be Real': The Dissident Forms of Black Expressive Culture." *Let's Get It On: The Politics of Black Performance.* Ed. Catherine Ugwu. Seattle: Bay, 1995. 12-33.

Grosz, Elizabeth. *Volatile Bodies: Toward a Corporeal Feminism.* Bloomington: Indiana UP, 1994.

Hartman, Saidiya. *Scenes of Subjection: Terror, Slavery, and Self-Making in Nineteenth-Century America.* New York: Oxford UP, 1997.

Homans, Margaret. "'Racial Composition': Metaphor and the Body in the Writing of Race." *Female Subjects in Black and White: Race, Psychoanalysis, Feminism.* Ed. Elizabeth Abel, Barbara Christian, and Helene Moglen. Berkeley: U of California P, 1997. 77-101.

———. "'Women of Color' Writers and Feminist Theory." *New Literary History* 25 (1994): 73-94.

James, Edwin. *Biography of Adah Isaacs Menken, with Selections from Infelicia.* New York: [1881?].

Johnson, Claudia. *American Actress: Perspectives on the Nineteenth Century.* Chicago: Nelson-Hall, 1984.

Johnson, E. Patrick. "'Quarying' Queerness, Queering Blackness: Reading Marlon Riggs' *Black Is, Black Ain't.*" University of California, San Diego. La Jolla, 24 Feb. 2000.

Kasson, Joy. "Narratives of the Female Body: The Greek Slave." *The Culture of Sentiment.* Ed. Shirley Samuels. New York: Oxford UP, 1992. 172-90.

Kendall, John S. "'The World's Delight': The Story of Adah Isaacs Menken." *Louisiana Historical Quarterly* (1938): 846-68.

Lauter, Paul, et al., eds. *The Heath Anthology of American Literature.* 2nd. ed. Vol. 1. Lexington: Heath, 1994.

Lesser, Allen. *Enchanting Rebel [The Secret of Adah Isaacs Menken].* New York: Beechhurst, 1947.

Lott, Eric. *Love and Theft: Blackface, Minstrelsy, and the American Working Class.* New York: Oxford UP, 1993.

Lyman, George D. *The Saga of the Comstock Lode: Boom Days in Virginia City.* New York: Scribner's, 1934.

McDowell, Deborah. "Recycling: Race, Gender, and the Practice of Theory." *Studies in Historical Change.* Ed. Ralph Cohen. Charlottesville: U of Virginia P, 1992. 246-63.

Mankowitz, Wolf. *Mazeppa: The Lives, Loves and Legends of Adah Isaacs Menken: A Biographical Quest.* New York: Stein, 1982.

Mazeppa; or, the Wild Horse of Tartary. A Romantic Drama in Two Acts. New York: [183?]. Special Collections Library, University of California, Los Angeles.

Menken, Adah Isaacs. *Infelicia. Collected Black Women's Poetry.* Ed. Joan R. Sherman. Vol. 1. New York: Oxford UP, 1988. 1-124.

———. "Notes of My Life." *New York Times* 6 Sept. 1868.

Modleski, Tania. "Doing Justice to the Subjects: Mimetic Art in a Multicultural Society: The Work of Anna Deavere Smith." *Female Subjects in Black and White.* Ed. Elizabeth Abel, Barbara Christian, and Helene Moglen. Berkeley: U of California P, 1997. 57-76.

Moi, Toril. *Sexual/Textual Politics: Feminist Literary Theory.* New York: Routledge, 1985.

Monfried, Walter. "The Negro Beauty Who Bewitched Two Continents." *Negro Digest* 14 (1965): 86-90.

Mullen, Harryette. "'Indelicate Subjects': African-American Women's Subjugated Subjectivity." *Sub/versions: Feminist Studies.* Santa Cruz: University of California, 1991. 1-7.

Painter, Nell. "Sojourner Truth in Life and Memory: Writing the Biography of an American Exotic." *Gender and History* 2.1 (1990): 3-16.

———. *Sojourner Truth: A Life, a Symbol.* New York: Norton, 1996.

Peterson, Carla. *"Doers of the Word": African-American Women Speakers and Writers in the North, (1830-1880).* New York: Oxford UP, 1995.

Roach, Joseph. *Cities of the Dead: Circum-Atlantic Performance.* New York: Columbia UP, 1996.

Robinson, Amy. "It Takes One to Know One: Passing and Communities of Common Interest." *Critical Inquiry* 20 (Summer 1994): 715-36.

Rourke, Constance. *Troupers of the Gold Coast; or the Rise of Lotta Crabtree.* New York: Harcourt, 1928.

Ryan, Mary. *Women in Public: Between Banners and Ballots, 1825-1880.* Baltimore: Johns Hopkins UP, 1990.

Smith, Valerie. "Black Feminist Theory and the Representation of the 'Other.'" *Changing Our Own Words: Essays on Criticism, Theory, and Writing by Black Women.* Ed. Cheryl A. Wall. New Brunswick: Rutgers UP, 1990. 38-57.

Sterling, Dorothy, ed. *We Are Your Sisters: Black Women in the Nineteenth Century.* New York: Norton, 1984.

Terry, Jennifer, and Jacqueline Urla. "Introduction: Mapping Embodied Deviance." *Deviant Bodies: Critical Perspectives on Difference in Science and Popular Culture.* Ed. Terry and Urla. Bloomington: Indiana UP, 1995. 1-18.

Twain, Mark. "The Menken—Written Especially for Gentlemen." *Mark Twain of the Enterprise: Newspaper Articles and Other Documents, 1862-64.* Ed. Henry Nash Smith with the assistance of Frederick Anderson. Berkeley: University of California, 1957. 78-80.

WPA. *San Francisco Theatre Research, Vol. 4, First Series, Abstract from WPA Project 8386 O.P. 465-03-286.* San Francisco: 1939. San Francisco Performing Arts Library, San Francisco.

Washington, Margaret, ed. *Narrative of Sojourner Truth by Olive Gilbert.* New York: Vintage, 1993.

Williams, Patricia. *The Alchemy of Race and Rights: Diary of a Law Professor.* Cambridge: Harvard UP, 1991.

Winter, William. *New York Tribune* 1 May 1866.

Yellin, Jean Fagan. *Women and Sisters: The Antislavery Feminists in American Culture.* New Haven: Yale UP, 1989.

Gregory Eiselein (essay date 2002)

SOURCE: Eiselein, Gregory. Introduction. Infelicia *and Other Writings.* By Adah Isaacs Menken. Ed. Eiselein. Peterborough: Broadview, 2002. 15-35. Print.

[*In the following essay, Eiselein examines the interplay between elements of Menken's private life, her stage career, and her poetry. Eiselein gives particular attention to the "elements of Jewish identity" in Menken's work from the late 1850s to the free verse prosody she likely adopted from Walt Whitman.*]

Learning about Adah Isaacs Menken's extraordinary life and writings is best done with an appreciation for questions and ambiguities rather than a need for definite or simple answers. When sorting through the facts about her life, an alert skepticism is also handy, though perhaps no amount of historical rigor could infallibly separate the facts from the legends that swirl around her.

The questions begin with her birth and the various, disputed stories about her parentage. In the version most common among her nineteenth-century biographers, Menken's father is James McCord, and she is born as Adelaide McCord on 15 June 1835 in Milneburg, Louisiana, near New Orleans. The original source for these details might be Menken herself, who seems to have given this or similar information to Thomas Allston Brown.[1]

Yet Menken's own personal narrative, the rather dramatic **"Notes of My Life"** [**"Some Notes of Her Life in Her Own Hand"**], claims she was born as Marie Rachel Adelaide de Vere Spenser on 11 December 1839 in New Orleans to a father named Richard Irving Spenser and a mother named Marie Josephine de Vere Laliette. Few biographers have ever accepted this version of her life story, in part because its narrative style makes extravagant use of formulas borrowed from popular fiction. At other times and places, Menken had different but equally romantic versions of her life story. In 1865 she revealed her real name as Dolores Adios Los Fiertes, the daughter of a French woman from New Orleans and a Jewish man from Spain, and moved the year of her birth to 1841. In an early encounter with the press about the details of her life, an 1860 series in the *New-York Illustrated News,* Menken said she was born in January 1839 and identified her father as Josiah Campbell. In addition to Adah, Adelaide, Ada, Marie Rachel Adelaide, Dolores, and Dolo, she also went by the names Ada Bertha, Ada Bertha Theodore, and Rachel Adah Isaacs.

Other nineteenth-century accounts of her life would have different "facts." *The American Year Book and National Register,* for instance, records her birthplace as Chicago in 1832, as does the *New-York Tribune.* Joaquin Miller, on the other hand, insists it was Cincinnati. Because he seemed passionate about biographical inaccuracies and indicated first-hand knowledge about her life, one might be inclined to accept Miller's story as possibly more reliable; but, according to his biographer, Miller didn't really know Menken.[2]

Twentieth-century researchers would find evidence for still other renditions of Menken's parentage and birth. A current and often accepted scholarly account of her life argues that Menken was born Philomène Croi Théodore on 3 May 1839 in New Orleans. Her mixed race father, Auguste Théodore, is described as a "free man of color," while her French Creole mother is identified as Magdaleine Jean Louis Janneaux. With this understanding of her family history and cultural background, scholars began treating Menken as an African American author. Another version of her life insists that Menken was Jewish from birth, locates her birth in Milneburg on 15 June 1835, but then concedes her parents are not precisely identifiable. Some have been persuaded by evidence that suggests she was born Ada McCord on 15 June 1835 in Memphis, while still others have adopted the view that she was born "Ada Bertha Theodore near New Orleans to a Creole father and a Jewish-Irish mother" in 1835.[3]

Bewildering as this beginning might be, with its surfeit of possible parents, birthdates, birthplaces, and ethnic identities (Irish, Jewish, Creole, African American, French, Spanish, British, and Scotch-Irish), Menken's later life is equally complex and often just as enigmatic. Wherever exactly she was born, New Orleans is the place Menken considered the hometown of her childhood. She had a sister who went by the name Josephine, Jo(e), or Annie (Campbell) Josephs and a brother called John Auguste, Augustus, or Gus. Her father died, it seems, in 1842, and her mother remarried a Josiah Campbell. As a child, she may have been a dancer and performer along with her sister.[4] Moreover, at some point in her life, Menken enjoyed an ample liberal education, particularly for a young woman. She was well read and knew several languages, not only the French and English of her hometown, but also Latin and German, Spanish probably, a little Hebrew, and purportedly even ancient Greek. Although she did not have the kind of comprehensive, systematic university education available to America's elite male authors, Menken's contemporaries often commented on her intelligence, wide reading, and her ability with languages. Her contemporaries described her as "well educated" and "very intelligent," and Adrian Marx took note of the breadth, if not depth, of her erudition: "she possessed a smattering of all human knowledge. She knew and talked on every subject with giddying facility, from the dialects of the New World to transcendental mathematics, from Latin to philosophy—from versification to theology."[5]

In 1855 Menken was living in East Texas, giving readings of Shakespeare, and writing poems and sketches for *The Liberty Gazette*. In February of that year in Galveston County, under the name Miss Adda Theodore, she married W. H. or Nelson Kneass (1823-68/69), the Philadelphia-born musician, composer (most famous for his music to the popular "Ben Bolt"), and founder of the Kneass Opera Troupe. Her marriage to Kneass might have been her first. It is the first documented. Yet there were also rumors about other early marriages—one about someone from Louisville, another about a man named "McA—" from New Orleans. Menken's own autobiography claims she wed Juan Clemente Zenea (1832-71), the Cuban poet and revolutionary, before seeing the marriage "legally dissolved" by the courts. Such a claim has seemed far-fetched to Menken biographers, but the exact mix of truth and legend in Menken biography has always been difficult to sort out. Zenea did remember Menken in his poetry; and José Lezama Lima, the great modern Cuban writer and one of the foremost authorities on Cuban literature, believes the teenage lovers had "una relación íntima" in Havana in 1850, one that Zenea recalled nostalgically for the rest of his life.[6]

Whether it was her first or second, her marriage to Kneass didn't last long. The following year, on 3 April 1856, in Livingston, Texas, she married Alexander Isaac Menken, another musician. Alexander was the son of Solomon Menken, a successful wholesale dry goods dealer and the head of a German Jewish family who had lived in Cincinnati since 1820. She took the last name, adopted Alexander's middle name and appended an "s," and added an "h" to her own first name, becoming and more or less remaining Adah Isaacs Menken. While married to Alexander, Adah began to develop a career as a professional actress, first on a New Orleans/southern Louisiana/eastern Texas circuit and later, after moving to Cincinnati in June 1857, through the Midwest. In Cincinnati, before Alexander's family and the Jewish community in general, Adah presented herself as Jewish from birth. She never converted in any formal or official manner, and there are reasons to doubt the view (promoted by Menken, some of her nineteenth-century contemporaries, and some twentieth-century scholars such as Allen Lesser) that she was born and raised Jewish. Nevertheless, she soon began writing exuberant, often serious Jewish-themed poems and essays for *The Israelite*, Cincinnati's Jewish newspaper, edited by the distinguished Rabbi Isaac Mayer Wise, the founder of organized Reform Judaism in the U.S. Moreover, the Menken family, Wise, and the Cincinnati Jewish community embraced Adah as Jewish. She studied Hebrew with Wise, applauded the admission of Baron Rothschild to the British Parliament, denounced

the Catholic church's kidnapping of a six-year-old Jewish boy, delivered a lecture on Judaism at a Louisville synagogue, published poems and essays in *The Jewish Messenger* (a New York weekly), and began work on a book of **"Tales and Poems on Judaism."** Yet, as Adah actively pursued her career, becoming a successful actress and an increasingly well-known celebrity, and as Alexander took to drinking, their marriage slowly deteriorated, until July 1859 when they were granted a rabbinical divorce and Adah left Cincinnati for New York.[7]

By September, Menken was performing in Albany and had begun publishing poems in the *Sunday Mercury*. She had also married again, this time to a famous boxer named John Carmel Heenan—or, as he was known to prizefighting fans, the Benicia Boy. By the new year, however, Heenan had abandoned his new and now pregnant spouse, leaving for England on 5 January 1860 to fight in a match for the heavyweight championship of the world and denying through his press agents and associates his marriage to Menken. The couple soon thereafter became the focus of a scandal covered in various national newspapers—a scandal that included charges of bigamy and revelations about Menken's previous marriage to Alexander, public statements affirming and denying the marriage of Menken to the Benicia Boy, and reports about the death of their infant son in the summer of 1860. During this tumultuous year, Menken began socializing with Walt Whitman, Ada Clare, and the rest of a group of bohemian writers and critics who gathered at Pfaff's beer cellar in New York City. No doubt influenced by Whitman and this circle of bohemian friends, she wrote a series of rather unconventional poems and essays for the *Sunday Mercury*. The year and a half from March 1860 through the summer of 1861 would be the most creative and prolific period in Menken's career as a poet. It was also the most painful and depressing period of her personal life. Following Heenan's desertion, the ensuing financial difficulties, the newspaper scandals and public humiliation, the death of her son and later her mother, a desperate and dejected Menken contemplated suicide and penned at the end of the year a note that explained, "I have suffered so much, that there can not be any more for me" (**"To the Public,"** 29 Dec. 1860).

She didn't, however, take her own life, and in the new year Menken would find her acting career blossom as never before. In June 1861, in Albany, Menken took the stage for the first time as the male lead in the dramatic version of Byron's *Mazeppa,* a role that would make her a world-famous celebrity. She later married the *Sunday Mercury*'s literary editor, the humorist and pundit Robert Henry Newell, known to the public by his pen name "Orpheus C. Kerr," in September 1862. During the midst of the Civil War, in 1863-64, the couple relocated to the West where Menken performed to packed houses in San Francisco, Sacramento, and Virginia City, Nevada, and in the process became the most highly paid actress of her time. She also met a new circle of literary friends, including Mark Twain,

Bret Harte, Ina Coolbrith, and Charles Warren Stoddard. She reunited with bohemian comrades from Pfaff's, Ada Clare and Charles F. Browne (better known as "Artemus Ward"), and began contributing to San Francisco's literary paper, the *Golden Era*. While her career prospered, her marriage failed; the modest, conventional, sometimes sullen, and often condescending Newell seems to have been a poor match for Menken. In 1864 she sailed to London after a brief stay in New York, and eventually the couple divorced.

Menken was a triumphant success in London, opening in *Mazeppa* on 3 October 1864. She also had a new boyfriend named Captain James Barkley, who was a gambler turned financier and, like Menken, a Southerner. Although she resisted marrying him for two years, the couple eventually wed, after learning of her pregnancy, in August of 1866. Three days later, Menken departed for Paris, never to see him again. In November, she gave birth to a son, Louis Dudevant Victor Emmanuel Barkley, who later died in the summer of 1867. Before his death, however, Menken became a star in Paris in a prosperous, long-running production called *Les Pirates de la Savane*.

During this period, Menken's celebrity and wealth permitted her to foster something of a literary salon in London composed of the bohemian writers, critics, artists, and intellectuals whose company she so enjoyed. There she mixed with critics like John Oxenford and writers such as Charles Dickens, Dante Gabriel Rossetti, and Algernon Charles Swinburne (with whom she allegedly had an affair in late 1867 and early 1868). In Paris as well, Menken loved socializing with writers like George Sand, Théophile Gautier, and Aléxandre Dumas. She enjoyed a close (some suggest erotic) relationship with Sand and an intimate (some suggest erotic) friendship with Dumas, which led to rumors of an affair following the public circulation of photographs of Menken and Dumas together. Although she wrote little poetry during the years she spent in London and Paris, she did begin to collect her poems for the volume that eventually became *Infelicia*. In May 1868, as the publication of her collection slowly moved forward, Menken grew ill, stopped performing, and drew up a will. Despite a period of convalescence and recuperation that summer and even some plans to return to the stage in *Les Pirates de la Savane*, Menken died in Paris on 10 August 1868 and was buried in the Jewish section of the Père la Chaise cemetery. The following week *Infelicia* was published.

* * *

In most of the biographies and criticism about Menken, her scandalous behavior and theatre career tend to overshadow how important literature was to her. Wherever she lived, she sought out writers. In New York, it was Whitman and the literati who frequented Pfaff's; in the West, it was Bret Harte and Mark Twain; in London, Swinburne and

the Rossetti's; in Paris, Sand and Dumas. Although she knew acting paid far better than poetry, Menken thought of herself as a writer and saw writing as essential to her identity and survival: "I am writing again, which is my only salvation," she wrote to her friend Ed James (qtd. in Mankowitz, 112-113). Moreover, while not a prolific poet, she did produce a significant body of work between 1855 and 1868, publishing almost twenty essays, around 100 individual poems, and a book of collected poems.

Menken's earliest work appeared in *The Liberty Gazette*, while she was living in east Texas in 1855. During the mid-1850s, Menken allegedly published a volume of poems titled **Memories** under the pseudonym "Indigena," yet no copy has ever been located, and scholars now seriously doubt it ever existed.[8] Her earliest extant efforts are mostly poems of love and devotion addressed to her family (like **"I Am Thine"**) and flirtatious light verse (such as **"New Advertisement!!!"**). In early pieces such as **"Wounded"** and **"A Twilight Whisper,"** however, Menken also writes about death and experiments with poetic personas: the speaker of **"Wounded,"** for example, is a male soldier at the moment of his death.

While married to Alexander Menken, the center of Adah's literary career was *The Israelite*. She kept authoring affectionate poems of admiration, now dedicating them either to members of the Menken family or to fellow writers for *The Israelite*. She also started sending essays and poems to *The Jewish Messenger* in New York. Unlike her early pieces, the poems from this period explore traditional Jewish themes such as the importance of reflection at Rosh Hashanah, God's presentation of the Law on Mount Sinai, and the death of Moses. With the exception of the republication of her essay on **"Shylock,"** her work for the *Messenger* focused primarily on spiritual themes, in particular the immortality of the soul. In *The Israelite*, however, her poems and prose pieces addressed religious as well as contemporary Jewish political issues, including antisemitism, the admission of Rothschild to Parliament, and the Catholic church's kidnapping of a six-year-old Jewish boy named Edgardo Mortara.

Menken's Jewish-themed work continued into the 1860s, in poems such as **"Hear, O Israel!"** and essays such as **"Affinity of Poetry and Religion."** Nevertheless, when Menken moved to New York, endured a distressing marriage to and divorce from Heenan, and began her association with the circle of writers who frequented Pfaff's, the form and content of Menken's verse changed. Her writings from the early 1860s, most of them appearing in the pages of the New York *Sunday Mercury,* tend to focus on love and lost love, sorrow and misfortune, intense unhappiness and despair. Some poems treat the agony of betrayal, the loss of hope, and the experience of death as a welcome release from the pain of life. Others represent an exhilarating return of courage, power, and even revenge. Still others are about the need to mask or hide one's identity in order to survive in a vicious world that has no place for women's passions or desires. The most striking aspects of these poems are the daring eroticism, the defiant declarations of female independence, and the thematizations of rage, vengeance, and wild despair. Formally, the poems range from the sentimental, to occasional poems and dedications, to what she called her "wild soul-poems" in free verse (see **"Notes of My Life"**). During these years, she also supplied the *Sunday Mercury* with translations of contemporary German and ancient and medieval Latin poetry as well as several prose pieces. The essays addressed topics ranging from Whitman's poetry (one of the first positive public assessments of his work), to the connection between creativity and Jewish spirituality, to the need for women's education and independence.

After she left New York for San Francisco in the summer of 1863, Menken wrote only about a half dozen new poems and revised some earlier work. In 1863 and 1864, she published three new poems and several revised or reprinted pieces in the San Francisco *Golden Era.* Later, she would publish a poem (**"Reply to Dora Shaw"**) in the *New York Clipper* and write a couple of poems that were never published in her lifetime, **"The Poet"** and **"Venetia."** The last years of her career as a poet were dedicated to collecting and revising poems for publication in her only book, *Infelicia.* Dedicated to her London acquaintance Charles Dickens, *Infelicia* remained in print through several editions from 1868 to 1902. Most of the reviews were negative or condescending, which isn't surprising. As Marie Louise Hankins's article on "The Female Writer" illustrates, women writers in the nineteenth-century encountered fierce public censure for their work, and Menken's very public career and her unconventional life, ideas, and poetic style all served to exacerbate such disapproval. Her work did manage to find some admirers, however, including writers like Rossetti and Miller.

* * *

Menken is the first poet and the only woman poet before the twentieth century to follow the revolution in prosody started by Whitman's *Leaves of Grass* (1855). Her adoption of free verse—her avant-garde use of poetic forms dependent on neither regular rhyme nor regular meter for their rhythms and patterns of sound—is truly exceptional. Although the majority of her poems were composed in a conventional, rhyming, accentual-syllabic verse, two-thirds of the poems she selected for *Infelicia* were in free verse; of those, all but one was written during the 1860-61 period when she was mostly directly influenced by Whitman and the bohemian literati at Pfaff's. Clearly she valued these poems, perhaps more than any of her other writings. In **"Notes of My Life"** she both distanced herself from these "wild soul-poems" ("they were to me the deepest mystery. ... I do not see in them a part of myself; they do not seem at all familiar to me") and then imagined their origins in the deepest and most spiritual part of herself ("the

soul that prompted every word and line is somewhere within me, but not to be called at my bidding—only to wait the inspiration of God").

Like Whitman's *Leaves of Grass,* Menken's free verse poems use images and rhythms gleaned from Ossian, the Old Testament, and popular oratory, in particular the sermon and the campaign or reform speech. Relinquishing fixed meters and rhyme schemes meant finding other ways to pattern sounds and generate rhythms, new ways for creating lyric order. Following Whitman, Menken relied heavily on forms of repetition besides rhyme and meter. In **"Where the Flocks Shall Be Led,"** for example, she deploys not only parallel sentence constructions, a series of interrogatives, but also anaphora, the repetition of the same word or words at the beginning of a line, to construct a rhythmic pattern:

> Must I pine in bondage and drag these heavy chains through the rocky path of my unrecompensed toil?
> Must I, with these pale, feeble hands, still lift the wreathed bowl for others to drink, while my lips are parched and my soul unslaked?
> Must I hold the light above my head that others may find the green pastures as they march in advance, whilst I moan and stumble with my bare feet tangled and clogged with this load of chains?
> Must I still supply the lamp with oil that gives no light to me?

In this poem, like others in *Infelicia,* she also makes use of what rhetoricians and literary critics call conduplicato, the repetition of words in a successive line or clause for emotional emphasis: "Answer me, ye who are ranged mockingly around me with your unsheathed knives. Answer me." Moreover, it should be noted, Menken sometimes incorporates conventional metered lines into her free verse poems, as if to blend conventional with unconventional rhythms or to mark her departure from them. Just as "Song of Myself" begins with the most familiar meter in English poetry, a line of iambic pentameter ("I celebrate myself, and sing myself"), **"Where the Flocks Shall Be Led"** opens with a four-beat line reminiscent of traditional English language hymns ("Where shall I lead the flocks to-day?") before deviating from the familiar pattern to explore other kinds of rhythm.

Though they ditch set end rhyme patterns, her free verse poems are nevertheless rich in prosodic techniques such as alliteration, assonance, and variations of conventional rhyme. In a pair of lines from **"Into the Depths,"** for example, Menken sings:

> Fleet of foot, they front me with their daggers at my breast.
> All heedless of my tears and prayers, they tear the white flowers from my brow, and the olive leaves from my breast, and soil with their blood-marked hands the broidered robes of purple beauty.

This short passage opens with a triplet of frame rhymes or what Wilfred Owen would later call pararhymes, words with differing vowel sounds but similar initial and final consonants (*fleet/foot/front*). But just as the alliteration of *f* sounds starts to sound overdone, the end of the line picks up on the pararhyme's less obvious *t* (a*t*/breas*t*), carries this emphasis over into the first part of second longer line (*t*ears/*t*ear/whi*t*e), and begins an alliteration of *s* sounds (dagger*s*/brea*s*t/heedle*ss*/tear*s*/prayer*s*/flower*s*/leave*s*/*s*oil/hand*s*/robe*s*). Yet, before that line becomes too thick with *t*'s and *s*'s, she slowly shifts again her emphasis to a clustering of plosive *b* and *d* sounds (*b*reast/*b*lood-marke*d*/han*d*s/*b*roi*d*ere*d*/robe*s*/*b*eauty) at the line's end. And in the clustering of "tears," "prayers," and "tear," each separated by a single unstressed syllable, she mingles consonant rhyme (te*ars*/pray*ers*), assonant rhyme (pr*a*yers/t*ea*r), and eye rhyme (t*ears*/t*ear*). In short, Menken does not so much dispense with meter and rhyme as make use of alternative patterns of sound and rhythm for the sonic textures and emphases of her free verse poems.

Such a free verse prosody is well suited to the extravagant representation of emotions, the most conspicuous feature of Menken's poetry. In **"Judith,"** for example, Menken combines short and long lines with Old Testament diction and rhythms to create a strikingly unconventional and emotionally charged poem. The speaker of the poem is Judith, the heroine from Jewish legend who saves her people by slaying the Assyrian general Holofernes. Many nineteenth-century images of Judith portray her as strong-willed and courageous, but nothing like the powerful, blood-craving, boastful, and erotic persona that comes to life in *Infelicia.* She promises to "revel" in her "passion," a breathtaking mixture of love and hate, and hold up the severed head of Holofrenes for a kiss:

> My sensuous soul will quake with the burden of so much bliss.
> Oh, what wild passionate kisses will I draw up from that bleeding mouth!
> I will strangle this pallid throat of mine on the sweet blood!
> . . . .
> I am starving for this feast.

Although Menken uses similarly lurid images of blood and violence in **"The Autograph on the Soul," "A Fragment,"** and **"Dying,"** the mixture of anger, threats, violence and blood, sadistic delight, and daring eroticism is quite unlike anything else in nineteenth-century women's poetry.

Although **"Judith"** is a highly unique poem, such affective intensity—which has been called "a torrent of force" and described as "hysterical," "spectacular," and most frequently "wild," "erratic," and "intense"—finds various forms throughout Menken's oeuvre. Indeed her exploration of emotional complexity and power is not limited to the free verse wild-soul poems, as perhaps her conventionally rhymed and metered **"Passion"** illustrates. This poem, like many of her poems, is about "the desire for bonding," which Joanne Dobson has called "[t]he principal theme of the sentimental text."[9] Yet the emotion in Menken's poetry does not always fit our customary understandings of sentimentalism. **"Passion"** begins with the language of sentimentality: the addressee was thought to be "true" and the speaker's love "pure"; the speaker (who is male in the Latin text upon which this poem is based) compares his love to the virtuous love parents feel for their children, and domestic affection is the sentimental affect par excellence. Yet from the very first troubling "*When* I believed thee true" (emphasis added), we know that this sentimental affection is set in the past. In the second stanza, the speaker borrows figures from sentimental discourse (such as knowing the other truly, concern for the heart) only to insist that "since all thy ways I know, / Thy heart is worthless in my eyes." What's interesting and unsentimental about this poem is that the discovery that one's beloved is faithless does not lead to heartbreak, piety, and renunciation but to a rather cruel devaluation of the beloved and a frank confession of heightened lust, now that the "chastening thought" that the beloved was "pure and good" no longer "represse[s]" the speaker's "high desires" and "fervent currents of the blood." The speaker admits that his formerly domestic affection for the beloved was based on repression, and now that the cause for that repression is gone, he admits to a rather dark, uncaring lust for the addressee. The poem is about the death of sentimental affection and, "in its seat," the triumph of audacious and cruel erotic passion. The speaker's view is pronouncedly pitiless, unsympathetic, and downright anti-sentimental.

Many of Menken's poems contemplate the difficulties of sexual/romantic relationships, but not all are so cruel as **"Passion."** In **"A Memory,"** for example, the speaker recalls with sad affection the dark, beautiful eyes of a woman she loved: "The stars . . . Are soft and beautiful, yet still / Not equal to her eyes of light." She remembers their meetings, kisses, but most of all her beloved's eyes:

> They may not seem to others sweet,
>   Nor radiant with the beams above,
> When first their soft, sad glances meet
>   The eyes of those not born for love;
> Yet when on me their tender beams
>   Are turned, beneath love's wide control,
> Each soft, sad orb of beauty seems
>   To look through mine into my soul.

Invoking central features of the discourse of romantic relationships, the poem depicts the women's wordless communication, which reaches past the eyes into the soul and confirms their unique, exclusive love for each other. According to G. Lippard Barclay, this poem was written for a young American Indian woman named Laulerack, whom Menken had met in Texas. This part of Barclay's biography has never been substantiated with any sort of reliable evidence; the story about Laurelack is almost certainly fictional. Still, the poem, whether based on a real encounter or not, exemplifies both Menken's handling of female-female romance and a far more tender form of erotic relation.

Nevertheless, the poem is not a happy one, as it ends with their separation and its lingering pain.

Indeed, the most often represented emotion in Menken's work is melancholy or despair, though her handling of these feelings is not always conventional. **"Saved,"** for example, a poem written in the summer of 1861 during the first year of the Civil War, portrays the death of a soldier. Yet the poem does not explicitly mourn his dying. Instead, in a kind of wild desperation, the speaker cradles his dead body, kisses "his pale, cold mouth," refuses to believe he has died, and promises in optimistic tones animated by a deranged denial that tomorrow the fallen soldier will "lead ye cheerily on to the attack!" **"Into the Depths,"** on the other hand, represents a grief that leads the speaker to believe that "All life is bitter," everything that matters is lost, every effort in vain. The final two sections of the poem turn momentarily hopeful as the speaker yearns for Eros, the "unspeakable, passionate fire of love," to rescue her from the pit of languid hopelessness, but the poem ends ambiguously: Does Eros arrive in time to restore passion? Does Eros arrive at all? Or does Love return just in time to hold the speaker's cold body as she drifts into death? In a poem such as **"Infelix,"** however, there is no release from despair, either through restored passion and life or the peacefulness of death. Instead, the despair is so thorough that it has transformed itself into a painful and seemingly endless regret:

> I stand a wreck on Error's shore,
> A spectre not within the door,
> A houseless shadow evermore,
>   An exile lingering here.

Thus, whether stimulated by an encounter with death or the loss of a beloved or a sense of aching regret, profound unhappiness courses its way through Menken's poetry, particularly the poems from the early 1860s.

Such unhappiness both generates and destroys identity, as perhaps the reference to "exile" indicates. An exile is simultaneously a kind of identity and the label for someone without an identity, someone who's been separated from or banished from the community that provides one with an identity. As one can gather from studying Menken's life and writings, identity is one of the key themes in her work. Yet attempts to understand identity in Menken in terms of binary designations like real/not-real, true/fake, or authentic/inauthentic are likely to miss exactly what is most fascinating about Menken's work. As Renée Sentilles argues, Adah performs Menken and her identities. Moreover, in explicit and implicit ways, Menken's writing is about not only the constitution and defense of specific identities but also the dissolution and often ephemeral nature of identity.

In her poems from 1857-59, Menken reproduces elements of Jewish identity through exhortations to maintain hope

in God, admonishments to defend Judaism against Gentiles, and a variety of references to tradition and history: the Law, the Patriarchs, Rosh Hashanah, etc. In phrases such as "our great and holy laws," *"our ancient race,"* and "OUR FAITH," Menken clearly and vigorously presents herself with Jewish culture. For Menken-as-a-Jewish-poet, threats to identity—whether from Islamic and Christian oppressors, for example, or hardships, or feelings of hopelessness and doubt—can be overcome by waiting patiently and placing faith in God. When she felt the Jewish people were under attack following the Mortara abduction case, Menken used her poem **"To the Sons of Israel"** to rouse her Jewish readers and to rail against "Popish rule."

However thunderous her declarations of Jewish identity, however passionate about her Jewish faith, Menken's publishing career also reveals a poet with doubts, or at least ambivalence, about her Jewishness. On more than a couple of occasions Menken plagiarized the work of her contemporaries. **"Dying,"** for instance, borrows from Alice Cary's "Perversity," while **"Spiritual Affinity"** poaches a line from Whitman's "Song of Myself." Some of Menken's plagiarisms are not as easily detected. Sentilles has discovered Menken's copying of passages from Margaret J. M. Sweat's *Ethel's Love-Life* in a personal letter to a fellow poet, Hattie Tyng, and portions of Rev. D. J. Pinckney's not especially well-known "Who Will Work?" make their way into Menken's essay titled **"The Mightiness of the Pen."** Menken's most egregious acts of plagiarism, however, involve a half dozen poems for *The Israelite.* One of them, **"Dream of the Holy Land,"** is a reworking of John Greenleaf Whittier's "The Holy Land," which happens to be a reworking of lines from Alphonse de Lamartine's *Voyage en Orient* (1835). The other five—**"Queen of the Nations," "The Sacrifice," "The Hebrew's Prayer," "The Sabbath,"** and **"Passover"**—she stole from hymns by Penina Moïse, a Charleston poet whose work was rather beloved within nineteenth-century Jewish communities in the United States. Unlike Menken's other instances of plagiarism—many of which were incidental, private, or obscure—her copying of these poems for republication in *The Israelite* was flagrant. Her pirating of Moïse's hymns is not subtle (it's often verbatim), and Whittier and Moïse would have been among the most recognized nineteenth-century American poets by Cincinnati's Jewish community in the 1850s. Predictably enough, in a June 1859 letter to *The Jewish Messenger,* Menken's plagiarism of Moïse was made public.[10]

It is not clear whether the conspicuousness of these plagiarisms indicate a certain irrationality impelled by a desire to impress others, or deep-seated doubts about her place within the Jewish community, or an ambivalence about that community and a certain wish to be discovered. Was she so eager to be accepted and admired as a Jew that she ventriloquized the words she believed the community wanted to hear? If admiration and acceptance were what she sought, why would she plagiarize in such an outrageous fashion, in ways likely to be recognized, and risk public humiliation? Or did Menken the actress-performer regard poems as lines from a play, available for speaking by whomever is to play the role, by whomever speaks the words most convincingly?

After the revelations about her theft of Moïse's hymns, Menken published just one more piece in a Jewish periodical, **"All Is Beauty, All Is Glory!"** in *The Jewish Messenger* on 19 August 1859. About a month earlier, Menken had moved to New York, and gradually her public identity and voice would become less identified with Jewish politics and culture and more with women's issues. Although she did not devote time to women's organizations or work within the movement, as did writers such as Lillie Devereux Blake, the New York press saw Menken as an advocate for women's rights:

> At length, the hobby of Horace Greeley and Adah Isaacs Menken Heenan; of Wendell Phillips and Fanny Wright; of Adin Ballou and Mrs. Jones of Ohio; is a success. Yes, Woman's Rights are a fixed fact, and a big thing. Let the conservatives weep, the henpecked husbands howl, and the irreverent scoffers of the press dry up.[11]

Vanity Fair's 1860 mock concession to feminist progress overlooked Menken's awfully submissive poems of love and devotion, from **"I Am Thine"** for Kneass and **"Karazah to Karl"** for Menken to the **"Why Do I Love You?"** for Heenan. Instead what probably captured the gossipy column's attention was Menken's position as a *public* woman (in an age when femininity was allied in a powerfully ideological way with the *private* sphere), details about her personal behavior (she smoked in public, visited bohemian night spots, wore unconventional and un-ladylike clothes), and her rather bolder writing that was appearing on weekly or bi-weekly basis in the *Sunday Mercury*. Her earliest work in the *Sunday Mercury* was not explicitly feminist, however, although she champions reform in general in **"Swimming Against the Current"** and in **"My Heritage"** expresses dissatisfaction with the cultural valorization of self-sacrifice, with having "To think, and speak, and act, not for my pleasure, / But others.'" Later, however, after *Vanity Fair* had named Menken to its list of women's rights activists, Menken's work turns even more decidedly feminist in tone and subject matter. She creates powerful and defiant female personas, such as Judith, and draws attention to the exploitation of working women in **"Working and Waiting."** In **"Women of the World,"** she addresses classic themes in eighteenth- and nineteenth-century feminist thought. Unlike Dinah Maria Mulock Craik, whose discussion of **"Women of the World"** emphasizes "the universal law, that woman's proper place is home," but rather more like Blake's "The Social Condition of Woman," Menken advocates more serious educational opportunities for women and criticizes the oppressiveness of fashion for its role in stifling solidarity between women and enfeebling women's intellectual curiosity. Moreover, Menken is forth-

right in her assertion that "There are other missions for woman than that of wife and mother." In other pieces, such as **"Self Defence,"** Menken's use of feminist rhetoric ("This weak little hand will strike its meagre weight against sin and oppression, and lift up the down-trodden colors of *woman's rights!*—her birth-rights—her rights of intellect—her rights of honor …") is aimed at the hypocrisy of the Victorian era's sexual double standard and its devastating consequences for women. While some might see this essay's concerns as more personal than political, other readers might be more interested in the ways the personal and political come together in a piece like **"Self Defence."**

Although her representations of Jewish and feminist identities are certainly emphatic, Menken's work suggests that identity is not always secure or easily known. Her essay titled **"Behind the Scenes,"** for instance, emphasizes the contrast between what appears to others in public and what forms of emotional agony remain unseen. In a poem such as **"Myself,"** she takes this theme a bit further and contends that survival depends on assuming a mask, for the world "lash[es] with vengeance all who dared to be what their God had made them." Thus, with sadness and some yearning that she's not quite able to stifle, the speaker accepts her mask ("Now I gloss my pale face with laughter") and waits for a kind of Messianic release from role playing.

Menken's ideas about identity are not typically clarified by contextualizing them in terms of what we know about her life.[12] In fact, interpreting her work and its thinking about and performance of identity with reference to her biography tends to complicate (rather than simplify or resolve) issues of identity and raise an array of interesting but difficult questions. What's the difference between assuming a public identity and creating a poetic persona, which some readers will understand to be the poet herself? If Menken is right about society's coercion of individuals, especially women, into wearing specific kinds of masks and assuming certain roles, how would this change our notions about authenticity, writing, and identity? How does it change our thinking about the morality of passing, masking, role-playing, and/or plagiarism? To what extent is plagiarism the theft of someone else's identity, the destruction of identity, or the re-creation of a new identity? If Menken were born into a mixed-race family, why and how did she pass as white? If she were born a Gentile, why would she adopt a Jewish identity in her private life, public life, and poems and essays—an identity she would carry with her to her grave? What do Menken's writings—her cravenly submissive love poems, rebellious feminist pieces, erotic passages, and same-sex love letters and poems—tell us about sexual identity? Are celebrities who self-consciously dramatize various identities in their lyrics and life (celebrities such as Byron, Madonna, or Menken) to be understood as texts or persons? as both or not exactly either? To what extent are such celebrities not really "real" people (like you and me)? To what extent are all of us necessarily performers of an always-evolving repertoire of identities?

Literary scholars who examine now overlooked writers sometimes imagine that earlier disdain or neglect can be explained as a past failure to appreciate what we can now recognize as daring, masterful, or significant. Yet, the fact is that as brutal and predictable as the criticism of Menken often was, many in her own era found Menken and her work supremely mesmerizing. Miller called her "the most entirely poetical of all women that have yet found expression in America" and described her poetry as "grand, sublime, majestic." What made her a captivating, popular writer in her own era—her attempts to adopt a Whitman-esque prosody, her gothic morbidity, her lurid sensationalism, her "erratic" or over-the-top style, her defiance of convention and traditional moralities, her attempt to viscerally invoke something as elusive as emotion—were also precisely the aspects of her work that brought her censure. Likewise, it is unlikely that Menken will suit the tastes or compel the interests of all twenty-first-century readers. Some may see her poetry as dated, a relic of a past era; others will find their own late modern interests and concerns resonating with various aspects of Menken's work, including its avant-garde formal experiments, its powerful expression of women's rage and desire, its feminist politics, as well as its performances of multiple racial, sexual, and religious identities and its questioning of fixed identity in general. Some will probably dislike or disparage these poems for their strange, emotional, and theatrical quality, and others will find them absolutely fascinating for precisely the same reasons.

Archives and Collections: Abbreviations

AJA   American Jewish Archives: Papers of Allen Lesser, the American Jewish Archives, Hebrew Union College, Cincinnati, Ohio.

AJHS   American Jewish Historical Society: Adah Isaacs Menken Collection, American Jewish Historical Society, New York, New York.

Notes

1. In 1861 Menken sent Brown biographical notes that she insists were "strictly *true*," notes that he probably used in his sketch of her life. Most of the biographical information in this Introduction is from the nineteenth-century biographical sources in Appendix A, the correspondence in Appendix B, and the works by Lesser, Mankowitz, and Sentilles listed in the Bibliography at the end of this volume.

2. "Menken, Adah Isaacs," *The American Year Book and National Register for 1869* (Hartford, 1869), 790-91; Obituary, *New-York Tribune* (12 Aug. 1868): 5; In *Splendid Poseur: Joaquin Miller—American Poet*

(New York: Thomas Y. Crowell Company, 1953), M. M. Marberry points out that "Menken was not in San Francisco when Joaquin was there in 1862" (49).

3. For respective instances of these twentieth-century versions of Menken's life, see Mankowitz, 34; Lesser, 248; Cofran, 54; Scharnhorst, 310. For examples of literary historians who have treated Menken as an African American writer, see Sherman; Gates and Sherman. For a critical examination of Menken's biographers, see Brooks. For the most insightful and reliable account of Menken's life and the complexities of her biography (and biographers), see Sentilles.

4. Little is known about her brother; and most biographers lose track of her sister after 1860 (see Lesser 251), though a letter at the AJHS indicates she died on 28 April 1862 in New Orleans. See Menken, to Henry Francis Keenan, 5 Sept. 1862, AJHS.

5. Obituary, *New-York Tribune* (12 Aug. 1868): 5; Charles Reade qtd. in Stoddard, 478; [Adrian Marx?], "Letter of Paris Correspondent," *New York World* (20 Aug. 1868?), from transcription at AJA.

6. José Lezama Lima, Prólogo, in Juan Clemente Zenea, *Poesía* (La Habana: Editorial Nacional de Cuba, 1966), 12. On the grounds of a chronological impossibility, Lesser and Mankowitz have each rejected Menken's claim that she married Zenea (Lesser, 247; Mankowitz, 31). But see Zenea, *Poesía,* especially Lezama Lima's introduction (11-12, 17 [7-19]) and Zenea's "Infelicia" (291-95), and "El Olvido Me Mató" ["The Forgetfulness Killed Me"] (37-38). Dollard also points to the Zenea-Menken connection, noting that Zenea's "biographers assert that the two met in Havana in 1850" (Dollard, 105n12).

7. About her lecture in Louisville, see *The Israelite*'s German-language supplement *Die Deborah* (24 Dec. 1858): 149. About the proposed volume of "Tales and Poems on Judaism," see *The Israelite* (16 Oct. 1857): 118; and *Die Deborah* (20 Nov. 1857): 109.

8. Barclay provides two early poems he claims appeared in *Memories,* "Wounded" and "'Milton wrote a letter to his lady love.'" See Barclay, 30.

9. Joanne Dobson, "Reclaiming Sentimental Literature," *American Literature* 69 (1997): 267. The descriptions of Menken's poetry can be found in Appendix C, though the term "hysterical" is from Sherman (182) and "spectacular" from Louis Untermeyer, to Allen Lesser, 29 May 1933, AJA.

10. "The Plagiarisms of Ada Isaacs Menken," *The Jewish Messenger* (10 June 1859): 174.

11. "The Result," *Vanity Fair* (7 July 1860): 21.

12. This has not prevented a number of nineteenth- and twentieth-century critics from attempting to discover the meaning of her poems in her biography or looking for the truth about her life in the poems. See also, for a twentieth-century example, Foster and Foster, 53.

Bibliography

Barclay, G. Lippard. *The Life and Remarkable Career of Adah Isaacs Menken.* Philadelphia, 1868.

Brooks, Daphne A. "Lady Menken's Secret: Adah Isaacs Menken, Actress Biographies, and the Race for Sensation." *Legacy* 15 (1998): 68-77.

Brown, T. Allston. *History of the American Stage.* New York, 1870.

Cofran, John. "The Identity of Adah Isaacs Menken: A Theatrical Mystery Solved." *Theatre Survey* 31 (1990): 47-54.

Dollard, Peter. "Six New Poems by Adah Isaacs Menken." *Louisiana Literature* 17 (2000): 97-118.

Foster, Barbara, and Michael Foster. "Adah Isaacs Menken: An American Original." *North Dakota Quarterly* 61 (1993): 52-62.

Gates, Henry Louis, Jr., gen. ed., and Joan R. Sherman, ed. *Collected Black Women's Poetry.* 4 vols. New York and Oxford: Oxford University Press, 1988. Vol. 1.

James, Ed. *Biography of Adah Isaacs Menken.* New York, [1881].

Lesser, Allen. *Enchanting Rebel: The Secret of Adah Isaacs Menken.* New York: The Beechhurst Press, 1947.

Mankowitz, Wolf. *Mazeppa: The Lives, Loves, and Legends of Adah Isaacs Menken.* New York: Stein and Day, 1982.

Miller, Joaquin. *Adah Isaacs Menken.* Ysleta, Texas: Edwin B. Hill, 1934.

Scharnhorst, Gary. "Adah Isaacs Menken." *Nineteenth-Century American Women Writers: A Bio-Bibliographical Critical Sourcebook.* Ed. Denise D. Knight. Westport: Greenwood Press, 1997. 310-13.

Sentilles, Renée. "Performing Menken: Adah Isaacs Menken's American Odyssey." Ph.D. diss., The College of William and Mary, 1997.

Sherman, Joan R., ed. *African-American Poetry of the Nineteenth Century.* Urbana and Chicago: University of Illinois Press, 1992.

Stoddard, Charles Warren. "La Belle Menken." *National Magazine* Feb. 1905: 477-88.

Swinburne, Algernon Charles. *Adah Isaacs Menken: A Fragment of Autobiography.* London: [privately printed], 1917.

Gregory Eiselein (essay date 2004)

SOURCE: Eiselein, Gregory. "Plagiarism, Passing, and Performance: Adah Isaacs Menken's Jewish Poetry." *Fakes and Forgeries.* Ed. Peter Knight and Jonathan Long. Amersham: Cambridge Scholars, 2004. 165-76. Print.

[*In the following essay, Eiselein discusses Menken's 1858-59 plagiarism of Penina Moïse, bringing nineteenth-century literary opinions and Postmodern discussions of identity to bear. Eiselein speculates about what may have led Menken to plagiarize, especially the conflict between her own unconventional behavior and the conservative expectations of her Cincinnati Jewish community.*]

A recent article describes Adah Isaacs Menken as "an American original," a tag that captures how unconventional and innovative she was as a poet, performer and personality.[1] Yet a careful study of her writings reveals she was also a plagiarist. Because of the ambiguity and apparent mutability of her public identity, such plagiarism might be understood as an act of passing or performance. Indeed, notions of performativity and passing have played major roles in recent interpretations of Menken's life and writings.[2] Such approaches may not be able to account for key particulars in this case of plagiarism, however; and such approaches overlook the ways plagiarism denotes not the forging but the undoing of identity. Suggesting some limitations of these two approaches, this essay provides an alternative perspective on Menken's plagiarism and examines the perhaps unexpected aftermath of her literary larceny.

MENKEN'S LIFE AND WRITINGS

The most highly paid actress of the 1860s, Menken was also a poet whose life constantly intersected with the prominent writers of her era: Walt Whitman, Mark Twain, Algernon Charles Swinburne, Charles Dickens, Dante Gabriel Rossetti, George Sand, Aléxandre Dumas and many others.[3] A compelling blend of originality, eroticism and exuberant representation of Jewish identity, her poetry was transformed in the early 1860s by her friendship with Whitman. She became the first poet and only woman poet before the twentieth century to work in the kind of free verse prosody Whitman had. Indeed, her use of poetic forms dependent on neither regular rhyme nor regular metre for their rhythms and patterns of sound is exceptional for the era.

Menken's biography is similarly exceptional, though it raises complicated and unanswerable questions that begin with the various, disputed stories about her parentage. In one version popular with nineteenth-century biographers, Menken's father is James McCord, and she is born Adelaide McCord on 15 June 1835 in Milneburg, near New Orleans. Menken's own narrative, however, claims she was born Marie Rachel Adelaide de Vere

Spenser on 11 December 1839 in New Orleans to Richard Irving Spenser and Marie Josephine de Vere Laliette. She later revealed she was really Dolores Adios Los Fiertes, the daughter of a French woman from New Orleans and a Jewish man from Spain, and moved her birth date to 1841. But in the *New-York Illustrated News,* Menken had said she was born in January 1839 and identified her father as Josiah Campbell.[4] In addition to Adah, Adelaide, Marie Rachel Adelaide, and Dolores or Dolo, she also went by the names Ada Bertha, Ada Bertha Theodore and Rachel Adah Isaacs.

Twentieth-century historians found evidence to support still other renditions of Menken. A recent version argues that Menken was born Philomène Croi Théodore on 3 May 1839 in New Orleans. Her mixed race father, Auguste Théodore, is described as a "free man of colour," while her French Creole mother is identified as Magdaleine Jean Louis Janneaux. Another account insists Menken was Jewish from birth, locates her birth in Milneburg on 15 June 1835, but then concedes her parents are not precisely identifiable. Some evidence suggests she was born in Memphis as Ada McCord, while other scholars have adopted the view that she was born "Ada Bertha Theodore near New Orleans to a Creole father and a Jewish-Irish mother" in 1835.[5]

This oversupply of possible parents, birthdates and ethnic identities (Irish, Jewish, Creole, African American, French, Spanish, British and Scotch-Irish) makes Menken's origins puzzling; but her later life is just as complex and enigmatic. She was a world-famous actress and an outspoken feminist who wore men's clothes, smoked cigarettes in public and hashish in private, and socialized with bohemian writers and artists throughout Europe and North America. She had affairs with men and women and married about six times: a Cuban poet (Juan Clemente Zenea), a musician-composer (W. H. Kneass), a musician-actor (Alexander Isaac Menken), a professional boxer (John Carmel "Benicia Boy" Heenan), a writer-editor (Robert Henry Newell), and a gambler turned financier (James Barkley).[6]

PLAGIARISM

This "American original" was also a plagiarist. Her textual appropriations were usually minor, perhaps unconscious, and not especially noteworthy. Her poem **"Dying"** borrows phrases from Alice Cary's "Perversity," while **"Spiritual Affinity"** steals a line from Whitman's "Song of Myself." Portions of Rev. D. J. Pinckney's obscure "Who Will Work?" (an essay from *The Ladies' Repository*) make their way into her **"Mightiness of the Pen."** In a slightly more extensive instance of plagiarism, Menken copied passages from the bisexual novel *Ethel's Love-Life* into a love letter to a fellow female poet, Hattie Tyng.[7]

In other instances, the evidence of plagiarism is inconclusive. For example, Menken's **"Adelina Patti"** is a revision, abridgement and rearrangement of "La Signora Vestvali"

by "Cinna Beverley," a poem that appeared in the New Orleans *Sunday Delta* in 1857. Menken may have stolen Beverley's work, but it's also possible that "Cinna Beverley" was another of the various names Menken used in the 1850s. Menken lived in New Orleans and contributed to *The Sunday Delta* in 1857; no known documents establish Cinna Beverley's existence.[8]

Nevertheless, Menken's most egregious plagiarisms involve half a dozen poems published in the Cincinnati *Israelite* in 1858-59. One of them, **"Dream of the Holy Land,"** is a reworking of John Greenleaf Whittier's "The Holy Land," which happens to be a reworking of lines from Alphonse de Lamartine's *Voyage en Orient.* The other five—**"Queen of the Nations," "The Sacrifice," "The Hebrew's Prayer," "The Sabbath"** and **"Passover"**—she stole from Penina Moïse, an American Jewish poet from Charleston. Unlike the other instances of plagiarism, which were incidental, obscure or private, her copying of these poems for republication in *The Israelite* was flagrant, often verbatim.[9]

PASSING

One way to see Menken's plagiarism is as an act of passing. Although Menken identified herself as Jewish throughout her public life and claimed Jewish parentage, some thought otherwise. Her friend and press agent, Ed James, begins his biography of Menken by indicating that he wants to clarify the facts of her life. The first truth he establishes is that "Menken was not born a Jewess." The distinguished Rabbi Isaac Mayer Wise, the founder of organized Reform Judaism in the United States and editor of *The Israelite,* also believed Menken was a Gentile.[10] And there is no evidence she ever converted in any official or formal manner. Nevertheless, from about 1856 (the year she married Alexander Isaac Menken) onward, the Menken family, Wise, and the Cincinnati Jewish community embraced Adah as Jewish. She studied Hebrew with Wise, applauded the admission of Baron Rothschild to the British Parliament, denounced the Catholic Church's kidnapping of a six-year-old Jewish boy, delivered a lecture on Judaism at a Louisville synagogue, published poems and essays in the New York *Jewish Messenger* and *The Israelite,* and began work on a book of **"Tales and Poems on Judaism."**[11] Perhaps then not born a Jew but wanting to be accepted as one, Menken plagiarised the poems of a Jewish writer in an attempt to convince others of the genuineness of her Jewish identity. In other words, she may have been so eager to be accepted and admired as Jewish that she ventriloquised the words she believed the community wanted to hear.

The notion of passing as a way to understand the racially and ethnically ambiguous Menken has had an appeal for several observers, from her nineteenth-century contemporaries to twentieth-century historians in search of the "real" Menken.[12] Yet such a view may be a bit too rigid in its approach to identity to explain adequately the protean Menken. It assumes perhaps an essentialist notion of identity: passing suggests a true self that one hides in order to deceive others into believing that one has some other identity. Although some theorists and critics have tried to use an analysis of passing as an "interrogation of . . . essentialism," the essentialism in the notion of passing seems inescapable, as Walter Benn Michaels, among others, has convincingly argued.[13]

The passing approach also flattens the complexity of Menken's identity and ignores the sequence of events in her life. Her most blatant plagiarizing happened in a defined eight-month period from August 1858 to April 1859. The evidence from this period does not indicate that others began to doubt or question her Jewishness. Though Wise believed Menken wasn't really Jewish, he never questioned her about it. Likewise, Moïse's family and friends, who discovered the plagiarism and protested about it, never complained that Menken was trying to pass. What the evidence from this period does suggest is that Menken's career and marriage were changing. As she became an increasingly famous actress working in cities throughout Ohio, Indiana, Pennsylvania, New Jersey and New York, her marriage became progressively more strained. The Menken family disapproved of Adah's public celebrity, and Adah's ever more successful career led eventually to a rabbinical divorce in July 1859. Nevertheless, a series of love poems to Alexander published in *The Israelite* from September 1858 to February 1859 suggest that Adah wanted, in this public forum at least, to mend her relationship.[14] During this period of public success and domestic difficulties before the divorce, Menken was attempting to improve her standing with her husband, his family and the close-knit German Jewish community of Cincinnati by publishing poems of Jewish faith, submission and tradition—exactly the kind of verse Moïse wrote. Menken's other Jewish-themed poems, written before and after this period of plagiarism, were typically more militant and public: praise poems about courageous Jewish heroes, outraged denunciations of Catholic and Turkish oppression, and determined exhortations about the need to carry on the difficult fight for Jewish truth in a Gentile world.[15] Thus, if one pursues the passing thesis, one would want to argue that she plagiarised not to pass as Jewish, but to pass as a quiet, devout and submissive Jewish wife who wrote poems to celebrate Jewish tradition. To say Menken was passing as white or Jewish is not a precise description of the identity others encountered.

PERFORMANCE

For a less reductive approach that breaks with the essentialism of passing, one might turn to performative theories of identity. To paraphrase Judith Butler, perhaps the most famous theorist of performative identity, there is no "true" or "false" Jewish identity behind Menken's use of Jewish verse; her Jewish identity is constituted by her expressions of Jewish identity. Butler's theory resembles the approach taken by Menken biographer Renée Sentilles, who argues that "Adah performed Menken; she created her as a separate person, who performed both a public and private life."[16] For Sentilles, it doesn't exactly matter whether Menken was really born Jewish or not, because Menken successfully performed Jewish identity. From such a perspective, it seems possible that Menken may have regarded poems as lines from a play, available for speaking by whomever is to play the role, by whomever speaks the words most convincingly.

This approach seems consistent not only with Menken's career as an actress but also the numerous, often differing accounts of her life. When talking about her life, Menken typically insisted that everything she said was "strictly *true*."[17] Yet the stories she told, often for the press, are not consistent with each other or even self-consistent. Thus, historians like Sentilles conclude that Menken deliberately invented versions of herself and performed them in her public and private lives. The performative approach also resonates with an important theme in Menken's work—the necessity of assuming roles, playing parts and wearing masks. **"Behind the Scenes,"** for instance, emphasises the contrast between the public face that others see and those forms of emotional agony that remain unseen. In **"Myself,"** she takes this theme further and contends that survival depends on assuming a mask, for the world "lash[es] with vengeance all who dared to be what their God had made them." Thus, with sadness and irony, the speaker accepts her mask: "Now I gloss my pale face with laughter / [. . .] After all, living is but to play a part!"[18]

Though less rigid than the passing approach, the performative perspective may blur important distinctions between theories that might seem similar. Sentilles argues that Menken intentionally created various identities for herself and performed them, whereas Butler's theory of performative identity does not restrict itself to those who deliberately craft public and private personas for themselves. Sentilles' work suggests that Adah's own choice and impersonating skills allowed her to perform various Menkens. Butler's theory, on the other hand, does not suggest individuals choose the identities they perform. Instead they repeat them. Identities for Butler are neither true selves nor self-selected roles to play but rather repeated acts of signification within already existing rule-governed discourses.[19]

Moreover, Menken herself distinguished performance from identity. According to Menken, individuals perform different identities for various reasons, from bad education to the social need to mask one's true self in order to survive. But she also insisted on the existence of a true self, a soul, a "real me." In other words, Menken did not equate identity with action, a "doing" with no essential "being" behind it, but instead distinguished between fictional roles she would perform (on stage, in courtships, in social venues) and her own real identity.[20]

In emphasising the forging of identity, the passing and performative approaches ignore the ways that plagiarism does not so much create or affirm identity as undo and disrupt it. Generally speaking, plagiarism *confuses* identity. The plagiarist poses as the originator of an utterance, and the connections between those words and the identity of the originating author are erased. In "Plagiarism and the Proprietary Self," Ellen Weinauer emphasises this "disruption of subjectivity accomplished by the act of plagiarism" and shows how not only "stolen words" but "authorial identity" itself are at issue in plagiarism.[21] Eclipsing Moïse's and Whittier's identities as poets to assert herself as an author, Menken doesn't simply construct a new identity for herself; she also undoes previous expectations about her own identity and muddles the audience's understanding of the identity of the poems' author(s). More specifically, this borrowing did not stabilize Menken's sense of self or her public image. Thus, because of its ability to exacerbate the instability of identity, such plagiarism might be seen more accurately as an expression of Menken's discordant sense of identity, an expression of the ambivalence she felt toward the roles she played in daily life.

As noted above, one might conclude that Menken plagiarised these poems so that she might appear to be a more submissive and religious wife in the eyes of her husband, in-laws and community. Yet if Menken had already demonstrated that she was capable of writing poems for Jewish newspapers, why would she want to publish poems by Moïse and Whittier as if they were her views and sentiments? Why wouldn't she simply write her own? One answer is that Menken did in fact have difficulty writing poems like **"The Sacrifice," "Passover"** and **"The Sabbath"**—poems that emphasise obedience, tests of faith, tradition, religious obligations and dreadful punishments: "tremble ye! who disobey / The mandate of the Lord."[22] In general, Menken seems to have found marriage, holiness and conventional middle-class life trying, if not impossible. She held unconventional views of marriage, ones laced with feminist irony: "I believe all good men should be married. Yet I dont [*sic*] believe in women being married. Somehow they all sink into nonentities after this epoch in their existence." And she admired those who resisted social norms; those "who have the valor and moral courage to swim against the current" were to her the true "Messiahs of humanity."[23] These kinds of insubordinate feminist and bohemian ideas, which circulate throughout her public and private writings, contrast sharply with the attitudes expressed in the plagiarised poems. In other words, uneasy about the social and domestic demand that she be not simply a faithful Jew but a conventional and submissive Jewish wife, Menken may have had difficulty with topics like dutiful submission and pious devotion and relied on the words of others to express such sentiments.

Her conflicted feelings about her role as wife, in-law and member of a restrained religious-ethnic community might also explain why she plagiarised so conspicuously.

In "The Psychology of Plagiarism," William Dean Howells wrestles with this question: why would an author pilfer another's literary work when "plagiarism carries inevitable detection with it"? Plagiarizers' names are permanently attached to the fenced material, and detectives for such crimes are numerous: "[t]he world is full of idle people reading books." Moreover, those who know the original author are often eager to prosecute such thefts, as indeed was the case with Menken's plagiarism (the nephew of Penina Moïse energetically exposed the plagiarism in a letter to *The Jewish Messenger*). Thus, Howells concludes: "Plagiarism is not the simple 'crime' or 'theft' that the lexicographers would have us believe. It argues a strange and peculiar courage on the part of those who commit it or indulge it, since they are sure of having it brought home to them."[24] In Menken's case, her "strange and peculiar courage" may have come not from an assurance that she would avoid detection or scandal but from a desire to be exposed. Unlike her other plagiarisms, where she may have borrowed a line unconsciously or stolen from another writer for a private letter or lifted portions of an obscure magazine article, Menken's plagiarisms in *The Israelite* were deliberate, sometimes precise copying of Whittier's and Moïse's poems. Whittier was one of the most well-known poets in the United States; and Moïse's work was rather beloved by Jewish Americans who attended synagogue and sang her hymns.[25] In other words, Menken's plagiarism was obvious, an invitation to others to reveal her literary theft. Plagiarising in a manner so likely to be discovered suggests a certain desire to be exposed, punished and/or renounced. Thus, to see Menken's plagiarism as an attempt at greater acceptance within the Cincinnati Jewish community ignores the ambivalence she felt about her place within that community, and it overlooks the possibility that the plagiarism was not a misguided attempt at greater assimilation but a (perhaps unconscious) part of an attempt at separation.

Her plagiarism may have also been an expression of the conflicts she felt about her identity as a poet. In the wake of Romantic conceptions of originality, genius and authorship, literary culture in nineteenth-century America became more sensitive to and more anxious about plagiarism and its implications. Poe, to cite a famous example, railed generally against the "sin of plagiarism" in the New York *Evening Mirror*, accused James Russell Lowell of stealing lines from Wordsworth, and engaged in a protracted harassment of Longfellow for plagiarism. Yet Poe was also a plagiarist, stealing from well-known British writers like Coleridge, popular poets, contemporary critics, natural history writers, newspapers and encyclopedias. Poe's biographer Kenneth Silverman has suggested that literary envy and self-doubt were at the root of Poe's plagiarisms; more generally, Weinauer has interpreted such plagiarism and anti-plagiarism as part of a "proliferating concern about plagiarism in the mid-nineteenth century."[26]

Though never a belligerent crusader against plagiarism like Poe, Menken experienced similarly conflicted feelings in which Romantic-artistic aspiration combined with uncertainty about one's identity or talent as a writer. She was a successful actress, but she yearned to be a poet and to be recognised and admired as one. Wherever she travelled, she sought out writers. In New York, it was Whitman and the literati who frequented Pfaff's beer cellar; in California, it was Twain and Bret Harte; in London, Dickens, Swinburne and the Rossettis; in Paris, Sand and Dumas. Indeed, Menken believed writing was essential to her identity and survival; as she explained to Ed James: "I am writing again, which is my only salvation."[27] Several of Menken's poems thematically treat artistic genius (**"My Heritage"** or **"Genius,"** for example), the talent of fellow artists (**"Adelina Patti," "To Nathan Mayer"**), and the nobility and responsibilities of the poet (**"The Poet"**). With confidence and bravado, she occasionally insists on the irrepressibility of poetic genius. More often, however, her poems lament her poetic failures: "All vainly I strive / Beauties like thine to portray." In **"Miserimus,"** she pleads with the apostrophized "Genius" and "Bards" to know why she has been led to poetry but denied the talent of a great poet: "You promised that I should create a new moon of Poesy / [...] why breaks there yet no Day to me? / [...] O Genius! is this thy promise? / O Bards! is this all?"[28]

Aspiring to the role of poet in a post-Romantic literary culture that worshipped originality and genius and fretted over issues of literary theft, Menken may have appropriated the poems of Moïse and Whittier out of admiration for their status as poets and insecurity about her own talents as a poet. Such plagiarism could be seen as imposture, though it would seem closer to emulation than passing or disguise. These literary appropriations were not, however, a confident attempt to forge a new identity. On the contrary, such plagiarisms epitomised Menken's self-doubt and her anxieties and uncertainties about being a poet, a Midwesterner and a wife; they were symptoms of a certain undoing of identity.

PERSONS, PERSONAS AND MENKEN'S TRUE SELF (AS SEEN BY THE CRITICS)

Despite her self-doubt, Wise's suspicions, the complaints about the plagiarism, the public revelation of her literary thefts and the general anxiety about plagiarism in nineteenth-century literary culture, Menken's plagiarism caused only a little scandal and few, if any, problems. Her literary crimes were soon forgotten, and they had no visibly negative impact on her career. After leaving Cincinnati for New York in 1859, Menken began the most successful, creative and prolific period in her career as a writer. Even M. Mayer, who had twice complained to Wise about Menken's plagiarism, pardoned her because she "found a sympathetic response in [his] heart, for 'to err is human, forgive divine.'"[29]

Such sympathy and forgiveness would have surprised neither Poe nor Howells. "When a plagiarism is detected," Poe observes, "it generally happens that the public sympathy is with the plagiarist." Howells acknowledges that authors, dictionaries, and anti-plagiarists often rail against such "crimes," yet society in general sees no great transgression: "as no penalty attaches to it, and no lasting shame, it is hard to believe it either a crime or a theft; and the offence ... is some such harmless infraction of the moral law as white-lying." Poe, of course, remains outraged ("how unjust!" he cries), and both seem unable to explain society's leniency toward plagiarism in light of literary culture's indignation over it.[30]

Yet one way to understand the unwillingness to prosecute plagiarism is that modern society tolerates, indeed needs, some degree of instability in identity—an instability that doesn't simply permit but actually produces passing, performative identities, and plagiarism. Despite the suspicions that surround passing, performance and plagiarism, modern society handles these possibilities for doubt by treating members of society as individual persons and as personas (or persons performing roles). The person is a kind of social object that orders expectations that can be fulfilled by that individual alone. Roles, however, are sets of expectations that may be fulfilled by various individuals. The necessity of playing different *roles* (poet, wife, synagogue member, etc.) does not usually occasion charges of identity theft, whereas a *person* who disappoints expectations located uniquely in herself may find herself accused of inauthenticity, deception or theft.[31] The performative approach would highlight the ways Menken created herself by playing multiple roles. The passing approach would seem to emphasise Menken as an individual person to whom a unique set of social expectations attaches. By plagiarising, she created a different or "fake" set of expectations and obscured the "real" identity of the original author. (This confusion of authorial identities, this erasure of Moïse's unique personhood, generated the objections or offence over Menken's plagiarism.) Yet modern society handles the diversity of individuals and the possibilities for doubting identity by treating individuals as both persons and personas. It expects one to be a unique individual at times *and* to play scripted roles in other circumstances. We move back and forth between our roles and our unique individuality, though social conditions (not individual choice) largely determine when we function as persons and when personas.

In her own time and in this particular case of plagiarism, Menken functioned as both a person and persona. Take, for example, Rabbi Wise's attitude toward Menken. On the one hand, when Mayer privately confronted him with that fact that Menken had plagiarised Moïse, Wise urged him "not to expose the matter." Menken was a celebrity and an outspoken advocate for Jewish causes. Wise needed a Jewish poet for *The Israelite*, and thus he actively promoted her literary productions, taught her Hebrew and tried to protect her from scandal. Though he treated Menken as a *persona,* as one fulfilling a certain social role in the Jewish community, he also kept track of the *person* he thought Menken to be. Five and a half years after her departure, he recalled that Menken wasn't really a Jew: "She is no Jewess, although she invariably calls the Hebrews 'our people,' and sympathizes altogether with them."[32] In other words, he publicly accepted Menken as a Jew in the 1850s because she played one for his newspaper; but he privately kept track to himself that the unique person he knew was not really a Jew at all. Publicly he encouraged her to perform her role and sought to protect Menken from charges of plagiarism, but privately he thought she was passing.

Wise was not ultimately able to protect her, but the public exposure of her plagiarism and the various suspicions that surrounded her "real" identity had little impact on critics' perceptions of her following her death and the release of her only book, **Infelicia,** in 1868. Indeed, most critics embraced this volume as an authentic reflection of the real Menken. *The New York Times* critic, for example, insisted on the "sincerity of her writings" and the fact that she never "claimed to be anything other than what she was." Rossetti also emphasized the sincerity of her expression: "Menken had a vein of intense melancholy in her character: it predominates throughout her verses … and was by no means vamped up for mere purposes of effect." Even her harshest critics who suspected inauthenticity found in Menken's "perpetual mask" the truth of her identity: "She unvails the secrets of her experience as unscrupulously as she went through the displays of the theater."[33]

Why would critics, with reasons to doubt, choose to embrace these poems as genuine expressions of Menken's real identity and deepest feelings? The poems' conventions certainly encourage readers to do so. The emphatic use of the first person, the confession of powerful emotions, and the thematic distinction between public role-playing ("living is but to play a part") and private, hidden feeling ("the shadowy depths of the Real") denote intimacy and sincerity; they appeal to the readers' desire to believe.[34] Yet her celebrity may have also played a role. Menken was a relatively well-known public figure about whom various, often contradictory, stories circulated. Even as they provided "information" about her to the public, newspapers and publicity also created questions and mysteries around Menken and fuelled or constructed the public's desire to know more, to know Menken's real story. When the poems appeared, they stood in contrast to the public stories in content, form and tone. Confessional verse rather than exposé prose, the poems were very melancholy, whereas the media stories were usually either humorously jaunty and adventuresome or moralistically condemnatory. This contrast, along with the close association of the poems with Menken herself (as her own private expressions), may have encouraged nineteenth-century readers and critics to see these poems as the key answer to the various uncertainties

surrounding the celebrity they had heard about from the newspapers, publicities and rumours.

Despite her reputation as a performer of roles, a teller of tales and a plagiariser of poems, Menken retained the power to mesmerise her audiences into believing that the words she uttered were most intimately and privately her own.

Notes

1. Barbara and Michael Foster, "Adah Isaacs Menken: An American Original," *North Dakota Quarterly* 61 (1993): 52-62.

2. Renée Sentilles pursues the performative approach in "Performing Menken: Adah Isaacs Menken's American Odyssey," Ph.D. diss., The College of William and Mary, 1997. (A revised version will appear soon as *Performing Menken: Adah Isaacs Menken and the Birth of American Celebrity* [Cambridge: Cambridge University Press, 2003].) An example of the passing assumption can be found in *Nineteenth-Century American Women Poets: An Anthology* (Oxford: Blackwell, 1998), where Paula Bernat Bennett concludes, "Menken knew that at bottom she was only Ada C. McCord, an Irish girl from Memphis" (199).

3. The biographical details in this article are drawn from nineteenth-century documents and recent scholarship. The crucial nineteenth-century sources for Menken's life are: G. Lippard Barclay, *The Life and Remarkable Career of Adah Isaacs Menken* (Philadelphia, 1868); T. Allston Brown, *History of the American Stage* (New York, 1870); Ed James, *Biography of Adah Isaacs Menken* (New York, [1881]); and Menken's correspondence and autobiography, reprinted in Adah Isaacs Menken, *Infelicia and Other Writings,* ed. Gregory Eiselein (Peterborough, Ont.: Broadview Press, 2002), 229-41, 199-209. Of the twentieth-century biographies, the most reliable are: Sentilles; Allen Lesser, *Enchanting Rebel: The Secret of Adah Isaacs Menken* (New York: The Beechhurst Press, 1947); and Wolf Mankowitz, *Mazeppa: The Lives, Loves, and Legends of Adah Isaacs Menken* (New York: Stein and Day, 1982). See also Eiselein, Introduction, *Infelicia and Other Writings,* 15-40.

4. See James, 3; Barclay, 19; Menken, "Some Notes of her life in her own Hand," *Infelicia and Other Writings,* 201-202; Lesser, 247; Mankowitz, 31; William Michael Rossetti, "Adah Isaacs Menken," *American Poems,* ed. William Michael Rossetti (London, 1872), 444-45; and Sentilles 37-38.

5. See Mankowitz, 34; Lesser, 248; John Cofran, "The Identity of Adah Isaacs Menken: A Theatrical Mystery Solved," *Theatre Survey* 31 (1990): 54; Gary Scharnhorst, "Adah Isaacs Menken," *Nineteenth-Century American Women Writers: A Bio-Bibliographical*

Critical Sourcebook, ed. Denise D. Knight (Westport, CT: Greenwood Press, 1997), 310.

6. See biographical sources listed in note 2.

7. The details of these plagiarisms are as follows. Section VI of "Dying" (*Infelicia and Other Writings,* 114) incorporates phrases from Alice Carey [*sic*], "Perversity," *Lyra and Other Poems* (New York, 1852), 41-42. "Spiritual Affinity" (*Sunday Mercury* [New York] [13 May 1860]: 1) borrows from Whitman's "Song of Myself," (1855), line 687. "The Mightiness of the Pen" (*Sunday Mercury* [10 Nov. 1860]: 6) takes ideas and words from Rev. D. J. Pinckney, "Who Will Work?" *Ladies' Repository* (Nov. 1851): 417-420. Portions of *Ethel's Love-Life* appear in Menken to Hattie Tyng, 21 July 1861, *Infelicia and Other Writings,* 230-33; cf. Margaret J. M. Sweat's *Ethel's Love-Life* (New York, 1859), 82-86.

8. See Menken, "Adelina Patti," *Infelicia and Other Writings,* 110-11; Cinna Beverley, "La Signora Vestvali," *Sunday Delta* (24 May 1857): 1.

9. Menken's "Dream of the Holy Land" (*Israelite* [13 Aug. 1858]: 45) plagiarizes "The Holy Land," *The Complete Poetical Works of John Greenleaf Whittier* (Boston and New York, 1892), 430. See also Alphonse de Lamartine, *Œuvres complètes de Lamartine,* 41 vols. (Paris, 1860-66), 6:20-21. Compare the other five plagiarized poems that appeared in *The Israelite* between 31 December 1858 and 22 April 1859 to *Secular and Religious Works of Penina Moïse* (Charleston: Charleston Section, Council of Jewish Women, 1911), 147-48, 1-2, 136-7, 164, 160-61.

10. James, 3. See *Die Deborah* [Cincinnati] (5 May 1865): 179; *Israelite* (30 Dec. 1864): 212.

11. See Lesser, 15-28, 39-40; Mankowitz, 31-32, 49-59; and Sentilles, 17-18, 82-121. See also Menken, "The Jew in Parliament" and "To the Sons of Israel," *Infelicia and Other Writings,* 174-76, 138-40. About her lecture in Louisville, see *Die Deborah* (24 Dec. 1858): 149. About the proposed volume of "Tales and Poems on Judaism," see *Israelite* (16 Oct. 1857): 118; and *Die Deborah* (20 Nov. 1857): 109.

12. For an analysis of Menken's biographers, see Daphne A. Brooks, "Lady Menken's Secret: Adah Isaacs Menken, Actress Biographies, and the Race for Sensation," *Legacy* 15 (1998): 68-77.

13. Elaine K. Ginsberg, "The Politics of Passing," *Passing and the Fictions of Identity,* ed. Elaine K. Ginsberg (Durham and London: Duke Univ. Press, 1996), 16. See Walter Benn Michaels, *Our America: Nativism, Modernism, and Pluralism* (Durham and London: Duke Univ. Press, 1995), 90, 132-35, 167n158, 181n241.

14. See Charles H. Moïse to the editors, 22 April 1859, *Jewish Messenger* [New York] (27 May 1859): 157; M. Mayer to the editors, 30 May 1859, *Jewish Messenger* (10 June 1859): 174; Lesser, 34-40; Mankowitz, 56, 62-63. The love poems were "Karazah to Karl," "What an Angel Said to Me," "A Heart Wail," *Infelicia and Other Writings,* 103, 137-38, 140; and "A Wife's Prayer," *Israelite* (17 Dec. 1858): 189.

15. See Menken, "Sinai," "Dum Spiro, Spero," "Moses," "Oppression of the Jews, Under the Turkish Empire," "Let There Be Light," "To Nathan Mayer" and "To the Sons of Israel," *Infelicia and Other Writings,* 127-32, 134-37, 138-40. See also her later poems "Hear, O Israel!" and "Where the Flocks Shall Be Led," *Infelicia and Other Writings,* 92-97.

16. Judith Butler, *Gender Trouble: Feminism and the Subversion of Identity* (New York and London: Routledge, 1990), 25; Sentilles, 4. In an interesting conflation of the passing and performative approaches, Pamela L. Caughie begins with the assumption that "all subjectivity is passing" and redefines "passing" as simply "the performance of identity." See *Passing and Pedagogy: The Dynamics of Responsibility* (Urbana and Chicago: University of Illinois Press, 1999), 2.

17. Menken to Thomas Allston Brown, 2 May 1861, *Infelicia and Other Writings,* 230.

18. Menken, "Behind the Scenes" and "Myself," *Infelicia and Other Writings,* 191-94, 68, 69.

19. See Butler, 144-45.

20. See Butler, 25. Menken addresses women's poor educations in "Women of the World," *Infelicia and Other Writings,* 188-91.

21. Ellen Weinauer, "Plagiarism and the Proprietary Self: Policing Boundaries of Authorship in Herman Melville's 'Hawthorne and His Mosses,'" *American Literature* 69 (1997): 698, 697.

22. Moïse, Hymn 155, *Secular and Religious Works,* 136-37; cf. Menken, "The Sabbath," *Israelite* (15 April 1859): 321. Although her changes to Moïse's work were not always extensive, the alterations suggest the important ways Menken differed from Moïse. In "Passover," for instance, Menken changes "Let piety redeem their souls" to a more stirring, less dutiful "Let songs of glory lift the souls." See Menken, "Passover," *Israelite* (22 April 1859): 330; Moïse, Hymn 183, *Secular and Religious Works,* 164.

23. Menken to Robert Reece, [1866?], *Infelicia and Other Writings,* 237; Menken, "Swimming Against the Current," *Infelicia and Other Writings,* 179.

24. William Dean Howells, "The Psychology of Plagiarism," *Literature and Life* (New York and London: Harper & Brothers, 1902), 276, 277. See Charles H. Moïse to the editors, 157. Howells and Menken both began their careers in the mid-1850s; he was a columnist for the *Daily Cincinnati Gazette* when Menken was writing for *The Israelite*.

25. A much-used nineteenth-century reference work says, "Of all American poets, with the single exception of Longfellow, Whittier has been the most popular." (*Appleton's Cyclopædia of American Biography,* ed. James Grant Wilson and John Fiske, rev. ed., 6 vols. (1889; New York: Appleton, 1900), 6:494.) Moïse's *Hymns Written for the Use of Hebrew Congregations* (Charleston: Congregation Beth Elohim, 1842) went through several printings from 1842 to 1875; her works were also frequently included in other nineteenth-century Jewish hymnals.

26. [Edgar Allan Poe], "Imitation—Plagiarism," *Evening Mirror* (15 Feb. 1845): 2; Weinauer, 700. For more on Poe and plagiarism, see Kenneth Silverman, *Edgar A. Poe: Mourning and Never-ending Remembrance* (New York: HarperCollins, 1991), esp. 70-72, 256-57.

27. Menken qtd. in Mankowitz, 112-113.

28. Menken, "Dreams of Beauty" and "Miserimus," *Infelicia and Other Writings,* 46, 86; the other poems mentioned all appear in *Infelicia and Other Writings.*

29. Mayer to the editors, 174.

30. [Poe], 2; Howells, 274.

31. For a discussion of the persons/roles distinction, see Niklas Luhmann, *Social Systems,* trans. John Bednarz (Stanford: Stanford University Press, 1995), 313-19.

32. Mayer to the editors, 174; Wise, *Israelite* (30 Dec. 1864): 212; Sentilles, 120.

33. "New Publications," *New-York Times* (21 Oct. 1868): 4; Rossetti, 445; "Adah Isaacs Menken's Poems," *New-York Tribune* (29 Sept. 1868): 6.

34. Menken, "Myself," 69, 68.

FURTHER READING

Bibliographies

Dollard, Peter. "A Bibliography of the Poems and Essays of Adah Isaacs Menken." *Bulletin of Bibliography* 58.4 (2001): 255-58. Print.

Provides a thorough bibliography of Menken's writings in nineteenth-century publications. Dollard includes a useful discussion of plagiarized pieces.

———. "A Guide to Core Critical Studies of Adah Isaacs Menken." *Bulletin of Bibliography* 59.2 (2002): 77-84. Print.

Offers a concise overview of work about Menken, from spurious biographies to theses and dissertations.

Whitley, Edward, ed. "Menken, Adah Isaacs (Bertha Theodore) (1835-1868)." *The Vault at Pfaff's: An Archive of Art and Literature by New York City's Nineteenth-Century Bohemians.* Lehigh U Digital Lib., n.d. Web. 3 Nov. 2012.

Provides a short biography of Menken and a solid list of primary and secondary source material, as well as information on her bohemian peers and access to the *Saturday Press.*

Biographies

Brooks, Daphne A. *Bodies in Dissent: Spectacular Performances of Race and Freedom, 1850-1910.* Durham: Duke UP, 2006. Print.

Argues that Menken emerged from the free people of color of New Orleans and traces her participation in popular entertainment on both sides of the Atlantic.

Foster, Michael, and Barbara Foster. *A Dangerous Woman: The Life, Loves and Scandals of Adah Isaacs Menken, 1835-1868, America's Original Superstar.* Guilford: Lyons, 2011. Print.

Comprehensive biography that sorts through claims made by Menken, her biographers, and her supporters and detractors to arrive at as faithful an account of her life as possible. The work also includes a useful bibliography of works about Menken.

Sentilles, Renée M. *Performing Menken: Adah Isaacs Menken and the Birth of American Celebrity.* London: Cambridge UP, 2003. Print.

Contends that Menken is significant because of her moment in history: the beginning of the cult of American celebrity. Sentilles provides important historical context for understanding how Menken viewed herself and her work as a writer and actress.

Criticism

Barnes-McLain, Noreen. "Bohemian on Horseback: Adah Isaacs Menken." *Passing Performances: Queer Readings of Leading Players in American Theater History.* Ed. Robert A. Schanke and Kim Marra. Ann Arbor: U of Michigan P, 1998. 63-79. Print.

Examines the evidence for a "queer reading" of Menken's poetry, noting that claims of a lesbian element in the poet's work rely on selective quotation. Barnes-McLain suggests that Menken, like latter-day pop icon Madonna, "flirt[ed] with a pansexual appeal" in a manner not necessarily indicative of her private feelings.

Elledge, Jim, ed. "Adah Isaacs Menken (1835-1868)." *Masquerade: Queer Poetry in America to the End of World War II.* Bloomington: Indiana UP, 2004. 64-7. Print.
> Includes three of Menken's poems: "My Heritage," "A Memory," and "Infelix." Elledge places these poems in the context of this collection, which explores lesbian, gay, bisexual, and transgender themes and allows the reader to consider gay interpretations of Menken's work.

Umansky, Ellen M., and Dianne Ashton, eds. "1842-1934: *Innovative Voices.*" *Four Centuries of Jewish Women's Spirituality: A Sourcebook.* Boston: Beacon, 1992. 99-178. Print.
> Includes Menken's poem "Drifts That Bar My Door" in the section on works from 1842 to 1934, a period the editors describe as producing more diverse spiritual literature than previous eras. In particular, Umansky and Ashton note "a strong sense of female religious self-identity" and "a stronger public voice," which is reflective of Menken's poetry and essays during her time in Cincinnati.

Additional information on Menken's life and works is contained in the following source published by Gale: *Literature Resource Center.*

The Antiquary
Sir Walter Scott

The following entry provides criticism of Scott's novel *The Antiquary* (1816). For additional information about Scott, see *NCLC,* Volumes 15 and 209; for additional information about the novel *Ivanhoe,* see *NCLC,* Volumes 69 and 241; for additional information about the novel *Waverley; or, 'Tis Sixty Years Since,* see *NCLC,* Volume 110.

INTRODUCTION

The Antiquary was the third in a series of twenty-eight historical novels that began with the anonymously published *Waverley* in 1814. All were written by the noted poet Sir Walter Scott, who had decided not to compromise his literary reputation through an association with popular fiction. He did, however, want to capitalize on the great success of his first effort as a novelist, and so subsequent volumes were attributed simply to "the author of *Waverley*." Although *The Antiquary* is less well known today than *Rob Roy* (1818), *Ivanhoe* (1820), and some of the other "Waverley novels," all were widely read and much admired in the nineteenth century. The novels typically feature colorful characters, vivid descriptions, and complicated plots, filled with adventure, romance, and generous helpings of period flavor. Scott, who was an enthusiastic collector of antiquities and a student of Scottish folkways, used the novels to preserve—or in some cases, invent—rich historical backgrounds, while at the same time touching on relevant political, cultural, and social issues current in the early nineteenth century. He also incorporated a wide range of quotations and literary allusions into the novels.

Although *The Antiquary* is set in the 1790s, less than twenty years before its date of publication, the work is "historical" not only because it refers to events (such as the French Revolution) that had taken place in recent history, but also because the novel is partly about ways of understanding history. *The Antiquary* is generally considered the most overtly self-reflexive of the Waverley novels, in part because the title character has much in common with Scott himself. Early critics praised Scott's skillful representation of working-class country people and their way of life but found fault with the novel's implausible, episodic plot and uneven characterization. European as well as British readers enjoyed the distinctive Scots dialect spoken by some of the characters, and touches borrowed from Gothic fiction—quite popular in Scott's time—also added to the novel's success. Beginning in the mid twentieth century, a revival of interest in Scott led critics to reexamine *The Antiquary* from a variety of literary, historical, and cultural perspectives.

PLOT AND MAJOR CHARACTERS

Set in the fictional town of Fairport, situated on the northeastern coast of Scotland, *The Antiquary* takes place during the last decade of the eighteenth century. The "antiquary" of the title is Jonathan Oldbuck, a cantankerous landowner who fancies himself an authority on history. His interest, however, is that of a collector, not a scholar, and although he has amassed a large stock of old objects, his ideas about them—along with his grasp of Scottish lore—cannot necessarily be relied upon. Oldbuck's opinions and assertions are often contrasted with those of Edie Ochiltree, whose status as a "licensed beggar" allows him to roam the countryside interacting with people of all classes, carrying news, and preserving traditions. As the last of his kind, Edie represents vanishing aspects of folk life in Scotland, just as Oldbuck represents the early stirrings of a new "scientific" approach to history. The two elderly men also symbolize, on the one hand, a life of interesting poverty, and on the other, a financially and domestically comfortable life that often seems to annoy Oldbuck more than it pleases him.

Both characters are unchanged by the end of the novel, but each serves as a catalyst for events in the related stories that make up *The Antiquary*. Oldbuck, who is something of a busybody, sets things in motion when he befriends a young man named Lovel. The two have met by chance, but Lovel shares Oldbuck's interest in history—and also, as it turns out, has a connection with the daughter of Oldbuck's friend Sir Arthur Wardour. Lovel, previously known to Isabella Wardour as Major Neville, had been rejected as a suitor for Isabella because of his presumed lack of social status. In the course of the novel, Lovel helps to rescue Sir Arthur and Isabella, who have been trapped on a cliff by rising water; experiences a dream vision while sleeping in a possibly haunted bedchamber; wounds Oldbuck's pompous nephew in a duel; disappears from the novel for quite some time; and is ultimately discovered to be the legitimate son and heir of the gloomy Lord Glenallan, who had been cruelly tricked by his family into believing his wife (Lovel's mother) was his own sister.

Meanwhile, an intersecting story line concerns Sir Arthur's financial problems, which he hopes to solve by finding a treasure buried in some nearby ruins. The naive nobleman is actually being duped by a German "magician" with the unlikely name of Dousterswivel. Ochiltree mischievously interferes with Dousterswivel's plan, and in the end, Sir Arthur is saved from his own gullibility. Although the various story threads are not causally related, and events seem to take place without any necessary connection, everything converges conveniently in the novel's conclusion. Wrongly believing that Fairport is about to be attacked by the French, everyone—from lowest to highest rank—assembles to defend the community, leading to a conclusion in which Lovel is recognized, restored to his rightful place, and betrothed to Isabella.

MAJOR THEMES

In a preface to *The Antiquary,* Scott confessed that he had been "more solicitous to describe manners minutely, than to arrange in any case an artificial and combined narrative," agreeing in advance with most critics that the novel does not have a unified thematic structure. It depends instead upon broad characterizations, melodramatic events, and an entertaining style. To keep readers engaged, Scott capitalized on the popularity of Gothic novels by borrowing motifs such as the lost heir, the family secret, and the mysterious ruin. He also catered to attitudes that were widespread in 1815, including continued antagonism toward the French, anxiety about the political and social effects of recent revolutions, and nostalgia for the rapidly disappearing Scottish folk culture. For good measure, he included ambiguous hints of the supernatural, an episode of genuine tragedy, and a patriotic finale that restores the Fairport community to wholeness.

This diversity of content has reinforced impressions that *The Antiquary* lacks coherent thematic development, but no one has argued that it lacks for themes. Among those that have interested critics are the nature of community and the role of the past in the present. Joan S. Elbers (1973) contended that "a series of thematic contrasts between isolation and community" provide an organizing principle for the novel. The main tension, according to Elbers, is "between man cut off emotionally and spiritually from the network of relationships that make up the social organism and man linked to his fellows through sympathetic understanding and a system of traditional duties and obligations." Both Lovel and Lord Glenallan are isolated from the community—Lovel, by his presumed illegitimacy, and Glenallan, by his guilt and depression. On the other hand, the Mucklebackits, a family of local fisherfolk, are fully integrated into the community, which turns out in support when young Steenie Mucklebackit is killed in a storm. The importance of community is demonstrated in the rescue of Sir Arthur and Isabella, which requires a series of actions involving Ochiltree, Lovel, Oldbuck, and the Mucklebackits.

The importance of the past is demonstrated when another of the Mucklebackits reveals the secret of Lovel's parentage, thus restoring the rightful Glenallan heir. Like Ochiltree, the aged Elspeth Mucklebackit represents the continuity of communal knowledge, which contrasts with the abstract, disconnected knowledge possessed by Oldbuck. Elspeth Mucklebackit's store of knowledge provides one example of how, as Paul Goetsch (1992; see Further Reading) explained, *The Antiquary* "concentrates on the dynamics of history and the processes by which traditions come into being, are destroyed, transformed, and rejuvenated." That theme may not be readily apparent, however, because it is often treated with humor—"poking fun at would-be analysts of history," Goetsch continued, "and revealing how much make-believe enters the collective consciousness and influences the self-definitions of social groups."

CRITICAL RECEPTION

Nicola J. Watson (2002; see Further Reading) summarized the problem of *The Antiquary* this way: "Although all the strands of the novel weave together at the climax, the tonal and generic disjunctions between the conversational comedy of the Oldbuck circle, the documentary realism of the Mucklebackits, the melodramatic Gothic of the Glenallan mystery, the slapstick of the Dousterswivel plot, and the mechanical *coup de theatre* of the denouement have persistently troubled critics." Even during the "Scott revival" that began in the 1950s, *The Antiquary* was viewed as a curiosity among Scott's fictional works. Opinions began to shift, however, as critics looked more closely at the literary values of the work. Edgar Johnson (1970; see Further Reading), for example, acknowledged the novel's faults, but concluded that, in many respects, *The Antiquary* is "triumphant," full of "the most varied and vivid pictures of human nature," and "rich in its portrayals of Scottish life."

In the latter part of the twentieth century, one important strand of critical commentary focused on whether there is a unifying principle in *The Antiquary,* and if so, what it might be. Robin Mayhead (1971) opened the question by examining "the problem of coherence" in *The Antiquary* and concluding that even though the novel seems to lack coherence when judged against conventional standards for the fiction of its time, it may have an *unconventional* coherence that "does not conform to familiar notions of unity in plot or consistency in tone." For Elbers, the underlying thematic structure concerns community, and for Kurt Gamerschlag (1985; see Further Reading), the novel constitutes a purposeful attempt "to probe the nature of history past and present." Other critics have explored community and history as interrelated, through what Goetsch characterized as a depiction of "tradition-making in process," and still others have studied how *The Antiquary* reflects issues current in the early nineteenth century through a portrayal of the 1790s. Miranda J. Burgess (2001), for example, asserted that "in Scott's hands, antiquarianism [became] a key tool in the historical production of Scotland's British modernity." Explorations of specific historical topics continued with Silvana Colella's (2003) essay on *The Antiquary*'s references to monetary modernization in Scotland, Mike Goode's (2003) consideration of the novel's role in the development of Romantic historicism, and Carolyn Buckley-Fletcher's (2004) examination of *The Antiquary* as Scott's most self-conscious and critical commentary on popular enthusiasm for the past and the primitive. Literary aspects of the novel have not been completely ignored, however, especially in the twenty-first century. Jennifer Parrott (2006) focused on Virginia Woolf's interest in Scott, and, in particular, on her use of *The Antiquary* as an element in the 1927 novel *To the Lighthouse*.

Cynthia Giles

PRINCIPAL WORKS

The Chase, and William and Helen: Two Ballads from the German of Gottfried Augustus Bürger. By Gottfried Augustus Bürger. Trans. Walter Scott. Edinburgh: Manners and Miller, 1796. (Poetry)

Goetz von Berlichingen, With the Iron Hand: A Tragedy. Translated from the German of Goethe. By Johann Wolfgang von Goethe. Trans. Scott. London: Bell, 1799. (Play)

The Eve of Saint John: A Border Ballad. Kelso: Ballantyne, 1800. (Poetry)

Minstrelsy of the Scottish Border. Ed. Scott. 2 vols. Kelso: Cadell and Davies, 1802. Expanded ed. 3 vols. Edinburgh: Longman and Rees, 1803. (Songs)

Sir Tristrem: A Metrical Romance of the Thirteenth Century; by Thomas of Ercildoune. By Thomas Learmouth. Ed. and completed by Scott. Edinburgh: Constable, 1804. (Poetry)

The Lay of the Last Minstrel. Edinburgh: Constable, 1805. (Poetry)

Ballads and Lyrical Pieces. Edinburgh: Constable, 1806. (Poetry)

Marmion: A Tale of Flodden Field. Edinburgh: Constable, 1808. (Poetry)

English Minstrelsy: Being a Selection of Fugitive Poetry from the Best English Authors. Ed. Scott. 2 vols. Edinburgh: Ballantyne, 1810. (Poetry)

The Lady of the Lake: A Poem. Edinburgh: Ballantyne, 1810. (Poetry)

The Vision of Don Roderick: A Poem. Edinburgh: Ballantyne, 1811. (Poetry)

The Bridal of Triermain; or, The Vale of St. John. In Three Cantos. Edinburgh: Ballantyne, 1813. (Poetry)

Rokeby: A Poem. Edinburgh: Ballantyne, 1813. (Poetry)

Waverley; or, 'Tis Sixty Years Since. As Anonymous. 3 vols. Edinburgh: Constable, 1814. (Novel)

The Ettricke Garland; Being Two Excellent New Songs on The Lifting of the Banner of the House of Buccleuch, At the Great Foot-Ball Match on Carterhaugh, Dec. 4, 1815. With James Hogg. Edinburgh: Ballantyne, 1815. (Songs)

The Field of Waterloo: A Poem. Edinburgh: Constable, 1815. (Poetry)

Guy Mannering; or, The Astrologer. 3 vols. Edinburgh: Constable, 1815. (Novel)

The Lord of the Isles: A Poem. Edinburgh: Constable, 1815. (Poetry)

The Antiquary. 3 vols. Edinburgh: Constable, 1816. (Novel)

Paul's Letters to His Kinsfolk. Edinburgh: Constable, 1816. (Fictional letters)

*Tales of My Landlord, Collected and Arranged by Jedediah Cleishbotham, Schoolmaster and Parish-Clerk of Gandercleugh. 4 vols. Edinburgh: Blackwood, 1816. (Novels)

Harold the Dauntless: A Poem. Edinburgh: Constable, 1817. (Poetry)

Rob Roy. 3 vols. Edinburgh: Constable, 1818. (Novel)

†Tales of My Landlord: Second Series, Collected and Arranged by Jedediah Cleishbotham, Schoolmaster and Parish-Clerk of Gandercleugh. 4 vols. Edinburgh: Constable, 1818. (Novel)

‡Tales of My Landlord: Third Series, Collected and Arranged by Jedediah Cleishbotham, Schoolmaster and Parish-Clerk of Gandercleugh. 4 vols. Edinburgh: Constable, 1819. (Novels)

Provincial Antiquities and Picturesque Scenery of Scotland. 10 parts. Edinburgh: Ballantyne, 1819-26. (History)

The Abbot. 3 vols. Edinburgh: Constable and Ballantyne, 1820. (Novel)

Ivanhoe: A Romance. 3 vols. Edinburgh: Constable, 1820. (Novel)

Miscellaneous Poems. Edinburgh: Constable, 1820. (Poetry)

The Monastery: A Romance. 3 vols. Edinburgh: Constable and Ballantyne, 1820. (Novel)

Kenilworth: A Romance. 3 vols. Edinburgh: Constable and Ballantyne, 1821. (Novel)

The Fortunes of Nigel. 3 vols. Edinburgh: Constable, 1822. (Novel)

Halidon Hill: A Dramatic Sketch. Edinburgh: Constable, 1822. (Play)

The Pirate. 3 vols. Edinburgh: Constable, 1822. (Novel)

Peveril of the Peak. 4 vols. Edinburgh: Constable, 1823. (Novel)

Quentin Durward. 3 vols. Edinburgh: Constable, 1823. (Novel)

St. Ronan's Well. 3 vols. Edinburgh: Fairburn, 1823. (Novel)

Redgauntlet: A Tale of the Eighteenth Century. 3 vols. Edinburgh: Constable, 1824. (Novel)

§*Tales of the Crusaders.* 4 vols. Edinburgh: Constable, 1825. (Novels)

A Letter to the Editor of the Edinburgh Weekly Journal, from Malachi Malagrowther, Esq.: On the Proposed Change of Currency and Other Late Alterations, as They Affect, or Are Intended to Affect, the Kingdom of Scotland. Edinburgh: Blackwood, 1826. (Letter)

A Second Letter to the Editor of the Edinburgh Weekly Journal, from Malachi Malagrowther, Esq.: On the Proposed Change of Currency and Other Later Alterations, as They Affect, or Are Intended to Affect, the Kingdom of Scotland. Edinburgh: Blackwood, 1826. (Letter)

A Third Letter to the Editor of the Edinburgh Weekly Journal, from Malachi Malagrowther, Esq.: On the Proposed Change of Currency and Other Late Alterations, as They Affect, or Are Intended to Affect, the Kingdom of Scotland. Edinburgh: Blackwood, 1826. (Letter)

Woodstock; or, The Cavalier. A Tale of the Year Sixteen Hundred and Fifty-One. 3 vols. Edinburgh: Constable, 1826. (Novel)

‖*Chronicles of the Canongate.* 2 vols. Edinburgh: Cadell, 1827. (Short stories)

The Life of Napoleon Buonaparte, Emperor of the French: With a Preliminary View of the French Revolution. 9 vols. London: Longman, Rees, Orme, Brown and Green, 1827. (Biography)

The Miscellaneous Prose Works of Sir Walter Scott, Bart. 6 vols. Edinburgh: Cadell, 1827. (Biographies, essays, fictional letters, and memoirs)

Tales of a Grandfather: Being Stories Taken from Scottish History. First-third series. 9 vols. Edinburgh: Cadell, 1827-30. (History)

#*Chronicles of the Canongate: Second Series.* 3 vols. Edinburgh: Cadell, 1828. (Novel)

Religious Discourses. By a Layman. London: Colburn, 1828. (Essays)

Anne of Geierstein; or, The Maiden of the Mist. 3 vols. Edinburgh: Cadell, 1829. (Novel)

Waverley Novels. 48 vols. Edinburgh: Cadell, 1829-33. (Novels)

The Doom of Devorgoil: A Melo-drama. Auchindrane; or, The Ayrshire Tragedy. Edinburgh: Cadell, 1830. (Plays)

The History of Scotland. 2 vols. London: Longman, Rees, Orme, Brown and Green, and Taylor, 1830. (History)

Letters on Demonology and Witchcraft. London: Murray, 1830. (Essays)

Tales of a Grandfather: Being Stories Taken from the History of France. 3 vols. Edinburgh: Cadell, 1831. (History)

****Tales of My Landlord: Fourth and Last Series, Collected and Arranged by Jedediah Cleishbotham, Schoolmaster and Parish-Clerk of Gandercleugh.* 4 vols. Edinburgh: Cadell, 1832. (Novels)

Miscellaneous Prose Works. 30 vols. Ed. John Gibson Lockhart. Edinburgh: Cadell, 1834-46. (Biographies, criticism, essays, fictional letters, and history)

The Waverley Novels: Centenary Edition. 25 vols. Edinburgh: Black, 1870-71. (Novels)

The Poetical Works of Sir Walter Scott, with the Author's Introduction and Notes. Ed. J. Logie Robertson. London: Frowde, 1894. (Poetry)

The Lives of the Novelists. London: Oxford UP, 1906. (Biographies)

Minstrelsy of the Scottish Border. Ed. Scott and Thomas Henderson. London: Harrap, 1931. (Songs)

The Letters of Sir Walter Scott. 12 vols. Ed. H. J. C. Grierson. London: Constable, 1932-37. (Letters)

The Journal of Sir Walter Scott. 3 vols. Ed. John Guthrie Tait and W. M. Parker. Edinburgh: Oliver and Boyd, 1939-49. (Diaries)

Private Letters of the Seventeenth Century. Oxford: Clarendon P, 1947. (Fiction)

The Life of John Dryden. Ed. Bernard Kreissman. Lincoln: U of Nebraska P, 1963. (Biography)

Sir Walter Scott on Novelists and Fiction. Ed. Ioan Williams. New York: Barnes and Noble, 1968. (Biographies and essays)

The Journal of Sir Walter Scott. Ed. W. E. K. Anderson. Oxford: Clarendon P, 1972. (Diaries)

The Prefaces to the Waverley Novels. Ed. Mark A. Weinstein. Lincoln: U of Nebraska P, 1978. (Prose)

The Letters of Malachi Malagrowther. Ed. P. H. Scott. Edinburgh: Blackwood, 1981. (Letters)

Scott on Himself: A Collection of the Autobiographical Writings of Sir Walter Scott. Ed. David Hewitt. Edinburgh: Scottish Academic, 1981. (Autobiography)

The Edinburgh Edition of the Waverley Novels. 28 vols. Ed. Hewitt. Edinburgh: Edinburgh UP, 1993-2009. (Novels)

*Comprises the novels *The Black Dwarf* and *The Tale of Old Mortality.*

†Comprises the novel *The Heart of Mid-Lothian.*

‡Comprises the novels *The Bride of Lammermoor* and *A Legend of Montrose.*

§Comprises the novels *The Betrothed* and *The Talisman.*

||Comprises the stories "The Highland Widow," "The Two Drovers," and "The Surgeon's Daughter."

#Comprises the novel *The Fair Maid of Perth.*

**Comprises the novels *Count Robert of Paris* and *Castle Dangerous.*

CRITICISM

John Wilson Croker (review date 1816)

SOURCE: Croker, John Wilson. Rev. of *The Antiquary,* by Sir Walter Scott. *Quarterly Review* 15 (1816): 125-39. Print.

[*In the following excerpted review, Croker criticizes the plot of* The Antiquary *but asserts that Scott "has not failed in the higher duty of the novelist—character, interest, eloquence." Croker places* The Antiquary *below the merits of* Waverley *but above those of* Guy Mannering.]

Having already delivered our opinion on the general character of *Waverley* and *Guy Mannering,* we have little or, indeed, nothing to add on that subject with regard to the present novel [*The Antiquary*], which professes to be a third brother of the same family. We doubt whether the voice of the public has ratified the preference which we so decidedly gave to *Waverley* over *Guy Mannering*; but a second perusal of both has convinced us that our judgment was not incorrect; and we are satisfied that the time is not far distant, if it be not already arrived, when the best claim of *Guy Mannering* on the attention of its readers will be the line of the title-page, in which it is described as the work of the author of *Waverley.*

The Antiquary is a work of precisely the same style; it unites to a considerable degree the merits of *Waverley* with the faults of the *Astrologer* [*Guy Mannering*]; and we have no hesitation in placing it, with the crowd of modern novels, below the former, and, with very few modern novels, above the latter.

The author tells us in his preface, that 'the present work completes a series of fictitious narratives intended to illustrate the manners of Scotland at three different periods. *Waverley* embraced the age of our fathers, *Guy Mannering* that of our own youth, and the *Antiquary* refers to the last ten years of the eighteenth century' (p. v). This may, in an occult sense, be true; but if it means, as it at first view imports to state, that the three novels have been written with this original intention, and that they were meant, in their first conception, to exhibit three different stages of society, we presume to doubt a little the literal authenticity of the statement.

In the first place we hardly think that so skilful an observer of manners could have imagined that in sixty years such changes could take place in national language, manners, habits, and character, as to warrant, *à priori,* the design of three distinct pictures. In the second place we find the author himself confessing that he has, '*especially* in his two last works, sought his principal personages in that class of society who are the last to feel the polish which assimilates to each other the manners of different nations' (p. vi); or, in other words, which change most slowly; and of course it follows that so far from endeavouring to illustrate the manners of three different periods, he has endeavoured to describe three different periods of which the manners were very much the same. And, finally, we appeal to our southern readers, at least, whether they can distinguish between the *Astrologer* and the *Antiquary,* and whether, with equal probability and appearance of truth, Jonathan Oldbuck, and his associates, might not have preceded in chronological order Guy Mannering and his dramatis personæ. We admit that, provided the author succeeds in amusing us, it is, in ordinary cases, of little consequence on what theory he may choose to proceed, or to say that he proceeds; but when he affects, as in the present instance, to write a work in some degree historical of men, and professedly historical of manners, it becomes our duty, as contemporaries, as well as reviewers, to withhold our testimony from what we consider a misrepresentation. We believe that the manners of Guy Mannering are as much the existing manners of the day as those of the Antiquary; and we are satisfied that the able and ingenious author, after having written these three very amusing romances, has indulged himself in a fanciful classification of them, and, waiving his higher claims, prefers the humbler one of writing on a *system,* which he never thought of, and in which, if he had designed it, we should have no hesitation in saying that he has, by his own confession, failed.

That, however, in which he has not failed is the higher duty of the novelist—character, interest, eloquence; something that hurries rather than leads you on; traits of feeling that melt, and strokes of humour that enliven the heart; all these he, in an eminent degree possesses; with them he combines so curious and accurate a delineation of human nature, that, through the Scottish garb, and the Scottish dialect, we distinguish the characteristic follies, foibles, and virtues, which belong to our own acquaintance, and to all mankind.

This is the peculiar merit of the author of these works, and no slight merit it is, for the want of it constitutes, as we have said on another occasion, the chief fault of some of our most eminent novelists, and the possession of it, the chief merit of the greatest poet that ever lived—of Shakespeare. His Romans, his Frenchmen, his Englishmen, are all *men*; the features of the national character are varied and amusing, but the great charm of his exhibitions of human life is, that, modified a little by their age and their country, his characters are all human beings, to whose pains and whose pleasures our own hearts are responsive, and to whose reasons and motives of action our own minds assent.

Our readers will recollect that our dissatisfaction with some parts of *Guy Mannering* was excited by the gratuitous introduction of supernatural agency, and that we said quodcunque ostendis mihi sic, incredulus odi. Even Shakspeare, who has been called the mighty magician, was never guilty of this mistake. His magic was employed in fairy land, as in the *Tempest,* and his ghosts and goblins in dark ages, as in *Macbeth* and *Hamlet.* When he introduces a witch in *Henry VI.* it is because, historically, his representation was true; when he exhibits the perturbed dreams of a murderer in *Richard III.* it was because his representation was morally probable; but he never thought of making these fancies actual agents in an historical scene. There are no ghosts in *Henry VIII* and no witches in the *Merry Wives of Windsor,* (except the merry ladies); and when, in one of his comedies, he chooses to wander out of nature, he modestly calls his drama a *Dream,* and mixes up fairies, witchery, mythology, and common life in a brilliant extravaganza which affects no historical nor even possible truth, and which pretends to represent neither actual nor possible nature. Not so *Guy Mannering,*— it brings down witchery and supernatural agency into our own times, not to be laughed at by the better informed, or credited by the vulgar; but as an active, effective, and real part of his machinery. It treats the supernatural agency not as a superstition, but as a truth; and the result is brought about, not by the imaginations of men deluded by a fiction, but by the actual operation of a miracle contrary to the opinion and belief of all the parties concerned.

From this blame the present work is not wholly free; there are two or three marvellous dreams and apparitions, upon which, we suspect, the author intended to ground some important parts of his denouement; but his taste luckily took fright, the apparitions do not contribute to the catastrophe, and they now appear in the work as marks rather of the author's own predilection to such machines, than as any assistance to him in the way of machinery.

This, then, is a manifest advantage which the present work has over *Guy Mannering*; and we own, that while we felt little or no interest in the fortunes of those whose fate was predestined, and whose happiness or woe depended not on their own actions, but on the prognostications of a beldam gipsy or a wild Oxonian, we are very differently affected for those who, like the characters in *Waverley* and the *Antiquary,* work out their own destinies, and must stand or fall (to use a common phrase) by their own virtue or folly, courage or weakness.

Some strong defects it must be admitted this work has; the story of the novel is not very novel, nor yet very probable. The heir of the earldom of Glenallan becomes enamoured of a relation, young, beautiful, and poor, who resides with his mother as a kind of companion. The countess, a proud and ferocious woman, indignant at the thoughts of so unprofitable an alliance for her son, to prevent it, imagines and propagates the monstrous story, that Miss Neville is— not the distant cousin of the young lord, but—his sister, an illegitimate daughter of his father. Although this horrible fiction came too late for the purpose of its inventor—for the marriage had already taken place—the horrors of the supposed discovery occasioned the premature birth of a boy, and the unhappy mother soon after puts an end to her own existence. The father, with a broken heart, and a restless conscience, estranges himself from the world, while the infant (escaping the fate to which it was doomed by its cruel grandame, by the humane treachery of one of her associates, and the secret generosity of its father's younger brother) survives to be restored, at the end of the third volume, to his rights, titles, and estates.

The protracted life of the dowager Lady Glenallan, and the fidelity of her copartners in guilt, deferred this explanation; and the brother of Lord Glenallan died in the belief that the boy, whom he educated as his own natural son, under the name of Lovell, was the offspring of the legitimate, but incestuous marriage of his brother and sister.

Circumstances had occurred to prove to the young Lovell that some strange mystery hung over his birth, and to create a resolution to endeavour to discover it. This led him to the neighbourhood of the family seats of his supposed father, and introduced him to the acquaintance of Jonathan Oldbuck, Esq. of Monkbarns, the Antiquary, and that of Sir Arthur Wardour, a gentleman of ancient family and encumbered fortune, whose daughter Isabella may be called the heroine of the piece, as she becomes in due season the wife of Lovell, who himself becomes Lord Geraldine, which (to the vehement indignation, no doubt, of all true Fitzgeralds) our author assigns as the second title to the House of Glenallan.

It will be seen from the summary, that though the antiquary gives his name to the work, he can hardly be called its hero; and, indeed, though the peculiarity of his character induces the author to produce him very frequently and forwardly in the scene, he has not any great share in the plot, and is evidently recommended to the high station which he occupies by his humour rather than his use. This character is, indeed, drawn with great truth and spirit; we should have praised its originality too, if we did not remember, with equal pleasure and affection, our admirable friend the Baron of Bradwardine, of whom Mr. Oldbuck sometimes reminds us, and never without at once gaining and losing a little by the recollection—gaining by his resemblance to that delightful portrait, and losing by a manifest inferiority to his striking original. In another character also, we have to observe a similar instance of self imitation—Edie Ochiltree, a kind of licensed beggar, is but a male Meg Merrilies; his character is, however, admirably drawn, and, in this case, we must confess, that we prefer the copy to the original. Edie is nothing supernatural, and therefore not so *striking* a personage as Meg; but there is great skill and great effect, as well as great simplicity and truth, in this portrait, and his contribution to the progress of the story is easy and probable, and, on that account, to us, more interesting, than the incantations and prophecies of the witch of the ashen wand.

We shall extract a description of Edie, not as the most amusing specimen we could produce, but because it is a living portrait of a singular class of the Scottish poor.

> He had the exterior appearance of a mendicant.—A slouched hat of huge dimensions; a long white beard, which mingled with his grizzled hair; an aged, but strongly marked and expressive countenance, hardened, by climate and exposure, to a right brick-dust complexion; a long blue gown, with a pewter badge on the right arm; two or three wallets, or bags, slung across his shoulder, for holding the different kinds of meal, when he received his charity in kind from those who were but a degree richer than himself,—all these marked at once a beggar by profession, and one of that privileged class which are called in Scotland the king's bedes-men, or, vulgarly, blue-gowns.

> —vol. i. p. 78

. . . . .

We hope we have now said enough to induce our readers to think this novel well worth reading, and we shall only add, that it is impossible to read it without feeling the highest respect for the talents, both gay and pathetic, of the author,

for the bold impartiality of his national delineations, and for the taste and discrimination with which he has rescued, from the overwhelming march of time and change of manners, these historical representations of a state of society, which even now is curious, but which in no long period will become 'a tale of other times'; and be examined not merely by the listless reader of novels but by the moralist and the antiquary.

It may be useful to apprise our readers (a circumstance which we unfortunately did not discover till we had got to the end of the third volume,) that there is there to be found a glossary, which is indeed almost indispensable to the understanding of nine-tenths of the work. Those ingenious persons, therefore, who begin to read novels by the latter end, have had, in this instance, a singular advantage over those who, like us, have laboured regularly on through the dark dialect of Anglified Erse.

If, as we expect, new editions of **Waverley, Guy Mannering,** and the **Antiquary,** should be required by the public, we suggest that the glossary should be placed conspicuously at the beginning of the first volume of the series.

J. R. Schultz (essay date 1913)

SOURCE: Schultz, J. R. "Sir Walter Scott and Chaucer." *Modern Language Notes* 28.8 (1913): 246-47. Print.

[*In the following essay, Schultz points out substantial inaccuracies in a quotation from Geoffrey Chaucer found in chapter 10 of* The Antiquary, *asserting that Scott's version of a stanza from "The Flower and the Leaf" is found in no published edition of the poem. Schultz provides a brief summary of other misquotations in various works by Scott.*]

In Chapter X of the **Antiquary,** Scott quotes a stanza from the poem formerly attributed to Chaucer, *The Flower and the Leaf.* Throughout the novel, as well as in others of his works, Chaucer is spoken of in terms of admiration, and even affection. A number of quotations from the *Canterbury Tales,* and from his other poems, are given in various places. In view of this evident fondness for Chaucer, it is interesting to note that the passage mentioned above is quoted incorrectly. His version follows:

> Lo! here be oakis grete, streight as a lime,
> Under the which the grass, so fresh of line,
> Be'th newly sprung—at eight foot or nine.
> Everich tree well from his fellow grew,
> With branches broad laden with leaves new,
> That sprongen out against the sonne sheene,
> Some golden red, and some a glad bright greene.

Compare this with Skeat's edition:

> In which were okës grete, streight as a lyne,
> Under the which the gras, so fresh of hew,
> Was newly spronge; and an eight foot or nyne

Every tree wel fro his felawe grew,
With braunches brode, laden with leves new,
That sprongen out ayein the sonnë shene,
Som very rede, and som a glad light grene.

It will be noted that there are several important differences, aside from mere variations in spelling. In lines 1 and 2, the change destroys the meaning, as well as the rime-scheme of the stanza. In the last line, *golden* is substituted for *very,* and *bright* for *light.* In line 3, *be'th* appears for *was,* and in 4, *everich* for *every.* In Scott, the stanza begins, *Lo! here be,* etc.; in Skeat, *In which were,* etc. In line 6, we read *against* for *ayein,* and *sheene* for *shene.* Of course the punctuation varies widely in different editions of Chaucer, but Scott's use of the period at the end of line 3 changes the sense entirely.

What, then, is the source of the novelist's version? Did his copy of Chaucer contain the stanza as he gives it? According to Miss Hammond's bibliography, there had been six editions of Chaucer, or collections of English poetry, containing *The Flower and the Leaf,* prior to the publication of the **Antiquary** in 1816. These editions were those of Speght, 1558 (reprinted in 1602 and 1687); Urry, 1721; Bell, in *The Poets of Great Britain,* 1782; Anderson, in *Works of the British Poets,* 1793; Chalmers, in *Works of the English Poets,* 1810; and Todd, in *Illustrations from the Lives and Writings of Gower and Chaucer,* 1810. To these may be added the modernization of Dryden, 1700. In none of these collections do the variations found in Scott's quotation appear. The spelling varies somewhat in these different works, but with reference to the instances given, as well as in certain other cases, Scott's reading does not reproduce any of them. It seems evident that Scott did not copy *verbatim* from any existing edition.

Did he, then, quote inaccurately from memory? An incident is related in Lockhart's *Life of Scott,* and also in Hogg's *Anecdotes of Scott,* which shows that he had an excellent memory for verse, being able to quote long passages with ease. This is incidentally confirmed by a letter of his, quoted by William Platt in *Notes and Queries* 6.4.279:

> The scraps of poetry which have been in most cases tacked to the beginning of the chapters of my novels are sometimes quoted, either from reading or memory, but in the general case, are pure invention. ... I drew on my memory as long as I could, and when that failed, eked it out with invention.

Is it possible that in the instance we are considering, he relied on his memory without verification, and failed to quote correctly?

It seems to be commonly agreed that Scott is not at all accurate in his historical facts. Among others who have pointed out historical errors are N. W. Senior in his *Essays on Fiction,* Yonge in his *Life of Scott,* and W. H. Hudson in his *Sir Walter Scott.* As to his scholarship in general, Rev.

G. R. Gleig, in his *Life of Sir Walter Scott* (p. 25) has this to say:

> He never took the trouble to make himself an accurate scholar. Enough for him if he could extract the meaning, or take in the beauties of his author. For whether it was an ancient book which came his way—whether an Italian, a Spanish, a German, or a Latin classic, his sole object in perusing it was to pick out from it the ideas which recommended themselves to his taste and judgment. In no single instance did he dream of making it the means of ascertaining far less of settling, the niceties of idiom or of grammar.

In several numbers of *Notes and Queries,* cases of misquotation in Scott's works have been pointed out. In 4.5.577, "F" cites a case where a passage from the *Gospel of Saint Matthew* is quoted inaccurately in both **Waverley** and the **Abbot,** differing in each place. He gives other misquotations, from the *Merchant of Venice* in the **Abbot,** and from *Macbeth* in the **Monastery.** In 4.5.486, the same writer cites two cases from the **Bride of Lammermoor,** and says there are many others in his novels. In 4.6.200, J. S. Udall notes a misquotation from *Saint Matthew* in the **Heart of Mid-Lothian,** and J. H. J. Oakley in 4.10.184 gives three Latin passages misquoted in the **Antiquary.** The last named writer remarks:

> When the author of **Waverley** described the Baron of Bradwardine as 'a scholar according to the scholarship of Scotchmen—that is, his learning was more diffuse than accurate, and he was rather a reader than a grammarian,' he has given us a pretty true account of his own scholarship.

An examination of other quotations in the **Antiquary** shows that several passages not hitherto remarked are also incorrect in detail. In quoting from *II Henry IV,* he has *fico* for *foutre;* five lines from *I Henry IV* are quoted correctly as a heading for Chapter XVI, but are given as from Part II. In Chapter III he quotes from *Hudibras,* and adds two lines which are not a part of the passage. Quotations from *King John, Romeo and Juliet,* and Wordsworth's *Fountain,* are also inaccurate. In **Woodstock,** elsewhere in the **Antiquary,** and in his review of Godwin's *Life of Chaucer,* quotations from Chaucer vary considerably from the standard editions.

Considering Scott's frequent allusions to Chaucer, he should have known the poet well. In the *Edinburgh Review* we find an extensive review of *Godwin's Life of Chaucer.* His comparisons are mainly with Tyrwhitt's edition, which is also mentioned in his review of Ellis' *Specimens of the Early English Poets.* But Tyrwhitt does not reprint *The Flower and the Leaf,* and mentions it only to doubt its authenticity. Scott mentions Warton's *History of English Poetry,* but this does not contain the poem, though there is a discussion of it. In his edition of Dryden's works, he expresses his admiration for *The Flower and the Leaf,* especially of Dryden's modernization.

If Scott occasionally misquoted, from undue reliance on his memory, he is not alone in this respect among English writers; but such extensive variations from his original as are disclosed by the passage from the *Antiquary* are not a little surprising.

Walter Graham (essay date 1915)

SOURCE: Graham, Walter. "Notes on Sir Walter Scott." *Modern Language Notes* 30.1 (1915): 14-16. Print.

[*In the following essay, Graham expands on J. R. Schultz's earlier observations concerning Scott's misquotations, providing additional information about Scott's use of chapter headings in* The Antiquary *and other novels.*]

In a recent article in *Modern Language Notes*[1] attention is directed to an interesting misquotation of Chaucer made by Sir Walter Scott in the *Antiquary.* The passage under consideration is the motto before the tenth chapter, and the author of the article reminds us that Scott was frequently inaccurate in quotation, especially in the matter of mottoes for chapter headings.

Another even more interesting example of this careless-ness in citation occurs in *Rob Roy,* his next novel, at the beginning of the eighteenth chapter.[2] The motto in this case is

> And hurry, hurry, off they rode,
> As fast as fast might be;
> Hurra, Hurra, the dead can ride,
> Dost fear to ride with me?

It is credited to Bürger (signed "Burgher" in the first edition), and the lines are from the *Lenore.* The quotation as Scott has used it is not to be found in his own rendering of the ballad (1796) nor in that of any other translator. Yet all the lines are found in different parts of Scott's trans-lation. The first two occur in the thirty-seventh stanza of *William and Helen* as

> And, hurry! hurry! off they rode,
> As fast as fast might be;[3]

and the only difference is in the punctuation. The last two lines of the motto are found in the forty-ninth stanza of the translation in inverted order and as the second and third lines of the quatrain. The entire stanza is

> Dost fear? dost fear? The moon shines clear,
> Dost fear to ride with me?—
> Hurrah! Hurrah! the dead can ride!—
> O William, let them be!

Scott's recollection of his own lines may have been modi-fied by a reminiscence of Taylor's version which was published the same year as his own, for in the latter the last two lines of the motto appear in the order quoted and, save for one word, in the same language.

> Hurrah! the dead can ride apace;
> Dost fear to ride with mee?[4]

Perhaps it may be possible to suggest a reason why Scott should be thinking of the ballad at this time. *Rob Roy* is considered to some extent autobiographical, and in Miss Vernon is generally recognized a sweetheart of Scott's youth. With this fact in view, I venture to suggest that the passage,

> 'There is a great deal of it,' said she, glancing along the paper and interrupting the sweetest sounds which mortal ears can drink in,—those of a youthful poet's verses, namely, read by the lips which are dearest to him.[5]

may have been based upon his own experience when the lady he was fond of read his translation of the *Lenore.* If there is any truth in this supposition, Scott may have had in mind the incident which occurs in *Rob Roy* only two chapters before the *Lenore* quotation, when he wrote the motto. The remarkable shuffling of lines can easily be accounted for by his habitual inaccuracy.[6]

Apropos of Scott's freedom in quotation, we are told by Lockhart[7] that in correcting the proof sheets of the *Anti-quary,* the novelist first began to give his chapters mottoes of his own invention. The biographer says:

> On one occasion he happened to ask John Ballantyne, who was sitting by him, to hunt for a particular passage in Beaumont and Fletcher. John did as he was bid, but did not succeed in discovering the lines. 'Hang it, Johnnie,' cried Scott, 'I believe I can make a motto sooner than you will find one.' He did so accordingly, and from that hour, whenever memory failed to suggest an appropriate epi-graph, he had recourse to the inexhaustible mines of '*old play*' and '*old ballad.*'

The motto alluded to is probably at the head of chapter thirty:

> Who is he?—One that for the lack of land
> Shall fight upon the water—he hath challenged
> Formerly the grand whale; and by his titles
> Of Leviathan, Behemoth, and so forth.
> He tilted with a sword-fish—Marry, sir,
> The aquatic had the best—the argument
> Still galls our champion's breech.
>
> *—Old Play*[8]

All the mottoes of the chapters preceding this, with the single exception noted above, are credited to known au-thors; but ten of the fourteen following are signed "Old Play." A further examination of the novels shows that only one motto was chosen from an unknown or fictitious source before Scott wrote the *Antiquary.* This one is before the forty-eighth chapter of *Guy Mannering,* and the signature, "Old Border Ballad," merely indicates that he had forgotten what he derived it from. As a matter of fact, he was quoting the thirty-fourth stanza of the ballad, *Kinmont Willie,* in-cluded in his own collection, **Minstrelsy of the Scottish**

Border.[9] In novels following the *Antiquary,* Scott quoted from "Old Play" ninety-one times, "Old Ballad" twenty times, "Old Song" seven times, "Anonymous" (which was probably employed in the same way) twenty-five times, "Old Poem" once, and "Ancient Drama" once; and in nearly every case the motto is believed by Dennis and other editors to be the novelist's own work.

Notes

1. J. R. Schultz, "Sir Walter Scott and Chaucer," *Mod. Lang. Notes,* XXVIII, 246.

2. I am indebted to Professor O. F. Emerson for this and other items.

3. *The Poetical Works of Walter Scott,* ed. John Dennis (Aldine Edition). London, George Bell & Sons, 1892, vol. V, p. 97.

4. Cf. *The Annual Register,* London, 1796; vol. XXXVIII, p. 499, St. 40. The two lines are repeated in St. 49 and St. 50. For this reference I am under obligation to Prof. Emerson's paper on the translations of Bürger's *Lenore,* read at the last meeting of the Modern Language Association.

5. *Rob Roy* (Centenary Edition), Edinburgh, Adam and Charles Black, 1890, p. 200.

6. See circumstances of his translating *Lenore*:—Lockhart, *Memoirs of the Life of Sir Walter Scott,* vol. I, chap. VII, pp. 216-7 (Cambridge Edition), 1902. See also Adam Scott, *Sir Walter Scott's First Love,* pp. 51-2. Edinburgh, 1896.

7. *Ed. cit.,* vol. III, p. 106 (chap. XXXVII).

8. The *Antiquary,* p. 280 (*ed. cit.*). The epigraph of chapter twenty-six, which later is signed "Old Ballad," appears without signature in the first edition.

9. *Guy Mannering,* chap. XLVIII, p. 344 (*ed. cit.*). *Minstrelsy of the Scottish Border,* vol. II, p. 64 (Ed. Henderson, Edinburgh, 1902). The epigraphs of chapters six and forty-five were not signed in the first edition. Later, they were credited to "*As You Like It*" and "*Shenstone.*" *Waverley* has no mottoes.

John Robert Moore (essay date 1944)

SOURCE: Moore, John Robert. "Scott's *Antiquary* and Defoe's *History of Apparitions.*" *Modern Language Notes* 59.8 (1944): 550-51. Print.

[In the following essay, Moore points out the similarities between an episode in The Antiquary *concerning a chest of silver bullion and a story told in Daniel Defoe's* History of Apparitions *(1727). Moore provides relevant passages from the two texts for comparison.]*

Critics have usually agreed in considering *The Antiquary* "a novel of contemporary life, a story of familiar charac-ters."[1] But on this showing, what explanation is one to give for the strange episode of the chest of silver bullion which was dug up amid the ruins of the old priory, together with the quest for "Search No. 2" into which Edie Ochiltree lured the Adept at midnight?

"This was a very romantic, foolish exploit," remarked the matter-of-fact Oldbuck. ". . . I think your contrivance succeeded better than such a clumsy one deserved, Edie."[2]

Like the "Supposed Apparition of Morton" which Scott himself said was "taken from a story in the *History of Apparitions* written by Daniel Defoe" (*Old Mortality,* Note 35), this episode seems to have been suggested by a tale in *The History of Apparitions.* A comparison of the incidents will serve to indicate the probable indebtedness:

The History and Reality of Apparitions[3]	*The Antiquary*[4]
A peddler was led by an apparition, late at night, to "a great stone." The next night the peddler returned to the indicated place with a spade and a pickaxe, and he dug until he struck a large chest. "He doubled his diligence when he came to the chest and, with great labour," he lifted up the chest and found it full of silver. He carried off both the silver and the chest, and afterwards he used the chest to make a hatch to his shop door. An old gentleman noticed on the new hatch (the former chest) an inscription in "old Saxon English in the ancient Gothic character," which might be read, Where this once stood, Stands another twice as good. The peddler was incited by this inscription to return to the original hiding place at night, and after digging deeper than before, he found another chest, "not so big as the other, but richer; for as the first was full of silver, so this was full of gold."	The mendicant Edie Ochiltree persuaded a searching party to dig with pickaxes and shovels below a "muckle stane" in the priory ruins. Five feet down, Edie struck some object with his pikestaff; and the laborers, who had deserted the pit, scrambled back and dug until they had unearthed a chest, so heavy that all hands were needed to lift it out. It was found to contain silver, which was carried away by the searching party. But Edie laid the lid of the chest aside, and when the others had left he pointed out to the Adept that the inscription on the lid "in the ordinary black letter" spelled "Search No. 1." When the adept surmised the existence of a "Search No. 2," Edie added that he had always heard that the legendary buried treasure contained much gold. If the second chest, he said, "be but—say the tenth part o' the size o' the kist No. 1., it will double its value, being filled wi' gowd instead of silver." At midnight Edie and the Adept came with pickaxe and shovel, and they dug in the original hole until the Adept broke the pickaxe against a foundation stone of the priory ruins.

It is characteristic of Scott that his version of the episode (despite its suspense, which sustains interest in the story while the principal events must mark time) was narrated in a tone of broad comedy, with its main emphasis on Edie's mischievous ridicule of the pretensions of the Adept. Furthermore, the mystery of the inscription on the lid was later explained away, when Oldbuck recalled that the king's ship on the coast (from which the chest had been landed) was named the *Search.*

Notes

1. John Buchan, *Sir Walter Scott* (London, 1932), p. 149.

2. *The Antiquary,* ch. 44 (Dryburgh ed., pp. 399, 400).

3. Tegg ed., pp. 378-382.

4. Chapters 23-25 (Dryburgh ed., pp. 218-236).

Robin Mayhead (essay date 1971)

SOURCE: Mayhead, Robin. "The Problem of Coherence in *The Antiquary." Scott Bicentenary Essays: Selected Papers Read at the Sir Walter Scott Bicentenary Conference.* Ed. Alan Bell. Edinburgh: Scottish Academic, 1973. 134-46. Print.

[*In the following essay, first presented at a conference in 1971, Mayhead provides an overview of relevant critical opinions regarding* The Antiquary *and then responds to the frequent charge that the novel lacks a principle of coherence. Mayhead regards the work as neither "happy" nor "unhappy" but rather as "a novel with a somber vision underlying much extravagant comedy."*]

It was almost inevitable, I suppose, that this discussion should start with a quick review of comments made on *The Antiquary* by gentlemen who are playing a very prominent part in this conference. For this book is in many ways the Cinderella of the Scottish *Waverley Novels.* I am not thinking of readers who have been frankly hostile towards it, or those who have patronized it as a work containing some marvellous 'bits' in a welter of incoherence. No, I have in mind the reader who rates it high, who may (like the author himself) have a special affection for it, but who may equally have serious reservations which make it rather hard for him to say convincingly just why he includes the book among Scott's best. I myself, at any rate, have been such a reader, and I want now to sketch my reactions to the following comments.

First there is Professor Robert C. Gordon in his valuable study *Under Which King?,* who closes his third chapter with these words: '*The Antiquary* is a very odd novel.' Indeed it is; and he tabulates with exemplary clarity the book's 'instances where "heterogeneous elements are yoked by violence together,'" and its 'discordant juxtapositions and "purposes mistook."' I am interested in Professor Gordon's view of the heterogeneity he so vividly brings out. 'These anticlimaxes, dissonances, obscurities suggest,' he says, 'a sort of careless mannerism, as though Scott were mocking the whole idea of coherence and perspective'; and he remarks a declining coherence of design 'in the conventional sense' through the first three *Waverley Novels,* observing that 'It would seem that the closer Scott came to his own age the more chaotic the world became for him.' He has, moreover, the useful suggestion that the book's oddities are connected with a basic 'discord' in the figure of Oldbuck himself: 'the authority on the past [who] does not know the past,' with the consequent reflection that 'the impulse to study the past may involve the use of tools that in themselves remove the past farther from us.'

That, I am sure, is one of the things this novel is telling us, but it does not take me as far as I feel I need to go. If I have the nagging impression that *The Antiquary,* odd though it is, really does have a principle of coherence somewhere, I do not think it is being inappropriately 'Jamesian' to want something rather more worked out and explained.

Now for Professor Daiches, in that famous essay of 1951, 'Scott's Achievement as a Novelist.' For him *The Antiquary* clearly presents no real problem of coherence. Its 'prevailing atmosphere,' he tells us, 'is comic'; and although the 'melodramatic Glenallan episode in this novel and the drowning of the young fisherman Steenie Mucklebackit give a sense of depth and implication to the action … they do not alter its essential atmosphere.'

No one is likely to play down the comedy in *The Antiquary,* but I wonder how many readers have queried pretty strongly, as I have, the contention that comedy constitutes the book's 'essential atmosphere.' Is it enough to 'fit in' the Glenallan and Mucklebackit strands of interest simply by saying that they 'give a sense of depth and implication'? May one not be right in suspecting that the book's 'atmosphere' (if one is going to use that word) is something both more complex and more compelling? And although I heartily agree with Professor Daiches that the 'plot' of *The Antiquary* hardly counts *as* plot, I find it hard to accept another of his views: that it is 'essentially a static novel.' Hard, because the oddities to which Professor Gordon rightly points engender in the book a textural 'irritation' and agitation quite incompatible, to my mind, with any notion of stasis. But I shall return to Professors Gordon and Daiches in a minute or two.

Professor Edgar Johnson, in his new biographical and critical study, offers a more persuasive reading of *The Antiquary*: more persuasive in that he makes the novel seem a more unified thing than does Professor Gordon, while he is at the same time more aware of its heterogeneity than Professor Daiches. He does not consider the book to be without flaws, but his over-all view is expressed in the contention that 'Far from being a cluttered ragbag of a story, like Oldbuck's study and its historical lore, the novel when truly understood is seen to have the clearest thematic unity.' He accepts the heterogeneity of the Glenallan business alongside so much that is comic, but insists that a coherent design is made out of it all: 'Both the melodrama of these events and the comedy of Monkbarns and Edie Ochiltree are in fact essentially fused into the significant action of the novel, which explores the way in which the present is rooted in the past and rectifies the errors of that present by putting it into a sound relationship with the past.' This, then, is the principle of 'thematic unity.'

Now, it would be both untrue and unfair for me to say that when I hear the word 'thematic' I reach for my revolver. Untrue because I would have to shoot myself; unfair because we must all be grateful to Professor Johnson, here and elsewhere in his critical chapters, for giving such sensible guidance as to what Scott's novels are well and truly *about*. I am sure, however, that he would agree that the thematic approach alone can cover a multitude of critical sins, or at any rate be at best a partial index to the kind of effect that a novel makes as a whole. To get our bearings by trying to say what a novel is most centrally about is the *start*; it can hardly be expected to do the whole job.

Professor Johnson makes it plain that he does not consider it as doing the whole job. He doesn't suppose that to proclaim *The Antiquary* unified on the principle of the present's being rooted in the past and the errors of the present being rectified by putting it into a sound relationship with the past is the ultimate critical insight which 'accounts for' the impression that book makes upon us. He is firm, or at least he tries to be, about real or suspected weaknesses in the book. He has something to say, for instance, about the apparently stilted language put into the mouths of Lovel and Miss Wardour, but although he is willing to agree that there is some reason genuinely to feel that Scott has not quite succeeded here, he reminds us that 'in imaginative literature all dialogue is a matter of convention and of adjustment to an established atmossphere.' That is well said, for it voices a truth too often forgotten, and I hope my saying this will remove possible offence from the remark of a moment ago that Professor Johnson is *trying* to be firm about the book's debit account. I was not meaning to patronize, but rather to draw attention to certain difficulties he seems to have in facing this admittedly odd novel as honestly as he can. Though he is inclined to feel that the language of Lovel and Isabel Wardour doesn't quite come off, his reminder about the conventional nature of all literary dialogue is an important qualification of that feeling. And take another item in his catalogue of the book's faults: 'For some readers the horseplay of Edie's tricks on Dousterswivel is too farcically out of tone with the more serious parts of the story and Dousterswivel so ridiculously transparent a swindler as to make Sir Arthur exaggeratedly credulous.' I underline those words '*For some readers*.' Professor Johnson is too honest a commentator to assert categorically that the Dousterswivel element definitely *is,* for *all* readers, a damaging flaw.

Clearly, despite his firmness about the book's 'thematic unity,' *The Antiquary* does present for him some problems of coherence, problems which the thematic approach does not completely solve. And for my part I have to say that although I find his comments very useful, Professor Johnson does not, for me, quite convey a sense of the book's 'established atmosphere,' to use his own phrase.

This brings us back to Professor Daiches, and his remark about 'the prevailing atmosphere' of *The Antiquary.* Well, 'atmosphere,' like 'thematic,' is a word which can cover a multitude of critical sins. I wonder how many of us here who are teachers have told our pupils to be drastically economical in its use—or even not to use it at all! Still, it is probably in this case the most useful general word, even if it is too vague to do duty for very long. The most useful general word, because to speak of this novel's prevailing or established 'tone' wouldn't do. For it seems to me that the main reason why we have to agree with Professor Gordon that it is 'a very odd novel' is that it contains so wide a variety of differing tones. It is not just a case of finding the Dousterswivel business 'out of tone with the more serious parts of the story,' but of finding umpteen things 'out of tone' with one another. Where, then, do we go from here?

It seems to me that each of the critics we have been looking at can give us a clue. First there is Professor Gordon's remark that the book's oddities 'suggest a sort of careless mannerism,' and I underline '*mannerism*' particularly. Then there is, once more, Professor Johnson's salutary reminder about literary 'convention and adjustment,' and I would here extend those words to apply to more things than dialogue, which he has specifically under discussion, especially the word '*convention*.' Thirdly comes a clue contained in Professor Daiches's claim that the book's 'prevailing atmosphere is comic.' If we query this, what do we substitute for the word '*comic*'? And what could one mean by 'the prevailing atmosphere,' if we accept that term for the meantime? Finally, back to Professor Gordon and his observation that the first three *Waverley Novels* are in declining order of coherence of design '*in the conventional sense.*' Suppose *The Antiquary* has a coherence that is quite *unconventional* in the sense that it does not conform to familiar notions of unity in plot or consistency in tone, but highly *conventional* in its own terms—in the sense, that is to say, that it is very firmly based on conventions of a kind different from those of the more familiar kind of eighteenth- or nineteenth-century novel, but still, very definitely, *conventions.*

There is little time for me to follow clues very far, but I shall try, in terms of the text, to suggest as many ways as possible of seeing where they lead us. I will start with the question of 'prevailing' or 'essential' atmosphere. Near the beginning of his excellent but all too short study *The Author of Waverley,* Mr. D. D. Devlin reminds us of 'a steady pessimism' colouring everything that Scott wrote, and the presence in his background of Dr. Johnson, especially the Johnson of *The Vanity of Human Wishes.* Now, consider this from Monkbarns in Chapter 16 of *The Antiquary*:

> ... To have lost a friend by death while your mutual regard was warm and unchilled, while the tear can drop unembittered by any painful recollection of coldness or distrust or treachery, is perhaps an escape from a more heavy dispensation. Look around you—how few do you see grow old in the affections of those with whom their early friendships were formed! Our sources of common pleasure gradually dry up as we journey on through the vale of Bacha, and we hew out to ourselves other reservoirs, from which the first companions of our pilgrimage are excluded;—jealousies, rivalries, envy, intervene to separate others from our side, until none remain but those who are connected with us rather by habit than predilection, or who, allied more in blood than in disposition, only keep the old man company in his life, that they may not be forgotten at his death—

There we find not only the spirit of *The Vanity of Human Wishes* but the cadences of *Rasselas,* and even something very like an echo of the first of the stanzas on the death of Robert Levett:

> Condemn'd to Hope's delusive mine,
> As on we toil from day to day,
> By Sudden Blasts, or Slow Decline,
> Our Social Comforts drop away.

It would, of course, be wrong to take Mr. Oldbuck's gloomy musings as an expression of Scott's 'central philosophy' or some such phrase. It is a commonplace that, if Monkbarns is in some ways very close to Scott, the author at the same time places him at a critical distance. I am not proposing, either, that we should invert Professor Daiches's statement and say that the prevailing atmosphere of *The Antiquary* is 'tragic.' I do suggest, however, that the note of Johnsonian pessimism in far more prevalent, and is far more of a unifying factor, than discussion of the book in terms of 'comedy of manners,' for example, would imply. We all know that comedy of manners is one major ingredient of the book. We note and enjoy the counterpointing of the different attitudes towards the past, and their social-historical implications, represented by Monkbarns and Sir Arthur Wardour. We laugh at the anachronistic notions of honour and gentility exemplified by Hector M'Intyre's insistence on a duel, its bluster and bravado so absurdly parodied in his attempt on the seal. These things, too, are all in keeping with what our three critics agree to be a central preoccupation of the book: wrong-headed or right-minded ways of looking at the past, and their bearing upon the present. But does comedy of manners, even with those important implications, account for this novel's remarkable emotional quality? It is precisely this element in *The Antiquary* that even the best critical discussions underestimate or even ignore. The objection is not that they underplay the Glenallan or Mucklebackit episodes, but rather that they do not really bring out the very important truth that such things are the most overtly 'serious' expression of what we might call a 'prevailing emotional atmosphere' in the novel; though

Professor Johnson does see them as thematically linked with the comic parts. And I suggest that this atmosphere is coloured throughout by the Johnsonian pessimism which, again, has its most overtly serious expression in the utterance of Monkbarns I quoted a minute or two back.

But let us now get away from the word 'atmosphere,' and talk in terms of the specific. What is it that unites so many episodes in the novel, so many activities, interests, convictions, and ambitions, over and above the thematic links brought out by Professor Johnson? Surely it is the feeling of *futility* which surrounds them. *The Antiquary* seems to me a far more powerful *Vanity Fair* than Thackeray's. Think of the catalogue. Mr. Oldbuck's antiquarian pursuits are not invariably misguided and futile (the point would be lost if they were), but how often they are, as he acknowledges from time to time himself! Sir Arthur Wardour is surrounded by futility, in his ancestral bluster, and in his gulling by Dousterswivel. The whole Glenallan story, until its final determination, has been a saga of futile passions and futile guilts. One of the most powerful scenes in the book is the opening of Chapter 34, where Monkbarns finds Mucklebackit making the futile attempt to work on his boat, as though no tragedy had befallen his family; and there is an echo of the bereaved father in *Rasselas* when we are told that 'Oldbuck, beaten from the pride of his affected cynicism, would not willingly have had any one by upon that occasion to quote to him his favourite maxims of the Stoic philosophy.' This scene is the tragic expression of that same 'vanitas vanitatum' which has its farcical manifestation in the contemptible antics of Dousterswivel, right at the other end of the gamut. Some readers with whom I have discussed *The Antiquary* have complained that there is no particular reason why the death of Steenie should have been introduced, seeing it as a gratuitous occurrence whose inclusion seems to be merely an injection of seriousness, of 'tragic relief,' to give the novel ballast, so to speak. But the drowning of Steenie is *meant* to be seen as gratuitous, as a piece of futile waste. Moreover, returning to the scene we were discussing, we can see how the episode links up with this book's concern with different ways of looking at the past. Sir Arthur's genealogy and Mr. Oldbuck's 'praetorium' represent two ways, and they look pretty silly, as do the latter's 'favourite maxims of the Stoic philosophy,' alongside Mucklebackit's overwhelming recollection of a past which has meant so much to him, in the context of a grey present whose full reality he can as yet hardly grasp. 'The large drops fell fast from [Oldbuck's] own eyes, as he begged the father, who was now melted at recollecting the bravery and generous sentiments of his son, to forbear useless sorrow, and led him by the arm towards his own home, where another scene awaited our Antiquary.' That other scene, of course, is his meeting with Lord Glenallan, and the juxtaposition of the Mucklebackit and Glenallan stories is interesting and important. It is a mistake to think of them as possessing the same kind of seriousness. The whole Glenallan story is 'serious' enough for the Earl and for old Elspeth, and the outcome is momentous for Lovel; but its farrago of squalid and ultimately futile intrigue puts it in a very different category from the stark catastrophe of the Mucklebackits' loss. The Glenallan story is melodrama; the other is not. If the two stories are at the most serious end of the scale that has Dousterswivel at the other extreme, the Glenallan theme is already well on the way down. And if these stories embody the sorrow and futility of wasted lives, in their different ways, we have another sort of futility in Chapter 30, which leads into those chapters where their full impact is felt; Chapter 30, in which Monkbarns and Hector M'Intyre discuss Ossian (a parody of useless scholarship) and the latter makes his attempt on the seal (a parody of heroic bluster). All these chapters, seen individually, are very different in feeling; yet what I have proposed as the book's over-all emotional quality permits them to cohere. And I suggest that the copresence of all this apparently heterogeneous material, not, however, 'yoked by *violence* together,' is the reason for the complex effect, the impression of being really 'stretched,' that a careful reading of *The Antiquary* produces.

Here I want to go back to Professor Gordon's remark about 'careless mannerism.' He does not, of course, mean 'careless' in the sense of 'slipshod,' but is thinking rather of the urbane ease of the writer introducing materials whose heterogeneity he is quite aware of, without overmuch concern for tidiness. Now, one needs to keep a sense of proportion when dealing with Scott. If one must beware of 'condemning the self-effacing Scott out of his own mouth,' as Professor Hart warns, one must also heed Professor Gordon's caution not to go to the opposite extreme of supposing him to be too self-conscious an artist. We know that he could be 'careless' in a quite ordinary sense, and relied on James Ballantyne to clear up the mess. But if he didn't plan his novels with the minuteness of a Henry James constructing his scenario for *The Ambassadors,* he was far from 'careless' about the *effect* a book would have, as his letters and *Journal* [*The Journal of Sir Walter Scott*] show. And if such concern is not a concern with *art,* in the most important sense, I do not know what is.

Perhaps I am asking too much of Professor Gordon's use of 'careless,' and in any case I said a while back that it was 'mannerism' I wanted to underline. I still want to, as it strikes me as pointing very happily to the way in which this book works. I am thinking of the word, as I take Professor Gordon to have been, as one uses it to refer to a type of painting, or architecture, or the French 'precieux' poets, or (with reservations, because of their variety) to the English Metaphysicals. Now, I am not about to claim that *The Antiquary* is a Metaphysical poem! At the same time I suggest that the ways in which Marvell's *Coy Mistress* or Donne's third *Satyre* 'stretch' the reader are not altogether absurdly remote from the impression produced by this novel. More to the point, though, is to think of writers Scott knew especially well: Swift, Dryden, Ben Jonson,

and, once again, the Samuel Johnson of *The Vanity of Human Wishes.* Blandly to dub them 'mannerist' would be extravagant; on the other hand they are all remarkable for compelling unity on very disparate materials, and demand of the reader particular flexibility and attentive vigilance. *The Vanity of Human Wishes* encompasses a great variety of tones. A long time ago T. S. Eliot quoted two couplets from it to demonstrate that Johnson himself was not averse to heterogeneity, whatever he said about the Metaphysicals.

If I made perhaps too much of the word 'careless' it is because Scott seems to me to have been very decidedly aware of what he was doing in *The Antiquary.* The novel abounds in little oblique references to its assorted ingredients. Take this, from Chapter 19, where Sir Arthur, Mr. Oldbuck, and Dr. Blattergowl are hard at it: 'But here the Baronet and Mr. Oldbuck having recovered their wind, and continued their respective harangues, the three *strands* of the conversation, to speak the language of a rope-work, were again twined together into one undistinguishable string of confusion.' Less bold, but still telling in this novel's context, is Oldbuck's lament in Chapter 22 on the loss of the poem he imagines Lovel to have conceived, 'with notes illustrative of all that is clear, and all that is dark, and all that is neither dark nor clear, but hovers in dusky twilight in the region of Caledonian antiquities.' Consider, moreover, the book's studied insistence upon the miscellaneous and incongruous in any number of applications. There is the wild miscellany of objects in Monkbarns's study in Chapter 3, to take the most obvious case; but hardly less striking is the incongruous appearance of his sister in Chapter 6:

> The elderly lady rustled in silks and satins, and bore upon her head a structure resembling the fashion in the ladies' memorandum-book for the year 1770—a superb piece of architecture—not much less than a modern Gothic castle, of which the curls might represent the turrets, the black pins the *chevaux de frize,* and the lappets the banners.

> The face, which, like that of the ancient statues of Vesta, was thus crowned with towers, was large and long, and peaked at nose and chin, and bore, in other respects, such a ludicrous resemblance to the physiognomy of Mr. Jonathan Oldbuck, that Lovel, had they not appeared at once, like Sebastian and Viola in the last scene of the 'Twelfth Night,' might have supposed that the figure before him was his old friend masquerading in female attire.

Less ridiculous than Monkbarns in drag, but still gloriously miscellaneous, is Griselda's ghost story about Rab Tull the town clerk and the 'marvellous communication about the grand law-plea between us and the feuars at the Mussel-craig,' with its linking of the supernatural and the most mundanely practical. And while we are on the subject of the Green Chamber, consider the contrast between Lovel's dream (if 'dream' it is), with all the rather stock 'Gothic' associations it conjures up, and the words of the song which wakes him—stock too, in their sentiments, but giving to the voice of Time crisply urbane Augustan accents far removed from the sensational:

Why sit'st thou by that ruin'd hall,
    Thou aged carle so stern and grey?
Dost thou its former pride recall,
    Or ponder how it passed away?

'Know'st thou not me!' the Deep Voice cried;
    'So long enjoyed, so oft misused—
Alternate, in thy fickle pride,
    Desired, neglected, and accused?'

On another level there is the meeting of incongruities when the Wardours meet Edie Ochiltree on 'The beach under Halket-head, rapidly diminishing in extent by the encroachments of a spring-tide and a north-west wind, ... a neutral field, where even a justice of peace and a strolling mendicant might meet upon terms of mutual forbearance.' It is something Edie is quick to underline, indeed, as the three seem to face certain death, in answer to a particularly sad piece of futility from Sir Arthur:

'Good man,' said Sir Arthur, 'can you think of nothing?—of no help?—I'll make you rich—I'll give you a farm—I'll'—

'Our riches will be soon equal,' said the beggar, looking out upon the strife of the waters—'they are sae already; for I hae nae land, and you would give your fair bounds and barony for a square yard of rock that would be dry for twal hours.'

Or, to return to comedy, take Mr. Oldbuck's disquisition on the meaning of a '*shathmont's-length,*' at the conclusion of the alarming episode. To explain it psychologically as the expression of relief at the conclusion of a harrowing affair may be sound enough, but that does not take away from its incongruity. I could list many more things of this sort, but there is no time for them, beyond reminding you of the circumstances attending the false alarm of invasion, a case of the beautifully incongruous, which Professor Gordon singles out for special comment.

Now, I am sure that some of you here want to protest that similar points could be made about *Waverley,* or *The Bride of Lammermoor,* or *A Legend of Montrose,* or *Redgauntlet*—and I would wholly agree, especially as regards *Redgauntlet.* I would still maintain, however, that although the miscellaneous and incongruous are repeatedly to be found throughout all Scott's best work, they are exploited in *The Antiquary* in a far more thorough-going way than elsewhere. Things assorted, sometimes absurdly, sometimes tragically—their use in this novel is so ubiquitous as to constitute a positive *convention,* a principle of organisation. To say which is not to argue that Scott thought out such a principle abstractly, but that it was the natural outcome of the vision of the 'vanity of human wishes' he is in this book projecting—a vision in which the best laid plans go wildly awry, in which fondly cherished theories turn out to be ludicrously hollow, in which random success sits cheek by jowl with equally random disaster, in which there is little to trust to or depend upon: just think of the Fairport post office, for example! Yes, the book ends 'happily,' but what has gone before is

enough to make us contemplate this with a certain wry amusement, or at least scepticism, though not with a sardonic chuckle. It is not surprising that *The Antiquary* should be Scott's most Ben Jonsonian work as well as his most Samuel Johnsonian, for the extremes of character and situation he here depicts lead to a use of 'Humour' characters, of representative types (and consider the naming of so many of them), which, again, we can find elsewhere in Scott, but not on such a scale. It is not for nothing that Monkbarns quotes from *The Alchemist* when he turns on Dousterswivel at the end of Chapter 23.

I have time for only one thing more, and as you might have predicted, it concerns Edie Ochiltree. I have avoided saying much about him so far, because, although I am second to none in my admiration for this particular creation of Scott, I am sure we need to get away from that notion of *The Antiquary* which sees it as charming muddle, with Edie's 'racy vernacular,' or some such phrase, as the richest ingredient. Don't let us play that down, but let us this time try to think of Edie in relation to the suggestions I have been making about the book as a whole. If I find Scott's Vanity Fair more powerful than Thackeray's, it is because all therein is *not* Vanity. *The Antiquary* contains irony enough, but it is not the 'bottomless' irony which in Thackeray makes it hard to believe that *anything* is really to be valued. And if we do not contemplate the book's happy ending with a sardonic chuckle, Edie has most to do with this. For he is the antithesis of the shortcomings of others. To complain that he is too conveniently 'on hand' to help out is to expect a realistic convention alien to this novel, for Edie is almost an allegorical embodiment of dependability where so many others lack it, and Scott presses the point home. Where others are hag-ridden by fantasy, whether it be about Roman encampments, or codes of supposed 'honour,' Edie is a realist. If Sir Arthur and Oldbuck can both be absurd about the past, and find it hard (especially the former) to adjust to the realities of the present, Edie is in tune with both past and present. He is the repository of any number of old tales and ballads, and he is also the inheritor of a tradition of rural usefulness which makes him almost an indispensable figure in the present of his locality. And his proud insistence on such points as not accepting too much in the way of alms is not an incongruity putting him into line with other characters, not a mere eccentricity or quirk, but a piece of realism showing a lively awareness of both past and present. For him to change would be at once to go against the tradition to which he proudly belongs, and to give himself an outwardly finer but essentially empty and meretricious present. He has no illusions about either past or present, and if he can at times be monumentally impressive, as in his protest to Lovel and M'Intyre before the duel, he is hardly an idealized figure, for all his worth. Nor, for all his apparent contentment, is he depicted as an ideally happy figure, a character out of pastoral convention; but it must immediately be said that he is no unhappy one either. He simply *lives,* facing situations astutely when they arise, and dealing with them as adequately as circumstances permit: this does not mean that he carries any invincible charm against misfortune.

If Monkbarns is to some extent a satirical self-portrait of the author in his antiquarian guise, Edie Ochiltree strikes me as being a kind of premonitory self-portrait. Obvious dissimilarities apart, he is very close to the Scott of the later years of disaster, bereavement, and sickness: by no means a 'happy' man in any ordinary sense, and yet certainly not 'unhappy' in feeling that he could face things and do the best he could with them. And I think, too, that the Mucklebackit whom Monkbarns meets trying to mend his boat in Chapter 34 is close to the Scott we meet in the *Journal* after the death of Charlotte. It isn't for nothing that Edie and Mucklebackit (and the Mucklebackits are by no means idealized) are the characters in the book least connected with sham or pretension.

A very odd novel, then. A novel with a sombre vision underlying much extravagant comedy: a vision which erupts once into melodrama, and once into tragedy. It is neither a 'happy' nor an 'unhappy' book. I think there are quite a few reasons why Scott had a special affection for it.

Joan S. Elbers (essay date 1973)

SOURCE: Elbers, Joan S. "Isolation and Community in *The Antiquary*." *Nineteenth-Century Fiction* 27.4 (1973): 405-23. Print.

[*In the following essay, Elbers argues that* The Antiquary *is not simply a collection of anecdotes, as critics have often asserted, but rather a unified work of art, organized around a series of thematic contrasts between "man cut off [from] the social organism" and "man linked to his fellows [through] a system of traditional duties and obligations."*]

In the "Advertisement" to *The Antiquary,* Scott, with his habitual modesty and self-deprecation, warns his readers that he has been "more solicitous to describe manners minutely, than to arrange in any case an artificial and combined narrative" and apologizes for his failure to unite "these two requisites of a good novel."[1] Since then criticism of *The Antiquary* has tended to follow Scott's dichotomy. Those critics who demand significant form have sometimes ignored and sometimes condemned the novel. Perhaps no work of a major writer has been subjected to anything like the hostility of E. M. Forster's merciless dissection and sneering dismissal of *The Antiquary.*[2] And even Francis Hart, Scott's sympathetic and sensitive modern interpreter, finds the novel to be flawed by a "lack of vital unity," "drastic shift of mood," and "the intrusive irrelevance of the historical setting."[3] But *The Antiquary* has found steadfast admirers among those critics who place truth and vitality of character and a pervasive infusion of generous and tolerant humanity above formal excellence. Apparently in later years Scott himself came to

hold a higher opinion of his novel; for on the eve of his last trip abroad he told Captain Hall, who had recently purchased the manuscript, that *The Antiquary* was his own favorite among the Waverleys.[4] John Buchan, typical of the lovers of Sir Walter Scott, admits the plot is "elaborate, artificial and unimportant" but delights in its humor and admires the "two or three humble figures who are invested with an heroic or tragic grandeur."[5] The most moving tribute to the novel's emotional power, however, is found in Virginia Woolf's description of Mr. Ramsey's enthusiastic appreciation: "This man's [Scott's] strength and sanity, his feeling for straightforward simple things, these fishermen, the poor old crazed creature in Mucklebackit's cottage made him feel so vigorous, so relieved of something that he felt roused and triumphant and could not choke back his tears."[6]

Does this critical dichotomy mean that we must give up either *The Antiquary* or our esthetic standards—that in order to appreciate Scott we must become, as Henry James not unkindly said, "credulous as children at twilight"?[7] I think not. Those critics who have condemned *The Antiquary* for its formal failures seem to me to have done so on the basis of an overly narrow definition which, explicitly or not, has tended to equate form with plot in the sense of a necessary or probable causal chain of events. Admirers have been equally circumscribed, failing to probe beneath their immediate responses to discover the formal sources of the novel's emotional appeal. For, however vital Oldbuck, Edie Ochiltree, and the Mucklebackits appear, they are in truth completely defined within the imaginative world of Scott's novel; and, if they convey to us something of the humanity and emotional power perceived by Mr. Ramsey, they do so because the novel as a whole possesses an underlying organization and system of values. *The Antiquary* is not a collection of humorous and pathetic anecdotes but a unified work of art organized around a series of thematic contrasts between isolation and community—between man cut off emotionally and spiritually from the network of relationships that make up the social organism and man linked to his fellows through sympathetic understanding and a system of traditional duties and obligations.

In the justly admired rescue scene (chs. 7 and 8) Scott composes a verbal picture that serves as an emblem, or symbolic visual presentation, of the theme of the novel and as a pattern for subsequent thematic contrasts. Viewed as a painting, the swelling sea rises in the foreground threatening to engulf the central figures of Sir Arthur and his daughter trapped on a narrow path of sand between the ocean and a background of precipitous cliffs. From one diagonal vector the tall, upright figure of the old Blue-Gown beckons them back. Coming toward them from above, on the opposite diagonal, Lovel scrambles along the cliffs carrying a rope, while in the distance on the cliff tops, Oldbuck and the villagers prepare a rescue operation. The composition captures both the danger and doubtful outcome of the baronet's predicament and suggests the possible sources of safety. Even on a first reading the emblematic arrangement of the figures implies meaning in the episode beyond the immediate representational content. A full realization of its significance, of course, depends on the total content of the novel, but enough preparation has been given in previous chapters to insure the reader's readiness to see the process of Sir Arthur's rescue as more than straightforward adventure.

Early in the novel, the continuity of traditional society is announced comically by MacKitchinson, the innkeeper, who has inherited a humorous Jarndyce and Jarndyce, "a ganging plea that my father left me, and his father afore left to him" (I.ii.13). Somewhat later we are made aware that the events of the story take place during a period when this traditional community is threatened both by insurrection within and invasion from without. Again, Scott's method is comic. Caxon, the aged barber and dresser of periwigs, comments: "nae wonder the commons will be discontent and rise against the law, when they see magistrates and bailies and deacons and the provost himsell, wi' heads as bald and bare as ane o' of my blocks" (I.v.54). The surface irony of Caxon's speech derives from the discrepancy between the seriousness of a popular uprising and the frivolity of the supposed cause—the failure of magistrates to wear periwigs; yet Caxon has metaphorically touched the cause of discontent, which proceeds, partially at least, from the failure of the governing classes—the aristocracy and the gentry—to maintain their traditional leadership during a period of change and social upheaval.

Sir Arthur's views on the necessity and manner of resisting France make this failure clear:

> ... an enemy who comes to propose to us a Whiggish sort of government, a republican system, and who is aided and abetted by a sort of fanatics of the worst kind in our own bowels. I have taken some measures, I assure you, such as become my rank in the community; for I have directed the constables to take up that old scoundrelly beggar, Edie Ochiltree, for spreading disaffection against church and state through the whole parish. He said plainly to old Caxon, that Willie Howie's Kilmarnock cowl covered more sense than all three wigs in the parish,[8]—I think it is easy to make out that innuendo. But the rogue shall be taught better manners.

(I.vi.69)

In this passage Sir Arthur makes explicit the connection between insurrection at home and the social ideals of the French Revolution. But he also reveals his own incapacity for leadership. His ludicrous contribution to the solution of the country's domestic problems is especially inept because his punitive action is perversely directed at the character in the novel most clearly identified with the traditional community. Edie's role in keeping the lines of communication open within the community—between man and man and class and class—is stressed from the moment he is introduced as a member of the ancient profession of licensed beggar who acts as news carrier, bard, historian, and even sage to the district. In turning on Edie, Sir Arthur assails the representative of the very community that supports his own hereditary rank and privilege.

At this point Scott has fully prepared the reader to respond imaginatively to the symbolic overtones of the material in the rescue episode. He has set his tale historically during the period following the Revolution when invasion from France was hourly expected and the idea of destroying existing institutions in order to reconstruct society rationally on the basis of the rights of man had captured the imagination of political thinkers; and he has suggested a connection between these ideas and the threat of popular revolt within the Scottish community of Fairport. He has established Sir Arthur Wardour as a pompous and somewhat foolish member of the landed gentry who, for all his patriotic delight in Scottish history and pride of rank and ancient descent, has little notion of the real value of the traditional community or of his true function within it. Finally, he has created in Edie Ochiltree, with his traditional role as messenger and news carrier, a representative of the sympathetic humanity necessary to weave individuals and classes into the larger community.

Chapter seven opens with the Wardours' decision to walk home from Monkbarns by way of the sands in order to avoid the necessity of asking Lovel to join them—"that young fellow, whom Mr. Oldbuck had taken the freedom to introduce them to" (82). The narration goes on to explain that Sir Arthur is incapable of the snobbish modern rudeness of cutting; yet, in deliberately choosing to avoid Lovel as an inferior acquaintance, the baronet is surely failing, as he had earlier in ordering Edie's arrest, to fulfill his traditional role as aristocrat. Integral to that role from ancient times has been the obligation of offering hospitality to the stranger. Sir Arthur should have been (to echo Yeats) Lovel's "heartiest welcomer"; instead, he resorts to an ignoble stratagem, the equivalent of crossing to the other side of the street. Isabella, too, though no blame can be attached to her resolution not to marry against her father's wishes, is yet, in rejecting Lovel, denying the wisdom of her own heart and evidence of true worth in favor of rank and legitimacy.[9]

Walking along the sands, Sir Arthur and Isabella view a somber and forbidding sunset: the disk of the sun rests on the sea like a "sinking empire and falling monarch" surrounded by misfortunes and disasters in the form of vaporous clouds (84). The sea itself is uncannily still lifting soundlessly into unnaturally high ridges before the storm wind is heard or felt on shore. Against this background of rock and sea, the human figures appear small and fragile, isolated beings helpless in the face of elemental natural forces. But given the historical setting of the novel and the terms of the simile describing the sunset, the storm suggests another danger. It comes across the sea out of the same quarter as the threatened invasion from France, accompanied by a lurid sunset which is likened to the fall of empires and monarchs, to threaten symbolically Sir Arthur and Isabella as members of the traditional ruling class.[10] In avoiding their obligations to society—in this case, hospitality to Lovel—the Wardours expose themselves not only to physical destruction as individuals but, as representatives of hereditary rank, to political destruction by the revolutionary ideas of equality spreading from the continent to Britain.

When Sir Arthur has at last begun to realize the seriousness of his and Isabella's position, Edie Ochiltree appears, advancing along the beach, to warn them to turn back and to offer to guide them to safety. Ironically, Edie, whom Sir Arthur had sought to arrest as a seditious person dangerous to church and state, comes in his role as mendicant and messenger to preserve the foolish representative of the hereditary ruling class. "It would have been utterly impossible for Sir Arthur Wardour or his daughter to have found their way along these shelves without the guidance and encouragement of the beggar" (88). Even so Edie's aid alone is not enough to save them from disaster; all three would have perished had not young Lovel appeared at the moment of gravest danger to lift them with the aid of his rope to temporary refuge above the reach of the waters.

Final rescue, however, depends upon the concern and cooperation of all members of the community of Fairport: Oldbuck anxious to save his friend and fellow antiquary in spite of their recent disagreement; Caxon determined to preserve intact the remaining periwigs in the parish; Mucklebackit and the other fisher folk ready to hoist Sir Arthur as they used "to bouse up the kegs o' gin and brandy lang syne" (I.viii.97), and half the men and boys from the nearby countryside out of "zeal or curiosity" (97). The mechanism that will bear the sufferers to safety consists of an armchair dependent "upon the security of a rope which, in the increasing darkness, has dwindled to an almost imperceptible thread" (98). This thread, like Lovel's rope and Edie himself as messenger, is an implement of communication and connection. Sir Arthur and Isabella are returned physically to the safety of the community, first, because they heed Edie's communication—his warning to turn back—and second, because the ropes provided by Lovel and the community prove strong enough to bear their weight. What is more, these ropes bear a further weight of significance: they suggest the strong yet tenuous links of loyalties, loves, and duties that bind the community into an organic whole. In the rescue scene and in *The Antiquary* in its entirety the links hold, but, as Oldbuck comically recognizes, the situation is precarious: "here a' comes—bowse away, my boys; canny wi' him; a pedigree of a hundred links is hanging on a tenpenny tow,—the whole barony of Knockwinnock depends on three plies of hemp" (101).

I have examined the rescue scene in some detail because the pattern of contrast between isolation and community

announced there is reiterated throughout the novel. It forms a basic structural device, organizing the work in spite of shifts in tone and weak causal development of plot into a coherent unity. Enriched through variation and repetition, it establishes the theme that man cannot with impunity cut himself off from involvement in communal life; and it furnishes the structural vehicle for a continuous probing of the ambiguous relationship of community to the past.

At times the contrast is presented emblematically as it is in the rescue scene. Driven to despair by the conviction that he has killed Hector M'Intyre—Oldbuck's highland nephew—in a duel, Lovel is pictured sitting despondently on the hermit's seat in the cave to which Edie Ochiltree has guided him in an escape from the sheriff. His bodily attitude reflects his reduction to a state of spiritual and emotional numbness, the result of committing an act representative of total isolation from the values of community—the taking of another's life. In the cave, at times the hideout of outlaws and once the cell of a hermit saint, Lovel reaches an extreme of isolation and indifference to the world around him. So great is his depression that Edie begins to fear for his survival and persuades the young man to ascend the monk's staircase to the chancel of the ruined Abbey of St. Ruth. There, in the free and mild air, sweet with the scent of wallflowers, the old beggar assumes the role of spiritual counselor and speaks to Lovel of the possibility of forgiveness.

Lovel is restored to participation in the world around him by overhearing Dousterswivel, the German confidence man, play on Sir Arthur's credulity and desperate need for money. Hope returns as he begins to wonder if the wound he gave M'Intyre was truly fatal; then his capacity to feel beyond his own misfortune is awakened. He reflects that, even if his innocence can never be restored, yet he can find reason for continued existence in active benevolence. Having passed through a kind of symbolic death during his visit to the underground cave, the young man is, in a sense, reborn when he finds himself capable of caring for the welfare of others without hope of reward for himself.

Earlier, disappointed in his courtship of Isabella and suspicious that he had been deceived about his parentage, he described himself to Oldbuck as "detached from all the world" (I.xiv.170) with few in whom he was interested and few interested in him. This state of emotional destitution gives him, he goes on to say, independence and the right to pursue his fortune according to his fancy. When Oldbuck remonstrates that, regardless of his personal isolation, he yet owes the service of his talents as a member of society, he replies impatiently that he asks nothing of society "but the permission of walking innoxiously through the path of life, without jostling others or permitting myself to be jostled. I owe no man anything; I have the means of maintaining myself with complete independence ..." (171). Here in a few lines of conversation is the deceptively modest creed of the laissez-faire economists and utilitarian philosophers, which during Scott's lifetime would prevent even men of good will from attempting to improve the wretched lot of the industrial poor. Any interference with freedom was bad; so men were free, when they could get work at all, to serve the machine in factories like prisons and live in jerry-built squatter's towns—or starve.[11] However much Lovel may misrepresent himself in this passage—and he is elsewhere shown to be a more feeling young man than he seems here—the contrast between this expression of a laissez-faire attitude toward social responsibility and his later discovery that only active benevolence and fulfillment of duty can give meaning to his continued existence is significant. Like the phoenix, to which he is compared throughout the novel, Lovel is reborn to a new self in the ruins of the abbey and is thus established as a fit inheritor of the aristocratic tradition of responsible leadership.

After the pivotal conversion scene—it occurs precisely halfway through the novel—Lovel will not appear again until the final scene of recognition and restoration. Throughout the second half he acts offstage in collaboration with Edie to save Sir Arthur and Isabella from financial ruin. When he does reenter the story directly, it is as Major Neville to announce that the invasion from France was a false alarm and as the lost heir of Glenallan to reintegrate the old nobility into the community.

For the ancient family of Glenallan illustrates a gothic form of isolation born of exclusive pride and preoccupation with the past that, left unchanged, can end only in the withering of their line. To Dousterswivel, alone in the abbey at midnight, the funeral of the Countess Glenallan appears an unearthly tableau. In the sacristy at the end of the one of the transepts, dark hooded figures, revealed in the smoky red glow of tall black flambeaus, bury the countess according to the ancient rites of the Catholic Church (II.iv.52-53). The funeral is conducted secretly at so strange an hour, not for fear of Protestant interference, but out of an ancient pride that forbids the family to show the grief of ordinary mortals. Theirs is an extreme of isolation that cuts the individual off not only from the general community but from those nearest in blood and affection. The Countess herself receives the news of the death of her second and once favored son with no more show of emotion than upon "perusal of a letter of ordinary business" (II.vii.84). And old Elspeth tells us that "the wives o' the house of Glenallan wailed nae wail for the husband, nor the sister for the brother" (II.vi.71).

The sepulchral formality of the Countess' secret rites contrasts pictorially and emotionally with the gathering for the funeral of Steenie Mucklebackit. (II.x.118-27). In the Mucklebackits' ramshackle cottage the young man's coffin lies within the wooden bedstead on which he had slept while alive; his father stands near the bed, lacerated by an almost unbearable grief, unable to look steadfastly at the coffin yet unable to keep his eyes from it. The mother,

Luckie Mucklebackit, sits weeping in a corner of the cottage, her apron covering her face. But the family are not alone; their cottage is filled with friends and relatives in best funeral black who have come to offer sympathy and to partake of the wheaten bread and wine, which mark the solemnity of the occasion even for so poor a Scottish family as the Mucklebackits. True, neither the sympathy of the mourners nor the traditional funeral fare or procession can lessen the parents' sorrow, yet these conventions perform the very real function of translating individual death into the public idiom of communal loss, and in doing so, reaffirm the supportive value of the organic community in times of personal crisis. The Countess of Glenallan's burial is the subject of rumor and whispered speculation; Steenie's is an event in the communal life of Fairport.

The family apartments of Glenallan House reflect the isolating pride and preoccupation with the past that characterize the Countess and her eldest son. In contempt of the times in which she lived the Countess had retained the decorations and furnishings of an earlier period before the union of the crowns of Scotland and England. Instead of landscapes and historical scenes, paintings depicting old sin and sufferings—martyrdom and saints—hang in tarnished silver frames along the hall (II.vi.81-82). The Earl's own isolation is rendered against the backdrop of his private chamber hung with heavy folds of black cloth and illuminated by broken light from a fourteenth-century stained-glass window representing the sufferings of Jeremiah. The only ornament in the room is a large painting by Spagnoletto of the Martyrdom of St. Stephen. As the Earl rises to greet Edie Ochiltree, he appears, though hardly past middle age, a "wreck of manhood"—gaunt and emaciated, broken in health by disease and mental misery (II.vii.85). His withered form, suffering under the burden of mysterious guilt, and the stifling atmosphere and formality of his household oppress the reader with the sense of having entered a wasteland of death and sterility.

Once the Earl's inhospitable domain is left behind both the narration and Edie's musings convey an almost kinetic sense of release: "It was a fine summer evening and the world ... lay before Edie Ochiltree, for the choosing of his night's quarters" (II.vii.95); and Edie, ruminating on where he will sleep, concludes that "the warst barn e'er man lay in wad be a pleasanter abode than Glenallan House, wi' a' the pictures and black velvet, and silver bonny-wawlies belonging to it" (95). Then, while the oppressive solitude of Glenallan House still lingers in the reader's consciousness, Scott pictures a scene of totally different atmosphere and tone. The isolation and formality of the manor are succeeded by the noisy involvement of a whole village in a game of long bowls on the common. The entire assembly—young men playing, elders making bets and arguing, women and children holding jackets or applauding, and Edie presiding as arbiter and umpire over all—presents an appropriate emblematic contrast to the Earl alone in his black, draped chamber.

It should be apparent at this point that Scott is a writer gifted with a highly visual imagination. The scenes I have examined—the storm and rescue, Lovel in the cave, the funerals of the Countess of Glenallan and Steenie Mucklebackit, the Earl of Glenallan's chamber and the villagers at long bowls—show Scott using pictorial description to embody thematic contrasts. In addition, he not infrequently suggests the tone of the scene by alluding explicitly to the works of known artists. Thus, David Wilkie is mentioned as the painter who could capture the interior of Mucklebackits' cottage on the day of the funeral; and the atmosphere of Glenallan House is indicated in part by referring to paintings by Domenichino, Velasquez and Murillo. Scott, of course, did not expect pictorial techniques to carry the full weight of his meaning. He was aware that in avoiding the then common practice of using explanatory rhetoric to reveal the significance of his narrative, he must depend like the playwright on "what the dramatis personae say to each other" to transfer the meaning of a scene.[12] His series of emblematic vignettes are, therefore, carefully reinforced by the terms in which his characters are conceived.

Edie Ochiltree has already been discussed as representative of the organic community, the repository of the folk wisdom and traditional knowledge that integrate the community in space and time. Elspeth Mucklebackit—Elspeth of the Craigburnfoot as she is known to the Glenallans—presents a contrasting pattern of almost complete isolation. Cut off from society by deafness and old age, she speaks as the dead to the living (II.v.64) or like a "mummy animated by some wandering spirit into a temporary resurrection" (II.vi.72). The spirit that animates old Elspeth comes out of the past—her own past of cruel deception and the feudal past of clan loyalty. Recalled to the present, her mind is vague and her speech incoherent; but when she speaks of bygone days, she speaks with an awesome authority:

> My dwelling at Craigburnfoot is before my een, as it were present in reality,—the green bank, with its selvidge, just where the burn met wi' the sea; the twa little barks, wi' their sails furled, lying in the natural cove which it formed; the high cliff that joined it with the pleasure-grounds of the house of Glenallan, and hung right ower the stream. Ah! yes, I may forget that I had a husband and have lost him; that I hae but ane alive of our four fair sons; that misfortune upon misfortune has devoured our ill-gotten wealth; that they carried the corpse of my son's eldest-born frae the house this morning,—but I can never forget the days I spent at bonny Craigburnfoot!

> (II.xi.135-36)

Ironically, the wrongdoing that makes her days at Craigburnfoot so memorable resulted from faithful adherence to the code of feudal loyalty. "They were stout hearts [she says] the race of Glenallan, male and female, and sae were a' that in auld times cried their gathering word of *Clochnaben*,—they stood shouther to shouther; nae man parted frae his chief for love of gold or of gain, or of right or of wrang" (II.xii.144). This is the code of Evan Dhu in *Waverley*—a warrior code, outmoded in the eighteenth century, yet able to command admiration and respect as late as the '45. But what was noble in the soldier following his chief to war becomes evil in the serving woman planning with her mistress a deception that engenders death and despair for the innocent. For Evan Dhu and the Sons of Ivor, feudal loyalty is the cement that binds the clan into a viable community; old Elspeth's loyalty isolates her from the community and from her family and binds her only to the dead past.

The relationship between adherence to the past and isolation from communal life apparent in the character of Elspeth Mucklebackit can be recognized in the delineation of other characters as well. The preoccupation of the Earl with the decisive event of his own past—what he believes to have been his incestuous marriage—prevents him from taking the place in society appropriate to his rank. He is, as he explains to Oldbuck, "without friends, unused to business, and, by long retirement, unacquainted alike with the laws of the land and the habits of the living generation" (II.xiii.161). Even more serious in a member of the landed aristocracy is his ignorance of the topography or even the names of some of his properties. But Jonathan Oldbuck, who expresses surprise at the Earl's ignorance, is himself tainted by an excessive involvement in the antiquarian past. In a comic vein, his collector's interest in antiquities makes him on occasion as unfit for business as Glenallan. More than once he has been taken in by the hope of acquiring some authentic remnant of olden times, and the town-clerk of Fairport finds no difficulty in getting his consent to bring the town water supply through Monkbarns by offering in return some stones from a decaying chapel.

Nor can it be said that Oldbuck's antiquarian interest in the past is always compatible with social involvement in the present. Despite his general goodwill, his basic tolerance and his charitable contribution to the welfare of his less fortunate neighbors, his objective curiosity prevents at times truly sympathetic participation in the traditional life of the community. Edie Ochiltree, with his usual perspicacity, sums up the dangers of this collector's interest in the past to a proper concern with human beings in the present: "Odd, I wish onybody wad make on antic o' me; but mony ane will find worth in rousted bits o' capper and horn and airn, that care unco little about an auld carle o' their ain country and kind" (II.ii.22). Once indeed Oldbuck comes close to losing his sense of the human importance of tradition in his antiquary's delight in survivals of the past. Caxon tells him that as landlord he is expected according to ancient custom to attend the funeral of Steenie Mucklebackit. Oldbuck of course approves of the tradition "founded deep in the notions of mutual aid and dependence between the lord and the cultivator of the soil" (II.ix.102-3); but his reaction is unemotional, objective, even clinical: "I assure you, you will see something that will entertain no, that's an improper phrase—but that will interest you, from the resemblances which I will point out betwixt popular customs on such occasions and those of the ancients" (II.ix.109). Such an attitude is as inappropriate to the sorrowful gathering at the Mucklebackits' as the toast of old Elspeth on the same occasion to more "such merry meetings" (II.x.121), and it cannot be sustained in the face of Saunders Mucklebackit's shattering grief. Oldbuck's human compassion overwhelms his affected cynicism and objectivity, and he undergoes a change of heart that leads to his spontaneous offer to carry the head of Steenie's coffin to the grave. He thus becomes a participant in the traditional rites he had earlier described so dispassionately. Nor is this new intensity of involvement merely temporary. The burial scene is followed, significantly, by the visit to Mucklebackit in which Oldbuck embraces the bereaved fisherman and sheds tears of compassion and by the meeting with Glenallan during which he is forced to confront a well-insulated part of his past and to feel again emotions he has long repressed.

For all the characters in *The Antiquary* a proper relationship to the past appears indispensable for satisfactory social engagement in the present. Characters as diverse as Elspeth and Sir Arthur or Oldbuck and the Earl are confronted by situations in which their preoccupation with the past dooms them to isolation or inappropriate action. Paradoxically, however, the organic community within which these people must ultimately find their salvation is itself the product of continuity with the past. Unlike the revolutionary society—constructed mechanistically according to some abstract blueprint of the rights of man—the community extolled by Burke and the Romantic conservatives is deeply rooted in the past, a living thing growing and changing while mysteriously maintaining its identity. If, like Glenallan, the traditional community should vegetate on the same spot, the end could be only withered foliage and a "decayed and dying trunk" (II.xiii.160)—a society ripe for insurrection at home and invasion from abroad.

Unfortunately, metaphorical description in terms of root and tree and leaf brings us little closer to a precise definition of what in *The Antiquary* constitutes a proper relationship between the good society or the good man and the past. What it is not has already been partially examined. It is not the isolating pride of birth and rank that leads the Glenallan family to deny the joys and sorrows common to all men, nor the preoccupation with past sin that destroys any emotion but remorse in the latest Earl of Glenallan. It is not Elspeth's single-minded and passionate adherence to an ancient code that places the loyalty of the vassal above concern with good and evil. On the other hand, the dispassionate curiosity about the past, characteristic of Oldbuck, though harmless in moderation, can, when indulged in too deeply, produce an isolation as serious though not so obvious as that of Elspeth or the Earl. But Sir Arthur's adaptation is even less satisfactory, consisting as it does of only so much historical learning as is necessary to make past deeds serve as reinforcements for present pomposity and prejudice.

Only Lovel and Edie Ochiltree assimilate the past to the present in a manner that survives critical examination. Lovel's successful integration of past and present is, however, largely symbolic. As Hart points out, "his role as a redeemer is simply that. He is extreme among Waverley heroes in the discrepancy between the significance of his role and the insignificance of his character."[13] His decision in St. Ruth's is the one positive act necessary to qualify him as worthy to redeem the hereditary governing classes represented by Sir Arthur and the Earl of Glenallan. Otherwise his personal fitness for the role is portrayed negatively—he doesn't, for example, display any of the self-importance or pride of rank characteristic of Sir Arthur and the Earl. Or it is merely announced by others—Oldbuck at one point eulogizes him as the "very prince and chieftain of the youth of this age" (II.xiv.172).

But however colorless Lovel may appear as a personality, his symbolic significance is unmistakable. It is reinforced by repeated references to him as a phoenix, symbol of rare value and rebirth, and explained by the unusual circumstances of his birth and upbringing. Though the legitimate heir of an ancient and aristocratic Catholic family, he believes himself a bastard and grows to manhood ignorant of the identity of his father. Brought up in England by his Protestant uncle, he is well provided for but taught to avoid any great expectations. On coming to Scotland, he is more or less adopted by Oldbuck, who responds to the young man as he might to a son of his own. At Monkbarns he is granted a vision of Oldbuck's ancestor, the Flemish burgomaster Aldobrand who printed the Augsburg Confession, "foundation at once and bulwark of the Reformation" (I.xi.136). In the vision Aldobrand sternly points out for Lovel's edification his motto expressive of "the independence and self-reliance, which scorned to owe anything to patronage, that was not earned by desert" (136). Lovel thus becomes heir to the two major strands of Scottish historical tradition—the one Catholic, Jacobite, and aristocratic and the other Protestant, Whiggish, and professional—one emphasizing hereditary right and continuity and the other individual ability and change. Yet he avoids the characteristic moral dangers of each, the isolating pride of the aristocracy and the narrow preoccupation with money-making of the middle class, uniting instead the virtues of each in a strong sense of social duty and active benevolence.

If history for Scott is, as Avrom Fleishman proposes, "the history of the Western European aristocracy from the early middle ages to his own time," then Lovel's background and character is an example of a "refinement of the aristocratic ideal"[14] suitable to the nineteenth century. In his happy succession to the Earldom of Glenallan and in his marriage to Isabella Wardour, we are symbolically promised a regeneration of the past through the union of the natural and hereditary aristocracies. But to understand the exact nature of a sustentative relationship of past to present, we must turn to Edie Ochiltree. The old Blue-Gown is the only character who voices reliable judgments about the role of the personal past in achieving internal harmony. First to Lovel after the duel with Hector, then to the Earl of Glenallan during his visit to Glenallan House, Edie expresses his faith in forgiveness—God's forgiveness of the repentant sinner and the forgiveness a man grants himself when he accepts his past but refuses to be defined by it. As a Christian Edie speaks of transferring the burden of his sins to Christ; yet his philosophy has a wider and secular application. It affirms the possibility of change and new beginnings and defends the fulfillment of the present against the destructive weight of an unfortunate past.

Francis Hart characterizes Edie as "committed to the humane use of the past in behalf of the present";[15] and this is an apt description of the thrust of his actions. His loving concern for the happiness and well-being of his friends is demonstrated throughout the novel—in warnings, advice, and in so small an act of mercy as his rescue of little Davie Mailsetter from the determination of a runaway pony. Nor does he hesitate to make use of his knowledge of the past to bring about a desired state in the present: the tale of Malcolm, the "love-begot," furnishes Edie with a symbolically appropriate hiding place for Lovel's anonymous aid to Sir Arthur and with an effective means of punishing Dousterswivel; the medieval hermit's cave and the abbot's alcove behind the chancel of St. Ruth's enable him to protect Lovel from arrest; most important, the time-honored privileges of his profession allow him to criticize with impunity the pretensions of the gentry.

Yet Edie is no radical, nor even a Whig, but the most eloquent of Burkean conservatives. What could be a more trenchant example of change as an extension of values already inherent in a society than his statement before the court of Bailie Littlejohn:

> Sae, neighbour, ye may just write down that Edie Ochiltree, the declarant, stands up for the liberty—Na, I maunna say that neither,—I am nae liberty-boy. ... Ay —write that Edie Ochiltree, the Blue-Gown, stands up for the prerogative ... of the subjects of the land, and winna answer a single word that sall be asked at him this day, unless he sees a reason for't.
>
> (II.xvi.198-99)

Edie claims as much freedom as any democrat, but he makes his claim not on the basis of abstract rights but on the basis of ancient privileges indigenous to his culture. Edie is further linked to organic conservatism through his traditional occupation. He has (if the phrase may be used without pejorative connotation) a vested interest in the lives of kings,[16] and his chief social function is to maintain the cohesiveness of the community. The ballads and tales, the traditional skills, even the gossip that he carries from one village or manor house to another constitute the basis for a consensus of values that permits the community to

endure even as it changes. In a novel organized around a series of contrasts between isolation and community Edie represents the value of sympathetic connection between man and man. And in a novel exploring the ways in which a sense of the past can destroy or nurture a sense of community he exemplifies the possibility of a life-supportive integration of past and present.

The Antiquary remains, none the less, what Robert C. Gordon has called it—"a very odd novel"[17]—not because it has no structure but because its structure is peculiarly static for a book so deeply concerned with time. Most of the determining action has taken place in the past outside the period covered by the novel, while the action in the present that is instrumental in producing the final resolution consists largely of incidents and in progressive uncovering of Lovel's true parentage. Conversely, much that gives the book its human interest and emotional intensity is only accidentally connected with the Lovel story. The function of scenes as different in tone and feeling as Steenie's funeral and the death of Elspeth on the one hand and the village game of bowls and the communal response of Fairport to the threat of an invasion on the other is not to thrust the reader forward in time toward the denouement but to deepen his understanding of the social organism.

Each scene manifests a slightly different aspect of community or isolation or continuity or change, and the variations of style to which some critics object appear to be the result not of artistic capriciousness but of Scott's attempt to realize the tone appropriate to each. Thus the storm off Halket Head is rendered in the language of romantic high adventure appropriate to the imminent physical danger of the sufferers and suggestive of the symbolic overtones of their plight, while the repetition of the same basic situation—rescue of the Wardours from the consequences of Sir Arthur's neglect of his proper role—toward the end of the book is treated with comic though compassionate realism. The parallel structure of the episodes is reinforced by the repetition of imagery of crag and precipice and by Edie's explicit comparison of the two incidents; but in the first the symbolic threat to the Wardours comes from France and the ideals and excesses of the French Revolution, while in the second Sir Arthur's ruin is announced in studied business jargon by Gabriel Grinderson, acting with bureaucratic solemnity "for self and partner" (II.xx.249), and put into execution by Saunders Sweepclean, the bailiff. Ultimately, the abstract cash-nexus definition of human interaction and morality, represented by the rising firm of Greenhorn and Grinderson and, on a farcical level by Sweepclean, poses as great a danger to the organic community of mutual rights and obligations as the abstract political philosophy of the Revolution; yet toward the end of a novel, soon to be resolved in redemption and restoration, the cash-nexus issue admits of the lighter treatment Scott has given it.

The Antiquary is no perfect unity—few novels are; nor is it without serious flaws. The inadequacy of Lovel's development as a character to the importance of his role as redeemer has already been discussed; a related fault is the insufficiently developed final scene—our sense of aesthetic completeness demands more than Scott's hasty dispensation of fortune. Neither, however, is *The Antiquary* the mindless and meaningless collection of incidents that E. M. Forster ridiculed. Only if we set up a rigid and parochial definition of the novel that automatically condemns any work lacking a necessary causal sequence of events can it be termed an artistic failure. Fortunately, the experimental fiction of the last few decades seems to have somewhat shaken the critical certainties of the first half century. From time to time one hears defenses of genre criticism or suggestions that the novel—prose fiction if you will—may be capable of developing as many kinds and modes as poetry. If so, Scott's novels with their peculiar blending of romance and comic realism may at last receive the kind of pragmatic and open-minded critical reading which Scott himself so generously gave to the works of others.

Notes

1. *The Antiquary,* introductory essay and notes by Andrew Lang, Border ed., 2 vols. (London: John C. Nimmo, 1893), p. vii. Citations in my text are to this edition; for convenience I cite volume, chapter, and page number.

2. *Aspects of the Novel* (New York: Harcourt, Brace, 1927), pp. 54-62.

3. *Scott's Novels: The Plotting of Historical Survival* (Charlottesville: Univ. Press of Virginia, 1966), p. 258.

4. Edgar Johnson, *Sir Walter Scott: The Great Unknown,* 2 vols. (New York: Macmillan, 1970), 2:1200.

5. *Sir Walter Scott* (London: Cassell, 1932), pp. 148-50.

6. *To the Lighthouse* (New York: Harcourt, Brace, 1927), pp. 179-80.

7. Henry James's review of Nassau W. Senior's *Essays on Fiction* (London, 1864), in *North American Review,* October 1864. This review was reprinted in James's *Notes and Reviews* (Freeport, N.Y.: Books for Libraries Press, 1968), p. 14.

8. The three wigs in the parish belong to Sir Arthur, Oldbuck, and Rev. Blattergowl respectively.

9. Apparently this is Edie's interpretation of her behavior when he advises her not to "sneer awa the lad Lovel" even though she is beautiful and good and possibly well-dowered (I.xii.151).

10. Oddly enough Scott makes his sun set in the east, an unusual error for an author so conscious of place and local geography. No one can know Scott's state of mind when he composed the scene, but carelessness about geographical realism might be expected if his concern was for the symbolic suggestiveness of the scene.

11. Sir Arthur Bryant, *The Age of Elegance: 1812-1822* (New York: Harper, 1950), pp. 335-39.

12. *Quarterly Review,* 16 (1817). Reprinted in *Sir Walter Scott on Novelists and Fiction,* ed. Ioan Williams (London: Routledge and Kegan Paul, 1968), p. 239.

13. Hart, p. 255.

14. *The English Historical Novel: Walter Scott to Virginia Woolf* (Baltimore: Johns Hopkins Univ. Press, 1971), p. 52.

15. Hart, p. 257.

16. As King's Bedesman Edie receives each year on the King's birthday a new cloak and as many shillings Scots as the King is years old.

17. *Under Which King? A Study of the Scottish Waverley Novels* (New York: Barnes and Noble, 1969), p. 214.

William A. Stephenson (essay date 1974)

SOURCE: Stephenson, William A. "Two Notes on Sir Walter Scott's *The Antiquary.*" *Studies in Scottish Literature* 11.4 (1974): 250-52. Print.

[In the following essay, Stephenson identifies an error in the chronology of The Antiquary *and also argues that contrary to the assumptions of most scholars, the story's fictional location is not in Forfarshire, but in Fifeshire. Stephenson bases his contention on compass directions mentioned in the novel.]*

1. AN ERROR BY SCOTT

As is well known, Sir Walter Scott's rapid composition occasionally led him into blunders. One mistake in *The Antiquary* has long been famous: in Chapter Seven, Scott describes the sun setting in the ocean—on the east coast of Scotland. So far as I know, another mistake in the same novel has never yet been noticed. In Chapter One, a handbill informs us that the date is Tuesday, July 15, 17—.[1] Lovel and Jonathan Oldbuck leave Edinburgh on that day, arriving in the town of Fairport "about two o'clock on the following day" (Chap. ii, p. 27). Lovel pays a visit to Oldbuck five days later (Chap. iii, p. 28). After an indeterminate passage of time, Oldbuck decides to give a dinner party. He accordingly sends to Sir Arthur Wardour and his daughter an invitation for "Tuesday the 17th" (Chap. v, p. 47). Lovel has also been invited, and he arrives "about five minutes before four o'clock on the 17th of July" (Chap. vi, p. 54). Thus, Scott places the party two days after the opening scene, even though the time lapse has clearly been greater than a week. Furthermore, we find that in the year 17—, both the 15th and the 17th of July fell upon a Tuesday.

2. An Error by the Critics

Most critics have placed the setting of **The Antiquary** in Forfarshire, Scott's town of Fairport being identified with Arbroath. Typical is W. M. Parker's statement in his introduction to the novel:

> Arbroath is generally accepted as being the Fairport of the novel. ... Hospitalfield, once a pilgrim's hospice near Arbroath, may have suggested Oldbuck's haunt. Auchmithie, farther north on the coast, answers more or less to the Mucklebackits' home, the Musselcrag, and yet farther north is Red Head, the scene of the escape of Wardour and Isabella, Ethie Castle, also to the north of Arbroath, may be taken as Knockwinnock, Wardour's residence.[2]

This interpretation of the novel's setting is plainly contradicted by Scott's own geographical details. The story takes place, not in Forfarshire, but in Fifeshire.

My view of the setting is supported principally by Scott's allusions to the directions of the compass. The coast of Forfarshire extends from Arbroath to the northeast, and previous critics have located the principal scenes of the novel on this northeast coastline. Yet Scott tells us that Monkbarns, the residence of Jonathan Oldbuck, was "secluded from the town by the rising ground, which also screened it from the north-west wind" (Chap. iii, p. 28). Thus, Monkbarns is located to the southeast of Fairport, which is entirely plausible if we identify Fairport with St. Andrews in Fifeshire. On the other hand, if we follow the northwest wind from Arbroath, we find that Oldbuck must have lived in the North Sea.

A few chapters later, Scott alludes to the direction of the wind once again:

> The wind began next to arise; but its wild and moaning sound was heard for some time, and its effects became visible on the bosom of the sea, before the gale was felt on shore. ...
>
> The beach under Halket-head [was] rapidly diminishing in extent by the encroachments of a spring-tide and a north-west wind, ...

(Chap. vii, pp. 69-70)

In this passage, the northwest wind is obviously blowing from the sea toward the land. It could do so on the coast near St. Andrews. The correspondence is better if we suppose the wind's direction to be somewhat north of northwest, but for the setting to lie near Arbroath, the wind's direction would have to be entirely opposite to that which Scott intended.

In still another passage, Lord Glenallan receives directions from the beggar, Edie Ochiltree. Speaking of old Elspeth, the Earl says, "She lives, I think, on the sea-shore, to the southward of Fairport?" Edie replies, "Just between

Monkbarns and Knockwinnock Castle, but nearer to Monkbarns" (Chap. xxviii, p. 266). If it were necessary, additional passages could be cited to show that Oldbuck and Wardour live to the south of Fairport. Furthermore, the bulk of the evidence indicates that the coastline extends from Fairport toward the southeast.

By now, it is clear that Forfarshire is not the correct setting. Of several other coastal shires, Fife is the most logical candidate for a number of reasons. Its coastline runs in the right direction, and it is about the right distance from Edinburgh.[3] As Scott specifies, it is within sight of the Grampian Mountains.[4] Finally, several place names in Fife are noticeably similar to those used by Scott. The Earl of Glenallan lives at some distance from the other main characters; his seat could well be Earlshall, located to the northwest of St. Andrews. The rising ground which separates Fairport from Monkbarns corresponds to the Boar Hills; these lend their name to the fishing hamlet of Boarhill. Transforming the boar into a marine creature and the hill into a crag, we have Scott's Musselcrag. Most convincing of all, both in nomenclature and in geographical location, is the correspondence between Scott's Monkbarns and the present-day hamlet of Kingsbarns.

Notes

1. Sir Walter Scott, *The Antiquary*, intro. by W. M. Parker (Everyman's Library ed.; London: J. M. Dent & Sons Ltd, 1907 [But Parker's Introduction is dated 1954]), p. 13. Subsequent quotations from the novel are taken from this edition.

2. P. x; see also, Andrew Lang, Editor's Introduction, *The Antiquary* (vol. III of *The Waverley Novels* [Border ed.; 1892; rpt. London: Macmillan and Co., Limited, 1900]), p. xxvii; and "Arbroath," *Encyclopædia Britannica*, 11th ed., II, 339.

3. Less than a twenty-four hour journey by coach (Chap. ii, p. 27).

4. Chap. iv, p. 39; and "Forfarshire," *Ordnance Gazeteer of Scotland* (6 vols., Edinburgh: Grange Publishing Works, 1883), IV, 403.

Miranda J. Burgess (essay date 2001)

SOURCE: Burgess, Miranda J. "Scott, History, and the Augustan Public Sphere." *Studies in Romanticism* 40.1 (2001): 123-35. Print.

[*In the following essay, Burgess situates* The Antiquary *in the complex historical, political, and economic context of Scott's own time. Burgess contends that "in Scott's hands, antiquarianism becomes a key tool in the historical production of Scotland's British modernity."*]

In December 1819, Walter Scott wrote to Lord Melville and Lord Montagu outlining plans for a militia of local smallholders and laborers to counter the approach of radical insurrection in Scotland and "civil war" in Britain.[1] The letters made two in a series Scott sent to his neighbors and colleagues, in which, in identical language, he preached the modern uses of a reinvented feudal loyalty and clothed himself romantically as the quasi-Highland chief of a "clan regiment" (*L* [*The Letters of Sir Walter Scott*] 6: 113). In seeking the support of his neighbors, Scott catalogued the benefits the militias would bestow:

> the influence on the morale of the common people by the display of such a force … will make loyalty the fashion with the young and able bodied check the progress of discontent and intimidate the radicals who will thus see enemies among those on whom they reckond as secret well wishers. …
>
> (*L* 6: 71)

> [W]e should give them a jacket & pantaloons of Galashiels grey cloth which would aid the manufacturers of the place—highland bonnets with a short feather their own grey plaids in case of sleeping out black crossbelts and musquets.
>
> (*L* 6: 61)

Scott's Scotland is caught between a past framed as Jacobite and a threatening Jacobin future. In response, he levels a Jacobite vernacular of belted plaids and tenant-soldiers against Jacobin aggression. What is apparent in his letters, as in his Waverley novels, is the insignificance of military force when compared with the mediated power of "fashion" and "display." The best defense against "national crisis" is for Scotland's "common people" to parade their "loyalty" to their British king and country, marshalled by cultural producers who orchestrate the cohesive processes of sympathy and emulation (*L* 6: 63). Thus in drawing up plans for his corps of volunteers Scott offers more details of the nostalgic uniforms he has invented than of recruitment, arming, or command. His plans demand that laboring-class militiamen and their gentlemen-sponsors alike buy into the cultural producer's fictions, conspicuously consuming the signs he authorizes, from the "paper pellets" of a literary "battery" to the theatrically traditional costume and weaponry of his projected Highland soldiers (*L* 6: 58). In this way Scott forges a cultural route out of the distinctive stalemate of his romantic Scotland and into a British modernity where Scotland's distinctness and history thrive precisely in their cosmopolitan consumption.

Scott was to realize his prescription for social order two years later, during the visit of George IV to Edinburgh in 1822. He planned a weeklong pageant, which he marketed to the intended participants in broadside poems and pamphlets that translated into popular, practical, reproducible terms the historical processes of reconciliation his novels depict.[2] The king paraded through streets lined by ordered rows of soldiers, Highland militiamen, gentlemen-volunteers, and dignitaries.[3] The sartorial distinction and spatial distribution of the players according to rank, class, trade, and place of origin emblematized both their loyalty to the British crown and their ethnic and class diversity.[4] Scott's staging of this festival of Britain iconographically confirmed the inclusive Hanoverian Britishness of Scotland while setting rigorous limits to protest and disruption.[5] Like the volunteers' riposte to radical dissent proposed in Scott's letters, these limits were simultaneously performative and economic. Rooted in production and consumption of avowedly historical costume and artifact, they stimulated the local economy and took part in the circulation of Scottish national sentiments throughout Britain in printed form.

This essay addresses the mix of tradition with economic and cultural production that characterizes Scott's practices of national identity. It brings together two turns in the cultural history of romantic Scotland. One is the moment at which economic production gives way to the cultural production it enables. But it is also here that the local performance of Scottish tradition begins to conduct the insertion of Scotland into an explicitly modern, inclusive conception of Britain. The practice that guides Scotland across both these intersections is antiquarianism, which I discuss in terms specific to Scott's thinking about the encounter of history with modernity, of economies with culture—about Scotland within Britain. As Scott theorizes it in his 1816 novel *The Antiquary,* antiquarianism is elegiacally national in its relation to the material fragments of the past, as Katie Trumpener and Yoon Sun Lee have noted.[6] Responding in pageantry to the Radical War of 1819-20, and in *The Antiquary,* as we will see, to the precursor threat of French invasion in the 1790s, antiquarianism pits what it declares is Scotland's traditional strength against a radicalism it invariably construes as foreign. But, in Scott's hands, antiquarianism is also cosmopolitan in its reconstruction and circulation of the fragments of the past, and commercial and literary in practice. As the historically self-conscious man of letters moves between the fields of commerce and letters, his antiquarianism bridges cultural preservation and cultural production, erasing the lines between them.

As a practice of cultural production, I will suggest, Scott's distinctive mix of the outward-, inward-, and backward-looking, and of commerce, letters, and antiquarian discovery, proved powerful, but not irresistible. Literary and commercial production worked together to shape a body of consumers of the past. These consumers, in turn, were required to appear in public as citizens, a function defined by what their purchases declared were their traditions of political consent, harmony across ethnic and class differences, and commercial free choice. The creation of such a British public from Scottish subjects demanded their acceptance—indeed, their embrace—of a coherent national history and of that history's status as a literary and commercial product. In Scott's hands, antiquarianism becomes a key tool in the historical production of Scotland's British modernity. As such, it is easily threatened by competitor histories that refuse their confinement within the fractured remainders of the past. These histories may be enacted by those who refuse to buy and display the artifacts of an invented traditional harmony, and who thus appear in public bearing signs of a history of their own making. Such reluctant performers reveal, by declining to take part, the fragility of the commercial relations that have been annexed by Scott's orchestrated displays of public consensus. Scott's cosmopolitan national public, the putative end of Enlightenment and progress, collapses as soon as consumer support is withdrawn: as soon as readers refuse to buy in.

In many, if not most, of the Waverley novels, Scott symbolically resolves questions of Scottish and British inheritance and legitimacy.[7] That he does so by means of cultural production names the reading public of his modern Britain, the participants in the marketplace, as the heirs of Scotland's traditional order, and places these works firmly on the border between Scotland's past and Britain's future (Duncan 118-19). In *The Antiquary,* these threads of inheritance and cultural production come explicitly together. In a restoration plot that mirrors that of the companion work *Guy Mannering* (1815), the lost heir to the earls of Glenallan is discovered and restored to his title and estate. But the restoration is not brought about, as in *Guy Mannering,* by sympathy between the hero's race-memory, his tenants' feudal loyalty, and the romantic visibility of inherited blood. Rather, it results from a self-conscious cooperation between traditional claims and literary production. Like the gypsy Meg Merrilies of *Guy Mannering,* the "sibyl" Elspeth Mucklebackit provides the oral-traditional knowledge needed to identify and restore the missing heir.[8] Ultimately, however, the heir's restoration is made possible by Scott's cultural production of the novel's resolution, which is enacted within the novel by the acts of cultural producers. He is legitimated by the artifacts and narratives of a historiography—at once archeological and highly literary, and thus antiquarian in Scott's sense—retailed by the titular antiquary in partnership with the heir, and with Scott himself.

The narrative of the heir's restoration in *The Antiquary* enacts in miniature Scott's narrative of Scotland in Britain. The novel's climactic moment, the revelation of its hero's birth, comes as a town on the northeast coast of Scotland convinces itself that the revolutionary French have landed and made contact with Jacobin radicals at home:

> The watch ... lighted the beacon ... which threw up to the sky a long wavering train of light, startling the sea-fowl from their nests, and reflected far beneath by the reddening billows of the sea. The brother warders ... caught and repeated his signal. The lights glanced on headlands and capes and inland hills, and the whole district was alarmed by the signal of invasion.

(A [The Antiquary] 6: 323)

The beacon fires of the local militia recall the signal for the gathering of the Jacobite clans in Scott's *Waverley* (1: 175-77, 2: 162-63). In response, the townspeople and gentry marshal their resources to repel an invading force. The community's response to the combined threat of French invasion and Jacobin rebellion unites historical with commercial impulses. The yeomanry and merchants group themselves into a series of "separate corps" under the direction of their landlords. The landowners outfit themselves nostalgically for command of their "volunteers," who are outfitted after the manner Scott was to revive in his letters to Montagu and Melville. Jonathan Oldbuck, staunch Whig and eponymous antiquary, unearths several ancient weapons before girding on "'the sword ... my father wore in the year forty-five'" against the Jacobite army (*A* 6: 323-24). He detaches the artifact of the Hanoverian past from the undifferentiated archive to which it has been consigned, and rededicates it to modern loyalist use. But his neighbor Sir Arthur Wardour, scion of a Jacobite line, is equally fervent in a new "lieutenancy uniform," and the Catholic arch-Jacobite Glenallan appears "in uniform" in command of his "feudal dependents"—"a handsome and well-mounted squadron ... of five hundred men, completely equipped in the Highland dress" (*A* 6: 325, 327-28). The lairds are aided by two career soldiers, Oldbuck's nephew and Glenallan's long-lost Protestant heir, both also in "handsome uniform" (*A* 6: 328).

The volunteers quickly learn that "the courage and zeal which they had displayed were entirely thrown away, unless in so far as they afforded an acceptable proof of their spirit and promptitude" (*A* 6: 329). Scott's military climax begets a military anti-climax. Yet, Scott suggests, the "spirit" of volunteerism, and its outpouring as "the substance of the wealthy, with the persons of ... all ranks," defines the strength of Scotland and thus British social order as well (*A* 6: 326). A "general confusion" initially prevails:

> The women of lower rank assembled and clamoured in the marketplace. The yeomanry, pouring from their different glens, galloped through the streets, some individually, some in parties of five or six as they had met on the road. The drums and fifes of the volunteers ... blended with the voice of the officers, the sound of the bugles, and the tolling of the bells from the steeple.

(A 6: 325)

But this blending of genders, classes, and origins gives way to "good order" once the participants are "assembled" in "the principal square": "the good sense and firmness of the people" make up for "the deficiencies of inexperience" (*A* 6: 326). The career soldiers find "the different corps in good order, considering the irregular materials of which they were composed, in great force of numbers, and high confidence and spirits" (*A* 6: 327). Uniformed and equipped according to their origin and profession, and with reference to the historical allegiances of their ancestors, the "general" mix of the people of Fairport resolves itself into a cohesive public before regrouping as a series of discrete but cooperating military bodies. The public and its constituent parts, Scott seems to suggest, are fully convertible and easily controlled by national sentiment, commerce, and pageantry.

There are two elements in this scene that I wish to stress in characterizing Scott's antiquarian nationalism. The first is the conflation of Jacobite and Jacobin impulses that precedes Scott's reduction of both to costume, consumption, and public display. For the imaginary invasion of Jacobins whose arrival occasions the Fairport volunteers depends on a Jacobite history. The watch on the cliffs is established on the belief that French forces may land on the Scottish coast because Franco-Scottish Jacobites did so in 1745, when Charles Edward Stuart commenced his invasion of Britain with a voyage from France to Glenfinnan. Without this history, the sea route from France to Scotland with a presumable goal of London is too circuitous to take seriously; with it, the belief that invasion has occurred assumes the legitimacy of a historical return.[9] The mixing of Jacobins with Jacobites is further complicated, moreover, when the expected invaders are met with the surviving artifacts of avowedly traditional Jacobite defenses—the beacons, the Highland-costumed volunteers, the fervent loyalties of Wardour and Glenallan. These artifacts are taken out of history to be revived and recontextualized as theatrical trappings of a Hanoverian Scotland. Scotland demonstrates its distinct character, and flexes its domestic economic muscles, in theatrically displaying its "general" fealty, the consensus of a diverse but unified people, to the British crown and Union. By collapsing Jacobite with Jacobin in his simulacrum of invasion and volunteerism, Scott breaks out of the opposition between them and reassigns Scotland's history to the evolutionary past of the British commercial present.[10]

Scott's break with this characteristic stalemate of Scottish romantic history, and with the oppositional version of Scottish nationhood the Jacobite-Jacobin dyad holds in place, is made possible, in turn, by an explicitly developmental economic history of Scotland:

> In a country which has neither foreign commerce, nor any of the finer manufactures, a great proprietor, having nothing for which he can exchange the greater part of the produce of his lands ... consumes the whole in rustick hospitality at home. ... A hospitality nearly of the same kind was exercised not many years ago in ... the highlands of Scotland.[11]

According to Adam Smith in *Wealth of Nations,* this hospitality has a military aspect, for the tenants of each estate make up a "highland militia" that "served under its own chieftains" to constitute "standing armies" (*W* 701). For Smith, however, Scotland has evolved into commercial modernity, in which a surplus of paper credit and an embrace of manufacture enable one another. He insists that it is

the enterprizing and projecting spirit of the people, their desire of employing all the stock which they can get as active and productive stock, which has occasioned this redundancy of paper money.

(*W* 941)

Union, with its concomitant opening of Scotland's economic borders, is the motor of the change. But it is also the occasion for a moment of nostalgia. "What all the violence of the feudal institutions could never have effected," Smith remarks,

> foreign commerce and manufactures gradually brought about. Those gradually furnished the great proprietors with something for which they could exchange the whole surplus produce of their lands, and which they could consume themselves without sharing it either with tenants or retainers. All for ourselves, and nothing for other people, seems, in every age of the world, to have been the vile maxim of the masters of mankind. ... For a pair of diamond buckles ... or for something as frivolous and useless, they exchanged the maintenance ... of a thousand men for a year, and with it the whole weight and authority which it could give them.

(*W* 418-19)

Like Scott, Smith insists that cultural transformation is more efficient than political or military force, and that commerce is the instrument of cultural transformation and progress. Yet he also mourns what is lost as progress moves ahead. The history of economic progress has run "contrary to the natural course of things," for the "childish vanity" of the landowners has made mercantile self-interest the primary agent of social and economic progress (*W* 422). Smith's history of economic progress is also an elegy for what he construes as Scotland's traditional, and now irrecoverable, forms of domestic authority and national civility.

As Scott revises Smith's economic history, he retains its caudalocephalic portrait of a Scotland evolving from Lowlands to Highlands and a Britain evolving from the commercial south to the north. The north and the Highlands appear, in *The Antiquary* as in *Waverley* and *Rob Roy,* as the last museumlike bastion of social arrangements once common to Saxon, Norman, and Gael (*W* 413). Throughout his portrait of the Fairport volunteers, Scott echoes Smith's praise of Scotland's enterprising "spirit." Unlike Smith, however, Scott does not mourn the hospitality or heroism of the past, but suggests instead that what defines tradition, and what gives it the continuing life that defines it *as* tradition, is the artifacts it leaves behind. The past for Scott is not, as for Smith, irrecoverably lost, though its artifacts are no use on their own, providing no metonymic window on tradition. Scott fills in gaps that Smith does not fill: he provides an account of the evolutionary process by which customary social relations give way to commerce and by which the relation of the past to the present becomes a national tradition. He insists that antiquarian remnants of the unproductive but hospitable and military past must be manufactured, retailed, and consumed by the enterprising present. The move from past to present is seamless, because the present reproduces and consumes the artifacts of the past. Authenticity, at least in the sense of historical provenance, is entirely beside the point.

The evolutionary movement of Scott's rewriting of Smith's economics is emblematized in the *éclaircissement* that follows the invasion scare and begins the conclusion of **The Antiquary.** The fires the watch believes to be French beacons are in fact the burning ruins of "machinery" built by Oldbuck and Wardour as dupes of the German confidence trickster Dousterswivel. The destroyed "engines, and wheels" have been produced for the purposes of gold mining, which Scott represents as one of Dousterswivel's alchemical sleights-of-hand, "convert[ing] ... lead into gold" (*A* 6: 267, 319). The French provide a catalyst for the coalescence of Scotland, that is, only as they appear in the shattered illusions of a Scottish landowner who gives up nostalgic dreams of "treasure" and "troops of liveried menials ... marshalled in his halls" to break and burn his machines for the production of specie (6: 265). What Fairport's citizens and landlords embrace instead is the modern apparatus of manufacture—the looms that produce tartan uniforms for local consumption and export, the forges that make weaponry for Britain's Scottish defenders. And what these latter machines make possible is a generalized public consumption of the trappings of nationhood. For Scott as for Smith, such a shared theatrical usage of the nation's artifacts is the *natural* end of national progress.

Highlighting the cultural character of Fairport's commercial production and consumption is the framing of Scott's scene within his thematic consideration, and his structural enactment, of the machines of literary manufacture that are a primary concern of **The Antiquary.** Scott emphasizes Oldbuck's role in producing the patriotic formation that characterizes Hanoverian Scotland, and a synecdochic relation ties Oldbuck's antiquarian activities to the work of the novel itself. For **The Antiquary** is an antiquarian novel, in Scott's dialectical sense, at least as much as it is a novel concerned with antiquarianism. Its affiliations are broadcast when Scott appears in his guise as "the author" to footnote his sympathy in Oldbuck's bibliomania (*A* 5: 41n). But Oldbuck is not driven to prove the authenticity of his ancient tracts or artifacts. Rather, the conjunction of Scott's with Oldbuck's antiquarian desire suggests that there is more to Oldbuck's love of fragmented, displaced ancient objects than the drive to recapture lost national glories, or to keep the past at bay by encountering it at a distance mediated by metonymy.[12] For even as Scott depicts what ought to be a crushing demystification of antiquarian fantasies, his narration recapitulates Oldbuck's easy acceptance of the failures. Oldbuck's consolations include Scottish bankruptcy law, an ancient "legal fiction" in which the king is said to be offended by debtors, who are declared "rebel[s]" and imprisoned for their country's good (*A* 6: 243). The narrator's own pleasure in this

fiction, and the commercial nationalist overtones of his pleasure, appear in a footnote avowing that "Scottish law is ... more jealous of the personal liberty of the subject than any other code in Europe" (*A* 6: 243n). Even Elspeth Mucklebackit "'speak[s] like a prent buke'" of ancient allegiances and genealogical memory (*A* 6: 72-73). The product of antiquarian failure to regain a heroic national past in this novel is a new ideological control of Scotland's past—which emerges in public out of the bond between cultural producer and consumer—and so of the British future as well. Oldbuck's will to unearth the genuine traces of history is displaced by his joy, and Scott's, in the power of imagination, and in the literary legitimation and print circulation of their shared imaginings.

The power of the cultural producer to move between past and present, and between artifact and manufacture, is made most explicit in Oldbuck's proprietory interest in the long poem, the *Caledoniad,* which he encourages Glenallan's son Lovel to write. Oldbuck offers to supply learned notes, framing Lovel's romantic fictions of the Scottish past with an air of authenticity, despite his insistence that the Scots as portrayed in the poem fight off Agricola's Roman invaders. The notes, modern cultural and commercial products, become artifacts backing up an invented antiquarian narrative of history, which (like Scott's own heavily annotated poems) will naturalize itself as national history in the imaginations of its readers. "'You are a poet,'" Oldbuck tells the scrupulous Lovel, "'free of the corporation, and as little down to truth or probability as Virgil himself—You may defeat the Romans in spite of Tacitus'" (*A* 5: 195). The defeat of antiquarian truth gives way to the most magisterial of nationalist, triumphalist historiographies precisely because it is the most avowedly artificial, demanding the acquiescence of writer and reader. The character of Scotland's self-imaginings is relocated from the discovery of buried histories to the nationalist author's production and circulation processes.

The *Caledoniad* is never written, but then, it doesn't need to be. By uniting the rediscovered heir to a Jacobite title with the iconoclastic descendant of Protestant printers, whose veins "run with printer's ink," in a network of what Scott calls "antiquarian societies" of "national concern," the poem has served its patriotic purpose (*A* 5: 44, 47, 275). The writers' union of Oldbuck and Lovel is founded on shared classical literacy, Protestantism, cultural production and "civility," which provide foundations for Scott's Scottish ideal of Britain's public. Scott carefully distinguishes this civility, "'a word that perhaps belongs only to a collector of antiquities'" and "'one of the old school,'" from sociability, a feminized trait that unites "the club of Royal True Blues" with the "society of the *soi-disant* Friends of the People" (*A* 5: 59, 152). The (literal) Augustanism of Oldbuck's preoccupation with Roman artifacts is best understood in this context. Oldbuck's, and Scott's, promotion of classic letters and civic virtue hearkens back to the early-eighteenth-century London of

Alexander Pope and Jonathan Swift, with its mix of literary professionalism and masculine coterie. For a nineteenth-century Britain modelled on Scottish public life, Oldbuck (and Scott) recapitulate that particular form of social relation.[13] Scott's civility, like Pope's and Swift's, is entrepreneurial and productive rather than corporate or speculative in its commercial sympathy—but no less commercial for that.[14]

The rubric of the community forged by the unwritten poem is the Oldbuck family motto, "Kunst macht Gunst" (*A* 5: 156). This motto names cultural production at once a rival "pedigree" to the "Saxon, Norman, or Celtic genealogies" claimed by Wardour and such forebears as Edmund Burke, William Gilpin, and Richard Hurd, and a counterweight to the radical corresponding societies, with their rejection of tradition.[15] In a double sense, the motto betokens "the diffusion of knowledge, not the effusion of blood" (*A* 5: 156). The union of Oldbuck and Lovel can produce no children save its cultural productions. Its masculine civic character, its union of men in a chain of productive imaginations, at once utterly local and "free of the corporation," undoes the necessity for inherited traditions of the kind mourned by Smith.[16] But it also supersedes the need for loyalist or patriotic violence. Because antiquaries "'are eternally exercising their genius and research upon trifles,'" it is "'impossible they can be baffled in affairs of importance,'" for "'the corps that is most frequently drilled upon the parade, will be most prompt in its exercise upon the day of battle'" (*A* 6: 195). There is less power in recovering, inheriting, or defending past traditions, or so Scott seems to conclude, than in the *invention* of them. It is not merely, for Scott, that an authentic history is unrecoverable, but that no history or artifacts exist before cultural producers draw up the marketing plan.

Taken together, the production narratives of the *Caledoniad* and the Fairport volunteers' festival enact the close ties between Scott's production of the Waverley novels and marketing of the royal visit of 1822. Scott, too, naturalizes in narrative and in public theater a traditionalized Scotland that lacks a demonstrably authentic source. Yet his Scotland, and the Britain to which it dedicates itself, is more than an imagined community. It is a culture produced and consumed in accordance with principles of sympathy and emulation outlined in Scottish Enlightenment accounts of human nature such as those of Adam Smith. Its influence, as Scott presents it, is almost irresistible. In the Magnum Opus preface to *Tales of the Crusaders,* even Dousterswivel reappears at the next stage of Smithian economic evolution: as a convert from coining to manufacture. He has adapted a "mechanical process like that by which weavers of damask alter their patterns" to literary labor on those "parts of the narrative . . . composed out of commonplaces."[17] When the "joint-stock company . . . for the purpose of writing and publishing the class of works called the *Waverley Novels*" reject the proposals Scott has called them together to consider, the

"Author of Waverley" castigates them for their "'modern antiques, and . . . antiquated moderns'" and departs in order to "write HISTORY" (*B* [*The Betrothed*] 37: xxxix). Scotland's historical and cultural character lies not simply in the mixing of modernity with antiquity, but rather in the seamless manufacture and naturalized consumption of the past by the cosmopolitan readers and writers of the British present.

Even so, the antiquarian cultural production and retailing of a public can have no effect without a paying audience, whose function is not only to observe but also to take part in the process of nation-formation. In positing volunteerism and production as an escape from the violent dichotomy between the Jacobite and Jacobin histories of Scotland, and a pathway to Scotland's British modernity, Scott's narrative acknowledges the possibility of resistance, and so forecloses the possibility of escaping Scotland's past. Oldbuck's willingness to acknowledge that the Scotland he desires is a product of his own imaginings, and that it depends on the support of its retailers and consumers, first appears as he attempts to bribe Edie Ochiltree, the "'news-carrier, the minstrel, and . . . historian of the district,'" to continue to circulate his antiquarian fictions even after Ochiltree announces that the Roman ruins on Oldbuck's estate are merely the remains of a twenty-year-old temporary shelter (*A* 5: 51-53). As a blue-gown mendicant, Ochiltree is the surviving artifact of the ancient patronage of Scotland's crown, but he refuses to become a museum piece. He is the chief purveyor, by means of old roads, of news and of class dissent in the form of gossip and balladry. His intrusion as Oldbuck shows off his pretorium to Lovel—"'Prætorian here, Prætorian there, I mind the bigging o't'"—is an "uncivil . . . interruption" that marks a strong contrast to the civility Oldbuck and Lovel share and makes him an alternative "public" figure (*A* 5: 49, 169). Ochiltree refuses to be drawn into Oldbuck's fictional production, however the latter tries to claim him for his feudal, and literary, demesne. As the "'privileged nuisance'" of the neighborhood, Ochiltree registers the failure of Scott's British Scotland wholly to generalize itself (*A* 5: 56).[18] His fate in the novel finally constrains him, his body bent and locked arthritically into place before his landlord's fire. Yet his restraint cannot wholly displace earlier images of his circulation through the countryside in a parallel, sub-commercial economy, trafficking in oral tales (Scott never repeats them) and refusing all but the tiniest sums of money. His modern laboring-class intransigence, wearing the antiquarian garb of a stubborn feudal survival, refuses to bow to Oldbuck's production of the present, in which production and an entrepreneurial print-culture replace, by incorporating, Scotland's histories, and in which the public consent is demonstrated by votes with the pocketbook.

Unlike Wardour's Jacobite pretensions, which are dismissed as "the shadow of a shade," Ochiltree's "voice from behind" appears as the voice of real history (*A* 5:

49). It endangers Oldbuck's version of a Scotland founded on the fantasy of defeating Agricola—on the merging of martial values and their commercial reinventions. It represents a free-ranging anxiety about the connections between Scotland's imperfectly metonymized past and its ongoing national and class dissension. The anxiety was to be realized in the counter-discourse to George IV's Edinburgh visit five years later, as Scott's opponents reproduced his Jacobite trappings for their own political purposes, and as Scott's unified public threatened to fracture under the pressure of competing histories dressed in identical clothes.[19] But the Highlanders, beggars, and gypsies who populate the Waverley novels are neither inevitably the carriers of Scott's national fictions nor the importers of Scotland's past into the literary and commercial present. In opting out of cultural consumption during the action of any novel, they can opt out of Scott's cultural production, even as Scott seeks to draft them back into his resolutions. Thus they market the possibility that readers might find and consume, even in Scott's fictions, competing versions of Scotland's, and Britain's past; that they might contest Scott's projected Scottish future, past, and public in politically diverse ways.

Notes

1. Walter Scott, *Letters,* ed. H. J. C. Grierson, 12 vols. (London: Constable, 1934) 6: 57. Subsequently in the text, abbreviated *L.*

2. Scott, *Hints Addressed to the Inhabitants of Edinburgh and Others, in Prospect of his Majesty's Visit, by an Old Citizen* (Edinburgh: Bell, 1822); *Carle, Now the King's Come* (Stirling: Macnie, 1822). For the Waverley novels as reconciling nostalgia with progress and the formation of Britain with Scottish nationalism, see Robert Crawford, *Devolving English Literature* (Oxford: Clarendon, 1992) 11-51; for the relation of reconciliation to Jacobitism, see James Kerr, *Fiction Against History: Scott as Storyteller* (Cambridge: Cambridge UP, 1989) 38, 43. James Buzard, "Translation and Tourism: Scott's *Waverley* and the Rendering of Culture," *The Yale Journal of Criticism* 8 (1995): 31, 53, and Ian Duncan, *Modern Romance and Transformations of the Novel: The Gothic, Scott, Dickens* (Cambridge: Cambridge UP, 1992), especially 13-15, address the potential for dialectical reversal latent in Scott's reconciliations.

3. See *Historical Account of His Majesty's Visit to Scotland* (Edinburgh: Oliver, 1822).

4. For a map, see *Edinburgh Gazette* (14 August 1822): n.p.

5. Buzard 41, traces a related dynamic in *Waverley.*

6. Katie Trumpener, *Bardic Nationalism: The Romantic Novel and the British Empire* (Princeton: Princeton UP, 1997) 123; Yoon Sun Lee, "A Divided Inheri-

tance: Scott's Antiquarian Novel and the British Nation," *ELH* 64 (1997): 539.

7. On Scott, fiction, and legitimacy, see Judith Wilt, *Secret Leaves: The Novels of Walter Scott* (Chicago: U of Chicago P, 1985) 18-48; Fiona Robertson, *Legitimate Histories: Scott, Gothic, and the Authorities of Fiction* (Oxford: Clarendon, 1994) 1-30.

8. Scott, *The Antiquary, Waverley Novels,* 48 vols. (Edinburgh: Cadell, 1829-32) 6: 72-73. Subsequently in the text, abbreviated *A.* On the role of peasant women, see Duncan 131.

9. The fear of Jacobite returns corresponds with the typological readings of Jacobitism that Murray Pittock discusses in *The Invention of Scotland: The Stuart Myth and the Scottish Identity, 1638 to the Present* (London: Routledge, 1991).

10. On the continuity of Jacobin with Jacobite in romantic fiction, see Nicola Watson, *Revolution and the Form of the British Novel, 1790-1825* (Oxford: Oxford UP, 1994); in Scott, see David Kaufmann, *The Business of Common Life: Novels and Classical Economics between Revolution and Reform* (Baltimore: Johns Hopkins UP, 1995) 113. On Jacobites as a figure for British culture, see Clifford Siskin, *The Work of Writing: Literature and Social Change in Britain, 1700-1830* (Baltimore: Johns Hopkins UP, 1998) 82-87.

11. Adam Smith, *Inquiry into the Nature and Causes of the Wealth of Nations, Works and Correspondence,* ed. R. H. Campbell and A. S. Skinner, vol. 2 (Oxford: Clarendon, 1976) 413. Subsequently in the text, abbreviated *W.*

12. See Trumpener 28; Lee 563.

13. On civility and its distinctness from sociability, which take on a conservative force by the late eighteenth century, see J. G. A. Pocock, *Virtue, Commerce, and History: Essays on Political Thought and History, Chiefly in the Eighteenth Century* (Cambridge: Cambridge UP) 69-70, 215-253. On nineteenth-century reclamations of civility, see Joyce Appleby, *Liberalism and Republicanism in the Historical Imagination* (Cambridge: Harvard UP, 1992) 334-38.

14. See Colin Nicholson, *Writing and the Rise of Finance: Capital Satires of the Early Eighteenth Century* (Cambridge: Cambridge UP, 1994).

15. See R. J. Smith, *The Gothic Bequest: Medieval Institutions in British Thought, 1688-1863* (Cambridge: Cambridge UP, 1987).

16. See Ina Ferris, *The Achievement of Literary Authority: Gender, History, and the Waverley Novels* (Ithaca: Cornell UP, 1991) 91-94, on the "masculinity" of Scott's sympathetic and reading communities.

17. Scott, *The Betrothed,* Waverley Novels (Edinburgh: Cadell, 1832) 37: xxxix.

18. His role resembles Theodor Adorno's cultural critic in "Cultural Criticism and Society," *Prisms,* trans. Samuel and Shierry Weber (Cambridge: MIT Press, 1992) 20, 29: the "salaried and honoured nuisance" of culture who can, nevertheless, "retain . . . mobility in regard to culture by recognizing the latter's position within the whole."

19. For example, J. L. Marks, *The English Irish Highlander* (London: Marks, n.d.); *A New Song* (n.p.p.: n. p., n.d.), *George IV's Visit to Scotland,* BL fol. 1876. E. 24.

Mike Goode (essay date 2003)

SOURCE: Goode, Mike. "Dryasdust Antiquarianism and Soppy Masculinity: The *Waverley Novels* and the Gender of History." *Representations* 82.1 (2003): 52-86. Print.

[*In the following essay, Goode approaches* The Antiquary *as important for understanding the role of Scott's Waverley novels in the development of Romantic historicism. Goode argues that contemporaneous debates over different forms of historical inquiry in general, as well as the cultural authority of the historical novel in particular, "frequently became contests over the manliness and sensibility of their practitioners' bodies."*]

Dominick LaCapra has been arguing for some time now that relationships between contemporary historians and their objects of inquiry are fundamentally transferential and, ideally, "dialogic."[1] Historians narcissistically project their discipline's controversies onto the past, and when things go well, the past's irreducibility to the terms of such controversies voices itself, disrupting those terms to the point that historians understand both the past and their discipline differently. If we provisionally accept LaCapra's model of the ideal historian—the historian as *"mentalité case,"* as he once characterized it—then we might argue that for contemporary historians of the discipline of history, one of the most disruptive dialogues ought to occur when studying an influential predecessor who practices and portrays other kinds of transferential history. Particularly provocative would be the dialogue with a predecessor who idealizes transferences with the past that involve the material realm of the body as much as they do the "mental" realm of disciplinary controversy. Such a dialogue would add a more blatantly physical component to scenes that we had grown accustomed to perceiving as just talking, perhaps complicating the view that the hallmark of modern historicism's development was the rise of a dialogic relationship to the past. Indeed, if this earlier transferential history were implicated in its age's own disciplinary controversies over history, it would inevitably alter our understanding of the discipline's history as well.

This essay initiates such revisions through a reading of Sir Walter Scott's *The Antiquary* (1816), among the most popular of Scott's immensely popular *Waverley Novels* during the nineteenth century (so solid was the novel's canonization by the early twentieth century that Virginia Woolf assumed that readers of *To the Lighthouse* needed only a small clue to identify it as the novel provoking Mr. Ramsay's tears, and E. M. Forster made it the butt of his famous distinction between "plot" and "story" in *Aspects of the Novel*).[2] In the novel, Scott interrogates the cultural legitimacy of various modes through which individuals know the past and live with that knowledge, and he does so while modeling individual relationships to history in terms that resonate with LaCapra's. But he also emphasizes the intimacy of those modes, portraying historical pursuits as sentimental and sexual ones too. Specifically, I mean to show that Scott's novel about the 1790s asserts the post-Waterloo relevance of that earlier decade's widespread concerns that historical inquiry can improperly sentimentally and sexually initiate—and, therefore, according to the logic of the period, also improperly gender—British men. Like participants in that earlier decade's debates over historical inquiry, the novel demarcates the field of history's legitimacy as one whose borders men literally ought to feel: it not only suggests that the sentimental and sexual constitutions of historically minded men are relevant when judging their competence as historical thinkers but also implies that the legitimacy of historical pursuits depends upon the manliness of the sentimental and sexual education that those pursuits impart.

As itself a kind of history, *The Antiquary* may only raise such concerns in order to commit them to the grave, deflecting them backwards onto 1790s antiquarianism and implying in turn that historical pursuits' affective propriety and manliness improved after that decade. I shall argue, however, that because such pursuits since the 1790s had come to include Scott's own novels, historical narratives that attended in part to realms previously associated with antiquarian research, the novel also gave those concerns continued life, particularly for historical novelists trying to grant their fictions cultural authority by way of association with history. This is clear in Scott's **"Dedicatory Epistle"** to *Ivanhoe* (1819), his famous meditation on the epistemological and methodological problems facing the historical novelist, which I read as an effort to defend the historical novelist's authority at the expense of antiquaries by establishing the greater affective propriety and manliness of the novelist's body.

Scholars have long recognized the *Waverley Novels'* importance to the rise of the novel and to the evolution of modern European historicism. Historians as early as Thomas Macaulay, Jules Michelet, James Anthony Froude, and Augustin Thierry cite them as a major influence on their work. If we accept this privileging—and given, as I argue, that *The Antiquary*'s terms for examining history's legitimacy are typical both of the *Waverley Novels* and of their age, I see no reason why we should not—then Scott's novel provides strong evidence that history's early move toward disciplinization was also a conscious work of disciplining men's feeling bodies. One goal of this essay, then, is to widen the terms in which contemporary scholars discuss Scott's historicism. While early-twentieth-century novelists like Woolf and Forster and critics like F. R. Leavis dismissed the *Waverley Novels* as boyish and sentimental, more and more scholars have been arguing that we ought to take that corpus seriously as history, and particularly as evidence that the field of history was being redefined in the early 1800s.[3] But these scholars also restrict that redefinition to a transformation in historical epistemology and concomitant changes in historical method, largely focusing their attention on how Scott's conception of the "problem" of representing culture derives from Scottish Enlightenment stadialist theories of uneven development; from early-nineteenth-century skepticism of essentialist conceptions of human nature; and from a more nuanced understanding of historical mediation and, by extension, of history's relationship to fiction. What such accounts neglect, and what this essay attends to, is the importance of the body within this new historicist epistemology as a medium or even organ of knowledge and, in turn, the cultural work performed on bodies in the domains of sentiment, sex, and gender as writers sought to give this historicism legitimacy.

Still more broadly, by reading *The Antiquary* as itself an authoritative history (of history in the 1790s), this essay also begins to correct for a general neglect of the same in accounts of historicism's emergence, accounts that inform this scholarship on Scott, not to mention LaCapra's ideal of the historian. Perusing many of the twentieth century's more influential histories of history—from R. G. Collingwood's *The Idea of History* (1946) and Georg Lukács's *The Historical Novel* (1937) to, more recently, Michel Foucault's *The Order of Things* (1966), Benedict Anderson's *Imagined Communities* (1983), J. G. A. Pocock's *Virtue, Commerce, and History* (1985), and James Chandler's *England in 1819* (1998)—one is apt to conclude that if historicism battled for its legitimacy at all while in its infancy, then this battle was waged solely on epistemological and methodological grounds. Foucault, for example, though he devoted his late career to examining the body's disciplining in nineteenth-century culture, never examines the work of bodily discipline that took place in the name of history's initial disciplinization (which he dates between 1775 and 1825) when he treats that topic in *The Order of Things*.[4] Perhaps more strikingly, Collingwood makes the same omission, despite insisting in *The Idea of History* that a genuine act of historical thought, or what he calls "scientific history," involves reenacting the past imaginatively in one's own person.[5] Surely, to the extent that he acknowledges that this reenactment involves "sensations and feelings" in addition to a "process of knowledge," that formulation suggests that scientific his-

tory can never be separated from the historical situation of its practitioner's own felt embodiment.[6] It further implies, then, that every scientific history is not only an expression, in part, of a feeling body but also, however consciously, an act of making and unmaking such bodies. Yet Collingwood's own history of scientific history's emergence never tells a story about the body, restricting that emergence to the discovery that "human nature" has a history or, as he puts it, that "the historical development of the science of human nature entails an historical development in human nature itself."[7]

Scholars familiar with *The Antiquary* may think it an odd place to reinterpret Scott's historicist project because the novel has long been read as a portrait of the Scotland that Scott knows in 1816 rather than of the Scotland "of the last ten years of the eighteenth century," as he claims in the novel's "Advertisement."[8] Fueling this impression has been a consensus that it lacks formal elements crucial to the other *Waverley Novels*' ability to represent history. Critics deny not only that Lovel, its protagonist, is a "mediocre hero"—Lukács's characterization of Scott's standard hero, a figure who mediates the conflicting social forces of a historical moment and, for Lukács, who thus stands in for the course of history—but also that its secondary characters fail to typify the kinds of competing social and national causes that their analogues represent in other Scott novels.[9] Obviously such criteria for assessing a novel's claim to be legitimately historical are unscientific and open to ideological reproach, but they do raise doubts about *The Antiquary*'s status as a historical representation to the extent that they generally have received praise as a way to describe Scott's particular historical method.[10]

In light of the evidence of Scott's **"Advertisement,"** however, this same point ought to prompt concern that the absence of identifiable historical types in *The Antiquary* simply means that critics have not known what they were looking for—that the novel, in short, tells us an unfamiliar history. David Hewitt recently paved the way for this recognition by pointing out that the novel's few national-historical references are entirely consistent with one another, dating its action very precisely to the mid-1790s.[11] I intend to show that the location of the novel's action in the 1790s is in fact historical in a quasi-Lukácsian sense—that it portrays representative types derived from the historical peculiarity of the mid-1790s as understood in 1816—and thus to help it reveal this unfamiliar history. If critics have recently denied that Scott's third novel *is* historical, they have been correct to point out that it is deeply *concerned with* the "historical"—concerned, that is, with the uses and limits of history as a field of study.[12] Indeed, I argue here that the unfamiliar history that the novel reveals is that of the 1790s struggle over what to accredit as history. What renders this history unfamiliar is that contrary to the "mentalist" bias of the histories of history with which we are now familiar, *The Antiquary* dramatizes the earlier struggle as a choice between different kinds of sentimentalized and sexualized men. Scott constructs his narrative around two stereotypes of the feeling historical man that 1790s thinkers routinely deployed—often when attacking Edmund Burke—in an effort to define the limits of proper historical study and the relationship between historical thought and prudent action. By way of juxtaposition with these types, Lovel then functions less as a mediocre hero than as an empty form for stating the case of the "historical" for post-1790s historiography.

Satirical portraits of men obsessed with history, particularly of antiquaries, abounded in the late eighteenth century.[13] Scott seizes upon perhaps the two most common of these for his main characters in **The Antiquary**: the modern-day Quixote (Scott's Sir Arthur Wardour), who turns to the past on deeply political and nostalgic grounds in an effort to sustain a chivalric order of things that not only is outmoded but also cannot exist in the form that the Quixote imagines; and the pedantic scholar-collector (Jonathan Oldbuck), whose interest in the past is so thoroughly detached from present concerns as to be misanthropic and even morbid. Both portraits reinforce charges of political irresponsibility with connotations that such men are social misfits, figures whose perverse affective constitutions make them, according to the logic of the age, barely recognizable *as* men. But in the context of a novel set in a community that fears the expansion of the French Revolution to Britain, such types also have broader resonance, for I shall argue that they were two of the stereotypes that 1790s radicals commonly applied to Burke when discrediting his opposition to France. In *Reflections on the Revolution in France* (1790), Burke had proposed that prudent political action depends upon competent historical understanding (something that he denies to the French and their British supporters) and that such competence both depends upon and reinforces a properly "manly" sentimental constitution.[14] These stereotypes were thus ideal fits, turning Burke against himself by implying that he was both out of touch with recent history and incompetent to his own historicist project on sentimental and gendered grounds. When Scott appropriates the types for his only novel set in the age of Burke, however, the resulting narrative reads as a vexed effort to rescue Burkean historicism from such types while also affirming their validity and, I conclude, their importance for keeping history, as well as the historical novel, disciplined.

For Sir Arthur, a knight of ancient Scottish blood, antiquarian inquiry is a profoundly sentimental enterprise, offering an outlet for Jacobite sympathies that, by the time of the novel's action, he feels more than he practices. "In all actual service and practical exertion he was a most zealous and devoted subject of George III," we read, but he opposes the "protestant succession" and "revolution principles" of 1688 in his studies, taking upon himself the role of "chivalrous assertor" of the "good fame of Queen Mary" (38-39). It is in fact this "chivalrous" role that

offers the best purchase on the sentimentality of those studies, for while Sir Arthur never seriously expresses a wish to restore an earlier historical moment, he does wish to preserve the chivalric system, a system whose ethical code is also a sentimental code, that secures hereditary "rank and privilege" (40).[15] His antiquarianism enacts this preservation insofar as he experiences his historical pursuits as chivalric ones, and in this respect, he clearly typifies the kind of historically minded subject that 1790s radicals famously charged Burke with being. Burke may update chivalry in *Reflections*, defending something closer to what Michael McKeon terms "conservative ideology" than to the "aristocratic ideology" that McKeon finds in medieval romance—defending, that is, the need to maintain the chivalric system of male sentimental deference to rank and sex because it has proven its worth as a prudent ethical and political code and not because rank and sex necessarily guarantee honor.[16] But for Burke's 1790s opponents, his historicism both defended and exhibited this older aristocratic ideology-based system of chivalric sentiment, just as, Scott suggests, Sir Arthur's antiquarianism does.

Those who sought to discredit Burke's competence as a historical thinker thus often caricatured him as a Quixote, implying that his chivalry-based historicist *apologia* for inherited cultural formations blinded him to the evidence of France's "true" state. Thomas Paine famously expresses this point in *The Rights of Man* (1791) when he locates Burke in "a world of windmills," arguing that his historical portrait of France resembles the world of "*plays*" and "tragic paintings" more than that of reality.[17] Scott similarly emphasizes that Sir Arthur's historical understanding is less sound epistemologically than his friend and neighbor Jonathan Oldbuck's and that his quixotic, chivalric sentiment-based faith in the probity of legends and received authorities is to blame. "The faith of Sir Arthur, as an antiquary, was boundless," he notes, whereas Oldbuck was

> more scrupulous in receiving legends as current and authentic coin. Sir Arthur would have deemed himself guilty of the crime of leze-majesty had he doubted the existence of any single individual of that formidable bead-roll of one hundred and four kings of Scotland, received by Boethius, and rendered classical by Buchanan, in virtue of whom James VI. claimed to rule his ancient kingdom.
>
> (38)

Sir Arthur's sentiment-based epistemological paradigm, that historical testimony's veracity correlates to the rank of its adherents (a transportation into historical method of the same principle of sentimental deference to "persons" over "principles" that Paine had criticized in Burke),[18] actually occasions a dispute when Oldbuck questions the evidentiary relevance of the fact that one of his friend's historical authorities is a "gentleman of high family and ancient descent" (50). In fact, Sir Arthur, whose "taste for antiquities" we are told is "neither very deep nor very correct" when compared to Oldbuck's, grows angry at intrusions of his neighbor's empiricist historical method—what Sir Arthur calls an "uncivil" method based on a "frivolous accuracy of memory" and "pettifogging intimacy with dates, names, and trifling matters of fact"—into his own romance-derived vision of the past (41).

For Burke's opponents, depicting him as a Quixote of course implied more than just an epistemological critique of his chivalric sentiment-based historicism. It borrowed his own correlation of historical understanding and political prudence to critique his historicism on moral and political grounds too, equating it with the injustices of the historical formations that he used it to defend. We find this in Paine's critique when, after detailing the abuses of the ancien régime, he suggests that Burke "pities the plumage but forgets the dying bird."[19] Political caricaturists made the equation more blatant, representing a quixotic Burke doing everything from riding the hydra of "monarchy" over the backs of "base born plebians" to wielding a "Shield of Aristocracy and Despotism." But the larger point to be made is that such images usually do less to indict Burke's historicism for being sentimental or chivalric than they do to imply that his sentimental chivalric constitution is malformed, that it misses the proper objects of sentiment. In *Reflections,* Burke had portrayed manliness, and manly sentiment in particular, as crucial to historical understanding and, in turn, to prudent action. Few of the era's portraits of Burke-as-Quixote—even Paine's—readily challenge that logic, representing him instead as historically imprudent because he is, quite simply, incompetent to his own sentimental project.[20] The properly feeling man would feel for the people whom the quixotic defender of monarchy crushes underfoot or emblazons on his shield. The atrophied nature of Burke's body in these and similar images (a body that is always out of place amidst the trappings of chivalry) only underscores the inadequacy of his bodily constitution to what Burke had implied are the mutually constitutive tasks of being manly, feeling properly, and prudently analyzing and acting in the present state of history.

The Antiquary similarly critiques Sir Arthur, matching his incompetence as a historian to his imprudence as a historical actor. Sir Arthur's fate is intertwined with that of Dousterswivel, a con man and possible spy for the French, who successfully preys upon the knight's ancestral pride and credulity in romance in order to prompt him to invest his family fortune in ill-advised business ventures. The result is that Sir Arthur's chivalric sentiment-based history nearly bankrupts his ancestral estate, shakes up the town's social hierarchy, reduces Britain's national wealth, and strengthens the French cause. Scott's sense of the threats that such possibilities pose—that Sir Arthur will, for example, inadvertently diminish the aristocracy's power and also increase Britain's vulnerability to revolutionary conspiracy—of course derives more from Burke's fears in the 1790s than from the views of his radical opponents. But

his equation of chivalric sentiment-based historicism with imprudence hearkens back to the earlier decade's caricatures depicting Burke as a Quixote.

Indeed, as in those images, Scott punctuates his portrait of Sir Arthur's incompetence as a historian and imprudence as a historical actor with various question marks about his manliness and sentimentality. In an early scene, for example, Sir Arthur assumes the role of the damsel in distress when he and his daughter are stranded on a cliffside by the tide. They must be rescued by Lovel, whose actions are then applauded as "manly" (74). In another early scene, Sir Arthur opens both his prudence and his sentiments up to suspicion by asking magistrates to round up Edie Ochiltree, an itinerant beggar, as a possible French spy. Not only does Ochiltree later help Lovel save Sir Arthur's fortune and protect Britain from French invasion, but in his roles as news-bringer, oral historian, and state-sanctioned object of sympathy, he is also the novel's most obvious emblem of sentiment's importance to national strength.[21] His name actually conjures up the oak tree, Burke's favorite metaphor for Britain's solidity: just as the community's tears sustain Ochiltree, Scott seems to imply, so they water the British oak.[22] Sir Arthur's failure to feel for Ochiltree thus contributes to the reader's sense of his incompetence as a historian, if not more generally to a sense of the incompatibility of Sir Arthur-like historical study in the 1790s with maintaining Burke's ideal political, sentimental, and manly order of things.

The historical understanding of Oldbuck, a landholder descended from early German printers, promises to avoid such problems given that the narrator indicates that it is more "scrupulous" and "correct" than Sir Arthur's. While Sir Arthur experiences his antiquarian pursuits as a deeply politicized defense and enactment of sentiment-based aristocratic ideology, Oldbuck imports a quasi-scientific empirical method and ideal of impartiality into his own.[23] The way he lives can "neither make nor mar [the] king" (47), he boasts, and indeed the relation of his historical study to his Whig politics never becomes entirely clear to the reader. But while that method and ideal may lend his histories a greater semblance of veracity, Scott makes it clear that they guarantee neither those histories' relevance nor their historian's social responsibility. In this respect, I would argue, Oldbuck revives the most prevalent late-eighteenth-century stereotype of the antiquary, a figure that Mary Wollstonecraft, Catherine Macaulay, and Paine also had applied to Burke in the 1790s in an effort to discredit his manliness and prudence.

When distinguishing eighteenth-century antiquarianism from the Scottish Enlightenment's "philosophical" historical project, contemporary scholars emphasize that the former, by privileging the particular over the general, the rare over the representative, and the empirical over the theoretical, raised questions about the politics and possibility of the latter's ideal of historical totalization.

Nationalist antiquaries, those who turned to oral tradition and the past's material remains so as to mourn and restore cultures colonized by the English, discounted Scottish Enlightenment stadialist models of historical progress as imperialist themselves.[24] Likewise, protracted debates between scientific antiquaries, gentlemen scholars who made a hobby of classifying and archiving ballads, artifacts, and ruins, tended to underscore not only the difficulty of producing stable knowledge of the past but also the inadequacy of existing philosophical histories to account for the raw materials the past had left behind.[25] As the epigraph on Sir Richard Hoare's *Ancient Wiltshire* (1810) tellingly boasts, "We speak from facts, not theory."[26] But by the turn of the century, such arguments had also given antiquaries a reputation for being unmanly on the grounds that they failed to produce forward-looking knowledge or policy. Many viewed them as men who, as Scott pointedly observed in his journal in 1826, "neglect what is useful for things that are merely curious": "trifling discussions about *antiquarian old-womanries*," he later writes, are "like knitting a stocking, diverting the mind without occupying it."[27] Some still valued antiquaries' insights for showing where philosophical histories—histories that acknowledge that every reflection of the past is also a selection of the past that gives it a direction—misdirect history by being inaccurate reflections. Indeed, Katie Trumpener has demonstrated antiquaries' importance for solidifying insurgent movements in Britain's peripheral Celtic states in the period.[28] But in general, antiquaries had acquired a reputation for neither selecting nor reflecting anything useful and, therefore, for rejecting historical "direction" in favor of the pleasure of historical reflection as an end in itself.[29] The popular image of the antiquary in the period was that of a man whose enjoyment in studying the past irresponsibly detaches him from present historical concerns, calling his manliness into question. It is certainly a mold into which Wollstonecraft and Macaulay inserted Burke in two of the earliest attacks on *Reflections*. Just after accusing Burke of having been "emasculated by hereditary effeminacy," Wollstonecraft depicts him in *A Vindication of the Rights of Men* (1790) as a man whose affinity for the ancient British constitution is akin to "rak[ing] amongst heterogeneous ruins" and to looking into "an ancient castle, built in barbarous ages, of Gothic materials."[30] Macaulay follows suit in *Observations on the Reflections of the Right Hon. Edmund Burke* (1790), writing that France's revolutionaries "do not profess to have any of the spirit of antiquarians among them," seeing "*none of those striking beauties* in the old laws and rules of the Gothic institutions of Europe, which Mr. Burke does."[31]

It is also the satirical image of the antiquary that Scott references when portraying Oldbuck. Oldbuck's taste for antiquarian disputes and consistent pleasure in the arcane perhaps imply a distance from believing in the possibility or the ideal of historical totalization.[32] But even if we reject this point, the novel consistently insists on the detachment

of his historical discourse from the "manly" project of directing the nation's present course. The opening scene of *The Antiquary* emphasizes precisely this detachment. We first encounter Oldbuck worrying about the state of Scottish infrastructure and threatening to sue when the public coach falls off schedule, but when he discusses his antiquarian researches with the coach's other occupant, we read that, *like a child,*

> the pleasure of this discourse had such a dulcifying tendency that, although two causes of delay occurred, each of a more serious duration than that which had drawn down his wrath ... , our ANTIQUARY only bestowed upon the delay the honour of a few episodical poohs and pshaws, which rather seemed to regard the interruption of his disquisition than the delay of his journey.

(10)

The episode sets up the subsequent aside that Oldbuck gave up a legal career in his youth and began a lifelong, monk-like confinement (he calls himself a kind of "coenobite"; 20) when his employer found that his great application and "pleasure" in tracing the history of legal casuistry could not be turned to "lucrative and practical purposes" (14). At times, this incompatibility between his pleasure in past cases and his ability to participate in present "causes" can be comic. But the novel as a whole implies that it is no laughing matter, emphasizing that Oldbuck's historical pursuits and pleasures interfere with other men's understanding of, and thus their ability to act prudently in, the nation's present historical situation. Early in the novel, for example, he dismisses fears of a French naval invasion, calling such fears a "military frenzy" and jokingly wishing the invasion "were made and over, that [he] might hear no more about it" (44, 120). Yet the novel legitimates that frenzy by its end: the French navy never lands, but only, the plot reveals, because the British army and navy have been preparing for such an event. When it emerges that Lovel, the novel's "manly" hero (74), has secretly coordinated the army's part in this effort to secure British shores, Oldbuck's earlier boast to Lovel that he is covertly excavating a "national concern" (a Roman battlefield that evidence suggests is probably a recent ditch) ironically points up the disconnection of the histories that he makes from the prudence and manliness that the latter shows as he, so to speak, makes history (29).

The metonymic relationship of this disconnection to the work of excavation in the scene also connects Oldbuck to another "unmanning" facet of the romantic-era stereotype of the antiquary. Throughout the period, writings by figures as diverse as Laurence Sterne, Jean-Jacques Rousseau, Robert Southey, George Crabbe, and William Hazlitt portray scholars—including antiquaries—as men who revive the dead to instruct the living.[33] Paine, who contends that Burke's sentimental deference to precedent maintains rights for the dead that he denies to the living, consistently links Burke to that project so as to suggest that the state he defends is "monstrous": such a state keeps its dead alive artificially and subjects the living to their authority.[34] But a more common implication in the period's antiquarian satires is that studying the past's material remains does not resurrect the dead so much as deaden the historian—that an interest and pleasure in nonvital or unrevivable material "unmans" a man by detaching him from the living. Certainly this is one of the ironies present, for example, in Thomas Rowlandson's early nineteenth-century caricature "Death and the Antiquaries." Death's presence in this scene, as in every other scene from the *Dance of Death* series from which this panel is taken, highlights the shared mortality of all ranks and walks of life. But in this case death also shares the interest that the antiquaries take in an exhumed body, mirroring them even in the pose that he assumes as he inspects the body.

This view of antiquaries is present too in Paine's attempt to discredit Burke and, later, in Scott's portrait of Oldbuck. "Dryness," "mouldiness," and "dustiness" are the era's most common tropes to evoke antiquarian morbidity, the implication being that dry bones, mold, and dust form not just the material but also the symbolic milieu of the antiquary. In the opening pages of *The Rights of Man,* Paine repeatedly depicts Burke's sentimental attachments to historical precedents (what Paine calls "the manuscript assumed authority of the dead") as nonvital antiquarian ones—that is, as less-than-human material attachments to "dry, barren" texts, "musty records," "mouldy parchments," and of course "the dead" themselves.[35] The same tropes, and perhaps even Paine's depiction of Burke, inform Scott's 1816 representation of Oldbuck's study (a space that Oldbuck's niece and maid are cleaning when he and Lovel enter it):

> "You'll be poisoned here with the volumes of dust they have raised," continued the Antiquary, "but I assure you the dust was very ancient, peaceful, quiet dust, about an hour ago." ... It was, indeed, some time before Lovel could, through the thick atmosphere, perceive in what sort of den his friend had constructed his retreat. It was a lofty room of middling size, but obscurely lighted by high narrow latticed windows. One end was entirely occupied by book-shelves, greatly too limited in space for the number of volumes placed on them, which were, therefore, drawn up in ranks of two and three files deep, while numberless others littered the floor and the tables, amid a chaos of maps, engravings, scraps of parchment, bundles of papers, pieces of old armour, swords, dirks, helmets, and Highland targets. ... The floor, as well as the table and chairs was overflowed by the same *mare magnum* of miscellaneous trumpery, where it would have been as impossible to find any individual article wanted, as to put it to any use when discovered.

(21-22)

The room resembles a church architecturally, but atmospherically, the "labyrinth of inconvenient and dark passages" at its entrance, along with its covering of artifacts and dust, more clearly evoke a tomb (20). The general impression is that this particular type of dry and dusty "study" (Scott clearly invites the double reading) is simply cut off from, out of place among, and useless to, the living. Indeed, the reader gets the sense, like Charles Lamb in a contemporaneous comment on Charron, that its contents are unavailable to resuscitation—that they are "scholastic dry bones, without sinew or living flesh."[36] If Sir Arthur evokes the 1790s stereotype of Burke that suggests his sentimental historical pursuits are imprudent, unmanly escapes from history and into romance, we might say that Oldbuck evokes the period's many portraits of the antiquary, including of Burke-as-antiquary, that suggest that he is imprudent, nonvital, and, thus, unmanly because his pleasures in historical pursuits lead him to live *too much* in history.

Scott's novel, set in a French Revolution-fearing Britain, thus reintroduces the terms and two key caricature types deployed in 1790s Britain's own French Revolution-inspired debates over history. But while it follows contributors to those debates in representing that decade's interrelated crises of historical understanding, political prudence, and national stability as crises of male feeling, it refuses to follow contributors—Wollstonecraft, for one—who contended that the crises lay in the very fact that British men feel.[37] A few recent commentators on the novel do note its celebration of sentiment, arguing that it asserts the dependence of national cohesion on sentimental interactions across social ranks and on those ranks' understanding of their traditional obligations to one another.[38] But such an account also falls short of acknowledging that the novel attributes Britain's 1790s stability as much to military action as to sentimental interaction and—and this is the key point given the way that the novel references 1790s political discourse—that it points to sentimental men as the key to Britain's success in both arenas. I would argue, that is, that *The Antiquary* retrospectively endorses one of Burke's implicit claims in *Reflections*—namely, that Britain's most manly and prudent historical subjects are those men whose teary eyes and tradition-based sentimental social ties not only strengthen the British oak directly but also enable them to recognize and prompt them to act when its waters need defending.[39]

For if Sir Arthur typfies the incompatibility of aristocratic ideology-based sentiment with manly and prudent historicism in the 1790s, then the character of Lovel, a sentimental man and capable army officer who rejects that ideology, looks like an attempt on Scott's part to assert the compatibility—even, the positive correlation—of other types of male sentiment with the same. The start of the novel clearly establishes Lovel as a "man of feeling": in addition to befriending Ochiltree, he is engaged secretly and, we are told, hopelessly to Sir Arthur's daughter Isabella; finds that his cheeks turn "scarlet" in her presence; spends most of his time alone; and worries much of that time about her well-being and their mutual feeling (43). Yet as the novel proceeds, Scott also suggests that he is both a competent historical thinker and a manly and prudent historical actor. As evidence of the former, Scott attributes to him the novel's only complex statement of the problem of historical epistemology. When, during a touring party led by Oldbuck and Sir Arthur, a question arises as to why more is known about medieval knights than abbots, only Lovel can supply a good answer:

> "The eras by which the vulgar compute time, have always reference to some period of fear and tribulation, and they date by a tempest, an earthquake, or burst of civil commotion. When such are the facts most alive in the memory of the common people, we cannot wonder," he concluded, "that the ferocious warrior is remembered, and the peaceful abbots are abandoned to forgetfulness and oblivion."
>
> (133)

This post-Scottish Enlightenment recognition, both that any historical representation is necessarily a culturally situated selection and reflection of culture and that the selection itself is a second-order reflection of culture, brings out the inadequacy of Sir Arthur's and Oldbuck's various appeals to representations to establish historical "facts." Moreover, Lovel matches this recognition with a capability—greater than those of the novel's other characters—to diagnose and act prudently in moments of local and national crisis: His quick thinking and physical prowess enable him to rescue Sir Arthur and Isabella; his assessment of Dousterswivel's motives allow him to save Sir Arthur financially; and on a larger historical scale, his skill and acumen as an officer insure Britain's safety from a naval invasion.

One could argue perhaps that the plot establishes Lovel's historical competence and prudence as if in spite of his sentiments insofar as he must perform these feats before he and Isabella can act on their feelings (his actions earn him Sir Arthur's respect and, thence, marital blessing). But given that the novel coerces the reader's sympathy for these sentiments, this denouement does more to assert, as Burke once had, that proper manly sentimental feeling (both for immediate loved ones and for the community at large) underwrites sound historical understanding, which the prudent historical actor in turn requires. This is not to say that *The Antiquary* repeats Burke's intellectual work in *Reflections*. Lovel's virtual absence from the second half of the novel prevents the reader from observing his development as a historical thinker, political agent, and sentimental man, thus making Scott's correlation of these developments much more mystical and arbitrary than Burke's. Rather, Lovel represents the validity of that Burkean correlation in the abstract for Scott, even as the figures of Sir Arthur and Oldbuck serve to acknowledge the difficulties, historically, of achieving that correlation. In turn, the reader is left with the sense that, while the novel portrays 1790s Britain's historical and historicist crises as problems of manliness, and specifically of

male feeling, the structure of its plot implies that these crises lessened with the emergence of a new generation of feeling men.

THE ANTIQUARIAN MIND'S DESIRE

The Antiquary does not limit the scope of these problems of feeling, however, to the terms in which I have just presented them. They are problems not strictly of men's sentiments and cognitive pleasures but of male sexuality too. Arguably, this is implicit in the novel's subject matter: the "man of feeling," whether revered or reviled, consistently emerges from 1790s debates over history as both a sentimental and a sexual type. Burke ensured this by erasing the line between male sentimental and heterosexual feeling in his "historical" performance in *Reflections*. He holds that France's national troubles stem from a paucity of sentimental men—men, for instance, who feel as he does toward Marie Antoinette—but prefaces the point with a passionate rhapsody on her beauty and an erotic tableau of an unsentimental mob driving her "half-naked" from her bedroom.[40] In an age in which caricaturists were wont to represent the "man of feeling" as a lascivious heterosexual type, *Reflections'* publication led them to insert Burke—particularly, in quixotic guise—into that formula. Others, like Wollstonecraft, interpreted male sentiment as a mark of unmanliness and sexual "equivocality," and charged Burke on these grounds with historical *in*competence and *im*prudence.[41] Given that Lovel's portrayal in Scott's novel suggests the Burkean point that sound historical understanding and manly, prudent historical action in the 1790s depended upon male sentiment and vice versa, the evidence of that decade's political debates over male sentiment suggests that perhaps we also ought to interpret the novel as establishing their dependence on men's "proper" sexual feelings too. That suggestion gains plausibility when we recall that the novel not only offers up marriage to Isabella as a reward for Lovel's manly, prudent historical actions but also invites our suspicion throughout that the motive for those actions is Lovel's desire for her.

But *The Antiquary* also explicitly correlates manly, prudent history-making with "proper" sexual feeling by establishing Lovel's historical career as a corrective to Oldbuck's. Earlier I argued that Oldbuck evokes the 1790s stereotype that antiquaries are unmanly, imprudent historical subjects because their pleasures detach them from the living. But I left out that this "dry" type can also be a male sexual type in the 1790s and in Scott's 1816 novel—indeed, throughout the period, many perceived antiquarian pursuits and pleasures as perverting men sexually, and even as evidence themselves of perversion. Romantic-era verbal and visual texts routinely represent antiquaries as nonvital men whose pleasures in the past's material presence compete with, or disqualify them for, "proper" sexual relations with the living. In the standard formulation, an antiquary does not just live among the dead; the past and its remains, even the act of examining and thinking about them, become a kind of replacement bedfellow.[42] As the wife laments in Francis Grose's satirical "Complaint of a wife at her husband's rage for Antiquities" (1791), ever since her husband joined the "Society of *Antic-queer-ones,*" he not only frequents "burial-places" more than "watering places" but also has lost interest in her sexually: appalled by the sum that he spent on an artifact because it was "eunuch" she concludes, in a phrase ripe with double entendre, "Folks must love those kind of cattle better than I do."[43] Burke's opponents sometimes linked him to this type too in their efforts to discredit his competence as a history-maker and to imply the unnaturalness of political systems that produce and depend upon such men. But caricatures and the *Reflections* fracas perhaps did less to solidify perceptions of antiquaries' perversity than did a roughly contemporaneous set of publicly canvassed events from the private life of Sir William Hamilton, the British Envoy to Naples and a renowned antiquary. Those events, though undoubtedly familiar to many readers, are nonetheless worth rehearsing in detail because their public representation not only affords a sustained glimpse at this sexual stereotype but also resonates with the cultural work that I take *The Antiquary* to perform through its juxtaposition of Oldbuck and Lovel.

In 1786, Emma Hart, the daughter of a blacksmith, became Hamilton's live-in mistress. He was a widower of nearly sixty; she was twenty and reputedly one of the most beautiful women in Britain.[44] What seemed to capture the public imagination about the relationship most, however, were not its startling differentials in age, education, social class, or physical attractions. It was that soon after it began, Sir William began having Emma perform for his friends a series of "attitudes," or poses taken from statues and frescoes familiar to antiquaries. By 1794, these astonishing *tableaux vivants* had spawned series of Frederick Rehberg sketches and Thomas Piroli engravings, as well as numerous public and private reports. Goethe describes Emma's pantomime, which he witnessed in 1787, in a passage that later appears in his *Die italienische Reise* (1816):

> The Chevalier Hamilton, so long connoisseur and student of Art and Nature, has found a counterpart in a lovely girl—English, and some twenty years of age. She is exceedingly beautiful and finely built. She wears a Greek dress becoming her to perfection. She then merely loosens her hair, takes a pair of shawls, and effects changes of posture, mood, gestures, mien and appearance that make one really feel as if one were in some dream. ... Her elderly knight holds the torch for her performance, and is absorbed in his mind's desire. In her he finds the charm of all antiques, the fair profiles on Sicilian coins, the Apollo Belvidere himself.[45]

In an essay on connoisseurship, Ann Bermingham supposes that these performances made Sir William appear as "merely a passive spectator in the thrall of feminine beauty."[46] But it was much the opposite that occasioned observations like Goethe's. Particularly striking in the passage is that Goethe in effect admits his own sexual pleasure in Emma's "finely built" female body but denies that pleasure to Sir William, attributing to him instead "a mind's desire" for the variously gendered "antiques" that she brings to life. And this attribution to him of pleasure not in the body of a living woman but in the body, so to speak, of history is not unique to Goethe. It informs most reports of Sir William, including Horace Walpole's quip, occasioned by news of his friend's second marriage in 1791, that "Sir William Hamilton has actually married his gallery of statues."[47]

If many already viewed Sir William as perverse before his marriage because they thought that he desired a woman most for her ability to transform herself into an archive, the subsequent events of his marriage did little to quell perceptions that he was unable to take or maintain sexual interest in women or, at least, in living women. In 1798, Emma began an open affair with Admiral Nelson, which lasted until his death at Trafalgar in 1805. She bore him two children, and in the two years prior to Sir William's death in 1803, Nelson, perhaps *the* national hero of Britain in his day, lived in the same house with the Hamiltons. This peculiar case, which perfectly encapsulated the tradition of seeing antiquaries as men who desire the past more than they do women, thoroughly solidified perceptions of antiquaries as "unmanly" and "perverse." Almost a decade after Sir William's death, the affair still filled the public imagination sufficiently to serve as the primary allusion for Rowlandson's *Modern Antiques* (c. 1811), probably the early-nineteenth-century's most famous caricature of the figure of the antiquary.

Rowlandson's image represents an artifact-filled cabinet in which an aged antiquary inspects the genitals on a male-figured sarcophagus while, nearby, a young woman and a naval officer employ another sarcophagus for a sexual liaison.[48] The sexual coupling inside the furniture of the tomb parallels the antiquary's relationship to that furniture such that the antiquary becomes the scene's comic butt. The parallel draws out the already present hint of the sexual nature of the antiquary's pursuits while registering their distance from, even their power to make him oblivious to, "proper"—that is, both heteronormative and vital—sexual impulses, such as those being indulged in his line of vision. That sexual perversion itself emerges as a kind of deathliness too insofar as the image's oxymoronic title marks the antiquary as less a person than an antique himself. At the same time, viewers receive no clues that they ought to see the antiquary as incompetent at his study or that they ought to disapprove of the liaison in the foreground, even if its "real-life" referent suggests it is adulterous. The effect is to suggest that antiquarian pursuits pervert men sexually or are evidence themselves of perversion; to correlate this perversion with deathliness; and, conversely, to correlate naval heroism with male sexual normalcy, vitality, and fecundity.

By juxtaposing Oldbuck's antiquarian type with a narrative of Lovel's fruitful careers as an officer and closet romantic, *The Antiquary* participates in the same tradition of 1790s anti-antiquarian thought that the Hamilton affair helped to consolidate and that Rowlandson's *Modern Antiques* encapsulates so perfectly. For there can be little doubt that Scott's portrait of Oldbuck not only conjures up the 1790s type of the antiquary as a man who is detached from the present state of the nation, living more among dry bones than among the living, but also taps into the sexual side of that type. We saw earlier that the novel opens with a coach journey during which "the pleasures of [antiquarian] discourse" distract Oldbuck from his historical situation (10). But before that discourse begins, the narrator has already sexualized Oldbuck's relationship to the archive by presenting him in flagrante delicto with a rare book, "undoing the parcel in his hand ... on which he gazed from time to time with the knowing look of an amateur, admiring its height and condition" (9). In this context, "amateur" of course connotes one devoted to or fond of something, and in fact, in a subsequent disquisition on the art of book collecting, Oldbuck himself emplots his antiquarian pursuits in the genre of the rake's narrative.[49] During the speech, he itemizes his conquests, celebrates his ability to coax others out of what they hold most sacred, recalls his nighttime searches for "trophies" on some famously seedy streets in 1790s Edinburgh, and all the while represents himself as an eager and impassioned "amateur":

> See this bundle of ballads, not one of them later than 1700, and some of them an hundred years older. I wheedled an old woman out of these, who loved them better than her psalmbook. ... These little Elzevirs are memoranda and trophies of many a walk by night and morning through the Cowgate, the Canongate, the Bow, Saint Mary's Wynd,— wherever, in fine, there were to be found brokers and trokers, those miscellaneous dealers in things rare and curious. ... [H]ow have I trembled, lest some passing stranger should chop in between me and the prize, and regarded each poor student of divinity that stopped to turn over the books at the stall, as a rival amateur, or a prowling bookseller in disguise!—And then, Mr Lovel, the sly satisfaction with which one pays consideration and pockets the article, affecting cold indifference, while our hand is trembling with pleasure!

(24-25)

Oldbuck's "rapturous voice" and "transport" as this disquisition continues cannot help but assume sexual overtones (25), particularly insofar as they echo the sexualized language and tone that the period's growing literature on book collecting consistently adopts to describe men's relationships to their books.[50] The best-known of these works, the lighthearted *Bibliomania* (1809), written by Thomas Frognall Dibdin, a friend of Scott's, provides several good examples of this, but richer still is John Ferriar's slightly earlier satire "The Bibliomania" (1809).[51] Ferriar's anti-antiquarian poem attacks the "Tyrant-passion" that turns a man into a "lettered fop," leading him to cast a "wistful glance" at books, to boast that the object of his "ardent mind" is "in red morocco dressed," and to regard bookcases as guardians of "tempting charms."[52] Even if such erotic overtones were to escape Scott's readers, however, Oldbuck makes them unavoidable by his speech's end. He concludes with the observation—one that resonates with stereotypes like Rowlandson's that depict antiquaries whose attachments to the material remains of the past substitute for, or provide alternatives to, heterosexual pleasures—that "the charms on which we doat are not so obvious to the eyes of youth as those of a fair lady" (26).[53]

Such self-posturing against traditional male heterosexual pleasures perhaps invites readers to interpret Oldbuck's historical pursuits and friendships as forms of homosexual practice, a reading made more compelling by Scott's own friendships with antiquaries like Richard Payne Knight, who had gained notoriety in 1786 for publishing a study on cults of priapus.[54] Indeed, Sir William Hamilton had collaborated on the study with Knight, a fact of which Rowlandson of course reminds his viewer when he portrays Sir William inspecting the male genitals on a sarcophagus. Nonetheless, as *The Antiquary* works to render Oldbuck's "dry" antiquarian career incompatible with a traditional heterosexual one, it also represents his eroticized relationship to the material remnants of the past less as a proxy for hetero- or homosexual relationships than as a sexual persuasion all its own, one that more often than not interferes with sexual interests in the living. In addition to depicting Oldbuck's study as a tomb, Scott consistently juxtaposes glimpses of Oldbuck's antiquarian pleasures with references to his "early disappointment in love, in virtue of which he had commenced Misogynist, as he called it" (15). When, for example, the reader first hears of this "disappointment"—a failed attempt to woo a woman named Eveline Neville—the discovery follows the suggestive observation that Oldbuck holds "little intercourse" with society at all and that his "studies and pleasures seemed to them alike incomprehensible" (15). It later turns out that these studies and pleasures themselves contributed to this failure insofar as they provided the rival suitor who ultimately married Eveline with ample opportunities for "indulging his levity at [Oldbuck's] expence" (270). That story of "disappointment" by itself brings the novel's portrait of Oldbuck into the proximity of the sexual discourse in which Rowlandson's drawing participates, and its appearance within the narrative of a military officer's success in the face of similarly disappointment-laden circumstances only heightens the connection. Lovel plays a kind of morally impeccable Lord Nelson (he is not an adulterer) to Oldbuck's sexually suspect and unmanly Sir William Hamilton.

Yet Scott also remakes a sexual critique like Rowlandson's as a history of male sexuality insofar as he uses these "proper" and "improper" male sexual types not in a synchronic image but in a diachronic historical narrative. *The Antiquary* provides little evidence of the kinds of historical changes that other *Waverley Novels* narrate, but I have already remarked that a sense of historical movement emerges within it in the form of a generational shift from affectively malformed antiquaries like Sir Arthur and Oldbuck to responsible history-making, sentimental men like Lovel. I am arguing here that Scott's novel suggests that this shift was one in male sexual norms too insofar as it maps these opposing sexual types onto different sides of the same generational divide—onto Oldbuck and Lovel, respectively. Given that Oldbuck refers to Lovel throughout as his "phoenix," the implication seems to be that the latter's marriage at the novel's end rises as if out of the dust of Oldbuck's sexual career, thus committing the old antiquary's "dry" sexual type to the grave. The metaphorical quality of Lovel and Isabella's marriage as generational rebirth is in fact made all the more blatant as it occurs just after Lovel discovers, as does everyone else, that he is the long-lost son of Eveline Neville, the woman who occasioned Oldbuck's early "disappointment": at the very moment that Lovel's sexual career appears most like a counterfactual version of Oldbuck's, Scott transforms him into the son that Oldbuck quite literally never had.

The Antiquary thus asks to be taken seriously as a historical portrait of the situation of history itself in and just after the 1790s, representing what we might call the "case" of history's disciplinary authority and legitimacy in that era in terms similar to those in which the era's own thinkers understood it. Recent histories of history would have us believe that during this period, the problem of defining the limits of legitimate historical inquiry primarily constituted an exercise in developing new epistemological forms. But when read as an authoritative history itself, *The Antiquary* draws into relief the extent to which the period's writers understood that problem to extend beyond epistemology. The problem was not just whether individuals could know the past, but whether the study of history could be made socially relevant and responsible. This latter concern had everything to do with what kind of sentimental and sexual education—in turn, what kind of man—people believed that study produced. There was even a sense that the epistemological problem of history derived from this problem of manliness, that only a properly sentimentally and sexually constituted man could ever truly know the past.

In addition, the novel begins to help us recognize that the period's stereotypes of antiquaries played an important role in defining and reflecting these concerns. As a history, *The Antiquary* reads largely as an effort to rescue the post-1790s historical thinker from the criticisms that such caricatures imply. Through the figure of Lovel, who avoids and compensates for the flaws of characters based on those caricatures, the novel endorses the Burkean position that competent historical thought should correlate with properly manly sentimentality and sexuality, and these, with prudent historical action. It may use such caricatures to highlight that correlation's difficulty, thus asserting their relevance to defining what count as proper ways to access

and relate to the past. But it also tries to commit that difficulty to the past, locating the relevant targets of such caricatures not only in an earlier historical moment but also, by way of juxtaposition with Lovel, in a residual position in relation to that moment. Lovel emerges from the novel as an empty form of a new historical man, a sparsely drawn figure whose outlines hold little more than the promise that between the 1790s and 1816 historical inquiry and practice successfully left their antiquarian forefathers' problems in the dust.

REOPENING THE CASE OF HISTORY IN 1816

Of course there would have been much to make Scott's readers skeptical about such a promise. In the decade preceding the novel's publication, there is plenty of evidence that attests to the continued vitality of 1790s stereotypes of antiquaries and, moreover, of that period's concerns over the manliness, sentimentality, sexuality, and political prudence of historical inquiry and education. Rowlandson's 1811 *Modern Antiques* is one of several surviving prints from this decade that rework the theme of the antiquary who neglects his wife; review essays of the 1810s on history and historical novels regularly discuss the importance of feeling to historical understanding and of vitality to historical representations;[55] and the period's political journalism and pamphleteering remain wedded to many of the same vocabularies and ideologies that structured the *Reflections* controversy.[56]

But the more important point in the context of the present essay is that there are also ways in which *The Antiquary* itself modifies the reader's conviction in the evenness of the generational shift in history-making that it narrates. To this point I have been discussing the novel as a history. In this section, however, I would like to suggest that Scott's investment in writing this history, particularly in promising that since the 1790s the Oldbucks and Sir Arthurs of the world had been safely marginalized in relation to the field of legitimate historical thought, derives from the fact that he is writing a novel. In other words, I mean to show that his concern with the 1790s, and with 1790s caricatures of antiquaries in particular, bespeaks his own concern over the authority and legitimacy of historical novels both as literature and as a form of history-writing, an anxiety that in fact underwrites many of Scott's efforts in the *Waverley Novels* to articulate his cultural project.

The key to this reading lies in the fact that, as so many readers of *The Antiquary* have remarked, Lovel's character never escapes being overshadowed by Sir Arthur's and Oldbuck's. This effect has been interpreted by some critics as a sign of the novel's "incoherence" and even "failure" as a plot.[57] But there is also a coherence and success to that effect: it does less to undermine confidence in the existence of a generational shift in history-making than it does to call into question the historical novel's own position in relation to that shift. Indeed, as *The Antiquary* turns Sir

Arthur and Oldbuck into residual figures within the landscape of post-1790s historical thought, the novelist comes to resemble the two aged antiquaries much more than he does Lovel. The ending, for example, arguably revives the same imprudent, incompetent mode of historical epistemology that it elsewhere attributes to Sir Arthur. In the last chapter, Lovel learns more than just his parentage: he finds out that he is heir to the title and estate of the Earl of Glenallan. If this use of the revealed parentage trope so familiar to readers of romance already reduces the plot's historical specificity, it also grafts the old knight's unhistoricist worldview onto the course of 1790s history. Far from upsetting Sir Arthur's correlation of true nobility with aristocratic nobility, along with the sentimental and ethical codes derived from it, Lovel's emergence as the right type for 1790s Britain revitalizes that correlation, effectively rendering his rightness as a type unspecific to any one time or place.

More strikingly, the ending also collapses the distance between the novelist and Oldbuck. Throughout the novel, Oldbuck tries to persuade Lovel to write a fictionalized account of an ancient Caledonian battle in Scotland, and, at the novel's end, he still "regularly inquires whether [Lovel] has commenced the Caledoniad, and shakes his head at the answers he receives" (365). But the closing sentence further indicates that he has "completed his [historical] notes" that will be appended to the project and that these are "at the service of any one who chuses to make them public" (365). In other words, the novel closes with Oldbuck writing, and Lovel abstaining from writing, Scottish historical fictions that resemble the *Waverley Novels* in form: Scott's own **"Notes to the Antiquary"** commence only a page after this sentence in most early editions. At the very least, Oldbuck's resemblance to Scott struck his contemporaries. Washington Irving, for example, wrote that "many of the antiquarian humours of [Oldbuck] were taken from [Scott's] own richly compounded character."[58] Scott even invited the comparison himself as his career unfolded. In his journals, he began referring to women as "ladykind" or "woman kind" (phrases he once had placed in Oldbuck's mouth), and he also entitled his catalogue of his antiquarian holdings *Reliquiae Trottcosianae, or the Gabions of the late Jonathan Oldbuck Esq.*[59]

Much of Scott's self-posturing as Oldbuck is tongue-in-cheek of course and, like Irving's own Geoffrey Crayon, even conventional for its day. Nonetheless, it does suggest how difficult he found it to separate his own relationship to the past and its remains from the attachments to the same that he critiques in *The Antiquary*. Since Macaulay's famous 1828 *Edinburgh Review* essay on "History," it has been a commonplace in Scott criticism to argue that the *Waverley Novels* encouraged professional historical inquiry's extension into fields previously examined only by antiquaries.[60] The flip side of that account must be that novels like *The Antiquary* reveal the extent to which Scott

understood his struggle for cultural legitimacy and authority outside of the field of traditional history-writing in terms of late-eighteenth-century antiquarianism's vexed struggle for the same. In turn, based on my argument to this point, we can expect that a key focal point for the former struggle was the manliness both of the Author of the *Waverley Novels*' sentimental and sexual constitution, and of the sentimental and sexual education that those novels offer.

Support for this argument can be found throughout the *Waverley Novels.* The legitimacy of applying it to the series as a whole gains particular credence, however, if we examine it through the **"Dedicatory Epistle"** to *Ivanhoe,* a text that critics often cite as Scott's most significant meditation on historiography. The **"Dedicatory Epistle,"** part of the prefatory matter to *Ivanhoe,* consists of a letter from *Ivanhoe*'s fictitious author asking permission to dedicate the novel (which is based on a manuscript owned by *The Antiquary*'s Sir Arthur Wardour) to the Rev. Dr Jonas Dryasdust, a fictional antiquary whose name first cropped up in *The Antiquary* as one of Oldbuck's colleagues (282). The text primarily defends the claim, one that Dryasdust purportedly disputes, that it is possible to write novels about English history that are as effective and interesting as Scott's novels about Scottish history. Yet, despite its specific focus on historical novels and not on history-writing per se, scholars have discussed the text almost unanimously as Scott's most detailed statement of the epistemological problem of knowing the past and the related methodological problem of making the past known through representations.[61] Lukács and Chandler even identify it as one of modern European historicism's foundational texts, the latter privileging it as "the literary instantiation of Romantic historicism's complex conceptual framework."[62]

These influential discussions, while insightful, nonetheless manifest the blind-spot that I attribute more generally to recent histories of history. Specifically, they pass over the fact that Scott formulates these epistemological and methodological problems as plights of feeling in the **"Dedicatory Epistle,"** squarely placing the blame for them on men's bodies and their material circumstances. For Scott, the acuteness of the artistic and historiographic challenge facing the novelist of English history lies in this physical realm:

> If you describe to him [the English novel-reader] a set of wild manners, and a state of primitive society existing in the Highlands of Scotland, he is much disposed to acquiesce in the truth of what is asserted. ... If he be of the ordinary class of readers, he has either never seen those remote districts at all, or he has wandered through those desolate regions in the course of a summer tour, eating bad dinners, sleeping on truckle beds, stalking from desolation to desolation, and fully prepared to believe the strangest things that could be told him of a people, wild and extravagant enough to be attached to scenery so extraordinary. But the

same worthy person, when placed in his own snug parlour, and surrounded by all the comforts of an Englishman's fireside, is not half so much disposed to believe that his own ancestors led a very different life from himself; that the shattered tower, which now forms a vista from his window, once held a baron who would have hung him up at his own door without any form of trial.[63]

Under this formulation, cognizance of historical difference depends on transportation, in all the Romantic-era ambiguity of that term. It requires an imaginative movement that is simultaneously an altered physical state and is thus particularly aided by sleeping in beds and inhabiting scenes that feel as if they belong to other places or times. The problem that the author of a novel about English history faces is that modern-day England is too "snug" a fit: Englishmen cannot remain in English beds and transport themselves *within* England. In turn, for Scott, knowing the past becomes a problem of a man producing what Chandler would call a "historical casuistry" of his own body.[64] A man attains historical consciousness, following the logic at work in the passage, only when he recognizes the case of his own embodiment—the historicity, in particular, of the relation of his feelings to the historical conditions defining his capacity to feel—and this requires assessing the relationship of that case to cases of embodiment in other times and places.

This conception of historical novel-reading and writing as a kind of physical education for men (one for which Scott also implies that certain male bodies have difficulty matriculating) sets the terms for what I take to be the **"Dedicatory Epistle**'s" overarching task—namely, that of distancing the *Waverley Novels*' artistic project from antiquarianism while also defending that project's legitimacy according to the criteria for evaluating historical thought that *The Antiquary* had endorsed three years earlier. Revisiting questions about the historical novelist that the ending of that novel had raised, Scott approaches this task by trying to establish the sentimental and sexual normalcy of the historical novelist's body and of the bodily works that his historical narratives perform. Toward that end, he further develops the comparison between novelists who write about Scotland's history and those who write about England's. Representing the historical archive as a set of fields strewn with corpses awaiting revival, he opposes the two on the basis of the kinds of fields and bodies on which each works. The former chooses a "recent field of battle," he writes, and is then "compelled to select" for revival "a body whose limbs had recently quivered with existence, and whose throat had but just uttered the last note of agony."[65] In such a scene of compulsions, quivering bodies, and notes of agony, historical novel-writing becomes a sentimental and even a seduced act—part response to a cry for help, part deathbed ministration and lamentation, and part attraction between bodies.

In contrast, Scott portrays the author of novels about English history as a man who "select[s] his subject amidst the dust of antiquity, where nothing [is] to be found but dry, sapless, mouldering, and disjointed bones."[66] If the scene's morbid dryness already implies that such writers and their narratives lack fecundity, its obvious invocation of the stereotype of the "dry" antiquary raises the possibility of their perversity too.[67] Indeed, Scott seems to confirm the distance of this scene of historical novel-writing from one of proper sentimental and sexual action and education when he comments explicitly on the abject nature of "dryness": he promises his readers not to tax them with "the *repulsive* dryness of mere antiquity."[68] It matters little, of course, that he goes on to suggest that this portrait of the English historical novelist need not be accurate. That suggestion alters only his judgment about the cultural legitimacy of such novels, leaving intact his correlation of legitimate relationships to the past with proper manly sentimentality and sexuality. Nor is the applicability of that correlation necessarily limited because it is applied only to historical novelists. His portrait of the author of historical novels about England, as well as the wry comments that he makes throughout the **"Dedicatory Epistle"** about Dryasdust's "grave" historical researches, imply that he thinks that the correlation also holds for establishing the claims of antiquarianism—and perhaps in light of the evidence of *The Antiquary,* those of any kind of historiography—to cultural authority and legitimacy within the field of history.

This last point is particularly revealing for understanding the *Waverley Novels*' role in relation to the discipline of history as the nineteenth century unfolded. Through a progressivist generational narrative set in the same nation (Scotland), *The Antiquary* had elevated an emergent manly historicist thinker over late-eighteenth-century antiquaries, the amateurism of the antiquarian fathers being supplanted, as it were, by the more manly feeling historicism of the son. The **"Dedicatory Epistle,"** like *The Antiquary,* works to establish a similar hierarchy—this time between the antiquary and the historical novelist—but it produces that hierarchy less through a narrative of generational succession than through one of uneven development. Scott, after all, maps the types of the dryasdustic English antiquary and the Scottish historical novelist onto different national spaces at the same moment in calendrical time. Although he also tries to deny the strict applicability of this model of uneven development along national lines, he nonetheless reasserts the applicability of the model to the space of the field of history by opposing historical novelists to dryasdustic antiquaries and then highlighting (through a passage that acknowledges the embattled nature of the historical novelist's claim to that field) the fact that both figures occupy that field at the same time. This model of uneven development of the field of history-writing of course need not negate the progressivist successional history of historicism and manliness that *The Antiquary* tries to develop—one of these figures may be more residual than emergent. But when contemplated alongside Scott's aforementioned portrayals of himself *as* Oldbuck as his career progressed, that model would seem, if not to enfold the successional model in Scott's own novel-writing body, then to mark that body as itself an unevenly developed space of competing feeling masculinities and modes of feeling history. This representation of an unevenly developed field of historical engagement enabled by, and productive of, the uneven development of masculinity in fact became the model that Victorian historians would later adopt when trying to stake claims to authority over their discipline for their own particular modes of history-writing.[69]

IS EVERYONE A SENTIMENTALITY CASE?

This essay thus uses the **Waverley Novels** to reveal some of the layers of tissue that, to adapt the title of Collingwood's classic study, flesh out "the idea of history" as it develops in Romantic-era Britain. In so doing, it shows that some unexpected—or, at least, recently unremarked—cultural work was being performed in the name of history's disciplinization in the Romantic era. The project of understanding the proper limits of historical enquiry often played out in the period's writings and caricatures as an effort to define masculinity's relationship to sentimentality and sexuality: masculinity served, in short, as a vessel for the period's thinkers to negotiate the relationship between, on the one hand, historical understanding and, on the other, sentimental and sexual feeling. Admittedly, that unexpected work has not gone entirely unremarked: a few feminist scholars have begun to respond to the neglect of sex and gender by historians of history and have done so in ways relevant to my concerns here. Bonnie Smith, for example, contends in *The Gender of History* (1998) that the professionalization of history in the 1800s involved gendering and, consequently, rejecting amateur histories as feminine.[70] Ina Ferris also makes the case in *The Achievement of Literary Authority* (1991) that the **Waverley Novels** lent the novel cultural legitimacy by borrowing some of the masculinity of historical discourse for a traditionally feminine genre that many critics believed overstimulated its readers' feelings.[71] But while I have sought, in part, to begin doing for our understanding of the role of the Waverley series in early-nineteenth-century historical discourse something analogous to the work that Ferris does for our understanding of its role in the novel's rise to "literary authority" in the same period, I have also been complicating her argument, not to mention Smith's. History's link to masculinity—and, in turn, its legitimacy—was itself far from secure in the 1790-1820 period, and I have tried to show here that its struggle for legitimacy and masculinity actually involved demonstrating its connection to certain types of sentimental and sexual feeling. **The Antiquary,** as a history, helps reveal that 1790s thinkers tried to gain authority for the discipline of history by defending its masculinity, and that they did so by distinguishing it from other modes of history-making—antiquarianism, particularly—that were not perceived as

dangerously feminine so much as sentimentally and sexually unmanly. Viewed through texts like **Ivanhoe**'s **"Dedicatory Epistle,"** the novel further reveals that Scott similarly understood the problem of establishing the historical novel's authority alongside, but also outside, the field of history-writing in the early nineteenth century. At the same time that he distances his post-Waterloo artistic project from antiquarianism, he also transfers its quest for cultural legitimacy into the terms of antiquarianism's struggles over the same in the 1790s.

In the context of discussing early reviews of **Waverley** (1814), Ferris notes that "the image of a new and abundant spring is typical of the idiom through which Scott's first readers articulated their experience of **Waverley** as an unexpected incursion of energy into a stale form: water in a dry season."[72] She is correct, I think, to cite this as evidence that early reviewers sought to give the novels an air of healthiness and manliness and thus to distinguish them from their "promiscuous" female-penned and read counterparts. But that metaphor of "water in a dry season" and its associated trope of resuscitation and rejuvenation—also a trope of impregnation given the link between "dryness" and impotency in the period's slang[73]—are even more typical of the way that Scott and many of his early readers conceived of the Waverley series as an incursion of positive energy into the sometimes imprudent, perverse, unmanly, and morbid realm of historical study.[74] In other words, what Ferris sees at stake in the **Waverley Novels'** negotiation of the divide between the genres of fiction and history—namely, sex and gender—was also already at stake in the period's attempts to define history itself as a field of study, and particularly to defend it from the types of charges that were being applied to antiquarianism. If the **Waverley Novels,** as Ferris herself notes, essentially brought the Scottish Enlightenment's project of historical generalization into contact with historical particulars that had traditionally been the antiquary's province, they also brought this crisis of sex and gender to a head in the process.[75] I have been arguing for **The Antiquary** as a privileged point of entry into that crisis insofar as it reads as an effort both to represent and to negotiate the purportedly "dry season" of 1790s antiquarianism. It remains to be seen whether my own critical intervention in doing so might have the power to make today's historians of history examine how their ability to think and argue as *mentalité* cases might be indebted to their forerunners' struggles to become *sentimentality* cases.

Notes

1. Dominick LaCapra, *Rethinking Intellectual History* (Ithaca, 1983); "Is Everyone a *Mentalité* Case? Transference and the 'Culture' Concept," in *History and Criticism* (Ithaca, 1985), 71-74; "Intellectual History and Critical Theory," in *Soundings in Critical Theory* (Ithaca, 1989), 182-209; and *Representing the Holocaust: History, Theory, Trauma* (Ithaca,

1994), 1-17. Similar transferential models of the relationship between the historian and history can be found in Hayden White's "The Historical Text as Literary Artifact" (1974), in *Tropics of Discourse: Essays in Cultural Criticism* (Baltimore, 1985), 86-87; Robert D. Newman's "Exiling History: Hysterical Transgression in Historical Narrative," in *New Historical Literary Study,* ed. Jeffrey N. Cox and Larry J. Reynolds (Princeton, 1993), 292-315; and Michel de Certeau's *The Writing of History* (1975), trans. Tom Conley (New York, 1988), 1-113.

2. Virginia Woolf, *To the Lighthouse* (London, 1927), chap. 19; and E. M. Forster, *Aspects of the Novel* (London, 1927), 46-56. Prominent nineteenth-century critics who place *The Antiquary* among the best of the Waverley series include Francis Jeffrey, John Wilson Croker, J. G. Lockhart, Leslie Stephen, Robert Louis Stevenson, John Watson, and G. M. Trevelyan; James T. Hillhouse, *The Waverley Novels and Their Critics* (Minneapolis, 1936), 45, 48, 163, 269; Leslie Stephen, *Hours in a Library* (New York, 1875), 199; John Watson, *Books and Bookmen and Other Essays* (1912; reprint, Freeport, N.Y., 1971), 169; and G. M. Trevelyan, Untitled 1937 Lecture to the Sir Walter Scott Society, in *Sir Walter Scott, 1771-1832: An Edinburgh Keepsake,* ed. Allan Frazer (Edinburgh, 1971), 33.

3. F. R. Leavis, *The Great Tradition* (London, 1948), 14 n. On Scott's reflection of the climate of historical thought in his age, see Sir Herbert Butterfield, *The Whig Interpretation of History* (London, 1931); Georg Lukács, *The Historical Novel* (1937), trans. Hannah Mitchell and Stanley Mitchell (Lincoln, Nebr., 1983), chap. 1; Duncan Forbes, "The Rationalism of Sir Walter Scott," *Cambridge Journal* 7 (1953): 20-35; Alexander Welsh, *The Hero of the Waverley Novels,* rev. ed. (Princeton, 1992); David Daiches, "Sir Walter Scott and History," *Etudes Anglais* 24 (1971): 458-77; Avrom Fleischman, *The English Historical Novel: Walter Scott to Virginia Woolf* (Baltimore, 1971), 16-36, 46-50; Peter Garside, "Scott and the 'Philosophical Historians,'" *Journal of the History of Ideas* 36 (1975): 497-512; and "Scott, the Romantic Past and the Nineteenth Century," *Review of English Studies* 23, no. 90 (1972): 147-61; David Brown, *Walter Scott and the Historical Imagination* (London, 1979), 196-98; Graham McMaster, *Scott and Society* (Cambridge, 1981), 49-77; and James Chandler, *England in 1819: The Politics of Literary Culture and the Case of Romantic Historicism* (Chicago, 1998), part 1.

4. Michel Foucault, *The Order of Things* (1966; reprint, New York, 1994), 217-21, 367-73.

5. R. G. Collingwood, *The Idea of History* (1946), ed. Jan van der Hussen, rev. ed. (Oxford, 1994), 282-302.

6. Ibid., 287.

7. Ibid., 84.

8. Walter Scott, *The Antiquary* (1816), ed. David Hewitt, Edinburgh Edition of the Waverley Novels (Edinburgh, 1995), 3. All subsequent citations refer to this edition and appear parenthetically in the text. Critics who suggest that the novel is not really about the past include David Daiches, "Scott's Achievement as a Novelist (Part One)," *Nineteenth-Century Fiction* 6 (1951): 157; Francis R. Hart, *Scott's Novels: The Plotting of Historic Survival* (Charlottesville, Va., 1966), 248; McMaster, *Scott and Society,* 165; Fleishman, *The English Historical Novel,* 75; Brown, *Walter Scott and the Historical Imagination,* 48, 65; Lars Hartveit, "'Silent Intercourse': The Impact of the Eighteenth-Century Conceptual Heritage on *The Antiquary* and *St. Ronan's Well,*" *English Studies* 1 (1996): 32; and Judith Wilt, *Secret Leaves: The Novels of Walter Scott* (Chicago, 1985), 168.

9. Lukács, *The Historical Novel,* 33-39.

10. On how Lukács's criteria "silence" certain histories, not to mention obscure some of Scott's ahistorical gestures, see Welsh, *The Hero of the Waverley Novels,* 194-96; Fleishman, *The English Historical Novel,* 50-51; Harry Shaw, *The Forms of Historical Fiction: Sir Walter Scott and His Successors* (Ithaca, 1983), 10, 43-46; Fiona Robertson, *Legitimate Histories: Scott, Gothic, and the Authorities of Fiction* (Oxford, 1994), 47-48; and Chandler, *England in 1819,* chap. 3. Support for Lukács's criteria as a description of Scott's historical method can be found in Fredric Jameson, *Marxism and Form* (Princeton, 1971), 191-96; Shaw, *The Forms of Historical Fiction,* 41-46; and Chandler, *England in 1819,* 255-57.

11. David Hewitt, "Historical Note," in Scott, *The Antiquary,* 444-46.

12. Daiches, "Scott's Achievement as a Novelist," 157; Hart, *Scott's Novels,* 246-58; Joan Elber, "Isolation and Community in *The Antiquary,*" *Nineteenth-Century Fiction* 27, no. 4 (March 1973): 418-19; James Reed, *Sir Walter Scott: Landscape and Locality* (London, 1980), chap. 5; Hartveit, "Silent Intercourse," 32-44; Robertson, *Legitimate Histories,* 197-205; and Wilt, *Secret Leaves,* 157-70.

13. Lucy Peltz and Martin Myrone, "Introduction: 'Mine Are the Subjects Rejected by the Historian': Antiquarianism, History, and the Making of Modern Culture," in *Producing the Past,* ed. Martin Myrone and Lucy Peltz (Aldershot, U.K., 1999), 2-3; and Lucy Peltz, "The Extra-Illustration of London: The Gendered Spaces and Practices of Antiquarianism in

the Late Eighteenth Century," in *Producing the Past*, 119.

14. Among the best recent scholarship on the subject are Claudia Johnson's *Equivocal Beings: Politics, Gender, and Sentimentality in the 1790s* (Chicago, 1995), 2-12, 23-46; and Tim Fulford's *Romanticism and Masculinity: Gender, Politics, and Poetics in the Writings of Burke, Coleridge, Cobbett, Wordsworth, De Quincey, and Hazlitt* (New York, 1999), chaps. 1-2. On the connection of prudence and manliness in Burkean political thought, see Welsh, *The Hero of the Waverley Novels*, 17. On the same in the Waverley Novels, see Wilt, *Secret Leaves*, 7-8; Welsh, *The Hero of the Waverley Novels*, 17-18, 112-17; and Ferris, *The Achievement of Literary Authority*, 247.

15. That is to say, he represents neither that type of pre-Victorian historian that Sir Herbert Butterfield identifies as a "Tory historian," nor the counter-imperialist "nationalist antiquary" that Katie Trumpener has shown to be a potent political figure in Britain's Celtic fringe in the late eighteenth century; Sir Herbert Butterfield, *The Englishman and His History* (Cambridge, 1944), chap. 2; and Katie Trumpener, *Bardic Nationalism* (Princeton, 1998).

16. Michael McKeon, *The Origins of the English Novel, 1600-1740* (Baltimore, 1987), part 2.

17. Thomas Paine, *The Rights of Man* (part 1, 1791) (London, 1966), 23. Paine in fact refers to Burke as a "Quixote" in the same passage.

18. Ibid., 23.

19. Ibid., 24.

20. Paine opposes Burkean sentimentality and chivalry on the grounds that they are "artificial" (i.e., unnatural) and not because he does not believe in natural sentiments and, even, a natural chivalry: this is the general thrust of his comment that Burke "is now a *case in point* with his own opinion that '*the age of chivalry is gone!*'"; Paine, *The Rights of Man*, 144. In fact, throughout the opening pages of *The Rights of Man*, Paine consistently celebrates various supporters of the revolution on the grounds that they are true men of feeling: see, for example, his comments on the secretary of the Archbishop of Thoulouse, Richard Price, and the Marquis de la Fayette; Paine, *The Rights of Man*, 5, 10, 17.

21. Ochiltree may have a historical original in Andrew Gemmels, an acquaintance of Scott's; W. S. Crockett, *The Scott Originals* (London, 1912), chap. 8; but as a symbol, he also has a clear original in William Wordsworth's "Old Cumberland Beggar" (1798).

22. On the oak's currency in the 1790s as an emblem of Britain, see William Ruddick, "Liberty Trees and Loyal Oaks: Emblematic Presences in some English Poems of the French Revolutionary Period," in Alison Yarrington and Kelvin Everest, eds., *Reflections of Revolution: Images of Romanticism* (London, 1993), 59-67.

23. Stuart Piggott finds such a method an ideal characteristic of seventeenth and much eighteenth-century antiquarianism. Deploying Collingwood's famous distinction between "facts" and "evidence," he characterizes these antiquaries as identifying "fossils or stone tools ... as an end in themselves" and not "as potential evidence from which wider inferences ... might be made." He also invokes Oldbuck explicitly as a literary example of this type of antiquary; Stuart Piggott, *Ruins in a Landscape* (Edinburgh, 1976), 110, 128, 157. Arnaldo Momigliano and Denys Hay express a similar view of the period's antiquarianism as "scientific," and Everett Zimmerman emphasizes its link to Enlightenment empiricism; Arnaldo Momigliano, "Ancient History and the Antiquarian" (1950), in *Studies in Historiography* (New York, 1966), 3, 20-21, 27; Denys Hay, *Annalists and Historians: Western Historiography from the Eighth to the Eighteenth Centuries* (London, 1977), 170; Everett Zimmerman, *The Boundaries of Fiction: History and the Eighteenth-Century British Novel* (Ithaca, 1996), 4, 17-18.

24. Trumpener, *Bardic Nationalism*, 27-28; and Piggott, *Ruins in a Landscape*, 120.

25. Momigliano, "Ancient History," 10-13, 20-21; Piggott, *Ruins in a Landscape*, chap. 6; and Everett Zimmerman, "Fragments of History and *The Man of Feeling*: From Richard Bentley to Walter Scott," *Eighteenth-Century Studies* 23, no. 3 (Spring 1990): 283-84.

26. Cited in Piggott, *Ruins in a Landscape*, 127.

27. Walter Scott, *The Journal of Sir Walter Scott*, ed. W. E. K. Anderson (Oxford, 1972), 170, 441.

28. Trumpener, *Bardic Nationalism*, passim.

29. Upon retiring from the Society of Antiquaries in 1784, Edward King, for example, upbraided many antiquaries for studying "without aiming at any one useful end"; quoted in Joan Evans, *A History of the Society of Antiquaries* (Oxford, 1956), 184. Some idea of the general currency of this opinion in the late eighteenth century can be obtained from Zimmerman, "Fragments of History," 283-85.

30. Mary Wollstonecraft, *A Vindication of the Rights of Men* (1790) (London, 1995), 41.

31. Catherine Macaulay, *Observations on the Reflections of the Right Hon. Edmund Burke* (1790), in

Political Writings of the 1790s, ed. Gregory Claeys (London, 1995), 1:131; emphasis mine.

32. On this point it is worth noting that most of the anti-quarian authorities whom Oldbuck cites in the novel, as well as the actual antiquaries upon whom Scott supposedly based Oldbuck—e.g., William Stukeley, Sir Robert Sibbald, Alexander Gordon, Sir John Clerk of Penicuik, etc.—are members of the tradition of scientific antiquarianism just described; Piggott, *Ruins in a Landscape,* 128, 134-145, 166.

33. Laurence Sterne, *Letters of Laurence Sterne,* ed. Perry Curtis (1935; reprint, Oxford, 1965); Jean-Jacques Rousseau, *Discourse on the Sciences and the Arts* (1750) in *The First and Second Discourses,* ed. Roger D. Masters, trans. Roger D. Masters and Judith R. Masters (New York, 1964); Robert Southey, "My Days Among the Dead are Passed" (c. 1828), in *The Poems of Robert Southey,* ed. Maurice H. Fitz-gerald (Oxford, 1909), 347; George Crabbe, *The Library. A Poem* (London, 1781); and William Ha-zlitt, "On the Conduct of Life" (1822), in *The Col-lected Works of William Hazlitt in Twelve Volumes,* (London, 1904), 12:429. On the seventeenth-century antecedents of this trope, see Scott Dudley's "Con-ferring with the Dead: Necrophilia and Nostalgia in the Seventeenth Century," *ELH* 66 (1999): 277-94.

34. Paine, *The Rights of Man,* 11, 13.

35. Ibid., 13, 20, 17, 12-13. For the continued currency of the trope of antiquaries' "deadness" at the time that Scott was writing *The Antiquary,* see William Haz-litt's "On the Conversation of Authors" (1820), in *The Selected Writings of William Hazlitt,* ed. Duncan Wu (London, 1998), 8: 38-39; and John Ferriar's satirical poem "The Bibliomania" (1809), which rep-resents the book collector (a figure generally con-flated with the antiquary) as a man for whom "books, neglected and forgot, / Excite his wish in many a dusty lot: / . . . He hovers eager o'er oblivion's shade"; John Ferriar, "The Bibliomania; being an epistle to Richard Heber, Esq.," (London, 1809).

36. Lamb, *Table-Talk* (1834), quoted in R. M. Leonard, ed., *The Book-Lovers' Anthology* (London, 1911), 121.

37. Wollstonecraft, *Vindication of the Rights of Men,* passim.

38. See Elbers, "Isolation and Community," 406-23, in particular, but also Peter Garside, "Scott, the Eigh-teenth Century, and the New Man of Sentiment," *Anglia* 103, no. 1/2 (1985): 84; Marilyn Butler, *Ro-mantics, Rebels, and Reactionaries: English Liter-ature and Its Background, 1760-1830* (New York, 1982), 110-11; and McMaster, *Scott and Society,*

161. Garside actually applies the same claim to the Waverley Novels in general as does John P. Farrell in *Revolution as Tragedy: The Dilemma of the Moder-ate from Scott to Arnold* (Ithaca, 1980), chap. 2.

39. On this point about the gender of the traditional Waverley hero, I take issue with Susan Morgan, "Old Heroes and a New Heroine in the Waverley Novels," *ELH* 50 (1983): 559-85. On the masculine regendering of sentiment in the Romantic era, see Johnson, *Equivocal Beings,* passim.

40. Edmund Burke, *Reflections on the Revolution in France* (1790) (Buffalo, 1987), 75-82.

41. Wollstonecraft, *A Vindication of the Rights of Men,* passim.

42. The formulation emerges in medieval discourse over book-love; F. Somner Merryweather, *Bibliomania in the Middle Ages* (London, 1933), 1-16, but it con-tinues to appear throughout the romantic period in texts such as Hazlitt's "On the Conduct of Life," 429, 438.

43. Francis Grose, "Complaint of a wife at her husband's rage for Antiquities," in *The Grumbler: containing sixteen essays, by the late Francis Grose, Esq. F.A.S.* (London, 1791), 49, 50.

44. For biographical accounts of these events, see Oliver Warner, *Emma Hamilton and Sir William* (London, 1960); Brian Fothergill, *Sir William Hamilton: Envoy Extraordinary* (New York, 1969); and Flora Fraser, *Emma, Lady Hamilton* (New York, 1987).

45. Goethe quoted in Warner, *Emma Hamilton and Sir William,* 99.

46. Ann Bermingham, "Elegant Females and Gentlemen Connoisseurs: The Commerce in Culture and Self-Image in Eighteenth-Century England," in *The Con-sumption of Culture, 1600-1800: Image, Object, Text,* ed. Ann Bermingham and John Brewer (Lon-don, 1995), 508.

47. Horace Walpole quoted in Warner, *Emma Hamilton and Sir William,* 110.

48. For a discussion of *Modern Antiques* in relation to the art of late 1700s political caricature in general, see Ronald Paulson, *Representations of Revolution, 1789-1820* (New Haven, 1983), 207-8.

49. The Edinburgh Edition of *The Antiquary* offers this definition of "amateur" (523). Scott refers to Old-buck and his colleagues as "amateurs" on four sep-arate occasions in the novel's first twenty-five pages (9, 23, 23, 24).

50. By emphasizing this aspect of Romantic-era discourse on bibliomania, I take issue with Philip Connell's

recent essay on the subject; Philip Connell, "Bibliomania: Book Collecting, Cultural Politics, and the Rise of Literary Heritage in Romantic Britain," *Representations* 71 (Summer 2000): 24-47. Connell argues that book collectors' emphasis on treating books as cultural treasures resulted in movements to build better and more complete libraries, in turn solidifying the idea of a national literary heritage and heightening a sense of national participation and belonging among readers and collectors of literature. No doubt this account of the political significance of this newfound interest in the materiality of books is accurate to some extent. Yet, it also passes over the fact that, more often than not, the age's writings on the subject express concern that the opposite is true—that book-obsession does not facilitate the circulation of books so much as impede it and that the book-obsessed man himself is less a part of national life than apart from it.

51. T. F. Dibdin, *Bibliomania; or Book-Madness; A Bibliographical Romance* (London, 1811). Writing of an ancient library, Leigh Hunt notes that "Dr. Dibdin should have existed in those days. ... But we doubt whether he could have borne the bliss. (*Vide* his ecstasies, *passim,* on the charms of vellums, tall copies, and blind tooling)"; Leigh Hunt, "Bookbinding and 'Heliodorus,'" in *Men, Women, and Books* (London, 1847), 2:78.

52. Ferriar, "The Bibliomania." A particularly dreadful 1790s example of the erotically and ecstatically overcharged verse that Ferriar satirizes can be found in Isaac D'Israeli's *Curiosities of Literature* (1791-1834), quoted in *The Book-Lovers' Anthology,* 226:

> GOLDEN volumes! Richest treasures!
> Objects of delicious pleasures!
> You my eyes rejoicing please,
> You my hands in rapture seize!

53. A bawdy joke in Daniel Terry's 1820 stage version of *The Antiquary* provides an indication of the extent to which readers *did* see something sexual in Oldbuck's dusty study. At one point, Jenny Rintherout, Oldbuck's maid, tells her master's hairdresser that Oldbuck, or Monkbarns, is one who "battles away at the auld iniquities." The hairdresser replies, "Antiquities you mean; ... —and Jenny, my lass, I'd advise ye no to let Monkbarns catch ye dusting his iniquities, as ye ca' them, a second time"; Daniel Terry, *The Antiquary; A National Drama founded on the celebrated novel of the same name, by the Author of "Waverley,"* &c. &c. as performed at the Theatre-Royal, Edinburgh* (London, 1820), 1.1.

54. Richard Payne Knight, *A Discourse on the Worship of Priapus* (1786), reprinted in *Sexual Symbolism: A History of Phallic Worship,* ed. Ashley Montagu (New York, 1957). For a reference to Knight by Scott, see Scott's *Journal,* 443.

55. Glimpses of these themes' prevalence can be attained from James Hillhouse's survey of early review essays on the Waverley Novels and the historical novel in general; James T. Hillhouse, *The Waverley Novels and Their Critics* (Minneapolis, 1936).

56. On the continuation of 1790s political discourse into the 1810s, see J. E. Cookson, *The Friends of Peace: Anti-War Liberalism in England, 1793-1815* (Cambridge, 1982); and H. T. Dickinson, *British Radicalism and the French Revolution, 1785-1815* (Oxford, 1985).

57. Forster, *Aspects of the Novel,* 46-56; Robin Mayhead, "The Problem of Coherence in *The Antiquary,*" in *Scott Bicentenary Essays: Selected Papers Read at the Sir Walter Scott Bicentenary Conference,* ed. Alan Bell (Edinburgh, 1973), 134-46; Daiches, "Scott's Achievement as a Novelist," 158-59; Robert C. Gordon, *Under Which King? A Study of the Scottish Waverley Novels* (New York, 1969), 35-44; Edgar Johnson, *Sir Walter Scott: The Great Unknown* (London, 1970), 536-43; A. N. Wilson, *The Laird of Abbotsford: A View of Sir Walter Scott* (Oxford, 1980), 70-74; and Brown, *Walter Scott and the Historical Imagination,* 47.

58. Washington Irving, *The Crayon Miscellany* (1835), rev. ed. (Philadelphia, 1872), 276, 288.

59. See, for example, the journal entries for Monday, 19 December 1825, and Tuesday, 24 March 1829, as well as the introductory matter to *Peveril of the Peak* (1822); Scott, *Journal,* 43, 539; and Scott, *Waverley Novels* (New York, 1902), 12: 22.

60. The classic twentieth-century interpretation of the Waverley Novels in these terms is Piggott, *Ruins in a Landscape,* chap. 7.

61. See Wolfgang Iser, *The Implied Reader: Patterns of Communication in Prose Fiction from Bunyan to Beckett* (Baltimore, 1974), chap. 4; Fleishman, *The English Historical Novel,* 25; Robertson, *Legitimate Histories,* 6, 63-64; and Brown, *Walter Scott and the Historical Imagination,* 173-81.

62. Lukács, *The Historical Novel,* 61-63; and Chandler, *England in 1819,* 135.

63. Walter Scott, "Dedicatory Epistle to the Rev. Dr Dryasdust, F.A.S., *Residing in the Castle-Gate, York,*" in *Ivanhoe; A Romance* (1819), ed. Graham Tulloch, Edinburgh Edition of the Waverley Novels (Edinburgh, 1998), 7.

64. On the "case" as the simple epistemological form for historical understanding in the period, see Chandler, *England in 1819,* chap. 4.

65. Ibid., 7.

66. Ibid.

67. Stephen Bann notes the lack of fecundity implied in the period's figure of the "dry" antiquary; Stephen Bann, "Preface," in Myrone and Peltz, *Producing the Past,* xxi. On the link between virility and manliness in the cultural imagination of early-nineteenth-century Britain, see Jeffrey Weeks, *Sex, Politics, and Society: The Regulation of Sexuality Since 1800* (London, 1981), 38-44.

68. Scott, "Dedicatory Epistle," 9.

69. In a forthcoming essay, I develop this point through readings of Victorian review essays on the historical novel and the study of history.

70. Bonnie Smith, *The Gender of History: Men, Women, and Historical Practice* (Cambridge, 1998), 37-69.

71. Ina Ferris, *The Achievement of Literary Authority: Gender, History, and the Waverley Novels* (Ithaca, 1991).

72. Ibid., 14, see also 242.

73. Recall the "Dedication" to *Don Juan* when Byron punningly likens poet laureate Robert "Bob" Southey's poetry to a "dry bob," or coitus without ejaculation; George Gordon, Lord Byron, "Dedication" (1818), *Don Juan,* line 24.

74. On the "dryness" of masculinity and "wetness" of femininity in Scott's *The Talisman,* see Margaret Bruzelius, "'The King of England ... Loved to Look upon A MAN': Melancholy and Masculinity in Scott's *Talisman,*" *Modern Language Quarterly* 62 (March 2001): 19-41.

75. Ferris, *Achievement of Literary Authority,* chap. 7. It should be noted, however, that Ferris describes the Waverley Novels more as efforts to "novelize" and expand traditional political history than as attempts to "antiquarianize" the novel.

Silvana Colella (essay date 2003)

SOURCE: Colella, Silvana. "Monetary Patriotism: *The Letters of Malachi Malagrowther, The Antiquary,* and the Currency Question." *Nineteenth Century Studies* 17 (2003): 53-71. Print.

[*In the following essay, Colella discusses the "mutually illuminating" ways in which certain of Scott's writings "investigate the Scottish connection between modernization and the paper pound," presenting stories in which gold is "symbolically depreciated." Colella notes that while* The Antiquary *is not explicit on this topic, it nevertheless connects gold with villainy.*]

Let them go and thrive by their "cash-credits," and let their paper-money poet, Walter Scott, immortalise their deeds.

—William Cobbett, letter of
30 September 1826, *Rural Rides* (1830)

Scotch logic floats on one-pound notes:
When rags are cash our shirts are ore:
What else would go to scare the crow
Becomes a myriad pounds and more.

—Thomas Love Peacock, "Lament of Scotch
Economists on the Extinction of the
One-Pound Notes," *Paper Money Lyrics* (1837)

The Douglas, Heron, and Company Bank was established in 1796 in the town of Ayr—or Air, as the name was spelled at that time. The phrase *Banking in Air* was printed on large quantities of banknotes issued by this unusually heedless Scottish company.[1] With the benefit of hindsight, one could argue that the unwittingly humorous inscription *Banking in Air* had an ominous ring to it. In less than three years, when the Ayr bank "achieved a spectacular insolvency,"[2] the fortunes of many stockholders vanished literally into thin air. Banking in Ayr proved to be a decidedly risky operation, yet another example of the kind of incautious gambling often associated with financial undertakings, speculative or otherwise. For was not air the (im)proper element of banking and commerce, always precariously suspended, in Adam Smith's phrase, "upon the Daedalian wings of paper money"?[3] Was not paper money, as John Wilson Croker said, a fragile construction of "airy and precarious pinnacles" that can never steadily support the "commercial fabric" of a country?[4]

Not always, and certainly not in every country, as Malachi Malagrowther, the fictional persona of Walter Scott (1771-1832), punctiliously demonstrates. Banking in air might very well be the essence of English banking—doomed by its very nature to frequent collapses. But it is not the essence of Scottish banking, despite the "solitary exception" represented by the Ayr bank (**Letters** [***The Letters of Malachi Malagrowther***], 1.24). Scott's nationalistic defense of the Scottish banking system in his controversial ***Letters of Malachi Malagrowther*** (1826) argues for the solidity of Scottish banks, the reliability and stability of Scottish paper. It celebrates the vigor of a century-old system of credit that had sustained the outstanding economic development of Scotland, a country that was growing, at that time, much faster than England, its richer neighbor.[5]

The peculiarity of the Scottish case, as Scott constructs it, lies at least partially in the reversal or disruption of associations that had been entrenched in British monetary discourse since the Financial Revolution—associations between speculation and gambling, banking and air, paper credit and the shadowy world of mock and ill-begotten riches.[6] By dissociating the Scottish banking system from this discourse, Scott demonstrates its superiority to be intricately linked to the very "Scottishness" that the English government had sought to eradicate. Thus, Scott mounts a political argument for nationalism, rooted in a kind of monetary patriotism. Defending the paper currency of Scotland from unwelcome attacks launched in the name of a misleading and misplaced "uniformity" principle, Scott stages his own intervention in the realm of political economy. He turns himself into a "patriot"[7] to produce what P. H. Scott ventures to call "the first manifesto of modern Scottish nationalism."[8]

N. T. Phillipson dismisses Scott's intervention in the realm of politics as "a fuss about nothing": Scott, he claims, "showed Scotsmen how to express their nationalism, by focusing their confused national emotions upon inessentials. ... By validating the making of a fuss about nothing. Scott gave to middle class Scotsmen and to Scottish nationalism an ideology—an ideology of noisy inaction."[9] P. H. Scott, by contrast, regards the banknote question as essential, yet, for him, the primary focus of *The Letters of Malachi Malagrowther* nonetheless remains political rather than economic: Walter Scott "was concerned not only with the currency question, which was the opportunity and the pretext, but much more with the whole problem of the relationship between Scotland and England, on which he had thought long and felt deeply."[10] Likewise, David Hewitt remarks that, "although the primary subject of *The Letters of Malachi Malagrowther* is the proposed curtailment of the rights of the Scottish banks to issue their own banknotes, the fundamental concern is the nature of the political conventions regulating the government of Scotland."[11] Hewitt and P. H. Scott tend to focus on those aspects of the text that seem to speak directly to late-twentieth-century political concerns. In a similar vein, although within a different theoretical framework, Caroline McCracken-Flesher's postcolonial interpretation of the "Malachi episode" emphasizes the political self-affirmation of the colonized Other, Scotland itself, which has triumphantly emerged as "a voicing body, a body capable of uttering resistance and even of shouting down the colonial narrative."[12]

Regardless of whether the political theme is more prominent than the monetary one, it is the correlation between the two that demands further investigation. Why did Sir Walter Scott, certainly no enemy of the Union, turn himself into a patriot, flaunting an unprecedented degree of (postcolonial?) nationalism, when writing about money? What kind of link does the text of the *Letters* establish between the defense of paper money (and free banking) and the nationalistic defense of the principle of "diversity"? Does money function in this text as a symbol of diversity? My contention is that economics and politics, the technicalities of free banking and the idealities of nationalistic feelings, are closely intertwined in Scott's text and that his economic arguments are, indeed, crucial to the construction of his political stance. His defense of

Scottish (and Irish, and English) diversity is not only triggered by, but also inextricably bound up with, his timely reflections on the peculiarities of a financial system—the *Scottish* system of *free* banking—that was, at that time, truly unique and uniquely Scottish.[13]

I also want to suggest that *The Letters of Malachi Malagrowther* is interesting in the way in which it assimilates and rewrites the traditional iconography of paper money in order to make its own plea for paper as more solid and nourishing than gold. I then turn to Scott's favorite novel, *The Antiquary,* published in 1816, ten years earlier, in which one finds oblique references to issues raised in the debates on money and bullion in the first few decades of the nineteenth century. I hope to show that paper money figures in this novel as an important element of that modernizing process ambivalently inscribed in the antiquarian "Romance of Property."[14]

In their introduction to the collection *The New Economic Criticism,* Martha Woodmansee and Mark Osteen remark that the "belief in the comparability of different cultural systems" is fundamental to all economic criticism.[15] Premised on the same assumption, my analysis is an attempt to trace a discursive continuum between Scott's texts and early-nineteenth-century monetary debates.[16] A comparative or interdisciplinary approach is almost mandatory in the case of *The Letters of Malachi Malagrowther,* a text that is squarely located at the intersection of fiction, economics, and politics. *The Antiquary,* on the other hand, does not engage with the discourse on money and banking as openly as does the *Letters.* The novel does, however, reproduce and complicate some of the most typical associations found in this discourse and especially in the monetary controversies of the 1810s. The bullion debate is by no means the only contextual discourse that impinges on Scott's novel, but the debate can be regarded as a particularly important one in the light of the nationalistic defense of paper money that Scott formulated later in the *Letters.* The idea of monetary patriotism is, I wish to argue, a culturally specific, historically determined formation that is interesting, not just as an example of Scott's ideological commitment, but also as evidence of the social and political significance of money itself.

A Republic of the Banks

Scott came to write *The Letters of Malachi Malagrowther* when his own financial situation was at its most disastrous. He himself marks this coincidence in the *Journal* [*The Journal of Sir Walter Scott*]: "I am turning patriot and taking charge of the affairs of the country on the very day I was proclaiming myself incapable of managing my own."[17] And, in case we fail to see the pertinence of this irony, Scott reminds us (the future readers of his journal) that to adopt the political identity of the patriot, at a time when his own private identity seemed inexorably to be tumbling toward disaster, was a clever way to avoid the most negative repercussions of this fall. "On the whole I am glad of this bruilzie as far as I am concerned," he comments, referring to the clamor aroused by the publication of his first letter:

> [P]eople will not dare talk of me as an object of pity—no more "poor manning." Who asks how many punds Scots the old champion had in his pocket when
>
> He set a bugle to his mouth
>   And blew so loud and shrill
> The trees in greenwood shook thereat
>   Sae loud rang ilka hill.[18]

Personal and national pride seem to work in tandem to boost Scott's anti-English monetary patriotism. To be regarded by the general public as a "poor broken-down man" in need of assistance is presumably a grimmer prospect than to incur the displeasure of a few English friends by denouncing their government for dealing with Scotland "very provokingly."[19] Whether or not these journal entries were written with an eye to posterity (as one editor believes),[20] they can be regarded as a kind of staging of patriotic feelings. They are a private performance of a "manly intervention"[21] in the twin realms of politics and economics, well timed to counteract the potentially laming effects of Scott's bankruptcy on his public reputation: "poor manning's" militant voice of action also works as a symbolic antidote to his financial paralysis. Of course, this is not to claim that Scott is merely serving his own interests—far from it.[22] Rather, it is to say that the performance of his patriotic role is precisely that: a public (the *Letters*) and private (the *Journal*) performance inseparable from the financial context, both private and public, in which it originated.

This context was overdetermined by the financial crisis of the mid-1820s and by the banking legislation of 1826, which included the proposal to suppress the issue of notes below the value of five pounds both in Scotland and in England. After the stock market crash of 1825 and the subsequent collapse of credit, England experienced an unprecedented series of bank failures and what Larry Neal characterizes as a "massive wave of bankruptcies in the rest of the economy." According to Neal, one of the chief determining factors in the crisis of 1825 was the problem of "information asymmetry."[23] But many contemporary observers blamed the overissue of small notes by the country banks for the speculative frenzy that led to the eventual collapse of the financial system. The government responded to the crisis by forbidding the issue of banknotes of small denomination, by establishing Bank of England branches throughout the country, and by encouraging competition between local country banks and joint-stock companies outside London.[24]

Unlike England, Scotland was not deeply affected by the financial panic of 1825. This was partly due to the differences between the financial systems of the two countries.

Since 1708, the Bank of England had enjoyed a monopoly on large-scale banking in the country. Private joint-stock banks with more than six partners were, in fact, barred from issuing banknotes. The business of providing the rural areas with notes of small denomination was left, Lawrence White remarks, to a "host of poorly capitalized, locally based banks," which often failed. It became common "to attribute the instability of these banks to their issues of small notes rather than their undercapitalization." In Scotland, on the other hand, the scene was dominated by three major joint-stock companies extensively branched throughout the country. The notes issued by these (and other, smaller) banks circulated freely, and "their value was secure and their acceptance by other banks commonplace."[25]

Most relevant to my discussion is another fundamental difference between the Scottish and the English systems of finance. Whereas coin was the common currency in England, paper was the principal medium of circulation in Scotland, and the greater bulk of business transactions were performed using one-pound notes. It is hardly surprising, then, that the proposal to suppress small notes met with so much hostility. Trivial as this proposal might seem, it did pose a potential threat to the prosperity of Scotland, which had been facilitated and sustained by the practice of free banking and by an efficient credit system in which the circulation of one-pound notes played a crucial part.[26]

Scott's *Letters* are constructed on a meticulous comparison between English and Scottish banking, in which the superiority of the latter stands out unequivocally, despite Scott's rhetorical concessions to British imperial pride. In comparing the shortcomings of English provincial banks and the successful performance of Scottish companies, Scott promotes an image of Scotland as the country where finance, banking, and paper money have never been synonymous with instability, speculative frenzy, and "airy" constructions. In Scotland, new credit instruments unknown in England (e.g., the cash accounts) have sustained an unprecedented degree of economic growth, and the public's preference for notes over specie has been rewarded in many tangible ways. Whereas "bubble buyers," "rags," "mock riches," "flimsy kite," and "paper mill" are emblems of the worthless emptiness of paper promises that would later be denigrated by Thomas Love Peacock (1785-1866) as specifically Caledonian,[27] such empty promises are much more typical of the English "malady" to which Scotland appears to be immune (*Letters*, 1.28). Professing himself "not adequate" to speculate "upon the wealth of nations," Malachi Malagrowther nevertheless produces a very accurate analysis of the peculiarities of the Scottish "experience":

> I assume, without much hazard of contradiction, that Banks have existed in Scotland for near one hundred and twenty years—that they have flourished, and the country has flourished with them—and that during the

last fifty years particularly, provincial Banks, or branches of the principal established and charactered Banks, have gradually extended themselves in almost every Lowland district in Scotland; that the notes, and especially the small notes, which they distribute, entirely supply the demand for a medium of currency; and that the system has so completely expelled gold from the country of Scotland, that you never by any chance espy a guinea there, unless in the purse of an accidental stranger.

(*Letters,* 1.20, 21)

These are the undisputed facts: the creation of credit in Scotland soars steadily and successfully on the wings of paper money. This money, unlike solid (and static) gold, can travel more easily even to the "most sequestered districts of the country." On the basis of these facts, a breathtaking vision of widespread prosperity is conjured up: "Through means of the credit which this system has afforded, roads have been made, bridges built, and canals dug, ... manufactures have been established, ... wastes have been converted into productive farms[.] the productions of the earth for human use have been multiplied twentyfold, while the wealth of the rich, and the comforts of the poor, have been extended in the same proportion" (*Letters,* 1.22). Who would dream of a return to gold when paper seems able to provide Scotland with its own version of El Dorado?[28]

This rhetoric of success is also meant to counteract the grotesque passivity[29] to which Scotland is being reduced through "experiments" conducted by the English government. Scotland has become "a subject in a common dissecting-room, left to the scalpel of the junior students." The image of Scotland as a healthy (and reluctant) body, being forced to take unnecessary remedies, prevails throughout the first letter, in which Scott is trying to establish the facts of the Scottish case and to undermine the principle of uniformity invoked by the English. "We are well," he concludes, "our pulse and complexion prove it— let those who are sick take physic." However, the passive female body, "bled and purged, ... and *talked* into courses of physic, for which she had little occasion," gives way in the second letter to a more assertive and defiant image of masculine valor: "The knife has gone to the very quick, and the comatose patient is roused to most acute possession of his feelings and his intellect. The heather is on fire far and wide" (*Letters,* 1.11, 28, 10, 2.4).

The second letter resonates with warlike evocations of the spirit of rebellion. "There is no room for compromise or surrender," writes Scott. "[O]ur Statesmen of today must be like our soldiers in ages past." There is a strategic allusion to the "ancient causes of quarrel" between England and Scotland in Scott's reference to the "present seven-leagued stride"; the aggression of the English is compared to an act of castration (the "well-known operation resorted to for taming the ferocity of such male animals as are intended for domestication"): and the threat

of a conspiracy between Ireland and Scotland is raised to scare the English out of their fixation on uniformity: "[S]tep this way, Pat—and see there is nobody listening— why should not you and we have a friendly understanding, and assist each other, as the weaker parties, against any aggressions, which may be made upon either of us, 'for uniformity's sake'?" (*Letters,* 2.21, 22, 22, 22-23, 24).

Given the belligerent tone of Scott's oration against English interference, it is hardly surprising that his words should have been hailed by P. H. Scott as "the first manifesto of modern Scottish nationalism." What demands further investigation, however, is not so much the representation of Scotland as a country of "true men and worthy patriots" always ready to engage in a good old fight in order to defend the rights of their nation (*Letters,* 2.21). What needs to be reassessed and emphasized is the vision of Scotland as an exemplary country, a model of social cohesion and well-deserved prosperity, an economic dream of stability and (self-)confidence amid recurrent, often unexplained financial collapses. This vision is relatively new, and it is nationalistic in its general orientation—"Saunders" has very little to learn from, and very much to teach to, "John Bull" as far as money and banking go. The representation thrives on the model of equilibrium successfully upheld by the Scottish "republic" of the banks:[30]

> The Banking Companies of Scotland, who take on themselves the issuing of notes, are, no doubt, independent of each other so far as they severally contract with the public: but a certain course of correspondence and mutual understanding is indispensable among themselves, and, in that respect, the whole Banks and Banking Companies in Scotland may be said to form a republic, the watchful superintendence of the whole profession being extended to the strength or weakness of the general system at each particular point. ...

> No new Banking institution can venture to issue notes to the public, till they have established a full understanding that these notes will be received as cash by the other Banks. ... The public have, in this manner, the best possible guarantee against rash and ill-concocted speculations.

(*Letters,* 2.34-36)

This republic efficiently combines a degree of competition (each bank is free to issue its own notes) with an even higher degree of cooperation (each bank participates in an effective note-exchange system). The republic is exemplary in the way in which it mitigates the potentially disruptive effects of a laissez-faire system through a series of internal "check[s]," beneficial to the general public, especially the poorest among them (*Letters,* 2.36, 37). But it is also exemplary in allowing for the expression of diversity within a system of mutual recognition and exchange. In this respect, the republic of the banks presents a specifically Scottish alternative to the English search for uniformity at all costs. Diversity rather than uniformity is, in fact, the distinguishing feature of the

Scottish monetary system, which, unlike the English one, is not constrained by the legal privileges bestowed exclusively on the Bank of England, "that immense Establishment, which, like a great oak, overshadows England from Tweed to Cornwall" (*Letters,* 1.37).

The one-pound note thus becomes the symbol of a particular type of "Scottishness," one that has little to do with the romantic or romanticized version of the Scottish past or with the martial tradition alluded to in the *Letters.* It is rooted, instead, in the relatively recent, post-Union history of modernization and economic development, which, in the sociological, Whig historiography of David Hume, John Dalrymple, and Scott himself, is unequivocally placed under the aegis of the "Anglo-British" identity.[31] In these letters, however, Scott's main line of defense is predicated on a significant divergence between the stability and efficiency of Scottish banking and the distressing "malady" of the English system. It is the Scottish alternative that most successfully embodies the British principle of free trade, a staple element of the modernization process: "I must say, it seems strange," Malachi observes ironically, "that, under a liberal system, of which freedom of trade is the very soul, we should be loaded with severe restrictions upon our own national choice, instead of being left at liberty to adopt that representative of value, whether in gold or paper, that best suits our own convenience!" (*Letters,* 2.53-54).

In other words, Scotland is ahead of England—moneywise at least—in its interpretation and realization of those very principles that lie at the heart of the English (and, hence, British) idea of "progress."[32] Needless to say, Scott also pays tribute to the dominance of England in the British context, depicting London, at one point, as the "head" of "fine gold" and Scotland as too poor to survive on a diet of gold (*Letters,* 2.51). But these concessions are not sufficient to overshadow the strong oppositional stance adopted in the *Letters.* There, the detailed illustration of the advantages of free banking and of the peculiarities of the Scottish model ensures that Scotland is constructed as an exemplum and England as a failure. "In England, unfortunately, things have been very different," Scott never tires of reiterating (*Letters,* 1.28). The insolvency of many provincial banks, the imposing presence and monopoly of the Bank of England, the frequent bank runs, the hazardous speculations of men "of sanguine hopes and bold adventure" that call themselves bankers, the widespread distrust of banknotes (*Letters,* 1.36)—these and other negative traits combine to render England itself a particular case, and a hopeless one, at that. By meticulously highlighting the details of the Scottish example—even the apparently trivial matter of the one-pound note—Scott throws into relief the relativity or particularity of the English case, further undermining the English attempt to impose its norm as universally valid.

Colin Kidd claims that, "by the time that Scott was explaining Scotland to the English, there was no grand narrative structure of national historiography by which to promote Scotland, other than that of her social retardation."[33] This may be true, but the popular narrative of social retardation, albeit not absent from the *Letters,* never goes unquestioned. It is constantly interrupted by the celebration of the Scottish "practice" (the Scottish "experience," the Scottish "case"), whose particularity and diversity not only contradict mainstream economic theories on the superiority of the metallic currency but also challenge the alleged "retardation" of Scotland. After all, it is not gold—Keynes's "barbarous relic"[34]—but paper that truly represents (however controversially) the novelty of modernization. And, at the beginning of the nineteenth century, paper money is very much a feature of Scotland, although not exclusively so, as Peacock and William Cobbett, staunch defenders of gold, were ready to admit. If the history of Scotland's social development could be (and was) framed according to the Anglo-British paradigm of retardation and assimilation, the specific history of Scottish banking could and did provide a discordant narrative strand—one in which Scotland could be recast in the successful role of the leader. It is precisely in these terms that Sir John Sinclair describes Scotland when urging Thomas Attwood to publish their learned correspondence on the currency question: "How fortunate would be the result," he soars, "if it led [the government ministers] to act *on that improved system of politics,* by which Great Britain would be rendered what Scotland now is—*Independent of Foreign Nations for Circulation and Food.*"[35]

English Gold and Scottish Paper

The ministers, of course, had no intention of granting so much. In the course of the nineteenth century, it was central banking, not free banking, that became the norm in Great Britain. And that is also the reason why "the record of free banking in Scotland is virtually a lost chapter in the history of monetary institutions."[36] However, the battle to promote paper money was not to be concluded until the first decades of the twentieth century, and Scott's creative contribution to it is certainly worth a second glance.

In the passage from the *Letters* most frequently cited by readers favoring the nationalistic hypothesis, Scott makes his plea for diversity, likening the sameness of nations to the indistinctness of metallic money: "For God's sake, sir, let us remain as Nature made us, Englishmen, Irishmen, and Scotchmen, with something like the impress of our several countries upon each! We would not become better subjects, or more valuable members of the common empire, if we all resembled each other like so many smooth shillings" (*Letters,* 2.81). Shillings, coins, the metallic medium of exchange, are here configured as the symbol of unacceptable sameness or mistaken uniformity.[37] By the same token, paper money, so eloquently defended against the proposed restrictions of the English government, might prove better equipped to bear the "impress" of national diversity. This argument is based on the implicit assumption that specie can be identified as English just as paper can be distinguished as Scottish or that English gold and Scottish paper are competing with each other in a common market.[38] In fact paper did circulate in England, albeit not as extensively as in Scotland. Scott's misrepresentation of the demand for money serves his nationalistic purpose in an oblique way: on the one hand, England is granted the "comparative excellence" of gold (*Letters,* 2.62); on the other hand, gold comes to be symbolically depreciated in Scott's narrative, and the gold standard, like the English standard, is denounced as unendurable.

The "smooth shillings" are just one link in the metaphoric chain of associations with which Scott constructs his own account of the efficacy of paper money. Admittedly, this is no easy task even for a Scottish thinker, given the overwhelming iconography of paper as the most dangerous of delusions.[39] In a famous cartoon by James Gillray (1757-1815) published in 1797—the year of the Restriction Bill, a measure to protect the Bank of England from a run on its gold in the panic ensuing on a French invasion[40]—the prime minister, William Pitt, is portrayed as Midas, sitting on top of the Bank of England's rotunda, where he transforms everything he touches, not into gold, but into paper. He flaunts a huge transparent belly stuffed with gold coins—the Bank's reserves—and is caught in the act of blowing paper from his various orifices. As the result of a corrupted and corrupting conspiracy between the government and the Old Lady (the Bank of England), paper money is, in more than one sense, worthless and untrustworthy, especially for the general public. What is also interesting in this and other cartoons is that gold appears in simultaneously a positive and a negative light. It is clearly a symbol of corruption, but it also provides the only form of substantial nourishment. Although the image of politicians gorging on gold is the epitome of public dishonesty, gold retains its connotation of solidity, making it preferable to paper money and its empty promises of payment.

In one instance in the *Letters,* at least, Scott reverts to the popular iconography of gorging, condemning the English proposal of "forcing gold down our throats" as a measure that will prove disadvantageous to "our devoted country" (*Letters,* 2.60). By shunning this unwholesome diet of gold, Scotland is also refuting the legacy of corruption that attends it. The return of gold might engender, as Scott suggests, a return to crime and dishonesty (see *Letters,* 2.59). But the most insistent connotations of the precious metal, evoked in the second and third letters, are concerned with its materiality. It is the inconvenient heaviness of gold, rather than its much esteemed solidity, that emerges in Scott's narrative when he tries to imagine the difficulties that would be faced by Scotland if it were compelled to adopt a metallic currency: "Our Bankers ... will be condemned to the labour of Sisyphus,—eternally employed in rolling a cask of gold up a Highland hill, at the risk of being crushed by it as the influence of gravity prevails, and it comes rolling down upon their heads." Gold is a burden

that will drag the country down. It is stationary and incapable of free circulation. Here, its very solidity, the trait that most endears it to the detractors of paper, is graphically transformed into a dubious asset: no "forcing-pump," no "new-invented patent pressure" could compel specie to circulate in the most "inaccessible regions" of the country (*Letters,* 2.52, 58).

Finally, in the third letter, gold is further debased by its connection with "broken tea-spoons and stray sugar-tongs, dismantled lockets and necklaces," and "stolen *sprech-erie*"—the kind of antique trash that delights Christopher Chrysal, the fictional character introduced here as the mouthpiece of political economy. Being connected, through his profession, to precious metals, "neighbour Chrysal has set himself up for a patron and protector of Gold and Silver." In fact, his views on bullion are recognizably mainstream: gold is a commodity that, "like all other commodities, will flow to the place where there is a demand for it." The water metaphor—gold flows freely like water—is inverted by Scott, who appeals to geography in order to confute Chrysal's theory: "Scotland, sir, is not *beneath* the level to which gold flows naturally. She is *above* that level, and she may perish for want of it ere she sees a guinea" (*Letters,* 3.6, 8, 6, 9, 16). The central ambiguity in this passage concerns the relative value of those terms emphasized by Scott himself: to be *above* the level of gold is, as the previous letters have already established, actually a "*twice blessed*" condition (*Letters,* 2.40). The geographic elevation of Scotland is also the emblem of its monetary superiority, of its ability to function quite well on the basis of a paper-money system that has proved more solid than cumbrous or trashy gold.

In fact, the final paragraph of the last letter pits practice against theory, contrasting the Scottish substance with the shadowy opinions of political economists, and undoing in one stroke the primacy of gold as "the ultimate money":[41]

> *Here* stands Theory, a scroll in her hand, full of deep and mysterious combinations of figures. ... *There* lies before you a practical System, successful for upwards of a century. The one allures you with promises, as the saying goes, of untold gold,—the other appeals to the miracles already wrought in your behalf. The one shows you provinces, the wealth of which has been tripled under her management,—the other a problem which has never been practically solved. Here you have a pamphlet—there a fishing town—here the long-continued prosperity of a whole nation—and there the opinion of a professor of Economics, that in such circumstances she ought not by true principles to have prospered at all. In short, good countrymen, if you are determined, like Aesop's dog, to snap at the shadow and lose the substance, you had never such a gratuitous opportunity of exchanging food and wealth for moonshine in the water.

> (*Letters,* 3.38-39)

Scott's rhetoric is at its most effective when he is campaigning for the Scottish "miracle." Such, in fact, it might have appeared, given the widespread preference for gold as the only reliable currency, especially in the first two decades of the nineteenth century, when, as the Bullion Report of 1810 testifies, gold was being reconfirmed as "the paramount asset."[42] In the conclusion to the third and final letter, by orchestrating a contrast, not between England and Scotland, but between papers on money (pamphlets, theories) and the practice of paper money, Scott once again reverses the familiar antithesis between shadow and substance. And he grafts it onto another, equally common binarism, that of theory versus practice. Scotland has consistently been on the militant side of practice in these letters. So too is paper money, which comes to represent the "miracles" of this country in Scott's patriotic rendering of the history of banking. The empty promises of theory—despite (or, rather, because of) their golden hue—must have sounded vague and inadequate against the tangible prosperity of a country that had profitably exploited the much-berated system of paper promises. It is no wonder that Scott's plea proved successful, the English government deciding to suspend its original proposal.

THE ANTIQUARY AND THE BULLION DEBATE

There is another side to Scott's reassessment of the primacy of gold that deserves to be mentioned here: its connection with "magic art" or trickery. In the *Letters,* this relation is revealed when Malachi asks Christopher Chrysal "by what magic art . . . our paper is to be changed into gold, without some great national distress, nay, convulsion, *in transitu?*" Moreover, guineas are somehow expected to appear and disappear "like the fairy goblets in Parnell's tale, '—that with a wish come nigh, / And with a wish retire' " (*Letters,* 3.14). If nothing less than magic is necessary to ensure the transition from paper to gold, that transition can never prove lasting or reliable. In *The Antiquary,* which anticipates the *Letters* by ten years, a similar transition, effected by means of legerdemain, captures the attention and the little remaining capital of Sir Arthur Wardour. Here, too, gold and silver coins appear supernaturally in the gothic setting of Saint Ruth's Priory. The financial plot, both story and scheme, revolves around a question of convertibility: the charlatan Dousterswivel promises to deliver fine gold, true and solid bullion, in exchange for "your dirty Fairport bank-note."[43]

Scott's novel was published in 1816, in the midst of a pamphlet war on the currency question that was unprecedented in the records of British monetary history. With some degree of raillery, it redefines the terms of this debate, establishing an opposition between the engrossing fascination of Sir Arthur with gold, metals, and precarious mining projects and the more down-to-earth, less speculative reliance of the antiquary, Jonathan Oldbuck, on his own "pocket-book" or paper money. Sir Arthur's dream, fueled by the promises and mysterious dealings of Dousterswivel, is a dream of convertibility in which "dirty" banknotes are transformed into bullion; and paper money,

recklessly invested in the German's mining adventure, yields an old-fashioned bounty of coins and precious metals. As the German swindler explains to a very skeptical Oldbuck: "If you join wid Sir Arthur, as he is put in one hundred and fifty—see here is one fifty in your dirty Fairport bank-note—you put one other hundred and fifty in de dirty notes, and you shall have de pure gold and silver, I cannot tell how much" (*Antiquary,* 187).

The main attraction of this shady investment scheme is clearly the metallic treasure, whether it comes in the shape of lead (should the mining project prove successful) or of gold and silver coins. It is bullion that Sir Arthur imagines as the source of his deliverance from imminent financial ruin. But it is paper money, wisely entrusted by Sir Arthur's son in the hands of Oldbuck, that finally guarantees Sir Arthur's solvency (*Antiquary,* 336).

What are the implications of the discourse on money expounded in this novel through the financial or German plot? First of all, the opposition between bullion and banknotes, or gold and paper money, echoes the more popular terms in which the currency question was being articulated after 1797, when the Bank of England suspended payments in specie. In February 1797, fears of a French invasion had precipitated a "rush to withdraw gold from the banking system." This eventually led the government to issue an Order in Council, later transformed into the Restriction Bill, that insured the Bank of England "against the legal consequences of refusing to pay out gold in exchange for the Bank notes."[44] The restriction period lasted twenty-four years, well beyond anyone's wildest predictions, and, during this time, the currency question commanded front-page attention. The Bullion Controversy, as it later came to be known, was a debate on gold, on inflation and overissuing, and on the value of the pound sterling. It questioned the role and proper function of the Bank of England and the very criteria for assessing the value of the "paper pound."[45] The bullionists argued for a prompt return to convertibility and the gold standard, capitalizing on the popular discontent about inconvertible and valueless "rags."[46] The antibullionists defended the paper-money system as being better equipped to support the commercial credit of the country. When, in response to the controversy, a parliamentary committee issued the Bullion Report in 1810, gold was reconfirmed as the ultimate currency and the most reliable standard of value (although the government still delayed the resumption of cash payments by another decade).[47]

By breaking the link between gold and Bank of England notes, the Restriction Bill rendered the topic of paper money even more controversial, more unsettled and resonant, than it already was.[48] When in *The Antiquary* Sir Arthur proposes to repay his standing debts in bullion, shunning paper promises "as one rejects the old-fashioned civility that presses food upon you, after you have eaten till nausea" (*Antiquary,* 182), Scott's narrative is positioning itself within the discursive boundaries of the currency question, even as it renegotiates those boundaries in a facetious way. It is noteworthy that, in *The Antiquary,* gold, bullion, and the metallic currency are associated with the gullibility of Sir Arthur, with the improbable undertakings of Dousterswivel, and with an all-too-conventional gothic artillery of midnight apparitions, ruins, and hidden treasures. Just as the English Parliament was declaring bullion to be the most reliable measure of value, urging the Bank of England to reestablish the monetary rationality of the gold standard, Scott was entertaining readers with a story of bullion magically retrieved and of "dirty" banknotes supernaturally exchanged at a profit for gold and silver. He was describing the enduring but misleading allure of precious metals and the delusions that attend the thirst for gold. In this sense, *The Antiquary* does not simply hint at one of the hottest public issues of the 1810s; it also comments on that issue by weaving a plot in which gold cannot possibly function as a standard of value, enmeshed as it is in Dousterswivel's machinations and in the kind of "mystical trash" indulged in by Sir Arthur (*Antiquary,* 102).

Gold and silver coins, as well as actual bullion, materialize in *The Antiquary* on two different occasions. A first casket of treasure, "containing a considerable quantity of coins, chiefly silver, but with a few gold pieces intermixed" (*Antiquary,* 183), is retrieved, in a patchy gothic fashion, by Dousterswivel and Sir Arthur in the ruins of Saint Ruth. The casket is clearly planted as bait to tempt Sir Arthur into investing more capital in the German villain's fraudulent project, but it seems, nevertheless, to realize the promises of convertibility held out by Dousterswivel. Unlike the Bank of England, which is unable to fulfill its own promises to pay, the German speculator does deliver gold and silver in the designated place, at the appointed time. Scott makes parodic use of gothic conventions: the midnight scene in which the casket is found is supervised by Edie Ochiltree, the old beggar, and Mr. Lovel, Oldbuck's young friend, who observe and comment on the mischievous dealings of Dousterswivel (see *Antiquary,* 170-74). Through this parody, Scott sheds humorous light, not only on Sir Arthur's penchant for speculation, but also on the very notion of convertibility, inscribing it in the superstitious register of the German's mumbo jumbo.

With the second apparition of a casket, Scott's novel once again seems to effect, by trick or magic, what the Old Lady, the Bank of England, is incapable of achieving. This time it is unminted silver bullion, "to the value of perhaps a thousand pounds sterling" (*Antiquary,* 193), that materializes. Within the gothic economic microcosm of *The Antiquary,* foreign (Mexican) bullion does eventually replenish, at least partially, Sir Arthur's empty coffers, to the astonishment of Oldbuck and Dousterswivel himself. The supernatural trick by which this bullion has been obtained remains unexplained until the final chapters, when Lovel admits to having planted the treasure himself, in an attempt

to rescue the Wardours from their imminent financial collapse. On the whole, the repeated treasure-hunting episodes do not simply create a generic parable on the risks of speculative undertakings or on the tragic consequences of ill-gotten wealth (as might be suggested by the fable of "Martin Waldeck," which interrupts the narrative [see *Antiquary,* 137-46]). Embedded as they are in the monetary jargon of the time, but reconfiguring the opposition between bullion and banknotes in ludicrous terms, these episodes turn the question of convertibility into a veritable gothic scam. It is noticeable that *The Antiquary,* written at a time when bullion was one of the most controversial economic topics, turns on a financial plot in which the allure of bullion and coins proves deceptive. But it is even more ironic that, in this plot, a German impostor seems to succeed where the Bank of England fails.

Nevertheless, the much-sought-after bullion proves incapable of preventing Sir Arthur's financial downfall. Neither gold nor silver but a bunch of papers and promissory notes, promptly delivered by post, serves in the end to guarantee Sir Arthur's indemnity (see *Antiquary,* 336). The fact that the financial plot reaches its denouement "upon the Daedalian wings of paper money" is further evidence of this novel's collusion with the less nostalgic ideologies of modernization, in which paper credit functions as a sort of economic deus ex machina.[49] Emerging from obscurity after the climax of the financial plot, Sir Arthur's son, Reginald, avails himself of new and powerful credit instruments to rescue his father—accomplishing this task far more effectively than Lovel contrived to do with his secret offer of silver bullion. Significantly, it is not Reginald's bodily presence but his creditworthy words, and the bills and legal papers that he sends along with his letter, that ensure the successful restoration of the Wardours' fortunes. The plot endorses Reginald's and Oldbuck's paper-money policy (the bills are entrusted to the antiquary) as more prudent and profitable than the gothic and mystical bullion policy of Sir Arthur.

By establishing a tie between "prudence" and paper money,[50] as exemplified by Oldbuck's impeccable financial record, Scott's narrative challenges another, more compelling symbolic configuration, in which paper is slighted by being linked to gambling, to speculative bubbles, and even to revolutionary politics. This connection is crucial, as Fiona Robertson rightly argues, if we want to understand Scott's representation of the Jacobite cause: "[T]he links [Edmund] Burke defines [in *Reflections on the Revolution in France* (1790)] between dangerous Frenchness, gambling, and paper money, and his forcible reminder of the importance of [the Scottish financial speculator] John Law [1671-1729], are also of key relevance to those inveterate gamblers, Scott's Jacobites."[51] However, although it is certainly true that *The Black Dwarf* (1816), *Rob Roy* (1817), and *The Fortunes of Nigel* (1822) explore the fatal attraction between speculative politics and paper money, *The Antiquary* points toward a symbolic legacy that differs from the one epitomized by John Law's utopian and eventually catastrophic schemes.[52]

This legacy is more in tune with the tradition of Scottish free banking that Scott was later to retrace in the *Letters.* As I have argued in the previous section, in this tradition paper is synonymous not with fictitious wealth or vaporous speculative projects but with stability and prosperity. Banknotes are not empty promises but a fully reliable medium of exchange that has successfully replaced gold. Paper money functions as a tautological system of representation in which the referent has, to all practical purposes, been eclipsed. And, just as in the *Letters* gold, the metallic money, is denounced as potentially destabilizing, so too in *The Antiquary* the thirst for gold and bullion proves disruptive because it is most closely related to gambling or to speculative dreams, which are best left undreamed. Scott unleashes the negative connotations of gambling in a story in which bullion, gold, and silver all play prominent roles as misleading objects of desire. Thus, he releases paper money from its degrading kinship with bubbles, mock riches, and grandiose but bungled schemes.

One could argue for the importance of a political over an economic theme in *The Antiquary,* by pointing out that Sir Arthur sympathizes with the cause of the Pretender: however, his Jacobite leanings are proclaimed at the onset of the story, only to be dismissed as inconsequential. The link between politics and finance is not relevant in this novel and does not constitute the main fault line along which to articulate the contrast between Oldbuck and Sir Arthur.[53] Such a fault line is provided, however, by the disputes about history that abound in *The Antiquary.*[54] It is also created by the "paper against gold" paradigm,[55] in which gold is repositioned on the speculative, fictitious, and fradulent side of the opposition. In fact, the antiquarian debates on the Scottish national past, which frequently occupy Sir Arthur and Oldbuck, are sometimes brought to bear on the monetary questions as well. In Oldbuck's view, for instance, the kind of speculation that attracts Sir Arthur coincides with a very flawed version of antiquarianism. "'Sir Arthur is a good honourable man,'" the antiquary admits, "'but, as you may see from his loose ideas concerning the Pikish language, he is by no means very strong in the understanding. ... This rapparee promised mountains of wealth, and an English company was found to advance large sums of money—I fear on Sir Arthur's guarantee." Sir Arthur's credulity in historical matters is matched by his gullibility in financial ones; the "embarrassed" fortunes of this exponent of the old aristocracy are complemented by his tendency to receive "legends as current and authentic coin" or his inability to tell a forgery (*Antiquary,* 102, 38). The style of Sir Arthur's historical knowledge, in other words, is ridiculed by its association with financial credulity—and vice versa.

As for Oldbuck's style, the text establishes another chain of connections, in which the solidity of his accumulated

patrimony—his secure reputation as a "ready-money man"—vouchsafes for the flights of his antiquarian imagination. Early on in the narrative, one of these flights is cut short by the observations of Edie Ochiltree, "one of the last specimens of the old-fashioned Scottish mendicant." Oldbuck is displaying to Lovel his new possession, the land where he believes "the final conflict between Agricola and the Caledonians" took place: "I was unwilling to say a word about it till I had secured the ground, for it belonged to auld Johnie Howie, a bonnet-laird here hard by, and many a communing we had before he and I could agree. At length—I am almost ashamed to say it—but I even brought my mind to give acre for acre of my good corn-land for this barren spot. But then it was a national concern; and when the scene of so celebrated an event became my own I was overpaid" (*Antiquary,* 15, 33, 28, 28-29).

When Edie appears, "unseen and unheard," he dismantles Oldbuck's romantic theory: "'I ... built this bit thing here ... for a bield [shelter] at auld Aiken Drum's bridal.'" But he also highlights the economic irrationality of Oldbuck's purchase, commenting that he never thought "'that his honour, Monkbarns [Oldbuck], would hae done sic a daft-like thing, as to gie grund weel worth fifty shillings an acre, for a mailing [tenant farm] that would be dear o' a pund Scots'" (*Antiquary,* 30, 31, 32). Although this episode is obviously intended as a comic commentary on Oldbuck's all-too-loose interpretation of history, it can also be seen as the occasion to expose the clash between two different systems of values. In Edie's popular and traditional view, value is conventionally related to the productivity of the land: a barren spot is worthless because it is barren. From Oldbuck's more modern perspective, economic or market value has an imaginary component, which, in this particular case, is independent of productivity.[56] To him, the Kaim of Kinprunes is worth every acre of his own productive land as long as it can be constructed as the site of an important battle. Its imaginary (and nationalistic) value, in other words, determines—and enhances—its exchange value.

Needless to say, in this particular instance, Oldbuck is proved wrong: his purchase turns out to be a bad deal. But the narrative does not entirely discard the antiquary's point of view. On the contrary, his ability to trade in imaginary values proves to be indispensable for his particular avocation. As he rapturously explains to his new friend Lovel, every item in his curious collection has been carefully secured "by skill and research" and not by sheer "force of money." Money comes in the bargain, of course, but it is the ability to determine the imagined value of any given object, and to foresee its future value, that distinguishes the true antiquary. "'See this bundle of ballads,'" Oldbuck explains to Lovel.

> not one of them later than 1700, and some of them an
> hundred years older. I wheedled an old woman out of

these, who loved them better than her psalm-book—tobacco, sir, snuff, and the Complete Syren, were the equivalent! For that mutilated copy of the Complaynt of Scotland, I sat out the drinking of two dozen bottles of strong ale with the late learned proprietor, who, in gratitude, bequeathed it to me by his last will. These little Elzevirs are the memoranda and trophies of many a walk by night and morning through the Cowgate, the Canongate, the Bow, Saint Mary's Wynd,—wherever, in fine, there were to be found brokers and trokers, those miscellaneous dealers in things rare and curious. How often have I stood haggling upon a halfpenny, least, by a too ready acquiescence in the dealer's first price, he should be led to suspect the value I set upon the article!

(*Antiquary,* 24)

The "romance of property," as Judith Wilt characterizes Oldbuck's romantic acquisitiveness vis-à-vis history itself, involves, on the one hand, a professional expertise in uncovering "the secret treasure" or hidden value of objects from the past[57]—the ability to price the past according to its present imaginary value—and, on the other hand, a willingness to invest one's own time and resources in cultivating human relationships, in creating connections that will eventually yield their expected returns. In this passage, Scott presents a style of speculation that differs significantly from the one exemplified by Sir Arthur's and Dousterswivel's mining project, a style that will stand Oldbuck in good stead when, in the second half of the novel, the plot swerves toward themes of legitimacy and recognition. After all, Oldbuck is the only character able to value and appreciate Lovel—the stranger who will later turn out to be the son of the earl of Glenallan—long before any disclosure of his real identity is made.

Most critics have remarked that *The Antiquary* is a novel of reconciliation and resocialization.[58] It is also a text in which the "common longing for a lost past that [the community members] remember, mourn, and re-create in very different ways" binds that community together.[59] Jane Millgate maintains that Oldbuck plays the most active part in the process whereby social cohesion is guaranteed or reconstructed: he "presides over the entire narrative exercise, the putting together of the Glenallan story that will supply Lovel with the name he is lacking at the outset and make possible a true reading of the Lovel text."[60] What demands further attention is the link between Oldbuck's antiquarian economics and his role in piecing the tragedy together. Among the old "worthies" (*Antiquary,* 40) paraded in this story—Sir Arthur, the earl of Glenallan, and even Edie—Oldbuck stands out both in his ability "to read the riddle" of Lovel[61] and in his profitable trades with "brokers and trokers." Oldbuck's capacity to credit the imaginary value of an objectified past—his own style of speculation that never impairs his patrimony—seems closely connected with his readiness to credit the value and moral worth of an unknown character, Lovel, whose past remains mysterious until the very end.

Thus, despite Sir Arthur's more overt tendency to gamble and speculate, it is Oldbuck who seems better equipped to embody that particular type of "personality" described by Kevin Barry in his discussion of paper credit and romantic aesthetics: a personality that is receptive to "signs that may represent or imitate nothing at all" and ready to cope with the "social demand for imaginary things."[62] Oldbuck is closer to this model of receptivity than is any other character in the novel. The peculiarities of his trade, his familiarity with new credit instruments (e.g., he holds a cash account), his skepticism as far as gold and bullion are concerned, all combine to create a character who feels at home in the "paper-pound" world. And, since, as Millgate remarks,[63] Oldbuck's perspective is the dominant one, this distinctly modern feeling emerges in the end as more satisfactory than the quaint, gothic quest after golden treasures.

* * *

The Antiquary and *The Letters of Malachi Malagrowther* are, in a sense, mutually illuminating. Both texts investigate the Scottish connection between modernization and the paper pound and articulate a story in which gold is symbolically depreciated. The equation between the gold and the English standards, which propels Malachi's cultural and political nationalism, is not an explicit concern in the fictional world of *The Antiquary.* But here, too, gold and villainy share the same territory and appear united, in one final comic stroke, in the very name of the villain—Mr. *Goldie*bird—who requests that Sir Arthur should settle his debts without further delay, precipitating the downfall of the old baronet. To be "preoccupied with the exchange of currency" is not new in Scott "or indeed in his contemporaries."[64] But what is interesting about *The Antiquary* is the discursive way in which this preoccupation is shaped. Echoing the terms of the Bullion Controversy, the financial plot anticipates, or points toward, the more antagonistic and militant narrative of Scottish paper money that is fully developed in the *Letters.* And, although *The Antiquary* makes no explicit case for nationalistic politics, it does offer a few comic insights into what must have seemed a peculiarly English obsession with "gowd" and "siller."

The Antiquary has often been read in relation to disputes over antiquarianism and the interpretation of history. My reading has tried to unravel a different configuration of meanings, albeit meanings that cluster mainly around the financial plot. In this plot, it is gold rather than paper that comes to be associated with ruinous speculative ventures, with gambling and incautious dreams of profit. Dousterswivel's promise to convert "dirty" banknotes into coins and bullion can best be understood in historical terms by placing it alongside the debate on inconvertible paper money that captured the public attention in the early years of the nineteenth century. *The Antiquary* offers an indirect commentary on the expectations and fears related to the popular perception of inconvertibility. The

(Scottish) process of modernization involves, as this novel seems to suggest, a more open, less detrimental understanding of paper money than the one most frequently inscribed in traditional financial discourse.

In the discourse on money with which both the **Letters** and **The Antiquary** engage, paper is often constructed as an insubstantial sign, a shadow, even when backed by solid gold. From 1797 until 1821, when the gold standard was suspended and paper money declared inconvertible (both in England and in Scotland), discussions of money centered insistently on the question of value: Is paper of any value once its relation to gold has been severed or suspended? Scott's monetary patriotism addresses the intertwined issues of value and paper in such a way as to question the popular association between value and the solidity of gold. It is significant, as Matthew Rowlinson remarks, that "this deployment of nationalism in defence of a particular material form of money should have been attached to paper rather than to metal currency."[65] Scott's reassessment of paper as the more efficient medium of circulation is predicated on a detailed analysis of the Scottish case and a defense of its "difference." What is most interesting in his construction of such a case is the reworking of familiar or traditional metaphors, of highly evocative symbolic associations recurring in the discourse on money since the Financial Revolution. The link between politics and economics, between nationalism and monetary concerns, is established in the **Letters** precisely by engaging with this powerful and long-standing rhetoric and by showing that the operations of money do differ from one country to another. Scott represents this difference in apparently ambivalent terms, especially when he links the use of a paper currency to what Colin Kidd describes as the narrative of the "social retardation" of Scotland. However, by relating the "excellence" of the gold standard to the arbitrary imposition of the English standard, Scott's text effectively undermines the alleged superiority of gold, questioning the validity of the principle of uniformity invoked by the English government. This intersection of political, monetary, and cultural issues is ultimately what renders **The Letters of Malachi Malagrowther** a fascinating text, both as a political "manifesto" and as a fictional intervention in the realm of political economy at a time when the frontier between literature and economics was still indistinct.[66]

Notes

1. C. R. Josset, *Money in Great Britain and Ireland* (Newton Abbot, Devon: David & Charles, 1971), 174.

2. Lawrence H. White, *Free Banking in Britain: Theory, Experience, and Debate, 1800-1845* (Cambridge: Cambridge University Press, 1984), 30.

3. Adam Smith, *An Inquiry into the Nature and Causes of the Wealth of Nations* (1776), ed. R. H. Campbell, A. S. Skinner, and W. B. Todd, 2 vols. (Oxford: Clarendon, 1976), 1:321.

4. John Wilson Croker, *Two Letters on Scottish Affairs from Edward Bradwardine Waverley, Esq., to Malachi Malagrowther, Esq.* (1826), in *Thoughts on the Proposed Change of Currency*, by Sir Walter Scott, and *Two Letters on Scottish Affairs*, by John Wilson Croker, with an introduction by David Simpson and Alastair Wood, facsimile ed. (Shannon: Irish University Press, 1972), 2.47.

Thoughts on the Proposed Change of Currency is the original title of the first pamphlet edition (1826) of Scott's letters on the currency question. However, these letters are commonly referred to as *The Letters of Malachi Malagrowther* (see, e.g., P. H. Scott, ed., *The Letters of Malachi Malagrowther* [Edinburgh: Blackwood, 1981]). Therefore, in this essay, I use this latter title (abbreviated where necessary as *Letters*). Subsequent documentation of the *Letters* is given in the text: quotations are taken from the Irish University Press facsimile, with citations keyed to letter number and page number of this discontinuously paginated edition.

5. On Scotland's outstanding economic performance in the early nineteenth century, see T. M. Devine, *The Scottish Nation, 1700-2000* (New York: Viking, 1999), 105-23; and Linda Colley, *Britons: Forging the Nation, 1707-1837* (New Haven, Conn.: Yale University Press, 1992), 123-24.

6. The rise of the system of public borrowing in the six decades before the Seven Years' War "was rapid enough, and important enough in both its main and secondary effects, to deserve the name of the Financial Revolution" (P. G. M. Dickson, *The Financial Revolution in England: A Study in the Development of Public Credit, 1688-1756* [1967; reprint, with a new introduction, Aldershot: Gregg Revivals, 1993], 12). For a study of the origins and operations of international capital markets in eighteenth-century Europe, see Larry Neal, *The Rise of Financial Capitalism: International Capital Markets in the Age of Reason* (Cambridge: Cambridge University Press, 1990).

7. Walter Scott, journal entry, 24 February 1826. *The Journal of Sir Walter Scott*, ed. W. E. K. Anderson (1972; reprint, Edinburgh: Canongate, 1998), 114.

8. P. H. Scott, "The Malachi Episode," introduction to Scott, ed., *The Letters of Malachi Malagrowther*, ix-xxxiv, xviii, and "'The Last Purely Scotch Age,'" in *The Nineteenth Century*, ed. Douglas Gifford, vol. 3 of *The History of Scottish Literature*, ed. Cairns Craig (Aberdeen: Aberdeen University Press, 1988), 13-22, 17.

9. N. T. Phillipson, "Nationalism and Ideology," in *Government and Nationalism in Scotland,* ed. J. N. Wolfe (Edinburgh: Edinburgh University Press, 1969), 167-88, 186.

10. Scott, "The Malachi Episode," ix.

11. David Hewitt, "Walter Scott," in Gifford, ed., *The Nineteenth Century,* 65-87, 82.

12. Caroline McCracken-Flesher, "Speaking the Colonized Subject in Walter Scott's *Malachi Malagrowther* Letters," *Studies in Scottish Literature* 29 (1996): 73-84, 83.

13. For the uniqueness of Scotland's free banking system, see White, *Free Banking in Britain,* 23.

14. As Judith Wilt notices, *The Antiquary* "is about the Romance of Property when the property is history" (*Secret Leaves: The Novels of Walter Scott* [Chicago: University of Chicago Press, 1985], 157).

15. Martha Woodmansee and Mark Osteen, "Taking Account of the New Economic Criticism: An Historical Introduction," in *The New Economic Criticism: Studies at the Intersection of Literature and Economics,* ed. Martha Woodmansee and Mark Osteen (London: Routledge, 1999), 3-50, 21.

16. For a lengthier discussion of the Woodmansee and Osteen collection and the project of the new economic criticism, see Silvana Colella, "Al margini dell'interdisciplinarita': Diritto, economia, e letteratura," *Nuova corrente* 47 (2000): 131-44.

17. Journal entry, 24 February 1826, Anderson, ed., *Journal,* 114.

18. Journal entry, 3 March 1826, ibid., 120. The editor glosses *bruilzie* as "broil."

19. Journal entries, 19 March and 17 February 1826, ibid., 137, 109.

20. Scott appears to have been "much franker—and ruder—in his correspondence than in his *Journal.* ... Obviously he had one eye on future publication, and had no wish to cause embarrassment to the people he wrote about" (W. E. K. Anderson, introduction to Anderson, ed., *Journal,* xxiii-xlv, xxiv).

21. I am referring here to Ina Ferris's analysis of the construction of Scott's historical fictions as a kind of "manly intervention" in the field of cultural production (see *The Achievement of Literary Authority: Gender, History, and the Waverley Novels* [Ithaca, N.Y.: Cornell University Press, 1991], 79).

22. Although Scott does consider the possibility that Scottish banks might well rejoice in his defense of *their* right to issue notes: "The Banks are anxious to have [the *Letters*] published. They were lately exercizing lenity towards me and if I can benefit them it will be an instance of the 'King's errand lying in the Cadger's gate'" (journal entry, 22 February 1826, Anderson, ed., *Journal,* 112).

23. Larry Neal, "The Financial Crisis of 1825 and the Restructuring of the British Financial System," *Federal Reserve Bank of St. Louis Review* 80, no. 3 (May-June 1998): 53-76, 65. "*Asymmetric information* is the term applied to the usual situation in which borrowers know more about the actual investment projects they are carrying out than do the lenders. Lenders, knowing this, charge a premium proportional to the uncertainty they feel about the borrowers in question. This situation, in turn, creates an adverse selection problem, in which higher-quality borrowers are reluctant to pay the high interest rates imposed by the market, while lower-quality borrowers are willing to accept the rates and to default if their ventures fail" (ibid., 74).

24. For a detailed analysis of the changes introduced by the 1826 banking legislation, changes that to a large extent, appear to have been inspired by the Scottish model, see Timothy L. Alborn, *Conceiving Companies: Joint-Stock Politics in Victorian England* (London: Routledge, 1998), 85-95.

25. White, *Free Banking in Britain,* 38, 39, 39.

26. "The period of Scottish free banking," writes White, "coincided with a period of impressive industrial development in the Scottish economy. The growth of Scotland's economy in the century prior to 1844 was more rapid even than England's. ... There is good reason to believe ... that Scotland's banking system played a major role in promoting the economy's growth" (ibid., 24). For an interesting overview of the social and economic history of the period under examination, see Bruce Lenman, *An Economic History of Modern Scotland, 1660-1976* (London: Batsford, 1977), 101-55.

27. See Thomas Love Peacock, *Paper Money Lyrics and Other Poems* (London: C. & W. Reynell, 1837), 26, 35, 28, 6, 15. Peacock had already attacked what in *The Misfortunes of Elphin* (1829) he called the "sacred thirst of paper-money" (Thomas Love Peacock, *The Misfortunes of Elphin and Crotchet Castle* [1924; reprint, London: Oxford University Press, 1937], 126). In his satirical novel *Crotchet Castle* (1831), he gave vent to his hostility toward the recently established discipline of political economy, represented in this text by Mr. MacQuedy. In *Paper Money Lyrics,* Scotchmen and paper money are the favorite target of Peacock's satiric wit: "Caledonia needs no bullion, / No coin in iron case; / Her treasure is a bunch of rags / And the brass upon her face; / With pellets from her paper mills / She

makes the Southrons trow, / That to pay her sole way / Is by promising to owe, / By making promises to pay / When she only means to owe" ("Ye Kite-Flyers of Scotland," in Peacock, *Paper Money Lyrics,* 40-41, 41).

28. Scott's impressive description of economic growth and prosperity at home provides an interesting contrast to the ill-fated Scottish dream of colonial expansion abroad. The Darien scheme (the attempt of the Company of Scotland, in the late seventeenth century, to found a colony in Central America, in order to trade simultaneously with the Pacific and the Atlantic) had proved, in fact, spectacularly disastrous. On the Darien expedition, see John Prebble, *The Darien Disaster* (1968; reprint, Edinburgh: Mainstream, 1978); and George Pratt Insh. *The Darien Scheme* (1947; reprint, St. Leonards on Sea: Andrew, 1986).

29. For a persuasive reading of the figure of the "grotesque body" in these letters, see McCracken-Flesher, "Speaking the Colonized Subject."

30. On the republican mode of self-government in the banking sector, see Alborn, *Conceiving Companies,* 92-95.

31. See Colin Kidd, *Subverting Scotland's Past: Scottish Whig Historians and the Creation of an Anglo-British Identity, 1689-c. 1830* (Cambridge: Cambridge University Press, 1993).

32. Scott's descriptions of the advantages accruing to the whole country from the adoption of a paper currency, and from the system of credit associated with it, are historically accurate. Before 1844, free banking proved by and large a better system than central banking—especially the kind of central banking practiced by the Bank of England—and more beneficial to the public (White, *Free Banking in Britain,* 43). However, the mainstream position of economic theory, at the time, was so much in favor of central banking that the Scottish "exception" was barely regarded as significant. In this respect, Scott's analysis goes against the grain of classical political economy.

33. Kidd, *Subverting Scotland's Past,* 266.

34. John Maynard Keynes, *A Tract on Monetary Reform* (London: Macmillan, 1923), 172.

35. Thomas Attwood and John Sinclair, *The Late Prosperity and the Present Adversity of the Country, Explained: The Proper Remedies Considered, and the Comparative Merits of the English and the Scottish Systems of Banking Discussed, in a Correspondence between Sir John Sinclair and Mr. Thomas Attwood* (London: James Ridgeway, 1826), 66.

36. White, *Free Banking in Britain,* 23.

37. For a discussion of coins as ideological links between thought and matter, see Marc Shell, *Money, Language, and Thought: Literary and Philosophic Economies from the Medieval to the Modern Era* (1982; reprint, Baltimore: Johns Hopkins University Press, 1993), 156-77. The mention in Scott's text of coins as symbols of homogeneity could be interpreted in a number of ways. The same holds true for his discussion of the one-pound note. However, what I am trying to demonstrate here is that the potentially unlimited semiotic value of coin and paper as (monetary and linguistic) signs is invariably restricted or contained by the discursive formations within which Scott's text positions itself. The cultural value of the Scottish one-pound note as a symbol of diversity is determined by the very specific political context in relation to which Scott's intervention comes to be situated. My attempt to historicize Scott's text is inseparable from the need to historicize money itself. It therefore seems essential to insist only on those meanings—values, connotations—that were most relevant and most disputed at the time when Scott was outlining his position on Scottish nationalism by reworking the traditional rhetoric of the unreality of paper.

38. "What becomes of the comparative excellence of the specie circulation to be established in England, if apprehensions are entertained that it cannot stand its ground against the reprobated paper system of Scotland? In God's name, are they afraid people will prefer paper to gold?" (*Letters,* 2.62).

39. The rich repertory of derogatory images associated with paper money has a long history. It would certainly be valuable to trace these images back to their roots, but such a history falls well beyond the scope of this essay, I shall mention only the bursting of the South Sea Bubble in 1720 as one of the most interesting symbolic loci where the conjunction of speculative manias, vaporous or insubstantial wealth, and the illusion of paper money came to be firmly established, these images gaining an unprecedented degree of cultural visibility. For a detailed analysis of Bubble literature, see Silke Stratmann, *Myths of Speculation: The South-Sea Bubble and Eighteenth-Century English Literature* (Munich: Fink, 2000). For a historical investigation into the eighteenth-century ambivalent rhetoric of corruption associated with finance, see J. G. A. Pocock, *The Machiavellian Moment: Florentine Political Thought and the Atlantic Republican Tradition* (Princeton, N.J.: Princeton University Press, 1975), 448-61. The indictment of the unreality of paper money was an integral part of the discourse on credit in the eighteenth century, as has been demonstrated by, among others, Colin Nicholson,

Writing and the Rise of Finance: Capital Satires of the Early Eighteenth Century (Cambridge: Cambridge University Press, 1994); and Catherine Ingrassia, *Authorship, Commerce, and Gender in Early Eighteenth-Century England: A Culture of Paper Credit* (Cambridge: Cambridge University Press, 1998). Shell's study of the monetary debate in America is also relevant here since it emphasizes the interconnections between discussions of paper money as an appearance or shadow and aesthetic concerns with symbolization (see Shell, *Money, Language, and Thought*, 5-23).

40. The Restriction Act is discussed in greater detail in the section "*The Antiquary* and the Bullion Debate" below.

41. Peter L. Bernstein, *The Power of Gold: The History of an Obsession* (New York: Wiley, 2000), 200.

42. Ibid., 211. The Bullion Report was issued by the parliamentary committe that had been appointed to inquire into the price of gold bullion and the state of the currency.

43. Walter Scott, *The Antiquary*, ed. David Hewitt (Harmondsworth: Penguin, 1998), 187. Page numbers for subsequent quotations will be given parenthetically in the text.

44. Bernstein, *The Power of Gold*, 199, 201.

45. See Edwin Cannan, ed., *The Paper Pound of 1797-1821: The Bullion Report, 8th June 1810*, 2d ed. (London: P. S. King & Son, 1925). For a thorough assessment of the theoretical, political, and cultural issues involved in the Bullion Controversy, see Jacob Viner, *Studies in the Theory of International Trade* (London: Allen & Unwin, 1937); Frank Whitson Fetter, *Development of British Monetary Orthodoxy, 1797-1875* (Cambridge, Mass.: Harvard University Press, 1965); and Gary F. Langer, *The Coming of Age of Political Economy, 1815-1825* (New York: Greenwood, 1987).

46. "The idea appeared increasingly," writes Fetter, "that banks had deprived the public of its natural metallic money and had created paper money as an instrument of oppression, in contrast to the view sometimes put forward in the late nineteenth and twentieth century of gold being the instrument by which banks exploited the people. A climate of opinion developed that inconvertible paper money should be abolished for reasons that went beyond the theoretical analysis on such matters as how much deflation might be expected from a return to specie payments. Men who were far apart on most points were in agreement that somebody was making too much money from the paper money system: the restrained criticism of Ricardo ... of the Bank's profits; ... the wholesale invective of Cobbett against bankers as a class; and the denunciations in Jonathan Wooler's *Black Dwarf*, in Leigh Hunt's *Examiner*, and in *Sherwin's Political Register*, where without benefit of economic analysis these radical journals reiterated that the paper money system was one of the oppressors of the people" (*Development of British Monetary Orthodoxy*, 69-70).

47. There is no doubt that the Bullion Controversy constitutes one of the most important chapters in the history of monetary theory. Discussions of the role of the central bank in a complex credit economy, e.g., were innovatory; the monetary aspects of the theory of international trade were reassessed in ways that proved path-breaking: the analysis of the relations between currency phenomena, exchange rates, and price levels achieved a high degree of sophistication. As David Laidler remarks: "It is hard to think of any other episode in the history of monetary economics when so much was accomplished in so short a period" ("Bullionist Controversy," in *The New Palgrave Dictionary of Money and Finance* [London: Macmillan, 1992], 255-61, 261). However, most pertinent to my analysis of *The Antiquary* is not monetary theory per se but the popular idea of inconvertibility and the kind of cultural disturbance that it generated in the first few decades of the nineteenth century.

48. For a very persuasive reading of the symbolic and aesthetic implications of the paper pound in the early decades of the nineteenth century, see Kevin Barry, "Crediting Power: Romantic Aesthetics and Paper Money, 1797-1825," *La questione romantica* 3-4 (spring 1997): 169-92.

49. This less nostalgic kind of ideology informs Henry Thornton's famous contribution to the bullion debate, his essay on paper credit published in 1802 (see *An Enquiry into the Nature and Effects of the Paper Credit of Great Britain*, ed. Friedrich August von Hayek [London: Allen & Unwin, 1939]). For an interesting analysis of Thornton's work, see Patrick Brantlinger, *Fictions of State: Culture and Credit in Britain, 1694-1994* (Ithaca, N.Y.: Cornell University Press, 1996), 110-39.

50. On the representation of *prudence* as a national characteristic in this novel, see Lars Hartveit, "'Silent Intercourse': The Impact of the Eighteenth-Century Conceptual Heritage on *The Antiquary* and *St. Ronan's Well*," *English Studies* 77, no. 1 (1996): 32-44, 43.

51. Fiona Robertson, "On Speculation and Return: Scott's Jacobites, John Law, and the Company of the West," *Scottish Literary Journal* 24, no. 1 (1997): 5-24, 13.

52. For an account of Law's international experiments with paper money, see James Buchan, *Frozen Desire: An Inquiry into the Meaning of Money* (London: Picador, 1997), 127-51. For the connection between changes in eighteenth-century political thought and the rise of new financial instruments, see J. G. A. Pocock, *Virtue, Commerce, and History: Essays on Political Thought and History, Chiefly in the Eighteenth Century* (Cambridge: Cambridge University Press, 1985), and *The Machiavellian Moment*. Most pertinent to my discussion, however, is Brantlinger's analysis of Burke's indictment of French paper money, the assignat, for its association with the revolutionary spirit and with gambling (see Brantlinger, *Fictions of State,* 118-20).

53. In the "Epistle to Bathurst" (epistle 3 of the *Moral Essays*). Alexander Pope highlights the role of money in disputes concerning the legitimacy of monarchs: paper credit "can fetch or carry Kings" (Alexander Pope, "Epistle to Bathurst" [1773], in *Epistles to Several Persons* [*Moral Essays*], ed. F. W. Bateson, 2d ed. [London: Methuen; New Haven, Conn.: Yale University Press, 1961], 75-125, 93). The link between speculative finance and politics, established almost paradigmatically in Pope's text, can also be traced in a number of Scott's novels, as Robertson ("On Speculation and Return") has brilliantly demonstrated. My contention is that, in *The Antiquary,* this connection is displaced by another set of associations. Sir Arthur's Jacobite sympathies are immediately marginalized within the text and are not intimately bound up with his speculative projects (*Antiquary,* 38). These projects, furthermore, hinge on the thirst for gold and precious metals, which in its turn is constructed as chimerical (if not fraudulent). In other words, it is not paper but gold that—via the German plot and the financial collapse in store for Sir Arthur—proves most deceptive in this text.

54. Trumpener's reading of these disputes as conducive to a heightened sense of "national solidarity" is interesting: "In Scott's narrative, the debates of the eighteenth century are taken up and argued on to infinity. Bard and antiquary, Johnson and Macpherson stand side by side, linked by well-worn, comfortably familiar paths of argumentation. Apparently destructive and disruptive arguments about the interpretation of tradition have themselves become a solidified, solidifying tradition" (Katie Trumpener, *Bardic Nationalism: The Romantic Novel and the British Empire* [Princeton, N.J.: Princeton University Press, 1997], 123-24).

55. William Cobbett, *Paper against Gold and Glory against Prosperity,* 2 vols. (London: J. M'Creery, 1815).

56. It is also worth noticing that Edie's attitude toward money is similarly anachronistic or, more precisely, rooted in a kind of nostalgia for the metallic medium. As a rule, he refuses to accept money, especially when offered in the form of banknotes: "'Were the like o' me ever to change a note,'" he explains to Miss Wardour, "'wha the de'il d'ye think wad ever be sic fules as to gie me charity after that?'" Later on, when Lovel wishes to express his gratitude by offering Edie some more money, the latter again refrains from accepting notes—"'take back your notes, and just gie me a lily-white shilling'"—presumably on the same grounds as before. But, when Lord Glenallan presents him with "five or six guineas," true and fine gold in Dousterswivel's parlance, Edie immediately pockets the money (*Antiquary,* 93, 177, 229).

57. Wilt, *Secret Leaves,* 157.

58. See Fiona Robertson, *Legitimate Histories: Scott, Gothic, and the Authorities of Fiction* (Oxford: Clarendon, 1994), 198-99; Jane Millgate, *Walter Scott: The Making of the Novelist* (Edinburgh: Edinburgh University Press, 1984): and Trumpener, *Bardic Nationalism.*

59. Trumpener, *Bardic Nationalism,* 123.

60. Millgate, *Walter Scott,* 101.

61. Ibid., 98.

62. Barry, "Crediting Power," 180. By bringing together romantic and economic discourses on money and credit, Barry is interested in assessing "a romantic textual process which attempts to suspend disbelief in *unreal* things: the functioning in commercial society of what we may call imaginary signs, paper pounds, promises to pay which may only be exchanged for further promises to pay." He goes on to ask what kind of personality "might be fashioned to accept such promises, to credit the reality of such imaginary things" (ibid., 173). During the "paper-pound" era, romantic aesthetics does, to a certain extent, contribute to the fashioning of such a personality.

63. Millgate, *Walter Scott,* 98.

64. David Punter, introduction to Scott, *The Antiquary,* ed. Hewitt, xiii-xxx, xxii.

65. Matthew Rowlinson, "'The Scotch Hate Gold': British Identity and Paper Money," in *Nation-States and Money: The Past, Present, and Future of National Currencies,* ed. Emily Gilbert and Eric Helleiner (London: Routledge, 1999), 47-67, 61.

66. On the close interrelation between political economy and literature in the early nineteenth century, see Philip Connell, *Romanticism, Economics, and the Question of "Culture"* (Oxford: Oxford University Press, 2001).

Helen Phillips (essay date 2004)

SOURCE: Phillips, Helen. "Scott and Chaucer: Ekphrasis, Politics, and the Past in *The Antiquary.*" *Poetica* 61 (2004): 25-42. Print.

[*In the following essay, Phillips examines chapter 10 of* The Antiquary, *which includes an ekphrasis—a graphic description of a work of visual art, used as a literary device. Phillips explores the connections between the tapestry described in the chapter and Geoffrey Chaucer's influence on Scott.*]

Scott mentions Chaucer only briefly in **The Antiquary** but his knowledge of Chaucer was deep. There are parallels in theme and structure between Scott's novel and Chaucer's *Book of the Duchess,* and the *Flower and the Leaf,* which Scott, like his era, believed to be by Chaucer.[1] Examination of these illuminates the most striking aspects of Scott's novel, its strange narrative style and its conflicted ideological stance, especially with regard to mourning for a lost past and the question of the fit leaders to rule in a modern society.

Chaucer's dream poetry, especially the *Book of the Duchess,* Scott's source for his dream episode in chapter 10, experiments with structures built on discordant juxtapositions and insertions, denying unity and easy closure or resolution of the problems raised in the texts. Those problems in the *Book of the Duchess* concern loss and mourning for the past, voiced by the Black Knight's mourning for his wife and also conveyed indirectly by other elements in the poem's design, attitudes which are challenged by more pragmatic (one might say, bourgeois) worldviews, expressed by the Dreamer in dialogue with the knight. As in the *Parliament of Fowls,* there is arguably implicit questioning of aristocratic attitudes, which are shown as debilitating though both poems appear also to revere them. Both Chaucer and Scott's narratives (especially given **The Antiquary**'s recurrent contrast of old and new religions, catholicism and protestantism) are built on complex oppositional themes. In both a similar structure keeps these in creative debate and the use of insertions and ekphrasis is an important tool in this. Is it chance that two authors using similar structural styles, and in Scott's case inspired by his medieval predecessor, are also both ambiguously conservative in politics, each celebrating and upholding the claims of the feudal class yet admitting into his writing provocative elements that challenge those claims?

In **The Antiquary,** chapter 10, Lovel, despairing of winning Isabella because of his obscure background, sleeps in the haunted Green Room. Its tapestry depicts a hunt, with quotations from the *Flower and the Leaf* and *Book of the Duchess*:

> Lo! Here be oakis grete, streight as a lime,
> Under the which the grass, so fresh of line,
> Be'th newly sprung—at eight foot or nine.

> Everich tree well from his fellow grew,
> With branches broad laden with leaves new,
> That sprongen out against the sonné sheene,
> Some golden red, and some a glad bright green.[2]

> And many an hart, and many an hind,
> Was both before me and behind.
> Of fawns, sownders, bucks, and does
> Was full the wood, and many roes,
> And many squirrells that ysate
> High on the trees and nuts ate.[3]

Lovel dreams about the hunt and a man in sixteenth-century dress who shows him a message in a, to him unreadable, language. The man is Aldobrand, a Reformation printer and the message is German, "Kunst macht gunst," meaning that skill will produce success.[4]

The dream and intertextual tapestries are ekphrasis: visual inset scenes. In a novel where the present seems always ruled by the past, they epitomise its recurrent restless interface between a feudal hierarchical past and a modern world which values individual effort. In *The Book of the Duchess,* just before the passage quoted in Scott's tapestry, Chaucer's narrator also has a dream and finds himself in a bedroom decorated with ekphrastic murals and stained glass decorated with scenes and quotations from antique texts, and—like Scott's dreamer—he hears and watches a dream-hunt. The illustrations in Chaucer's bedroom come from the *Roman de la Rose* and *Roman de Troie,* narratives respectively of sexual desire and knightly battles in an ancient setting. Chaucer's influence on Scott's use of ekphrasis seems clear, here and also in the intertextual stained glass and painting in the hall of Scott's own mourning "man in black," the Earl of Glenallan.

Lovel's dream of past things—past texts—in a haunted chamber in an antiquary's abode is a figure of the way the past confronts the modern throughout the novel. On a simple literal level it foretells the happy ending: a promise more decipherable by the reader at this stage than the hero. Both the pre-Reformation Chaucerian poems contain consolatory messages for a despairing lover, while both the *Flower and the Leaf* and Aldobrand's story promise success as the reward of merit.[5] The dream's elements (the two Chaucerian poems and Aldobrand) also encapsulate central tensions of **The Antiquary,** tensions drawn from history which are also, more widely, opposed worlds and discourses, politically, spiritually, and psychologically: between the feudal and modern, Catholic and Reformation, privilege and merit, and between mourning for the past and a rational, positive attitude towards loss. The central debate in the *Book of the Duchess* between the inconsolable knight in black and his lower-class interlocutor, counselling more pragmatic, moderate approaches, seems adumbrated in several aspects of the novel.

Ekphrasis has a profound role in **The Antiquary.** It is part of the continuous shifting between different narrative levels and styles, and contributes symbolism and a repetition *in parvo* of central patterns. The plot, juxtaposing feudal and modern worlds, and different classes, is conveyed through a corresponding stylistic patchwork of literary styles, genres, allusions, different languages, inset songs, pictures, and tales: an unrestful, provocative narrative style engendering a sense that themes are being problematized, not just presented. The stylistic diversity and juxtapositions take readers into dichotomies at the heart of Scott's political vision: questions about the relevance of models from the past to issues of political order, religion, and masculine identity. Like Chaucer's dream poems, the text provides no easy unifying, resolutions, despite its plot's happy conclusion. Scott's political model is that of a social reformation that succeeds to the past rather than destroying it, a rescue of feudalism not its overthrow. Yet much in this novel condemns its characters representing the old regime and puts the energy of the bourgeois characters, Lovel and Oldbuck, attractively centre-stage. The denouement reveals a dynastic history that has been misinterpreted and removes a guilt hanging over legitimate rule, yet this re-interpretation and resolution itself is presented in an indirect and fragmentary way.

A later ekphrasis further illustrates the novel's preoccupations and methods. In chapter 28 the bereaved Earl of Glenallan sits in a black-hung hall beneath window illustrating "the life and sorrows of the prophet Jeremiah" and a painting of St Stephen's martyrdom (226). The obvious message is of mourning. Yet, just as the chapter 10 tapestries present, on the surface, the picturesque Romantic charms of nature and the antique but have deeper intertextual implications which point in oppositional directions, referring to past and future, these biblical subjects betoken simultaneously mourning and hope, tragic past and hopeful future. Using texts that, for Christian tradition, show the Jewish old religion succeeded by Christianity, this ekphrasis symbolises pervasive political themes in the novel, the replacement of Catholicism by Protestantism and feudalism by the modern socio-economic world.

The Book of Jeremiah contains a famous line: "Rachel weeping for her children, refused to be comforted," 31.15, an inconsolable bereavement paralleling both Lord Glenallan, and the black knight's mourning in *The Book of the Duchess*. There is a contrasting link back from the Earl's black chamber to chapter 10's cheerful leafy illustrations in the green bedchamber of Lovel who, unbeknowns, is his lost son.[6] Chaucer had made a contrast of dark and light, Black and White, mourning and a bright morning with hunting in a forest, all contributing to the implicit message of consolation offered by his poem's structure.

Scott specifies both the "sorrows," as well as the life of Jeremiah (226) and the Lamentations of Jeremiah begins "How doth the city sit desolate that was full of people!": the heirless Glenallan estate resembles desolate Jerusalem. Yet Jeremiah also prophecies the Messiah, parallel to the true heir, the Protestant Lovel/Neville/Lord Geraldin,

who will take over ancient privilege, just as (in Christian eyes) this Old Testament text is fulfilled in a reformed religion, the new covenant. An earlier reference to Rachel weeping for her children, occurs in chapter 17: the bachelor Oldbuck's image not for a human, family bereavement but for antiquarians' mourning the loss of documents from the past, those destroyed from monastic libraries by the protestant Dissolution.[7]

Similarly Stephen's death, though tragic, was the occasion for a sermon about the Messiah and God's favour passing to a new religion (Acts 7). It parallels Steenie's death, and Chaucer's dialogue about bereavement surely inspired chapter 34's dialogues about mourning what is lost, between Oldbuck and both "stoic," workingman Meiklebackit and melancholic aristocratic Glenallan.

Scott's Tory model of a new age reforming the past yet inheriting power structures from it is visually symbolised when, within Lovel's dream, the pre-Reformation Chaucerian texts and their image of knightly hunting give way to the figure of the Reformation craftsman printer with his message of meritocratic achievement.

The *Flower and the Leaf* teaches that the knights of the Leaf, symbolising chastity, constancy, and the active pursuit of honour, will triumph despite vicissitudes, whereas those dedicated to idle pleasure, the company of the Flower, find only short-lived happiness.[8] Dryden's modernisation in his *Fables* further emphasised this message (and Scott had edited Dryden). The poem became enormously popular in the nineteenth century, with the *Book of the Duchess* and other dream poems, establishing Chaucer as a type of poet familiar to Victorian taste, a Nature poet.[9] Scott's use of his two tapestry texts predates this Victorian reading of them, and his allusions to the *Flower and the Leaf* in several works show interest in it primarily as a model for masculine identity, endeavour, and virtue. Although Nature is certainly a theme in the Green Room's ekphrasis, the *Flower and the Leaf* has its own message, like Aldobrand, of meritocracy: the men of the Company of the Leaf show their prowess in a tournament, and their moral and practical superiority to the irresponsible Company of the Flower whom they rescue from a storm. Though a fifteenth-century poem about knights, the *Flower and the Leaf* expresses something like a protestant work-ethic and combines a chivalric model of masculinity with one of endurance and effort compatible with Scott's own political ideals. Aldobrand's story shows him as a representative man of the ensuing modern, Protestant and rational world: no chivalric knight but a printer and chemist, a skilled man of the Reformation, reason, and science.

Lovel, depicted at this stage as a modern bourgeois young man making his own way in the world, has, like the knights of the Leaf, shown heroic endeavour in the previous scene (whose style envelops him paradoxically in

Gothic glamour), by rescuing Isabella and her arrogant aristocratic father from a storm, a danger created by the irresponsibility of Sir Arthur—clearly a moral descendant of the feckless Company of the Flower who are rescued by the prudent Company of the Leaf.

The *Book of the Duchess* also contains a storm scene, taken from Ovid, which parts the lovers Ceys and Alcyone. As with Isabella and Lovel's separation after their storm-scene, which will end in their reunion, there is a happy ending in store for Ovid's Ceyx and Alcyone, which Scott would have known also from Dryden's *Ceyx and Alcyone* in the *Fables*. Lovel's happy ending includes marriage, and love is the central subject of *The Book of the Duchess*: its hunt, the subject of Scott's tapestry, is a symbol of desire. Chaucer's poem offers a further consolation appropriate for Scott's hero: its inset tale of a high-born lady's acceptance of an assiduous constant wooer. The juxtaposed sections of Chaucer's complex design present a range of other potential consolations.[10] Scott and Chaucer's poems both employ a disconcerting structure of insertions and intriguing juxtapositions, a structure that puts responsibility on readers rather than the author for finding unity or conclusions out of the texts' cross-currents.

The delay in interpreting the import of chapter 10's mysterious book alerts Scott's readers to their need to interpret. Chapter 15's scene in Fairport post office, where unopened letters are scrutinised and the messages they might contain discussed, symbolises the novel's presentation of its own material and structure as virtually a set of unsorted fragments in need of interpretation—through its miscellaneous narrative style, its unsolved and misinterpreted mysteries from the past, its themes of archaeology and the pursuit of antiquarian relics and texts, and its deeper questioning of whether the political structures inherited from history should be left unchanged or reinterpreted. Mingling past and present is an aesthetic pattern in Scott's text as in Chaucer's, and also an image of Scott's political vision, a project of fusing apparently oppositional social structures from the medieval and modern worlds.

Is the social order of the past, an inherited presence in the modern world, to remain a loved but inert collection of unrelated, useless, unproductive relics, like an antiquary's museum, or should we submit it to interpretation and synthesis, some form of *grand récit* for today? Does a past like the feudal aristocracy, that may need to be rejected in its own terms for modern politics, nevertheless have a value if reintegrated in reformed ways into a modern dispensation? Lovel, seemingly the outsider, will embody Scott's answer: an enlightened, energetic inheritor of old privilege. Scott's patchwork narrative style juxtaposes competing forces, religious, political, and psychological. The tapestry and dream, with their ekphrasis and intertextuality, like the biblical illustrations in Glenallan's hall, are representations of two worlds held in dialogic tension throughout *The Antiquary*: two forms of the past, and these are psychological and spiritual as much as social or political. The first can be summed up as with what is feudal, Catholic, chivalric, "Gothic," irrational and supernatural, and is given over to mourning, and mourning over the past. This is epitomised by the tragic Earl Glenallan (his own history has been misrepresented and will be healed and reinterpreted by the plot's merging of feudal and modern in the person of Lovel/Lord Geraldin).[11] The second is associated with middle-class work, the Reformation, Protestant rationality, concrete factuality, objectivity, and with a confidence in the future. Like the Church's succession to the heritage of Israel, the novel depicts a group with ancient, God-given, special status—the nobility, whom Scott makes parallel to Israel by his ekphrastic allusions to Jeremiah and Stephen—renewed by modernity and Protestant bourgeois enterprise and rationality.

Chapter 10 juxtaposes these two pasts in its medieval and Reformation *mélange* of tapestry and dream, knighthood and meritocracy. Scott moves his Chaucerian tapestries forward in time, into Reformation Europe, saying they were woven by sixteenth-century "looms of Arras" (75), and Chaucer inspired a "Flemish artist" (76). This elides Scott's two worlds of the past. Lovel is revealed to be a distinguished soldier—like a medieval knight—and also a modern man of courage, modesty, and integrity. Though the novel, published 1816, is set in 1794, that represents conceptually the modern post-Reformation world. It is set amid conflicts germane to Scott's religious and political preoccupations: one is the war against Catholicism, in the form of France (Lovel fought in Flanders: a geographical metonymy, like Aldobrand and Martin Waldeck's Germany, for the Reformation); another is the repression of radicalism, France being a revolutionary power. The international conflict thus parallels national conflict: agitation in Britain for reform and the government's repression of this.[12] It is an era "threatened with invasion from abroad and insurrection at home" (46). Personally, it was the time when the young Scott loved and lost Williamina Belsches (encountered, like Isabella Wardour, at the sea-side), fought political battles against radicals, and went ballad-collecting among the peasantry, an authorial past that perhaps haunts *The Antiquary*.[13]

The Chaucerian texts, depicting knightly leisure, belong to the Catholic Middle Ages, whereas Aldobrand was a self-made craftsman and active Protestant, the printer of the Augsburg Confession. The Green Room is haunted by two pasts which the dream shows merging. The consolatory, amatory, and elegiac associations here, as elsewhere in the novel and Scott's oeuvre, straddle feudal and modern worlds, and offer a double model for masculine identity, pride, and success, and a marriage, literal and metaphoric, of privilege and enterprise, will be the novel's happy denouement.

This is not reached easily: the central chapters form a debate on class as much as steps in a plot. The dream's marriage of the feudal and meritocratic disappears once the narrative re-emerges out of the presciently haunted Green Room into the present-day world next morning. Chapter 10's ekphrastic interlude is sandwiched between two episodes where Lovel's endeavours, though heroic enough to suit a Gothic novel or medieval romance, are rejected because of class barriers erected by the survival of a restrictive feudal past personified in the Jacobite, snobbish, and pro-Catholic Sir Arthur Wardour. The socially despised man's heroism in chapters 7 and 8, the evening before the dream, took place amid darkness, towering cliffs, storm and sea: figures of the Gothic and the imaginary (which paradoxically validate them further in Scott's aesthetics). His rejection by Sir Arthur, a rejection rooted in antique hierarchies, is manifested by the cold light of morning in a modern drawing room (chapter 13). The interpenetration and aesthetic conflict of romantic and anti-romantic modes in these surrounding chapters, 7, 8 and 13, 14, centres on Lovel: and the conflict between a feudal and meritocratic social model will finally be resolved in his person. This happy ending, as fantastic as any hauntings and dreams, can be taken (if not discounted as one of Scott's wish-fulfilment endings) as representing the persistent strength of Scott's desire to work in both worlds. Lovel is a modern young man of the 1790s, dispossessed of any prospects except his own efforts and self-governance, but also heroic, passionate, and (a fact occluded till the end) heir to an ancient Catholic earldom.[14]

The Flower and the Leaf, that fable of a proto-Protestant work ethic, offers images attractive also to Scott's conservatism. His tapestry quotation describes trees, "leafy boughs of the forest trees, branching over the tapestry ... The branches of the woven forest were crowded with fowls of various kinds," (75-6) making it the "Green Room." Scott used the tree often to symbolize national stability through traditional social structures.[15] The tapestry celebrates *The Flower and the Leaf,* whose Company of the Leaf symbolise masculine constancy and prowess. Scott evokes here a group of ideas with associated Chaucerian references found also in *Rokeby* (1813) and *Ivanhoe* (1819). *Rokeby,* whose plot is partly inspired by Chaucer's *Knight's Tale,* cites the *Flower and the Leaf,* and again less for the natural description beloved of the Victorians than for its theme of a tournament, representing individual masculine enterprise and perseverance rewarded. In canto VI, xxv, before a confrontation between enemies and supporters of Matilda, Scott calls for poetic inspiration equal to Chaucer's descriptions of tournaments in the *Flower and the Leaf,* and the *Knight's Tale,* where Palamon and Arcite fight for the hand of Emily.[16] The lovers of *Rokeby* and *The Antiquary* have similarities: their travails and constancy will be rewarded with love and a feudal inheritance, Lovel turning out to be Lord Geraldin and *Rokeby*'s Redmond (another lost son) being descended from noble Irish families, including the

Geraldines. The repeated name suggests Scott is working with common patterns of allusion and theme.

In *Ivanhoe* (1819) he cites the *Flower and the Leaf* again in terms of its tournament, as a chivalric poem like the *Knight's Tale.* Extracts from *Palamon and Arcite,* Dryden's modernisation of *The Knight's Tale,* introduce chapters 7 and 8 about the tournament.[17] The next chapter, in which Rowena is crowned queen of the tournament, has a quotation from *The Flower and the Leaf,* describing the Lady of the Leaf. The tournament's second day, chapter 10, returns to the *Knight's Tale, Ivanhoe*'s hero, displaced from his feudal rights, fighting back to success, marriage and high status through his own efforts, is the same model of hero found in *The Antiquary*: another political fable about a meritocratic feudalism producing social healing. Ivanhoe, nobly-born, exiled, and fighting injustice, is endowed by Scott with many motifs traditionally associated with the rebellious Robin Hood while being a figure who safely neutralizes the potentially radical or disruptive elements in reform or outlawry.[18]

Scott provides *The Antiquary* with a similar neutralization of the *wrong* sort of Protestant work-ethic and success. It is the inset tale of Martin Waldeck, volume 2, chapter 3. "Martin" suggests Luther, and this is another narrative imbued with the spirit of the Company of the Leaf: Waldeck means "nook of the wood," and the Harz demon is conceived as a Green Man or wild man of the woods.[19] The tale of upward mobility is told as the company sits "*fronde super viridi,*" 'upon the green leaf,' under "a huge oak tree called the Prior's Oak," (136) a name nicely mixing medieval Catholicism and greenery, while exemplifying Scott's liking for ancient trees as symbols of the politically wise respect for tradition. The symbolic leafy greenery from *The Flower and the Leaf* continues in this tale about the evil dangers of lower-class upstarts usurping aristocratic privileges. It explores themes associated together in *Rokeby, Ivanhoe* and *The Antiquary.* This inset episode, like chapter 10's scenes, is in dialogue with surrounding episodes, and holds in tension catholic and protestant worlds. The fortunes of Waldeck a forester, though he is courageous and ambitious, are ill-gotten; his upward mobility is even presented as demonic. Although he gains a patent of nobility, becoming Baron von Waldeck, his attempt to enter into a tournament is resisted by the real aristocracy: he "had the arrogance to appear among the chivalry of the province and demand permission to enter the lists ... a crime only inferior to sacrilege or regicide" (Scott's jocular style conveys unmistakable ambivalence). "We will have no cinder-sifter mingle in our games of chivalry" is aristocracy's contemptuous response (144-45). Martin, enraged, commits murder—aptly on a herald, warder of the symbols of ancient inherited nobility. Banished from his former rank and arms, punished by losing his right hand, the former artisan ends his days first mocked by the vengeful wood-demon, threatening the fires of hell, and then, though in his heyday he had been a rabid

Protestant, returning to Catholicism and confessing his sins before expiring.

Punter sees this tale as an instance of the way Gothic and supernatural are woven into the pot-pouri of genres and modes in *The Antiquary,* but, like the intrusions from the pre-modern examined earlier (Glenallan's pictures, the Gothic style of the cliff rescue, and the medieval scenes from the tapestry), it also conducts us to the heart of the political anxieties that are at work in the novel's mixed genres, disconcerting juxtapositions, and jumbled, fantastical plot.[20] The tale is a prophylactic warning of an unacceptable type of individual ambition, and the potential for social peril, even damnation, in the political and social values associated with upward mobility, radical challenges, and Protestantism, when these are unconstrained by traditional social order and hierarchy. Waldeck's dual profession, forester and charcoal-burner, figuratively combines affinities with the assiduous Company of the Leaf and punishment in hellfire: upstart individual enterprise allied to and leading to perdition. To complete the fable's complexity, Scott surrounds it with a strange mixture of ownership: written by the aristocratic Miss Wardour; read aloud by Lovel, whose despised lineage prevents him from crossing the class barrier and marrying her; its truth vouched for only by the superstitious Dousterswivel, whose view is treated with contempt. Oldbuck the rationalist dismisses it but says a sound moral emerges from it. This is explicitly anti-radical: "the miseries attendant upon wealth, hastily attained and ill-employed, exemplified in the fortunes of Martin Waldeck" (146).

The Waldeck fable, with its woods and tournament—those *Flower and the Leaf* motifs again—and the disdain from the traditional knightly community for modern upstarts entering it, prefigures events that follow: a modern-day tournament between Lovel and Hector MacIntyre, representing the new world and the old world of unchallenged feudal privilege. After the tale, the significantly named Hector, an army captain of aristocratic highland lineage, rivals Lovel for Isabella's affections. Scott signals this episode's almost schematic symbolism by verbally identifying Hector with a chivalric knight, "cavaliere servente," "knight-companion," "Hotspur," and so on. Lovel's lack of pedigree is mocked, yet Scott, in revealing him to be a valiant soldier as well as poor man, underlines his hero's fusion of ancient chivalric and modern models of masculine enterprise. Lovel, like Ivanhoe, is the right kind of leader for Scott's social vision. His merits, while temporarily displaced into the role of a man without social recognition, justify his fitness for inherited leadership when it comes. The need for hierarchical order is raised in a dialogue curiously inserted at this point, between Lovel and Oldbuck, where the latter claims that the overthrowing of traditional symmetry and order in architecture in the seventeenth century produced "primitive confusion," which he calls "dishonourable," "enormities," "disgraceful," created "at immense expense" by a "barbarous, fantastic, and ignorant architect," (148) words suggesting riot, social disruption and upstart vulgarity. Lovel takes Oldbuck's criticism of non-traditional architecture as an attack on his own suit and ambitions. Scott used the architectural political analogy in his anti-Whig propaganda, *The Visionary* (1819), where Mr Vitruvius Whigham tries to spoil the grand old mansion with its ancient garrets (the traditional political system, including rotten boroughs), aided by a rabble led by Rob Radical: a Robin Hood figure. Here, as in *The Antiquary,* large oaks are images of Tory principles: the *Visionary*'s radicals create a landscape denuded of trees; their leader brandishes a club made out of an uprooted sapling (like Waldeck's demon this recalls German wild man woodcuts) but the dreamer, waking from this revolutionary nightmare, returns thankfully to a waking world to find the huge oak that protected him still flourishing.[21]

Hector, deriding Lovel's lowly origins (150-51), snarls, "does the valorous knight aspire to the hand of the young lady he has redeemed from peril?—It is quite the rule of romance," (150) boasting a "pedigree of fifteen unblemished descents." The young men have a modern-style tournament: first a verbal duel as Hector impugns Lovel's regimental credentials only for Lovel to vindicate them (152-53); then Hector throws down his glove and challenges him to a pistol duel which Lovel wins. These events seem animated by the pattern of associations drawn from Scott's reading of *The Flower and the Leaf* already seen in *Rokeby,* as well as linking back to the tournament from the just-finished Waldeck tale, with its class prejudice against a self-made man. Sir Arthur's pride in his ancestor, Gamelyn de Guardover, is another medieval literary allusion that offers the promise of the possibility of a marriage between inherited rank and individual enterprise and merit (*Gamelyn* appeared as Chaucer's in some editions such as Bell's of 1782.) Like Lovel and Ivanhoe, Gamelyn is deprived of his noble ancestral rank and has to make his own way in the world. He ends with his inheritance restored and a happy marriage, acclaimed for his prowess and leadership.

The Antiquary contrasts images of masculine identity as well as social, religious and political attitudes.[22] If the age of knights is past what are the images to mould and inspire modern men? In modern society must men's instinct for aggression and wild freedom always be a form of social outlawry? In Scott's plots the aggressive male is typically contained, embedded in a minor role, with his social wildness and bellicosity exaggerated or rendered incongruous with the more civilised modes of the novel's main protagonist, to the point where it seems an unacceptable or comic, archaic, throwback. Examples include *Rob Roy,* Denzil the outlaw in *Rokeby,* the Children of the Mist in *A Legend of the Wars of Montrose,* and here, as a mild equivalent amid the polite modern society of Fairport, MacIntyre the mindlessly proud and belligerent highlander. Ian Duncan sees Scott in *Rob Roy* using a collection of contrasting masculine characters to represent tensions, anxieties and suppressions in "nineteenth-century masculine subjectivity," and this seems true of *The Antiquary*.[23] The novel's ideal of a union between individual merit and inherited rank, is symbolised in the craftsman's motto "Kunst macht gunst" carved on the ancient gold wedding ring of the new "Lord Geraldin." Yet much in the narrative celebrates sober individual effort. Lovel's military—chivalric—career takes place off-stage. Of his two other identities (defined on page 351 as "pacific Lovel" and "brave Major Neville") it is humble pacific Lovel who is the hero of adventures that are actually shown to the reader. Oldbuck, the very man who deplores overthrowing traditional order in architecture, praises the professional honour of a hard-working lawyer, without pretensions to be a gentleman, above gentleman lawyers and the claims to automatic honour via inheritance represented by MacIntyre. He ripostes that MacIntyre's family has its reputation for honesty "by patent" (338). Oldbuck, whose name, paired with young Lovel's, suggests his misogyny derives not from lack of sexuality but a complicated relationship to his own masculinity in the past, is an intriguing bundle of paradoxes on gender issues. Just as the larger plot hinges on a hidden sexual sin from the past, filtered in through disconnected narrative fragments, so Oldbuck, the character who unifies the novel, is conceived by Scott as a man retreating into pedantic hypermasculinity as a cover for a buried sexual failure in youth. This too is revealed only through fragments and incongruities. His anti-emotional, anti-women, exterior is explained as a defence for an affectionate heart in chapter 34, which reveals his long-past love for Eveline. Humiliating mockery from a male rival of higher, more military, rank caused the calcification of his personality: "The pride of his affected cynicism" (268). As the novel exposes its aristocrats as unimpressive, so it shows Oldbuck's academic studies to be a useless hobby that he vaunts aggressively above the useful tasks of his female household. Isabella's rationality and practicality similarly contrast with Sir Arthur's perilous folly.

Like its ambivalent attitudes to aristocracy and superstition, the novel's presentation of the two sexes' relative power is contradictory. The plot's surface, full of conflicting forces and claims, is dominated by males but the hidden powers driving it are revealed ultimately to be strong, ruthless women; these brought Glenallan and Lovel to their positions of weakness: Elspeth, Teresa and Joscelin ("they were a doughty and a dour race the women o' the house o' Glenallan," 213). They control interpretation of the fragments from the past: "the dreadful hints" Glenallan begs Elspeth to explain (258), the "doubtful hints," sometimes thrown out in paradoxical style by Joscelin (262). Elspeth, who excavates crucial buried truths piece-meal, in baffling fragments and elusive traditional songs, is the voice of the past ("it's awesome to hear your gudemither break out in that gait—it's like the dead speaking to the living," 214); she chronicles the Glenallan family, showing them bound by a family past, as her inset tale of the night-time burial of

the Great Earl (213-4), and ballad of Roland Cheyne (310-12) illustrate.

Oldbuck, whom the reader (implicitly masculine) is clearly assumed to find sympathetic underneath his eccentricities, denigrates women as a rank below him to be exploited (employing female domestics because they are paid less), attempting to negotiate his way through a self-evidentially contradictory range of attitudes to women offered by masculinist history:

> Let them minister to us, Sir Arthur—let them minister, I say—it's the only thing they are fit for. All ancient legislators, from Lycurgus to Mohommed, corruptly called Mohomet, agree in putting them in their proper and subordinate rank, and it is only the crazy heads of our old chivalrous ancestors that erected their Dulcineas into despotic princesses.

(1. 6 44)

Grizzel's Chaucerian name is another allusion that conveys ambiguous political attitudes, in this case towards male domination. The instability of Oldbuck's masculinist fantasies (and Scott's characteristic tendency—like Chaucer—to introduce dialogic challenges to conservative discourses that his texts otherwise support) is further underlined by ekphrasis: his wall depicts the romance of *Gawain and Dame Ragnell,* an allusion expressing his misogyny while also destabilising it, since in this romance it is a socially despised, ugly, but sagacious woman who saves the knight's life (chapter 3). Oldbuck's national and sexual politics represent the instinct to leave things as they are, as they have been left from the past, without [re-]interpretation. As antiquarian collector he personifies the collage-like mode of the novel, its assemblage of themes from history. Even his language resembles a miscellany of treasures from the past.

Sutherland compares Scott's collage-like structures to archaeological levels of culture and literature: "layered narrative deposits, strata embedded in stories that offer progressive redescriptions of their materials." She sees traditional songs as the deepest historical layer, so that Scott's reader passes progressively "through the mediating half-fictions of the prefaces, into the confrontation of historical forces against which private dilemmas are enacted, and beyond that to an unreadable core, a fragment of song or a paradigmatic tale, which teases and evades the reader's skill."[24] Literal archaeology is part of this novel, whose title suggests resemblance to a museum or assembly of disconnected remains from the past. To questions about what sort of role survivals of the past have, and ought to have, in the present, Oldbuck represents the simple approach, arrested at the stage of collecting a miscellany, not constructing a *grand récit*.[25] Elbers says the novel, though often criticised for weak plotting and shifts of mood and style, is "a unified work of art organised round a set of thematic contrasts."[26] Furthermore, I suggest, whatever conceptual and aesthetic unity is found will be produced by the reader, deciding to pick up a particular thematic nexus of ideas and intertextual implications, or reading, as I have done here, as a dialogic structure, in its insertions, allusions and stylistic contrasts. Like the book Lovel cannot read in chapter 10, or speculation over sealed envelopes at the post office, or the disputed ancient inscriptions, the text is not fully *lisible* in its own terms. With its inset tales and songs, ekphrases, juxtapositions, and generic shifts, as well as its political multiplicity of views, it is an assemblage, like Chaucer's *Duchess,* offered for interpretation to readers as they progress through the narrative, a good example of narrative as construal rather than constructed.[27]

Chapter 10 claims history itself is like this. Scott precedes the dream with Oldbuck's musings about historical relics, asking whether what is recalled from the past into the present, can remain the same and preserve its meaning intact, when we, the observers, are different (75).

The inserted songs, though initially baffling to any attempt to relate them to surrounding narratives, have intimate connections with the novel's themes. Antiquaries in Scott's period collected texts from the past as well as objects, as in the ballad collections of Percy, Ritson, and Scott himself. He distinguishes between mere collecting and interpretation when Elspeth sings an ancient ballad at a time of intense loss (3.11). This strikes Edie as tragic but excites Oldbuck's de-emotionalised passion for collecting.[28] Elspeth's song, like much in the novel, is both as a proleptic celebration of the House of Glenallan's happy ending, and part of Scott's political message: it promises that "stout and good" knights can succeed against terrible odds. The unthinking aristocrat Hector despises it. A. N. Wilson observes that Scott makes Oldbuck, like James Cargill, the phenomenon of a man who, having failed to succeed in love in youth, turns to the pursuit of historical knowledge thereafter. In him the manic pursuit of hard "objective" knowledge appears a retreat into a stereotypical masculinist self-image (like the equally gender-stereotyped activity of collecting) to escape unmanageable masculine sexual fears and self-doubt.

There are deep affinities between Scott and Chaucer, these two complex conservatives, especially in the political and structural discontinuities in their fictions. Narrative frames, insertions, and ekphrasis construct those "competing levels of authority," observed by Fiona Robertson in Scott and equally evident in Chaucer.[29] These foster political dialogism in both writers. Middle class in origin, successfully upwardly mobile towards aristocratic echelons of society, both authors wrote in praise of chivalric ideals and feudal culture while living in time of rapid socio-economic change, the beginnings respectively of English commercialism and of industrial Britain, and also in the aftermath of revolutions: the 1381 Rising and French Revolution. These two political challenges both had their most impor-

tant repercussions in Britain not in regime change but in the fears and responses of the ruling classes during ensuing decades. Scott and Chaucer present themselves deprecatingly as entertainers not didacticists; Chaucer's aim, he protests, with the caution of one living in dangerous times, is "game" not "ernest"—any provocative social message derived from his fictions must be the reader's responsibility.[30] They mock and dissemble their own seriousness, move quickly between solemnity and comedy. In comparison with their contemporaries, they excel in a wide social canvas, mingling diverse classes and social viewpoints, bringing the traditional and innovative tendencies of their own periods into contact, conflict, and provocative juxtaposition.[31] Both show acute awareness of the social dimension of language and its capacity to put disparate world-views into dialogue.

Chaucer and Scott seem irresistibly drawn to revealing deep instabilities in aristocratic dominance. The melancholy of Lord Glenallan, Sir Arthur's shallow sourness and irresponsibility, Hector's rashness, and Chaucer's suicidal Black Knight exemplify damaging psychological states in men unprofitably imprisoned in a conventional and class-based self-image, and each text contains a challenge in the form of the pragmatic, wiser, and more stoic men of lower rank. Robertson calls Scott's novel a tale of "restored legitimacy," yet by the time Lovel's rank is restored the value of such rank has been so thoroughly questioned, and the concept of succeeding through individual effort and endurance so celebrated, that the politics of this denouement are themselves rendered dialogic.[32]

The Antiquary (like *To the Lighthouse* for which it is an intertext) is set on the edge of the sea, between the worlds of land and tempestuous ocean. Images of sea-creatures, especially amphibious ones, recur; notably the seal or *phoca,* first appearing in chapter 30. In a scene probably inspired by *The Book of the Duchess,* from Chaucer's inserted Ovidian tale of Ceyx and Alcyone, and also from Dryden's versions of *Ceyx and Alcyone* in the *Fables,* Lovel dreams of himself and Isabella metamorphosed: he feels alternately a fish and a bird, and she is a syren (an alluring marine bird-woman) and bird of paradise. Her father is a triton (half-man, half-fish) or sea-gull; Oldbuck a porpoise or cormorant. These ambiguous, amphibious creatures cross boundaries. The images of Isabella suggest both a supernatural realm and earth—much as the novel interweaves the supernatural and the rational.

The symbolic potential of the sea/land contrast is multiple. McMaster sees political symbolism: contrast between the hard lives of Scotland's "sea-going poor" and "home-keeping gentry."[33] Lovel's bird/fish dream also recalls the preceding episode, Isabella's near-drowning and rescue. The phantasmagoric chaos of the dream sequence seems an epitome, an acknowledgement, of the way the Gothic and sensational imagination is occasionally licensed to break free at points throughout Scott's text.

The boundary-crossings by dream-creatures into which the four actors from this previous episode are transmuted could be interpreted, like the inrushing tide during the seashore emergency, as symbols of loosening of restraints, and the threat of past and destructive emotions, taboos, and hidden guilts, uncontainable within the bounds of normal ordered experience. Fear, the past, and fear of the past haunt the plot of **The Antiquary.**

The plot turns on false reading of the past: the tale of incest and illegitimacy in the noble family. The novel is disconcerting in its style of conducting narrative but also surprisingly open, conveying at times a scepticism about the possibility of arriving at true readings of past events. The comic image of this is Oldbuck's projected *Caledoniad*: he can provide the historical materials but cannot construct them into a narrative, and—the last page confirms—that narrative will never be concluded. Pessimism about the limitations of human interpretation is strengthened by intimations of mortality (another theme of the two Chaucerian intertexts), in Glenallan's bereavement and Steenie's death, and also inset elements like the song, "Why sit'st thou by that ruin'd hall," in chapter 10. This gives a universal perspective to the novel's theme of the meaning of the past within the present. Another, spiritual, approach to reassessing the past is confession, a recurrent Catholic motif ambiguously introduced, into Waldeck's story and the confessions or half-confessions of Elspeth, Teresa, and Mr Neville.

For both Scott and Chaucer, juxtaposition, generic shifts, ekphrasis, and insertion are techniques which allow maximal interpenetration and conflict between different times, emotional modes, and political or spiritual world-views, allowing their narratives to contain oppositional tendencies. Reviewing Godwin's *Life of Chaucer* (1803), Scott derided Godwin for, he claimed, exaggerating Chaucer's respect for women and his historical importance in the political circles of his time.[34] If Scott downplayed the importance of politics and gender in Chaucer's worldview, perhaps it was partly because these produce irreconcilable conflicts and discontinuities in his own fictions. Beneath the success both authors have had throughout the centuries as entertainers, as portrayers of a wide social canvas, and of comedy mingled with tragedy, it is these two issues— attitudes towards feudal structures and gender issues— together with the further question of how the new artist fits within the established literary past (new genres and discourses using old genres and discourses), that above all bring recalcitrant, discordant, materials into their narratives, and with it greater profundity and complexity. Such internal conflicts respond best to fictional structures based less on the smooth control of linear plotting than on a provocative patchwork of elements, shifting in style, mood, and time: structures in which disparate materials can comment on, contradict, and modify each other. Such structures Scott may have learnt, or been encouraged to use, from reading Chaucer, while his views on the compatibility of meritocratic and inherited social leadership seem to have been influenced, here and elsewhere in his writings, by apocryphal Chaucer, *The Flower and the Leaf.*

Notes

1. A general outline is offered in Jerome Mitchell, *Scott, Chaucer, and Medieval Romance: A Study of Sir Walter Scott's Indebtedness to the Literature of the Middle Ages* (Lexington, 1987).

2. *Flower and the Leaf,* 29-35, Bell's edition of Chaucer (London, 1782). Quotations from *The Antiquary* are from the edition by David Hewitt, Edinburgh Edition of the Waverley Novels (Edinburgh, 1995).

3. *The Book of the Duchess,* Bell's edition, 427-32. Other Chaucer quotations from *The Riverside Chaucer,* ed. Larry D. Benson (London and New York, 1987).

4. Oldbuck translates "skill, or prudence, in availing ourselves of our natural talents and advantages, will compel favour and patronage, even where it is withheld, from prejudice or ignorance," 85. Dryden's *Flower and the Leaf* says "Lawrel is the Sign of Labour crown'd; / Which bears the bitter Blast, nor shaken falls to Ground: / From Winter-Winds it suffers no decay, / For ever fresh and fair, and ev'ry Month is May. / Ev'n when the hoary Head is hid in Snow; / The Life is in the Leaf . . . ," *The Poems of John Dryden,* ed. James Kinsley, 4 vols (Oxford, 1958), vol. 4, 578-85.

5. Another prefiguration is the tale of Malcolm Misticot's return to his ancestral home, vol. 2, chap. 9.

6. "Refrain thy voice from weeping . . . there is hope in thine end, saith the Lord, that thy children shall come again to their own border," 16-17.

7. Vol. 2, chap. 2 (chap. 17), 131.

8. Skeat put apocryphal works in a separate volume in his revised edition of Bell, 1878.

9. Amply illustrated especially for c. 1815 to c. 1870, in *Five Hundred Years of Chaucer Criticism, 1357-1900,* ed. Caroline Spurgeon, 3 vols, Chaucer Society, 50-2 (London, 1921).

10. See Helen Phillips, "Structure and Consolation in the *Book of the Duchess," Chaucer Review* 16 (1976): 107-18.

11. On Scott and feudalism see Alexander Welsh, *The Hero of the Waverley Novels* (New Haven, 1963); Avrom Fleishman, *The English Historical Novel: Walter Scott to Virginia Woolf* (Baltimore, 1971), 47.

12. See Historical Note, Hewitt's edition, 358-61.

13. Fiona Robertson, *Legitimate Histories: Scott, Gothic and the Authorities of Fiction* (Oxford, 1994), 197, suggests the 1790s sets the novel in a modern era associated with the Gothic, a taste for tales of the supernatural, and ballad collecting.

14. During Scott's lifetime, Kathryn Sutherland observes, upward mobility between the middle classes and aristocracy was easier in Scottish than English society: "Fictional Economies: Adam Smith, Walter Scott and the Nineteenth Century Novel," *ELH* 54 (1987), 97-127.

15. E.g. in *Ivanhoe*: the opening forest scene; the tree-like associations of the Saxon palace, Rotherwood; the oak under which the outlaw sits in state flanked by his King and the Saxon lord; and that "huge oak-tree" under which King Richard is enthroned when his outlaws have become his orderly retinue (chap. 41); see note 24.

16. *Rokeby, The Poetical Works of Sir Walter Scott,* ed. J. Logie Robertson (London, 1904): canto VI.

17. *Palamon and Arcite, Poems,* ed. Kinsley (1958), vol. 4, bk. 3, 11, 453-63, 580-6. See Helen Phillips, 'This Mystique Show: Dryden and *The Flower and the Leaf,*' *Reading Medieval Studies,* 29 (2003), 51-70.

18. On political implications in this reworking of the Robin Hood legend, see Stephen Knight, *Robin Hood: A Complete History of the English Outlaw* (Oxford, 1994), 175-8.

19. Scott calls him a false interpretation of forest in a superstitious age, "tutelary daemon," "woodland goblin," "wild man, of huge stature, his head wreathed with oak leaves, and his middle cinctured with the same, bearing in his hand a pine torn up by the roots," 138. Scott seems to be recalling sixteenth-century printed German representations of the Wild Man or woodwose: R. Bernheimer, *Wild Men in the Middle Ages: A Study in Art, Sentiment, and Demonology* (Cambridge, Mass., 1952), plates 11-18, 27, 47-48.

20. See Punter, xiv-xv.

21. *The Visionary,* ed. Peter Garside, Regency Reprints 1 (Cardiff, 1984); on the oak's political symbolism, see Introduction, viii.

22. The antiquarians' fervour resembles battle: another cultural form that masculine self-assertion takes, vol. 2 chap. 4 (chap. 19); "The Antiquary, starting like a war-horse at the trumpet sound, plunged himself at once into the various arguments," 149-50.

23. *Rob Roy,* ed. Ian Duncan (Oxford, 1998), Introduction, xiii.

24. Sutherland, "Fictional Economies," 121.

25. E.g. chap. 4.

26. Joan S. Elbers, "Isolation and Community in *The Antiquary,*" *Nineteenth-Century Fiction* 27 (1972-3), 405-23, p. 406.

27. See Mark Currie, *Postmodern Narrative Theory,* Transitions (Basingstoke, 1998), 2-3.

28. "a genuine and undoubted fragment of minstrelsy!—Percy would admire its simplicity—Ritson could not impugn its authenticity," 310.

29. Robertson, *Legitimate Histories,* 133.

30. *Canterbury Tales* 1 (A), 3186.

31. See Peggy Knapp, *Chaucer and the Social Contest* (New York and London, 1900).

32. Light is cast on New Tory ideas associated with the invention of Lovel/Neville/Lord Geraldin, by a passage in Scott's "Essay on Chivalry": he quotes from Jonson's *New Inn* Lord Lovel's praise of the ancient practice of educating young men as pages, to follow "the noblest way / Of breeding up our youth in letters, arms, / Fair mien, discourses, civil exercises, / And all the blazon of a gentleman," *Essays on Chivalry, Romance and the Drama,* 28.

33. Graham McMaster, *Scott and Society* (Cambridge, 1981), 153-4.

34. *Miscellaneous Works,* 17 (Edinburgh, 1870), 79.

Carolyn Buckley-Fletcher (essay date 2004)

SOURCE: Buckley-Fletcher, Carolyn. "Sir Walter Scott and the Beginnings of Ethnology." *Nonfictional Romantic Prose: Expanding Borders.* Ed. Steven P. Sondrup, Virgil Nemoianu, and Gerald Gillespie. Amsterdam: Benjamins, 2004. 107-13. Print.

[*In the following essay, Buckley-Fletcher contends that Scott's historical novels go beyond mere reaction to reflect "subtle changes in the intellectual landscape of the European mind" and suggests that Scott responded to a cultural crisis by creating a new genre of fiction. Buckley-Fletcher discusses* The Antiquary *as Scott's most self-conscious commentary on emerging enthusiasms for the past and the primitive.*]

Around the middle of July 1802, a meeting took place between a young Edinburgh lawyer, a border shepherd, and his mother. The lawyer was Walter Scott, who was gathering material for the ***Minstrelsy of the Scottish Border.*** His host was a self-educated poet named James Hogg, who had been copying down ballads from the oral tradition of his family and community ever since coming across the first two volumes of the ***Minstrelsy*** in the spring of that year. In Hogg's thatched cottage his mother, Margaret

Laidlaw, recited to their guest the traditional ballad "Auld Maitland." Scott was delighted and asked if it had ever been in print:

> "O, na, na sir," she replied, "it never was printed I' the world, for my brothers an' me learned it an' many mae free auld Andrew Moor and he learned it free auld Baby Mettlin, wha was housekeeper to the first laird of Tushilaw. She was said to hae been another nor a gude ane, an' there are many queer stories about hersel', but O, she had been a grand singer o' auld songs an' ballads.
>
> Ay, it is that sir! It is an auld story! But nor that, excepting George Warton an' James Stewart, there war never ane o' my sangs prentit till ye prentit them yoursel', an' ye hae spoilt them awthegither. They were made for singing an' no for reading; but ye hae broken the charm now, an' they'll never be sung main An' the worse thing of a', they're nouther right spell'd nor right settee down."

(Hogg 136-37)

This meeting well symbolizes the changes taking place in the relationship between the oral and print cultures in England. Scott, self-appointed archivist, historian, and antiquarian and later recognized as one of the fathers of British anthropology and archaeology, is one of the seminal figures in that cultural transition. The same impulse that shaped the emergent social sciences—the impulse to preserve, to record, to commemorate—animates his literary work. In the introduction to **The Minstrelsy of the Scottish Border,** Scott voices his hope that by "such efforts, feeble as they are, I may contribute somewhat to the history of my native country; the peculiar features of whose manners and character are daily melting and dissolving into those of her sister and ally" (cxxii). In the preface to the Waverley novels, he remarks that his fiction begins in the interest of the preservation of ancient manners and customs, concerns shared by history and ethnology. It ends in a reflection and commentary not only on the crisis facing traditional cultures, but on the intellectual dilemmas of his own contemporaries, dilemmas inherent in literate attempts to salvage a largely preliterate past. It is a commentary remarkable for its candor and insight into the enterprise at large.

Scott's role is in part determined by the historical and geographical accidents of his birth. Scott was born in the second half of the eighteenth century to middle-class parents in Edinburgh, a city particularly distinguished by its progressive character in a nation where primitive, even atavistic tribal traditions had persisted long after their eclipse in Europe and England to the south, a country also distinguished by its fierce divisions and fiercer loyalties of clan, church, and kin. Scotland was a kingdom uniquely marked by its own internal polarities. Emerging from the northern edge of Europe, where cultures collided head on, where the practices of industrialism and the tenets of the Enlightenment had taken root and had grown with a remarkable rapidity, in seeming inverse proportion to the

rapid eclipse, even annihilation of Scotland's ancient traditions, Scott's work gives form to the very extremities of his time and place.

While the claims of Scott's birth and history along with the enthusiasms of his contemporaries go far in explaining the subjects of his work, they do not fully account for his manner of rendering of them, but his education does: the comparative method he learned at the University of Edinburgh became the basis for later developments in ethnology and anthropology. (Particularly important in this regard, notes Marinell Ash, was the influence of Ferguson and Dugald Stewart, whose comparative approaches to the study of societies past and present are reflected in Scott's student work, notably his 1789 paper to the student Literary Society, **"On the Origins of the Feudal System,"** where Scott argues for the cross-cultural appearance of feudalism in widely disparate cultures [443].) At the time Scott was writing, several distinct approaches to the study of earlier or primitive cultures had appeared. At the opening of the nineteenth century, the antiquarianism and mythography that had dominated much of the eighteenth century began to give way to an early ethnology and a proto-anthropology, which were not, however, fully defined until well into its second half of the century. (John Pilkey describes the position of Scott's work within larger developments in the nineteenth-century social sciences.) In 1802 James Hogg and Margaret Laidlaw clearly recognized Scott's leading role in antiquarian and folklore pursuits. By mid-century, his part in the growth of ethnology and archaeology as well as a nascent anthropology was widely, even officially, recognized. In 1851 Daniel Wilson, pioneer of both Scottish and American archaeology, opens *The Archaeology and Prehistorical Annals of Scotland* in praise of Scott:

> The zeal for Archaeological investigation which has recently manifested itself in nearly every country in Europe, has been traced, not without reason, to the impulse which proceeded from Abbotsford. Though such is not exactly the source which we might expect to give birth to the transition from profitless dilettantism to the intelligent spirit of scientific investigation, yet it is unquestionable that Sir Walter Scott was the first of modern writers to teach all men this truth, which looks like a truism, and yet was as good as unknown to writers of history and others, till so taught—"that the bygone ages of the world were actually filled with living men."

(xi)

Modern critics have agreed. Pointing to Scott as a seminal figure behind the work of Wilson and others, Marinell Ash seconds Wilson noting that the achievements in early archaeology and related studies "would not have been possible without the intellectual legacy that Scott transmitted to the historians—and prehistorians—of the nineteenth century" (441). In his study of the persistence of the oral tradition in nineteenth-century Great Britain, David Vincent notes the importance of Scott's contribution to the antiquarian tradition and the archaeological work that followed it. Comparing Scott's work north of the border to Brand's in the south, Vincent cites them together as the fathers of British archaeology, pioneers in the development of modern inquiry into peoples and cultures (22). By the middle of the nineteenth century, Vincent continues, "an army of middle-class antiquarians was at work following the guidelines laid down by Scott and Brand, and adding to the material collected in their pioneering volumes" (23).

Other critics have noted the impress of these developments on Scott's own work. John Pilkey suggests that "Scott's good fortune was to stand at a crossroads in the progress of the British interpretation of human origins" (iv), a crossroads where the traditions of the eighteenth-century British mythographers and antiquarians begin to yield to the emerging social sciences. In a 1986 study, "Dialectic, Rhetoric, and Anthropology in Scott's *Waverley*," Louise J. Smith explores the intersection of eighteenth-century antiquarianism and nineteenth-century anthropological historicism in Scott's fiction. Both note that Scott's work is distinctly conscious of its position. Scott's work bears them out.

The obvious text here is Scott's **Antiquary**, where these pursuits supply much of the action and character of the novel. The weaknesses of antiquarianism and the frauds of mythography are profiled in the genial caricature of Jonathan Oldbuck and the more grotesque figures of Herman Dousterswivel and his dupe, Sir Arthur. In their persons the novel pokes fun at the credulity of antiquarianism and condemns the pseudo-mythical claims of mythography. While the assumptions of both studies are basically discredited—and by the same agent (Old Edie, who of all the characters has his feet most firmly on the ground)—the distinction is clear. The antiquarian, while crusty and overcredulous in his pursuit of antiquities, shows sound feeling and judgment in all else. Dousterswivel and Sir Arthur, on the other hand, are not attractive characters in any sense. The character of Sir Arthur is distorted by a range of selfish passions; Dousterswivel's, by pure greed. He is little more than a common swindler. Antiquarianism, if sometimes foolish, Scott shows us, is at least honest in its intentions and is born of a real enthusiasm for history and tradition. Pseudo-mythical pursuits like those of Dousterswivel, which claim to discover or reveal hidden truths or treasures of that past, are, the novel suggests, inevitably tainted with opportunism, self-seeking, and a whole range of base and reprehensible motives.

The Antiquary is recognizably Scott's most self-conscious and critical treatment of contemporary appetites for past and primitive. But Scott's work is much more than a caricature and commentary on these pursuits. It is not merely reactive, but rather responds to more subtle changes in the intellectual landscape of the European mind. In its texts, the self-conscious activity of the social scientist and scholar seems to merge with the creative activity of the literary artist. Its issue is a new and uniquely malleable genre responsive to the encounters convulsing European society along historical, cultural, and intellectual frontiers. It is a genre that, in the comparative freedom of fiction, explores the subjective experience codified in the "objective" disciplines of history, ethnology, and anthropology.

As a historian, antiquarian, and ethnologist, Scott responds to a cultural crisis. As a novelist, he comments on that response by creating a genre that expresses European society's deepest anxieties about its past and present, anxieties that shape the new disciplines, anxieties that take on tangible form and substance in these texts, and anxieties that are joined in the fictional text with the larger literary conventions of romanticism. In this fiction, the encounter with past and primitive—an experience distanced and objectified in the narratives of history and ethnology—is expressed with a freedom and clarity found nowhere else, and it is consciously linked to an experience now called romanticism. These are narratives of those encounters, which explore their dangers and attractions and strike a deeply responsive chord among Scott's contemporaries by expressing the dilemmas inherent in the differentiation of self and other at the heart of work in the emergent social sciences.

The genre begins in the play of identities. The first of Scott's heroes, Edward Waverley is introduced while rapt in daydreams of legendary family heroes—medieval and Jacobite—of Sir Wilibert the Crusader and William Waverley, the young Jacobite—and is drawn irresistibly into the Highlands—a regressive process rendered with an almost archetypal clarity. Waverley passes first from the Hanoverian base at Dundee into the medieval feudal enclave of Cosmo Comyne Bradwardine, and from there into the hands of Highlander and clansman Evan Dhu MacCombich, who leads the youth into the encampment of Donald Bean Lean and his nomadic robber band—a steady progression from the realities of the contemporary world back through time to the cave itself. In the process, Edward's identity becomes blurred as it merges with that of other atavistic individuals and groups. He puts off his British clothing and assumes the "garb of old Gaul," the Highland gear of "a son of Ivor" or clansman (**Waverley** 112). Abandoning king and country, he joins the Highlanders in a rebellion that itself marks a regressive movement in the national and collective psyche. But it all has a distant fairy-tale quality about it—an air of unreality. Amidst the swelling war cry of the attacking clan, Edward Waverley is suddenly seized by a feeling of alienation. Looking at his tartan, his weapons, and his companions in disbelief, he internally dissociates himself from the scene. The remainder of the novel chronicles his return to contemporary society through a kind of depressurization, as he passes through a series of five transitional identities in order to reenter contemporary society safely with position, property, and privilege intact.

The novel closes with the image of an Edward pardoned and restored standing in the midst of his wedding party while gazing at a sentimental portrait of himself in rebel's bonnet and Highland tartan arm-in-arm with his brother in rebellion, Fergus—arch-rebel and last chieftain of the Highland clan of Vich Ian Vohr, a less fortunate figure disemboweled, dismembered, and decapitated. The danger of that encounter is transmuted and framed in the art of portrait and text. The immersion in past and primitive is contained and deliberately mystified by an authorial sleight of hand.

Romanticism is implicated in all this. The idealization of past and primitive associated with romanticism is, in fact, the very subject of the first historical novel, **Waverley.** The titular hero's adventures chronicle the impulse toward a more primitive past and the harsh chastening of that impulse, of those yearnings for a more primitive—a more "heightened" way of life—which, faced with the barbarities and cruelties native to those traditions and with the equally barbarous and cruel policies of a modern imperialism, draws back in horror. Set in the midst of a world dominated by Machiavellian movements, movements that catch him up, spin him about, and spit him out exhausted, disheveled, gasping for breath, still not knowing what hit him, the protagonist escapes with his life only with the help of a kind of *deus ex machina,* the intercession of a friend or relation intimate with the winning side. Fergus, his Highland counterpart and "brother" is literally torn to pieces—limb from limb—by the ferocity of history. Edward, the survivor, having seen all this and briefly tasted its horror, is happy to stay by the fireside henceforth, arm-in-arm with his Rose. His immersion in the landscape of his imagination almost cost him his life. He survives, but lets fall those romantic dreams and embraces the simpler and certainly more conventional life of husband, proprietor, and citizen. His high purpose is abandoned for a more pedestrian peace and quiet. Waverley and his literary descendants launch their quest for the past and primitive in the teeth of political, social, and cultural realities that come crashing in on them. Having run the gauntlet formed by the collision of the earlier idealized vision of history with a brutal reality, the hero makes his peace with his own time and place. It is a kind of renunciation of the earlier quest and an acknowledgment of the claims of the present. Dreams of political apocalypse and cultural utopia fade into the blurred outline of memory—into that sentimental portrait of Edward and Fergus, itself a visible symbol of Scott's own rendering and enframing of the romantic quest of past and present.

Springing from a later romanticism, its hopes for social and political utopia chastened and conditioned by the cataclysms through which it had passed—a romanticism whose exaltation of the primitive as a model for modern man had met bitter defeat again and again—the genre is one way in which romanticism assesses itself, acknowledges its own limits, and writes its own eulogy. But the tragedies that close the revolutionary action in **Waverley** mark the immolation not only of Flora and Fergus as well as the youthful romantic impulse, but also of the primitive, elder culture from which they sprang. The MacIvors are extinct; the apocalyptic and utopian hopes, the dream of reviving an idealized past, are spent. This is the discourse after the flood recording the great changes that had taken place, recording not only the demise of romantic hopes, but also the demise of a culture and people wiped off the face of the earth—the discourse of a nascent ethnology. Scott's work is not only a part of this, but is also a profoundly self-conscious part tracing the trajectories of all these contemporary approaches to past and primitive— romanticism, antiquarianism and mythography, and the emergence of the modern anthropological disciplines.

What gives these novels their wide appeal is perhaps not their conservative "happy" endings, but the element of risk—the threat of annihilation or absorption. Even in the most cautious of these chronicles or adventure stories—novels like **Rob Roy** or **Waverley**—the heroes momentarily lose their identity. Their survival hinges on its recovery. He, or more rarely she, must contend with a host of shadow selves, not only the individual double—the hermit, the beggar, the idiot, the outlaw or rebel, the criminal, the traitor, and all the "others," the marginal figures who populate the text—but also the collective doubles as well—shadow figures of contemporary culture such as the Highlander, Cossack, or Mohican—who are all projections of modern consciousness and culture at risk. What emerges is a kind of shadow play of desire and differentiation, cultural and individual.

It is a cathartic experience. Part of what makes the historical novel so dynamic, what gave it such phenomenal force in its own time is its direct representation of this play of identities at the borders of history, culture, and self in the personal experience of the protagonist. There is a focus, familiarity, and intimacy in the fictional reading that reveals what remains unspoken, though not concealed in the scientific text; it reveals the fascination with the other. Indeed, it could not be concealed. It is the mainspring of the narratives concerned with past and primitive, which emerge from the first half of the nineteenth century.

In the larger narrative of differentiation, there is a narrative of desire—a hunger for alternate experience—a response to the call of past and primitive. This impulse to explore and define the relationship between self and other, past and present, as well as primitive and modern is at the bottom of the early discourse of the social sciences. Theirs are disguised or distanced "scientific" narratives of the conflict and confrontation of identities expressed so freely in the figure and adventures of the protagonist—a youth on the brink of adulthood, the persona of a nation and a culture moving into the modern world—turning back to confront its own past and primitive self. The genre that seems to spring full-grown from the mind of Sir Walter Scott, amateur antiquarian, ethnologist, and historian turned novelist, is an expression of this fascination with the other—past and present—paired with the need to differentiate, to explore the boundaries of the self, a fascination implicit in the emergent discourse of ethnology, history, and psychology. Drawn to the shadow side, venturing into foreign universes, the scientific narratives maintain a cautious distance—through the persona of the historian, the ethnologist and the antiquarian. The novel's protagonist, noted for his typicality and passivity, emerges as the persona of this modern consciousness—a focal point for the concerns, anxieties, and aspirations of the age, an expression of the emergent, even neophyte consciousness of modern Europe. His desire to explore alternate worlds and alternate experience without losing his own privileged cultural identity is a metaphor for the larger ventures of the intellectual community exploring beyond the boundaries of self, but careful about the safety and integrity of its person and property.

The early historical novel is only one episode in a larger chronicle of literary encounters and inversions, but it is particularly intriguing because it emerged roughly simultaneously with scientific "narratives" in ethnology, history, and even psychology, which share a common subject matter—the past and primitive—and a common medium—the prose narrative. It is surely no coincidence that these begin to emerge and take on a disciplinary identity and a common discursive mode at roughly the same time. It is a symptom of an underlying disease in culture and consciousness. The shadow self of man and culture is projected and constructed in a narration of distance and differentiation that becomes "science," taking on an air of authority and authenticity, and acquiring the directing and ordering potency associated with "disciplinary" activity. Born of the tension between the impulse to recapture a more primitive experience and the necessity to repudiate that condition, a tension spawning a new wave of narrative discourses, both literary and scientific, the historical novel explores in personal terms the workings of larger cultural imperatives and gives a face and a name to the impulse at work in the emergent disciplines. Ethnology, history, and other emergent disciplines like psychology arise as modes of self-definition—communal and individual. They allow contemporary consciousness to observe at a safe distance its own past and primitive experience, while all the while maintaining those boundaries seemingly so critical to modern consciousness and that distance formalized in the concept of scientific objectivity, which affords the individual an opportunity to enter alternate worlds without compromising the integrity of his modern identity—the freedom and detachment of the tourist, the voyeur, the professional, the author. This is the subject of the Waverley novels. Edward Waverley, Frank Osbaldistone, and Darsie Latimer are all implicated. First drawn to the past and primitive, they pull back to regroup seeking a safe distance as those cultures move toward their inevitable end. Theirs is, in this sense, an act of bad faith repeated in text after text across Europe.

From where she sat, Laidlaw was right. Scott's work, however sincere, must remain from her perspective an act of betrayal, albeit a highly self-conscious and articulate one. Committed to commemorating and preserving the forms of a passing culture, Scott's work is, for all its efforts, predicated on the death of that culture. But from where she sat, Laidlaw was missing half the picture. What Laidlaw could not have seen was Scott's role not only as conservator and commemorator, but as commentator and critic of the whole enterprise. Laidlaw's accusation was aimed at Scott's archival work. What might she have said of the historical novel? Perhaps she would have damned it too. Or perhaps she would have said that there at least Scott himself conceded that act of betrayal—that act of bad faith—and that the genre made an honest man of him, if not his generation.

References

Ash, Marinell. 1983. "A Past 'Filled with Living Men': Daniel Wilson and Scottish and American Archaeology." *Scott and His Influence.* Ed. J. H. Alexander and David Hewitt. Occasional Papers 6. Aberdeen: Association for Scottish Influence. 443-54.

Hogg, James. 1983. *Familiar Anecdotes of Sir Walter Scott.* Ed. Douglas S. Mack. Edinburgh: Scottish Academic Press.

Pilkey, John Davis. 1974. "Walter Scott's Fiction and British Mythographic and Ethnological Movements." Diss. University of Kansas.

Scott, Sir Walter. 1910. *The Antiquary.* London: J. M. Dent & Sons.

———. 1813. *Minstrelsy of the Scottish Border Constituting of Historical and Romantic Ballads, Collected in the Southern Countries of Scotland, with a Few of Modern Date, Founded upon Local Tradition.* Philadelphia: M. Carey.

———. 1985. *Waverley.* Ed. Andrew Hook. New York: Viking Penguin.

Smith, Louise Z. 1986. "Dialectic, Rhetoric, and Anthropology in Scott's Waverley." *Studies in Scottish Literature* 21: 43-52.

Vincent, David. 1982. "The Decline of the Oral Tradition in Popular Culture." *Popular Culture and Custom in Nineteenth-Century England.* Ed. Robert D. Storch. New York: St. Martin's Press. 20-47.

Wilson, Daniel. 1851. *The Archaeology and Prehistorical Annals of Scotland.* Edinburgh: Sutherland and Knoc.

Jennifer Parrott (essay date 2006)

SOURCE: Parrott, Jennifer. "'Slaves of the Imagination': Sir Walter Scott in the Works of Virginia Woolf." *Virginia Woolf Miscellany* 70 (2006): 32-4. Print.

[*In the following essay, Parrott analyzes Virginia Woolf's interest in Scott, noting the role played in her childhood by Scott's work and pointing out references to Scott in her writing. Parrott suggests that Woolf wanted to reclaim Scott's reputation and proposes a reconsideration of both authors.*]

On the surface, it is a strange pairing indeed: Virginia Woolf, a feminist and a modernist who is writing in a style that, through carefully crafted stream-of-consciousness, attempts to get at the texture of an ordinary mind on an ordinary day, and Sir Walter Scott, a materialist and an elitist whose novels demonstrate a greater concern with intellectualism and plot twists than with the internal lives of his characters. Woolf consciously writes against the tradition, the style, the gender, and the entire outlook that Scott represents. His is the outlook that she defines herself against in both her essays and her fiction, and, along with contemporaries such as Arnold Bennett and John Galsworthy, Scott exemplifies in fiction what Woolf strove to move beyond.

In contrast, however, to the harsh treatment and constant derision that she heaped upon these "materialists" (286), Bennett, Galsworthy, and other "unscrupulous tyrants," Woolf demonstrated affection for and reverence toward Scott. She shows a surprising preoccupation with him. Scott appears in various places throughout her novels, diaries, and letters, and she wrote several essays specifically on Scott, including her essay on his novel *The Antiquary*.

Scott's importance to Woolf was both autobiographical and critical. Louise DeSalvo suggests that Woolf uses Scott to come to terms with her family and her childhood. DeSalvo convincingly argues that, in wrongly describing the relationship between the Earl of Glenallan and Evelina Neville in *The Antiquary* as incestuous, Woolf unconsciously links herself to Evelina because of her incestuous relationship with her half-brother. In addition, DeSalvo associates Miss Neville's suicide with Woolf's later suicide, concluding that "the similarities between *The Antiquary* and Woolf's life, and her later use of the novel, suggest that *The Antiquary* was immensely important to Woolf—that she used it to understand her father, to explain her own ambivalence about parental figures—but that somehow she projected her own experiences onto Evelina Neville" (226-27). Woolf refers to Scott more than twenty times in her diaries, and she directly references his work in *The Voyage Out, Night and Day,* and *To the Lighthouse.*[1] *Orlando, Three Guineas,* and *Between the Acts* can be read as responses to nineteenth-century realism, and, more specifically, as responses (of varying degrees) to Scott's work, particularly to his linear approach to history and narrative plot.

Initially, it appears that Woolf rejects Scott, particularly his plot structure, his sense of history, and the realism characteristic of nineteenth-century fiction. Judith Wilt writes: "It is exactly this notion of history as a great drama passed from fathers to sons [...] that Virginia Woolf wishes to reject" (476). Woolf rejects the chronological, alphabetical, egotistical notion of history as reserved for men only, a secret between fathers and sons, by manipulating both chronology and her characters' gender in *Orlando* and *Between the Acts.* In *To the Lighthouse* she frustrates the linear plot, as she dwells on particular moments and subsequently skips a decade with the turn of a page. Woolf brings the reader into the Ramsays' world through the thoughts and impressions of her characters rather than depending upon a third person narrator to package neatly the experience. But despite her divergence from Scott's style of writing, Woolf, in an essay on the greatness of Dickens, remarks, "It can only be a question whether any other English novelist, save Scott, has a right to be called Shakespearean" (*Essays* 26). Woolf's allusions to Scott in *Night and Day* and in some of her non-fiction pieces further suggest that she is not merely interested in working against him; the relationship between Woolf and Scott is more complex than just a memory from her childhood or a collection of texts she associates with her parents. She uses Scott as a bridge between the male and the female, and, to an extent, the Victorians and the modernists.

That complexity shows itself in connections between Leslie Stephen, Scott, and *To the Lighthouse*'s Mr. Ramsay. Much like Mr. Ramsay, Leslie Stephen was a writer who thought and worked in a linear fashion, as evidenced by his position as editor of The Dictionary of National Biography, a project in which he literally worked through the alphabet as he edited the biographies of Britain's most notable citizens, the majority of whom were men. Woolf connects the linear, masculine perspectives of her father, Mr. Ramsay, and Scott by using Scott's *The Antiquary* in the "The Window" section of the novel, immediately after the climactic dinner scene. This vital chapter is the final one of the first section and marks the last time we see Mrs. Ramsay alive in the novel. Furthermore, it is the only moment of true connection that we observe between husband and wife. The chapter begins as Mrs. Ramsay watches her husband. She:

> looked at her husband (taking up her stocking and beginning to knit), and saw that he did not want to be interrupted—that was clear. He was reading something that moved him very much. He was half smiling and then she knew he was controlling his emotion. He was tossing the pages over. He was acting it—perhaps he was thinking himself the person in the book. She wondered what book it was. Oh, it was one of old Sir Walter's she saw,

adjusting the shade of her lamp so that the light fell on her knitting.

(118-19)

Mrs. Ramsay observes her husband become one with the characters in the novel, displaying yet maintaining control over the emotion that his family so often finds lacking in him. As she does throughout this chapter, Woolf illustrates how interacting with art is a means of connecting Mr. and Mrs. Ramsay. Both at the level of content and form, art draws them together. Reading Shakespeare's *Sonnet 98,* Mrs. Ramsay allows the beauty of the words to draw her toward her husband; reading **The Antiquary,** Mr. Ramsay allows himself to be overcome with emotion through empathizing with those who mourn young Steenie's death.

In **The Antiquary** Steenie's death ultimately unites his parents. Steenie's mother, Mucklebackit's "masculine wife, virago as she was, and absolute mistress of the family, as she justly boasted herself, on all ordinary occasions, was by this great loss terrified into silence and submission, and compelled to hide from her husband's observation the bursts of her female sorrow" (229). In Woolf's novel, the emotional roles are reversed in terms of gender. In Scott's novel, it is the peasant woman who runs the family who must hide her grief in order to maintain the virago image; in contrast, in Woolf's novel it is Mr. Ramsay who feels the need to hide his emotion behind the pages of Scott's novel. But ultimately, both Mrs. Mucklebackit and Mr. Ramsay resign themselves to their grief.

Woolf's allusion to the funeral scene from **The Antiquary** occurs at a crucial point in the narrative, as it marks the moment in which Mr. and Mrs. Ramsay are finally united after a day spent apart:

> Then, knowing that he was watching her, instead of saying anything she turned, holding her stocking, and looked at him. And as she looked at him she began to smile, for though she had not said a word, he knew, of course he knew that she loved him. He could not deny it. And smiling she looked out of the window ... (thinking to herself, Nothing on earth can equal this happiness).

(124)

This silent connection between husband and wife occurs only after their individual engagement with Shakespeare on one hand and Scott on the other; it is Steenie's death (and not Mrs. Ramsay's carefully arranged dinner) that brings Mr. Ramsay back to his wife and breathes new life into his relationship with his family.

Woolf mirrors the Ramsays' union through the continual shifting of point-of-view throughout the scene, as she subtly moves from wife to husband and back again:

> Oh, it was one of old Sir Walter's she saw, adjusting the shade of her lamp so that the light fell on her knitting. For Charles Tansley had been saying [...] that people don't read Scott any more. Then her husband thought, "That's what they'll say of me"; so he went and got one of those

books. And if he came to the conclusion "That's true" what Charles Tansley said, he would accept it about Scott. (She could see that he was weighing, considering, putting this with that as he read.) But not about himself.

(120)

Throughout the novel, Mr. Ramsay and Charles Tansley continually discuss their work, Mr. Ramsay his latest book and Tansley his dissertation, and in these discussions Ramsay constantly questions the permanence of his writing, comparing his own work to Scott's. He constantly reevaluates his own work, questioning whether it will endure. Ultimately, Mr. Ramsay decides that Scott's work will endure, and he finds comfort in this conclusion, thinking, "Well let them improve upon that, he thought as he finished the chapter. [...] They could not improve upon that, whatever they might say; and his own position became more secure" (120). Here Woolf connects the linear, masculine pursuits of Mr. Ramsay and Scott.

Through his reading of Scott, Mr. Ramsay pardons himself for being unable to reach Z in his pursuit of intellectual perfection, concluding, "Somebody would reach it—if not he, then another. This man's strength and sanity, his feeling for straightforward simple things, these fishermen, the poor old crazed creature in Mucklebackit's cottage made him feel so vigorous, so relieved of something that he felt roused and triumphant and could not choke back his tears" (120). Mr. Ramsay attempts to raise the book "to hide his face," but he ultimately lets it fall and "forgot himself completely, [...] forgot his own bothers and failures completely in poor Steenie's drowning and Mucklebackit's sorrow (that was Scott at his best) and the astonishing delight and feeling of vigour that it gave him" (120). If only momentarily, Mr. Ramsay takes himself out of the alphabet in order to resign himself to the emotional dimension of life.

In this scene, Woolf breaks down the boundaries between her work and Scott's, between the experience of her generation and the one that preceded it. Scott's linear, masculine perspective must have intrigued Woolf because it so directly opposed her own. She undoubtedly had respect for it—partially because she loved her father and was influenced by him, but also because she sensed complexity and sophistication in a mind different from her own. Yet why did Woolf turn Bennett and Galsworthy into straw figures whom she viewed as constraining and restrictive, while she continued to breathe life into Scott, reserving room for him as a substantial presence in her life and work?

Woolf herself provides some answers to this difficult question in her 1921 review of *The Intimate Life of Sir Walter Scott,* a biography in which the writer, Archibald Stalker, concludes that Scott's writing is far less important than his life. Woolf's praise of Scott is tempered by an acknowledgment and understanding of his shortcomings, but she also refers to him as "a confirmed writer, with a prodigious gift for the calling" (302). She concludes that,

"Anyone who wants to come near the character of Scott, or to analyse the nature of his charm, must give full weight to the fact that he spent hours every day during the great part of his life with the creatures of his imagination" (303). While his technique and outlook are admittedly different from Woolf's, she acknowledges their shared occupation as artists and their shared existence as "slave[s] of [the] imagination" (303). Much as Mr. Ramsay does, Woolf rises to Scott's defense, and by the end of the review she has long forgotten Stalker's book and rouses readers to return to Scott, proclaiming that "each epithet and scene and incident serves to make us more and more sure that we know Sir Walter and are not to be argued out of our knowledge" (304). This impulse in Woolf suggests that she wants to reclaim Scott's reputation and argue for his placement among the literary greats. Whether we attribute her interest in Scott to the role that his texts played in her childhood or to her desire to embrace a writer who (at least on the surface) could not be more different from her, it certainly compels us to reconsider both Woolf and Scott.

Note

1. Woolf's father was a fan of Scott and read all 32 volumes of the Waverley novels aloud to his children (starting again once he had finished the last); Woolf's mother shared her husband's passion for Scott (Kelley 37, 48) and Woolf writes that "for a birthday present she chose all of the works of Scott, which her father gave her in the first edition—some remain, others are lost. She had a passion for Scott" (*Moments of Being* 80).

Works Cited

Cohan, Steven. "Why Mr. Ramsay Reads *The Antiquary.*" *Women and Literature* 7:2 (1979): 14-24.

DeSalvo, Louise. *Virginia Woolf: The Impact of Childhood Sexual Abuse on Her Life and Work.* Boston: Beacon, 1989.

Kelley, Alice van Buren. *To the Lighthouse: The Marriage of Life and Art.* Boston: Twayne, 1987.

Scott, Sir Walter. *The Antiquary.* New York: Oxford UP, 2002.

Wilt, Judith. "Steamboat Surfacing: Scott and the English Novelists." *Nineteenth-Century Fiction* 35:4 (1981): 459-86.

Woolf, Virginia. *The Essays of Virginia Woolf.* Vol. 2. Ed. Andrew McNeillie. San Diego: Harcourt, 1988.

———. "Modern Fiction." *The Virginia Woolf Reader.* Ed. Mitchell A. Leaska. San Diego: Harcourt, 1984. 283-91.

———. *Moments of Being.* 2nd ed. Ed. Jeanne Schulkind. Orlando: Harvest, 1985.

———. *To the Lighthouse.* 1927. San Diego: Harcourt, 1981.

FURTHER READING

Bibliographies

Barnaby, Paul. "Recent Publications." *The Walter Scott Digital Archive.* Edinburgh U Lib. 25 Oct. 2012. Web. 2 Nov. 2012.

Provides an annotated bibliography of Scott scholarship and criticism from 2000 to the present. The site also includes a descriptive bibliography of Scott's works, links to manuscript collections, e-texts of many of Scott's more obscure works, and links to over 300 free e-texts.

Corson, James Clarkson. *A Bibliography of Sir Walter Scott: A Classified and Annotated List of Books and Articles Relating to his Life and Works, 1797-1940.* London: Oliver and Boyd, 1943. Print.

Provides annotated listing of criticism and scholarship published from 1797-1940.

Rubenstein, Jill. *Sir Walter Scott: A Reference Guide.* Boston: Hall, 1978. Print.

Provides annotated listing of criticism and scholarship published from 1932-77.

———. *Sir Walter Scott: An Annotated Bibliography of Scholarship and Criticism, 1975-1990.* Aberdeen: Assoc. Scottish Lit. Studies, 1994. Print.

Provides annotated listing of criticism and scholarship published from 1975-90.

Biographies

Johnson, Edgar. *Sir Walter Scott: The Great Unknown.* 2 vols. New York: Macmillan, 1970. Print.

The standard twentieth-century biography. Called "minutely detailed," the study thoroughly covers Scott's life and works, but has been criticized for lack of discrimination in detail and an uncritical approach to Scott's writings.

Lockhart, John Gibson. *Memoirs of the Life of Sir Walter Scott.* 7 vols. Edinburgh: Cadell, 1837-38. Print.

The standard nineteenth-century life of Scott by his son-in-law. This detailed study of his life relies heavily on passages from Scott's letters and journals, and passes judiciously over many more intimate details that have been filled in by later biographers.

Sutherland, John. *The Life of Sir Walter Scott: A Critic's Biography.* Oxford: Blackwell, 1995. Print.

A scholarly study that has been praised for its "shrewd, unillusioned" biographical detail and its critical analysis of Scott's works.

Criticism

Alexander, J. H., and David Hewitt, eds. *Scott and His Influence: The Papers of the Aberdeen Scott Conference,*

1982. Aberdeen: Assoc. for Scottish Lit. Studies, 1983. Print.

> Collects diverse essays dealing with various aspects of Scott's work, some of special relevance to *The Antiquary,* including an essay by Robin Gilmour.

Brown, David. "*The Antiquary.*" *Walter Scott and the Historical Imagination.* London: Routledge and Kegan Paul, 1979. 47-67. Print.

> Examines the relationship between the past and the present in Scott's work.

Daiches, David. "Sir Walter Scott and History." *Études Anglaises* 24.4 (1971): 458-77. Print.

> Discusses Scott's perception of history, including discussion of *The Antiquary.*

Gamerschlag, Kurt. "The Non-Explosive Mixture: Historical Analysis and Social Ideals in Scott's *The Antiquary.*" *Studies in Scottish Fiction: Nineteenth Century.* Ed. Horst W. Drescher and Joachim Schwend. Frankfurt am Main: Lang, 1985. 65-81. Print.

> Argues that *The Antiquary* is not "just a good example for primitive story-telling and extemporizing" but rather "a work of conscious art trying to probe the nature of history." Gamerschlag suggests that the structure of the novel reflects two aspects of Scott's experience—life as "unpredictable, confusing, contradictory" and life as relatively well-ordered.

Garside, Peter. "Scott, the Eighteenth Century and the New Man of Sentiment." *Anglia* 103.1-2 (1985): 71-89. Print.

> Considers both eighteenth and nineteenth-century aspects of Scott's work. Garside contends that *The Antiquary* can be seen as "a vindication of the experience of the 1790s," even though its presentation is "highly coloured by the tensions and presuppositions of a later age."

Goetsch, Paul. "Scott's *The Antiquary*: Tradition-Making as Process." *Literatur im Kontext—Literature in Context: Festschrift für Horst W. Drescher.* Ed. Joachim Schwend, Susanne Hagemann, and Hermann Völkel. Frankfurt am Main: Lang, 1992. 91-107. Print.

> Approaches *The Antiquary* as a self-reflexive work that "concentrates on the dynamics of history and the processes by which traditions come into being, are destroyed, transformed, and rejuvenated." Goetsch focuses on "how Scott uses different kinds of oral and written knowledge in the novel."

Gottlieb, Evan. "Sir Walter and Plain Jane: Teaching Scott and Austen Together." *Approaches to Teaching Scott's Waverley Novels.* Ed. Gottlieb and Ian Duncan. New York: Modern Language Assoc., 2009. 97-104. Print.

> Describes the benefits of teaching Scott's novels in conjunction with those of Scott's contemporary, Jane Austen. Gottlieb illustrates the strategy through a comparative discussion of *The Antiquary* and *North-*

anger Abbey (1817), both of which employ conventions associated with the gothic novels popular in the 1790s.

Hart, Francis. "*The Antiquary* as a Modern Test Case." *Scott's Novels: The Plotting of Historical Survival.* Charlottesville: U of Virginia P, 1966. 246-58. Print.

> Pays special attention to the relationship between form, plot, and character in Scott's fiction with particular focus on *The Antiquary.*

Hewitt, David. "Essay on the Text." *The Antiquary.* By Walter Scott. Ed. Hewitt. Edinburgh: Edinburgh UP, 1995. 357-93. Print.

> Includes an overview of the genesis and composition of *The Antiquary,* compares successive iterations of the text from Scott's original manuscript through multiple printings and revised editions, and comments on Scott's unconventional punctuation and orthography.

Jackson-Houlston, C. M. "'Scoundrel Minstrels': Some Allusions to Song in Two Scott Novels." *Scott in Carnival: Selected Papers from the Fourth International Scott Conference, Edinburgh, 1991.* Ed. J. H. Alexander and David Hewitt. Aberdeen: Assn. for Scottish Lit. Studies, 1993. 97-109. Print.

> Compares *The Antiquary* with Scott's 1826 novel *Woodstock,* noting that both are structured as "cultural antitheses" represented by "different kinds of intertextual allusion and quotation." Jackson-Houlston focuses on references to William Shakespeare and patterns of allusion to popular song.

Johnson, Edgar. "Time Looms Gigantic." *Sir Walter Scott: The Great Unknown.* New York: Macmillan, 1970. 520-43. Print.

> Summarizes the plot of *The Antiquary,* enumerates its strengths and weaknesses, and briefly relates it to the two previous Waverley novels. Johnson concludes that despite the novel's uneven characterization and unlikely plot, it triumphs in its rich portrayals of Scottish life and its "varied and vivid pictures of human nature."

Lee, Yoon Sun. "A Divided Inheritance: Scott's Antiquarian Novel and the British Nation." *English Literary History* 64.2 (1997): 537-67. Print.

> Contrasts the "antiquarian mode of producing historical knowledge" with a type of "patriotic historicism" that reached its peak during the period in which *The Antiquary* is set. Lee attempts to correct the "unreflective alignment of antiquarianism with political conservatism."

Malley, Shawn. "Walter Scott's Romantic Archaeology: New/Old Abbotsford and *The Antiquary.*" *Studies in Romanticism* 40.2 (2001): 233-51. Print.

> Characterizes *The Antiquary* as a "meta-archaeological novel" that capitalizes on "the psychology of historical desire." Malley connects the novel's genealogical and

antiquarian themes with the ideological foundations underpinning Scott's approach to building Abbotsford House.

Parker, David. General Introduction. *The Antiquary.* By Walter Scott. Ed. David Hewitt. Edinburgh: Edinburgh UP; New York: Columbia UP, 1993. xi-xvi. Print.

Discusses *The Antiquary* and its place in Scott's career.

Robertson, Fiona. "Phantoms of Revolution: Five Case-Studies of Literary Convention and Social Analysis." *Legitimate Histories: Scott, Gothic, and the Authorities of Fiction.* Oxford: Clarendon P, 1994. 197-244. Print.

Discusses the challenge of integrating various plots and stylistic components in *The Antiquary* and suggests that the Glenallan story forces a recognition that Scott's novels are not "seamless endorsements of the rational" but rather "experimental, questioning, and aesthetically disruptive" texts. Robertson also considers political aspects of the novel in relation to its historical context.

Watson, Nicola J. Introduction. *The Antiquary.* By Walter Scott. Ed. Watson. Oxford: Oxford UP, 2002. vii-xxvii. Print.

Provides a comprehensive overview of *The Antiquary,* summarizing the plot, the early critical response, and the novel's place in Scott's canon. Watson also discusses major themes such as identity and inheritance, as well as aspects of language and genre.

Wilt, Judith. "The Salted Mine of History: *The Antiquary, Woodstock, The Talisman.*" *Secret Leaves: The Novels of Walter Scott.* Chicago: U of Chicago P, 1985. 153-84. Print.

Explores the idea of "legitimacy" and the "past" in *The Antiquary.*

Additional information on Scott's life and works is contained in the following sources published by Gale: *Authors and Artists for Young Adults,* **Vol. 22;** *Beacham's Guide to Literature for Young Adults,* **Vol. 2;** *British Writers,* **Vol. 4;** *Children's Literature Review,* **Vol. 154;** *Concise Dictionary of British Literary Biography: 1789-1832; Dictionary of Literary Biography,* **Vols. 93, 107, 116, 144, 159, 366;** *DISCovering Authors; DISCovering Authors: British Edition; DISCovering Authors: Canadian Edition; DISCovering Authors Modules: Most-Studied Authors, Novelists* **and** *Poets; Gale Contextual Encyclopedia of World Literature; Gothic Literature: A Gale Critical Companion,* **Vol. 3;** *Literature and Its Times,* **Vol. 1;** *Literature Resource Center; Nineteenth-Century Literature Criticism,* **Vols. 15, 69, 110, 209, 241;** *Novels for Students,* **Vol. 31;** *Poetry Criticism,* **Vol. 13;** *Reference Guide to English Literature,* **Ed. 2;** *Reference Guide to Short Fiction,* **Ed. 2;** *St. James Guide to Horror, Ghost and Gothic Writers; Short Stories for Students,* **Vol. 10;** *Short Story Criticism,* **Vol. 32;** *Supernatural Fiction Writers; Twayne's English Authors; World Literature and Its Times,* **Vol. 3;** *World Literature Criticism,* **Vol. 5;** **and** *Yesterday's Authors of Books for Children,* **Vol. 2.**